Reading French P

In this book, Dana Birksted-Breen and Sara Flanders of the British Psychoanalytical Society, and Alain Gibeault of the Paris Psychoanalytical Society, provide an overview of how French psychoanalysis has developed since Lacan. Focusing primarily on the work of psychoanalysts from the French Psychoanalytical Association and from the Paris Psychoanalytical Society, the two British psychoanalysts view the evolution of theory as it appears to them from the outside, while the French psychoanalyst explains and elaborates from inside the French psychoanalytic discourse. Seminal and representative papers have been chosen to illuminate what is special about French thinking. A substantial general introduction argues in favour of the specificity of 'French psychoanalysis', tracing its early influences and highlighting specific contemporary developments.

Sections are made up of introductory material by Alain Gibeault, followed by illustrative papers in the following categories:

- the history of psychoanalysis in France
- the pioneers and their legacy
- the setting and the process of psychoanalysis
- phantasy and representation
- the body and the drives
- masculine and feminine sexuality
- psychosis.

An excellent introduction to French psychoanalytical debate, *Reading French Psychoanalysis* sheds a complementary light on thinking that has evolved differently in England and North America. It will be ideal reading for beginners and advanced students of clinical theory as well as experienced psychoanalysts wanting to know more about French psychoanalytic theory, and how it has developed.

Dana Birksted-Breen is a Training and Supervising Psychoanalyst of the British Psychoanalytical Society. She is the General Editor of the New Library of Psychoanalysis and the Joint Editor-in-Chief of the *International Journal of Psychoanalysis*.

Sara Flanders is a Training and Supervising Psychoanalyst of the British Psychoanalytical Society.

Alain Gibeault is a Training and Supervising Psychoanalyst of the Paris Psychoanalytical Society and Director of the E. & J. Kestemberg Centre for Psychoanalysis and Psychotherapy.

THE NEW LIBRARY OF PSYCHOANALYSIS
General Editor   Dana Birksted-Breen

The New Library of Psychoanalysis was launched in 1987 in association with the Institute of Psychoanalysis, London. It took over from the International Psychoanalytical Library, which published many of the early translations of the works of Freud and the writings of most of the leading British and Continental psychoanalysts.

The purpose of the New Library of Psychoanalysis is to facilitate a greater and more widespread appreciation of psychoanalysis and to provide a forum for increasing mutual understanding between psychoanalysts and those working in other disciplines such as the social sciences, medicine, philosophy, history, linguistics, literature and the arts. It aims to represent different trends both in British psychoanalysis and in psychoanalysis generally. The New Library of Psychoanalysis is well placed to make available to the English-speaking world psychoanalytic writings from other European countries and to increase the interchange of ideas between British and American psychoanalysts.

The Institute, together with the British Psychoanalytical Society, runs a low-fee psychoanalytic clinic, organizes lectures and scientific events concerned with psychoanalysis and publishes the *International Journal of Psychoanalysis*. It also runs a prestigious and internationally admired training course leading to qualification in the British Psychoanalytic Council and in the International Psychoanalytic Association, the body which preserves internationally agreed standards of training, of professional entry, and of professional ethics and practice for psychoanalysis as initiated and developed by Sigmund Freud. Distinguished members of the Institute have included Michael Balint, Wilfred Bion, Ronald Fairbairn, Anna Freud, Ernest Jones, Melanie Klein, John Rickman and Donald Winnicott.

Previous General Editors include David Tuckett, Elizabeth Spillius and Susan Budd. Previous and current Members of the Advisory Board include Christopher Bollas, Ronald Britton, Catalina Bronstein, Donald Campbell, Sara Flanders, Stephen Grosz, John Keene, Eglé Laufer, Juliet Mitchell, Michael Parsons, Rosine Jozef Perelberg, Richard Rusbridger, Mary Target, David Taylor, and Alessandra Lemma, who is Assistant Editor.

ALSO IN THIS SERIES

Impasse and Interpretation Herbert Rosenfeld
Psychoanalysis and Discourse Patrick Mahony
The Suppressed Madness of Sane Men Marion Milner
The Riddle of Freud Estelle Roith
Thinking, Feeling, and Being Ignacio Matte-Blanco
The Theatre of the Dream Salomon Resnik
Melanie Klein Today: Volume 1, Mainly Theory Edited by Elizabeth Bott Spillius
Melanie Klein Today: Volume 2, Mainly Practice Edited by Elizabeth Bott Spillius
Psychic Equilibrium and Psychic Change: Selected Papers of Betty Joseph Edited by Michael Feldman and Elizabeth Bott Spillius
About Children and Children-No-Longer: Collected Papers 1942–80 Paula Heimann. Edited by Margret Tonnesmann
The Freud–Klein Controversies 1941–45 Edited by Pearl King and Riccardo Steiner
Dream, Phantasy and Art Hanna Segal
Psychic Experience and Problems of Technique Harold Stewart
Clinical Lectures on Klein and Bion Edited by Robin Anderson
From Fetus to Child Alessandra Piontelli
A Psychoanalytic Theory of Infantile Experience: Conceptual and Clinical Reflections E. Gaddini. Edited by Adam Limentani
The Dream Discourse Today Edited and introduced by Sara Flanders
The Gender Conundrum: Contemporary Psychoanalytic Perspectives on Femininity and Masculinity Edited and introduced by Dana Breen
Psychic Retreats John Steiner
The Taming of Solitude: Separation Anxiety in Psychoanalysis Jean-Michel Quinodoz
Unconscious Logic: An Introduction to Matte-Blanco's Bi-logic and Its Uses Eric Rayner
Understanding Mental Objects Meir Perlow
Life, Sex and Death: Selected Writings of William Gillespie Edited and introduced by Michael Sinason
What Do Psychoanalysts Want? The Problem of Aims in Psychoanalytic Therapy Joseph Sandler and Anna Ursula Dreher
Michael Balint: Object Relations, Pure and Applied Harold Stewart
Hope: A Shield in the Economy of Borderline States Anna Potamianou
Psychoanalysis, Literature and War: Papers 1972–1995 Hanna Segal
Emotional Vertigo: Between Anxiety and Pleasure Danielle Quinodoz
Early Freud and Late Freud Ilse Grubrich-Simitis
A History of Child Psychoanalysis Claudine and Pierre Geissmann
Belief and Imagination: Explorations in Psychoanalysis Ronald Britton
A Mind of One's Own: A Kleinian View of Self and Object Robert A. Caper

Psychoanalytic Understanding of Violence and Suicide Edited by Rosine Jozef Perelberg
On Bearing Unbearable States of Mind Ruth Riesenberg-Malcolm
Psychoanalysis on the Move: The Work of Joseph Sandler Edited by Peter Fonagy, Arnold M. Cooper and Robert S. Wallerstein
The Dead Mother: The Work of André Green Edited by Gregorio Kohon
The Fabric of Affect in the Psychoanalytic Discourse André Green
The Bi-Personal Field: Experiences of Child Analysis Antonino Ferro
The Dove that Returns, the Dove that Vanishes: Paradox and Creativity in Psychoanalysis Michael Parsons
Ordinary People and Extra-Ordinary Protections: A Post-Kleinian Approach to the Treatment of Primitive Mental States Judith Mitrani
The Violence of Interpretation: From Pictogram to Statement Piera Aulagnier
The Importance of Fathers: A Psychoanalytic Re-Evaluation Judith Trowell and Alicia Etchegoyen
Dreams That Turn Over a Page: Paradoxical Dreams in Psychoanalysis Jean-Michel Quinodoz
The Couch and the Silver Screen: Psychoanalytic Reflections on European Cinema Edited and introduced by Andrea Sabbadini
In Pursuit of Psychic Change: The Betty Joseph Workshop Edited by Edith Hargreaves and Arturo Varchevker
The Quiet Revolution in American Psychoanalysis: Selected Papers of Arnold M. Cooper Arnold M. Cooper. Edited and introduced by Elizabeth L. Auchincloss
Seeds of Illness, Seeds of Recovery: The Genesis of Suffering and the Role of Psychoanalysis Antonino Ferro
The Work of Psychic Figurability: Mental States Without Representation César Botella and Sára Botella
Key Ideas for a Contemporary Psychoanalysis: Misrecognition and Recognition of the Unconscious André Green
The Telescoping of Generations: Listening to the Narcissistic Links Between Generations Haydée Faimberg
Glacial Times: A Journey Through the World of Madness Salomon Resnik
This Art of Psychoanalysis: Dreaming Undreamt Dreams and Interrupted Cries Thomas H. Ogden
Psychoanalysis as Therapy and Storytelling Antonino Ferro
Psychoanalysis in the 21st Century: Competitors or Collaborators? Edited by David M. Black
Recovery of the Lost Good Object Eric Brenman
The Many Voices of Psychoanalysis Roger Kennedy
Projected Shadows: Psychoanalytic Reflections on the Representation of Loss in European Cinema Edited by Andrea Sabbadini
Feeling the Words: Neuropsychoanalytic Understanding of Memory and the Unconscious Mauro Mancia

Encounters with Melanie Klein: Selected Papers of Elizabeth Spillius Elizabeth Spillius
Yesterday, Today and Tomorrow Hanna Segal. Edited by Nicola Abel-Hirsch
Constructions and the Analytic Field: History, Scenes and Destiny Domenico Chianese
Psychoanalysis Comparable and Incomparable: The Evolution of a Method to Describe and Compare Psychoanalytic Approaches David Tuckett, Roberto Basile, Dana Birksted-Breen, Tomas Böhm, Paul Denis, Antonino Ferro, Helmut Hinz, Arne Jemstedt, Paola Mariotti and Johan Schubert
Time, Space and Phantasy Rosine Jozef Perelberg
Rediscovering Psychoanalysis: Thinking and Dreaming, Learning and Forgetting Thomas H. Ogden
Mind Works: Technique and Creativity in Psychoanalysis Antonino Ferro
Doubt, Conviction and the Analytic Process: Selected Papers of Michael Feldman Michael Feldman. Edited by Betty Joseph
Melanie Klein in Berlin: Her First Psychoanalyses of Children Claudia Frank
The Psychotic Wavelength: A Psychoanalytic Perspective for Psychiatry Richard Lucas

TITLES IN THE NEW LIBRARY OF PSYCHOANALYSIS
TEACHING SERIES

Reading Freud: A Chronological Exploration of Freud's Writings Jean-Michel Quinodoz
Listening to Hanna Segal: Her Contribution to Psychoanalysis Jean-Michel Quinodoz
Reading French Psychoanalysis Edited by Dana Birksted-Breen, Sara Flanders and Alain Gibeault

THE NEW LIBRARY OF PSYCHOANALYSIS: TEACHING SERIES

3

General Editor: Dana Birksted-Breen

Reading French Psychoanalysis

Edited by Dana Birksted-Breen, Sara Flanders and Alain Gibeault

With selected material translated by David Alcorn, Sophie Leighton and Andrew Weller

LONDON AND NEW YORK

First published 2010
by Routledge
27 Church Road, Hove, East Sussex BN3 2FA

Simultaneously published in the USA and Canada
by Routledge
270 Madison Avenue, New York, NY 10016

Routledge is an imprint of the Taylor & Francis Group, an informa business

Copyright © 2010 Selection and editorial matter, Dana Birksted-Breen, Sara Flanders and Alain Gibeault; individual chapters, the contributors

Copyright © Translation of introductions by Alain Gibeault; chapter 40, key terms, tables and author biographies, David Alcorn

Copyright © Translation of chapters 13, 16, 22, 23, 28, 29, 31, 32, 33, 34, 36, 37, 38, 39, Sophie Leighton

Copyright © Translation of chapters 1, 2, 9, 10, 11, 14, 20, 21, 26, Andrew Weller

This book is supported by the French Ministry of Foreign Affairs, as part of the Burgess programme run by the Cultural Department of the French Embassy in London. (www.frenchbooknews.com)

Translated with the assistance of the French Ministry of Culture – National Book Centre [Ouvrage publié avec le concours du Ministère français chargé de la culture – Centre national du livre]

Typeset in Bembo and Helvetica by RefineCatch Limited, Bungay, Suffolk
Printed and bound in Great Britain by
TJ International Ltd, Padstow, Cornwall
Paperback cover design by Sandra Heath
Paperback cover photograph: © AFP/Getty Images

All rights reserved. No part of this book may be reprinted or reproduced or utilised in any form or by any electronic, mechanical, or other means, now known or hereafter invented, including photocopying and recording, or in any information storage or retrieval system, without permission in writing from the publishers.

This publication has been produced with paper manufactured to strict environmental standards and with pulp derived from sustainable forests.

British Library Cataloguing in Publication Data
A catalogue record for this book is available from the British Library

Library of Congress Cataloging-in-Publication Data
Reading French psychoanalysis / edited by Dana Birksted-Breen, Sara Flanders and Alain Gibeault ; translated by David Alcorn, Sophie Leighton, and Andrew Weller.
p. cm.
Translated from the French.
Includes bibliographical references and index.
1. Psychoanalysis – France – History.   2. Lacan, Jacques, 1901–1981.   3. Freud, Sigmund, 1856–1939.   I. Breen, Dana.   II. Flanders, Sara, 1944–.   III. Gibeault, Alain, 1942–
BF175.R37 2009
150.19'50944 – dc22
2009011663

ISBN: 978-0-415-48502-9 (hbk)
ISBN: 978-0-415-48503-6 (pbk)

CONTENTS

Acknowledgements	xv
Note on the paperback cover image	xix
Filiations in French psychoanalysis	xx
1926–2009: The development of psychoanalytic societies in France	xxi

General Introduction　　1
Dana Birksted-Breen and Sara Flanders

Section I
History of psychoanalysis in France　　53

Introduction　　54
Alain Gibeault

1　Some distinctive features of the history of psychoanalysis in France (2004)　　60
Alain de Mijolla

2　What has become of the lines of advance in psychoanalysis? The evolution of practices in France (2001)　　73
Daniel Widlöcher

Section II
The pioneers and their legacy　　87

Introduction　　88
Alain Gibeault

3　The mirror stage as formative of the function of the I as revealed in psychoanalytic experience (1949)　　97
Jacques Lacan

4　The non-verbal relationship in psycho-analytic treatment (1957)　　105
Sacha Nacht

5	Technical variation and the concept of distance (1958) *Maurice Bouvet*	115

SECTION III
The setting and the process of psychoanalysis — 135

	Introduction *Alain Gibeault*	136
6	From the fundamental rule to the analysing situation (2001) *Jean-Luc Donnet*	155
7	Preliminary remarks on the present state of psychoanalysis of children (1972) *René Diatkine*	173
8	Narcissistic aspects of the analytic situation (1977) *Bela Grunberger*	190
9	The uncanny, or 'I am not who you think I am' (2009) *Michel de M'Uzan*	201
10	The role of the countertransference (1982) *Serge Viderman*	210
11	Countertransference and psychoanalytic thought (1974) *Michel Neyraut*	218
12	Transference: Its provocation by the analyst (1992) *Jean Laplanche*	233
13	Speaking and renouncing (2008) *Jean-Claude Rolland*	251

Section IV
Phantasy and representation — 267

	Introduction *Alain Gibeault*	268
14	Object relationships in children (1961) *S. Lebovici*	286
15	Fantasy and the origins of sexuality (1964) *Jean Laplanche and J.-B. Pontalis*	310

16 The prelude to fantasmatic life (1971)   338
    Michel Fain

17 The work of the negative (1986). Negative hallucination (1993)   355
    André Green

18 Working as a double (1995)   367
    César Botella and Sára Botella

19 The illness of mourning and the fantasy of the exquisite corpse
    (1968)   388
    Maria Torok

20 Listening to the telescoping of generations: The psychoanalytic
    pertinence of the concept (1988)   405
    Haydée Faimberg

21 'Speech in psychoanalysis': From symbols to the flesh and back
    (2007)   421
    Julia Kristeva

Section V
The body and the drives   435

   Introduction   436
   Alain Gibeault

22 Operational thinking (1963)   449
    Pierre Marty and Michel de M'Uzan

23 Essential depression (1968)   459
    Pierre Marty

24 Psychosomatic solution or somatic outcome: The man from
    Burma – *psychotherapy of a case of haemorrhagic rectocolitis* (1993)   463
    Marilia Aisenstein

25 Functions of the skin ego (1985)   477
    Didier Anzieu

26 The death drive: Meaning, objections, substitutes (2007)   496
    André Green

27 (Erotogenic) Masochism and the pleasure principle (1982)   516
    Benno Rosenberg

28 Sexualisation and desexualisation in psychoanalysis (2004) *René Roussillon*	528
29 The Croatian cravat: The narcissism of small differences and the process of civilisation (1993) *Gilbert Diatkine*	543

Section VI
Masculine and feminine sexuality — 553

Introduction *Alain Gibeault*	554
30 Feminine guilt and the Oedipus complex (1964) *Janine Chasseguet-Smirgel*	563
31 Poor men – or why men are afraid of women (1998) *Jean Cournut*	601
32 The feminine and femininity (1998) *Monique Cournut-Janin*	623
33 Primary homosexuality: A foundation of contradictions (1982) *Paul Denis*	641
34 The beautiful differences (1973) *Christian David*	649
35 Plea for a measure of abnormality (1978) *Joyce McDougall*	668

Section VII
Psychosis — 683

Introduction *Alain Gibeault*	684
36 The shield of Perseus or psychosis and reality (1971) *Francis Pasche*	694
37 The fetishistic object relationship: Some observations (1978) *Evelyne Kestemberg*	706
38 Suffering and surviving in paradoxes (1991) *Paul-Claude Racamier*	724

39 Retreat into hallucination: An equivalent of the autistic retreat? (1985) 738
Piera Aulagnier

40 Schizophrenia and soul murder: Psychoanalytic psychodrama with 'John', the man 'saddled with that/the id' (2008) 752
Alain Gibeault

Glossary 765
Index 791

ACKNOWLEDGEMENTS

We are grateful to all those who have, over the years, been part of a Franco-British dialogue. This book has been germinating somewhere over those years.

A special thanks to the three translators – David Alcorn, Sophie Leighton and Andrew Weller – who have translated most of the material in this book and have been part of some discussions and difficult decisions about the translation of certain concepts. Evelyne Séchaud, John Churcher and Alessandra Lemma read earlier drafts of the introductions, and we thank them for their comments.

Eric King was of great assistance with his careful copy-editing of the manuscript, and we are very grateful to him for his patience and thoroughness.

We would like to thank the following for their kind permission to reproduce copyright material:

Cathy Miller Foreign Rights Agency for permission to reproduce Appendix 2 of *Travail du negatif* (1993/1999) by André Green.

Agence Eliane Benisti for permission to reproduce 'La culpabilité féminine' (1964) by Janine Chasseguet-Smirgel.

Dunod for permission to reproduce 'A l'écoute du télescopage des générations: pertinence psychanalytique du concept' (1988) by Haydée Faimberg and *Le moi-peau* (1985) by Didier Anzieu.

Éditions l'Esprit du Temps for permission to reproduce 'Que sont devenues les voies de la psychanalyse? L'évolution des pratiques en France' (2001) by Daniel Widlöcher, in A. de Mijolla (Ed.), *Évolution de la clinique psychanalytique* (pp. 41–57), © L'Esprit du Temps 2001.

Gallimard for permission to reproduce 'Le rôle du contre-transfert' by Serge Viderman, © Editions Gallimard, Paris, 1982.

The International Psychoanalytical Association for permission to reproduce 'Quelques particularités de l'histoire de la psychanalyse en France' (2004) by Alain de Mijolla, in A. Gibeault & A. Rossokhin (Eds.), *Anthologie de la psychanalyse contemporaine, école psychanalytique française: théorie, méthode et pratique* (in Russian).

International Universities Press, Inc. for permission to reproduce 'Plea for a Measure of Abnormality' (1980) by Joyce McDougall, © by IUP.

Presses Universitaires de France for permission to reproduce: 'Narcissistic Aspects of the Analytic Situation' (1977) by Bela Grunberger; 'L'inquiétante étrangeté ou "Je ne suis pas celle que vous croyez"' (2009) by Michel de M'Uzan; 'Le contre-transfert et la pensée psychanalytique' (1974) by Michel Neyraut; 'Parler renoncer' (2008) by Jean-Claude Rolland; 'La relation objectale chez l'enfant' (1961) by Serge Lebovici; 'Prélude à la vie fantasmatique' (1971) by Michel Fain; 'Parler en psychanalyse' (2007) by Julia Kristeva; 'La pensée operatoire' (1978) by Pierre Marty and Michel de M'Uzan; 'La dépression essentielle' (1968) by Pierre Marty; 'Masochisme mortifere et masochisme gardien de la vie' (1991) by Benno Rosenberg, translated by Ann Levy; 'La cravate croate: narcissisme des petites différences et processus de civilisation' (1993) by Gilbert Diatkine; 'Le pauvre homme ou pourquoi les hommes ont peur des femmes' (1998) by Jean Cournut; 'La boite à secret et sous couvert de féminité' (1988) by Monique Cournut-Janin; 'Homosexualite primaire, base de contradiction' (1982) by Paul Denis; 'Le bouclier de Persée ou psychose et réalité' (1971) by Francis Pasche; 'La relation fétichique à l'objet' (1978) by Evelyne Kestemberg; 'Souffrir et survivre dans les paradoxes, la douleur et la souffrance psychiques' (1991) by Paul-Claude Recamier.

Taylor & Francis Books UK for permission to reproduce: 'The Mirror Stage as Formative of the Function of the I' (1949) from *Ecrits: A Selection by Jacques Lacan*, copyright © 2001 by Routledge; and 'Working as a Double' (2004) by César Botella and Sára Botella, in C. Botella and S. Botella, *Work of Psychic Figurability*, © 2004 by Routledge; 'Transference: Its Provocation by the Analyst' (1992) by Jean Laplanche, in J. Laplanche, *Essays on Otherness*, translated by Luke Thurston, © 1992 by Routledge.

University of Chicago Press for permission to reproduce: 'The Illness of Mourning and the Fantasy of the Exquisite Corpse' by Maria Torok, Chapter 4 in *The Shell and the Kernel – Renewals of Psychoanalysis, Vol. 1*, ed. Nicolas Abraham and Maria Torok, edited and translated and with an introduction by Nicholas Rand. University of Chicago Press, Chicago and London, 1994.

Wiley-Blackwell for permission to reproduce (all from *International Journal of Psychoanalysis*): 'The Non-Verbal Relationship in Psycho-Analytic Treatment' (1957) by Sacha Nacht; 'Technical Variation and the Concept of Distance' (1958) by Maurice Bouvet; 'From the Fundamental Rule to the Analysing Situation' (2001) by Jean-Luc Donnet; 'Preliminary Remarks on the Present State of Psychoanalysis of Children' (1972) by René Diatkine; 'Fantasy and the Origins of Sexuality' (1964) by Jean Laplanche and Jean-

Bertrand Pontalis; 'Psychosomatic Solution or Somatic Outcome: The Man from Burma – Psychotherapy of a Case of Haemorrhagic Rectocolitis' (1993) by Marilia Aisenstein.

W. W. Norton & Company for permission to reproduce 'The Mirror Stage as Formative of the Function of the I' (1949) from *Ecrits: A Selection by Jacques Lacan*, translated by Alan Sheridan, copyright © 1966 by Editions du Seuil. English translation copyright © 1977 by Tavistock Publications. Used by permission of W. W. Norton & Company, Inc.

We would also like to thank Dr Denys Ribas, Editor of the *Revue Française de Psychanalyse*, who has given us permission to reproduce many papers from the journal, and Mrs Marion Colas of the PUF, who has helped us a great deal with the issue of copyright and the request for a grant from the Centre National du Livre.

NOTE ON THE PAPERBACK COVER IMAGE

Marie Bonaparte and Sigmund Freud

In this photograph, taken on 5 June 1938 at the Paris Gare de l'Est, we see Princess Marie Bonaparte welcoming Sigmund Freud, as he emigrated from Vienna to London. That image is symbolic of the birth of psychoanalysis in France, because Marie Bonaparte, the only daughter of Napoleon's great-nephew, Prince Roland Bonaparte, and herself Princess of Greece and Denmark, began her analysis with Freud in 1925 and was instrumental in the founding in 1926 of the Paris Psychoanalytical Society and, a year later, of the *Revue Française de Psychanalyse*. Herself a 'lay analyst', she was a faithful representative of Freudian psychoanalysis in France, and Freud's spokeswoman in the task of ensuring the development of a form of psychoanalysis that would follow the principles laid down by its inventor: the necessity of a training analysis, a non-academic charter that would accept the practice of psychoanalysis by non-medical practitioners, affiliation to the International Psychoanalytical Association. Her published work, especially on Edgar Allan Poe and on female sexuality, as well as her translation into French of many of Freud's writings, enabled psychoanalysis to become more widely known in France. In 1938, thanks to her financial support and her own personal involvement, she made it possible for Freud and his immediate family to leave Nazi Austria after the *Anschluss* and settle in London. Her generosity was a significant factor also in setting up in 1954 the library and premises of the Paris Institute of Psychoanalysis.

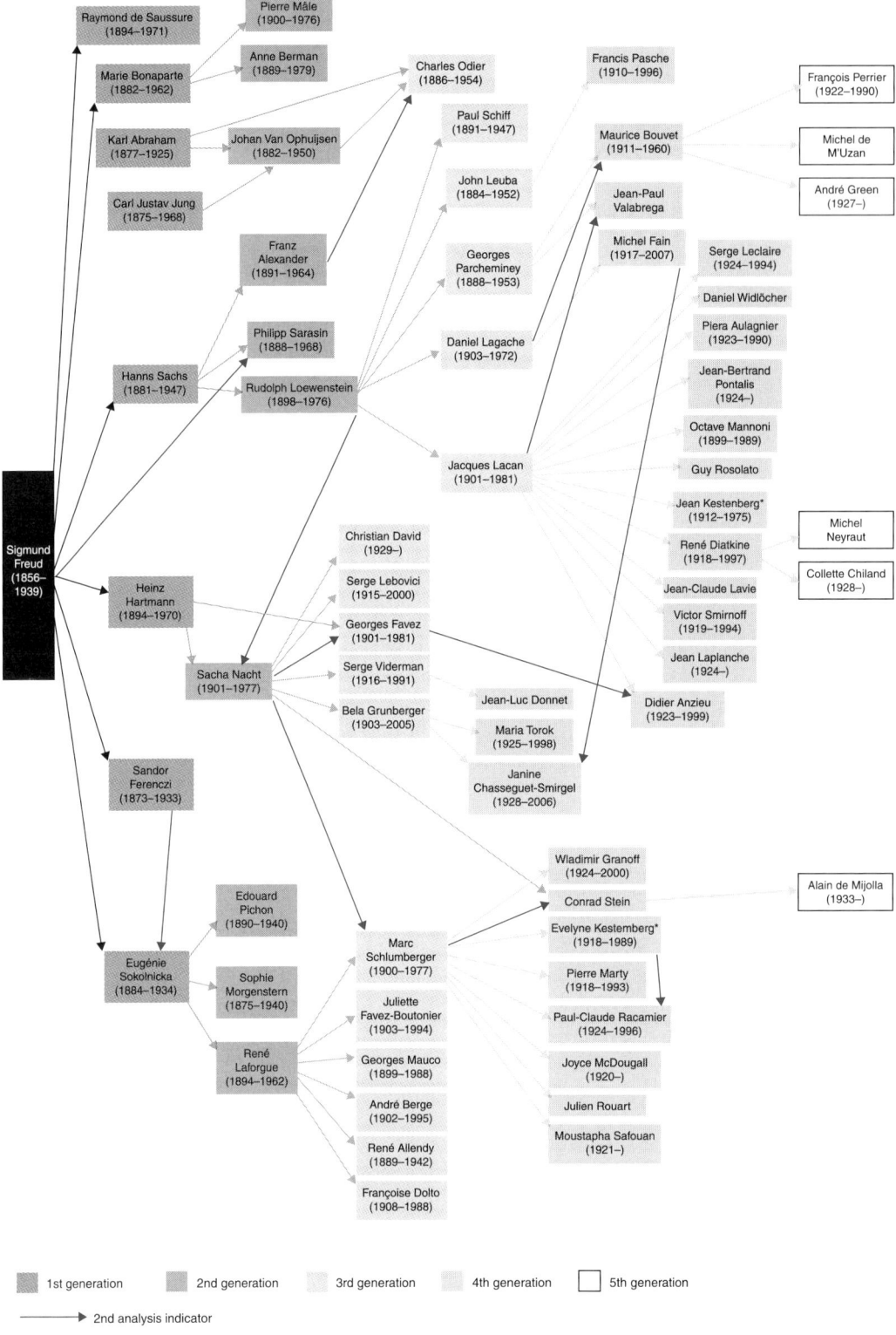

1926–2009: The Development of Psychoanalytic Societies in France

The Paris Psychoanalytical Society [SPP – *Société psychanalytique de Paris*], which was the very first psychoanalytical society in France, was founded in 1926 and is still in existence. In 1953, however, after some disagreement among its members as regards training procedures for future analysts, a dissident group (including Jacques Lacan) set up their own association, the French Psychoanalytic Society [SFP – *Société française de psychanalyse*]. That association was disbanded in 1964. Some of its former members then founded the French Psychoanalytical Association [APF – *Association psychanalytique de France*], which is still in existence, while Lacan set up the Freudian School of Paris [EFP – *École freudienne de Paris*]. In 1980, that association split into several Lacanian societies which have continued to break up, regroup, combine with or oppose one another for the same reason: the issue of how psychoanalysts should be trained.

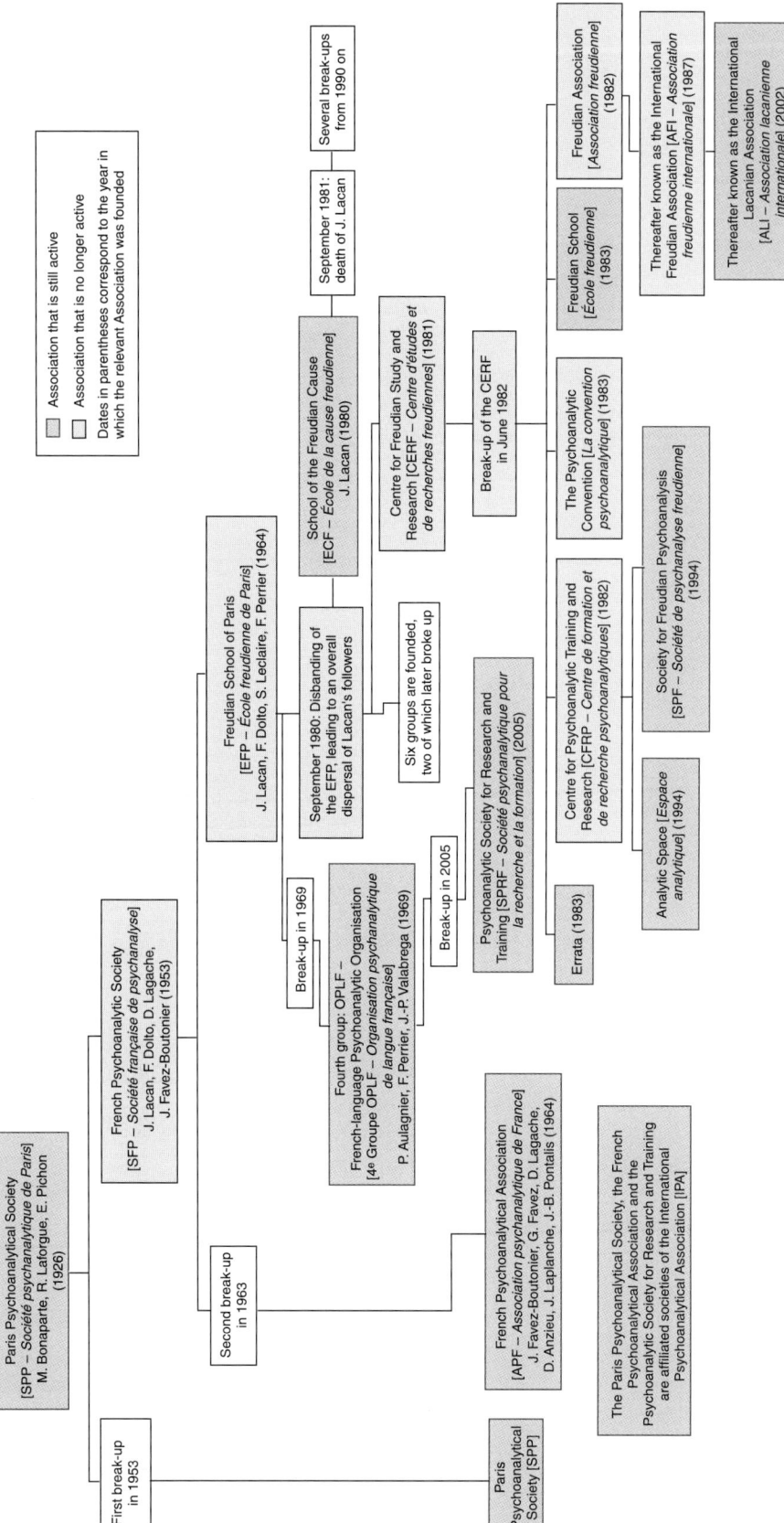

This diagram can be viewed online at www.routledgementalhealth.com/reading-french-psychoanalysis-9780415485036

GENERAL INTRODUCTION

Dana Birksted-Breen and Sara Flanders

While psychoanalysts all over the world recognise their Freudian origins, it is undeniable that psychoanalysis has developed along different lines of interest in different geographical areas due to cultural phenomena and to the influence of important or charismatic figures. It can be argued that this even overrides to some extent the different 'schools' in that a French Kleinian or a French Winnicottian will sound very different from his or her British counterpart.

We will not be representing in this book all groups who call themselves psychoanalysts in France. A project that included all the splinter groups and the Lacanian school is beyond the scope of this book, which is meant as an introduction to the work of colleagues from the two Societies that belong to the International Psychoanalytical Association (IPA): the Paris Psychoanalytical Society (SPP: Société psychanalytique de Paris) and the French Psychoanalytical Association (APF: Association psychanalytique de France).[1,2] An exception is the paper written by Piera Aulagnier (chapter 39), who belonged to the 'Quatrième groupe', which is now the closest to the other two groups.[3] In fact, the Quatrième groupe has itself divided recently (2006), over the issue of training, one section asking to join the IPA; this section is called the Psycho-analytic Society for Research and Training (SPRF: Société psychanalytique pour la recherche et la formation) and is now an IPA Study Group and should become in the near future a third French IPA component Society. Here, as when Lacan split from the original SPP in 1953, and when again, in 1964, his own SFP (Société française de psychanalyse) split in two, and the APF was formed, the issue has centred on training and membership in the

---

[1] The SPP is by far the larger of the two societies, with about ten times more members.
[2] It should be remembered that there are also some dialogues between analysts from the Lacanian schools and IPA analysts both in France and elsewhere, but these are on a much smaller scale, more to do with individual interests.
[3] Nathalie Zaltzman left the Freudian School of Paris (EFP: École freudienne de Paris) in a disagreement over training and founded the Quatrième groupe with Piera Aulagnier, Jean-Paul Valabrega and François Perrier.

IPA.[4] It should be noted, however, that while no contribution to this collection has been written by a member of a Lacanian psychoanalytic school, a number of the contributors are psychoanalysts who either originally trained with Lacan as their analyst or belonged to the society that split off from the Paris Psychoanalytical Society between 1953 and 1963 along with him, or who participated in his famous seminars in the 1960s, the best known of whom in the English-speaking world is André Green. The wish to foster dialogue between the Societies of the IPA justifies our approach, but our readers should be aware that there are other important writers who have broken from Lacan but do not belong to the IPA. For instance, in 1974 René Major opened a dialogue, forming a group, Confrontation, which refuses to recognise any institutional allegiance and out of which a journal, *Confrontation*, was born.[5,6]

In France, the close ties between psychology and philosophy, the piecemeal and slow translation of Freud, and the role of Lacan have all coloured the development of the field, while in Britain, the separation of psychology and philosophy, the trust and reliance on empiricism and clinical evidence, and the influence of Klein have left their mark.

In recent years there has been an increasing cross-fertilisation, both theoretically and clinically, but those differences between France and Britain are still apparent. It is always easier to see the characteristics from outside rather than inside a culture and to see where explanations are required; therefore, the two editors of this collection who come from the British Psychoanalytical Society have written this General Introduction from the point of view of outsiders who have also had to work at understanding French theory. The third editor, who belongs to the Société psychanalytique de Paris, has a more thorough knowledge of the texts and will therefore introduce the different sections. All three editors were involved in structuring the book and selecting the texts. This selection is inevitably not as exhaustive as we would have wished, due to practical constraints, and some well-known authors have unfortunately had to be left out. We hope, however, to be presenting a sufficient number of important papers to give the reader a panorama which they can be motivated to go on exploring.

As the two outsiders to the French tradition, we have come to think that the single most important influence marking the unique development of French psychoanalysis has been Lacan's original and revolutionary intrusion into the psychoanalytic culture, bringing also with him a philosophical tradition. His

---

[4] For Lacan a person simply had to declare themselves ready to be a psychoanalyst and there was no assessment. '*La passe*' marked this passage.
[5] A 1984 issue of *Psychoanalytic Inquiry* (Vol. 4, No. 2) records a Franco-American meeting which took place with members of Confrontation, in particular François Roustang, Michèle Montrelay, René Major and Nathalie Zaltzman, none of whom belong to the two IPA Societies.
[6] The journal *Confrontation* has closed down.

direct influence appears to have been underplayed by French psychoanalysts belonging to the IPA, but we see his influence surviving in many areas of contemporary French psychoanalysis: Lacan's focus on unconscious processes, his insistence on the importance of language,[7] and the specific non-linear temporality of *après-coup* inform some of the most creative contributions in French psychoanalysis. It was Lacan who emphasised the distinction between drive and instinct, the separation of psychic from biological, it was Lacan who emphasised the ubiquity of the Other in the formation of the ego, as well as the centrality of the Oedipus complex and, in particular, the role of the father and the formative significance of castration. And it was Lacan who originally attached such great importance to reading Freud, though mainly to the early Freud, the one for whom psychoanalysis was to liberate the individual from repression, and it was his own way of reading Freud which was transmitted to French psychoanalysts. Only recently has Gilbert Diatkine (1997) admitted in a little book he has written on Lacan for the Presses Universitaires de France – and as if surprised himself – that 'We are often Lacanians without knowing it. One must read him to realise the influence he has had on us' and he quickly adds 'in order to free ourselves from it.' It is because they have been so eager to distance themselves from Lacan's practice (in particular, his not keeping to the constancy of setting), and from some aspects of his theory which accompany it, that these psychoanalysts have been slow to recognise how much they have been and still are influenced by his writings. From their 'insider' point of view, they have moved far away.

Those aspects of Lacan which were not questioned have taken root and their origin masked. Other aspects have been openly questioned. The debates which ensued are also part of Lacan's role in shaping current thinking. The questioning has often come from those who were in direct contact with his teaching, and it has produced, in antithesis, a specifically French reassertion of the significance of the body, of the primacy of affect, of the importance of the drives; it has lead to the resurrection of the *infans* (a Latin word used by French psychoanalysts to refer to the pre-verbal child) and to the pre-verbal in psychic life as well as to the importance of the setting. For instance, a kernel of two of André Green's books, *Le discours vivant* (1973, translated in 1999 as *The Fabric of Affect and Psychoanalytic Discourse*) and *On Private Madness* (1986), is a critique

---

[7] Montrelay, a member of Confrontation, writes (1984): 'One of the most distinctive aspects of current French psychoanalysis is the importance a relatively large number of practitioners attach to language. Lacan's influence can be measured in the clinical situation in this way. Not that Lacan invented a technique of words, but he emphasised the fact that Freud did. And that this had been a bit forgotten. This is why analysts of the Freudian and Lacanian schools use Freud's opinion that words are the main "tool" of psychoanalytic treatment as a point of reference. Perhaps this is as much as all these French analysts agree on. Words belong to everyone, but each person has a way of using them that is unlike any other' (p. 193). In her clinical paper she demonstrates an approach to language and, in particular, to the importance of the patient's actual names.

of the central Lacanian position which disregards affects in favour of representations (*Vorstellungen*, ideas).[8] In this, Lacan develops a theme traceable to Freud, who particularly in his early writing follows the distinct and different fates of representation and affects in psychic processes (Laplanche & Pontalis, 1967). Green, for whom there is a primary non-distinction between affect and idea, suggests that if Freud placed an emphasis in his early writings on representations rather than affect, it was because of his concern initially with demonstrability and scientific status and a wish to keep psychoanalysis separated from hypnosis and catharsis (Green, 1993). He also points out that Freud, in his later writings (those Lacan disregarded), gave an increasing place to affects.

If French psychoanalysts of the three IPA Societies (the Paris Psychoanalytical Society, the French Psychoanalytical Association and the new Psychoanalytic Society for Research and Training) have been reluctant to admit the extent of Lacan's influence, it is above all because of his manipulation of the setting with his introduction of the practice of variable-length analytic sessions ('*séances scandées*'; Lacan, 1973). Even this can be said to have had a repercussion in the frequent references to *le cadre* (the setting, in its reference to the fixed length of the sessions – in France, 45 minutes), something which is taken more for granted on our side of the channel.[9]

In our account, seen from a British and a historical perspective, we will be coming back quite frequently to Lacan in order to make sense of the current positions. However, we want to stress that Lacan comes up infrequently in modern French psychoanalytic papers and discourse, and mention of him has been frowned upon by many of our French colleagues who have been eager to dissociate themselves from his practice and have rejected the underpinning of his theory with structural linguistics. Up until the 1990s, there was a total

---

[8] Representation and the absence of representation are central issues for French psychoanalysts, but it is important to note that they make a distinction between two words used by Freud: *Vorstellung*, which is to do with an idea about something, and *Darstellung*, which is to do with the image of something.

In Laplanche and Pontalis (1967/1973, p. 200), *Vorstellung* is given as the German translation of 'Idea (or Presentation or Representation)'. According to Mark Solms (personal communication), 'Strachey translated *Vorstellung* with a bewildering array of English equivalents: but "idea" and, to a lesser extent, "presentation" were the most common. The latter term was used mainly in the context of *Word-*, *Ding-*, *Sach-* and *Objekt-Vorstellungen*. He almost always translated *Darstellung* by "representation".'

However, French psychoanalysts tend to use the French word '*representation*' for *Vorstellung* only, while British psychoanalysts tend to use the English word 'representation' in a more generic way, for both idea and image – *Vorstellung* and *Darstellung*. For *Darstellung*, the French use the word '*figuration*'. It is in particular in speaking about the dream and the considerations of representability [*Rücksicht auf Darstellbarkeit*] that they use the term '*figurabilité*'.

It is probably in order not to risk a confusion that, in his section introductions, Alain Gibeault sometimes uses 'ideation' to translate the French '*representation*' when meaning *Vorstellung*.

See also Alain Gibeault's introduction to section IV.

[9] Although the variable lengths of psychoanalytic sessions is rejected, a reflection on the setting is one which leads to a consideration of different treatment settings as appropriate for different types of mental functioning. Bouvet's work on the distance to the object is important in this respect (see chapter 5).

rejection of Lacan in the SPP, apart from a few people like André Green, who kept the relevance of his ideas alive. The APF had a more uncomfortable and ambivalent relationship to Lacan as their forefather.

In recent years we have noticed a greater and more positive citation of his work, as if, with time, it has become possible to give him a more balanced place and overcome the 'trauma' of the role he played personally, theoretically and institutionally in French psychoanalysis.

We also want to stress the many developments which have taken place since Lacan's early influence, and this includes British and American contributions as well as those of other IPA societies around the world. Nevertheless, the more philosophical and theoretical level of discussion, always with Freud in counterpoint, gives these new developments – even when they come closer to British developments – a typically French flavour.

French–British reciprocal influences

British psychoanalysis has been of interest to French analysts at least since the post-war development of psychoanalysis in France. In Lacan's 'The Topic of the Imaginary'[10] (1954b), one of the seminars given as part of the training at the SPP in 1953 (the same year Lacan and his group left the society) he utilises Melanie Klein's 1930 paper, 'The Importance of Symbol Formation in the Development of the Ego', to illustrate his theory of the significance of language in what he calls the constitution of the subject. Insofar as this seminar follows one entitled 'Discourse Analysis and Ego Analysis: Anna Freud or Melanie Klein' (1954a), he is framing his seminar as an entry into the controversy which dominated psychoanalysis in England during and after the Second World War. But Lacan is using that controversy to further his own argument with ego psychology, as he perceived it developing in France. He clearly aligns himself with Melanie Klein's radicalism, her originality, and her genius and criticises Anna Freud for what he regards as the fundamentally mistaken focus of ego psychology on the affects and defences of the patient within the transference relationship to the analyst. Lacan is interested in locating the fundamental structure of the patient's unconscious, and in his view the ego is not an ally in this research.

Lacan compares Anna Freud's caution and her sensitive attunement to her six-year-old neurotic patient with Melanie Klein's more radical approach to a very disturbed child patient who offers no apparent connection with her or to language, to toys or to his nurse. With appreciative gusto Lacan describes a Melanie Klein, whose 'animal instinct' (1954b, p. 69) allows her 'to bore

---

[10] The translation of '*topique*' by 'topic' makes reference to a philosophical language since Greek antiquity in which the term 'topography' means a theory of 'places' (Greek: τόπος), and it is consistent with how this has been translated in Aristotle's work, for instance. Topic is thus a spatial notion (topography) rather than a subject matter.

through a body of knowledge which was up to then impenetrable', and, facing the void of the child's development, she does not, he says, interpret, 'she just tells him *Dick little train, big train daddy train*' and thereupon the child starts to play. In response to her naming of the trains, he speaks, 'the word *station.* . . . Melanie Klein plays this back to him, *the station is mummy, Dick is going into mummy.* . . . From this point on, everything starts firing' (1954b, p. 85). It is Melanie Klein's articulation – in which, Lacan writes, she 'plastered on the symbolisation of the Oedipus myth' – that reaches into the heart of the child's disorganisation and confusion, providing him with the structure missing in his development. In response to her verbalisation, characterised as brutal, Dick 'calls' for his nurse, who had previously been ignored, and so he enters into speech, into symbolic functioning and into an acknowledgement of dependence. In Lacan's words, at that moment Dick has become a subject, a speaking subject, a human subject. Indeed, for Lacan, it is language, identified with the naming of the father by the mother, which is formative of the subject. According to his reading, Melanie Klein has introduced her patient to language, a place in the Oedipal structure, and a place in the world of relationship and difference. Her direct, brutal speech has rescued him from the chaos of his omnipotence, his denial of attachment, meaning, desire, loss. Even if Lacan viewed Klein's imposition of meaning on the toys as brutal, not a true interpretation, he favourably contrasts her effort to establish a 'discourse analysis' which helps bring her patient into a world structured and humanised by language and simultaneously into the Oedipal structure (something always imposed from the outside), with Anna Freud's prioritising of an analysis of defence and a focus on affect within the transference situation.

In his comparison of Melanie Klein with Anna Freud, he uses an example from *The Ego and the Mechanisms of Defence* (1936), in which Anna Freud puzzles over her six-year-old patient's contemptuous relationship to her own feelings whenever Anna Freud brings them to her attention. Anna Freud, like many analysts today, assumes a transference meaning to this behaviour. Eventually she understands it as the patient's resistant identification with an idealised dead father who used to encourage her not to dwell on unhappiness – a father with whom, we might now say, ironically, following Melanie Klein, her young patient was in projective identification. Lacan portrays Anna Freud's understanding of this identification – which she starts out as seeing as a defence against painful affect, eventually finding it a defence against mourning the death of her father – as too narrow and missing the point. He believes that she eventually highlights something which has a deeper meaning, that of the fundamental structuring of the ego through the identification with the father, an essential concern of the analytic process. He asserts that Anna Freud's preoccupation with affect and defence is 'too intellectualist', and this leads her, in his view, into putting forward a conception of an analysis which must be conducted from a 'median, moderate position, which would be that of the ego'. For her, he states, everything starts with the education or the persuasion of the ego, and everything must come back to that. Ironically, again, he has chosen to illustrate this educationalist approach with Anna Freud's quite rigorous analytic work, in which symptomatic behaviour is first interpreted in the transference and then understood as a problem in mourning. The analytic work is not 'educationalist', as was Anna Freud's first approach to child psychoanalysis (1926), and it does not strike one as dated. For Lacan, however, such sensitivity to the patient's ego, and to the patient's affective state, appeases the agency which has constructed the symptom in the first place. His admiration and his bid for allegiance rests with Klein, whose inspired interpretative bravery he perhaps associated with his own personal flamboyance; he called her, it has been said, *'une tripière de génie'*.[11] Her genius, in his view, is that she does not reason with her cut-off little patient, she does not pander to his ego, she cuts through his defences and introduces him to the structuring power of language, just as an interpretation ought to do, according to Lacan, in any analytic process. There is no doubt of the brilliant results of Melanie Klein's radical experimental intervention on her very much more disturbed child patient. And there is nothing naïve in the theory regarding symbolic acquisition which developed out of her work with Dick.

Through Klein, Lacan lay down the gauntlet to the French psychoanalytic establishment and to ego psychology, represented in particular by his own analyst, Rudolph Loewenstein, who emigrated to the United States where he followed a distinguished career, joining with Heinz Hartmann and Ernst Kris to form a solid foundation for the ego psychology which thrived there. There remained, of course, classical, even ego psychologists in France, among them Sacha Nacht, Lacan's psychoanalytic sibling.

Like Klein in Britain, Lacan regarded himself as the true inheritor of Freud's project, and, like Klein, he inserted a message into the understanding of the mind and mental functioning and the project of psychoanalysis which would have a continuing direct and indirect impact on the development of theory and practice in France, as it would for Klein in Britain. French psychoanalysis is unique because the dialectic of its growth and development is specific to the entry of Lacan onto the scene.

Klein herself was not destined to have a direct influence on the development of French psychoanalysis. In spite of Lacan's contempt, the ego psychology that he used her to attack would continue to have a creative place in the clinical life of the SPP, from which he separated in 1953, the year of the Seminar just quoted.[12] Klein will re-enter the French discourse indirectly via

---

[11] This is a reference to the fact that Melanie Klein explored the unconscious archaic fantasies of the child, concerning the womb, with its viscera [*les tripes*], its excrements and its imaginary monsters. It may be an oral legendary saying, because everybody has heard this but no one is able to point to an actual reference.

[12] Nevertheless, it should be noted that she was known in France. In the early 1950s the French philosophers Maurice Merleau-Ponty and Daniel Lagache were the first to speak of Klein's works in the university, while the child psychoanalysts Serge Lebovici and René Diatkine showed the importance of her findings in the psychoanalytic treatment of children.

D. W. Winnicott, who became an important influence on many of the analysts who were students of Lacan in the 1960s (Pontalis, 2005). Winnicott learned from Klein, and he certainly grasped from her the significance of children's play as well as the violence of infantile emotional life. But unlike Klein he was very taken up with the impact of the (m)other and the interpersonal context through which the baby enters into life ('the facilitating environment'). Lacan was not interested in the baby or the interpersonal. His emphasis was on the moment of acquisition of language, the acquisition of the given, the inheritance of an order from without, 'the symbolic' – a specific reference to the sign system of language and not to symbolisation based on imagery. Winnicott, on the other hand, was interested in the acquisition of the capacity to play, a capacity which predates and accompanies the development of language and develops out of a relation to the mother. Winnicott gave priority to the mother–child relationship, the therapeutic relationship, the importance of affects, as well as creativity (Gibeault, 2005). The first two of these qualities had been the concern of the ego psychologists – those who would call Anna Freud the 'plumb line' of psychoanalysis – and of those struggling to fathom the implications of the object relations which can be found in the later Freud, in, for instance, 'Mourning and Melancholia' (1917e [1915]), 'On Narcissism' (1914c), or *The Ego and the Id* (1923b). The inclusion of Nacht (chapter 4) and Bouvet (chapter 5) in this volume balances the picture of clinical psychoanalysis in France during the years of Lacan's celebrity, bringing in the role of affect and of the relationship to the object, which Lacan had excluded.

British psychoanalysts have been slower in showing an interest in French psychoanalysis than their French counterparts have been with them. French psychoanalysis was thought for a long time to be synonymous with Lacan, and Lacan's very elusive writing, and the clinical scandal of his shortened sessions which drove his expulsion from the IPA, combined to turn British analysts away from reading Lacan. His appeal was primarily to academic circles to which practising British psychoanalysts did not usually belong (such a split between academia and psychoanalytic Institute is not present in France). It is primarily, though not entirely, after the introduction and assimilation of Winnicott by some French analysts, notably André Green, and the latter's active interest in a dialogue with British analysts and publication in the English language that they have been more able to take an interest in the French contribution. André Green is probably the most widely read of French psychoanalysts in the English-speaking world, though Laplanche and Pontalis, through their dictionary, *The Language of Psychoanalysis*, are the most relied on. But it is still a problematic affair. In his introduction to André Green's recent book, *The Work of the Negative* (1993/1999), Otto Kernberg advises the English-speaking reader to skip the chapter on Freud and Hegel and return to it later, fortified by an encounter with the less philosophically challenging chapters. Green's use of Hegel links current French psychoanalytic thinking to the same conceptual sources utilised by Lacan, particularly in his earlier, more accessible stages.

The importance of Hegel to Lacan's conceptualisation of subjectivity derives from the famous Kojève lectures on Hegel in 1933–34 which were attended by Lacan, as well as by Lévi-Strauss and other luminous and subsequently influential French intellectuals (Roudinesco, 1990). The emphasis on a de-centred subject, defined in a relation to the Other; the alienation of the subject in the Other, as described in the master–slave relationship; the definition of human desire as desire of the Other's desire; the role of the negative in a dialectical evolution of a subject – these are some of the themes drawn from Hegelian philosophy. This influence is particularly evident in the earlier work of Lacan, the thinking of his seminal paper, 'Le stade du miroir' (1949 – see chapter 3, this volume), and is still profoundly resonating in the later work of André Green. It is true to say that beyond and before Lacan, Hegel had a profound influence on French thinking which might have made itself felt even if Lacan had not been there, as philosophy is an important part of French culture. Laplanche and Pontalis, for instance, both analysands of Lacan, are philosophers as well as psychoanalysts. Pontalis (2005) recognises his debt in particular to Merleau-Ponty. One of the difficulties for British psychoanalysts in understanding French psychoanalytic writings is that these often assume a knowledge of philosophy, particularly continental traditions.

The historical situation in France

As both de Mijolla (chapter 1) and Widlöcher (chapter 2) explain in their papers, the Lacanian revolution did not take place in a vacuum, but in the depleted, institutionally fragile if personally ambitious psychoanalytic culture of post-war France.[13]

Narcissistically 'wounded' by a devastating war, France watched the exodus of many psychoanalysts from Europe, the vast majority of whom went to a newly powerful, newly dominant America, a country which came out of the Second World War with its landscape intact, its people relatively unscathed, and its industry robust, vastly improved by the war effort. Its population welcomed a psychoanalysis tailored not to disturb its sleep, but to promote the 'pursuit of happiness' as opposed to the acceptance of 'ordinary unhappiness', which was one Freudian definition of cure. Here Hartmann, appointed emissary of Freud,

---

[13] Roudinesco notes that 'Perhaps in France, for reason of the historical and political circumstances surrounding the cultural implantation of Freudianism, only a non-Jew – an atheist, but culturally a Catholic – could occupy the place of a founder analogous to Freud's in the first Viennese Society' (1990, p. 123). Lacan's charismatic, messianic appeal was apparently enormous. Freud's own writings were difficult to access, as few of the texts had been translated. 'In his seminars and in his writings Lacan constantly sought to create the impression of scholarly familiarity with the German text. The sacred terminology of Freud was thus used to authenticate Lacan's own idiosyncratic psychology' (Webster, 2002, p. 15).

popularised what became known as ego psychology, which emphasised the later Freud, 'the structural model of the mind'.[14]

In the face of an increasingly complex picture of human dependency, identity, sexuality and aggression, which is one way of reading the later Freud, Hartmann posited a more 'adaptive' ego capable of 'conflict-free' functioning and a psychoanalysis which could be helpful, positive (Jacoby, 1986). Lacan's contemptuous caricature of American ego psychology presents it as a comic and humiliated European servant compliantly assisting the strengthening of the ego rather than interrogating and exposing its 'misrecognitions' (Roudinesco, 1990). Of course, there were in France a substantial number of classical analysts who would carry the tradition of ego psychology into the post-war psychoanalytic scene, and in this volume, the paper by Nacht (chapter 4) – analysand of Loewenstein as was Lacan, but also of Hartmann – illustrates that less vocal, modest but continuous thread of psychoanalytic thinking.

The wholesome, arguably social Darwinist project of ego psychology did not fit comfortably in the surrealist avant-garde intellectual world in which Lacan moved, and which would be the context in which psychoanalysis flowered in France. It would certainly not meet the preoccupations which inspired Lacan, from his first forays into the meaning of paranoid thinking in his doctoral dissertation as a young psychiatrist, to his last obscure absorption in linguistics and mathematics. Lacan was intrigued to find meaning in the delusions and disguises in the language of his psychotic patient. For this analysis of language, he called upon the early Freud, the Freud of *The Interpretation of Dreams* (1900a) and of *The Psychopathology of Everyday Life* (1901b), the Freud who discovered the unconscious processes in jokes and slips of the tongue. Lacan's famous challenge for French psychoanalysts to 'return to Freud' meant a return to the early Freud, the Freud who uncovered the ego's problem with the truth, which nonetheless could be discovered through listening to the speech of the patient.

---

[14] It is interesting to note in passing that the term 'structural model' appears to have been first coined by Kris in 1943 and has become of such common usage in the Anglo-Saxon literature that it is often assumed that Freud himself used the term. It was never adopted in France, where the terms '*première topique*' and '*deuxième topique*' are used (which André Green's English translator has translated more faithfully as 'first topography' and 'second topography', as has also the translator of Laplanche & Pontalis's *The Language of Psychoanalysis*). While in Britain reference is mainly to the second topography (the structural model), in France it is not seen as replacing the first topography but as coexisting with it, as two different descriptive approaches with their specific uses. For this reason, some French papers can seem very foreign and difficult to understand because they use the language and theorisation of the topographic model and of the early Freud writings only. This was also the Freud that Lacan remained faithful to, ignoring later developments. The very central notion in French writings of 'representation' is understood in reference to the first topography (topographic model); 'representation' is discussed in more detail in the introduction to section IV. Many French analysts, however, also move easily between the two models and two sets of concepts. Some have recently proposed a notion of a 'third topography' to conceptualise the intersubjective approaches of Ferro, Ogden, Baranger and others (Brusset, 2006), showing the contemporary continuing French openness to other approaches. Being Freudian also means being open to development, as Green pointed out at a recent congress in Barcelona in 2007.

Hartmann's very different Freud was the Freud to which Lacan's analyst, Loewenstein, attached himself. Loewenstein left France for America during the Second World War in 1942, having analysed three of the most powerful and ambitious and soon to be dominant figures in the French analytic movement: Jacques Lacan, Sacha Nacht and Daniel Lagache. He left them to fight it out, over the next twenty years, while he became the third in the triumvirate of Hartmann, Kris and Loewenstein. In many ways, the analysts in this volume represent different syntheses of a unique French dialectic, some writers closer to Lacan, others to Nacht and to Lagache – himself a pivotal figure in establishing what would become the APF, the second IPA Society, the association of Lacan's creative but independent students, Laplanche, Pontalis, Anzieu, Widlöcher, Lavie, Granoff and Smirnoff.

In the first split in 1953, which lead to Lacan's creation of the SFP, both Lagache and Nacht played pivotal roles. Rebelling against the dominance of Nacht in the SPP, founded in 1926, Lagache, Lacan's students and Lacan himself split off from it to form the SFP. A pivotal concern then, as later in 1963, was Lacan's practice of variable length sessions. In 1964 Lagache and a group of analysts decided to separate from Lacan in order to become affiliated to the IPA, which had excluded Lacan on account of his short sessions. This forced Lacan to found his own school, the Freudian School of Paris (EFP: École freudienne de Paris), whose name suggests that it saw itself as the true inheritor of Freud. Lagache and his colleagues formed the APF, which joined the IPA. Lacan had a greater influence on the APF than on the SPP for these historical reasons. To this day differences remain between these two (oldest) IPA French Societies, the SPP and the APF. To generalise, it appears that the APF includes members who are more closely tied to the universities and an academic approach (such as Laplanche) and often have a style of writing and analytic work which is more allusive and a style of practice which is more silent. For some of these analysts, the unconscious 'speaks' through the patient's words as long as the analyst does not interfere with interpretations but instead facilitates the associative process, the deepening of associations until the patient arrives at his or her own interpretation (Rolland, 2006).

Widlöcher (chapter 2), also a member of the APF, describes some of the features of what he wisely calls the French culture rather than the theory of psychoanalysis which bear the mark of Lacan. He singles out the often observed attitude of silence on the part of French analysts, which receives numerous theoretical justifications, including those which are criticisms of what is regarded as too much interference through interpretations, too much provision of an object in some practices, essentially British. He suggests that the attitude of silence is primarily justified by a Lacanian theory of the process, which is eventually the disillusionment of the desire which disguises a lack which can never be filled; this is in contrast to an interpretation of drives and defence. Practice has intertwined with theory, migrated back and forth between Lacanians and non-Lacanians, but silence remains a feature of much, though by no means all, French psychoanalytic work. It is interesting that the quality of silence is the subject of one of Nacht's papers (presented here in chapter 4), whose concerns were very much opposed to his analytic sibling, Lacan. While Nacht understands silence as supporting the ego, which he thinks is a positive thing, for Lacan, supporting the ego amounts to supporting '*méconnaissance*', the false knowing which it is the task of the analysis to undo.

British psychoanalysts are in general less silent than their French counterparts. One British argument against silence is that it leaves the patient with too much uncontained anxiety. Reducing anxiety is infrequently the stated aim of the French psychoanalyst.

The return to Freud

French psychoanalysis is much more grounded in Freudian metapsychology and Freudian concepts than is British psychoanalysis and reflects the powerful and sustained influence of Lacan's early call for a 'return to Freud', away from what he identified as the revisionist ego psychology that had become dominant in America immediately after the war. Widlöcher (chapter 2) notes the irony that this return to Freud was also used by many to liberate themselves from Lacan. Laplanche and Pontalis, both of whom were analysed by Lacan, but who effectively separated from Lacan in the upheavals of 1963, published their *Vocabulaire de la psychanalyse* in 1967. With its publication in English in 1973 as *The Language of Psychoanalysis*, they introduced English-speaking readers to the disciplined, philosophically grounded and Lacan-inspired French reading of many Freudian conceptualisations, tracing each entry through its various, changing manifestations in the work of Freud. The Freud re-discovered by Laplanche and Pontalis is larger than the Freud to whom Lacan was drawn, as Lacan turned his back on many of the later writings which were so central to the thinking of ego psychologists. For all students of Freud everywhere, clinical and academic, *The Language of Psychoanalysis* has set a standard for Freudian study which has informed all subsequent thinking and is probably the most important single influence coming from France. As has been noted elsewhere, though Laplanche and Pontalis extended the Freud which was known and discussed in France, their work leaves out essential concepts. In their prodigious work, there is, for example, no entry on the subject of mourning nor on melancholia or depression, although there is an entry for the 'depressive position', a Kleinian concept, a concept which does seem now to be freely used by French psychoanalysts.

The grounding of Laplanche and Pontalis in rigorous argument informs their patient and careful attention to the Freudian text. This attention to the text, the search for new meanings in it and especially the painstaking attention to the evolution of ideas and concepts throughout Freud's work are specific features of French psychoanalysis. This fascination probably explains why, while there is as yet no complete standard edition of Freud in France, there are competing translations of important texts. In particular, a literary translation by Pontalis contrasts with a translation by Laplanche which claims to be more literal but has attracted criticism for creating neologisms such that the text is difficult to read and is inaccessible to the ordinary reader.

As for Lacan himself, his 'return to Freud' became more a reinvention of Freud (Turkle, 1978), for which he used linguistic structuralism as the underpinning of his approach. However, his emphasis on the importance of reading the text of Freud – if necessary, over and over – to inhabit the process of his thinking in addition to grasping the argument of his conceptualisation made a permanent mark on the French culture of psychoanalysis, as Evelyn Séchaud has pointed out.[15]

'Le stade du miroir': Lacan's narcissistic baby

In 1936, before Loewenstein left with so many European analysts for America, Lacan read to the 14th IPA Congress in Marienbad a first version of his revolutionary 'Le stade du miroir', in which he presented his conceptualisation of the ego, disclosing how far from mastery and adaptation he placed it. In his study of the barely standing, not quite walking infant seizing on its image in the mirror, he describes what he sees as a fundamental human vulnerability: a potential young subject is ensnared by an image of himself that does not correspond to his altogether more chaotic, disorganised and fragmented being in the world. The intact body in the mirror is wonderfully different and contrasting with the frequently out-of-control body of the infant and child in reality. The sharp contrast with the marvellous wholeness of the image in the mirror, so different from the body of experience, intensifies anxious images of a body fragmented in bits and pieces, the Lacanian 'fragmented body' ['*corps morcelé*'], and drives the developing subject into identification with the image in the mirror. This intact image forms a crucial element in what Lacan calls 'the imaginary' [*l'imaginaire*]. The imaginary is a product of the fundamental

---

[15] Séchaud writes: '. . . Jacques Lacan . . . urged French analysts to read Freud often in German, with a view to following as closely as possible the elaboration of his thinking, since it is very true that thinking cannot be separated from its language of origin. This reading, in which the analysts of my generation were trained, enabled us to follow Freud's approach, the birth, the occultation and resurgence of concepts which are often caught up in the unconscious thing itself – that is to say, they suffer displacements, repressions and the return of the repressed. We thus learnt to "make Freud work" [*faire travailler Freud*], as Jean Laplanche's expression and point of view, by reading and re-reading Freud in an attempt to identify with the approach that enabled its author to discover hitherto unknown phenomena whose nature is such that they still resist disclosure. There is undoubtedly a need to subject Freud's discoveries to a critical examination today in the light of contemporary scientific acquisitions, but this implies and requires a great knowledge of what is developed or outlined in the Freudian text' (Séchaud, 2008, pp. 1011–1012).

misunderstandings, the illusory 'misrecognition' [*méconnaissance*] associated with the ego. Winnicott will later be influenced by Lacan's paper when he writes about the mirror-role of the mother's face in each individual's ego development (1967). The way he develops this, however, highlights the very different perspectives. For Winnicott, what the baby sees in the mother's face is him/herself if the mother is not depressed, and this will enable the child to develop a sense of self and to feel real. The baby will know about him/herself via the mother – that is, through a relationship to her. For Lacan, however, unification is via *the image* of the self in the mirror, which is fundamentally alienating.[16]

Lacan's argument is with Freud the author of *The Ego and the Id*, of 1923, the conceptualiser of the body ego, and not simply with the ego psychologists who drew heavily on this seminal work. Lacan's *corps morcelé*, not unrelated to Melanie Klein's vision of the infant's early world of part-objects, does not develop into the bodily foundation of a strengthened ego, because it remains split between experience and image. Lacan's compelling and disturbing but also profound and challenging version of the body ego is one with which most French analysts have had to grapple in one way or another. Anzieu, an analysand of Lacan, posed an antithesis to Lacan's sceptical view of the relation between body ego and body image. Anzieu's inspired conceptualisation and elaboration of the *moi-peau* (1974, 1985), drawing on the work of the Kleinian Esther Bick (1968), of attachment theorists, as well as of many classical psychoanalysts, explores the origins of a body ego in development from the beginning of the mother–child relationship, the product of the caregiver's communicative touch. Anzieu's work, like that of many of the French writers in this collection, shows an indebtedness to the rigorous challenges of Lacan, against which his works stands in argument. Indeed, Anzieu returns to Freud, drawing, as Lacan did *not*, on the later Freud and utilising the work of Winnicott, Klein, and Bion and also, unusually, that of Esther Bick and of Bowlby, to produce a fresh synthesis and deepening psychoanalytic understanding of the conception of

---

[16] Lacan has been accused of not crediting the French psychiatrist Henri Wallon, who first wrote about the role of the mirror in the development of the sense of a unified self and the acquisition of symbolic function (Wallon, 1933). Barzilai (1995) makes the point, however, that Lacan's view is at times antithetical to that of Wallon. For Lacan the mirror may be a real one, but it may also be a metaphorical one: '. . .it is noteworthy that Lacan transforms the real mirror that Wallon posed before his experimental subjects into a metaphor for a metapsychological concept of human genesis' (p. 4), which makes Lacan's approach closer to Winnicott's views than to Wallon's. But in contradistinction to Winnicott, the mirror for Lacan has nothing to do with the mother. And Barzilai suggests further: 'To a largely secular and skeptical readership, Lacan's mirror stage presents a new myth of genesis . . . in Lacanian theory, the function of the I does not emerge as a result of any parental intervention. The birth of the ego takes place in and through the looking glass. In Lacan's view, the mirror is the mother of the ego. But the mother is not in the mirror' (p. 9).

But here again, it may be possible to trace a remnant of this fundamental role of the mirror for Lacan in the importance of primary narcissism and primary homosexuality in French psychoanalysis, and also in recent developments such as the Botellas' notion of the 'double' (1984) and the 'work as a double' (chapter 18).

the body ego. His exploration of the complex functions of the skin, the boundary of the body ego, separating inside from outside, self from other, has been very influential in France.

The Lacanian ego or self is permanently alienated from itself, like Narcissus, enchanted with an image that is far more organised than the perceiving subject at the time of its adoption. In Lacan's view, this uncomfortable split, at the heart of human personality, is the true Freudian legacy. From the British perspective, one might say that it is a view of the ego permanently moving into projective identification with its own ideal, a perspective not without value in thinking about narcissistic pathology and here shown clearly in Lacan's description of the baby. The bad news, according to Lacan, is that the human ego is always precocious, always guilty of a premature appropriation, always coloured with narcissistic compromise, fundamentally wedded to a lie. The hard-working realist of Hartmann's adaptation only appears if it is sufficiently enslaved to an ideal it calls its own. For many analysts, this view was at bottom too dark.

In many of the papers which are gathered in this collection it is possible to trace the influence of this seminal paper of Lacan's, a paper written, indeed, before the splits in the French institutions which occurred 20 and then 30 years after its first publication. Lacan's highlighting of the universal human susceptibility to a defensive narcissism, including phallic narcissism, informs the thinking of the feminists of the 1970s, among them Chasseguet-Smirgel, as well as that of the theorists of narcissism, like Bela Grunberger, with his own emphasis on the conflict between narcissistic self-image and the humiliations of the drives. At the same time, the Freudian primary non-defensive narcissism plays an important part in French psychoanalysis. In contrast to Klein and nearer to Winnicott, and to the ego psychologists, this narcissism is considered necessary and positive, and its theory was developed by Grunberger (1979) amongst others. In particular, the psychoanalytic process is considered to rest on the possibility of a narcissistic regression.

A possible legacy of this fundamental paper discussing the birth of the ego is a particular interest of French psychoanalysts in processes of 'subjectivation', and of alienation, something which is also, of course, traceable to French philosophers before Lacan. British analysts will tend to be interested in such issues as splitting of the ego, or notions of self-esteem or of masculine or feminine identity, or of false self, but they do not tend to discuss how the sense of an 'I' comes about. Inasmuch as there is concern about the development of a sense of self – or as Winnicott puts it, a 'psychosomatic unity', a feeling of 'continuity in time' – the focus is on an integrated rather than divided self.

Winnicott in France

Through the introduction of Winnicott in the 1960s and 1970s, the psychoanalysts who had been close to Lacan but who separated themselves from the Lacanians in 1963 found support for their effort to look earlier in the individual's history for the origins of the development of language and the relation to symbolisation. Winnicott's particular originality had much to do with his own integration of the insights that Melanie Klein brought to the psychoanalysts in England. Accepting many of her hypotheses about the instinctual and emotional life of infants, he promoted the exploration of the mother–child relationship, famously insisting that there is no infant without a mother. He specifically explored the development of the infant's acquisition of a capacity to symbolise within the mother–child matrix, an acquisition underpinned by an early experience of a sufficient omnipotence with only gradual disillusionment. Winnicott did not emphasise an induction into language, the '*Nom du Père*', the law of the father, the rescue from the imaginary fantasy world, as in Lacan's conceptualisation. Winnicott emphasised a slow evolution, beginning with maternal primary preoccupation, the support of an illusion of omnipotence, only a gradual surrender of the omnipotence, the crucial establishment of an intermediate area of experience – a space for play, creativity, symbolic activity – through attachment to 'transitional objects'. Pontalis, a former student and colleague of Merleau-Ponty and an analysand and student of Lacan – whom he still characterises as a great awakener, 'awaking us up from the dogmatic sleep into which psychoanalysis risked lapsing' – describes the relish which accompanied his encounter with Winnicott. He 'freed me – freed us from Lacan'. Pontalis (2005) describes the English author's imaginative liberation of the world of the '*infans*':

> By infans I mean one who lacks words, one who even when he finds words, is still searching to regain that which escapes language. I prefer to imagine that he feels that access to verbal language will accentuate the gap between that which he hallucinates and the object of desires. . . . Our intense emotions, like our instinctual urges, can hardly be translated into words. How often are we surprised in analysis by the fact that it is exactly in those moments when words fail us – both patient and analyst – that we come closest to the intimate, the unknown, the hidden distress that is buried beneath words and even perceptible affects?

Winnicott's notion of a transitional space has particularly touched a French post-Cartesian sensitivity. His description of the infant's finding of the breast which he has created has turned into a French psychoanalytic term '*le trouvé-créé*' (the found-created) and used without quotation marks or reference. *Transitional* has also been made into a noun (*la transitionnalité*) and comes in to French discourse as a significant modality.

To this day, French psychoanalysts make much use of Winnicott and also of Bion in their writings, and considerably less of Klein, although they quite regularly use the notion of a 'depressive position'. It is also true to say that the very style of the writing of both Bion and Winnicott – more poetic than Klein's, and also willing to hold ambiguity when describing phenomena beyond the rational and respecting a sense of an unknowable – appeals to French sensitivity.

André Green's exploration of the role of affect in *Le discours vivant* (1973), a challenge to Lacan for whom there is nothing relevant to psychoanalysis before and outside of language, is inspired and informed by Winnicott's understanding of the mother–child relationship, which 'carries to the maximum that supersession of the representation–affect opposition in order to confront the affective basis of the sense of existence' (1973/1999, p. 77). That is, Winnicott looks to the affective foundation of the origins of the self, and he locates it in the first year of life. Kristeva continues this with her exploration of the embodied origins of the early 'semiotic' pre-symbolic communication – that is, the primitive modes of communication grounded in the body, before the development of language (Kristeva, 1974). The French theoreticians of psychosomatic illness, Michel Fain and Pierre Marty, consider those illnesses in terms of a failure to link affect and idea, and their focus also takes them to the early mother–child relationship; they followed the thinking of Maurice Bouvet, who as one of the most important post-war pioneers of French psychoanalysis described the regressions to oral and anal object relationships of 'pregenital' subjects with a 'weak' ego. While Bouvet worked on pathological states like phobia, obsessions, psychosis or perversions, the psychosomaticians (Pierre Marty, Michel de M'Uzan, Michel Fain, Christian David) became original and fascinating students of those early object relationships which can also lead to somatisations.

The contribution of Winnicott rescued the psychoanalytic baby from the position created by the Lacanian emphasis on its alienation by the image in the mirror. The initial entrapment of the Lacanian baby is that of being ensnared in the imaginary construct of the mother, the extension of the mother's desire, being, in Lacan's words, her phallus. This is a reading of primary narcissism, and the human subject is driven by a nostalgia for a return to this idealised state, and it is from this project that psychoanalysis can free him. Serge Leclaire, a committed Lacanian, published a paper in a small volume with the provocative title, *On tue un enfant* [A child is being killed] (1975). He describes a patient who is not unfamiliar to most analysts: a patient who was a replacement baby, whose name as well as *raison d'être* referred to the previous birth. The aim of his analysis was to 'kill the baby' who represented the maternal phallus and the impossible narcissism of this position. It is the aim, he suggests, of every analysis. This fundamental suspicion of the narcissistic position of 'his majesty the baby' and of the analyst's 'desire' informs a scepticism which runs through much of French thinking about the analytic situation – a dominant concern about the suggestibility of the patient who listens in too carefully to the wishes of the analyst. A concern not to gratify this destructive and narcissistic wish to be the mother's phallus occupies a central place in the thinking of many French analysts. It can be seen in the caution with which words are used in sessions, the awareness of the dangers of suggestibility and indoctrination, which is a very important theme in psychoanalysis in France (see, for example, Donnet, chapter 6). It is also present in Anglo-Saxon thinking, though the conceptual basis is different, through Winnicott's concern with authenticity versus compliance, true versus false self, or the classical concern with transference resistance in treatment, or, for example, Betty Joseph's preoccupation with patients who are hard to reach (Joseph, 1975). However, in France, unlike Britain, this has led to separating radically the psychoanalysis of the future analyst from his or her training. There is no 'training analysis' in France, and the training analysts have such a status only in relation to selecting and supervising the candidates. The aim of the analysis of the analyst, according to Donnet, is a disidentification and the de-idealisation of institutional objectives (Duparc, 2001).

The role of the Other in the formation of the unconscious

Lacan's reorientation to the study of the construction of the human subject through the acquisition of language shows the subject forming around a logic which comes from outside the self. Language is Other. But language is not the only Other. Lacan's early absorption, perhaps love of Hegelian dialectic, has left its mark on French psychoanalysis in the complex and elusive ubiquity of the Other, which appears in Lacan's writing in many guises. He uses the notion of Other in different ways at different times. It appears as the unconscious, Freud's 'other place' of the *Interpretation of Dreams*. The Other also appears as language, existing as it does outside and a priori to the individual. Woman is also the Other, as seen in the linguistic system (Evans, 1996). The first Other is the mother, inasmuch as she is the first receiver and giver of messages.

The concept of Other migrates into the thinking of French psychoanalytic thinkers in many ways, but it has been systematically elaborated and linked to Freudian metapsychology by Jean Laplanche. For Laplanche, transmission from the outside onto the child is central to the psychoanalytic understanding of the unconscious, and he links transmission specifically to the precocious intrusion or transmission of adult sexuality through the infant's encounter with the maternal unconscious. This marks a famous return to Freud's early seduction theory, but it places the traumatic beginnings in the earliest relation to the mother, a mother who here is not conceived of as holding or containing, the Winnicottian or Bionian mother. Laplanche returns to the seduction theory not only as the origins of potential neurosis, but also as the original overloading of the psyche which results in the formation of the unconscious. The infant cannot meet the first overpowering impact with adult desire (unconscious desire), which nonetheless marks him forever. The primal phantasy, the origins of the unconscious, and the quality of the drives are shaped in this encounter. This original seduction is not seen as pathological but as constitutive of the psyche and rests on 'a universal fact: the intervention of the adult other, with his sexual unconscious' (1997, p. 660). Laplanche calls it '*la théorie de la séduction généralisée*' [general theory of seduction] in order to reflect its larger role in the formation of the unconscious now seen as involving enigmatic messages received from the other. The adult 'makes a sign' (*faire signe à quelqu'un* – calling someone's attention) to the child. Laplanche criticizes both Freud and Klein for not recognizing this normative sexual message:

> The way Freud and all his followers – Melanie Klein, adepts of object relations, etc. – theorise the first experiences of the child, is cruelly marked by the absence of precisely this 'sign making' relation. This is the case concerning the breast: whether in what Freud calls the 'experience of satisfaction' or in the Kleinian theorisation, the breast remains an 'object', good or bad, a representation for the child, isolated by it from the *Umwelt*. The idea that the breast transmits to the child a message and that this message is sexual – any attention paid to the fact that the breast is firstly sexual for the mother, that it forms part of her sexual life as an erogenous zone – such an idea, such attention, are practically never found.
>
> (p. 660)

For Laplanche, an enigmatic sexual message is conveyed from the maternal unconscious, in verbal and non-verbal ways the meaning of which is not conscious to the mother. Repression is seen as the partial failure to translate these messages. The role of maternal subjectivity in this owes much to Lacan's conceptualization, but is conceived specifically as an *enigmatic other*, a carrier of an enigmatic message which will be awakened in the transference (Laplanche, chapter 12). Laplanche returned to Freud to re-orientate Freudian theory in a powerful and original way, utilising Lacan's conceptualisation of the impact of the Other.

Throughout French psychoanalytic thinking, emphasis on the impact of the maternal unconscious constitutes a significant trend and is a heritage of the Lacanian contribution. A French sensitivity to identifications with past significant figures, and to the Oedipal configurations of both parents, has some links with the thread which colours an understanding of what is more likely to be seen as projective identification from a Kleinian-influenced object-relations position. André Green's famous conceptualisation of the Dead Mother, his study of the impact of a maternal depression on the formation of identity, has found its way into the thinking of many psychoanalysts, on both sides of the channel, and represents another creative synthesis, here of object relations theory and sensitivity to the impact of maternal subjectivity.

A different line of influence has been important in French thinking, which centres on communication and around the notion of 'paradox'. The notion of paradox was first introduced by the British-born anthropologist Gregory Bateson and his colleagues working in California in the 1950s (Bateson, Jackson, Haley, & Weakland, 1956). While Lacan was inspired by structural linguistics, Bateson and his collaborators leaned on theories of communication and cybernetics to describe pathological family systems of communication in the families of schizophrenics. They describe in particular a form of communication they call the 'double bind', in which a person is receiving simultaneously two contradictory messages. In England this was taken up and developed by R. D. Laing, while in France '*paradoxicality*' was introduced into the psychoanalytic discourse by Anzieu (1975) and by Racamier (chapter 38, this volume). The paradoxical characterises an organisation more primitive than Klein's paranoid-schizoid position, in which the ego uses the more developed defences of splitting and idealisation. This mode of functioning differs radically from Winnicott's register of the transitional, which holds opposites in a forward movement (Caillot, 2002).

The paradox is a survival defence, a 'supreme defence'. 'It appears that ultimately paradox is that which organises the insoluble' (Racamier, chapter 38, p. 729). Anzieu suggests that some situations of impasse in psychoanalysis rest on paradoxical transference and paradoxical countertransference which need to be spelt out to the patient.

Nachträglichkeit or *après-coup*

As we saw, Green's study of affect marked a disagreement and a challenge to Lacan's emphasis on language and representation. For Lacan, pre-verbal experience takes on meaning retrospectively only – that is, it is language which structures the pre-verbal, and it is language we interpret in the psychoanalytic situation. The Oedipus complex is always present in the culture and imposes itself on the child from outside via the father and his 'law' – which is identified with the word, or the 'name of the father'. Castration is understood in this way by Lacan. It is only with language that the law of the father reorganises previous experiences (loss of the breast, loss of faeces) into the 'knowledge' that the penis too can be lost. So the sight of the girl's missing penis, which had little meaning to the very young child, now takes on the meaning that castration can take place if the incest taboo is not respected. In insisting on the retrospective attribution of meaning to pre-genital experience, Lacan, following the early Freud (1905d, 1918b [1914]) established in French psychoanalysis – and not only amongst Lacanians – the theme of *Nachträglichkeit*, or in French '*après-coup*', which refers to a re-interpretation at a later stage of earlier events, in particular those before language and before the Oedipal phase. It was Lacan who recognised the importance of this form of temporality.

It is now generally recognised that Freud's notion of *Nachträglichkeit* was poorly translated by Strachey as 'deferred action', and perhaps because of this it was not picked up as important in the Anglo-Saxon literature. Laplanche and Pontalis (1967) also suggest that the importance of the concept of *Nachträglichkeit* was not recognised partly because the same word was not used throughout in the translation of Freud (this is the case both in English and in French), and this because the meaning of it given by Freud varies between different usages (Laplanche, 1998). In discussions with French analysts today, the recurrent reference to phenomena as '*après-coup*', ultimately from one moment to the next, even within a given session (Faimberg, 1981), has become a distinguishing feature of French discourse and has formed the basis for a conception of non-linear time, one which awakens the interest and curiosity of English-speaking psychoanalysts. In British analysis, it is implicit in notions of reorganisation via the mutative interpretation (Sodre, 1997) and in the interpretation in the 'here and now' (Birksted-Breen, 2003), although the reference to sexual trauma or development (one of the meanings central for certain French authors as well as for Freud) is, for some, absent.[17]

Après-coup, its specificity as a concept, is sometimes hailed as a French contribution to psychoanalysis (in particular by French psychoanalysts), and we have seen its centrality in Lacan's understanding of the constitution of the ego in the mirror stage, where the retrospective dread of fragmentation is understood to be a product of the recognition of the idealised whole, as well as in his emphasis on the capacity of language to organise retrospectively the relationship to the Imaginary and to the Real. Indeed, the concept of *après-coup* is illustrated in the fate of the term itself in French psychoanalytic discourse.

Sexuality

Freud posited that there is no natural heterosexuality, that sexuality is always constructed over time within the Oedipal configuration, and that both heterosexuality and homosexuality are part of the sexuality of all individuals. In his supposed 'return to Freud', Lacan, ignoring the fact that biology does have a certain role in Freudian theory, and using the Saussurian structural-linguistic theory, took this up in an extreme form, saying that there is no such thing as a pre-given male or female subject, that 'masculine' and 'feminine' only exist as a division in language, where 'feminine' is the negative pole and refers to 'lack' and to the 'Other'.

---

[17] Perelberg (2006) proposes that in this respect a distinction should be made between 'descriptive *après-coup*' and 'dynamic *après-coup*'.

As part of the separation of the biological from the psychic, Lacan also highlighted – basing himself on Freud's 'phallic stage', when only one genital organ is known – the notion of the phallus. He made a distinction between 'penis' the anatomical organ and 'phallus' the symbolic representation. The phallus, for Lacan, is the signifier of the desire of the Other, originally the desire of the mother, for whom the phallus signifies her completion (this is a rephrasing of Freud's idea of the equivalence of penis and child, and the woman's wish for a child to replace her missing penis). Both men and women aspire to be the phallus, to be what the mother wants and to complete her, and in that way it comes to represent a lack. The father is a representative of language by giving his name to the child, who thus becomes part of a paternal filiation. When the child has the name of the mother, it still refers to the name of her own father, hence a paternal filiation. It is the name of the father, given to the child, which introduces 'the third' by naming the father as the object of the mother's desire, and separating thus mother and child. Lacan plays on the homophony of '*le nom du père*' (later written as *Nom-du-Père*) and '*le non du père*', the father who lays down the incest taboo in the Oedipus complex. This is the 'symbolic father' who is part of the 'symbolic order' without which the individual is thrown into psychosis.

In the 1920s, the debate which came to be known as the 'Freud–Jones controversy' centred on female sexuality and implicitly on the issue of the role of the body. Klein, Jones and others questioned the idea that the girl starts off as 'a little man', and they argued for the important role of pre-verbal experiences in relation to the mother as the foundation to female sexuality. British analysts on the whole lost interest in this debate in the 1930s; the extensive influence of Klein's theories meant that the dominant view was that there is a natural male and female sexuality, and interest in sexuality was not at the forefront again, being replaced instead by interest in specific mechanisms like introjection, splitting and projection, particularly in the context of separation anxiety. Nevertheless there were some important contributions on the subject by non-Kleinian psychoanalysts such as William Gillespie, Moses and Eglé Laufer, and Mervin Glasser.

In France, sexuality never left the scene. Specific interest in the question of feminine sexuality was renewed in the 1960s, and this came partly as a reaction to Lacan's views. Chasseguet-Smirgel published her collection *Recherches psychanalytiques nouvelles sur la sexualité féminine* in 1964. Like Lacan, Chasseguet-Smirgel proclaimed her faithfulness to Freud but suggested it was time to 're-examine the theories of female sexuality using the Freudian approach to the unconscious' (1964/1970, p. 3). The authors in that collection questioned sexual monism in both sexes whereby only one genital – active and penetrative and hence male – is known and penis-envy is central to feminine development. Here we see again the important influence of British psychoanalysis, in that Chasseguet-Smirgel's re-examination is done in the light of the writings of those whose views on female sexuality were opposed to those of Freud when it came to female sexuality, in particular Melanie Klein and Ernest Jones. For these authors, there is a primary femininity which is a given and is not constructed over time from an early masculine position, the vagina is known from early on and the phallic phase is defensive.

Some French Lacanian women psychoanalysts – for example, Luce Irigaray (1985) – while retaining Lacan's larger model, also refuted the centrality of the phallus and asserted that there is a feminine sexuality which is beyond the phallic definition. The legacy of Lacan, however, in the area of sexuality as elsewhere is still noticeable. In French psychoanalysis, the role of the penis and its symbolic counterpart the phallus is central, whether or not analysts subscribe to the theory of phallic monism. They recognise, however, a duality between a (phallic/narcissistic) femininity referring to the external appearance and a femininity which refers to the internal feminine organs, a position also taken by Birksted-Breen in England (1993, 1996). It should be noted that in French '*envie*' can mean both desire and envy, which brings closer the notion of wanting to possess as an attribute and the desire to receive.

French psychoanalysts, unlike their British counterparts, have never stopped being interested in femininity and masculinity. Again starting from Freud's notion of the 'repudiation of femininity' (Freud, 1937c), they discuss the importance of integration or non-integration of the feminine in both sexes and of a healthy psychic bisexuality (Bergeret, 2002; Bokanowski, 1995; David, 1975; Guignard, 1997).

Cournut-Janin (chapter 32) develops the idea that a message (a prohibition) is conveyed by the mother to her daughter to make herself 'feminine', which means beautifying her whole body as a '*leurre*' [a lure] in order to avoid arousing the castration anxiety of the father (much as the constitution of the fetish in the man), while repressing her sexual organs (see also 'The feminine' in the Glossary). And Cournut (chapter 31) discusses specific masculine anxieties, which he separates into anxieties in relation to both '*le féminin maternal*' and '*le féminin érotique*'.

Schaeffer (1997) talks about the 'work of the feminine' [*le travail du feminin*]. For the woman this involves overcoming her hatred of what is felt as a defeat, in order to be able to give in to her erotic masochism and to accept and allow entry to what is other, different, familiar and disturbing.

What appears as difference between French and British discourse can also sometimes be put down to a figure of speech. For instance, the extensive use French analysts make of 'castration' has to do with the much broader significance they attribute to the word, as can be seen for instance in this quote from McDougall (1974): 'The mythical moment in which the fusional identity with the mother is relinquished requires a mother who herself is prepared to accept the loss of the magical union. This loss might be considered as the primordial castration in an individual's life' (p. 438). When French psychoanalysts speak of 'castration', they refer to the castration anxiety related to the Oedipus complex but also to the loss of omnipotence, which concerns pregenital anxieties. Here there has for some time been an overlapping of Lacanian and non-Lacanian analysts. For Lacan, the notion of 'lack' was fundamental and related to the illusion of wholeness, represented by the phallus.[18] Françoise Dolto, a Lacanian who enjoyed wide public influence as one of the earliest French child analysts, pioneered and popularised the understanding of development as the progress of successive symbolic castrations, on oral, anal and genital levels. These experiences, if not too traumatic, lead to the development of the unconscious body image and, at the same time, generate the development of symbolic capacity (Dolto, 1984).[19] When the phallus is understood as a symbol of narcissistic wholeness (see Chasseguet-Smirgel, chapter 30, this volume) all narcissistic fears become equivalent to castration because of the narcissistic value given to the phallus by both sexes. While for some this is a given, others, like Chasseguet-Smirgel, look for the basis of this. She writes: 'Realization that possession of the penis presents the possibility of healing the narcissistic wound imposed by the omnipotent mother helps to explain some of the unconscious significance of the penis, whether it is that of a treasure of strength, integrity, magic power, or autonomy' (p. 584).

While the relation to the maternal breast has dominated British thinking about narcissistic omnipotence, a French influence may have contributed to the greater importance attached to the father and to the role of the primal scene in the last decades in British Kleinian psychoanalysis (see, for instance, Britton, 1989).

McDougall (1972) and Chasseguet-Smirgel (1974) have discussed the consequences of the denial of the role of the genital penis and the concomitant idealisation of pregenitality in the perversions. Chasseguet-Smirgel also notes that the denial of the vagina is not only due to the fear of castration; it is a denial of the role of the father's penis in the primal scene, the recognition of which is a recognition of Oedipal failure and a narcissistic blow to the boy. 'The sexual pervert and related personality structures will always, in one way or another, search to realise the fantasy that underlies the theory of phallic monism in infantile sexuality: that is to say, the twofold negation of the difference between the sexes and the generations' (1974, pp. 354–355).

The expression 'differentiation between sexes and generations' originated in France, according to Chasseguet-Smirgel (1991). This expression has hit a

---

[18] In a paper on Lacan and Winnicott, Luepnitz (2009) aptly writes: 'For Lacan, an interpretation should be "halfway between a quotation and an enigma" – not a "good feed". For Winnicott, the central drama will turn around the infant's loss or feared loss of maternal connection. For Lacan, while loss is obviously important, something more profound is at stake – the *lack* built into subjectivity by the mere existence of the unconscious' (p. 964).

[19] Dolto became a member of the SPP in 1939, followed Lagache in the first split in 1953 and joined Lacan's Freudian School (École freudienne) in 1964. Her field, the subjectivity of the child, popularised psychoanalysis in France, as Winnicott had done in England.

chord with British psychoanalysts who now also use the term, with its bearing on the relationship to the primal scene. Chasseguet-Smirgel notes a point of rapprochement with the post-Kleinian position and writes: 'One wonders whether it may not be possible, on the one hand, to replace the notion of an early Oedipus complex by that of an Oedipus complex which is structurally inherent in the mental apparatus, and on the other hand, whether certain moves in the direction of a more or less fully developed Oedipus complex may not make it possible to bridge the gap between the "classical" conception of the Oedipus complex and the (post) Kleinian conception' (1991, p. 729).

It remains that, for French psychoanalysts, no area of the mind is free of sexuality, sexuality understood as infantile sexuality, or of enigmatic sexual messages or in terms of the theory of the drives in which the sexual drive is opposed to the self-preservative drive or the death drive. At the same time, Roussillon points out (chapter 28), while sexuality is of major importance in French psychoanalysis, even perhaps part of its identity, defining what is meant by it is far from clear. He suggests the need to distinguish between sexuality as a behaviour (*sexualité*) and sexuality as a psychic process involved in symbolisation and subjectivation (*le sexuel*). It is the latter which makes a psychoanalytic contribution to an understanding of sexuality, and it is within the psychoanalytic process that this can be identified.

Genital sexuality is also given a bigger place in French psychoanalysis than in Kleinian-influenced British psychoanalysis. When André Green came to London in 1995 to present a Sigmund Freud birthday lecture, he gave his paper the provocative title: 'Has Sexuality Anything to Do with Psychoanalysis?' In it he questions the way in which direct discussion of sexuality seems to have declined in presentations, replaced instead by a focus on object relations, pre-genital fixations and borderline pathology – particularly in British psychoanalysis – and his aim is to restore the importance of genital sexuality and the Oedipus complex. He writes: 'In fact, the sexual and genital fixations were like the heart of an onion covered by many layers. . . . In the eyes of others, patients wanted to appear as if these problems were non-existent or trivial.' He goes on: '. . . I cannot conceive of the unconscious differently from Freud's view, that is of not being rooted in sexuality and destructiveness' (1995a, p. 873).

Green argues that there is a tendency to focus on manifest features and the primitive fixations they seem to reveal rather than on the latent unconscious fantasies. Behind the regressive nature of behaviours and fantasies lies the core meaning, which has to do with the genital aims 'with all their conflicting connotations: the difference of the sexes and the difference of the generations, the tolerance of otherness, the conflict between desire and identification with the object, the acceptance of the loss of control in sexual enjoyment etc.' (Green, 1995a, p. 874). Elsewhere he also suggests that it is not just in Britain that there has been a diminishing importance given to sexuality, but also in France. He writes in *The Chains of Eros* (2001) that the diminishing importance of sexuality and the drives in post-Freudian psychoanalysis is due to two things:

on the one hand, to the interest in borderline cases and object relations theory brought by Klein and her followers, and, on the other, in France, to the influence of Laplanche, who, according to Green, separates sexuality from the id and the body, a position Green calls 'neo-Lacanian'.

An emphasis on sexuality can also be found in the importance given to the notion of 'primary homosexuality'. Primary homosexuality concerns both sexes in relation to the 'pregenital mother' and is an evolution from a primary identification, or oneness with the mother. In the case of the boy, there is also a primary homosexuality in relation to the mother in the early phase, when the mother is conceived of as being like the self. It refers to the state of sameness with the mother, dependent on the development of the affect of tenderness (Denis, 1982). This is an example of the way in which French analysts speak of 'sexuality' where British analysts would speak simply of, for instance, a primitive relationship to the mother or of a fusion with the mother, depending on their theoretical stance.

French psychoanalysts are also more concerned with avoiding any normative ideas in relation to sexuality. McDougall, who has written extensively on sexual deviations, writes in her *Plea for A Measure of Abnormality*: 'It is not the analyst's function to decide what his analysands are to do with their lives, their children, or their sex' (1978/1980, p. 477). Freud's description of the goals of analysis as to do with being able to work and to love are indeed very open ended. French psychoanalysts, who have often stayed closer to the early Freud of the topographic model, have put more emphasis on the liberation of sexuality from repression than have British psychoanalysts. That being said, Colette Chiland (1997), who studied transsexualism, understanding it as an identity problem corresponding to a denial of one's own biological sex and a defence against psychosis, found that psychoanalytic treatment of such patients was difficult because of the collusion between the request for changing sex and the medical and social possibilities of carrying out such a transformation.

Les pulsions (the drives)

Again, it was Lacan who first clearly rejected the Strachey translation of *Trieb* as 'instinct' (Diatkine, 1997), a term which had been adopted in France, as it had been in England, prior to Lacan's indignant attack on the misrecognition of Freud's intention. Lacan proposed to replace it with '*pulsion*', a less biologically based term, more in keeping with Freud's notion of it being 'a concept on the frontier between the mental and the somatic, as the psychical representative of the stimuli originating from within the organism and reaching the mind, as a measure of the demand made upon the mind for work in consequence of its connection with the body' (Freud, 1915c, p. 122). The word *pulsion* carries in French a greater sense of a movement towards a realisation than does the word instinct. Increasingly, in England too, largely through the influence of French writing, 'drive' is replacing 'instinct', as indeed will be the case in the updated translation of the *Standard Edition*.[20] Lacan's early identification of *pulsion*, or drive, as one of the four key concepts in psychoanalysis (alongside the unconscious, repetition and transference) placed it high in the theoretical canon, where it has stayed in France. Lacan himself eventually abandoned the subject of drive in favour of the more complex conceptualisation of 'desire', which is further removed from the body and is formed in the more narcissistic wish to satisfy the desire of the Other. In this he has not been followed by most French psychoanalysts, except inasmuch as most French psychoanalysts continue to be more conservative in their interpretative style because they are concerned to interpret but not to provoke the patient's wish to please his analyst.

Supported by the rigorous and rich tradition of the 'return to Freud' in France, '*les pulsions*' occupy a central place in French psychoanalytic thought, which distinguishes it from most English or American thought, where the debate about drives carries much less urgency and commands much less profound theoretical meditation than it does in France (Scarfone, 2004, p. 103). In Britain the importance of the object has overshadowed the importance of the drive, although the two do not have to mutually exclude each other if it is considered that a drive always has an object (Freud, 1905d) or that the object of the drive contributes to defining the drive (Denis, 2006). Green (2008) himself now writes: '... today I think we do not have to choose between a drive model and an intersubjective one. I think that the correct method should be a drive-object model, not the one without the other. No object without the drive, no drive without the object' (p. 1039). Notwithstanding this, French analysts have been more interested than British analysts in thinking about the status of the drives and their implication.

The centrality of the drive for French psychoanalysts connects with the importance they give to Freud's economic model, according to which psychic processes consist in the distribution or redistribution, and increase or decrease, of instinctual energy.

While Kleinian psychoanalysts tend to focus on secondary narcissism and analyse its destructive defensive nature because of their fundamental idea that there is no drive without an object from the very beginning, French psychoanalysts see as fundamental to development Freud's conceptualisation of a normal primary narcissism (1914c).

French theory follows Freud; as Freud himself pointed out, the twin pillars of his thinking, the two major works he returned to, were *The Interpretation of Dreams* (1900a), fundamentally a theory of the representation of unconscious processes understood to be motivated by repressed wishes, and the *Three Essays*

---

[20] We will use the term 'drive' unless quoting from Strachey's *Standard Edition* or unless the French author chooses to retain the word 'instinct' (as does Marty, in chapter 23).

on the Theory of Sexuality (1905d), in which he offers the first definition of the drives (Gibeault, 1980). There he makes his claim that the drives, by which he meant at this time sexual drives, are present and active from infancy and are defined as 'the psychical representative of an endosomatic, continuously flowing source of stimulation . . . a concept . . . lying on the frontier between the mental and physical'. Writing in 1933, in *The New Introductory Lectures*, Freud confers a magisterial, but still ambiguous, honour on this theory of the drives. It is, he says, 'our mythology . . . instincts, our mythical entities, magnificent in their indefiniteness. In our work we cannot for a moment disregard them, yet we are never sure that we are seeing them clearly' (1933a, p. 95).

Many French psychoanalysts are comfortable with this ambiguity. Other French psychoanalysts have tackled this myth and, following Lacan, critiqued the biologism of the mythology. Widlöcher argues (1984, p. 30) that it is not necessary to hypothesise the drives if one accepts the tendency of all acts, including all acts of thought, to realise themselves.[21] If the body is the primary agent of action, he goes on, what is needed is a theory of association of thoughts to action, rather than a theory of drives. Laplanche (1989), in his own development of a Freudian Lacanianism, finds the intrusive invasion of the adult unconscious, the first maternal seduction, as discussed above, as formative of the sexual drive, which is therefore always precocious and always by its nature traumatic. Both Widlöcher and Laplanche belonged to the SFP, the society which Lacan formed at the time of the first split. Their arguments bear witness to the creative tension in French thinking between, on the one hand, the wish to remove the biological from the field of psychoanalysis, as first imposed by Lacan, and, on the other, a determined, ultimately non-Lacanian commitment to the Freudian emphasis on the embodied drives as fundamental to the formation of the unconscious and the establishment of subjectivity. We can therefore see that a major debate in France has been structured around the impact of Lacan: Laplanche – more Lacanian – reduces the importance of the biological dimension in favour of the role of the Other and in particular maternal desire, seduction and enigmatic messages, while André Green always emphasises the central importance of the drives and of the id and the phenomenology of object relationships.

As mentioned earlier, Lacan's interest and theorising developed from the early Freud, and this had a marked influence on many French analysts. The acceptance of the notion of a death drive – a product of the later Freud – has been a point of controversy in France, as indeed it has also been in Britain. André Green is the chief proponent of a conceptualisation of the death drive whose aim, he understands, is to reduce all tension by severing all links to objects and representations. He links it to the id rather than to the unconscious, as the latter would imply that it has some representation. Green uses the notion of 'objectalisation/disobjectalisation' ['*objectalisation-desobjectalisation*']

---

[21] Mentioned in Scarfone (2004), p. 105.

to describe the push from the life drive towards a link to objects and of the aim of the death drive which is to sever that link. Pointing out that Freud did not continue his work on narcissism after 1920, implicitly considering it to be part of the life drives, Green explores this link between narcissism and the destructive or death drives in his concept of 'death narcissism' (1983). This notion can be compared to Rosenfeld's notion of 'destructive narcissism' (1971), but it differs in that for Rosenfeld object relations are central and form a pathological organisation in which there is a stranglehold from parts of the personality (the gang) on the dependent and needy parts of the personality. Green's description, on the other hand, tends more towards nothingness, a state of no object, describing 'death narcissism' as 'a culture of void, emptiness, self-contempt, destructive withdrawal, and permanent self-depreciation with a predominant masochistic quality' (2002).

Other French psychoanalysts reject Freud's theory of life and death drives. Paul Denis (2002), for instance, proposes instead that 'life instinct and death instinct (or life drive and death drive) are in fact principles of functioning that oppose an organising principle to a disorganising principle' (p. 1805). Developing his conceptualisation from an earlier Freud, he suggests that each drive has its own possibility of becoming aggressive. For him, each drive has two currents – an erogenous current linked to the erogenous zones, and a current which aims at possession linked to motricity and the sense organs – both components being libidinal. 'It is the combination of these two currents, as the experience of satisfaction is accomplished, that goes to form the drive' and, further, he adds that 'this association creates a representation in the psychic apparatus' (Denis, 2006).

Gibeault (1980) describes a French conceptualisation of the drives, which has roots in very early Freud (Freud, 1950 [1892–99], Draft E, pp. 192–193), where the libidinal drive is understood to push towards representation but is not assumed to be linked with a representation from the start, or a phantasy, and is therefore assumed only to become psychic when it achieves, in Freud's text, the required *linkage*. This is a point of view at odds with the notion of the ubiquity of unconscious phantasy, particularly as understood by Klein, and as articulated by Susan Isaacs in the seminal paper which launched the Controversial Discussions (Isaacs, 1952; King & Steiner, 1991) in England during the Second World War. For Klein, the drive always has a phantasy linked to it, whereas French psychoanalysts stay again closer to Freud in considering the linkage of the drive to an idea, a phantasy, to be an achievement which rests on a theory of *après-coup*. Representation for the French is an achievement, a linking of an affect or sensation or drive with a thing-presentation, an unconscious phantasy, an image, or hallucination, which finally can become linked to a word-presentation. It then becomes available for thinking, in and out of the psychoanalytic process. All this linking binds the drives. The notion of 'binding' – again a Freudian concept not so often referred to in the British school – is considered fundamental in France. It is in particular developed in the work of André Green in relation to Freud's latest theory of the drives, in which the drive of Eros is seen as a drive towards representation and objects, as opposed to the death drive, seen as the drive which unbinds, undoes connections and destroys relationships and representations.

Unbinding is one of the negative forces which Green gathers up under the important French notion of 'the negative'. Green argues the ubiquity of 'the work of the negative' in psychic life (Green, 1993).[22] In this respect, Freud's late papers – which Lacan ignored – are considered fundamental: 'Negation' (1925h), 'Fetishism' (1927e) and *Beyond the Pleasure Principle* (1920g).

In his thinking about drives, when drawing on the later Freud, Green highlights the implications for the central French concern with the fate of representation. The psychoanalytic preoccupation with the interconnection of the drive and its representation (as Gibeault points out in his Introduction to section IV) is based on Freud's earliest recognition of the splits between representation and affect or wishes in the mind of hysterics and dreamers. Green theorises the development of the second topography, or structural model, creating a new conceptualisation of the relationship between drives and representations. He describes how in Freud's first model, the unconscious was made of representations, representations of the objects of desire. The pursuit and interpretation of these representations made up the fundamental material of the psychoanalytic project, which was the illumination of the ego's activity in repressing the representation of unacceptable desires and hatreds. But treatment proved more elusive than is promised in this conceptualisation. The negative therapeutic reaction – the failure to change in spite of illumination – argued a force in the personality preventing change, a negative force, what Freud in 1920 identified as the death drive. In Green's reading, from 1920 on Freud re-introduces and re emphasises the drives. What is important is the fate of the id impulses: either they are able to transform themselves into *unconscious object-representations* or they will discharge (2008). We see Green's appreciation of Winnicott and of Bion in his description of how it is Bion's alpha function and maternal reverie and Winnicott's access to the transitional phase that enable id impulses to transform into unconscious representation.

The study of 'the work of the negative' opens on to a very wide field, in which the death drive finds a place, and is crucial to the theorising of the treatment of non-neurotic patients. Green writes that his view of pathological situations is close to Winnicott's. In the case of unbearable separation, there is

---

[22] The wider theoretical conceptualisation of the negative has its roots, as Green points out, in the philosophy of Hegel and in early pioneers of structural linguistics and precursors of Lacan. Baudry (1989) finds 'the independent development of the interest in the negative in France from fields allied to psychoanalysis: language, philosophy and literary criticism' (p. 502).

In his concept of 'the negative' and 'the work of the negative', Green includes both normal positive aspects of the negative and pathological aspects. The negative can refer to something which is not present – for instance, the transitional object, which is the first 'not-me' possession; or 'the analytic third', which is not visible; or the unconscious, which implies the idea of a 'latent operating behind the scenes, invisible though active' (1997).

a decathexis of the object – 'a fading of the internal representation' for Winnicott and for Green himself, 'a destructive negative hallucination of the object' (Green, 1997, p. 1081).

This version of the destructiveness of the death drive is indebted to the work of the French school of psychosomatics (see below) who identified in the death instinct a process of withdrawal of investment and what Green calls 'disobjectalising', which leads to an impoverishment of representation. The drive towards life, the drive towards objects, is what leads to representation (1993/1999, p. 85).

French thinking is usually framed within a psychoanalysis that does not stray far from the focus on the drives. The ubiquity of the drive in French theorisation of clinical phenomena is very evident in Benno Rosenberg's paper (chapter 27), which develops the theory of masochism to underpin the establishment of ego functions not often associated with drive.

Rosenberg links psychic achievements associated with the capacity to delay gratification, and so ensure the development of a thinking capacity, to a masochistic contribution, an integration finally of the two drives, life and death. He shows how the investment of primary masochism in the unpleasure linked to the hallucinatory wish-fulfilment in the absence of the object offers the possibility to invest the wish to obtain a real satisfaction and thus to invest a capacity for waiting and looking for an object.

Representation

The focus on the Freudian conceptualisation of *representation* occupies a pivotal place in French theory, for a number of reasons. Much of it, we think, has to do with the response to Lacan, who both insisted on the return to Freud and paradoxically produced a Lacanian Freud in which psychoanalysis is understood in theory and practice to be a linguistic enterprise. Words are its medium, the process is a discourse, words produce the illumination which is its product. More radically, Lacan claimed that the unconscious is structured like a language. Influenced by Lacan's still resonating emphasis on the role of speech in psychoanalysis but troubled by the narrowness of his focus, a number of French psychoanalysts beginning with Laplanche (Roudinesco, 1990, pp. 312–314) returned to Freud, particularly to metapsychological papers, specifically 'The Unconscious' of 1915, to establish a foundation to challenge Lacan's concept of the unconscious.

In the 1915 paper, Freud states explicitly that the unconscious contains representations, what Strachey translated as 'thing-presentations', *Vorstellungsrepräsentanz*, ideas and images representative of the repressed drive experience. Thing-presentations have never reached consciousness, or they have been repressed. They can only find their way into consciousness if the thing-presentations – memory traces of sensory experiences that develop into images

– become linked to word-presentations in the preconscious and so become available to consciousness and to thought. Freud's conception is that language is a function of the preconscious and consciousness. It is a secondary process not primary, it is topographically different, and it develops later. First, there are thing-presentations in the unconscious; later, there are words in the preconscious which may become linked to them and so form a 'hypercathexis' (1915e) of the thing-presentation. Words can be treated as things, they can be subjected to a primary process, in wit or in dreams or in psychosis, but word-presentation is a development of consciousness. A deepened and careful appreciation of Freud's sometimes elusive thoughts on representation, how it evolves, and particularly, the relationship between representation and emotional experience, becomes a foundation for a French contribution to the study of the place of affect in psychoanalysis, the role of the drives, non-verbal representation and communication, and the role of words in the psychoanalytic process. *The failure to achieve representation in the unconscious*, pertaining to the hallucinatory activity of infancy and dreams, or the impoverishment of representation in the operational thinking of psychosomatic patients (Marty & M'Uzan, chapter 22) or the failure to represent in psychotic functioning (Botella & Botella, chapter 18), marks a specific focus in French thinking. The fundamental importance of the achievement of representation in the unconscious – a representation of drive, sensation and affect – is central to French conceptualisation of mental functioning. The use of the word 'representation' by British analysts has blurred this as it is used loosely to speak of conscious images or ideas and often as equivalent to the word 'symbolisation'.

Representations and affects

In their careful reading of Freud, French psychoanalysts use and develop Freud's distinction between representation and affects, the separate fates of which defined his early understanding of hysterical symptoms and dream formation. However, the psychoanalysts included in this volume do not follow Lacan in the virtual elimination of affect from the psychoanalytic field. André Green's monumental consideration, *The Fabric of Affect in the Psychoanalytic Discourse* (1973/1999), is an encyclopaedic effort to trace and examine the consideration of affect in Freud's writing, bringing the role of affect back theoretically, and clinically, to the forefront of French theory, where it informs the discourse today. Affect is central to the psychoanalytic process, although tracing its fate in Freud's understanding is a complex process, as Green's work painstakingly shows. Qualitatively different from a representation, affects do not follow the same path as the representation to which they are originally linked. Affects are more amorphous, a representation more reliable and, in that way, less problematic or confusing, as Lacan affirms, in his emphasis on the signifier. His still-resonant effect on the philosophical foundations of French psychoanalysis is, we think, evident in an assertion of Green's in 2005: when he proposes to characterise the essential paradigm of psychoanalysis, he situates it 'without hesitation, on the side of representation'. 'Affect' he places second. Assessing the relation between affect and representation from a developmental point of view, Lebovici (chapter 14) argues that the object is invested with affects first and only secondarily with representations (ideas). As Gibeault points out in his Introduction to section IV, the emphasis on the gap between representation and affect differs from the Kleinian coincidence of affect and phantasy. The emphasis on the differences and the tension between affect and representation, between the experience of the object and its representation, between sensation and perception, argue the basis for the ubiquity of the wish for a reduction of that tension in a 'narcissistic regression', the fusion with the object which the drives are always seeking.

Representation and phantasy

Just as the movement towards representation comes from the pressure of the drives, so the development of representation into phantasy is understood as a process, an achievement rather than a given. Hallucination of an object of desire, a phantasy, develops as a product of experience of the satisfaction of need, coupled with memory traces of the object. Out of the experience of the satisfaction of need, memory traces develop that link to a good experience, a wished-for experience. The wish for the breast emerges out of an auto-erotic moment. Phantasy is the *mise en scène* of this desire. In order to construct a phantasy, there has to be a capacity for figuration, *Darstellung*, or *Darstellbarkeit*. Sensations must take the shape of images, which have emerged from the need-satisfying experience recalled and desired. There is in this erotic production of a phantasied image an element of loss, because the thing-presentation exceeds the binding power of the image.

The rhythms of bearable differences between presence and absence are implicit in this model of the development of a capacity to phantasise: some absence is required for the infant to generate his own auto-erotic phantasy, which Laplanche and Pontalis (chapter 15, this volume) see as the origins of sexuality as such. This facilitation of representation out of bearable quotas of absence is a feature of Braunschweig and Fain's (1975) discussion of the night-time baby, where again, the mother is seen to give the child the opportunity to construct a phantasy by virtue of her absence (*'la censure de l'amante'*; Fain, 1971).

Freud's idea of auto-erotism preceded his conceptualisation of narcissism. The notion of *auto-erotism* is one which is often used by French psychoanalysts, introducing the notion of pleasure, which remains throughout life as an important aspect of sexual life.

Laplanche and Pontalis in their *Language of Psychoanalysis* write that 'the "origin" of auto-erotism is thus considered to be that moment – recurring constantly rather than fixed at a certain point in development – when sexuality draws away from its natural object' (1967/1973, p. 46), which is the feeding breast combining nourishment and pleasure. This initiates a distinction between need and desire – that is to say, the need for nourishment and the pleasure of sucking.

Gibeault (1980) underlines that, for the human being, 'pleasure dependent upon the object is always *traumatic* in contrast to the pleasure he seeks to give to himself'. French psychoanalysts' appreciation of this trauma and the ways of dealing with it informs their understanding of psychic functioning and behaviour. The task of the psychoanalyst is to enable the patient to represent that trauma and make it less overwhelming.

The adaptive and defensive requirement to construct a phantasy out of the disturbances produced in contact with, rather than in the absence of, the mother is developed by Laplanche, who finds a base for primary phantasy in the 'enigmatic messages' which come from the maternal unconscious. The impact of the sexually mature, structured adult disturbs the equilibrium of the infant and requires some defensive metabolisation. Laplanche applies this idea clinically in his paper on the transference (chapter 12, this volume).

Pasche (chapter 36) describes the necessity of a shield between mother and child to protect from too much excitation and to enable the infant to see the mother without feeling devoured or invaded by her desire. The metaphor of Perseus's shield depicts the relation to the mother via an intermediary (shield), whereby her presence appears in a less blinding way, only as a reflection in the mirror. When this shield is absent, the individual is prey to psychotic fears of non-differentiation and annihilation. This paper is fundamental to French psychoanalysts and is often referred to in different contexts. In pointing to the danger of the maternal desire (the Medusa), Pasche, like Lacan and Laplanche, puts the emphasis on what originates from the other, in contrast to a Kleinian emphasis on infantile projections. The image made possible by the reflection is the representation which protects from psychosis and from a traumatic encounter with reality. This bears some similarity to the 'dream screen' described by Lewin (1946), a screen on which images are projected; it also connects with Winnicott's transitional space, as Gibeault points out in his introduction to section VII.

The role of the impact of maternal environment on the origins of the capacity to represent (i.e., of connecting sensation and affect with idea or image) has been explored by Kristeva (in her work on semiotics), by Marty and the psychosomaticians Fain, David, and de M'Uzan, as well as by André Green. The role of the mother as the facilitator of the capacity to represent shows indebtedness to the influence of Winnicott and Bion, the respective development of notions of holding or reverie and containment certainly influencing the work of André Green and Pontalis and enhancing such conceptualisations as that of Lebovici (chapter 14), who draws largely on object relational theory in his understanding of infantile development.

The failure to represent

The pioneers of the French consideration of the failure to achieve representation were the psychosomatic practitioners, psychoanalysts who worked in hospital with physically ill children and adults. It was here that somatic illness was discovered to be the consequence of a failure to *mentalise* experience, the body offering up an organ to bind a disintegration, a progressive disorganisation which was seen as the product of an overwhelmed and disabled psyche. The progressive disorganisation was identified by Marty and his colleagues, with the death instinct, the psychosomatic symptom, the illness, substituting for the mentalisation. The diseased organ provides a kind of binding, halting the progressive disintegration into death. The failure of the mind in this process, in both its image-making and thinking capacity, has been integrated into Freud's second topography, by André Green. He links the movement of disintegration with the death drive. The death drive, or *pulsion de mort*, is charged with a negative energy, rather than simply being a manifestation of a failure of the life instinct, or Eros, which would be closer to Marty's view. Green's death drive benefits from the later Freud's conceptualisation of the id, the death drive posing a constant pressure on the erotic attachments, an attack on the investment in objects or on the binding of the drives through representation. In Green's synthesis, following the later Freud, it is the drives which determine whether a subject moves in the direction towards objects and representation – what he calls *objectalisation* – or towards negation, and death. The death drive *is unbinding*. In the second topography, unconscious representation, always understood as an achievement of the psyche in the French reading of Freud's theory of representation, now is understood to be the result of psychic work *against* the unbinding power of the death drive. Included in this volume is one of Green's many contributions to the theory of the negative (chapter 17), the development of the idea of a 'negative hallucination', a defensive negation which provides the background for the more positive hallucination, a retrieval of connection to the object through the image-making capacity of the mind. In that sense, this 'negative' has a positive value in that it creates a background or space for the representation of the object. At its most positive, this idea is reminiscent of Lewin's 'dream screen' (1946). It is also reminiscent of Bion's reading of Freud, where Bion conceives of a 'no-breast' becoming a thought and thus promoting the development of an 'apparatus for thinking' (Bion, 1962). Both Bion and Green follow Freud in the emphasis on the capacity for tolerating frustration and delay as the requirement for thinking. They both are concerned with that which takes place before 'thinking' (Bion) or 'representation' (Green).

In the writing of César and Sára Botella, the word 'figurability' refers to the image-making capacity of the mind, with reference primarily to hallucination in dreams, and to the scene-making capacity of phantasy (Botella & Botella, 2001). Their word 'figurability', the neologism *figurabilité* in French, is their translation of *Darstellbarkeit*, which was translated as 'representability' in Strachey's English Freud, where it appears significantly in chapter 6 of the *Interpretation of Dreams*. There, Freud addresses the 'Considerations of representability', which in French is translated as '*prise en consideration de la figurabilité*', hence the Botellas' choice of '*figurabilité*' to refer specifically to a visual representation, such as dream imagery. They chose to use '*figuration*' [*Darstellung*] and '*figurabilité*' in order to avoid the more generic 'representation' to make it clear that they are referring to image and image making, something more specific than primitive drive representations but more archaic than words (see also the footnote in Alain Gibeault's introduction to section IV).

Like Piera Aulagnier (1975), who conceived of the 'pictogram' as the fundamental visual representation of early experience, the Botellas have studied psychotic mental functioning, especially that of children. They hypothesise the greatest dread to be that of losing the capacity to represent (in the sense of *figurabilité*) rather than that of losing the object. Even persecution is object-related and better than the inexpressible terror of the non-object, a catastrophic 'decompensation'. They show how in these situations the analyst, through tolerating a regression himself, can bring forth images which can help the patient to represent that which had formerly remained unrepresentable because of a traumatic origin. It is in this sense that Green writes that psychoanalysis has moved from an analysis *of* representation to an understanding of the analytic process as a *work of representation* (Green, 1995b).

In contradistinction, Kleinian psychoanalysts posit phantasy as an invariable concomitant of the drives, and Kleinians do not refer to a state without some kind of representation. When a representation of the object is missing, it is usually seen as the result of an attack on the object giving rise to its evacuation. However, Bion's notion of 'nameless dread' (1962), although putting the accent more on there being no language, no name for a powerful anxiety, moves towards an idea of non-representation. So, too, does Winnicott's concept of primitive archaic, unthinkable anxiety (1962, p. 57; 1965, p. 86).

Representation and symbolisation

Although certainly a symbol is a representation, representation is not the same as symbolisation, and it is not equated with symbolisation in French thinking. Representation, required in order to symbolise, is a less developed phenomenon, its origins predating the achievement of symbolisation. Symbolisation in French thinking usually carries the Lacanian reference to the father, the Oedipal triad, which he was the first to link with the entry into the symbolic.

The Lacanian symbolic is always equated with language, the entry into culture; the sensitivity to language remains a French preoccupation, even when Lacan is repudiated. As we have pointed out elsewhere in this introduction, Winnicott's influence transformed and enriched the understanding of symbolic functioning generally and, in particular, its developmental trajectory. However, the classical study of the relationship between the thing-presentation and the word-presentation in Freudian metapsychology (1915e) continues to underpin the thinking of French psychoanalysts about the symbolic, alongside both the Lacanian equation of the Oedipal with the symbolic and the Winnicottian understanding of the role of transitional phenomena in the development of symbolisation (Gibeault, 1989; Roussillon, 1995).

In French psychoanalysis, the gap between the word or the image and 'the thing' is understood to be a product of a complex development, a recognition of the otherness of the other, and a corresponding decline in infantile omnipotence. We find that French psychoanalysts refer to 'the thing' in a way which does not quite match the English language 'concrete', a more explicit and far less mysterious notion, less redolent of a remote realm of archaic experience.

Hannah Segal (1957), drawing on Klein's conceptualisation of the work of mourning in the depressive position, has linked the achievement of symbolic thinking with a mourning process in her analysis of the difference between symbolic equation and symbolisation proper. In fact, a tone of mourning colours the French understanding of the gap between any image and the experience it represents, such that there will always be a wish for a narcissistic regression, a fusion with the object, and the drives will always seek to reinstate that illusory position. There is, on the other hand, a sense – again following Freud – that the joining of the thing-presentation with words actually has the power to restore some affective resonance to the image, and this capacity of words – in particular, the metaphorical capacity of words – is the subject of Kristeva's article (chapter 21, this volume). There she focuses on the centrality of this function of words within the analytic process to restore the links between image or idea and affect.

Psychosomatics

Whether referred to or not, in the writings of many French thinkers the pioneering work of Pierre Marty, along with that of the other founding members of the Paris Psychosomatic School, Fain, David and de M'Uzan, informs any consideration of the relationship between drives and representation, the capacity to think, imagine, free-associate, metabolise feelings. There is no real equivalent in the English-speaking tradition of psychoanalysis, although there is, amongst the French, respect paid to Franz Alexander (1950) and, later, Nemiah and Sifneos (1970) in America. As early as 1956, Pierre Marty located a process in which the drives fail to achieve psychic representation, and he identified somatisation as the alternative to 'mentalisation' (Debray, 1998, pp. 14–23). At the time that Lacan was placing language and linguistic analysis at the centre of the psychoanalytic process and psychoanalytic understanding of unconscious processes, Marty was turning his attention to the body, not only as the source of the drives which may fail to reach psychic elaboration, but as the alternative field to which the psyche returns when the mental elaboration of the drives, fundamentally due to trauma and the overwhelming of the psychic apparatus, breaks down. In 1962, Marty and his collaborators, Fain, de M'Uzan and David, presented the concept of 'operational thinking' ['*pensée opératoire*'],[23] a form of thinking split radically from the level of phantasy, which is to say, libidinal life, or dream life (Marty & M'Uzan, 1963 – see chapter 22, this volume). '*Pensée opératoire*' is two-dimensional thought without the penumbra of associations which enriches psychic functioning – thought without relationship to the imaginary, cut off from unconscious processes, indeed, thought which seems to lack any 'reference to a living interior object' (Debray, 1998, p. 24). Marty declared this form of thought, a form of not thinking, not imagining, not dreaming, as typical of the psychosomatic patient, whose only method of discharge is action, behaviour or illness. Marty subsequently offered another conceptualisation central to the psychosomatic process, that of the '*dépression essentielle*', or essential depression (Marty, 1968 – chapter 23, this volume), a depression without an object, a disappearance of libidinal and narcissistic investment, a flattening of affect, and a corresponding breakdown of psychic processes. Essential depression, he emphasised, is different from melancholia, which is fundamentally object related, a struggle with an object, libidinal or narcissistic. Even a psychotic depression is a way of hanging on to the object relationship. Essential depression lacks this quality of struggle, ultimately between the life and death instincts. Rather, as Marty wrote dramatically in 1968, the two defining qualities of the essential depression are, in his view, the disappearance of the libido and the 'functional fragmentation' ['*morcellement fonctionnel*'], by which he seems to mean the dissolution of the psychic capacity to function, to represent experience. And this, he continues, is the definition of the death instinct: it is a movement in the direction of a progressive disorganisation that ultimately ends in death. Marty does not use the language of *pulsion*, or drive, in reference to the death instinct. His conceptualisation of the death instinct seems more to do with the actuality of death, a radical subtraction of life, rather than with a drive. In less extreme situations, this process towards disorganisation is bound, contained by a temporary physical symptom. Such a symptom, even when it appears, as it often does, in

---

[23] '*Opératoire*' is sometimes translated as 'operative' and sometimes as 'operational'. It refers to the realm of action as opposed to the realm of phantasy and oneiric thinking and to a deficiency of the preconscious. Thus Marty and his collaborators refer to operational thinking, operational life, operational functioning and even operational dreaming (in relation to certain types of dreams in which symbolic elaboration is minimal). In order to keep a consistency of translation, we have chosen 'operational' as the translation for *opératoire* in all the texts, as it is the more usual translation.

the functioning of less damaged, more neurotic personalities, is seen not to express a conflict but to halt the progressive unbinding unleashed in the movement towards disorganisation, which is the response to the overwhelming of the ego. The body offers a physical place which, one might say, 'patches' – as Freud said of delusion (1924b [1923]) – the hole in the psychic shield. Marty finds the psychosomatic regression a feature of life, a product of traumatic encounter, frequently a temporary response to an overwhelming psychic blow. Severe psychosomatic illness, characterised by the robotic *'pensée opératoire'*, is the manifestation of a process that is more destructive, pervasive and unreachable.

It is a distinguishing feature of French psychoanalysis that the field of psychosomatics, which continues to be a focus of profound meditation and controversy, concentrates the minds of so many important thinkers. It is of interest that this theorising of the disintegration or disorganising of the mind derives from the study of psychosomatic illness, whereas in the English-speaking world the emphasis on the destruction of psychic links in the mind has been one of the central contributions of Bion and has been studied as a characteristic of psychotic functioning. Bion's application has been primarily to the metabolising of affect and the relation to the object, rather less to the relationship to the libidinal drives and the body. The violence of Bion's depiction of the attacks on linking in psychotic functioning contrasts with Marty's portrayal of the almost passive surrender to the destruction of life in the disorganisation, in which he sees the psychosomatic illness as both manifestation and defence. The body pays in illness to save the mind from disintegration. For Marty, the symptom discloses a loss of meaning, the surrender to the death instinct manifesting itself in the cutting of links to object and representation. This conceptualisation is different from that of the French psychoanalyst Joyce McDougall (1989), who sees the somatic symptom as the result and expression of conflict, more reminiscent of Freud's theory of hysteria and, though differently conceived, similar to Rosenfeld's conceptualisation (1965, pp. 187–188), who also sees the somatic symptom as the product of conflict.

Marty's bold conceptualisation, like Bion's, is susceptible to reification and trivialisation, but it also carries unforgettable impact. The problematic of the death instinct – challenged by both Lacan and Nacht, the two founding fathers of French psychoanalysis (Diatkine, 2005) – was placed firmly on the theoretical and clinical map of psychoanalytic thinking by Marty, where it continues to inspire disagreement and controversy in clinical and theoretical debate in France (see chapters by Green, Laplanche, Rosenberg, Aisenstein, Gibeault, etc., this volume). His emphasis on the failure of representation provides a significant foundation for André Green's conceptualisation of 'the negative', one aspect of which is *'la psychose blanche'*. Evelyne and Jean Kestemberg, who were pioneers in the psychoanalytic treatment of psychotic patients, introduced at the same time the hypothesis of a 'cold psychosis' to describe non-delusional psychoses which are very close to borderline states (Kestemberg, 2001).

The psychoanalytic process and the setting

In French, a psychoanalysis is referred to as '*la cure*'. It is important to note that the word '*cure*' in French does not have the same meaning as 'cure' in English; the two words are what is called '*faux amis*'. The French analyst, reminded again by Lacan, adheres to Freud's belief that the therapeutic gains come as a by-product of the uncovering of psychic truth. The uncovering of truth is the only aim, and this is what heals. However, contrary to the Lacanians, French Freudian psychoanalysts have always stressed the importance of linking the issue of *knowledge* to the *therapeutic* aims of psychoanalysis, aims which, however, go beyond the resolution of symptoms (the English meaning of 'cure'), as Freud himself underlined.

In fact it is difficult to translate '*la cure analytique*'; it has been translated as 'the psycho-analytic cure' (e.g., in Laplanche & Pontalis, 1967), which is misleading, but there seems no adequate equivalent. It is not 'the psychoanalytic treatment', unless we keep it separate from a medical model and removed from the more Anglo-Saxon notion of specific outcome goals. '*La cure*' implies a span of time as its central feature; it is used for such things as rest cures or thermal baths.[24] *La cure analytique* is something which takes place over time and has as its central aim the freeing of the associative process. A British analyst might consider the relationship to the analyst and its modifications to be of central importance – 'making contact with the patient' will be the sort of expression used – but for the French analyst, what is central is enabling the free associative process and working-through to take place.

Donnet (2001 – chapter 6, this volume) compares the psychoanalytic situation with what La Fontaine describes in his fable 'The Labourer and His Children'. In this, a rich farmer on his deathbed tells his children that they must not sell the land left by their parents because on it is hidden a treasure, and they must work the land if they wish to find it. The father dies and they get to work. At the end of the year, thanks to their efforts, the land becomes more productive. Then comes the moral of the fable: there was no hidden money, but before dying the father had shown his children that work is the treasure. In other words, 'the goal is the journey'; there is no other goal. In '*la cure*', the

---

[24] It is interesting to note that in Freud's pre-psychoanalytic paper on 'Hysteria' (1888b), he writes: 'In recent years the so-called "rest-*cure*" of Weir Mitchell (also known as Playfair's treatment) has gained a high reputation as a method of treating hysteria in institutions, and deservedly so. It consists in a combination of isolation in absolute quiet with a systematic application of massage and general faradisation; the attendance of a trained nurse is as essential as the constant influence of the physician. This treatment is of extraordinary value for hysteria, as a happy combination of "traitement moral" with an improvement in the patient's general nutritional state. It is not to be regarded, however, as something systematically complete in itself; the isolation, rather, and the physician's influence remain the principal agents, and, along with massage and electricity, the other therapeutic methods are not to be neglected. The best plan is, after four to eight weeks of rest in bed, to apply hydrotherapy and gymnastics and to encourage plenty of movement' (p. 55; italics added). A footnote mentions that 'At a later date Freud recommended a combination of Weir Mitchell's rest-cure with Breuer's cathartic treatment'. On this model of the hydrotherapy 'cure', Freud saw his patients for periods of months.

open-ended process without a predetermined outcome is the only goal – a Freudian notion which Bion has also picked up on when he writes that what is required of the analyst 'is a positive act of refraining from memory and desire' (1970, p. 31). For the French psychoanalyst, however, the psychoanalytic patient needs to have the potential for associative work – that is, the capacity for symbolisation. Hence, for many French psychoanalysts, only neurotic patients are suitable for psychoanalysis. This again was Lacan's view, since there was no analysis outside of language and only the neurotic patient is capable of the symbolic activity required for the analysis of 'signifiers'. To non-neurotic patients (psychosomatic, borderline or psychotic) French analysts will propose either psychotherapy face to face in order to avoid regression and potential disintegration, or a very French form of treatment, psychodrama, described by Gibeault in chapter 40. Sometimes this comes as a prelude to a classical analysis, what they call a 'cure-type'. In the 'cure-type', the interpretation goes from one preconscious to another, with the aim of enhancing the associative process and enabling the de-condensation of meaning while maintaining an enigmatic dimension and a dose of uncertainty which pushes the process forward. The practice of sparse, short and sometimes enigmatic interpretations is based on this theoretical premise. The British practice of frequent, long and more explanatory interpretations addressed to the conscious ego is considered to be a more psychotherapeutic approach by French psychoanalysts, who reserve this for the more borderline patients and consider it to be 'supportive' rather than psychoanalytic.

French psychoanalysts are very interested in conceptualising the difference between psychotherapy and psychoanalysis. For them, regression is what characterises psychoanalysis. They are concerned to distinguish those patients who are able to use psychoanalysis from those who should be offered psychotherapy. In their view, narcissistic regression (regression to primary narcissism, i.e., the wish to fuse with the object in order to be completely satisfied) is possible only on the couch, and only patients able to manage such regression are suitable for psychoanalysis. This assumes a capacity to use representation instead of action. In psychotherapy, on the other hand, there is the assumption that the patient lacks the capacity to use topographical and formal regression.

In France, the indication for psychoanalysis is more restricted than in Great Britain, where the lack of capacity to symbolise is not necessarily taken as a contraindication, because it is thought that this capacity can develop within a traditional setting. Hence the British psychoanalyst will treat patients who would be treated in psychotherapy by the French psychoanalyst. From the French point of view, the British psychoanalyst is much more active and uses language in order to 'hold' the patient and hence prevent regression, which would be too disorganising ('malignant regression') for these patients. However, they believe that this way of practising psychoanalysis tends more towards what they would consider to be psychotherapy.

Taking off from the notion of narcissistic regression, de M'Uzan (1994; see also chapter 9, this volume) specifies an experience of controlled depersonalisation in the session during this regression, which will enable a reconfiguration of identity and the boundaries of the self, as well as of the integration of psychic bisexuality.

It should be noted that British analysts may consider that patients whom French psychoanalysts call neurotic and suitable for psychoanalysis are really borderline. British analysts will often focus on the psychotic parts of the personality of otherwise neurotic patients, which to French colleagues make such patients sound more disturbed, while they believe that their French colleagues are not seeing or are ignoring those aspects of their patients which are not neurotic. The practice of the five-times-a-week analysis, as opposed to three times a week in France, also brings to the foreground claustro-agoraphobic anxieties typical of borderline patients. In fact, one of the justifications for the practice, in France, of three-times-a-week analysis is that it introduces 'the third' through the importance of the breaks between sessions and thus reduces the psychotic anxieties. French psychoanalysts also believe that the patient needs to be encouraged to be independent, to have days when he or she will take over the 'analysing function', which they see as the ultimate aim, and to have time for 'working through' in the *après-coup*. The British stress on separation anxiety and the acceptance of dependency needs is not usually a concern of theirs, the focus being more on sexuality in the wider sense of the word, or on representation. The relationship to language itself is different. While for British psychoanalysts the language used by the analyst is primarily thought of as a tool, for the French analyst language is 'the third'.

It should be noted that French psychoanalysts have, in more recent years, shown interest in treating more disturbed patients on the couch, probably influenced by their reading of Winnicott and Bion. Previous to that, the post-war French analysts such as Sacha Nacht, Paul-Claude Racamier, Serge Lebovici, René Diatkine and Jean and Evelyne Kestemberg also worked with psychotic and borderline patients in the 1950s and 1960s, developing other settings and a theory of technique quite different from the one developed by British psychoanalysts and which is still in use today (see section VII).

We are here, of course, having to make some generalisations which do not cover the many nuances and individualities. It is also interesting to recognise that similar issues are discussed within cultures, although addressed differently. For example, the issue of what is 'supportive' and what is 'psychoanalytic', what is 'gratifying' and what is 'the truth' comes up repeatedly in the psychoanalytic field and is a point of debate between various theoretical positions. While French psychoanalysts sometimes consider a Kleinian technique to be supportive and psychotherapeutic, some Kleinians consider a Winnicottian or a Kohutian approach to be supportive and non-psychoanalytic.

French psychoanalysts often emphasise the role of '*le cadre*', the setting. The literal translation of '*le cadre*' is 'the frame', as in the frame of a painting, a meaning which puts an emphasis on the distinction between inside and outside the analytic situation, but also on the necessity of a rigidity at the frontier between inside and outside. It is for French psychoanalysts a reference to the third, while in Britain the setting is sometimes conceived of more as a maternal container. Marion Milner (1950) has explicitly used the metaphor of the frame of a painting but only to describe the delineation, spatial and temporal, of outside from inside as enabling a creative illusion to take place.

The '*cadre*' is also a reference to the frequency of weekly sessions and the use of the couch, and it touches on 'rules', 'the fundamental rule' of free association without censorship, which French analysts usually remind their patients of whereas British analysts might not. A frequent reference to '*le cadre*' by French psychoanalysts is a counterpoint to Lacan's breaking of the time frame.

The metaphor of the theatre is a recurring theme in French psychoanalysis. Psychoanalysis is conceived of and represented as a three-dimensional space, a theatre where unconscious scenes are staged. The idea that patient and analyst are, in a sense, both spectators to this stage conveys a rather different conception to the more frequent British notion of the relationship between patient and analyst as the focus of attention. Winnicott's notion of 'playing alone in the presence of someone' (1958, p. 418) may be nearer to it, a notion of the analyst as provider of a space for the patient free from intrusion – and French psychoanalysts often make reference to this notion of Winnicott's. This is also reflected in a concern by French psychoanalysts not to intrude with their theories. Winnicott's notion of transitional space also influences a notion of the analytic space as a space which does not belong to either analyst or patient but is transitional and a joint creation.

The Lacanian, very silent analyst, who makes only very brief enigmatic comments mirroring the enigmatic unconscious, has given the image of French psychoanalysts as almost completely silent. This is not true of contemporary psychoanalysts who do not belong to the Lacanian school. Green writes against too much silence: '. . . excessive silence abandons the patient to dereliction. . . . Worse still would be if the patient's "organisation" were to respond to the analyst's silence by a sort of narcissistic indifference in which he puts himself out of reach' (2005, p. 85). However, it remains true that, in general, French analysts speak less than their British counterparts.

The concern with an experience free from intrusion is developed foremost by Donnet (2001 – chapter 6, this volume). He writes about the transference onto the setting in which the setting becomes idealised for unconscious reasons, something which may not be noticed by the analyst if he or she has a similar countertransference to the setting. Donnet argues that this transference onto the setting needs to be worked through and dissolved.

Laplanche (chapter 12, this volume) conceived of the analytic situation as structured by a first seduction from the analyst who offers an analysis, paralleling the first seduction by the mother towards the child. It is in this sense that

Neyraut (1974 – chapter 11, this volume) writes that the countertransference precedes the transference. This seduction by the analyst is as necessary as the seduction of the mother by her own desire which is structuring of the psyche.

The role of the (m)other in shaping the psyche has also given rise to the interest of a number of French psychoanalysts in the notion of the 'field', a unity or system in which both analyst and patient are participants. The notion of bipersonal field developed by Madeleine and Willy Baranger (1961–62), psychoanalysts of French origin who trained and settled in Latin America, refers to an unconscious phantasy of the patient-and-analyst couple to which each contributes. According to Duparc (2001), the notion of the field was perhaps inspired by Lagache's borrowing from behaviourism in the 1950s and was developed, independently from the Barangers, in France by Viderman around 1967.[25] Neyraut, de M'Uzan, Faimberg and d'Urtubey are amongst those whose theories also rely on this way of thinking in which can be found the ideas of Laplanche and his Lacanian origins. For instance, de M'Uzan describes the '*chimèra*', an image coming into the mind of the analyst in a state of 'formal regression' and a pure construction of the specific analytic situation. This specific interest in the mode of communication with the patient via the formal regression of the analyst, which enables the analyst to capture images which may be made explicit to the patient in order to foster representation, is also central to the work of César and Sára Botella, with their notion of '*figurabilité*'.

A specific French contribution is a significant contemporary development centring around the work of Green and the Botella and which is concerned with mental states in which there is no representation (as idea or image). This rests on a model which sees representation as an active psychic development rather than a given, together with a notion of a death drive which pushes towards nothingness, as described earlier. 'Blank psychoses' [*psychose blanche*] do not include an object; they follow the trajectory of the death drive in Green's formulation, in which the movement is away from objects, from links and from representations.

The Botellas (chapter 18) describe a clinical stance in which the analyst in a state of formal regression lends himself to 'working as a double' [*travail en double*], a state in which the work of representation (forming images) can take place in the mind of the analyst where it could not in the mind of the patient.

---

[25] Duparc, in a paper on the countertransference scene in France (2001) in the *International Journal of Psychoanalysis*, interestingly suggests that in reviewing the literature he came to see that Lacan's disparagement of the use of the word countertransference, in vogue in the English-speaking countries, became an impediment for all the authors he influenced, for some time. Noting the same kind of influence that we have commented on more generally in French psychoanalysis, he writes: '. . . Lacan's idiosyncratic practice and the liberties he took with session length and the classical setting, by sparking a fierce debate within French psychoanalysis, usefully drew attention to the link between countertransference and the treatment setting, an interesting trend in the French literature on the countertransference. This however, in effect called for a period of mourning – on the part of Lacan's pupils and enemies alike – for the positive or negative idealisation aroused by his thought' (p. 153).

In that way the analyst can lend him/herself to do the work which it is not possible for the patient to do. They call this work 'figurability' [*figurabilité*], making reference to Freud's *Darstellung* [figuration, image]. 'The analyst's work of figurability arising from the formal regression of his thinking during the session, proves to be the best and perhaps the only means of access to this state beyond the mnemic trace, which is memory without recollection' (Botella & Botella, 2001/2005, p. xv). This interest in conceptualising the experience of nothingness seems at least in part to belong to a French philosophical tradition which gives French contemporary psychoanalysis its particular flavour. The work of Bion supplemented this. This departs from the Lacanian influence insofar as Lacan was not interested in what is outside representation. At the same time, the notion of the double and 'working as a double' is interestingly reminiscent of the role of the mirror for Lacan, as a founding moment in the apprehension of the self from the outside.

This concern with representation as discussed earlier also stems from the extensive interest of French psychoanalysts in patients suffering from psychosomatic disorders without any awareness of psychic conflict or distress. This focus may be the product of the greater cooperation between the medical profession, the hospital services and psychoanalysts in France.

The title of Joyce McDougall's book *The Theatres of the Body* (1989) reflects that understanding of an unconscious scene played out in the body and which the psychoanalyst needs to relocate in the mind via the analytic situation. With such patients, the French psychoanalysts work for a long time in face-to-face psychotherapy until a proper psychoanalytic setting can hopefully be started (see Aisenstein, chapter 24, this volume).

Concluding remarks

In this introduction we have wanted to give a general map of French psychoanalysis as seen from our perspective, showing the impact of Lacan on the development of the French psychoanalytic scene and the specific debates within it. The interest in and influence of the work of Winnicott and of Bion in particular have been part of this debate and reaction against Lacan. This has led to developments towards an interest in the more disturbed states, in particular states and pathologies in which there is a deficiency of representation (blank psychosis, cold psychosis, psychosomatic states, 'essential depression'). The study of the analytic work necessary for representation to develop (*'travail de figurabilité'*), the study of specific states within the psychoanalytic situation ('controlled depersonalisation') and the development of specific treatment modes (psychodrama) are the product of this focus. We have argued in favour of the specificity of 'French psychoanalysis', to describe the early influences from within France and, later, from outside of France, leading together to these specific contemporary developments.

We arrived at the choice of papers in discussion with Alain Gibeault and from there came a decision about the structure of the book. A majority of the papers chosen are translated into English here for the first time.

Following the sections on the History of Psychoanalysis in France (section I) and The Pioneers and Their Legacy (section II), we divided the book into a further five sections which we thought best represented the main areas of concern of French psychoanalysts: The Setting and the Process of Psychoanalysis (section III), Phantasy and Representation (section IV), The Body and the Drives (section V), Masculine and Feminine Sexuality (section VI), and Psychosis (section VII). This division could obviously be done differently, but it grouped the important papers in a way which for us made sense and allowed the introductions to the sections to coalesce around a meaningful theme that could be fruitfully developed by Alain Gibeault.

At the end of the book we have added a glossary of concepts developed by some of the authors presented in this book and which cannot be found in Laplanche and Pontalis's *The Language of Psychoanalysis*.

References

Alexander, F. (1950). *Psychosomatic Medicine: Its Principles and Applications*. New York: W. W. Norton.

Anzieu, D. (1974). Le moi-peau [The skin ego]. *Nouvelle Revue de Psychanalyse*, *3*: 195–208.

Anzieu, D. (1975d). Le transfert paradoxal. De la communication paradoxale à la réaction thérapeutique négative. *Nouvelle Revue de Psychanalyse*, *12*: 49–72. [Paradoxical transference. *Contemporary Psychoanalysis* (1986), *22*: 520–547.]

Anzieu, D. (1985). *Le moi-peau*. Paris: Dunod. [*The Skin Ego*. New Haven, CT: Yale University Press, 1989.]

Aulagnier, P. (1975). *La violence de l'interprétation. Du pictogramme à l'énoncé*. Paris: Presses Universitaires de France. [*The Violence of Interpretation: From Pictogram to Statement*, trans. A. Sheridan. London: Routledge, 2001.]

Baranger, M., & Baranger, W. (1961–62). La situación analitica como campo dinámico. *Revista Uruguaya Psicoanálisis*, *4*: 3–54. [The Analytic Situation as a Dynamic Field. 1961–1962. *International Journal of Psychoanalysis*, *89* (2008, No. 4): 795–826.]

Barzilai, S. (1995). Models of Reflexive Recognition. *Psychoanalytic Study of the Child*, *50*: 368–382.

Bateson, G., Jackson, D. D., Haley, J., & Weakland, J. (1956). Toward a Theory of Schizophrenia. *Behavioral Science*, *1*: 251–264.

Baudry, F. (1989). Negation and Its Vicissitudes in the History of Psychoanalysis – Its Particular Impact on French Psychoanalysis. *Contemporary Psychoanalysis 25*: 501–508.

Bergeret, J. (2002). Homosexuality or Homoeroticism? 'Narcissistic Eroticism.' *International Journal of Psychoanalysis*, *83*: 351–362.

Bick, E. (1968). The Experience of the Skin in Early Object Relationships. *International Journal of Psychoanalysis*, *49*: 484–486.

Bion, W. R. (1962). A Theory of Thinking. *International Journal of Psychoanalysis*, *43*: 306–310. Reprinted in *Second Thoughts*. London: Heinemann, 1967.

Bion, W. R. (1970). *Attention and Interpretation*. London: Tavistock Publications.

Birksted-Breen, D. (1993). *The Gender Conundrum*. New York: Routledge, 2007.
Birksted-Breen, D. (1996). Unconscious Representation of Femininity. *Journal of the American Psychoanalytic Association, 44S*: 119–132.
Birksted-Breen, D. (2003). Time and the après-coup. *International Journal of Psychoanalysis, 84*: 1501–1515.
Bokanowski, T. (1995). The Concept of Psychic Homosexuality. *International Journal of Psychoanalysis, 76*: 793–804.
Botella, C. & Botella, S. (1984). L'homosexualité inconsciente et la dynamique du double en séance [Unconscious homosexuality and the dynamics of the double in the session]. *Revue Française de Psychanalyse, 48* (3): 687–708. [Revised and extended version reprinted as: 'Working as a Double'. In *The Work of Psychic Figurability: Mental States without Representation*, trans. A. Weller, with M. Zerbib. London: Routledge, 2005.]
Botella, C., & Botella, S. (2001). *La figurabilité psychique*. Paris/Lausanne: Delachaux et Niestlé. [*The Work of Psychic Figurability: Mental States without Representation*, trans. A. Weller, with M. Zerbib. London: Routledge, 2005.]
Braunschweig, D., & Fain, M. (1975). *La nuit, le jour. Essai psychanalytique sur le foncionnement mental*. [Day, night: A psychoanalytic essay on mental functioning]. Paris: Presses Universitaires de France.
Britton, R. (1989). The Missing Link: Parental Sexuality in the Oedipus Complex. In: R. Britton, M. Feldman, & E. O'Shaughnessy *The Oedipus Complex Today: Clinical Implications* (pp. 83–101). London: Karnac.
Brusset, B. (2006). Métapsychologie des liens et troisième topique [The metapsychology of linking and a third topography]. *Revue Française de Psychanalyse, 70* (5, Special Congress Issue): 1213–1282.
Caillot, J.-P. (2002). *Dictionnaire international de la psychanalyse* [International Dictionary of psychoanalysis]. Paris: Calmann-Lévy.
Chasseguet-Smirgel, J. (1964). *Recherches psychanalytiques nouvelles sur la sexualité feminine*. Paris: Presses Universitaires de France. [*Female Sexuality: New Psychoanalytic Views*. Ann Arbor, MI: University of Michigan Press, 1970; reprinted London: Virago, 1981.]
Chasseguet-Smirgel, J. (1974). Perversion, Idealization and Sublimation. *International Journal of Psychoanalysis, 55*: 349–357.
Chasseguet-Smirgel, J. (1991). Review of *The Oedipus Complex Today: Clinical Implications*. *International Journal of Psychoanalysis, 72*: 727–730.
Chiland, C. (1997). *Changer de sexe* [Changing sex]. Paris: Editions Odile Jacob.
David, C. (1975). La bisexualité psychique: éléments de réevaluation [Psychic bisexuality: Elements of re-evaluation]. *Revue Française de Psychanalyse, 39* (5/6): 713–856.
Debray, R. (1998). *Pierre Marty*. Paris: Presses Universitaires de France.
Denis, P. (1982). Homosexualité primaire. Base de contradiction [Primary homosexuality: A foundation of contradictions]. *Revue Française de Psychanalyse, 46* (1).
Denis, P. (2002). Un principe d'organisation–désorganisation [A principle of organisation–disorganisation]. *Revue Française de Psychanalyse, 66* (5): 1799–1808.
Denis, P. (2006). *The Power of the Drives*. Paper presented at conference on Freud Today, University College London.
Diatkine, G. (1997). *Jacques Lacan*. Paris: Presses Universitaires de France.
Diatkine, G. (2005). 'Beyond the Pleasure Principle.' In R. Perelberg (Ed.), *Freud: A Modern Reader*. London: Whurr.
Dolto, F. (1984). *L'image inconsciente du corps* [The unconscious image of the body]. Paris: Editions du Seuil.
Donnet, J. (2001). From the Fundamental Rule to the Analysing Situation. *International Journal of Psychoanalysis, 82*: 129–140.

Duparc, F. (2001). The Countertransference Scene in France. *International Journal of Psychoanalysis*, *82* (1): 151–169.

Evans, D. (1996). *An Introductory Dictionary of Lacanian Psychoanalysis*. London: Routledge.

Faimberg, H. (1981). Listening to Listening. In *The Telescoping of Generations*. New Library of Psychoanalysis. Hove: Routledge, 2005.

Fain, M. (1971). Prélude à la vie fantasmatique [Prelude to fantasmatic life]. *Revue Française de Psychanalyse*, *35*: 291–364.

Freud, A. (1926). Introduction to the Technique of Child Analysis. In *The Writings of Anna Freud*. New York: International Universities Press, 1966.

Freud, A. (1936). *The Ego and the Mechanisms of Defence*. London: Hogarth Press.

Freud, S. (1888b). 'Hysteria' and 'Hystero-Epilepsy'. *S.E.*, 1.

Freud, S. (1900a). *The Interpretation of Dreams*. *S.E.*, 4/5.

Freud, S. (1901b). *The Psychopathology of Everyday Life*. *S.E.*, 6.

Freud, S. (1905d). *Three Essays on the Theory of Sexuality*. *S.E.*, 7.

Freud, S. (1914c). On Narcissism: An Introduction. *S.E.*, 14.

Freud, S. (1915c). Instincts and Their Vicissitudes. *S.E.*, 14.

Freud, S. (1915e). The Unconscious. *S.E.*, 14.

Freud, S. (1917e [1915]). Mourning and Melancholia. *S.E.*, 14.

Freud, S. (1918b [1914]). From the History of an Infantile Neurosis. *S.E.*, 17.

Freud, S. (1920g). *Beyond the Pleasure Principle*. *S.E.*, 28.

Freud, S. (1923b). *The Ego and the Id*. *S.E.*, 19.

Freud, S. (1924b [1923]). Neurosis and Psychosis.*S.E.*, Vol 19.

Freud, S. (1925h). Negation. *S.E.*, 19.

Freud, S. (1927e). Fetishism. *S.E.*, 21.

Freud, S. (1933a). *New Introductory Lectures on Psycho-Analysis*. *S.E.*, 22.

Freud, S. (1937c). Analysis Terminable and Interminable. *International Journal of Psycho-Analysis*, 18: 373–405.

Freud, S. (1950 [1892–99]). Extracts from the Fliess Papers. *S.E.*, 1.

Gibeault, A. (1980). Les *Trois Essais*: auto-érotisme prépubertaire, choix d'objet précoce, étayage; narcissisme et définition de la pulsion [The three essays: Pre-pubertal auto-eroticism, early object-choice, anaclisis and the definition of drive]. In *Les pulsions. Amour et faim, vie et mort* [Drives: Love and hunger, life and death] (pp.53–88). Paris: Tchou.

Gibeault, A. (1989). Destins de la symbolization [The vicissitudes of symbolization]. *Revue Française de Psychanalyse*, *53* (3, Special Congress Issue): 1517–1617.

Gibeault, A. (2005). *D.W. Winnicott and France: A Love Story*. Paper presented at the Third International Congress on the Work of Donald W. Winnicott, Milan (17–20 November).

Green, A. (1973). *Le discours vivant. La conception psychanalytique de l'affect*. Paris: Presses Universitaires de France. [*The Fabric of Affect in the Psychoanalytic Discourse*. The New Library of Psychoanalysis. London: Routledge, Kegan and Paul, 1999.]

Green, A. (1975). Has Sexuality Anything to Do with Psychoanalysis? *International Journal of Psychoanalysis*, *76*: 871–883.

Green, A. (1983). *Narcissisme de vie, Narcissisme de mort*. Paris: Minuit. [*Life Narcissism, Death Narcissism*. London: Free Association Books, 2001.]

Green, A. (1986). *On Private Madness*. London: Hogarth Press and The Institute of Psychoanalysis.

Green, A. (1993). *Le travail du négatif*. Paris: Editions de Minuit. [*The Work of the Negative*, trans. A. Weller. London: Free Association Books, 1999.]

Green, A. (1995a). Has Sexuality Anything to Do with Psychoanalysis? *International Journal of Psychoanalysis*, *76*: 871–883.

Green, A. (1995b). De l'objet non unifiable à la fonction objectalisante [From the non-unifiable object to the objectalizing function]. In *Propédeutique. La metapsychologie revisitee* [Propaedeutics: Metapsychology revisited]. Seyssel: Editions Champ Vallon.

Green, A. (1997). The Intuition of the Negative in *Playing and Reality. International Journal of Psychoanalysis*, *78*: 1071–1084. Reprinted in: *The Dead Mother: The Work of André Green*, ed. G. Kohon. London: Routledge, 1999.

Green, A. (2001). *The Chains of Eros*. London: Karnac.

Green, A. (2002). A Dual Conception of Narcissism: Positive and Negative Organizations. *Psychoanalytic Quarterly*, *71*: 631–649.

Green, A. (2005). *Key Ideas for a Contemporary Psychoanalysis*. The New Library of Psychoanalysis. Hove: Routledge.

Green, A. (2008). Freud's Concept of Temporality: Differences with Current Ideas. *International Journal of Psychoanalysis*, *89* (5): 1029–1039.

Grunberger, B. (1979). *Narcissism: Psychoanalytic Essays*. Madison, CT: International Universities Press.

Guignard, F. (1997). *Èpître à l'objet* [Epistle to the object]. Paris: Presses Universitaires de France.

Irigaray, L. (1985). *The Speculum of the Other Woman*, trans. B. C. Till. Ithaca, NY: Cornell University Press.

Isaacs, S. (1952). *The Nature and Function of Phantasy in Developments in Psychoanalysis*. London: Hogarth Press.

Jacoby, R. (1986). *The Repression of Psychoanalysis*. Chicago: University of Chicago Press.

Joseph, B. (1975). The Patient Who Is Difficult to Reach. In *Psychic Equilibrium and Psychic Change*, ed. M. Feldman & E. Bott Spillius. New Library of Psychoanalysis. London: Routledge.

Kestemberg, E. (2001). *La psychose froide* [Cold psychosis]. Paris: Presse Universitaires de France.

King, P., & Steiner, R. (1991). *The Freud–Klein Controversies 1941–1945*. New Library of Psychoanalysis. London: Routledge.

Klein, M. (1930). The Importance of Symbol Formation in the Development of the Ego. In *Love, Guilt and Reparation*. London: Hogarth Press, 1975.

Kris, E. (1943). Some Problems of War Propaganda – A Note on Propaganda New and Old. *Psychoanalytic Quarterly*, *12*: 381–399.

Kristeva, J. (1974). *La révolution du language poétique*. Paris: Editions du Seuil. [*Revolution in Poetic Language*, trans. M. Walter. New York: Columbia University Press, 1984.]

Lacan, J. (1949). Le stade du miroir comme formateur de la fonction du Je telle qu'elle nous est révélée dans l'expérience psychanalytique. In *Écrits*. Paris: Editions du Seuil, 1966. [The Mirror Stage as Formative of the Function of the *I* as Revealed in Psychoanalytic Experience. In *Ecrits*, trans. A. Sheridan. London: Tavistock, 1977.]

Lacan, J. (1954a). Discourse Analysis and Ego Analysis. In *The Seminar of Jacques Lacan, Book I*, ed. J.-A. Miller. Cambridge: Cambridge University Press, 1988.

Lacan, J. (1954b). The Topic of the Imaginary. In *The Seminar of Jacques Lacan, Book I*, ed. J.-A. Miller. Cambridge: Cambridge University Press, 1988.

Lacan, J. (1973). *Le Séminaire, Vol. XI*. Paris: Editions du Seuil.

Laplanche, J. (1989). Towards a General Theory of Seduction. In *New Foundations for Psychoanalysis* (pp. 104–116), trans D. Macey. Oxford: Blackwell.

Laplanche, J. (1997). The Theory of Seduction and the Problem of the Other. *International Journal of Psychoanalysis*, *78*: 653–666.

Laplanche, J. (1998). *Notes sur l'après-coup*. Standing Conference on Psychoanalytical, Intracultural and Intercultural Dialogue, Paris (27–29 July).

Laplanche, J., & Pontalis, J.-B. (1967). *Vocabulaire de la psychanalyse*. Paris: Presses Universitaires de France. [*The Language of Psychoanalysis*, trans. D. Nicholson-Smith, New York: Norton, 1973.]

Leclaire, S. (1975). *On tue un enfant*. Paris: Points-Editions de Seuil. [*A Child Is Being Killed: On Primary Narcissism and the Death Drive*. Stanford, CA: Stanford University Press.]

Lewin, B. (1946). Sleep, the Mouth, and the Dream Screen. Psychoanalytic Quarterly, *15*: 419–434.

Luepnitz, D. (2009). Thinking in the Space between Winnicott and Lacan. *International Journal of Psychoanalysis*, *90*: 957–981.

Marty, P. (1968). La dépression essentielle [Essential depression]. *Revue Française de Psychanalyse*, *32* (3): 345–355. [Also in: *Revue Française de Psychanalyse: Textes 1926–2006* (pp. 205–208). Paris: Presses Universitaires de France, 2006.]

Marty, P., & M'Uzan, M. de (1963). La pensée opératoire [Operational thinking]. *Revue Française de Psychanalyse* (1968), *32* (3): 595–598.

McDougall, J. (1972). Primal Scene and Sexual Perversion. *International Journal of Psychoanalysis*, *53*: 371–384.

McDougall, J. (1974). The Psychosoma and the Psychoanalytic Process. *International Review of Psychoanalysis*, *1*: 437–459.

McDougall, J. (1978). *Plaidoyer pour une certaine abnormalité*. Paris: Gallimard. [*Plea for a Measure of Abnormality*. New York: International Universities Press, 1980.]

McDougall, J. (1989). *Théâtres du corps*. Paris: Gallimard. [English: *Theatres of the Body*. London: Free Association Books.]

Milner, M. (1950). *On Not Being Able to Paint*. London: Heinemann.

Montrelay, M. (1984). On Folding and Unfolding: An Example of Dream Interpretation in Analysis. *Psychoanalytic Inquiry*, *4*: 193–219.

M'Uzan, M. de (1994). *La bouche de l'inconscient* [The mouth of the unconscious]. Paris: Gallimard.

Nemiah, J. C., & Sifneos, P. (1970). Affect and Fantasy in Patients with Psychosomatic Disorders. In *Modern Trends in Psychosomatic Medicine, Vol. 2*. London: Butterworth

Perelberg, R. (2006). The Controversial Discussions and Après-Coup. *International Journal of Psychoanalysis*, *87*: 1199–2220.

Pontalis, J.-B. (2005). *Notable Encounters*. Paper presented at the British Psychoanalytical Society.

Rolland, J. C. (2006). The Analyst at Work: A Young Woman's Distress. *International Journal of Psychoanalysis*, *87* (6): 1433–1443.

Rosenfeld, H. (1965). The psychopathology of hypochondriasis. In *Psychotic States*. London: Hogarth Press, 1982.

Rosenfeld, H. (1971). A Clinical Approach to the Psychoanalytic Theory of the Life and Death Instincts: An Investigation into the Aggressive Aspects of Narcissism. *International Journal of Psychoanalysis*, *52*: 169–178.

Roudinesco, E. (1990). *Jacques Lacan & Co: A History of Psychoanalysis in France, 1925–1985*. London: Free Association Books.

Roussillon, R. (1995). La métapsychologie des processus et la transitionnalité [The metapsychology of processes and transitionality]. *Revue Française de Psychanalyse*, *59* (Special Congress Issue): 1351–1519.

Scarfone, D. (2004). *Les Pulsions* [The drives]. Paris: Presses Universitaires de France.

Schaeffer, J. (1997). *Le refus du féminin* [The repudiation of the feminine] (4th edition). Paris: Presses Universitaires de France, 2003. New edition: *Le refus du féminin (La sphinge et son âme en peine)* [The repudiation of femininity (The Sphinx and its lost soul)]. Paris: Presses Universitaires de France, 2008.

Séchaud, E. (2008). The Handling of the Transference in French Psychoanalysis. *International Journal of Psychoanalysis*, *89* (5): 1011–1028.

Segal, H. (1957). Notes on Symbol-Formation. *International Journal of Psychoanalysis*, *38*: 391–397.

Sodre, I. (1997). Insight et après-coup. *Revue Française de Psychanalyse*, *61*: 1255–1262.

Turkle, S. (1978). *Psychoanalytic Politics: Freud's French Revolution*. London: Burnett/Basic Books.
Wallon, H. (1933). *Les origines du caractère chez l'enfant* [Origins of character in children]. Paris: Presses Universitaires de France, 1949.
Webster, R. (2002). *The Cult of Lacan: Freud Lacan and the Mirror Stage*. Available at www.richardwebster.net/thecultoflacan.html
Widlöcher, D. (1984). Quel usage faisons-nous du concept de pulsion? [What do we do with the concept of drives?]. In D. Anzieu, R. Dorey, J. Laplanche, & D. Widlöcher, *La pulsion pour quoi faire?* [Drives – What use are they?]. Paris: Association Psychanalytique de France, Colloque de l'Association Psychanalytique de France, 12 May.
Winnicott, D. (1958). The Capacity to Be Alone. *International Journal of Psychoanalysis*, *30*: 416–420. [Also in *The Maturational Processes and the Facilitating Environment*. London: Karnac, 1990.]
Winnicott, D. (1962). Ego Integration in Child Development. In *The Maturational Processes and the Facilitating Environment*. London: Karnac, 1990.
Winnicott, D. (1965). A Clinical Study of the Effect of a Failure of the Average Expectable Environment on a Child's Mental Functioning. *International Journal of Psychoanalysis*, *46*: 81–87.
Winnicott, D. (1967). Mirror Role of Mother and Family in Child Development. In *Playing and Reality*. London: Tavistock, 1971.

Section I

HISTORY OF PSYCHOANALYSIS IN FRANCE

I HISTORY OF PSYCHOANALYSIS IN FRANCE

Introduction

Alain Gibeault

In a letter addressed in March 1932 to the presidents of the various psychoanalytic societies, Freud wrote: 'The analyst must not want to be English, French, American or German, before becoming an adept at Analysis; he will have to place the common interests of the latter above national interests' (Mijolla, 1982, p. 31). Yet even by then certain trends in psychoanalysis could be seen as challenging Freud's conception; among the best-known of his followers, Jung, Ferenczi and Adler spring immediately to mind, even if we leave aside national characteristics that tended to throw an odd light on Freud's writings. Given that context, should we be talking of 'French psychoanalysis' – or would it not be better to discuss 'psychoanalysis in France'?

As in all countries, that history is part of a dynamic movement in which scientific and literary culture intersects with – and sometimes runs counter to – that of medicine. That is the point of view put forward in this volume by Alain de Mijolla, the founder of the International Association for the History of Psychoanalysis and an expert in the history of psychoanalysis in France (Mijolla, 2004 – chapter 1, this volume). He has painted here a broad picture of its development, in which he differentiates two trends. The first of these, prevalent in literature and the media, contributed to psychoanalysis becoming more widely known in French culture, while the second, more medical and psychiatric, encouraged – and continues to encourage – the development of psychoanalytic training and practice.

That dialectic belongs indeed to the definition that Freud himself gave of psychoanalysis in the famous encyclopaedia article that he wrote in 1923:

> Psycho-analysis is the name (1) of a procedure for the investigation of mental processes which are almost inaccessible in any other way, (2) of a method (based upon that investigation) for the treatment of neurotic disorders, and (3) of a collection of psychological information obtained along those lines, which is gradually being accumulated into a new scientific discipline.
>
> (1923a [1922], p. 235)

As a science aiming both to interpret civilisation and to be seen as a method of treatment, psychoanalysis could not avoid evoking both enthusiasm and rejection.

France did not escape that dialectic. Initially, medical and psychiatric circles in France rejected psychoanalysis in the name not only of the 'Latin' culture that was shocked by Freud's pansexualism, but also – and above all – of the anti-German feeling that was so characteristic of the situation in France between the two world wars. It was in fact the Surrealists – not particularly concerned with psychoanalysis as a treatment method – who at that time welcomed Freud's ideas. Freud commented on this in 1925: 'In France the interest in psycho-analysis began among the men of letters. To understand this, it must be borne in mind that from the time of the writing of *The Interpretation of Dreams* psycho-analysis ceased to be a purely medical subject' (Freud, 1925d [1924], p. 62). In a footnote to her 1950 French translation of Freud's *Autobiographical Study*, Marie Bonaparte writes, not without humour:

> The French have, as a national characteristic, certain features that make understanding psychoanalysis more difficult for them. . . . Primitive processes, which are specific to the unconscious and revealed by psychoanalysis, clash head-on with 'common-sense' points of view, logical reasoning, 'good taste' and sensitiveness; they easily scandalize the French spirit, which then forgets that Nature's phenomena are not always in 'good taste', a fact that 'does not prevent them from existing' as our Charcot used to say.

Nevertheless, the Paris Psychoanalytical Society (SPP: Société psychanalytique de Paris) – the first and therefore the oldest of the French psychoanalytic societies – was founded in 1926 and rapidly joined the International Psychoanalytical Association (IPA) founded by Freud in 1910. The credit for that belongs primarily to Marie Bonaparte, who began her analysis with Freud himself in 1925; he saw in her his special representative within psychoanalytic circles in France. As a psychoanalyst who had not trained as a medical practitioner, Marie Bonaparte played a significant role in making Freud's ideas more widely available in France, thanks to her translation of many of his books and papers; she firmly opposed those French psychiatrists who advocated a form of psychoanalysis 'made in France' – that is, cleaned of its Germanic residues such as the importance of infantile sexuality in unconscious mental life. In July 1927, she was one of the founders of the *Revue Française de Psychanalyse*, which is to this day the most important psychoanalytic journal in the French language.

It was only after the Second World War that a new generation of psychoanalysts enabled that science to develop rapidly in France; that expansion soon became one of the major trends in psychoanalysis throughout the world. At that time, Marie Bonaparte was still playing an important role in psychoanalytic circles: she was the only person in France to have been analysed by Freud (who, indeed, had entrusted her with the fate of psychoanalysis in France), and in 1938 she had been instrumental in helping Freud leave Austria after the Nazi occupation of that country, a fact that earned her the respect and gratitude of psychoanalysts throughout the world. She was not, however, in any way the guardian of any doctrine that would have enabled her to personify a French school of psychoanalysis.

Paradoxically enough, French psychoanalysis was born of two contradictory trends: the influence that psychoanalysis had in the English-speaking world, and the radical rejection of that movement as expressed in Britain and America. In post-war France, pioneers such as Serge Lebovici, Daniel Lagache and Maurice Bouvet welcomed the developments introduced by Anna Freud, Melanie Klein and D. W. Winnicott, who were indeed invited to Paris to meet their French counterparts. Child analysts such as Serge Lebovici and René Diatkine bore witness to the importance of the influence that these colleagues had on their own thinking – this was particularly the case of Winnicott's concepts of the transitional object and the potential space for play. From that point of view, the relationship between Winnicott and France was truly a story of love (Gibeault, 2005).

At that time, in the early 1950s, Jacques Lacan played a major role in stigmatising the ideas of the English-speaking psychoanalytic world – particularly those of Heinz Hartmann, Ernst Kris and Rudolph Loewenstein, the official representatives in the United States of the ego psychology school. This deep-rooted anti-Americanism had probably something to do with Lacan's transference with respect to his analyst, Loewenstein, one of the co-founders of the SPP in 1926, who fled to the United States in 1942 in order to escape the Nazi occupation of France. From that point of view, Lacan's report, 'The Function and Field of Speech and Language in Psychoanalysis', delivered to the Congress of Romance-Language Psychoanalysts in 1953, was quite obviously an anti-American manifesto and marked the beginning of that 'return to Freud' which would become a characteristic feature of the French psychoanalytic scene. That report, perhaps more familiar under its alternative title 'Discourse of Rome', marked a real turning-point. There were three aspects to the document: it was, simultaneously, a fierce argument against American developmental psychoanalysis, an invitation to undertake a careful re-reading of Freud's own papers and the premise of a theory that, for the next thirty years, would dominate French psychoanalysis (Smirnoff, 1979).

Even though this 'return to Freud' contributed to calling into question the psychoanalytic setting (shortening the length of sessions, in what he called 'scansion') and led to Lacan's exclusion from the SPP in 1953 (and, consequently, from the IPA), it remains to this day a specific feature of French psychoanalysis, with its fundamental reference to Freud's thinking, in its appraisal of psychoanalytic theory and clinical practice. More than for any other school of thought in psychoanalysis worldwide, the link between Freud and French psychoanalysis is a special and fundamental relationship, because the reference to Freud's concepts has a direct influence on our clinical understanding. In other countries, Freud's thinking is seen as belonging to the past, whereas in France it is still considered to be very much alive and topical; from that point of view, France could be seen as the loyal heir to Freud's thinking.

That loyalty has less to do with the man himself than with his life's work, hence the ease with which the fundamental concepts of psychoanalysis came to be examined. As Lacan himself pointed out: 'The meaning of a return to Freud is a return to Freud's meaning' (Lacan, 1955/2006, p. 337). That well-known Lacanian expression condenses the various directions taken by French psychoanalysis during the golden age which ran from the 1950s all the way through to Lacan's death in 1981. A whole generation of very well-known French psychoanalysts, many of them former analysands of Lacan (Jean Laplanche, Jean-Bertrand Pontalis, Daniel Widlöcher, Piera Aulagnier, René Diatkine, Jean Kestemberg, Didier Anzieu) contributed, each in his or her own way, to that psychoanalytic revival in France – a *renaissance* that could perhaps be seen as its true birth.

> The concept of **subjectivation** was introduced into psychoanalytic thinking in France in the early 1990s by Cahn (1991) in his description of the psychoanalytic treatment of adolescents. In the 1950s, Lacan had already insisted on the importance of differentiating between 'the subject' and 'the ego'. However, Lacan's linguistic approach led him to dispossess the concept of subject of any link with the body and affects.

The only way to discover 'Freud's meaning' was to go back to Freud's early writings, his early concepts, the very first papers that form the basis of his discoveries such as the 'Project for a Scientific Psychology' (1950 [1895]), *The Interpretation of Dreams* (1900a) and *Three Essays on the Theory of Sexuality* (1905d). Hence the paradox: 'It was thanks to that allegiance to Freud's Vienna that, in 1955, psychoanalysis became French' (Smirnoff, 1979).

The emphasis that American psychoanalysis laid on Freud's structural model (ego, id and superego) came therefore to be displaced onto his earlier topographical model (the unconscious, preconscious and conscious systems). The autonomous ego, separated from the instinctual drives and corresponding to the ideas of ego psychology, was pushed aside in favour of the 'other scene', that of the unconscious, corresponding to the hidden meaning of what one says. This is a shift from 'ego psychology' to the problem situation encountered by the *subject*, called into question by the logic of the signifier; this can still be seen today when mental phenomena are viewed in terms of **subjectivation and de-subjectivation**.

In their respective chapters, Alain de Mijolla and Daniel Widlöcher show that the charismatic Jacques Lacan had a major influence on the history of post-war psychoanalysis and gave French psychoanalysis a quite specific dimension. Widlöcher emphasises in chapter 2 (a paper which was written in 2001) also the fact that many French psychoanalysts later distanced themselves from Lacan's ideas, particularly as regards the aims of psychoanalytic treatment, transference and interpretation.

Indeed, as time went by, the 'return to Freud' gradually became a 'going towards Lacan' (Green, 2006) through his invention of a whole new terminology – the Other with a capital 'O', the Name-of-the Father [*Nom-du-Père*], the object *a* [*objet a*], etc. – and of new categories – the Real [*Réel*], Imaginary [*Imaginaire*] and Symbolic [*Symbolique*] dimensions – which were close to the French structuralist movement inspired by Ferdinand de Saussure's approach to linguistics. This approach to the 'unconscious structured like a language' led Lacan to put aside all reference in psychoanalysis to the affects, the body and the instinctual drives – thereby succumbing to the very trend he had castigated in American psychoanalysis. The return to Freud was intended as a counter-measure against '. . . the eclipse in psychoanalysis of the liveliest terms of its experience – the unconscious and sexuality, which will apparently cease before long to even be mentioned . . .' (Lacan, 1953/2006, p. 204). In fact, as this Lacanian adventure drew to a close, sexuality and the drives would also find themselves evacuated.

Nonetheless, that 'return to Freud' was the driving force behind the huge effort that was put into defining Freud's concepts more precisely, studying how they developed in his own writings and translating them into French in as relevant a way as possible. That is one of the positive effects of the importance given to written and oral language; it is not by chance that two of Lacan's analysands, Jean-Bertrand Pontalis and Jean Laplanche, were the initiators of the *Vocabulaire de la Psychanalyse* (1967), which has been translated into several languages, including English (*The Language of Psychoanalysis*).

That said, the scrupulous attention paid to the translation of psychoanalytic concepts also had a negative effect: the translation of Freud's complete works into French has still not been completed and is the object of an ongoing controversy in France between the advocates of a 'literary' translation that takes into account the spirit of the French language (J.-B. Pontalis) and the supporters of a 'literal' translation, with their utopian ideal of an almost-perfect match between German and French; here, the price to pay is that of creating neologisms in French in order to translate Freudian concepts that were expressed in ordinary, everyday German – so, *Hilflosigkeit* [helplessness] becomes *désaide*, 'loss of help'; *Versagung* [frustration] becomes *refusement*, 'refusing'.

References

Freud, S. (1900a). *The Interpretation of Dreams*. S.E., 4/5.
Freud, S. (1905d). *Three Essays on the Theory of Sexuality*. S.E., 7.
Freud, S. (1923a [1922]). Two Encyclopaedia Articles. (A) Psycho-Analysis; (B) The Libido Theory. *S.E.*, 18: 235 & 255
Freud, S. (1925d [1924]). *An Autobiographical Study*. S.E., 20: 3
Freud, S. (1950 [1895]). Project for a Scientific Psychology. *S.E.*, 1.
Gibeault, A. (2005). *D. W. Winnicott et la France. Une histoire d'amour*. Unpublished paper read at the Milan Congress on D. W. Winnicott (16–20 November).
Green, A. (2006). *Présence de l'histoire* [The presence of history]. Unpublished paper read at the Symposium on Lines of Advance in Psychoanalysis, commemorating the 150th anniversary of Freud's birth and the 80th anniversary of the foundation of the Paris Psychoanalytical Society. Paris (18–19 November).
Lacan, J. (1953). Fonction et champ de la parole et du langage en psychanalyse. In *Écrits*. Paris: Editions du Seuil, 1966. [The Function and Field of Speech and Language in Psychoanalysis. In *Ecrits*, trans. B. Fink. New York: Norton, 2006.]
Lacan, J. (1955). La chose freudienne ou sens du retour à Freud en psychanalyse. In *Écrits*. Paris: Editions du Seuil, 1966. [The Freudian Thing, or the Meaning of the Return to Freud in Psychoanalysis. In *Ecrits*, trans. B. Fink. New York: Norton, 2006.]
Laplanche, J. & Pontalis, J.-B. (1967). *Vocabulaire de la psychanalyse*. Paris: Presses Universitaires de France. [*The Language of Psychoanalysis*, trans. D. Nicholson-Smith. London: Hogarth Press, 1973; reprinted London: Karnac, 1988.]

Mijolla, A. de (1982). La psychanalyse en France (1893–1965) [Psychoanalysis in France, 1893–1965]. In R. Jaccard (Ed.), *Histoire de la psychanalyse* [A history of psychoanalysis] (vol. 2). Paris: Hachette.

Mijolla, A. de (2004). *Quelques particularités de l'histoire de la psychanalyse en France* [Some distinctive features of the history of psychoanalysis in France]. Unpublished manuscript.

Smirnoff, V. (1979). De Vienne à Paris. Sur les origines d'une psychanalyse 'à la française' [From Vienna to Paris. On the origins of psychoanalysis '*à la française*']. *Nouvelle Revue de Psychanalyse, 20:* 13–58.

Widlöcher, D. (2001). Que sont devenues les voies de la psychanalyse? L'évolution des pratiques en France [What has become of the lines of advance in psychoanalysis? The evolution of practices in France]. In A. de Mijolla (Ed.), *Evolution de la clinique psychanalytique* [The evolution of clinical practice in psychoanalysis]. Bordeaux-Le Bouscat: L'Esprit du temps.

1 SOME DISTINCTIVE FEATURES OF THE HISTORY OF PSYCHOANALYSIS IN FRANCE

Alain de Mijolla

> **Alain de Mijolla** is a psychiatrist, full member of the Paris Psychoanalytical Society, the enthusiastic president and founder of the International Association for the History of Psychoanalysis, and a member of the Conceptual Research Sub-Committee of the International Psychoanalytical Association. His main research area has to do with identification fantasies and the processes by which they are handed down from generation to generation. He is the author of *Les visiteurs du Moi. Fantasmes d'identification* [Visitors of the ego: Identification fantasies] (Les Belles Lettres, 1981); *Les mots de Freud* [Freud's words] (Les Belles Lettres, 1989); *Freud, fragments d'une histoire* [Freud: Fragments of a history] (PUF, 2003); and *Préhistoires de famille* [Family prehistories] (PUF, 2004). With S. Shentoub, he wrote *Pour une psychanalyse de l'alcoolisme* [The psychoanalysis of alcoholism] (Payot, 1973 & 1981) and co-edited, with Sophie de Mijolla-Mellor, the standard reference work, *Psychanalyse* [Psychoanalysis] (PUF, 1999). He is the architect of the monumental *Dictionnaire International de la Psychanalyse* (Calmann-Levy, 2002) [*International Dictionary of Psychoanalysis* (Thomson Gale, 2005)]. He is at present writing what will be a very important book: *Histoire de la psychanalyse en France* [A history of psychoanalysis in France].

The history of the penetration – one might even say the 'intrusion'[1] – and development of psychoanalytic theories and practices in the different countries in which it has taken root has always been characterised by phenomena of rejection and assimilation, succeeding one another with greater or lesser regularity and intensity. Although apparently similar, anyone who studies them in terms of the sociocultural and historical parameters of each nation state will find that there are subtle differences between them.

---

[1] The International Association of the History of Psychoanalysis devoted its 4th International Meeting, in Brussels in September 1992, to the theme: 'The Comparative History of the Beginnings of Psychoanalysis in Europe (1900–1945)'.

France is an old nation and hence marked by its traditions. Sometimes it is too passionately interested in its history and the influence that it has exerted during previous centuries in the domains of politics, science and the arts for one to be surprised by the distinctive features, at once invigorating and deadly, which have characterised the destiny of psychoanalysis there (Mijolla, 1982; Roudinesco, 1982, 1986). It is also a sufficiently complex nation, behind its exhibitionist tendencies, for us not to be wary of being taken in, as we seek to write the history of psychoanalysis, by the most noisy appearances, by the most superficial anecdotes (notwithstanding their claim to hypothetical interpretative virtues), or by the gesticulations of those that successive fashions have thrust onto the front of the stage or the cathode-ray screen before sweeping them away again, sometimes permanently.

This does not mean that we should overlook the French appetite for charismatic personalities who know how to seduce with words, or the apparatus with which they surround themselves, or the heroic identifications to which they give rise, such as Jean d'Arc, the Sun-King, the Emperor Napoleon, General de Gaulle, the illusionists like Cagliostro or Robert Houdin, or again, in our more modest and recent domain, Jean-Martin Charcot, Gaëtan Gatian de Clérambault or Jacques Lacan. Acknowledging the impact of this influence, often of a hypnotic order, does not, however, imply succumbing to it in turn, but situating it where its role has proved efficacious and profitable – that is, as the motor of research work and clinical practice that is also being elaborated and developed in other places at the same time.

Psychoanalysts do not need reminding that ambivalence is universal and that Manichaeism leads back to the most archaic judgements: 'This is good, I'll keep it . . . this is bad, I'll get rid of it . . .'. It will hardly come as a surprise to anyone that these were the sorts of reaction the French had simultaneously and alternately to the psychoanalytic pill that the developments in the world and thought of the twentieth century obliged them to swallow. Nor will anyone suppose that they were going to accept any more easily than others, in 1900, the 'narcissistic wound' that Freud was conscious of inflicting on his contemporaries, reproaching them for not having received his ideas with howls of enthusiasm. The pioneers of the psychoanalytic adventure in the inter-war period can hardly be expected to have suddenly abandoned their white coats and reservations as psychiatrists.

At the time when they were gradually becoming aware of Freud's theories – for we must not forget that translations of Freud's works were absent until 1920 – the French prided themselves on a medical aristocracy of world renown, especially in the psychopathological domain in which Freud had just turned everything upside down. They were also proud of an intellectual elite which boasted a rich past and was as quick to criticise as to heap praise on any novelty appearing in the field of philosophy or literature. They were persuaded that they possessed well-established knowledge in the three domains designated by Freud in his definition of psychoanalysis as a depth-psychology, a therapeutic procedure and a means of understanding cultural facts.[2] They considered there was no reason to accept as 'true' in their totality (which was what Freud claimed) hypotheses which rendered their traditional knowledge obsolete. especially as these hypotheses came to them in the German language, the language of the victors of both Napoleons, of the 'barbarians' of the war of 1870, of the occupiers of Alsace-Lorraine, and of the authors of vast rival medical and psychiatric treatises – a language, moreover, which transmitted a culture whose richness thwarted the one in which they took such pride.

Once Charcot's empire had collapsed with the Master's death, it was the work of his pupil Pierre Janet that was put forward to block Freud and his shocking 'pansexualist' theories. Why look beyond one's own borders for that which is explained even better within them, and which is free, above all, of considerations that were considered to be pornographic, or purely speculative, and even mystical, by the supporters of Claude Bernard's experimental method as well as by the supporters of saucy allusions or of Cartesian rationalism? For decades, Freud was to be confronted with statements such as: 'Your theories are stupid and shocking' and, in a contradictory vein, 'We discovered all that before you', while 'the dangerous transference' and the profanation of innocent childhood would be repeatedly condemned.

After the first presentation, accompanied by numerous reservations, of 'Psycho-Analysis' in the treatise by Emmanuel Régis and Angélo Hesnard (1914), at a time when the canons of the First World War meant that everything coming from Germany and its allies was considered as deadly, one had to wait a while for young psychiatrists to take cognisance of Freud's theories and the interest they presented for their daily practice and their understanding of enigmatic mental disturbances. These theories were studied during the 1920s, a time when the after-effects of the war led to the breakdown of the old social and moral references and offered youth and women new and previously unthinkable perspectives, created by the places left vacant by the millions of men who had died on the front in the name of moral ideals that were now widely challenged.

It was now that, following Eugénie Sokolnicka, a former patient of Freud and Sándor Ferenczi, the journalistic and literary milieu, coaxed by André Gide and the authors of the *Nouvelle Revue Française*, pushed under the spotlights their discovery of the scandalous and juicy stories of psychoanalysis, which would soon be followed, and even surpassed, by André Breton and the fiery agitators of Surrealism. 'In France the interest in psycho-analysis began among the men of letters', Freud (1925d [1924], p. 62) wrote, not without a certain bitterness that some have since taken pleasure in emphasising.

---

[2] According to the definition he gave of it in 1923 for the *Encyclopaedia Britannica* (1923a [1922], 235–254).

A different view of the situation can be taken, however, if we distinguish roughly among those structures within which this interest has manifested itself up until the present day, two distinct, but constantly interacting levels, each driving and stimulating the other.

On the one hand, we have the parade, fad and infatuation of those who believe they have found in psychoanalysis the miraculous key to their problems, a source of new ideas, or even a means of attracting attention and gaining an audience, celebrity or money. Most of them only have brief contact with analytic practice and, being quickly disappointed, lose no time in seeking out some new, more consumable cultural gadget. Yet, at the same time, they have often been the first to make Freud's name known publicly, singing the praises of what they believe they have understood of theories that they are capable of subjecting just as noisily to ironic and bitter attacks (Mijolla, 1984). They inhabit the realm of illusion, opening the way to gurus who are always ready to dazzle the naïve, whom they can easily manipulate, and to the all too many disappointed ones who do not fail to reproach psychoanalysis for not having lived up to its promises of omnipotence which they themselves had attributed to it. However, illusion is not only negative and often proves to be the motor of fresh undertakings and discoveries. Thus, in one and the same breath, Freud's noisy admirers or denigrators did not fail to attract among their public the attention of hospital professionals or academics, thanks to whom psychoanalysis in France would take root and develop, though not without difficulty, on both clinical and theoretical levels.

The spectacular cure of numerous 'nervous' disorders was the best introduction to psychoanalysis for young French psychiatrists exasperated by the powerless nature of traditional methods. But they were less convinced by the psychoanalytic theoretical corpus as a whole, which, at the time, was changing rapidly, since Freud had only just begun to develop his considerations on the death drive and to propose a model of the psychic apparatus consisting of the ego, id and superego. In 1925, they even founded a society, and a journal called *L'Évolution Psychiatrique*, which today still represents the sector of medicine in France interested in a dynamic vision of psychiatry. But they have proved to be reticent about making a radical commitment to any form of school, especially when it is foreign in origin.

There is a way of speaking about the history of psychoanalysis in France that sometimes takes a rather scornful view of the small cautious steps of this penetration of psychoanalysis and that takes pleasure in stressing the incomprehension of the young doctors who were the first elements of it. It is sustained by an anachronistic a priori which assumes that the beginners of the 1920s were able to read and absorb Freud's ideas with the benefit of the experience of those who would write about them seventy years later. It bears witness to a quasi-religious illusion that was to grow and culminate in the 1980s, creating the image in the media of a French psychoanalysis that was puffed up with self-importance and apparently, though falsely, becoming increasingly detached from the daily and modest reality of its practice.

These first studies, and the discussions they raised, give a good idea of the passionate and lively milieu – albeit one that was conflictual from the outset – which allowed psychoanalysis to take root in France. Alongside the followers of the Viennese master, such as Marie Bonaparte (Mijolla, 1988b) or Rudolf Loewenstein, who fought for sexual aetiology, the recently theorised death drive, didactic analysis, the recognition of lay analysts, and the cultural extension of the psychoanalytic approach, doctors such as Édouard Pichon, René Allendy, Angélo Hesnard or René Laforgue, in spite of a situation of marginality which had led them towards the psychoanalytic adventure, insisted on distinguishing the qualities of 'the Freudian method' from the obscurities of 'the doctrine'.

However, even if the threat of a split remained permanent within the Paris Psychoanalytical Society (SPP: Société psychanalytique de Paris), founded in 1926, progress was achieved, albeit slowly: consultations were set up in some general hospitals, and the psychoanalytic approach to children was developed. The diverse critiques and attacks elicited responses which bore witness to the efforts being made to extend and deepen knowledge. Notwithstanding newspaper articles in which Freud appeared sporadically as a nice old man but a bit of a guru, or as a rather salacious psychologist, or, in June 1938, as a victim forced into exile by Hitler, the psychoanalytic impregnation of medical and philosophical thought progressed. A second generation was in ascendancy, with Sacha Nacht in the domain of hospital psychiatry, with Daniel Lagache, a student of the École Normale Supérieure, who was destined for a brilliant academic career, and with Jacques Lacan, who was also a psychiatrist but was fascinated by Hegelian philosophy and Surrealist witticisms.

The Second World War and the occupation of France by German troops put a sudden check on these developments. Psychoanalysis, the 'Jewish science', had no other choice but to survive in the shadows, which subsequently gave it an exalting aura of having participated in the 'Resistance to Nazism', synonymous with 'Liberation'. René Laforgue's efforts to create a French annex of the German Psychotherapy Society, which, headed by Mathias Goering, was swallowing up psychoanalysis in those countries that were under the Nazi boot, were destined to failure (Mijolla, 1988a). They nonetheless had significant consequences insofar as they discredited this pioneering analyst after the end of the war and placed his analysands in a difficult transferential situation; this in turn had institutional repercussions with the split of 1953, of which they were the principal artisans. The traces of a 'psychoanalytic filiation' were thus already noticeable and would become more marked from generation to generation and from couch to couch.

The end of the war saw the rebirth in France, as in the rest of the world, of a psychoanalysis that had undergone considerable modifications. Freud was dead, and with him the supreme judge of who was worthy or unworthy of being recognised as a psychoanalyst, or of what deserved to be called psychoanalytic. Henceforth, this role fell to institutions whose training goals would become a source of conflicts and would relegate purely theoretical quarrels to the background. The 'Controversies' between Anna Freud and Melanie Klein in England marked the turning-point between the two eras.

Furthermore, the emigration of the majority of Jewish European analysts to America placed the supreme temporal seat of power in the United States and conferred on the International Psychoanalytical Association (IPA) an increasingly important function of arbiter, and then judge. But, at the time, America meant 'imperialism' both for a Soviet bloc consolidated by the Cold War and for a certain number of psychiatrists – owing to their submission to the instructions in Zhdanov's report to the Cominform[3] – grouped together during the Resistance under the banner of the French Communist Party. These confrontations led the public to have contrasting images of psychoanalysis, which in some quarters saw itself designated – in conformity with Freud's fears, at the time he was speaking of *Weltanschauung* – as a 'reactionary and bourgeois ideology', a slogan often repeated, among other more violent insults, by communist intellectuals and doctors from 1949 up to about 1965. Once this period was over, the new theories of Jacques Lacan, considered more 'scientific' owing to their links with linguistics, triggered a spectacular reversal of opinion. In the same way, and at the same time, following the more open positions taken by Pope Pius XII, Catholics who had formerly rejected Freud's 'materialistic' theories with violence were now won over to them.

Thus the double register was back in place: psychoanalysis was increasingly a subject of discussion – mainly of a pejorative or ironic turn initially – in newspapers, films, and novels. Radio, in its turn, popularised it (Serge Moscovici's magisterial 1961 book remains an unequalled instrument of study in this domain). For many, psychoanalysis seemed embellished with the colours of the 'American dream', imported with Hollywood films in the euphoria of the post-war period, when the sun of freedom seemed to be shining in the West. At the same time, the psychoanalytic movement was reorganising itself

---

[3] Andrei Alexandrovich Zhdanov (1896–1948) was a Soviet politician in charge of the Soviet Union cultural policy. In 1947, he organized the Cominform, designed to coordinate the Communist parties of Europe. The French Communist Party followed his instructions which were aimed at fighting against the new enemy of the USSR, American imperialism. Three French journals – *La Nouvelle Critique*, *L'Humanité* and *Les Lettres Françaises* – associated psychoanalysis with the dollar and Coca-Cola and accused it of being a corrupting agent aimed at anaesthetising the class struggle. Many French psychiatrists who were later to become well-known psychoanalysts, such as Serge Lebovici, Jean and Evelyne Kestemberg, and Salem A. Shentoub, were members of the French Communist Party at the time, having been involved in the resistance against the Nazis in the Second World War. In 1949 they signed an article in *La Nouvelle Critique* attacking psychoanalysis. Shortly afterwards they left the Party and denounced the article. However, for many years they continued to be reproached for having signed this text, their opponents forgetting the year of the publication, the age of the signatories at the time (in their 30s) and their many years of clandestine struggle against the German Occupation.

on a new basis: young psychiatrists were taking increasing interest in a dynamic approach to mental disorders, and they were soon followed by students who were beginning to explore the new field of 'psychology', organised under the leadership of Daniel Lagache, with the creation in 1947, of a *licence de psychologie* (a degree in psychology).

During a period that extended from 1945 to 1953, these modifications were carried out without causing too much fuss in the media. French psychoanalysts reorganised themselves more than they innovated and, faced with the increasing demand for 'didactic' analyses, were essentially preoccupied with training conditions. Moreover, the creation of the Institut de Psychanalyse in Paris triggered, in June 1953, the first split in the French psychoanalytic movement (Mijolla, 1996). The outcome of the split was that only the SPP, under the leadership of Sacha Nacht, was recognised as having training status in the eyes of the IPA, whereas the secessionists, led by Françoise Dolto, Juliette Favez-Boutonier, Jacques Lacan and Daniel Lagache, formed the French Psychoanalytic Society (SFP: *Société française de psychanalyse*) and had to fight for ten years before being reintegrated within the international community, at the price of the exclusion of Jacques Lacan and Françoise Dolto. A new split followed in 1963 (Mijolla, 1995).

Even if these ten years of conflict initially met with few echoes outside the professional circles concerned, where the battles were lively, they were decisive for the French psychoanalytic movement in that they gave it a creative impetus such as it had never known before. The need for each of the two rival societies to impose itself in medical and academic circles as the best, if not the sole, repository of 'Psychoanalysis', led to numerous creations and publications, each of them blithely failing to mention in their bibliographies the work of their adversaries.

No domain was neglected by the other side: the treatment of psychotic patients, child and adolescent psychoanalysis, psychosomatic medicine, addictions, institutional psychoanalysis. The radical expansion of psychoanalytic practices and modes of thinking thus went ahead without interruption in the medico-social and academic fabric of the country. The names of Piera Aulagnier, Maurice Bouvet, Janine Chasseguet-Smirgel, René Diatkine, Michel Fain, Wladimir Granoff, André Green, Bela Grunberger, Jean Laplanche, Serge Lebovici, Serge Leclaire, Joyce McDougall, Pierre Marty, Jean-Bertrand Pontalis, Victor Smirnoff, Conrad Stein, Jean-Paul Valabrega and Serge Viderman, amongst many others, became increasingly familiar to the players in the sector of public health and psychological research, just as they appeared more and more frequently on the shelves of specialised bookshops. After the mini-storm of the split of 1953, psychoanalysis in France seemed to rapidly take up again the course of a history marked by its persistent and triumphant conquest of the traditional hospital and academic bastions. Behind the institutional dissonances, this development even allowed it to make its voice heard to some extent on the international scene, strongly dominated at the time by British Anglo-Saxon authors around Melanie Klein, Donald Winnicott and W. R. Bion, or Americans who, with a view to promoting ego psychology, were grouped around Heinz Hartmann, Ernst Kris and Rudolf Loewenstein.

But the totally unforeseeable sociocultural phenomenon triggered in the 1960s and 1970s by the charismatic personality of Jacques Lacan and his invigorating thought would have consequences that went beyond anything that one could imagine in terms of a progressive but relatively quiet implantation. His boldness, his taste for provocation, in the best as well as the worst sense, and above all his philosophical culture, which distinguished him from the 'average doctor', made him a public figure. He attracted an increasingly large section of the French intellectual elites and, bringing a certain kind of discourse to the foreground, imposed an image of psychoanalysis which gradually became excessive, even if, it should be emphasised, behind the scenes his very extravagance obliged the French psychoanalytic community as a whole to call itself into question.

Among psychoanalysts, even those from whom he separated in 1953 or those who would separate from him ten years later in order to rejoin the IPA, very few could avoid the questions raised by his practice as well as his theories. Very few could claim to be unscathed by his way of speaking about Freud or about psychoanalytic training, or by the liberties he took in opposing the international consensual discourse by proposing a neo-Freudianism which would be designated as *à la française*, one that he would impose inside and outside the country in spite of, or because of, the derision and opposition to which his seductive methods gave rise.

This was the period of slogans such as the 'return to Freud', 'cure as an additional benefit', 'the analyst is authorised only by himself', among others, that were passed around by word of mouth. It was at this time that theoretical proposals were put forward in sufficiently obscure terms for a whole generation of young psychiatrists and psychologists to have to struggle hard to understand them, just as they would have to open themselves to the literary and philosophical culture in which the discourse of the Master was impregnated. These would soon be followed by the figure of the 'Moebius strip', which everyone hastened to cut and paste, 'graphs' and 'Borromean knots'. Just as Jacques Lacan's own mind was restless, no one who listened to him could preserve their own peace of mind.

Let me repeat: the phenomenon was unique in the history of psychoanalysis. A living figure became a popular personality representing psychoanalysis in France in the eyes of the world, just as the baguette or the Basque beret still characterise the average Frenchman in the eyes of foreigners. And so for the first time his person, and the destiny of the Freudian School of Paris (EFP: *École freudienne de Paris*) which he founded in 1964, would synthesise for the next twenty years these two levels which, as I have said, had hitherto only been complementary.

I have already pointed out that the French Communist Party immersed itself, in the wake of Louis Althusser,[4] in this new psychoanalysis whose theories now seemed usable, thanks to the preponderant role given to linguistics and to abstract formulae acceptable to scientific materialism. In their turn, Christians showed themselves to be receptive to Lacanian teaching which did not threaten their faith as did the non-religious, scientific and, above all, fiercely atheistic *Weltanschauung* which Freud had hoped would be associated with his psychoanalysis. Each year, between 1965 and 1980, ever-increasing numbers came to join in the big 'mass' in the form of Jacques Lacan's weekly *Seminar*, with his servants, his hierarchy of deacons and sub-deacons, eager to serve the officiant distilling his words to a floor of subjugated followers whose tape-recorders recorded the Master's heavy silences and the slightest, highly significant clearings of his throat.

This description, naturally, is somewhat of a caricature and, even if it is substantially true, does not do justice to the unique phenomenon recognised above. Jacques Lacan was not just the personage whose outbursts, tics, insolence and affectation the public at large became familiar with through the press, a personage sufficiently fashionable for the publication of his *Écrits* in 1966 – a large theoretical book, particularly arduous to read – to become a media event and to be followed by a commercial success worthy of a best-selling novel. He was a 'cultural bulimic' with a passion for philosophical reflection, an eager investigator who pursued week after week the announcement of a revelation that would never come but whose advent everyone was waiting for, like that of the Messiah, at the next Seminar. Attracting more and more intellectuals of high quality, such as Jean Hippolyte or Maurice Merleau-Ponty, who was involved in the then triumphant structuralist movement, he obliged his audience to read little-known authors whom he liked to cite, thereby compelling a generation of psychiatrists to steep themselves in a culture for which their medical studies and very often their social milieu had not prepared them at all. In this way, too, his influence on French psychoanalytic thought was preponderant, for naturally the non-Lacanians, not wishing to be left out, began to read and conceptualise a psychoanalysis that was increasingly considered outside France as overly intellectual, whereas in reality it was much more subtle than that.

The years 1953–1980 were the most productive and fruitful in the history of the French psychoanalytic movement, owing to the ardent rivalry between psychoanalytic institutions claiming allegiance to the IPA, such as the SPP and the French Psychoanalytical Association (APF: *Association psychanalytique*

---

[4] Louis Althusser (1918–1990) was a French Marxist philosopher and a lifelong member and sometimes strong critic of the French Communist Party. In his philosophical works he tried to reconcile psychoanalysis and Marxism in referring himself to the structuralist conception of psychoanalysis introduced by Jacques Lacan. Althusser is commonly referred to as a Structural Marxist, although his relationship to other schools of French structuralism is not a simple affiliation and he is critical of many aspects of structuralism.

de France), and others such as the EFP and the 'Quatrième groupe' or French-Language Psychoanalytic Group (OPLF: *Organisation psychanalytique de langue française*), created in 1969 out of the Lacanian group.

But everything fell apart when Lacan, ageing and ill, decided in January 1980 to dissolve the EFP, the vicissitudes of which had mobilised the French public to such an extent. He declared that he was handing over the reins to his son-in-law, Jacques-Alain Miller, whose influence has grown increasingly over the years, in respect both of ideas and of institutional issues. This announcement came as a bombshell, and its effects were reflected in all the main newspapers, just as the latter would give constant coverage to the indignation aroused in Lacan's first disciples, who were furious to see themselves dispossessed in this way, eventually taking the matter to court. Many of these same newspapers announced the death of Jacques Lacan on 9 September 1981, on their front page, as if it were an event of national importance. An essential chapter of the history of psychoanalysis in France closed, in effect, with his death, which led to the atomisation of the Lacanians into increasingly unstable groups, all persuaded that they were the true heirs of the Master's thought, though in fact they were often less united by this claim to fidelity than by their rejection and opposition to the School of the Freudian Cause (ECF: *École de la cause freudienne*). In the name of Lacan, and then in his own name, put forward increasingly with consummate skill, Jacques-Alain Miller initially gave the latter a more international than national dimension, South America having exchanged its Kleinian preferences for these new theories which also had the attraction of having been rejected by North American psychoanalysis.

In the years that followed, without a new charismatic leader, the infatuation of the French public for psychoanalysis began to wane, but on the national scale, the first analysands of the Lacanian movement, some of whom were already famous and had been on the Master's couch, came with time to fill key posts in the most diverse branches of the public and private sectors of French political, economic and cultural life. Through their networks of friendship in the domains of publishing, the press or the diverse sectors of radio and television, they assured a certain continuity in the propagation of the Lacanian myth, but on a scale that bore no comparison with the fanfare of earlier times.

This was how the two 'psychoanalyses', both forms of which still persist today (in the 2000s), were reconstituted during these decades. On the one hand, we have a brilliant psychoanalysis, handling with elegance and intelligence language and its games, always ready to show itself publicly, to open itself extensively to the public, from Françoise Dolto's first radio programmes[5] to

---

[5] Françoise Dolto (1908–1988), a French pediatrician and psychoanalyst, was a pioneer of and specialist in child psychoanalysis. In 1950, she participated with a teacher, a psychiatrist and a priest in radio programmes on the sexual education of children. She continued these broadcasts until 1978 and thus played a very important role in the diffusion of psychoanalysis to the public.

Serge Leclaire's 'Psy Show',[6] and, taking things to extremes, as Gérard Miller[7] would do, the image of the highly gifted psychoanalyst who dabbles in everything, without fear of sometimes appearing ridiculous. The 'duty psychologist' [psy de service] has become common currency, and his or her intervention for just about anything seems to have become the pet theme of many French evening television shows, accrediting in the eyes of the public at large an image which ultimately can only appear extremely ambiguous, half-clownish, half-omniscient. Alternatively, the newspapers or televised news programmes speak about it in order to decry it or to rediscover merits in it that are sometimes excessively exaggerated. On the other hand, groups and associations have formed and multiplied in the background, whose members are united around the same theoretical and practical affinities. Many of them are doing more discreet work in the field of treatments as well as in the domain of possible extensions of Freudian, Kleinian, Ferenczian or Lacanian hypotheses, just to cite a few of the directions which post-Freudian psychoanalysis has taken.

The multiplicity and diversity of practices exercised by the large numbers who have emerged from Lacanian movements have nonetheless given increasing importance to everything that sees itself classified under the term 'psychotherapies', a label that also covers the supporters of heteroclite methods that are supposed to 'cure' psychic disorders rapidly and without difficulty. In a world where people increasingly expect happiness, in which the pace of life is accelerating and the competitive pressure in professional life is increasing, the classical 'psychoanalytic treatment' with its demands on time and both affective and financial investment has gradually lost the exclusive importance that it had during the first eighty years of its existence. The 'short sessions' inaugurated by Jacques Lacan, or their reduced frequency from four times a week to once a week in the best of cases, coupled with the increasing preference for the face-to-face setting over the use of the couch – even though it was considered indispensable by Freud (as a means of excluding visual contact during the session) – and a whole series of modifications of the 'setting' as he had defined it in 1904, have contributed to creating a psychoanalytically inspired psychotherapeutic entity in which interpretations of a general 'symbolic' nature and the elimination of the symptom are privileged. Cognitivism, behaviouralism, hypnotic suggestion or the development of the use of

---

[6] Serge Leclaire (1924–1994) was the first follower of Lacan, from whom he eventually distanced himself by creating his own psychoanalytic theory. When he was a candidate at the Paris Psychoanalytical Society, he followed Jacques Lacan first in the French Psychoanalytic Society and then in the Freudian School of Paris. In 1983, he agreed to participate in a prime-time television programme called the 'Psy Show', in which he was invited to do live analysis. He left very quickly after realising that this show was exploiting audience voyeurism: an anonymous couple came to the show to talk about their sexual problems.

[7] Gérard Miller (1948–), a French Lacanian psychoanalyst, is much involved in the media – radio, television and newspapers. He is the brother of the French psychoanalyst Jacques-Alain Miller, son-in-law and intellectual legatee of Jacques Lacan. Like the latter, he considers himself a follower of Freud and Lacan.

chemical substances going hand in hand with progress in the neurosciences are some of the different therapeutic procedures which are presented in turn as being 'more efficient' than the psychoanalytic approach and its rivals, whereas in fact they have a role that is contiguous and sometimes even complementary in the vast menu of currently available procedures in the domain of mental health. But this is on the rarely fulfilled condition of stating more clearly who does what and for what ultimate aims.

For there is room for everyone under a sun that cannot be reduced to projectors solely riveted on constantly changing items of news. We should not, however, overlook the specificity of psychoanalytic training, which, away from the easy methods of the media, has constantly called itself into question, even if the ambiguities of the criteria of recognition of the EFP have led hundreds of self-proclaimed therapists to take advantage of a public easily misled by skills that others only acquire after long and laborious training.

It can be seen that during the successive waves which have characterised the history of the French psychoanalytic movement – with regularly proclaimed announcements of the decline or even the death of psychoanalysis in France – only one event is needed (for instance, the recent vague desires of the French State to regulate 'psychotherapy') for the continuity of the most rigorous psychoanalytic transmission to surface once again, demonstrating by the sudden increase of renewed public interest that it arouses that the implantation of psychoanalysis in its diverse forms is still very real and present.

French psychoanalysis cannot, however, be presented as a model. First, because there cannot be a general model in such complex domains where each individual must find his or her own original path of development; and second because, owing to its contradictions and particularities, it is too bound up with its sociocultural history as well with the personalities and events that have characterised its development.

But there are lessons to be drawn from its evolution, from the reflections that have marked and enriched its eighty years of existence, from the alternation between exhibitionist seduction and discreet work on the terrain of psychic suffering, as well as from its inclinations for philosophical questioning which continually tempers clinical experiences. For these are always acting behind the scenes as a bulwark against the most intellectualist speculations. '*La théorie, cela n'empêche pas d'exister*' ['If only one knew *what* exists!'], Charcot used to take pleasure in saying, and French psychoanalysts do not forget this lesson from their past. Even at the heart of their most abstract jousting, they are permanently confronted – both in the silence of their private practices and in the harsh reality of their daily life in hospitals or in the various healthcare institutions where they practise – with the actuality of human relations in respect of which what Freud has taught them about the transference and countertransference remains the ferment of a psychoanalytic practice that has been kept alive over the years and transmitted throughout the generations.

References

Freud, S. (1923a [1922]). Two Encyclopaedia Articles. *S.E.*, 18: 235–262.

Freud, S. (1925d [1924]). *An Autobiographical Study. S.E.* 20: 7–70.

Mijolla, A. de (1982). La psychanalyse en France, 1893–1965. In R. Jaccard (Dir.), *Histoire de la psychanalyse*, vol. II. Paris: Hachette, pp. 9–105; Livre de Poche, 1985, pp. 5–118. [France (1893–1965). In P. Kutter (Ed.), *Psychoanalysis International, A Guide to Psychoanalysis throughout the World*, R. Hoffman, W. Sobanski & T. Klein (trans.), vol. 1. Stuttgart: Frommann-Holzboog, 1992, pp. 66–113.]

Mijolla, A. de (1984). Quelques avatars de la psychanalyse en France. Lecture du Disque Vert, juin 1924. *L'Evolution Psychiatrique, 49* (3): 773–795.

Mijolla, A. de (1988a). La psychanalyse et les psychanalystes en France entre 1939 et 1945. *Revue Internationale d'Histoire de la Psychanalyse, 1*: 167–223.

Mijolla, A. de (1988b). Quelques aperçus sur le rôle de la princesse Marie Bonaparte dans la création de la Société Psychanalytique de Paris. *Revue Française de Psychanalyse, 5*: 1197–1214.

Mijolla, A. de (1995). Les scissions dans le mouvement psychanalytique français de 1953 à 1964. *Topique, 57*: 271–290. [Splits in the French psychoanalytic movement between 1953 and 1964. In R. Steiner & J. Johns (Eds.), *Within Time and Beyond Time, A Festschrift for Pearl King*. London: Karnac, 2001, pp. 1–24.]

Mijolla, A. de (1996). La scission de la Société Psychanalytique de Paris en 1953, quelques notes pour un rappel historique. *Cliniques Méditerranéennes, 49–50*: 9–30.

Moscovici, S. (1961). *La psychanalyse, son image, et son public* [Psychoanalysis, its image and its audience]. Paris: Presses Universitaires de France.

Régis, E., & Hesnard, A. (1914). *La psychoanalyse des névroses et des psychoses. Ses applications médicales et extra-médicales* [The psychoanalysis of neuroses and psychoses: Medical and non-medical applications]. Paris: Félix Alcan.

Roudinesco, E. (1982). *La bataille de cent ans. Histoire de la psychanalyse en France*, vol. I. Paris: Ramsay; Paris: Fayard, 1994.

Roudinesco, E. (1986). *Histoire de la psychanalyse en France. La bataille de cent ans*, vol. II. Paris: Le Seuil; Paris: Fayard, 1994.

2 WHAT HAS BECOME OF THE LINES OF ADVANCE IN PSYCHOANALYSIS?
The evolution of practices in France

Daniel Widlöcher

Daniel Widlöcher was the head of the department of psychiatry and professor in the Pitié-Salpétrière hospital group from 1980 to 1986. A member of the French Psychoanalytical Association, he is at present the president of the International Psychoanalytical Association. Emeritus Professor of the Pierre and Marie Curie University, he is a former president of the European Psychoanalytical Federation, as well as a Ph.D. *honoris causa* of both the Catholic University of Louvain (Belgium) and the University of Lima (Peru). Influenced by Lacan's 'return to Freud', he explored in detail the major concepts of Freudian psychoanalysis, beginning with two issues which he considered to be fundamental: that of change – *Freud et le problème du changement* [Freud and the problem of change] (PUF, 1970) – and that of the drives, challenging the attempt to see them as purely or mainly biological in nature – 'Quel usage faisons-nous du concept de pulsion?' [What use do we make of the concept of drive?], in *La pulsion pour quoi faire?* [Drives: For doing what?] (APF, Editions Colloques, 1984). More recently, he has made an in-depth study of the theory of infantile sexuality: 'Amour primaire et sexualité infantile: un débat de toujours' [Primary love and infantile sexuality: An eternal debate], in *Sexualité infantile et attachement* (PUF, 2000) [*Infantile Sexuality and Attachment* (Other Press, 2001)].

He is a strong supporter of interdisciplinarity, is keenly interested in how psychoanalysis develops in different countries and has facilitated the renewal of discussions with Lacanian psychoanalysts.

Among other books, he has written: *Le psychodrame chez l'enfant* [Psychodrama with children] (PUF, 2003); *La dépression* [Depression] (with M.C. Hardy-Baylé; Hermann, 1989); *Métapsychologie du sens* [Metapsychology of meaning] (PUF, 1986); and *Les nouvelles cartes de la psychanalyse* [The new state of psychoanalysis] (O. Jacob, 1996). In addition, he coordinated the publication of *Traité de Psychopathologie* [A treatise on psychopathology] (PUF, 1994); with Alain Braconnier, he edited *Psychanalyse et psychothérapie* [Psychoanalysis and psychotherapy] (Flammarion, 1996), and with Nicole Delattre he edited *La psychanalyse en dialogue* [Psychoanalysis in dialogue] (O. Jacob, 2003). More recently, he was principal editor of *Choisir sa psychothérapie* [A guide to psychotherapy] (O. Jacob, 2006) and *Les psychanalystes savent-ils débattre?* [Psychoanalysis and its great debates] (O. Jacob, 2008).

Alain Braconnier wrote a concise biography of Daniel Widlöcher for the 'Psychanalystes d'aujourd'hui' series (PUF, 2003).

The idea that the practice of psychoanalysis should evolve over the course of time is not a new one. Freud had already suggested as much at the International Congress held in Budapest in 1918.

Two important points in these discussions, held scarcely twenty years after the birth of psychoanalysis, are noteworthy. The first is that the factor of change is external to psychoanalysis; it depends on social events. The debate was about extending the indications of psychoanalysis to a larger section of the population. Second, the model of the therapeutic process is only called into question by the addition of techniques external to the method. Hence Freud's constantly cited statement concerning the need to alloy the pure gold of psychoanalysis freely with the copper of suggestion. Freud subsequently showed, however, that what he saw as the young science of psychoanalysis was open to progress. Shortly before the Marienbad Congress, his reply to his pupils, who had chosen the processes of change in the treatment as a theme, was that these processes were already quite well known and that it would be better to discuss the resistances to change. In fact, Freud's thought had always progressed by studying resistances, as can be seen from the principal milestones of *Beyond the Pleasure Principle* (1920g), the addendum to *Inhibitions, Symptoms and Anxiety* (1926d [1925]), and finally 'Analysis Terminable and Interminable' (1937c). In order to study resistances in greater depth and so to treat them more adequately, the setting must be maintained as well as all the rules that guarantee the conditions required for analysing the transference.

The situation was to change radically in the middle of the century, after the Second World War. There were two reasons for this: the first was connected with Freud's death, which had the effect of liberating the diverse tendencies of the movement illustrated by the Freud–Klein controversies (1941–1945) within the British Psychoanalytical Society. The second reason was linked to Freud's expectations: psychoanalysis quickly acquired an important place in the field of mental health and, more generally, in the optimistic ideology of a new society that was victorious, democratic and pacified. Psychoanalysis now appeared to be an essential therapeutic agent for establishing this very society which sought to assure the well-being of each citizen and to eradicate violence. But it was these two conditions, the pluralism of its theories and its place in the new society, which were to be at the origin of the changes in practice we have observed over the last forty years.

If external pressures are more or less the same from one country to another, from one continent to another, internal debates have been, and remain, closely associated with local situations. The history of ideas and of the psychoanalytic movement have had a diverse influence on practices in different countries, and, in the face of external pressures, this local history has given rise to different solutions and modes of adaptation. It is these points of view that I would like to illustrate from the history of psychoanalysis in France over the last fifty years or so.

External pressures

Let us consider first the pressures exerted by the developments of the technical and social environment on practices. Psychoanalysis, which was called upon to occupy a recognised and important place in the new society, found itself subject to changing demands on the part of the politics of care in mental health, the health budget, the university as a place of teaching and research and, finally, the collective ideas of society.

I do not have space or time here to re-examine these external pressures. They have varied from one country to another, from one epoch to another, but always seem to develop in two phases. The first is characterised by an increasing demand for psychoanalysis to offer ever more in terms of care, training, research and the diffusion of ideas. The second is marked by a drop in demand, which seems to involve different factors: rival therapies, the need to economise and rationalise the provision of treatment, and the dwindling interest for a discipline considered as outmoded by young professionals as well as by the public at large. The pressures of demand are immediately followed by restrictions and rejections. This development seems to follow the same path from one country to another, but with a gap in time, which means that the USA and Western Europe already seem to be faced with a terminal stability beyond decline whereas others, like Eastern Europe, seem to be just at the beginning of the process.

My first remark is to say that the consequences for practice are partially the same. The development of psychoanalytically inspired psychotherapies is a response both to the expanding demand of an increasing number of potential clients and to the continued presence of psychoanalysis in treatment centres when the drop in demand makes itself felt. In the first stage, the pure gold of psychoanalysis is protected by the diffusion of practices and the steady stream of candidates for training, whereas in the second stage survival must be ensured. In other words, in the first stage psychoanalysts train other psychoanalysts and psychotherapists; in the second, it is the latter who survive by practising psychotherapies.

This evolution, presented in somewhat schematic way, is well illustrated by the distinction that has to be made between the practice of psychoanalysis and psychotherapy. For Freud, the question did not occur. There existed a new psychotherapy – psychoanalysis – and the new lines of advance under consideration were those offered to psychoanalytic treatment itself. So it was possible to propose a psychoanalysis of the psychoses (in which Freud had scarcely any belief), of delinquents, of melancholics, and so on. And the familiar debate concerning child psychoanalysis simply consisted in knowing whether one could apply psychoanalysis from the outset or whether it was necessary to prepare the ground, so to speak, using pedagogical measures.

After the Second World War, on the other hand, the issue was to invent new methods, inspired by psychoanalysis, by modifying the technical parameters and modes of intervention. This led to a description of technical variations and, above all, to their differentiation from the strictly classical definition of psychoanalysis. This gap was in turn reinforced by an institutional separation. Psychotherapeutic methods were applied, giving rise to research studies and specific forms of training. Private clinics and public treatment centres, in France as elsewhere, contributed to this development. Scientific societies were created to meet the research and training objectives (the Society for Group Analytical Psychotherapy, family therapies, etc.). During this whole phase of ascension, however, psychoanalytic societies lost interest entirely in this domain of application. With the recession [in the 1970s], and the need to conform increasingly to certain requirements of the State, they were now obliged to address this issue. By continuing to refuse to consider the need for a training scheme in psychotherapy, they were exposing their candidates to a split, because the latter were training in a psychoanalytic institution for a discipline that gave them a status, but one that did not always correspond to their practice. The danger was that they would come looking for the pure gold in the institution but then resort, above all, to the alloy with copper which they could find in diverse centres of treatment or in specific societies. This paradox is all the more regrettable in that, during this whole period, the greatest discoveries in psychoanalysis have come from treatments applied to severe pathologies (I am thinking here both of Kohut and Bion).

There is one major reason, I think, for this situation. The question of the status of psychoanalytic psychotherapies is directly linked to that of psychoanalysis. The constant questioning about the nature of the pure gold of psychoanalysis encourages one to remain vague about the copper to be added to it. The issue would be easily resolved if we stuck to what Freud had in mind when he spoke about the copper of direct suggestion. The clinical example he gives is clear: it is a question of making it clear to the patient what he must do or think. But directivity is not the only criteria we can satisfy ourselves with.

The reference to pure gold clearly has a metaphorical meaning. A precious metal *par excellence*, gold reminds us of the value we place on psychoanalytic listening and on the psychic work which takes place not only in the patient but also in the analyst. Moreover, the idea of renunciation or compromise continues to play an important role in any reflections on psychotherapy and on its very practice. If we take interest in it, are we not being too easily satisfied (i.e., with psychotherapy), thereby showing that we do not know how to be satisfied with what should satisfy and fulfil us (i.e., psychoanalysis)?

Beyond the metaphor, one may ask: what does gold consist of? The definition of a pure psychoanalysis – that is, without alterations for psychotherapeutic ends – remains uncertain. Criteria of a technical nature, the definition of the analytic setting, are debateable. No parameter (frequency, duration, the patient's position, payment, etc.) is decisive. We generally refer to a body of variables in order to define not one, but minimal, criteria. But if these are necessary for our institutional coherence, they only have minimal validity. Certain analyses, conducted according to rigorous criteria, do not result in any psychic activity which corresponds to our expectations; on the other hand, authentic and rich psychoanalytic experiences can develop within other less rigorous settings. The definition of minimum criteria implies that, beneath this minimum, psychic work cannot be expected to take place which satisfies the criteria of a psychoanalytic process. The whole difficulty lies in the term 'possible'. The term minimum should perhaps be replaced by the term optimum. When someone requests analysis, we need to ask which setting will provide the subject with the best opportunity of developing an authentic and rich analytic experience? What risks do we take in offering him/her a setting that falls short of this optimum?

The setting serves the analytic process – that is to say, the psychic transformations that we expect to see operating in the treatment. Before such a process occurs in the patient's mind (or, rather, at the same time as it occurs), it develops in the analyst's mind. Are we in a position with a given patient to think 'psychoanalytically' – that is, to develop an associative activity which allows us to identify the effects of the transference and the countertransference, the creations of the unconscious, our resistances and those of the patient? The 'psychoanalytic' is defined in the co-thinking that is constructed between us. This means a 'pure psychoanalysis' can scarcely be decreed before it unfolds. It is only during the treatment itself, in each individual case, and according to our own dispositions, that we can decide on the 'purity' of our psychoanalytic practice.

Only too often, psychotherapy, in contrast with psychoanalysis, is defined in terms that seem to be not a 'plus' but a 'minus'. Psychotherapies are then defined as 'lighter' forms of psychoanalysis: this concerns both the setting (frequency, length of sessions) and the mode of intervention (less and less reference to the transference, to unconscious internal conflicts), or the process (less abstinence, less transference).

In reality, these compromises are related to external considerations: motivational weakness and the cost in time and money. The risk is to imagine one has obtained as much as one would have done by doing a psychoanalysis, while sparing oneself the constraints inherent to the latter. In many cases, the results do not live up to expectations. It is in this sense that we speak of a 'light' psychoanalysis. But such modifications are clearly of interest to the State: why undertake a long and often costly analysis if the results expected are roughly the same?

Whether it is a case of intervening more directly or of making the conventions of the setting more flexible, at what point do we leave the specific field of psychoanalysis? Do we leave it when we no longer refer to the Freudian paradigm of neurotic conflict? Or, conversely, should we consider, with Lacan (1966/2006, p. 329), that 'a psychoanalysis, whether standard or not, is the treatment one expects from a psychoanalyst'? It can be seen just how far theoretical issues can have an important bearing on individual as well as institutional practices.

A more general aspect of this evolution of practices, linked to external pressures, is the frequency of sessions. Let's return here to the pure gold and the price to be paid for having access to it. It seems that it was in France, in the 1950s, that the habit of practising psychoanalysis, and in particular a training analysis, on a three-times-a-week basis, developed. There is no trace of this in written texts or in administrative documents, but it is a practice that established itself progressively outside Lacanian circles. Lacan, moreover, did exactly as he liked with regard to the time of the sessions, but generally maintained the rhythm of four sessions a week. The habit had become so well established that when, in 1973, the International Psychoanalytical Association (IPA) decreed in writing that the criterion for the training of psychoanalysts was four or five sessions, a restrictive clause had to be inserted to respect French practices.

In fact, this practice is found elsewhere, in particular in American societies that are not part of the American Psychoanalytic Association (APA). We may assume that it was already employed before the war and that it was linked to the influence of certain psychoanalysts, some of whom were émigrés. The court case that took place between certain of these independent societies and the IPA and the APA had the effect of rekindling the question. The rule of four or five sessions was thus reinforced as a 'standard' criterion within the IPA in spite of the French exception. However, it is commonly acknowledged that this rule is far from being respected everywhere, principles notwithstanding, and recently a movement from Latin America has challenged these principles. Whatever institutional solution is proposed, the question deserves to be raised in all its complexity: what does this tendency to reduce the frequency of sessions reside in? What arguments justify it or oppose it? And above all, on what methodology is the search for the solution to be based?

It is interesting to note that if the practice of doing a training analysis on a three-times-a-week basis coincided with the phase of expansion of psychoanalysis, this practice is currently gaining ground or being reinforced during a phase of contraction. During the period of expansion, a small number of psychoanalysts had to meet the high demand for training and treatment. With the economic recession, the already rare demand for psychoanalysis becomes even rarer if more frequent sessions are necessary. In countries where psychoanalysis is reimbursed by a system of insurance, the argument advanced by the State for reimbursing only a small number of sessions is that no 'empirical' study has shown that a greater frequency of sessions gives a better result. It is true that in this case one could satisfy oneself with two sessions – or even one session – per week! It is clear that the absence of a methodology for finding an empirically based solution is sorely lacking, both for answering the State and consultants as well as psychoanalysts themselves. Comparative studies are being carried out to evaluate the results of therapies in respect of whether they are long or short term, and in terms of the frequency of sessions (between one and three). Unless they are applied to psychoanalysis, the risk is that we will be confined to answers of an administrative nature. French psychoanalysts often point out, moreover, that although the frequency of sessions has been reduced, the treatments are longer. This argument will appear to many as an admission of weakness, but the advocates of the principle of three sessions a week will reply that it is the very quality of the psychoanalytic work accomplished over a longer duration that authorises this reduction of the number of sessions. In my view, the only general criterion that one can adopt is one of probability. Greater frequency makes it more likely that the experience of the analytic process will occur in the best conditions. Reducing the sessions runs a greater risk of failure. This risk has to be evaluated in the light of each individual case and, above all, has to be situated in relation to the other constraints of the situation. A particularly perverse argument would be to claim that the quality of the psychoanalyst or of the group alone authorises a reduced frequency.

The question of the frequency of sessions, as can be seen, is closely bound up, in a period of recession and declining influence, with the question of money. Has there been any evolution in practices concerning this issue? We have to distinguish here between the just remuneration of work (who pays?), the place of financial payment in the contract (how does one pay?) and the place of money in fantasies and the transference (money as a symbol). It will be recalled that so-called free analysis, mentioned by Freud in 'Lines of Advance in Psycho-Analytic Therapy' (1919a [1918]), was already practised in the 1920s at the Vienna Ambulatorium and at the Berlin Institute. The expression in France of diverse practices and diverse points of view can be found in the work of the Alfred Binet Mental Health Centre (that of E. Kestemberg and of A. Gibeault, in particular) in Paris. If certain psychoanalysts stick strictly to the principle of direct payment without recourse to a third party, others accept more flexible arrangements. But, generally speaking, French psychoanalysts remain opposed to any negotiation with the State and insurance funds.

Thus in France, as elsewhere, psychoanalysts have had to respond to external pressures. But we shall see that the answers they have given to the questions raised are inseparable from the theoretical presuppositions linked to what I will call a certain psychoanalytic culture that is specific to the French situation and to the local history of the movement.

A French psychoanalytic culture?

Viewed from the outside, distinctive practices and theoretical perspectives are confused under an umbrella of terms that are sometimes critical and sometimes laudatory, but which all refer to a French style. Can one speak of exception? The history of the international psychoanalytic movement is comprised of local histories marked by the conflicts between different schools and currents of thought. The adversaries of psychoanalysis are often ironical about these 'squabbles'. I think that independently of all the pathological factors from which neither psychoanalysts nor their institutions are protected, this diversity, and the debates or rather the controversies that it nourishes, are an important factor in the progress of psychoanalysis, both theoretically and practically. A real deepening and enrichment of our methods grows out of this theoretical pluralism. The confrontation of models is without doubt the most fruitful means we currently have at our disposal for developing and refining our practices.

Psychoanalysis is a modern science. This means it is a twentieth-century science, but one, to cite Lacan (1966/2006, p. 361), which finds its place

> at the centre of the vast conceptual movement which in our time – restructuring so many sciences that are improperly called 'social', changing or refinding the meaning of certain sections of the exact science *par excellence*, mathematics, in order to restore the foundations of a science of human action insofar as it is based on conjecture – is reclassifying the body of sciences of intersubjectivity under the name 'human sciences'.

It is not a science which results from new techniques but one that is applied to social practices. Like political science, economic science or the science of education, psychoanalysis develops from the articulation between a theoretical model, devised to describe observed processes, and clinical practice.

The double movement closely linking model and practice is thus not confined to psychoanalysis. The manner in which practice and theory develop and evolve in tandem is found precisely in these other sciences of modernity. The confrontation between models marks the development of these disciplines. Theoretical pluralism has given birth to models which sometimes complete and sometimes modify the Freudian model, modifying practices in the process. To be sure, the general framework and fundamental rules remain the same, but the mode of listening and the interpretations and the manner in which they are formulated vary from one psychoanalytic school to another.

To illustrate this movement, I propose to examine, by way of example, the influence exerted in France by the Lacanian culture. This choice is dictated obviously by my personal experience but also seems justified by the interest and criticisms frequently expressed with regard to the 'French model', often mixing the Lacanian model with other currents of thought and practice.

The term 'culture' seems to me to be more appropriate than those of theory, practice or model, inasmuch as it applies to a broader milieu than the group of Lacan's successors. It is also preferable to the term 'school' in that it is sufficiently vague to cover sometimes highly dissimilar practices which are nonetheless inspired by Lacan, while taking into account the positive and negative influences exerted by the latter, and by his pupils, on French psychoanalysts as a whole.

My purpose here, then, is not to present my own version, however brief and schematic, of the theory of the treatment in Lacan's work, but to isolate certain essential aspects of it in order to show the consequences they have on clinical practice. I will confine myself to three aspects here, concerning the aims of the treatment, the transference and interpretation.

In the Freudian model, the fundamental aim is the treatment of intrapsychic conflict. This principle remains at the basis of all the models arising from theoretical pluralism. The Lacanian model clearly breaks with it. By substituting the concept of the drive with that of desire, Lacan introduces much more than a semantic nuance. The object of desire has nothing to do with the object of the drive. The latter is what the drive seeks. Satisfying the drive means finding the object to meet the aim of the drive. The object of desire, in the Lacanian sense of the term, is not the complement sought by desire but its signifier. In the example of the dream of 'the abandoned supper party', reported by Freud in *The Interpretation of Dreams* (1900a), the smoked salmon is the symbol of the object desired by the rival, just as she herself desired the caviar. This caviar, which she had asked her husband not to give her, symbolises an aspect of her relationship with him, just as the supper party she could not give symbolises the gift she did not want to give her friend – the friend her husband thought so highly of – and the fact that she had to abandon this dinner expresses both her rivalry and her wish to identify with her. From Lacan's point of view, the caviar and smoked salmon are signifiers of a fundamental lack of being. The smoked salmon does not symbolise the object of desire but the desire itself; it signifies it – or, to be more exact, by representing it in the dream, the subject identifies with it. The aim of analysis is no longer the quest for illusory objects (those that cannot satisfy the sexual drive), but the recognition by the subject of this fundamental lack of being, and the recognition of it in the signifier which is its rhetorical figure, in this case metonymy.

The transference, from this perspective, is conceived of as being beyond the transference neurosis – that is to say, beyond the play of instinctual drive objects displaced in the psychoanalytic situation, becoming instead the fundamental relation to the other, to whom the question of the subject is addressed. The transference is thus an absolute lure since the demands that are addressed to the other can only express the fact that no object can respond to this lack of being. Consequently, the aim of interpreting the transference is not to identify the objects that the drives give themselves in psychic reality, but to 'fill the emptiness of this standstill with a lure' (Lacan, 1966/2006, p. 225), to mark the instant in which the subject, who has been unable to recognise this void in the signifier which expresses it, tries to nourish the illusion of an object. In abstinence, the analyst, by his radical non-response, will enable the subject to recognise the futility of his demand.

This non-response should not be understood only as a response to the transference but, in its very materiality, as silence. Interpretation in the Freudian sense of the term no longer exists in the Lacanian model. How do we interpret the unconscious, asked J.-A. Miller a few years ago, when the unconscious itself is interpretation, the signifier of a discourse that comes from elsewhere, the expression of a lack of being the message of which each individual receives in the speech addressed to him or her by the other?

When, at the beginning of the 1960s, a certain number of us, among Lacan's pupils, broke with him to join the IPA, we did it to dissociate ourselves from practices that we considered incompatible with psychoanalytic ethics, but we dissociated them from the theory. Those who remained faithful to Lacan thought, on the contrary, that to remain in agreement with the theory it was necessary to accept these shortcomings. They tolerated ethical failings and technical anomalies to protect their adhesion to the theory. Only Lacan strived to justify his practice by his theory. At the time, we took this position to be a rationalisation, especially as Lacan promised to bring us evidence of it, but always at a later date, in the future. We were wrong. In fact, already in the 1950s, in several fundamental texts and in his oral teaching, we could find the arguments that I have just briefly enumerated. The same misunderstanding can be found today, sometimes fostered by Lacan's followers who say, in effect: let's leave technical divergences in the background and concentrate on theoretical developments. A part of the Lacanian culture today takes the same stance as we took at the time and minimises the clinical consequences of the theoretical model. And yet they are inseparable. By substituting the recognition of a fundamental lack of being for the analysis of intrapsychic conflicts, and relegating instinctual drive objects to the status of an illusion that has to be thwarted in the analytic experience in favour of this recognition of lack, clinical practice finds itself radically modified. The transference loses all importance, and interpretation no longer has any meaning. All that remains is the frame, which forces the subject to have an experience of disillusionment, a release from the imaginary psychic world in favour of the recognition that we are radically obliged to be the subject of a desire which will never find its satisfaction and can simply be recognised as the signifier of this lack.

In practice, for many of those who claim allegiance to the Lacanian culture, the strict application of the Lacanian model has been tempered by the permanence of the Freudian model. The latter sometimes even remains the principal field of reference, Lacanian principles constituting more an implicit tendency than a recognised rule. But what is no doubt more important is the opposite effect – that is to say, the influence of the Lacanian model on the practices of those who do not claim allegiance to it and who even show clear hostility towards it.

Let us consider first the aims of the treatment. Apparently the 'non-Lacanians' and the 'Lacanians' are in total opposition here. A fundamental question of psychoanalytic ethics is at stake, and the divorce on the level of praxis seems absolute. But we have already seen that, in Lacanian circles, the opposition was not so clear-cut and that the interpretation of interpersonal or intrapsychic conflicts was not radically excluded, but simply regarded as a preliminary stage, the interpretation of the domain of the lure 'setting the whole process in motion anew' ('Presentation on Transference', 1966/2006, p. 225). On the other hand, for psychoanalysts who situate themselves outside Lacanian circles, the analysis of intrapsychic conflicts remains the essential principle. It even makes it possible to differentiate psychoanalysis clearly from every other psychotherapy. Lacan's aphorism according to which cure is only an additional benefit is, however, understood in a very general sense and, let it be said, trivialised: the issue is not to intervene directly at the level of the symptom but to have confidence in the process. Thus they mistrust practices which are aimed too directly at the symptom and seem too 'psycho-therapeutic'. Interpreting ego defences or archaic anxieties or the need for narcissistic reparation too soon seems to them to be turning one's back on listening to psychic formations of unconscious origin, on listening to psychic reality.

For the non-Lacanians, too, analysis of the transference remains a priority; it is the very frame of analytic work, and, in this respect, they are explicitly opposed to Lacanian practices, which they consider as a form of manipulation of the transference, an indirect form of suggestion. However, they mistrust transference interpretations that are formulated, and thus conceptualised, in terms of interpersonal relations ('in thinking of that, you are thinking of me . . .') – hence the lively opposition that exists currently to the so-called trend of intersubjectivity. Referring to the relations between the patient and the analyst seems to them to be reductive and to overlook the presence of a symbolic third, the triangular dimension of fantasy life which for them forms part of the Oedipal structure. The issue, then, is not to reject the figures of the imaginary order in favour of the symbolic order, as Lacan proposed, but to recognise a dialectic between the two, the symbolic order guaranteeing a structuring elaboration of the Oedipus complex. It is true that this elaboration has to be conceived of within the subject's individual history, within his relations to instinctual drive demands and not within a play of signifiers coming from the discourse of the Other.

When all is said and done, at the most immediate level of practice it is the rejection of interpretation and the almost absolute silence within which the Lacanian analyst is believed to enclose himself that is reproached. But, outside France, this reproach is often directed at the French psychoanalyst in general. The silent attitude of French psychoanalysts is associated with the practice of three sessions a week, not because the psychoanalyst does not listen to psychic reality but because he does not dare to communicate interpretations unless he knows he will have the 'return' in a session that follows soon after – a remark that I readily concur with, but one that can be inverted by explaining that the psychoanalyst can make do more easily with less frequent sessions if he 'interprets less'. Several theoretical constructions, beyond strictly Lacanian references, may be used, moreover, to back up this practice of 'using interpretation sparingly'. It is argued, for instance, that it is preferable to leave to the patient the privilege of finding the meaning rather than suggesting it to him, or that one must open up the path to the patient and not travel along it in his place. Finally, in the articulation between the frame and interpretation, the accent is often placed on the former. My work as a supervisor has very often shown me that 'young' psychoanalysts are first and foremost concerned to establish the frame, which, it seems to them, is almost sufficient to guarantee the unfolding of the analytic process. They are less concerned to communicate to the patient the interpretative work which is going on in their mind. The very clear influence exerted by Winnicott and Bion on French psychoanalysts has reinforced the notion of the analyst's 'containing function'.

Thus, apart from the radical differences existing between 'Freudian' and 'Lacanian' practices, clearly perceived by French analysts, a progressive evolution has led the latter to less contrasting practices than it would seem. For many of them, Lacan asked some good questions, even if he did not give acceptable answers. Lacan's direct influence as well as that of some of his pupils is undeniable. We should not forget that during more than a decade, this influence was exercised in the name of a 'return to Freud', a return that was supposed to find in the spirit of practice its principal justification. Alongside this direct influence, however, it is certainly necessary to take into account a certain common ground whose history needs to be traced. Let us not forget that when it re-emerged at the end of the Second World War, French psychoanalysis was an 'orphan' analysis; its principal training analysts, exiles from central Europe, were dead (Eugenie Sokolnicka, Sophie Morgenstern), or had taken up the path of exile again before the Nazi occupation (Hartmann, Loewenstein). Lacan's ambition found its place initially within a movement of no particular charisma. The old chauvinism of a psychoanalysis *à la française* rose easily from its ashes. The rapid integration of Freudian thought in the culture of the time, and the fact that its place was quite quickly recognised within psychiatry and clinical psychology, facilitated this evolution of practices and the relative isolation of French psychoanalysis in relation to the major movements of international psychoanalytic thought, in particular in the English-speaking world.

I have chosen to take the example of the effects of a certain Lacanian culture on French psychoanalytic practices. I have shown that these effects resided partly in the direct influence of the Lacanian model but also in the concern to differentiate oneself from this model or even clearly oppose it. The history of the French psychoanalytic movement cannot be reduced to Lacan. Child psychoanalysis, group psychoanalysis and psychosomatics have given birth to original models that are recognised internationally. But, even if they have inspired fruitful technical innovations and fresh clinical perspectives, they have not influenced practices as was the case for Lacanian culture.

This influence can, moreover, be discussed from two different standpoints. Those who are opposed to this culture can contest the weight that I give to it. After all, Lacan's positions did not emerge out of a void. Others have posed similar questions (on the drive, the transference or interpretation) but without ever embarking along such a radical path. As for the analysts belonging to the Lacanian movement, it is possible that they will contest, not the theories that I have concentrated on, but their place in Lacanian theory in general. I have not tried to discuss an overall model but have submitted for clinical debate the consequences of certain elements of this theory, elements which nonetheless seem to me to be essential for understanding the model and its technical implications.

French psychoanalysts are often reproached for their 'fixation to' Freud's work. This concern to retrace, each one in his own way, the movement of the Freudian discovery seems to me to be very directly linked to Lacan. Not because he advocated the 'return to Freud' but, for many, because this return has made it possible to free oneself from Lacanian solutions to questions which, after all, are not absent from Freudian thought.

The evolution of psychoanalytic practices in France has thus been marked by the confrontation between a Freudian model which viewed the treatment as an 'interminable' search for individual pathological expressions of unconscious thought and a Lacanian model which viewed the treatment as a revealing experience of the incompleteness of the subject prey to desire. What I have tried to show is that this fundamental opposition had led to technical positions that are less antinomical than it would seem. Is it a good thing or a bad thing? To what extent, in underlining certain similarities, have I underestimated the differences?

What I have wanted to show is that the theoretical and technical debates, the plurality of schools, and thus the plurality of models, gave – and gives – life to psychoanalytic practice. What is just as important as marking difference is to understand its meaning.

References

Freud, S. (1900a). *The Interpretation of Dreams. S.E.*, 4/5.
Freud, S. (1919a [1918]). Lines of Advance in Psycho-Analytic Therapy. *S.E.*, 17.
Freud, S. (1920g). *Beyond the Pleasure Principle. S.E.*, 18: 1–64.
Freud, S. (1926d [1925]). *Inhibitions, Symptoms and Anxiety. S.E.*, 20: 75–174.
Freud, S. (1937c). Analysis Terminable and Interminable. *S.E.*, 23: 209–253.
Lacan, J. (1966). *Écrits*, trans. B. Fink. New York: Norton, 2006.

Section II

THE PIONEERS AND THEIR LEGACY

II THE PIONEERS AND THEIR LEGACY
Introduction

Alain Gibeault

Jacques Lacan, Sacha Nacht and Maurice Bouvet are the three pioneers who gave a new impetus to French psychoanalysis after the Second World War and highlighted the specific nature of the approach and concepts adopted by French analysts. Lacan and Nacht were both born in 1901, at the dawn of the twentieth century, the former in France, into a middle-class Catholic family, the latter in Romania, into a rural Jewish family that had converted to the Orthodox religion and remained very attached to French language and culture. Lacan was analysed by Rudolph Loewenstein, who had settled in France. Nacht had initially wanted to be analysed by Freud, but since his knowledge of German was somewhat inadequate, he undertook analysis with Heinz Hartmann, first in Vienna then in Paris, once Hartmann had settled there after fleeing the Nazi regime. Thus it was that those who were to become the eminent representatives of ego psychology were also the 'fathers' of the first great post-war French psychoanalysts.

It is, therefore, not surprising that French psychoanalysis developed in a context of controversy with respect to American psychoanalysis. Lacan and Nacht started off as 'brethren' and friends in the Paris Psychoanalytical Society, then in the early 1950s became 'estranged' with respect to issues to do with training. With his shortened sessions, Lacan quickly became the training analyst who had the greatest number of trainees; it was to counter that somewhat questionable practice in a psychoanalytic Society affiliated to the International Psychoanalytical Association (IPA) that, in 1954, Nacht founded the Paris Institute of Psychoanalysis, advocating the now-typical practice in French psychoanalysis of three 45-minute sessions per week.

According to Bela Grunberger, who was analysed by Nacht, the latter, like Freud, initially proposed five or six sessions per week. From 1954 on, however, he recommended that analysts in training should be offered three sessions per week, thus making it possible to analyse two candidates in any given week. It was mainly for these reasons – training policy and, to some extent, the sibling rivalry between Nacht and Lacan – that training analyses in France have been carried out on the basis of three sessions per week, while in Britain different historical reasons have maintained a rhythm of five sessions per week for training analyses. Later, the identificatory processes at stake as regards the personal analysis of French analysts-to-be preserved that way of doing things and contributed to developing certain ideas on the theoretical and clinical issues involved in it; this, too, was a significant difference with respect to the procedures adopted by other psychoanalytic societies affiliated to the IPA.

Disagreements on technique such as those led to Lacan's expulsion from the Paris Psychoanalytical Society in 1953 – the famous 'split'. Before then, in fact, a certain number of differences of opinion had become obvious in the psychoanalytic theorisations of the two protagonists. The two papers included in this collection bear witness to these: Lacan's famous 'mirror stage' paper (chapter 3) dismisses the non-verbal specular relationship with the object in favour of language and discourse, while Nacht's article on the non-verbal relationship in psychoanalytic treatment (chapter 4) emphasises the importance of the analyst's silent 'presence' and of non-verbal aspects.

If we examine Lacan's ground-breaking paper on the mirror stage (1949), it is interesting to note that it was first read at the 1936 IPA Congress in Marienbad. The story goes that Ernest Jones stopped Lacan's presentation after ten minutes – a fact which no doubt was hardly conducive to developing a positive relationship between Lacan and the English-speaking psychoanalytic world. Lacan, however, did not give up hope of defending his point of view, and he presented another version of his paper at the 1949 IPA Congress in Zurich.

That paper represents one of the basic tenets of Lacanian thinking and gives a direct description of the characteristic features of that approach. Lacan discusses the notes that psychologists – in particular, Henri Wallon (1934) in France – had made as they observed the infant's experience when looking at a mirror. When they recognise their image in a mirror, infants are jubilant, and Lacan sees in this the primary crystallisation of the '**specular image**' (chapter 3, p. 99), an intuitive form thanks to which the subject fulfils the search for unity. This 'jubilant assumption' (p. 99) reveals the possibility for the infant to go beyond a motor image that is still fragmented towards a visual one in which his or her body is already global: the anticipated image of the body as a totality puts an end to that of the 'fragmented body'.

In that paper, Lacan claims to have fathered the concept of the 'fragmented body' (chapter 3, p. 101), a term which, he says, he introduced into 'our system of theoretical references'. However, in 1966, when *Écrits* was published, he acknowledged how much he owed to Melanie Klein, who had earlier spoken of images of the

> **Specular image** refers to the experience Lacan (1949) described in his classic paper, first read in 1936, on the 'mirror stage': between the age of six and eighteen months, infants – who are still in a state of motor helplessness because of their neoteny – anticipate in an imaginary manner being in control of their bodily unity through the perception of their own image in a mirror and by identification with the image of a visual likeness [*semblable*] in terms of a whole unit. It is a narcissistic identification that Lacan calls *imaginary*, because the child identifies with a '*double*' of him/herself.

Introduction 89

fragmented body. 'They are confirmed by the assertion of fantasies of the so-called paranoid phase in the phenomenology of Kleinian experience' (Lacan, 1966/2006, p. 55).

Although Lacan is referring to a maturational moment in the infant's life, he eschews any developmental reference and makes of it a structural event in mental life: the mirror stage, as the title of his paper makes clear, is a 'formative' moment of the I function which is at the same time revealed by it. As such, the ego is no longer the agency involved in perceiving reality; it is drawn into a '*function of méconnaissance*' (chapter 3, p. 103), in which it is alienated with respect to the Other as a self or with respect to the self as an Other. In his willingness to engage in dialogue with the English-speaking world, Lacan makes reference to Anna Freud – but in words that are not his own, and all the time he calls into question the hypothesis of the 'autonomous ego' so fundamental to the American concept of ego psychology.

That perspective was to set in motion all sorts of research in France on narcissism, on the difference between the ideal ego and the ego-ideal, in terms of a distinction borrowed from Hermann Nunberg (1932), and on the problem of the 'double', which evokes both the fantasy of primary narcissism and the destructive violence that is inherent in this primal fantasy of returning to undifferentiated unity.

According to Lacan, the mirror experience makes obvious the decisive role of the *Imaginary* dimension in the construction of the ego; it is one of the 'three registers of human reality', the other two being the *Symbolic* and *Real* dimensions; together they form the framework for Lacan's theory as a whole. In the Imaginary register, the ego identifies with the Other as with its own image and identifies the Other with itself, with its own image; this brings to mind certain aspects of what Melanie Klein called projective identification. The Imaginary would therefore seem to lie somewhere between the Real and the Symbolic. On the one hand, it is a defence against the abyss of the Real dimension of primeval time, with its idea of an unknown factor (in the mathematical as well as psychoanalytic sense) that is both something one does not wish to know about and that unknown factor represented by the primitive mother figure, a source of anxiety and engulfment. On the other hand, one has to go beyond the Imaginary dimension via entry into the Symbolic Order that constitutes a reformulation of the Oedipal situation in terms of having access, thanks to the paternal figure, to the universe of the Law, of participation in social and cultural *mores* and of being acknowledged as a subject in one's own right in return for respecting certain fundamental prohibitions. Lacanian theory has a great deal to do with the structuralist movement of the 1960s and bears witness to the influence of Claude Lévi-Strauss, for whom the elementary structures of kinship were the fundamental institution of any form of society.

From that point of view, the Real dimension lies outside any symbolic reference and is all the more threatening in that it eludes every attempt at fantasising and symbolisation. The Real dimension is therefore distinct from *reality*, which corresponds to a filtering or processing of real elements by means of the Imaginary and Symbolic registers. All through his work, Lacan maintained what he saw as a fundamental trilogy; in his final lectures, he laid great emphasis on Borromean knots –

those inseparable rings which, if they are broken apart, collapse: a metaphorical representation of the catastrophic situation that would ensue for the individual, for theory and for human relationships.

That image of how the mind works sees the Real dimension as something impossible and irreducible, at the very limit of what is thinkable. That idea is close to Bion's point of view in which the mind is constantly being called upon to transform beta elements, which cannot be symbolised, into alpha elements that can be thought about thanks to the mother's reverie; if this is not done, the infant may be overwhelmed by 'nameless dread'. In Lacan's theory, however, the hiatus between Imaginary and Symbolic works against that process of transformation involving the body and affects which Bion's idea of 'feeling' (1963, p. 95) enables us to grasp much more easily.

Lacan's emphasis on the pre-eminence of Culture as an intermediary between Nature and Society had as one of its aims the struggle against Marxist thought, which at that time in France was widespread. It did, however, lead to the introduction into his theory of a radical hiatus between the Imaginary and Symbolic dimensions, between Nature and Culture, between the drive-activated body and language, between mother and father. The mirror stage, from that point of view, lies at the origin of an opposition between Imaginary and Symbolic rather than of any articulation between them. The reason for this is as follows: Lacan confused *imaginary* and *specular*. The Imaginary dimension is not something that will simply lock the individual into a narcissistic form of capture; on the contrary, as Winnicott (1971) pointed out in his reading of Lacan's paper, it may well enable access to the world of culture and creativity. Winnicott is absolutely correct when he says: 'In individual emotional development, *the precursor of the mirror is the mother's face*' (1971, p. 111); if the mother's gaze can be a source of alienation, it can also guarantee the existence of a capacity for symbol formation. Lacan (1960) did not dismiss the idea that the mother's gaze may carry with it some reference to a third party; in so doing, he was close to what many French psychoanalysts, among them André Green, would later discuss in terms of *thirdness* and the negative.

> For the Other where discourse is situated, which is always latent in the triangulation that consecrates this distance, is not latent as long as it extends all the way ... to the gesture by which the child at the mirror turns toward the person who is carrying him and appeals with a look to this witness; the latter decants the child's recognition of the image, by verifying it, from the jubilant assumption in which *it* [elle] certainly *already was*. But this 'already' should not mislead us as to the structure of the presence evoked as a third party here: it owes nothing to the anecdotal personage who incarnates it. All that subsists here is the being whose advent can only be grasped by no longer being.
> (Lacan, 1960/2006, p. 568)

In that approach, there is a hiatus rather than a dynamic articulation between presence and absence, and between positive and negative.

Introduction

> French psychoanalysts, who always go back to Freud, have not entirely rejected Freud's view of femininity and feminine development. Chasseguet-Smirgel (1964) and her colleagues questioned some of these assumptions, considering penis envy to be essentially defensive rather than primary. Others have developed and added to the Freudian theory. **The feminine** is a concept used by French analysts in order to describe the feminine identifications, not only in girls but also in boys.

In that pioneering period, Lacan saw himself as the defender of the negative and of absence, whilst his 'brother', Nacht, focused on the positive dimension and on presence. Indeed, Nacht published a certain number of his writings in a book entitled *La présence du psychanalyste* (Nacht, 1963a). The paper published in the present collection (chapter 4) is the final chapter (1963b) of that book. The comparison with Lacan's theoretical and clinical standpoint is highly revealing: Nacht's aim is to put forward a conception of theory and practice that is, to all intents and purposes, the opposite of Lacan's. Although he does emphasise the importance of the talking cure and of verbal interpretations, Nacht sees in silence a highly useful factor: in his view, silence is not to be looked upon, as it is in classical theory, as a resistance with respect to the transference, but as a positive experience of absolute union with the mother figure. Lacan emphasised the 'law of the father', the role of which is to enable the patient to accept separation from the mother. Nacht, however, sought to draw attention to the intense joy of *being* rather than of *having*, which is a source of conflict. This can be likened to Winnicott's (1971) description of primary identification as the experience of *being*, with its relevance to **the feminine** dimension, as opposed to that of *doing*, which is more typical of the masculine dimension.

This supposes on the analyst's part 'a certain *quality of presence* rooted in inner availability and openness' (Nacht, chapter 4, p. 110), thus enabling the patient to have an experience similar to that of Winnicott's found–created object; Nacht (1971, p. 223) conceptualises this as what enables the analyst to 'make contact with a conflict-free area in which the autonomous ego can blossom'. A conflict-free area means one that is not drive-related, part of what Nacht (1971) called 'narcissism as guardian of life', corresponding to primary narcissism which deploys its protective function from birth all through life (p. 202). When we lose this positive narcissism, we become 'more vulnerable to everything that attacks life' (p. 203), such that the road to all sorts of psychosomatic disorders lies open. From that point of view, Nacht was something of a forerunner as regards the psychosomatic theories that would later be put forward by Marty, Fain, de M'Uzan and David, the founders of the Paris School of Psychosomatics. The idea of primary narcissism as a positive form of narcissism also foreshadows Bela Grunberger's work on narcissism – Grunberger was analysed by Nacht – as well as that of André Green (life narcissism) and of Benno Rosenberg (masochism as preserving life).

Nacht goes even further in his therapeutic approach when he advocates, as he does in this paper, a 'gratifying presence' (chapter 4, p. 112); that would open the door to challenging the analyst's neutrality. In order to facilitate the experience of absolute union with the mother figure, Nacht does not exclude the possibility of stretching the rules of the analytic setting – he would agree to changing the times of sessions, to letting them last a few minutes longer than usual, etc. That therapeutic attitude cannot fail to recall Winnicott's 'enactments' in the course of certain analyses.

Lacan steadfastly opposed any narcissistic alliance with the 'good maternal object', but Nacht is not far from the idea that the analyst should be a good object, even if this entails calling into question the setting as a third party/intermediary: on the one hand, then, the uncompromising Law of the Father that may be expressed as persecutory absence; on the other, a Mother who, with her benevolent presence, may well encourage incestuous collusion. Another indication of the contrast between their positions is that, for Lacan, psychoanalysis had nothing to do with any therapeutic aims – recovery could be no more than an 'extra' – whereas Nacht insisted on the importance of the therapeutic aspect of psychoanalysis, as the title of one of his books, *Guérir avec Freud* [Healing with Freud] (Nacht, 1971), makes clear. Thus it was that in France a whole series of debates on the therapeutic value or otherwise of psychoanalysis took place, contrasting *self-knowledge* with *recovery*. Paradoxically, however, although they started out in different directions, Lacan and Nacht came together in order to consider a relationship with the object that would be separate from the drives, in spite of their contrasting views on the issue of the 'autonomous ego'.

In any history of the post-war 'pioneers' of psychoanalysis, Maurice Bouvet must figure as a major contributor. He was about ten years younger than Lacan and Nacht and, for French psychoanalysis, is a classic reference. Bouvet introduced a theory of object relations that remained linked to that of the drives; this enabled him to develop his thoughts on the indications for psychoanalysis that would take into account the various ways in which the mind functions. Much more of a theorist than Nacht, Bouvet influenced a whole generation of French psychoanalysts; in particular, he opposed Lacan's ideas on the psychoanalytic process (Bouvet, 1954; Lacan, 1955).

The paper included in the present collection (chapter 5) was initially read to the 1957 IPA Congress, in Paris. It is the summary of a much longer article published in the *Revue Française de Psychanalyse* in 1958; Bouvet himself said that the latter text was more representative of his views than the paper he read at the Paris Congress. Bouvet conceptualised the possibility of introducing technical variations on the basis of the idea of distance; this emphasises the need to take into account the relationship between setting and process, and it leaves the door open for proposing psychoanalytic work to patients whose mental structure is not unequivocally neurotic. Hence the idea of 're-arranging' the setting not only as to its physical layout (on the couch or sitting face to face, rhythm of the sessions) but also with respect to the work of interpretation. In that way, Bouvet established the French approach to psychoanalysis through his careful preservation of the conditions underpinning the analytic process, whatever the actual technical setting. Bouvet focuses in chapter 5 mainly on the activity of interpretation, but the points that he raised led those who came after him to think deeply about issues concerning the actual physical setting.

Following in the footsteps of Freud and Abraham, Bouvet adopted a psychopathological outlook that distinguished between pregenital and genital object relations; this enabled him to make a connection between the structure of the ego and the consequences of loss of the object. In chapter 5, although his definition of the object has mainly to do with external objects, it necessarily echoes the kinds of fantasy object relations that are set up and, therefore, also concerns internal objects. Bouvet introduced the concept of 'distance' with respect to the object as a technical means of evaluating the kind of object relations that patients present, whether in preliminary interviews or in the course of their analysis. The definition he gives of this notion in the present chapter is fundamental: distance is '*the gap* which separates the way in which a subject expresses his instinctual drives from how he would express them if the process of "handling" or "managing" (in French: *aménagement*) these expressions did not intervene' (chapter 5, p. 116; emphasis added).

The distance/nearness pairing is thus the spatial and temporal instrument that enables the analyst to follow, step by step, the development of the transference–countertransference relationship. Bouvet was criticised for leaving aside the 'topographical point of view' and for initially giving more importance to the external object than to its internal counterpart. Bouvet's theory, however, focuses principally on technical matters, and, as Bernard Brusset (1988) quite rightly points out, the idea of distance offers the clinical practitioner an instrument that is easy to use, has a direct link with the transference and gives rise to an effective reduction that, as Bouvet argued, is transnosographical (Brusset, 1988, p. 91). Brusset adds that it is this that makes the notion of distance invaluable in bringing together and differentiating between the various 'morbid entities' – the neuroses, perversions, psychoses and above all borderline states, in the identification of which, says Brusset, Bouvet was a true pioneer.

Bouvet was André Green's analyst and thus helped Green to do his own research into borderline states; he was instrumental also in encouraging Pierre Marty's (1958) work on the 'allergic object relationship' in psychosomatics. In French psychoanalysis, the semiology of distance with respect to the object thus contributed to research on how to evaluate mental functioning from the economic and dynamic points of view – and this, of course, made for quite a contrast with the Lacanian approach, which focused mainly on the topography of the mind and on knowledge. Contrary to Nacht, however, Bouvet was much more reticent as regards the use of 'active methods' in the clinical work of psychoanalysis, precisely because of what was at stake in the idea of distance with respect to the object. Bouvet makes it clear in chapter 5 that excessive satisfaction or frustration can lead to unbearable 'rapprochers'.

Finally, Bouvet highlights in his chapter the fact that symptoms of depersonalisation may arise 'when the relation to the object is not kept at an optimum distance' (pp. 117–118). The last major paper that Bouvet wrote was read, just a few weeks before he died, at the Congress of Romance-Language Psychoanalysts in April 1960 on the subject of depersonalisation and object relations (Bouvet, 1960). In that paper, Bouvet points out that the object relation that is a typical feature of phenomena such as depersonalisation is 'marked by affective dependence upon the narcissistic object and the intensity of the need to maintain the affective bond with it' (1960, p. 428) and, as such, is a defence against psychosis. First and foremost, according to Bouvet, there is a change in the patient's vision of the self and the world which is specific to each individual; the dominant feeling is one of strangeness, of unfamiliarity. This basically fluctuates from day to day and from hour to hour (p. 304). This state of 'ego breakdown' has to do with a reduction in the arrangements that keep a proper mental distance between the object and the self, with the object coming closer and closer to the place it occupies in the individual's unconscious fantasies. The character of the object relation turns it into a 'narcissistic object', the loss of which brings about an upheaval in the individual's sense of self. Michel de M'Uzan, who was analysed by Bouvet, continued this line of research, in particular through his studies of how controlled depersonalisation can become manifest in psychoanalytic treatment as a fundamental factor for change and for integrating psychic bisexuality in the work of an analysis. In this way, Bouvet did indeed contribute to defining a specifically French approach to psychoanalysis.

References

Bion, W. R. (1963). *Elements of Psycho-Analysis*. London: Heinemann; reprinted London: Karnac.

Bouvet, M. (1954). La cure-type [The standard form of psychoanalytic treatment]. In *Œuvres psychanalytiques II, Résistances transfert. Écrits didactiques* [Psychoanalytic writings II. Resistances, transference: Didactic texts] (pp. 9–96). Paris: Payot, 1968.

Bouvet, M. (1958). Les variations de la technique (Distance et variations). In *Œuvres psychanalytiques I, La relation d'objet. Névrose obsessionnelle, dépersonnalisation* [Psychoanalytic writings I. The relationship to the object: obsessional neurosis, depersonalisation]. Paris: Payot, 1968. [Technical Variation and the Concept of Distance. *International Journal of Psychoanalysis*, 39 (1958): 211–221 (shorter version of the paper in French).]

Bouvet, M. (1960). Dépersonnalisation et relations d'objet [Depersonalization and object relations]. In *Œuvres psychanalytiques I, La relation d'objet. Névrose obsessionnelle, dépersonnalisation* [Psychoanalytic writings I. The relationship to the object: obsessional neurosis, depersonalisation] (pp. 295–435). Paris, Payot, 1968.

Brusset, B. (1988). *Psychanalyse du lien. La relation d'objet* [Psychoanalysis of object relations]. Paris: Le Centurion.

Lacan, J. (1949). Le stade du miroir comme formateur de la fonction du Je telle qu'elle nous est révélée dans l'expérience psychanalytique In *Écrits*. Paris: Editions du Seuil, 1966, p. 93. [The Mirror Stage as Formative of The *I* Function as Revealed in Psychoanalytic Experience (trans. B. Fink). *Ecrits*. New York: Norton, 2006, p. 75.]

Lacan, J. (1955). Variantes de la cure-type. In *Écrits*. Paris: Editions du Seuil, 1966, p. 323. [Variations on the Standard Treatment. In *Écrits*, trans. B. Fink. New York: Norton, 2006, p. 269.]

Lacan, J. (1960). Remarque sur le rapport de Daniel Lagache: Psychanalyse et structure de la personnalité. In *Écrits*. Paris: Editions du Seuil, 1966, p. 647. [Remarks on Daniel Lagache's Presentation: 'Psychoanalysis and Personality Structure'. In *Écrits*, trans. B. Fink. New York: Norton, 2006, p. 543.].

Lacan, J. (1966). *Écrits*. Paris: Editions du Seuil. [*Ecrits*, trans. B. Fink. New York: Norton, 2006.]

Marty, p. (1958). The allergic object relationship. *International Journal of Psychoanalysis*, *39*: 98–103.

Nacht, S. (1963a). *La présence du psychanalyste* [The psychoanalyst's presence]. Paris: Presses Universitaires de France.

Nacht, S. (1963b). De la relation non-verbale dans le traitement psychanalytique. In *La présence du psychanalyste* [The psychoanalyst's presence]. Paris: Presses Universitaires de France. [The Non-Verbal Relationship in Psycho-Analytic Treatment. *International Journal of Psychoanalysis*, *44*: 334–339.]

Nacht, S. (1971). *Guérir avec Freud* [Healing with Freud]. Paris: Payot.

Nunberg, H. (1932), *Allgemeine Neurosenlehre auf psychoanalytischer Grundlage* [General theory of the neuroses on a psychoanalytic basis]. Berne: Hans Huber.

Wallon, H. (1934). *Les origines du caractère chez l'enfant* [The origins of character in children]. Paris: Presses Universitaires de France, 1987.

Winnicott, D. W. (1971). *Playing and Reality*. London: Tavistock Publications; reprinted London: Routledge, 1982.

3 THE MIRROR STAGE AS FORMATIVE OF THE FUNCTION OF THE I AS REVEALED IN PSYCHOANALYTIC EXPERIENCE[1]

Jacques Lacan

> **Jacques Lacan** (1901–1981) was a psychiatrist and psychoanalyst, a full member of the Paris Psychoanalytical Society (SPP: *Société psychanalytique de Paris*) in 1934 and president of that Society in 1953. He then broke away from the SPP because of differences of opinion concerning how analysts should be trained and how long sessions should last. With Françoise Dolto, Georges Favez and Daniel Lagache, he resigned from the SPP and set up his own association, the French Psychoanalytic Society, over which he then presided. In 1964, expelled from the International Psychanalytical Association, he could no longer be a training analyst; he therefore decided to set up, on his own initiative, the French School of Psychoanalysis which in the first roster was renamed the Freudian School of Paris. As a result of dissension within that association, he decided to disband it on 5 January 1980. He immediately set up the School of the Freudian Cause and 'adopted' it officially in January 1981. Lacan died that same year.
>
> Lacan was a prolific writer, although much of his material is dispersed throughout a considerable number of journals. In 1966, a significant part of his writings was published in a 912-page volume called *Écrits* (Seuil, 1966; Norton, 2006); this has become a psychoanalytic best-seller in spite of the fact that Lacan's thinking is by no means easy to understand.
>
> His teaching was for the most part oral, although his Seminars (1953–77, Seminars I to XXVII) have appeared in print from 1975 on; many of them, however, are still unpublished.
>
> Gilbert Diatkine wrote an account of Lacan and his work for the 'Psychanalystes d'aujourd'hui' series (PUF, 1997).

The conception of the mirror stage that I introduced at our last congress, thirteen years ago, has since become more or less established in the practice of the French group. However, I think it worthwhile to bring it again to your attention, especially today, for the light it sheds on the formation of the *I* as we

---

[1] Delivered at the 16th International Congress of Psychoanalysis, Zurich, 17 July 1949.

experience it in psychoanalysis. It is an experience that leads us to oppose any philosophy directly issuing from the *Cogito*.

Some of you may recall that this conception originated in a feature of human behaviour illuminated by a fact of comparative psychology. The child, at an age when he is for a time, however short, outdone by the chimpanzee in instrumental intelligence, can nevertheless already recognize as such his own image in a mirror. This recognition is indicated in the illuminative mimicry of the *Aha-Erlebnis*, which Köhler[2] sees as the expression of situational apperception, an essential stage of the act of intelligence.

This act, far from exhausting itself, as in the case of the monkey, once the image has been mastered and found empty, immediately rebounds in the case of the child in a series of gestures in which he experiences in play the relation between the movements assumed in the image and the reflected environment, and between this virtual complex and the reality it reduplicates – the child's own body, and the persons and things, around him.

This event can take place, as we have known since Baldwin,[3] from the age of six months, and its repetition has often made me reflect upon the startling spectacle of the infant in front of the mirror. Unable as yet to walk, or even to stand up, and held tightly as he is by some support, human or artificial (what, in France, we call a '*trotte-bébé*'), he nevertheless overcomes, in a flutter of jubilant activity, the obstructions of his support and, fixing his attitude in a slightly leaning-forward position, in order to hold it in his gaze, brings back an instantaneous aspect of the image.

For me, this activity retains the meaning I have given it up to the age of eighteen months. This meaning discloses a libidinal dynamism, which has hitherto remained problematic, as well as an ontological structure of the human world that accords with my reflections on paranoiac knowledge.

We have only to understand the mirror stage *as an identification*, in the full sense that analysis gives to the term: namely, the transformation that takes place in the subject when he assumes an image – whose predestination to this

---

[2] Wolfgang Köhler (1887–1967) was a German psychologist who, with Max Wertheimer and Kurt Koffka, founded Gestalt psychology. *Gestalt psychology*, or *gestaltism* (German: *Gestalt* – 'shape' or 'figure'), of the Berlin School, is a theory of mind and brain positing that the operational principle of the brain is holistic, parallel and analogue, with self-organising tendencies, or that the whole is different from the sum of its parts. The *Gestalt effect* refers to the pattern-forming capability of our senses, particularly with respect to the visual recognition of figures and whole forms instead of just a collection of simple lines and curves. In psychology, gestaltism is often opposed to structuralism and Wundt. [*Eds., this volume*]

[3] James Mark Baldwin (1861–1934) was an American philosopher and psychologist. His most important contributions were those to developmental psychology. His stepwise theory of cognitive development was a major influence on the later, and much more widely known, developmental theory of Jean Piaget. He is well known for the experimental study of infant movement and its role in mental development. In the experimental framework, every practice of an infant's movement intended to advance the integration of behaviour favourable to development appeared to be selected from an excess of movement in attempts at imitation. [*Eds., this volume*]

phase-effect is sufficiently indicated by the use, in analytic theory, of the ancient term *imago*.

This jubilant assumption of his specular image by the child at the *infans* stage, still sunk in his motor incapacity and nursling dependence, would seem to exhibit in an exemplary situation the symbolic matrix in which the *I* is precipitated in a primordial form, before it is objectified in the dialectic of identification with the other, and before language restores to it, in the universal, its function as subject.

This form would have to be called the Ideal-I,[4] if we wished to incorporate it into our usual register, in the sense that it will also be the source of secondary identifications, under which term I would place the functions of libidinal normalization. But the important point is that this form situates the agency of the ego, before its social determination, in a fictional direction, which will always remain irreducible for the individual alone, or rather, which will only rejoin the coming-into-being [*le devenir*] of the subject asymptotically, whatever the success of the dialectical syntheses by which he must resolve as *I* his discordance with his own reality.

The fact is that the total form of the body by which the subject anticipates in a mirage the maturation of his power is given to him only as *Gestalt*, that is to say, in an exteriority in which this form is certainly more constituent than constituted, but in which it appears to him above all in a contrasting size (*un relief de stature*) that fixes it and in a symmetry that inverts it, in contrast with the turbulent movements that the subject feels are animating him. Thus, this *Gestalt* – whose pregnancy should be regarded as bound up with the species, though its motor style remains scarcely recognizable – by these two aspects of its appearance, symbolizes the mental permanence of the *I*, at the same time as it prefigures its alienating destination; it is still pregnant with the correspondences that unite the *I* with the statue in which man projects himself, with the phantoms that dominate him, or with the automation in which, in an ambiguous relation, the world of his own making tends to find completion.

Indeed, for the *imagos* – whose veiled faces it is our privilege to see in outline in our daily experience and in the penumbra of symbolic efficacity[5] – the mirror-image would seem to be the threshold of the visible world, if we go by the mirror disposition that the *imago of one's own body* presents in hallucinations or dreams, whether it concerns its individual features, or even its infirmities, or its object-projections; or if we observe the role of the mirror apparatus in the appearances of the *double*, in which psychic realities, however heterogeneous, are manifested.

---

[4] Throughout this article I leave in its peculiarity the translation I have adopted for Freud's *Ideal-Ich* (i.e., '*je-idéal*'), without further comment, other than to say that I have not maintained it since.
[5] Cf. 'L'efficacité symbolique' (Lévi-Strauss, 1958).

That a *Gestalt* should be capable of formative effects in the organism is attested by a piece of biological experimentation that is itself so alien to the idea of psychical causality that it cannot bring itself to formulate its results in these terms. It nevertheless recognizes that it is a necessary condition for the maturation of the gonad of the female pigeon that it should see another member of its species, of either sex; so sufficient in itself is this condition that the desired effect may be obtained merely by placing the individual within reach of the field of reflection of a mirror. Similarly, in the case of the migratory locust, the transition within a generation from the solitary to the gregarious form can be obtained by exposing the individual, at a certain stage, to the exclusively visual action of a similar image, provided it is animated by movements of a style sufficiently close to that characteristic of the species. Such facts are inscribed in an order of homeomorphic identification that would itself fall within the larger question of the meaning of beauty as both formative and erogenic.

But the facts of mimicry are no less instructive when conceived as cases of heteromorphic identification, in as much as they raise the problem of the signification of space for the living organism – psychological concepts hardly seem less appropriate for shedding light on these matters than ridiculous attempts to reduce them to the supposedly supreme law of adaptation. We have only to recall how Roger Caillois[6] (who was then very young, and still fresh from his breach with the sociological school in which he was trained) illuminated the subject by using the term '*legendary psychasthenia*' to classify morphological mimicry as an obsession with space in its derealizing effect.

I have myself shown in the social dialectic that structures human knowledge as paranoiac[7] why human knowledge has greater autonomy than animal knowledge in relation to the field of force of desire, but also why human knowledge is determined in that 'little reality' [*ce peu de réalité*], which the Surrealists, in their restless way, saw as its limitation. These reflections lead me to recognize in the spatial captation manifested in the mirror-stage, even before the social dialectic, the effect in man of an organic insufficiency in his natural reality – in so far as any meaning can be given to the word 'nature'.

I am led, therefore, to regard the function of the mirror-stage as a particular case of the function of the *imago*, which is to establish a relation between the organism and its reality – or, as they say, between the *Innenwelt* and the *Umwelt*.

In man, however, this relation to nature is altered by a certain dehiscence at the heart of the organism, a primordial Discord betrayed by the signs of uneasiness and motor unco-ordination of the neo-natal months. The objective

---

[6] Roger Caillois (1913–1978) was a French intellectual whose idiosyncratic work brought together literary criticism, sociology and philosophy by focusing on subjects as diverse as gems, play and the sacred. He was also instrumental in introducing Latin American authors to the French public. In 1935 he wrote a paper, 'Mimétisme et psychasthénie légendaire', to which Lacan refers in this paper. [*Eds., this volume*]

[7] Cf. 'L'agressivité en psychanalyse' (Lacan, 1966).

notion of the anatomical incompleteness of the pyramidal system and likewise the presence of certain humoral residues of the maternal organism confirm the view I have formulated as the fact of a real *specific prematurity of birth* in man.

It is worth noting, incidentally, that this is a fact recognized as such by embryologists, by the term *foetalization*, which determines the prevalence of the so-called superior apparatus of the neurax, and especially of the cortex, which psycho-surgical operations lead us to regard as the intra-organic mirror.

This development is experienced as a temporal dialectic that decisively projects the formation of the individual into history. The *mirror stage* is a drama whose internal thrust is precipitated from insufficiency to anticipation – and which manufactures for the subject, caught up in the lure of spatial identification, the succession of phantasies that extends from a fragmented body-image to a form of its totality that I shall call orthopaedic – and, lastly, to the assumption of the armour of an alienating identity, which will mark with its rigid structure the subject's entire mental development. Thus, to break out of the circle of the *Innenwelt* into the *Umwelt* generates the inexhaustible quadrature of the ego's verifications.

This fragmented body – which term I have also introduced into our system of theoretical references – usually manifests itself in dreams when the movement of the analysis encounters a certain level of aggressive disintegration in the individual. It then appears in the form of disjointed limbs, or of those organs represented in exoscopy, growing wings and taking up arms for intestinal persecutions – the very same that the visionary Hieronymus Bosch has fixed, for all time, in painting, in their ascent from the fifteenth century to the imaginary zenith of modern man. But this form is even tangibly revealed at the organic level, in the lines of 'fragilization' that define the anatomy of phantasy, as exhibited in the schizoid and spasmodic symptoms of hysteria.

Correlatively, the formation of the *I* is symbolized in dreams by a fortress, or a stadium – its inner arena and enclosure, surrounded by marshes and rubbish-tips, dividing it into two opposed fields of contest where the subject flounders in quest of the lofty, remote inner castle whose form (sometimes juxtaposed in the same scenario) symbolizes the *id* in a quite startling way. Similarly, on the mental plane, we find realized the structures of fortified works, the metaphor of which arises spontaneously, as if issuing from the symptoms themselves, to designate the mechanisms of obsessional neurosis – inversion, isolation, reduplication, cancellation and displacement.

But if we were to build on these subjective givens alone – however little we free them from the condition of experience that makes us see them as partaking of the nature of a linguistic technique – our theoretical attempts would remain exposed to the charge of projecting themselves into the unthinkable of an absolute subject. This is why I have sought in the present hypothesis, grounded in a conjunction of objective data, the guiding grid for a *method of symbolic reduction*.

It establishes in the *defences of the ego* a genetic order, in accordance with the wish formulated by Miss Anna Freud, in the first part of her great 1936 work, and situates (as against a frequently expressed prejudice) hysterical repression and its returns at a more archaic stage than obsessional inversion and its isolating processes, and the latter in turn as preliminary to paranoic alienation, which dates from the deflection of the specular *I* into the social *I*.

This moment in which the mirror-stage comes to an end inaugurates, by the identification with the *imago* of the counterpart and the drama of primordial jealousy (so well brought out by the school of Charlotte Bühler[8] in the phenomenon of infantile *transitivism*), the dialectic that will henceforth link the *I* to socially elaborated situations.

It is this moment that decisively tips the whole of human knowledge into mediatization through the desire of the other, constitutes its objects in an abstract equivalence by the co-operation of others, and turns the I into that apparatus for which every instinctual thrust constitutes a danger, even though it should correspond to a natural maturation – the very normalization of this maturation being henceforth dependent, in man, on a cultural mediation as exemplified, in the case of the sexual object, by the Oedipus complex.

In the light of this conception, the term primary narcissism, by which analytic doctrine designates the libidinal investment characteristic of that moment, reveals in those who invented it the most profound awareness of semantic latencies. But it also throws light on the dynamic opposition between this libido and the sexual libido, which the first analysts tried to define when they invoked destructive and, indeed, death instincts, in order to explain the evident connection between the narcissistic libido and the alienating function of the *I*, the aggressivity it releases in any relation to the other, even in a relation involving the most Samaritan of aid.

In fact, they were encountering that existential negativity whose reality is so vigorously proclaimed by the contemporary philosophy of being and nothingness.

But unfortunately that philosophy grasps negativity only within the limits of a self-sufficiency of consciousness, which, as one of its premises, links to the misrecognition [*méconnaissances*] that constitute the *ego*, the illusion of autonomy to which it entrusts itself. This flight of fancy, for all that it draws, to an unusual extent, on borrowings from psychoanalytic experience, culminates in the pretention of providing an existential psychoanalysis.

At the culmination of the historical effort of a society to refuse to recognize that it has any function other than the utilitarian one, and in the anxiety of the

---

[8] Charlotte Bühler (1893–1974) was a Jewish German psychologist who emigrated to the United States during World War II. Her methods for testing little children, which resulted from systematic observations and research, were very advanced for child psychology.

individual confronting the 'concentrational'[9] form of the social bond that seems to arise to crown this effort, existentialism must be judged by the explanations it gives of the subjective impasses that have indeed resulted from it; a freedom that is never more authentic than when it is within the walls of a prison; a demand for commitment, expressing the impotence of a pure consciousness to master any situation; a voyeuristic–sadistic idealization of the sexual relation; a personality that realizes itself only in suicide; a consciousness of the other than can be satisfied only by Hegelian murder.

These propositions are opposed by all our experience, in so far as it teaches us not to regard the ego as centred on the *perception–consciousness system*, or as organized by the 'reality principle' – a principle that is the expression of a scientific prejudice most hostile to the dialectic of knowledge. Our experience shows that we should start instead from the *function of méconnaissance* that characterizes the ego in all its structures, so markedly articulated by Miss Anna Freud. For, if the *Verneinung* represents the patent form of that function, its effects will, for the most part, remain latent, so long as they are not illuminated by some light reflected on to the level of fatality, which is where the *id* manifests itself.

We can thus understand the inertia characteristic of the formations of the *I*, and find there the most extensive definition of neurosis – just as the captation of the subject by the situation gives us the most general formula for madness, not only the madness that lies behind the walls of asylums, but also the madness that deafens the world with its sound and fury.

The sufferings of neurosis and psychosis are for us a schooling in the passions of the soul, just as the beam of the psychoanalytic scales, when we calculate the tilt of its threat to entire communities, provides us with an indication of the deadening of the passions in society.

At this junction of nature and culture, so persistently examined by modern anthropology, psychoanalysis alone recognizes this knot of imaginary servitude that love must always undo again, or sever.

For such a task, we place no trust in altruistic feeling, we who lay bare the aggressivity that underlies the activity of the philanthropist, the idealist, the pedagogue, and even the reformer.

In the recourse of subject to subject that we preserve, psychoanalysis may accompany the patient to the ecstatic limit of the '*Thou art that*', in which is revealed to him the cipher of his mortal destiny, but it is not in our mere power as practitioners to bring him to that point where the real journey begins.

---

[9] '*Concentrationnaire*' – an adjective coined after the Second World War (this article was written in 1949) to describe the life of the concentration camp. In the hands of certain writers it became, by extension, applicable to many aspects of 'modern' life [*Trans.*].

References

Caillois, R. (1935). Mimétisme et psychasthénie légendaire [Mimicry and legendary psychasthenia]. *Minotaure*, 7.

Freud, A. (1936). *The Ego and the Mechanisms of Defence*. London: Hogarth Press.

Lacan, J. (1966). L'agressivité en psychanalyse. In *Écrits* (pp. 101–124). Paris: Editions du Seuil. [Aggressivity in Psychoanalysis. In *Ecrits: A Selection* (pp. 10–30), trans. B. Fink. New York: W. W. Norton, 2002.]

Lévi-Strauss, C. (1958). L'efficacité symbolique. In *Anthropologie structurale* (pp. 205–226). Paris: Plon. [The Effectiveness of Symbols. In *Structural Anthropology* (pp. 186–205). New York: Basic Books, 1963.]

4 THE NON-VERBAL RELATIONSHIP IN PSYCHO-ANALYTIC TREATMENT[1]

Sacha Nacht

> **Sacha Nacht** (1901–1977) was a neuro-psychiatrist, psychoanalyst and full member of the Paris Psychoanalytical Society. In 1929, he initiated the decrease in the length of sessions to 45 minutes and reduced their frequency in training analyses (three sessions a week instead of five or six). He was president of the Society in 1947 and in that position accomplished a great deal: in 1951, he founded the Paris Institute of Psychoanalysis, of which he was made director, and created the advanced seminar for psychoanalysts in 1958. He was vice-president of the International Psychoanalytical Association from 1957 to 1959.
>
> In addition to his institutional work, his theoretical and technical conceptions were particularly influential and remained so for some 30 years. He wrote many papers and authored the following books: *De la pratique à la théorie psychanalytique* [Psychoanalytic practice and theory] (PUF, 1950), *La présence du psychanalyste* [The Psychoanalyst's Presence] (PUF, 1963) and *Guérir avec Freud* [Healing with Freud] (Payot, 1971).

At first it seems paradoxical to talk of the non-verbal relationship in psycho-analytic treatment when classical analytic technique rests entirely on the dialogue between analyst and patient. The relationship established between them, which is at times the very substance and at others the activating force in the therapeutic procedure, can only be clarified and interpreted by the use of words.

It would certainly be absurd, therefore, to deny the importance of words in the analytic relationship. By the use of words the patient makes himself known to the *Other*, the analyst, and thereby learns to know himself too; he learns to express his desires and his fears; he assesses what he thinks he possesses and what he lacks – what he is and what he would like to be. But talking in analysis

---

[1] Presented at the Fourth Latin-American Psycho-Analytical Congress, July 1962. Translated from the French.

is even more than this, as we know: it is a continuous search, a veiled demand to be listened to, reassured, understood – in brief, to be recognised as a person and to be loved.

We also know that this demand, which cannot be fully satisfied in the analytic situation, will lead the patient through the vicissitudes of the treatment process to the end when he leaves the analysis and the analyst to look for a more satisfying object in an outside world which has at last become real to him.

It seems unnecessary to linger on the subject of the fluctuations which occur as the analysis progresses and which every analyst knows well. Throughout the treatment we see words used by the patient not only to express his thoughts and to reveal himself, but to appease, seduce, and disarm the analyst as object – particularly when the latter is unconsciously feared.

We recognise, then, that words are the vehicle of all the affects underlying the analytic relationship. And it is just because they express or provoke these affects that certain words take on particular values at different moments during the course of treatment. For instance, I remember a cyclothymic patient I had in treatment for a long time, whose progress was slow and painful, until the moment when in showing her (as I had indeed already shown her many times) the restricting power of her Oedipal fears, I spoke of her fear of being a *usurper*. This word, no doubt crystallising a great deal of preparatory work, seemed to release a trigger in her. It was as if a veil had been torn apart. And so it was that the real liberating process began, which proved decisive.

I should, however, like to draw the reader's attention to another aspect of the role of speech in psycho-analytic treatment. We have just seen how speech establishes an essential bond between patient and therapist. Now it follows that if speech can form such a link between patient and therapist, it is also possible, in the patient's unconscious, for it to become a barrier profoundly *separating* them.

In analytic dialogue the patient talking to the therapist as *object* well knows that, in this relationship between two, the object is *separated*, *distinct* from him, and that the words addressed to the *Other* can only confirm a separation which, for the unconscious, is painful. For the human being – so it appears to me more and more clearly – harbours two fundamental and contradictory aspirations: one towards separation (perceived at the time as a kind of liberation) and the other towards complete and absolute union.

In the analytic relationship the patient expresses in different ways, through the transference, his need to be understood, accepted, loved by the *other*; but separation is nevertheless experienced by him as a natural fact, rationally accepted. However, in spite of himself, something at the deepest level inside him *refuses* separation and strives blindly towards a union in which subject and object would be no longer distinct but *one*. The patient cannot, however, express this wish, for two reasons: firstly because he does not recognise it, and secondly because this need for union, or shall we say *fusion*, plunges him down to a level in his development at which speech has not meaning and language is as yet unknown. The subject has to reach the object-relations level – and it is precisely at this turning-point in development that he feels himself separate from the object – before language, and, at the same time, the functions of the ego, begin to appear.

The ego acts, we know, as a controlling agent, as a superintendent, and as a filter for demands coming both from external reality and from internal, unconscious reality. The ego confirms this separation as if it marked the frontier between the internal and external worlds. We also know that these ego functions can be exercised too strongly, and the ego (a term which I have always thought too anthropomorphic) then becomes tyrannical and entirely inundates mental life.

When the infant reaches the object-relations stage and feels himself separated from the object, he then has only one means of reaching this object, of trying to possess it, and that is language; language which indeed at that stage is not more than rudimentary, as little developed as the other motor functions by reason of the immaturity of the nervous system.

What is the meaning of speech, and to whom are the first inarticulate babblings addressed if not to the mother – to this object from which the child feels himself separate but tries to find once more? For it is man's nature to try to separate himself, to free himself from the object on whom he depends, in order to open out on his own and at the same time to try to reach and hold once more the object from which he has separated himself. These two drives, apparently contradictory, are found in exactly the same way in the analytic situation. At least this is the view I have put forward many times.

Accession to a world resting on this subject–object duality has the fatal implication for man of *separation*. This external world gives rise to needs and wishes which are nothing but an illusory pursuit of the sole object, in various guises. Nothing can satisfy the subject except the possession which can wipe out separation. That is why the world of external reality – that of separation – gives rise to a throbbing need to *have*, to possess – a need which the world of multiplicity can only reinforce but never satisfy. For what the subject wants is far beyond that multiplicity: he could only find peace in a union with the object so complete that it would imply a *fusion*. Freed, by this union, from the need to *have*, the subject would spread his wings in the sole joy of *being*.

How is this fundamental need for union manifested during the course of analysis? Precisely when the flow of words ceases, giving way to silence, to a silence experienced in security, in tranquillity. Experience has shown me many times that the patient in the midst of this silence finds again at times an internal state of union with the object-analyst, through which he again reaches in the innermost depths of his unconscious the original where the subject–object duality is no more. It sometimes happens that he reaches a point where indeed he feels himself at one with the world and as if confounded with a wholeness in which the limitations inherent in the human condition become wiped out.

He then wants nothing more, pursues nothing more, but experiences the intense joy of being.

If readers see here only metaphysical speculations, foreign to psychoanalysis proper, I should like to quote something that one of my patients, who knew nothing of metaphysics, said one day. After a silence lasting for the greater part of a session he said: 'I have not talked today – I was giving myself up, in this silence, to something extremely good, healing, as if I had plunged into a deliciously warm bath. To feel that you were there, in this silence gave me a wonderful sense of well-being.' The symbolism of the warm bath and the delight in the silence do not, I think, need explanation. But beyond this unconscious return to the maternal bosom there appeared to me another, more important meaning – that of the return to an original state of union – absolute and without restriction.

Another of my patients, after a long, perfectly calm silence at the beginning of a session, looked at the sky through the window in front of her and said, 'I feel so blissful in this silence . . . as if I were united with the sky and the sun, melted into the Cosmos.' Obviously these are just images, but the choice of these images is in itself symbolic. If certain deep truths are not accessible to us except in the guise of symbols, I am tempted to believe that firstly this is because the symbolised truths are sometimes of a kind difficult to express, and secondly – perhaps this is the most important reason – because these truths, expressed in this way, are less frightening to us. The chosen symbol itself is a representation familiar to the human mind – an image which brings the mind back to what is known; whereas the truth can never be perceived in its entirety: some part of it is always submerged in the unknown. It is in fact the non-verbal relationship which takes this indefinable part into account. That is why the necessary condition for it to arise is that fear be first overcome and eliminated from the mind. It is this point in particular that I would like to stress here.

Anyone who is frightened cannot bear silence. Because of this, the non-verbal relationship is not always possible in any analysis, and particularly not at any particular moment in an analysis. Besides, is it possible to talk about a non-verbal *relationship*? Does not this term 'relationship' rather imply the use of language, arising from the separation of subject and object and the attempt to remedy this separation? What we are rather incorrectly calling 'non-verbal relationship' is the establishment of the person on a level at which there is no separation: therefore, no two-person *relationship*, but a *union*. The subject–object duality is wiped out, dissolved into a whole in which there are no more distinctions.

Among all the well-known motivations for the sexual act (over-determined, like most human behaviour), there is also included the need to abolish separation in union. We read in Genesis: 'They shall be one flesh'; and human love, when it goes beyond the sole need to possess the object, is directed towards a complete union, to that ideal fusion which alone can fully satisfy it. That is why union can only be communion. It excludes 'relationship' in the true sense, that which implies a kind of bridge thrown between subject and object; that is to say, a communication which maintains the separation between subject and object as such.

The communication necessary for a relationship is established by the use of language. But it is by silence and in silence that a two-person relationship can dissolve into communion. I am using the word 'communion' here in the sense in which Kelman (1958, 1959, 1960) uses it. However, if I appreciate some of Kelman's ideas on this subject, I must say that I find it difficult to follow him in the conclusions that he draws from his clinical experience. In fact, I find the constant presence of fear, or the shadow of fear, in the situations he describes. Now fear seems strictly to exclude any possibility of achieving the state of union which he calls communion.

For silence to be beneficial it must be made tolerable to the patient; in fact, he can bear silence only if he feels perfectly at ease in the analytic situation – that is to say, if fear and tension have been eliminated or at least attenuated. This tranquillity is not possible for the patient unless the analyst by his own deep inner attitude – and not only by the words he utters – reassures him and protects him against fear in order to give him the opportunity himself to eliminate fear little by little. It is this deep inner attitude on the part of the analyst which in fact can only be revealed to the patient in silence and gives the silence a fullness and a therapeutic impact. It is in this sense that I take up again the term 'non-verbal relationship', which now seems more explicit.

Some authors have indeed already studied the non-verbal relationship. But so far as I know, they have thought of it particularly in its negative aspect: in short, what the patient cannot express in words he translates into gestures, play-acting and general bodily attitudes, etc. (Greenson, 1961). Others have centred the problem of the non-verbal relationship on silence – silence which to them means either an inability on the patient's part to give way to a discharge of an affective or emotional tension (Loewenstein, Zeligs, & Arlow, 1961) or the fear of expressing transference manifestations (Glover, 1955). Did not Freud himself consider silence to be a first resistance to the transference? Silence is, moreover, usually understood as resistance and is interpreted as such in the analytic relationship ('passive-masochistic attitude' – Glover, 1955).

Finally, when I sent a résumé of this paper to Dr Kemper (necessary for the preparation of the Congress), he had the kindness to inform me that he had himself published an article dealing precisely with the problem of silence in the analytic relationship (Kemper, 1948). In that article he distinguishes first the kind of silence which consists in 'dropping into silence', and then the kind of silence that is consciously motivated and the silence which is unconsciously motivated. This last kind of silence would betray in early stages, amongst other processes, the fear of contact, unless it is the disappointing nature of the contact with the analyst.

But the most interesting part of Kemper's article has very much the same perspective as my own – namely, the 'productive' character of some forms of silence. Through the transference the patient can, by silence, make a step forward in his development, in the sense that his silence is a way of measuring himself against the analyst and of challenging him, even if it is still only a frightened way of doing so, somewhat as a child would stand up to an adult.

The technical implication of all this is summed up in the questions Kemper asks himself when confronted with a patient, and which seem important: how is he silent, why is he silent, and above all why precisely *at this moment* – that is to say, at such and such a point in the treatment?

Ever since I have understood the therapeutic importance of the non-verbal relationship, I have been careful not to take all silences up immediately nor to interpret them systematically as manifestations of resistance during the course of treatment, as classical theory would have it. When a patient does not talk, I do not in any way incite him to do so. If he says 'I have nothing to say' or 'I do not want to talk', I reply simply 'All right, don't talk'. It is understood that for the silence to be fruitful not only the patient, but the analyst also, must be able to bear it perfectly calmly – that is to say, without unconscious fear. If the therapist finds he has a need to light a cigarette at the precise moment, for example, or to wind his watch, or to cough, or make some such movement, he will be betraying a certain lack of ease brought about by a kind of fear which the patient perceives intuitively. Union – or communion – is not possible then, since between the subject and the object stands an insidious fear. The object is not then perceived by the subject merely as distinct, separate, but even more as dangerous, being himself overcome by uneasiness.

For the patient to be able to let himself go in that special kind of deep union which he unconsciously desires, it is more than ever necessary for the analyst to bring a certain *quality of presence* rooted in inner availability and openness. This quality can only be beneficial if it arises from an authentic inner attitude; any semblance of it would be without value, without bearing, and without significance. What significance would such an attitude have, and what would be its efficacy, if it were not based on a truly profound interest on the part of the doctor for his patient, a constant and unconditional understanding?

I must add here, however, that this gratifying attitude cannot be adopted directly in an analysis: it could be not only useless but might even constitute a risk to the satisfactory progress of treatment as long as the patient's aggression has not been reduced – because aggression implies guilt, and as long as the patient is unconsciously full of guilt he cannot accept from the analyst an attitude felt as gratifying without his guilt being aggravated. This would lead to his becoming more aggressive as a defensive reaction, and then to his feeling more guilty, and there would then be a serious risk of his becoming involved in an unshakeable transference neurosis with its implication of interminable analysis.

That is why I still consider the classical attitude of neutrality to be useful during certain phases of treatment, the phases in which a climate of frustration skilfully administered is necessary for the development of the transference neurosis. It must be borne in mind, however, that the transference neurosis should be only a stage in the course of treatment. If this stage is too prolonged and becomes fixed, it will then become incapable of resolution, since then the patient is settled into a sado-masochistic relationship which is a repetition of the pathogenic relationships of his childhood – that is, the infantile neurosis. A new illness, as Freud said, has then replaced the old one.

If I remind the reader of all these ideas which are certainly familiar to him, it is so that I can add here that if we wish to avoid the serious mishap of an irreducible transference neurosis, there is a moment in the analysis when it is necessary to avoid a rigid conception of neutrality. Without ever falling into the still more dangerous hazard of gratifying the patient with affectionate words or gestures, it is necessary, however, for the analyst to have a different *presence* in the analytic situation, maintained by this deep understanding attitude; I would even say an attitude of authentic benevolence. I have advocated this particular 'presence' on the part of the analyst for a long time past (in fact, since 1949).

It is only this other quality on the part of the analyst which allows the patient to find, in silence and tranquillity, this special state of union to which he aspires. It permits him to renounce the myth into which he had put the therapist and to strip him of all the fantasies he had about him, particularly the aggressive fantasies, charged with fear. It is only when the analyst has ceased to be a terrifying object that a non-verbal relationship can be established in security – one in which this kind of 'union' so much desired can be arrived at.

In the paper that I was asked to present at the Edinburgh Congress (Nacht, 1961) on curative factors, I insisted above all on the fact that the curative factors so often cited – such as the modification of the superego, the reinforcement and strengthening of the ego, and even the necessary gradual insight into unconscious processes – cannot lead to an effective cure unless the deep inner attitude of the analyst is as it should be. For if what the analyst says, if the interpretations that he gives, are to be of value to his patient, it is, rather, in what the patient unconsciously perceives from the unconscious of his therapist that he finds – or does not find – the source of security he is looking for. The words of the analyst and the interventions that he makes are only effective in so far as they open up a path to the patient. But the latter cannot set himself upon that path, follow it, and finally emerge from it, unless he feels himself secure in the non-verbal unconscious-to-unconscious relationship. That, I feel, is the key to happy progress in analysis. That is why it does not seem desirable to preserve the rule of neutrality rigidly throughout the treatment, without taking into account the stages in its development.

The transference neurosis, in my opinion, should be present only at the culminating stage in the analytic process, and should last as short a time as possible if the treatment is not to become bogged down in a hopeless labyrinth. If this danger, which amounts to a failure, is to be avoided, it seems necessary at the appropriate moment gradually to replace the classical neutral attitude by one which I shall describe as a *gratifying presence*, in which the patient perceives a deep-down attitude of availability and hearty attentiveness. In such a climate it is sometimes sufficient to give a word of encouragement underlining a progress accomplished, or even a simple acceptance of a requested change of times, or yet a prolonging of the session, be it only for a few minutes, so that these gratifications can take on the significance of a 'gift'. Thus a new relationship is instituted: from now on the object – in this situation, the analyst – ceases to be feared, and the subject can at last allow to be revealed in himself this fundamental need for union which leads all men to rediscover, beyond any love object, the original source of all life.

If the non-verbal relationship which I am attempting to describe does not come about, if the process of treatment extends only to the bringing of unconscious material to consciousness (in my view, a limited approach to the unconscious, at all events in one essential direction), the instinctual forces will certainly be better used by the patient to adapt himself to everyday life; but he will remain deprived of a world of great richness which is spread out on a less generally known side of the unconscious. To limit the unconscious to instinctual drives alone seems to impoverish it a great deal. It seems necessary to find in it a complementary dimension, to reach back further to certain sources of life itself, born not in the tumult of the instincts, but according to Aldous Huxley's image, in 'the peace of the depths' where a whole part of the mind lies immersed.

In this way we are led to distinguish two very different functions in an analysis which proposes to establish the patient in the fullness of his potentialities: the first would be the attempt, by methods familiar to us, to reinforce the ego by bringing instinctual forces to awareness. This reinforcement leads, as we know, to a better and more harmonious adaptation to the external reality of the world of the senses, and this permits the patient to benefit more from the outside world. The second function would be to open up, by an extremely quiet communication, the access to another part of the unconscious which anchors man in a permanence which escapes the continuous ebb and flow of multiplicity, the troubles of history and social conditions. In this way man can arrive at a complementary dimension of knowledge – an approach similar to the 'Noein' of Parmenides, transcending the 'reasoning reason' which cannot escape the subject–object duality.

The question is by no means to encourage the subject to establish mainly a type of non-verbal relationship during the treatment, for he would then run the risk of sinking into a regressive unsatisfactory relationship. I have already made a preliminary formulation of these ideas in an article entitled 'Du monde pré-objectal dans la relation transférentielle' (1959). I pointed out in that article the danger of allowing a patient to become fixed in this so-called union, in such a way that the analyst may not be able to free him from it. If we can arrive at and tolerate in the analytic situation this profoundly peaceful silence in which a non-verbal relationship is established (satisfying an essential need in the patient, as I see it), we must nevertheless not allow the patient to become fixed in a regression so delectable to him that it prevents his making a healthy adaptation to reality. In my view the establishment of this non-verbal relationship ought to mark certain important points in the analysis, just like the transference neurosis at its strongest, but both present the same hazards if we allow the patient to indulge in them indefinitely.

It must be emphasised again how important it is for the patient to be able to experience this desire for union in a profound quiet – a desire for an *impersonal* union, as it were, extending at least beyond the person of the analyst. At the same time, the analyst must be on his guard against this being an enriching experience which never becomes a kind of relationship, to which the patient attaches himself too firmly. Because, in fact, nothing ought to turn the patient away from the world of reality, in which he must learn to live as full a life as possible. That is why, if the deep inner attitude of the analyst can permit the patient to reach this silent region and to enjoy there the satisfaction of a kind of fusion, to which he unconsciously aspires, this attitude must also enable the analyst to control it in such a way that it can bring the patient back to external reality and thus underline the *necessity for separation* implied in all object life. In short, once fear has been liquidated and ego functions reinforced, it is a matter of allowing the patient to become aware of other sorts of need which are situated at a level other than that of the instinctual forces and, at the same time, carefully emphasising the still greater importance of making a necessary adaptation to everyday life. What is more, this procedure can only bring about an increase of richness. Only certain fears, generally not recognised but none the less powerful, lead a man to believe that different aspirations are contradictory and irreconcilable, driving him to cut himself off from this one or that. If the analysis can help him first to recognise these aspirations and then to accept them in their various kinds, without being torn apart by illusory contradictions, he will reach a quality of fullness which is certainly the most worthy aim that psycho-analytic treatment can set itself.

References

Glover, E. (1955). *The Technique of Psycho-Analysis*. London: Baillière.
Greenson, R. (1961). On the Silence and Sounds of the Analytic Hour. *Journal of the American Psychoanalytic Association, 9*.
Kelman, H. (1958). Communing and Relating. Part I: Past and Current Perspectives. *American Journal of Psychoanalysis, 18*.
Kelman, H. (1959). Communing and Relating. Part II: The Mind Structure of East and West. *American Journal of Psychoanalysis, 19*.
Kelman, H. (1960). Communing and Relating. *American Journal of Psychoanalysis, 14*.
Kemper, W. (1948). Der Patient schweigt [The patient is silent]. *Psyche, 1*.
Loewenstein, R. M., Zeligs, M. A., & Arlow, J. A. (1961). Contributions to Symposium on The Silent Patient. *Journal of the American Psychoanalytic Association, 9*.

Nacht, S. (1949). Réflexions sur le transfert et le contre-transfert [Reflections on transference and countertransference]. *Revue Française de Psychanalyse*, *13*.

Nacht, S. (1959) (with S. Viderman). Du monde pré-objectal dans la relation transférentielle. *Revue Française de Psychanalyse*, *23*. [The Pre-Object Universe in the Transference Situation. *International Journal of Psychoanalysis*, *41* (1960).]

Nacht, S. (1961). Curative Factors in Psycho-Analysis. (Presented at the 22nd IPA Congress.) *International Journal of Psychoanalysis*, *43*.

5   TECHNICAL VARIATION AND THE CONCEPT OF DISTANCE[1]

Maurice Bouvet

> Initially a medical practitioner, **Maurice Bouvet** (1911–1960) became a full member of the Paris Psychoanalytical Society in 1948 and president in 1956. He seemed at the time to be the only member of the Society whose thinking could match that of Lacan, who was then reaching the height of his fame; Lacan made no secret of his mockery of Bouvet. Bouvet's major work had to do with object relations and is both a significant landmark and essential reading for those interested in the theoretical and clinical fields that he explored. Two of his primary works are: *La relation d'objet* [Object relations] (Payot, 1967) and *Résistances-transfert* [Transference-resistances] (Payot, 1968). In 1962, the Maurice Bouvet Award was set up in his memory; it is awarded each year to the author of the most significant paper published in the *Revue Française de Psychanalyse*.

Introduction

Dr Loewenstein's paper (1958) raises a number of questions on the possible variations within the framework of an analytic practice, for which he does not give the criteria, but which seem nevertheless to be strictly classical.

Thus he is interested in 'variations' rather than 'modifications', and it is of course evident that the outcome of an analysis may depend upon just such small variations. However, the 'modifications' with which he contrasts the 'variations' are also important in view of the fact that many of the cases with which we have to deal are borderline cases. On the other hand, both modifications and variations can be gauged only by reference to a criterion which is not formal but dynamic in nature – that is to say, to the development of the transference neurosis and its ultimate dissolution.

For this reason I find it difficult to separate variations from modifications.

---

[1] Contribution to the Panel Discussion on Variations of Classical Psycho-Analytic Technique, read before the 20th Congress of the International Psychoanalytical Association, Paris (July–August, 1957).

We might with reason refer to them as small and large variations, and it seems to me that the difference between them rests upon artificial distinctions. The more so since, as Loewenstein has already pointed out, there remain many obscurities in our technique and each analyst in addition has his own style. As an example of this I need only cite the difference between the active and passive attitudes in analytic technique.

I was recently required to write a work on a standard analytic treatment where I was to explain and uphold the most commonly recognised technical rules of psychoanalysis. But to do this I was constantly obliged to demonstrate the deviations which intuitive insight imposes upon these rules, and indeed in order to avoid giving any impression of rigidity in their formulation. But the term 'intuitive insight' when used to justify technical variations appears rather too vague, and I would like today to present a point of view which I hope will prove more precise.

The different object relations

I have already referred to the need for testing any technical variation from the standpoint of the development of the transference neurosis, and here I would wish particularly to draw attention to certain concepts I developed some time ago in the study of object relations, and to the fact that the object of transference, the analyst, is of prime importance in any study of technical variation.

I would define as an object everything which makes up the environment of the subject with which he establishes a relationship fashioned by his unconscious conflicts. In so far as internal objects (i.e., the superego) are concerned this would still apply, since these are projected on to external objects, or, more precisely, on to those external objects which are cathected to a greater or lesser degree, with specific significance. It must be recognised that there is always a certain distance in the relationship between subject and object. I would define 'distance' as the gap which separates the way in which a subject expresses his instinctual drives from how he would express them if the process of 'handling' or 'managing' (in French: *aménagement*) these expressions did not intervene. In other words this 'managing' represents one aspect of the ego's defences, and this term seems to me useful since it draws attention to the exterior aspect of the ego's activity, while 'defence' characterises more particularly its internal aspect.

The distance which a patient will take from his analyst varies constantly during the analysis, but in general it tends to diminish as the analysis progresses, until it disappears. It is this point which I call the '*rapprocher*' (which signifies in French: drawing close, but progressively). Once attained, this partial rapprocher can be jeopardised by other conflicts, but appears to be more easily re-established, and to lead finally to a more general rapprocher.

At a later stage, the distance which the patient takes from his analyst gives the appearance of growing wider again. In favourable cases this distance is only apparent since the conflict has been liquidated and reintegrated in the ego. This phase corresponds to a much fuller development of ego activities and the dissolving of a relationship which has now become obsolete. It is the terminal phase of analysis. But in less favourable cases either the distance is never really broken down but is, instead, maintained by more discrete methods of adaptation which give the impression of a rapprocher, or it may become greater again through the reappearance of habitual defensive activities, or again the distance becomes fixed at an intermediary level which is insufficiently close for the conflict to be clearly apparent.

The clinical signs of this rapprocher show up in a readiness to integrate the conflict and are here seen in the material through a muscular or psychic relaxation; we find, for example, an absence of postural rigidity or of stereotyped movement, or the patient will freely associate to a transference dream whose significance has not yet been recognised, etc.

The source of distance in relationships is projection. Since projection is unconscious, and is almost always present, the significant object is transformed into a likeness of the subject, or of his internal objects. It remains unconscious but, through the defences, makes itself felt in those object relations which are the most carefully arranged and handled. But even in those cases where projection is the most accentuated, it does not render all perception of the true nature of the object impossible. If this were the case all analytic action would be incomprehensible. However, this accurate perception is slow in developing and remains in jeopardy for a considerable period of time.

Object relations fall into two main categories, which represent two extremes, although bridged by various intermediate forms. They remain, however, two distinct clinical entities, doubtless stemming from a quantitative factor – the degree of fixation. These are: (i) the pregenital object relation; (ii) the genital object relation.

Object relations of the first type are stereotyped from the moment they emerge as significant, since they are able to take on symbolic displacement indefinitely. The expression of emotion has an undifferentiated character due to a lack of development and of genitalisation of the different drives, thus conferring upon all of them the same significance. They are carefully handled and kept in place by a dilemma which excludes on the one hand a satisfactory instinctual release and on the other any independence of the object. The first term of the dilemma is the result of projection which has transformed the other into a likeness of the subject, and this combined with an absence of genitalised drives makes the object a destructive being whom it is impossible to possess directly, since he has become bad in himself, as is the subject. The second term of this dilemma, a state of unbearable remoteness, is the result of the fundamental weakness of an ego impoverished by its inability to integrate its primitive drives. Serious symptoms of depersonalisation make their appearance when the relation to the object is not kept at an optimum distance. The result is that such a relationship, in those cases where fixation is more important than regression, is not normally capable of resolution, and the management of the defence cannot do other than persist if the analytic object is not finally perceived as different from the subject in spite of projection, as already noted above.

The structural characteristics of the genital object relation are completely different. They are varied, differentiated and usually sensitive to the reaction of the object as a consequence of the variety of affects and emotions, and the limitation of symbolic thought. There is no dilemma, direct instinctual gratification is possible, and the subject is able to break off relationships without endangering the structure of his ego, since he has already acquired a complete structural independence. Projection still plays a part, but genitalisation of the drives makes a rapprocher possible, since the object is not felt to be fundamentally dangerous.

In such object relations there is less management of the situation, and what there is is more easily given up, even when a failure in the Oedipal conflict obscures the picture. In effect these remain, basically speaking, reality relationships, and the essential characteristics of the drives and the ego are not changed.

As we can see, this concept of object relations is in line with Freudian teaching and regards the sexual conflict as of prime importance. The outstanding characteristic is the attempt to describe a movement, a continual movement of approach and retreat in the interactions of subject and analytic object, and this movement can be inscribed in time – that is, the development of the distance.

Since technical variation if taken in its widest sense must imply a question of time, then it will be most readily understood in relation to the 'moment' in the analysis, and it is this which I would now like to demonstrate after having recalled the essential features of this point of view. Those who are interested in pursuing the subject further will find fuller accounts in earlier publications (Bouvet, 1956).

Object relations and variations in technique

The practical situation with which we are faced is quite different in two types of object relation. Let us take, for example, the pregenital object relation, which offers the greater difficulty. At the beginning, any intervention on the part of the analyst is liable to be regarded by the patient as if a dangerous object were coming towards him, and thus to set in motion a movement of recoil, in order to keep a safe distance. Can we say then that it is the immobility, or even more the immutability, of the analyst which is alone beneficial? Immutability needs then to be carefully defined. It is not necessarily silence on the part of the analyst, since this could be an intolerable frustration for the patient. Paradoxically enough, it could be reassurance. In reality it can be clearly defined only in terms of distance. It consists in leaving the patient in complete liberty to establish his contact with his analyst at what is for him a suitable distance, avoiding all frustrations and also gratifications which could disturb him in this freedom. A gratification, for example, can be experienced as intolerable advance, while a frustration, by heightening the desire which is frustrated, may provoke in the patient a rapprocher which cannot be sustained.

Every movement in the analysis can be measured in this way – the smallest modification in the pattern of the relationship or in the behaviour of the analyst, the simplest remark or the most superficial of interpretations. Obviously we are here primarily concerned with the idea of relative measurement in both directions. What is too much for one is not so for another, but quite the contrary. It is just relativity, a strictly individual measurement, which justifies this study.

Any variations on the classical technique would in the beginning have as their aim the avoidance of a premature rapprocher, since this would only be followed by a defensive recoil.

This is particularly evident with schizophrenics[2] where the innumerable parameters introduced into the treatment seem to have as their end, however specialised the technical exigencies of psychosis may appear, to help the subject establish a distance. This clearly underlies those techniques which consist in adapting oneself passively to the reactions of the subject. We see the same thing in those active measures which guess at and satisfy the patient's immediate needs. What holds for the psychotic is equally true of the regressed neurotic (see Bergler, 1947; Bouvet, 1953; Jacobson, 1954; Weigert, 1954).[3] The doctor in keeping to the precise distance needed by the patient facilitates the establishment of the transference, which does not seem to me to be a rapprocher in the true sense of the term, since in this case the therapist is not a highly cathected object but corresponds, rather, to the projection of a beneficial image of an idealised kind, which will help the patient throughout his analysis. This becomes very marked in the case of schizophrenics, where the whole clinical picture will change once a real rapprocher has been achieved.

At this stage the analysis of defences and the setting up of inevitable frustration have their place, but they must be introduced with great discretion so that the rapprocher may be gradual, in consideration of the rapid intervention of projective anxiety, as has already been mentioned.

---

[2] My remarks here are based on what I have observed in the personal analyses of schizoid cases, and in the analysis of a schizophrenic, controlled by me. Dr. Racamier, who has had considerable experience in the treatment of schizophrenics, confirms my viewpoint.

[3] Jacobson (1954) and Weigert (1954) in their recent papers on technique, with regard to depressive neuroses of different kinds and to character neuroses, have made observations similar to those which permitted me to formulate in 1953, in a paper on obsessional neurosis, the thesis to which I here refer, and which I have applied more widely since, to psychopathological structures in general, and in particular to those neuroses where fixation and severe regression are important.

Afterwards, when a rapprocher becomes possible, or has already begun, the variation in technique is generally directed towards quickening this. It reinforces the combined action of the defence and of frustration. Even the most minimal change in the analyst's behaviour (and here, properly speaking, we are not dealing with variations but modifications in attitudes often instigated by the analyst's intuition of the patient's need for a rapprochement, or a need for discretion, or perhaps due to something outside the analytic situation) is perceived with acuity by the patient, and felt as a variation. The effects of such modifications must always be analysed, and the dynamic effect of interpreting them in terms of distance is considerable. At the beginning of analysis they would have remained out of the field of discussion, and their effect would have scarcely been felt, sometimes even remaining unconscious to the patient. The dynamics of the situation are as follows: projection is at a maximum, and any action taken by the analyst, or even a lack of action, is interpreted in terms of the projection. On the other hand, the latent positive transference which began in the preceding phase makes its action silently felt, identification with the analyst is intensified, and the reaction to any analytic action is expressed and is not controlled. Extremely violent changes in affect follow as a result. For example, the spontaneous addition of the patient's name to the customary 'Good-bye', which before was a reassurance of distance, might now precipitate an intense feeling of rejection. But since these reactions are now exteriorised, their analysis becomes possible and fruitful. Deliberate variations of a purely technical order, such as, for example, recourse to reversed interpretation[4] to stimulate projection in the transference, are often indispensable. It is during this phase that we find most of the large variations of an 'active' type, such as the invitation to struggle against a phobic situation, whose effect, among others, is to precipitate the rapprocher. They correspond to the parameters of Eissler (1953). On the other hand, variations deemed necessary in the first phase of treatment may be badly tolerated here, and may hold up the development of the transference neurosis. Thus, too great a distance can be artificially maintained, owing, for example, to a persistence in the analyst of a too-stereotyped attitude in his welcome and farewell to the patient – an attitude which at the beginning was necessary and indeed reassuring.

In the last stages of an analysis, variations are not used to re-establish a distance, but to bring to an end an object relationship which has now become obsolete. The attitude advocated by Nacht (1954) has a similar significance. It is

---

[4] I refer here to the type of interpretation which through a regressive fantasy makes conscious the pregenital instinctual satisfaction and not the defensive functions. As this latter is always given first, I have called the former type 'reversed' because its meaning and direction is in fact the reverse of the interpretation of defence. Since 1952 I have attempted to demonstrate the importance of this in relation to obsessional neuroses. Given at the opportune moment, such interpretations alone will allow the anxieties protecting pregenital feelings to be 'digested'. Jacobson (1954) has made similar observations, and I am in agreement with her findings that the therapeutic results obtained are markedly superior to those obtained by interpreting only the defence against the anxiety surrounding the genital conflict.

only in exceptional cases (Bouvet, 1956) that the variations are directed towards establishing a real distance. These latter are not opposed to those already described so far as their form is concerned, but only in their meaning in terms of distance.

Thus a variation in technique at any of the various phases of an analysis is directed towards different ends. To know even in a very general fashion what one expects as a result of this seems to me to facilitate the consideration of its timeliness, its real value, and, once introduced, the understanding of its effect.

General considerations

If we apply all that can be learnt from a systematic study of object relations to the problem of technical variations we find the following:

i. That it is difficult to distinguish between variations and modifications in technique. They can in fact only be distinguished in a formal way, and must be submitted to the same dynamic criteria.

   a. We are obliged to regard as analytic all variations large and small which contribute first to the fullest development, and later to the reduction of the transference neurosis in the full sense of the word: the technique of 'managing' relational situations and instinctual constellation. Formulated in this way we imply that a deliberate technical variation is introduced only when absolutely indispensable, that it is strictly limited, that its effects in overcoming certain resistances are duly analysed, and that it is maintained only for as long as is warranted. In other words, this formulation coincides with the laws of Eissler and can be shown here in a particularly vivid fashion.
   b. Any variations which do not conform to this general pattern cannot truly be regarded as analytic.

ii. Any discussion of the analytic character of a variation in technique can only be undertaken in consideration of the general movement of the analysis at a given moment. It is easy to foresee that one variation, however small, will at different times carry dynamically a totally different meaning.

iii. Movement invariably includes an idea of time. Thus in my opinion we can best estimate a variation against the situation in the development of the object relationship in the analysis, and are enabled to understand its dynamic significance better, and even to forecast its effect. The question is whether the subject as a consequence will be able to establish himself freely at whatever distance from the analyst he can support, or will he be precipitated into a rapprocher where there will be a direct or more direct expression of his instinctual drives in their unconscious form, and will this rapprocher then cause a secondary movement of retreat (Bouvet, Marty, & Sauguet, 1956) (i.e., strengthening of the resistance)?

iv. Generally speaking, at the beginning these variations are intended to facilitate the patient's control of his distance from the analyst (a distance which of course varies constantly) and to avoid the frustrations and gratifications which could upset this freedom. During this time a transference which is not a true rapprocher installs itself, and this gives the subject some support. When an atmosphere of rapprocher is achieved, imperceptibly or otherwise and often as a result of a deliberate or spontaneous variation which crystallises it, small and large variations may now be directed towards defining and stimulating the rapprocher. Towards the end of analysis they tend to facilitate the patient's detachment from the analyst.

v. The description given here is largely schematic. Each phase of an analysis is marked by an irregular alternation of approach and retreat, so that certain variations intended to retard a rapprocher, which may have as its consequence a reinforcing of the defences, become clearly necessary. Let us take an example drawn from the second phase of an analysis where a partial interpretation is deliberately given to a transference dream which normally could bring to consciousness the desire for an amorous relation with the analyst. The patient is phobic with considerable regression and oral fixation and would certainly react to an irruption of her concealed wish by an abreaction which would be dispelled subsequently by a true repression, thus taking away any therapeutic benefit from this massive and premature rapprocher.

It is at this point that complementary ideas in terms of the concept of distance, drawn from the study of the defences appropriate to each main psychopathological structure, become important. I shall make allusion in passing to the difference between the hystero–phobic neuroses where passive avoidance is habitual and the obsessional type of neuroses where active intellectual mastery is constantly striven for (Federn, 1952). In the first case, the rapprocher, if one wishes it to be lasting and to correspond to a real integration, will be facilitated by interpretations which are for a long time concerned only with the periphery of the conflict, making perceptible partial resemblances between the object and the actual conscious feeling (analyst and transference), and the object and past feelings (father and Oedipal feeling), in such a way as to avoid too severe an abreaction and subsequent repression. In the second case, the necessarily slow abandonment of the various processes of management which result from bringing into play all the resources of the thinking process, plus the nature of active defence itself in which the psychological ego is hardly excluded at all, are such that it is possible to give certain interpretations touching the heart of the conflict (such as a desire for incorporation) without any risk of subsequent repression.

vi. I may perhaps be accused here of taking into account only a part of analytic therapy and its variations, that I treat it as though we were concerned only with the emotional aspect of the problem. This is only apparently so. There is no more scotomisation here of the other aspects than when one brings analysis back to the transference neurosis. The concept of distance is equally applicable to interpretation. Interpretation is given when one sees that a rapprocher exists, at whatever level.

This is above all the case with so-called mutative interpretations which lead to an enlightenment through experience, or a coming together (Richfield, 1954), which establishes the identity between a present emotional experience and its prototype in the past, and requires the coming together of the unconscious of analyst and patient, thus making possible a revelation which affirms the rapprocher. It is frequently preceded by preparatory remarks in the same way that the general rapprocher in treatment is the result of painstaking work. The tone and the form in which it is expressed are dictated by the necessity of not breaking this rapprocher, still in a potential state, but, on the contrary, of reinforcing it. Of equal importance, as already noted in other terms by Loewenstein, referring to Hartmann (1951), is the avoidance of compromising through an interpretation, even though accurate, the gradual development of the analysis as a whole. The need for preserving the rapprocher in general is more important than a partial integration. It is a question of taking a step which can be followed by other steps. There is always a sense of movement, and the concept of the rapprocher has the merit of adding to the content value of an interpretation its value in terms of its being a movement towards the patient by the very fact of its being given, thus making up a whole which enables one to judge its effect more easily. Thus at a certain moment a simple affirmative will suffice to underline the importance of a destructive phantasy, while its integration in the transference would not be well tolerated.

A little later this same integration will be proved indispensable for the progress of the analysis, and if it were lacking would even be felt as a lack of understanding on the part of the analyst. One could say the same thing for all varieties of analytic intervention – the question, for example, which can be felt by the patient as an inquisition as much as an invitation to lift repression.

vii. To discuss a technical variation in its normal setting makes the elements of the countertransference more obvious. It is naturally very easy to make rationalisations, but it is nevertheless the case that the inadequacy of a variation is significant. Through this means I was able successfully to help a candidate understand the effect of her own impulsiveness in her relationship to her patient. She had given an interpretation which was in fact correct but was expressed through the use of a current slang phrase, whereas the patient was seeking through her a reassuring image more tolerant than that of his own mother, but no less correct in her manners. The candidate was trying to make too rapid a rapprocher as a consequence of her own character pattern.

This example serves to show how by applying this theory of the object relation an analyst may better adapt to the individual characteristics of his patient. His own personality will naturally lead him to adopt either an attitude tending to the active (analysis of defences) or tending towards the passive (Reik, 1948), whatever the extent of his own personal analysis. No single attitude is suitable to every patient. Some will react, to an analysis of their technique of coping with situations, as an intolerable intrusion, a perpetual reproach, and will strengthen the resistance; on the other hand, they may feel an abstention on the part of the analyst as remoteness and use this as a reason to shut themselves up in defensive behaviour. This feeling of a distance which remains fixed or which increases will guide the analyst in his adaptation to his patient. Thus, in my opinion all the variables in the analytic situation are affected by the object relation. It may seem that this study is no more than a paraphrase of what is already well known about the transference neuroses and the analysis of defence. However, I believe that to see the analytic process constantly in terms of distance, of rapprocher in relation to the general drift of the analysis and the timing of interpretations, can help us to judge the utility of a small or large variation. There is no doubt that intuition plays a part here, but it is for this very reason that to proceed from this standpoint increases greatly the sureness with which we use this fundamental tool in our analytic work.

This perspective will also help us understand the use of *tact* in the analytic situation, in the sense in which Loewenstein has for so long used this term, which he has rightly considered as one of the essential factors in analytic practice – that subtle and intuitive understanding at every moment of the drift of the analysis, and the response which is called for. The concept of distance in the analytic relationship can here serve as a sure guide and, in my opinion, enables us to place more effectively any variation in technique, whatever the reasons (for example, a particular type of ego structure) which underlie the form it may take.[5]

---

[5] A more detailed work on the same topic, illustrated with clinical material, will appear in the *Revue Française de Psychanalyse* (Bouvet, 1958).

Case material

The following brief excerpts from two cases are intended to clarify the concepts of *distance* (the gap which separates at any given moment the expression of a subject's drives from what they would be if the processes of management in the relationship to the object did not intervene), and *rapprocher* (movement which tends to diminish distance as well as the state in which distance is practically nil).

Case no. 1

To exemplify the idea of distance, I cannot do better than quote the following excerpt. A woman thirty years of age came to see me because she had difficulty in making contact with people. Prior to coming to see me she had had about four years' analysis, which had helped her to a certain extent.

Sexual difficulties still continued, and in addition her contact with people was unsure to the point that one had the impression that her thought processes were disturbed.

i. From the very first sessions with me she provided many accurate interpretations, and it must be remarked that she understood well the meaning of her reactions.

   I paraphrased some of her interpretations without in any way adding to them. I wished simply to confirm her views, but proceeded with extreme caution in view of the mental disturbances I had noticed in our first interview and which had now completely disappeared.

   They reappeared suddenly.

   At that point I simply encouraged her with an approving affirmative, when circumstances warranted. Once more, the thinking disturbances completely disappeared.

   Not wishing to give her too much gratification, I intervened less and less and finally kept silent.

   At this moment her troubled mental state reappeared. She lost the thread of what she was saying, forgot the beginning of her sentences, her thoughts wandered, and she stopped suddenly in the middle of simple phrases.

   When I was completely silent, she felt that I was utterly indifferent to her, and she felt this as an unbearable rejection. When I began to paraphrase her interpretations, she reacted to this as an intolerable intrusion into her psyche which destroyed everything. I understood subsequently that this brief affirmative which I had kept to for several weeks was all that she could stand and exactly what she wanted from me at this stage of her analysis.

   I was at just the right distance. If I did not keep to it, her intellectual functioning was impaired, her personality structure underwent a kind of disintegration,

while in addition her feelings about herself were considerably altered. She immediately became withdrawn.
ii. After her reaction to this rapprocher, and to what she considered to be an excessive withdrawal of the object, had been analysed, her analysis went ahead particularly well.

This example seems to illustrate clearly the concept of distance in the analytic object relation, the role which it plays in the analytic situation, and the difficulties which may arise from the failure to recognise it. I believe that if I had persisted in giving too much or too little satisfaction, her analysis would have encountered the very greatest difficulties.

In this case the analytic progress would appear to be favourable. The traumatic situations responsible for her sudden but relative decathexis of external objects have become clear, some particular sensitivities discovered, and her general behaviour is considerably improved.

The technical variation here consisted in keeping to a fixed distance for a certain period of time which enabled some contact to be established and eventually allowed for the analysis of the effects of this period.

Case no. 2

I have chosen this example because it required throughout the use of many variations rendered necessary by the vicissitudes undergone by the object relationship.

I am only able to give a very brief summary here, particularly in view of the fact that this observation is not a recent one. The patient was severely obsessional with pronounced schizoid characteristics, which had led to a diagnosis of simple schizophrenia.

She had undergone a series of biological treatments, and several prominent psychiatrists were in agreement in recommending a bilateral lobotomy.

When this patient finished her analysis she had become competent in a profession which had always interested her, and one which brought her into continual contact with a difficult clientèle, and she had had several sentimental adventures. This was two or three years ago, and I have heard nothing from her since. Considering the satisfactory manner in which her analysis was concluded, I have every reason to believe that if any new difficulty had arisen, she would have come back for help.

Towards the end of analysis she had become a very attractive young girl who, apart from a certain sensitiveness, no longer presented any symptoms. On the other hand, when the treatment finished she had not yet had any sexual relationships.

In fact, she was just nearing the end of her adolescence when she first came to see me. Up till then she had accepted without question the domination of a devouring, anxious, and rigid mother who was so involved with her that when the young girl was able to free herself from this domination, the mother became profoundly depressed.

The mother's interference made certain technical variations necessary. She did her best, sometimes consciously, to interrupt her daughter's treatment.

First parameter. – I had to accept various visits from the mother for the first two years, or she would otherwise have ceased treatment immediately. In addition, at this time, the patient presented several severe obsessions, which appeared as an intractable agoraphobia. And in addition, at home she demanded continual supervision.

She had an extremely labile ego structure, and was terrified (which motivated in a superficial manner her agoraphobia) that in a secondary or unconscious state (to use her own terminology) she might commit acts that would be dangerous to those around her.

This state of mind favoured the interference of her mother, and, besides, the patient was completely in league with her mother and manifested a total hostility towards me. I was obliged to do a little psychotherapy with the mother during my interviews with her, and refused systematically but gently to give her any idea of what was discussed in her daughter's sessions, this having been already agreed on between myself and my patient.

Second parameter. – It was during this period that I had to be particularly careful to keep silent about what I learnt from my patient. For example, that she was instructed to hide certain things from me, and that she was being dragged, in spite of her protests, to every psychiatrist in Paris, as well as to different kinds of faith healers in and around Paris. Thus this unfortunate young patient was often undergoing two psychotherapies at the same time – a situation for which she herself was partly responsible.

I was able to show her that this served as a protection against her anxiety over passively giving in to me, and that by her conduct she castrated me to a certain extent and put me to the test.

I was able to analyse the reasons underlying these repudiations.

Her attitude began to change. From being completely negative she became more confiding, but little else. She gradually admitted certain obsessions, listened attentively to my remarks, asked advice, and asked me to join with her in several 'undoing' rites. I was no longer regarded as a charlatan, a sham doctor interested only in her money and that of her family, but I had still not become a sexual object (idealised transference).

She was at this time very attached to a patient from the rest-home where she had been staying and with whom she had had what amounted practically to an imaginary relationship.

Much later a positive transference which was at the same time regressive and destructive began to develop, but before it could be established we had to work through a triangular relationship, about a year after the beginning of treatment, which was accompanied by a revival of the Oedipal situation with some unrepressed memories and, in particular, certain dream material to which she resolutely refused all interpretations. It was in this atmosphere that I established the third parameter.

During the establishment of this parameter, I was led to tolerate the psychotherapeutic actions of others in order to respect the contract made with my patient but, more particularly, by the realisation that she could not – given the nature of her object relations – put up with this sudden intrusion into her personality, which the so-called extra-analytic acts represented, and above all aided by my knowledge of the development of her object relations. The way in which my patient reacted to the faith-healers confirmed this standpoint. All those whom she consulted gave her up one after the other, and I was able to analyse the reasons underlying these renunciations.

Third parameter. – Some time later I suggested she might try to fight her phobia of travelling alone. I must add here that her treatment required the whole family to rally around. Her mother waited in my waiting-room, her father brought her in the car, and her sister acted as an auxiliary supervisor.

I asked her to give up the reassuring presence of her mother in the waiting-room, but it was I who had to make this request. The mother reluctantly accepted, and the patient subsequently felt much relieved. This 'admirable' mother weighed heavily upon her. As my patient put it, she felt that my insistence on this point was 'rational', but that she herself would never have dared lend her voice to it. She now came alone, but the family all waited together for her out in the street. It was at this time that she worked out a series of masochistic fantasies, such as that I was Dr. Petiot, the mass murderer, etc. However the rapprocher in the object relationship continued to develop.

Some months later she presented a typical obsessional relationship to me. She was afraid she might kill me, and equally that she might die as a result of ingesting faecal matter deposited either on her hands or on mine. A series of defence mechanisms manifested themselves here.

This was all able to be analysed in the transference.

The exclusion of the mother from the treatment was the determining factor in this phase. It was made possible as a result of my firmness in keeping the secrets of her analysis and, at the same time, in helping her avoid an acute conflict in reality.

Her transference continued to evolve. She became unable to overlook its destructive character, and thus found herself in an impasse. If I were to love her I would become belittled and diminished, and thus she would no longer be able to love me. Besides which, she wished to merge completely with me, and to lose all consciousness. But then she would become nothing, and could give nothing, and it is not possible to love nothing.

Here one found the transposition of her phantasy of being poisoned by faeces.

Fourth parameter. – I will not deal at length with the handling of the transference during this period, except to say that I was many times led to use the form of interpretation which I describe as 'reversed'.

Although the interpretation of a regressive fantasy is usually intended to bring to light its defensive nature in relation to a genital situation, in this case the interpretation tends to the direct re-living of a fixation conflict, and of projected anxieties. It is for this reason that I apply the term 'reversed' to this type of interpretation. It can only be used effectively when all the defensive functions of the fantasy have been completely understood.

I have corroborated in my own experience the findings of Jacobson, although based on a different type of patient – namely, that the most marked and lasting success is obtained when such fantasy productions have been fully 'relived, understood, and digested'.

With patients such as the one presented here, such fantasies are accompanied by an extreme anxiety and are spontaneously charged with affect and emotion. Others which are rigorously isolated are revealed to be as rich as the former, once the isolation is dealt with. This is the case even outside the typically obsessional relation. When the defensive character of these fantasies has been adequately demonstrated, in my opinion it is important to analyse them in their pregenital context. Experience shows that this is a necessary rapprocher. Depersonalisation phenomena often make their appearance at this point, and the proof that these are not an artefact of the analysis is to be found in the fact that the patient has spontaneously presented similar phenomena prior to any analysis.

Fifth and sixth parameters. – Shortly afterwards, my patient manifested towards me the same tyrannical behaviour which betrayed itself in her attachment to her relatives, and which originally must have been her attitude during her early childhood. She required me to give in to her at any price, demanding, for example, that I join her in her undoing ritual. Then in the face of my implicit refusal she turned to acting out in the analysis – for example, by refusing to leave the consulting room unless I pronounced certain formulas which she had endowed with magical power. I was often obliged to use my authority even when her demands took on a pseudo-rational aspect. It was important not to infringe the law of abstinence, except when her state of mind rendered it absolutely necessary – either because she was anxious over a long separation (for example, during my vacations), or because between two sessions she had to face a situation which appeared to her as terrifyingly dangerous (for example, meeting a young man who interested her, or leaving with her father on a car trip, etc.). It was equally important to distinguish among the various underlying motivations, such as the desire to protect herself, to be punished, or to force me to give in to her. On such occasions she could be as stubborn as a little child, and would stamp her foot and prevent me from opening the door.

I always interpreted in one sentence the meaning of her demands, which varied according to the moment, even on the occasions when she was unable to surmount her anxiety and I found it necessary to give her some gratification. When I had to return to the summing up of her behaviour, it was always with a smile, without impatience or change of manner, but nevertheless very clearly stated.

I believe that it was because of her correct understanding of the significance of her demandingness that she did not seek in this situation substitute gratifications which would impede her analysis.

She began to come alone from the suburbs, then to work, choosing a profession which she had always wanted to practise and which required artistic talent. This was far from easy. The first time she was confronted with an entirely nude male model, she underwent a critical period of depersonalisation analogous to those partial states of depersonalisation she had experienced in her relation to me.

Here I gave her solid support by explaining the significance of these symptoms which deprived her of her most elementary powers of perception, of her most simple thoughts, and which altered so markedly her feeling of self-awareness. She felt she was becoming 'transparent, empty, and lacking in bodily substance'.

During this period she brought to the surface an extreme hostility to the masculine sexual organs, wanting to tear them off and to eat them; according to the moment, she wanted to make them disappear or to keep them preciously inside herself, and thus become strengthened and feel a pleasure that would be absolute, unreal, and totally passive. This form of love relationship in which the man lost his virility either way stimulated more fear and guilt than did the desire for pure destruction.

I was able to analyse the meaning of these two aggressive phantasies: rejection and love. Here again, the ideal of 'distance', of 'movement', and of 'rapprocher' helped me considerably.

It was at this point that her position in the Oedipal situation was re-awakened. It had already been widely explored at the beginning of her analysis, but this time the initial situation was reversed – positive towards her mother and accompanied by a genuine release of repressed ideas and the appearance of a real tenderness towards her father.

Seventh parameter. – The transference became a typically genital-Oedipal one and slowly lost its regressive character, while she built up phantasies of a liaison with me.

Also at this time she was able to arrange to live alone in Paris, having made a definite affective break with her mother. She began to have a series of sentimental adventures in a very free milieu for which she was in no way prepared.

These relationships had only one meaning to begin with: they were intended to make me give up my neutrality towards her. Later they were cathected in their own right, and this became a difficult therapeutic period.

She was, in fact, completely defenceless, ignorant, and without any judgement whatsoever of the real value of the relationships she engaged in, and to which her reactions were excessive.

I considered it necessary to intervene with interpretations which would invariably have an effect on her outside life. This constituted the seventh and last parameter of the treatment.

However, I said as little as possible and only when her behaviour was manifestly incoherent. It was necessary to show her, without playing a forbidding role, the neurotic determinants of her behaviour, For example, her impulsiveness due to a terror of being abandoned, her need to assert herself, her flight from difficult situations, her aggression motivated by guilt or anxiety about getting 'too close'. I knew she would not be able to stand an unforeseen event, or a profound disappointment. This expectation was borne out when she produced symptoms of depersonalisation and an extremely acute anxiety reaction to an imagined pregnancy. To sum up, after many errors, dangers, transitory reactivation of her obsessions, and above all after having overcome the difficulties inherent in her inhibitions, her magic beliefs, her demands and susceptibility, she seemed to attach herself to a boy to whom she had an ever-increasing relationship of affection and sexual interest. She wished to get married and have children.

The treatment ended at this stage by common agreement, two years ago. The patient had a steady profession, had formed a number of professional friendships, and had managed to pay for her analysis from her salary. Physically there was no longer any resemblance between the girl as she first came – her features deformed by metabolic disturbances, her behaviour stereotyped, mannered, and discordant, and giving a falsely masculine impression – and the young woman who left me, crying but without excessive demonstration and in a normal fashion.

★ ★ ★

To sum up: I was obliged to use many parameters. All were transitory and necessary, and each was analysed. The end of the treatment, although suggested by me, does not seem justifiably designated as a parameter. Parameters (i) and (ii) fulfilled the requirement of avoiding a premature close relationship. Parameters (iii), (iv), and (v) were the periods of her coming alive in the treatment, while (vi) represented the 'management' of the rapprocher in our relationship, since it satisfied a need of the patient. For if the magical aspect of my intervention might account for the accentuation of the rapprocher, in reality I only confirm a situation which existed prior to any analysis. She used to deal with her mother in this way, and I gave her no help in the projection of her negative feelings – a true rapprocher.

As for Parameter (vii), it was directed at reducing the transference, since it helped the patient on a reality level to enter into a worthwhile relationship outside the analysis. It will be seen that on the whole these variations correspond well in their direction to the schema I have presented and make explicit the preceding considerations.

The concept of 'distance', of 'rapprocher', and of 'management' aided me considerably to adopt towards my patient the attitude which best permitted the transference neurosis to evolve fully, and later to be normally reduced. I would have liked to demonstrate this in detail, but for the reasons previously stated this is not possible. However, it is clear that I would have accepted much less well the presence of the mother and the extra-analytic psychotherapies if I had not been able to interpret them aright as to their function – namely, as devices for handling or managing her object relationship in the transference. This situation had to be respected as long as she was not able to project on me an idealised image, and to develop this sufficiently to support the consequences of a true instinctual cathexis.

Parameters (i) and (ii): These two parameters were obviously imposed by circumstance, but I would have felt much less free in my own reactions if I had not been guided by the feeling that these concessions were necessary, and had their place in the normal development of the transference neurosis.

Parameter (iii): Here in the same way, it would have been much more difficult for me to decide the moment when I could ask the patient to fight against her phobia with some chance of succeeding.

This was proposed to her at a moment when she was beginning to develop a strongly cathected relationship to me, but without this being so predominant as to render the struggle against the phobia impossible. This might have been the case had the idealised transference been covered by the intensity of the anxieties accompanying such cathexes.

Parameter (iv): I also wonder whether I would have seized the right moment at which to use the 'reversed' interpretations if I had not regarded the transference situation from this standpoint. Here it was a question of an indispensable rapprocher to which, of course, she was led by the analysis of the Oedipal situation, as it presented itself then: that is to say, very superficially, any true release of repression, but which it was important to precipitate by placing her face to face with her possessive needs in their archaic and destructive form – destructive both for the object and for herself, the object being basically 'bad' owing to the projection of her own characteristics.

This moment occurred during a complete impasse in her love-relationship with me. The only way out, since the causes of the regression had been analysed as far as possible, was that she accept her wish for incorporation and that it no longer be accompanied by this destructive and aggressive tension which the frustration of her wishes provoked, at the same time aggravating her need. This tension projected on the object resulted in the impasse referred to.

This is precisely what seems to happen with direct and continued analysis of fixations and, in fact, is what happened with the patient after a long period.

Parameters (v) and (vi): I need not emphasise the extent to which the notion of movement in the transference relationship helped me to judge the responses which would be adequate in the face of her infantile demands. Was she drawing close to me as idealised image, beneficial and now more cathected in order to be protected against an overwhelming danger, or was she on the other hand making me bear the burden of a caprice? In the first case, her demand could be met, justified by the gravity of the danger, and this in turn was judged in consideration of her external object relations, for example; the more she was attracted to someone the greater her fear.

In the second case it was important not to give in under any circumstances, for this would have amounted to 'loving' her by consenting to a veritable castration, and thus would even have destroyed her sense of security. On the contrary, it was necessary to remain a strong masculine figure while allowing her to express fully her aggressive outburst, without punishing her.

Parameter (vii): There remained only the termination, and here again the concepts already discussed enabled me to sense the moment when an outside relationship began to establish itself, not in relation to a transference wish. The rapprocher was accomplished, and the transference which had taken a more and more genitalised form then became increasingly less intense. The patient's interest in outside objects became keener, and her inexperience combined with the neurotic relics which affected her picture of the world came to the fore. It was then that I helped her as already mentioned.

I have chosen this illustration not only because it demonstrates a number of small and large variations in technique, but also because it completes the first example, which showed clearly how, in a limited situation, the concept of distance can help the analysis.

References

Bergler, E. (1947). Specific Types of Resistance in Orally Regressed Neurotics. *Psychoanalytic Review, 34* (1).

Bouvet, M. (1953). Le moi dans la névrose obsessionnelle [The ego in obsessional neurosis]. *Revue Française de Psychanalyse, 17* (1/2): 111–196.

Bouvet, M. (1956). La clinique psychanalytique. La relation d'objet [The psychoanalytic clinic: The object relationship]. In *La psychanalyse d'aujourd'hui* [Psychoanalysis today] (pp. 41–121). Paris: Presses Universitaires de France.

Bouvet, M., Marty, P., & Sauguet, H. (1956): Transfert, contre-transfert et réalités [Transference, countertransference and reality]. (Communication au Congrès International de Genève, 1955.) *Revue Française de Psychanalyse, 20* (4).

Bouvet M. (1958). Les variations de la technique (Distance et variations). [Variations of technique (distance and variations)]. *Revue Française de Psychanalyse, 22* (2): 145–189.

Eissler, K. (1953). The Effect of the Structure of the Ego on Psychoanalytic Technique. *Journal of the American Psychoanalytic Association*, *1*: 104–143.

Federn, P. (1952). *Ego Psychology and the Psychoses*, ed. E. Weiss. New York: Basic Books.

Hartmann, H. (1951). Technical Implications of the Psychology of the Ego. *Psychoanalytic Quarterly*, *20*.

Jacobson, E. (1954). Transference Problems in the Psychoanalytic Treatment of Severely Depressive Patients. *Journal of the American Psychoanalytic Association*, *2* (4).

Loewenstein, R. M. (1958). Remarks on Some Variations in Psychoanalytic Technique. *International Journal of Psychoanalysis*, *39* (2–4): 202–210.

Nacht, S. (1954). Colloque sur la fin du traitement psychanalytique [Colloquium on the end of psychoanalytic treatment]. *Revue Française de Psychanalyse*, *18*: 328–364

Reik, T. (1948). *Listening with the Third Ear: The Inner Experience of a Psychoanalyst*. New York: Grove Press.

Richfeld, J. (1954). An Analysis of the Concept of Insight. *Psychoanalytic Quarterly*, *23*: 390–408.

Weigert, E. (1954). The Importance of Flexibility in Psychoanalytic Technique. *Journal of the American Psychoanalytic Association*, *2* (4).

Section III

THE SETTING AND THE PROCESS OF PSYCHOANALYSIS

III THE SETTING AND THE PROCESS OF PSYCHOANALYSIS

Introduction

Alain Gibeault

The clinical and theoretical work done by the post-war pioneers of French psychoanalysis gave rise to a great deal of research into the issues involved in classical psychoanalysis and its variations: individual psychotherapy, individual and group psychoanalytic psychodrama, psychoanalytic relaxation therapy, etc. Hence the question: is there one single conception of the analytic process or many?

The relationship between psychoanalysis and psychotherapy immediately comes up against a semantic difficulty, insofar as the terms themselves can have different meanings. It is fairly easy to draw a distinction between psychoanalytic psychotherapy and non-psychoanalytic procedures: the specific feature of psychoanalytic treatment is that it seeks to uncover the unknown and unconscious aspects of mental life by means of a particular method – free association – and a rule which applies to both patient and analyst – that action is to be replaced by words and no satisfaction in reality is to be sought. This perspective thus rules out any therapeutic technique based on suggestion, hypnosis, education or manipulation.

Although that distinction between psychic reality and external reality is in principle a simple one, the history of psychoanalysis shows that it has not always been easy to preserve the specific nature of the psychoanalytic approach against every action on the patient's external reality. This is particularly the case when we consider the relationship between psychoanalysis and psychoanalytic psychotherapy. Not so long ago, the difference between the two was marked precisely by the opposition between psychic reality and external reality. Freud, for example, contrasted 'the pure gold of analysis' with 'the copper of direct suggestion' which was characteristic of 'psychotherapy for the people' (Freud, 1919a [1918], p. 168). Although psychoanalysis had to follow the fundamental principles that Freud discovered, psychoanalytic psychotherapy did at times appear to be a less strict technique that could include certain instructional and manipulative approaches that represented a direct challenge to Freud's invention.

If we put to one side the distinction between psychoanalysis and psychoanalytic psychotherapy based on the contrast between psychic reality and external reality, we can then take as our basis certain extrinsic criteria that have to do with technical parameters: rhythm and length of sessions, patient lying on the couch or sitting facing the therapist. It is nevertheless well known that such a perspective in fact leads to a certain vagueness as regards the very definition of psychoanalysis: in France, analytic treatment with three sessions per week and the analysand on the couch is considered to be psychoanalysis, whereas in the United Kingdom this would be seen as psychotherapy; conversely, in France, psychotherapy would imply less frequent sessions (one or two per week), while in the United Kingdom psychoanalysis would necessarily imply a frequency of some four or five sessions per week. For Freud, of course, psychoanalysis meant six sessions per week; it was only quite late on that he agreed to psychoanalysis with five sessions per week in order to allow a foreign colleague of his to begin analysis – the only possibility Freud had was to ask his other patients to reduce the number of their weekly sessions from six to five, which they agreed to do! As we have seen, in France issues concerning the training of psychoanalysts led to changes in the analytic setting.

Given that the extrinsic criteria are relatively unsatisfactory, it might be helpful to define the *intrinsic* criteria that correspond to the aims of psychoanalytic work. Psychoanalysis implies the unfolding and subsequent dissolution by means of interpretation of a regressive transference neurosis in a situation of technical neutrality. That somewhat narrow definition, however, does not take into account the broadening of the aims of psychoanalysis and its utilisation in psychopathological states other than the 'transference psychoneuroses', in accordance with developments in psychoanalytic theory that began with Freud and have continued to the present day. If we broaden the definition of psychoanalysis, the frontier between psychoanalysis and psychotherapy becomes less and less clear, so that we may end up with nothing more than a tautology: psychoanalysis is what a psychoanalyst does.[1]

The debate concerning psychoanalysis and psychotherapy thus gives rise to the need to reflect upon the dialectic between the *setting* and the *analytic process*. What means are employed, and to what end? For Freud, cure was the ultimate objective, and, as we know, he saw some manifestation of healing in the fact that his patients had recovered their capacity to love and to work. From the outset, all the same, Freud was wary of any kind of flight into health through a quick lifting of symptoms that left the unconscious reasons untouched; he was more interested in the paths that led from process to symptoms. These paths may be many in number, and the means employed in following them may be quite different. Hence the importance given to evaluating change in the course of treatment in terms of the topographical, dynamic and economic criteria that characterise the metapsychological approach to mental phenomena: this implies focusing on the nature and purpose of the analytic process.

From that point of view, the chapter by Jean-Luc Donnet (2001 – chapter 6, this volume) bears witness both to this debate and to the theoretical and clinical solutions devised in order to resolve the dilemmas to which the relationship between the

---

[1] In France, a great deal of research has gone into exploring the differences between psychoanalysis and psychotherapy. See in particular Brusset (1991), Gibeault (2001), Green (2006) and Roussillon (1991).

> The concept of **acted scansion** concerns the changes that Lacan introduced into the psychoanalytic treatment setting in the early 1950s. His intention was to promote the idea of variable-length sessions and the interpretative value for the analyst of ending sessions unexpectedly. This challenge to the idea of fixed-length sessions triggered the principal schisms that agitated psychoanalytic institutions in France – first in 1953, then in 1963.

setting and the analytic process gives rise. Donnet (1995) was initially influenced by Lacan, but he distanced himself from him when Lacan's technique of 'acted scansion' seemed to Donnet to be a kind of suggestion which attempted to reconcile – 'at last!' – in a magical way psychoanalysis and suggestion (Donnet, 1995, p. 22). A close friend of André Green's, Donnet co-authored with him in 1973 a book entitled *L'enfant de ça* [The child of that/of the id], introducing the concept of 'blank psychosis':[2] this describes a form of psychotic functioning that is not delusional but is characterised by a complete emptiness of thought. Donnet was influenced above all by Winnicott, and in particular by the latter's concept of transitionality.

Donnet's paper 'From the Fundamental Rule to the Analysing Situation' (chapter 6) is both highly condensed and subtle; his argument, he felt, failed to connect with a non-French audience, and he elaborated his theory in a book, *La situation analysante* [The analysing situation] (2005).

In his paper, Donnet highlights the dilemma that is inherent in the psychoanalytic method: on the one hand, a discourse *about* the method, with respect to a theory of technique that comes under the secondary process; and, on the other, a discourse *against* the method, in the sense that the analysand's free associations and the analyst's evenly suspended attention call into question the secondary-process functioning of the participants in the treatment in their encounter with the unconscious. Hence the paradox: the fundamental rule set forth at the beginning of every analysis is both the basis of the method and an applicable instruction that cannot but be immediately disqualified. It was that element, indeed, that led Ferenczi (1928) to suggest that free association expressed as part of the fundamental rule was in reality obtained only at the end of an analysis and, as such, was one of the criteria for deciding when to bring an analysis to a close.

From that point of view, the discourse against the method enables the gap between theory and practice to be maintained, thereby safeguarding analytic work from being a 'simple application of what we know already' and keeping open the paths to the unconscious. That point of view led Donnet to replace the setting/process pairing with that of the analytic site/analysing situation (Donnet, 2005, p. xi). This is one way of challenging any attempt at reifying the setting by insisting solely on extrinsic criteria in order to justify its intangibility and to decide upon the value of any given analytic process. The 'site' covers not only the *material aspects* of

---

[2] The indeterminate pronoun 'ça' ('that' or 'it') is also the technical term in French for the 'id'. 'Blank psychosis' translates the French expression '*psychose blanche*', the word '*blanche*' meaning both 'blank' and the colour 'white'.

the setting (the rhythm and length of the sessions) but also the *overall arrangement* (use of the couch or sitting facing each other, psychodrama), the *analyst's position* including his or her countertransference, theory and sociocultural representations of psychoanalysis in any given context (Donnet, 2005, p. 35), as well as the *fundamental rule* with the paradox that is an integral part of it (chapter 6, this volume). The 'structure' of this site may then be the object of a 'construction', leading to an 'analysing situation' that in fact corresponds to what is at issue in the psychoanalytic process. The analytic situation thus becomes an analysing situation corresponding to *a process in movement*, as emphasised by the present participle; 'the analysing situation results, haphazardly, from the sufficiently adequate encounter between the patient and the site. It implies the subjectivised use, through the experience of "found-created", of the resources of the site and their singular configuration by the patient' (chapter 6, p. 168).

Donnet (2005) develops and continues Bouvet's work on the technical variations of the setting. He looks first of all at the analysing situation 'in its optimal or ideal form: the unfolding and dissolution of the transference neurosis' (Donnet, 2005, pp. xii–xiii). He attaches considerable importance to psychoanalytic work with borderline patients who challenge the site that has to be constructed and who insist on 'exchange modalities' that Donnet likens to Winnicott's *squiggle*.

Donnet's thoughts about issues concerning interpretation in analytic work are also highly relevant here. He argues, for example, that in some analysing situations, the *content* of an interpretation is equated with the *act* of interpreting (a similar idea to Hanna Segal's notion of the symbolic equation: Segal, 1957), thus giving rise to a therapeutic deadlock: the split between present and past creates a de-symbolisation of the analysing situation, such that interpretation too is obliged to lock itself into a persecutory 'here-and-now relationship' that resembles the 'hypnotist's position' and hypnotic suggestion (Donnet, 2005, p. xvi). What Donnet has to say about interpretation and suggestion reminds us of the discussions that took place in the English-speaking world concerning mutative interpretations. In his seminal paper on 'The Nature of the Therapeutic Action of Psycho-Analysis', Strachey (1934) emphasised the idea that mutative interpretations are fundamentally transference interpretations, enabling patients to become aware of the fact that their drive-related cathexis with respect to the analyst has really to do with a primary fantasy object. Others, such as John Klauber (1972), have emphasised the need to make use, over and above explicit mutative interpretations, of their 'implicit' counterparts, which are just as vital; implicit mutative interpretations have to do with a relationship in which the transference–countertransference interplay is uppermost. This was a salutary reminder of the potential impact of *suggestion* and *construction* in analytic work, as opposed to *remembering* and *reconstruction*, together with the important role of the countertransference in the development of the analytic process.

Following Winnicott, Donnet emphasises the importance of play in the work of analysis, arguing that its role in the 'exploration of the site' is a major one; he is here referring to the exploration of the 'gap between play and the rules governing it' through 'subjectifying it' (Donnet, 1995, p. 31). From that point of view, in a tradition that reminds us of the Independent Group within the British Psychoanalytical Society, the analyst is more of a 'guardian of play' than a 'guardian of the setting' (Donnet, 2005, p. xxiii; Parsons, 2009). For Donnet what matters is the internal setting ('the site'), which, unfettered by rigid rules, is open to analytic work with different modalities of treatment to cover a wide spectrum between neurotic and psychotic functioning. The distinction that Winnicott drew between *play* and *game* is, in this context, of considerable significance as regards any description of the work of analysis. From that point of view, the French idea of talking about 'psychoanalysis in a face-to-face setting or on the couch' rather than contrasting 'psychoanalysis or psychotherapy' is part of this issue.

The question is not one of abolishing all differences between the various modalities of analytic work but of furthering the idea that the analytic process or analysing situation can take place in a large variety of analytic sites. Green provided support for this view when he proposed that the analytic process rests on 'a tripod', but not the one which can be seen in Freud's early work, 'transference psychoneurosis/transference neurosis/infantile neurosis'. Green proposed an alternative tripod on which the process rests: 'setting/the dream/interpretability' (Green, 2002/2005, p. 38). This is another way of thinking about the analytic session on the basis of oneiric regression and of its three types of regression in order to take into account any differences between the classical form of treatment and the variations that have been brought about in it.

If, like Freud, we see in the couch/armchair situation the archetype of the psychoanalytic approach, we must also remember that the psychoanalyst's interpretation has a mutative and therapeutic value only because it is made within a formal setting which, as we know, was inherited from hypnosis: the interruption of visual perception of movement provides the conditions under which regression can take place in its three dimensions: topographical, formal and temporal.

What does that imply? The hallucinatory aspect of dreams lies at the heart of the basic construction of psychoanalytic theory – the experience of satisfaction typical of the infant at the breast. That basic premise, according to which hallucination equals satisfaction, cannot be verified by experience, but it does in fact determine the psychoanalytic approach to mental functioning. From that point of view, without being identical to oneiric regression bringing something to life through hallucination, regression in the analytic situation nevertheless enables us to get in touch with the origins of mental functioning and therefore, perhaps, to give a new impetus to its dynamic aspect.

In accordance with the dream model (Freud, 1900a), regression in this situation is *topographical*, since, given the way the mind works, unconscious excitation which cannot be released through motor activity regresses to the perception–conscious (Pcpt.–Cs.) system along a path that goes from remembering to hallucination. This is at the same time a *formal* regression, because this backward movement entails a change in psychic substance, from 'thought identity' to 'perceptual identity' – in other words from thinking to memory images or even hallucinations. The fundamental rule as stated at the outset of the analysis – to say everything that comes into mind, following the method of free association – implies that work is being done simultaneously on two kinds of mental functioning: the one prevalent during the day, thought identity, and the other during the night, perceptual identity. It is this that gives rise to the feeling of loss of control and of the uncanny. From that point of view, the work of analysis would seem to be the gradual integration of topographical and formal regression, as well as that of conflict and the means adopted to cope with the anxiety which is thereby generated.

Regression is not only topographical and formal, it is also *temporal* insofar as the conditions under which the work of association proceeds give rise, as Freud pointed out (1916–17, p. 342), to 'a return of the libido to earlier stopping-places in its development'. This revival of the past takes place in three different ways, because temporal regression may be simultaneously object-related, libidinal and narcissistic – in other words, there may be a return to the original cathected objects and earliest libidinal structures, all the way back, indeed, to primary narcissism. This movement backwards is sometimes said to be a return to an earlier state; another way of looking at it is in terms of a fantasy of going back to one's origins. The analytic situation immediately brings the analysand face to face with the quest for something absolute that haunts all human beings, a foreshadowing of the possibility of a completely satisfying union with oneself and with other people. The analytic process thus implies for the individual a conflict in which that temptation, with its nostalgia for absolute satisfaction, will have to be negotiated in a variety of ways.

In French psychoanalysis, the *raison d'être* of the unity of the analytic process lies in this dialectical movement between the model and its variations, the aim of which is always, as Donnet puts it, to seize hold of the 'analytic site' in an 'analysing situation', thanks to the analyst's benevolent neutrality and the analysand's capacity to create/find the analytic situation. A process could therefore be defined as a movement that takes place over time and acquires unity with respect to an end-point. The process is psychoanalytic when it enables the individual to conceive of psychic change as described by Freud in terms of its topographical, dynamic and economic aspects. We may choose to see in that process a movement that becomes organised on a certain basis, while leaving considerable leeway for unpredictability, uncertainty and the unknown. That approach corresponds to the free-association method invented by Freud, echoed as it is by the analyst's evenly suspended attention. It is all the same necessary to see in the analytic process a movement *towards* something corresponding to the need to replace an immediate drive-related discharge with the possibility of transforming this into representations, fantasies and thoughts.

It was that same outlook that influenced the way in which the analytic process in child and adolescent psychoanalysis would be thought of. In a paper he read at the first European Psychoanalytical Federation congress in Geneva in 1970, René Diatkine, who, with Serge Lebovici, was one of the initiators of child analysis in France, showed that he was in agreement with that tradition in French psychoanalysis. The overall theme of the Congress was 'The Role of Child Analysis in Psychoanalytic Training'; among the keynote speakers were Anna Freud, Hanna Segal and René Diatkine, thus enabling a comparison to be made between different psychoanalytic approaches. According to Diatkine, who trained several generations of child analysts in France, the purpose of the analytic process is to encourage the child to identify with the analyst's interpretative function; this '... development of a certain insight and above all of the new pleasure found by the child in this interest in his inner reality must be considered as one of the most positive results to be obtained in child analysis' (chapter 7, this volume, p. 183). Child psychotherapy, as distinct from child psychoanalysis, says Diatkine, is able, thanks to the medium of play, to bring about economic and dynamic changes; there is no topographical change, however, related to the introjection of the analyst's words.

In Diatkine's view, the difference does not lie in the rhythm of the sessions. In one of his books, *La psychanalyse précoce* [Psychoanalysis with young children] (Diatkine & Simon, 1972), there is an account on a session-by-session basis of a 3½-year-old girl in analysis with Janine Simon, one of Diatkine's closest colleagues and, as a child analyst, one of the most gifted of her generation. That analysis took place on the basis of one session per week. Without criticising the value of child analyses with several sessions per week, Diatkine argues in favour of a flexible relationship between the analytic process in children and the rhythm of the sessions. With some children, he says, verifying the permanent nature of the object requires only very little actual experience – that is, it can be done with few sessions. That choice, he goes on to say, does not imply that he is an out-and-out advocate of a small number of weekly sessions – quite the contrary. Such empirical and formal criteria, however, should not be seen to be an adequate basis for studying what transpires within the therapeutic relationship (Diatkine & Simon, 1972, pp. 266–267).

In the discussion that followed Diatkine's presentation, Anna Freud and Hanna Segal disagreed on how the analytic process in children should be defined. The difference between psychoanalysis and psychotherapy requires another set of criteria. According to Anna Freud (1970), psychotherapy has more to do with resolving external conflicts between the child and his or her immediate circle, whereas psychoanalysis is an option only if it then becomes possible to tackle internal conflicts. It is at that point that true analytic work can begin and the analytic process be initiated. Hanna Segal (1970) highlighted the importance of play in child psychoanalysis, and went on to say that it is only when the analyst is able to interpret the whole process – and that implies non-participation in the play – that any change which occurs in the treatment situation becomes a psychoanalytic mutation (p. 31). Child psychoanalysts in France followed the same criteria as in adult psychoanalysis for evaluating the analytic process, distancing themselves from the conditions of the setting both materially (rhythm of the sessions) and in their interpretative approach.

Flexibility in the setting or in the analytic site does not, all the same, imply that the contractual conditions of the analytic situation are laid aside, as Nacht (1963) had suggested. The clinical example of an analysis that Donnet gives at the end of his paper (chapter 6, this volume) bears witness to the danger, highlighted by Bouvet, that is entailed by modifying the distance between analyst and analysand in an arbitrary manner. He relates the anxiety experienced when lengthening the time of a session becomes a possibility for the representation of a demand for love linked to the power of hallucination inherent in the fantasy of unconscious desire. We see here the issues involved in the fantasy of primary narcissism and in the quest for limitless love.

It is that conception of narcissism that Bela Grunberger developed in his work. Unlike his predecessors, who saw in narcissism a negative element in the analytic process and something that could hinder the development of an object-related transference, Grunberger argued that narcissism is *the* essential energy factor, the *primum movens* of the analytic process. In one chapter – 'Narcissistic Aspects of the Analytic Situation' – of his book on narcissism, Grunberger (1971) introduced the idea that there is a *narcissistic elation* at the beginning of every psychoanalytic treatment; this ties in with non-conflictual regression, thereby giving the analysand an inkling that, in the analysis, there may be a possibility of fulfilling his or her wish to be loved in a limitless manner. After a few months of analysis, that regression becomes conflict-ridden, and this contributes to the development of ambivalence.

In order to fulfil this role as a driving force, narcissism needs the energetic dimension of an instinctual drive, which it finds mainly in the oral component that lies at the heart of this desire for unlimited satisfaction. Grunberger emphasises the importance of the setting for inducing narcissistic regression: lying on the couch, the invisibility of the analyst who thus becomes, as it were, simply a function with no material basis; the fundamental rule of free association also contributes to opening up limitless possibilities by means of words. This specific and non-conflictual regression then facilitates the establishment of a transference relationship; this, however, represents an object-related and conflictual regression. If the narcissistic cathexis of the analytic situation can be preserved, the negative transference will not jeopardise the unfolding analytic process.

In his paper, Grunberger makes the significant comment that the dizziness and disorientation experienced at the end of a session bears witness to this narcissistic regression. Ferenczi (1914) had already pointed this out when he said that vertigo such as this had to do with the sudden change in the analysand's physical and mental attitude at the end of a session, in the perhaps brutal movement from the pleasure principle to the reality principle. The vertigo of Grunberger's hypochondriac patient may have had something to do with the loss – experienced as permanent – of a narcissistic object, which Danielle Quinodoz (1994) has described as the source of pathological vertigo and the experience of infinity. The narcissistic regression in psychoanalytic treatment could, if that were the case, lead to an experience of the uncanny, as Freud himself described this (1919h) in situations that call into question the ego's functions.

In several of his papers, Michel de M'Uzan has examined the issues surrounding narcissistic regression in the course of an analysis. Following Maurice Bouvet, whose analysand he was, Michel de M'Uzan has offered a novel interpretation of the analytic method, in particular through his insistence on describing its specificity based on experiences of controlled depersonalisation in the course of an analysis. In the chapter published in the present collection, de M'Uzan (2009 – chapter 9, this volume) describes an important point in the analytic process that has to do

> The concept of *vital-identital* was introduced by de M'Uzan (2005) and corresponds in part to Freud's concept of self-preservation.

with the integration of the 'non-sexual, self-preservative field of identity (*vital-identital*)' and 'sexual drive functioning' (psycho-sexual). De M'Uzan makes use of Freud's first theory of the instinctual drives, in which the self-preservative drives are contrasted with the sexual ones, in order to highlight the importance in analytic work of challenging the analysand's sense of self so as to make way for 'the integration of what is new'. However he does not accept Freud's hypothesis of the self-preservative drives and insists on considering only the 'psycho-sexual' as being based on drives. On the way to narcissistic regression, the mind has to cope with experiences of the uncanny closely related to depersonalisation phenomena. This challenge to the frontiers of the ego, and therefore to the individual's whole being, is necessary, argues de M'Uzan, if seminal and sustainable psychic change is to be brought about through psychoanalytic treatment.

De M'Uzan (1996, 2006) is here restating his hypotheses as regards the psychoanalytic process, which can only provide conditions for change if it allows the analysand to experience a '**spectrum of identity**'. De M'Uzan defines this as the possibility for the analysand to experience fluctuations in his or her sense of identity in the course of the treatment, 'a kind of transitional space'. 'The I is not wholly in the ego, nor on the contrary in the other – i.e. in the representation of the object'; he goes on: 'The I is spread all through the fringes of the spectrum, the spectrum of identity, defined by the *loci* and quantities cathected by narcissistic libido from an internal pole (the representation of the actual individual) to an external one that coincides with the image of the other' (1996, p. 51).

> The **spectrum of identity** is a concept invented by de M'Uzan (1994) to define the various positions that narcissistic libido may take up – or, more precisely, the *loci* and quantities cathected by narcissistic libido. Thus the 'I' is not in the ego, nor completely in the other person – it is distributed all along the fringes of this spectrum of identity.

> De M'Uzan's notion of **paradoxical system** is taken from the term '*sommeil paradoxal*', which refers to REM sleep. The **paradoxical system** is a mode of mental functioning in the analyst. During the session, the analyst is invaded by strange representations corresponding to as yet undetected mental processes that are taking place in the analysand. The fundamental feature of this phenomenon is that the analyst is some steps ahead both of what can be understood from the material, and of the fantasies that the patient is able to formulate. De M'Uzan designates this phenomenon as *paradoxical countertransference*.

Free association depends, therefore, on the possibility the analysand has of unfolding this spectrum of identity; for the analyst, evenly suspended attention depends on the development of a very specific modality of mental functioning that de M'Uzan (1976, 1996) has called a **paradoxical system**, in an allusion to that paradoxical form of sleep called REM sleep which favours dreaming. These ideas are based on the clinical observation of his own mental processes during a session. He was listening to his patient when his attention was distracted by strange representations, colourful images and daydreams that apparently had nothing to do with what the patient was saying. Instead of seeing this as the analyst's negative countertransference, de M'Uzan considered it to be a positive experience in his countertransference, comparable to a feeling of floating that resembles a slight degree of depersonalisation related to an experience of something uncanny.

These thoughts and images correlative with the analyst's evenly suspended attention corroborate the idea that, underpinning mutative interpretations in the work of analysis, there lies a paradoxical countertransference. The form of these interpretations is quite different from that of interpretations/explanations which, more in line with secondary processes, can go no further than the censorship that lies between consciousness and the preconscious. Mutative interpretations are allusive, highly condensed, close to primary processes and dream-work; they can therefore draw near to the censorship between preconscious and the unconscious.

These ideas on mutative interpretations are in tune with what Dennis Duncan (1989) has written on the importance of making interpretations within the flow of associations. Michael Parsons (2009) has also emphasised the importance of allusive interpretations that encourage further developments in the associative process and the introjection of the analyst's interpretations.

This kind of analytic work, argues de M'Uzan, leads to the creation of a psychological ***chimera***, a monster as it were, upon which will be constructed a particular aspect of the transference neurosis (1996, p. 51). That conception of the analytic process requires both that the analyst is able to function in primary-identification mode and that the analysand can process his or her capacity for narcissistic regression.

It is for this reason that regression in analysis has to be thought of in terms of all three aspects – topographical, formal and temporal – as offering the individual the possibility of integrating the necessary passivity or receptiveness of human experience, corresponding to active mental work. It is probably the possibility of experiencing that regression without losing oneself that has to be assessed whenever a decision on whether to offer analysis is being contemplated; this is what led Freud to speak of the biological bedrock that was inaccessible to any attempt at changing it. Here, it is more of a psychological bedrock, given the difficulty, encountered in some analyses, of integrating that primeval passivity that Freud (1937c) described in terms of resistance of the id and the refusal of femininity in both sexes.

This conception of the analytic process based on issues involving narcissistic regression as a condition of psychic change makes for a number

> The **chimera** is a theoretical and clinical concept introduced by de M'Uzan (1994) to designate a new kind of organism that emerges from the encounter between two unconscious systems, that of the analysand and that of the analyst: it appears as a monster that possesses its own ways of functioning.

of differences between French psychoanalysis and that of the English-speaking world. De M'Uzan (1988) describes a *tactical* conception of analysis which stays closely in touch with what transpires in the transference; the interpretative generosity of this approach, in the here-and-now situation, as illustrated by the Kleinian technique, means that the analysand is continuously supported in his or her attempts to cope with anxiety. The contrary conception of analysis, says de M'Uzan, would be a *strategic* one, more Freudian in nature, that is based on letting time pass in silence, an approach impregnated by ideas of waiting and of positioning which accepts more easily the anxiety that emerges as a necessary condition for narcissistic regression. Hence the idea that one must know how to waste time in order to gain any. Although in both cases the idea is to process issues belonging to the childhood past, it is obvious that the conception of that past is not the same and that its interpretation based on the here-and-now situation does not relate to the same setting or analytic site. In the one, the idea is to contain drive-related impulses through providing a significant number of sessions (four or five per week) and the intensity of the interpretative work, while in the other, the analysand is left with some 'room for manoeuvre' by focusing on 'interpretative periods' on the basis of less frequent sessions (three per week).

From that point of view, there is a close relationship between the analyst's countertransference and the analysand's transference, even though there lies within it an asymmetry between the two protagonists of the analytic 'partnership'. De M'Uzan evokes the idea of co-creation within the work of analysis, which does not, all the same, imply that there is no difference between analyst and analysand. That outlook on the transference and countertransference is part of a specifically French tradition in which these two aspects of the analytic work are seen as forming an indissociable unit.

That conception of the analytic process is illustrated in France particularly through the work of Serge Viderman, who introduced the idea of 'the construction of the psychoanalytic space' – the title of the book he published in 1970, of which a particularly evocative extract dealing with the French approach to the transference–countertransference relationship can be found in the present collection (chapter 10).[3] This conception runs counter to the classical theory in which the analyst is ideal and objective, with the countertransference being looked at with suspicion – the attitude that Freud adopted. In the opening paragraphs of his paper, Viderman takes issue with the idea of the analyst-as-mirror whose neutrality must be absolute; that conception, he argues, is based on a negative view of the countertransference.

Viderman takes issue also with the idea that the analyst has to be absolutely benevolent; that notion, he says, underlies another theory of the countertransference, the modern totalistic one in which the countertransference is the creation of the patient. In that view, the analyst is a receptacle ready to receive the analysand's

---

[3] Viderman's hypothesis concerning the 'construction of the analytic space' influenced Donnet's idea of the 'construction of the analytic site'. Donnet himself acknowledged how much he owed to Viderman, who was his analyst (Donnet, 1995, p. 27; 2005, p. xii).

affects and projective identifications, without adding anything personal of his or her own (cf. Urtubey, 1994). Several papers by Michael and Alice Balint (1939), Paula Heimann (1950) and Leon Grinberg (1962) bear witness to this positive conception of the countertransference.

Viderman suggests that we think about the paradox contained in the very idea of the analyst's 'benevolent neutrality'; this implies that the analyst's countertransference is at least as valuable as the transference, and that analyst and analysand share a commitment to the analytic situation, which Viderman calls the 'analytic space'. As Luisa de Urtubey (1994), who agrees with that point of view, makes clear, this conception of the work of analysis corresponds to that of Madeleine and Willy Baranger (1961–1962) who, ten years previously, in Argentina, had introduced the idea of analyst and analysand both involved in the 'analytic situation': the dynamics of that situation depend as much on the analyst and on the analyst's personality, technique and theories as on the patient's ability to face up to his or her conflicts and resistances. Hence the Barangers' idea of a 'bipersonal field' in which the patient's fantasies are created through a collaboration between the unconscious of both participants; this is what, in his theory, de M'Uzan calls the construction of a chimera. Interpretations are made on the basis of this transference–countertransference intersection that brings to mind Winnicott's 'intermediate area of experience'.

Nevertheless, the idea of co-creation of the analytic field did not lead the Barangers or Viderman to suggest that there is some kind of symmetry between the protagonists of psychoanalytic treatment, as some of those who follow the North-American intersubjectivist school of thought would have us believe. Viderman (1970) agrees that the countertransference is at least as important as the transference, but goes on to emphasise the fact that the countertransference is not the analyst's transference: in other words, the asymmetry between analyst and analysand attests to the difference between countertransference and transference. The gap between these positions thus forms the basis for the process of symbol-formation in psychoanalytic treatment.

Viderman therefore suggests the idea of working at building up a narrative truth that aims at reinstating and restoring the patient's mental cohesion and continuity. That idea springs from a comment Freud made in his paper 'Constructions in Analysis' (1937d), in which he stated: 'the truth of the construction . . . achieves the same therapeutic result as a recaptured memory' (1937d, p. 266). That theoretical and clinical view also includes a technical option insofar as it promotes the importance of here-and-now interpretations – that is, with respect to what analyst and analysand are experiencing in the present time of their shared history.

In the early 1970s, that point of view gave rise to much debate in France, focused on Viderman's arguments. In a symposium of the Paris Psychoanalytical Society, Francis Pasche (1974) criticised Viderman's point of view and stressed Freud's earlier idea of reconstructing a historical truth that contained within it a universal structural value, insofar as its roots lay in a rediscovered concrete reality – that is, that of recollecting traumatic memories dating from childhood. Thanks to that hypothesis, the analyst can avoid being accused of making arbitrary constructions –

the reproach that Jung had addressed to Freud – and stay clear of any subjective interpretation that could be intrusive as far as the patient is concerned. That objective conception of psychoanalysis thus lays emphasis on interpretation of the analysand's past.

Freud never really came to a decision on that issue; the development of French psychoanalysis over the past forty years could be seen as an attempt to resolve that aporia. It could even be said that the question concerned the world-wide psychoanalytic community, because many papers and symposia, in North America as well as in Europe, took as their topic the issue of construction and/or reconstruction in psychoanalysis (cf. *Psychoanalysis in Europe*, 1988; *Psychoanalytic Inquiry*, 1983).

The theory according to which the countertransference is a constituent part of the analytic situation was explored also by Michel Neyraut (1974) in his now-classic book on the transference. He begins, somewhat paradoxically, with a chapter on the countertransference, an extract from which can be found in the present volume (chapter 11). According to Neyraut, the countertransference in fact *precedes* the transference, and this on three levels. In the history of psychoanalytic thought, the actual concept of transference appears only retroactively, as an *après-coup*, in Freud's writings; it was seen initially as an obstacle, an accident in the *corpus* of an already-constituted theory and technique. It is in second place also in the unfolding of an analysis because it appears at a time when the analytic process is already on-going, and assumes that, at an earlier point in time, the analyst expressed the wish to have that other person as his or her patient: it follows that, although the countertransference has been seen as a response to the analysand's transference, it should be considered as relating to the initial request for analysis. The patient's seductiveness thus makes the analyst a co-desirer, obliged to live through a paradoxical situation of listening both in an interested and in a disinterested manner. The countertransference could thus be defined as 'the analyst's implication', an anticipation of transference repetition, thereby constituting both a resistance and the necessary condition for the interpretative processing of the transference.

The idea that the countertransference precedes the transference also influences analytic thinking. What lies at the heart of this, of course, is the analyst's thoughts about the psychoanalytic treatments that have been carried out, but at the same time these reflections modify the way in which analysts listen attentively to their patients; they are therefore part of the countertransference – the theoretical aspect. Like Viderman, Neyraut does not agree with the idea of a neutral analyst whose countertransference serves simply to reveal his or her resistance as regards the patient's transference. In this broader theory of the countertransference, the analyst is already closely involved in an identification with the patient that will determine how the analysis unfolds – although a capacity to dis-identify with the patient still remains, in keeping with the asymmetrical conception of the analytic situation.

Jean Laplanche (1992) goes further into this idea of the countertransference preceding the transference. In that paper, which is published in the present volume, he asks: 'Are we able to conceive that it is the offer of analysis, the offer of the analyst, which creates . . . what? Not analysis, but its essential dimension, transference. Not, perhaps, the whole of the transference, but its basis . . .' (chapter 12, p. 244). It is thus the analyst who 'inaugurates . . . the transference' by offering analysands the hollow in which they can lay down their own primary relationship with the enigma in order to reprocess it. This is what Laplanche calls the 'hollowed-out transference' as opposed to the complete or 'filled-in transference' which refers to the usual conception of repetition in the transference.

> The concept of **enigmatic message** was introduced by Laplanche (1987) in his description of what he called the 'fundamental anthropological situation' corresponding to a fundamental asymmetry between adult and infant as regards the act of communication. Laplanche suggested a theory of *generalised seduction*, in which the mother becomes the seducer who addresses to her infant messages that are pregnant with unconscious sexual signification.

Lacan had emphasised the anxieties that have to do with the mother's desire; Laplanche (1987) reworked that approach and outlined what amounted to a true theory of seduction: between child and adult there is a primary seduction through which the adult offers the child both non-verbal and verbal signifiers, or even complementary ones impregnated with unconscious sexual meaning (1987, p. 125). Laplanche introduced the hypothesis of 'enigmatic signifiers' – which has to do with the idea of something that *signifies to*, addressed to the child – but preferred the term **'enigmatic messages'**, thus distancing himself from Lacan's conception of the signifier.

The psychoanalytic situation, from this point of view, is the *locus* in which that primary seduction comes again to the fore, inasmuch as, through the offer of analysis, the analyst inevitably takes the place of the adult addressing messages to the child. Hence the idea that the transference is provoked by the analyst, who is by that very fact the 'guardian of the enigma'. The analyst's benevolent neutrality is the 'hollow' that enables the treatment to be the *locus* in which the infantile situation, with its enigmatic dimension that requires to be reprocessed, is deposited. The fate of that primary seduction may be either the *implantation* of sexuality in the child or an *intromission* that leads to a non-metabolisable sexual irruption. The end of an analysis leads not to a dissolution of the transference, but to a 'transferring of the transference', the aim of which is to signify the fact that, after the analysis, the relationship to the enigma continues.

In her reflections on Laplanche's 1992 paper, Haydée Faimberg (1994) shows that her own approach is similar to that of Laplanche. She came to France from Argentina in the 1970s, having followed in the tradition of the Barangers and of other Argentinian analysts who had emphasised the importance of the 'bipersonal field' in psychoanalytic treatment. The hypothesis concerning enigmatic messages echoed her own conceptualisation of what analysis is all about, pre-dating that of Laplanche. For Faimberg, analysis is a process mobilised by the unconscious wish to resolve an enigma posed by the transference (p. 213). From that point of view, the analyst's provoking a hollowed-out transference is a possibility, as long as he or she does not intrude into the patient's mind nor give rise to alienating unconscious identifications.

The analyst's positive function as object of the transference consists in defining the analysand's message as enigmatic insofar as it is the unconscious spokesperson of intergenerational unconscious identifications. 'By means of an interrogative construction, the analyst interprets what the patient says *in* the transference; the situation may then be interpreted as enigmatic *in* the transference and as an enigma *of* the transference' (p. 219). The dissymmetry between analyst and analysand thus forms the basis of the work of *construction* in the analysis, which proves its validity through the resolution of a transference–countertransference enigma which can quite as easily be understood as a *reconstruction* of the past in the course of the analytic treatment. Seen in this light, the controversy between Viderman and Pasche could be resolved in an interesting way through this encounter between the South-American and French schools of thought, each of which offers the international psychoanalytic community a new approach to the transference–countertransference relationship.

The idea, in fact, is to go beyond the alternative 'historical truth' *or* 'narrative truth' by considering analysis as a retroactive processing of past history within a new relationship – that is, between analysand and analyst. It is this that may make the past appear in a different light or perhaps as a potentially new dimension. From that point of view, French psychoanalysis, beginning with Lacan and then involving many other analysts, highlighted the importance of seeing in an *après-coup* ['deferred action'][4] the possibility of validating psychic causality by taking it to mean, not a direct and linear cause-and-effect relationship between past and present, but a retroactive causality from present to past. This dialectic conception of the psychoanalytic relationship enables us to see in the analytic process something more than a confrontation between objective reconstruction and subjective construction and, thereby, to discover the *latent* history at the point where transference and countertransference meet.

It is that meeting-point between transference and countertransference that Jean-Claude Rolland explores in his paper on the relationship between hallucinatory vision and speech (2004 – chapter 13, this volume). In so doing, he distances himself from the Lacanian approach to the unconscious and language, highlighting the essentially affect-based dimension of the movements and shifts between hallucinatory wish-fulfilment, based on perceptual identity and that of images, and the need to *renounce* that 'envisioning' in order to have access to speech and language. Freud described this as the acceptance of a delay before fulfilment and the access to thought identity. Going from the pleasure principle to the reality principle requires processing in the very depths of the mind in order to accept the loss of the object and of its hallucinatory revival. Freud described cathecting language as a 'substitute' for hallucinatory satisfaction, and Rolland emphasises this in his evocation of the

---

[4] The traditional English translation of '*après-coup*' by 'deferred action' has been called into question by many French analysts, as it does not make clear the importance of the *retroactive* aspect of that action. See the General Introduction by D. Birksted-Breen and S. Flanders, this volume, pp. 20–21.

renunciation that is an integral part of any attempt to use words. He quite correctly argues that this is a mental processing that follows the dictates of an 'economic constraint'. From that point of view, speech, conscious thought and thinking processes all have to do with the same process of transformation of the contents of the mind from image to thought.

The work of analysis also invites the analysand to move in the opposite direction – renouncing 'speech activity' and re-cathecting the child's capacity for 'envisioning' typical of unconscious fantasising. Like many other French psychoanalysts, Rolland describes the issues involved in formal and topographical regression during analytic treatment as lying at the very core of temporal regression. The clinical example he gives throws light on those issues and furthers our understanding of what the analytic process involves: a change in mentality is possible only if the analyst is capable of 'unconscious participation', which Rolland likens to empathy, defined as a capacity for primary identification with the way in which the analysand's mind works. Like de M'Uzan, Rolland bases that countertransference experience on the analyst's capacity to be in touch with a feeling of relative depersonalisation in the course of the analysis: the analyst must be ready to fall in with 'the time necessary for the working-through, the incarnation of the analysing subject's lost or concealed objects' (chapter 13, p. 260).

Rolland's clinical illustration enables him to emphasise the value of the work of analysis, based on what he calls 'satellite signifiers' – that is, preconscious word-presentations which enable unconscious thing-presentations to have access to the possibility of becoming conscious and to the lifting of repression. By contrast, repression works in the opposite direction, making use of language but removing from it its linguistic function of communication. Rolland helps us to understand the 'efficacy of the analytic method' from the point of view of French psychoanalysis based on Freud's approach to his topographical model of the mind: it is not a question of choosing between the visionary experience of images and the experience of speech, but of showing how they are in a close and continuous relationship all through the analytic process. A mutative interpretation is one that acknowledges the polysemous value of the word-presentations tied to unconscious ideas and allows them to have access to the preconscious.

From that point of view, psychoanalysis has more to do with *semiotics* in Peirce's (1932) sense – that is, a science of signs that open on to a heterogeneous variety of signs (indices, icons and symbols), as opposed to *semiology* in de Saussure's (1916) sense, which is based to a greater extent on linguistic signs. Rolland's references to semiotics bear witness to the fact that French psychoanalysis has distanced itself somewhat from Lacan and his return to Freud – which, by assimilating the unconscious and language in fact made the link between them disappear. Rolland's paper has the signal merit of demonstrating the 'solidarity' between language and the unconscious without losing sight of the differences between them.

References

Balint, M. & Balint, A. (1939). On transference and counter-transference. *International Journal of Psychoanalysis*, *20*: 223–230.

Baranger, M., & Baranger, W. (1961–1962). La situation analytique comme champ dynamique. *Revue Française de Psychanalyse* (1985), *49* (6): 1543–1571. [The analytic situation as a dynamic field. 1961–1962. *International Journal of Psychoanalysis*, *89* (2008, no. 4): 795–826.]

Brusset, B. (1991). L'or et le cuivre (la psychothérapie peut-elle être et rester psychanalytique?) [Gold and copper (can psychotherapy be and remain psychoanalytic?)]. *Revue Française de Psychanalyse*, *55* (3): 554–579.

Diatkine, R. (1970). Remarques préliminaires sur l'état actuel de la psychanalyse d'enfants. *La Psychiatrie de L'enfant* (1971), *14:* 7–29. [Preliminary Remarks on the Present State of Psychoanalysis of Children. *International Journal of Psychoanalysis*, *53* (1972): 141–150.]

Diatkine, R. & Simon, J. (1972). *La psychanalyse précoce* [Psychoanalysis with young children]. Paris: Presses Universitaires de France.

Donnet, J.-L. (1995). *Le divan bien tempéré* [The well-tempered couch]. Paris: Presses Universitaires de France.

Donnet, J.-L. (2001). From the Fundamental Rule to the Analysing Situation. *International Journal of Psychoanalysis*, *82*: 129–140.

Donnet, J.-L. (2005). *La situation analysante* [The analysing situation]. Paris: Presses Universitaires de France.

Donnet, J.-L. & Green, A. (1973). *L'enfant de ça. Psychanalyse d'un entretien: la psychose blanche*. [The child of that/of the id. The psychoanalysis of an interview: Blank psychosis]. Paris: Editions de Minuit.

Duncan, D. (1989). The Flow of Interpretation – The Collateral Interpretation, Force and Flow. *International Journal of Psychoanalysis*, *70*: 693–700.

Faimberg, H. (1994). L'énigme que pose le transfert. Pour une solution non solipsiste [The enigma posed by the transference. For a non-solipsistic solution]. In J. Laplanche et al., *Colloque international de psychanalyse, Montreal, 3–5 July 1992* [International symposium on psychoanalysis]. Paris: Presses Universitaires de France.

Ferenczi, S. (1914). Sensations of Giddiness at the End of the Psycho-Analytic Session. In *The Selected Papers of Sandor Ferenczi, Vol. II. Further Contributions to the Theory and Technique of Psycho-Analysis*. London: Hogarth Press, 1950.

Ferenczi, S. (1928). The Problem of the Termination of the Analysis. In *The Selected Papers of Sandor Ferenczi, Vol. III. Final Contributions to the Problems and Methods of Psycho-Analysis*, ed. M. Balint, trans. E. Mosbacher et al. London: Hogarth Press and the Institute of Psychoanalysis; New York: Basic Books, 1955.

Freud, A. (1970). Discussion paper. *La Psychiatrie de L'enfant*, *14* (1971, no. 1): 29–35.

Freud, S. (1900a). *The Interpretation of Dreams*. *S.E.*, 4/5.

Freud, S. (1916–17). *Introductory Lectures on Psycho-Analysis*. *S.E.*, 15/16.

Freud, S. (1919a [1918]). Lines of Advance in Psycho-Analytic Therapy. *S.E.*, 17: 159.

Freud, S. (1919h). The 'Uncanny'. *S.E.*, 17: 219.

Freud, S. (1937c). Analysis Terminal and Interminable. *S.E.*, 23: 209

Freud, S. (1937d). Constructions in Analysis. *S.E.*, 23: 257.

Gibeault, A. (2001). Du processus analytique en psychanalyse et en psychothérapie. De l'interpersonnel à l'intrapsychique [On the analytic process in psychoanalysis and in psychotherapy: From interpersonal to intrapsychic]. *Revue Française de Psychanalyse*, *65* (Special Issue): 49–65.

Green, A. (2002). *Idées directrices pour une psychanalyse contemporaine*. Paris: Presses

Universitaires de France. [*Key Ideas for a Contemporary Psychoanalysis. Misrecognition and Recognition of the Unconscious*, trans. A. Weller. London: Routledge, 2005.]

Green, A. (Ed.) (2006). *Les voies nouvelles de la thérapeutique analytique. Le dedans et le dehors* [New developments in analytic therapy. Inside and outside]. Paris: Presses Universitaires de France.

Grinberg, L. (1962). On a specific aspect of counter-transference due to the patient's projective identification. *International Journal of Psychoanalysis, 43*: 436–440.

Grunberger, B. (1971). *Le narcissisme*. Paris: Payot. [*Narcissism: Psychoanalytic Essays*, trans. J. S. Diamanti. New York: International Universities Press, 1979.]

Heimann, P. (1950). On Counter-Transference. *International Journal of Psychoanalysis, 31*: 81–84.

Klauber, J. (1972). On the Relationship of Transference and Interpretation in Psychoanalytic Therapy. *International Journal of Psychoanalysis, 53*: 385–391.

Laplanche, J. (1987). *Nouveaux fondements pour la psychanalyse*. Paris: Presses Universitaires de France. [*New Foundations in Psychoanalysis*, trans. D. Macey. Oxford: Blackwell.]

Laplanche, J. (1992). Du transfert. Sa provocation par l'analyste. *Psychanalyse à L'université, 17* (65): 3–22. Also in *Le primat de l'autre en psychanalyse*. Paris: Flammarion, 1997. [Transference: Its Provocation by the Analyst. In *Essays on Otherness*, ed. J. Fletcher. London: Routledge, 1998.]

M'Uzan, M. de. (1976), Contre-transfert et système paradoxal [Countertransference and paradoxical system]. In *De l'art à la mort* [From art to death] (pp. 164–181). Paris: Gallimard.

M'Uzan, M. de. (1988). Stratégie et tactique à propos des interprétations freudiennes et kleiniennes [Strategy and tactics with respect to Freudian and Kleinian interpretations]. In *La bouche de l'inconscient* [The mouth of the unconscious]. Paris: Gallimard, 1994.

M'Uzan, M. de. (1996). A propos de la formulation de l'interprétation [Formulating interpretations]. *Psychanalysis in Europe. Bulletin of the European Psychoanalytical Federation, 47*: 45–54.

M'Uzan, M. de. (2006). Invite à la fréquentation des ombres [Invitation to frequent the shadows]. *Psychanalysis in Europe. Bulletin of the European Psychoanalytical Federation, 60*: 14–28.

M'Uzan, M. de. (2009). L'inquiétante étrangeté ou 'Je ne suis pas celle que vous croyez' [The uncanny, or 'I am not who you think I am']. Unpublished paper read at an internal symposium of the Paris Psychoanalytical Society (25 March).

Nacht S., (1963). *La présence du psychanalyste*. Paris: Presses Universitaires de France.

Neyraut, M. (1974). *Le transfert* [The transference]. Paris: Presses Universitaires de France.

Parsons, M. (2009). Als estrangers tan pao que valgon [To the strangers, whatever they're worth!]. In: *Inquiétante Etrangeté* (pp. 75–78), ed. L. Danon-Boileau. Paris: Presses Universitaires de France.

Pasche, F. (1974). Le passé recomposé [The past reconstructed]. *Revue Française de Psychanalyse, 38* (2–3): 171–182.

Peirce C. S. (1932). *Collected Papers of Charles Sanders Peirce, Vol. 2: Elements of Logic*, ed. C. Hartshorne & P. Weiss. Cambridge, MA: Harvard University Press.

Psychoanalysis in Europe. (1988). Construction and Reconstruction: 3rd Symposium of the European Psychoanalytical Federation. *Psychoanalysis in Europe. Bulletin of the European Psychoanalytical Federation, 31*: 3–89.

Psychoanalytic Inquiry. (1983). Special Issue: Construction and Reconstruction in Psychoanalysis. *Psychoanalytic Inquiry, 3* (2).

Quinodoz, D. (1994). *Le vertige entre angoisse et plaisir*. Paris: Presses Universitaires de France. [*Emotional Vertigo: Between Anxiety and Pleasure*, trans. A. Pomerans. London: Routledge, 1997.]

Rolland, J.-C. (2004). Parler, renoncer [Speaking and renouncing]. *Revue Française de Psychanalyse*, *68* (3): 947–962.

Roussillon, R. (1991). Épreuve d'actualité et épreuve de réalité dans le face à face psychanalytique [Actuality-testing and Reality-testing in the psychoanalytic encounter]. *Revue Française de Psychanalyse*, *55* (3): 581–596.

Saussure, F. de (1916). *Cours de linguistique générale*. Paris: Payot, 1949. [*Course in General Linguistics*, ed C. B. & A. Sechehaye, trans. R. Harris. La Salle, IL: Open Court, 1983.]

Segal, H. (1957). Notes on Symbol-Formation. *International Journal of Psychoanalysis*, *38*: 391–397.

Segal, H. (1970). Discussion Paper. *La Psychiatrie de L'enfant*, *14* (1971): 29–35.

Strachey, J. (1934). The Nature of the Therapeutic Action of Psycho-Analysis. *International Journal of Psychoanalysis*, *15*: 127–159.

Urtubey, L. de. (1994). Le travail de contre-transfert [The work of the countertransference]. *Revue Française de Psychanalyse*, *58* (5): 1271–1372.

Viderman, S. (1970). Le rôle du contre-transfert [The role of the countertransference]. In *La construction de l'espace psychanalytique* [The construction of the psychoanalytic space]. Paris: Denoël.

6 FROM THE FUNDAMENTAL RULE TO THE ANALYSING SITUATION[1]

Jean-Luc Donnet

> **Jean-Luc Donnet** is a psychiatrist, full member of the Paris Psychoanalytical Society and a former director of the Jean Favreau Centre for psychoanalytic treatment. Much of his work has focused on the analytic setting, as regards both its material and its interpretative dimensions.
> With André Green, he wrote *L'enfant de ça. Psychanalyse d'un entretien: la psychose blanche* [The child of that/of the id. Psychoanalysis of an interview: Blank psychosis] (Minuit, 1973). He has also published *Surmoi, le concept freudien et la règle fondamentale* [Superego, the Freudian concept and the fundamental rule] (*Revue Française de Psychanalyse* Monograph, PUF, 1995), *Le divan bien tempéré* [The well-tempered couch] (PUF, 1995) and *La situation analysante* [The analysing situation] (PUF, 2005) (now published in English (Karnac, 2009)).

For André Green
'Though this be madness, yet there is method in't.'
Hamlet, Act II, ii

Some key aspects of the method

1) Any attempt to define the analytic method is immediately confronted with the contrast between what the term method suggests in the way of controlled organisation, and the renunciation of control implied by free association. No doubt this paradox of *methodic unreason* was necessary if the Ucs. was to open itself to rational investigation.

   In its immanence, the method cannot be distinguished from the manner in which the psyche proves itself capable of producing an

---

[1] This paper was presented at the 42nd Congress of the International Psychoanalytical Association in Nice, 23–27 July 2001. It was translated by Andrew Weller.

associative sequence and of discerning an unconscious logic in it afterwards. When one thinks about it, the method cannot easily be separated from the theory of the psyche, which makes it possible to interpret the sequence and think about the hypothesis of the *Ucs*. In this respect, by writing *The Interpretation of Dreams* (1900a), Freud went to the very heart of the matter: the telling of dreams and their interpretation finds its continuation in the theorisation on the work that produces them.

2) At another level, the method provides the link between this Freudian invention, its scientific reference (positivist) and the demands of clinical practice, which needed to demonstrate its validity as an applicable medical technique. Thus in accordance with the project of an analytic cure, the method consists in carefully creating the conditions in which free association proves to be practicable, interpretable and beneficial. A contradiction emerges at the heart of these conditions between those based on acquired knowledge, theoretical and practical, and those that prescribe the suspension of this knowledge so that the encounter with the *Ucs.* is authentic. Knowledge does tend to predetermine the finality of the experience, and even to give the method a quasi-programmatic dimension. Hence the importance of the capacity to function *negatively* in order to preserve the loss of the ordinary references of meaning that the shared associative process entails and also the hazardous dimension of the *après-coup* in which there is an attempt to find meaning through interpretation. In addition to evenly suspended attention, a learned ignorance (Lacan, 1961) or negative capability (Bion, 1970) are also qualities said to characterise the analyst in his work. This contradiction reveals the need for the element of thirdness, for which the method is the safeguard.

3) Retrospectively, certain initial aspects of the method now appear to have been more or less adequate responses to this requirement, which became all the more imperative because analysis needed to shake off the hypnotic 'influence'.

   a) Freud's preference for a method operating *per via di levare* corresponded in part to his assertion that the analyst and the situation should introduce nothing foreign into the patient's mind. This asepsis meant that the method simply allowed unconscious processes to manifest themselves, and that interpretation merely revealed the meaning of what was already there in the repressed. Nowadays, no one doubts that the analyst and the analytic situation participate, *nolens volens*, in the structuring of the phenomena in process.

   b) In the first place, the method postulates a conscious ego-subject, capable of observing a part of his internal world in order to make it an object of investigation. The very development of the method would show how this ego is subverted by the *Ucs.* and how precarious the observer–observed distinction is (for the analyst as well).

It was difficult to get beyond these initial responses, which were often institutionalised. Evidence of this may be found, for instance, in Freud's attachment to the material truth of memories, before he was able to authenticate the conviction arising from a construction, and its indirect associative confirmation, and then sift out the notion of historical truth. Conceived of as a neutral agency of objectivisation, the method seemed, in effect, to guarantee the objective validity of the knowledge acquired and the results obtained. Is it not the case that there is still a widespread conviction that the truth of analysis can be validated by studies aimed at objectivising the initial development?

Psychoanalysis is currently exploring what it can learn from other scientific models (self-organisation, determinist chaos, new conceptions of history, etc.) that are compatible with the specific requirements of its own discipline.

4) The function of the third party can no longer provide any sort of prior guarantee. Its specific role is one of *producing thirdness* (Green, 1989), an essential factor in the dynamics of a process that sometimes causes it to disappear.

The adventure of transference situates the desire for alienation, inherent in the intersubjective relationship, at the heart of analytic activity. There is always a risk that the experience will comply with the analyst's desire and his theoretical preconceptions. Freud draws attention to the unavoidable ambiguity of this when he says that, at a certain level, a hypothesis can no longer be distinguished from the phenomenon it relates to. This is why it is necessary to confer a specific value on the *gap between theory and practice in analysis*; for it is not *de facto* but involves an ethical prescription that is related to the respect for otherness.

This gap is the object of a constant conflict in inter-analytic exchanges between the 'scientific' desire to fill it and the humanistic requirement to confirm its irreducibility.

5) Because of the increasing complexity of the psychoanalyst's function, descriptions of method tend to be focused on his functioning, the modalities of which are sustained by his particular gifts, his own analysis and training, and ultimately inform his interpretative creations.

This description is rendered all the more accessible and open to theoretical elaboration in that the analyst combines within himself both subjective experience and his/the theorisation. But for this very reason, it activates the self-referential danger that threatens psychoanalysis and the temptation to turn the psychoanalyst into an omnipotent 'technical subjectivity'.

a) This is illustrated, for instance, by modern theories of countertransference. Originally, countertransference was conceived of as something disturbing the analyst's function: this was a narrow point of view, but one which drew attention to the gap between subject and function, the symbolic support of the function. A wider theoretical outlook takes into account the structural character of the psychoanalyst's subjective involvement, as well as the principle of the potential functioning of that part of it which is accessible to him. This unquestionably results in broadening the basis of the function. But there is an increased danger of the gap between subject and function disappearing; either because, for example, the analyst ends up candidly making a function out of his subjectivity; or, because he thinks of his function as being indefinitely relevant and malleable, once the countertransference capacities are there. Yet, is it not necessary for the method to place an elaborative reference point (dialectical) between the limits of the analyst and the limits of the analysis – which after all are the correlate of its consistency?

b) Moreover, faced with a commonplace impasse in the transference–countertransference situation, the analyst quickly sees that the *Ucs.* remains the *Ucs.*, and that his capacity to use his countertransference and self-analysis is strictly limited. What can he learn, then, from the method? Quite simply, by returning to the beginning by doing another period of analysis or supervision. In so doing, he rediscovers the original challenge – that is, speaking by associating in order to give a chance to the interpretative *après-coup*.

The listening situation, then, is part and parcel of the method: it is an inter-analytic annex of the analytic situation in which countertransference can take the place of transference.

6) Centring the method on the analyst goes hand in hand with the temptation of merely seeing the patient as his beneficiary in order to describe the effects he has on him. One of the moving forces of my work has been to draw attention to the fact that the first meaning of the rule – making the patient the active agent of the method – survives the vicissitudes of transference, and that it is the analysand, primarily, who makes the analyst an analyst. My experience as an analyst and consultant has made me particularly sensitive to the attachment that patients – even the most difficult ones – show towards the analytic situation with regard to *its specificity*, the logic of its functioning and its ethics; a sense of attachment that is distinct from – and sometimes in conflict with – that which they show towards the analyst. For them, it is a question of playing

by the rules of the game, a key element in the function of creating thirdness. Something essential in the method is at play in the process of self-appropriation through which the patient becomes an analysand.

From the procedure to the rule

1) It will be worthwhile to return to the definition Freud gave of psychoanalysis in his *Encyclopaedia* article of 1922 (1923a [1922], p. 233). He both linked and distinguished:

    - the procedure for the investigation of mental processes which are almost inaccessible in any other way;
    - and the method '(based upon that investigation) for the treatment of neurotic disorders'.

    The transition from investigation to treatment corresponds to the shift from procedure to method:

    - the procedure of free association can be used for pure investigation;
    - the method lays down the procedure, which has become the fundamental rule in the 'structured' situation, resulting in a process of *transformative* investigation. This is why the method can be used *for* a treatment: the psychoanalytic cure consists of *additional* indirect effects, of psychic transformations inherent in the process. Notwithstanding the complexity that has been introduced, we still find the founding postulate of a truth that heals.

2) Freud replaced the panoramic memory of the hypnotised subject with free association. It was up to the patient to actively suspend the exercise of his reason in order to grasp and communicate his incidental *unwelcome* thoughts. The procedure was only introduced originally to investigate an enigmatic phenomenon that was already there – that is, that of symptoms and dreams whose meaning needed elucidating. There was a clear distinction, then, between this *fixed* object and the subject who participates, with the analyst, in investigating it.

    This limitation of the procedure reflected that of the *Ucs.* conceived of as a lacuna.

3) In spite of the simplicity of its formulation, the rule contained all the ambiguities that would lead to the analytic situation and its complexity.

    a) By suggesting to the patient that he should say everything that comes into his mind, even if it seems nonsensical, unimportant or disagreeable, the rule combines the positive proposition to speak spontaneously, i.e. 'freely', and the *negative* prescription not to shut out incidental thoughts. It makes the *already existing* object of investigation disappear, which implies conventionalising the spatio-temporal limits of the session; and, it suspends the implicit difference between those moments when the patient is speaking in his own name and others when he is talking nonsense while associating. However, it does not prevent the patient from bringing, at the beginning of the session, an object of investigation (an account of a dream, for instance) to which he will have some associations.

b) At the same time, however, announcing the rule favours psychic and discursive factuality in the *here and now*; it places the session under the *virtual* aegis of free association. The analyst, for his part, finds himself immediately in a position to listen associatively to the process of the session; there is thus a gap between the two protagonists that is part of the structural asymmetry of their positions. The crucial question, with regard to the method, is to know how this asymmetry can lead to a division of labour that is functional and not hierarchical, since this gap involves a risk of alienation. Which analyst has not been troubled by the observation that he has just heard a transparent associative process during a session in which the patient seems not to have wondered if he was saying something different from what he had intended to say?

c) This danger is inherent in the fact that the rule stipulates implicitly that the object of investigation will be produced in or as a result of the session. The patient's activity becomes, then, both the actual vehicle and the specific object of the investigation. How can the method ensure that concomitance exists between the production and the investigation of an object? Stated in this way, the question elicits but mediocre answers.

The first would be that of alternation. With the psychoanalyst's tacit agreement, the patient rediscovers the initial logic of the procedure: associative investigation follows the presentation of an object.

The second, a caricature, would be that of a permanent split, as in the metaphor of a train journey during which a traveller sitting next to the window describes to the person next to him the changing views he sees outside. The patient ensures there is a disjunction, without interference, between the associative production of a psychic film and a purely informative account collaborating with the investigation.

The third solution would be that of a permanent division of labour, the principle of which is that the analyst's listening *applies the rule* to the patient's functioning. Is it not the case that Freud expected the rule, in an objectivising mode and in the third person, to provide an impartial guarantee that the forces involved in the conflict could be fully manifested? For the experienced analyst, the rule is an analyser of the whole of the patient's psychic functioning.

From this point of view, it is the psychoanalyst's interpretation that constitutes, retroactively, the object of investigation, as a result of the choice of 'material' made in the session.

It can be seen that the division of labour makes the patient the producer, and the analyst the investigator. The patient is assumed to be subject to an internal split between subject and object (of investigation), since, in the final analysis, the interpretation has to be addressed to a part of his ego that has remained an observer.

d) The weakness of these responses shows that the rule introduces a rupture with the principle of objectivising the procedure. The distinction between an immobilised object of investigation and its investigation by a conscious subject is erased when confronted with the intra- and intersubjective logic of an investigation that transforms what it encounters and is itself transformed by the encounter. The process involves the subject's indefinite experience of being decentred. The rule supposes that, through the heterogeneity of the signifiers employed (Green, 1973) and the diversity of the forms of enunciation, associative activity is no longer only a means: informed by the subject's self-division, it provides the opportunity for a tangible and troubling perception of *the other scene*; the experience of this drifting takes only one direction: 'the goal is the journey'. As in La Fontaine's fable, 'The Labourer and His Children', associative exploration can end up substituting the value of working-through for the discovery of the hidden treasure – the *predetermined* finality of the initial procedure.

Transference

The primacy conferred by the rule on here-and-now factuality inevitably implied that the transference would become the object of investigation produced *in* the session. But it also contained the idea that, as it was produced *by* the session, its interpretation required a renewed conception of the analytic situation.

1) Within a short space of time, Freud stated first that the theme of transference should only be interpreted once it had turned into a resistance; and then, that it proved possible to give a new transference meaning to all the symptoms of the transference-neurosis (1914g, p. 154). From resistance to interpreting, transference thus became the medium of an interpretative function that was obliged to comply with it 'methodically'. But we may wonder whether this progress was not paid for by a slightly restrictive systematic dimension ('succeed in').

2) In 'The Dynamics of Transference' (1912b), Freud refers to the 'immense disadvantage in psychoanalysis as a method' when speaking of the fact that transference, generally speaking the strongest factor in success, can turn into the most powerful vehicle of resistance. I do not want to go back over the way in which he proved that this was only a matter of appearance and showed how the obstacle is changed into a vehicle of success. But it is not difficult to detect the signs of unease that transference and the exigency of interpreting it constituted for the theory of analytic method as he had conceived of it. I would like to highlight two of these signs:

   a) After pointing out that the stoppage of associations is always linked to a transference-idea and observing that as soon as the 'explanation' is given to the patient the stoppage is removed, Freud writes that in case of failure the situation is changed from one in which the associations fail into one in which they are being kept back (1912b, p. 101).
   b) At the end of the article, and in a manner which stands out from the rest of the text, he emphasises that the highly regressive form taken by the transference actualisation is due to the psychological situation in which the treatment places the patient (p. 107); and, as if to justify its necessity, he concludes it is impossible to destroy anyone '*in absentia* or *in effigie*' (p. 108). It is clear that resistance in the transference raises the issue of the violence of interpretation as well as that of countertransference, the cause and consequence of the turmoil affecting the method.

   It is not very difficult to demonstrate this turmoil. To illustrate the 'acting out' of transference (*agieren*), Freud cites as an example the case of a man who became mute when the fundamental rule was imparted, owing to the displacement onto the analyst of a conflict with parental authority. It can be seen, then, that the rule, which is supposed, *a priori*, to further the investigation of an intrapsychic conflict, loses its status as a tool and becomes its unconscious factor on the analytic stage. It has lost its referential value of thirdness.

   But it has not lost its functional relevance, since the patient has produced an interpretable transference symptom.

   Nonetheless, a problem arises with regard to its eventual interpretation, particularly in the absence of an adequate associative context. Is there not a danger of it manifesting the analyst-father's knowledge and power, and of it being perceived – like the formulation of the fundamental rule – as resulting from the position that he occupies in the transference?

   Thus, not only does transference disqualify the rule's function as a third party, but it tends to unite the interpreter and the transference-object, and to turn resistance towards analysis into resistance towards the analyst. This is surely an immense disadvantage for the method.

The objectivising distance was indispensable for transference to be understood as a symptomatic phenomenon. By the same logic, its interpretation was seen as containing the principle of its resolution. But if transference is turned against transference, it also means suggestion is turned against suggestion (Freud), in which the reference to thirdness tends to be lost in the dual relationship, and meaning gives way to force.

If transference lends itself so readily to resistance, is it not also because its interpretation is too closely tied up with the aim of lifting its resistance and, perhaps, of denying the analyst's desire? Exaggerating slightly, Lacan said that there is no other resistance to analysis than that of the analyst himself. You will recall the metaphor Freud (1916–17, Lecture 19) employed to illustrate the impossibility of allowing the patient the right of reserve or asylum. Resistance would make its home there just as criminals would take refuge in churches if there were a round-up that respected their sanctuary in such places. Is it not the case that the exigency of relating everything that happens to the transference contributes to making transference the favoured refuge of resistance, in response to the round-up approach of the method?

The analytic situation

1) The dialectics of transference and its interpretation constitutes a source of methodological malaise owing to the ambiguity it introduces into the conception of the analytic situation. It was noticeable in a certain outlook that prevailed at the time of my training, which claimed that the situation was as neutral as the analyst and his mirror-function. It was supposed to guarantee the spontaneity of transference, itself a condition of its analysability. However, this notion of spontaneity has long been marked by a striking ambiguity, for it has been understood as meaning that the analyst and the situation 'play no part' in the development of transference (instead of simply pointing out that the reserve of the former and the invariance of the latter make it easier to understand). Thus, in 1950, Macalpine caused a sensation by describing transference as induced (Macalpine, 1950), rediscovering what Freud had written in 1912. This occultation, which can be interpreted as an after-effect of the mourning of neurotica, was the demand – necessary if one was to objectivise the psychic reality of the transference fantasy – that no seducer should be subject to incriminations.

In correlation with this, because the method was preoccupied for the most part with the lifting of infantile amnesia and reconstructing the past, transference was inevitably considered from the angle of its purely repetitive dimension; accordingly, its interpretation was supposed to uncover the contents of its amnesic memory (Green, 1993). From this point of view, interpreting the transference necessarily implied an aspect of refutation, rectifying its illusion by means of the 'neutral' reality of the situation.

2) Insofar as the actualisation of transference represents the vehicle of analytic action, a more open and complex conception – but also more ambiguous – of the analytic situation is both required and permitted. It raises in a different way the question of creating thirdness.

   a) On the one hand, there is no reason to describe transference as pure repetition; it displaces, invests, introjects and projects in a (more or less) discriminating manner. It is psychic work that is symbolic or potentially symbolising. It introduces *difference into repetition*, which was even more evident for Freud when, *a contrario*, he encountered transferences in which reproductions emerged of an 'unwished-for exactitude' (1920g, p. 18), evoking a compulsion to repeat going beyond the pleasure principle.

   The spontaneity of transference can be seen in the way it erupts, takes advantage of circumstances and *creates a happening*. I am tempted to generalise Freud's metaphor on transference-love: a cry of fire is raised during a theatrical performance; for a while, one does not know whether it is part of the performance or whether the theatre is going to catch fire. Once one has decided not to call in the fire brigade, the problem is how to let the performance continue while modifying it so as to be able to integrate the event afterwards. The precious ambiguity of transference is to give tension, more or less intensely, to the continuity of the plot and the discontinuity of the event. For Freud, the analytic situation falls halfway between fiction and reality; one should add, between the 'here-and-now' and the 'then-and-elsewhere'. With his concept of the transitional area, Winnicott showed why it was essential that transference not be faced with the dilemma of being a real or a false fire: what matters is the spirit of play in which the ethics of transference is sometimes difficult to distinguish from the principle of the method.

   b) On the other hand, the analytic situation is not 'neutral', in the sense of a pure projective surface. It is active in two ways: negatively, because it repudiates through the constraints it imposes; and, positively, because it contains something gratifying and appealing too. Behind the necessary reserve of the manifest offer lurks a latent mixture of frustration and gratification: by proposing his two successive active techniques, Ferenczi simply accentuated what already existed.

The analyst and the situation are both involved in the structuring of the transference process: the principle of a permanent demarcation between the observer and observed is untenable. Moreover, there is scarcely any sense in claiming to be able to describe in an objective manner a direct causal effect of the instruments of analysis: the same element (the couch, the analyst's silence) can, depending on the patient and the moment in question, assume different, even contrary, meanings.

3) The process is thus the result of an *encounter* that cannot be reduced to determining factors: an encounter between the demand – the suffering – of the patient, and the analyst in question. But, in the last resort, it is an encounter *between two differences: that which sustains the transference and that which distinguishes the analytic situation from any other life-situation.*

The dynamics of transference stem from the potential of the encounter: they are nourished by what the situation has to offer to transference investments, quite apart from the analyst's contribution as a person. The investigation by the patient of his internal world can scarcely be separated from the use he makes – for the most part in silence – of the resources of the *site*.[2] One can thus speak of a *situation analysis*[3] (as one speaks of a situation comedy) linked to the mobilisation of a *compulsion to represent* (Rolland, 2006) that is simply sustained and accompanied by stating the rule.

This compulsion occurs at all levels of psychic *représentance*,[4] from that which is nearest to the psychical delegation of id impulses, or alpha function (Bion), to that which depends on the systems (ego–superego) connected with language. It is remarkable that already in *The Interpretation of Dreams*, Freud had described an antagonistic equilibrium in the session between the narcissistic regressive tendency of figurative thought processes, attracted by hallucinatory fulfilment, and the anti-regressive tendency of objectalising speech. He did not separate, therefore, the *psychisation*[5] of the drive and the socialisation of the psyche, repudiating in advance the false dilemma between drive and object.

On the contrary, the acting out of transference marks speech with the stamp of hysterical acting. Its major concern is to introduce a portion of

---

[2] The term 'site' might perhaps have been translated as 'setting'; however, for the author, particularly as a French speaker, the word 'site' has an echo with the term *situation analytique*; and, furthermore, his original use of it carries a signification which he feels is broader than the term 'setting' (cf. Donnet, 1985). [*Trans.*]
[3] The French here is: '*analytique de situation*'. [*Trans.*]
[4] A general category including different types of representation and which implies the activity, the movement, of representation. [*Trans.*]
[5] The process of rendering psychic. [*Trans.*]

the hallucinatory charge of unconscious phantasy into speech. It is this factor that gives the analytic situation and interpretation their specific economic and dynamic dimension.

An enactment that is so charged with affective potential presupposes that all the means provided by the situation are used – that is, figurative regression, which makes the session an equivalent of the system sleep-dreams, makes use of the site, the couch and the environment, even if only in order to negativise them perceptively. Speech implies addressing the invisible other and, in so doing, makes a demand on him (Lacan), which means transference. But the enunciation invaded by acting and affect implies a transference *on to speech*: a temporary transformation of the psychic apparatus into a language apparatus (Green, 1984).

'Situation analysis' realises the singular, variable configuration of these various forms of transference, and the question of knowing whether and how transference on to the analyst may be distinguished from transference on to the analytic situation is crucial for the method and the function of thirdness.

4) If I am insisting on situation analysis, it is because the particular use the patient makes of the resources occurs relatively independently of the analyst's interventions, enabling him, in a sufficiently autonomous manner, to become an *analysand*.

We know how far attempts to teach the patient his task as an analysand, to explain how to use analysis, are more or less in vain. In order to account for an appropriation that constitutes a reinvention, it is necessary to refer to the *paradoxical nature of Winnicott's idea of 'found–created'*, which basically corresponds to the creativity involved in the spontaneity of transference.

The analyst's role in this appropriation is, first and foremost, not to hinder it; but there are no guarantees. Although one of the most constant functions of his silent listening is to be found here, it has to be noted that an 'additional' effect of interpretative interventions is to show the patient that he is using the situation advisedly, even if negatively.

Here, I am doing no more than to point out the extent of the methodological problem posed by including the interpretative function among the resources of the site, particularly where the transference interpretation uttered by the analyst is concerned.

The extent of the problem can be measured in terms of what separates, beyond their understandable differences, two extreme models:

– in the first model, which is very widespread in France, a sort of renunciation of interpreting has resulted in making the silence of the analyst's listening the essential aspect of his role;

- in the second, an intensive and systematic interpretative activity indicates a sort of *obligation* to interpret, the correlate of which is that the analyst then has to find in his theory the means to defend it.

By laying emphasis on the autonomy the patient has in making personal use of situation analysis, I certainly do not mean to justify the analyst's fetishistic silence. On the contrary, the patient's autonomy may enable the essential resource of interpretation to free itself from an obligation that meant that free association would only consent to give up control over meaning if it could be made up for later on.

In fact, interpretation, when it is mutative – whether it originates from the analysand or from the analyst – comes when it wants: it is a matter of *après-coup*, and its emergence is uncertain and unpredictable. Even if it falls within the continuity of the process, it takes effect through the discontinuity of its emergence, of its metaphorical significance. Its additional effect, then, is to rediscover, to *produce* the disjunction between the analyst as interpreter and the analyst as transference-object. This effect of creating thirdness is jeopardised, and even annulled, when the transference does not introduce an element of symbolising difference into what is being repeated. One of the fundamental questions concerning the analytic method is to know whether interpretation can make transference analysable, or if the situation must rely on presymbolic effects.

If interpretation is not to acquire the addictive value of providing meaning, it is necessary, as we have seen, that the patient has been able to invest the couple activity–passivity specific to associative activity, even when the latter serves the work of remembering, (re)constituting his own history and self-interpretation. The analysand does not attempt to apply the rule, but he reinvents it by giving meaning to the dimension of play it offers, the unknown outcome of which remains to be discovered. Perhaps he senses rather quickly that the implementation of the rule is an outcome of the process, and that its deepest implications are closely tied up with the principles of mental functioning that are the foundation of the theory of the analytic method.

The analysing situation

As it is commonly used, the term 'analytic situation' quite rightly combines the analytic action and the space-time in which it unfolds.

I think it would be useful, nonetheless, to distinguish between the analytic *site* and the analysing situation:

- the analytic site contains the ensemble of what the offer of an analysis constitutes. It includes the analyst at work.
- the analysing situation results, haphazardly, from the sufficiently adequate encounter between the patient and the site. It implies the subjectivised use, through the experience of 'found–created', of the resources of the site and their singular configuration by the patient.

Why the analysing situation?

First, this is in order to stress the depth of the metapsychological issues involved in appropriating the site and the self-representations implied: for instance, the analyst's silence sustains the crucial experience of solitude in the object's presence. But this experience is not necessarily made explicit or interpreted. As with an iceberg, only a small part of the density and complexity of the process appears on the surface. The tendency of discourse on the method is to ignore the silent process of working through on the intrapsychic level. The notion of the analytic situation is an attempt to get beyond – by integrating it – the dialectic 'transference neurosis–working alliance' in which the role played by the alliance appears to be too reasonable.

Second, it is to underline the specific functional unity constituted by the ensemble 'analysand–analyst–situation'. That is to say, a binding unity between the patient's intrapsychic processes and their externalisation on the stage of transference; but also between the mental processes of the two protagonists, to the extent of realising, through the interplay of transference and counter-transference, an activity of co-thought, a field (Baranger), a partial fusion, by bringing into play primitive identificatory processes – that is, a shared area of play.

The analytic framework makes it possible to contain the complexity of these entangled processes; however, the bilateral internalisation of what it represents symbolically is what enables it to ensure, through its materiality, the vicariousness of the element of thirdness at the height of transference–counter-transference crises and the extreme situations they give rise to (Roussillon, 1991).

Through the self-regulated interplay of these exchanges, the analytic situation takes the form of a structure integrating the analysand–analyst couple in its capacity for self-organisation, as well as the dynamic processes of its disorganisations–reorganisations.

Third, and finally, it is to indicate that this structure is the vehicle of a self-investigating dynamic, arising from the potential of the encounter. The process unfolding within the analysing situation has its own trajectory and is informed by the immanence of a terminable analysis. Ultimately, this end can only be defined by *the exhaustion of the resources of the site*, as it has been actualised, at a given moment in the relationship between such and such a patient and his analyst. This temporality, which is included in the very dynamics of the transference experience of illusion–disillusion – which is so lacking in interminable analysis – ensures the latent presence of a function creating thirdness that is actualised through interpretation.

It sheds meaning on the paradoxical words of a patient at the heart of his transference process: I come to my session to ask myself why I come. The process owes temporality its capacity to be the exploration through speaking of the transference experience (Rolland, 2006).

Addendum

In memory of S. Viderman:
To illustrate the way in which the rule works, here is a scene from the beginning of my own analysis, forty years ago: my memory of it has retained the intensity of a screen-memory.

1) It concerns a session that was to end at eight p.m. Sensing or anticipating that it was about to end, I stopped talking. In the silence, the church tower nearby marked out eight strokes. The sign I was expecting was not forthcoming, and instead my anxiety increased. I exclaimed: But I don't want you to give me more than my time. I was both surprised and reassured by what I had just said. My analyst then ended the session.
2) I would like to draw attention here to those aspects of my recollection that remain for me the most striking.

    a) the *contrast*, first of all, between my conviction that I had used the situation in a way that was both new, improvised and in accordance with its potentialities and, what was for me, the altogether enigmatic dimension of the scene. This contrast shows that the feeling of being an analysand is not necessarily linked to providing meaning through interpretation;
    b) my conviction was based, on the spur of the moment, on the actualisation of all the different elements of the site – that is, the framework (the set time for ending the session); the setting (the scene is unthinkable without the couch and the immanence of the standing position); the analyst (the supposed guardian of the framework and object of the transference); and finally, the rule (I will come back to this).
    This unexpected conjunction of circumstances gave me the feeling that I was the author of the whole scene, that I had created what was already there.
    c) My conviction was also based on the memory-trace of the transformation that had occurred and been provoked by my enunciation:

at the beginning, I was addressing my analyst through action; at the end, I felt that my enunciation had emerged from somewhere far off and had touched me closely, but it was enigmatic and not unpleasant; I can recall just how much the experience of this process needed the support of the analyst's silence.

3) Some comments retrospectively:

a) Later on in my analysis, as a result of interpretation and working through, I was able to discover the various facets of the seduction fantasy of/by the adult that had been actualised on the stage of transference and expressed transparently under the cover of negation. It was no easier to integrate the traumatic resonance of the eight strokes of the clock, evoking the inexorability of time, separation and death.

It seemed to me, then, that in the scene, what I had said had had the effect, through my identification with the voice of the superego ideal, of making me the one who decided the moment of ending in order to avoid being subjected to it.

My pleasant feeling of being an analysand was perhaps above all an expression of my satisfaction at having taken the place of the one who was safeguarding the frame. Was this a maniacal defence or an experience of 'found–created'?

In any case, the analysand's autonomy cannot be located – any more than the working alliance – outside the field of transference and its interpretation. It can, occasionally, be interpreted as a defence against the experience of dependency; but who would this interpretation be addressed to if this transference dependency were not given metaphorical form by the transference itself?

b) In the scene itself I did not say (scrupulously) to my analyst, 'I am feeling anxious about the idea that . . .', and even less 'I have just had the fantasy that . . .'. My enunciation had the status of acting out. How, then, did this form of acting out use the analytic situation more fully than the two others that would have been the expression of an insight?

First of all it involved the experience of confusing, projectively, the analyst with the other – whoever it was who wanted to keep me – before I refound the person of whom I would not have gone as far as saying that I 'had always known' that he was going to end the session, and that by identifying with me, he was leaving me the time to say: nothing can replace the fact that returning to oneself comes about by making a detour through the other (Green, 1981).

It was also the complexity of what was happening in the gap between psychic factuality (the affect of silence, hearing the clock, increasing anxiety) and speech:

- first, the anxiety was enigmatic and the enunciation ego-syntonic (I know what I do not want);
- second, my enunciation, which relieved my anxiety (repression), then became enigmatic and, in this sense, it was offered to the analyst by the analysand. It assumed the value of a *signifier*. It is the ensemble of this 'mix-up' that has an irreplaceable subjectivising significance.

The underlying issue here is that of a privileged mode of overcoming the barrier of repression: from the point of view of interpretation, this is accomplished through the associative linking occurring between anxiety and the denied representation of a demand for love. But compared with a mere insight, acting out involves an instinctual introjection; it transfers on to the act of speaking the hallucinatory power inherent in the unconscious wishful fantasy. *Speaking hysterically is an ersatz for hallucinatory satisfaction.*

The transference actualisation underlies the possibility of conceiving the effect of interpretation as being similar to a *wave of symbolisation*, containing an optimal conjunction of force and meaning.

References

Bion, W. R. (1970). *Attention and Interpretation.* London: Tavistock Publications; reprinted London: Karnac, 1984.
Donnet, J.-L. (1985). *Le divan bien tempéré* [The well-tempered couch]. Paris: Presses Universitaires de France.
Freud, S. (1900a). *The Interpretation of Dreams. S.E.*, 4/5.
Freud, S. (1912b). The Dynamics of Transference. *S.E.*, 12.
Freud, S. (1914g). Remembering, Repeating and Working-Through. *S.E.*, 12.
Freud, S. (1916–17). *Introductory Lectures on Psycho-Analysis. S.E.*, 16.
Freud, S. (1920g). *Beyond the Pleasure Principle. S.E.*, 18.
Freud, S. (1923a [1922]). Two Encyclopaedia Articles. *S.E.*, 18.
Green, A. (1973). *The Fabric of Affect in the Psychoanalytic Discourse.* London: Routledge, 1999.
Green, A. (1981). Vue de la Société Psychanalytique de Paris. Une conception de la pratique. *Revue Française de Psychanalyse, 52*: 569–593.
Green, A. (1984). *Le langage dans la psychanalyse* [Language in psychoanalysis]. Paris: Les Belles Lettres.
Green, A. (1989). Du tiers, de la tiercéité. In *La psychanalyse, questions pour demain* [Psychoanalysis: Questions for tomorrow] (pp. 243–279). Paris: Presses Univeritaires de France, 1990.
Green, A. (1993). *Le travail du négatif.* Paris: Editions de Minuit. [*The Work of the Negative*, trans. A. Weller. London: Free Association Books, 1999.]
Lacan, J. (1961). La direction de la cure et les principes de son pouvoir. In *Ecrits*. Paris: Editions du Seuil, 1966. [The Direction of the Treatment and the Principles of Its Power. In *Ecrits* (pp. 489–542), trans. A. Sheridan. London: Tavistock, 1977.]

Macalpine, I. (1950). The Development of the Transference. *Psychoanalytic Quarterly*, *19*: 501–539.
Rolland, J.-C. (2006). *Avant d'être celui qui parle* [Before being the person who speaks]. Paris: Gallimard.
Roussillon, R. (1991). *Paradoxes et situations limites de la psychanalyse* [Paradoxes and borderline situations in psychoanalysis]. Paris: Presses Universitaires de France.

7 PRELIMINARY REMARKS ON THE PRESENT STATE OF PSYCHOANALYSIS OF CHILDREN[1]

René Diatkine

> **René Diatkine** (1918–1997) trained as a psychiatrist before becoming a full member, and then president, of the Paris Psychoanalytical Society. He was also a professor at the University of Geneva (1972–1995), then professor *honoris causa* (1991). His far-reaching work prepared the ground for child analysis. In 1958, with S. Lebovici and P. Paumelle, he created the Mental Health Association of the 13th *arrondissement* of Paris and, in 1963, with S. Lebovici, founded the Alfred Binet Centre. He created the journal of that Centre, *Les Cahiers du Centre A. Binet*, and in 1964 he was the initiator of the Symposium of the Paris Psychoanalytical Society, held each year in Deauville.
>
> He founded several major series such as *La Psychiatrie de l'enfant* (PUF, 1958) with S. Lebovici and R. Crémieux and added a sub-collection, devoted to working with children, to the 'Fil Rouge' series (PUF) with J. Ajuriaguerra and S. Lebovici.
>
> The book he wrote with J. Simon, *La Psychanalyse précoce* [Psychoanalysis with young children] (PUF, 1972) is a landmark work because it gives the reader a true understanding of the psychoanalytic process in children. With M. Soulé and S. Lebovici, he wrote a *Nouveau traité de psychiatrie de l'enfant et de l'adolescent* [A new treatise on child and adolescent psychiatry] (3 vols., PUF, 1985, 1996).
>
> Florence Quartier-Frings wrote a concise biography of René Diatkine for the 'Psychanalystes d'aujourd'hui' series (PUF, 1997).

In the last few decades, the application of psychoanalysis to children has been considerably extended in several directions. Psychoanalytic treatment of children has increased in accordance with the theoretical and technical options of the various schools of thought, while the psychoanalytic comprehension of mental functioning has added a new meaning to child psychiatry as well as to

---

[1] Presented at a Symposium on 'The Role of Child Analysis in the Formation of the Psychoanalyst', organised by the European Psychoanalytical Federation, Geneva, 27 and 28 June 1970.

pedagogy. If nowadays no one doubts the importance of the contribution of the psychoanalysis of children to the elaboration of psychoanalytic theory – the vehemence of discussion on this subject is testimony enough – the modes of application of psychoanalysis to children have at times evoked a certain suspicion among analysts who, for various reasons, wondered if one could legitimately retain the term 'psychoanalysis' for techniques that did not seem to follow the adult psychoanalytic cure on certain decisive points.

The difficulties brought out by the application of psychoanalysis to other disciplines concerning the child reinforced this doubt. The limit was no longer clear between the technical variations indispensable in the application of psychoanalysis to children and the psychotherapeutic or educational uses entrusted to specialists of various formations who utilise psychoanalytic concepts but risk introducing important distortions if they do not practise psychoanalysis. This risk has not gone unnoticed by any of the schools of child psychoanalysis and has resulted in a deepening of the theory, as well as a growing concern for the proper formation of child analysts. In the long run these difficulties have been a factor of progress, and we meet together today to evaluate this progress and the prospects deriving from it.

Let us not forget, however, that the problems which we shall debate have practically all been brought up since the publication in 1909 of the Little Hans case history (Freud, 1909b). His father's very special attitude and interventions aroused a mobilisation of forces which are analogous to the psychoanalytic process, but this analogy posed serious problems from the very first. The use of the father as a therapist throws us directly back to the controversy of a child's capacity to develop a transference relation.

However, it allowed an immediate demonstration of the particular interest for the development of psychoanalytic theory of the interpretation of the latent content in the child's productions (symptoms, dreams, fantasies). As you well know, this child had been the subject of what we call today a 'direct observation', and the information gathered by the parents had only been used by Freud as a testimony confirming the theory of child sexuality worked out from adult material, when in fact the analysis of the phobia of this young boy had directly contributed new material vital in the development of psychoanalysis.

It seems to us that a discussion on the actual positions of child psychoanalysis should go along the following points: (1) the specificity of the psychoanalytic process in the child; (2) the finality of this process, which implies definite positions concerning the problem of the indication for psychoanalysis with children as well as with regard to the use of the concepts of 'normality' or 'pathology'; (3) the comparison between the psychoanalytic process in the child and the psychotherapeutic effects of other techniques: action on the environment, psychotherapeutic, educational and re-educational activities. The mechanism of these effects is to be seen in the light of psychoanalysis.

Specificity of the psychoanalytic process in the child

For a long time, emphasis was put on the fact that a child is rarely conscious of suffering from his own mental functions, which already differentiates him from the adult. In the latter, the desire to be cured would constitute an important factor of the 'therapeutical alliance', generally understood to be necessary in order to begin the analytic process. But if one goes beyond the phenomenological aspect of the 'consciousness of being ill' or the desire to be cured, the opposition between adult and child is less clear-cut than it would seem at first sight. The adult patient has no consciousness of the benefits drawn from his symptoms and from his initial mode of mental functioning. If he desires to be rid of some embarrassing manifestation, if he expects to be able to accomplish some of his remote desires, he has indeed no way of realising what analysis could do for him; one of the effects of elaboration through interpretation is to allow him to discover a possibility of a new functioning and a new 'ego pleasure'. The same is true of the child. However conscious of his difficulties he may be, he expects nothing from the psychoanalyst and immediately displaces on to him a cathexis which is the product of his earlier experiences. The negative aspect of this cathexis is emphasised and facilitated by the fact that, although the analyst may be a person very much like his parents, he is not actually one of them.

But each new experience cannot be reduced to a simple repetition, and from the very first session, psychoanalysis presents the child with an experience that is as new and original as for the adult patient: someone – and what is more, an adult – will devote his attention to him unconditionally for a constant length of time and, moreover, without accompanying that interest with the usual conditions of demands and restraints which usually define the child–adult relationship. Let us underline at once the conditions of 'neutral benevolence' that are special to the young child. In adult psychoanalysis, listening in itself constitutes an intense as well as an unusual mark of interest, a sign of being cathected by another person forever nostalgically awaited as corresponding to the primary narcissistic fantasy – whereas giving attention to the child's play, taking him into consideration, demands a certain participation in his play that is rather incompatible with the immobile and relaxed position of the adult psychoanalyst. One can be an excellent adult psychoanalyst and yet be bored with looking at a child who plays or draws. This boredom, which the child always senses, puts him back in a well-known situation: the psychoanalyst will have 'played the game' of the child, in the connotation used by Fenichel (1945, 1953–54), and will thereby himself have barred the development of the psychoanalytic process. If the need to play easily with children does not permit one and all to become child psychoanalysts, it is nevertheless certain that this activity, which is unusual within the framework of the 'neutral benevolence', makes the practice of our profession especially difficult. This situation produces effects of countertransference that can hinder the psychoanalytic process just as easily. In any case, our practice requires an elaborated comprehension, not only of the unconscious meaning of the child's production, but of the essence of the psychoanalytic process in the child and what for him should be the working-through process, the '*Durcharbeiten*'.

The possibility of inferring the latent content of the child's production already constitutes a decisive step, and in spite of diverging opinions which persisted for a long time, this new possibility of comprehending the child's drawings and games represented for the psychoanalysis of children a historical role comparable to that of *The Interpretation of Dreams* (1900a). But our capacity to apprehend the unconscious fantasies must not detract our attention from the conditions of elaboration of the child's manifest production during the sessions. One can no longer maintain that children's psychological conflicts are principally determined by their parents' sexual taboos and their refusal to approach the subject with their child; thus one must not see in the child's production a disguised attempt to enter a forbidden dialogue, but, on the contrary, the visible result of an ego activity tending to control the situation in a quite different way.

Whether or not the child suffers from his mental functioning prior to psychoanalysis, this close exchange with an adult who takes an interest in him puts into question his processes of regulation, dependent on the pleasure principle and its corollary, the reality principle. The usual attitude of adults in care of a child tends to favour – if only by stimulating his projections through demands and restraints – his process of defences and the counter-cathexis allowing the repression of the drive representatives, whereas the attitude of the child psychoanalyst has the opposite effect, which immediately mobilises the functioning of the patient's ego.

This results in a movement which can follow in two directions: the first is determined by the tendency to repetition, in an effort to master the object projected on the psychoanalyst so as to draw him into a familiar situation. The child can thus multiply his provocations in order to make the psychoanalyst finally respond by a restraint or a demand and in so doing react as everybody else. The other tendency is a new ego production permitting a better repression of unconscious desires stimulated by the gain of libido deriving from the privileged situation of the child in relation to this adult who takes him into consideration. The child's play, whatever its form, must, from this viewpoint, be considered as a reaction formation destined to maintain far from his consciousness the drives and cathected representations, the activity of which is to be spotted by the psychoanalyst through the comprehension of the latent content in terms of which the drawing and playing are organised. These two tendencies are not exclusive of each other, especially as the child dealing with symbols (when drawing or handling toys) believes at first that what he expresses has no meaning for him and hence that he is not doing or thinking what should be expected of him.

One could be satisfied with giving the child this experience and believe that the unconditional benevolence of the adult faced with these transgressions would provoke a *corrective emotional experience*, and we shall see that some approaches aiming at a psychotherapeutic goal go no further. But if the tendency to repetition predominates, more and more provocative acting outs will greatly undermine the situation by forcing the therapist to abandon his permissiveness or by giving the situation a quality of strange unreality devoid of all therapeutic value. In other cases, the repressive effect of the play activity can succeed, i.e. can provoke a progressive withdrawal of cathexis from the situation and the therapist; it is just another way of rendering void the specificity of the experience. We shall return, in the third part of this paper, to those psychotherapies which use absence of constraint as the only therapeutic agent.

The child's productions during sessions initially permit him to control affects which threaten to overwhelm him in this close relationship, unavoidably felt as an experience not very far from a seduction. Consequently, it is not surprising that we should find in it a symbolic representation of the primal scene, a latent content easy to recognise behind its manifest content, whether it concerns games with small cars or with animals or drawings of houses and any other maternal symbols.

Since the repressed drive representatives include regressive elements as well as highly evolved elements, the reaction formation which develops during the session is heavily overdetermined. From this point of view, the child's play and his drawings are to be elaborated in analysis, as is the manifest content of dreams, taking into account the effect of primary and secondary processes in the transformation, thus allowing passage from the material produced in session to unconscious fantasies. Moreover, it can easily be shown that the characters and symbols are the product of the process of displacement and especially *condensation*, thus all interpretative attempts resembling a distribution of roles as in an imaginary theatre run the risk of bringing the situation to a dead-point, impoverishing it and thereby preventing the psychoanalyst from following the unfolding of the transference, thanks to mechanisms of defence common to both child and therapist.

On the contrary, the most immediate effect of an elaboration of the manifold meanings and structure of the child's play and drawings is to give him the feeling of a certain gratuitousness of his production, which, besides, facilitates it. The child feels both implicated and relatively free (this being a general characteristic of play activity). He draws from this situation a certain pleasure, completing the one described above. It is no longer thinkable to use this pleasure in order to seduce the child by offering him an exceptional play material. Now the interventions of the psychoanalyst will permit the play activities to become meaningful for the child in relation to his own history and his own conscious and unconscious mental functioning. The modes of approach differ according to the theoretical concepts of the psychoanalyst concerning the child's psychic organisation. Some, for example, would point out to the child that a specific character in the game or the drawing could have feelings similar to his own, thus establishing a relationship between the imaginary output and the psychic reality of the child. Others would insist on the necessity of rapidly interpreting unconscious fantasies in their aspect most conducive to anxiety. Naturally, these divergences in technique do nothing but mask differences in interpretation concerning concepts of object relation and transference. But it is worthwhile to question the general effects of elaboration through interpretation, while remaining conscious of the fact that this question brings up more difficulties in child than in adult psychoanalysis. The words of the psychoanalyst provoke a mobilisation of preconscious ideoverbal associations, and it is through this mobilisation that the differences in unconscious cathexis can occur. The usual poverty of verbal associations expressed by the child results in this relative obscurity for the psychoanalyst. This leads to a seeming solution of continuity between the words of the psychoanalyst and their observable effect on the patient. To perceive what the child has heard already necessitates an elaboration in which the theoretical options play a decisive role at once.

This point being stated, let us question ourselves on the dynamic and economic effect of the interventions and interpretations. What happens, in particular, in the best cases where their effect tends to diminish the isolation of the play material? How can one distinguish in child psychoanalysis a fruitful interpretation from a 'wild' one? An interesting clue to this discussion is the above hypothesis which gave to the child's production in the session the value of a reaction formation. The repression of the drives mobilised by the psychoanalytic situation indicates the very early existence of a superego aggressing the ego and forcing it to elaborate the play compromise within which the repression can be maintained. We shall not enter here into a detailed discussion about the nature of this early superego, prior to the final introjection of the Oedipal image. Whatever the age of the child, psychoanalytic practice shows that this persecuting agency is projected on to the analyst, all the more intensely as he is at the same time the object of libidinal cathexis. Our own experience, as well as what we can learn from published reports of cures carried out by others, leads us to believe that the interventions which bear upon the fantasied dangers of being aggressed by the psychoanalyst and which lead the child, through their verbalisation, to elaborate this danger in a new way allow the patient's ego to cease functioning in a repetitive way and to elaborate new modes of functioning that are expressed by new productions and a certain interest on the part of the child in his own mental activities. The new pleasure from this situation results in a tendency entirely specific to the psychoanalytic cure when once truly established; it is a tendency towards the introjection of the psychoanalyst who gives interpretations. Whether these are at first consciously considered by the child as strange though fascinating words, whether they are rapidly invested in a very ambivalent way – 'Don't say "nervous" words to me today', said a 4-year-old girl to her analyst – or whether they are in the end the means of apprehending psychic reality, the impact of interpretations (and interventions, which, however, have at times a limited manifest content) gives an indispensable clue to distinguish child psychoanalysis and psychotherapy.

Not all the interventions inducing a modification of the associative process and of what is expressed in relation to the therapist have an identical value; thus the interpretation of certain deeply guilty, unconscious desires reinforces at times very evidently the projections of the superego on to the therapist, which leads to a rejection of his words. Such reinforcements of negative transference are inevitable, but if they are the exclusive reactions of the child to interpretations, this situation can constitute an insurmountable obstacle to the unfolding of the analytic process.

The introjection of the interpreting analyst reinforces the libidinal aspect of transference in both its object and its narcissistic dimensions, thereby showing its importance in the actualisation and accentuation of conflicts. It plays a role identical to the narcissistic elation at the beginning of the cure; whereas the latter could turn short by the arousal of usual defensive processes, the opposition between the new factors and the repetitive and regressive tendencies permits the pursuit of the elaboration through interpretation.

Let us not forget that this opposition between progredient elements (specific to the unusual situation in analysis) and repetitive factors has already been underlined by all those who have studied transference in adults. Beyond the obvious and visible differences, this analogy should be stressed.

It is important that from the very beginning of the cure the psychoanalyst should be for the child the source of both pleasure and aggression and that this ambivalence should not cease to develop thereafter. This ambivalent cathexis of a single person traces back to the establishment of the object relation in its continuity and to the defensive processes used by the child in order to escape passive dependence in relation to this object. The outcome of the relation with the psychoanalyst and its effects on the mental functioning of the child as a whole depends on the new capacity of the libidinal drives, partially turned to the service of the ego, to modify the destructive drives. As usually happens from the very first object relation, one of the principal mechanisms will be the separation of the sources of pleasure and unpleasure. This phenomenon of relative isolation can take on various aspects, depending upon the child's preceding development and the elaboration through interpretation. But the fact that the child finds in the words of his analyst, besides any repetitive process, a new source of pleasure at the level of his ego allows him to differentiate the two terms of the ambivalence and to acquire a certain control over this contradiction. It is precisely when this control is lacking that a certain way of splitting the object transforms the psychoanalyst into a phobic object and the child's usual environment into a counterphobic object; clearly, then, such a situation makes the unfolding of the analytic process difficult. On the other hand, the interpretations permit the child to elaborate the double cathexis of the psychoanalyst, both as a libidinal object and as a forbidding agency. The Oedipal triangle is all the more easily spotted in the productions permitting the child to elaborate acceptable compromises in the session, as the process of introjection of the psychoanalyst will have developed by the effect of the interpretations.

We must now make a brief theoretical return to the organisation of the child's object relations, in order to avoid excessive disagreements or misunderstandings over the subject of transference. From the time the object relation takes on its basic characteristic of continuity – a single form perceived as external to the subject is the source of both pleasure and displeasure, and these affects develop through the continuity of self – the processes of displacement, of introjection and projection, thanks to which the displeasure is brought back to its lowest level, organise an intricate system of cathexis, making very precociously necessary the distinction between the metapsychological concepts of objects, imagos and cathected persons. Very soon, the parents themselves become differentiated from the parental imagos, if only because of their structuring and repairing role. The parents' educational role could be evaluated with regard to the possibilities which they offer the child to deal with his parental imagos. The cathexis of all new persons entering the child's environment is the result of a projection of his internal objects.

As we have seen, at the beginning of the analysis the cathexis of the analyst is only a special case of this general way of mental functioning. The specificity of the transference, allowing a new control over the ambivalence, is the product of the activity of the analyst. This capacity for transference is accepted today as being very precocious. The ways and means of transference are modified when the introjection of the superego at the peak of the Oedipal complex marks the beginning of the latency period, but the tendency to project imagos already internalised can be seen in analysis carried out with the youngest children.

Because of the manifold sources of the child's production in the session, the choice of meanings to be interpreted to the child has often been discussed. Rather than restrict ourselves to topographical metaphors which are all partly true – interpreting at the level of the ego, of consciousness or, on the contrary, at the very core of anxiety – we have already seen that the dynamic and economic effect of interpretations on the conflict between the ego and the superego has permitted us a certain understanding of the action of these interventions. In line with this, one should not forget that the appearance of anxiety is determined by the contradiction between the diverse systems. Thus the secondary Oedipal identifications are held in check by the desire to incorporate the objects belonging to the image to which the child attempts to identify himself. By the action of pre-genital regressions the identifications of the phallic stage are rendered precarious and the fantasies proceeding therefrom represent the dramatisation of the conflict between the ego and the superego, be it during the first years of life or during the latency period. Therefore, child psychoanalysts often attend particularly to the elaboration of these very conflicts, in spite of their differences in theoretical orientation.

In adult psychoanalysis, remembrance of the past is considered one of the important dimensions of the psychoanalytic process. This recollection certainly has its limits; certain important stages of the past are reconstructed only through screen memories or fantasies. It also frequently happens that the childhood amnesia is not completely overcome, but that the analytic work nevertheless ends with the disappearance of a certain isolating process which had prevented the patient from valuing an event whose formal remembrance only persisted, the affects linked with it having been forgotten, i.e. repressed. For the adult, the thread of the forgotten drama is his child neurosis and a result of this past drama, present anxieties partly take on their meaning. The situation is different with children. The psychoanalyst often has the impression of being confronted with the result of a preceding elaboration, in relation to the child's past, if only because of the coherence in the latent content of the child's productions. But, at the same time, the actualisation within the transference situation leads to interpretations in the present, whether in reference to transference or to the relation with the parental imagos. Indeed, this past seems present. In spite of the differentiation between objects, imagos and parents in their existence exterior to the patient, the past seems forever present, probably because of the structuring role of the parents, as we have outlined above. A certain tendency to minimise the importance of the original situations has always existed, especially in child psychoanalysis, since for the adult the child neurosis and the Oedipal complex constitute a sufficient reference to the past. But this tendency does not modify in any way the actualisation; at times it might lead to a simplification of the theoretical understanding of the concept of regression and to certain facilities in the reconstruction of the past which not everyone could approve of.

In any case, this form of psychoanalysis in the present brings out important differences between child and adult psychoanalysis, since the former is not based upon remembrance either at the stage of the constitution of the Oedipal complex or at the latency period. Just as in the first dream of the adult, the psychoanalyst perceives in the first games or drawings of the child the product of his unconscious fantasies, at their most evolved as well as at their most regressive level. Through the elaboration of the reciprocal relations of the phallic and pre-genital expression of the Oedipal complex, by the remembrance of the past – recognised as such by the young patient – the psychoanalytic process will evolve.

If one takes into account the modifications of transference provoked by each intervention, one realises the importance of studying closely the goals pursued in a psychoanalytic cure during which the past is not recalled and the future is so distant that it remains purely conjectural. Before asking ourselves when a child can be considered sufficiently analysed, it is indeed indispensable to ask ourselves what we are seeking to obtain.

The finality of the analytic process in the child

If the consideration of evolution and regression of the id and the ego permits the understanding of the variations in mental functioning, one must not tend to schematise in an evolutionistic way the appreciation of the unfolding of psychoanalysis. Child psychoanalysis does not suppress the tendency to regression. The modification in the cathexis of the original repressions can make the power of attraction of the points of fixation less intense, without suppressing them entirely. On the other hand, the mobilisation of the child's ego before the reactivation of the partial drives modifies itself, and in this sense the only criteria for the success of child psychoanalysis is the patient's recovery of a better developmental capacity. A metapsychological definition of the finality of child analysis – that is, the metapsychological conditions of this developmental recovery – should be agreed upon if a coherent theory of the technique is to be elaborated.

With the child, even more than with the adult, one must give up aphorisms such as 'to render conscious what is unconscious'. Such an expression does not take into account what we now know about mental functioning. It is well known that early child treatments follow the fate of child amnesia and that in the latency period the activity of secondary repression has the same effect on the child's conscious discoveries of unconscious meanings; this repression will grow in intensity as the patient progresses. Child analysis must be studied in relation to its effect upon the ego. But one must not be satisfied with vague and purely symptomatic descriptions found in various authors. Failing the usual aphorism applied to adults – love and social success – one frequently finds still more imprecise formulae implicating a symptomatic recovery or a modification of behaviour: better playing capacity, better school work, improved possibilities of making friends, etc. Such successes are in no way significant in the child whose symptoms disappear spontaneously during growth and whose behaviour can be modified by various psychotherapeutic or educative measures.

Another criterion that is valid for adult analysis but cannot be applied to child analysis is the disappearance of the transference neurosis. It is one of the particularities most generally recognised in the child's transference not to be brought to an end in a correct way. The latter would indeed demand a capacity for autonomy and a control over regressions of which the child, by his very nature, is not capable. If certain analyses are interrupted by the prevalence of negative transference, experience shows that in other cases, once the treatment is ended, the analyst remains an idealised figure long after the child has forgotten the content of the sessions. Furthermore, it is to be noticed that for many authors and in many articles, child analysis ends because of external circumstances and rarely through the analyst's having decided that the cure has come to term. At times the disappearance of the child's symptoms and the improvement of his behaviour lead the parents to interrupt the treatment on the pretence of normalising the child's social life. If one is to arrive at a certain rigour in the descriptions of the psychoanalytic process, i.e. its finality, it is necessary to return to the initial elements that led to the decision to start an analysis. We shall not study here the psychoanalytic cure at the end of the latency period and in adolescence. Indeed, at that age the patient's suffering and the organisation of his personality allow only a relatively narrow range of developments and thus permit one to specify the indications for psychoanalysis much as one would for the adult. With the younger child, whether at the period of the organisation of the Oedipal complex or at the latency period, the eruption of symptoms does not make psychoanalysis indispensable, since their more or less spectacular aspect has no prognostic value. We think that what constitutes one of the most important prognostic criteria is the ego's capacity to organise new activities or, on the contrary, its tendency to exhaust itself within repetitive defensive processes. Most of the indications of child analysis show this necessary modification in the relative equilibrium of these two tendencies of the ego.

Symptom formations must be studied in relation to their effect on the entire mental functioning. From this viewpoint, traditional symptomatology is certainly misleading, since the important thing is not to recognise the existence of such a phobia or such a compulsion, but to detect its effects. There are cases where the organisation of symptoms allows a focalisation of anxiety leaving the child a certain liberty in cathexis, thus contributing to the modification of the cathexis of internal objects, whereas with other children all the libidinal energy is absorbed by the symptom, which remains the only source of pleasure for the ego. Such a situation reinforces fixations and renders the developmental possibilities precarious.

This mode of approach to various ways of the child's mental malfunctioning permits one to understand the effect of the above-described analytic process. The capacity for elaboration resulting from the introjection of the interpreting analyst opens a way to new ego activities. In this light it is clear that no child arrives at a capacity for self-analysis, long considered as one of the goals of adult analysis, but that the development of a certain *insight* and above all of the new pleasure found by the child in this interest in his inner reality must be considered as one of the most positive results to be obtained in child analysis. The denial of the inner reality recognised as such is not only due to the prevalence of manic defences; it is often the consequence of projection, one of the foremost mechanisms of the latency period. If this projection permits an unconditional submission of the ego to the superego – the young patient feels innocent and persecuted by the others, especially by ill-willed adults – the persistence of the passivity implied by this position reinforces the patient's fantasies of powerlessness, from castration anxieties all the way to the deepest depressive tendencies. This position certainly constitutes the starting point of the most stubborn resistances to psychoanalysis, and the elaboration in psychoanalysis must tend towards the overcoming of these resistances. According to us, if the disappearance of symptoms and the progress in behaviour cannot in themselves be considered as the goal in child analysis, the appearance of this insight certainly seems to be a sign of the greatest importance. We have described above the double movement which results from this insight: whereas the ego arrives at new compromises, the awakening of the libido related to this introjection leads to new anxieties and regressions. If the elaboration through interpretation is correctly pursued, these new conflicts are progressively mastered by the ego, and this mastery, by reinforcing the introjection of the psychoanalyst, prepares the possibility for terminating the analysis, in spite of what we have said about the impossibility of completely liquidating the transference. The transformation of ego activity is often perceptible at the beginning of the cure, but a premature interruption would throw the child back to his previous mode of functioning, for the loss of the analyst would reawaken the most anxiety-laden fantasies and confer a negative value on the words of the analyst. Insight then disappears with the analyst, and the child has no recollection of the experience.

We believe that to end analysis in good conditions is possible only if one takes into account the new dynamic and economic activities which the child organises outside of treatment, owing to the progress of analysis. An example would be the non-compulsive development of cognitive activities and epistemophilic tendencies during the latency period. They are not a goal in themselves, but are witness to a certain freedom of the ego, and, besides, the resulting pleasure permits a better distribution of pleasant and unpleasant affects. But, realistically, one must admit that this movement towards identification, which we have spoken of as the introjection of the analyst giving interpretations, is only found in cures which evolve in the most favourable conditions, and that without this identification, the development of *insight* – which we have defined as specific to the psychoanalysis of children – does not occur. Such treatments can nevertheless have a beneficial effect not only on the child's mental functioning, but on his future development, and we are quite naturally led to question ourselves on the comparative mode of action of psychotherapies and other psychological therapies upon the child.

Psychoanalysis of children, psychotherapy, environmental modifications, educative and re-educative measures

While all treatments aspiring to be authentic child analyses are not able to set in motion a psychoanalytic process such as we have described above, nevertheless beneficial effects are often observed in cures during which the child has apparently acquired little or at times no insight. It is about such cures that the theory of the techniques becomes less precise and their differentiation from the psychotherapeutic practices becomes unclear. And yet, there are numerous cases where the therapeutic effect is not only the disappearance of symptoms, but also an obvious modification of the evolution of mental functioning.

Thus, we must question ourselves upon the action of such a process. On this subject, two proposals can be formulated:

a. In all psychotherapy, as in all psychoanalytic attempts, the consideration of the child's mental productions creates an entirely new situation, occasioning a narcissistic gain which constitutes the moving force of the therapeutic situation. As we shall see, this acceptance of the child as a valid party is a general condition in all therapeutic or educational efforts. But in child analysis, as well as in all psychoanalytic psychotherapy, the product of the elaboration of fantasies (i.e. the result of the ego's effort at arriving at a compromise between the pressures of the id and the demands of the superego) is the object of the therapist's attention. A possibility for identification of a very specific nature is hence opened, thereby modifying the submissiveness of the ego to the superego.
b. We have described above the rebound of this economic modification: the actualisation of conflicts and the reinforcing of the tendency to repeat, both resulting in important regressions. Faced with this surge of anxiety, the ego tends to break off with the new situation and reconstitute its habitual former relationships. In order for the relation with this new person to be therapeutic, the break must not be actualised, either by an interruption of treatment or by the withdrawal of cathexis of the therapist. Two ways are open. We have seen how the psychoanalytic process permits the child's ego actively to secure the continuity of the transference relation. In all cases where this ego activity is not the obvious result of the analytic elaboration, it is the therapist's activity that makes up for it. We shall not describe here the various procedures usually put into practice, especially as the manifest expression of the therapist's activity is probably less important than the reality of his interest for the child's production and for the cure. In this connection, one can note that certain interventions, more or less repetitiously offered, provoke modifications of the associative flow without at any moment seeming to be truly internalised by the child, without arousing denial or the patient's interest. And yet the effect of this interpretative activity is far from being constant. In the best of cases, the child undeniably reacts to the libidinal gain conveyed by the interpretation, a proof of the therapist's sustained interest. Certainly it is difficult to demonstrate the exact means through which this continuous action modifies the subject's structural equilibrium because of the child's scarce verbalisation and lack of insight. The importance of the cathexis of the situation by the therapist, on the other hand, is easily demonstrable. Indeed, interpretations, pertinent though they may be in their content, but repeated without conviction by a therapist for whom they represent only dry

intellectual formulae used according to abstract indications, only convey an aggressive charge. They have no therapeutic effect because, without realising it, the therapist falls in with the unconscious demands of the child. Hence the evolution of psychotherapy or psychoanalytic attempts which do not arrive at a true psychoanalytic process depends on two factors: the intensity of the child's tendencies to regression and repetition, and the therapist's capacity to resist these tendencies and maintain the relation at an equal level.

Another frequently observed pattern should also be studied. At times both the child and the adult arrive at a compromise permitting them both to find sufficient guilt-free pleasure in the therapeutic relation. This pattern can be found within the treatments of psychotherapists or psychoanalysts of several schools of thought. A certain complicity can be established at the level of the interpretation – when the latter tends over-systematically to respect the conflicts most charged with anxiety – or at the level of the child's production, his games and drawings. The child is very glad to come to his sessions and at times expresses very positive feelings for the therapist. The situation is then very comparable to certain resistances through transference described in adult analysis. And yet, the effect of these compromises is not as radically negative as with adults, to the extent that this complicity can favour the identification mentioned above. But it is clear that if the patient's mental structure can progress owing to the dynamic and economic effects of this identification, this progress only manifests itself very slowly within the sessions themselves. It is as if the therapeutic relation constituted a new symptom, allowing the focalisation of anxiety and thus the perturbed development to take a new course. But the ritualisation of the sessions for long renders them static. In many similar cases, the treatment is interrupted, either by the child himself for whom this neo-symptom is no longer necessary, or by the parents, who, in certain cases, rejoice in the child's progress or, in others less fortunate, find a pretext in the relative stagnancy of the situation.

We shall review briefly the possibilities of action upon the environment. We shall only mention a few obvious truths, which nevertheless cannot be passed in silence. All action limited to the child presupposes that, in one way or another, he will be able to generalise the results of the experience – limited in time and space – of his association with a psychoanalyst or a psychotherapist. For this generalisation to take place, the patient's ego must be capable of a certain activity and autonomy. It is our belief that this tendency towards autonomy manifests itself very early, as soon as the child struggles by his own means against his submission to the object, a submission that represents a continual threat of depression. Because of this hypothesis, we believe child psychoanalysis to be often necessary and at times possible.

It is nevertheless true that for a long time the child remains subjected to the structuring parental influence, whose effect is determined by their system of object and narcissistic cathexis as a whole. This structuring effect can go in the direction of the psychoanalytic or psychotherapeutic process, but more often it acts in just the opposite way.

Everyone agrees that a psychotherapeutic approach of the parents is necessary, except, of course, when one treats exclusively the children of psychoanalysts themselves, whose own analysis should suffice. In spite of the fact that at times undertaking a treatment can modify the most profound parental attitudes in a favourable way by restoring their hope – that is, by permitting them to find once more their lost ego ideal – experience shows that, more often, unforeseeable reactions occur that get in the way of the child's treatment. We shall only mention here two points that seem to us essential.

Whatever the child's state of dependency, the parents must not be confused with the child's parental imagos. They can play a most important restorative or traumatic role, but they are not the original 'objects' of the child, for the elaboration of object relations begins very early. The effect of therapy must be to give them the possibility of a better restorative action; it must not aim at the utopian goal of making them conform to an image of ideal parents.

Their profound attitude and their system of projection on the child are taken over by the organisation of their character defences, a situation which should orientate the therapeutic action. Since character neurosis can only be reached by a long psychoanalysis that is started only after a depressive episode, the ambitions of therapists dealing with parents should be limited. To consider the child as a symptom is not a state of mind conducive to accepting a radical transformation. More often, the psychotherapeutic approach of the parents owes its effectiveness only to the displacement of cathexis – relative and limited in time – provoked by the establishment of a relation with the therapist. The most useful and most spectacular effects are obtained through the improvement of hysterical depressive conditions easily obtained from the outset of the therapeutic relation with the mothers, as well as through the breaking of repetitive attitudes, not strongly cathected, for which the very existence of a dialogue is a sufficient opening. If the parents' mental functioning has a structuring effect upon the psyche of the child, one must not forget that the child in turn structures his parents and that this essential aspect of reciprocity should not be neglected. One could describe the particularly pathogenic effect of those parents who do not allow themselves to be modified in any way by the mental development of their own children; but it would be vain to expect important transformations of the parents' reactions when the latter are subjected to the repeated traumas which the aggressions and projections of certain psychotic children represent. The constitution of self-maintained systems of reciprocal aggressions justifies in certain cases the necessity of placing the psychotic child in a therapeutic institution. But one must then be conscious of the very great difficulty encountered in preventing the psychotic child from reconstituting the same system within the institution.

Lastly, we would not have completely outlined the boundaries of child psychoanalysis if we did not define the specific differences separating child psychoanalysis from various educational and re-educational techniques. We are not concerned here with the traditional methods of education, but specifically with the most modern forms of these activities. Psychoanalytic concepts are at times used in the educator's theoretical approach, sometimes with questionable success, often with regrettable confusion. Educational experiences that are free from all restraints are justified by the necessity evoked above in connection with institutions for psychotic children. But we often slide from the necessity not to perpetuate mutual aggressions to a conception of permissiveness in education considered as an active therapeutic means. Education then becomes a form of group therapy, whose justification becomes progressively weaker. This in itself would not be too serious if the results were not so often disappointing.

Thus it is necessary to underline a few differences, fundamental to a psychoanalyst, between the educational approach and the psychoanalytic attitude. Doubtless both demand the taking into consideration of the child and his productions, but actually, as we have mentioned in passing, the productions concerned are not the same. Beyond this similarity are differences that are to be taken into account even in the most progressive educational system. Whereas the psychoanalyst expects nothing from his patient, the educator offers him an activity. By permitting the child to identify himself with him, the adult leads him to adopt his skill, but this movement brings a meaning to the elaboration of the conflicts. The projection of the child's superego upon the educator constitutes an efficient defensive process, and the external conflict produced by the adult's desire that the child conform to his wish greatly diminishes the pressure of his inner conflicts. The skill offered by the educator or re-educator also permits the child's ego to find a new pleasure, but this pleasure is of a quite different nature than in psychoanalysis, if only because it facilitates repression by reinforcing the symbolic activities. One cannot deny that the educational relationship possesses a psychotherapeutic potential whose far-reaching effects are considerable, but the specific means of its action must not be forgotten.

In concluding this introduction to the discussion, let us note that the application by psychoanalysts of the psychoanalytic theory to children has considerably enriched not only our knowledge of mental development, but also our means of action and our comprehension of their specific effects. We have left aside the important problem of the respective contributions of child psychoanalysts and direct observation, which in itself would deserve another debate. Without a coherent theory of the psychoanalytic process in the child, it hardly seems possible to differentiate child psychoanalysis from the numerous psychotherapeutic approaches now developing. Whether in its very nature or in its finality, this theory relates back to the adult's mental functioning at every step of its development.

References

Fenichel, O. (1945). *The Psychoanalytic Theory of Neuroses.* New York: W. W. Norton.
Fenichel, O. (1953–54). *The Collected Papers of Otto Fenichel.* New York: W. W. Norton, 1998.
Freud, S. (1900a). *The Interpretation of Dreams. S.E.*, 4/5.
Freud, S. (1909b). Analysis of a Phobia in a Five-Year-Old Boy. *S.E.*, 10: 5–149.

8 NARCISSISTIC ASPECTS OF THE ANALYTIC SITUATION

Bela Grunberger

A psychiatrist and full member of the Paris Psychoanalytical Society, **Bela Grunberger** (1903–2005) is known for his original and illuminating explorations of the narcissistic dimension in psychoanalytic treatment, demonstrating its importance, challenging as he did so a great number of received ideas. Some of his most important writings are: *Le narcissisme* (Payot, 1971) [*Narcissism: Psychoanalytic Essays*. International Universities Press, 1978]; *Narcisse et Anubis* [*Narcissus and Anubis*] (Editions Des Femmes, 1989); *Narcissisme, christianisme, anti-sémitisme* [*Narcissism, Christianity and anti-Semitism*] (with P. Dessuant; Actes-Sud, 1997).

Pierre Dessuant wrote a concise biography of Bela Grunberger for the series 'Psychanalystes d'aujourd'hui' (PUF, 1999).

> Sitting in the grass, his arms clasped around his knees, Pierre looked at the river, his line, the cork. Something new had just happened; he had enjoyed talking about himself. The memory of his childhood had come naturally to his lips, no doubt because it was not a happy memory. Such abandon was not without irony, but it was especially pleasant not to be understood, to talk to this man as he would have talked to the river or to an echo, since all that mattered was the sound of his own voice. The words that it pronounced gained nothing by being understood. 'If one day I should discover a friend,' thought Pierre, 'this is how it will happen. In a chance meeting, a man will lend me a willing ear. All that I wouldn't dare tell to someone who knows me, I will tell to him. When I have finished, I will leave, counting on never seeing him again.' Any new meeting could only be disappointing, for everything will have been perfect the first time.
>
> Jean Bloch-Michel, *Le Trottoir de droite*

Most patients – as we all know from experience – quickly settle into the analytic situation, and for a longer or shorter period of the analysis, depending on the case, they talk volubly and easily throughout the sessions. They speak fluently and derive genuine and obvious pleasure from this verbal flow. I have noticed that in life such patients – I shall speak of the others later – maintain a close correspondence with partners whose role at base is precisely that of communicator or mailbox between the patient and himself. I had in analysis a patient who came to see me for anxiety neurosis and symptoms of hypochondria; he talked throughout the sessions without my being able to get a word in edgewise. This patient, whose occupation was in no way intellectual, lovingly carried on a correspondence whose content – even the subjective content – surely did not justify the time and attention he devoted to it. Others keep journals or diaries which are for them clearly *equivalents* of analysis. I had in treatment a woman writer who flatly declared, as if it were self-evident, 'Writing or coming to analysis, it's all the same thing.'[1]

The pleasure such patients derive from analysis is unquestionably a narcissistic pleasure. Although the subject's pleasure appears in the guise of a specific confrontation with his 'alter ego,' the analyst, it comes from the narcissistic contemplation of himself in which he indulges. The analyst's role is that of a mirror according to Freud's classic analogy which has lost none of its validity. If it is to serve its purpose this mirror must remain a pure function, without material support, and invisible,[2] with the analyst behind the analysand, for otherwise the presence of an object would drive the analysand from his narcissistic position. In the analytic situation, he is alone, yet without being completely so; his position contains *in posse* another position, that of object relations. Object relations can be gradually established, proceeding through the various phases of development. The process will be a slow one and attended by difficulties, which the analysand must learn to face up to. The analytic situation offers an intermediate position,[3] which is what characterizes analysis and makes it unique (compared to other types of psychotherapy and aberrant forms of 'psychoanalysis').

Something else we have all observed is how patients characteristically behave at the end of a session, especially the very early sessions. When the patient gets up from the couch, he glances about vacantly; he seems disoriented and in doubt, as if he felt a little dizzy. Some stagger and clasp their forehead, like someone trying to collect his thoughts. This disorientation is not only spatial; they seem to lose all sense of time as well, and on getting up they may say, 'Really, the hour is up? I would have sworn only a few minutes had

---

[1] The narcissistic equivalents just mentioned (as well as many others – namely, keeping a diary or carrying on an egotistical correspondence (to borrow a term from that great narcissist Stendahl)) are activities of adolescence, the narcissistic age by definition (Rank).

[2] I had a patient who, after two years of analysis, was unaware of the kind of chair I use; in short, he had never seen me. For him – despite my presence – the analytic situation had never really lost its narcissistic character.

[3] The position is that of Narcissus gazing at himself in the water along with – in the background, like the analyst – the nymph Echo (still another mirror), as depicted by the painters of Pompeii, for example, whose works are preserved in the Museum of Naples.

passed.' Such behavior is entirely independent of the content of the session; sessions prove very tiring for patients, but only *a posteriori*. 'I am terribly shaken,' said one woman, 'I feel as if I'm about to faint. And yet I told you only things that I have told others before without being bothered in the least.' Once this little crisis had passed, however, she felt fine, indeed euphoric, and on her way home she went strolling and shopping, indulging in pretty things. Another patient (again a woman, this behavior being less marked in men, sometimes scarcely noticeable) told me, 'After a session, I felt dead, burned out, exhausted,' and this feeling resembled a real illness; once she had to go into a tea room to seek refreshment, and the waiter asked her, 'Aren't you feeling well, Miss?'

Patients experience this feeling *after* the session — which tends instead to be euphoric on the whole[4] — and they describe the feeling differently, depending on the case: 'I had a weird sensation, as if I were quaking in my bones,' or 'It was as if I had been drinking,' or again, 'I felt changed, more air was going into my lungs.'

A patient whom I saw only once, a hypochondriac with paranoid delusions,[5] exhibited the *end-of-session syndrome* in a particularly acute manner. Getting up from the couch (I had him get up after a short quarter-hour), he began to totter, almost collapsing on the spot, and I had to support him, then literally drag him along to the waiting room. It was only after ten minutes, and then still in a groggy state, that he was able to make it out of the door and bundle himself into a passing taxi. During those ten minutes, his face betrayed no suffering; on the contrary, all one could discern was that vaguely libidinal hebetude that one sometimes notes in the frozen masks of the insane.

Thus we can see that the phenomenon in question is similar in nature, irrespective of whether it involves transference neurotics or *narcissistic* neurotics — to use one of Freud's later terms, now more or less discarded by psychiatrists — designating those whom we call simply 'psychotics.' The difference is only quantitative, as Freud remarked in reference to healthy individuals and neurotics. Basically, both types of neurosis involve *narcissistic regression*.[6]

Regression during analytic treatment is a classical notion; the patient in analysis turns to the past in order to relive his preoedipal and oedipal conflicts. That view, then, links the regression to object relations (preoedipal and oedipal), whereas we have just seen that the patient's position is a narcissistic one, at least during the early phase of analysis and in the analytic situation

---

[4] In this connection, Lagache (1954) has spoken of 'elation with a new feeling of inner freedom and capacity for self-fulfillment,' which has a certain narcissistic ring, though he attributes it to transference.

[5] I accepted the patient for a session on the couch after the briefest of interviews, for he had been referred to me with a diagnosis of benign neurosis.

[6] For practical reasons and to avoid confusion, however, I shall speak of narcissistic position or state or of narcissistic relationship or rapport, since our discussion concerns analysis; I shall reserve the term narcissistic regression for serious cases, as a rule, for psychotics.

outlined above. The regression described in the classical formulation is a conflicted and object-related regression; those who hold that view therefore ignore the element of euphoria or *elation*,[7] though it is manifest, even strikingly so with all its accompanying phenomenology, the whole being typically narcissistic,[8] hence non-objectal and unconflicted.

If one only stops to consider, one can discover the most diverse manifestations of this narcissistic state.[9] It becomes evident at the beginning of analysis, well before transference is established, and, contrary to transference, which can be somewhat of an obstacle, especially early in analysis (the tendency to act out conflicts instead of remembering them being a source of transference *resistance*), this narcissistic state proves to be the prime mover of the analytic process. The elation that accompanies the analytic situation is what makes it possible for oedipal elements to penetrate the conscious, slowly, sporadically, and superficially at first – for there is still resistance to act as a brake – then more distinctly.[10] In uninhibiting the patient, narcissistic elation acts similarly to

---

[7] Or else it is broadly attributed to 'transference,' a term that is applied too widely in my opinion (in point of fact, transference implies the existence of an object conflict 'transferred' from one object to another), a true catch-all of analytic theory, a notion that embraces 'everything that goes on between the analyst and the analysand,' which is practically equivalent to 'everything that goes on in analysis.'

[8] Macalpine (1950) has expressed surprise that in the analytic situation transference can take on the intensity that we know it does, and that it can be considered a general phenomenon. For her, 'analytic transference is actively induced in a "transference-ready" analysand by exposing him to an infantile setting to which he has gradually to adapt by regression' (p. 528). True transference indeed develops gradually, but *the narcissistic phenomena in question occur immediately, in the first session – that is what characterizes them*. It is a specific narcissistic regression, related not to transference, which is not established until later, but to the analytic situation as such.

The narcissistic pleasure that the patient experiences *during* a session marked by the end-of-session syndrome can be compared to sexual pleasure with its concomitant fatigue and regression; indeed, at a certain layer of the unconscious, that is surely one of its meanings, for it seems to be abundantly overdetermined. In the analytic situation we are discussing here, however, this pleasure is typically narcissistic and hence by definition outside transference.

[9] Sometimes a patient indulges in an unconscious fantasy of masturbation during a session, or even in a more or less unconscious masturbatory act in either a direct or substitute form, which he projects onto the analyst, saying, for example, 'You are masturbating.' When the patient dares to *express* this projection, however, he is already at an advanced stage of the analysis, and the projection serves to cancel out the aggressive component that is inherent in the masturbatory act, which is then very close to consciousness.

[10] Which proves, incidentally, that the regression has nothing to do with transference. This 'transference' at the beginning of analysis (Bouvet, 1954, cites W. Reich 'who denies the genuineness of positive manifestations of transference at the outset of an analysis'), this analytic 'honeymoon,' is generally interpreted as *pregenital maternal transference* (see Greenacre, 1954, for example), whereas the real 'content' of this transference, if one may call it that, is usually *clearly oedipal*, to the point that it has become an established rule that 'one begins with analysis that is superficial, oedipal.' Patients themselves recognize the importance of the narcissistic element in relation to the Oedipus complex. A very intelligent woman suffering from hysteria said to me: 'I seem to be coming to like you more and more. And yet I know nothing about you; in short, I like you only in relation to myself – you are nice, understanding, and so on. *Thus it is myself that I am coming to love through you.*' In this connection, it could be said that – seen in this perspective – a great deal of narcissism might be found in love itself. Indeed, that is surely the case, and many writers are of that opinion (see, for example, Jekels & Bergler, 1934).

alcohol, eliminating censorship.[11] In addition, the oedipal elements seem to merge into the narcissistic background and take on its characteristics in the sense that they lack solidity.

At this stage, objects tend to be phantomlike, and analysis of the Oedipus complex at the beginning of treatment – barring certain exceptional cases – usually amounts to no more than preliminary groundbreaking. Effective investigation of the Oedipus begins when the analysis has been enriched by preoedipal contributions. Alexander (1927) cited cases in which superficial and purely oedipal analysis was able to achieve very satisfactory results; they were cases of 'actual trauma,' according to the author, in which simple clarification was sufficient. Still, one may sometimes wonder whether, when seemingly analyzing the Oedipus, one is not analyzing, indirectly, pregenital conflicts.

Freud said that analysis should be characterized by frustration and that the patient should not derive pleasure from the analytic situation. Certainly from the oedipal standpoint, the patient is frustrated throughout analysis, from beginning to end; however, from a narcissistic viewpoint, which is typical of the period under consideration, he is far from being frustrated.[12] The narcissistic pleasure that the patient derives from the analytic situation is precisely the condition needed for that situation to become firmly established and the therapy to be successful, for the fate of the two are inexorably linked. The analysand should not be denied that pleasure, unless it becomes obvious after a while that the regression is remaining at the same level, that the patient is settling in for a long stay and cultivating his regression, indulging in 'art for art's sake' so to speak. Even then, there are situations in which one must be cautious, for a patient may have reasons for perpetuating this situation, which he will not reveal until later.[13]

Infiltration of oedipal elements into consciousness may occur early on, even simultaneously with narcissistic regression. I have already commented on the nature of those elements. Frequently I have recorded patients' oedipal dreams that also contain their entire conflict constellation, sometimes even in the first therapeutic session. A valid analysis then often requires years. If one examines such dreams closely, one always finds some small detail that testifies to the presence of a strong narcissistic component.

---

[11] On the other hand, this elation retains its specificity, its full 'validation' depending on a more or less parallel maturational process, the development of object relations. That is why it serves no purpose to try to interfere with the process, which can only cause harm (narcoanalysis or hypnosis). Hypnosis is an artificially induced narcissistic state of fusion, quite apart from genital maturation and ego formation. As for narcoanalysis, it constitutes an equally artificial regression that also falls outside normal development.

Needless to say, one must take care that narcissistic regression (according to the forms it assumes) does not become pathological regression, if only from the analytic point of view (narcissistic fixation).

[12] A somewhat similar conclusion, though pertaining to object relations and transference, was reached by Luquet (1957, p. 197), who noted 'a frustrating human relationship in regard to object relations that are relatively well developed but are *gratifying at an extremely primitive level*' (italics added).

[13] The functioning of the ego is inconceivable without narcissism, and for the analytic process, one of the aims of which is to heal the ego, it is all the more essential.

One of my patients – a woman suffering from severe hysteria with obsessional defenses – reported the following dream during the first session: 'I was in my bed. My father and the cleaning woman [the mother] were sitting in a corner of the ceiling and cleaning it with a big black brush. I felt impatient, when my father threw me the brush.' And then she added, using the phrase of the Sun King, which she immediately recognized, '*Finally! I very nearly had to wait!*' – narcissistic omnipotence.

Transference that is markedly oedipal from a historical standpoint can prove to be a narcissistic account: 'I like you because you have blue eyes like my father. . . . To tell the truth, I'm the one who has blue eyes. My father had brown eyes.' The 'transference' that has been compared to love is much blinder than love; it is *quasi-delusive* in nature, and even Freud was astonished at the bizarre situations between analysand and analyst that can grow out of it. The absence of the 'sense of reality' again shows that we are dealing with a deep regression governed by the primary process, the pleasure principle, and that there is nothing that has been transferred – that is, no object-related conflict.

It is not by chance that the analytic method, the most restrained and passive of all forms of psychotherapy or any other type of treatment, is the method that is most favorable for narcissistic cathexis on the part of the patient. In fact, patients find that the approach of the analyst who never bothers them or interferes provides ideal conditions for narcissistic expansion. Transference may occur with one's dentist or one's cardiologist,[14] for in those cases there are true relations, object relations. During analysis, at first it is the analytic situation that is cathected, and this cathexis will withstand all the vicissitudes of objectual transference, which will be established later with the analyst.[15] Furthermore, this cathexis will be intense, and the importance that a patient's analysis assumes in his life reveals the archaic primal source of its cathexis. Among all the medical methods, only analysis can take on the quality of an *initiation*, of a *conversion*, of *redemption*, or of *first love*. The patient chooses not only his analyst but, more important, analysis as such, and his narcissism should not be injured in this positive or negative choice. We know that we can analyze only those who willingly consent to it and that the most highly 'indicated' analysis from an objective viewpoint can (and most often does) fail if it is imposed on the analysand.

---

[14] Freud showed that transference is a common phenomenon, and that in life we are continually projecting everywhere (repetition compulsion).

[15] In the case of 'negative transference,' the analysand will have a hostile and deprecatory attitude toward the analyst, but only toward the analyst as object; *the analytic situation will be shielded from this attitude and will remain positively invested*. If, for example, the patient flees because he can no longer bear his guilty feelings toward the analyst as object, he will seek another analyst. Some will even go to several, one after the other, just as patients who need to maintain their narcissistic regression while undergoing medical treatment but are always changing doctors because they are incapable of maintaining a stable object relation.

It is the analysand who directs the analysis, for it is he who controls its flow by opening the flood-gates of his unconscious to let the material come out, it is he who prepares the ground for interpretations and sometimes even makes discoveries. Jones has related how Freud discovered the free-association method with the help of one of his patients: Freud was about to intervene with an interpretation when his patient cried out, 'Don't interrupt me!'

In regard to the choice of analyst, the patient does the choosing, and his choice may be highly significant in the case of a didactic analysis, for example. One may have very decided ideas on the subject before even knowing one's analyst. In that case, then, should we speak of 'transference at a distance?' Certainly not. What can be said in that case is that the analysand forms a favorable preconception of one analyst over another, so that analyst becomes *his* analyst, and from then on the analysand will overestimate him and bestow a strong narcissistic cathexis on him. His analyst will be the best and will remain so, come what may. Whatever his analyst may do or not do, say or not say, will be interpreted favorably by the analysand, *as if it were a question of his own actions*. And in fact, it is he who is concerned, for the cathexis is narcissistic. It is in this same narcissistic way, moreover, that the child invests his father, *to whom he attributes his own narcissistic omnipotence* (Freud), which he has lost but recuperates in this manner. One is reminded of the narcissistic scenario of the love-struck – 'With him (or her), I could do anything' – or that of the parent – 'My child will succeed where I have failed.'

The narcissist loves himself because he derives pleasure from himself and because he is omnipotent and unique. He will rediscover all these feelings through the medium of his analyst, not by identifying with him, for identification is part of another process, that of object relations, but *by projecting his ego-ideal onto the analyst*. If 'the subject continues to perceive a common nature shared by the analyst and himself' (Bouvet, 1954), it can only be because of his projection. As for the nature in question, it can only be his own nature; the role of the analyst is comparable to that of the priest, a mediator (mirror) between the subject and his own narcissistic projection, which is idealized, magnified, and glorified, or, as the case may be, detested, repudiated, and reviled. Despite appearances, the analyst's role is theoretically a contingent one, which is not at all inconsistent with the enormous role he seems to play in the analytic process; indeed, the believer dwells in the shadow of and in total subjection to him – God or the Devil – who is merely the projection of his own ego-ideal and 'omnipotence.'[16]

Nacht has said that 'what counts in analysis is not so much what the analyst "does" or "says" as what he "is"' (1956, p. 84). In the perspective that we are

---

[16] The neurotic needs this narcissistic projection. Anna Freud (1954) observed the terrible anxiety that the rise of the Hitler regime provoked in her patients, when in their eyes she suddenly changed from God-analyst into a despicable pariah. It is true that the 'faith' of some of her patients was not shaken so easily, and one of them continued to consider her as powerful as ever, in fact, even more powerful than Hitler and the British government put together; he was a civil servant.

developing here, the analyst, a mere reflection of the analysand, can only be what the latter is or, more precisely, would like to be. The patient does not know the analyst otherwise, nor should he. How else could he maintain his projections – whether perfectionist and idealistic, or suffused with almost paranoid[17] hostility? The analyst is the vehicle of the drives and defenses of the analysand and only that. When the patient is struggling against his impulses, the analyst is the warder onto whom he projects his severe superego; when he wants to yield to his impulses, the analyst becomes 'permissive,' even seductive. I once had a young patient who said to me at the beginning of analysis, 'Doctor, I came to you because I am a drunkard, a gambler, a homosexual, and a pimp, but I would like to change.' A few sessions later he told me, 'You know, doctor, I no longer gamble, I have stopped drinking, I am leading a completely different life – *just like you told me to.*' Well I had, of course, told him nothing, at least nothing of that sort. Another patient interpreted all my gestures (real or imagined) in an almost delusive narcissistic sense. Everything I did was linked to his treatment in one way or another; gestures that I was subtly and intentionally calculating were always for his benefit. As for negative transference, the analysand consistently interprets everything in paranoid fashion, so to speak, a projection that must be repeatedly corrected – that is, interpreted as such.

The analysand's narcissism is always on guard, and one must avoid injuring it by discussing it with him or criticizing it. Even if he does not show it, he will react by producing new unconscious sadistic fantasies, which will increase his sense of guilt. The patient should enjoy complete narcissistic freedom in the sense that *he should always be the only active party*. The analyst has no real existence of his own in relation to the analysand. He doesn't have to be either good or bad – he doesn't even have to *be*.[18] If the analyst were to begin living in his own behalf in analysis, he would only disrupt the free fantasy formation of the analysand, just as adults disrupt the play of children, who also live in a narcissistic world. Analysis is thus not a dialogue at all; at best it is a monologue for two voices, one speaking and the other echoing, repeating, clarifying, interpreting correctly – a faithful and untarnished mirror.[19]

I should like to cite a phenomenon that occurs in a number of analyses and that also has its roots in this same narcissistic foundation: I am thinking of those patients who immediately establish a very euphoric, even impassioned,

---

[17] 'Paranoid' as pertaining to *délire d'interprétation* – in French psychiatric terminology, *paranoiaque*.
[18] That is – of course – an ideal that is difficult to achieve, the problem being one of countertransference. Certain exceptions to this rule will be considered later.
[19] Since the process that binds the analysand to the analyst is at base narcissistic, we can also understand why the analyst should not be afflicted with any conspicuous infirmity, for its existence in reality might interfere with the projections of the analysand. The analyst is a looking glass in the hand of the analysand, and the latter should be satisfied with the sight of his own perfection reflected in the mirror. In a crippled analyst, the patient will see his own castration. Yet the entire process is essentially a means for him to transcend that castration.

This analytic mirror can also be compared to a converging lens with the analysand at its focal point; each time he tries to escape, the analyst will relentlessly bring him back face to face with himself.

'transference.' Such an analysis proceeds at a brisk pace, with the patient going from admiration and delight to ecstasy; he is brimming with joy and makes his treatment the focal point of his life. Then one day, after a few weeks of analysis, he suddenly declares that he is cured, more than cured, and consequently announces to the analyst that he is going to leave treatment. It is a difficult moment that tests the tact and ability of the analyst who is confronted by this complication, this 'cure' that is attributed to transference. What is paradoxical is that the impulse to flee is also attributed to transference (fear of transference). The fact is that this crisis passes and soon gives way to a very different analytic situation, in which the patient's behavior is noticeably changed. What, then, has happened?

At the outset, the patient enters into a specific state, the source of highly gratifying narcissistic emotions. This 'elation' enables him to overcome certain inhibitions but not resistance, which remains intact and undiminished, as is proven by the fact that interpretations given at this point in the analysis bring about no structural change. Yet the patient, interpreting his feeling of euphoria – a state that could, relatively speaking, be compared to a sort of mania – is convinced that he is cured. Actually, it is a narcissistic pseudo-cure, corresponding to archaic narcissistic satisfaction, which the child tries to achieve in a hallucinatory mode and which the analysand seeks in therapy. We shall return to this subject later, and we shall also see that *the uniqueness of Freudian analytic therapy lies precisely in its refusal to maintain this narcissistic illusion of omnipotence; on the contrary, it leads the patient to develop a more advanced system of relations, that of object relations, for that is the crux of the matter.*

In this state of elation, essentially all the patient gets from the analyst is the opportunity to admire himself in the analyst and to derive pleasure from the analytic situation, which makes that possible (but a situation that nevertheless contains – *in posse* – all the elements of therapeutic progress). At a certain point, however, the subject becomes aware that beneath this unconflicted (preambivalent) satisfaction, the analytic situation is gradually shifting him toward another position as object relations begin to develop. This new position frightens him, and this fear is what moves him and sometimes even compels him to leave treatment. In short, what has happened up to this point has been like a game, but now he is going to have to get involved in transference and begin the analysis; the two situations are fundamentally different. In a way, then, it is right to say that the patient fears transference; what is wrong is to link his flight to an *increase in the intensity* of that fear. The fact is that the *beginning* of transference is what gives rise to fear, the preceding state being outside transference, which shows, incidentally, that of these two factors, it is narcissism that energizes the analytic situation, whereas transference serves resistance ('transference-resistance').[20]

---

[20] M. Balint (1935) described an analytic sequence that is quite similar, but it occurs toward the end of analysis, and the conclusions he reached are different from mine ('*Neubeginn*'); however, he did draw attention to the narcissistic character of the episode in question.

The analysand's narcissism enables and encourages him to form with the analyst a double image of himself (mirror). This tendency is probably what has been interpreted as 'transference readiness' (Nunberg, 1951) or 'desire for transference' (Ferenczi & Rank, 1924); true transference rapport, which is established later, must be bound up with object relations. In fact, we are confronted with an essentially superficial process, inconsistent and fleeting,[21] which will not change – for reasons that will be discussed later – except in analysis. The narcissist is continually in search of a mirror, and he will always seize on any new possibility for narcissistic satisfaction precisely because he would like to go beyond this position (save in cases of narcissistic perversion or total regression); he would like to establish an object relationship, but he feels incapable of doing so. Because narcissism constitutes the beginning of the process and serves as the primer for what follows, it will commence and recommence again and again, but will not be able to develop beyond a certain point.

When we speak of identification, we must remember that there are different kinds of identification and even pseudo-identification. The pseudo-relation of the narcissist is the latter. One can see this quite clearly in certain famous narcissists (artists, politicians, etc.), who very readily form a relation with no matter whom, without the least affinity for the person in question, provided that that person affords them an opportunity for narcissistic gratification, which they constantly need. Such bonds are superficial in nature, however; there is no object relation. The narcissist does not love, he lets himself be loved.

That is what happens in the narcissistic analytic relationship. At the beginning of treatment, the analysand is carried away in narcissistic ecstasy, and to stabilize his position in relation to the analyst, he will play at identification, as it were, simply to stay in the good graces of the latter. Looked at objectively, it could not be otherwise; the analysand knows nothing about the analyst, except in certain didactic analyses.[22]

---

[21] I am speaking of the process in general; narcissism transcends the psychopathological framework and follows the individual from birth to death.

[22] If 'the subject continues to perceive a common nature shared by the analyst and himself' (Bouvet, 1954, p. 84), it could only be a delusive-projective hallucinatory perception. Bouvet, who places this position near the *end* of therapy and makes the cure contingent upon it ('One then speaks the same language, and the analyst becomes that "good object," permanent possession of which is the necessary point of departure for the development, or I should say growth, of the ego'), seems to contradict himself, for at the same time he makes it the *point of departure* of a development (the growth of the ego) that he considers, moreover, to be the essence of the analytic process.

References

Alexander, F. (1927). *The Psychoanalysis of the Total Personality: The Application of Freud's Theory of the Ego to the Neuroses*. New York: Nervous and Mental Diseases Publishing Co., 1930.

Balint, M. (1935). The Final Goal of Psycho-Analytic Treatment. In: *An Outline of Psychoanalysis* (revised edition, pp. 423–435), ed. C. Thompson, M. Mazer, & E. Wittenberg. New York: Random House, 1955.

Bouvet, M. (1954). La cure-type [The standard form of psychoanalytic treatment]. In *Œuvres psychanalytiques II, Résistances transfert. Ecrits didactiques* [Psychoanalytic writings II. Resistances, transference: Didactic texts] (pp. 9–96). Paris: Payot, 1968.

Ferenczi, S., & Rank, O. (1924). *The Development of Psychoanalysis*. New York: Nervous and Mental Disease Publishing Co., 1925.

Freud, A. (1954). The Widening Scope of Indications for Psychoanalysis: Discussion. In *The Writings of Anna Freud, Vol. 4* (pp. 356–376). New York: International Universities Press, 1968.

Greenacre, P. (1954). The Role of Transference: Practical Considerations in Relation to Psychoanalytic Therapy. *Journal of the American Psychoanalytic Association*, *2*: 671–684.

Jekels, L. & Bergler, E. (1934). Transference and Love. *Psychoanalytic Quarterly*, *18* (1949): 325–350.

Lagache, D. (1954). La doctrine Freudienne et la théorie du transfert [Freudian doctrine and the theory of transference]. *Acta Psychotherapeutica, Psychosomatica et Orthopaedagogica*, *2*: 228–249.

Luquet, P. (1957). A propos des facteurs de guérison non verbalisables de la cure analytique [Non-verbal curative factors in psychoanalysis]. *Revue Française de Psychanalyse*, *21*: 182–224.

Macalpine, I. (1950). The Development of the Transference. *Psychoanalytic Quarterly*, *19*: 501–539.

Nacht, S. (1956). Psychoanalytic Therapy. In: *Psychoanalysis of Today* (pp. 78–98). New York: Grune & Stratton, 1959.

Nunberg, H. (1951). Transference and Reality. *International Journal of Psychoanalysis*, *32*: 1–9.

9 THE UNCANNY, OR 'I AM NOT WHO YOU THINK I AM'

Michel de M'Uzan

> **Michel de M'Uzan** is a psychiatrist, former full member of the Paris Psychoanalytical Society and a former director of the Institute of Psychoanalysis. He is one of the founding members of the Paris Psychosomatic Institute and co-editor of the 'Fil Rouge' series (PUF). He has written some thought-provoking and creative books, characterised by his exceptional aesthetic sensitivity. His work on interpretation and its mutative potentiality, on memory, on the mechanisms of artistic creation and on female sexuality is both original and cohesive.
>
> A list of his writings would include: *De l'art à la mort* [From art to death] (Gallimard, 1977 & 1994) and *La bouche de l'inconscient* [The mouth of the unconscious] (Gallimard, 1994). In his most recent book, *Aux confins de l'identité* [The frontiers of identity] (Gallimard, 2005), he explores, in some depth, issues relating to the sense of identity, drawing a clear distinction between the non-drive-related *vital-identital* sphere and the psycho-sexual dimension, which has to do with the drives and encompasses narcissism. He has written several works of literature, among which are: *Les chiens des rois* [The kings' dogs] (Gallimard, 1954), *Anthologie du délire* [An anthology of delusion] (Editions du Rocher, 1956), *Le rire et la poussière* [Laughter and dust] (Gallimard, 1962), and *Celui-là* [That one] (Grasset, 1994).
>
> Murielle Gagnebin wrote a concise biography of Michel de M'Uzan for the 'Psychanalystes d'aujourd'hui' series (PUF, 1996).

'I am not who you think I am.' Here, this formulation is not the reply of a hypocritically prudish young girl to the propositions of an honest man sensitive to her lures. No, it is the *uncanny* that proffers it . . . provided, that is, the latter is endowed with speech. In any case, one could suppose that the expression lends itself, from the outset, to being inscribed in a universe of words. At the very beginning of his study, Freud devotes many pages to a linguistic approach to the term '*unheimlich*', citing terms which define related emotions: fright, fear, anxiety, horror. Sensitive to his example – but I am exposing myself to introducing nothing more than a worthless parenthesis, even if what follows will show that this is not at all the case – I note that, in the list, a word is missing. It is the word *bizarre*, borrowed from the Italian around 1549. What is missing is often very instructive, isn't it? It is perhaps the case here, because Paul Robert's *Dictionnaire de la langue française* states that the word *bizarre* was first employed as a feminine noun, '*une bizarro*', and, qualitatively, to designate a *singular* person or thing. Would the feminine, and the question or questions that it raises, have some part to play in the matter?

Freud thinks so, noting that 'it often happens that neurotic men declare that they feel there is something uncanny about the female genital organs' (1919h, p. 245). And it was while I was thinking about this remark that I recalled the extreme turmoil experienced one day by a gynaecologist – the profession clearly aggravates the singularity of the emotion. One day, then, while he was having intimate relations with his partner, he was arrested by the thought: 'So that's what she's got at the bottom of her belly' (*C'est donc ça qu'elle a au bas du ventre*).

We do not really know here if the *that is only that*. It would be tempting to limit ourselves to the inscription of the matter within the context of a problematic of sexual identity. And yet, even when this position is convincing, one cannot overlook those 'experiences' that are *at the very least closely related* to the uncanny, in which anxiety is sometimes absent and where the sexual does not seem to be involved, or at least not regularly. I am thinking, among other things, about the phenomena of depersonalisation. So would one not be justified in saying that the uncanny forms part of, or is just a moment of, an infinitely larger or different domain than one had imagined? Pushing this proposition to its extreme, it would hardly be a provocation to claim that a situation would be '*unheimlich*' precisely when it is free of all strangeness! Would strangeness be in the process of taking precedence over the uncanny? At any rate, we owe it to ourselves to pursue the quest for a common factor at work in the phenomena in question.

In order to take these considerations further, it is worth recalling, in a very condensed fashion, Freud's basic contention. Having set aside, as a determining factor, the role of intellectual uncertainty alleged by E. Jentsch (1906), as well as the impact of the confrontation with the double inherited from Otto Rank (1914) and regarded as only a predisposing factor, Freud – as we know – argues that the uncanny proceeds from the return of the repressed and castration anxiety: 'The fear of castration itself contains no other significance and no deeper secret' (1919h, p. 231). The matter cannot be stated more clearly. It is even with a certain boldness, and almost provocation, that he adds: 'I hope the majority of readers will agree with me' (p. 227). Or better still: 'I would not recommend any opponent of the psycho-analytic view to select this particular story of the Sand-Man to support his argument that anxiety about the eyes has nothing to do with the castration complex' (p. 231). So we have been warned! But in spite of that, Freud is more ambiguous when he nonetheless recognises the role of perception at another point in the text. And he even declares that 'we must be prepared to admit that there are other elements besides those which we have already laid down as determining the production of uncanny feelings' (p. 247). One cannot underestimate the significance of this correction, whose trace can be found, for example, in the text 'A Disturbance of Memory on the Acropolis', written in 1936, thus a long time after the one we are concerned with, where the feeling of uncanniness is referred to notably without any reference to sexuality. Freud recognises that, in front of the Acropolis, he had (or might have had) a momentary feeling that what he saw was not real, and he continues: 'Such a feeling is known as a "feeling of derealization" . . . just as when "the subject feels that a piece of his own self is strange to him"' (1936a, pp. 244–245). Following the same train of thought, Freud asserts in the text we are concerned with that when 'the subject identifies himself with someone else . . . he is in doubt as to which his self is, or substitutes the extraneous self for his own. In other words there is a doubling, dividing and interchanging of the self' (1919h, p. 234). In a footnote, Freud makes an allusion to something similar when he cites two observations by E. Mach in which the subject at first takes the reflection of his image in the mirror for someone else's face (p. 248).

'The "Uncanny"', then, is certainly not simply a work that has been left in a drawer and rescued from oblivion, as Freud claims in a letter to Ferenczi (dated May 12, 1919). Furthermore, the effort he devotes to studying the phenomenon – one some would consider as almost marginal compared with the other issues that psychoanalysis is faced with – shows that this is not at all the case. Consequently, the uncanny – which, I would add in passing, transcends in any case the specific domain of aesthetics – largely justifies a closer study.

In response to this challenge, and after the points that I have just made, I want to say again that the term that should be given priority is *strangeness*. Strangeness is an impression that is affirmed each time 'natural distinctions' tend to become erased – that is, distinctions between the inside and the outside, the ego and the non-ego, the subject and the object, the familiar and the alien. This is true to the point that the uncanny, which does not tolerate being confined within an overly restrictive notional framework, will become a term that characterises a relationship in which the *disturbing* and the *fascinating* are contrasted. Once again, it is the idea of strangeness that predominates: strangely disturbing, strangely fascinating. Such is the *plus* that must be given to the *new* for these two moments to be visible. This plus is also a minus since what tends to get lost is the intimate feeling of the ego's specificity. An opportunity arises for introjection, especially as, in the tension between the fascinating and the disturbing, the experience of a correlative vacillation, not necessarily or always accompanied by anxiety, echoes something of the primordial state of being. It is precisely in this connection that I recall Maurice Bouvet's report, in 1960, during the Congress for French-Speaking Analysts, when, in my intervention, I argued that phenomena of depersonalisation could occur without being accompanied by anxiety but, rather, by a sort of exaltation, as can be observed during so-called creative activities or during technical sports exercises that are mastered perfectly.

At this point in my exposition, it seems appropriate to relate certain circumstances encountered in life or in analytic practice which will lend support to what I have just asserted. We will see the important role played in them by perception, a role that Freud at times wanted to reduce, and yet what is experienced is largely induced by phenomena of a sensory order. I remember, then, the peculiar emotion I felt one day upon hearing, at twilight, the unique cry of a black bird perched on the roof. In an earlier text (M'Uzan, 1974, p. 26/1977, p. 155), I studied a situation in which the observation of a relation of strict symmetry with an interlocutor who was facing me across a small table showed that the latter was simply a double, and that consequently it meant that one could be dead without knowing it.

I also recall the dream of a young girl who was hospitalised after making a suicide attempt. It was a recurrent dream. *Walking down a deserted road at night, she hears someone walking behind her. As the footsteps get closer, she starts to run . . . and at that point wakes up in an acute state of anxiety.* The anxiety was very real. In certain respects this is an ordinary dream in which the determining role of sexuality will easily be recognised. But that is not the end of the matter, because the young girl, still intrigued and moved, hoped, each time she had the dream, to turn round one day, in the dream itself, and to discover the identity of her pursuer. Well, one day this happened, but what she then saw, with a mixture of horror and terror, was herself: very old, with dishevelled white hair falling across her face, a sort of reflection of her demented mother. Though there are many interesting points one could comment on here, I would like above all to emphasise the swing from castration anxiety towards an order where sexuality, even narcissistic, is no longer involved. What is involved is something quite different. In another dream reported to me recently by a patient who has been in classical analytic treatment with me now for just a few months, the pursuer was the patient herself. She was pursuing a young woman 'who had a reputation for mistreating children'. She managed to catch up with the fleeing woman, who suddenly turned round . . . and my patient, utterly horrified, recognised that it was no other than herself.

Not hesitating to broaden the field in which the uncanny manifests itself, I will mention a curious experience, occurring more or less sporadically, in those moments when the memory of precise events, sometimes amongst the oldest, is exacerbated to the point of hallucinatory clarity, even though at the same time, and with equal force, there is a powerful impression of never having been anything more than a witness to them. It is an experience completely devoid of anxiety, as if the activity of perception had supplanted every other activity or function.

We know how it is often wise to be careful when reporting a sequence arising from our practice. This is particularly necessary for some of these 'vignettes', as we call them, when we have been led to introduce technical variations, or to make, as Michael Parsons[1] proposes, allusive, 'open' interpretations that are capable of 'undergoing all sorts of surprising transformations in the patient's mind'. Uncanny phenomena can occur during a session, whose fruitfulness may be compared with undergoing episodes of depersonalisation. In his time, Maurice Bouvet already took this view, regarding it as a decisive instrument for integrating that which is new.

A female patient, whom I spoke about recently, and who has been in analysis with me for several years, had barely settled down on the couch when she said in a somewhat embarrassed voice:

'I don't know what colour your hair is.'
A: 'Which hair?' (this may seem a rather surprising question)
P: 'Well, the hair you have on your head.'
A: 'So I have hair on my head.'
P: 'Oh, I don't know now . . .'

The episode was free of all anxiety. On the other hand, in this strange, uncanny atmosphere, a certain curiosity, perplexity and uneasiness were undoubtedly being expressed. But what should be noted above all is that this exchange was the initial phase and motor of a large movement of organic integration of sexuality and identity.

As one proceeds further in the study of the uncanny, one notes a constantly changing perspective in oneself whereby one seeks alternately either to discover what would be in line with Freud's will, a narrow and fundamental specificity of the phenomenon, or to recognise its effects in very diverse domains, as I have argued on several occasions. This leads me to relate the adventure, if I may put it like that, of a young woman during a train journey at night in which uncanniness *connotes perversion*, another domain altogether. Leaving her seat, the young woman went out into the corridor to stretch her legs. It was years ago when trains had compartments and corridors. She stopped, with her forehead pressing against the rain-streaked window. The young woman watched the lights breaking, now and then, through the darkness. A young man, who at first was standing at some distance from her, now approached her. The only unusual thing about him was the large and dark pair of sunglasses he was wearing. Very politely, he asked her what time the train was due to arrive in Paris. She replied, telling him what he wanted to know. However, he persisted, saying that there might be some delay. She suggested he should speak to the ticket inspector. Apologising, the man repeated his request and, to justify doing so, explained that he worked as a make-up artist for radio and television and had to be there at a precise time,

---

[1] Lecture given at the Paris Psychoanalytical Society in 2006.

which was why he was so anxious. The young woman was now getting a bit impatient, when the man suddenly removed his glasses, revealing his heavily made-up eyes and long false eyelashes. In an extreme state of shock, the young woman let out a cry and rushed to the other end of the corridor, where another man was standing. She grabbed him by his jacket, saying: 'Quick, quick, say something to me quickly.' It was as if a sound, speech of any kind, another perception, would wrench her away from the depersonalisation that was overcoming her. She almost no longer knew who she was or where she was.

Whether the experience of uncanniness is expressed in a flamboyant or, alternatively, a furtive manner, one can infer without excessive boldness that the phenomenon manifests the continuity of those times when indecision characterised a natural state at the frontiers of being – a state, as Freud said, that 'strictly speaking is never surmounted'. The uncanny commemorates, celebrates, a crucial phase in the development of psychic functioning, *a moment when the uncanny finds its primordial basis*, a moment when the indeterminate nature of identity, the daughter of the naturally uncertain character of the frontiers of being, projects into the future an occasional return, a return that is even more insistent than one would imagine it to be, in the form of troubling or disturbing experiences of uncanniness. It is from this situation of a continuum between the inside and the outside, between the self and the non-self, that an evolution occurs towards distinctions, even though they will never acquire a frank and affirmed character. This evolution may be considered as a 'psychisation' – that is to say, an inscription in the psycho-sexual register, with the aim of objectalisation. So it is indeed through the intervention of castration anxiety that 'the operation of the uncanny', and the mechanics that underlie it, induce the integration, the organic aggregation of the dimensions of identity [*l'identitaire*] and the psycho-sexual. As an instrument and witness to this psychisation of a primordial state, the uncanny is situated at the intersection of two orders; moreover, it sustains, while translating it, an activity of *negotiation*, a negotiation between what I call, to be precise, the self-preservative, non-instinctual dimension of identity and sexual drive functioning. I must add, as I have often argued, that the term drive should be reserved for object and/or narcissistic sexuality alone. The dimension of identity belongs to the self-preservative order: let's keep the expression, provided we remember that the term self-preservative defines a programme of development of being – a programme that is essentially genetic, endowed with a duration of application that is limited by the planned extinction of its activity, without the intervention of any kind of drive activity. It is on the basis of this so-called self-preservative programme that maternal seduction (in Jean Laplanche's sense of the term) gives birth to erogenous zones whose activity will demand the psychic activity which is called *drive functioning*. Among others, it is at these moments, or when they return, and almost throughout the whole of life, that the uncanny finds the opportunity of manifesting itself more or less spectacularly. In the negotiation in question, we can see a shift of emphasis from the quantitative towards the qualitative with, to boot, a gain in meaning. In analytic treatments, it is essential to identify the precise stage of this negotiation. Otherwise, the analyst is in danger of thwarting the integration of what is new, which persists alongside experiences of uncanniness. In addition, and perhaps more seriously, the analyst runs the risk of not intervening at the essential moment, but elsewhere.

At this point, I want to return once again to uncanny phenomena in the treatment, as Michael Parsons proposes, and in particular to the sorts of technical initiatives that I referred to earlier when answering my patient with the question, 'Which hair?' It was an intervention, it is true, that some would rightly consider destabilising. Well, yes indeed, it is even by virtue of saying things of this kind that *a new path emerges in the psychoanalytic approach to the other*. You may remember that, a long time ago, in 1991, in a paper entitled 'Du dérangement au changement' [From disturbance to change] concerning the management of the most classical psycho-sexual difficulties, I argued that, prior to any hermeneutic preoccupation, it was useful to provoke an economic scandal in the higher psychic systems. That is to say, it is useful to get the psychic energy flowing again where it has become 'immobilised' by the regime of binding. Otherwise, no interpretation can be invested, except as an aggravating factor of resistance.

In a similar way, it is advisable to trigger what I shall call a *scandal of identity* – to trigger and even aggravate it, for there is much less to be feared than one imagines. It is a question of intervening in the non-sexual self-preservative field of identity ('*vital-identital*'),[2] of disturbing (disorganising), undoing as a reference, the famous 'sense of uniqueness of an integrated organism which should recognize others without ambiguity' (Greenacre, 1958). It is a state, it is worth noting, that resists all fundamental change. In fact, what is involved is the *recognition that the psychoanalytic treatment has another responsibility* alongside that which proposes to give access to drive mastery, while according a maximum of satisfaction compatible with reality. Another responsibility which is of cardinal importance when one has in mind the most authentic aspect of the individual – the liberation of his most intimate, primordial self, of permitting or guaranteeing the subject the possibility of acceding to a state of *permanent restlessness*, as I suggested at the last Congress of the European Federation. Psychoanalysis is not what you think it is. I constantly point out, almost to the extent of pleading on its behalf, the importance of linking up with the point where the uncertain – and even more or less secretly durable – and aleatory character of the frontiers between all the orders must be recognised as a fundamental fact of being.

---

[2] The '*vital-identital*' is a neologism introduced by Michel de M'Uzan. It stands in opposition to Jean Laplanche's term 'the sexual'. Self-preservation is one of the functions of the '*vital-identital*'. This term replaces the term '*identitaire*' which can lead to confusion with its usage in other disciplines, notably philosophy. [*Trans.*]

Phenomena of uncanniness are thus not to be seen simply as accidents, even meaningful ones. They must be considered as the trace of an essential activity of the mind. They participate, let us remember, in the constant negotiation operating between two orders (the dimensions of identity and the psycho-sexual) by revealing a particular and new dimension of psychoanalytic science – that is to say, a dimension in which the uncertain and aleatory occupy a nuclear place. And once the hermeneutic dimension tends, even provisionally, even partially, to become 'marginalised', one finds a legitimate place for psychoanalysis in the domain of hazy frontiers, alongside what has been called the 'science of indefinite boundaries'.[3] I will just give one or two examples. Biology, towards which analysts are sometimes prepared to turn, tells us that the distinction between the *inert* and the *living* is aleatory. Think of quantum physics – Sylvie Faure and Georges Pragier (2007) refer to it, as I have also done on several occasions – which suggests that 'God might indeed play with the dice'. Even mathematics has discovered that there are elements which can belong *more or less* to an ensemble 'and that there exists a continuous transition between this ensemble and those elements that do not belong to it'.[4]

Let us stop there as if, in the very course of our reflection, a powerful call had summoned us to step back from the universe, where the universe is without certain and defined limits or, rather, had invited us to lean on it in order to allow for a demand for *significance* that is better inscribed in the 'psychoanalytically familiar' – namely, the psycho-sexual. And this movement brings us back, brings me back, to the beginning of my paper, to my modest young girl and her charms, to my '*bizarro*'. To my well-behaved young girl who assures the sleeping fetishist of eternity that there is nothing to see . . . except what she has pinned on her blouse, while letting him know that everything is there and that he can trust her. 'I am not who you think I am', she says. But am I not the one now who is proffering these words? What a relief – with the triumph of castration anxiety, perhaps the file opened on the uncanny can now be closed? How tempting it would be to be able to say so. But strangely – yes, strangely, let's keep the term – at this very instant, an invitation appears on the horizon. At this very instant, at any moment, someone will arrive and suggest that his fellow man should stand in front of a mirror and contemplate at length the reflection of a bather in celluloid, the naked bather of former times, pressed closely against the mirror beside his own.

---

[3] *Pour la science*, December 2006 (French edition of *Scientific American*).
[4] Ibid., p. 1.

References

Bouvet, M. (1960). Dépersonnalisation et relations d'objet [Depersonalisation and object relations]. In *La relation d'objet, Vol. 1* (pp. 295–435). Paris: Payot, 1967.

Faure-Pragier, S., & Pragier, G. (2007). *Repenser la psychanalyse avec les sciences* [Rethinking psychoanalysis with the sciences]. Paris: Presses Universitaires de France.

Freud, S. (1919h). The 'Uncanny'. *S.E.*, 17: 217–252.

Freud, S. (1936a). A Disturbance of Memory on the Acropolis. *S.E.*, 22: 239–250.

Freud, S., & Ferenczi, S. (1996). *The Correspondence of Sigmund Freud and Sándor Ferenczi, Vol. 2, 1914–1919*, trans. P. Hoffer. Cambridge, MA: Belknap Press.

Greenacre, P. (1958). *Emotional Growth*. New York: International Universities Press.

Jentsch, E. (1906). Zur Psychologie des Unheimlichen. *Psychiatrisch-Neurologische Wochenschrift*, 8. ['On the Psychology of the Uncanny', trans. R. Sellars. *Angelaki*, 2 (1995, no. 1): 7–16.]

M'Uzan, M. de (1974). S.J.E.M. *Nouvelle Revue de Psychanalyse*, 9: 23–32. Reprinted in *De l'art à la mort* (pp. 155–163). Paris: Gallimard, 1977.

M'Uzan, M. de (1991) Du dérangement au changement [From disturbance to change]. *Revue Française de Psychanalyse*, 60 (2): 325–337. Reprinted in *La bouche de l'inconscient* [The mouth of the Unconscious] (pp. 115–128). Paris: Gallimard, 1994.

Rank, O. (1914). *The Double: A Psychoanalytic Study*, trans. Harry Tucker Jr. Chapel Hill, NC: 1971, University of North Carolina Press.

10 THE ROLE OF THE COUNTERTRANSFERENCE

Serge Viderman

Serge Viderman (1916–1991) trained as a psychiatrist and became a full member of the Paris Psychoanalytical Society in 1960. With Christian David and Michel de M'Uzan, he was one of the founding members and co-directors of the general 'Fil Rouge' series (PUF). His major ideas, in particular those he developed in *Construction de l'espace analytique* [The construction of the psychoanalytic space] (Denoël, 1970) and in *De l'argent en psychanalyse et au-delà* [Money in psychoanalysis and beyond] (PUF, 1992), introduced a true epistemological break in the classic conception of psychoanalytic treatment: his main focus was on the fact that what predominates is truly an act of creation. He emphasised the role of construction in psychoanalysis as distinct from that of reconstruction. He was also one of the first psychoanalysts in France to highlight the major role played by the countertransference.

André Bauduin wrote a concise biography of Serge Viderman for the 'Psychanalystes d'aujourd'hui' series (PUF, 1999).

If the analytic situation is conceived of as an ideal, experimental setting, whose rigorous coordinates guarantee the truth that will be inscribed there, it is necessary to be as discreet as possible with regard to the role that the psychoanalyst plays in it. It is as if the setting or frame arose from a sort of objective necessity – the need to establish in as rational a manner as possible the protocol for an experience in which the purity of the result will be measured by the absence of any manifestation that might trouble it. As it was difficult to do away with the psychoanalyst, his existence in it had to be (practically) virtual, i.e. a pure projection, a product of the analysand's fantasy, a mirror, a screen – a concealed figure. In order to meet such a challenge, the movements stemming from the countertransference had to be reduced to the minimum. It was almost deplorable that the analyst existed; without his presence, and above all without the interventions whose countertransferential purity can never be guaranteed, we might have had a good chance of suddenly seeing the patient's past emerging in the analytic space, like in the magic mirror of Oriental tales, with a sort of dazzling and undisputable presence.

Such a conception not only leaves out of consideration the obvious fact that it is by virtue of the analyst's unilateral decision that such a frame (or setting) has been imposed, but also (and this is also the most important and consequential point) that it is on his attitude and his decisions that the way in which the treatment unfolds depends. That the transference neurosis is an authentic manifestation, revealing the deep unconscious structure of the subject, is not in question. But the method that reveals it, along with its artifices, is inseparable from what the method has revealed. In this sense it is not possible to separate the means from the ends – in other words, it is not possible to separate what has been obtained from that by which and by whom it has been obtained. The illusions we nourish with regard to the absence of the psychoanalyst's responsibility in the process of the transference dynamics stem from the fact that most of the conditions of his action are defined negatively. So, his refusal to play a role is itself a role which clearly has a positive aspect to it: the psychoanalyst plays the role of one who refuses to play a role; the patient clearly perceives the meaning and content of his neutrality, his benevolent attitude (put to so many tests) and his silence (subjected to so many nuances and variations).

If it is true that the transference phenomenon is at the centre of the treatment on which it depends, it is also true that the countertransference response assumes at least as much significance. To believe that the analyst does not respond is to avoid posing the problem, a problem on which the actual understanding of the analytic process depends. The analyst tries to escape the dilemma in which he is trapped by his alleged imaginary transparency and tries to convince himself that there is no response on his part. This is not really conceivable when one considers his behaviour in analysis: his silence and the transition from silence to speech; his multiple subtle ways of breaking or maintaining silence; the range of possibilities at his disposal for frustration or gratification; the choice of the timing and tone of an intervention or interpretation; the need for silence, prolonging it or interrupting it; the nature of the intervention, whether brief or parsimonious, well thought out or spontaneous, gratifying or frustrating; and the patient's demand, which sometimes meets with silence and sometimes with a response. However rational we hope these variations and these nuances are, no doubt owing to the analyst's experience, ability or lucidity acquired through endless self-analysis, they necessarily elude any possible stock-taking, any possibility of rationalisation. It is not so much with his knowledge and experience (the role and importance of which are not to be denied) as with his countertransference that the analyst conducts the analysis. It is by virtue of this countertransference that every interpretation is given and that the alternations between speech and silence are subject to scansion, the technical justifications for which will only be sought *a posteriori*. It is always possible to remonstrate with oneself (after the event), telling oneself that no doubt one could have said in three words what one formulated in twenty; if at the moment in question we did not find the brief formulation that would have been more appropriate, it is not so much because it was more difficult to find as because, *at that moment*, we needed unconsciously to say twenty words instead of three, because our own silence frustrates us (it is not certain that it frustrates the analysand *at the same moment*), because we feel narcissistically that the twenty words uttered were better than the three that would have been preferable. No amount of advice, even the advice we give ourselves, can prevail against this pressure in us which deludes us with regard to the value of our own speech. We share with the patient the same magic belief in the power of words.

The paradox of the analyst's situation lies in the difficulty he has of finding a position where the balance between observation and participation is not constantly threatened. No science of observation would survive under the conditions in which the analyst has put himself. He must both observe and know how to utilise the means of scientific reasoning to benefit from his observation; he must also participate and be emotionally involved, but equally he must remain neutral;[1] to the patient's free associations he brings his evenly suspended attention which is complementary to it, allowing his own unconscious contents to emerge in response to the unconscious material brought by the patient's associations. The meeting between two unconscious minds in the analytic situation, one of which is allowed to structure itself freely in the transference, while the other is subject to the strict limitations of the countertransference without even being able to imagine seriously that he has eliminated it or even being sure that it is to his advantage if he succeeds in doing so, shows clearly how much uncertainty hangs over discovery of meaning in the analytic situation – and without there being any possibility of imagining an efficient means of countering the situation.

We know that when observing a planet, there is no disturbing interference of the observer on the system studied. In the case of the behaviour of the electron, the interference is of the utmost importance: the relation is one of objective indetermination. This same difficulty arises each time that the subject observed and the act – the operation or the agent by which he is observed – are of the same order of magnitude. Here we come up against one of the specific difficulties of any kind of study of man by man. One can imagine, then, the difficulties the analyst encounters in a situation where

---

[1] And this neutrality will have to be benevolent at the same time. Have we given sufficient attention to the contradiction in terms involved in the paradoxical situation of the psychoanalyst who is required to sustain an impossible juxtaposition between two mutually exclusive attitudes? One cannot be both neutral and benevolent: one has to choose. One can only be neutral if one claims, in spite of everything, to be a pure mirror devoted to reflection – and one risks reflecting badly. One can only be benevolent if one both runs and takes the risk of not being so. There is no positive quality that is not sustained by an element of negativity. Both mirror and angel, the psychoanalyst clearly does not choose the easy way out.

the subject's unconscious can only be heard by another unconscious; where unconscious resistances can only be perceived, analysed, and overcome within the framework of a narrow relationship where emotional interferences remain extremely intense (whatever the analyst may claim and in spite of the snare in which he himself, at times, is caught) – in short, between two unconscious minds tuned intimately in a closed situation of the same order of magnitude.

The transference neurosis does not develop in an affectively empty space. For a long time it was hoped that the elimination of any emotional implication or involvement of the analyst, of any reaction or countertransferential response, would allow us to read on a perfectly transparent screen, without the analyst's shadow getting in the way, the patient's pure projection in which a past conserved in indelible signs would be relived in the present. The experimental study of the transference neurosis is impossible when the coordinates of the analytic situation contribute to creating it. The transference neurosis is organically linked to the existence, to the action of the analyst and to the conditions in which it manifests itself and on which it is based. Whatever precautions – and they are great and largely justified – are taken by the analyst to preserve his effacement, thereby allowing maximum space for the patient's projections, and notwithstanding his passivity, his silence and all the other artifices of his technique, nothing will prevent him from being the second organiser of the analytic field around which the patient will necessarily organise his 'game', which is not played out in advance and which will not simply be a replay.

It goes without saying that the psychoanalyst is not a technician. Technical rules can be learnt; they are neither difficult nor numerous. One can know everything about colours, how to mix them, the canvas, oil, water and charcoal, but that has never produced a painting. We all know how to speak, but that has never produced a poem. Why does interpretation seem to be so difficult, since for technicians who are skilled and used to such exercises, the snares of reconstruction should be well within their reach? The fact is that neither the analyst nor the analysand is in an indifferent situation of linguistic communication. One cannot say to the patient just any old thing, at any old time, and in any old way, and simply content oneself with linking up within a meaningful discourse that which surfaces here and there through associations, dreams or memories. The analyst cannot say what would make the most sense, because it is not just meaning that determines whether he is heard or not. It is not enough for interpretation to carry meaning; someone else must receive it at the same instant with as little alteration as possible. At each moment, the analyst must take into account the patient's affective state, the character of the transference, the degree of resistance, the progress of the treatment, the moments of insight already achieved, their quality, the work and time that are necessary for the patient to integrate them, so that they can be put to the test in many other transferential and historical situations than those in which the interpretations were given. And this is not an exhaustive list of the parameters which must be included in our appreciation of the situation. The factors which the analyst will have to take into account cannot be reduced to intellectual and objective apprehension. They depend on a situation saturated with affects, on an intense and shifting emotional sensibility that undergoes constant reshaping – a situation in which it would be illusory (and surely harmful as well) to require the analyst always to keep a cool head and heart. The countertransference is not a disturbance that one can hope to eliminate (except in the myth of the 'completely' analysed analyst). The complementary disturbances of the transference/countertransference are linked to the very structure of the analytic space, the cumulative effects of which are a gauge of the refractive index of the milieu in which the experience unfolds.

As for wanting to delimit the field of the countertransference, the task is anything but easy. Between the neurotic residue that the analyst's own analysis has not touched and the universal disposition to transference which is to a large extent irreducible, the analyst is not always in the best position to do this. Of the unconscious – his own as well as the analysand's – the analyst perceives no more than the depth of the furrow traced in the field by the plough, which is very little compared with the rest. There is no countertransference that is not also governed by some blind spot. It is because of the countertransference that things elude us; it is thanks to the countertransference that we perceive all the other things. The strong narcissistic cathexis of the situation by the analyst (and equally by the patient) makes the analysis possible, but at the same time equips us poorly for objectivity.

The more we have stressed the draconian character of the rules, the more we have made the setting in which the analysis unfolds inflexible, and the harder the core of resistances becomes in the transference neurosis. We had imagined an ideal situation within which the patient could speak as freely as possible, but we have created a situation in which he can only act. The strength of the transference affects risks being so disconcerting that we can no longer even retrace their distant origin, and we have even less chance of getting the patient to recognise it. Compared with the sparkle of the present, the past will be as dull and faded as the lustre of the pearl compared with the grain of sand from which it was formed. We have imagined a situation that should have allowed the patient to speak; but in fact what we observe is the invasion of the entire analytic space by the transference, with the effect that the patient tends to abandon the speech which is asked of him in favour of the act of transference which is refused. This is why the rational arrangements of the analytic setting escape the rationality which establishes them in order to manage an unconscious necessity which cares little for reason.

The lying-down position was designed to allow the patient the maximum liberty of speech; but it has become an absolute constraint (exercised by the analyst: it is not the intentions which are in question, but the effects) which he can only avoid by intensifying the transference regression, by multiplying the silences and the acts of transference. The analyst's position, which complements the patient's, was supposed to increase the patient's liberty; but it accentuates the disparity between the forces that determine the organisation of the analytic situation. The analyst's silence was intended to allow the patient to have the maximum time to speak, but it also becomes the surest means of frustration. Only the analyst's silence is legitimate. He speaks unexpectedly, without warning, when he wants and as he wants, either just a little or quite a lot according to necessity (theoretically); and his mood is variable depending on the luck of the moment or on his own unconscious needs – how can one know? Both of these factors mark the deep, irrational reality of a situation that was initially conceived with highly rational intentions.

There is no transference neurosis outside the analytic situation; there is no countertransference outside this situation. The countertransference is not the analyst's transference. Outside this situation he would not have – and did not have in the past, either when he was an analysand or in any other non-specific transference situation – the reactions which characterise his countertransference, and which are strictly linked to the analytic situation. The spontaneous disposition for transference, the dynamics of which are common to both protagonists, is differentiated in a specific manner by the diametrically contrasting positions they occupy in the analytic space. It is the position that determines how each of them evolves transferentially.

Yes, the countertransference can be harmful – like the transference. It is like Epictetus' basket; it has two handles – so why hold it by the one that hurts your hand?[2] It is not good for the analyst to settle quietly into a position that is intellectually comfortable. Nor is it a good thing if he lives in fear of the menace hanging over him in the form of his countertransference. We are in the presence here of very lively transferential manifestations, born in and through the setting that has been created for them, and refracted in a space in which the analyst occupies the second essential dimension, and whose very activity both reveals and breaks the continuity of a history, just as water breaks up the piece of wood that has been plunged into it.

If this is one of the aporia (and not the least) of the analytic situation, it is necessary either to change our technique or to make compromises to deal with the difficulty. We will not succeed without making some concessions or sacrifices, as a result of which the pure Freudian schema will lose something of its purity. Interpretation is at the heart of psychoanalysis; psychoanalytic technique is based on it. As soon as one attempts to diminish its influence by shifting the accent onto the one who gives it (a development of technical ideas

---

[2] Epictetus (ca. 55–135) was a Greek Stoic philosopher who focused more on ethics than did the early Stoics. Repeatedly attributing his ideas to Socrates, he held that our aim was to be masters of our own lives. The role of the Stoic teacher, according to Epictetus, was to encourage his students to learn, first of all, the true *nature of things*, which is invariable, inviolable and valid for all human beings without exceptions. He is well known for his aphorisms. [*Eds., this volume*]

that began with Wilhelm Reich[3] and was reinforced by Edward Glover,[4] for whom interpretation is of less importance than the one who gives it), it becomes clear that even though one continues to claim allegiance in all essential matters to Freud's conception, all that remains of the latter is a form emptied of all content. This does not imply in any way that the authors who have tried to put the analyst in the foreground of the process of the treatment, to the detriment of interpretation, have not understood an important phenomenon of analysis. They have simply not taken their examination of it far enough. It is not interpretation that should have been relegated to the background while simply noting the fact that it is subordinate to the analyst's attitude. The evident importance of the latter does not imply that one should link all the effects of the analysis to the analyst's person, which would clearly ruin psychoanalysis as we have conceived of it since Freud, making way, in forms slightly better cloaked, for a relational psychotherapy which would be nothing other than a more refined form of suggestion. Hence it becomes all the more urgent to form a sound appreciation of the analyst's role, and of the disturbance that he introduces into the character of interpretation, to the extent that the latter is considered to be of cardinal importance. Placing more emphasis on the analyst's personal role, at a time when the role of interpretation is being reduced so much, also facilitates a change of perspective which results in prescribing definite aims for the analyst's action which no longer depend on a theoretical model but on normative rules. According to this trend, it is necessary to modify, correct and reform that which has been deformed; to repair narcissistic wounds and remodel ego-distortions, etc. The fact that the analyst plays a role even when he refuses to do so is something analysis cannot avoid. The extreme consequences of playing a role deliberately, and as a matter of principle, can be clearly seen in the case of Franz Alexander.[5] Modifying, correcting, reforming, remodelling the patient's ego are all mechanistic temptations. If the analyst must *do* something, it will always be at the expense of what should be *said*. And the act, which is prohibited for the patient, must equally be excluded for the analyst. The patient's associations must be met by the analyst's interpretation. Psychoanalysts are sure that the countertransference designates irrational zones of their personality. If they must (as they do) explore the irrational zones of their patient's

---

[3] Reich's 1933 *Character Analysis* (New York: Farrar, Straus & Giroux, 1980) was a major step in the development of what today would be called 'ego psychology'. Reich considered that a person's entire character, not just the individual symptoms, could be looked at and treated as a neurotic phenomenon. [Eds., this volume]

[4] See Glover's *The Technique of Psycho-Analysis* (New York: International Universities Press, 1958). [Eds., this volume]

[5] Alexander (1891–1964), a Hungarian American psychoanalyst and physician, is considered to be one of the founders of psychosomatic medicine and forensic psychoanalysis. He was one of numerous analysts between the 1930s and the 1950s who were engaged with the question of how to shorten the course of therapy but still achieve therapeutic effectiveness. [Eds., this volume]

unconscious personality, there can be no doubt that the rational zone of their own personality will only be of little assistance to them.

Imagine two beacons, turning in opposite directions, whose lights intersect periodically. It is when transference and countertransference intersect that the brightest moments occur. They are privileged moments in which the truth of interpretation is dazzling.

Editors' added bibliography

Glover, E. (1958). *The Technique of Psycho-Analysis*. New York: International Universities Press.

Reich, W. (1933). *Character Analysis*. New York: Farrar, Straus and Giroux, 1980.

11 COUNTERTRANSFERENCE AND PSYCHOANALYTIC THOUGHT

Michel Neyraut

Michel Neyraut is a psychiatrist and full member of the Paris Psychoanalytical Society. His work on the transference–countertransference relationship has brought about significant developments in our understanding of psychoanalytic treatment.

With his independence of mind and innovative thinking, he has written the now-classic text *Le transfert* [The transference] (PUF, 1974), as well as *Les logiques de l'inconscient* [The logic of the unconscious] (Hachette, 1978) and *Les Raisons de l'irrationnel* [The reasons of the irrational] (PUF, 1997).

Sylvie Dreyfus wrote a concise biography of Michel Neyraut for the 'Psychanalystes d'aujourd'hui' series (PUF, 1999). Michel Neyraut is at present writing *Alter Ego*, to be published by the Éditions de l'Olivier.

> 'The question often arrives a terribly long time after the answer.'
> Oscar Wilde

On the precession of the countertransference

The reader may well be surprised to see a psychoanalytic study on the transference begin with its antinomical term: the countertransference.

But this is only an apparent paradox, if one considers that the transference as a concept only appeared '*après-coup*' in Freud's work, and that it appeared as an obstacle, an accident on the path of a body of thought and technique that had already been constituted. The transference is thus preceded by something.

Furthermore, the transference is not only second in the history of analytic thought; it also appears to come second in analytic treatments – that is to say, it appears after a certain delay. The transference *occurs* or appears in the course of a dynamic process called the psychoanalytic process, i.e. within a specific context. The problem of knowing if it only appears there, or if it was already there, will be discussed further on.

What can we say, then, about this context?

If, on the one hand, we assign it an intrapsychic origin by declaring, for example, that the transference is second in relation to primary narcissism, on the other hand – and as soon as we envisage this context as dialectical – we will have to consider that, as a concept, the transference must be noticed, identified, and thought about and that this 'conception' implicates the analyst and analytic thought.

Finally, the nature of the transference itself is to break repetition in the here-and-now, like waves breaking on a rock; if this repetition is not interpreted, it may repeat itself indefinitely.

Among these values of the here-and-now, the analyst occupies an essential place – he or she is directly or personally implicated and must eventually elucidate this implication.

Both this implication and this thought are part of the context in which the transference appears.

For the time being, I am calling this context the countertransference, leaving it until later to define its limits and extensions. I will just note at this stage that the countertransference, so defined, as context and implication goes beyond its traditional accepted meaning.

This traditional meaning is no other than that of the analyst's *passion*. Passion in all the senses of the term: both Christ-like passion ... and passion of the soul; passion in the passive sense of *suffered*, even if this passion is expressed through some sort of acting out or ... active technique.

The traditional and ambiguous status of the countertransference thus seems to denote 'technical mistake' and 'substance' of interpretation.

This sense of technical 'mistake' stands in contrast with a sort of ideal analysis, in which thinking and listening would be free. This point of view must also be upheld and proves, moreover, to be a corollary of the first. It throws light on the function of presumptuousness in the exposition of all those theories of the treatment which claim to be situated beyond this guilt.

Restricted meaning

The etymological composition of the term countertransference, which is quite a faithful transposition of *Gegen-Übertragung*, suggests a precise and limited meaning whereby the countertransference is opposed to the transference, comes after the transference, and is determined by it: it is essentially secondary and reactive.

This rather limited sense remains perfectly acceptable if one refers to Freud's first impressions on discovering the transference, when he was obliged to admit that in addition to the *restitutio ad integrum* of the 'text' of neurosis, of anamnesis and of the filling in of memories, something suddenly appears in the full actuality of the treatment – namely, new psychic manifestations which, this time, concern the personal relations between the doctor and his patient – and that these new manifestations, which are perfectly importunate, unexpected and unforeseeable, regularly complicate the task of the therapist who has hitherto been busy reconstituting the thread of memory from its vestigial traces.

Insofar as the transference displaces in its wake heavy affective charges, the doctor then finds himself in the unfortunate situation of having to acknowledge that he is the object of these manifestations.

Consequently, one can measure by the reticence he feels or by the difficulty he has in simply 'observing' the occurrence of these manifestations, a certain resistance that has shifted towards the therapist, obliging him to consider this resistance as his own.

This resistance allows us to form an initial idea of the countertransference as being strictly opposed to the transference and determined by it. The first effect of the countertransference belongs to the domain of blindness and disturbance. The activity of analytic thinking, which was hitherto serene, is now compromised by the unexpected occurrence of affective manifestations, the inevitable result of which will be that of having 'a deaf ear'.

I will come back to this traditional understanding of the countertransference which arose when it was initially discovered. But I should point out now that, even if countertransferential phenomena seem to me to go beyond, and above all, to precede the acceptation of their strict opposition to the transference, this moment of their appearance remains fundamental. The reactive and secondary aspect of the countertransference seems to me to be essential even if I consider it to be primary in other ways.

The analyst's implication

The analyst's countertransference begins, then, with *his implication*; it is because he suddenly recognises himself as the object, and perhaps already as the instigator of affective expressions coming from his patient, that he notices in himself the effect of a resistance. Does this mean that the analyst is only implicated through the transference or simply that the transference, owing to its essential character of 'address', implicates the analyst more directly, more personally, and that he then has no other option than that of interpreting the meaning of this address, of recognising himself in it, or of disowning it.

I prefer this last hypothesis, since the analyst's presence is required not only by the transference, but also by all the other solicitations that are engendered by the analytic situation. These solicitations are of all kinds, and among them a significant place belongs to those that emanate from the analyst himself, from his demands and his thinking.

Extensive theory

This last remark introduces us to an extensive theory of the countertransference, the sense of which is broadened to include all the manifestations, ideas, fantasies, feelings, interpretations, actions or reactions of the analyst. If, theoretically, such an acceptation is imaginable (and even if, for my own part, I have a tendency to extend the notion of countertransference much further than its usage in strict opposition to the transference), I think that it is only of relative interest and fails to account for the conflictual, affective and dynamic relationship (in the sense of the *Papers on Metapsychology*: Freud, 1915) which is formed in the analytic situation and only assumes its value in this situation.

So another paradox of the countertransference that needs to be grasped is that it can be conceived of both as preceding the analytic situation proper (preliminary didactic analysis, training, distortions or orthodoxies of all kinds) and as assuming its true dimension only through being confronted with the internal solicitations arising from the analytic situation.

A problem exists, then, concerning the specificity of analytic countertransference, since many other disciplines apart from analysis borrow a part of its theory, use its concepts, draw inspiration from its formation and, in a general way, have access to the theoretical knowledge of psychoanalysis.

If psychoanalytic thought constitutes a context in which transference can occur, this 'preliminary condition' is shared by other disciplines, and insofar as such thinking is bound up with the countertransference, in what respect can the creation of the analytic situation lay claim to specificity?

Philosophers and the psychological field

Many philosophical works or essays which come under the umbrella of the 'human sciences' and discuss psychoanalysis, psychoses or any form of alienation, begin by stating that the arguments advanced (e.g. by Ricoeur, de Waehlens, Deleuze, Sartre, etc.) are in no way linked to analytic practice, that the authors are not psychoanalysts, or that they have never seen a schizophrenic in their life, etc. Having acknowledged this, they continue their investigations and share with us their discoveries and their enquiries.

This attitude is entirely reasonable and, moreover, does not require any justification, which the above-mentioned authors have understood perfectly well.

So it is reasonable to wonder what differentiates such an approach from another which would be strictly psychoanalytic, since the proposition can be the same in both cases.

Specificity of the psychoanalytic field

This difference – and this is what I want to demonstrate – resides precisely in the countertransference. What I mean by that is that any manifestation of the analyst, in particular, and in the strict sense of the term, any publication, any piece of writing, any epiphany, even though it may appear to be *outside* the analytic situation, *outside* its specific field, proceeds in reality from this field and are internal to it.

Psychoanalytic thinking necessarily forms part of a response. This is because the analytic situation originates with a demand. In this sense, the scientific writings formulated by the analyst may be considered as a counterpoint or rejoinder. By definition, we must take them as the equivalent of a response – unconscious or deliberate; or of a response to the precise solicitations of a particular analysis.

Not only will we assume that psychoanalytic thinking constitutes a response, but that it is constituted by this response; that it cannot escape its essential status of arising from a specific confrontation that we call the analytic situation, and that this analytic situation originates in a demand and implicates the analyst in such a way that he will be unable, either before or after the event, to clarify the meaning of the unconscious elements that have appeared in it except by elucidating this implication.

If psychoanalytic thinking is essentially constituted by a response, we will have to acknowledge that sometimes the response precedes the question, and that this is a first form of countertransference.

It is not simply a question here of opposing the 'practice' of analysis with the 'non-practice' of it, as one would oppose the operation and the armchair strategy,[1] because in the operation, as in the armchair strategy, there is a practical field and a non-practical field.

Limits and contradictions of this field

The issue is to understand that psychoanalytic thinking, through the contingencies of its practice, the requirements of its theory, and the specific nature of what we call the countertransference, is subject to limitations and extensions which determine and specify its particular way of looking at the psychological field.

It has no particular rights with regard to this psychological field but, on the contrary, is limited in its expression by the doctrinal and countertransferential constraints of its practice. This contradiction is illustrated by one of the first technical prescriptions of Freud, which stipulates that the analyst must under

---

[1] 'Armchair strategy' – a French expression used during the Second World War – refers to pseudo-strategists who never get their boots muddy. [*Eds., this volume*]

no circumstances consider the treatment as scientific work, which would prejudice the freedom of his listening:

> It is not a good thing to work on a case scientifically while treatment is still proceeding – to piece together its structure, to try to foretell its further progress, and to get a picture from time to time of the current state of affairs, as scientific interest would demand. . . . The correct behaviour for an analyst lies in swinging over according to need from the one mental attitude to the other, in avoiding speculation or brooding over cases while they are in analysis, and in submitting the material obtained to a synthetic process of thought only after the analysis is concluded.
> (Freud, 1912e, p. 114)

This 'swinging over from one mental attitude to another' seems to me to characterise one of the specific moments of psychoanalytic thinking. It supposes amongst other things a 'suspension', a bracketing [*epoché*] even more radical than that required by Husserl's phenomenology, since it must be extended to the domain of unconscious representations. In one sense, which is nothing more than jest, the real phenomenology is to be situated more on the side of analysis than on the side of phenomenological reflection.

Thus psychoanalytic thinking gets out of its armchair and returns to it. This contingency is, if I may so, essential.

If, between these two moments, it needs to speak, to write, to deepen the theory and even to demolish it or transmit it, it means that it does not find in the analytic situation enough to satisfy it entirely; but in any case it is in relation to this analytic situation that it must judge itself, and in so doing, it implicates the analyst in person because it takes account of his demands.

Countertransference and the historical development of psychoanalytic thought

The response, as I have said, can precede the demand and constitute a first form of countertransference. There are three ways of looking at this: the first is to consider psychoanalytic thinking from the angle of its historical development. In this sense, for example, the 'Project for a Scientific Psychology' (1950 [1895]) and the work that preceded the exposition of Dora's case may be attributed to a resistance to the discovery of the transference or, more exactly, to the concept of the transference.

I would say that, in this work, psychoanalytic thinking was structured, the perspective of the treatment was envisaged and the conception of the psyche was constructed in such a way that the transference was *then* discovered as an obstacle, a hindrance, a surprise, an unexpected phenomenon. Freud's boldness, his absolute confidence in himself, was then necessary to affirm that the transference is an obstacle, that it *is in its very nature to be* an obstacle.

This precession of psychoanalytic thinking in relation to the discovery of the transference, a precession that I am considering here from a kind of retroactive perspective – that is, *après-coup* – delimits an 'external' field of the countertransference and an 'internal' field, it being understood that it is simply for the sake of convenience of exposition that they are so distinguished. In reality, they are indistinguishable beforehand or retrospectively because, at a given moment, they are confronted with the implications of the analytic situation.

The 'external field of the countertransference' imposes on analytic thinking, and on any given analyst, limits whose nature pertains to sociological and political disciplines.

It is in this way that all the theories which denounce the dated, social, normative, religious, dogmatic and historical character that is linked to the here-and-now situation of a specific analyst, and of analysis in a given social context, are introduced.

One cannot find an example, in fact, of a sociocultural context that has not influenced the general direction, the aims and the conception of analysis itself. *The ethical subordination of analysis to the implicit ideals of a specific society is a discernible fact*, even if analytic theory draws on concepts of universal value.

But the problem is to see that the unconscious only appears and, above all, only reveals itself in specific contexts and conditions which provide a basis for the manifest text.

If Freud determined in his own context the best technical conditions for the unconscious to appear and reveal itself, it does not suffice to denounce these historical conditions to be rid of the unconscious.

The epoch always supplies the terms of the manifest text.

Reducing the manifest expression to the latent meaning is in itself an a-chronic procedure. This does not mean that the moral values of a particular epoch do not appear during this unveiling, but it is unlikely that the sociocultural modifications that have occurred since Freud's discoveries have sufficient weight to necessitate technical modifications in such a way that it could be said that now technical conditions should be modified so that the unconscious can appear and be interpreted more adequately.

If such modifications do take place, they will not occur as a result of a prescription *ex cathedra*, of a noisy conversion, but rather, insidiously, through the imperceptible modification of the ideals specific to a society.

It is not part of my purpose here to explore in more depth the external field of the countertransference, for the reason that its study belongs to other disciplines than those of analysis itself.

From the standpoint of the historical development of psychoanalytic thinking, we have seen that the response could precede the question and that the countertransference could constitute a historical antecedent in the recognition and discovery of the transference. This same precession is found during the establishment of the analytic situation itself.

Countertransference in the analytic situation

Among the concrete modalities concerning the setting (the analyst's invisibility), this situation – which, moreover, recognises other arrangements – was conceived so as not to have to tolerate being face to face with the patient for twelve hours a day.

This setting allows the analyst to conceal any form of response which, even if not articulated verbally, would nonetheless be expressed by some facial expression or gesture.

There is no doubt that this situation outlines in the concrete space of the setting the traits of an attitude which concerns the countertransference. It facilitates the rule of silence and supports the containment of emotional expression, but in so doing it simply renders the analyst's emotional implication tangible.

This involvement, as we know, goes beyond the emotions to the reasons for these emotions, or if you will, to the 'body of offence' (*corpus delicti*). We will have the opportunity of coming back to the different modes of the analyst's involvement, since we will see how it is impossible to speak of the countertransference without introducing the countertransferential elements.

One only has to recall the first of the implications that we have noted – namely, that the analyst is forced to consider himself as the object of the transferential manifestations – in order to understand the amplitude of this implication. These transference manifestations must be understood both directly as the expression of immediate seductions and indirectly via the detour of the complex configurations evoked.

Freud warns on many occasions against the dangers of direct seduction (in the widest sense of the term), referring to immediate provocations, explicit requests and precise entreaties. Such demands are ordinarily illustrated by an attractive woman seeking signs of affection.

Although Freud constantly traced these misplaced requests back to their infantile origins, these warnings are situated in the full actuality, in the full reality, in the perfect immanence of their need for satisfaction. The rule is not to give way to them at all, which is to be understood in the most real and tangible way possible.

In a certain way these prescriptions seem naïve with regard to Freud's multiple implications in the case of Dora, where one can see that seduction can be exercised without resorting to explicit demands, and where the satisfactions hoped for are acquired at degrees of reality that belong to psychic reality.

It would be a mistake, however, to neglect these 'realistic' prescriptions which, however realistic they may be, nonetheless remain the model for all seductions, precisely because seduction keeps on the horizon of its desire some very tangible aspects of reality.

Listening to the flattest discourse, the dullest narrative, exposes the analyst to a huge field of instinctual solicitations, as we shall see later on.

All the levels of seduction overlap and transcend the resistances. The narrative or discourse, for example, inasmuch as it constitutes itself as resistance, is more resistance because it seems seductive than resistance proper. Conversely, the discourse can be boring in itself but seductive in its content.

Every allusion, every associative pattern which refers to an erogenous zone, is a seduction. Seduction is always directly due to the very fact of being heard. Consequently, it is multiple and appeals to the analyst's desire both through the enunciation of its own desire and through the dramatisation of any given fantasy. Seduction establishes the analyst as co-desiring just as much by constituting itself as the object of his desire, by choosing him as object, and by facing him with a third desire, *as by only invoking the indeterminate object of the desire.*

There is no such thing as neutral listening, there is no 'disinterested' listening, but only free listening, and it is free insofar as it knows in advance how to interest itself and disinterest itself at one and the same time. Nor is there any such thing as listening without identification and without 'disengaging from identification'. Identification must be understood here both at the global level of an understanding 'on the basis of common points', which, moreover, may be unconscious, and at the level at which the analyst is 'identified' with this or that desirable or hateful object.

Identification, which is otherwise commonplace, is only countertransference here to the extent that it is inscribed within a situation that is favourable both for elucidating unconscious phenomena and for resisting their comprehension. It is only countertransference in the psychoanalytic sense of being inscribed within a technical situation that depends on explicit prescriptions which limit or even condemn, or tolerate, and in any case regulate, the response which can be made to any demand through the channel of this or that identification.

By 'regulation', I mean both external regulation, which, by means of didactic training, the pressure of schools and allegiances of all kinds, modifies the course of analytic thinking, as well as internal forms of regulation which only proceed from a subject for the reason that if the analyst prohibits himself from responding, or simply does not feel the need to do so, this limitation governs the analytic situation, to the extent that it has no other aim than that of elucidating the unconscious, and that this elucidation of desire involves the necessity of suspending the response.

That this suspension, which the analysand experiences concretely as an interpretation in waiting (and which is interpreted by some as a virtue of frustration), is necessary to confound the very essence of the disguise of the unconscious, is another way of saying that this disguise, this displacement or this condensation of the representable elements of the unconscious is only so well disguised because it is addressed to someone else who hears it and responds to it, and that it needs this response to confirm, perfect and even constitute its disguise.

It will be understood from this that the most unassailable core of resistance (whether considered from the standpoint of the transference or of the countertransference) will be made up of fantasies in which the answer is implied in the question – in other words, repetition in treatments conducted according to relational models, where the analyst is involved in such a way that his response is no longer waited for but anticipated, that is to say, implicated in the demand.

The analyst's implication in the analysis of character

This sort of resistance can be linked up with character resistance.

Much emphasis has been rightly laid on the defensive aspect of character and not enough on the lowest level of libido that it guarantees.

In the face of any given danger, situation or ordeal, character ensures a sort of vital minimum of satisfaction. But this satisfaction can only be conceived of if the protagonist of the ordeal or the agent of the danger is implicated in such a way that he responds in advance to this satisfaction, and without prejudice to the narcissistic satisfaction that is inevitably consumed in the process.

Character resistance does not only reside in the defensive strength that is revealed in it, whether this strength is defensive in relation to internal drives or in relation to a danger perceived as external, or whether, and primarily, it is defensive in relation to unconscious instinctual satisfactions which find their expression in a relationship that is already represented, repeated over and over again, and constantly adjusted.

It can be seen that, conceived in this way, character is strangely similar to the transference, which, as it is also caught up in a thoroughly actual situation, transposes the elements of an infantile relationship on to a contemporary conflict. Their essential difference lies in the fact that the transference, even in its aspect of pure repetition, maintains the possibility of a new response.

It questions a figure of childhood in a way that is sometimes stereotyped, but it really does question.

Beyond its peremptory assignations, the transference maintains a sort of indecision of roles, drawing on the contrast of the opposing drives. It is more the analysis of the transference and its elucidation which will then make it possible to designate the exact meaning of the process of questioning or of the demand.

Character, on the other hand, does not accept indecision or the questioning of an instinctual vicissitude, does not run the risk of noticing the danger of a reversal or the transformation of a passive aim into an active aim. Its compromises are self-imposed, and it pushes symptoms as far away as possible. To do this, it necessarily involves the analyst in a definite, inalienable and timeless role, and it responds on his behalf in spite of any interpretation, since this interpretation is already 'caught' in the context of a response formulated in advance.

The countertransferential problem of character, which is perfectly evident in Reich or Ferenczi, always engenders the same type of metaphors taken from a tale of chivalry – namely, shield, armour, defence, smashing.

If my memories are exact, Lacan speaks for other reasons, which are perhaps the same, of blazon. But more clearly in Ferenczi than in Reich, we can see that the real problem is one of a *correspondence* of characters.

Character calls forth character because it implicates the analyst in such a way that only archaic modes of relating seem to be able to thwart it. Moreover, *this problem of the similarity of structures goes beyond that of character and concerns all countertransferential relations*. To be persuaded of this one only has to think about the criteria an analyst uses when referring a patient to another analyst.

Irrespective of all the other contingent problems, one will see that, even without realising it, he will make his decision in terms of similar or contrasting structures. The effect of too great a similarity between these structures will be akin to the effect produced by the vibration of identical frequencies, just as a sound can shatter crystal.

As the analyst does not want to shatter the 'characteropathic shell', character-analysis can be conducted up to a certain point, beyond which it is sometimes more advisable to learn to 'use' the character by making it conscious. In so doing, one acknowledges its value as the guardian of a minimal level of libidinal satisfaction. If we take the example of characteropathic conformism, it is no doubt a result of improper objectification that we designate such a mode of thinking as characteropathic. But the fact is that character calls for objectification by the insistent nature of its style, and, furthermore, it is only character inasmuch as it responds in advance to what is expected of it: that it manifests itself and has constituted itself so that is, precisely, what one expects of it and nothing else. But if, having decided not to tackle it head-on, nor to analyse it as such, since that would lead to objectifying it in one way or another, we analyse it by the detour of anal erotism, we may discover that it is in order to conform eternally to the maternal desire to produce a perfect turd that our conformist condemns himself to ready-made ideas, but ideas that are in keeping with what is expected.

But this interpretation will be accepted (this one, or another) through conformism. The characteropathic circle is thus closed, from which it is impossible to escape, since, to be able to hear conformism, one has to be in conformity with it.

It is in this respect that character is character, and is expressed by an invincible resistance. This resistance involves the analyst in sorts of trials of strength, as can be seen in the case of Reich, where all the 'tact' and 'touch' in the world will not change the fact that the analyst has tried to force the issue. We can see that here the answer is contained in the question. If the patient questions the analyst while showing him perpetually that he is in compliance, it is because he considers unconsciously that he only has to conform to be loved. The answer that he expects is indeed that he is loved as he is – that is, insofar as he conforms. Any other detour will only lead him to reiterate his conformism, since by conforming he obtains the answer that he expects.

The example of character is only given here to point up the implication of countertransferential thinking, or, more exactly, one of its impasses. It illustrates the second point of view that I referred to earlier: namely, that in the analytic situation, as in the historical development of analytic thinking, the countertransference shows how the analyst is implicated or involved at all levels – either because, owing to his own demands or the ethical constraint that he imposes, his thinking seems to precede the birth of the transference and to respond to it in advance, or because, being confronted finally with the necessities of identification, of seduction or rejection, he cannot resolve the enigmas that he has as a rule himself posed as enigmas, except by leaving the response in abeyance.

This response constitutes the very essence of what is solicited in the analytic situation. We can see in the example of character that resistance can be interpreted as an imbrication of the response and the demand, whether this imbrication is due to the patient or to the analyst.

The countertransference is confronted not only by the transference but by all the solicitations entailed by the setting-up of the analytic situation. The latter is only sustained by the suspension of interpretation, which constitutes either a hope or a danger for it.

Every rupture of silence is an interpretation. Interpretation is on the horizon of all the tensions and all the demands which occur. From this it is understandable that unless one denies the analyst's involvement in the analytic situation and takes his neutrality for non-existence, countertransferential thinking – whose only reason for being is to suspend its articulated expression – is subject to implosions, new outcomes, lost associations, silent catastrophes or hidden triumphs. For the large part, countertransference thinking is not expressed, and, furthermore, interpretation cannot, either by right or in reality, constitute a discharge of it.

With regard to this silent confrontation, the transference stands in opposition, among other elements of the analytic situation, to the countertransference. But in view of its eminently heuristic character, the indecision of the response that it expects and the insistence with which it solicits immediate satisfaction in the name of a much older desire, it constitutes a remarkable possibility for opening up the intrapsychic conflict. At the same time as it outlines and creates the limits of a specific field of opposition – that of the transference–countertransference – it contributes to or even founds this field and this opposition as dialectical. In other words, it outlines in a veiled manner forms of 'animation' where the historical figures that have contributed to giving it the possibility of a psychic displacement seem to be set in motion; where instinctual demands, even if they are begged for in the here and now and addressed to the most immediate listening, are nonetheless formulated in archaic terms; and where, by means of this immediate demand, it is possible to identify the permanent modalities, the obligatory channels and the privileged structures through which these demands are unfailingly repeated.

The transference is not opposed to the countertransference more than any other form of solicitation; it is simply that it imposes itself more directly and clearly because it is more blind; and as it is more blind, it utilises precisely the *here-and-now* elements of the concrete analytic situation which are the most favourable for resistance – that is, those that reintroduce the most efficiently the most insistent archaic modes of relating.

These archaic modes of relating, which constitute the structures of the transference, are organised all the more dramatically in that they borrow the forces which animate them from the fundamental Oedipal structure, and the organisation of the transference-neurosis – which can occur at a very early stage – only finds its true dimension in the Oedipal expression of jealousy. It thus sets a new trap in which the countertransference gets stuck by responding too well to it.

Countertransference as demand

It goes without saying that so far we have assimilated the countertransference to a response, *but its true nature is to constitute itself as a demand*, and this is precisely the kind of response that is expected of it.

To constitute itself as a demand, it infringes a fundamental rule which is not formulated anywhere but which everyone nonetheless tries to observe. If the analyst expresses a demand, the analytic situation is destabilised, and yet everything is organised so that he ends up by formulating it. The strictest purism coincides here with the purest naïvety in believing that via interpretations the demand does not show through in any way; in this connection it is worth pointing out that the demand for payment can only be dissimulated as a demand by being formulated as an exigency. However, it is an implicit demand that sustains the analytic situation, and what Freud calls the sublimation of the transference is based on this demand. This demand is sustained both by the analyst and by the patient and is the basis of the alliance.

Countertransference and reflective thinking

I shall now consider a third point of view in order to illustrate the interaction of the demand and the countertransferential response. It completes the first two and concerns the reflective moments which comment on the analytic situation. These reflective moments are also part of psychoanalytic thinking and, like it, share the limitations of the countertransference.

Whether one speaks, as Freud does, of the theory of the technique, or whether one refers to the speculations of analytic thinking on the nature of religions, the future of any other illusion, or of interpreting this or that discontent in civilisation, these speculations, however far removed from the contingencies of the treatment they seem, do not belong to any other field than that of the analytic situation itself. Even in the so-called speculative theories such as that of the death drive, the analytic situation remains the fundamental reference, and the negative transference is at once the evidence and the model of an invincible *resistance* attributed to this drive. We can thus see that a theory of the death drive can be qualified as countertransferential in the same way as another theory that opposes it in the name of the same arguments.

Unless they are brought back to the analytic situation, and particularly to the transferential field which guarantees resistance, the so-called speculative Freudian texts, such as *Civilization and its Discontents* (Freud, 1930a), if they are studied as such for their ideological value, can only give the grotesque image of a *trompe l'oeil*. If it is really a matter of passing judgement on communism or the accumulation of capital, these texts offer a very poor example of what analytic thought can constitute, unless, that is, they are transferred and distorted by the invisible eye of the unconscious which is looking at them.

Links between the countertransference and psychoanalytic thought

But what does psychoanalytic thought mean? Why am I linking psychoanalytic thought and countertransference? My aim is to demonstrate the unity of this thought both in the history of analytic theory and in the actual practice of a treatment, as well as in the moments of reflection which comment on the analytic situation.

What is meant here by thought?

Thought can be considered from several points of view in Freud's work: (1) From a general point of view, when it is the evolution of thought in the history of humanity that is being considered. This term replaces the pejorative and outmoded term of 'mentality' (in the sense of primitive mentality). Thus he speaks of animistic thought, religious thought or scientific thought. (2) From the particular point of view of the world of dreams, and coinciding with the opposition latent–manifest, he speaks of latent thoughts in contrast with the manifest text and with the associations themselves. (3) From the point of view of nature itself and of the function of thought in the mind in general. This point of view concerns the opposition between primary process and secondary process and is developed particularly in 'Formulations on the Two Principles of Mental Functioning' (1911b), the article on 'Negation' (1925h) and in 'The Mystic Writing-Pad' (1925a [1924]). To this third group can be added Freud's considerations on 'perceptual identity' and the 'thought identity', already presented in the *Interpretation of Dreams* (1900a).

References

Freud, S. (1900a). *The Interpretation of Dreams.* S.E., 4/5.
Freud, S. (1911b). Formulations on the Two Principles of Mental Functioning. *S.E.*, 12: 215
Freud, S. (1912e). Recommendations to Physicians Practising Psycho-Analysis. *S.E.*, 12: 109–120.
Freud, S. (1915). *Papers on Metapsychology.* S.E., 14: 105–258.
Freud, S. (1925a [1924]). A Note upon the 'Mystic Writing-Pad'. *S.E.*, 19: 227–232.
Freud, S. (1925h). Negation. *S.E.*, 19: 233–239.
Freud, S. (1930a). *Civilization and its Discontents.* S.E., 21.
Freud, S. (1950 [1895]). Project for a Scientific Psychology. *S.E.*, 1.

12 TRANSFERENCE: ITS PROVOCATION BY THE ANALYST

Jean Laplanche

A graduate of the prestigious École Normale Supérieure and professor at the Sorbonne, **Jean Laplanche** turned first to psychiatry then to psychoanalysis both as a practitioner and as a theoretician. The path that he followed is above all an internal trajectory, characterised by a quest that would lead him to challenge all kinds of received ideas; the rigour of his approach has radically changed psychoanalytic thinking over the past four decades. He is one of the founders of the French Psychoanalytical Association, over which he presided from 1969 to 1971. In May 1968, he participated in freeing the clinical human sciences from the hegemony of experimental psychology. As a university professor between 1970 and 1993, he supervised several remarkable theses, including some in the field of psychoanalysis: he was one of the founders of the Teaching and Research Units in clinical human sciences in the French university system.

Among his published works are: *Hölderlin ou la question du père* (PUF, 1961) [*Hölderlin and the Question of the Father*. ELS editions, 2007]; *Vocabulaire de la Psychanalyse* (with J.-B. Pontalis; PUF, 1967) [*The Language of Psychoanalysis*. Hogarth Press, 1973]; *Fantasme originaire, fantasmes des origines, origines du fantasme* [Primal fantasies, fantasies of origins and origins of fantasy] (with J.-B. Pontalis; Hachette, 1964); *Vie et mort en psychanalyse* [Life and death in psychoanalysis] (Flammarion, 1970); the series 'Problématiques' [Problematics] (I to V, PUF 1980–1997); *Le fourvoiement biologisant de la sexualité chez Freud* [Biologically related going-astray in Freud's view of sexuality] (Les Empêcheurs de Penser en rond, 1993); *Le primat de l'autre en psychanalyse* [The primacy of the Other in psychoanalysis] (Flammarion, 1997), a collection of his major papers written between 1967 and 1992; this was followed by *Entre séduction et inspiration. L'homme* [Between seduction and inspiration: Man] (PUF, 1999), a selection of later writings between 1992 and 1998.

As an editor, too, Laplanche has been very active. He is the editor of the PUF series 'Bibliothèque de Psychanalyse' [Library of psychoanalysis] and 'Voies nouvelles en psychanalyse' [New paths in psychoanalysis] (a series of early writings by research graduates). He created the journal *Psychanalyse à l'Université* (1975–1994), and since 1988 he has been scientific editor of the new French translations of Freud's *Complete Works* (PUF). He received the Sigourney Award in 1995.

Dominique Scarfone wrote a concise biography of Jean Laplanche for the 'Psychanalystes d'aujourd'hui' series (PUF, 1997).

> *Analyst:* You are taking me for someone else, I'm not the person you think.
>
> *Analysand:* But the other in the originary relation was, precisely, not the person I thought. So I'm perfectly right to take you for someone else.

The transference, or more particularly the accounts which are given of it, has always been a source of dissatisfaction to me. The formulations I have set forth correspond to a broader view, that of the theory of seduction. Terms like 'transcendence of the transference', 'hollowed-out transference',[1] 'transference of the transference' or even 'originary transference' are formulations open to discussion and 'work'. It is often difficult to work over one's own formulas.

If I have adopted, as an introduction to this presentation, the opposition between 'ordinary' and 'extraordinary' transference, this is not to add two supplementary categories, two new concepts; it is more a possible guiding thread, which I have grasped as such, in a series of lectures on 'ordinary and ideal psychoanalysis'. The binary ordinary/extraordinary can have at least two meanings: it is one and the same transference – ours, that of psychoanalysis – which can be described as both ordinary and extraordinary, familiar when it appears, disconcerting when one tries to think about it: at the same time *heimlich* and *unheimlich*.[2] Also perhaps, from another perspective, there exists somewhere an ordinary transference, and elsewhere an extraordinary variety of the same species – something which is less surprising because the word 'transference' itself implies the transportation of the same thing to somewhere else.

I will return later to this second formulation, which concerns the opposition between transference within psychoanalytic treatment and transference outside it. For the moment, I will pause over this notion that a single transference constitutes our ordinary quotidian experience, even if, for Freud, it was extraordinary, the moment of a divine – or rather diabolic – surprise: a moment

---

[1] [Laplanche makes a distinction between 'filled-in' transference – '*en plein*' – and 'hollowed-out' transference – '*en creux*'. The former is a positive reproduction of childhood imagos and behaviours, while the latter is a reproduction of the originary relation to the enigma of the adult other to which the former is in some sense a response and a translation, which must be worked through so as to allow the latter relation to emerge. See J. Laplanche, *New Foundations for Psychoanalysis* (1987), trans. D. Macey (Oxford: Basil Blackwell, 1989), pp. 160–162. Editor's note.]

[2] [The German terms for canny and uncanny. For Freud's discussion of the ambiguities and shifting relations between them, see 'The Uncanny' (1919h, S.E., 17), p. 219. Editor's note.]

which seems, moreover, to have become a thing of the past. For Breuer, in his misadventure, it was something diabolic; but it was, too, for Freud, this transference he considered a 'cross', an 'unwanted devotion' which blocked remembering. Let us recall *Beyond the Pleasure Principle* (1920g, S.E., 18): transference is one of the major reasons – *the* major reason – for positing a 'repetition compulsion' which would escape the pleasure principle. Let us also recall 'Observations on Transference-Love' (1915a, S.E., 12), an article often discussed, at least since Octave Mannoni.[3] The article appears thoroughly *dramatic*, in the true sense of the word, since it concerns a theatrical performance where suddenly, on stage, a fire breaks out: the fire of real love. Will I provoke objections if I say that this article is most often used as a pretext for this bit of rhetoric, a way of scaring ourselves a little, of recalling how, in practising what is termed the 'cure by love', we are handling explosives? It is also a means of showing that Freud was – just as we still are ourselves (which reassures us) – trapped when it comes to distinguishing normal from pathological, love from transference-love. As far as clinical practice goes, however, we seem to manage not so badly with transference-love, at any rate when it is contained within non-psychotic limits (but in the case of psychosis, should we not also speak of transference-hate?).

In analysis, our day-to-day experience – the existence or even the declaration of transference-love – often appears immediately, which confirms, if confirmation were necessary, its 'lightning' quality. It is rare for us to draw back, or encourage someone in supervision to do so, and not to engage with this development in the treatment. A certain vigilance is current, a certain attention to structural dimensions, for instance the 'mirroring' aspects of the relationship. In passing – is it not remarkable that Freud does not, in that article, make any reference to the principal text in which he introduces precisely the problem of love, amorous passion, *Verliebtheit* – that is to say, the text on narcissism? One has to check the dates and to rub one's eyes, so to speak, on realising that the text on transference-love is from 1915, and that it nevertheless contains not a word about the developments concerning love in 'On Narcissism: An Introduction' which dates from 1914.

I will continue with the 'ordinary' transference. Guy Rosolato, in a quite remarkable article, 'La pratique: son cadre, ses interdits',[4] gives us in summary a description of what usually takes place, as opposed to what is said. What takes place, that is, in France, in what he terms a 'basic practice' reckoned to be orthodox, average, marked (but in a considered fashion) by Lacan's influence,

---

[3] Octave Mannoni (1899–1989), a French psychoanalyst, was inspired by Lacan and published several psychoanalytic books (e.g., *Clefs pour l'imaginaire ou l'Autre Scène* [Key for the imaginary or the Other Scene] – Paris: Editions du Seuil, 1969) and articles. Arguably his most well-known work, *Prospero and Caliban: The Psychology of Colonization* (New York: Praeger, 1956), deals with the psychology of the coloniser and the colonised. [Eds., *this volume*]

[4] *Psychanalyse à l'Université* (1987), vol. 12, no. 47, pp. 469–485.

but not the practice of true-believers. The description is done with humour, but like all forms of humour, it bears traces of sympathy, even in its criticism. Actually, Rosolato's description only refers to transference in passing, not that it is absent for it impregnates the whole, but the author mentions it explicitly only a few times. Is this not also the result of our clinical exchanges, centred in an important way on cases in supervision? The location of the transference, together with a discreet allusion to the countertransference, is considered vital; but one never insists either to oneself or to the other on what, for decades, was called the technical management – the *Handlung* or *handling*[5] – of the transference, and still less (a point to which I will return) on its dissolution.

Let us regard this 'basic practice' Rosolato talks of with the same benevolence as he does, a benevolence which is not unquestioning. Let us say that on the whole we have moved from the analysis *of* transference to analysis situated *in* transference. This implies a 'basic' transference, which would be in the end the very *milieu* of analysis, in the sense of its surrounding environment. One ends up getting used to a *milieu*, no longer noticing it. The very idea that the transference has to establish itself, evolves, disappears, becomes blurred. Transference, it has been correctly remarked, is present straight away, from the first interview; it is often noticed even before the beginning of the treatment, for instance in a dream, and is frequently observed in the period which elapses between the first interview and the beginning of analysis. One notices a *milieu* less when one is plunged in it; more so when it is rather briskly altered or when one leaves it. Thus the interest there has been in what is called 'lateral transference'. Is this a term of Freud's? It is not clear. Lateral transference, acting out, an infidelity to the analytic relation – what is to be done with it? It may be drawn back into that relation, interpreted, in sum, as a *transference of transference*: 'What you could not, did not wish to tell me, you have signified, enacted, outside'.

Characteristic of this perspective is an interpretation, or rather a persistent misinterpretation, of the Freudian term *Übertragungswiderstand* (transference resistance). This misinterpretation has been pointed out by Lagache, Pontalis and myself; the term always means the resistance *of* the transference, in other words, the resistance which the transference opposes to the treatment: transference as one of the major resistances. For it is a mistake to think that Freud ever speaks of resistance *to* transference: such a notion absolutely fails to occur to him. Now, this mistranslation should give us pause for thought. It indicates a crucial development since Freud, for transference has become the outright equivalent of the treatment, so that resistance to one is identical to resistance to the other. Is this to say that we do not speak about transference in the

---

[5] [The terms are in German and English in the original. *Translator's note*.]

treatment, that we fail to analyse the transference? It is certain that we exercise the 'caution' underlined in the first place by Rosolato. If we interpret a transferential movement, it is not to attack it as a defence, nor to resolve it; it is in the end to make it evolve, to help in its evolution.

Like the terms 'resistance of transference' and 'resistance to transference', the term 'dynamic' would provide interesting material for our reflection. Freud's article 'The Dynamics of Transference' (1912b, S.E., 12) is a big disappointment if one hopes to find anything in it about 'dynamics' in the modern sense of the term: a dynamic movement internal to transference. What Freud describes is the determination of the transference by forces, thus the unconscious dynamics which produce it; but as for dynamics as movement, as evolution, as the changing relation of forces, as 'dynamism' – there's no question of this in the article. Rosolato connects the 'basic practice' he describes[6] to what he terms the 'logodynamic' axis. Adopting what he says fairly freely, I will propose something along these lines: speech in the transference reveals the unconscious, but is also the bearer of new meaning. In this second sense of the word 'dynamic', precisely that of logodynamics, there is very little that is dynamic in Freud.

Interpreting the transference is enabling it to develop. The notion of *Lösung*, resolution or dissolution of the transference, which is so important for Freud and whose presence was so strong for a long time in analysis, seems to have taken a secondary place in our concerns. Not without justification, perhaps: isn't the dissolution of the transference sawing through the branch one is sitting on? Analysis remains analysis up until the last second, which means that until the last second there will be transference. Not without justification, then. But also not without error, if the almost instantaneous dissolution of the transference as an 'illusion' has to give way, in our time, to a sort of gradual disappearance of the limits of analysis, a process of attenuation too frequently embodied in certain ways of ending analysis: one moves on to two sessions, then one session; why not to a half-session or a quarter-session? One moves from lying-down to sitting; why not, in caricature, have a couch equipped with a crankshaft which would progressively bring the patient into a sitting position?

Briefly, this problem of ending replays, precisely, the whole problem of analysis. The move from the extraordinary situation of analysis to the ordinary one of life can be conceived in at least three ways: as a radical shift of level (from illusion to reality), as an imperceptible transition, or – and this will be my proposal – as *transference*.

Whatever its nature, there is no question of demolishing this basic practice to which I have just added a little on the topic of transference, nor of

---

[6] The five axes on which Rosolato situates all psychoanalytic practice are: logodynamic, transgressive, ideal-inducing, technical and negative (ibid., p. 483).

aggressively reforming it. It is tried and tested, but in a certain way it lacks *real* examination, lacks self-reflection. It always refers, to be sure, to Freud, but this reference can become reverence. Yet its differences, even its divergences, from Freud are major. What remains of Freud is no doubt an essential element, but one which is not necessarily well theorised – rather an intuition or a lived experience: the specificity, the unprecedented character of what takes place in analysis. The certainty that sexuality is at work, and not only psychological transference in general, is connected to this extraordinary quality.

The last great reference to Freud, the last coherent explanation of the Freudian position, is clearly the great '*Rapport*' of Daniel Lagache.[7] This report may seem at a certain distance from contemporary practice, but nevertheless it is not out of date in so far as the problematic it sets out has not been given any theoretical renewal. This problematic, as you know, is that of the unity of psychology, and I would immediately stress my differences with Lagache, for I think it is precisely a duality of psychology, or a duality of the psyche, which should be spoken of if one is to understand anything at all about transference. By duality, I mean simply the opposition between self-preservation and sexuality. To talk of the unity of psychology is to return the unfamiliar to the familiar, the extraordinary to the ordinary, the psychoanalytic transference to the psychological transference of habitual behaviour, which is the unavoidable common destiny of all humans, even of all living beings.

I will not follow this work of Lagache's in detail; I did this a few years ago in my book on transference.[8] It constitutes an historical step, one of whose most important moments is assured by the transition from Freud to an author who was a contemporary of Lagache, and who is perhaps now rather forgotten, Ida Macalpine. According to Freud, the specificity of analytic transference is due to the specificity of the neurotic. It is neurosis – unresolved, unconscious conflict – which produces transference. Neither the analyst nor the situation do so in the slightest. This 'clearing' of the analyst is strongly denounced by Lagache, precisely following Ida Macalpine. For her, by contrast, it is the analytic situation, analysis *as situation*, which creates transference.[9] This is certainly an important step, to be hailed as such; but a step whose failure, I should immediately state, is due to its inadequate exploration of what is properly the analytic situation. Ida Macalpine defines the situation as unreal, infantilising, regressive. In analysis, she says, the subject regresses because he adapts to a situation which is itself regressive. The formula cannot be contested in behavioural or object-relations terms. Nor is this incontestable formula con-

---

[7] D. Lagache, 'Le problème du transfert'. Communication à la XIV Conférence des Psychanalystes de Langue française, 1951, in D. Lagache, *Oeuvres III. Le transfert et autres travaux psychanalytiques* (Paris: Presses Universitaires de France, 1980), pp. 1–114. See Lagache's two essays on transference in *Selected Writings*, trans. Elizabeth Holder (London: Karnac, 1992).

[8] *Problématiques V: Le baquet: transcendance du transfert* (Paris: Presses Universitaires de France, 1987), especially pp. 13–29.

[9] Ida Macalpine, 'The Development of the Transference', *Psychoanalytic Quarterly* (1950), vol. 19.

tested by its advocate, Ida Macalpine: transference, she says, is an infantile reaction, but one which, given the situation, is perfectly justified. One can help it to evolve further; its 'resolution' is doubtful – or to tell the truth, it is out of the question.

For his part, even if Lagache is on board with Ida Macalpine at first, at a certain point he disembarks. I am doubtless schematising his thought, but it is very clear that he cannot follow Macalpine the whole way. Once on board with the 'relation' and the 'situation' defined as regressive, how is one to get off? In the name of what? In the name of what should really be called an act of violence: the return – in order to pass judgement on a transference considered, all the same, to be *true* to a situation which is itself derealising – of another norm, in the form of an adaptation to a present and actual situation: a reasonable relation to the 'real analyst'. The term 'interpretation as confrontation', created by Daniel Lagache, is perfectly explicit. It is this which, in a certain sense, I aimed at in the little dialogue which I used as my epigraph: 'I'm not the person you think, you are taking me for someone else'.

Finally, is this idea of 'confrontation' out of date? It could be said that in a sense it has left everyday use, and *thus* it is not part of concrete practice. Nevertheless, it is by no means certain that it does not remain present at the heart of current practice and, even more so, in every psychoanalyst's conviction. At the most intimate level of practice, it remains as the guarantee of a division between the pathological and the normal, the imaginary (or fantasy) and the real, the atemporal and the present, and so on. Probably (or at least we hope so), the contemporary analyst is not so fatuous as to present himself as 'the measure of all things'. The idea of reality-testing or the examination of reality is no longer an explicit axis of practice. Apprenticeship to reality remains more implicit.

Let us be irrational together – says Daniel Lagache – and then, at a second moment: let us now be rational! The formula is democratic, if it states that on both sides there is both irrationality and rationality. Yet despite everything, what is infantile, atemporal, transferential – in short, irrational – remains, according to this conception I would criticise, what has to be more or less reduced, that which should diminish. The infantile is, despite everything, considered as a 'minus'.

At this point my short opening dialogue ought to foreshadow the nub of what I am proposing: beyond all the splits which can be traced at the heart of the transference – between past and present, unreal and real, unadapted and adapted – there is the primordial split, which means quite simply that *the other is other*, but with this paradox or amphibology: he is other than me because he is other than himself. External alterity refers back to internal alterity.

However, before following that path of the relation between analysis and the originary situation, I will take a detour. My reason for returning to the theme of transference was a recent conference on 'Psychoanalysis Outside the Clinic [*hors cure*]', and a round-table discussion entitled 'Transference and

Countertransference in Psychoanalysis Outside the Clinic'.[10] Four things I was not satisfied with, four questions, which were connected, led me to formulate, first to myself, then to the round table, a sort of response.

1. Whatever the formulation chosen – psychoanalysis *hors cure*, 'extramural' [*hors les murs*], transposed or exported psychoanalysis – we never get away from the schema of *application*. Witness the very title of the discussion. It is always a question of finding a clinical paradigm (here, the paradigm of transference and countertransference) and seeing how it can be transported beyond this setting, in other words into a *second* location.
2. Nevertheless . . . hasn't psychoanalysis found one of its most productive aspects in its relation to culture? Can it not be maintained that it is *originally* at home in its reflections on Sophocles, on Shakespeare, on jokes? In *culture*, therefore.
3. Whatever the unprecedented character of Freud's inaugural gesture in founding analytic treatment, is it possible to think the psychoanalytic relation has no antecedents in human history, or correspondences beyond the clinical? If one thinks that is not possible, if one admits that the foundation of psychoanalysis took place as a rupture on the basis of a continuity, one is then led to posit and search for predecessors of, or correspondences to, transference, beyond the clinical. But in such a search, the reverse claim is no less mistaken if it is given an inappropriate generalisation: that repetition in psychoanalysis is nothing but a particular case of the repetition proper to all human beings, or rather to all living beings. If, in the broadest sense, everything is 'transference', everywhere and always – as Lagache reminds us[11] – and if it is vain to think that we can transport ourselves somewhere else, without taking our habits with us, then analytic transference, dissolved into a 'psychological' transference, totally loses its specificity. Now, for us it is not so much a question of such a psychologisation, such a generalisation of transference, as of the need to find a kinship between what is most specific to the clinical situation and what is produced, not everywhere, but in some privileged places existing outside it.
4. Finally, the last unsatisfactory point. We cannot accept the schematic reduction of transference to a transition between only two points in

---

[10] Conference of 24–25 November 1990; the *table ronde*, in which Roger Dorey, André Green, Guy Rosolato and Gérard Bonnet (chair) participated, has been published in *Psychanalyse à l'Université* (1991), vol. 16, no. 64, pp. 3–28.

[11] 'If one takes transference in the largest sense, it becomes difficult to set its limits. All conduct is in fact a blend of the assimilation of the present situation to old habits, and the adjustment of old habits to the present situation. In man, the notion of absolutely new conduct, which would not in any way involve the transference of old habits, is unthinkable; what can be new is the organisation of old habits on whose repertoire the individual has drawn.' Lagache, *Oeuvres III. Le transfert*, p. 80 [translator's translation].

time; between these two points, alongside them, there must certainly be intermediary stages; and beyond them, succeeding points.

I then said to myself, in the course of this discussion (perhaps too rapidly): perhaps we are looking for something which has already been found. Or perhaps we are looking the wrong way round: we wish to transpose the model of clinical transference onto what lies beyond it (psychoanalysis 'outside the clinical'), but maybe transference is already, 'in itself', outside the clinic.

If one accepts that the fundamental dimension of transference is the relation to the enigma of the other, perhaps the principal site of transference, 'ordinary' transference, before, beyond or after analysis, would be the multiple relation to the cultural, to creation or, more precisely, to the cultural message. A relation which is multiple, and should be conceived with discrimination, but always starting from the relation to the enigma. There are at least three types of such a relation to be described: from the position of the producer, from that of the recipient,[12] and from that of the recipient-analyst.

Putting Victor Hugo, Jules Verne or Leonardo 'on the couch': the approximate, journalistic character of such a formula is clear. Of course, the author is always absent, definitively or not; but is he perhaps *essentially* absent, whether or not he is dead? The author, allegedly psychoanalysed by Freud or by one of us, cannot respond to the interpretation with new associations. Where is the 'logodynamics'? On his side or on that of the reader? André Green has drawn from this a conclusion which takes things forward: 'In applied psychoanalysis', he says, 'the analyst is the analysand of the text'. The formulation has the merit of putting back into question a too-easy equation (the analysis of Dora = the analysis of Leonardo). But perhaps this is to rush too far ahead. Before asking, concerning the cultural domain, what is the position of the recipient-analyst and where analysis is situated, one should first investigate the position of the recipient (the reader) *in general* and ask where – not analysis – but transference is situated; for transference is not the whole of analysis.

Der Dichter und das Phantasieren, 'the poet and the activity of fantasy':[13] it is a rich text, but it is limited, and it leaves us on our guard. It shows the origin of the *content* of the imaginative work marvellously, then it skims over, in the last two pages, the so-called question of *means* or of effects. Doubtless some recollection of seduction is tracing itself out, but only in a faint outline. But Freud, as always, keeps to the major, and wholly inadequate, opposition between content and form, or fantasy and technique. Nowhere is the question asked: what, quite simply, drives the *Dichter* – *sit venia verbo* – to 'dicht'?[14] Why create *in order to* communicate, and communicate through creating? And above all, why communicate *in this way* – that is, by addressing no one, aiming beyond any determinate person?

---

[12] On the choice of this word [*réceptionnaire*], see p. 242.
[13] 'Creative Writers and Day-Dreaming' (1908e, S.E., 9).
[14] [In other words: 'what . . . drives the Poet – pardon my saying so – to "poetize"?' – *Trans.*]

Modern studies of language have clearly shown that communication is a pragmatics: to communicate is to manipulate, to produce an effect on someone. There is no question of denying that cultural production has its own effects as well, realistic, self-preservative effects – glory and profit. Let us go further. Cultural production can be partially submitted to a directly sexual pragmatics. A jazz saxophonist said, in a recent interview: 'Don't forget to tell those who don't know which instrument to choose, one thing: girls can't resist a saxophone.' Here, it is a question of what I call 'restrained' seduction. No doubt the sax enables conquests; so do the novel and painting. But what a laborious path, what an extraordinary going-beyond it takes to get there. Going beyond oneself, but above all going *towards* another who is no longer determinate, and who will only incidentally be the object of an individual sexual conquest. Going-beyond, transcendence towards an other = X.

Through this dimension, cultural production is situated from the first *beyond all pragmatics*, beyond any adequation of means to a determinate effect. The problem of the addressee, of the anonymous addressees, is an essential part of any description of the poetic situation. The addressee is essentially enigmatic, even if he sometimes takes on individual traits. So it is with Van Gogh's Theo, who is as much an analyst without knowing it as is Fliess for Freud, for behind him looms the nameless crowd, addressees of the message in a bottle.

Am I in the process, here, of describing an elitist phenomenon, the privilege of certain people, and not a constant human dimension? I do not think so, for what can be termed 'the cultural' exists from the moment the human becomes human: cave-paintings, idols and probably music and poetry. What can be isolated here as characteristic of the cultural is an address to an other who is out of reach, to others 'scattered in the future', as the poet says. An address which is a repercussion, which prolongs and echoes the enigmatic messages by which the *Dichter* himself, so to speak, was bombarded: 'A quiet piece, fallen down here, of an obscure disaster'.[15]

What name should we give to the one who welcomes in, gathers up, the cultural work? 'Consumer' is too prosaic, taking us back to self-preservation. 'Addressee' implies a relation of direct address to an individual in order to have effects on him. 'Reader' only applies to writing. '*Amateur*', perhaps? 'Recipient' is the term which I would choose. It is of the essence of the cultural product that it reaches him with no pedigree, and that it is received by him without having been explicitly addressed to him. The recipient's relation to the enigma is thus different from the author's, a partial inversion of it. But here too, this relation is essential, a renewal of the traumatic, stimulating aspect of the childhood enigma.

---

[15] A renewed study of the phenomenon of 'inspiration' could take as its guiding thread the idea that here we have a transference of the relation of primal seduction. [The quotations here are from Mallarmé's poem, 'Le tombeau d'Edgar Poe': 'Calme bloc ici-bas chu d'un désastre obscur', *Mallarmé*, ed. with trans. by Anthony Hartley (Harmondsworth: Penguin Books, 1965), p. 90. – Ed.]

What I have just proposed, sketched out concerning the cultural, is too hasty; one would have to add to it the situation of the recipient-analyst (or simply 'art critic'), who is, in turn, caught between two stools: the enigma which is addressed to him, but also the enigma of the one he addresses, his public (for it is too easy to forget that one always does non-clinical psychoanalysis in order to write about it, to communicate it in turn).

It is the offer which creates the demand: a constant proposition in the culture domain. The dominance of human needs, undeniable but truly minimal in the domain of biological life, is completely covered over by culture. The biological individual, the living human, is saturated from head to foot by the invasion of the cultural, which is by definition intrusive, stimulating and sexual. How has analysis been able to lose sight of this truth, which was ready to emerge alongside the theory of seduction?

This forgetting, and the long going-astray which was its result, can be verified both in the psychoanalytic theory of the human being and in its conception of transference and the treatment. In both cases one cannot escape from a monadological, auto-centred conception. Everything is constructed from the centre, all mechanisms are conceived with, as subject, the person in question – Pierre, let's say, or Sigmund. It is Pierre who does the transference, Pierre who projects. And even if the movement is centripetal, it is still Pierre who introjects.

With Freud, transference has a subject fully equipped with his conflicts; with Klein, someone burdened with instincts and objects, who brings them along to analysis. With Ferenczi, perhaps the notion of reciprocity is introduced, but only ever to relate two monads, about which *from that moment* that author is right to wonder why one should be termed the analyst, the other the analysand. Reciprocity, mutuality, the response of the shepherd/countertransference to the shepherdess/transference, and the other way around – all of this stems from the fact that the arrow of analytic asymmetry has not been noticed. With Lacan, one sometimes seems to have emerged from monadology. But the Hegelian formulations on desire as desire of the other easily become circular (the desire of desire of desire . . .); an endless circle which favours the assimilation of the unconscious to a language, and the claim that it is transindividual. No doubt things are opening up in Lacan, but it is an opening onto all the winds of language. As for the categories of need, desire and demand, henceforth easily accepted, integrated, rendered banal in today's clinic, they lend themselves only too well to monadological recentring. The desire or the demand *of* the analysand: departure-points for *his* transference.

Is it possible for us to succeed in this intellectual conversion, this unimaginable 'version'? to abandon the centrifugal arrow, free ourselves from the idea that everything is already in Pierre's pouch, in that 'indestructible percipiens' Lacan speaks of – an expression which is from one of his inspired moments, his article on psychosis? There he is right to denounce the primacy accorded to projection, which is assumed by the conception of hallucination. Everything would be in the internal 'convenience store', and would be reduced to the simplistic question of 'moving the inside to the outside'.[16]

Is it possible for us to conceive that the arrow, the originary vector, goes in a reverse direction? Reversing the arrow is not to fall back into the symmetry of transference and countertransference, not to ask which desire of the analyst's would correspond to the analysand's desire. The 'desire of the analyst' – no doubt there is one, even several, and very diverse; but my question is a different one. Are we able to conceive that it is the offer of analysis, the offer of the analyst, which creates . . . what? Not analysis, but its essential dimension, transference. Not, perhaps, the whole of the transference, but its basis, the driving force at its heart, in other words, the re-opening of a relation, the originary relation, in which the other is primary for the subject. A re-opening, because the entire process of the constitution of the subject takes place through a closure, which is, precisely, repression, the formation of topographical agencies, the internalisation of the other and its enclosure in the form of the unconscious.

What does analysis offer? What is the analytic situation? It can be formulated, reformulated, again: I have attempted to do so at length, with the image of the tub.[17] Here, I will propose three dimensions, three functions of the analyst and of what he inaugurates: the analyst as the guarantor of constancy; the analyst as the director of the method and the companion of the primary process; the analyst as the one who guards the enigma and provokes the transference.

The first two functions are correlative: the guarantor of constancy and the director of the method. Without these, there is no analysis; more precisely still, without the second, there is no analysis. This is what Freud says: analysis is a method to gain access to phenomena which would otherwise be more or less inaccessible. The method is precisely decomposition, which is steered

---

[16] Jacques Lacan, *Écrits*, trans. Alan Sheridan (London: Tavistock, 1977), pp. 187–189. Lacan's failure to succeed fully in the radical de-centring required, as well as the fact that he does not truly formulate it in his seminar on transference, is due, we think, to two reasons: (1) An abstract and purely linguistic conception of the signifier, the 'Other' being reduced to the 'treasury of signifiers' in a completely impersonal way. (2) The total misrecognition of the seduction theory, which alone enables the so-called 'supremacy of the signifier' to be put back into its originary frame: the real primacy of the concrete adult over the child.

[17] Laplanche, *Problématiques V: Le baquet*, especially pp. 30–46. [Laplanche locates the model of the tub – *le baquet* – as one of a series of homeostatic models of enclosure in Freud's work whether of the living organism or vesicle, the psychic apparatus, the ego or the dream. The analytic situation is also modelled in similar terms as an enclosed space, artificially constructed, from which is bracketed out through the fundamental rule and associated conventions the everyday realm of needs and interests; a space in which fantasy, the sexual drives and their derivatives can be brought into play through speech. The difference from these other models of enclosure is that it includes the analyst and his offer of analysis and so incites the re-establishment of the situation of primal seduction and its relation to the originary enigma of the other. – *Ed.*]

according to the current, or the currents, of the primary process. It analyses, that is, it dissolves. It is governed by the 'zero principle', setting in motion what Freud, in his way, designated as the 'death drive'; which has nothing to do with biological death, but which, potentially, leads to the dissolution of all formations – psychical, egoic, ideological, symptomatic. But as a counterbalance to this force of unbinding, this liberation of psychical energies, psychoanalysis offers itself as a guarantor of constancy; of containment, as it has been called; of support. It offers the constancy of a presence, of a solicitude, the flexible but attentive constancy of a frame. The principles of *constancy* and of *zero* are, for me, the true principles of psychical functioning.[18] The images of the cyclotron, the tub and the dream link up here: in the dream, the ego takes up a wholly peripheral place, that of the desire to sleep, leaving the field open to the primary process. On this very point, the same takes place in the analytic situation: it is only because there is containment that analysis is possible. It is because the principle of constancy, of homeostasis, of *Bindung* is maintained at the periphery that analytic unbinding is possible.

The dream as model: André Green has taken note of this in order to set out a critique – that the analytic session is conceived by Freud in terms of a solipsistic model, that of chapter VII of *The Interpretation of Dreams* (1900a). But I'm not sure that a model which would be 'intersubjective' could fully remedy this. Here, I must return to the idea of the 'offer', and to the third function of the analyst: as the one who guards the enigma and provokes[19] the transference. What is *offered* is a place for speech, for free speech, but not, properly speaking, the place of an exchange. There is an essential dissymmetry in the relation. Lacan was already talking of 'subjective disparity'. But one must go further, towards something which is difficult to think, as difficult to think as the priority of the other in the constitution of the sexual subject. I have also attempted to take up again the formulation of 'the subject supposed to know', noting how little elucidation Lacan had given it. Let us try it, then!

What is put forward with the offer of analysis in so far as it is social, everyday, banal is certainly a response to the patient's questions: What do I have? What should I do? I would add Kant's third question: What am I permitted to hope? What is proposed is a certain path towards truth, supposed to lead towards the good, towards well-being. But analysis is not a guru, nor a preacher, nor an oracle – despite the impression given by certain practices. It does bring

---

[18] Cf. 'Les principes du fonctionnement psychique' in *La révolution copernicienne inachevée* (Paris: Aubier, 1992).

[19] The term *Reiz*, so difficult to translate in its double usage, is our guide here. The *Reiz*, in neurophysiology and in Freudian metapsychology, is a stimulus: that which attacks from the exterior, and provokes change. But it is also the *Reiz* of a person: attractiveness, seductiveness, *sex-appeal*, temptation (a temptress . . .). In Germanic, *wraitjan* means, to be exact, 'to cause to break up' (*reissen machen*), 'to cause someone to come out of himself'; cf. also *herausfordern*, to challenge, provoke, unhinge. The French word *provocation* would take in both meanings, in line with the theory of seduction.

experience and knowledge – that of the method – but also a radical refusal to know the good of its patient, to know the truth about his good.

Benevolent neutrality – two terms which are one, and which take us deeply into paradox. Benevolence: 'to want the good' of the other without ever claiming to know what it is, without manipulating the patient, even for his supposed good. With the word neutrality, things are even less in focus, and this goes back to Freud. The image of neutrality is inevitably that of the blank screen or, rather, the mirror. Offering projection as much room as possible, allowing solipsism its full space, finally to overthrow it in a confrontation: you clearly see that *it's you that*.... In short: *you have projected, and I give you back your projection, I counter-project*. This is neutrality's artificial, almost experimental conception of the mirror: it should be possible to deduct the conditions of the experience or experiment, and for everyone to get back his marbles.

One must arrive at a positive, creative conception of neutrality, productive of the enigmatic dimension. It is here that we should complete our short dialogue, with this response from the analyst:

> *Analyst:* Yes, you can take me for an Other, because I am not what I think I am; because I respect and maintain the other in me.

It is maintaining the dimension of interior alterity which allows alterity to be set up in the transference. Interior relation, relation to the enigma, 'the relation to the unknown': 'If the relation is free enough . . . it becomes for the psychoanalyst the support of his alertness regarding his own psychical reality, his theory and his analysands. For the latter it guarantees access to the diversity of their desires.' I have quoted Guy Rosolato.[20] I will not indicate here my slight differences *vis-à-vis* this notion of the relation to the unknown;[21] but I find there something corresponding to what, for me, is the maintenance of the analyst's interpellation by the enigma; the maintenance which not only guarantees access to the diversity of desires, but truly *creates, provokes transference*.

'Filled-in transference', 'hollowed-out transference'. It is something simple, in the end, which I have tried to express in this way. We offer the analysand a 'hollow', our own interior benevolent neutrality, a benevolent neutrality concerning our own enigma. The analysand can place there something 'filled-in' or 'hollowed-out'. If it's something filled-in, he empties his pouch into it; if hollowed-out, *another hollow*, the enigma of his own originary situation, is placed there. So we are sent back to the originary infantile situation. The sexual enigma is presented to the child by adults in an *address*, and this address is enigmatic in so far as the other (the one who sends it) does not entirely

---

[20] Laplanche quotes the title of Guy Rosolato's book, *La Relation d'Inconnu* [Relation of/to the unknown] (Paris: Gallimard, 1978), p. 15. [*Trans. translation*]
[21] In particular: that the unconscious is not necessarily, in my opinion, on the maternal side.

know what he is saying: he is other to himself. It is in this sense that I have spoken of the *transcendence of the transference* and the transcendence of the originary situation. This originary situation could be called, paradoxically, '*originary transference*'. It is not, of course, the transfer of another thing, but it can nonetheless be given this name, by a sort of movement to the limit – because it already contains the driving force of transference, that is, the doubling, the diplopia which is proper to it. The adult's sexual, provocative, traumatising enigma is, for the child, what has to be ceaselessly mastered, translated, brought back into constancy. All development takes place, therefore, in the direction of a double closure to the message of the other. The closure on the side of what can be translated, theorised, in other words, more or less given ideological form; and also closure through the sealing-off, the repression of the anamorphic residue of messages, that is, of what resists symbolisation.[22]

Analysis offers – and perhaps in this it is allied to the site of culture – a reopening of the dimension of alterity. In this opening, of course, something must also take up its place: that which, precisely, had been sealed off.

Taking up a place to open things out, but also to analyse things. For what is new in analysis, in relation to culture, is not transference, it is . . . analysis – that is, *Lösung*. Again, I come back to this definition of Freud's: analysis is before anything else a method of access to unconscious processes. *Lösung*: analysis, solution and resolution, dissolution; a term which unfortunately cannot be translated into French, with all its compounds (*Auflösung, Erlösung, Ablösung* . . .). There is no dissolution of the transference as such; there is the resolution or dissolution of 'filled-in' transference into 'hollowed-out' transference.

From this point on, in that outcome which I consider to be the most analytic, what becomes of the 'hollowed-out' transference? This leads me to conclude with my notion of the 'transference of transference'.[23] If transference, like our interpellation by the enigma, exists before and outside analysis, if it is a fundamental dimension of the human being, any outcome worthy of analysis cannot entail an end to that opening.[24]

---

[22] In the face of the alterity of the other, the methods of defence are immutably the same: attempt at assimilation, denial of difference, segregation, destruction. These are quite clearly found again in attitudes to cultural and ethnic differences. But what is lacking in all the analyses of 'racism' is any consideration of the internal split inherent in the other himself: it is this *internal alterity* which is at the root of the anxiety provoked by external alterity; it is this that one seeks to reduce at any price.

[23] I have noted, very much in passing, that these words were first used by Reich, who wished them to indicate that the analytic process was the assumption of, the arrival at, genitality and the orgasm, and once the analysand had reached this point, he was to transfer himself beyond this recovered genitality. There is, in fact, between this conception of Reich's (transference of one 'fullness' to another) and my way of proposing the terms 'transference of transference' a total antinomy. Hollowed-out transference is not the result of a development or a process. It cannot be measured in terms of normality and abnormality. Its irreducible dimension of alterity is the basis of transference.

[24] Lagache, it is well known, wished to relate transferential repetition to the 'Zeigarnik effect': unfinished tasks tend to be better remembered and more often taken up again than finished tasks (cf. Lagache, *Oeuvres III. Le transfert*, pp. 93, 135, 166). The only meaning we can give to this relation is that the transference cannot aim at closure, since it is the return to, the re-elaboration of, our relation to originary enigmas – a relation, in essence, unfinished.

In other places – during analysis, outside analysis – other possibilities of 'transference' are available to the analysand, other poles for the elaboration of an individual destiny. This complex situation, where discrimination is necessary, cannot be envisaged without considering a principal factor, which until now has been ignored: the cyclical character of the dynamics of transference. This fact of experience – that the subject's elaboration passes periodically through points, memories, fantasies whose sequences are organised in analogous ways – finds an exact correspondence in the 'translation' theory we are developing: there is no new translation which does not first pass through the old translations, in order to detranslate them in the interests of a new translation. The process could be purely repetitive, with the same furrows or ruts being indefinitely retraversed. Hollowed-out transference – the point of attraction which constitutes the enigma, and which is re-activated by the analyst – although it is the very origin of the movement of gravitation, is no guarantee that an orbit should not remain stationary, either temporarily or indefinitely. Further cycles, on the other hand, carry the certitude of some gap, some change of level. The same themes are, to be sure, gone through again, 'retranslated', but the 'target language' is enriched; in exceptional cases, it is changed.

I introduce here, concerning the transference, a model familiar to me, the spiral.[25] The circle and the spiral both define gravitational movements. With the former, the movement takes place around a point; with the latter, along an axis. But the spiral can only move forward by passing through, on the horizontal axis, the same enigmatic signifiers (ES):

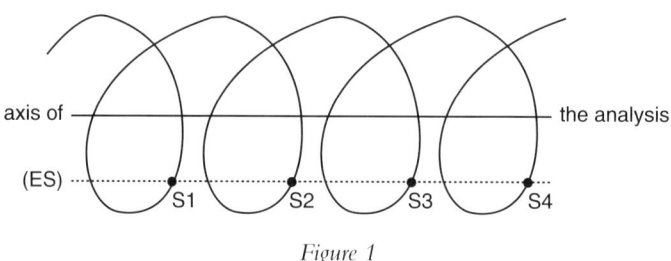

Figure 1

In astronautics, the precise lapse of time when the launching of a spaceship is possible is called a 'window'. It would be a question either of going into orbit from the earth, or the departure, from a satellite already in orbit, of a vessel aiming to leave the earth's gravitational system.

Likewise for departures from analysis: there are favourable windows, which it can be judged opportune to take advantage of – failing which, gravitation re-asserts its pull for another turn of the spiral.

---

[25] In rigorously mathematical terms, it is in fact a 'helix'.

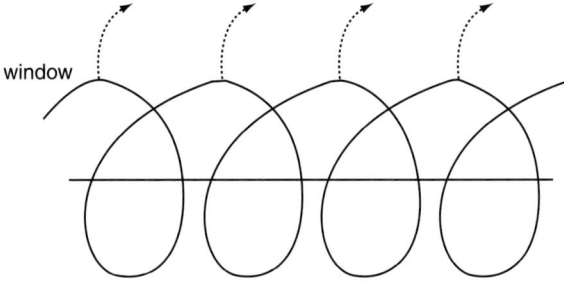

Figure 2

The parameters at stake, nevertheless, are no less complex – and above all, more conjectural and aleatory – than those of interstellar navigation. Will one more turn be a turn for nothing, pure repetition, or is a certain potential for elaboration still present in the analysis? Likewise, that which 'makes a sign' outside can take on diverse meanings: saturation; the arrival at a given point; valencies released by the hollowed-out transference and leading to a new and eventually definitive closure; lateral transference, which perhaps appears under the sign of something new but at the price of breaking, out of time, the current spiral; the transference of transference, in which is set out, outside the treatment, a true site for the confrontation of the enigma.[26]

To distinguish these different modalities can be considered one of the analyst's major tasks, when it comes to proposing the termination of analysis, or acquiescing in one. Again, it must be admitted that often the ways out are not sharply outlined, nor easily predictable. On the other hand, the analyst's narcissism may risk blinding him, belittling the perspectives available outside for the pursuit of elaboration. Ultimately, the mastery of the analyst, at the end of the process as well as in its pursuit, is largely illusory; but a mastery which recognises its limits and acknowledges its own testimony is something different from one which strains itself and, in the end, fails.

Among the kinds of transference which exist 'before' analysis (before an individual analysis, and before the historical creation of analysis), we have accorded a privileged place to the multiple relations to the cultural, taken in the widest sense. Now, post-analytic transference will not be absolutely the same as pre-analytic transference, nor totally different from it. That is once again to say that the site of the cultural, as the site of an enigmatic interpellation, with many voices and ears, remains privileged in that it concerns the transference of transference.

---

[26] We have no hesitation in considering, among the circumstances favourable to the end of the analysis, not only the internal dynamics (turns and windows) but also the external situation. To be still more precise: not only the subject's capability to face up to new difficulties and conflicts (cf. 'Analysis Terminable and Interminable', 1937c, S.E., 23), but also the new poles of gravitation, or the 'provocations' which might impinge from the outside. This is the reverse of a conception – monadological again – which would only take account of 'internal' modifications in the structure of the personality.

To this must be added an essential factor: analysis cannot fail to take into account the fact that it is itself also present, in a privileged way, in that 'culture', which has been informed and transformed by its very intervention. I proposed, a few years ago,[27] the idea that, with psychoanalysis, sublimation *changed*: that not only our way of conceiving it, but the essence of sublimation itself changed. In other words, we could no longer speak of sublimation as an eternal and unchanging process: sublimation 'was no longer what it was', it had *drifted* because of the irreversible introduction of analysis into the culture, through all the modalities of analytic praxis, of which the practice of analytic treatment is the most eminent, without perhaps having the greatest impact. The analysand, having emerged from treatment to get involved in new gravitational forces, inevitably encounters, at the cultural sites of transference, the expanding presence of analysis. It is not necessary to think – as Lacan wished to – that the only analysis worthy of the name is that which leads to the practice of analytic treatment, in order to affirm that the analytic experience cannot be a simple parenthesis, which opens one day and closes another, in the human individual's destiny; and this is so even if he does not himself become a practising psychoanalyst.

Editors' added bibliography

Freud, S. (1900a). The Interpretation of Dreams. *S.E.*, 4–5.
Freud, S. (1908). Creative Writers and Day-Dreaming. *S.E.*, 9.
Freud, S. (1919h). The Uncanny. *S.E.*, 17.
Freud, S. (1937). Analysis Terminable and Interminable. *S.E.*, 23.
Lacan, J. (1966). *Écrits*. Paris: Le Seuil. [*Écrits*. London: Tavistock, 1977.]
Lagache, D. (1952). Le problème du transfert. In *Œuvres III, le transfert et autres travaux psychanalytiques*. Paris: Presses Universitaires de France, 1980, 1–114.
Lagache, D. (1992). Two essays on transference. In *Selected Writings*. London: Karnac.
Laplanche, J. (1980). *Problématiques III, La sublimation*. Paris: Presses Universitaires de France.
Laplanche, J. (1987). *New Foundations for Psychoanalysis*. Cambridge, MA/Oxford: Basil Blackwell, 1989.
Laplanche, J. (1987). *Problématiques V – Le Baquet; transcendance du transfert*. Paris: Presses Universitaires de France.
Laplanche, J. (1992). *La révolution copernicienne achevée*. Paris: Aubier.
Macalpine, I. (1950). The development of the transference. *Psychoanalytic Quarterly, 19*.
Mannoni, O. (1956). *Prospero and Caliban: The Psychology of Colonization*. New York: Praeger.
Mannoni, O. (1969). *Clefs pour l'imaginaire ou l'autre scène* [Key for the imaginary or the other scene]. Paris: Le Seuil.
Rosolato, G. (1907). La pratique, son cadre, ses interdits. *Psychanalyse à l'Université, 12* (47): 469–485.
Rosolato, G. (1978). *La relation d'inconnu* [Relation of/to the unknown]. Paris: Gallimard.

---

[27] *Problématiques III: La sublimation* (Paris: Presses Universitaires de France, 1980), part II, 'Faire dériver la sublimation' (especially the concluding pages).

13 SPEAKING AND RENOUNCING

Jean-Claude Rolland

> **Jean-Claude Rolland** is a psychiatrist, full member and former president of the French Psychoanalytical Association. He is co-editor with Catherine Chabert of *Libres Cahiers pour la Psychanalyse* (In Press editions) and the author of *Guérir du mal d'aimer* [Recovering from the pain of love] (Gallimard, 1998) and of *Avant d'être celui qui parle* [Before being the person who speaks] (Gallimard, 2006).

Before being a speaker, the human being is a seer. To this relationship of continuity, linking two essential mental activities – vision and speech – I might have preferred a genetic or causal relationship and stated that to become a speaker, the human being had to be a seer, or, alternatively: because a gift of envisioning threatens to block his access to the world, it is imperative that he has recourse to speech.

I do not accord any force of truth, or any scientific import, to these rudimentary formulations: they are random thoughts on which I am lingering for a moment longer, before confronting the indomitable unknown spirit of language, which Hölderlin (1995) calls:

> The spirit of night,
> The aggressor of the sky, a fast talker who has deceived
> Our country of many indomitable languages . . .

I am lingering, first to situate speech as an operation required by psychic life, a necessity that can only permissibly be escaped by implementing some powerful and costly pathological strategies – for, contrary to the claim of every thought-system that is not completely secular, there is no 'gift of tongues'. Then to situate speech activity as the resumption, in an existential sphere defined by the abstraction of its productions and the arbitrariness of its signs, of a mental activity characterised by the materiality of the experiences it generates and by the frenetic *mimesis* that connects the signs it produces with the 'things' that animate it.

To situate these two activities – vision and speech – in relation to each other, we must immediately renounce the genetic category of origin or the temporal category of anteriority. We must – and this is inconvenient, it may even be the greatest complication we will confront – restrictively conceive this relationship in spatial terms. 'Psyche is extended; knows nothing about it', writes Freud (1941f [1938], p. 300), at the very end of his works, unusually for him, in an aphorism.

Psychic space has a depth and a surface. According to where it unfolds, psychic activity processes the same material but does not allocate it the same forms. To accede to the surface (and this does not refer only to consciousness) to test its (drive) demand at the requirement of (external) reality, representation – familiar from the depths – must undergo a mutation of which the linguistic signifier, which gives speech its skeleton, is only the final stage. There is something spectacular and vertiginous in the prescription we are given to imagine our mental representations having to carry out or undergo this paradoxical crossing of the psychic space, in the absolute continuity of their ideational contents, and the radical discontinuity of their formal organisations.

For spontaneously we only accord a secondary, contingent, importance to form; the logical thinking that directs every thought, even when it seeks to think against itself, being applied, always and primarily, to the content, which it identifies with the essence. We will rediscover in this psychoanalytic approach to speech the same complication that confronted Freud in his psychoanalytic approach to the psyche, faced with the conflict, with no immediate possibility of resolution, between the logic of the preconscious and the drive-related irrationality of the unconscious. Except that this complication will be displaced for us on to the gap, as subtle as exhausting, as difficult to define as it is painful to conceive, which isolates as it were both the perfect identity of content and the evident formal disparity between what we will designate following Freud as the 'thing-presentation' that forms the substance of the unconscious and the 'word-presentation' that speech activates in discourse.

The human being has to speak to divest himself of this gift of envisioning that has fallen to him like a destiny. We do not enquire as to its origin: we have no means of responding to it. Let us be content with affirming its reality. We can first observe that we only find this envisioning so strange because at one time in our existence it was perfectly familiar to us and remains so in the deepest states of our mental life. I am referring here to *phantasieren*, the representational activity – to which we will accord the status of a thought activity – which realises the most secret desires, playing on the most primitive imagos, and only unfolds – which is why it remains outside our logical understanding – in this specific penumbra that play, dreams, daydreaming, symptomatic expressions and perhaps also works of art can all create in their own way.

But I now need to make a particular use of this notion of *phantasieren*, which is so central to psychoanalytic thought, a use that maintains both its strangeness and its capacity for concealment. I need to avoid both mining all its meta-psychological significance and using a far too descriptive phenomenology for it. To leave it in the penumbra that is its natural environment.

To state that the human being has an envisioning capacity does not refer to the quality of his vision. *Phantasieren* remains alien to the category of perception, even if the 'whatever material', to use Freud's expression, that carries his vision originates, as we will have to concede a little later, from perceptual memory. The human being envisions in the sense that he is a visionary, he is a *Seher*, as was said of Hölderlin, in the sense that he sees what does not exist, because what he sees is 'that which insists', and is invisible in nature. In fact, what has become invisible, in the precise sense in which what has been, for a while, there, present, valuable, cathected by him as an object of desire immanent in his very life, has suddenly disappeared. What I call envisioning is this capacity of the psyche to reverse into its opposite the fact of the object's disappearance, making it reappear.

Let us leave there the causes of this disappearance, the effective loss or repudiation of the object required by psychic development and the reality principle. Let us only remember that through the visionary power that falls to him as a destiny, the human being resolves the distress into which he is thrown by a direct inscription in the space of object relationships, and thereby confronts their precarity and instability. The human being's envisioning, which can be called a gift in the sense that it binds what Freud referred to as *Hilflosigkeit*, the primal helplessness of the human subject, and in the sense that it moderates its economy by inscribing it in a pair of opposite psychic impulses, is more the invocation of what is invisible than of its opposite. It is the invocation of the image, whether plastic, resonant or gestural, against pain. It consists less in seeing than in bringing out, making 'appear' what has disappeared. And in that it partakes of magic [*magie*], this word that as Lyotard (1971) among others has observed is anagrammatically identical to 'image' [*image*]. In such a way that, in its realisation, the nature of the material that incarnates the appearance and revival of a lost bond matters less than the quality of the 'objectal' presence and meaning with which desire, upholding the envisioning, cathects it. Etymologically, the word 'fantasy' comes from the Greek *phainen*, to make see, to make appear, to shine, from which are also derived the words '*fanal*' (headlamp), phantom, epiphany and even phenomenon . . . Envisioning, a glimmer in the night of absence.

Let us consider this envisioning in terms of psychic automatism. Let us classify it with the homeostatic principle that directs the entire apparatus of the soul, more strictly to the part of this apparatus that remains under the control and organisation of the ego. Its production is activated as soon as the essential frustration impedes desire in its drive demand – what Freud termed *Triebanspruch* – in which even as foreigners we cannot help but hear the root *sprechen*, the German for 'to speak'. It is tolerated by the ego to the extent that it can – through splitting – allow it to coexist with its adherence to the demands of reality – *Realitäteinspruch*, according to Freud's formula (1940e [1938], p. 275), containing the same root, *sprechen*. It is tolerated by the ego for the appeasement and consolation it brings to the drive masses, which accordingly relax the pressure they exercise over it. Perhaps it is even slightly more than tolerated: it exercises a fascination over the ego through this cunning quality – '*kniffig*', says Freud (ibid.) – which is due to its capacity to fulfil the desire immediately, almost magically, and is also due to the formidable economy of means achieved by this complete short-circuiting of satisfaction.

This means that although for the logical thought that orders our discursive activity the clandestine and invasive insistence of this visionary thought, this hallucinatory activity, remains outrageous and becomes the object of a refusal to see (which would add further emphasis to this strange dialectic of the invisible and vision), its reality contains nothing enigmatic for the person who can understand what is hidden behind the words every time they are uttered at the closest place to being and are dedicated to expressing the depths of the inner world, nor for the person who consents to combine his hearing with an activity, even slightly visionary, echoing that of the speaker.

What is, however, enigmatic is the fact that the human subject has to renounce it. I return here to my starting formula: the human being must speak. The enigma does not reside so much in its 'prescriptive' significance – 'must' – which does not have to be elevated as a law or as mysticism to be legitimised. Speech, and this is what we will seek to establish together, shares in the same psychic automatism as hallucination, providing the same homeostatic function at the surface of the apparatus as that provided by envisioning at a deep level. The 'must' refers only to an endopsychic necessity, an economic constraint.

The enigma resides rather in the 'how': how does Psyche renounce such a resolutive, efficient and fascinating envisioning activity? The formula proposed at the outset seems to yield the answer: by speech. Of course, we do not understand it in this way: this would be going too far too fast, it would even be unseemly. What this formula seeks to show is simply that the birth of speech in the human subject, examined from the viewpoint of its necessity rather than the mystical perspective of a 'revelation', remains enigmatic. It is as enigmatic as the renunciation by which this same subject abandons a representational activity centred on the incarnation of his ghosts and the preservation of a first infantile sexual activity, to substitute for it – at the cost of a certain amount of pain and frustration – a perceptual activity directed at the world and the objects of reality.

My formula anticipates that a coincidence, even an identity, unites these two enigmas. Two thoughts then immediately strike us, which seek to resolve the question, or eliminate it. The first would consist in stating that speech is born in the wake of the mind's renunciation of its visionary representational activity and thereby revealed as a psychic production in its own right, emerging as the sign by which the mind attests its openness to the world. The second consists in stating that language, as a symbolic agency, external to the subject, forces the mind to sublimate its formations of desire into a discursive activity. These are hypotheses that cannot immediately be rejected, because we cannot refrain from thinking them. They remain suspect to us, however, because they are too strongly imprinted by the hallmark of a 'common-sense' logic. This would trivialise the enigma by substituting it with an indecision.

In fact, the enigma does not have to be resolved. Let us consider it to be a psychic 'event' that leads to two questions: What is speaking? What is renouncing? For example, what event is occurring when, in a conversation or a treatment, a patient utters his mother's first name that he has kept silent until then or when, after telling a dream, an association links a particular detail of this dream with an event in his childhood history that he has so far overlooked? What transformation has occurred at the interface between communication with an Other, Freud's *Nebenmensch*, and an intrasubjective and inter-agency dynamic, the barrier of a particular repression having been shaken in the brilliance, a transformation that is 'crystallised' in speech by the addition of a word or a sentence to the discourse? And, for another example, of what is a patient divesting himself in his treasure-trove of childhood fantasies, talking to the obscure interlocutor behind him, to whom he represents he knows not what, when having said that his Mum didn't want his sister and him to have children and after a certain silence allowed the time for the unconscious representation to reach the surface of his psyche, he hears, as a judgement with no further right of appeal, the Oedipal significance of this desire?

It seems that both speaking and renouncing involve the same outpouring from the mind, that they are both in themselves and indistinctly the constituents of conscious thought, the only form with which we can reasonably reckon in our contradictory aspiration to be both what we are and what the world prescribes to us to be. It also seems that, as an outpouring of the mind, speaking and renouncing are the principles that ultimately best qualify 'thinking'. Less as a psychic production, defined positively by a specific content, than as an impulse of the soul's apparatus, which, like an earthquake, breaks up a certain organisation of representations, to reconstitute it, differently and at another level, by assigning it a form that is something more than a receptacle and contributes to the 'transubstantiation' of its content . . . And in saying that, we return to the intuition of the poet who most deeply explored these experiences of vision, language and silence, Hölderlin, asserting that 'enigma is the pure outpouring'.

For this play of representations made of resonant, plastic or coenaesthetic images, animated by a secret and ever-specific passion, unfolds, probably constantly, in the depths of the soul, sometimes appearing in broad daylight, for example in dreams, when all attention has been withdrawn from the psychic surface and the mirror function of language has been eliminated, when summoned, in the waking state, to reflect exclusively the facts of the external world. Let us accord this *phantasieren* the status of a thought even if it is an act, the psychic act *par excellence*. For what it realises in the satisfaction of desire, in rediscovery and conquest of the object, forms part of the same movement, as a system of signs, addressed from the id to the ego, for example, so that it informs as to its reality and its nature. An effect of communication from one agency to the other animates this experience and elevates it to expression. That the presence – in retreat – of an impartial, benevolent interlocutor should be necessary to instigate this slight displacement of the 'experience' into 'expression' is probably as necessary as the presence of a mother, eliminating herself before her object, for her infant to develop a satisfactory auto-erotic activity.

Let us therefore grant this *phantasieren* a status of thought, because the act that is manifested there indicates its intention and assumes a value or a meaning faced with its respondent, its object in the sense of *Gegenstand* – whether it is himself or an Other. We will discover, examining conscious thought, but in inverse proportions, the same combination, which can only be disconnected to a certain point, between what constitutes its status as an 'act' and what constitutes its status as a 'sign'. From this perspective, 'thinking' would always be 'doing something and indicating what thinking does'.

It is probably due to this predominance of the act over the sign that unconscious thought, the thought of fantasy, accedes only in an oblique and faltering way to the expressivity that is reduced there to a semiotic: its signifiers remain iconic, they are scarcely separate from the objects they represent; its syntax is elementary, in accordance with the partiality of the drive that carries it; it says fundamentally only what it does, in proportion with the massivity of its action. This is what Freud very clearly indicates, when building a bridge between what he calls 'the language of the oldest – the oral – instinctual impulses' and our common language; he translates the semiotic of orality in these terms: ' "I should like to eat this", or "I should like to spit it out"; and, put more generally: "I should like to take this into myself and to keep that out." That is to say: "It shall be inside me" or "it shall be outside me"' (1925h, p. 237).

Unconscious thought is established in a semiotic through the use of unambiguous metaphors that are 'spectacular' in that they are revealed by the accomplishment of unequivocal acts that offer themselves to be felt: a mouth, and a breast or a penis, which are connected by sucking or vomiting. Or again, to follow Freud in his desire to transpose qualmlessly the idiomatic meanings of the unconscious into the signifiers of conscious thought, this formulation he gives of the second stage of the fantasy: 'I am being beaten by my father'. This is a phase that he explains as follows: 'in a certain sense [that] it has never had a real existence. It is never remembered; it has never succeeded in becoming conscious. It is a construction of analysis, but it is no less a necessity on that account' (1919e, p. 185). Except that – and this we can and must now add to Freud's first advance – the unconscious thought that in its native state was ordered around two metaphors, the father and the female sex, and an act, the spanking, gave rise in the little girl to a 'vision' from which she was partly distanced by the fictions she constructed of them. Just as it gave rise, in the analyst who recognised it, to a similar if not identical 'vision', a shared vision that nurtured the construction by which he protected himself from it.

What we now have to examine is the way in which the visionary activity that expresses unconscious life forms the deepest affinities with the constructions that the analyst constantly builds when he listens to his patients, and how the envisioning of *phantasieren* rediscovers a distant echo in the most sophisticated theoretical construction. We should first note that we may not have paid enough attention to the role that falls to this semiotic import of unconscious thought in establishing the phenomenon of empathy, which Freud described as 'an inference which we draw by analogy from their observable utterances and actions, in order to make this behaviour of theirs intelligible to us' (1915e, p. 169). Let us turn to some specific examples.

After many years of analysis, this patient rediscovered the existence of a maternal grandfather, who had disappeared from his mental horizon, as in fact he had disappeared, even before his death, from the family discourse. The old man lived alone, in an isolated house, doing small jobs around the place all day. The patient retrieved the memory of staying with him there, remembered his surprise mingled with fright at this figure, who struck him as an 'eccentric', and his admiration at many sheds full of tools that he was forbidden to enter. With this rediscovery was gradually mingled another: his mother, at a certain period of his life – when he was very young – passionately set about doing odd jobs around the house from time to time, which he did not like because he felt she was particularly absent at these times, as if she had 'become another person'. I told him that he was probably thinking about this grandfather when he saw his mother turning into someone else while doing odd jobs. He amplified this interpretation with this memory fragment: what made her different then was the posture she adopted, that of an old man, and the shaky gait that was exactly the same as his grandfather's.

Like the child in Hans Christian Andersen's story *The Emperor's New Clothes*, who discerns that the Emperor is naked under his new clothes, the child that this adult used to be recognised, without having the means to think it, in this sort of 'trance' with a domestic application, the phantasmatic experience to which his mother was surrendering by identifying melancholically with this father, concealed from her. And the passionate attachment that he felt to her appeared to be rooted in this vision he shared with her of a specific female suffering.

The child is granted a gift of envisioning that the adult, to enter fully into the reality of the world, partly renounces. In another situation, the analysand lost her mother during her analysis. I could not ignore, listening to her, the fact that in revealing the immense pain this caused her, she associated fairly regularly about her very young daughter who, she said, called incessantly for her grandmother. On the morning of the anniversary of her mother's death, the four-year-old girl took hold of a stick as soon as she got up and used it all day to walk. The patient thought, without expressing it to herself in any way, that her mother used a walking stick in the final years of her life. That night, the patient had a dream that involved a sword that the analyst easily recognised as the famous stick. She could then clearly formulate a joint denial of the mourning for the beloved mother that had been in play from her daughter to her through a shared vision of the reincarnation of her person.

What are we to make of this semiotic of unconscious thought, structured like a theatrical action? That the little girl was specifically addressing her mother, or that her mother, recognising her own pain and denial in her daughter, raised this empathy into a communication system? We have no way of answering this question. Let us only note that this example perfectly illustrates two specific features of the unconscious semiotic, which provide it with the essentials of its expressive significance: the elective address to an object calling for recognition in it, and the dimension of an offering. For there is no doubt that the timely consolation brought by this little girl, at this solemn moment, is for her mother a gift of love. In such a way that what characterises this unconscious semiotic is due not only to the fact that its signifying metaphors exist in the closest mimesis with the objects they represent, but to the fact that the syntax between them is nothing other than the libido itself, a primal libido that has not undergone any desexualisation to be constructed as a sign. 'I, your daughter with a stick, am your mother who loves you': this is how the child expresses herself; this is how her mother hears her.

We will see shortly when we go on to address speech how the libidinal transformation impacts in the transition from the unconscious semiotic to the semiology of discourse. The sexual drive that saturates unconscious thought is not opposed to its expressivity. It simply returns it to a single interlocutor, designated as the beloved, to the exclusion of any other. Whereas, as we find it in conscious thought, the drive – which still shares its syntax by providing it both with its capacity to connect semantemes in a certain phrasing and its faculty to articulate its tropes in a certain affective direction and according to a certain meaning – will have had to undergo many deep transformations, so that speech no longer withdraws jealously to the beloved alone but opens up to the entire community of human beings. These transformations that we witness in analysis, which the highly enigmatic concept of sublimation professes to designate, remain fundamentally mysterious to us.

'He was afraid of the mysteries that lurk in the shadows, the evil forces that seem to threaten life, the swarming of monsters, that give rise to horror in every child's mind and mingle with everything he sees: probably last traces of a vanished wildlife, hallucinations from early days near to nothingness.' We can judge from these lines from Romain Rolland's novel *Jean-Christophe* the strange and disturbing proximity that united Freud and Rolland, confronted with the deep phenomena of the child's soul. A visionary activity invades the child, which the adult that he is becoming largely renounces, so as to submit to the world and its reality.

It is for the analyst to recathect this child's 'faculty', to attune himself to the early sexual experiences reactivated by the transference, which have caused the analysand's neurosis. The analyst must therefore, more or less according to each moment of the treatment, partly renounce his speech activity (both with the passive listening aim and the active interpreting aim) and engage his presence with the analysand through an identification with the latter's phantasmatic, or through a counter-identification, in the sense that the unfolding of the object relationship requires that the analyst, as the late Pierre Fédida (1976) so well expressed it, 'self-represents himself' there and incarnates this object.

The third situation concerns the movement of the treatment itself in its most radical intimacy between transference and countertransference. It involves a very ordinary, fluent and rewarding analysis for both its partners. Quite simply, at an advanced moment in its development, a small storm occurred: the patient remained totally silent for several sessions, then did not attend the same number of sessions. It was difficult for me to exclude the possibility that this analysis was going to be broken off, although for reasons that remained mysterious to me I was not truly able to worry about it. On her return, the analysand nevertheless asserted in the treatment and in her speech that she had been tormented by a strong desire to stop the work with me. Then there was another productive moment, when the patient discovered that in her highly conflictual relationship with her father an essential role was played by the spectre of her dead mother. And also discovering that 'if she was told now that her mother was going to come back that would be highly disagreeable to her because she had set her mind from then on being without her . . .'. The session fragment that I want to report took place shortly afterwards. She reports two dreams: in one she is gorging herself on some thick syrup that her father has given her, in which she recognises the most obvious sign of her neurosis, consisting in bulimia and obesity; in the other, she becomes reconciled with a couple of bad-tempered neighbours and drinks an aperitif with them.

The figure of speech that repeats the same signifier 'drinking' in two different contexts has no 'linguistic' quality in the communicative sense; it has, however, in my view an immense quality in relation to a particular 'psychic' function of speech to which we will return later. This is what I called the production of analogies (Rolland, 2003) – a sort of linguistic symptom – which signals that at the frontier between unconscious and preconscious a conjunction occurs between thing-presentations and word-presentations. 'Both dreams contain the same idea of drinking', I tell her. She clearly dislikes this interpretation, which puts her in a bad mood. I must say that I did not like it myself, finding its content prosaic and rather commonplace. But in the position I am in, it is language that directs my being and not the other way round. She protests that 'drinking the aperitif' does not especially refer to 'drinking' but, rather, to a form of friendly bond that she readily favours. Then she lapses into a long, deep silence, at the end of which she finally tells me 'I am right though', because a dream she had long ago came back to her as soon as I spoke to her: 'we – she and I – were in a bar or a club, a flashing light radiated a blue, sensual glow; we were drinking cocktails of a similar blue colour.'

We will make nothing more of the dream in this session, nothing beyond her stating it, and my hearing it and relating its content to the enigmatic moments that we had recently experienced. I thought that this dream illustrated the unconscious thought that had been animating her transference for a while. Or rather, I supposed that this dream, for as long as it could subsist in the penumbra of silence, revealed to her ego, from the psychic depths that eluded her control, the phantasmatic scenario that attached her to the analysis: a fantasy of desire that disguised a 'primal scene' that was completely fulfilled while she remained silent in my presence, and against which she was defending herself, phobically, by avoiding our meetings. And that, now that a certain psychic revision had forced her to utter it, she revealed it to me. From the dreamt dream to the narrated dream, we had moved from the visionary experience to the speech experience.

But of course this visionary experience, this phantasmatic pleasure that was knowingly protected or maintained by a certain 'strategy' of silence, was not hers alone. I have to acknowledge that – through a certain quality of my presence that mingled the discomfort of not understanding and the passivity of waiting with confident certainty that a secret intrigue had been woven and was to unravel – I undoubtedly shared it. Lévy-Bruhl (1965) gave the term 'unconscious participation' to the close and deep empathy between the members of a particular tribe and their ancestors (deified or otherwise). He regarded this affective and representative solidarity as the true spirit of the primitive soul. I would certainly apply the term 'unconscious participation', in my turn, to this level of the analytic experience, its 'nodal point', at which transference and countertransference merge, and where the analyst, at the cost of a certain depersonalisation, allows himself the time necessary for the working-through, the incarnation of the analysing subject's lost or concealed objects.

This participation is necessarily unconscious and it is therefore inevitably concealed from us. But there is one detail I must provide to you that gives clear evidence of it: for a long time, blue was the main colour of my office, until I redecorated it about a year before this session took place. The metonymic continuity, so unequivocal and lucid, between the dream material and a transferential residue should have paved the way for its interpretation. This is also what provided the unconscious thought with the necessary verbal bridge both to be illustrated in a dream and to be addressed to the Other that is the analyst. Now this association, which 'springs to my mind' now that I am presenting this situation, did not then cross my consciousness for an instant. It is as if in this subterranean phase in which the thought germinated, to which two minds necessarily had to contribute, an unconscious desire – borne by the most acute nostalgia – had prepared, in its progression towards speech, for its renunciation. Then had delayed it by being fulfilled one last time in what can be considered a shared dream activity, a shared vision.

For this patient, 'blue' is certainly a signifier representing loss, which links, in this precise sense, both the current situation (the previous colour of my office) and a traumatic situation in childhood – the loss of her mother – of which the first is the transference. It is strange that for this transference to unfold, I had to rid myself of this signifier, in both my thought and in my discourse, had to repress it, lose it temporarily. I even feel, retroactively, a distinct displeasure at having undergone this amputation. But 'blue' is also a signifier that represents sensuality, and in that sense it naturally enters the patient's conscious discourse. It is likely that 'blue' also refers to some more obscure representations, which are not currently finding access to her speech, but which are already appearing in my internal discourse – that is to say, in my general construction of her psychic situation: her mother died in childbirth, taking with her the twin boys she was carrying and who in this family of three girls were being fervently anticipated and whose absence she believes her father still regrets. It is, furthermore, the particular circumstances of this death that resulted for this little girl, then well into the Oedipal phase, in her mourning taking a strongly neurotic turn. And in the associations that the patient went on to develop from the dream report in this session there appears, fairly clearly and for the first time, the 'obstetrician' figure, whom her father regarded as his wife's murderer.

Concerning the polysemy of the 'blue' signifier at this point in the progress of the treatment, we can observe that different meanings do not have the same psychic status: some are known to both the patient and myself; others are consciously known only to me; and there is a third kind, related to absence, of which we are both unconscious. The homogeneity of the signifier, in the linguistic sense of the term, has almost shattered. The general signifier 'blue' has broken down into part signifiers, some of which remain in the flow of speech while others are as if sunk into the depth of the apparatus. They work, as we will soon see, to organise semiotic metaphors that accord phantasmatic experience its expressivity.

I would be inclined to give these signifiers, which have become unconscious, the term 'satellite signifiers' to emphasise the mobility that characterises them from now on and to indicate that despite the topographical regression to which they are subject they retain their linguistic structure. They continue to belong to the spirit of language while having in a timely way surrendered part of their materiality – resonant, plastic – to the exclusive use of the semiotic figuration. They remain 'signs' because their inscription in language is only suspended; they have become, for unconscious desire, the very 'thing' that accomplishes it. They are what Freud called 'mixed bloods'. I am not sure it is necessary to overburden our analytic theory with new concepts, and I would willingly bow to the view of those among you who would classify these mobile signifiers under the very Freudian term 'word-presentations', given that they oppose and connect with 'thing-presentations'. Or, alternatively, under the label 'demarcation signifiers', by which Guy Rosolato (1985) opened such a productive line of enquiry into language as 'Symbolic'.

I have the vague sense that with this case presentation, I have left the domain of envisioning and returned surreptitiously not yet into the domain of speech but into the intermediate and paradoxical one of 'unconscious discourse'. For what this situation leads us to consider is something more than this breakdown of signifiers that analytic discourse reveals to us, by thus presenting a specifically 'psychic' use of language that has only the most tenuous connections with the 'linguistic' usage to which we believe language is exclusively devoted.

What it also directs us to consider is that for an unconscious experience to be revealed, to form the object of a hallucinatory activation, to cathect, through the mediation of a dream, a symptom or a game, the perceptual–motor apparatus, it must be organised around a signifier that is necessarily semiotic in nature. For representation to accede to vision, it requires the addition of a satellite signifier. I fear that this assertion may prove controversial; I even fear it may be in contradiction with what I was just suggesting about the semiotic quality of unconscious expressivity.

Unless, that is, we should consider that the unconscious representation, in its archaic state, as it forms around the first awakenings of the drive and the establishment of the earliest object relations even before the human child's appropriation of language, remains as it were dormant, admittedly subtracting a considerable quantity of psychic energy from the active part of the apparatus and thereby generating a major source of inhibition, but that it is deprived as if negatively of this capacity for *agieren* [acting out] that we are bound to accord to phantasmatic activity. The unconscious representation accedes to expressivity through the combination of its hypothetical materiality (the famous mnemic traces that the psyche simultaneously registers and erases, like a magic notepad – Freud, 1925a) and a 'fallen' signifier of language, this satellite signifier, snatched from the holism of language, from the strongly articulated organisation of the preconscious.

If this hypothesis proved to be justified, it would not be the unconscious but the 'repressed unconscious' that would have to be considered a creation of discourse and its specific activity, speech. Repression – I am moving on quickly, but for the purposes of my demonstration I cannot avoid the model of the labyrinthine apparatus of the soul – therefore only repudiates representations rejected by the ego and its censorship. Confronted with the energy with which they are charged, it must counter-cathect them, and it is very probably the elements of language, its semantemes, that provide it with the medium of this counter-cathexis.

The binding of an unconscious representation to a satellite signifier impedes its access to utterance, the only psychic operation that can accord a representation the quality of 'consciousness'. It opens up to it instead the access to sensory perception and motricity. For the hallucination to occur requires, in fact, a percept that constitutes its support or its sensory material. The signifier provides it with this: 'blue' in the above-quoted example gives the dream its spirit and colour, its content and form. But along with its material, the signifier provides a certain communicative dimension to the hallucination: it allows it to be expressed in whatever kind of plastic or gestural semiotic.

Repression operates by drawing support from language, which it uses like a repressive surface, and from speech, which it leads to sacrifice, to the benefit of unconscious formations, a part of its linguistic function. It ultimately leads to enmeshing these two psychic agencies or categories of language and the unconscious. Repression can be said to work both to expel and to incorporate the unconscious representation. So that in the relationship between language and the repressed representation, there is sometimes a 'relationship of negativation' that is manifested in speech as a lack of saying and signifying and, at the level of the unconscious, as an excess of *agieren*, of oneiric or psychoneurotic production. Sometimes, and here we will conclude, there is a 'relationship of representation' (which includes negation – Rolland, 2000) when, in a formation of discourse, organised around a particular signifier and a particular syntax, the fantasy of the subterranean desire has transferred to the psychic surface.

Furthermore, the disparity between the visionary experience and the speech experience is not as wide as we initially thought. The hallucination by which the fantasy manifests its visionary power over the psychic apparatus is neither prior nor alien to the experience of speech: it is adjacent to it. When a word is missing from the fabric of discourse on which this develops, there appears in its place a depressive impulse, a pain or a phobia or, alternatively, when this speech belongs to the sleeper, a dream. The psychic signifier to which this word has regressed has established a continuity between a certain unconscious thought and the perceptual apparatus, and has organised, like a perception that has come from outside, from the world, a representation that has emerged from the interior, from Psyche. Green (1997) has given a good demonstration of the indecision that besets some borderline patients in distinguishing between a real representation of the world, a percept, and what belongs to an internal representation, a formation of desire.

From this perspective, the satellite signifier attests a certain indulgence towards this highly impersonal agency of language for the highly intimate subjectivity of desire. For better and for worse. Hallucinatory activity, for example, draws its strength from this perceptual procedure that confuses what is desired with what is seen or heard, according to the strictest identity and the most 'optative' mode: 'That what I see should be what I am lacking!' It is the same, with only a little more inspiration, and through a more elaborated procedure, with aesthetic activity. As Freud said: 'the artist . . . finds the way back to reality, however, from this world of phantasy by making use of special gifts to mould his phantasies into truths of a new kind, which are valued by men as precious reflections of reality' (1911b, p. 224).

This semantic continuity between the visionary experience and the speech experience is ultimately the source of the efficacy of the analytic method itself. What do we do when we interpret, who is really operating, and what is common to us all, whatever the particular style in which we organise our work? We work to 'displace' the satellite signifier attached to the unconscious representation and restore it to its place, both in the polysemous hierarchy of the word from which it has originated and in the strict organisation of the preconscious. In terms of its effects in the depths of the psyche, interpretation carries out a fundamentally indirect action of which the analogical interpretation (which is why I find it so valuable) is the provisional version: it summons in the patient a new utterance that inscribes the lost signifiers of subjective language in the holism of discourse and thus liberates the perceptual-motor apparatus from the pressure exerted on it by unconscious representations connected to the satellite signifiers. Accordingly, it restores the controlling and duplicating function that the preconscious system normally carries out in relation to the perceptual system by giving it the means to differentiate what comes from inside from what comes from outside the apparatus.

I may have moved too quickly by embarking on what is enigmatic about the presence of the root *sprechen*, to speak, in the Freudian terms of *Anspruch* (the drive demand) and *Einspruch* (the prohibition of reality), designating very deep and very obscure operations of psychic functioning. In this semantic choice that borders on *Witz*, witticism, is Freud not suggesting the part played by language in the organisation of every psychic formation and the indecision into which it throws us in discerning that which in mental productions bears witness to an act or a sign? Like every speech formation and like every psychic formation, interpretation partakes both of the sign and of the act: it leads the patient to utter, and therefore to renounce, turning the person who sees into a person who speaks.

References

Fédida, P. (1976). 'L'objeu' (III et IV). Objet, jeu et enfance. L'espace psychothérapeutique [The '*objeu*' (play object), play and childhood. The psychotherapeutic space]. *Psychanalyse à l'Université*, 2 (5): 17–48. Reprinted as: L'objeu, jeu et enfance. L'espace psychothérapique. In *L'absence* (pp. 97–195). Paris: Gallimard, 1978.
Freud, S. (1911b). Formulations on the Two Principles of Mental Functioning. *S.E.*, 12.
Freud, S. (1915e). The Unconscious. *S.E.*, 14.
Freud, S. (1919e). 'A Child Is Being Beaten'. A Contribution to the Origin of Sexual Perversions. *S.E.*, 17.
Freud, S. (1925a). A Note upon the 'Mystic Writing-Pad'. *S.E.*, 19.
Freud, S. (1925h). Negation. *S.E.*, 19.

Freud, S. (1940e [1938]). Splitting of the Ego in the Process of Defence. *S.E.*, 23.
Freud, S. (1941f [1938]). Findings, Ideas, Problems. *S.E.*, 23.
Green, A. (1997). The Intuition of the Negative in *Playing and Reality. International Journal of Psychoanalysis*, *78*: 1071–1084. Reprinted in: *The Dead Mother: The Work of André Green*, ed. G. Kohon. London: Routledge, 1999.
Hölderlin, F. (1995). Le plus proche, le mieux [The closer, the better]. In *Anthologie bilingue de la poésie allemande* [Bilingual anthology of German poetry]. Paris: Gallimard, Bibliothèque de la Pléiade.
Lévy-Bruhl, L. (1965). *The Soul of the Primitive*, trans. L. Clare. London: Allen & Unwin.
Lyotard, J. (1971). *Discours, figure* [Discourse, figure]. Paris: Editions Klincksieck.
Rolland, J.-C. (2000). La loi de Lavoisier s'applique à la matière psychique [The application of Lavoisier's law to psychic material]. *Libres Cahiers pour la Psychanalyse*, *2*.
Rolland, J.-C. (2003). L'analogie dans la cure. Un processus. Le théâtre des mots [Analogy in the treatment: A process. The theatre of words]. *Libres Cahiers pour la Psychanalyse*, *7* (Spring).
Rosolato, G. (1985). Le signifiant de démarcation et la communication non verbale [The demarcating signifier and non-verbal communication]. In *Eléments de l'interprétation* [Elements of interpretation]. Paris: Gallimard, Connaissance de l'inconscient.

Section IV

PHANTASY AND REPRESENTATION

IV PHANTASY AND REPRESENTATION
Introduction

Alain Gibeault

The French conception of the psychoanalytic process bears witness to the importance it gives to Freud's thinking on his first (topographical) model of the mind and on a kind of regression similar to that which occurs in dreams. It is based on the concept of 'idea' as part of a long tradition in philosophy and psychology, although the psychoanalytic approach gives a specific dimension to the concept by relating it basically to that of the instinctual drives. The difference can be thought of on two levels: the horizontal axis would correspond to the philosophical and psychological level in which a representation or idea is an exact replica of external reality, following a process correlative with the *Pcpt.-Cs.* system, while the vertical axis would correspond to the psychoanalytic approach, in which an idea is the psychic representative of a drive, hence the immediate distinction between the idea of an internal object and the perception of an external object. That is why the introduction of the concept of drive was a fundamental element in defining the psychoanalytic conception of representation in Freud's work; that definition was taken up in French psychoanalysis.

The discovery that affects and ideas follow different paths in hysterical symptoms (Freud, 1895d) and in dreams (Freud, 1900a) led Freud to suggest the hypothesis of the unconscious and to put forward his theory of the psychic representatives of the drives [*psychische Triebrepräsentanzen*]. In his metapsychological papers of 1915, Freud defines the drives in terms of a somatic process that has two psychic representatives: the idea in the strict sense of the term [*Vorstellung*] or 'ideational representative' [*Vorstellungrepräsentanz*] of the drive, and a quantity of energy, the 'quota of affect'. That theory was an attempt to clarify the reasons behind psychic conflict in neurotic symptoms, in which repression attempts to separate the idea from the affect, seen as a quantity of excitation that could overwhelm the individual. In his paper on 'The Unconscious', Freud (1915e) explains the differences between the psychic systems based on the concept of idea: the unconscious contains only thing-presentations – that is, thoughts relating to psychic objects – while the preconscious–conscious system contains both thing-presentations and word-presentations – that is, language. Freud's aim was to understand the process by which something becomes conscious, especially since the difference between what is *heard* and what is *experienced* in the course of analysis is a significant one. The analytic process, with the lifting of repression, only develops when interpretations do not focus merely on language-based ideas (word-presentations) located in the preconscious, but enable links to be made with unconscious thing-presentations.

In various ways, French psychoanalysts have highlighted the fundamental role of the preconscious in the process by which things 'become conscious' and psychic change is brought about. From that point of view, language is a constituent part of the secondary process and of making things conscious, because unconscious thing-presentations have less to do with images than with 'thoughts' about things, 'ideas' about things that have lost all the sensory liveliness of perception. Similarly, these ideas enter into a process of association with other ideas, thereby constituting a thought process; according to this model of the psychic apparatus, thoughts have, by definition, no specific quality. Hence the need to resort to language, in order to restore to unconscious thoughts the sensory liveliness that they have lost. Freud (1923b) did not, however, exclude the possibility that unconscious thoughts may become conscious directly – that is, without having to go through language, as we see in dream-images and in hallucinations [*Darstellung*].[1] He added, all the same, that these non-verbal thoughts are a very imperfect means for making thoughts conscious, as we can see in their attempt to represent logical relationships in dreams (Freud, 1900a, p. 312).

Verbal thinking is indeed the preferred instrument of the psychoanalytic experience because it enables all parts of the psychic apparatus to be accessible to thinking processes at all times. The impartiality of language means that the two demands of the pleasure principle – both the tendency to avoid ideas that generate unpleasure and the tendency to stay with those that evoke pleasure – can be put on hold by purposive ideas (Freud, 1950a [1887–1902], p. 270). It is that property of language which led Freud to hypothesise that language or word-presentations, as a process of 'hypercathexis' of unconscious thoughts or thing-presentations, 'makes it possible for the primary process to be succeeded by the secondary process' (1915e, p. 202) and brings about 'a higher psychical organization', the preconscious.

---

[1] The topographical difference between idea [*Vorstellung*] and representation [*Darstellung*] made by Freud in his discussion of dream-work and mental functioning has given rise to many problems of interpretation and translation. Freud uses the word *Vorstellung* to describe unconscious thing-presentations, which are thoughts, and *Darstellung* to take into account the transformation of these into the sensory images that are typical of dreams, hallucinations and artistic creation. In French, the term *Vorstellung* is translated as '*représentation*', while *Darstellung* is translated as '*figuration*' or '*présentation*'. In English, in the *Standard Edition*, *Vorstellung* is translated mainly by 'idea', which points to the fact that in the unconscious there are only thoughts, and to a lesser extent by 'presentation' when used in the context of *Wort-, Ding-, Sach- und Objekt- Vorstellungen* [word-, thing-, object-presentations]; neither idea nor presentation necessarily implies an image or perception. *Darstellung* is translated in the *Standard Edition* as 'representation', which would then be reserved for their transformation into images. These issues show how difficult it can be to translate Freud's concepts into other languages, and they highlight the problems that may be encountered by psychoanalysts from different cultures, depending on the extent to which they make reference to Freud's metapsychology in their understanding of clinical issues. In English, the recent use of 'representation' to translate both *Vorstellung* and *Darstellung* seems to ignore the topographical movement implicit in the transformation of an unconscious idea into a conscious depicted image (see 'figurability' in the Glossary).

However, in *An Outline of Psycho-Analysis* (Freud, 1940a [1938]), written at the very end of his life, he narrowed that idea down somewhat and argued that language does not in itself constitute the preconscious, even though it is one of its major features. 'The inside of the ego, which comprises above all the thought-processes, has the quality of being preconscious. . . . It would not be correct, however, to think that connection with the mnemic residues of speech is a necessary precondition of the preconscious state. On the contrary, that state is independent of a connection with them, though the presence of that connection makes it safe to infer the preconscious nature of a process' (p. 162).

This obviously implies that, from a developmental point of view, the secondary process and the ego are structured before language is set up; pre-verbal thinking correlative with the economic equilibrium between the principle of inertia and the principle of constancy must therefore precede language. In his *Outline*, Freud writes of the opposition between free energy and bound energy, thus confirming the importance at an early level of the work of binding done in the preconscious–conscious system before the arrival of language. The work done by that system can be thought of as binding affects by means of ideas. Preconscious thinking would therefore appear to depend on the setting up of categories of space, time, causality and permanence in the first two years of life; language development is based on those categories.

It is not simply a matter of describing a developmental sequence; the point here is to underline the metapsychological aspect of what constitutes the mind. This is an important issue, because what is at stake is the status of language with respect to the discovery of the unconscious and infantile sexuality. Lacan argued that language is a necessary condition for the existence of the unconscious and insisted on the idea that 'it is the world of words that creates the world of things' (Lacan, 1953/2006, p. 229) in order to account for the mental activity required for the building-up of the object. For many of the French psychoanalysts who criticised Lacan on this point (e.g., Green, 1973), it is the unconscious that is a necessary condition of language, and the organisation of the topography of the mind precedes and explains the emergence of language.

The issue here is the status of thing-presentations in Freud's theory. It is true that, in many of his papers, he saw thing-presentations simply as reproductions of things in the sense that empiricist psychology gives to the word; the concepts of images and memory traces would appear to lend support to that idea. French psychoanalysts, however, have always been suspicious of that empiricist conception, preferring the definition that Freud himself gave in his paper 'The Unconscious' (1915e), in which he wrote: 'the presentation of the *thing* . . . consists in the cathexis, if not of the direct memory-images of the thing, at least of remoter memory-traces derived from these' (1915e, p. 201). Drive-related cathexis immediately creates a difference between the internal world and the external one. In that definition, Freud draws on everything that he had been able to discover about the psychic apparatus, the contrast between perception and memory, and the succession of memory systems. In that model, the mind has a spatial structure in which ideas are connected together according to different kinds of association – 'associations by simultaneity' in the *Pcpt.-Cs.* system or 'arranged according to other (perhaps causal) relations' in the unconscious system, corresponding to what Freud called 'conceptual memories' (1950a [1887–1902], p. 234) – thoughts rather than images. It follows that ideas are less meaningful individually than with respect to the network in which they are encoded.

From the very beginning of his work with patients suffering from hysteria, Freud (1895d) described 'groupings of similar memories into collections arranged in linear sequences . . . stratified concentrically round the pathogenic nucleus' (p. 289). The 'talking cure' method (1895d, p. 30; 1910a [1909], p. 13) had made him aware of the resistances that attempt to oppose the recollection of those pathogenic memories at the origin of hysterical symptoms: 'The deeper we go the more difficult it becomes for the emerging memories to be recognized, till near the nucleus we come upon memories which the patient disavows even in reproducing them' (1895d, p. 30). From a psychoanalytic point of view, thing-presentations are not so much a direct replica of the object as the inscribing in the psychic systems of certain aspects of the object that have to do with drive-related cathexes.

It is in the difference between cathected external objects and objects which correspond to the processes of introjection and projection (these concern external objects) that the idea of thing-presentations takes on a specific importance in psychoanalysis: they have to do with the mental work of internalisation and the re-cathecting of memory traces, work which, by representing the object, forms the basis for fantasising, rooted in a cathexis that precedes the perception of the object. Freud explained that conception of idea with reference to his model of hallucinatory wish-fulfilment, according to which – following the dream model – hallucination brings satisfaction: the hungry infant hallucinates the maternal breast and can, for a short time at least, wait for mother's return, thanks to that hallucinatory activity which includes affects and ideas related to the experience. Basically, it is this hallucinatory work that defines the psychoanalytic view of ideas as the 'psychical representative of the drives'. The work of cathecting and of imagining defines thing-presentations in terms of a process that connects an experience based on affects and sensations (the hallucination of satisfaction) with one that is organised around the perception of the mother as a whole object (hallucination of the object). When word-presentations connect with that, they take over from hallucinatory wish-fulfilment while preserving the motor aspects inherent in that experience.

In this way of looking at the situation, the distinction between sensation and perception becomes extremely important when we consider the idea of thing-presentations, because the 'thing' in question – a psychic object – is manifested initially through the medium of an affect; it can never be completely or adequately represented by an image or expressed in words. As unconscious ideas become conscious, 'affects . . . correspond to processes of discharge, the final manifestations of which are perceived as sensations' (1915e, p. 178); this dimension prevents repression from being completely lifted, in terms of both language and the almost-hallucinatory revival of certain memories (Freud, 1937d).

The extract from Serge Lebovici's 1961 paper published in this collection (chapter 14) bears witness to the attempts by French psychoanalysts to reflect on the relationship between drives and ideas in the creation of object relations. It illustrates the French approach to developmental psychoanalysis, following in the steps of those British and American analysts who have studied the subject (Anna Freud, ego psychology, René Spitz). Trained as a paediatrician and analysed by Nacht, Lebovici followed in that tradition which attached considerable importance to pre-verbal relationships. On the theoretical level, Lebovici is well-known because of a famous phrase of his that really caught on in those French psychoanalytic circles close to his way of thinking: 'The object is cathected before being perceived' (1961, p. 151). As regards clinical practice and technique, he was, along with René Diatkine, one of the pioneers of child and adolescent psychoanalysis in France. Lebovici always wanted French psychoanalysis to reach out to the international psychoanalytic community, and he played a major role in introducing to the French the work accomplished by some of the greatest British psychoanalysts (Anna Freud, D. W. Winnicott, Melanie Klein, etc.); as the first French president of the International Psychoanalytical Association, he participated actively in the scientific life of many countries.

Lebovici's paper has to this day remained essential reading because of the synthesis it suggests and the avenues it opens up on these still-topical themes. The idea of object relation enables connections to be made between psychoanalytic data and neurobiological studies of development and illustrates the role of the object in the formation of the ego. Adopting a very Freudian point of view on the genesis of object relations, Lebovici distinguishes between a pre-object stage and an object one. That distinction is extremely important because it accounts for the conflict inherent in the emergence of the sexual drives and acknowledges the part played by the affects in all relationships with the object. Before the infant recognises the mother as a whole object, hallucinatory wish-fulfilment opens the door to the act of desiring. In *The Interpretation of Dreams*, Freud puts it thus: 'The first wishing seems to have been a hallucinatory cathecting of the *memory of satisfaction*' (1900a, p. 598; italics added). The satisfaction of a need is hallucinated before the disjunction between meeting the need and the emergence of fantasising. Hallucinating the satisfaction of a need must therefore be differentiated from hallucinating the object. At a pre-object level, wishes are not linked to any representation of the object; developmental research has shown that, from the point of view of the affects, cathecting the object precedes any image-based representing of it. Perception of faces at three months of age comes before perception of the feeding-bottle or of the breast; furthermore, that perception is meaningful only with respect to the affects of pleasure and unpleasure linked to the satisfaction of needs.

When the whole object is perceived as such – according to Freud, this occurs at the period when infants are cutting their teeth – wishes acquire continuity, linked to the permanent nature of the whole object, thus bearing witness to the continuity of the ego. At the same time, however, the infant hallucinates the part-object that should provide as much satisfaction as in the case of satisfaction of his or her needs. As Freud argued in 'Instincts and their Vicissitudes' (1915c, p. 118), drives become a constant force, so that there is no way of escaping them; this would be meaningless unless the relationship with the permanence of the object is taken into account.

For Lebovici, that way of approaching object relations implies that any fantasising which has to do with the idea of the whole object is retroactive in its effect of making meaningful the affect-based experiences relating to the pre-object stage. Contrary to Klein, for whom drives and fantasies were linked together from birth onwards, with a temporal disjunction between the idea of part-objects and that of whole objects, for Lebovici it is important not only to preserve a dialectical relationship between part-objects and whole objects but also to acknowledge the part played by external objects and by those cognitive processes connected with affect cathexes. That is why Lebovici's writings made a significant contribution to research into the early interactions between mother and child; their aim was to explore further and in a more detailed manner the connection between direct developmental observation of children and child and adult psychoanalysis, integrating the developmental perspective with the mainstream psychoanalytic approach. Right up to the end, Lebovici tried to broaden the scope of psychoanalysis by taking into account intersubjectivity, intergenerational transmission and the analyst's capacity for empathy.

In a paper that has also become a classic text of French psychoanalysis, Jean Laplanche and Jean-Bertrand Pontalis (1964 – chapter 15, p. 310) develop their ideas on the genesis of fantasy, based on Freud's concept of anaclisis [*Anlehnung*]. They describe the metapsychological sequence that enables a connection to be made between history and structure: the birth of the sexual drives is correlative with the 'mythical' moment when 'sexuality is detached from any natural object, and is handed over to fantasy, and, by this very fact, starts existing as sexuality' (chapter 15, p. 310). Freud's discovery of the choice of object in childhood and of infantile sexual theories, which bear witness to fantasy activity taking place at an early age, showed that over and beyond the search for a specific organ-pleasure, the aim of the sexual drives is to seek satisfaction; this is highlighted by the life-preserving function that underpins them, but the sexual drives are at the same time very different from that function and undergo transformations with respect to it. Freud (1905d, p. 198) argues that the aim of the oral sexual drives is the incorporation of the object. This is an entirely new point of view: between ingesting food and incorporating the object there is a gap that bears witness to a fantasy activity which includes ideational elements that are all the same far removed from their bodily prototype. As Laplanche and Pontalis (1967/1973, pp. 214–216) point out, there is an analogical and metaphorical displacement from the aim of the eating function to a sexual one, as well as a metonymic displacement between the object of physical need – warm milk – and that of the oral drive – the maternal breast.

Freud (1905d) had already observed that this transformation, which goes under the name of auto-erotism, occurs at a time when the object is lost: the real object, that of the function, is lost (i.e. the warm milk), but auto-erotism indicates the symbolisation of that loss, in the shape of the fantasy of losing the maternal breast. There is therefore a conjunction between a *structural schema* and an *event*: part of the object (the maternal breast) is fantasised about and becomes the symbol of auto-erotic satisfaction at a point in time when the whole object (the mother) is perceived in reality. Part-object and whole object, fantasy object and real object emerge in this 'event' that is auto-erotism, which marks not only the qualitative excitation of an erotogenic zone but also the fact that the object which brings satisfaction – the maternal breast – is taken up into the fantasy, as well as the defensive struggle to reduce the unpleasure linked to the cathexis of that object.

In this, the disjunction between need and sexuality lies at the origin of fantasy. However, like Lebovici, Laplanche and Pontalis disagree with Klein's idea that fantasy appears as a consequence of the drives; they argue that in drive-related processes both fantasy and the 'seducing' object have a part to play. As is well-known, Laplanche went on to develop this issue of the mother 'seducing' her infant. Without at that point choosing between the idea of drive, fantasy and object coming simultaneously into existence or that of some kind of circular causality, they emphasised the importance of the structural dimension with respect to Freud's hypothesis of 'primal fantasies' [*Urphantasien*].

Laplanche and Pontalis thus remind us of a major issue in Freud's discovery: is the emergence of symptoms and neuroses the result of a traumatic seduction or due to infantile sexuality? In his wish to differentiate the impact of psychic reality from that of external reality, Freud (1918b [1914]) took heed of Jung's (1911–12) criticism as regards the arbitrary aspect of individual interpretations. Laplanche and Pontalis tried to show that Freud (1915f) had introduced his theory of primal fantasies – primal scene, seduction, castration – in order to emphasise the demands of a structure that transcended individual initiative. He would later add the narcissistic fantasy of a return to intra-uterine life. In Freud's concepts, the prefix *Ur-* can refer to something originally primal in accordance with the scenario he described in *Totem and Taboo* (1912–13) concerning the prehistory of humanity. Laplanche and Pontalis deserve all the more credit for pointing out that these fantasies have more to do with origins – that is, with what gives experience its conditions of possibility in accordance with Kant's transcendental *a priori*. That interpretation would thus resemble the distinction that Lacan drew between the **Real, Imaginary and Symbolic** dimensions; Laplanche and Pontalis quite rightly point out, however, that these primal fantasies are not simply

> **Real, Imaginary and Symbolic** were introduced by Lacan in the 1950s when he described his conception of the topography of the mind and his structural approach to the unconscious 'structured as a language'. The concept of the **Real** dimension is a reference both to the philosophical notion of the thing-in-itself that cannot be known and to Freud's concept of psychic reality. The **Imaginary** dimension designates a dual relationship with a visual likeness; it is the *locus* of the ego with its phenomena of illusion, alienation and deception correlative with narcissistic identification with the mother. The term **Symbolic** involves a *structure*, the elements of which are to be described not in themselves but through their reciprocal relationships, like signifiers in language; it designates the register to which that structure belongs – that is, the *symbolic order*. The idea is to make reference to a *law* of functioning.

an *a priori* structure like Lacan's symbolic order – they are, above all, fantasies that are built up from elements which belong to the individual's own history.

That difficulty can properly be understood only if we take into consideration how the concept of drives works out with respect to the ambivalence of object relations. Stranger anxiety at eight months of age and negative responses to strangers are in fact an anti-depressive mechanism: the primal-scene fantasy is simply a development of the same process. If we are to avoid considering primal fantasies as unchanging contents of the unconscious (phylogenetic traces or transcendental schemata), we must see them – as Diatkine and Simon (1972) quite rightly pointed out – as a defensive working-through that alleviates the painful consequences of object-related ambivalence (p. 389). They went on to say that it is precisely because 'object cathexis is ambivalent from a very early stage that fantasizing cannot be seen as an effect of the pleasure principle alone'. It is not only the emergence of fantasising that constitutes a defence against the absence of the object; the internal organisation itself is a defensive working-through.

This helps us to understand the role of primal repression, described by Freud as enabling a drive to be attached to an idea, the only mechanism of which is counter-cathexis. Its aim is to contain the tendency to absolute discharge of excitation and to defend itself against the hallucination of satisfaction by creating a process of fantasising and setting up primal fantasies. At the same time, this fixation is the starting point for the 'influence of the compulsion to repeat' (Freud, 1926d [1925], p.153) and for 'the attraction exercised by unconscious prototypes' (p. 159) that Freud spoke of in his discussion of the resistance of the id. In this psychic work, the mother plays the part of a protective shield against stimuli; she leads her infant towards being able to control both excitation and anxiety and contributes to the creation of bodily frontiers by binding the excitation she gives to the infant's erotogenic zones and skin. By encouraging auto-erotism, she enables her infant to defend him/herself against the ordeals that reality inflicts by hypercathecting pleasure and the erotogenic zones.

It is this economic function of the mother that Michel Fain describes in his papers based on the hypothesis of the censorship of the woman-as-lover. Fain, who trained as a medical practitioner, was analysed by Daniel Lagache shortly after the war. His theory is based on clinical work on traumatic dreams in adults and on psychosomatic disorders in children (insomnia in infancy, merycism, early forms of asthma, etc.). A close colleague of his brother-in-law, Pierre Marty, and of the well-known paediatrician, Leon Kreisler, he played a major role in the development of the Paris School of Psychosomatics. In his famous paper 'The Prelude to Fantasmatic Life' (Fain, 1971) – an extract from which is included in chapter 16 – Fain describes the psychic moment when the mother turns away from her infant to become once more the father's erotic object. In so doing, she makes it possible for her infant to construct an auto-erotism rich in fantasy activity. The construction of the three primal fantasies bears witness to that activity: the potentially traumatic seduction is bound only through its connection with the fantasies of the primal scene and of castration.

The concept of the censorship of the woman-as-lover thus gives us a clearer understanding of what is involved in pre-object relations and shows what may facilitate or hinder the tendency to create a space for ideation within object relations. In an important book Fain co-authored with Denise Braunschweig, he developed his thinking on the subject by differentiating between the mother's cathexis of a 'day baby' confirming filiation with respect to a father in reality and that of a 'night baby' corresponding to the mother's incestuous fantasy as regards her own father (Fain & Braunschweig, 1975). Hence the importance for proper mental functioning of the mother's ability to counter-cathect the imaginary child, the night baby, in order to allow the real child, the day baby, to exist in his or her own right. Fain (Fain & Braunschweig, 1975) could therefore argue that he had modified somewhat the concept of anaclisis as defined by Laplanche and Pontalis: drive-related cathexis of objects is not carried out *with the help* of the self-preservative drives but *in spite of* them, because the latter set up resistances to the sexual drives when the 'censorship of the woman-as-lover' creates a certain number of counter-cathexes, the aim of which is to bind drive-related excitation (physical contact, caresses, rocking movements, etc.). In other words, the mother who maintains her sexual bond to her husband/lover can take care of her infant's needs without sexualising that relationship, thereby allowing the child to exist in his or her own right.

The French approach to ideas and fantasies is therefore close to Bion's theory of the mother's reverie and to Winnicott's potential space for play that lies at the heart of transitionality. French analysts, however, emphasise the discontinuity between idea and perception, encouraged by the fluctuation between mother and lover that introduces the absent third party. André Green's papers on the work of the negative and on negative hallucination are a development of that idea. In the two papers published together here in chapter 17, Green (1977, 1986) argues that these concepts have both a positive function, that of being a necessary condition for the individual's ideational capacity, and a negative one, linked to the destructive drives.

The concept of the **work of the negative** introduced by André Green (1986) is described in the first part of chapter 17 as a process which has to do with the mechanisms of defence of the ego, as well as with all the agencies of the psychic apparatus. This can lead to the negative and destructive manifestations of the mind, such as **negative narcissism**, pathological negative hallucination, negative therapeutic reaction, blank

> The **work of the negative** is one of the major concepts of Green's thinking. It has to do with all the negative and destructive manifestations of the mind: negative or death narcissism, pathological negative hallucination, blank psychotic nucleus, dead mother. However, in parallel with the destructive effect, Green emphasises the positive role of the negative dimension in the mind; he shows that the capacity for representing and fantasising is related to that of setting up a *negative hallucination*.

> Green's concept of **negative narcissism** is a clarification of his idea of the disobjectalising function of the death drive. The regressive movement that decathects every significant cathexis, following the principle of inertia or Nirvana principle described by Freud, is seen here as attempting to discharge all excitation and reduce it to zero.

psychosis, the dead mother. But the work of the negative also has a positive aspect in contributing to the process of representation of the object by negating the mother's presence; this gives to negative hallucination a positive meaning in mental functioning, involving a positive aspect of some mechanisms of defence.

In the second paper published in chapter 17, Green (1977) describes the origin of the concept of negative hallucination in psychotic functioning, in which negative hallucination is the 'sign' of the annihilation anxiety that follows on from denial and de-cathexis of external reality. Positive hallucination is therefore part of the process of recovery and of re-cathexis of reality within the delusion; hence Green's idea that it is therefore the 'symptom' of that void. He thus makes clearer a footnote that Freud (1917d [1915]) added to his 'Metapsychological Supplement to the Theory of Dreams': 'I may add by way of supplement that any attempt to explain hallucination would have to start out from negative rather than positive hallucination' (p. 232 n.).

Green adds a metapsychological annotation to the concept of negative hallucination, making it the 'precondition for any theory of representation'. In so doing, he underlines the importance of discontinuity between hallucination and perception in order for the process of ideation to become organised. The economic aspect of mental functioning thus lies at the heart of the differences between the psychic systems – an idea that was already present in Breuer's hypothesis, which Freud accepted, of the distinction between memory and perception in mental functioning. Freud's paper, 'A Note upon the "Mystic Writing-Pad"' (1925a [1924]), shows how important these two moments in time are – they are consecutive, not simultaneous: perception appears *in place of* a memory trace, for they cannot both exist at the same time. Simultaneity is never absolute; where they do coexist, as in psychosis, topographical splitting takes place, not regression. From that point of view, negative hallucination, as Green points out, is indeed the common matrix of dreams and positive hallucinations, as well as of ideational activity in neurosis and psychosis.

Following Green, César and Sára Botella (1984 – chapter 18, this volume) have added further developments to the theory of negative hallucination, confirming the clinical relevance of that concept. In the paper of theirs included in the present collection, they show how destructiveness aimed at the object brings about its de-cathexis, which corresponds both to the 'white of negative hallucination and the black of the terror of *non-representation*' (chapter 18, p. 380). The fundamental anxiety of human beings is not that of losing the object but of losing all *representation* of the object, which follows on from the threat of non-existence because of the object's disruptive presence. Positive hallucination is thus the outcome both of a drive-related wish and of the fear of non-representation.

The psychic solution for that anxiety – which resembles what Bion called 'nameless dread' and Winnicott described as 'primitive, archaic (unthinkable) anxiety' – lies, say the Botellas, in the narcissistic cathexis of a 'double'. It was Lacan who first studied that kind of issue, with his idea of the specular double; the Botellas treat the problem differently, thanks to their hypothesis of a narcissistic double that enables the individual to accept temporarily the necessary differentiation with respect to the

> The concept of **primary homosexuality** was introduced by Kestemberg (1984). In both sexes, primary homosexuality can be defined as cathecting the maternal object in a first attempt at differentiation in terms of a 'double'.

object. Other analysts, such as Evelyne Kestemberg (1984), have suggested that **primary homosexuality** plays a similar structuring role, corresponding to a cathexis of someone resembling the particular individual in the shift from primary to secondary identification (cf. chapter 37, this volume).

In his paper on 'The "Uncanny"', Freud (1919h) had emphasised the importance of cathecting a 'double' – which he saw both as an 'assurance of immortality' in order to protect oneself against annihilation anxiety and as 'the uncanny harbinger of death' (p. 235). César and Sára Botella underline the positive dimension of cathecting the double and give a very clear clinical illustration of the issues involved. Narcissistic regression in the course of an analysis confronts the analysand with this anxiety about the unthinkable, which can be likened to de M'Uzan's description of the experience of depersonalisation (chapter 9). Like de M'Uzan, the Botellas emphasise the importance of the analyst's countertransference in processing the 'double' in the course of an analysis; this is a paradoxical countertransference, as de M'Uzan also points out, which enables the kind of fantasy activity that facilitates interpretation of these narcissistic issues.

The Botellas describe the analyst's 'work of **figurability**', an attempt to ward off the anxiety of non-representation that the analysand experiences in the session. They would later develop that hypothesis in their book *The Work of Psychic Figurability* (2001/2005), in which they explore the metapsychological notion of the hallucinatory dimension. This leads them to describe a permanent process of mental life, the 'instinctual representative of a drive', that accompanies affects and ideas. In a session, this may be expressed as an almost hallucinatory, but not psychotic, re-experiencing which justifies, in Freud's terms, 'constructions' in analysis that are therapeutically effective; these are different from 'reconstructions' based on remembering and representing. That notion enables what the patient finds non-representable or unthinkable to be made meaningful in the course of an analysis.

> The notion of **figurability** is important in French psychoanalysis: 'Figuration (or presentation) is the operation which transforms the latent content into a hallucinatory production through the work of the dream: unconscious desire is thus presented visually, that is figuratively, through a specific movement of formal regression using primary process mechanisms' (Bourdin, 2009, p. 543). The focus is on the work of figuration, which obeys the conditions of representability.

Maria Torok's 1968 paper on the illness of mourning (chapter 19, this volume) foreshadowed the studies of the hallucinatory dimension that Green and the Botellas were instrumental in exploring. It has since become a classic text in French psychoanalysis, promoting a better understanding of the question of transmitting secrets from generation to generation. Born in Hungary, Torok adopted Ferenczi's hypothesis about the difference between *introjection* as a process involving the instinctual drives and enabling an awakening of the ego and *incorporation*, which corresponds more to a fantasy by which the process of introjection makes itself known to the ego. Incorporation of an object does indeed correspond to object loss and marks its installation in the ego as a replacement for the lost object in order to preserve the pleasure that was linked to it. Pathological mourning processes thus bear witness to these incorporated objects, the function of which is to recall not only the loss of the loved object but also the prohibited sexual desire relating to that object. Incorporation of an object takes place in a kind of hallucinatory mode, its aim being to recover an object that had not accomplished its role of 'mediating the introjection of desires'. For Maria Torok, the pain that attaches to mourning cannot be explained simply, as in Klein's theory, by evoking aggressiveness and destructiveness; there is also a libidinal satisfaction that is prohibited. With her husband Nicolas Abraham, Maria Torok went further into the question of incorporated objects (Abraham & Torok, 1978), with reference to concepts such as ghosts, crypts and intrapsychic tombs, which correspond to the work done in the unconscious on the unmentionable secret of another person; their perspective here is close to that of Ferenczi, with his idea of the confusion of tongues and the unconscious messages that the adult addresses to the child.

From the 1970s on, a great deal of research work was done in France concerning secrets and the absence of symbolisation when certain elements are handed down from one generation to the next. Haydee Faimberg, a psychoanalyst who came to France from Argentina in 1976, highlighted the links between Argentinian thinking in the 1950s and how ideas in France were developing in the 1970s. Although she had not heard of Torok and Abraham's work on 'ghosts', she discovered that there was some considerable agreement between their points of view and her own research. However, rather than take as her basis the question of mourning, Faimberg hypothesised the existence of alienating unconscious identifications that are transmitted from one generation to the next – what she called 'the telescoping of generations'. That problem situation exists in every analysis, she argued, and she then went on to study the narcissistic dimension of the Oedipal configuration.

In her 1988 paper, which forms part of the present collection (chapter 20), Faimberg argues that it is very important not to draw a simple parallel between that issue and the mourning situation, in order that the 'resistance to acknowledging the difference between generations' can be properly addressed, and with it the narcissistic cathexis of the object. The clinical case of 'Mario', which she again discusses in this paper, had already been described in her 1987 paper and appeared again in her book published in 2005. Although one could see in that case that the patient's father found it impossible to accomplish the work of mourning, Faimberg prefers to leave that aspect aside in order to explore the concept of narcissistic object regulation. Her intention is to discuss the wider problem situation, one that does not depend solely on the reality of mourning; she raises the question of the relationships between the idea of psychic death or psychic absence and the work of mourning. She does not over-emphasise the physic reality of the parents or their representation in fantasy, focusing more on the transference–countertransference construction of the object based on '*what the patient does not know he knows and what the analyst is completely unaware of*' (chapter 20, p. 413). Validating that construction depends on the resolution of a transference–countertransference enigma that has to do with unconscious identifications with the object over two or more generations. Faimberg prefers the term 'intergenerational' to 'transgenerational' in order to avoid anything that might evoke a sociological approach; she insists on the intrapsychic dimension of this process.

This way of approaching the object in terms of the 'internal parents' does, all the same, lead her to issue a word of warning against any reification of the object, a criticism that could be levelled at Klein's concept of the internal object. This is close to the French approach, in which, as René Diatkine (1989) points out, 'the object is neither a person, nor the fantasy content or body area of that person, even although reference is made to this all through the work of the analysis'. Diatkine continues:

> It is the unconscious element that gives a certain continuity to the cathexis of different kinds of representation evoked by what the patient says; that continuity is constructed by the analyst through a representation of what is going on in the mind of the person he or she is listening to. The only relevance which that has is the unexpected response that it brings about in the patient and the analyst's capacity to continue advancing while taking into account the new elements that are thereby discovered.
>
> (Diatkine, 1989, p. 1039)

'Object' in psychoanalysis designates a relationship and a modification constructed on the basis of what the patient says at the point where transference and countertransference come together, thus giving rise to something new and surprising.

It is this specificity of language in psychoanalysis that Julia Kristeva (2007 – chapter 21, this volume) discusses in her paper. A French philosopher, psychoanalyst and writer of Bulgarian extraction who has lived in Paris since the 1960s, Kristeva took part in the great literary, philosophical and psychoanalytic movements of the 1960s; her international fame comes from her many writings in domains as diverse as linguistics, semiotics, literature, psychoanalysis, ethics, and political theory and commitment. She was influenced by Lacan's theories and by his structuralist view of the unconscious, but she later distanced herself from these and became a training analyst with the Paris Psychoanalytical Society.

Her paper, on speech in psychoanalysis, bears witness to these various interdisciplinary currents through its philosophical and literary references, while aiming to bring out a psychoanalytic approach to language that is quite distinct from that of Lacan. The paper was originally read at the Congress of French-speaking Psychoanalysts in Paris in May 2007, on the subject of 'The Talking Cure'. This discussion paper followed on from the presentation of reports by two other French psychoanalysts, Laurent Danon-Boileau on 'The Power of Language' (2007) and

Dominique Clerc on 'Listening to What Is Said' (2007). In her paper, Kristeva follows the French tradition of including both verbal and non-verbal communication in the psychoanalytic understanding of mental functioning. She advocates a distinction between metamorphosis and metaphor: *metamorphosis* corresponds to the hallucinatory dimension and an object cathexis based on sensations and affects, while *metaphor* has to do with the dimension of linguistic signs and an object cathexis based on perceptions and representations. She suggests a theory of sublimation in which there are echoes of Freud's dichotomy between pre-object auto-erotism and object-related auto-erotism – as developed by Serge Lebovici and other psychoanalysts. According to Kristeva, the act of speaking as a primary sublimatory act means that object-related auto-erotism becomes part of the symbolic field between those participating in the dialogue, through the mediation of language – to begin with, of one's native language.

The fact that Kristeva emphasises a translinguistic semiotics which is different from the linguistic symbolic dimension enables her to explore the 'sensory substratum of language', which, in her view, acts as a 'point of relay between signs and drives'. She makes use of the example given by Danon-Boileau, following Diatkine, who said that the extract quoted from *Mr Seguin's Goat*[2] was an excellent illustration of the link between language and sensation:

> The affect that one feels when listening to a story, whether it be that of a patient or a literary narrative, may constitute what becomes of a sensation that arises out of the words used, provided all the same that those words do not designate it directly. In order to be summoned up, transmitted and in the end shared (which is precisely what makes it into an affect rather than remain a sensation), that sensation must be brought into play transversely and in a deflected manner, via a mechanism that circumvents any direct reference to what it really is, yet without following on from the margins of the apparatus of language. . . . Thanks to the words used in that description [i.e. the portrayal of the surrounding landscape which suggests anxiety], the reader *feels* something. The writing 'transmits' what is happening inside the animal without describing it – indeed, precisely because it does not describe it.
>
> (Danon-Boileau, 2007, p. 1391)

Danon-Boileau, who is both a linguist and psychoanalyst, took that opportunity of underlining the fact that a given literary style may evoke sensations and, in a similar manner, what patients say may – to a varying extent, if at all – lead to feeling something, then to constructing an affect that can be shared and finally to representing the world as well as themselves within it (p. 1394).

That example enabled Julia Kristeva to show that 'metaphor metamorphoses the reader by placing him in a chiasmus, in the "flesh of the world"' (chapter 21, p. 424).

---

[2] In Alphonse Daudet's *La Chèvre de Monsieur Séguin* [Mr Seguin's Goat], the goat in question is tied by a rope to a stake driven into the ground. The animal is terrified, because its role is to act as bait for the marauding wolf.

In other words, the style of a discourse may recall the idea that the philosopher Maurice Merleau-Ponty (1945, 1964) developed all through his writings – that is, the importance of an experience of the antepredicative unity of the world, which lies below the level of any objectifying judgement that contrasts subject and object; it is both a recovery of the world through the body and its sensations and an opening-up towards the world in its existential reality. Kristeva agrees with Merleau-Ponty in his description of how the anonymous experience of the body enables things and the world to be always *for me* (immanence) but no less *in themselves* (transcendence). Kristeva, all the same, introduces the dimension of desire, of the drives and of their ambivalence – parameters that are not at all taken into consideration by phenomenology or by Merleau-Ponty. The idea of 'the flesh of the world', with its reference to philosophy that Kristeva incorporated into her own thinking, enabled her to give its full metapsychological meaning to the experience of pre-object auto-erotism. That point of view is in agreement with Bion's (1963) idea of substituting 'feeling' for 'thinking', the better to bring out the emotional content of that experience of sensations and affects which precedes any kind of representation of the object.

Language is therefore a 'language of contact', an expression first used by Dominique Clerc and taken up by Kristeva, because 'the contacts of words are the contacts of bodies ... the sexual contact of bodies' (Clerc, 2007, p. 1296). The concrete nature of words enables us to find our way back to sensations and emotions while allowing them to be put into words and admitted to. Hence the difference between the dimension of *fantasy*, which presupposes a scenario, a dramatisation, with a subject, verb and object, and another dimension which has not yet reached ideation or fantasy and which has sometimes been described as that of the *formal signifier* (Anzieu, 1987), expressed as a sensation or physical feeling with no differentiation between inside and outside, or as a **pictogram** (Aulagnier, 1975), a complementary object-zone, the illusion that every erotogenic zone auto-engenders the object that conforms to it in accordance with what the body feels.

Kristeva is part of that French tradition which aims to restore to language its full meaning as being capable of putting words on the 'unmentionable' aspect of the drive-motivated body. Her reference to the two clinical examples given by the congress speakers emphasises the importance, for the way in which analysts listen to their patients, of getting in touch with not only the defensive aspects but also the sublimatory elements of any recourse to sensoriality through language and also, when interpreting these, of taking into account the appeal launched towards the father as third party. Her distinction between the father of 'the prehistory of the individual' (as Freud put it in *The Ego and the Id*: 1923b, p. 31) and the 'Oedipal

> The term **pictogram** was used by Aulagnier (1975) to describe a primal form of representation. It is not a representation of the object as such, but of the partial experience of an encounter between a sensory zone and an object that perhaps will make it complete. The concept has to do with the beginnings of the self-reflexive capacity and with the possibility, at a primal level, of self-representation.

father' – a distinction that is seldom referred to in contemporary psychoanalysis – is ample evidence of that. 'Speech in psychoanalysis' does indeed imply that there is a to-and-fro movement from language to sensoriality and from sensoriality to language with constant reference to the Oedipal situation, 'a formulation concerning the Oedipus complex, not to be confused with a formulation that can be reduced to the Oedipus complex' (chapter 21, p. 427).

References

Abraham, N. & Torok, M. (1978). *L'écorce et le noyau*. Paris: Aubier-Flammarion. [*The Shell and the Kernel*, trans. N. T. Rand. Chicago: University of Chicago Press, 1994.]

Anzieu, D. (1987). Les signifiants formels et le moi-peau [Formal signifiers and the skin ego]. In *Les enveloppes psychiques*. Paris: Dunod. [*Psychic Envelopes*, trans. D. Briggs. London: Karnac, 1990.]

Aulagnier, P. (1975). *La violence de l'interprétation. Du pictogramme à l'énoncé*. Paris: Presses Universitaires de France [*The Violence of Interpretation: From Pictogram to Statement*, trans. A. Sheridan. London: Routledge, 2001.]

Bion, W. R. (1963). *Elements of Psycho-Analysis*. London: Heinemann; reprinted London: Karnac.

Botella, C., & Botella, S. (1984). L'homosexualité inconsciente et la dynamique du double en séance [Unconscious homosexuality and the dynamics of the double in the session]. *Revue Française de Psychanalyse*, 48 (3): 687–708. [Revised and extended version reprinted as: 'Working as a double'. In *The Work of Psychic Figurability: Mental States without Representation*, trans. A. Weller, with M. Zerbib. London: Routledge, 2005.]

Botella, C., & Botella, S. (2001). *La figurabilité psychique*. Paris/Lausanne: Delachaux et Niestlé. [*The Work of Psychic Figurability: Mental States without Representation*, trans. A. Weller, with M. Zerbib. London: Routledge, 2005.]

Clerc, D. (2007). L'écoute de la parole [Listening to what is said]. *Revue Française de Psychanalyse*, 71 (5): 1285–1340.

Danon-Boileau, L. (2007). La force du langage [The power of language]. *Revue Française de Psychanalyse*, 71 (5): 1341–1409.

Diatkine, R., (1989). Introduction à une discussion sur le concept d'objet en psychanalyse [Introduction to a discussion on the concept of the object in psychoanalysis]. *Revue Française de Psychanalyse*, 53 (4): 1037–1044.

Diatkine, R., & Simon, J. (1972). *La psychanalyse précoce* [*Psychoanalysis with young children*]. Paris: Presses Universitaires de France.

Faimberg, H. (1987). Le télescopage des générations. A propos de la généalogie de certaines identifications [The telescoping of generations: On the genealogy of certain identifications]. *Psychanalyse à l'Université*, 12 (46): 181–200.

Faimberg, H. (1988). A l'écoute du télescopage des générations. Pertinence psychanalytique du concept [Listening to the telescoping of generations: The psychoanalytic pertinence of the concept]. *Topique*, 42: 223–238.

Faimberg, H. (2005). *The Telescoping of Generations: Listening to the Narcissistic Links between Generations*. London: Routledge.

Fain, M. (1971). Prélude à la vie fantasmatique [Prelude to fantasy life]. *Revue Française de Psychanalyse*, 35: 291–364.

Fain, M., & Braunschweig, D. (1975). *La nuit, le jour. Essai psychanalytique sur le fonctionnement mental* [Day, night: A psychoanalytic essay on mental functioning]. Paris: Presses Universitaires de France.
Freud, S. (1895d). *Studies on Hysteria. S.E.*, 2.
Freud, S. (1900a). *The Interpretation of Dreams. S.E.*, 4/5.
Freud, S. (1905d). *Three Essays on the Theory of Sexuality. S.E.*, 7: 125.
Freud, S. (1910a [1909]). Five Lectures on Psycho-Analysis. *S.E.*, 11: 3.
Freud, S. (1912–13). *Totem and Taboo. S.E.*, 13.
Freud, S. (1915c). Instincts and their Vicissitudes. *S.E.*, 14: 111
Freud, S. (1915e). The Unconscious. *S.E.*, 14: 161.
Freud, S. (1915f). A Case of Paranoia Running Counter to the Psycho-Analytic Theory of the Disease. *S.E.*, 14: 263.
Freud, S. (1917d [1915]). A Metapsychological Supplement to the Theory of Dreams. *S.E.*, 14: 219.
Freud, S. (1918b [1914]). From the History of an Infantile Neurosis. *S.E.*, 17: 7.
Freud, S. (1919h). The 'Uncanny'. *S.E.*, 17: 219.
Freud, S. (1923b). *The Ego and the Id. S.E.*, 19: 3.
Freud, S. (1925a [1924]). A Note upon the 'Mystic Writing-Pad'. *S.E.*, 19: 227
Freud, S. (1926d [1925]). *Inhibitions, Symptoms and Anxiety. S.E.*, 20: 77.
Freud, S. (1937d). Constructions in Analysis. *S.E.*, 23: 257.
Freud, S. (1940a [1938]). *An Outline of Psycho-Analysis. S.E.*, 23: 141.
Freud, S. (1950a [1887–1902]). Extracts from the Fliess Papers. *S.E.*, 1: 175.
Green, A. (1973). *Le discours vivant. La conception psychanalytique de l'affect.* Paris, Presses Universitaires de France. [*The Fabric of Affect in the Psychoanalytic Discourse*, trans. A. Sheridan. London: Routledge, 1999.]
Green, A. (1977). L'hallucination négative. In *Le travail du négatif*. Paris: Editions de Minuit, 1993. [Negative hallucination. In *The Work of the Negative* (pp. 269–274), trans. A. Weller. London: Free Association Books, 1999.]
Green, A. (1986). L'hallucination négative. In *Le travail du négatif*. Paris: Editions de Minuit, 1993. [Negative hallucination. In *The Work of the Negative* (pp. 274–279), trans. A. Weller. London: Free Association Books, 1999.]
Jung, C. G. (1911–12). *Symbols of Transformation: Collected Works of C. G. Jung, Vol. 5.* Princeton, NJ: Princeton University Press, 1976.
Kestemberg, E. (1984). 'Astrid' ou homosexualité, identité, adolescence. Quelques propositions hypothétiques ['Astrid' or homosexuality, identity, adolescence: Some hypothetical propositons]. In *L'adolescence à vif* [Adolescence laid bare]. Paris: Presses Universitaires de France, 1999.
Kristeva, J. (2007). 'Parler en psychanalyse'. Des symboles à la chair et retour. (Paper read at the Congress of French-Speaking Psychoanalysts, Paris, 17–20 May.) *Revue Française de Psychanalyse, 71* (5): 1509–1520.
Lacan, J. (1953). Fonction et champ de la parole et du langage en psychanalyse. In *Écrits*. Paris: Editions du Seuil, 1966, p. 237. [The function and field of speech and language in psychoanalysis. In *Ecrits*, trans. B. Fink. New York: Norton, 2006, p. 197.]
Laplanche, J., & Pontalis, J.-B. (1964). Fantasme originaire, fantasmes des origines et origine du fantasme. *Les Temps Modernes, 215*: 158–182. [Fantasy and the origins of sexuality. *International Journal of Psychoanalysis, 49* (1968): 1–18.]
Laplanche, J., & Pontalis, J.-B. (1967). *Vocabulaire de la psychanalyse.* Paris: Presses Universitaires de France. [*The Language of Psychoanalysis*, trans. D. Nicholson-Smith, New York: Norton, 1973.]
Lebovici, S. (1961). La relation objectale chez l'enfant [Object relationships in children]. *Psychiatrie de L'enfant, 3* (1): 147–226.
Merleau-Ponty, M. (1945). *Phénomènology de la perception*. Paris: Gallimard. [*Phenomen-

ology of Perception, trans. C. Smith. London: Routledge & Kegan Paul, 1962; reprinted, 2002.]

Merleau-Ponty, M. (1964). *Le visible et l'invisible*. Paris: Gallimard. [*The Visible and the Invisible*, trans. A. Lingis. Evanston, IL: Northwestern University Press, 1968.]

Torok, M. (1968). Maladie du deuil et fantasme du cadavre exquis. *Revue Française de Psychanalyse*, 32 (4): 715–733. [The illness of mourning and the fantasy of the exquisite corpse. In *The Shell and the Kernel*, trans. N. T. Rand. Chicago: University of Chicago Press, 1994.]

14 OBJECT RELATIONSHIPS IN CHILDREN

S. Lebovici

Serge Lebovici (1915–2000) was a psychiatrist, psychoanalyst, full member of the Paris Psychoanalytical Society, director of the Institute of Psychoanalysis (1962–67), president of the International Psychoanalytical Association (1975–79), president of the International Association for Child and Adolescent Psychiatry and Allied Professions (1966–70), president of the World Association for Infant Psychiatry and Allied Disciplines, and emeritus professor of child and adolescent studies in the University of Paris XIII. He contributed to all the major innovations in psychoanalysis in the second half of the 20th century, and together with his close friend René Diatkine, he founded a considerable number of institutions.

As early as 1948, he made use of psychoanalytic psychodrama in the treatment of child and adolescent psychosis. In 1961, with Diatkine, he inaugurated the Alfred Binet Centre, a pioneering institution in which child analysis played a dominant role. He was one of the main initiators of the direct observation of early complex interactions between mother and infant; his writings opened up new pathways between the psychoanalytic traditions of French-speaking countries and the developmental theories of the English-speaking world. An associate professor in the Paris-Nord University, he created the child psychiatry unit in the Avicenne Hospital.

Known the world over for his work in child analysis, he wrote an impressive number of papers and books, including: *La connaissance de l'enfant par la psychanalyse* [Learning about children through psychoanalysis] (with Michel Soulé; PUF, 1975), and *Traité de psychiatrie de l'enfant et de l'adolescent* [Treatise on child and adolescent psychiatry] (with Michel Soulé & René Diatkine; PUF, 1985). His interest in autism and psychosis led to his writing *Un cas de psychose infantile. Une étude psychanalytique* [A case of infantile psychosis: A psychoanalytic study] (with Joyce McDougall; PUF, 1960).

Françoise Coblence wrote a concise biography of Serge Lebovici for the 'Psychanalystes d'aujourd'hui' series (PUF, 1996).

The genetic study of object relations

1. The narcissistic stage

The description of this stage refers to the state of the neonate. There would be no reason to place it at the beginning of a study on the genesis of object relations if one did not have to refer to certain texts of Freud devoted to the study of narcissism as opposed to object relations.

In his *Papers on Metapsychology* (1915), he opposes the narcissistic stage and the object stage:

> Let us imagine ourselves in the situation of an almost entirely helpless living organism, as yet unorientated in the world, which is receiving stimuli in its nervous substance. This organism will very soon be in a position to make a first distinction and a first orientation. On the one hand, it will be aware of stimuli which can be avoided by muscular action (flight); these it ascribes to an external world. On the other hand, it will also be aware of stimuli against which such action is of no avail and whose character of constant pressure persists in spite of it; these stimuli are the signs of an internal world, the evidence of instinctual needs. The perceptual substance of the living organism will thus have found in the efficacy of the muscular activity a basis for distinguishing between an 'outside' and an 'inside'.
>
> (p. 119)

> Originally, at the very beginning of mental life, the ego is cathected with instincts and is to some extent capable of satisfying them on itself. We call this condition 'narcissism' and this way of obtaining satisfaction 'auto-erotic'. At this time the external world is not cathected with interest (in a general sense) and is indifferent for purposes of satisfaction. During this period, therefore, the ego-subject coincides with what is pleasurable and the external world with what is indifferent (or possibly unpleasurable, as a source of stimulation). If for the moment we define loving as the relation of the ego to its sources of pleasure, the situation in which the ego loves itself only and is indifferent to the external world illustrates the first of the opposites which we found to 'loving'. In so far as the ego is auto-erotic, it has no need of the external world, but, in consequence of experiences undergone by the instincts of self-preservation, it acquires objects from that world, and in spite of everything, it cannot avoid feeling internal instinctual stimuli for a time as unpleasurable. Under the dominance of the pleasure principle, a further development now takes place in the ego. Insofar as the objects which are presented to it are sources of pleasure, it takes them into itself, 'introjects' them (to use Ferenczi's term); and on the other hand, it expels whatever within itself becomes a cause of unpleasure.
>
> (pp. 134–136)

It is also in this text that we can read the following important note:

> Indeed the primal narcissistic state would not be able to follow the development [that is to be described] if it were not for the fact that every individual passes through a period during which he is *helpless* and has to be looked after. . . .
>
> (p. 135)

This narcissistic stage corresponds, then, to the first period of life during which the newborn exists in a state of relative indifference to the external world, against which he is protected to a certain extent by a high stimulus threshold. His needs, which arise from internal stimuli, are expressed through his discomfort on awakening, and his cries, and acquire a rhythmic character linked to the early stages of conditioning. At this stage the infant cannot discriminate any object. The external world, and in particular the mother, is not an object, though she feels she is an object of attraction for a subject whose reactions are beginning to acquire distinctive features for her because she can hear and understand his cries. In any case, in the environment the formless object satisfies the rhythmic needs of the newborn infant.

Narcissistic cathexis has its vicissitudes which were subsequently clarified in Freudian doctrine. I will come back to this later and we will see the role that it plays in certain object-choices of the child and the adult.

I will assume somewhat schematically that this narcissistic stage corresponds to the first weeks of life and lasts for 8 to 12 weeks.

Spitz's term of 'non-differentiation' is useful for defining it. The infant cannot differentiate himself from his surround, and he experiences the maternal breast as a part of himself. The 'I' is not yet distinct from the 'Non-I'.

Since at this stage all perception is linked to interoceptive needs, the infant's responses depend on the perception of needs which are expressed through this system, and external stimuli are only perceived insofar as they break through the stimulus barrier, provoking reactions which can scarcely be described as unpleasure.

We know that Spitz does not accept the famous trauma of birth – exploited so abundantly by Otto Rank (1924) – as the prototype of these reactions of unpleasure. However, Margaret Ribble (1938) has shown that the oxygen needs of the newborn lead to reactions that could be considered as the prototypes of anxiety.

At any rate, if it is possible to speak of unpleasure in the first days of life, the counterpart of this affect could be called quiescence. These binary physiological bases underlie the development of the foundations of psychic life, throughout the whole developmental process of the pre-objectal relationship, and then of the object relationship, as we shall see further on.

Yet the newborn's responses already correspond, according to the laws of conditioning, to those of the environment. From this point of view, it is not out of place to speak of the first signals coming from the object, not as a libidinal object, but insofar as it acts on deep sensitivity: in other words, changes of equilibrium occur which have been observed by Spitz (1957, p. 47), after Hetzer and Ripier (1930), whose work Spitz cites:

> If after the eighth day, one lifts a breast-fed child from the crib and places it in one's arms in the nursing position (that is, *horizontal* position), the infant turns his head in the direction of the chest of the person, male or female, who is lifting him. By contrast, if the same infant is lifted from his crib in a *vertical* position, the turning of the head does not take place.
>
> The signals become increasingly specific, but until the beginning of the 2nd month the infant only recognises food when he is hungry.
>
> Towards the end of the 2nd month, the adult begins to exist in the infant's surround: he/she is now perceived visually and the narcissistic stage gives way to the next phase: if an adult approaches the hungry, crying baby at feeding-time, the baby will become quiet and open his lips. This reaction only occurs, however, if he is hungry. The disappearance of the buccolingual directional reflex described by André Thomas in the case of gastric repletion should be interpreted in the same way, as Ajuriaguerra and his collaborators (1956) have shown. The main point is that 'the infant reacts to the external stimulus only when it coincides with the baby's interoceptive perception of hunger. At this stage the perception of the surround is predicated on tension generated by an ungratified drive'.
>
> (Spitz, 1965, p. 16)

2. The anaclitic stage

This is the stage of the pre-objectal relationship when the object is not as yet recognised as such. In Spitz's terms it is a precursor and is constructed around the first organisers. I have employed the Freudian term 'anaclitic relation' to show that the infant's relations are still relations of need (Lebovici, 1955).

According to Spitz, this stage is characterised by a specific reaction of the infant to the human face – namely, smiling. It will be recalled that Spitz conducted experiments which showed that the smiling-response occurs on the condition that the adult offers his face straight on to the infant, in such a way that his eyes are visible, and that this is accompanied by movement. Once again, this is a signal linked to a privileged *gestalt* which plays a role in the genesis of the constitution of the object.

So the infant's first perceptions are not linked to the mother's breast or to the baby's bottle. They generally occur during nursing, but are produced by a 'pre-perception' of the human face.[1] A bond is thus established in the first perception between the breast and the human face.

These first perceptions only occur when this activity is set in motion interoceptively, when the infant is hungry, and above all thirsty. Suckling, which soothes the sensations of discomfort, and the human face determine a buccolingual-directed activity which is generally accompanied by palmodigital activity. We can also mention here the coincidence of the two primitive buccolingual and palm reflexes of *grasping*.[2] The first perception is thus both visual (the human face) and oral (mastery of the movements of sucking and deglutition). The first imprecise *gestalt* associates the mother's face and oral contact with her.

These first perceptions in contact with the oral-visual *gestalt* of the pre-object are linked to need – that is, to an affect which could be described as an absence of quiescence or as unpleasure. With the reduction of tensions, the possibilities of perception decrease. In any case, it is the delay between need and satisfaction, according to a rhythm that will become one of pleasure–unpleasure, which enables the infant to develop a tolerance for frustration, which is a necessary basis for understanding the origin of thinking (Freud's secondary system).

We will see why the breast is the *first object* in the real sense of the term. It is reconstituted in the infant's first fantasies as the support of satisfaction or of non-satisfaction. But it is not the *first object perceived*. The first perceptions of contact are furnished by three organs: (1) the hand, which participates in the nursing act, and whose activity becomes more coordinated as this extremity of the body is increasingly cathected; (2) the labyrinth, if we recall the directional reflexes described in the preceding phase, at the narcissistic stage. When changes of position occur, it may be assumed that the infant experiences a combination of vestibular and auditory excitation that is interoceptive, vague, noisy and worrying in character; and (3) the outer skin surface, if we assume that the infant rediscovers in the form of his cot the skin protection which was supplied up to delivery by the amniotic fluid; contact with air inevitably creates a state of excitation, which is also charged with affect. So it is probable that these three organs are united indissolubly at the moment of need, in order to represent the moment of satisfaction, in particular through food.

The experience of nursing thus involves a certain number of activities which will become increasingly coordinated and meaningful:

(1) Factors of a physiological rather than psychological nature, which are linked with an unpleasant tension and with its reduction during nursing;

---

[1] These views are set out in René Spitz's paper 'The Primitive Cavity' (1955), in which he explores the genetic signification of the phenomenon of the blank dream (Lewin) and the phenomenon of the bodily image (distressing and disagreeable modifications) while falling asleep or during illness (Isakower).
[2] In English in the original.

(2) Motor factors which will organise themselves in a directed and psychological manner starting from the uncoordinated and diffuse activity which characterises this period;
(3) Perceptual factors of the experience of feeding (sucking and deglutition) which determine the activation of the proprioceptive organs of the oral cavity;
(4) Sensory and simultaneous experiences of the hand and the whole of the skin surface;
(5) Simultaneous experiences of an interoceptive character which must be activated by labyrinthine stimulation.

All these factors, whose organisation originates in the affect triggered by need, determine an immediate perception at the moment of the experience of feeding. This is the basis for the organisation of distance perception which is at the origin of cognitive processes. The first perceptual elements, as we have seen, are diffuse, and rest on proprioceptive elements: this is why palmodigital responses do not correspond to any coordinated movement and result in a manual 'overflow' during the nursing act. The oral cavity and the hands form a whole, 'the primal cavity', which is capable of forming a perceptual element at the moment of nursing – that is, when the cycle between needs and their satisfaction is established. At this point visual experience is merged with the total experience of feeding and the infant is certainly not able to distinguish what is inside him from what is outside him. With maturational progress, he is no doubt capable of understanding what waiting for food means for him. The mother's face, which is now familiar to him, signifies, he knows, *provision-of-food-and-in-the-mouth*. The distance perception thus becomes both the mother's face and the food that she provides. At the same time, the infant perhaps begins to have a vague awareness of his oral and manual activity.

Two factors intervene, then, in the elaboration of this perceptual mode: (a) the perception of that which is external and mediated by our sensory system; and (b) intero- and proprioceptive perception. The essential fact is that an instinctual gratification is associated with these perceptions: what gives them the value of experience is the presence of an affect.

We can therefore attempt to identify the various levels of perceptual and cognitive integration which can be achieved by an infant of three months: it is possible to speak here of 'thinking in images'. To start with, there is a coenesthetic organisation characterised by perceptions in totalities, mediated by the coenesthetic system and the intero- and proprioceptive receptors. At three months, the infant is most probably capable of diacritic distance perception on the basis of visual images, which, it may be assumed, leave ephemeral memory-traces.

The rudimentary ego, so defined, is called by Spitz the central steering organisation, which permits the infant to coordinate his first intentional actions in the service of defence and mastery. It dispenses with the need for a protective barrier against external stimuli: in effect, the infant emerges from his state of interoceptive receptivity and begins to perceive. Affects determine memory-traces and discharges of activity. Action itself contributes to the development of the ego. As a reality perceived verbally and extra-verbally, the object must be envisaged in the sense of Freudian theory: it is a support for the instinctual drives. As it is not yet recognised as object, it merits the name of pre-object, towards which the libidinal and aggressive impulses are directed; the pre-object which satisfies needs or which refuses their satisfaction is not worthy of the name libidinal object. It only acquires its value because of the cathexis attached to the instinctual affect: hence it is only functional. But this defusion of the instinctual drives, which is linked to the conditioning governed temporally by internal need, explains the organisation of the part-object fantasies which have been revealed by Melanie Klein's (1932) psychoanalytic observations with young children, the genesis of which I have attempted to explore with René Diatkine.

The object's permanence will only be distinguished from the environment when the infant's maturational progress allows it to recognise it, and when the instinctual drives can be fused with it. It is understandable that a portion of the affects is desexualised. Hartmann, Kris and Loewenstein (1946) prefer to speak here of neutralisation, an important process for the development of the ego whose so-called autonomous cognitive functions are decathected from the conflict created with them by the instinctual drives which determine the state of need. This process, as we shall see, must not be confused with the later one of sublimation.

In spite of the complexity of the processes in operation, in spite of the fact that the infant is not entirely passive, and in spite of the disappearance of archaic reflexes and protopathic reactions, the infant's field of perception remains very limited. Exchanges are established between the libidinal pre-object and the infant: verbal and extra-verbal on the mother's part and infra-verbal on the infant's part. Our knowledge of the reality of these processes, whose richness we can infer from ethological observations, remains limited.

Yet, in their paper 'Psychanalyse et neurobiologie', Ajuriaguerra, Diatkine and Garcia-Badaracco (1956) have made a careful study of the stages of maturation and the progress of the first rudiments of the ego. These authors have insisted on the limits of the infant's possibilities of perception and expression at this period: his perceptual field is limited, at least in our culture, to a reduced portion of space, since he is almost constantly lying in his cot. Moreover, he is still sleeping for a great part of the day and is not capable of prehension. It may be possible, though, that certain noises connected with deglutition or expulsion give him an opportunity for infra-verbal expression.

The infant's helplessness is thus the central fact of this pre-objectal stage. His action on his surroundings, in spite of the possibilities of what might be called pre-communication, is essentially characterised by simple diffuse 'discharge':

cries, tears and agitation. Nevertheless, by means of the specific smiling-response, the infant *organises the object*.

Spitz (1965) describes this period as one of *transitional relations* between infant and mother, speaking of continuous and often violent transitions. I would like to add that they are *transitive*, because unmediated. It is with the development of language and signals that they become *intransitive*. During this period of transitional relations, it is impossible to refer to adult experiences in order to understand the world the infant lives in: if he can resist certain stimuli of privation that would be unbearable for the adult, it is still the case that he is closely dependent on his environment. He is on the point of entering a period when a lack and privation of provisions will be experienced as the loss of an object – an object that is from now on quite different from a support for instinctual drives. But in the face of the object, the ego strives to emerge from the self: it will structure itself precisely because of the lowering of the threshold of perception which makes the control of stimuli indispensable.

3. The object stage

In their paper of 1956, Ajuriaguerra, Diatkine and Garcia-Badaracco describe the maturational progress of the infant: he is now able to sit, and his perceptual field is increasing considerably; at the same time his possibilities of acting on his surroundings are increasing, thanks to progress in the spheres of motricity and prehension.

We can understand that the maternal object now exerts its influence outside periods of nursing and care. It becomes part of the perceptual world of the infant, who can influence it through pre-language: cries, lallation, expulsive noises, etc.

It is at this period – which extends throughout the whole of the second half of the first year of life – that Spitz situates the 'second organiser', which is constituted around the affect of unpleasure provoked by the mother's absence. This is the phase of *eighth-month anxiety*.

Here is a brief summary of the author's thesis: affects of pleasure provoke the specific 'social smiling-response' around three months. Affects of unpleasure play an increasingly clear role after six months and are just as indispensable as affects of pleasure in ego-formation. At this period, the infant responds to his mother's friendly presence but responds to the stranger differently by hiding, crying or remaining inhibited. It is on the basis of this discrimination and its consequences that Spitz bases the description of eighth-month anxiety.

He envisages three successive stages in the genesis of this reaction which lead from unpleasure to anxiety, passing through a stage of fear. States of tension, prototypes of unpleasure, organise themselves at the narcissistic stage, whether or not one accepts that there is in fact a trauma at birth. The state of unpleasure gradually emerges in relation to certain stimuli and provokes increasingly expressive manifestations which the mother perceives ever more clearly.

At the anaclitic stage, we can speak of fear of certain unpleasant experiences: tension and unpleasure corresponded initially to a lack of internal equilibrium; fear occurs when there is a change in the animate or inanimate surroundings. A new perception provokes a reaction of flight from the danger, that is to say fear, in the sense in which Freud (1926d [1925]) contrasted it with anxiety.

Now the infant no longer reacts to the perception of a disagreeable experience with a stranger; he recognises the stranger, the unknown person who causes in him a state of apprehension, especially in his mother's absence. According to Spitz, the infant is disappointed by the stranger because he had hoped to find his mother: his anxiety is linked to the internal tension caused by his expectations. This reaction, which acquires sharp focus around three months and is the prototype of anxiety, indicates that the infant can distinguish his mother from others, just as he recognises himself because he knows her: the object exists in the perceptual domain, but it is a libidinal object. It is now possible to speak of an object relationship proper.

We need to explore in more depth the maturational bases which make recognition of the object possible, and the consequences that this situation has for ego-formation. As I have said, the perceptual field has increased greatly, while the possibilities for motor activity and expression are commensurate with the development and integration of nervous functions.

We may assume that the memory-traces which accumulate permit the various systems of discharge to coordinate themselves into directed action. It is now that one can speak of an *ego*, conceived of as an apparatus of equilibrium which not only permits need-satisfaction but the organisation of secondary circuits through a series of exchanges of actions between the ego and the object. Hitherto there had only been the self and the surrounding world of fusion and defusion. Now, the ego finds a state of equilibrium with the surrounding world through its negotiations with individuals and things on the one hand, and with internal stimuli on the other. This is the origin of the defence mechanisms which have been systematically described by Anna Freud (1936). The organisation of the secondary systems of discharge permits the decathexis of drive energy which is partially neutralised, following the fusion, mentioned earlier, of the *libido* and aggression with the object, hence the efficiency of the so-called autonomous sectors of the ego (Hartmann, Kris, & Loewenstein, 1946).

Along with Diatkine, I have tried to show the formative role of these so-called manifestations of anxiety (Lebovici & Diatkine, 1954). They allow the infant to have a real experience of 'manipulating' the object, which is expressed through certain playful and ritualised forms of manipulation. The most classic example, already mentioned by Freud, is the game in which the infant causes an object to fall out of his cot, obliging the adult to go and pick it up for him, thus having an experience of manipulating him: he learns that what disappears can return.

The beginnings of fantasy life can thus also be situated at this period. When the object is absent, the infant can 'hallucinate' it. This hallucinatory satisfaction shows that the infant is aware of the object's permanence. In this way he establishes the foundations of his own bodily image. We can also imagine that this constantly relived experience of the 'all-or-nothing nature of the object' awakens traces of fragmenting traumatic experiences of an object which both gives satisfaction and refuses it, and explains the origin of fantasies of the part-object.

So by recognising that the object exists outside the periods when he needs it, the infant recognises himself as existing in the world. Through knowledge of the other, he establishes the knowledge of his own existence and continuity.

In his monograph (1965), Spitz discusses at length the progress linked to this second phase of organisation: understanding of prohibitions and commands – participation in the rudiments of social games – knowledge of tools, very particular to man – the inception of defence-mechanisms, in particular identification with the aggressor, or rather the frustrator – the beginning of imitation of the adult (identification through gestures).

4. The stage of differentiated object relations

In the second year of life, the child's means of perception and action develop with astonishing speed. He walks, takes hold of objects, understands the language of adults and begins to speak. Diatkine, for example, has shown the extraordinary progress symbolised by the first sentence in which the verb indicates that the action concerns two objects, the subject and the complement. For his part, Spitz, in his monograph devoted to the study of *No and Yes* (1957), has shown how the acquisition of 'No' as an expression and its association with the gesture of negation – in short, its semantification – attests to a new organisation (the stage of the third organiser). The child has passed from action to communication.

Under the term transitional object, Winnicott (1954) has described the objects invested during this second year of life, which reproduce the human image in a rudimentary fashion. We know how young children take a prolonged interest in teddy bears and other typical animals that they like to handle and go to sleep with. These objects are the support for projections in which the first defensive mechanisms are externalised: identification with the frustrator, projective identification, or even identification with the aggressor.

The object is first maternal, or at any rate maternalised: though the object is in fact differentiated – that is, a factor of identification – there is not as yet a clear distinction between the role of the father and that of the mother. Diatkine and I have spoken of fantasies of 'oedipification' which seem to characterise this period. Identification is in effect subtended during this period by early mechanisms of introjection and incorporation. The child cannot fail, then, to imagine that his father desires and obtains from the mother what he never obtains – namely, the fusional and destructive incorporation of the object. Thus he comes to see that his desires are frustrated by the father whose existence he gradually becomes aware of.

This paternal frustration only assumes its full significance with the triangulation of object relations which specifies more precisely the role of the protagonists in the drama that the child goes through owing to his development. At the end of the second year he can say: 'I want', thereby asserting his relative autonomy. The I stage corresponds to an advanced development of the ego, which justifies the convenient description of psychoanalytic topography. The ego is now fully differentiated from the id, that is, from the ensemble of the drives whose expression it controls, and from the superego, which acquires its structure through the process of identification which will allow the Oedipal conflict to be overcome.

★ ★ ★

The description that I have just outlined of the first stages of the object relationship is necessarily schematic. The individualisation of certain stages is convenient for shedding light on their genesis. As we have seen, Spitz introduced the notion of organisers to show their structuring embryological character.

There would be many disadvantages, however, in forming an overly static conception of the processes of development. The object relationship is a mutual relationship that is constantly developing. There is a relation between the maturational progress, which only permits us to distinguish discontinuous stages because the constant progress and successive integrations give an impression of stages and new forms, and the modifications of the relationship in which the object is cathected, then perceived, and therefore structuring: these new forms take shape, then, against the discontinuous background of development.

Spitz (1965), who reminds us that the mother–child relation develops before our very eyes, expresses himself as follows:

> Among the peculiarities of this relation is that, before our very eyes, a state of social unrelatedness, a purely biological bond, is transformed, step by step, into what is eventually to become the first social relation of the individual. What we witness is a transition from the physiological to the psychological and social. In the biological state (*in utero*) the fetus's relations are *parasitical*. But in the course of the first year of life, the infant will pass through a stage of psychological *symbiosis* with the mother, from which he will graduate to the next stage, in which social, i.e. hierarchical interrelations are developed.

An equally peculiar and perhaps unique aspect of the mother–child relation is that the psychic structure of the mother is fundamentally different from that of her child. Aside from the somewhat comparable relation of a human being with a domesticated animal (a pet, for instance), such a high degree of disparity in two as closely associated and interdependent individuals is not found anywhere else in our social organisation. I believe that the first sociologist who called attention to the possibilities of sociological investigation of the mother–child group (which he called a 'dyad') is George Simmel. He stresses that in this relation one could find the germ of all subsequent development of social relations. . . .

(pp. 11–12)

This conception of the genesis of the object relationship, which is held by so-called genetic psychoanalysts, particularly American, and by child psychoanalysts of the Paris school, can be briefly formulated as follows: the infant becomes aware of the object as his maturation progresses in a given culture; but the recognition of the object is itself a factor of maturation.

It thus reduces the place of instinctual drive mechanisms, and R. Diatkine (1959) has explained himself clearly in this connection:

During the first month of life, the instinctual behaviour of the human being is very similar to the behaviour of animals described by ethologists. This activity is characterised by:

(1) Its precise biological finality, and in any case by the fact that it corresponds strictly to defined levels of humoral balances. The state of dissatisfaction is a real state of need.
(2) External stimuli, on the other hand, have a particular value. They are barely differentiated . . . they only have effect during the state of need . . . They are thus stimuli of a nondifferentiated and discontinuous value. This discontinuity and this nondifferentiation of the activity can be found in many animal behaviours.

. . . From the eighth month, the establishment of the object relationship implies a fundamental structural modification and Spitz rightly considers the ensemble of the phenomena unfolding at this moment as the 'second organiser' of psychic life. In effect, we can define the appearance of the object relationship as being characterised by the fact that, in all circumstances, the infant reacts to the perception or the non-perception of a privileged and always identified *gestalt* (the face of the mother or her substitute). When the infant sees his mother's face, he shows signs of satisfactions which are the continuation of the phenomena of quiescence triggered by the ingestion of food; the mother's absence or departure can provoke behaviour very similar to that which was caused by hunger at the beginning of life. This is why it is correct to speak of oral cathexis of the maternal object. This links up with the two stages of the oral phase described by Abraham: the auto-erotic stage and the object-stage. But one cannot emphasise enough the fundamental difference between these two modes of instinctual drive activity. The object-cathexis is now freed of any kind of biological finality; it is in no way linked to the internal humoral state; the infant manifests oral satisfaction on seeing his mother even if he is not hungry and her facial expression does not signal that it is feeding-time.

I think that this transition from the discontinuous to the continuous, from the necessary to the unnecessary (at the vital level, of course), is the characteristic element of the beginning of human psychic organisation, in the strict sense of the term, and I believe that it is only from this point that one can speak of pleasure, a word which indicates going beyond the notion of the satisfaction of a biological need.

. . . This value conferred upon a particular *gestalt* also explains the fact that the object can never be totally satisfying, since it will never have an actual feeding role. It is in this respect that it has been said that the early object relationship is essentially psychotic, and that one can see the emergence of fantasies of incorporation, the first compromise between the libidinal drive and reality . . .

The differentiated object relationship thus bears witness to a new organisation on the basis of which one can speak of the ego. The cathected object is one of its formative forces. The ego structures and organises itself in order to master the stimuli originating in the object, which come both from the outside and from within.

★ ★ ★

This genetic study of object relations, envisaged from a neurobiological and environmental perspective, requires us to dwell for a moment on the problems of object-cathexis. Perception is, in effect, preceded by affect, and object-cathexis precedes its perception.

As Spitz points out, in the dyadic mother–infant system, the affective climate plays a more important role than a whole series of more or less traumatising events, which, moreover, are difficult to distinguish.

This climate comprised of processes, intentions and undoubtedly affective perceptions is, in a way, ahead of ego-development.

The processes of object relations precede during the first year of life the perception of objects in the sense of 'thing'. If we assume that the smiling-response to the gestalt of the human face is indeed the first organiser, we must remember that this face, associated with the experience of feeding, is recognised before the feeding-bottle which the baby handles several times a day.

With the development of language, a much more elaborate means of communication, semantic signals assume their full importance and weaken those of postural signs.

★ ★ ★

It is here that the study of communication in the development of the object relationship has its logical place. The point is not to indulge in the pleasure of explaining its genesis with the help of a convenient and widely used theory. The emphasis that I am putting on it can be more readily explained by an observation that I have already made: because the object relationship was first studied by adult psychoanalysts in stages of development, the object was first considered as an internal reality, before acquiring any characteristic of typological structures. In the genesis of the object relationship, we have seen that the cathexis of the object precedes its perception and its knowledge; in turn, this perception structures the infant's ego. This means that the object relationship cannot be studied in one direction only. Within the mother–infant dyad, a series of circular processes develop continuously which express the actions and reactions of both members of the couple studied. The influence of the mother on the child's development has been studied extensively. Much less effort has been made to discover how the baby influences its mother, who, in turn, may modify her affective attitude depending on the way that she experiences this relationship which engages her narcissistic energies.

Communication theory, which generally employs terminology relating to problems studied in mathematics in information theory, provides us with terms that are convenient for showing the reality of the reciprocal and circular processes between the mother and the infant.

I am not closing my eyes to the disadvantages of a hasty comparison between infinitely subtle and complex facts on the one hand and the schematic data which belong to mathematical hypotheses. We cannot content ourselves with approximations that are intellectually satisfying: this would result in a reification which any complete and dramatic description must avoid. But it seems to me that formulating certain phenomena observed in the progress of the object relationship in terms used by communication theory enables us to reach a deeper understanding. To employ a reference that belongs to this theory, let us say that certain images have a 'symbolic' value which is appealing and attests to certain 'relations' between the explanatory systems. A genuine phenomenon of resonance then occurs which culminates in the integration of new data which are useful for a practical understanding of the phenomena that structure the dyadic relations between the mother and the baby.

A certain number of examples will illustrate the importance of such a study. The first refers to a widely known fact: during the first days of its life, the infant expresses his discomfort and his needs through cries. It is only much later that these manifestations will acquire their value as signals for him. Yet the mother perceives them as signs; she recognises her infant's cry and gives it the signification of a call for help. Thus a manifestation that is insignificant for the infant is significant for the mother.

In her study on the errors of prediction in longitudinal studies on child development, Marianne Kris (1957) shows how certain basic facts are likely to influence the mother's attitude and to modify the prognosis that could be inferred from studying her personality. One would expect, for example, from certain rigid, obsessional and perfectionist mothers, pathogenic attitudes during sphincter training. Now we know that the quality of appetite seems to belong to the equipment. The child who doesn't eat much often drives his mother to despair, whereas the child who is a vigorous eater seems to her to be in perfect health and makes her feel relaxed. A fact as basic as the weight at birth seems to have some sort of correlation with this quality of appetite. Thus children who are a bit fat and good eaters are likely to make anxious and perfectionist mothers feel relaxed. While they were expected to have rigid attitudes, meals that are quickly consumed in mutual satisfaction can contribute to narcissistic supplies, which then modify certain aspects of the relationship.

The same is true if one studies the personality of mothers of psychotic children. It seems undeniable that most of them are pathogenic owing to their anxiety and their difficulty in contributing valid sensory and affective experiences to the relationship with their child. But conversely, how can we not take into account the psychotising role of certain forms of encephalopathy, of certain disharmonies in development which inflict deep narcissistic wounds on mothers who are already highly sensitive owing to the structure of their personality?[3]

Thus a thorough study of early object relations must culminate in the description of certain clinical types, which René Spitz tried to characterise. I will come back to this, but I should say right away that these descriptions – which introduce us to the field of psychosomatic praxis – give an account above all of variations in the maternal attitude. Thus the description of the reciprocal object relation still has to be tackled.

Freud had anticipated its importance, and Spitz is undoubtedly right to insist on a sentence in 'The Project' (Freud, 1950 [1895]) which he renders as follows: 'This path of discharge thus acquires an extremely important secondary function – viz: of bringing about understanding'[4] (Spitz, 1965, p. 129). In this truly premonitory remark, Freud shows that the problem of communication lies in the hiatus which separates primary processes (of immediate discharge) from secondary processes, where semantification, the specific characteristic of the human animal, is situated.

---

[3] This perhaps justifies the term 'progressive encephalopathy' which has sometimes been employed to define certain psychotic states in childhood (on this subject, see Lebovici & McDougall, 1960).

[4] There is a footnote here which reads: 'which in this context refers primarily to communication'. In the original German, Freud (1950 [1895]) used the term *Verständigung*. [*Trans.*]

Communication theory, in its biological applications, is based on an obvious and fundamental observation: an organism must be distinguished from the milieu in which it lives. The reciprocal conditions of these two entities are changing. In certain circumstances, the milieu can exert influence on the organism and direct its behaviour. The stimuli must have a certain organisation to act. In verbal communication, they are semantic signs, words. In order to have value as communication, these stimuli, specific to man, must also be organised. The efficacy of the stimulus is translated by a response of the organism which may be likened to a 'reward'.[5] Finally, communication is characterised by the fact that *information is transmitted from one point to another.*

In this system where information is transmitted through a *channel* or chain, the components (source and destination) must be distinct in time and space. The *transmitter* and the *receiver* carry out a constant work of *coding* and *decoding*, which obviously presupposes not only the heterogeneity of the two components of the system, but also their eventual resonance.

It is important to insist on the progression of the manifestations which can be emitted at the level of the source of information. They follow the following progression:

a) The indicator (perception naturally linked to the experience of an object or a situation);
b) The sign (linked with the experience of perception and replacing it);
c) The signal (perception linked to an experience);
d) The symbol (a sign which stands for an object).

On the basis of these very general definitions, we must assume the existence of a system of communication between the mother and the child on the one hand and the child and his mother on the other.

During the narcissistic and anaclitic phases of the pre-objectal relationship, we have seen that the infant learns to have contact with something by touching it before seeing it, since he touches the food object in a *continuum* which must consist of his oral cavity, his poorly controlled fingers and sensations of a coenesthetic order: his mother only has value for him when he needs her; tension is thus followed by discharge. But after a few weeks, the infant sees his mother's face. So the maternal 'pre-gestalt' is a pre-object, seen and touched, where the face and the breast are in continuity, even though they only acquire meaning and shape during the experience of nursing.

The primal perception is structured, then, out of a primary experience. At this moment, the infant's motor discharges are pure expression: though they are not meaningful for him, they become so for the mother and form the basis of a *pre-verbal communication* in the direction infant–mother.

---

[5] The expression is Miller's (see Miller, *Language and Communication*, 1951).

But in the first weeks of life the infant also experiences, as I have just said, and then perceives something of his mother during the moment of tension. So communication in the direction mother-child is largely *extra-verbal*.

Thus pre-verbal communication, based on the signals of the infant and the extra-verbal communication originating from the mother's perception, define the basis of the earliest object relation. In the direction of the infant towards the mother, communication is based on non-semantic signals. At this same period, one can speak of a communication from the mother towards the infant, if one refers to the notion of coded indicator, which I spoke about earlier.

Later on, the semantification of communication in the differentiated object relation is translated by a slow antithetic process. From the moment the infant is capable of 'hallucinating' his mother, he begins to imitate her gestures.[6] The acquisition of semantic signs means that the infant no longer has to use motor discharge alone as a means of expression.

In his monograph devoted to the study of the genesis of object relations, Spitz (1965) tries to clarify the nature of the structuring forces within this communication. The object relation is global and involves two totalities. On the side of the infant, the affects he experiences form the basis of the formative forces that come from the mother. Her presence is the fundamental fact. But her slightest actions have the value of informative stimuli. The mother learns to discern what gives her infant pleasure. Conversely, any activity on the baby's part will generally be agreeable for her. Thus the mother's unconscious attitudes can be the most efficient; at the same time, and reciprocally, the mother learns to recognise the infant's pre-signals.

The intimate nature of the phenomena underlying this first communication remains mysterious: ethological studies on the lure remind us that in certain animals, communication depends on postural signs and structural configurations. These stimuli trigger motor behaviours which have expressive value.

Thus one can imagine that the earliest forms of pre- and extra-verbal communication depend on the experience of certain extra-verbal affects and are expressed through expressive, but pre-verbal discharges. The information emitted by the infant is both a sign and a signal; the information emitted by the mother becomes a signal. In the infant, the reception of these extra-verbal signals causes diverse effects, in all probability coenesthetic. They belong to diverse sources, among which we may mention: rhythm, equilibrium, skin warmth, etc.

Affect, it must be repeated, is the basis of communication. The channel of communication is thus constantly functioning and models both the infant and his mother in an interplay of circular and reciprocal interactions. On the side of the infant, a 'modelling' or 'moulding' process occurs, to use Spitz's expression. Thus the term *transactional relationship* is justified to define this aspect of the

---

[6] Spitz puts particular emphasis, as we know, on the gesture of negation (see *No and Yes*, 1957).

object relation.[7] The term transactional interaction seemed to me to be useful to the extent that it symbolises (and consequently informs us) the constant inter-reaction which operates between the two partners of the object relationship, culminating in a series of equilibriums that are constantly challenged. Let us remember that we can call it *transitional*, because it is evolving. It remains transitive, as long as it is pre-verbal. Language, by virtue of the distance it introduces, makes it *intransitive*.

Drawing on the theory of conditioned reflexes on the one hand and on the theory of communication on the other, Spitz (1965) explains the role of maternal *behavioural matrixes* in the process of *learning*: they are translated by an anticipatory affective response: 'it is the mother who offers these signals during the first year to the child. The child responds to these signals during the first trimester by a series of conditioned reflexes. After the third month, one sees the emergence of a special process of learning that I have called "*learning according to the human pattern*"' (p. 236). It parallels the organisation level of the child's ego. This learning process is linked on the one hand to the maturation of the child's perceptual capacities and, on the other, to the signals that his mother offers to him in any situation of pleasure, unpleasure or discrimination. 'These signals originate in the mother's affective attitude. Though they may be scarcely perceptible to the adult observer, these signals serve to elicit anticipatory affective responses in the child' (p. 237).

The inconsistency of maternal signals or their incoherence is the cause of a transmission of anxiety to the child and explains the particular structuring of egos which Spitz describes in the so-called psychotoxic syndromes of the child.

From this same perspective, Spitz goes on to speak about identification with the unconscious tendencies of the mother: the rejecting attitude of the depressive mother, for instance, is experienced by the child as a loss of the object and would explain the compensatory coprophagic tendencies observed in the anal stage.

★ ★ ★

[Pp. 201–209] So if the entire classical theory of the genesis of object relations is indeed based on the hypothesis that I have evoked several times – namely, that *the cathexis of the object precedes its perception* – the theory of narcissism leads to an inverse proposition which also needs to be taken into consideration: *the cathexis of the ego founds the object*. These two situations are indistinguishable, in fact, during the first days of life, when the narcissistic state defines the life of the newborn.

★ ★ ★

---

[7] To the best of my knowledge, in information theory, the word transaction has a double meaning: (1) The system A has an effect on B, and B on A. The resulting mutual equilibrium is the transaction. (2) In this interaction of A→B and B→A, A and B play a role in the milieu which in turn has an effect on A and B, just as A and B have an effect on the environment.

But now that it is time to conclude the theoretical study of the object relationship based on the synthesis of a large number of writings by adult psychoanalysts and genetic psychoanalysts, a place needs to be given to certain authors who, like Fairbairn (1941, 1944, 1946), reject the hypothesis of the libido.

Fairbairn starts out from the study of schizoid and manic-depressive subjects and recognises in them the importance of the two oral phases described by Abraham (1916). In neurotics, on the contrary, it is the oral conflict that seems to him to be pathogenic, and the developed Oedipal material seems to him to translate a defensive genitalisation which is elaborated secondarily. However, it should be noted that the libidinal stages are not described in terms of objects, but in terms of developing phases of the libido. Reference is made to the oral stage (developing phase) and not to the breast stage (objectal term).

Thus this author would like the theory of development to be formulated henceforth in terms of object relations. For example, one should not say that in the adult the libido is genital, but that the genital relation is libidinal. It is because the adults' object relations are satisfying that genital sexuality can be attained.

The erotogenic zones do not translate stages but modalities of the fundamental phenomenon of the incorporation of the object. The way this is handled internally at different levels is at the origin of variations in the object relationship.

The development of the object relation is characterised by the transition from the relationship of dependency on the object (identification) to the relation of differentiation from the object. The long phase of transition which separates these two states corresponds to the two anal phases and to the phallic phase. It is necessarily dominated by the rejection of the dichotomised object, according to the Kleinian theory set out above.

Hence the following schema, which relegates libidinal development to the background:

I. Stage of infantile dependency → behaviour = taking.

   (a) Early oral phase: sucking and incorporating (pre-ambivalence).
   (b) Late oral phase: biting and incorporating (ambivalence).

II. Stage of transition → between infantile dependency = taking and adult dependency = giving.

   → Transitional object.
   → Rejection of the incorporated object.

III. Stage of adult differentiation → Attitude of giving.

   → Externalisation of the differentiated object.

In this theory, as we can see, the development of the organism is not linked to the pleasure principle: 'The libido is object-seeking and not pleasure-seeking.' This is the most complete formulation of the theory of object relations. The persistence of the internalised good and bad objects explains psycho-pathological structures, constituted on the basis of the pseudo-automatism of repetition. The Freudian death drive can be formulated in terms of relations with bad objects. In psychoanalytic technique, moreover, one cannot separate the drives from their objects. The theory of ego development must, then, be reformulated, for the repression of the instinctual drives acts against the bad objects, which are organisers of structures. The primary structure of the ego – or Fairbairn's 'central ego'– is linked to aggression against the bad object, but it is divided and split by this aggression (schizoid position), whereas the resulting 'subsidiary egos' are the object of secondary aggressions by the bad incorporated objects.

Finally, in line with scientific principles which make the opposition between drives and structures absurd, Fairbairn rejects the Freudian concepts of ego and superego. Originally, the organisation of the dynamic ego leads to the central ego, and to the libidinal ego, which is dependent on the incorporated bad object (this corresponds to the id), as well as to the 'internal destructive' ego attached to the rejecting part of the bad incorporated object (this is the superego).

★ ★ ★

Fairbairn's theory, which has important clinical extensions, is situated well outside the usual formulations, to which I will now return, with the aim, on the one hand, of attempting a synthesis in a comparative table (Table 1) and, on the other, of presenting some critical reflections.

1. The first Freudian reconstructions were confirmed, astonishingly, by the so-called early analyses of children and subsequently by the direct observation of children: this is a remarkable fact, and it is worth dwelling on it for a moment.

For my part, for example, in the study I carried out with Diatkine on the fantasies of children (Lebovici & Diatkine, 1954), we believed we were in a position to show that the productions described by Melanie Klein are only the elaboration of the primary situation experienced by the child in his mother's presence. His immaturity leaves him fragmented in front of a mother whom he can only experience as fragmented. The evolving structures of the ego lead to the fear of castration, which can always transform itself into fragmentation anxiety, owing to the prevalence of primary situations. The most disturbed structures of the ego hinder the integration of these primitive fantasies which are operative in psychosis: they externalise the psychotic object relation in which neo-organisations are established, designed to avoid fragmentation anxiety. The fantasy of exchanging the part-object corresponds, as we shall see,

Table 1

	Stages			Genetic evolution					Communication theory			
	Freud	Abraham	Melanie Klein	Genetic evolution of object relations	Stages of the subject	State of the object	Function of the object	Relation	The subject		The object	
									Mode of information	Information received	Information received	Mode of information
Auto-erotism	Oral stage	1st oral stage (objectless)	1st oral stage	Narcissistic stage (0–3 months)	Self / 1st organiser = socialised smile	Pre-object	Physiological function	Pre-objectal relation	Indicator	Affect		Signal
Auto-erotism		2nd oral stage	Persecutory stage	Anaclitic stage (3–6 months)	I // non-I	Precursor of object	Fusional pre-object	→ Desexualisation	Indicator	Extra-verbal primary experience	Infra-verbal percept	
Auto-erotism	Anal-sadistic stage	1st anal stage: taking in the object		Object stage (6–12 months)	2nd organiser = 8th month anxiety / Ego (Id)	Differentiated object	Mother	Neutralisation	Sign	Perception	Perception	Signal
Auto-erotism		2nd anal stage: rejection of the object	Depressive stage	Stage of the differentiated object	3rd organiser = no	1° Transitional object / 2° Maternalised object	Father = mother	↑	Verbalised symbol	Perception	→	→
Hetero-erotism	Phallic stage	Post-ambivalent genital stage	Genital stage		I (ego–id–superego)	Oedipal triangulation	Mother + father / Mother ≠ father	Object relation				Verbalised symbol
Hetero-erotism	→	→	→	→	→			→	→			→

to the search for protective fusion. It has thus been said with good reason that the study of the fantasy productions of infants and of psychotic adults is a good way of acquiring verbalised material that teaches us about the earliest relational experiences of the child.

For their part, as I have already mentioned, Ajuriaguerra, Diatkine and Garcia-Badaracco (1956) have shown the contradiction between the notion of part-object, which belongs to fantasy elaboration, and that of the object that is cathected and perceived by the child, which is whole and global.

In any case, as I have pointed out, following Diatkine, in my study devoted to regression (Lebovici, 1956), the clinical picture which reveals the early structures of the ego cannot be observed in any child or in any adult. It is no doubt in the deepest disorganisations of the ego, in the psychoses, that the Oedipal content is most obvious: as I have said, there is no superposition between pre-Oedipal and Oedipal developments on the one hand and pregenital and genital developments on the other (Nacht, 1953).

2. Under these conditions, the following hypotheses can be made concerning the contradiction which I have just defined with regard to the coincidence and divergences of the results of the investigations of adult psychoanalysts, child psychoanalysts and genetic psychoanalysts.

(a) As regards direct observation, comprehension of the genesis of the whole object through the pre-object and the part-object is possible. But the succession of the oral and anal stages is not obvious. At the pre-objectal stage, there is no oral zone but, rather, a preliminary organisation of the ego that Spitz has defined as 'the primal cavity' (1955). The first organiser translates the relation to a *pre-gestalt*, in which the mouth of the pre-object is part of a more complex ensemble. Recent studies by Bowlby (e.g., 1951) – even if one views them critically – nonetheless show that the ethological reference leads us to adopt a wider point of view than one that is confined to the purely oral sphere of interests.

(b) Fantasies of the part-object relation reconstruct the pre-objectal and narcissistic experience that is elaborated subsequently. Fairbairn's critique of the classical conceptions of the stages valorised the importance – already underlined by Freud – of the erotogenic zones. We cannot help noticing the existence of these fantasies, but we can also only understand them if we follow Melanie Klein, who puts aside the relationship to speak instead of instinctual conflicts. The part-object presupposes both incorporation and rejection – that is, the cathexis of oral and anal zones. Thus the part-object fantasy is in fact contemporaneous with the period when Melanie Klein practised so-called early psychoanalytic treatments, around the age of three years, an age when the erogeneity of the anal zone is not in question.

(c) Adult psychoanalysts find material in the treatment of neuroses and psychoses, which is often, though not always, stratified, genital, anal and oral. They are always neo-organisations which result both from the destructuring and restructuring which is commonly called regression. But it should be pointed out that the 'conflictualisation' of each stage of fixation is a clinical fact. For example, the anal material can often only be understood in the light of a fear of genital castration. The very frequent richness of the oral material often only translates the mastery of the anal object: one has to be able to find the anal material through the continuity of oral–genital material.

3. In the genetic theory of object relations, reference is commonly made to non-psychoanalytic theories: conditioning, communication and ethology are the references I have used in this paper. We should not, however, underestimate the danger involved of approximation and eclecticism. Integrative claims must avoid superficial assimilations, even if they are satisfying as hypotheses of general significance.

Many psychoanalysts have warned against the temptation to integrate psychoanalytic material, which has its own originality and belongs to a specific experimental field, with more general hypotheses belonging to a more extensive and heterogeneous operational sector.

It has also been said that recourse to these theories risks making obsolete the energetic hypothesis which is fundamental in psychoanalysis. A superficial reading of the somewhat laborious texts of Hartmann, Kris and Loewenstein, and the description of the autonomous ego based on desexualisation or, rather, neutralisation, can effectively lead one to think this.

4. Thus studies of the development of the object relation and of the ego are inseparable from those that are devoted to the so-called narcissistic cathexis of this agency. As for genesis, the fundamental hypothesis according to which the cathexis of the object precedes its perception leads to the axiom according to which the object founds the ego. But how can we suppose the recognition of the object without the existence of a rudimentary ego? So in order to avoid the illogicality of this position, it is necessary to recognise the importance of the cathexes of the ego which alone permit the differentiation of the I and the Non-I, and thereby the recognition of the external world and the precursors of the object (Freud, Federn).

5. The theory of object relations can only lead to a new metapsychological formulation of the drives, a notion that is ambiguous and often criticised by ethologists. Freud defined the vicissitudes of the drives in terms of energetic cathexes, of libido and aggression. Instinctual behaviours are more specific. As Diatkine has said, the object is founded on their mutation: it could even be said that the psychological object is created by the disappearance of the instinctual necessity which was associated with it.

References

Abraham, K. (1916). The First Pregenital Stage of the Libido. In *Selected Papers of Karl Abraham*, trans D. Bryan & A. Strachey. New York: Basic Books, 1953.

Ajuriaguerra, F. de., Diatkine, R., & Garcia-Badaracco, J. (1956). Psychanalyse et neuro-

biologie [Psychoanalysis and neurobiology]. In *La psychanalyse d'aujourd'hui* [Psychoanalysis today] (pp. 437–498). Paris: Presses Universitaires de France.
Bowlby, J. (1951). *Maternal Care and Mental Health*. New York: Schocken.
Diatkine, R. (1959). Intervention dans la discussion sur le rapport de R. de Saussure: 'Métapsychologie du plaisir' [Response to R. de Saussure's paper on the 'Metapsychology of pleasure']. *Revue Française de Psychanalyse, 23* (5): 563–566.
Fairbairn, W. R. D. (1941). A Revised Psychopathology of the Psychoses and Psychoneuroses. *International Journal of Psychoanalysis, 22*: 250–279.
Fairbairn, W. R. D. (1944). The Endopsychic Structure in Terms of Object-Relationships. *International Journal of Psychoanalysis, 25*, 70–92.
Fairbairn, W. R. D. (1946). Object Relationships and Dynamic Structure. *International Journal of Psychoanalysis, 27*: 30–36.
Freud, A. (1936). *The Ego and the Mechanisms of Defence. The Writings of Anna Freud, Vol. II* (revised ed.). New York: International Universities Press, 1960.
Freud, S. (1915). *Papers on Metapsychology. S.E.*, 14: 105–258.
Freud, S. (1926d [1925]). *Inhibitions, Symptoms and Anxiety. S.E.*, 20: 75–174.
Freud, S. (1950 [1895]). A Project for a Scientific Psychology. *S.E.*, 1: 283–413.
Hartmann, H., Kris, E., & Loewenstein, R. (1946). Comments on the Formation of Psychic Structure. *Psychoanalytic Study of the Child, 2*: 11–38.
Hetzer, H., & Ripier, R. (1930). Frühestes Lernen des Säuglings in der Ernährungssituation [Earliest learning of the infant in the feeding situation]. *Zeitschrift für Psychologie, 118*.
Klein, M. (1932). *The Psycho-Analysis of Children. The Writings of Melanie Klein, Vol. II*. London: Hogarth Press, 1975.
Kris, M. (1957). The use of prediction in a longitudinal study. *Psychoanalytic Study of the Child, 12*: 175–189.
Kubie, L. (1958). *Integrating the Approaches to Mental Disease*, ed. H. Kruse. New York: Harper Books.
Lebovici, S. (1955). Les aspects précoces de la relation objectale [The features of the early relationship to the object]. *Bulletin de l'Association belge des Psychanalystes*.
Lebovici, S. (1956) Une observation de psychose infantile. *L'Evolution Psychiatrique, 4*: 843–863.
Lebovici, S., & Diatkine, R. (1954). Etude des fantasmes chez l'enfant [The study of phantasies in the child]. *Revue Française de Psychanalyse, 18* (1): 108–155.
Lebovici, S., & McDougall, J. (1960). *Un cas de psychose infantile* [A case of infantile psychosis]. Paris: Presses Universitaires de France. [*Dialogue with Sammy*. London: Hogarth Press, 1966.]
Miller, G. A. (1951). *Language and Communication*. New York: McGraw-Hill.
Nacht, S. (1953). Discussion au colloque sur l'interprétation prégénitale [Discussion from the colloqium on the interpretation of the pregenital]. *Revue Française de Psychanalyse, 17*: 452–457.
Rank, O. (1924). *The Trauma of Birth*. London: Routledge & Kegan Paul.
Ribble, M. (1938). Clinical Studies of Instinctive Reactions in Newborn Babies. *American Journal of Psychiatry, 95*: 148–160.
Spitz, R. A. (1955). The Primal Cavity: A Contribution to the Genesis of Perception and its Role for Psychoanalytic Theory. *Psychoanalytic Study of the Child, 10*: 215–240.
Spitz, R. A. (1957). *No and Yes: On the Genesis of Human Communication*. New York: International Universities Press.
Spitz, R. A. (1965). *The First Year of Life: A Psychoanalytic Study of Normal and Deviant Development in Object Relations*. New York: International Universities Press.
Winnicott, D. (1954). Transitional Objects and Transitional Phenomena. *International Journal of Psychoanalysis, 34* (2): 89–97.

15 FANTASY AND THE ORIGINS OF SEXUALITY[1]

Jean Laplanche and J.-B. Pontalis

For **Jean Laplanche's** biography, see pp. 233–234.

A philosopher who has written many books and articles and edited journals, **Jean-Bertrand Pontalis** is a full member of the French Psychoanalytical Association, of which he was one of the founding members. With Jean Laplanche, he wrote *Vocabulaire de la psychanalyse* (PUF, 1962–1967) [*The Language of Psychoanalysis* (Hogarth, 1973)] and in 1970 created the *Nouvelle Revue de Psychanalyse*. He translated Winnicott's writings into French, thus contributing to making the latter's ideas more widely known.

A theoretician of the negative dimension, of language and of images, his psychoanalytic writings include: *Entre le rêve et la douleur* (Gallimard, 1983) [*Between the Dream and Psychic Pain* (Hogarth, 1981)]; *Perdu de vue* [Lost from sight] (Gallimard, 1988); *La force d'attraction* [Force of attraction] (Le Seuil, 1990); *Ce temps qui ne passe pas* [Time which does not go by] (Gallimard, 1997). Among his more literary writings, there are two novels: *Loin* [Far away] (Gallimard, 1980) and *Un homme disparaît* [A man disappears] (Gallimard, 1996). His autobiography, *L'amour des commencements* (Gallimard, 1986) [*Love of Beginnings* (Free Association Books, 1993)] won the Prix Femina-Vacaresco in 1986. He has recently published *La traversée des ombres* [Going through shadows] (Gallimard, 2003) and *Frère du précédent* [The previous person's brother] (Gallimard, 2007).

Claude Janin wrote a concise biography of Jean-Bertrand Pontalis for the 'Psychanalystes d'aujourd'hui' series (PUF, 1997).

From its earliest day, psychoanalysis has been concerned with the material of fantasy. In the initial case of Anna O., Breuer was apparently content to plunge

---

[1] Translated from the French, 'Fantasme originaire, fantasmes des origines, origine du fantasme'. *Les Temps Modernes*, 19 (1964, no. 215).

The English title *should* be translated as 'Primal fantasy, fantasies of origins, origin of fantasy'. The translation of 'Fantasy and the origins of sexuality', published in the *International Journal of Psychoanalysis* and reproduced in this volume, does not take into account the nuances of the original French title, especially with regard to the difference between the *structure* ('primal fantasy') and the *history* ('origin of fantasy').

into the patient's inner world of imagination, into her 'private theatre', in order to achieve catharsis through verbalisation and emotive expression. 'I used to visit her in the evening', he writes, 'when I knew I should find her in her hypnosis, and I then relieved her of the whole stock of imaginative products which she had accumulated since my last visit' (Freud, 1895d, p. 30).

It is remarkable to note, when studying this case, how Breuer, unlike Freud, is little concerned to recover the elements of experience which might underlie these daydreams. The event which provoked the trauma is considered to contain an imaginary element, a hallucination leading to trauma. There is a circular relationship between the fantasy and the dissociation of consciousness which leads to the formation of an unconscious nucleus: fantasy becomes trauma when it arises from a special hypnoid state but, equally, the panic states it induces help to create this fundamental state by a process of 'autohypnosis'.

If Breuer worked from within the world of imagination and tried to reduce its pathogenic force without reference to extrinsic factors, the same can be said of the methods of certain contemporary analysts, notably the followers of Melanie Klein. First, the imaginary dramas underlying the verbal or behavioural material produced by the patient during the session – for instance, introjection or projection of the breast or penis, intrusions, conflicts or compromises with good or bad objects and so on – are made explicit and verbalised (no doubt in this case by the analyst; Klein, 1960). A successful outcome to the treatment, if it does lead eventually to a better adaptation to reality, is not expected from any corrective initiative, but from the dialectic 'integration' of the fantasies as they emerge. Ultimately, the introjection of the good object (no less imaginary than the bad), permits a fusion of the instincts in an equilibrium based on the predominance of the libido over the death instinct.

Fantasy, in German '*Phantasie*', is the term used to denote the imagination, and not so much the faculty of imagining (the philosophers' *Einbildungskraft*) as the imaginary world and its contents, the imaginings or fantasies into which the poet or the neurotic so willingly withdraws. In the scenes which the patient describes, or which are described to him by the analyst, the fantastic element is unmistakable. It is difficult therefore to avoid defining this world in terms of what it is not, the world of reality. This opposition antedates psychoanalysis by many centuries, but is liable to prove restrictive both to psychoanalytic theory and practice.

Psychoanalysts have fared rather badly with the theory itself, all too often basing it on a very elementary theory of knowledge.

Analysts such as Melanie Klein, with techniques devoid of any therapeutic intention, are, more than others, careful to distinguish between the contingent imagery of daydreams and the structural function and permanence of what they call 'unconscious phantasies'. (We shall discuss this distinction later.) Yet in the last resort they maintain that the latter are 'false perceptions'. The 'good' and 'bad' object should, for *us*, always be framed in quotation marks,[2] even though the whole evolution of the patient will occur within this framework.

Turning to Freud, we shall find a marked ambiguity of his conceptions as new avenues open out to him with each new stage in his ideas. If we start with the most accepted formulation of his doctrine, the world of fantasy seems to be located exclusively within the domain of opposition between subjective and objective, between an inner world, where satisfaction is obtained through illusion, and an external world, which gradually, through the medium of perception, asserts the supremacy of the reality principle. The unconscious thus appears to inherit the patient's original world, which was solely subject to the pleasure principle. The fantasy world is not unlike the nature reserves which are set up to preserve the original natural state of the country:

> With the introduction of the reality principle one species of thought-activity was split off; it was kept free from reality-testing and remained subject to the pleasure principle alone. This activity is '*fantasying*'.
>
> (Freud, 1911b, p. 222)
>
> The strangest characteristic of unconscious processes is due to their entire disregard of reality testing; they equate reality of thought with external actuality, and wishes with their fulfilment.
>
> (p. 225)

This absence of the 'standards of reality' in the unconscious may lead to its being depreciated as a lesser being, a less differentiated state.

In psychoanalytic practice any inadequacy of the conceptual background cannot fail to make itself felt. It is no purely formal necessity to recall how many techniques are founded on this opposition between the real and the imaginary, and which envisage the integration of the pleasure principle into the reality principle, a process which the neurotic is supposed to have only partially achieved. No doubt any analyst would find it incorrect to invoke 'realities' external to the treatment, since the material must be developed in the context of the analyst–patient relationship, the transference. But unless we are careful, any interpretation of the transference 'You are treating me as if I . . .' will imply the underlying '. . . and you know very well that I am not really what you think I am'.

Fortunately we are saved by the technique: we do not actually make this underlying comment.[3] Speaking more fundamentally, the analytic rule should be understood as a Greek εποχπ, an absolute suspension of all reality judgements. This places us on the same level as the unconscious, which knows no such judgements. A patient tells us that he is an adopted child, and relates fantasies in which, while searching for his true mother, he perceives that she is a

---

[2] 'Good' and 'bad' objects are 'imagos which are a phantastically distorted picture of the real objects upon which they are based' (Klein, 1934).

[3] It is fascinating to observe how Melanie Klein, who provides an uninterrupted interpretation of the transference relationship, never brings in any 'in reality', or even an 'as if'.

society woman turned prostitute. Here we recognise the banal theme of the 'family romance', which might equally well have been composed by a child who had not been adopted. In the course of our 'phenomenonological reduction' we should no longer make any distinction, except to interpret, as a 'defence by reality', the documents which the patient brings to prove his adoption.[4]

Preoccupied, understandably, by the urge to discover at what level he was working, Freud does not come out so well when he has to justify the suspension of reality judgements in the course of treatment. At first he feels it almost his duty to show the patient what is under the counter. But, caught like the patient himself between the alternatives real–imaginary, he runs the double risk of either seeing the patient lose all interest in the analysis, if he is told that the material produced is nothing but imagination (*Einbildung*), or of incurring his reproaches later for having encouraged him to take his fantasies for realities (Freud, 1916–17, p. 368). Freud has recourse here to the notion of 'psychical reality', a new dimension not immediately accessible to the analysand. But what does Freud mean by this term?

Frequently it means nothing more than the reality of our thoughts, of our personal world, a reality at least as valid as that of the material world and, in the case of neurotic phenomena, decisive. If we mean by this that we contrast the reality of psychological phenomena with 'material reality' (Freud, 1916–17, p. 369), the reality of thought with 'external actuality' (p. 225), we are in fact just saying that we are dealing with what is imaginary, with the subjective, but that this subjective is our object: the object of psychology is as valid as that of the sciences of material nature. And even the term itself, 'psychical reality', shows that Freud felt he could only confer the dignity of object on psychological phenomena by reference to material reality, for he asserts that 'they too possess a reality of a sort' (p. 368). In the absence of any *new* category, the suspension of reality judgements leads us once more into the 'reality' of the purely subjective.

Yet this is not Freud's last word. When he introduces this concept of 'psychical reality', in the last lines of the *Interpretation of Dreams*, which sums up his thesis that a dream is not a fantasmagoria, but a text to be deciphered, Freud does not define it as constituting the *whole* of the subjective, like the psychological field, but as a heterogeneous nucleus within this field, a resistant element, alone truly real, in contrast with the majority of psychological phenomena:

> Whether we are to attribute reality to unconscious wishes, I cannot say. It must be denied, of course, to any transitional or intermediate thoughts.

---

[4] However, we have found in the case of actual adoption to which we are referring clinical manifestations quite obviously different from those encountered in adoption fantasies: an actualisation, quickly blurred, of fantasies of the recovery of the mother, episodes where the attempts to rejoin the *true* mother, are worked out symbolically in a kind of secondary state, etc. Even in treatment, from the very beginning, many elements such as dream contents, the repeated occurrence of sleep during the session, showing a massive working out of a far-reaching tendency, demonstrated the disjunction between crude reality and verbalisation.

> If we look at unconscious wishes reduced to their most fundamental and truest shape, we shall have to conclude, no doubt, that psychical reality is a particular form of existence which is not to be confused with material reality.
>
> (1900a, p. 620)[5]

There are therefore three kinds of phenomena (or of realities, in the widest sense of the word): material reality, the reality of intermediate thoughts or of the psychological field, and the reality of unconscious wishes and their 'truest shape': fantasy. If Freud, again and again, finds and then loses the notion of 'psychical reality', this is not due to any inadequacy of his conceptual apparatus: the difficulty and ambiguity lie in the very nature of its relationship, to the real and to the imaginary, as is shown in the central domain of fantasy.[6]

The years 1895–99 which completed the discovery of psychoanalysis are significant not only because of the dubious battle taking place but also because of the oversimplified way in which its history is written.

If we read, for instance, Kris's introduction to the *Origins of Psycho-Analysis* (Freud, 1950),[7] the evolution of Freud's views seems perfectly clear: the facts, and more especially Freud's own self-analysis, apparently led him to abandon his theory of seduction by an adult. The scene of seduction which until then represented for him the typical form of psychological trauma is not a real event but a fantasy which is itself only the product of, and a mask for, the spontaneous manifestations of infantile sexual activity. In his 'History of the Psycho-Analytic Movement', Freud (1914d) thus traces the development of his theory from his experience:

> If hysterical subjects trace back their symptoms to traumas that are fictitious, then the new fact which emerges is precisely that they create such scenes in fantasy, and this psychical reality requires to be taken into account alongside practical reality. This reflection was soon followed by the discovery that these fantasies were intended to cover up the autoerotic activity of the first years of childhood, to embellish it and raise it to a higher plane. And now, from behind the fantasies, the whole range of a child's sexual life came to light.

---

[5] The successive reformulations of this principle in the various editions of the *Traumdeutung* show both Freud's concern to define accurately the concept of 'psychical reality', and the difficulties he experienced in so doing – cf. Strachey's note to this passage.

[6] One further word about the suspension of judgement in the analytic rule: 'Verbalize everything, but do no more than verbalize.' This is not suspension of the reality of external events for the *benefit* of subjective reality. It creates a new field, that of verbalisation, where the difference between the real and the imaginary may retain its value (cf. the case of the patient referred to above). The homology between the analytic and the unconscious field, whose emergence it stimulates, is not due to their common subjectivity, but to the deep kinship between the unconscious and the field of speech. So it is not: 'It is *you* who say so', but 'It is you who *say* so'.

[7] Especially the section entitled 'Infantile Sexuality and Self-Analysis'.

Freud would, in these lines, be admitting his error in imputing to the 'outside' something that concerns the 'inside'.

The very words, *theory* of sexual seduction, should arrest our attention: the elaboration of a schema to explain the aetiology of neuroses, and not the purely clinical *observation* of the frequency of the seduction of children by adults, nor even a simple *hypothesis* that such occurrences would preponderate among the different kinds of traumas. Freud was concerned theoretically to justify the connection he had discovered between sexuality, trauma and defence: to show that it is in the very nature of sexuality to have a traumatic effect and, inversely, that one cannot finally speak of trauma as the origin of neurosis except to the extent that sexual seduction has occurred. As this thesis becomes established (between 1895 and 1897), the role of the defensive conflict in the genesis of hysteria, and of the defence in general, is fully recognised, although the aetiological function of trauma is not thereby reduced. The notions of defence and trauma are closely articulated one to the other: the theory of seduction, by showing how only a sexual trauma has the power to activate a 'pathological defence' (repression), is an attempt to do justice to a clinically established fact (*Studies on Hysteria*, 1895d), that repression concerns specifically sexuality.

We should consider a moment the schema propounded by Freud. The action of the trauma can be broken down into various time sequences and always implies the existence of *at least two events*. In the first scene, called 'seduction scene', the child is subjected to a sexual approach from the adult ('attempt' or simply advances), without arousing any sexual excitation in himself. To try to describe such a scene as traumatic would be to abandon the somatic model of trauma, since there is neither an afflux of external excitation nor an overflow of the defences. If it can be described as sexual, it is only from the point of view of the external agent, the adult. But the child has neither the somatic requisites of excitation nor the representations to enable him to integrate the event: although sexual in terms of objectivity, it has no sexual connotation for the subject, it is 'presexually sexual' (Freud, 1950, letter 30). As for the second scene, which occurs after puberty, it is, one might say, even less traumatic than the first: being non-violent, and apparently of no particular significance, its only power lies in being able to evoke the first event, retroactively, by means of association. It is then the recall of the first scene which sets off the upsurge of sexual excitation, catching the ego in reverse, and leaving it disarmed, incapable of using the normally outward-directed defences, and thus falling back on a pathological defence, or 'posthumous primary process'; the recollection is repressed.

If we dwell on concepts which might, at first sight, appear only of historic interest since they seem to presuppose an innocent child, without sexuality, thus contradicting undeniable later findings, it is not solely to outline the various stages of a discovery.

This explanatory schema, which Freud described as *proton pseudos*, is of remarkable value in considering the significance of human sexuality. In fact, it introduces two major propositions. On the one hand, in the first stage, sexuality literally breaks in from outside, intruding forcibly into the world of childhood, presumed to be innocent, where it is encysted as a simple happening without provoking any defence reaction – not in itself a pathogenic event. On the other hand, in the second stage, the pressure of puberty having stimulated the physiological awakening of sexuality, there is a sense of unpleasure, and the origin of this unpleasure is traced to the recollection of the first event, an external event which has become an inner event, an inner 'foreign body', which now breaks out from within the subject.[8]

This is a surprising way to settle the question of trauma. The question often arises, whether it is an afflux of external excitation which creates the trauma or whether, on the contrary, it is the internal excitation, the drive, which, lacking an outlet, creates a 'state of helplessness'[9] in the subject.

However, with the theory of seduction, we may say that the whole of the trauma comes *both* from within and from without: from without, since sexuality reaches the subject from *the* other;[10] from within, since it springs from this internalised exteriority, this '*reminiscence* suffered by hysterics' (according to the Freudian formula), reminiscence in which we already discern what will be later named fantasy. This is an attractive solution, but it is liable to collapse when the meaning of each term deviates: the external towards the event, the internal towards the endogenous and biological.

Let us look at the seduction theory more positively and try to salvage its deeper meaning. It is Freud's first and sole attempt to establish an intrinsic relationship between repression and sexuality.[11] He finds the mainspring of this relationship, not in any 'content', but in the temporal characteristics of human sexuality, which make it a privileged battlefield between both too much and too little excitation, both too early and too late occurrence of the event: 'Here we have the one possibility of a memory subsequently producing a more powerful release than that produced by the corresponding experience itself' (1950, Draft K). Hence the re-partition of the trauma into two stages, as the psychological trauma can only be conceived as arising from something *already there*, the reminiscence of the first scene.

---

[8] In *Studies on Hysteria* we already find the idea that psychological trauma cannot be reduced to the once-and-for-all effect on an organism of some external event. 'The causal relation between the determining psychical trauma and the hysterical phenomenon is not of a kind implying that the trauma merely acts like an *agent provocateur*, in releasing the symptom which thereafter leads an independent existence. We must presume rather that the psychical trauma – or more precisely the memory of the trauma – acts like a foreign body which long after its entry must be regarded as an agent that is still at work' (1895d, p. 6).

[9] The problem is constantly present in these terms in such works as Freud's *Beyond the Pleasure Principle* (1920g), *Inhibitions, Symptoms and Anxiety* (1926d), and Rank's *Trauma of Birth* (1924).

[10] 'It seems to me more and more that the essential point of hysteria is that it results from *perversion* on the part of the seducer, and *more and more* that heredity is seduction by the father' (Letter 52).

[11] He never ceased to assert this relationship (cf. 1940a [1938], pp. 185–186), but without stating the theory.

But how can we conceive the formation of this 'already there', and how can this first scene, which is 'pre-sexually sexual', acquire a meaning for the subject? Given a perspective which tends to reduce temporal dimensions to chronology, one must either embark on an infinite regression in which each scene acquires sexual quality solely through the evocation of an earlier scene without which it would have no meaning for the subject or, on the other hand, one must stop short arbitrarily at a 'first' scene, however inconceivable it may be.

No doubt the doctrine of an innocent world of childhood into which sexuality is introduced by perverse adults is pure illusion: illusion, or rather a myth, whose very contradictions betray the nature. We must conceive of the child both as outside time, a *bon sauvage*, and as one already endowed with sexuality, at least in germ, which is ready to be awakened; we must accept the idea of an intrusion from without into an interior which perhaps did not exist as such before this intrusion; we must reconcile the passivity which is implied by merely receiving meaning from outside with the minimum of activity necessary for the experience even to be acknowledged, and the indifference of innocence with the disgust which the seduction is assumed to provoke. To sum up, we have a subject who is pre-subjectal, who receives his existence, his sexual existence, from without, before a distinction between within and without is achieved.

Forty years later Ferenczi (1933) was to take up the theory of seduction and give it analogous importance. His formulations are no doubt less rigorous than Freud's, but they have the advantage of filling out the myth with two essential ingredients: behind the facts, and through their mediation, it is a new *language*, that of passion, which is introduced by the adult into the infantile 'language' of tenderness. On the other hand, this language of passion is the language of desire, necessarily marked by prohibition, a language of guilt and hatred, including the sense of annihilation linked with orgastic pleasure.[12] The fantasy of the primal scene with its character of violence shows the child's introjection of adult erotism.

Like Freud in 1895, Ferenczi is led to assign a chronological location to this intrusion, and to presuppose a real nature of the child before seduction. One

---

[12] From the beginning Freud rejected the banal thesis which attributed the unpleasure provoked by sexuality to a purely external prohibition. Whether they are of internal or external origin, desire and prohibition go hand in hand. 'We shall be plunged deep into the riddles of psychology if we enquire into the origin of the unpleasure which is released by premature sexual stimulation and without which the occurrence of a repression cannot be explained. The most plausible answer will recall the fact that shame and morality are the repressing forces and that the neighbourhood in which nature has placed the sexual organs must inevitably arouse disgust at the same time as sexual experiences. . . . I cannot think that the release of unpleasure during sexual experiences is the consequence of a chance admixture of certain unpleasurable factors. . . . In my opinion there must be some independent source for the release of unpleasure in sexual life: if that source is present, it can activate sensations of disgust, lend force to morality, and so on' (Draft K).

might, on the other hand, be tempted to close the discussion once and for all by introducing the concept of myth: the seduction would become the myth of the origin of sexuality by the introjection of adult desire, fantasy and 'language'. The relationship of the myth to the time factor (the event) is present and, as it were, embedded in the myth itself. But we cannot rest there. This myth (or fantasy) of the intrusion of the fantasy (or myth) into the subject cannot but occur to the organism, the little human being, at a point in time, by virtue of certain characteristics of his biological evolution, in which we can already distinguish what is too much or too little, too early (birth) and too late (puberty).

In 1897 Freud abandoned his theory of seduction. On September 21st he wrote to Fliess: 'I will confide in you at once the great secret that has been slowly dawning on me in the last few months: I no longer believe in my neurotica. . . .' He adduces a number of arguments. Some were factual: the impossibility of conducting analyses to their conclusion, that is, back to the first pathogenic event; even in the deepest psychosis – where the unconscious seems the most accessible – the key to the enigma is not available. Others were of a logical nature: one would have to generalise the father's perversity even beyond the cases of hysteria, since when hysteria supervenes it entails the intervention of other factors. On the other hand, and this is the point that interests us, '. . . there are no indications of reality in the unconscious, so that one cannot distinguish between the truth and fiction that is cathected with affect'. Two solutions are mentioned by Freud, either to consider fantasies of childhood as only the retroactive effect of a reconstruction performed by the adult (which would amount to the Jungian concept of retrospective fantasies [*Zurückphantasieren*] which Freud rejected), or to revert to the idea of hereditary predisposition. If this second possibility – which Freud admitted he had always 'repressed' – returns to favour, it is because the search for the first scene has led to an impasse. But it is also because Freud, momentarily at a loss, did not succeed in isolating the positive element, lying beyond the realistic chronological approach, in the seduction theory. If the event evades us, then the alternative factor, constitution, is rehabilitated. Since reality, in one of its forms, is absent, and proves to be only fiction, then we must seek elsewhere for a reality on which this fiction is based.

When the historians of psychoanalysis tell us, picking up Freud's own version of his evolution, that the abandonment of the seduction theory in the face of facts cleared the ground for the discovery of infantile sexuality, they oversimplify a much more involved process. To a contemporary psychoanalyst, to Kris as to us, infantile sexuality is inseparable from the Oedipus complex. And in effect, at the very moment of the 'abandonment' of seduction, we find three themes predominant in the correspondence with Fliess: infantile sexuality, fantasy, and the Oedipus complex. But the real problem lies in their interrelation. And we find that inasmuch as real trauma and the seduction scene have been effectively swept away,[13] they have not been replaced by the Oedipus complex but by the description of a spontaneous infantile sexuality, basically endogenous in development. Libidinal stages succeeding each other in a natural and regular evolution, fixation considered as an inhibition of development, genetic regression, form at least one of the perspectives suggested in the *Three Essays on the Theory of Sexuality* (1905d). In this direction, we must notice that the second essay, on 'Infantile Sexuality', discusses neither the Oedipus complex nor fantasy. An article which appeared at the same time as the *Three Essays* is typical of this point of view: in it Freud is able to discuss his 'Views on the Part Played by Sexuality in the Aetiology of the Neuroses' (1906a) without a single word about the Oedipus complex. The sexual development of the child is here defined as endogenous, and determined by the sexual constitution:

> Accidental influences derived from experience having thus receded into the background, the factors of constitution and heredity necessarily gained the upper hand once more; but there was this difference between my views and those prevailing in other quarters, that on my theory the 'sexual constitution' took the place of a 'general neuropathic disposition'.

It may however be objected that it was also in 1897, at the very moment when he abandoned the seduction theory, that Freud in his self-analysis discovered the Oedipus complex. We should emphasise, though, that in spite of Freud's immediate recognition of its importance, the Oedipus complex was, for twenty years, to lead a marginal existence alongside his theoretical syntheses. It was deliberately set apart in a section devoted to 'the choice of objects of puberty' (in the *Three Essays*), or to studies of 'typical dreams' (in *The Interpretation of Dreams*). In our opinion the discovery of the Oedipus complex in 1897 was neither the cause of the abandonment of the seduction theory, nor clearly indicated as its successor. It seems much more probable that, being encountered in a 'wild' form in the seduction theory, the Oedipus complex nearly suffered the same fate of being replaced by biological realism.

Freud himself recognised, much later, all that was positive and foreboding in the seduction theory: 'here I had stumbled for the first time upon the Oedipus complex' (1925d [1924]) or again,

> I came to understand that hysterical symptoms are derived from fantasies and not from real occurrences. It was only later that I was able to recognize in this fantasy of being seduced by the father the expression of the typical Oedipus complex. . . .[14]
>
> (1933a, Lecture 23)

---

[13] It would be easy to demonstrate that Freud, throughout his life, continued to insist on the reality of the fact of seduction.
[14] And no longer the expression of the child's spontaneous, biological sexual activity.

At that time (1897) Freud had on the one hand discarded the idea, contained in the seduction theory, of a foreign body which introduces human sexuality into the subject from without, and, on the other hand, discovered that the sexual drive becomes active before puberty. But for some time he was not able to articulate the Oedipus complex with infantile sexuality. If the latter existed, as clinical observation undoubtedly proved, it could henceforward only be *conceived* as biological reality, fantasy being no more than the secondary expression of this reality. The scene in which the subject describes his seduction by an older companion is, in fact, a double disguise: pure fantasy is converted into real memory, and spontaneous sexual activity into passivity.[15] One is no longer justified in attributing 'psychical reality' – in the stricter sense sometimes employed by Freud – to the fantasy, since reality is now totally attributed to an endogenous sexuality, and since fantasies are only considered to be a purely imaginary efflorescence of this sexuality.

Something was lost with the discarding of the seduction theory: beneath the conjunction and the temporal interplay of the two 'scenes' there lay a pre-subjective structure, beyond both the strict happening and the internal imagery. The prisoner of a series of theoretical alternatives, subject–object, constitution–event, internal–external, imaginary–real, Freud was for a time led to stress the first terms of these 'pairs of opposites'.

This would suggest the following paradox: at the very moment when fantasy, the fundamental object of psychoanalysis, is discovered, it is in danger of seeing its true nature obscured by the emphasis on an endogenous reality, sexuality, which is itself supposed to be in conflict with a normative, prohibitory external reality, which imposes on it various disguises. We have indeed the fantasy, in the sense of a product of the imagination, but we have lost the structure. Inversely, with the seduction theory we had, if not the theory, at least an *intuition* of the structure (seduction appearing as an almost universal datum, which in any case transcended both the event and, so to speak, its protagonists). The ability to elaborate the fantasy was, however, if not unknown, at least underestimated.

It would be taking a very limited view to describe as follows the evolution of Freud's ideas during the period around 1897: from historical foundation of the symptoms to the establishment of an ultimately biological theory, to the causal sequence, sexual constitution → fantasy → symptom. Freud never makes the theory entirely his own until he is obliged to present his aetiological views in systematic fashion. If we intended, which we do not, to present a step-by-step account of the development of his thought, we should have to distinguish at least two other currents in this central period.

The one derives from the fresh understanding of fantasy which is effective from 1896 onwards: fantasy is not merely material to be analysed, whether appearing as fiction from the very start (as in daydreaming) or whether it remains to be shown that it is a construction contrary to appearances (as in

---

[15] 'I have learned to explain a number of fantasies of seduction as attempts at fending off memories of the subject's *own* sexual activity (infantile masturbation)' (Freud, 1906a, p. 274).

screen-memory), it is also the result of analysis, an end-product, a latent content to be revealed behind the symptom. From *mnesic symbol* of trauma, the symptom has become the *stage-setting of fantasies* (thus a fantasy of prostitution, of street-walking, might be discovered beneath the symptom of agoraphobia).

Freud now starts to explore the field of these fantasies, to make an inventory, and to describe their most typical forms. Fantasies are now approached from two aspects at once, both as manifest data and latent content; and, located thus at the crossroads, they acquire in due course the consistency of an object, the specific object of psychoanalysis. Henceforward analysis will continue to treat fantasy as 'psychical reality' whilst exploring its variants and above all analysing its processes and structure. Between 1897 and 1906 appear all the great works which explore the mechanisms of the unconscious, that is to say, the transformations (in the geometric sense of the word) of fantasy, namely, *The Interpretation of Dreams* (1900a), *The Psychopathology of Everyday Life* (1901b), *Jokes and Their Relation to the Unconscious* (1905c).

But, and here is the third current, the development of Freudian research and psychoanalytic treatment display at the outset a regressive tendency towards the origin, the foundation of the symptom and the neurotic organisation of the personality. If fantasy is shown to be an autonomous, consistent and explorable field, it leaves untouched the question of its own origin, not only with regard to structure, but also to content and to its most concrete details. In this sense nothing has changed, and the search for chronology, going backwards into time towards the first real, verifiable *elements*, is still the guiding principle of Freud's practice.

Speaking of one of his patients, he writes in 1899: 'Buried deep beneath all his fantasies we found a scene from his primal period (before twenty-two months) which meets all requirements and into which all the surviving puzzles flow' (Letter 126).

A little later we come across these lines, eloquent of his passion for investigation, pursued ever deeper and with certainty of success, and the resort to a third person, if necessary, to verify the accuracy of his enquiry:

> In the evenings I read *prehistory, etc., without any serious purpose* [our italics], and otherwise my only concern is to lead my cases calmly towards solution.... In E's case the second real scene is coming up after years of preparation, and it is one that it may perhaps be possible to confirm objectively by asking his elder sister. Behind it there is a third, long-suspected scene....
>
> (Letter 127)

Freud defines these scenes from earliest infancy, these *true* scenes, as *Urszenen* (original or primal scenes). Later, as we know, the term will be reserved for the child's observation of parental coitus. The reference is to the discussion in 'From the History of an Infantile Neurosis' (1918b [1914]) of the relationship between the pathogenic dream and the primal scene on which it is based. When reading the first draft of the clinical account composed during 'the winter of 1914/15, shortly after the end of treatment', one is struck by the passionate conviction which urges Freud, like a detective on the watch, to establish the reality of the scene down to its smallest details. If such concern is apparent so long after the abandonment of the seduction theory, it is surely a proof that Freud had never entirely resigned himself to accepting such scenes as *purely* imaginary creations. Although discarded as concerns the seduction scene, the question re-emerges in identical terms twenty years later, in the case of the observation of parental coitus by the Wolf Man. The discovery of infantile sexuality has not invalidated in Freud's mind the fundamental schema underlying the seduction theory: the same deferred action [*Nachträglichkeit*][16] is constantly invoked; we meet once more the two events (here the scene and the dream), separated in the temporal series, the first remaining un-understood and, as it were, excluded within the subject, to be taken up later in the elaboration of the second occasion.[17] The fact that the whole process develops in the first years of infancy affects nothing essential in the theoretical model.

It is well known that before publishing his manuscript Freud added, in 1917, two long discussions which showed that he was disturbed by the Jungian theory of retrospective fantasy [*Zurückphantasieren*]. He admits that since the scene is, in analysis, the culmination of a reconstruction, it might indeed have been constructed by the subject himself, but he nevertheless insists that

---

[16] *Editors' note:* The English translation of *Nachträglichkeit* in the *Standard Edition* by James Strachey is 'deferred action'. This translation has been criticized by a number of people and better translations have been proposed, such as 'retroactive resignification' (Mehler, 1992), or 'afterwardness' (Laplanche, 1991). French psychoanalysts have shown that *Nachträglichkeit* was used by Freud in different ways. The French term *après-coup* is now often adopted in English when referring to the retrospective attribution of meaning from the present onto the past (see General Introduction by D. Birksted-Breen and S. Flanders, pp. 20–21).

This paper is one of the papers previously translated and published in English, and is reproduced here as it originally appeared. Today we would write *après-coup* rather than deferred action.

[17] There is an obvious similarity between the Freudian schema of *Nachträglichkeit* and the psychotic mechanism of 'repudiation' [*forclusion*] described by Lacan: that which has not been admitted to symbolic expression ('repudiated') reappears in reality in the form of hallucination. This non-symbolisation corresponds precisely to the earliest time described by Freud. As Lacan and Freud illustrate their theory by the case of the Wolf Man, it may be asked whether Lacan may not have treated as specifically psychotic what is really a very general process, or whether Freud has not taken the exception to be the rule, when basing his demonstration on a case of psychosis.

Freud's demonstration is strengthened by the fact that in this particular case the primal scene is very probably authentic. But one might conceive of such absence of subjective elaboration or of symbolisation, normally characteristic of the first stage, as not a prerogative of a truly experienced scene. This 'foreign body', which is to be internally excluded, is usually brought to the subject, not by the perception of a scene, but by parental desire and its supporting fantasy. Such would be the typically neurotic case: in the first stage (not locatable in time, since it is fragmented into the series of transitions to auto-erotism (cf. p. 331)), a pre-symbolic symbolic, to paraphrase Freud, is isolated within the subject who will, at a later stage, recover and symbolise it. In psychosis the first stage would consist of naked reality, and is evidently not symbolised by the subject, but will offer an irreducible nucleus for any later attempt at symbolisation. Hence, in such cases, the failure, even the catastrophe, of the second stage. This offers an approach to a distinction between repression (original) and the psychotic mechanism which Freud tried to delimit throughout his work (more particularly by describing it as *Verleugnung*: denial), and which Lacan called '*forclusion*'.

perception has at least furnished some indications, even if it were only the copulation of dogs. . . .

But, more particularly, just at the moment when Freud appears to lose hope of support from the *ground of reality* – ground so shifting on further enquiry – he introduces a new concept, that of the *Urphantasien*, primal (or original) fantasy. The need for a theoretical foundation has now undergone a veritable transmutation. Since it has proved impossible to determine whether the primal scene is something truly experienced by the subject, or a fiction, we must in the last resort seek a foundation in something which transcends both individual experience and what is imagined.

For us too it is only at a deferred date (*nachträglich*) that the full meaning of this new direction of Freud's thought becomes apparent. Nothing appears to be changed: there is the same pursuit of an ultimate truth, the same schema is used once more, the dialectic of the two successive historical events, the same disappointment – as if Freud had learned nothing – as the ultimate event, the 'scene', disappears over the horizon. But simultaneously, thanks to what we have described as the second current, there is the discovery of the unconscious as a structural field, which can be reconstructed, since it handles, decomposes and recomposes its elements according to certain laws. This will henceforward permit the quest for origins to take on a new dimension.

In the concept of original fantasy,[18] there is a continuation of what we might call Freud's desire to reach the bedrock of the event (and if this disappears by refraction or reduction, then one must look further back still), and the need to establish the structure of the fantasy itself by something other than the event.

The original fantasies constitute this 'store of unconscious fantasies of all neurotics, and probably of all human beings' (Freud, 1915f, p. 269). These words alone suggest that it is not solely the empirical fact of frequency, nor even generality, which characterises them. If 'the same fantasies with the same content are created on every occasion' (1916–17, p. 370), if, beneath the diversity of individual fables we can recover some 'typical' fantasies,[19] it is because the historical life of the subject is not the prime mover but, rather, something antecedent, which is capable of operating as an organiser.

Freud saw only one possible explanation of this antecedence, and that was phylogenesis:

> It seems to me quite possible that all the things that are told to us in analysis as fantasy . . . were once real occurrences in the primaeval times of the human family [what was factual reality would, in this case, have become

---

[18] We might be accused of exaggeration in speaking of concept. 'Original fantasy' does not, of course, form part of the classical psychoanalytic concepts. Freud uses it marginally in his very precise study of the question whose development we have traced. The phrase therefore has the value of an 'index' and requires clarification.

[19] An ever-present concern of Freud's (cf. Draft M): 'One of our brightest hopes is that we may be able to define the number and species of fantasies as well as we can those of the "scenes".'

psychological reality] and that children in their fantasies are simply filling in the gaps in individual truth with prehistoric truths.

Thus once again a reality is postulated beneath the elaborations of fantasy, but a reality which, as Freud insists, has an autonomous and structural status with regard to the subject who is totally dependent on it. He pursues this some considerable way, since he admits the possibility of discordance between the schema and individual experiences, which would lead to psychological conflict.[20]

It is tempting to accept the 'reality' which inspires the work of imagination according to its own laws, as a prefiguration of the 'symbolic order' defined by Lévi-Strauss and Lacan in the ethnological and psychoanalytic fields, respectively. These scenes, which Freud traces back in *Totem and Taboo* (1912–13) to the prehistory of man, are attributed by him to primaeval man [Urmensch], to the primal father [Urvater]. He invokes them, less in order to provide a reality which escapes him in individual history, than to assign limits to the 'imaginary' which cannot contain its own principle of organisation.

Beneath the pseudo-scientific mask of phylogenesis, or the recourse to 'inherited memory-traces', we should have to admit that Freud finds it necessary to postulate an organisation made of signifiers anteceding the effect of the event and the signified as a whole. In this mythical prehistory of the species we see the need to create a pre-structure inaccessible to the subject, evading his grasp, his initiatives, his inner 'cooking pot', in spite of all the rich ingredients our modern sorceresses seem to find there. But Freud is in fact caught in the trap of his own concepts; in this false synthesis by which the past of the human species is preserved in hereditarily transmitted patterns, he is vainly trying to overcome the opposition between event and constitution.

However, we should not be in a hurry to replace the phylogenic explanation by a structural type of explanation. The original fantasy is first and foremost fantasy: it lies beyond the history of the subject but nevertheless in history: a kind of language and a symbolic sequence, but loaded with elements of imagination; a structure, but activated by contingent elements. As such it is characterised by certain traits which make it difficult to assimilate to a purely transcendental schema, even if it provides the possibility of experience.[21]

---

[20] 'Wherever experiences fail to fit in with the hereditary schema, they become remodelled in the imagination. . . . It is precisely such cases that are calculated to convince us of the independent existence of the schema. We are often able to see the schema triumphing over the experience of the individual; as when in our present case, the boy's father became the castrator and the menace of his infantile sexuality in spite of what was in other respects an inverted Oedipus complex. . . . The contradictions between experience and the schema seem to supply the conflicts of childhood with an abundance of material' (Freud, 1918b [1914], pp. 119–120).

[21] We are not here trying to develop a coherent psychoanalytic theory which would involve the relationship between the level of the Oedipus structure and that of the original fantasies. One would first have to define what was meant by the Oedipus structure. Indeed the structural aspect of the Oedipus complex – considered both in its basic function and in its triangular form – was worked out much later

The text in which Freud first mentions primal fantasies ('A Case of Paranoia', 1915f) leaves no doubt in this respect. In it he describes the case of a woman patient who declared that she had been watched and photographed while lying with her lover. She claimed to have heard a 'noise', the click of the camera. Behind this delirium Freud saw the primal scene: the sound is the noise of the parents who awaken the child; it is also the sound the child is afraid to make lest it betray her listening. It is difficult to estimate its role in the fantasy. In one sense, says Freud, it is only a provocation, an accidental cause, whose role is solely to activate 'the typical fantasy of overhearing, which is a component of the parental complex', but he immediately corrects himself by saying: 'It is doubtful whether we can rightly call the noise "accidental". . . . Such fantasies are on the contrary an indispensable part of the fantasy of listening.' In fact, the sound alleged by the patient[22] reproduces in actuality the indication of the primal scene, the element which is the starting point for all ulterior elaboration of the fantasy. In other words, *the origin of the fantasy is integrated in the very structure of the original fantasy*.

In his first theoretical sketches on the subject of fantasy, Freud stresses, in a way which may intrigue his readers, the role of aural perception.[23] Without placing too much importance on these fragmentary texts, in which Freud seems to be thinking more particularly of paranoid fantasies, one must consider why such a privileged position was accorded to hearing. We suggest there are two reasons. One relates to the *sensorium* in question: hearing, when it occurs, breaks the continuity of an undifferentiated perceptual field and at the same

---

by Freud: it does not appear at all, for instance, in the *Three Essays* (1905d). The so-called generalised formulation of the complex appeared first in *The Ego and the Id* (1923b), and the generalisation in question cannot be taken in any formal sense: it describes a limited series of concrete positions within the inter-psychological field created by the father–mother–child triangle. From the point of view of structural anthropology, one might see this as *one of the forms* of the law governing human interchanges, a law which in other cultures might be incarnated in other persons and in other forms. The prohibitory function of the law might, for instance, be expressed by an agency other than the father. By adopting this solution the analyst would feel he had lost an essential dimension of his experience: the subject is, admittedly, located in a structure of inter-relationship, but the latter is transmitted by the parental unconscious. It is therefore less easy to assimilate it to a language system than to the complexities of a particular speech.

Freud's concept of the Oedipus complex is, in fact, remarkable for its realism: whether it is represented as an inner conflict (nuclear complex) or as a social institution, the complex remains a given fact; the subject is *confronted* by it: 'every new arrival on this planet is faced by the task of mastering it' (1905d, p. 226, fn.). Perhaps it was the realism of the concept which led Freud to allow the notion of original fantasy to coexist alongside the Oedipus complex, without being concerned to articulate them: here the subject does not encounter the structure, but is carried along by it.

[22] According to Freud it is, incidentally, a projection, the projection of a beat in her clitoris, in the form of a noise. There would be a new, circular, relationship between the pulsation which actualises the fantasy, and the drive which arouses it.

[23] 'Built up out of things that have been heard about and then *subsequently* turned to account, they combine things that have been experienced and things that have been heard about past events (from the history of parents and ancestors) and things seen by the subject himself. They are related to things heard in the same way as dreams are related to things seen' (Draft L). And again: 'Fantasies arise from an unconscious combination of things experienced and heard' (Draft M).

time is a sign (the noise waited for and heard in the night), which puts the subject in the position of having to answer to something. To this extent the prototype of the signifier lies in the aural sphere, even if there are correspondences in the other perceptual registers. But hearing is also – and this is the second reason to which Freud alludes explicitly in the passage – the history or the legends of parents, grandparents and the ancestors: the family *sounds* or *sayings*, this spoken or secret discourse, going on prior to the subject's arrival, within which he must find his way. Insofar as it can serve retroactively to summon up the discourse, the noise – or any other discrete sensorial element that has meaning – can acquire this value.

In their content, in their theme (primal scene, castration, seduction . . .), the original fantasies also indicate this postulate of retroactivity: they relate to the origins. Like myths, they claim to provide a representation of, and a solution to, the major enigmas which confront the child. Whatever appears to the subject as something needing an explanation or theory is dramatised as a moment of emergence, the beginning of a history.

Fantasies of origins: the primal scene pictures the origin of the individual; fantasies of seduction, the origin and upsurge of sexuality; fantasies of castration, the origin of the difference between the sexes.[24] Their themes therefore display, with redoubled significance, that original fantasies justify their status of being already there.

There is convergence of theme, of structure, and no doubt also of function: through the indications furnished by the perceptual field, through the scenarios constructed, the varied quest for origins, we are offered in the field of fantasy the origin of the subject himself.

Since we encounter fantasy as given, interpreted, reconstructed or postulated, at the most diverse levels of psychoanalytic experience, we have obviously to face the difficult problem of its metapsychological status, and first of all, of its topography within the framework of the distinction between the unconscious, preconscious and conscious systems.

There are certain tendencies in contemporary psychoanalysis to settle the question by making a theoretical transposition, which seems inevitable in practice, between the fantasy as it presents itself for interpretation and the fantasy which is the conclusion of the work of analytic interpretation (Isaacs, 1948). Freud would thus have been in error in describing by the same term,

---

[24] If we ask what these fantasies mean to *us*, we are embarking on a different level of interpretation. We then see that they are not only symbolic, but represent the insertion, mediated by an imagined scenario, of the most radically formative symbolism, into corporeal reality. The primal scene represents for us the conjunction of the biological fact of conception and birth with the symbolic fact of filiation: it unites the 'savage act' of coitus and the existence of a mother–child–father triad. In the fantasies of castration the conjunction of real and symbolic is even more apparent. With regard to seduction, we should add that it was not only, as we believe we have shown, because Freud had come across numerous actual cases, that he was able to use a fantasy as a scientific theory, and thus, by a roundabout way, hit on the true function of fantasy. It was also because he was trying to account, in terms of origins, for the advent of sexuality to human beings.

Phantasie, two totally distinct realities. On the one hand, there is the unconscious *Phantasie*, 'the primary content of unconscious mental processes' (Isaacs), and on the other, the conscious or subliminal imaginings, of which the daydream is the typical example. The latter would be only a manifest content, like the others, and would have no more privileged relationship to unconscious *Phantasie* than dreams, behaviour or whatever is generally described as 'material'. Like all manifest data, it would require interpretations in terms of unconscious fantasy.[25]

Freud's inspiration is shown by his persistent employment of the term *Phantasie* up to the end, in spite of the very early discovery that these *Phantasien* might be either conscious or unconscious. He wishes thereby to assert a profound kinship:

> The contents of the clearly conscious fantasies of perverts (which in favourable circumstances can be transformed into manifest behaviour), of the delusional fears of paranoics (which are projected in a hostile sense on to other people), and of the unconscious fantasies of hysterics (which psychoanalysis reveals behind their symptoms) – all these coincide with one another even down to their details.
>
> (Freud 1905d, pp. 165–166)

That is to say, that the same content, the same activation can be revealed in imaginary formations and psychopathological structures as diverse as those described by Freud, whether conscious or unconscious, acted out or represented, and whether or not there is a change of sign or permutation of persons.

Such an affirmation (1905d) does not come from any so-called proto-Freud. It is of cardinal importance, particularly in the period 1906–1909, when much research was devoted to the subject (in *Gradiva*, 1907a; 'Hysterical Phantasies and their Relation to Bisexuality', 1908a; 'On the Sexual Theories of Children', 1908c; 'Creative Writers and Day-Dreaming', 1908e; 'Some General Remarks on Hysterical Attacks', 1909a; 'Family Romances', 1909c). At this time the unconscious efficacy of fantasy was fully recognised as, for instance, underlying the hysterical attack which symbolises it. Freud however takes the conscious fantasy, the daydream, not only as paradigm, but as source. The hysterical fantasies which 'have important connections with the causation

---

[25] The proposal to eliminate the unfortunate confusion by the graphological device (using 'ph' for unconscious fantasies and 'f' for the daydream type) has been declared at times to be real progress, the result of half a century of psychoanalysis. Whether or not this distinction is in fact justified, it seems undesirable to use it in translations of Freud's work. It betrays little respect for the text to render words such as *Phantasie* or *Phantasieren*, which Freud invariably employed, by different terms according to the context. Our opposition to this terminological and conceptual innovation rests on three grounds: (i) the distinction should not be introduced into translations of Freud's work, even if the interpretation of his thought were correct; (ii) this interpretation of Freud's thought is incorrect; (iii) this distinction contributes less to the study of the problem than Freud's concept.

of the neurotic symptoms' (we must be dealing with unconscious fantasies) have as 'common source and normal prototype what are called the daydreams of youth' (Freud, 1908a). In fact it is conscious fantasy itself which may be repressed and thus become pathogenic. Freud even considers fantasy as the privileged point where one may catch in the raw the process of transition from one system to another, repression, or the return of repressed material.[26] It is indeed the same mixed entity, the same 'mixed blood' which, being so close to the limits of the unconscious, can pass from one side to the other, particularly as the result of a variation of cathexis.[27] It may be objected that Freud is not here taking fantasy at its deepest level, and that we are not dealing with a true fantasy, but simply with a subliminal reverie. But Freud does describe the process of dismissal as repression, and the frontier of which he speaks is indeed that of the unconscious in the strict, topographical, sense of the term.

We do not of course deny that there are different levels of unconscious fantasy, but it is remarkable to note how Freud, when studying the metapsychology of dreams, discovers the same relationship between the deepest unconscious fantasy and the daydream: the fantasy is present at both extremities of the process of dreaming. On the one hand it is linked with the ultimate unconscious desire, the 'capitalist' of the dream, and as such it is at the basis of that 'zigzag' path which is supposed to follow excitation through a succession of psychological systems: 'The first portion [of this path] was a progressive one, leading from the unconscious scenes of fantasies to the preconscious' (Freud, 1900a, p. 574), where it collects 'the day residues' or transference thoughts. But fantasy is also present at the other extremity of the dream, in the secondary elaboration which, Freud insists, is not part of the unconscious work of the dream, but must be identified 'with the work of our waking thought'. The secondary elaboration is an *a posteriori* reworking which takes place in the successive transformations which we impose on the story of the dream once we are awake. This consists essentially in restoring a minimum of order and coherence to the raw material handed over by the unconscious mechanisms of displacement, condensation and symbolism, and in imposing on this heterogeneous assortment a façade, a scenario, which gives it relative coherence and continuity. In a word, it is a question of making the final version relatively

---

[26] 'In favourable circumstances, the subject can still capture an unconscious fantasy of this sort in consciousness. After I had drawn the attention of one of my patients to her fantasies, she told me that on one occasion she had suddenly found herself in tears in the street and that, rapidly considering what it was she was actually crying about, she had got hold of a fantasy to the following effect. In her imagination she had formed a tender attachment to a pianist who was well known in the town (though she was not personally acquainted with him); she had had a child by him (she was in fact childless); and he had then deserted her and her child and left them in poverty. It was at this point in her romance that she had burst into tears' (Freud, 1908a).

[27] 'They draw near to consciousness and remain undisturbed so long as they do not have an intense cathexis, but as soon as they exceed a certain height of cathexis they are thrust back' (Freud, 1915e, p. 191).

similar to a daydream. Thus the secondary elaboration will utilise those ready-made scenarios, the fantasies or daydreams with which the subject has provided himself in the course of the day before the dream.

This is not necessarily to say that there is no privileged relationship between the fantasy which lies at the heart of the dream, and the fantasy which serves to make it acceptable to consciousness. Preoccupied by his discovery of the dream as the fulfilment of unconscious desire, it was no doubt natural for Freud to devalue anything close to consciousness which might appear to be defence and camouflage, in fact, the secondary elaboration.[28] But he quickly returns to a different appreciation:

> It would be a mistake, however, to suppose that these dream-façades are nothing other than mistaken and somewhat arbitrary revisions of the dream-content by the conscious agency of our mental life. . . . The wishful fantasies revealed by analysis in night-dreams often turn out to be repetitions or modified versions of scenes from infancy; thus in some cases the façade of the dream directly reveals the dream's actual nucleus, distorted by an admixture of other material.[29]
>
> (Freud, 1901b, p. 667)

Thus the extremities of the dream, and the two forms of fantasy which are found there, seem, if not to link up, at least to communicate from within and, as it were, to be symbolic of each other.

We have spoken of a progression in Freud's thought with regard to the metapsychological status of fantasy. It does, of course, move towards differentiation, but we believe we have already shown that this goes without suppression of the homology between different levels of fantasy, and above all there is no attempt to make the line of major differentiation coincide with the topographical barrier (censorship), which separates the conscious and preconscious systems from the unconscious. The difference occurs within the unconscious:

> Unconscious fantasies have either been unconscious all along or – as is more often the case – they were once conscious fantasies, daydreams, and have since been purposely forgotten and have become unconscious through 'repression'.
>
> (Freud, 1908a, p. 161)

---

[28] There must of course be a dismantling of the secondary elaboration in order to be able to take the dream element by element. But Freud does not forget that by *setting everything on the same level*, which is one of the aspects of psychoanalytic listening, the structure, the scenario, becomes itself an element, just as much, for instance, as the global reaction of the subject to his own dream.

[29] Freud seems also to have indicated that, generally speaking, desire can be more readily discovered in the *structure* of the fantasy than in the dream, unless the dream has been much restructured by the fantasy, as is particularly the case in 'typical dreams'. 'If we examine the structure [of fantasies] we shall perceive the way in which the wishful purpose that is at work in their production, has mixed up the material of which they are built, has re-arranged it and has formed it into a new whole' (1900a, p. 492).

This distinction is later, in Freudian terminology, to coincide with that between original fantasies and others, those that one might call secondary, whether conscious or unconscious.[30]

Apart from this fundamental difference, the unity of the fantasy whole depends, however, on their mixed nature, in which both the structural and the imaginary can be found, although to different degrees. It is with this in mind that Freud always held the model fantasy to be the reverie, that form of novelette, both stereotyped and infinitely variable, which the subject composes and relates to himself in a waking state.

The daydream is a shadow play, utilising its kaleidoscopic material drawn from all quarters of human experience, but also involving the original fantasy, whose *dramatis personae*, the court cards, receive their notation from a family legend which is mutilated, disordered and misunderstood. Its structure is the primal fantasy in which the Oedipus configuration can be easily distinguished, but also the daydream – if we accept that analysis discovers typical and repetitive scenarios beneath the varying clusters of fable.

However, we cannot classify or differentiate different forms of fantasy[31] as they shift between the poles of reverie or primal fantasy, simply, or even essentially, by the variability or inversion of the ratios between imaginary ingredient and structural link. Even the structure seems variable. In terms of daydream, the scenario is basically in the first person, and the subject's place clear and invariable. The organisation is stabilised by the secondary process, weighted by the ego: the subject, it is said, lives out his reverie. But the original fantasy, on the other hand, is characterised by the absence of subjectivisation, and the subject is present *in* the scene: the child, for instance, is one character amongst many in the fantasy 'a child is beaten'. Freud insisted on this visualisation of the subject on the same level as the other protagonists, and in this sense the screen memory would have a profound structural relationship with original fantasies.[32]

'A father seduces a daughter' might perhaps be the summarised version of the seduction fantasy. The indication here of the primary process is not the

---

[30] We suggest the following schema:

Urphantasie (original unconscious)	Phantasie (secondary)	
	unconscious (repressed)←	conscious →(daydream)

The repression which returns secondary fantasies to the unconscious would be that described by Freud as 'secondary repression' or 'after-pressure'. A further type of repression, more mythical and obscure, which Freud called 'primal repression' [*Urverdrängung*] corresponds to the constitution of the primal fantasies or their reception by the individual. We attempt later to indicate an approach to this subject. Cf. also Laplanche & Leclaire (1961).

[31] Amongst which we should obviously include screen memories and infantile sexual theories.

[32] Freud saw in this characteristic of screen-memories that they were not true memories, yet of all conscious fantasies, they are the only ones to claim reality. They are *true* scenes, the screens of primal fantasies or scenes.

absence of organisation, as is sometimes suggested, but the peculiar character of the structure, in that it is a scenario with multiple entries, in which nothing shows whether the subject will be immediately located as *daughter*; it can as well be fixed as *father*, or even in the term *seduces*.

When Freud asked himself whether there was anything in man comparable to the 'instinct in animals' (Freud, 1915e, p. 195), he found the equivalent, not in the drives (*Triebe*) but in primal fantasies (Freud, 1918b [1914], p. 120 n.). It is a valuable clue, since it demonstrates indirectly his unwillingness to explain fantasy on biological grounds: far from deriving fantasy from the drives, he preferred to make them dependent on earlier fantasy structures. It is also valuable in clarifying the position of certain contemporary concepts. Finally, it leads us to investigate the close relationship between desire and fantasy involved in the term *Wunschphantasie* [wish-fantasy].

Isaacs, for instance, considered unconscious fantasies to be 'an activity parallel to the drives from which they emerge'. She sees them as the 'psychological expression' of experience, which is itself defined by the field of force set up by libidinal and aggressive drives and the defences they arouse. Finally, she is concerned to establish a close link between the specific forms of fantasy life and the bodily zones which are the seat of the drives, though this leads her to underestimate one part of the Freudian contribution to the theory both of fantasy and of drives. In her view, fantasy is only the imagined transcription of the first objective of any drive, which is a specific object: the 'instinctual urge' is necessarily experienced as a fantasy which, whatever its content (desire to suck, in a baby), will be expressed, as soon as verbalisation is possible,[33] by a phrase consisting of three parts: subject (I), verb (swallow, bite, reject), object (breast, mother).[34] Of course, insofar as the drives are, for the Kleinians, in the first place in the nature of relationships, Isaacs shows how such a fantasy of incorporation is also experienced in the other sense, the active becoming passive. Furthermore, this fear of a return to sender is a constituent element of the fantasy itself. But it is hardly enough to recognise the equivalence of eating and being eaten in the fantasy of incorporation. So long as there is some idea of a subject, even if playing a passive role, are we sure to reach the structure of deepest fantasy?

---

[33] According to Isaacs, 'primary phantasies are ... dealt with by mental processes far removed from words'. It is only through practical necessity that we express them in words, but we thereby introduce a 'foreign element'. Isaacs, using one of Freud's expressions, speaks of 'the language of drives', and it is true that it is not its verbal or non-verbal character which defines the nature of language. But if Isaacs confuses language and the power of expression, perhaps this leads here to a failure to appreciate the originality of Melanie Klein's concepts: her attempt to describe a language which is non-verbal, but nonetheless structured, on the basis of pairs of opposites (good–bad, inner–outer). The audacity of the technique does at least assume a reference, not to the mobile expression of instinctual life, but to some fundamental oppositions.

[34] Cf. the variants formulated by Isaacs: 'I want to eat her all up', 'I want to keep her inside me', 'I want to tear her to bits', 'I want to throw her out of me', 'I want to bring her back', 'I must have her *now*', etc.

For Isaacs, fantasy is the direct expression of a drive, and almost consubstantial with it, and can, in the last resort, be reduced to the relationship which links subject to object by a verb of action (in the sense of the omnipotent wish). This is because, for her, the structure of the drive is that of a subjective intentionality and inseparable from its object: the drive 'intuits' or 'knows' the object which will satisfy it. As the fantasy, which at first expresses libidinal and destructive drives, quickly transforms itself into a form of defence, so finally it is the whole of the subject's internal dynamic which is deployed in accordance with this unique type of organisation. Such a concept postulates, in agreement with certain Freudian formulations, that 'all that is conscious has passed through a preliminary unconscious stage', and that the ego is 'a differentiated part of the id'. One is therefore obliged to provide every mental operation with an underlying fantasy which can itself be reduced on principle to an instinctual aim. The biological subject is in a direct line of continuity with the subject of fantasy, the sexual, human subject, in accordance with the series: some → id → fantasy (of desire, of defence) → ego mechanism: the action of repression is difficult to grasp, since 'fantasy life' is more implicit than repressed, and contains its own conflicts by virtue of the co-existence within the psyche of contradictory aims. There is, in fact, a profusion of fantasy, in which it is impossible to recognise the special type of structure which Freud tried to distinguish and where the elusive but elective relationship which he established between fantasy and sexuality also dissolves.

It is a little surprising that Freud, at a time when he fully recognised the existence and extent of sexuality and fantasy in the child, should have continued, as for instance in a footnote to the *Three Essays* in 1920 (1905d, p. 226), to consider the period of maximum fantasying activity to occur in the period of pubertal and pre-pubertal masturbation.[35] It is perhaps because to him there was a close correlation between fantasy and auto-erotism, which was not sufficiently accounted for by the belief that the second is camouflaged by the first. In fact he seems to be sharing the common belief that in the absence of real objects the subject seeks and creates for himself an imaginary satisfaction.

Freud himself did much to authorise this viewpoint when he tried to establish a theoretical model of desire, both in its object and purpose.[36] The origin of fantasy would lie in the hallucinatory satisfaction of desire; in the absence of a real object, the infant reproduces the *experience* of the original satisfaction in a hallucinated form. In this view the most fundamental fantasies would be those

---

[35] More often than not masturbation implies, of course, an imaginary relationship with an object: thus it can only be described as auto-erotic from an external standpoint, to the extent that the subject obtains satisfaction by resorting solely to his own body. But an infantile auto-erotic activity, such as sucking the thumb, in no sense implies the absence of any object. What makes it eventually auto-erotic is, as we shall show later, a special mode of satisfaction, specific to the 'birth' of sexuality, which lingers on into pubertal masturbation.

[36] 'The first wishing [*Wünschen*] seems to have been a hallucinatory cathecting of the memory of satisfaction' (Freud, 1900a, p. 598).

which tend to recover the hallucinated objects linked with the very earliest experiences of the rise and the resolution of desire.[37]

But before we try to discover what the Freudian fiction [*Fiktion*] is really intended to cover, we must be clear about its meaning, more particularly since it is rarely formulated in detail, but always presupposed in Freud's concept of the primary process. One might consider it a myth of origin: by this figurative expression Freud claims to have recovered the very first upsurgings of desire. It is an analytic 'construction', or fantasy, which tries to cover the moment of *separation* between *before* and *after*, whilst still containing both: a mythical moment of disjunction between the pacification of need [*Befriedigung*] and the fulfilment of desire [*Wunscherfüllung*], between the two stages represented by real experience and its hallucinatory revival, between the object that satisfies and the sign[38] which describes both the object and its absence: a mythical moment at which hunger and sexuality meet in a common origin.

If, caught in our own turn by the fantasy of origins, we were to claim to have located the emergence of fantasy, we should start from the standpoint of the real course of infantile history, and the development of infantile sexuality (see from the viewpoint of chap. 2 of *Three Essays*), and we should relate it to the appearance of auto-erotism, to the moment of what Freud calls the 'pleasure premium'. This is not a pleasure in the fulfilment of function, or the resolution of tension created by needs, but a marginal product, emerging from the world of needs, these vitally important functions whose aims and mechanisms are assured and whose objects are pre-formed.

But in speaking of the appearance of auto-erotism, even when taking care not to transform it into a stage of libidinal development, and even stressing its permanence and presence in all adult sexual behaviour, one is liable to lose sight of all that gives the notion its true meaning, and all that can illuminate the *function* as well as the *structure* of fantasy.

If the notion of auto-erotism is frequently criticised in psychoanalysis, this is because it is incorrectly understood, in the object-directed sense, as a first stage, enclosed within itself, from which the subject has to rejoin the world of objects. It is then easy to demonstrate, with much clinical detail, the variety and complexity of the links which, from the beginning, relate the infant to the

---

[37] Cf. for instance Isaacs's interpretation of Freud's hypothesis of the first hallucination: 'It seems probable that hallucination works best at times of less instinctual tension, perhaps when the infant half-awakes and first begins to be hungry. . . . The pain of frustration then stirs up a still stronger desire, viz. the wish to take the whole breast into himself and keep it there as a source of satisfaction; and this in its turn will for a time omnipotently fulfil itself in belief, in hallucination. . . . This hallucination of the internal satisfying breast may, however, break down altogether if frustration continues, and hunger is not satisfied, the instinct-tension proving too strong to be denied.'

It is obvious that the author is in difficulty about reconciling a hallucinated satisfaction with the demands of a frustrated instinct. How indeed can an infant *feed itself* on wind alone? The Freudian model is incomprehensible unless one understands that it is not the real object, but the lost object; not the milk, but the breast as a signifier, which is the object of the primal hallucination.

[38] The breast, wrongly named 'object of desire' by psychoanalysts.

outer world and, particularly, to its mother. But when Freud, principally in the *Three Essays*, speaks of auto-erotism, he has no intention of denying the existence of a primary-object relationship. On the contrary, he shows that the drive *becomes* auto-erotic, only after the loss of the object.[39] If it can be said of auto-erotism that it is objectless, it is in no sense because it may appear before any object relationship,[40] nor because on its arrival no object will remain in the search for satisfaction, but simply because the natural method of apprehending an object is split in two: the sexual drive separated from the non-sexual functions, such as feeding, which are its support [*Anlehnung*[41]] and which indicate its aim and object.

The 'origin' of auto-erotism would therefore be the moment when sexuality, disengaged from any natural object, moves into the field of fantasy and by that very fact becomes sexuality. The moment is more abstract than definable in time, since it is always renewed, and must have been preceded by erotic excitation, otherwise it would be impossible for such excitation to be sought out. But one could equally state the inverse proposition, that it is the breaking in of fantasy which occasions the disjunction of sexuality and need.[42] The answer to the question of whether this is a case of circular causality or simultaneous appearance is that however far back one may go they originate from the same point.

Auto-erotic satisfaction, insofar as it can be found in an autonomous state, is defined by one very precise characteristic: it is the product of the anarchic activity of partial drives, closely linked with the excitation of specific erogenous zones, an excitation which arises and is stilled on the spot. It is not a global, functional pleasure, but a fragmented pleasure, an organ pleasure [*Organlust*] and strictly localised.

It is known that erogeneity can be attached to predestined zones of the body (thus, in the activity of sucking, the oral zone is destined by its very physiology to acquire an erogenous value), but it is also available to any organ (even

---

[39] 'At a time at which the first beginnings of sexual satisfaction are still linked with the taking of nourishment, the sexual instinct has a sexual object outside the infant's own body in the shape of his mother's breast. It is only later that the instinct loses that object, just at the time, perhaps, when the child is able to form a total idea of the person to whom the organ that is giving him satisfaction belongs' (Freud, 1905d, p. 222). The passage is also invaluable as a further indication that the very constitution of the auto-erotic fantasy implies not only the partial object (breast, thumb or substitute), but the mother as a total person, withdrawing as she becomes total. This 'totalisation' is not to be understood as in the nature of a *Gestalt*, but by reference to the child's demand, which may be granted or refused by the mother.

[40] Described by some psychoanalysts as an 'objectless' stage, on a genetic basis, which one might call totalitarian, since it confuses the constitution of the libidinal object with that of objectivity in the external world, and claims to establish stages in the development of the ego as 'organ of reality', stages which they also hold to be correlative with those of the libido.

[41] Elsewhere (Laplanche & Pontalis, 1967), we are developing this notion which is fundamental to the Freudian theory of instincts.

[42] In one of his first reflections on fantasy, Freud notes that the *Impulse* could perhaps emanate from fantasy (Draft N).

internal organs), and to any region or function of the body. In every case the function serves only as support, the taking of food serving, for instance, as a model for fantasies of incorporation. Though modelled on the function, sexuality lies in its difference from the function: in this sense its prototype is not the act of sucking, but the enjoyment of going through the motions of sucking [*Ludeln*], the moment when the external object is abandoned, when the aim and the source assume an autonomous existence with regard to feeding and the digestive system. The ideal, one might say, of auto-erotism is 'lips that kiss themselves'.[43] Here, in this apparently self-centred enjoyment, as in the deepest fantasy, in this discourse no longer addressed to anyone, all distinction between subject and object has been lost.

If we add that Freud constantly insisted on the seductive role of the mother (or of others), when she washes, dresses or caresses her child,[44] and if we note also that the naturally erogenous zones (oral, anal, uro-genital, skin), are not only those which most attract the mother's attention, but also those which have an obvious exchange value (orifices or skin covering) we can understand how certain chosen parts of the body itself may not only serve to sustain a local pleasure, but also be a meeting place with maternal desire and fantasy, and thus with one form of original fantasy.

By locating the origin of fantasy in the auto-erotism, we have shown the connection between fantasy and desire. Fantasy, however, is not the object of desire, but its setting. In fantasy the subject does not pursue the object or its sign: he appears caught up himself in the sequence of images. He forms no representation of the desired object, but is himself represented as participating in the scene although, in the earliest forms of fantasy, he cannot be assigned any fixed place in it (hence the danger, in treatment, of interpretations which claim to do so). As a result, the subject, although always present in the fantasy, may be so in a desubjectivised form – that is to say, in the very syntax of the sequence in question. On the other hand, to the extent that desire is not purely an upsurge of the drives, but is articulated into the fantasy, the latter is a favoured spot for the most primitive defensive reactions, such as turning against oneself, or into an opposite, projection, negation: these defences are even indissolubly linked with the primary function of fantasy, to be a setting for desire, insofar as desire itself originates as prohibition, and the conflict may be an original conflict.

[43] Cf. also in 'Instincts and Their Vicissitudes' (1915c), the analysis of the pairs of opposites, sadism–masochism, voyeurism–exhibitionism. Beneath the active or passive form of the phrase (seeing, being seen, for instance), we must assume a reflexive form (seeing oneself) which, according to Freud, would be primordial. No doubt this primordial degree is to be found when the subject no longer places himself in one of the different terms of the fantasy.

[44] 'A child's intercourse with anyone responsible for his care affords him an unending source of sexual excitation and satisfaction from his erotogenic zones. This is especially so since the person in charge of him, who, after all, is as a rule his mother, herself regards him with feelings that are derived from her own sexual life, and quite clearly treats him as a substitute for a complete sexual object' (1905c, p. 223). It is, however, customary to say that Freud took a long time to recognise the link with the mother.

But as for knowing who is responsible for the setting, it is not enough for the psychoanalyst to rely on the resources of his science, nor on the support of myth. He must also become a philosopher.

Summary

1. The status of fantasy cannot be found within the framework of the opposition reality–illusion (imaginary). The notion of *psychic reality* introduces a third category, that of structure.
2. Freud's theory of seduction (1895–97) is re-examined from the point of view of its pioneering and demonstrative value: it permits the analysis of the dialectic relationship between fantasy productions, the underlying structures and the reality of the scene. This 'reality' is to be sought in an ever more remote or hypothetical past (of the individual or of the species), which is postulated on the horizon of the imaginary, and implied in the very structure of the fantasy.
3. Freud's so-called abandonment of the reality of infantile traumatic memories, in favour of fantasies which would be based only on a biological, quasi-endogenous evolution of sexuality, is only a transitional stage in the search for the foundation of neurosis. On the one hand, seduction will continue to appear as one of the data of the relationship between child and adult (Freud, Ferenczi); on the other hand, the notion of *primal* (or *original*) *fantasies* [*Urphantasien*], of 'inherited memory traces' of prehistoric events, will in turn provide support for individual fantasies.

    The authors propose an interpretation of this notion: such a pre-history, located by Freud in phylogenesis, can be understood as a pre-structure which is actualised and transmitted by the parental fantasies.
4. Original fantasies are limited in their thematic scope. They relate to problems of origin which present themselves to all human beings [*Menschenkinder*]: the origin of the individual (primal scene), the origin of sexuality (seduction) and the origin of the difference between the sexes (castration).
5. The origin of fantasy cannot be isolated from the origin of the drive [*Trieb*] itself. The authors, reinterpreting the Freudian concept of the *experience of satisfaction*, locate this origin in the auto-erotism, which they define not as a stage of evolution but as the moment of a repeated disjunction of sexual desire and non-sexual functions: sexuality is detached from any natural object, and is handed over to fantasy, and, by this very fact, starts existing as sexuality.
6. The *metapsychological* status of this mixed entity, the fantasy, is finally established. The authors refuse to accept the main line of separation between conscious and unconscious fantasies (Isaacs). They place this division between the original and the secondary fantasies (whether repressed or conscious) and demonstrate the relationship and the profound continuity between the various fantasy scenarios – the stage-

setting of desire – ranging from the daydream to the fantasies recovered or reconstructed by analytic investigation.

References

Ferenczi, S. (1933). Confusion of tongues between the adult and the child. In *Final Contributions to the Problems and Methods of Psycho-Analysis*. London: Hogarth Press, 1955.
Freud, S. (1895d) (with Breuer, J.). *Studies on Hysteria, S.E.*, 1.
Freud, S. (1900a). *The Interpretation of Dreams, S.E.*, 4–5.
Freud, S. (1901a). *On Dreams. S.E.*, 5.
Freud, S. (1901b). *The Psychopathology of Everyday Life. S.E.*, 6.
Freud, S. (1905c). *Jokes and Their Relation to the Unconscious. S.E.*, 8.
Freud, S. (1905d). *Three Essays on the Theory of Sexuality. S.E.*, 7.
Freud, S. (1906a). My Views on the Part Played by Sexuality in the Aetiology of the Neuroses. *S.E.*, 7.
Freud, S. (1907a). *Delusions and Dreams in Jensen's Gradiva. S.E.*, 9.
Freud, S. (1908a). Hysterical Phantasies and Their Relation to Bisexuality. *S.E.*, 9.
Freud, S. (1908c). On the Sexual Theories of Children. *S.E.*, 9.
Freud, S. (1908e). Creative Writers and Day-Dreaming. *S.E.*, 9.
Freud, S. (1909a). Some General Remarks on Hysterical Attacks. *S.E.*, 9.
Freud, S. (1909c). Family Romances. *S.E.*, 9.
Freud, S. (1911b). Formulations on the Two Principles of Mental Functioning. *S.E.*, 12.
Freud, S. (1912–13). *Totem and Taboo. S.E.*, 13.
Freud, S. (1914d). On the History of the Psycho-Analytic Movement. *S.E.*, 14.
Freud, S. (1915c). Instincts and Their Vicissitudes. *S.E.*, 14.
Freud, S. (1915e). The Unconscious. *S.E.*, 14.
Freud, S. (1915f). A Case of Paranoia Running Counter to the Psycho-Analytic Theory of the Disease. *S.E.*, 14.
Freud, S. (1916–17). *Introductory Lectures on Psycho-Analysis. S.E.*, 15–16.
Freud, S. (1918b [1914]). From the History of an Infantile Neurosis. *S.E.*, 17.
Freud, S. (1920g). *Beyond the Pleasure Principle. S.E.*, 18.
Freud, S. (1923b). *The Ego and the Id. S.E.*, 19.
Freud, S. (1925d [1924]). *An Autobiographical Study. S.E.*, 20.
Freud, S. (1926d). *Inhibitions, Symptoms and Anxiety. S.E.*, 20.
Freud, S. (1933a). *New Introductory Lectures on Psycho-Analysis. S.E.*, 22.
Freud, S. (1940a [1938]). *An Outline of Psycho-Analysis. S.E.*, 23.
Freud, S. (1950 [1887–1902]). *The Origins of Psycho-Analysis*. London: Imago, 1954.
Isaacs, S. (1948). The Nature and Function of Phantasy. *International Journal of Psychoanalysis, 29*.
Klein, M. (1934). A Contribution to the Psychogenesis of Manic-Depressive States. In *Contributions to Psycho-Analysis*. London: Hogarth Press, 1949.
Klein, M. (1960). *Narrative of a Child Psycho-Analysis*. London: Hogarth Press.
Laplanche, J. (1991). Specificity of terminological problems in the translation of Freud. *International Review of Psycho-Analysis, 18*: 401–406.
Laplanche, J., & Leclaire, S. (1961). L'inconscient, une étude psychanalytique [The unconscious: A psychoanalytic study]. *Les Temps Modernes, 183*.
Laplanche, J., & Pontalis, J.-B. (1967). *Vocabulaire de la psychanalyse*. Paris: Presses Universitaires de France. [*The Language of Psychoanalysis*, trans. D. Nicholson-Smith, New York: Norton, 1973.]
Mehler, J. A. (1992). Love and male impotence. *International Journal of Psycho-Analysis, 73*: 467–480.
Rank, O. (1924). *Trauma of Birth*. London: Kegan Paul, 1929.

16 THE PRELUDE TO FANTASMATIC LIFE

Michel Fain

A psychiatrist, full member and former president of the Paris Psychoanalytical Society, **Michel Fain** (1917–2007) worked very closely with Pierre Marty and was one of the founders of the Paris Psychosomatic Institute. His published work is complex and wide-ranging, and he had a significant and long-lasting impact on psychoanalytic technique thanks to his understanding of the functional value of dreams and fantasies. One of his major articles is 'Prélude à la vie fantasmatique' [A prelude to fantasmatic life] (*Revue Française de Psychanalyse*, 1971, no. 5). With Denise Braunschweig, he wrote *Eros et Antéros* [Eros and Antéros: Psychoanalytic thoughts on sexuality] (Payot, 1971) and *La nuit, le jour* [Night, day: A psychoanalytic essay on mental functioning] (PUF, 1975); with M. Soulé and L. Kreisler, he wrote *L'enfant et son corps* [The child and his or her body] (PUF, 1974). Another of his books is *Le désir de l'interprète* [The desire of the interpreter] (Aubier-Montaigne, 1982); and with C. Dejours he wrote *Corps malade et corps érotique* [Ill body, erotic body] (Masson, 1984).

Marilia Aisenstein wrote a concise biography of Michel Fain for the 'Psychanalystes d'aujourd'hui' series (PUF, 2000).

Presentation

I am fortunate in having an extremely learned cousin. One day I asked him for a definition of the concept of entropy that I would find accessible. He reflected for a moment and replied: 'Entropy is the degree of disorder in a system.' When I met him again a couple of years later, he reminded me of this definition and told me it contained one significant omission: a definition of order. I was taken aback by this, as I am whenever I feel I have been working on the basis that something is self-evident. Be that as it may, this learned cousin told me that the higher the level of improbability attained by a system, the more it is a locus of order. It must be said that this explanation suited me particularly well, given the point I had reached in my research on mental functioning.

The work I have had the honour of presenting to you undertook to examine some conditions of appearance of actors asked to move around in a set that is not constructed alone. The conclusion can continue the second definition quoted above: the higher the level of improbability attained by the symbolic order, the more effective it becomes. In this sense, the entropy of this system transpires in a probability that dons the mask of repetition. Thus in the course of a human life many things occur that seem trivially everyday, which make the person's way of perceiving, thinking about and acting on them, of allowing himself to think and act, attain a higher or lower level of improbability. Thus, this work has had a bearing on a limited number of factors from which I will seek to draw some points for discussion.

1. A certain sensitivity to things is debilitating. This occurs when this sensitivity is due to the maintenance or the re-emergence of a reality that has rediscovered all its primary raw quality.
2. A certain mode of psychomotor activity, termed 'the hypercathexis of the factual' by David and de M'Uzan (Marty, M'Uzan, & David, 1963) and 'operational life' by Marty (Marty & M'Uzan, 1963), gives some protection against the previous possibility by blunting this sensitivity through a particular use of a characteristic of the death instinct.
3. A certain sensitivity to things makes it possible to live well. The things in question are then organised according to a high level of improbability.

Nevertheless, this high level of improbability is attained by means of a fact, simple at first glance, which has an extraordinary potential for resonance on the representative faculties: the human offspring matures better if within a desired time-span he does not impede the father's desire, which I see no reason not to call the other's desire.

This reality requires a receptive and attentive mother who within the same desired time-span will be able to emerge as a lover who knows how to prepare herself to become welcoming to the man's desire. This emergence gives rise to a censorship that is met by a need for compensatory representations. Censorship and representations then lead to the maintenance of the child's sleep – sleep that will distance him from the father's desire – this latter, however, then indirectly generating the dream-work, a mental work with results that are practically impossible to foresee.

In fact, another resonance then intervenes: between the primal fantasies and the other's desire. The foundations of the symbolic order are in place. It is no accident that the circumstances leading to this high level of improbability are those that incorporate, as Pasche discussed, all the propositions that are inscribed in Freud's works.

For this high degree of improbability to be maintained, the energy of the system needs to be partly borrowed from another system that nevertheless tends to reduce the first one to its simplest expression. This amounts to using some of that energy that originates from an unsymbolised raw reality as a spur.

This is another point that requires discussion.

There is a central dynamic phenomenon in psychoanalytic matters. It is that which is best perceived through the sleep–dream system. The ego's desire to make its cathexes regress to the level of primary narcissism is always opposed by a desire to maintain the object cathexes that have been thwarted. Serge Viderman (1970) has given a remarkable account of this impulse during the psychoanalytic treatment. This concerns a particular phenomenon. Every time an apparent aspiration towards narcissism, whether primary or secondary, manifestly operates, it is obscurely juxtaposed by an erotic refusal to follow this path.

The mother's cathexis of the newborn is accompanied by a narcissistic retreat that extends to maternalising the environment. Many authors have placed particular emphasis on the baby's mental development in this environment, the general quality of this environment being judged in terms of good and bad – that is, with a low level of improbability.

In fact, the maternal cathexis is also subject to the above-mentioned rule, and a part of her libido remains overtly erotic. A woman survives somewhere. The representation of this woman clinging to her erotic objects is expelled beyond the mothering environment, and its existence is one of the reasons for the mother's distrust towards the world in general. Thus, the representation of a hallucinatory satisfaction of the other's desire, prefiguring a later primal scene, is depicted outside the mothering environment. However, in relation to the primary identification formed by the mother and child, this representation is not distinguished from the primary raw reality, and the protective-shield system – the role of which is essentially provided by the mother – takes charge of insulating the baby from all this. It is the chaos preceding the genesis from which the baby is protected in a way that justifies the comment 'he won't know'. In other words, there is an effort to prevent this chaos that incorporates both the raw reality and the many human emotions from exerting any influence, having any effect on the baby, whereas protection is exercised in an infinitely subtler way over the effects deriving from this baby's internal drive source. The energy that manages to get through the protective-shield system has no tendency towards either exhaustion or satisfaction. The child's own drive source is located inside the mothering system and within the primary identification; the child's id becomes the mother's ego – only in part – because some of the erotic libido of the woman who refuses to become a mother is 'outside the perimeters', although it quickly begins to make unexpected appearances. When the woman regains right of mention, she creates a forbidden zone in the mothering environment, namely the couple's bedroom – I purposely do not say 'the parents' bedroom'. This place has only brief, too brief, moments of complete existence. Admittedly, the external walls still exist, but the constitution of a forbidden zone means that at certain times the mother who is becoming a woman again breaks the primary identification and consequently liberates the drive potentials of the child's ego. This is what led me to indicate the censorship of the lover initially exercised over these potentialities that can obstruct the father's desire. Accordingly, in favourable conditions the child's ego is confronted at an early stage with the father's desire. If the child's unawareness concerning perception of this desire nonetheless persists, its efficacy is fully exercised over this same child. Unawareness and the efficacy of an unperceived force are familiar entities to psychoanalysts. From the modern-day perspective, the child's mental productions – initially censored – require in turn the conditions of elaboration. The fact that this encounter occurs is already laden with a future elaboration in resonance with primal fantasies. Although just now I could say that the mother cathected her child's id as her own ego, the decathexis, by discovering id potentialities that were initially censored to give free rein to the father's desire, leads to the formulation of representations that in their resonance with primal fantasies will constitute the core of the unconscious.

I have also examined what might impede such a development; how a deficiency in the mother's protective-shield role risks perpetuating the primitive and undifferentiated chaos, presenting the individual with an impossible integrative task because of the need to confront an inexhaustible source. The persistence of excessively large breaches in the primitive protective shield tends to reopen their gap at the slightest lapse in defences. This leads to a tendency for the subject to invent mountains where only crevasses exist. This is what led me to exaggerate, by reducing multiple solutions to one single large mechanism, primary fetishisation – a denial mechanism that deploys methods of formulating the excitation that springs from the crevice that characterises a splitting. I feel this over-extension is highly questionable and needs to be debated. The other defensive solution stems from the use of reductive properties incorporated in the death instinct. The sleep obtained by rocking young early insomniacs represents the acme of the calming effect procured by a specific excitation. The effect ceases with the rocking. I have directly related the psychomotor activity that characterises the operational life of psychosomatic patients to this mechanism. I think this viewpoint should be improved by the discussion.

This is what has led me to describe in outline some facts that, aside from some exceptional cases, never appear in a pure state and that are found to a greater or lesser degree within every structure.

There is one final point for discussion that I am inclined to challenge in advance. My contribution to this colloquium[1] was made following a central theme of works characterised by an imbalance in terms of metapsychology. The economic dimension intrudes there and, as Pasche (1965) recalled, the meaning is obstructed by the economic. This study relates to some modes of

---

[1] Colloquium of the Paris Psychoanalytical Society, 20 and 21 December 1970.

reinforcement that strive to alter the high level of improbability according to which a latent meaning comes to expression.

★ ★ ★

Discussion

Clinical data

It is always adult psychoanalytic treatments that have enabled me to understand what was happening with children, which is not a rule but a characteristic of my own. The question of representation arose acutely in the analysis of a case that involved among other things a doubt as to the existence of the penis. This doubt originated from repressed female tendencies represented by an unconscious desire to metamorphose into a woman. The idea, for example, of being seen with a hole in his trousers filled the patient with anxiety. I will not discuss his clumsy tendencies to appear masculine that lapsed each time into a failure that enabled him to play masochistically on a feminine mode, but the remarkable clarity of phallic symbols in his dreams and his vivid memory of this symbolism in contrast with everything reminiscent of the vagina, always reported in a vague, indistinct way, and usually forgotten. Now, this patient's failure, as he remained in a narcissistic phallic organisation, was obvious. His sexual life did not contain any fetishism beyond what is normally observed in men. It was the precision and the clarity that appeared in the memory of the dream that were striking. There was always a spectacle that included some vivid impressions. There was an evident counter-cathexis of the influences exerted by the female sex, which were conceived as evidence of the threat of castration. Although it was possible to reconstruct, through the fear of having a hole in his trousers, his own childhood fear on catching his elder sister naked, it appeared that the perception of this 'void' had been experienced as a sudden, colourful, noisy impression, qualities found in the phallic symbolism of his dreams. Following dreams that accompanied the traumatic neurosis, these lively qualities appeared in his dreams, confined as it were in a phallic representation then playing the role of mastery usually devolved to the anus. These dreams were frightening. It then became apparent that the phallic representation had no reassuring effect on this patient and that an associative chain between the female sex, lack of penis, bright colours and noise existed in the background. The phallic symbols had in no way succeeded in their soothing function. We are justified in saying that in such cases the representation has failed to attenuate a traumatic memory. An example of this kind also shows that it is necessary to determine whether a representation does not intrinsically contain, as a result of its general symbolism, a fetishistic element, that is containing a denial, which is not necessarily the role of a symbol. Be that as it may, the essential quality to emphasise in this case is that the phallic symbols appearing in the dream narratives were not forgotten in the same way as other material; we might say that they never bored holes in the discourse, that these representations failed in their attempt at denial and that their colourful and noisy quality was associated more with the absence of the penis than its presence. The image of a volcanic eruption, a blazing, noisy eruption springing from the hole in the trousers, is ultimately reminiscent of a more regressive symbolism of an anal type.

Be that as it may, the nightmarish quality of these dreams also showed the failure of the censorship and protective-shield functions, a failure characterised by the incapacity of the phallic symbol to ensure the fetishistic denial of an absence.

A preliminary commentary is required: all the previously experienced situations of absence are connected with the absence of the penis in the female sex. Now, as we have seen following Freud, it is absence that sets in motion the hallucinatory realisation of desire. In this patient's case, an absence seems to have given rise to a failure in the hallucinatory realisation. The Kleinian system seems to dominate: the hole, the noise and the light seem to fuel persecutory anxieties, the representation loses its efficacy, and we find ourselves in the highly mysterious domain of the unrepresentable. In this case, the failure of the phallic representation can impact as the disappearance of a containing form. The above patient has more than one string to his bow and can then organise an anal representation of volcanic eruption, recreate a more regressive form that allows him to hold on; nevertheless, there exists alongside the absence a vivid sensory impression that has not been diminished by censorship.

If the above observations seem to lead naturally into a discussion of infants, of less than three months old, presenting an almost total insomnia that cedes only to a continual rocking, resuming as soon as this rocking ceases, the mother's failure in her protective-shield role becomes obvious.

Already in the study of early insomnia undertaken at Kreisler's initiative in collaboration with Soulé (Kreisler, Fain, Soulé, 1967), the mother's massive failure in this protective-shield role was evident in this condition, a failure translated by a cathexis that was not absent but so vitiated that the baby did not succeed in reconstituting, as is seen in other cases, an autonomous protective-shield system. We were then struck by the rocking action, a specific form of excitations that enabled sleep to continue. The rocking mother was then the guardian of sleep, although she bore no similarity to a dream. When this type of excitations stopped, the infant awoke and the wailing resumed. This is why I stated at the Lisbon Congress in my commentary on Jacqueline Loriod's psychosomatic clinical observation how it was essential to distinguish between the soothing mother and the satisfying mother, and that we could anticipate the primary identification with the mother becoming increasingly complicated. Taking up the study of the sobbing spasm from the perspective of an affective illness with Denise Braunschweig in relation to an intervention concerning Green's paper and commenting on the fact that all the cases studied had presented early insomnias to varying degrees, we inferred that the rocking by the soothing mothers represented almost in its pure state the protective-shield action described by Green in relation to the death instinct (Braunschweig & Fain, 1970). A later sexualisation of this maternal action led to the sobbing spasm. In fact, this specific detail concerning the soothing mother entailed *ipso facto* a modification in the libidinal quality of sleep, which could follow on from libidinal satisfaction or encouragements with a soothing tendency, leading to the silent action of the death instinct.

★ ★ ★

Having reached this point, we still have a long way to go. What is the reason for this apparent tendency of excitation to overwhelm representation? I have used the term 'hiatus' in this connection, as if ultimately the excitation, whatever its origin, did not manage to subsist in any form. This would imply that the representation that the patient complains of as persecutory is only the secondary elaboration of another complaint, connected with the failure of the representation in question to protect against a traumatic emergence of stimuli. The example of our last patient shows that this emergence can even overwhelm the oneiric function, a supremely representative function, recathecting a primitive sensoriality of which the very exercise indicates a deficiency. Chasseguet-Smirgel (1968) has described similar phenomena with regard to her theory of the phallic mother. It is possible that, when the excessive excitation comes from the mother figure, rather than from the failure of this figure, this excitation can be better attached to the mother figure through phallic symbolism. It is then a vitiated cathexis, but a cathexis nonetheless. The question still arises as to whether this is not a doomed attempt to formulate stimuli that have regressively resumed an anarchic and discordant tonality.

Clinical examples of early insomnia do not show sadistic mothers, but women who cannot organise their maternal instinct and are consequently the source of discordant messages in which the tendency to constitute the primary identification coexists with an equivalent tendency to rejection. In some sense, this type of mother eliminates herself while also preventing the child from developing an early protective-shield system, as is seen in other cases. It only achieves its efficacy through the rocking, which attenuates the undifferentiated stimulation that is constantly undergone by the baby, coming not only from her but also from the external world. Here we find the notion of the raw unsymbolisable reality introduced by Laplanche and Pontalis (1964). Thus reaching the notion of a primary, global, undifferentiated stimulation, a notion linked by Freud (1926d) to the birth trauma, then addressed exclusively by Rank (1924), we end up at the notion of a primary sensorium, the very exercise of which connotes a deficiency in the maternal protective-shield function. I have purposely avoided any reference to paranoid anxiety. In developing a viewpoint, we cannot allow ourselves to switch from one viewpoint to another. For Freud, the ego becomes differentiated in contact with reality; for Klein it exists from the outset but to a certain extent the dice are thrown, the capacity to love and to constitute oneself are already a solid fact. For Freud it is the primal fantasies initially held apart from the ego that are constituted and that assume an important role in symbolic development. I repeat, in terms of the Freudian system the Kleinian viewpoint exists only in a conflictual perspective – that of the general and the perceptible, seeking to reduce and deny what is intelligible, complex and differentiated.

This is the conflict I have described at length with Braunschweig between the maternal instinct and Oedipal structuring. For the mother with a normally developed maternal instinct, the baby has an ego, his own, and a capacity to love, his own, and she is right. The characteristic aspect of both Klein's and Winnicott's work is the disappearance of the woman, who at a certain point would not hesitate to get rid of her child to enjoy her partner's penis. She has only one legitimate means of getting rid of the baby, which is to get him to fall asleep. The mother and the woman will always remain implacable enemies. When the mother is present, she cathects her baby's id, which as a result becomes his ego. This is the 'innate' ego posited by Klein. Its existence is not in question. But if this mother becomes a woman again, her child's id will return to being an id that has to be silenced and neutralised. If the father's penis is then projected on to the breast, this is no surprise, while being less simple than that. The real trauma comes from the fact that this breast is no longer feeding; it wants to be caressed, it corresponds to the existence of the vagina. The father's penis in the maternal breast is 'the full vagina' (Braunschweig & Fain, 1970), symbolising the decathexis of the child, who has temporarily been orphaned and exposed to the external world.[2] It is not parents who have sexual relations – at least if they like making love – only a couple that has broken all its libidinal ties with every group, including the family, makes love. All the psychoanalytic theories focused on the child's genetic development are marked by the desire to maintain the full force of maternal instinct, and they consequently have an anti-erotic aspect. Thus splitting as described by Klein or Winnicott leaves in the shadow a metamorphosis that occurs more or less rapidly depending on the woman and her dual personality as mother focused on her child and woman who no longer knows anyone but her male partner, and whose child therefore becomes a stranger at this precise moment. Let us also remember that the father is present and plays a decisive role in this metamorphosis, either hastening or delaying it. All these considerations lead us to auto-erotism, which has so far been remarkably absent. I have just touched on some consequences connected with the maternal role with regard to the undifferentiated global stimuli, with her absence due to the resurgence of her sexual desires or, in more vivid terms,

---

[2] This viewpoint accords with the fantasy of the abandoned child 'exposed to the outside world'.

the transformation of the maternal breast into the erotic breast that then longs for the man's hand and mouth and rejects the baby, who has become a source of annoyance and a stranger. What is the exact meaning of this shift? Quite simply that when the mother fails in her optimal protective-shield role, she introduces an obstacle, creates an early triangulation, which at the level of primary narcissistic needs is an obstacle that is not the sexual father. When, decathecting her baby, she becomes a woman again, it is for the sexual father, and she then remains in the path of symbolic organisation. She substitutes for the feeding-breast part-object a system that with Braunschweig I have called primary genital. There again, in our view, Klein is mistaken to think that early genital agitations lead to autism; it is the genital agitations of the mother-turned-lover that drive the child into a symbolic organisation that is echoed by his primal fantasies.

Thus, President Schreber's father (Freud, 1911c [1910]), who early imposes sadistic educational rules on his son, appears as an obstacle to a more adequate mothering, but he is repudiated as a sexual father, at least with regard to his wife. He is prematurely sexed for his son. The stimuli to which he subjects him are erotised and turn the child into an object. These are not traumatic effects resulting from the absence of a protective-shield system, and this is why the President's delusions are ultimately more mystical than persecutory.

From a utopian perspective, then, the mother having assumed her protective-shield role temporarily decathects her child as soon as desire transforms her into a woman. She seeks to benefit from the baby's sleep, which through its characteristic regression should resume the protective-shield role, since the baby's sleep is an autonomous form of primary identification. This is in fact a formal description. The woman's desire has banished the mother before the child sleeps and the baby has experienced physical contact with an absent mother, and with the woman and former mother's desire something appears in the child that certainly cannot manifest as a constituted desire but already as a clinging to an object that is simultaneously absent and present, a clinging that can entail the refusal to regress into sleep. Can we say that elements of a hallucinatory realisation of the desire in the form of a dream are in place at an early stage? It is in this regard that the term 'fantasy' does not take account of the nuances that can be observed in the facts. With Kreisler, I have shown the essential differences that pertain between one baby who, while asleep, makes sucking movements with his lips, another who sleeps with his thumb in his mouth, and finally one who frenetically sucks his thumb and no longer sleeps. There is no doubt that these three modes of auto-erotism show qualitative differences being transposed into a motricity-representation equilibrium that corresponds to different distributions of narcissistic libido and of libido that remains clinging to an object. The first is close to representation, a representation that reinforces sleep by a hallucinated discharge of the excitation that can almost be calculated in time; the second requires a real excitation that is already much longer; while the third appears to be thrown into an infernal and apparently endless cycle of discharge. These examples lead us to conclude that while mnemic traces exist from the outset, they only acquire a representative value very gradually, although in an individual's psychic life the unconscious knowledge of an unrepresentable auto-erotism can only be constituted as an effective mnemic trace through a regression that has involved loss of the representation.

Let us return to this baby in connection with the desire of his former mother who has returned to being a lover. This latter will rock him to make him sleep and eliminate him as an object and refuse to remain his object. The former mother's narcissism is henceforth mobilised for itself, to become welcoming to the father's penis. This rocking thus contains all the elements of a censorship being exercised over the clinging to the object that has occurred in the child. Even if in an initial stage the auto-erotism through which the child responds can be considered as an excitational discharge without representation, this auto-erotism is situated in a context that contains all the elements of the Oedipal situation, elements against which a censorship is beginning to be exercised. This is why the concept of unrepresentability cannot simply be a genetic notion based on lack of maturation. The unrepresentability is also connected with the father's desire, who is somewhere offstage. Thus, this auto-erotism, which, as just described, is what appears in optimal conditions, exists in resonance with primal fantasies to some extent, and consequently emerges in the symbolic path that leads to the Oedipal conflict. It is that of the first baby above, who makes some sucking motions during his sleep. This example, utopian in fact, clearly shows the distinction between censorship and the protective-shield system. The latter belongs to the mother, while the censorship is carried out by the lover.

However, the early childhood pathology that is already so varied shows in fact that matters are infinitely more complicated. Two conditions (Kreisler, Fain, & Soulé, 1967) – one that is mild, the first-term colic, the other infinitely more serious, a form of early asthma that appears only in the mother's physical presence (Fain & Kreisler, 1970) – indicate that the mother's continual cathexis of the child, preventing the development of primary auto-erotism, which involves *ipso facto* its distancing from the symbolic chain, reveals the vicissitudes of this hypercathexis. This maternal attitude, accompanied by a certain lack of paternal authority, does not only affect the development of the auto-erotism that she crushes along with her own desire and that of her husband. What becomes of her protective-shield role? The pathological effects that ensue from her attitude point to the fact that despite appearances, she has also failed in this role. It is likely that too great a barrier against the excitation constitutes an intense source of excitations, perhaps in fact by default. Furthermore, we have more precise information on this subject. The mothers of allergics (Fain, 1969) prevent the development of an entire sector of their children's personalities, at least of those who go along with it. Satisfaction is tolerated only in contact with them, preventing the development that is instigated by auto-erotism.

We have postulated that these mothers have retained in their unconscious a tendency to want to return the child to the foetal state, in their womb. It seemed to us that this fact only represented an intensification of a habitual attitude that is generally overcome by the desire to see the child grow. In our view, this attitude plays an important role in the constitution of primary repression. The study of a particularly instructive case has shown us (Fain & Kreisler, 1970) literally the representation by the opposite that merycism constitutes in relation to early asthma. This immediately introduces many complications. We have just seen the censorship of the lover that becomes differentiated from the protective shield initially provided by the mother, and now we are faced with a desire that makes this protective shield regress to the level of that which existed during the pregnancy! Thus, instead of a censorship of the lover, which places the child in the symbolic order, we have a protective shield that seeks to compensate in a particular way for a specific lack experienced by the mother.

To clarify our ideas about these complications, I will make a brief digression into that strange condition known as merycism, while focusing only on the questions that concern us here. Merycism is an unnatural auto-erotic activity, as Soulé has emphasised, which can be regarded either as a true perversion, with organic libido, cathecting the mouth–oesophagus–stomach system, being of a purely erotic nature, or as an infringement of biological laws, which would bring this disorder close to a psychosis. We can in any case, through the exaggeration that lends it a caricatural aspect, separate from this disorder the essential aspects of the auto-erotisms. The authors who have observed it have invariably noted the breakdown in relations with the surrounding environment experienced by these children during their auto-erotic activity, and have even applied the term 'autism'. In fact, this autism only exists during the auto-erotic activity, with young merycists generally preserving strong aptitudes for re-establishing relations with maternal substitutes. From my perspective, I will say that the subject has constituted for the exercise of his erotism a prematurely autonomous protective-shield system that allows a certain narcissistic concentration on the exercise of auto-erotism. What characterises this closed-circuit system is its consumptive quality, with the narcissistic libido constantly allied with the death drive to fuel a pleasure that strives for a discharge towards the zero level. From this alliance also emerges a complex abnormal functioning, as if abnormal capacities to use the body were being released by this isolation. (These actions are already highly complex, certain cases having shown in their organisation the condensation of an oral erotism that is forcibly suppressed by 'psychogenic' vomiting episodes.) In fact, the above description is rather theoretical; the merycist retains amid his activities a certain capacity for narcissistic recharging, his sleep generally remaining good. Whatever the case may be, merycism spectacularly illustrates that a positive exercise of auto-erotism requires the constitution of an autonomous protective-shield system that can create a decathexis of the sensorium for the period in which it occurs. It also shows that the constitution of this protective-shield system in an early mode – because of a certain environmental lack – tends to form an entity that strives towards exhaustion. This is why self-destructive acts sometimes carried out by young insomniacs are in no sense auto-erotic, since the very disorder that characterises these young patients is the total absence of any protective-shield system. These acts are literally fuelled by a constant influx of undifferentiated stimuli. The merycist seems to provide a true demonstration of the splitting of the ego, as described by Klein. He detaches himself completely from his mother, with whom he should at least temporarily still be constituting a fusional unity. In fact, we have introduced in its place in our most recent works the conception of a splitting, not of the ego, a notion that presupposes the existence of an ego from birth, but of the drive. This latter can in fact be satisfied by physical contact with the object or be stimulated auto-erotically to struggle against the negative effects of the object's absence. The drive has been identified as a site of splitting because it seems to occur within the primary identification before the ego is truly constituted. I do not hesitate today to apply to myself the above criticism concerning the term 'splitting'; the description given can just as easily give rise to inaccuracies because it means something different from the term used by Freud.

Already in a first commentary on merycism, comparing this disorder to the *fort–da* game, I demonstrated its self-enclosed, repetitive and ultimately deadly nature. It is obvious that the emergence of such a deformation cannot be due to the mother's metamorphosis into a lover but something different altogether. Such a case does not involve censorship of the lover seeking to get the child to sleep but, instead, the merycist's own censorship of the world around him. The very existence of the 'unnatural' activity shows the mother's incapacity to prevent this development, perhaps a complicit incapacity that indicates that the mother plays a normative role in the child's erotic development. In the course of merycism, a spectacular reversal of the situation occurs: it is the mother who powerlessly witnesses her baby's erotism. It is common to find unconscious maternal manifestations that have helped to establish such a situation, normal auto-erotism – for example, thumb-sucking – having been interpreted by the mother as an actual Oedipal masturbation, incurring a suppression by methods of restraint. I have already indicated that this suppression, which misconstrues the baby's level of libidinal development, is not enough in itself and that it requires to be allied to another disorder incurred by manifestations of rejection. Whatever the case may be, it is still surprising to observe that the projection carried out by the mother, whose misconstruction posits her baby's libidinal evolution as complete, can lead this child into an erotic death. This leads us to re-emphasise the dual nature of the famous mother–child dyad. This duplication plays a vital role in the constitution of these children's fantasies. Here too there are grounds for criticising the concept of splitting.

In summary, then, the merycist child separates from his mother, in contact with whom he experiences a state of uneasiness, and he constructs an autonomous protective shield that notably isolates him from this mother, which enables him to develop in a deformed way an auto-erotic system linking Eros and Thanatos to the point of extinction. This auto-erotism, like any other, struggles against the absence of an object, an absence that is the result of a denial. Let us emphasise immediately that merycism, an auto-erotism born of a denied absence, thus resembles fetishism. This similarity reconciles us with the notion of splitting, since we can add to it the notion of a fetish. In the case of merycism, we can state that this partial activity replaces everything, although at the same time it fortunately retains the capacity to resume contact with objects.

It must be said that something eludes us in merycism. What is it that enables the child to construct such an effective closed system? Everything occurs as if the conflict chose the oral system as a site – the oesophagus–stomach primal cavity is the site that gives rise to the earliest drive relations, this part of the body constituted by the mouth, oesophagus and stomach being the first to be situated as a place in which the external object is perceived, paradoxical as that may seem. The decathected sensorium, however, denies any separation by rejecting any stimulus. Thus, another caricatural aspect takes shape in this caricatural disorder, a separation between the world of the drives, site of the oral drive, and the sensorium, site of stimulation from the external world. From direct observational findings (Spitz, 1955), we can observe that the circuit closes by excluding those very sensory elements that constitute a *Gestalt* with the mouth–oesophagus–stomach drive path: the human face seen during feeding, sensations in the palms of the hands. In a development that exists within normal bounds, the sensations in question affecting sensorimotricity become connected with the drive path, and consequently become capable of providing the elements of a representation. Thus, this pathological example shows the closure of the circuit at two points – one where the auto-erotism fails to correspond to the appearance of a penis bearing the father's desire offstage, a penis to which the mother responds by becoming a lover, in a transformation that comprises the differentiation of a censorship based on the protective shield; the other where the premature resumption of an autonomous protective-shield system closes the exit towards the 'sensory' elements of the *Gestalt* that leads to the 'first organiser' according to Spitz. This indicates a transition-point between the structural viewpoint and genetic observation. Already, with Braunschweig (Braunschweig & Fain, 1971), I have observed that although objectively Spitz (rather than Lewin) is right in demonstrating that the blank screen is not the breast but the mother's face seen during feeding, subjectively he is wrong, for the human face seen opposite does not form part of the breast–faeces–penis symbolic chain. I went even further than this. The human face seen opposite at which the baby smiles – a fact that I previously interpreted as the end of the primitive splitting of the drive, the auto-erotic attitude connecting with an object-representation and then terminating the solitary nature of the drive – attests to a hallucinatory realisation constituted not with this manifest human face but the paternal penis that exists offstage without appearing, which has such an efficacious impact on the mother as to banish her. The hallucinatory realisation that manifestly deploys the human face latently contains a primary goal concerning the penis, whether the baby is a girl or a boy, although this goal is more pronounced in the girl for reasons specific to her (Braunschweig & Fain, 1971).

Because of the denial of maternal absence it permits through a complete invasion of the libidinal field, by transforming a satisfaction that should only be partial and temporary into a definitive goal, I have accorded this abnormal auto-erotic activity the status of a primary fetishism. I believe that here too we can pose the question: might there not exist, less ostentatiously than in merycism, systems of primary fetishisation that are true impasses short-circuiting the symbolic organisation? These systems would manifest every time a splitting occurred and have the function, with potential for success or failure, of denying the disintegrative effects of absence.

As I recall, this commentary began with examples in which the fetishistic representation failed. The characteristics of the failure are indicated by the stark, enduring quality of the sensory impressions. The example of certain cases of temporary arterial hypertension reveals the emergence of a hallucinatory system short-circuiting the dream, re-cathecting during sleep a true primary sensoriality, of which the emergence demonstrated a deficiency in the protective shield. To the failure of the denial corresponds a difficulty in binding the excitation to a representation, and in this regard I have indicated a hiatus between the excitation and the representation that does not manage to bind it. The reason for this difficulty is the mother's inadequate mediation between the undifferentiated stimuli not transformed into the death drive, which not only are silent but impose silence. Our extremely tense patient's hallucination, which wakes him, resembles a sudden invasion of excitations of the kind that appear in the young insomniac as soon as his mother stops rocking him. The reverberation of meaning shows an abortive attempt at representation. This leads us to compare the hiatus to the space that emerges and brings an intolerable excitation when the mother ceases the rocking. This case is symmetrical to that of the merycist who, separated from the external world, then escaping its influence, lives only through a deformed development of an external world situated solely inside his body, a world of external origin, purely drive-related and constituting an end in itself. The right environment certainly exists somewhere between the two, the future outcome being the path of the symbolic order that is potentially present as soon as the couple's sexual desire reappears. But in the meantime? When the mother decathects her child to become the lover again, she only seldom manages, through the intervention of the baby's sleep with which she integrates her death drive, to confer on him an adequate protective shield, and she therefore discovers not only the erogenous zone that will serve to produce auto-erotism, but also the capacity for invasion by stimuli. This constitutes a phenomenon that goes beyond sensoriality, and, while I am using the concept of a primary sensoriality, this is solely in terms of

Freud's view that the reality ego pre-exists the pleasure ego. This reintroduces a supplementary element that both overloads and complicates the economy. This element, if its power exceeds a certain norm, can make the primal scene more traumatic for several reasons:

1. To the specific effects of the primal scene that play on a drive register are added the traumatic stimulus activated by the couple's decathexis of the child.
2. The lack of an adequate protective-shield system or one that is insufficiently differentiated from the censorship of the lover complicates the conditions for exercising auto-erotism.
3. The need to integrate these stimuli will come up against the limits of the binding capacity of auto-erotism.
4. This necessity tends to develop systems that build up at the expense of the representation and to the benefit of motor systems. If the latter predominate, there is a tendency to fetishistic solutions in an impasse that seeks to deny the damage caused by the decathexis. It is difficult to confer an open symbolic significance on such solutions.
5. Pasche has rightly demonstrated that fetishistic solutions are generally only transitory – provided that some means is found of emerging from them. It is therefore likely that a linear evolution is extremely rare and that this evolution is characterised by a series of more or less acrobatic emergences from impasses.

Following these reflections, we are led to postulate a conclusion: in the hiatus that can occur between auto-erotism, intensified by the stimulus, and representation, this hiatus is negatively symbolised: it is the gap, the void, which allows the traumatic impact to pass. This negative symbol is reactivated during the castration complex, while anal symbolism manages in fact to integrate it more or less entirely. It is necessary to understand what can constitute a negative symbol. In our view, it is that which leads to an impasse situated outside the symbolic order. With reference to fetishism, Pasche has shown that the fetish can be developed and refined, while still remaining a part that is affirmed as a whole. I think this is a fact that merits extensive elaboration based on data from associative chains of individuals in analysis. It seems to me that mental development centred on a specialisation of the mind contains a fetishistic core in the sense of a fetishism that I will in fact call primary – that is to say, in relation to a threat of traumatic irruption literally springing up from a hiatus, a disparity between the sum of excitations to be integrated and the representation. To describe as phallic a woman who causes a terror that comes from a series of gaps she induces in the subject by the specific lack of which she is at the origin is the prototype of an intrinsically fetishistic form of reasoning. I see this as the deep origin of the violent clashes between proponents of different psychoanalytic theories, differences that admittedly are then elaborated, just as I also see there the success in psychoanalytic matters of proponents of mediocre psychoanalytic theory. Psychoanalysts are constantly confronted with Freud's genius and cannot help feeling a hiatus or a disparity between their limited knowledge and that of the Viennese master, which reactivates their childhood traumas. This is what explains the success in the psychoanalytic field of very ordinary individuals, individuals who become true fetishes hiding the deep abysses of our deficient understanding, abysses that we fear will give rise to an irruption of traumatic stimuli.

Although I have just shown that I reserve the term 'splitting' for a situation that leads to a denial by fetishisation with all its inherent limitations, I would nevertheless criticise Freud for having led psychoanalysts in relation to fetishism in a direction that, like the fetishism he described, ends in a certain impasse.

Psychoanalysts influenced by Freud's paper on fetishism (1927e) have forgotten what the term fetishism used to mean in the everyday sense. Although officially it comes from the Latin *facticia*, the term 'fetishism' originates from the Portuguese *fatiçao* which, as a result of the pronunciation, is phonetically pronounced *fétichéo*. The Portuguese, who combine tolerance with their wayfaring characteristics, did not behave in the same iconoclastic way as everyone else but deduced, observing primitive tribes, that the idol, fundamentally a symbol, had lost that quality and was God itself. There was therefore a confusion between the symbol and the representation. Thus there was no space left between the symbol and the representation, a space from which Zeus' lightning bolt could have sprung. We can thus begin to understand how the confusion between the symbol and the representation can in some cases assume such force and be sustained by such aggression, since this confusion, through its intrinsic denial, conceals a deficiency in a protective-shield system, a hole in the armour, through which a primary sensoriality could be re-cathected directly in contact with undifferentiated stimuli, attesting the resurgence of a hypersensitive reality ego.

References

Braunschweig, D., & Fain, M. (1970). Intervention sur le rapport de 1970 de A. Green. *Revue Française de Psychanalyse, 34* (8): 5–6.

Braunschweig, D., & Fain, M. (1971). *Eros et Antéros*. Paris: Payot.

Chasseguet-Smirgel J. (1968). Réflexions sur l'envie de pénis [Reflections on penis envy]. *Revue Française de Psychanalyse, 22* (2): 273–278.

Fain, M. (1969). Intervention sur le texte de Sami Ali. *Revue Française de Psychanalyse, 33* (2).

Fain, M., & Kreisler, L. (1970). Discussion sur la genèse des fonctions représentatives, à propos de deux observations pédiatriques. *Revue Française de Psychanalyse, 34* (2).

Freud, S. (1911c [1910]). Psycho-Analytic Notes on an Autobiographical Account of a Case of Paranoia (Dementia Paranoides). *S.E.*, 12: 3.

Freud S. (1926d). *Inhibitions, Symptoms and Anxiety. S.E.*, 20: 87–174.

Freud, S. (1927e). Fetishism. *S.E.*, 21.

Kreisler, L., Fain, M., & Soulé, M. (1967). La clinique psychosomatique de l'enfant. Les états frontières dans la nosologie [The psychosomatic clinic of the child: Borderline states in the nosology]. *Psychiatrie de L'enfant*, *10* (1): 157–198.

Laplanche, J., & Pontalis, J.-B. (1964). Fantasme originaire, fantasmes des origines et origine du fantasme. *Les Temps Modernes*, *215*: 158–182. [Fantasy and the origins of sexuality. *International Journal of Psychoanalysis*, *49* (1968): 1–18.]

Marty, P., & de M'Uzan M. (1963). La pensée opératoire [Operational thinking]. *Revue Française de Psychanalyse*, *27* (Special Issue): 345–356.

Marty, P., M'Uzan, M. de, & David, C. (1963). *L'investigation psychosomatique. Sept observations cliniques* [Psychosomatic investigations: Seven clinical observations]. Paris: Presses Universitaires de France.

Pasche, F. (1965). Notes sur l'investissement [Notes on cathexis]. In *A partir de Freud* [Starting with Freud] (pp. 243–248). Paris: Payot.

Rank, O. (1924). The trauma of birth in its importance for psychoanalytic therapy. *Psychoanalytic Review*, *11* (3): 241–245.

Spitz, R. (1955). The primal cavity – a contribution to the genesis of perception and its role for psychoanalytic theory. *Psychoanalytic Study of the Child*, *10*: 215–240.

Viderman, S. (1970). *La construction de l'espace analytique* [Construction of the analytic space]. Paris: Denoël.

17 THE WORK OF THE NEGATIVE. NEGATIVE HALLUCINATION

André Green

A psychiatrist and full member of the Paris Psychoanalytical Society, **André Green** is a former president of that Society and a former director of the Institute of Psychoanalysis. He was Freud Memorial Professor at the University of London (1979–80). A prolific writer, he has published many books and papers on a great variety of subjects: the affects, borderline states, language in psychoanalysis, literature and art. He has been instrumental in bringing together within the confines of a well-defined metapsychology both the main post-Freudian contributions (Winnicott and Bion) and the various trends of French psychoanalysis, including some of Lacan's most interesting ideas.

Several of Green's books have become classics in their own right; in particular: *Le discours vivant. Une conception psychanalytique de l'affect* (PUF, 1970) [*The Fabric of Affect in the Psychoanalytic Discourse* (Routledge, 1999)]; *Narcissisme de vie, narcissisme de mort* [Life narcissism, death narcissism] (Editions de Minuit, 1983); *La folie privée. Psychanalyse des cas limites* (Gallimard, 1990) [*On Private Madness* (International Universities Press, 1993)]; *Le travail du négatif* (Editions de Minuit, 1993) [*The Work of the Negative* (Free Association Books, 1999)]; *Idées directrices pour une psychanalyse contemporaine* (PUF, 2002) [*Key Ideas for a Contemporary Psychoanalysis* (Routledge, 2005)]; *La lettre et la mort* [Writing and death] (Denoël, 2004), a series of discussions with Dominique Eddé on literature; and in 2007 he wrote a book with the somewhat controversial title *Pourquoi les pulsions de destruction ou de mort?* [Why are there destructive or death drives?] (Panama, 2007).

François Duparc wrote a concise biography of André Green for the series 'Psychanalystes d'aujourd'hui' (PUF, 1996).

An international tribute was paid to him in 2000 via the publication of a book in his honour with papers from several contributors: *Penser les limites. Écrits en l'honneur d'André Green* [Thinking about limits. Essays in honour of André Green] (ed. César Botella; Delachaux et Niestlé, 2000).

The work of the negative[1]

Several years ago I proposed to designate as 'the work of the negative' all the psychic operations of which repression is the prototype and which later gave rise to distinct variations such as negation, disavowal and foreclosure. This expression, borrowed from philosophy, no longer owes anything to its Hegelian origins. Moreover, it has been adopted by numerous analysts. Should the work of the negative be related to the ego alone and its mechanisms of defence? One might think so at a first approach. I would maintain on the contrary that the work of the negative extends to the agencies of the psychic apparatus as a whole. In other words, an analysis of it leads us to distinguish the no of the ego, the no of the super-ego and the no of the id. I shall also envisage the effects of the object's response on the constitution of yes–no relations. These problems are not purely theoretical since they raise technical questions about analysability.

In his article on 'Repression' of 1915, Freud, who envisaged two possible vicissitudes of representation, its disappearance from consciousness when it was conscious or keeping it away from consciousness when it was on the point of becoming conscious, wrote: 'the difference is not important; it amounts to much the same thing as the difference between my ordering an undesirable guest out of my drawing-room (or out of my front hall), and my refusing, after recognising him, to let him cross my threshold at all.' He adds in a note: 'This simile, which is thus applicable to the process of repression, may also be extended to a characteristic of it which has been mentioned earlier: I have merely to add that I must set a permanent guard over the door which I have forbidden this guest to enter, since he would otherwise burst it open.'[2]

The comparison is revealing and comprises several registers. Alongside those aspects we are familiar with, that is, dynamic, topographical and economic (an allusion to the trauma of the door being burst open), its anthropological aspect is particularly striking. Representation is symbolised by the undesirable guest – and repression is a good illustration of the idea of the little man within man – who is subject to other divisions (master of the house and guard), endowed with a power of recognition based on labels (desirable–undesirable) which apply a yes and no logic to them depending on whether they accept or refuse, thus sorting, selecting, orienting like a real Maxwell demon governing particles. Furthermore, the sorting, discrimination and distribution are unconscious. What determines the access of the unconscious into consciousness is itself unconscious. Does such anthropomorphism owe nothing to the model on which repression is built?

---

[1] Due to a lack of space I am obliged to put forward only one argument the justifications for which necessitate a more lengthy treatment. I propose to come back to this on another occasion.
[2] S.E., 14: 153.

In treatment, what has operated as repression appears in the form of resistance. The fundamental rule of not filtering and of not selecting is transgressed consciously and unconsciously. It implies the lifting of moral and rational censure. Yet, contemporary analytic practice enables us to attribute different meanings to repression:

- Resistance may indicate a fear of being judged, condemned or punished. This can range from the threat of the loss of love to the anxiety of mutilation.
- Resistance opposes the danger of disorganisation through a loss of control of speech and through speech which gives rise to a fear of madness.
- Resistance suggests a fear of annihilation consecutive to an unbinding of predominantly destructive drives.

These three examples, among others, can all be interpreted as the expression of the ego's defensive activity. However, they can also be understood as the expression of a no originating from the superego, the ego and even the id. This last point deserves discussion, the unbinding of the drives opposing the formulation of a desire towards an object which is reduced here to its most undifferentiated state.

Now, all of a sudden, the reasons for repression and resistance can be seen more clearly. They have three aims:

- To control the violence of the drives.
- To organise the ego by establishing links, which presupposes investments of a certain constancy, subject to minimal variations.
- To guarantee the object's love and, secondarily, that of the superego.

Repression is therefore inevitable, necessary and indispensable for the structuring of human desire. However, no criterion exists to determine precisely what must be repressed and what can be spared from repression. The result of this is that one always represses too much or too little, just as one resists too well or too badly. The obstacle of the resistances met with in treatment and the analyst's temptation to overcome them, albeit by their analysis, involved a danger of returning to hypnosis. To say to a patient, 'You are resisting!', even in the most subtle way, was not much different from the formula 'You are counter-suggesting' coming from the hypnotist's mouth. Similarly, there is perhaps nothing one can say to a patient presenting a negative therapeutic reaction more traumatising than 'You don't want to change!', whereas he himself has the feeling he cannot do otherwise. In order to avoid this kind of impasse, when Freud was faced with resistance he sometimes resorted to traps. Even if this practice is questionable, we can at least learn certain things from it. He discusses it in his 1925 article on 'Negation': ' "What", we ask, "would you consider the most unlikely imaginable thing in that situation? What do you think was furthest from your mind at that time?" If the patient falls into the trap and says what he thinks is most incredible, he almost always makes the right admission.'[3]

In fact Freud is saying to his patient, 'Since your no is opposed to a near yes which you cannot admit consciously, tell me instead what the no is which is furthest from this near yes but inaccessible.' And he concludes by answering that this no which is the furthest away is the near yes which cannot be admitted.

This example brings into play categories of opposing pairs, some of which are explicit, imaginable–unimaginable, believable–unbelievable, near–far; and others implicit, agreeable (in the sense of what can be accepted)–disagreeable, present–past (to the extent that it is a question of obtaining a piece of repressed unconscious material) and no doubt too, good and evil (recognition can be barred by moral disapproval). Thus the opposition yes–no depends on a number of factors distributed throughout the entire psychic apparatus, from the surface to the depths as well as from the oldest to the most recent.

'A negative judgement is the intellectual substitute for repression', says Freud. This intellectual substitute which is linked to desire is the product of a symbolisation by means of language and an economy which saves energy. The no appears to be a label of repression. But before language and repression itself, 'expressed in the language of the oldest drive impulses' (oral), judgement consists in saying 'I would like to eat that' or 'I would like to spit it out'. Thus there is a translation of an ego language which speaks, into an id 'language' which swallows or spits. There is therefore a no of the id which is expressed through the drive motion. Repression is a psychological mechanism; Freud never fails to remind us of it, whereas what is described on the level of the drives of the id is not, at least to his mind. The question which then arises concerns the relation between the psychological mechanism which is connected with speech and the one which is related to another use of the mouth through oral impulses. In other words, do the statements: 'I would like to eat or I would like to spit out' originate from the id or from an archaic primitive ego? If we follow Freud, since the ego differentiates itself from the id, the archaic primitive ego and the id are scarcely discernible.

I would like to dwell a moment on the destiny of these oral impulses. Eating and spitting out involve on the one hand incorporation (of the object) and, on the other, what I have called excorporation, a mechanism which is prior to projective identification, in my view. I spit out or I vomit. Freud uses a verb which is translated by eject. It is generally understood as an action which puts what is inside outside, bringing us back to the boundary between inside–outside. The postulate of this original boundary is based on the existence of an ego reality at the start which is in a position to detect the internal or external origin of excitations. This hypothesis seems to me to be too costly.

---

[3] *S.E.*, 19: 233.

The excorporation in which I see the prototype of a no of the id in the forms of 'I am spitting out' or 'I am vomiting', does not imply the existence of an object in the space which receives what is expelled. We may even wonder if the expelled products do not disappear in the process. In any case, the identification of the space seems to me to be prior to that of the objects it might contain. (I am thinking of the noticeably hostile atmosphere in certain delusions before the persecutor is designated.) Furthermore, I do not think that we can infer that there is a boundary between inside and outside. All that exists is the idea – if one can put it this way – of expelling as far away as possible. There is no justification for speaking of a 'not-ego' at this stage because the ego–not-ego boundary has not been established. It is the consequences of the expulsion which allow it to be established. Expelling what is bad allows for the creation of an internal space in which the ego as an organisation can come into being, setting up an order founded on the formation of links related to experiences of satisfaction. This organisation facilitates recognition of the object as separate in the space of the not-ego as well as the reunion with it.

But even when this recognition and separation have been achieved, the ego itself is obliged periodically to take over from the work of the negative which formerly only concerned the drives. In order to be able to say yes to oneself, one must be able to say no to the object. This work can only be carried out on two conditions, at least:

- that the object continues to take care of the infant's ego by sparing it what is excessively unpleasant;
- that the object takes the place of the undifferentiated space in order to take in what we designated earlier as excorporation and which now deserves to be called projection, by consenting to be experienced as bad while seeking to transform these projections and return them to the infant. (The mother does not have more belief in the baby's badness than in her own.)

In order for the formation of baby's ego to occur, allowing him to say yes to himself, the mother must accept that he can say no to her. And not only in the form of 'you are bad', but also occasionally 'you don't exist'.

This is manifested in analysis not only by hostile projections onto the analyst but also, of course, onto the mother, at a distance – far off – and ultimately by the exclusion of transference.

Excorporation is an illusion, for how can the psyche get rid of what encumbers it? The object's assistance is needed if it is to be possible. Hitherto, we have only taken into account spatial considerations. But temporal considerations play an equally important role, as Winnicott has shown. If the response is immediate, without delay, symbiotic omnipotence sets in, depriving the infant's ego of the possibility to say no to the object and therefore yes to itself. The idealisation of the maternal object goes hand in hand with the suppression of the subject's own desire. On the other hand, when the delay is too great, it is despair, stamped by the experience of pain, which makes one say no to everything (including oneself). Linking is destroyed, intolerance of frustration is increased and excessive projective identification occurs. The work of the negative takes on the form of a radical exclusion, and the negative aspect of relationships (Winnicott) gains the upper hand. This exclusion probably affects even the drive, before there is any question of Freudian *Verwerfung* or Lacanian foreclosure.

It is only when the object's response comes with a sufficient and tolerable delay and in a form which can be assimilated (the mother's capacity for reverie, Bion), that the infant's ego can say to itself 'it's not wonderful, but it's all right'. And it is from this point on that repression can come into effect. Repression is thus carried out on the model of the object's acceptances and refusals. Freud's anthropomorphic comparison cited at the beginning of these reflections is now more understandable. The little man within man is in fact a little mother. What is pleasant or unpleasant for the ego is based on what is accepted or not accepted by the object. The relation to the object has been internalised, the yes and the no have been introjected. Primal repression establishes the boundary between the *Cs.–Pcs.* on the one hand and the *Ucs.* on the other.

These theoretical remarks arise from clinical experience and analytic technique. For it is by means of the latter that the analyst learns to modulate the timing of his interventions and to offer these in a form which is acceptable to the patient. Maintaining distance from the object and evaluating the period of delay which is tolerable go hand in hand. Between the two extremes of successful repression and rejection (foreclosure or *Verwerfung*), the work of the negative can take intermediate paths such as splitting or disavowal in which recognition and denial, yes and no coexist.

The work of the negative in disavowal cannot simply be characterised by the coexistence of yes and no. For such a coexistence can be conjunctive or disjunctive. When conjunctive, it occurs under the primacy of Eros. The same is true of the transitional object which is and is not the breast or the mother; judgement of existence does not apply to it, any more than it has to be decided if it was created as a subjective object, or found, as an object which is objectively perceived. Regarding spatiality, let us note that it is situated at the intersection of the internal space and the external space in the intermediate area. The intense investment it receives shows that this coexistence is thoroughly positive. When the coexistence is disjunctive, the work of the negative is carried out under the auspices of the destructive drives. This is the case of splitting and disavowal, concerning which some have claimed that it is difficult to distinguish it from foreclosure. The difference from the earlier case is that instead of bringing about a union, the work of the negative separates and obstructs all choice and positive investment. In this case, it is not yes *and* no, but *neither* yes *nor* no. A well-known example of this is the case of the 'Wolf Man' (who 'won't have it' – that is, castration – which, in spite of his sexual performances, is demonstrated in the analyses that came after those he did with Freud), and his tortuous thought processes; 'He always had at least two opinions on the same subject', said one of his therapists. There is nothing in this case which can be linked with obsessional doubt, but, rather, to an incapacity to decide if a thing is good or bad (analysis for example) or again, in his choices of identification and his symptoms, whether he is a man or a woman. But in this case the ego, paralysed by ambivalence in its relation to psychic reality as well as material reality, can only accept the coexistence if it can respond with neither a yes nor a no. This response takes its roots in drive life. What is expressed at the level of the ego is simply a reflection of this (what I have called bi-logic). The responses of its objects have doubtless only aggravated the situation. They have been marked neither by a capacity to receive its destructive projections by returning them in an acceptable form nor by the decision to confront it, on another level, with a structuring 'no'. They have preferred to play the role of a prosthesis upholding the disavowal of castration, right to the end. As far as we know, at least. Yet the example of the 'Wolf Man' is not unique. Many analysands presenting a negative therapeutic reaction reveal in the transference that the agonising struggle between yes and no is a vitiation of the work of the negative. What they show us in fact is that the refusal to choose, the refusal to believe, the refusal to invest is nothing other than the refusal to live.

Negative hallucination

Let us consider two examples taken from Freud. They concern a psychotic structure without hallucinatory clinical phenomena, but have the advantage of allowing us to compare an isolated hallucination and a central dream in the same subject. You will have guessed that I am alluding to the 'Wolf Man', to his hallucination of the severed finger and to his wolf dream. Concerning the hallucination of the severed finger, the 'Wolf Man' recounts: 'I was playing in the garden near my nurse, and was carving with my pocket-knife in the bark of one of the walnut trees that come into my dream as well.[4] Suddenly, *to my unspeakable horror*, I noticed that I had cut through the little finger of my (right or left?) hand, so that it was only hanging on by its skin. I felt no pain, but great fear. I did not venture to say anything to my nurse, who was only a few paces distant, but I sank down on the nearest seat and sat there *incapable of casting another glance at my finger*. At last I calmed down, took a look at the finger, and saw that it was entirely uninjured.' Freud interprets this event by comparing it with the experience of Tancred as told by Tasso, and relates the hallucinatory wound to the mother's haemorrhages which are evocative of castration. But

---

[4] Here, Freud inserts a note: 'Cf. "The Occurrence in Dreams of Material from Fairy Tales".' In telling the story again on a later occasion he made the following correction. 'I don't believe I was cutting the tree. That was a confusion with another recollection, which must also have been hallucinatorily falsified, of having made a cut in a tree with my knife and of *blood* having come out of the tree.' S.E., 17: 85.

immediately afterwards, he links the origin of the hallucination to a story that a female relation of his had been born with six toes and that the extra one had immediately been chopped off with an axe.

If we analyse this fragment, many associations will come to mind. First, the interpolation of a false recollection, the cutting of the tree, which belongs to another context 'hallucinatorily falsified'. This false recollection fills a void. For what the young child was doing and thinking at that moment, we cannot know, and so this is the first blank. Be that as it may, this false recollection forms a bridge between the memory of the hallucination of the severed finger and the walnut trees in the wolf dream. Then, in a state of inexpressible terror, comes the hallucination of the severed finger. Now what is remarkable in this hallucination *is not the sight of blood – there is no question of that – but the void which separates the finger from the hand so that it was only attached by a fragment.* No pain, but fear: the feeling of pain is replaced by that of fear. A moment of silence follows, then a collapse, and an incapacity to cast the slightest glance at the finger . . . Finally, there is a return of normal perception and feeling, along with a state of calm. The origin of the event shows us that the *one too few* which threatens the hand finds its source in the *one extra*, the relation's sixth toe which was chopped off with an axe, an instrument used for felling trees. Here we come across an enigma relating to the drawing of the dream in which five wolves are represented, whereas the account of the dream mentions six or seven (six or seven: one extra, in fact two in relation to the drawing, whereas compared with the dream the drawing represents one too few, at least). *The hallucination of the severed finger is preceded by the negative hallucination of the extra finger hidden in the hallucinatory content; the latter simply positivises, on the basis of this negative hallucination, an amputation which has already been carried out on the level of thought.* The traces of it are: the void which separates the finger from the hand, the absence of pain, the silence, the state of collapse and above all the inability to look.[5]

Now let us turn to the dream. The fairy tale forms a bridge between them. I shall not expand further on this dream which has already been analysed at length by generations of psychoanalysts following Freud. I shall simply cite the opening sentence: 'I dreamt that it was night and that I was lying in my bed.'

---

[5] Here I would like to add a personal observation. A patient suffering from infantile asthma which resulted in strengthening a repression of infantile amnesia spent endless nights suffering during which she would scrutinise the deserted landscape and the starry sky waiting for daybreak which would bring relief. She had no memory of her parents' bedroom, which was adjacent to the one where she spent her sleepless nights. During her analysis with me, she told me the following: one morning, seeing that her young son looked worried, she asked him what was troubling him. The child then told her that he had spent a sleepless night because he had had a terrible nightmare. He had dreamed that his head only remained attached to his body by a bit of skin. He had woken up in horror and, gripped by the powerful effect of this dream, he had spent the rest of the night awake, immobilised, for fear that his head might be separated from his body completely. Hence the worried look he still had in the morning. The event was quickly forgotten during the following day. But as a result of the dream, the mother had a skin allergy on her chest.

This is a strange thing: the wolf man dreams that it is night, that is to say that he is dreaming; in his dream he sees the dark night: the invisible. And Freud interprets, not without reason, 'it was night' as a deformation of 'I had been asleep.' This means the dream, obeying the conditions of representability, *imagines* – in the strict sense of the word – the unimaginable, *the non-imaginable in sleep*. The imaginary world of dream imagines the image of blackness where there is an absence of any image. Hence the interpretation of the opening of the window as representing the sleeper waking up: 'Suddenly I woke up *of my own accord*' (my italics). The wolf dream is therefore a dream within the dream, an imaginary dream within the dream of the unimaginable. Then the walnut tree appears with its seven white wolves. For Freud the colour white alludes to the whiteness of the seven goats in the fairy tale which is echoed by the white of his parents' bedclothes and underclothes. This interpretation is undoubtedly right, but it calls for a theoretical commentary.

Bertram Lewin has made us aware of the existence of the dream screen and blank dreams. In his opinion, the dream screen is a visual representation of the sleeper's wish to sleep which is empty, blank, without stimulation. He interprets these blank dreams as a repetition of the fulfilment of the wish to sleep – let us bear in mind that this is the dreamer's ultimate desire according to Freud – in its full form, to fall into a deep sleep after being fed. He believes that we are dealing with a relatively uniform experience, with a physiological basis comparable to a reflex, which is completely independent of the structure of the ego; consequently, any idea which suggests that the baby is defending itself against something is out of place. We might wish to discuss with Lewin whether the representation of the blank is necessarily related to the after-image of the breast; in any case, what is fundamental is the representation of the absence of representation which deep sleep implies.

These remarks thus lead me to insist on the *constituting structure of negative hallucination*, or to be more exact, *on its containing function of representation*. Negative hallucination is not a pathological phenomenon. It is not the absence of representation as is suggested by the absence of the image in the mirror, but the *representation of the absence of representation*. Negative hallucination is the theoretical concept which is the precondition for any theory of representation, whether it is dreams or hallucination which is concerned. Undoubtedly dreams and hallucination cannot be superimposed. Negative hallucination is their common matrix. In psychosis, hallucination has to be related not only to wish-fulfilment but to *wishful thoughts*, as I argued with J. L. Donnet in *L'enfant de ça*, where we described *blank psychosis* as a fundamental[6] psychotic kernel. I can only refer readers to it. I would simply point out that structured thought is only established in discontinuity and that this structuring discontinuity involves, in the spaces, the blank which constitutes any chain of thought. In

---

[6] J. L. Donnet & A. Green, *L'enfant de ça* [The child of that/of the id] (Paris: Minuit, 1973).

psychosis, this blank is materialised by the *blank thought* whose empty space is urgently filled by hallucination, occupying the space with drive offshoots.

Let us take another well-known example: President Schreber. Fortunately, we have access both to Freud's work and its unabridged source, the President's *Memoirs*.[7] Freud rightly notes the often-repeated observation, one should say the leitmotif, of the *Memoirs* which is the withdrawal of divine rays which Schreber attracts in an almost magnetic way by his supernatural powers of attraction. But what he then describes in great despair is the emptiness which he feels. 'Every time that my intellectual activities ceased, God jumped to the conclusion that my mental faculties were extinct and that the destruction of my understanding (the idiocy), for which He was hoping, had actually set in, and that a withdrawal had now become possible.'[8] It is necessary to follow Schreber's developments in order to see how in fact he carries out an inversion of psychic events: the withdrawal of the divine rays is the repetition of the emptiness which precedes the hallucinatory phenomenon, an emptiness which is replaced by a supernatural erotic power. This calls for a detailed analysis, which I will undertake on another occasion. But reading the *Memoirs* has other surprises in store for us. There has been a constant tendency to confuse – and this continues to be the case – two kinds of data: the first relate to *chaos* to which Schreber's delusion attempts to restore the Order of Things through healing; the second concern the nothingness of which chaos is never more than *the least imaginable evil*, albeit at the sacrifice of thought. *It is of this nothingness that negative hallucination is the sign and positive hallucination the symptom. The voluptuousness of the soul is nothing other than the ghost of the soul-murder condemning it to narcissism by pushing it to homosexuality, as a temptation to meet up again with the same, who is lost.* With regard to paranoid psychoses Freud says, 'Paranoia decomposes just as hysteria condenses.'[9] One might add: hallucination decomposes whereas dreams condense. What this division of hallucination amounts to is the positivising of negative hallucination which transforms the zero into two, short-circuiting the subject's unity, albeit illusory. Nothing, not even God, who is responsible for the world's unity, can escape division into two according to Schreber. And when at the end of the *Memoirs* he seems only to be one, it is so that Schreber can affirm that henceforth God, the saviour, cannot do without him. The hallucinations are the creations – in the strict sense of the word – the children of Schreber's mind. Generation is found both in Schreber's semantics as well as in his syntax. Negative hallucination is its precondition.

Freud understands this well and writes:

> The distinctive character of paranoia (or of dementia paranoides) must be sought for elsewhere [than in the paternal complex] – namely, in the

---

[7] *Memoirs of My Nervous Illness* (London: Dawson, 1955).
[8] *S.E.*, 12: 25.
[9] Ibid., p. 49.

particular form assumed by the symptoms; and we shall expect to find that this is determined, not by the nature of the complexes themselves, but by the mechanism by which the symptoms are formed or by which repression is brought about.[10]

In the end, his analysis leads him to posit an ultimate stage in the various propositions relating to delusion (concerning which linguistic conclusions have been drawn which go beyond the bounds of our subject here), 'I do not love at all – I do not love anyone', for which Freud substitutes 'I love only myself.' But this last statement is only a minimal step back from the earlier one, which is the basis of negative hallucination. Thus projection is simply the reaction against chaos to which the threat of nothingness is subordinated. That is, the abolition of the inside makes room for the return of what is outside.

Yet we would scarcely be justified in allotting negative hallucination with the essential function we have attributed to it without evidence to substantiate it. This proof is difficult to provide since the psychic phenomenon we are talking about originates in what is negativised and therefore not easily accessible to examination. Nonetheless, the strangest aspect of these negativising phenomena is that they generally manage to represent themselves in the form of discreet signs. The rays are obliged to go to Schreber because their 'thoughts are lacking'.[11] It is indeed this projection of emptiness requiring to be filled which underlies the state of bliss. But we have to consider the representation even of this constitutive blank which materialises against the background on which all figures appear. So, when Schreber finds himself prey to the 'frightening miracles' by which he is persecuted, he counter-attacks by becoming in turn the agent of similar miracles: 'I can even provoke the frightening miracles or something very like it: if I put my hand in front of a white surface, perhaps the white-painted door of my room or the white glazing of the stove, I can see very peculiar distortions of shadows obviously caused by certain changes in the light rays of the sun.' And he adds, protesting, not without reason, 'I am quite certain that these phenomena are not only my subjective sensations ("hallucinations" in the sense of Kraepelin's psychiatry), as with every frightening miracle my attention is particularly drawn to it by directing my gaze (turning my eyes).'[12]

Thus Schreber sees himself in turn as a psychiatrist, correcting Kraepelin. We could almost be taken in if we were not careful. For although he is quite right to distinguish the production of his frightening miracles from 'visual hallucinations', since he recognises himself to be the agent of this visual production and not subjected to its effects, he risks leading us astray by directing our attention, just as he directs his gaze, to the positivity of the phenomenon, to

---

[10] Ibid., p. 59.
[11] *Memoirs of My Nervous Illness* (London: Dawson, 1955), p. 207.
[12] Ibid., p. 190.

the form rather than its background. For it is thanks to this 'white surface' that the phenomenon can occur, this screen whose existence we are unaware of. At the cinema, the film makes us forget that without it there would be nothing for us to see. What is projected, then, is not the figures of the imaginary world as psychoanalysis has long believed, i.e., fantasies, but *processes*. To be more exact, these imaginary figures are mimes and figures of thought. Freud had caught a glimpse of this, but only a glimpse, when he wrote at the end of his study, 'Since I neither fear the criticism of others nor shrink from criticising myself, I have no motive for avoiding the mention of a similarity which may possibly damage our libido theory in the estimation of many of my readers. Schreber's "rays of God", which are made up of a condensation of the sun's rays, of nerve-fibres, and of spermatozoa, *are in reality nothing else than a concrete representation and projection outwards of libidinal investments; and they thus lend his delusions a striking conformity with our theory*.'[13]

Thus the function of hallucination which divides the mind is to condense external perceptions (sun rays), bodily representations (nerve-fibres) and sexual productions (spermatozoa), that is to say, to give a hallucinated representation in the positive form of the negative hallucination of thought. This being so, the delirious patient and the analyst cease to be radically different from each other; the first represents what the other has to content himself with thinking abstractly. Each of them makes use of the negative in his own way; the delirious patient positivises it, the analyst negativises it a second time in order to represent not thought, but meaning. A bridge thrown between the two allows them to meet mid-way, i.e., the dream which is projected onto the blank screen of sleep.

Editors' added bibliography

Donnet, J. L., & Green, A. (1973). *L'enfant de ça* [*The child of the id*]. Paris: Minuit.
Freud, S. (1915). Repression. *S.E.*, 14.
Freud, S. (1925). Negation. *S.E.*, 19.
Schreber, D. P. (1903). *Memoirs of My Nervous Illness*. London: Dawson, 1955.

---

[13] *S.E.*, 12: 78. My italics.

18 WORKING AS A DOUBLE[1]

César Botella and Sára Botella

> **César and Sára Botella,** both of whom are child and adult psychoanalysts in private practice, are full members of the Paris Psychoanalytical Society. They are particularly well-known for broadening our conceptions of how the mind works within the analytic session and contributing some original ideas to that functioning. They introduced the concept of the hallucinatory dimension, defined as the spontaneous and permanent tendency of the activity of the unconscious. Their innovative idea of the 'analyst's work of figurability' as a means of gaining access to the non-representable aspect of trauma, particularly in borderline states, is highly regarded.
>
> Several of their papers have been published in a book with the title *La figurabilité psychique* (Delachaux et Niestlé, 2001) [*The Work of Psychic Figurability: Mental States without Representation* (Routledge, 2005)]. In 1983 they received the Maurice Bouvet prize for their paper 'On the Auto-Erotic Deficiency of the Paranoiac'.

> Psyche is extended; knows nothing about it.
> Freud, 1941f [1938]

We do not doubt the importance of the close relationship between transference and countertransference forming the central axis of the analysis in any treatment. However, in this chapter, we will primarily be concerned with elucidating the existence of certain psychic processes that are covered over most of the time by the transference–countertransference dynamic. We shall also be trying to identify situations where a shared complicity – frequently an unconscious homosexual complicity – between the two protagonists of the

---

[1] The title in French is 'Le travail en double'. This chapter is based on an article of 1984, 'L'homosexualité inconsciente et la dynamique du double en séance', *Revue Française de Psychanalyse*, 4. It was revised and extended in 1995, 'La dynamique du double en séance', in *Monographies de la Revue Française de Psychanalyse*. [*Trans.*]

session impedes the emergence of a certain mode of relating that, owing to its unusual or strange nature, is experienced as disturbing or even disorganising. A feature of this mode of relating is that an area of the psyche of which the subject was hitherto unaware strives to find its way into consciousness. In the first place, our intuition will be based on an idea halfway between scientific hypothesis and fiction, concerning the evolution of Freud's thought and his successive transferences on to Fliess, Jung, then Romain Rolland, and finally Moses, at the end of his life.

The orientation of our research into the notion of homosexual investment may be compared with the attitude Freud (1900a) recommended to analysts in a footnote of 1925 in relation to the dream:

> I used at one time to find it extraordinarily difficult to accustom readers to the distinction between the manifest content of dreams and the latent dream-thoughts. . . . The need to interpret it would be ignored. But now that analysts at least have become reconciled to replacing the manifest dream by the meaning revealed by its interpretation, many of them have become guilty of falling into another confusion which they cling to with equal obstinacy. They seek to find the essence of dreams in their latent content and in so doing they overlook the distinction between the latent dream-thoughts and the dream-work. . . . It is the *dream-work* which creates that form, and it alone is the essence of dreaming – the explanation of its peculiar nature.
>
> (Freud, 1900a, p. 506 n.)

More than the content, manifest or latent, it is the 'work of homosexual transference' that is of interest to us here.

The evolution of Freud's thought and the double

Let us tackle this 'work of homosexual transference' at work in every treatment by drawing the now classic parallel between Freud's homosexual transference onto Fliess and the discovery of psychoanalysis. Notwithstanding Jones's different point of view, we imagine that Fliess loved more the man Freud than his ideas, that he loved him above all with an erotic investment and that his ideas represented for Fliess an elegant finery rather than the fundamental reason for his friendship. Having said that, Freud's homosexual investment of Fliess was more than an end in itself, a means of making Fliess a double in the service of the blossoming of his thought. Fliess's libidinal gaze, the response of the double nourishing Freud's narcissism, enabled the latter to throw himself headlong, without fear, into the auto-erotic movement inherent to all original thought. It may be said that Fliess represented a sort of detour via reality, a reality test, a materiality enabling Freud to overcome the fear of vertigo, the fear of the auto-erotic madness of unbridled thought. And yet original thought requires a rupture.

Indeed, the development of Freud's thinking seems to have been a long journey oscillating between gaining reassurance from his investments in 'material' doubles and the need to free himself from them so as to be able to continue to create. Freud knew this very well: 'It seems certain that homosexual love is far more compatible with group ties, even when it takes the shape of uninhibited sexual impulses – a remarkable fact, the explanation of which might carry us far' (Freud, 1921c, p. 141). This is a complex matter, for although the 'materialisation' of the double, with the aid of the hook of homosexuality, offers a protection against the vertigo of thought, the price to be paid is the adhesion, the collage of thought to the double, the sacrifice of differences. And it was the transition from the relationship to a 'material' double, to the relationship to an autonomous, internal double, as a result of analysing homosexuality, that would give Freud's thinking all its originality. *The Interpretation of Dreams* was not born of Freud's homosexual transference towards Fliess; on the contrary, it came into being when he surpassed it by beginning his self-analysis in 1897. Before that, there was the 'Project', reflecting Fliess' biologising outlook. Between the two there was a painful rupture.

Our feeling is that Freud's homosexual dream concerning Fliess, which was repeated several nights in a row during the summer of 1904 when they had fallen out definitively, and regarded in *The Interpretation of Dreams* (Freud, 1900a, p. 145, n. 1) as a hypocritical dream, for it disguises the wish to break up his friendship with Fliess by feigning the contrary, expresses, through its hypocritical homosexuality, a wish other than that of blocking out aggressivity. It attempts to hide the universe of solitude emerging after the disappearance of the 'material' double, to deny the gaping hole opened up by withdrawing his investment from Fliess and to fend against the insufficiency of the internal double. It was an attempt destined to failure. A few weeks later, Freud suffered a psychic disturbance on the Acropolis, which he could only analyse in 1936 in a letter to Romain Rolland, an echo of his investment of Fliess reverberating in the present.[2]

At the end of the year 1911, as he was once again 'absorbed' by the investment of the double, incarnated now by Jung, Freud complained bitterly about the lack of originality in his thinking: 'I always find it hard to conform completely to another's thoughts. . . . I am working hard on the psychogenesis of religion, finding myself on the same track with Jung's "*Wandlungen*"' (letter to E. Jones, 5 November 1911: Jones, 1955, vol. 2, p. 394).

Moreover, it was a fresh attempt to free himself from the 'material' double, by continuing with the analysis of his own homosexuality – after fainting in front of Jung in November 1912, an event that was reminiscent of a similar

---

[2] Nevertheless, Freud lets it be understood in 1927 (*The Future of an Illusion*) that he has already interpreted the disturbance on the Acropolis.

disturbance in front of Fliess in the same place – that would enable Freud to emancipate his thinking. The months that followed saw the birth of a first study of the double ('The "Uncanny"') (editor's note, *S.E.* 17, p. 218; letter to Ferenczi, 12 May 1919: Brabant, Falzeder, & Giampieri-Deutsch, 1993–2000) not published until much later (1919h), the 'Theme of the Three Caskets' (1913f), the fourth and final part of *Totem and Taboo* 'which will perhaps hasten my breach with Jung' (letters to E. Jones, 9 April 1913, and Ferenczi, 8 May 1913: Jones, 1955, vol. 2, p. 396) and the first approach at a study of Moses ('The Moses of Michelangelo', 1914b), constituting the ferment of a future crisis. Moreover, as a result of being released from the double Jung/Fliess, Freud was able to go beyond Fliess' biological concept of periodicity in favour of the psychic compulsion to repeat – 'Fausse Reconnaissance ("déjà raconté") in Psycho-Analytical Treatment' (1914a) and 'Remembering, Repeating and Working-Through' (1914g) – and in October 1913 (Jones, 1955, vol. 2, 116), with a fervour comparable to that of *The Interpretation of Dreams*, to conceive of the complete draft of his text 'On Narcissism: An Introduction' (1914c), which represented a radical revision of his theory.

When, at the end of his life, Freud reinvested Moses, he found his thinking was once again impeded. He was assailed by doubt, 'the historical novel won't stand up to my own criticism. I need more certainty', he wrote to Arnold Zweig on 6 November 1934. One month later, on 16 December, he was discouraged: 'Don't say any more about the Moses book. The fact that this, probably my last creative effort, should have come to grief, depresses me enough as it is' (E. L. Freud, 1970, p. 98). The courage and certitude he sought did not come through scientific discoveries but through his relationship with Romain Rolland, the least 'material' of his doubles (they only met once). With regard to the pacifist writer admired for qualities Freud could equally apply to himself – his 'love of truth', his 'courage as a thinker' (1936a, p. 239) – he was finally able to tackle, 32 years later, the gaping hole opened up by the 'dematerialisation' of the double Fliess and to analyse his disturbance on the Acropolis. The fragment of self-analysis, constituting his open letter to Romain Rolland in January 1936, freed Freud further from his passive homosexual position towards the father and allowed him to escape from the impasse of Moses by transforming the 'founding father' (who had faced him with 'quite special difficulties – internal doubts as well as external obstacles') into an internal double (a text in which the themes of uncanniness and the double appear again).

Freud was then in a position, in the summer of 1936, to rewrite his work on Moses, and to abandon himself at last, without fear, to a relationship with an internal double. His thinking was now able to function through perceptual identity providing the much wished for certitude of the soundness of his views. From the materiality of his homosexuality, Freud had moved on to a sense of assurance in his psychic functioning. A vast work of figurability, on the model of an internal mirror work, with reflected images, led Freud to 'the perception of historical truth', arousing in him the intimate conviction of the historical reality of his intuitions. The 'truth' was no longer only 'external', material, following the logic of reflections governed by secondary processes, but 'internal', intimate, arising from the force of the impact of perception awakened by a work of figurability, the only means of awakening external truth.

We believe that this new relation to Moses, via the intermediary of Romain Rolland, awoke in Freud hitherto relegated – and not 'dried up' – psychic possibilities, and that the culmination in the perception of the 'historical truth', in intimate convictions, released a new dynamic of thought, enlightened Freud and led him to fresh perspectives on the analyst–analysand relationship. We see evidence of this in the change that occurred in Freud between his two technical writings of 1937. The new relation to Moses enabled Freud, over a period of a few months, an interval during which he finished *Moses* (E. L. Freud, 1970; Freud, 1939a [1937–39]), to move from the conception of the biological bedrock, of which the 'repudiation of femininity' (Freud, 1937c, p. 250) is part, limiting the possibilities of the analytic process and the action of the analyst, to that of 'Constructions in Analysis' (published in December 1937), where the analyst is no longer a person handicapped by the weight of biology, the limits of secondary processes and the recollection of memories but, on the contrary, by virtue of his psychic functioning alone, can bring the treatment to its resolution. A few months after his text on the impossibility of terminating an analysis, Freud put forward an idea, which, it seems to us, was revolutionary – namely, that the conviction aroused in the analysand by the work of the analyst 'achieves the same therapeutic result as a recaptured memory'. He then added: 'The problem of what the circumstances are in which this occurs and of how it is possible that what appears to be an incomplete substitute should nevertheless produce a complete result – all of this is matter for a later enquiry' (Freud, 1937d, p. 266). From thereon, analysis could no longer be considered simply as a work of remembering.

Freud's thought, then, re-emerged invigorated by a mode of functioning involving an internal double during the study on Moses; a mode of functioning that gave him the certitude that the analyst's intuitions through perceptual identity can contain the psychic 'truth' of the analysand. This is possible – and herein lies our thesis – when this work of the analyst, consisting notably of figurability, originates in community with the analysand's psychic functioning. The conviction, emerging initially in the analyst, in reality belongs to both. *The conviction of today is no longer the suggestion of yesterday, but the product of a common work.*

The analyst's work of thinking, as we imagine its evolution in Freud, oscillates during the analytic encounter between the homosexual transference–countertransference dynamic, revealing the history of the analysand's infantile neurosis and the dynamic of the double through perceptual identity, and is directly in tune not with the analysand's mechanisms and unconscious phantasies – as is customary in analytic work – but with their weak spots, opening up flaws, gaping holes, in his functioning. This mode of thinking reveals, in particular, aspects of the analysand's infantile history with which it has not been possible to work; hence its importance, its necessity, in the analyses of borderline cases. As this mode of thinking is obscured most of the time by the unconscious homosexual dynamic and the efforts of the preconscious ego to avoid it because it is a source of feelings of uncanniness, we call it *functioning or working as a double* ('*travail en double*').

Florian

The following case is an extreme scenario, involving a turbulent and, fortunately, rather rare session, whose analytic understanding requires us to consider a certain number of facts and mental processes operating in the analyst, which are the consequence and reflection of 'flaws', of the absence of any possibility of intelligibility on the analysand's part.

It was an apparently ordinary neurosis that brought Florian into analysis, but at certain moments of the regression, originating in the analytic situation, his system of neurotic defences proved insufficient and he was forced to use means of coping other than those characteristic of neurosis.

At the beginning, as at the end of each session, Florian was constantly observing the analyst, not in a mistrustful way, but, one might say, without sufficient conflict, without any inhibition. His expression was neither curious nor guilty, but seemed to be clinging to his perception of the analyst. Once he was lying down, Florian would cling to the perception of a noise, an object, a light, or whatever and would then construct rational associations and commentaries in connection with them. This was how he accomplished his work in the session while, at the same time, his muscles would tighten up to the point of causing him pain. Rediscovering his muscular tension and clinging to a perception were the mechanisms Florian used less as a defence to avoid a possible emergence of repressed ideas than a means of survival against emptiness, against the disorganising effect of losing his perception of the analyst.

In the session prior to the one we shall be discussing in detail, Florian related a dream, which was a rather rare occurrence. '*We are together . . . you are going to have a shower . . . I don't follow you*', but he did not bring any associations. Being a man, the analyst's associations naturally suggested themes of communal showers between men. He said vaguely to himself something like: Florian is beginning to emerge from a regressive state, from an overly archaic mode of relating; perhaps this dream, with its homosexual content, represents a turning point in his analysis and foreshadows the alleviation of a lateral investment in operation from the beginning. For, the day after the first meeting, Florian had formed a passionate friendship with a man who had some points in common with him, i.e. with a 'material' double.

This dream was the culminating point of a movement in the treatment. And yet the analyst had a barely perceptible, almost intangible feeling, alerting him to the presence in his analysand of another universe sustaining his economy. This was perhaps due to Florian's readiness to relate his dream and to the analyst's satisfaction; or alternatively, it may have been due to the homosexual countertransference that became manifest slightly too easily, too hastily.

In the next session, Florian did not need to go looking for perceptions; they came to him on a massive scale: 'I saw you this morning . . . You were on the Boulevard Saint-Michel!' (The analyst had indeed been on the Boulevard Saint-Michel that morning, but what Florian had not noted was that the analyst was accompanied by his wife.) A few minutes of silence followed. Then, strangely enough, Florian was seized with doubt: 'It was you that I saw, wasn't it?' With intervals of silence, the sense of doubt continued, becoming more accentuated, accompanied by rising anxiety: 'I thought I saw you . . . I did, didn't I? I'm not sure any more if I saw you . . . You were wearing dark glasses, weren't you?' He was increasingly tense, anxious, then gave up: 'I don't know any more if I saw you or not . . . You were wearing dark glasses, weren't you?'

Meanwhile, the impressions emerging from what Florian had been saying aroused in the analyst an increasingly sustained feeling of 'derealisation'. He was struck by the discrepancy between the embarrassing picture of himself that was being imposed on him as he was listening to the analysand and the pleasant memory that he had of his morning, a sunny morning on which he had been out for a relaxing walk. Surreptitiously, he was infiltrated by an image accompanied by a word that did not come from the analysand and one he did not normally use: 'hieratic'.

His work of figurability could be summed up with the phrase: 'hieratic ego with dark glasses'. Vague thoughts came to him; surprisingly, like the analysand's, they were shrouded in doubt: 'Dark glasses . . . but do we say dark glasses? Don't we say sunglasses? Dark glasses – the glasses used by a blind man . . .? It's strange, dark glasses . . . Ah, glasses for mourning!'

'Hieratic ego? What does hieratic mean? Solemn? Is the image solemn? It's more rigid than solemn. Rigid ego . . . Dead!? . . . A living corpse . . . Ego, menacing and indestructible like the living dead in the film of the same title[3] and, at the same time, on the point of turning me into dust.'

A struggle was going on in the analyst, although he was barely conscious of it: his narcissism held on firmly to his pleasant recollection of the morning, but it was as if there was a force resisting it. Under the influence of what the analysand had told him, a sinister image of the morning forced itself on him, stuck to him like the shadow of his own experience. He was prey to a double self-representation: 'Relaxed-ego, hieratic-ego', the first of which, only, was recognised as belonging to him, as something familiar, whereas if the figuration

---

[3] The title in French is *Les morts-vivants*, and in English *The Night of the Living Dead* (1968), directed by George A. Romero. [*Trans.*]

'hieratic-ego' had not been controlled by a diurnal ego but produced by the regressed ego of the sleeping state, it would have had all the characteristics of a nightmare. Two representations, then, depicting in fact two parallel modes of work in the same psyche.

The analyst got himself out of this state by means of humour. The terrifying living corpse with dark glasses assumed a peaceful, relaxed appearance, sunbathing like any other holidaymaker. A corpse on vacation! Now he was able to laugh! The analyst's black humour clearly enabled him to recover. It was a triumph for his narcissism trying to save the unity of his identity at that moment, a way of making the incompatible double representation evolve towards a compromise solution, a condensation, in which the pleasant nature of his memory could link up with, and overcome, the horror of the nightmare.

But Florian went on speaking, and the analyst's pleasure associated with his note of humour did not last very long. It was as though listening to the analysand was drawing him once again towards a world of terror. And when the analyst heard Florian say again in an intransmissible, flat voice 'Dark glasses . . . You had dark glasses?' he felt his nightmare welling up again. There followed a heavy silence, longer, more pregnant than usual, which was interrupted by the analyst, practically without his realising it, by a questioning mumble. Erm? 'I don't know any more if I saw you or not . . .' said Florian; and he added the astonishing formula: 'I don't know any more if I saw you . . . I am looking for you in the image and I can't find you any more.'

In other words, the analyst had disappeared in Florian's hallucinatory memory. Can such a withdrawal of investment from the representation of the object be qualified as a negative hallucination? What is certain is that at the same time as this psychical phenomenon took place in Florian, there occurred in the analyst a work of figurability in the form of a nightmare. Are there not grounds for thinking, then, on the basis of this clinical observation, that there is a correspondence between the void of the analyst's disappearance from the analysand's 'image' and the fullness of the means of figuration employed by the analyst's nightmare? Further, that the analyst's nightmare is the counterpart, the complement, the positive of the analysand's negative hallucination? And moreover that the analyst's psyche served as a 'darkroom' revealing what could only be inscribed negatively in the analysand?

Once he had recounted his hallucination of the absence, Florian calmed down a bit and then recalled the dream of the session before. The analyst had forgotten his nightmare; he was only too happy to turn his thoughts to the shower! Florian said to him: 'If I don't follow you into the shower, it is because something prevents me.' And quite naturally, the analyst was on the verge of making an intervention on the subject of homosexuality. Suddenly, as if it was an ordinary session, repression took over again as in the case of a usual negative Oedipal complex. But, simultaneously, and almost imperceptibly, he had a vague feeling he was being baited by his analysand, and so he kept silent. Then Florian did not know what more to add on the dream or what to talk about.

Perhaps he felt frustrated by the fact that the analyst was not saying anything. 'Shall I tell you about my duty period [he had been on duty at the hospital] . . . Since I have nothing else . . . I had three deaths.' The words came out brutally, bluntly and the forgotten nightmare came back to the analyst equally brutally: three deaths; three weekly sessions. Then Florian spoke about an elderly couple, former deportees; the widow had particularly irritated him because he felt she had been relieved by her husband's death; although, as he had cancer, it was better for him that he had died. 'It was perfectly obvious that she did not want to follow him', commented Florian. The idea immediately sprang to the analyst's mind: 'Ah! The point is that he didn't want to follow me into the shower either . . . into death!' The analyst then had the impression that the whole session was falling into place and acquiring meaning. 'Following me into the shower', the negative hallucination, and 'hieratic-ego' were thus connected by the notion of death. The analyst now understood his intuition that the analysand's homosexual transference was a lure and how his own homosexual countertransference, denying Florian's destructiveness, suited him. Destructiveness was the kingpin holding together the negative hallucination and the nightmare. Operating against this world of ego disorganisation, of terror, were homosexual investments, in both analysand and analyst, functioning as a lifebelt.

While Florian was speaking about deportation, the idea of death in the shower took on a terrifying dimension for the analyst; and, as Florian, whose infantile history had no connection with the Nazi horror, returned immediately to the dream, the analyst heard himself saying: 'The shower is a gas chamber.'

The analyst's *work as a double* (*travail en double*) ended here. He was finally able to formulate in words what, until then, had only been possible to grasp through affects and images. His words rendered the colour of his nightmare and finally gave Florian's foreclosed affects, and his nightmare that had remained blank, the right to exist. Heavily charged with visual imagery, expressed through perceptual identity, the intervention led to liberating, violent sobbing from Florian, which he was unable to control during the rest of the session and with a great deal of difficulty once he was on his feet again.

This opening up of the containing dyke against affects seemed to be closer to the economic solution of a straightforward discharge than to a symbolic meaning of a hysterical order. And if one accepts the idea that Florian's noisy sobbing was the echo – albeit somewhat out of step – of his own affects, which until then had been foreclosed in him, but which, contrariwise, caused the analyst to have a nightmare, is there not good reason for thinking that two psyches were necessary in order to construct a single psychic object?

Theoretical and clinical commentaries

The latent content of Florian's dream calls for some reflection. Do the words 'I don't follow you' or, to be more precise, the negation of 'I follow you', really represent a repression of homosexuality, or, rather, are they a sign, along with the negative hallucination, of the difficulty of homosexual investment, and even ultimately of the difficulty of being able to invest the object in any real way? It is as though Florian were caught between the need to invest the analyst as a narcissistic, homosexual double and his terror of losing his boundaries in doing so, of passing over on to the other side of the mirror. In a later session, he was finally able to express this drama himself in words, to condense it in a succinct phrase: 'Either I take interest in you and forget myself entirely, or I negate you.'

From the point of view of analytic technique, one may consider that, in the initial period of the session, the absence of any intervention by the analyst concerning the dream was judicious. Not only because the dream represented the return towards the analyst of libido that had hitherto been lost in a lateral movement, in a passionate friendship with a double, but also because it was the first time that homosexuality had appeared clearly in the material of the treatment. By the same token, should he not perhaps have intervened when the analysand began to doubt his memory, to depersonalise himself? Instead of letting himself be carried away by Florian's state, and accompanying him in his regression, instead of identifying with him to the point of becoming his reflection, his complement, instead of functioning as a double, should the analyst not, for instance, when his analysand became depersonalised, have simply recalled the dream of the session before? That is to say, should he not have intervened as closely as possible to the ego by giving, for instance, an interpretation such as: 'If you are hesitating about whether you saw me or not, it may be because the possibility of meeting me outside the session was the equivalent for you of following me into the shower'? He might then have added: 'Just as when you were a child, you both wanted to take a shower with your father, and yet were afraid of doing so.' Or he might have said something about the denial of the primitive scene. Such interpretations were available to the analyst and would certainly have had the virtue of reducing Florian's anxiety. The latter would have disappeared the moment the analyst had named it, had given the disarray a meaning, a content. Such an interpretation would have avoided Florian's distress at the same time as stopping the uncanniness and the retrogressive course of the analyst's thinking; it would have avoided the analysand's negative hallucination as well as the analyst's nightmare. An intervention of this sort would surely have had a soothing effect, but our reproach is that attributing a homosexual meaning would have suffocated the material which led to the association 'shower–gas', revealing a particularity of Florian's structure, of the drama of his impossible homosexual quest. It was the figuration of this world of homosexuality, a disorganised world, a source of terror, which made it possible to get the analytic process moving again at its true conflictual level. In fact, the sudden confrontation in reality with a primitive scene overwhelmed, as a result of its intensity, the precarious interplay of Florian's Oedipal investments. The dark glasses may certainly be seen as representing his castrating wishes towards the analyst and may be likened to the 'widow', representing a coveted Oedipal mother, but the investment of these representations was unable to resist the economic/dynamic situation that had been triggered. The flaw in Florian's secondary auto-erotism, with its repercussions on the constitution of his alterity, meant that his transference desires could not be organised and the analyst could not be invested either as a loved father or as a feared rival, a 'sandman', or one who 'tears out eyes', symbolising castration. Florian was thus subjected to such a disorganising level of tension, to such a destructive experience, that he would try to get out of it, if he could, by decathecting the analyst and the analysis.

Now we can imagine that on seeing his analyst in the street (who, consequently was no longer invested with the same narcissistic characteristics in duplicate; he was simply an external object), and while referring to him as he told the story, a sense of danger was awakened in Florian faced with the picture of the analyst who had become too autonomous, too concrete, involving the risk for Florian of being absorbed by it and of forgetting himself in the process. Threatened with the danger of not existing, as much by the presence of the object as by his tendency to disinvest it, Florian came within a hair's breadth of the danger of *non-representation*, hence the extraordinary hallucinatory surge transforming the memory into the sensory power of a negative hallucination. Being obliged both to deny and recognise the object's presence at one and the same time, he succeeded in doing so perfectly with his dazzling negative hallucination.

Nevertheless, alternative possibilities were available to Florian other than this radical solution corresponding to an exceptional economic situation; he could employ the mechanism of negation in a more nuanced fashion, as the dream shows. And although the negative hallucination totally denied the object's presence, the dream, by way of contrast, bore witness to a certain acceptance of its existence. Florian's dream represented, above all, the enactment of his new, recent affirmation: the statement 'I don't follow you' could be understood as a 'I am not you'. By means of the negation of 'I am you', a negation in front of the emergence of the double, Florian marked the beginning of an alterity, a mirror alterity, it is true, but alterity nonetheless; for the animistic continuity – in which the subject is the double of an object that is the double of the subject – was broken.

The dynamic of the double: animistic, auto-erotic, narcissistic

> The idea of the 'double' does not necessarily disappear with the passing of primary narcissism, for it can receive fresh meaning from the later stages of the ego's development.
>
> Freud (1919h), p. 235

It is above all in French psychoanalytic publications that the notion of the double has been developed. The authors who have influenced us most in this connection are Christian David (1971) and André Green (1974). (See also Braier, 2000.)

Since the works of Rank and Freud, there has been a tendency, initially, to consider the double as a unitary and invariable notion: a specular image, a hallucinatory projection outside, of a bodily representation of oneself the primitive function of which is an 'energetic denial of the power of death' (Rank, 1914, p. 235). But beyond this most wide-ranging and representative sense of the double, one can find in contemporary psychoanalytic literature all the complexity of an original dynamic. Freud himself had already had a glimpse of it. Thus, in 'The "Uncanny"' (1919h) he puts forward the idea, as we recalled in the epigraph, that 'the idea of the "double" does not necessarily disappear with the passing of primary narcissism, for it can receive fresh meaning from the later stages of the ego's development'. Namely, the agency of 'moral conscience' and the fact that man is capable of self-observation that 'renders it possible to invest "the old idea of a double"', Freud adds, 'with a new meaning and to ascribe a number of things to it – above all those things which seem to self-criticism to belong to the old surmounted narcissism of earlier times. . . . But it is not only this latter material, offensive as it is to the criticism of the ego, which may be incorporated in the idea of a double. There are also all the unfulfilled but possible futures to which we still cling in phantasy, all the strivings of the ego' (pp. 235–236). These avatars of the double, self-observation, ego ideal, moral conscience, constitute an ensemble which later on, in the *New Introductory Lectures on Psychoanalysis* (1933a), Freud includes under the name of superego.

But that is not all. Along with the idea of a double progressively taking on itself a variety of contents, one encounters in Freud descriptions concerning different constitutions and forms of the double. It is not so much a question of this or that stable form as a fundamental organisational mode of inter- and intrapsychic reality, capable of assuming sometimes one form of the double and sometimes another. Indeed, in 'The "uncanny"', the double is defined as 'a creation dating back to a very early mental stage', belonging to an animistic world and considered at that time as having a 'more friendly aspect'. But 'when this stage [of assurance against death] has been surmounted', the double can transform itself into the terrifying image of a 'harbinger of death'. It is in *Totem and Taboo* that Freud develops his conception of the animistic character of the double:

> A general overvaluation has thus come about of all mental processes ... things become less important than the idea of things ... the reflection of the internal world is bound to blot out the other picture of the world – the one which *we* seem to perceive.
>
> (1912–13, p. 85)

An animistic world 'which caused us to see copies of our own consciousness all around us' (Freud 1915e, p. 171), 'invented' to use Freud's expression, by primitive man with the help of his animistic capacities in order to struggle against death anxiety. According to our hypothesis, to this creation of the double in phylogenesis there corresponds an ontogenetic counterpart inherent to the functioning of every psyche; it is inseparable from the traumatic effect of the perception of absence on the 'primary narcissism which dominates the mind and of primitive man' (Freud, 1919h, p. 235). The double may be said to emerge in response to the fear of psychic death, in response to the risk of *non-representation*, doubled by a non-perception, whether this occurs in the small child faced with the absence of the object or in the adult each night during the narcissistic regression of sleep arousing the fear of *non-representation*, of *non-perception*; hence the pressure towards a hallucinatory representation of the subject himself (a double) in the dream.

The animistic double

The *animistic double* is thus a mode of thinking in which representation, perception and motility are equivalent and undistinguishable. A product of retrogressive processes, this animistic double, overflowing with sensory experience, is under the dominance of the perceptual and/or hallucinatory register and is ignorant of alterity. It is a psychic state that only understands the world in terms of what it is itself; the world being simply a mirror for it in which it is reflected through projection.

When Freud describes, in *The Ego and the Id* (1923b), primary identification as 'a direct and immediate identification and takes place earlier than any object-cathexis' (p. 31), one is justified in wondering if, at this level of psychic non-differentiation, Freud's use of the term identification, which by definition, presupposes a relation to a distinct object, is valid. At least if one accepts the existence of a psychic capacity before animism, a *pre-animistic psychic stage* (doctrine of R. R. Marett, 1909, cited by Freud in *Totem and Taboo*, to which we shall return) in which the intrapsychic cannot be differentiated from the non-psychic.

The auto-erotic double

It would seem that the emergence from animism corresponds to the appearance of another modality of the double, the *auto-erotic double*. The psyche, always eager to be reflected and complemented, captures something of this undifferentiated world and internalises its animistic double. For lack of a better term and without claiming any temporal succession, [elsewhere] we qualified this movement of 'captation', which is fundamental for psychic growth, as secondary auto-erotism, for it bears the mark of the object even though the latter has not yet been recognised as distinct. Secondary auto-erotism organises the transition from animistic continuity to the auto-erotic double. This means the subject constantly reinvests the erotogenic body, appropriating his own members, his erotogenic zones, which have opened out precisely through contact with the animistic object, whence their quality of both separation and union. The body ego, and one's self-image, are dependent on them.

Notwithstanding its narcissistic characteristics, secondary auto-erotism works in favour of maintaining the sense of alterity. During waking life, by virtue of its permanent activity of returning to itself, the auto-erotic double represents an endopsychic mirror which, like Perseus's reflecting shield facing the Gorgon, removes the terror of the danger of *non-representation* and gives support to reality testing. The internal play of reflections of the auto-erotic double, where the subject is both an observed passive object and an observing subject – a miraculous return of the subject to himself – leads Francis Pasche to say in respect of Descartes: 'Thus when I say, "I think, I am", I am split, detached from my thinking self, in order to be able to watch myself thinking' (Pasche, 1981).

The narcissistic 'material' double

But at certain moments this internal mirror can be effaced, making way for a narcissistic regression, which, beyond a certain degree, eclipses the interplay of internal reflections and awakens the terror of an animistic continuity driving the subject to search desperately on the outside for this 'mirror' that he is lacking on the inside and to cling to the perception of a *narcissistic 'material' double*.

The session that we have just analysed is an example of this. The flaw in his secondary auto-erotism reduces Florian to an analytic relation with a narcissistic 'material' double, to functioning in terms of 'psychic life or death': the white of negative hallucination and the black of the terror of *non-representation*, of animistic continuity, projected into dark glasses. If the analyst had manifested himself by giving an essentially Oedipal interpretation relating to homosexuality, as the analysand and his countertransference wished, so as to blot out a world of terror by 'leaning', so to speak, on the erotogenic body, he would have shortcircuited the possibility of understanding Florian's problem of alterity; the analyst's intuitive representation (*figurabilité*), 'the shower is the gas chamber', evoking both homosexuality and terror, a nightmarish double of 'I don't follow you', would not have occurred. It was this way of *working as a double* that allowed an 'I am me', a body ego, to emerge, a locus of penetration and conservation, of limit and expulsion, making it possible to consolidate the endopsychic, auto-erotic double, a link and separation between the subject and the object cathexis.

As he had hitherto been without any secondary auto-erotic anchoring, Florian had to cling to a 'material' double, to the analyst's perception, in order to avoid the animistic continuity representation–perception; or alternatively to gather, to concentrate himself in his tense muscular attitudes, which, although painful, served to delineate his bodily limits at the price of a certain erotogenic masochism. This was an auto-erotic minimum for the psychic survival of his alterity. However, we cannot deny that Florian longed for a homosexual object investment. The day after the stormy session, he said he felt a weight had been lifted from him and repeated with fascination the intervention 'the shower is the gas chamber', like a child who, in order to be able to go to sleep peacefully at night without having nightmares, needs to be told a horror story inscribing his erotogenic masochism within an object relationship. Likewise, he came back to the dream and said boldly: 'There must be something sexual in it.' By that he meant that he could at last call out desperately for his homosexual, narcissistic double, for he now possessed, in place of an auto-erotic 'I am me', this 'I am not you', the negation we spoke of earlier, the indispensable minimum alterity enabling him to see himself in the analyst without feeling terrified.

State of session

At certain moments, the analyst is brought face to face in his practice with the problem of the regression of his thinking. As early as *The Interpretation of Dreams*, Freud, announcing the fundamental rule, associates free association with a particular state of the psyche in which self-observation is possible: 'a psychical state which bears some analogy to the state before falling asleep' (1900a, p. 20). Thus, the economic and dynamic conditions of the analytic encounter are such that the ego's functioning, which, in principle depends on the mode of activity of the waking ego, is at moments akin to the ego's night-time functioning. A complex situation in which the ego of the session that is losing its assets of the waking state – motility, action and perception being in a large measure abandoned as during the sleeping state – does not, like the night-time ego, have the advantages that derive from the opening up of the hallucinatory path; we call this the *state of session* in order to emphasise its temporary, even absurd and monstrous character, halfway between the waking and sleeping state. Moreover the ego, thus disconcerted, has to suffer the libidinal closeness inherent to the session, the re-sexualisation, at the heart of the treatment, of social investments and an increase in instinctual tension owing to frustration; a real instinctual overload whose impossible realisation leads inevitably to an increase in psychic tension, to a plethora. And when the paths of discharge specific to the session – free association, the work of figurability and speech – prove insufficient, this economic ensemble puts the session in an economic situation akin to that of actual neurosis. It may be supposed, then, that just as psychoneurosis admits of a kernel of actual neurosis, there exists in every analytic relationship a certain aspect that is actual. *Just as psychoneurosis tries to elaborate its kernel of actual neurosis, transference neurosis must absorb its actual component inherent to the here-and-now of the session.*

Faced with this problem, the ego in the session, which is neither diurnal nor nocturnal, in order to find a way out, tries to make use of two modes of functioning as best it can. The lesser evil represented by this gymnastics, for which the ego is not prepared, has its consequences; for the convergence of the two modes of psychic functioning, daytime and night-time, which are normally meant to be separate, raises a state of uncanniness. The state of the session and the proximity of the animistic world that it imposes will entail different adjustments in each partner.

During the session, as thinking proceeds in a progressive direction, one can observe at certain moments, and sometimes continuously in the background, the effects of retrogressive tendency 'which makes possible the cathexis of the system *Pcpt*. in the reverse direction, starting from thoughts, to the pitch of complete sensory vividness' (Freud, 1900a, p. 543) and, as a consequence, 'an idea is turned back into the sensory image from which it was originally derived' (p. 543). The formal regression of thought facilitates the tendency to immediate discharge: the cathexis of the intensity of the ideas overrides the cathexis of the 'connecting paths' (p. 280) and can even result in the predominance of the perceptual quality. In this way, by virtue of its unaccustomed thrust towards hallucinatory figurability, by virtue of its proximity to animistic thought, the formal regression of the session can collaborate in the development of the uncanny, indicating a weakening of the auto-erotic double.

One way for the analysand to resorb the state of the session, and putting a break on hallucinatory figurability, is to over-invest the object-analyst. We have seen it at work – and above all through its absence – in the guise of a clinging to the perception of an external self-projection, to a 'material' double. Nevertheless, narcissistic though it is, this libidinal investment of the analyst as a double represents, in contradistinction to the animistic double described earlier, a minimum of alterity, a detour via material reality. In fact, the cathexis or investment of the 'material' double is a sure means of eliminating the hallucinatory solution and of maintaining a work via thought identity.

From this perspective, recollection is another means of achieving this, for it can be seen as having a double function: of (a) leading to the resolution of conflicts and to the liquidation of the psychoneurosis, and (b) resisting, like a defensive rampart, the continuation of formal regression, of 'bringing regression to a halt so that it does not proceed beyond the mnemic image' (Freud, 1900a, p. 566). In effect, the analysand will spontaneously avoid the risk of the formal regression of his thought by taking refuge in mnemic images, formations capable of inhibiting animistic regression, especially as their vividness, which at times is remarkable, can take charge of the hallucinatory tendency awakened by regression. Thus, remembering (transference being a form of it) reveals the infantile history with its repressed wishes, while setting itself up as a defensive formation against animistic regression by providing the ego with a reassuring sense of *déjà vu*. The complexity of psychic functioning in the analytic situation never ceases to surprise us. Let us add that the point here, in our opinion, is not to relativise remembering and transference; on the contrary, we wish to underline their economic and dynamic weight and the vast field that they cover.

In the light of these considerations, the fact that every transference neurosis involves a homosexual transference could be explained, beyond the dynamic peculiar to infantile object-relations in connection with the auto-erotic double, by the reactivation, at the sexual and narcissistic level, of the animistic tendency originating in the here-and-now of the state of the session; the animistic double will be more or less covered by the narcissistic double, bearing the ideal ego, and by the homosexual object-love, depending on the Oedipal quality of the infantile neurosis. This means that while the *transference and the transference neurosis organise themselves within the upward tendency of the repressed wishes and the infantile neurosis, they are no less facilitated, and even triggered, by the actual neurosis peculiar to the state of the session.*

Working as a double

If, as we have just seen, the analysand is led along different paths to use his analyst as a narcissistic and/or homosexual double, the analyst, for his part, is not led to invest the analysand in this way. For, owing to his own analysis, as well as to the experience of practising analysis, he is used to coping with formal regression and his animistic tendency; and, depending on the particular economic conditions and moments of the session, he will have at his disposal the possibility of working both via perceptual identity and via thought identity, of functioning as an animistic double and as an auto-erotic double. In effect, if the analyst's thinking can tolerate the movement of regression, without having recourse to defensive solutions such as investing the analysand narcissistically, analytic theories, 'ready-made' ideas, or again, memory, i.e. the reinvestment of his own memory traces culminating in a countertransference meaning that turns the relationship into something 'already known', he finds himself faced with the formal regression of his thought with the unknown (see Rosolato,

1978, 1985, 1996, 1999). He is then not very far from the child faced with the traumatic unknown – namely, sexual difference, the arrival of a newborn child, the mother's withdrawal of investment. And, like the child he used to be, the analyst in his regression, will have the tendency to transcend this by means of a work of figurability taking the form that is peculiar to the thought of the infantile sexual theories impregnated with animism. Without the obstacle of the countertransference and the field of pre-conscious memory, remaining as close as possible to the unknown of the analysand that is a triggering cause of the state of quality of his thinking, interpretations of a particularly intuitive nature can come to the analyst. These interpretations, which are formed along the direct path of regression, give access to unrepresentable areas of the analysand's mind that would otherwise remain unreachable. Under these conditions, the analyst's work of thinking is in continuity with the analysand's psyche and corresponds to the model of the relationship of the dream-work with the day residues and momentary sensory impressions. The analyst's work of figurability, arising from a regressive mode of functioning as an animistic double, has its roots both in the analysand's unconscious and in the analyst's own capacity to tolerate the regressive movement of his thought, making it possible to create new connections, new contents. As a counterpoint to countertransference elements, the analyst's work of figurability represents both the reflection and the complement of the analysand's psychic functioning.

Just as the countertransference is the counterpart of the act of transference, that is, a manifestation of the analyst's unconscious along the progressive waking path, the analyst's capacity to pursue, at certain times, the regressive path of animistic thinking is the counterpart of the analysand's regression in dreams. If we follow Freud in his *Papers on Metapsychology* (the chapter on 'The Unconscious', where he affirms that, 'unconscious mental activity appears to us . . . as a further expansion of the primitive animism'; 1915e, p. 171), we are bound to admit that analysis can only reach the animistic form of infantile wishes through a hallucinatory–perceptual process, at least where primary repressions are concerned. At certain privileged moments, the transferring analysand, and the analyst in formal regression, are together in a position to approach, or organise, the model of animistic continuity representation–perception constituting the unconscious system. Without this encounter, the analytic process would remain limited; the unconscious, the animistic nature of the repressed aspects of the psychoneurosis, would still remain largely veiled.

This way of *working as a double* thus operates between two psyches. One of them, demonstrating a remarkable degree of momentary plasticity, reflects what is only potential in the other. The need for complementarity is sometimes such that the psychic object is only complete, as Green says, in 'the union of the work of two psyches' (Green, 1974). It is a complex act involving both passiveness and appropriation, revealing and even creating psychic data.

Certainly, this mode of *working as a double* does not often manifest itself openly, and most of the time it escapes the analyst's attention; which partly explains the paucity of publications on its role in analytic treatment. Among them, we have been particularly interested in those already cited – Christian David (1971), André Green (1974) – and in those that concern paradoxical thought in the work of Michel de M'Uzan (1976).

Let us return now to the session with Florian. The formal regression of the analyst's thought, his *work as a double*, allows him to discern, beyond what is manifest, more than a content, thought or unconscious phantasy, something in the order of a traumatic element, a rupture, in the analysand's representational order. The 'living corpse' was not the translation by the analyst of a murderous unconscious wish of Florian stemming from his infantile neurosis; it arose, on the contrary, in the latter's absence, in the face of the failure of his infantile neurosis, under the effect of a traumatic discontinuity. The analyst's nightmare emerges from this discontinuity and gives a meaning to the analysand's *non-representation*. From this same point of view, the analyst's interpretation 'the shower is the gas chamber' does not correspond either to an unconscious wish of Florian, in spite of the representations 'three dead', 'deportation' and 'widow', which it is tempting to consider as associations that have their origin in the unconscious problematics of the dream. In the session in question, Florian's associations represent, above all, attempts to elaborate his affects of terror arising from the proximity of *non-representation* triggered in the here-and-now of the session and absorbed in part by the flash of the negative hallucination. The figurations 'living corpse' and 'gas chamber' are the echoes of this in the analyst. Arising from the regressive functioning of the analyst's thinking, as an animistic double, they bear the mark of what he has been able to pick up of the analysand's terror of non-representation. It is only after they have been evoked in the interpretation offered that Florian's so precarious auto-erotic continuity is given new impetus, that his internal mirror is reconstituted and that he will be able to form an idea of his distress that hitherto had been unrepresentable. By appropriating the connection between the representation 'shower', coming from his dream, and the representation 'gas chamber', coming from his analyst, he is able to get beyond the fracture caused by his weak narcissism.

The *work as a double* inevitably awakens an effect of uncanniness, and the analyst's psyche will have the tendency to defend itself against it, to minimise it or even to forget it immediately. We have read a striking example in which the analyst and the analysand had the same dream on the same night, with a practically identical manifest content. Only the analyst did not want to publish this 'strange' occurrence until 25 years later when the analysand was already dead and he himself was terminally ill, he adds, as if to excuse himself for a misdeed, as if it were shameful to say openly what should remain secret (Rascovsky, 1976). Thus in order to blot out such an event in an analysis, in order to avoid the sense of strangeness, there will be a tendency to consider this mode of *working as double* in ways that are already known, quickly making the uncanny product fit into reassuring pre-established moulds, transforming the strange into the familiar, the sense of uncanniness into its 'positive counterpart', into the *déjà vu*. Sometimes, then, we will be led to think of the notion of countertransference and as we often, if not always, find a few elements reflecting our own conflicts, we will quickly put the matter aside. Sometimes the phenomenon will be understood as a manifestation of habitual mechanisms; and, depending on each person's theoretical leanings, this mode of functioning as a double will be seen and suffocated under the cover of a hysterical identification, through community or, alternatively, in the form of a projective, or even adhesive, identification, or again as a residue of primary identification. In fact the specificity of this *work as a double* cannot be reduced to a mechanism of identification, even if it is primary identification, although it can be sustained by it; for, in this mode of functioning, identification properly speaking does not exist; rather, there is an immediate, primitive perceptual capacity, comparable to the figurability, to the endopsychic perception of a dream.

To conclude, it has to be said that the problem of the distinction between the mechanisms discussed in this chapter and the mode of *working as a double*, which is theoretically evident, is not simple in daily practice, especially as the operative mechanisms depending on each person's structure will occupy the foreground most of the time. The best indicator of its specificity is its hallucinatory character, for this represents the culmination of the formal regression necessary for the expression of a psychic work of this kind.

References

Braier, E. (2000). *Gemelos. Narcisismo y dobles*. Buenos Aires: Paidos.
David, C. (1971). *L'état amoureux* [The amorous state]. Paris: Payot.
Freud, E. L. (Ed.). (1970). *The Letters of Sigmund Freud and Arnold Zweig*, trans. E. W. Robson-Scott. New York: Harcourt, Brace and World.
Freud, S. (1900a). *The Interpretation of Dreams*. *S.E.*, 4–5.
Freud, S. (1912–13). *Totem and Taboo*. *S.E.*, 13.
Freud, S. (1913f). The Theme of the Three Caskets. *S.E.*, 12.
Freud, S. (1914a). Fausse Reconnaissance ('déjà raconté') in Psycho-Analytical Treatment. *S.E.*, 13.
Freud, S. (1914b). The Moses of Michelangelo. *S.E.*, 13.
Freud, S. (1914c). On Narcissism: An Introduction. *S.E.*, 14.
Freud, S. (1914g). Remembering, Repeating and Working-Through. *S.E.*, 12.
Freud, S. (1915e). The Unconscious. *S.E.*, 14.
Freud, S. (1919h). The 'Uncanny'. *S.E.*, 17.
Freud, S. (1921c). *Group Psychology and the Analysis of the Ego*. *S.E.*, 18.
Freud, S. (1923b). *The Ego and the Id*. *S.E.*, 19.
Freud, S. (1927c). The Future of an Analysis. *S.E.*, 21.
Freud, S. (1933a). *New Introductory Lectures on Psychoanalysis*. *S.E.*, 22.
Freud, S. (1936a). A Disturbance of Memory on the Acropolis. *S.E.*, 22.
Freud, S. (1937c). Analysis Terminable and Interminable. *S.E.*, 23.
Freud, S. (1937d). Constructions in Analysis. *S.E.*, 23.

Freud, S. (1939a [1937–39]). *Moses and Monotheism. S.E.*, 23.
Freud, S. (1941f [1938]). Findings, Ideas, Problems. *S.E.*, 23.
Green, A. (1974). The Analyst, Symbolization and Absence in the Analytic Setting. In *On Private Madness*. London: Hogarth Press, 1986.
Jones, E. (1955). *The Life and Work of Sigmund Freud, Vol. 2.* London: Hogarth Press.
Marett, R. R. (1909). *The Threshold of Religion*. London: Longman.
M'Uzan, M. de (1976). *De l'art à la mort* [From art to death]. Paris: Gallimard.
Pasche, F. (1981) Métaphysique et inconscient [Metaphysics and the unconscious]. *Revue Française de Psychanalyse, 1.*
Rank, O. (1914). *Le double*. Paris: Payot. [*The Double: A Psychoanalytic Study*. London: Karnac, 1989.]
Rascovsky, I. (1976). Un sueño de dos y dos sue nos de uno. *Revista de Psicoanalisis*, 1.
Rosolato, G. (1978). *La relation d'inconnu* [The relationship to the unknown]. Paris: Gallimard.
Rosolato, G. (1985). *Eléments de l'interprétation* [Elements of interpretation]. Paris: Gallimard.
Rosolato, G. (1996). *La portée du désir ou la psychanalyse même* [The significance of desire, or psychoanalysis itself]. Paris: Presses Universitaires de France.
Rosolato, G. (1999). *Les cinq axes de la psychanalyse* [The five axes of psychoanalysis]. Paris: Presses Universitaires de France.

19 THE ILLNESS OF MOURNING AND THE FANTASY OF THE EXQUISITE CORPSE

Maria Torok

Of Hungarian origin, **Maria Torok** (1925–1998) trained as a psychologist before becoming a full member of the Paris Psychoanalytical Society. She studied in particular the concepts of introjection and incorporation as they developed from Ferenczi's work through to that of Melanie Klein; with Nicolas Abraham, she formulated the theory of the 'crypt within the ego' that involves the incorporated object. Among their other writings, two of their books are particularly interesting: *Le verbier de l'Homme aux loups* (Aubier-Flammarion, 1976) [*The Wolf-Man's Magic Word* (Minnesota Press, 2005)] and *L'écorce et le noyau* (Aubier-Flammarion, 1978) [*The Shell and the Kernel* (Chicago, 1994)].

A revelatory misunderstanding

An astonishing exchange of letters between Sigmund Freud and Karl Abraham brings attentive readers to the origins of my topic and illustrates its immediately disturbing aspects.[1]

> Berlin-Gruenewald, 13.3.22
>
> Dear Professor,
>
> Incorporation of the love-object is very striking in my cases. I can produce very nice material for this concept of yours, demonstrating the process in all its detail. In this connection I have a small request – for a reprint of 'Mourning and Melancholia,' which would be extremely useful to me in my work. Many thanks in anticipation.

---

[1] *A Psycho-Analytic Dialogue: The Letters of Sigmund Freud and Karl Abraham*, ed. H. C. Abraham & E. L. Freud, trans. B. Marsh & H. C. Abraham (London: Hogarth Press, 1965), pp. 328–331.

One brief comment on this paper. You, dear Professor, state that you find nothing in the course of normal mourning which would correspond to the leap from melancholia to mania. I think, however, I can describe such a process, without knowing whether this reaction is invariably found. My impression is that a fair number of people show an increase in libido some time after a period of mourning. It shows itself in heightened sexual need and appears to lead relatively often to conception shortly after a death. I should like to know your opinion and whether you can confirm this observation. The increase of libido some time after 'object-loss' would seem to be a valid addition to the parallel between mourning and melancholia. . . .

Bergasse 19, Vienna, 30.3.22

Dear Friend,

After more than a fortnight I reread your personal letter, and came across your request for a reprint, which for some reason escaped my attention when I first read it.

I plunge eagerly into the abundance of your scientific insights and intentions; I only wonder why you do not take into account my last suggestion about the nature of mania after melancholia (in 'Group Psychology'). Might that be the motivation for my forgetting about 'Mourning and Melancholia'? No absurdity is impossible for psychoanalysis. I should like to discuss all these things, particularly with you, but it is impossible to write about them. In the evening I am tired, . . .

Berlin-Gruenewald, 2.5.22

Dear Professor,

. . . Your letter of March 30 is still waiting for a reply, but I have already thanked you for your reprint of 'Mourning and Melancholia.' I fully understand your forgetting it. Your failure in sending the paper I asked for was meant to indicate that I should first of all study the other source ('Group Psychology'). I am, however, quite familiar with its contents concerning the subject of mania and melancholia but, in spite of going through it once again, I cannot see where I went wrong. I can find no mention anywhere of a parallel reaction after mourning in normal cases which can be compared to the onset of mania (after melancholia). I only know from your remark in 'Mourning and Melancholia' that you were aware of something lacking and I referred to this in my observation. The increase of libido after mourning would be fully analogous to the 'feast' of the manic, but I have not found this parallel from normal life in that section of 'Group Psychology' where this 'feast' is discussed. Or have I been so struck by blindness that I am unable to see the actual reference? . . .

Bergasse 19, Vienna, 28.5.22

Dear Friend,

With Eitingon's help I discovered to my amusement that I completely misunderstood you through no fault of yours. You were looking for a normal example of the transition from melancholia to mania, and I was thinking of the explanation of the mechanism.

With many apologies,

This series of misunderstandings cannot be ascribed to pure chance.
Karl Abraham senses the fruitfulness of his discovery, he insists, and I understand him. But what to make of the extent of Freud's resistance to a clinical observation? It demonstrates the reluctance we all feel when, in a sacrilegious move, we want to grasp the inmost nature of mourning. It is not surprising that, without encouragement from the professor, Karl Abraham is led to minimize the importance of this subject. He accords it only limited space in his crucial essay of 1924 ('An Outline of the History of the Development of the Libido Based on the Psychoanalysis of Mental Disturbances') and does not come to the theoretical and clinical consequences the problem most assuredly implies.

'Normal mania' and the illness of mourning

Still, clinical observation brings forward a preliminary fact. All those who admit to having experienced such an 'increase in libido' when they lost an object of love, do so with shame, astonishment, hesitation, and in a whisper. 'My mother was there, dead. And at a time when people should feel the most intense grief, be doleful and forlorn, at a time when the arms and the legs should give way, when the whole frame should be prostrate, sinking to the floor – I can hardly bring myself to say it – at that moment I had sensations, yes, carnal sensations,' says a voice. Another voice says, 'I've never understood how something like that could have happened to me; I've never forgiven myself . . ., but a giddy song coursed through my mind and wouldn't leave me. It continued during the entire vigil. I tried on the black veil like a bride preparing for the big day.'
These admissions definitely concur with Karl Abraham's ideas. His intuition seems to me fully confirmed by clinical experience. In this essay I will draw the lesson from his preliminary observation by casting new light on all the cases psychoanalysis teaches us to designate as 'illness of mourning.'
Why are these patients overwhelmed with self-reproach and inhibitions, why are they subject to exhausting ruminations, physical diseases, constant depression, fatigue, and anxiety? Why do they suffer from disinterest in objectal

love? What dulls their creativity and makes them sigh nostalgically: 'I might if I could . . .'? It is *very* rare that the connection between their state of mind and the originating event becomes conscious. To effect this realization is the task of analysis. 'He pursued me intensely and I wanted to marry him. But an inner voice said to me: "You would then have to abandon your dead." This sad and insistent voice would return and for a long time I heeded its call. The world was an immense desert for me.' Or this: 'I've never forgiven myself for something. The day my father died I had intercourse with my husband. It was the first time I felt desire and satisfaction. Shortly thereafter we separated because . . .' (here she gives some 'good reasons'). This handful of examples characterizes the core around which the illness of mourning is constituted.

The illness of mourning does not result, as might appear, from the affliction caused by the objectal loss itself, but rather from the feeling of an irreparable crime: the crime of having been overcome with desire, of having been surprised by an overflow of libido at the least appropriate moment, when it would behoove us to be grieved in despair.

These are the clinical facts. A measure of libidinal increase upon the object's death seems to be a widespread, if not universal, phenomenon. Karl Abraham's intuition leads me to see manic reactions as only one of the pathologically exaggerated forms of such an increase of libido. (It should be added that this sudden increase in libido can also lead to the emergence of a latent neurotic conflict.) How are we to understand the untoward arrival of this kind of libidinal invasion? A complex set of problems is tied up in this question, and I will attempt to highlight some of its strands. First I will discuss conflictual introjection and the auto-aggressive reactions that derive from it, in addition to the economical problems they may engender. Next, I will consider the specific form of repression that manifests itself in the therapeutic process through a particular content: incorporation. Finally, and in a more general way, I will try to delimit the various neurotic trends that might be termed neurosis of transition. Strictly speaking, the illness of mourning appears to be a restricted form of this larger category of neurosis.

Ferenczi's concept of the introjection of drives contrasted with the concept of the object's incorporation

a) Some transformations of the concept of introjection

Whoever approaches the problem of mourning or depression is required to muddle through a conceptual terrain studded with obstacles, for example 'introjection.' Ever since Sándor Ferenczi introduced the concept in 1909 – first Freud and then Karl Abraham took it up, handing it down to Melanie Klein and others – the term 'introjection' has undergone so many variations in meaning that its mere mention is enough to arouse in me the suspicion of confused ideas, not to say verbiage. The initial and rigorous meaning of this concept must be revived if we are to avoid such pitfalls. The concept gives shape to the first great discovery Ferenczi made, being filled with wonder before the phenomenon of psychoanalysis. Only when its initial and precise meaning is restored will the concept of 'introjection' reveal its effectiveness in clarifying the clinical facts noted above, as regards both their genesis and evolution.

Freud, Karl Abraham, Melanie Klein, and others are quite willing to consider Ferenczi as the father of the concept of introjection. Nevertheless, it is remarkable that none of these authors attempts an in-depth analysis of the original concept, travestied from the start despite the clarification in Ferenczi's brilliant 1912 article 'On the Definition of Introjection.' Immediately adopted because of its pithiness, the concept became muddled – departing from its initial sense as an explicative synonym for 'transference' – on account of its lexical structure (intro-jection: casting inside) and ended up being given entirely other, even mutually exclusive meanings. The confusion is such that the term 'introjection' is often used to denote a mechanism characterized by the impossibility or the refusal to introject, at least in the sense originally intended by Ferenczi.[2]

We know that the study of psychosis and the emphasis placed on the narcissistic forms of the libido between 1913 and 1917 gradually enriched the libido theory (see *S.E.*, 14). Freud's views on identification – narcissistic forms of incorporation as opposed to incorporation in the neuroses – continued to gain in complexity and came to constitute the pivotal point in his enonomic understanding of the work of mourning in the 1919 article 'Mourning and Melancholia.'[3] According to Freud, the trauma of objectal loss leads to a response: incorporation of the object within the ego. The incorporated object, with which the ego would identify partially, makes it possible both to wait while readjusting the internal economy and to redistribute one's investments. Given that it is not possible to liquidate the dead and decree definitively 'they are no more,' the bereaved become the dead for themselves and take their time to work through, gradually and step by step, the effects of the separation.

Karl Abraham has established (and Freud recalled this in his study on mourning) that incorporation of the object and separation from it occur in the form of oral-cannibalistic and anal-evacuative processes. Given that they make use of Ferenczi's term 'introjection,' we might think that neither Freud nor K. Abraham would stray far from Ferenczi's original conception. Yet this initial impression fades as we examine Freud's interpretation of the concept. For example, he equates introjection with identification. Moreover, Freud equates introjection with the recovery of investments placed either in a lost object (the

---

[2] This paragraph followed the next two in the original and was moved here at Maria Torok's request. [*Ed. of the American collection from which the paper is taken*]

[3] 'Incorporation' and 'introjection' in this historical overview reflect Freud and K. Abraham's use of these terms; Torok's definitions follow in the next two sections. [*Ed., as above*]

ego becomes what it cannot leave) or in an inaccessible ideal object (the ego sets itself the ideal of becoming what it cannot yet be). Both of these processes – the identification with the relinquished object and the rival's so-called 'introjection' into the superego, which is also the double requirement for the dissolution of the Oedipus complex – are justified through the loss of love objects in Freud's *Group Psychology and the Analysis of the Ego* and *The Ego and the Id*. In the essay on 'Denial,' the same theme of introjection, allegedly compensating for a loss or a lack, is found. We will see that completely different ideas inspired Ferenczi's concept.

b) Ferenczi's text and its significance

It will be useful to stop and consider for a moment this basic text, worthy of being read and reconsidered. In any case, it constitutes the keystone of my theoretical elaboration.

> I described introjection as *an extension to the external world of the original autoerotic interests, by including its objects in the ego* [emphasis mine]. I put the emphasis on this 'including' and wanted to show thereby that I considered *every sort of object love* (or *transference*) both in normal and in neurotic people (and of course also in paranoiacs as far as they are capable of loving) as an extension of the ego, that is as introjection.
>
> In principle, man can love only himself; if he loves an object he takes it into his ego. . . . I used the term 'introjection' for all such growing onto, all such including of the loved object in, the ego. As already stated, I conceive the mechanism of *all transference onto an object*, that is to say *all kinds of object love*, as *an extension of the ego*.
>
> I described the excessive proneness to transference of neurotics as *unconscious exaggeration of the same mechanism*, that is, as addiction to introjection. . . .[4]

What does an analysis of this text teach us? First and foremost, in the sense Ferenczi gave this concept, 'introjection' is comprised of three points: (1) the extension of autoerotic interests, (2) the broadening of the ego through the removal of repression, (3) the including of the object in the ego and thereby 'an extension to the external world of the [ego's] original autoerotic interests.' In the writings of Ferenczi's contemporaries, this initially threefold meaning of introjection is reduced to a single superficial aspect: taking possession of the object through *incorporation*, that is, by putting it into the body or the psyche. Yet the difference is considerable and must be sustained by a clear distinction

---

[4] S. Ferenczi, *Final Contributions to the Problems and Methods of Psycho-Analysis* (New York: Brunner/Mazel, 1980), pp. 316–317.

between the two concepts. In defining the illness of mourning more precisely, I want to eliminate the misleading synonymy between introjection and incorporation. I will adhere strictly to the proper semantic specificity of each as it manifests itself in clinical work and as should appear clearly in what follows.

Ferenczi's text implies that introjection cannot have as its cause the actual loss of an object of love. No violence is done to his concept by the statement that introjection operates like a genuine instinct. Like transference (that is, like its mode of action in therapy), introjection is defined as the process of including the Unconscious in the ego through objectal contacts. The loss of the object will halt this process. Introjection does not tend toward compensation, but growth. By broadening and enriching the ego, introjection seeks to introduce into it the unconscious, nameless, or repressed libido. Thus, it is not at all a matter of 'introjecting' the object, as is all too commonly stated, but of introjecting the sum total of the drives, and their vicissitudes as occasioned and mediated by the object.

According to Ferenczi, introjection confers on the object, and on the analyst, the role of mediation toward the unconscious. Moving back and forth between 'the narcissistic and the objectal realms,' between auto- and hetero-eroticism, introjection transforms instinctual promptings into desires and fantasies of desire, making them fit to receive a name and the right to exist and to unfold in the objectal sphere.

c) Incorporation: The secret magic aimed at the recovery of the object of pleasure

Most of the characteristics falsely attributed to introjection in fact apply to the fantasmatic mechanism of incorporation. This mechanism does suppose the loss of an object in order to take effect; it implies a loss that occurred before the desires concerning the object might have been freed. The loss acts as a prohibition and, whatever form it may take, constitutes an insurmountable obstacle to introjection. The prohibited object is settled in the ego in order to compensate for the lost pleasure and the failed introjection. This is incorporation in the strict sense of the term.

Incorporation may operate by means of representations, affects, or bodily states, or use two or three of these means simultaneously. But, whatever the instrument, incorporation is invariably distinct from introjection (a gradual process) because it is instantaneous and magical. The object of pleasure being absent, incorporation obeys the pleasure principle and functions by way of processes similar to hallucinatory fulfilments.

Furthermore, the recuperative magic of incorporation cannot reveal its nature. Unless there is an openly manic crisis, there are good reasons for it to remain concealed. Let us not forget that incorporation is born of a prohibition it sidesteps but does not actually transgress. The ultimate aim of incorporation is to recover, in secret and through magic, an object that, for one reason or another, evaded its own function: mediating the introjection of desires. Refusing both the object's and reality's verdict, incorporation is an eminently illegal act; it must hide from view along with the desire of introjection it masks; it must hide even from the ego. Secrecy is imperative for survival. Here we see one more difference between incorporation and introjection. True to its spirit, introjection works entirely in the open by dint of its privileged instrument, naming.

The specificity of each of these two movements now appears clearly.

While the introjection of desires puts an end to objectal dependency, incorporation of the object creates or reinforces imaginal ties and hence dependency. Installed in place of the lost object, the incorporated object continues to recall the fact that something else was lost: the desires quelled by repression. Like a commemorative monument, the incorporated object betokens the place, the date, and the circumstances in which desires were banished from introjection: they stand like tombs in the life of the ego. Clearly, the mechanisms of introjection and incorporation are at odds. To call these two movements – the introjection of drives and the incorporation of the object – by the same name can hardly contribute to clarity in communication.

d) Incorporation, its origin, and its telling nature

There is an archaic level on which the two mechanisms, though subsequently opposed, could still be fused. Let me illustrate this with the early form of the ego which is made up of the oral libido's introjection. This type of process *signals* its meaning to itself by way of a *fantasy* or ingestion. Comprised exclusively of the oral libido's introjection, the ego consists at this stage in the use it makes of ingestion and its variants (salivation, hiccups, vomiting, etc.), in symbolic expressions, such as asking for or refusing food *regardless of the actual state of hunger* or, alternatively, fantasizing the consumption and refusal of food by means of the same mechanism but when the object is absent. The latter corresponds quite precisely to what is usually described as the mechanism of incorporation.

The fantasy of incorporation is the first lie, the effect of the first rudimentary form of language. It is also the first instrument of deception. Satisfying need by offering food does not satiate the actual and persistently active hunger for introjection. The offer of food only serves to deceive it.

(A gesture of this type occurs in the manic position too, but in relation to oneself.) Thirsting for introjection despite an insurmountable internal obstacle, the ego tricks itself with a magical procedure in which 'eating' (the feast) is paraded as the equivalent of an immediate but purely hallucinatory and illusory 'introjection.' Manic persons announce with fanfare to their unconscious that they are 'eating' (an act signifying the process of introjection and satisfaction for the ego). Yet, this is nothing but empty words and no introjection. When deprived of progressive libidinal nourishment, the ego regresses to this archaic level of magical attainment.

Inasmuch as it is merely a language *signalling* introjection, without actually accomplishing it, the fantasy of incorporation lends itself to wide-ranging, even opposite contexts. At times it signals the desire for an impossible introjection as in penis envy; at other times its claim is that introjection has already occurred, for example in phallic displays; or else it signals the displacement of introjection, pointing to the oral zone when in fact another zone is meant. Realizing that incorporation is a form of language, which merely *states* the desire to introject, marks an important step forward in psychoanalytic therapy. This language is striking in the vocabulary of dreams. A patient who has never masturbated dreams: 'My mother is serving a dish of asparagus and hands me the fork.' (I wish she would relinquish her power over my penis and hand it over into my own hand, authorizing me to introject my desire for her.) Another patient dreams: 'I am eating and vomiting blood flow and periods.' (This recalls a gynecological examination during her puberty at which her father was present.) Any number of examples could be marshalled; they occur daily in clinical work. The same function of language can be found also in the 'clinical' study of myths and traditions. Consider Popeye eating spinach; love potions; the fruit of knowledge whose ingestion by the first mythic couple conferred on it genital sexuality; various cannibalistic rites; and the incorporative function of first communions, etc.

All these examples illustrate the point that, unlike lay people, analysts do not understand incorporation as a request to be granted or hunger to be satisfied, but as the disguised language of as-yet unborn and unintrojected desires.

Fixation and the illness of mourning

Having established the difference between Ferenczi's concept of introjection and my own concept of incorporation, it is now time to return to our original problem, Karl Abraham's idea of 'normal mania.' An increase in libido, leading at times to orgasm, is a reaction to a death. I will now proceed with a metapsychological reconstruction of this moment, experienced and repressed upon the death of the object. Here we will reach the core of the illness of mourning.

It is clear now that, in the course of its organization and also in transference, the ego makes use of the object (or the analyst) to achieve its libidinal awakening and nourishment. Playing, as it does, the part of mediator between the ego and the unconscious in the introjection of drives, the object's function is not to serve as a complement to instinctual satisfaction. Since it is a pole of the developing ego, the object is the more intensely invested because it carries the promise of introjection. This is manifestly the meaning of the passionate love characteristic of both childhood and transference. Supposedly in possession of all that the ego requires for its own growth, the object long remains its focus of attention. When the process of introjection is complete, the object can descend from the imaginal pedestal where the ego's need for nourishment has placed it. If there is a death, the nature of the bereavement will be a function of the role the object played at the time of the loss. If the desires concerning it were introjected, no breakdown, no illness of mourning or melancholia should be feared. The libido invested in the object will be recovered eventually and the ego, in accordance with Freud's description, will become available once more in order to fix itself on other objects that might be necessary for its libidinal economy. Surely, the work of mourning is a painful process even in these cases, but the ego's integrity guarantees the outcome.

The same is not true in the other case – a rather frequent occurrence – in which the process of introjection was incomplete. Because the unassimilated portion of the drives has congealed into an imago, forever reprojected onto some external object, the incomplete and dependent ego finds itself caught in a self-contradictory obligation. The ego needs to keep alive at all costs that which causes its greatest suffering. Why this obligation? It is understandable if we consider the following. The imago, along with its external embodiment in the object, was set up as the repository of hope; the desires it forbade would be realized one day. Meanwhile, the imago retains the valuable thing whose lack cripples the ego. 'My wife took my potency to the grave. She holds my penis there, as though it were in her hand.' The imagoic and objectal fixation is cemented precisely by the contradictory and therefore utopian hope that the imago, the warden of repression, would authorize its removal. The object invested with such an imaginal role ought never to die. We sense the disarray into which the object's disappearance throws the ego. Its destiny having been fixation, the ego is henceforth condemned to suffer the illness of mourning.

An attempted reconstruction of the metapsychological moment of loss

The initially mysterious increase in libido at the moment of loss becomes understandable in light of the metapsychological analysis of introjection. The increase in libido is a desperate and final attempt at introjection, a sudden amorous fulfilment with the object. Here is how it can be explained.

When patients describe their being overcome with libido (for example, Breuer's Anna O. overcome with 'serpents,' one of my patients with 'fleas,' another one with 'frivolous' songs), they recount the astonishment they felt at this completely unexpected event. The libido breaks in on them like an unbridled tidal wave, giving no heed to the imago guarding repression. The 'surprise' is no doubt a disclaimer: 'It's not my fault. It occurred without my being there to intend it.' The event is never totally repudiated, however: 'It was a dream and yet not a dream.' Faced with the imminent threat that it might be too late, the ego regresses to the archaic level of hallucinatory satisfaction. In that realm, as we saw earlier, introjection and incorporation still constitute two aspects of the same mechanism. Not being able to remove repression and thus remaining unfulfilled, the long-contained hope is cornered in a desperate dilemma: deadly renunciation or fallacious triumph. Regression permits the latter, substituting fantasy for the real thing, magic and instantaneous incorporation for the introjective process. The hallucinatory fulfillment exults in orgasm.

Obviously, such a regression to magic does not match the ego's present conformation. In consequence, this fleeting fulfillment is struck with explicit condemnation and immediate repression. The ensuing amnesia concerns the concrete context of the moment in which the regression and the orgasm occurred. Should those ill from mourning consciously recall an orgasm (for which they secondarily blame themselves), its link to a desire for the dying or dead object is always severely censored. The novelty of the illness of mourning in relation to any underlying infantile neurosis is precisely the repression of this particular link. Which is why the relation between the orgasmic moment and the illness of mourning fails to be recognized.

The additional repression placed on the hallucinatory fulfillment of desire is responsible for the particularly intense resistance encountered in the analysis of these cases. The resistance here is comparable to that displayed by patients who, prior to psychoanalysis, have undergone therapy by narcosis. Placed all too abruptly before their desire, without previously having had the chance to deconstruct their imago gradually, these patients awaken in the same situation as those ill from mourning; both carry the buried *memory* of an instant of illegitimate sexual delight.

In both these cases, repression not only separates, but also has to *preserve* carefully, although in the unconscious, the wish the ego can only represent as an 'exquisite corpse' lying somewhere inside it; the ego looks for this exquisite corpse continually in the hope of one day reviving it.

Those patients of mourning who choose psychoanalysis seem to know nothing of their attempt to recapture a precise moment. Everything unfolds as though a mysterious compass led them to the tomb wherein the repressed problem lies.

A character in the verse of Edgar Allan Poe comes to mind here, a character who, unaware of the secret aim of his journey, notwithstanding the admonishments of his Psyche, walks under an ashen sky in a desolate and dank region to his beloved Ulalume's tomb, buried on that very night in the previous year. This poem is psychoanalytical ahead of its time since it symbolizes openly, for the first time in literature, the action of the unconscious. The return of the repressed occurs inescapably through the fatality of acted remembrance. I can say for my part that what drives the Narrator to relive the moment of loss with the blind force of the unconscious is the delight that silenced all prohibition at that supreme moment. The involuntary commemoration a year later exemplifies the revival of the unforgettable moment when the object's death permitted its magical conquest in the rapture of orgasm.

A clinical example

Only in rare cases can the diagnosis of illness of mourning be made quickly. This characterization usually comes at an advanced stage of the analysis when a substantial amount of material has collected around a death.

'Leaving here, I was shaken up. I sobbed. I don't know what I cried over. I feel as if I've just buried my mother. You reminded me of what I said at the beginning: I had to leave that very evening. And that evening she died. She had already been dying for days. I knew, I expected it. I was fleeing. I didn't want to know anything. No, that's not it. Not quite. There is something mysterious. She was dying and I – I'm upset saying it – I had desires, yes, carnal desires actually overcame me.'

'What I said at the beginning': Thomas is a young journalist of Alsatian extraction who came to analysis wrenched by anxiety, fatigue, and depression. Gradually, he discovered some regularity in the appearance of his depressive states. They occurred on Thursdays, the day he lost his mother. The analysis showed that this beloved and loving mother contributed a great deal to the formation of an imago: a violent sea [*mer: mere:* mother] that uproots trees, a kind of hard man-woman who withholds money, etc.

The incorporation of the imago, obstructing phallic and genital introjections, took place thus: 'When I was a little boy, mom used to wash me in a tub. One day, my penis got really big. She took hold of it abruptly, saying: "See, if a woman is attacked, she can overpower a man by taking hold of his penis."' The desire of the little boy and the mother met for an instant then, but for an instant only. The hardly reassuring idea suggested by the erection revealed at once the mother's desire and her superego's aggression toward the penis. This contradiction led to the boy's imaginal incorporation of both the desire and the mother's superego. Fixated on the imago, Thomas never stopped looking for this moment in order to overcome the prohibitive superego, hoping to carry off his mother's and his own desire in a common triumph.

Numerous dreams about rain, flooding, and bathing recall the mother 'washing.' 'A small path. In the middle there was a toilet. I relieved myself. "How old is the little boy?" asked someone. I wanted to get away. But in front of the door there were some washerwomen. I don't know whether they were taking care of me or not. They were working, laughing and laughing.' Thomas said on another occasion: 'Your area is completely flooded with water. I like your area of town. I like the antique shops, the little garden in your courtyard.' (I like you; wash me as my mother used to like to do.) But as soon as their common desire emerges, the internal mother's superego surfaces to erase it. 'A stingy, rude, masculine kind of woman who gives you trouble. Why pay an analyst rather than a plumber?' Yet, Thomas rebels against this imago. He has Chinese men [*chinois:* penis – *Trans.*] come to Paris in his dreams who spread tar on the ground and make faces with their heads between their legs. 'I like people who are assertive, who have their way, saying "I, me."' (As for me, I really want my mother to recognize her desire for me.)

The Christmas vacation is drawing closer. Thomas remembers how much he used to like his mother's bed. She would get up and he would slide between the sheets. His rebellion is beginning to bear fruit. Thomas is drawing closer to his desire for his mother just as the internal mother also recognizes her own repression and sexual fear. 'I would probably have trouble overseeing a child's sex education. I would be afraid' (like his mother). His depression intensifies. We are two sessions away from the vacation and Thomas says he feels ruined. All he can talk about is his ill health, his anguish, and his failures. But, at the end of the session, he tells me this dream: 'A curious image, very clear and distinct, as though suddenly in a spotlight. How could I dream such a thing? I'll tell it because here you have to say everything. Otherwise, I would do my best to forget it. I see her ill on her bed and, despite her age, she appears to be a lustful woman, someone who still has carnal desires. Her eyes are full of . . ., she's out of breath . . ., her thighs are wide open. She is like an old prostitute. Then rails, rails, rails (alluding to the flow occurring at the moment of agony). And while I was watching her, I ruined, ruined, ruined. No! I urinated.' Ever since his mother's death Thomas has been ruining himself for having 'urinated' that day, for having unearthed their common desire, bringing victory to it by 'ruining' his mother's superego. Thomas is astonished when I remind him of this moment. 'Yes, I left in a hurry and suddenly, I was seized with intense desire in an incomprehensible way.' And now the repressed content revives in the transference: the analyst-mother is leaving and 'dies.' Thomas says to this old woman in the throes of death: I wish you could be a prostitute for me (and caress my penis in the tub) *since you desire it too.* Shaken after this session, Thomas can finally mourn for his mother and thereby somewhat lighten the load of his imaginal fixation.

The pain of mourning and the fantasy of the exquisite corpse

The triumphant libidinal intrusion attendant upon objectal loss offers matter for renewed thought about the pain inherent in the work of mourning. Taking up Freud's question as to why the work of mourning is such a painful process, Melanie Klein suggests an answer. Every objectal loss entails a manic sadistic triumph over the object. Such a feeling of triumph seems to be badly tolerated in most cases and the ego allegedly does everything in its power to turn a blind eye to this proof of its ambivalence. The rejection or denial of triumph blocks the work of mourning either temporarily or permanently. The remorse and the guilt felt on account of aggressive fantasies would then explain the pain of mourning. This is so because, according to Melanie Klein, every time a love object is lost, the original situation of objectal loss is revived along with the ego's archaic attitude, namely the depressive position. The latter manifests itself above all in the fear that the child's own sadism might actually have caused the loss of the good and indispensable maternal object. The specific anguish, in this position, of having done the irreparable makes the child lose the prospect of ever being able to restore or reinstate the object permanently in order to guarantee the harmony and cohesion of the internal world.

However rigorous and plausible the Kleinian conception may be, it provides only a partial answer to the question at hand. Neither the dialectic of aggression directed at the 'good' object (no doubt found in all patients), nor the repudiated fact of sadistic triumph manages to clarify the true source of the pain of mourning. A distinction is needed here between an internal object and the imago. The former is the fantasmatic pole of the introjective process, whereas the latter is precisely all that resisted introjection and that the ego took possession of through other means, namely through the fantasy of incorporation. Melanie Klein seems to have focused, justifiably, on cases in which this type of fixating imago exists. Its dual nature needs to be kept in mind from now on. First of all, this imago was born of a failed introjective relation to an external object, and second, its effect is always to prohibit sexual desire. Clinical experience shows that the imago forms after a satisfaction was initially granted and then withdrawn. The presence of an imago in the subject attests to the fact that a desire became retroactively reprehensible and unspeakable before it could be introjected. The 'bite' of remorse no doubt refers to aggression. But psychoanalytic elaboration showed very early on that remorse and rumination arise at the libidinal spring of prohibited sexual desire. No wonder that, despite the suffering it causes, self-torture does not relent, since in it desire concerning the object is both revived and satisfied.

We now see that, upon the death of the object, for an instant hallucinatory regression gratified desire. In cases of fixation the intense pain tied up with the work of mourning concerns this precise moment. Though denying it, the pain testifies to this moment as well as to the objectal fantasy which furnished its content. With every libidinal outburst, with every unconscious revival of the exquisite moment, pleasure takes on the appearance of pain because of repression. The subject of so many sessions, this pain is highly instructive. A genuinely 'exquisite' pain, it constitutes a valuable tool for analysis when it is understood in the medical sense of the term, not only because it derives from a desire but also because it points to the place where one needs to operate in order to unearth repression.

Leading us to the tomb where desire lies buried (the pain being a kind of 'here lies,' an inscription on which the name of the deceased long remains undecipherable), the pain of self-torture is an invitation extended to the analyst to proceed with the exhumation as well as an appropriate directive for this stage of the analysis: 'Accuse me.'

These kinds of analyses present many special features, but I will mention only one here because it appears constantly and also because it constituted my study's point of departure. The analysis of the ill from mourning often yields a nightmarish dream that patients say brings some relief although it is troubling. The following example captures this type of sometimes recurrent dream. 'I *am being accused*. I committed a terrible crime. I ate someone and then buried him. I'm on the site of the crime with someone who is charged with disinterring and examining the remains. This person is accusing me. I don't know who it is I ate and buried. I only know that I myself committed the crime. For this reason I have to spend the rest of my life in prison.'

'I ate *then* I buried', a macabre *yet* palliative dream . . . and a twofold contradiction. Its meaning comes to light when the transference is analyzed. In these dreams the analyst is cast in the role of the accuser. At a time when patients cannot name their desire – so as to recognize it as being legitimately their own – and cannot relive it in the transferential relation, a single avenue remains open: inviting the analyst to don the judge's robes. Let us not be misled by such a request. It is simply a maneuver. Wishing to see the crime proven, and the guilty indicted, patients demand that the 'crime of repression' ('the burial of the corpse') that followed the satisfaction ('I ate someone') be placed on trial. This particular 'crime' explains the feeling of oppression: having to spend one's entire life in prison, locked up in neurotic suffering as a result of repression.

The analyst-judge also acts as a morphologist: they have to reconstruct the event from a few scattered body fragments. Whether they play morphologist or judge, analysts – consulted because of the pain of mourning – are called upon to unmask the 'crime' of repression and to identify the victim: the orgasmic moment experienced upon the object's death. That is why, in the dark hours when patients feel they are at an impasse, a dream of this type, though apparently macabre, can bring relief and the hope of finding a way out. Patients ask their analysts: Help me find that moment so that I can come out of the impasse of my interminable mourning.

Thérèse has feelings of sensuality each time she feels she is acting as a 'nurse.' When asked to visit a bedridden family member or friend, she feels embarrassed ahead of time: 'It's going to happen again and I don't know why.' And yet she is mysteriously attracted into friendships with people she rightly or wrongly suspects of being ill. Thérèse has been blocked in her work of mourning over ten years. The suffering and the embarrassment that had led her into analysis turned out to be of the same nature as the 'pain of mourning.' Analysis has shown a massive repression of the father's death through a scene whose memory she has not stopped wanting to recapture at her ill friend's bedside.

In the course of her analysis Thérèse brought a dream triptych that I also found in other patients of mourning: marriage with an inaccessible man, an indictment for having eaten a corpse, a dentist predicting the exposure of her receding gumline, followed by the total loss of her teeth ('exposure' is an allusion to the father's corpse being dressed for the funeral). The much desired though deeply repressed union in love with her father was consummated hallucinatorily during the last rites. Thérèse's added repression of the moment of magical satisfaction directed her development toward an illness of mourning that endangered both her romantic relationships and her professional pursuits.

The vicissitudes of transition and the illness of mourning

In addition to the constantly recurring dream of the 'exquisite corpse,' we also need to note the existence of another type of dream in illnesses of mourning: dreams about 'teeth,' about their growth or loss, their mending or their exposure due to a receding gumline (as in Thérèse's case), etc. While dreams about 'eating and burying a corpse' characterize the illness of mourning, dreams about 'teeth' reach beyond this frame; they are found in nearly all analyses.

What does the language of 'teeth' tell? Patients evoke this symbol each time a conflict born of the passage from one stage of introjection to the next is discussed. Teething marks the first great transition, hence its symbolic value in the evocation of transitions in general. Whether it is the Oedipal passage, adolescent growth, the attainment of adulthood, or progress toward menopause, 'teeth' always lend themselves to symbolizing the vicissitudes of libidinal reorganization. 'You expect your first period like your teeth,' says a patient. For another patient the recurrent dream in which she loses her teeth expresses the loss (in the strong sense of the term) of the Oedipal mother when she passes into adolescence.

When dreams about 'teeth' appear, they can offer a helpful clue if we know how to take advantage of them for the organization of dispersed material.

A sudden and severe form of adolescent anorexia is set off by a teacher's comment: 'You're too big.' The boy stops chewing for several months. His passive silence also hides his now adult voice. A dream about 'teeth' fortunately throws light on the conflict of adolescent transition and bears fruit in the psychoanalytic process. The dream is a nightmare about 'mice who bite' and persecute him. (The boy hears the 'biting' comment made by the teacher, the jealous father's substitute image, as follows: 'Your penis grew too large when you first ejaculated.') He runs away bewildered from these 'beasts with powerful and sharp teeth,' is paralyzed, and wakes up in anguish.

For those who might ask whether the illness of mourning is an autonomous formation or merely an episode in a prior neurotic problem, the recurrent dreams about teeth, indicating conflicts of transition, authorize an answer. The illness of mourning is a special case of a wider and more inclusive framework of disturbances that generally characterize periods of transition.

Libidinal irruptions occur precisely in moments of transition when the new drive (experienced as pleasant) 'cuts through' and forces the ego to reorganize itself and its objectal relations. There really is an intrinsic problem, reminiscent of fixation, in transitional periods. Although mindful of the sweetness of its new drive, the ego is not always ready to accommodate what 'the gods give it.' The ego remains ambivalent for a more or less lengthy period as regards this newcomer. In cases where the object helps the child ever so slightly to introject the drive, giving it back to the child in objectalized forms, the transition need not degenerate into an insurmountable conflict. Introjection should proceed quite smoothly. If, on the other hand, the object is absent, lacking, or has performed a seduction, the introjection of new drives will be blocked and imaginal fixation will inevitably follow. This is why, as libidinal forces appear, new transitions create a favorable breeding ground for inhibitive developmental disturbances. How is the object who inhibits the ego's growth experienced? Clearly, as someone who is cut off from his or her own desire (as in the case of Thomas's mother). If in addition, the object fleetingly welcomes the child's (that is, its own) desire for an instant *and then rejects it*, the object effectively sets the stage for infantile conflict due to its own conflict. The fixation feeds on the child's unwavering hope that one day the object would once again be *what it was* in the privileged moment. For the child, after all, is not the object comparable to itself, it too being subject to a superego's prohibition, but also, just like the child, an exclusive lover in its heart of hearts?

There is a difference, however, between objectal loss linked to fixation – the loss of a moment of satisfaction and its being buried like a corpse – and the illness of mourning. Loss here consists in the actual death of the object.[5] Paradoxically, the object who is dead because of real death revives momentarily the 'exquisite corpse' that together the dead and the survivors had both long before consigned to the grim tomb of repression.

Editors' added bibliography

Ferenczi, S. (1933). *Final Contributions to the Problems and Methods of Psycho-Analysis* (pp. 316–317). New York: Brunner-Mazel.
Freud, S. (1915). *Papers on Metapsychology. S.E.*, 14.
Freud, S., & Abraham, K. (1907–1926). *A Psycho-Analytic Dialogue: The Letters of Sigmund Freud and Karl Abraham*. London: Hogarth Press, 1965.

---

[5] In his study 'If I Were Dead' (in *De l'art à la mort* [From art to death]; Paris: Gallimard, 1977), Michel de M'Uzan describes the *work of passing away* at the point of death. The dying person experiences an increase in relational appetite in the form of renewed creative impetus. The analysis of people ill from mourning shows the many revivals of these moments in which the respective introjections of both parties converge and the impulse of the survivor coincides with the 'last muster' ('let us muster up life') of the dying person; these impulses manifest themselves in an anguished state of confused identity, if not in pain. [This footnote was inserted by Torok in the French edition of *The Shell and the Kernel* in 1978, ten years after she originally published her essay. – Ed., as above]

20 LISTENING TO THE TELESCOPING OF GENERATIONS

The psychoanalytic pertinence of the concept

Haydée Faimberg

A medical doctor and psychoanalyst, originally from Argentina, **Haydée Faimberg** is a training and supervising analyst of the Argentine Psychoanalytical Association and of the Paris Psychoanalytical Society. As vice-president of the International Psychoanalytical Association, she created the Standing Conference on Psychoanalytical Intracultural and Intercultural Dialogue. Her keen interest in international discussions led her to set up a clinical Forum within the European Psychoanalytical Federation and, from 1993 on, to co-chair, with A.-M. Sandler, the annual Franco–British clinical meetings. The main focus of her work has involved the study of intergenerational issues centred on the transference process, on listening to anachronisms in the unconscious and on the (re)construction of historical truths in psychoanalysis. The 'listening to the [patient's] listening' function of the analyst gives access to the unconscious alienated narcissistic identifications (where there is a condensation of three generations: 'telescoping of generations') which constitute a link between generations. She has contributed one or more chapters to each of fourteen books and has published *The Telescoping of Generations: Listening to the Narcissistic Links between Generations* (Routledge, 2005). Among her numerous essays she has formulated a broader concept of *après-coup* by articulating it, in 1998, with Winnicott's concept of 'fear of breakdown' and in 1977 wrote about Lewis Carroll (both published in *The Telescoping of Generations*). In her essay in 1989 on Italo Calvino, she refers also to temporality ('Time Zero: Waiting').

In 2005, Dr. Haydée Faimberg received the Haskell Norman International Award for her 'outstanding achievements as a clinician, teacher and theoretician'.

Introduction[1]

The baby looks at the way he is seen by his mother. Winnicott's notion suggests how the subject is constituted initially, and it helps us to see clearly how Freud's metaphor of 'the analyst as a mirror' can be understood, while avoiding empiricism. This idea, highlighting intersubjectivity, arose from a stimulating dialogue between Winnicott and Lacan. At the beginning of his article 'Mirror-Role of Mother and Family in Child Development' (1967), Winnicott tells the reader *how he has read* Lacan's study, 'Le stade du miroir' [The mirror stage] (1949 – see chapter 3, this volume). Having acknowledged his sources, he is quite free to think it through again and, in so doing, to grant the reader the same liberty. By putting the reader immediately in the position of recognising the otherness of the two authors, he saves him from having to 'suspect' the text by thinking, for example, that 'it was one of Lacan's ideas'.

This dialectical matrix proposed by Winnicott in the form of a dialogue between psychoanalysts constitutes for me an ideal of creation. On the one hand, it avoids the pitfall of eclecticism, since Winnicott respects the essential structure of Lacan's thinking, and, on the other, Winnicott remains faithful to his own conception of psychic formation. The result of this is that the theory of the object relation can be articulated with the concept of the intersubjective relation. Moreover, by citing his sources, Winnicott is not afraid of exposing himself to seeing the originality of his thinking challenged. In fact, the identity of his thinking is strengthened. It seems to me that *the function of recognition* is the source of creation.[2]

---

[1] On Sunday, 25 October 1987, Micheline Enriquez and I were due to meet – the appointment had been made in June – to speak about the presentation of my article 'Le téléscopage des générations' at her seminar. The Sunday before, she was killed in a car accident.

When Piera Aulagnier kindly invited me to participate in a volume by way of tribute to Micheline Enriquez, I first thought that I would write up some notes, imagining a dialogue with Micheline about the article in question. I subsequently gave up my initial project, saying to myself that one could pay tribute to an author just as well by not making her say what she might not have said. This was how I overcame my scruples about only presenting my own ideas in a volume whose purpose was to pay tribute to her.

What follows is the presentation that I would have made at her seminar on my article 'Le téléscopage des générations'. In fact it is a new reading of this article. 'Le téléscopage des générations' was written in 1979–1980 and discussed at the time in a group run by André Green. I read an abridged version of it in 1981 at the Paris Psychoanalytical Society under the title 'La résistance narcissique à la reconnaissance de la différence des générations et de l'altérité' [Narcissistic resistances to accepting difference between generations and otherness]. The full version was first published in Spanish in *Revista de Psicoanálisis* (1985), *42*, pp. 1042–1056, under the title 'El telescopaje de generaciones: genealogía de ciertas identificaciones', and in French in *Psychanalyse à l'université*, (1987), *12* (46), pp. 181–200; it constitutes chapter 1, 'The Telescoping of Generations: A Genealogy of Alienated Identifications', in *The Telescoping of Generations: Listening to the Narcissistic Links between Generations* (Faimberg, 2005). The notes of the present publication refer to this 2005 book.

[2] My reflection is grounded in two sources: on the one hand, the study seminars of Freudian texts conducted by Guillermo Maci; and on the other, the generous oral and written transmission (from different standpoints) by Willy Baranger, José Bleger, André Green, Jean Laplanche, David Liberman, Jorge Mom and Enrique Pichon-Rivière.

When Winnicott's ideas were not recognised by an author, he would write to him to point this out and would go on to say: now that I have told you how I think, I feel free to consider *your* ideas. By making this gesture, Winnicott also liberated the forgetful.[3]

The complexity of factors that play a part in the destiny of the recognition of an idea does not escape me. For instance, the same Winnicott, citing Marion Milner, says that she has recently discussed the idea that he is proposing to develop. This recognition in no way hindered the subsequent evolution of Marion Milner's ideas. Indeed, while every analyst knows the concepts of transitional space and transitional object, few recall Marion Milner's very fine article 'The Role of Illusion in Symbol Formation' (1952).

I have conceived of the problem of '*listening to the [patient's] listening*' drawing on two authors as a source of inspiration: if my notion of listening to listening is linked up with Winnicott's notion of intersubjectivity, it also takes account of Enrique Pichon-Rivière's notion of dialectical spiral.[4]

Psychoanalytic pertinence of the concept of the telescoping of generations

By the telescoping of generations, I mean the appearance, during a psychoanalytic treatment and within the strict frame of the session, of a special type of alienating narcissistic[5] unconscious identification which condenses three generations and *reveals itself in the transference*.

In psychoanalytically oriented family psychotherapies, during interviews with the parents of patients (children, adolescents and psychotics),[6] in the testimonies of subjects who have survived catastrophic situations (the Shoah, for example), and in other contexts, problematic issues appear that are sometimes closely related to the theme we are considering. Such a fact, which is so conducive to dialogue, must not make us lose sight of the perspective from which I developed the concept of the telescoping of generations. Not confusing the fields of discourses and respecting the pertinence of each concept allows, I think, for an equally pertinent and stimulating interdisciplinary discourse.

Consequently, I wish to return to what I have already said about the concept of the telescoping of generations by underscoring the rigorous *conditions* in

---

[3] The collection of Winnicott's letters bears the title *The Spontaneous Gesture* (Winnicott, 1987).
[4] For this notion, see Faimberg, Corel, & Wender (1982).
[5] I qualify these unconscious identifications as alienating because they are part of a history which belongs in part to someone else, and as narcissistic because they concern the patient's being. It is worth noting the importance that Piera Aulagnier also gives to this notion of alienation.
[6] This in no way means that children, adolescents and psychotics or any other kinds of patients cannot be approached by psychoanalysis (as they certainly are, with success). It just means that each time we compare experiences, they need to be contextualised in relation to the particular frame in which the experience took place.

respect of which I have delimited the psychoanalytic pertinence of this concept.

(1) I consider the concept of the telescoping of generations as a specific concept of *psychoanalytic experience, a psychoanalytic clinical concept.*

(2) A clinical concept is *neither descriptive nor empirical.*

(3) The telescoping of the generations concerns *unconscious narcissistic alienating* identifications.

(4) I have shown that unconscious identifications have a *cause* and are not merely an initial datum that requires no explanation. This is because I am not situating myself on the descriptive or empirical level but on the level of psychoanalytic clinical experience. Such a criterion also helps to *free the notion of unconscious identification of any pre-Freudian, non-psychoanalytic baggage.*

(5) These unconscious identifications are initially *inaudible*, maintain themselves, and *must* maintain themselves as such for a long time in the psychoanalytic treatment.

(6) The countertransference–transference axis (stated in that order) is fundamental for the consideration of what follows. Indeed, the analyst must be able to contain, in the countertransference, the anxiety of not knowing, and of not knowing that he (or she) does not know. This is the very condition that allows for the silent maintenance of these identifications. *In this way, the analyst avoids resorting to a method for deducing a genealogy of identifications on the basis of his/her theory, without taking account of what the patient is saying.*

In the contrary case, the analyst runs the risk with his theory of intruding on the patient's psyche.[7] I have studied in detail the clinical conditions that allow one to be (almost) sure that the unconscious identifications brought out by the analysis *really belong to the patient's mind.*[8]

(7) As a corollary of the preceding points, two different ways of treating the problem of identifications may be defined.

The first, which I have adopted, consists in *inferring* the existence of unconscious identifications on the basis of what the patient says. The patient *speaks and listens on the basis of unconscious identifications.* When the analyst listens to how the patient has heard his (or her) interpretations, he is able, on the basis of what he believes he has said, and of what has actually been heard by the patient, to infer the analysand's unconscious identifications. Thus, *misunderstanding becomes one of the essential motors of the analysis.* This function of 'listening to listening' has been discussed elsewhere (see in particular, Faimberg, 1981/2005, pp. 24–30). From this point of view, unconscious identifications come to the fore where neither the patient nor the analyst expect them: hence the effect of surprise.

A second perspective, which I do not share, consists in taking into account only the representations of the identifications that the patient and the analyst

---

[7] Jean Cornut is interested in the effects of the analyst's intrusion.
[8] See in particular Faimberg (1981 [1985]/2005), pp. 7–8.

form for themselves. In this case, the decentring due to repression, which follows from the first perspective, does not occur. This second perspective is based on introspection alone.

Consequently: *respect for the psychoanalytic method, which permits the unconscious identifications linked to the telescoping of generations to emerge in the transference, is a necessary criterion for defining the telescoping of generations as a psychoanalytic concept.*

The transference–countertransference[9] constitutes the privileged aspect of this study.

In reality, for the telescoping of generations to be a psychoanalytic concept, *it must meet the requirements of any psychoanalytic concept* – namely, it must account for a clinical fact (neither descriptive nor empiric, as we have seen); and it must manifest itself through the patient's discourse (in the strict framework of the treatment) *and only through the patient's discourse. This does not mean that everything can be said. It just means that the unspoken may be heard by the analyst through what the patient is able to say.*

In the case in question, the situation is enigmatic. How can two people speak about something when one of them – the patient – does not speak about this thing, because he does not associate to it during the session and does not think that it concerns him, and when the other – the analyst – is unaware of the existence of this thing or, if he knows what it is, does not know how it is articulated in the patient's psyche?

What must we do to avoid short-circuiting the psychoanalytic process and to remain in the pertinent field of psychoanalysis? In my view, this difficulty is inherent to every psychoanalytic treatment.

Consequently, the psychoanalytic pertinence and the clinical conditions of the discovery of the telescoping of generations are two indissociable aspects of the same problem.

On reading Michel Tort's (1986) article 'L'argument généalogique', which is situated at an epistemological level, I wondered why I had never had the idea of using the term 'transgenerational'.[10] In light of what has gone before, the answer is straightforward: my conception of the telescoping of generations fits in with usual analytic practice and the framework of my usual theoretical

---

[9] 'I place the countertransference at the intersection of three narcissisms of the analyst on the one hand, and of the patient's narcissism on the other (which includes the narcissism of the internal parents)' (see Faimberg, 1981/2005, p. 29).

[10] [Note added for this publication:] On the basis of further analytic experience as developed in *The Telescoping of Generations* (Faimberg, 2005), I proposed a definition of the 'intergenerational relationship' included in an article I wrote for the *International Dictionary of Psychoanalysis* on the notion of 'Intergenerational' ('*Intergénérationnel*') – where the term is always used as an adjective: 'The concept of an "intergenerational relationship" refers to a process of (re)construction whereby a particular dimension – (which we may metaphorically call an "original dimension" [*l'originaire*]) – is brought retroactively (*après-coup*) into existence in the history of the transference. This "original dimension" then becomes an enabling condition for the initiation of a process of "historicization" of the analysand in relation to two or more previous generations' (Faimberg, 2002/2006).

position. Furthermore, my central hypothesis is that the telescoping of generations is discovered in *every analysis* conducted rigorously. In this context, I have not needed to resort to a concept which implies a notion of the unconscious that is different from the psychoanalytic notion of unconscious which I usually employ.

Antecedents

The first article, as far as I know, to deal with the subject that interests me was Guy Rosolato's 'Trois générations d'hommes dans le mythe religieux et la généalogie' (1967).

The second work that appeared on this theme was a study of so-called applied analysis by Alain de Mijolla, *Les visiteurs du moi* (1986), in which the author proposes the concept of fantasy of unconscious identification.

Nicolas Abraham and Maria Torok (1978) have taken interest in the problem of mourning, and propose the concepts of ghost and crypt. Implicitly, they refer to a similar problem to the one that I am concerned with and that I will be developing further on.

The studies devoted by Piera Aulagnier (1975) and Micheline Enriquez (1986) to this subject are centred on psychosis. The articulation of their ideas and mine will be the subject of another article.

I will not give a survey here of the abundant literature that is currently available.[11] My contribution will just focus on those points which, to the best of my knowledge, have not been treated elsewhere:

(1) Firstly, the *clinical conditions* that are necessary for facilitating the revelation of unconscious identifications bound up with a history *condensing three generations*. These clinical conditions constitute in turn the criterion which allows us to consider the psychoanalytic pertinence of the concept of the telescoping of generations: my reflection is focused on the transference–countertransference.

(2) As a central hypothesis, I propose to consider the telescoping of generations as a universal phenomenon present in *every analysis* provided that the problem is taken into account and that *the clinical conditions of its discovery are respected*.

(3) I consider that the functions of appropriation and intrusion are characteristic of the narcissistic object regulation (and that they are a personal contribution for understanding this kind of regulation).

---

[11] But I shall recall the contributions by Jean Guillaumin, who in his paper of 1982, at the Paris Psychoanalytical Society, quotes the function of appropriation that I propose and prefers to name the resulting identifications as 'identifications *en abîme*'; in 1988, in his report to the 48th Congress of French-Speaking Analysts 'L'objet de la perte dans la pensée de Freud', he links the identifications *en abîme* to a problem of 'interlocking identifications'.

Telescoping of generations and transmission of history: Functions of appropriation/intrusion

I have linked the way the parents transmit their history to their mode of saying and not saying (Faimberg, 1981 [1985]/2005, pp. 113–115). But which parents are we speaking about during an analysis? The analyst knows nothing about the real parents. The character of the parents' reality is put between parentheses (*epoché*) during the session. A hypothetical reality of the parents can be inferred from that which insists in the transference as a remainder. In this sense, it is not material reality but a notion of reality that subsists as a remainder.[12] This theme of reality in psychoanalysis, which is very complex and important, will not be discussed here.[13]

My conception of these parents corresponds to theoretical choices that cannot be elaborated within the context of one article.[14] I shall simply allude to them by means of the following anecdote: in 1977, in a cycle of lectures organised by Piera Aulangier at the Hopital Saint-Anne, Micheline Enriquez presented a fine paper on the function of writing in some of her patients. I found her work admirable and I was in agreement with her on all the points she made. But when we tried to understand the reasons for our agreement, we were unable to agree. I understood much later that the ideas set out around this same time by Piera Aulagnier (1975) in *La violence de l'interprétation* had an explanatory function for Micheline Enriquez equivalent to the one I found in Bion and Winnicott.[15]

At the same moment, I had begun – in the light of certain writings of Freud – a re-evaluation of the concepts of Winnicott and Bion.[16] It is worth recalling here that already in 1956 the Argentinian psychoanalyst Enrique Pichon-Rivière[17] was questioning the conception that attributes to the mother the initial exclusive role in the baby's psychic make-up.

The parents I am speaking about are the parents as they are inscribed in the patient's psychic reality. I recognize this inscription in the way the patient speaks and in the way he/she hears the analyst's interpretations and silences.

I have called these parents 'internal parents', not without some concern about the possible reification of the concept which this terminology could entail. Actually, I am designating thereby a third term situated between

---

[12] Perhaps what 'remains' overlaps with the category of 'the Real' defined by Lacan.
[13] For a discussion of this theme, see Faimberg & Corel (1989).
[14] [Note added for this publication:] My theoretical choices are developed in *The Telescoping of Generations* (Faimberg, 2005).
[15] This may explain why Piera Aulagnier's ideas were accepted so quickly in Argentina.
[16] I had the opportunity of listening to André Green, during his first visit to Argentina in 1974, presenting his original ideas on Winnicott and Bion.
[17] It is also worth noting that for Pichon-Rivière (in his 1960s seminars given at his School of Dynamic Psychiatry) the triangular situation is the impassable epistemological limit in psychoanalysis. He said that, in the session, each of the official participants brought his Oedipal situation.

what the patient says and what the analyst hears. This same third term reappears between what the analyst thinks he says and what the patient actually hears.

This third term does not coincide, and cannot coincide, with the parents of material reality. These internal parents do not coincide either with the idea that the patients have of their parents. The parents that interest me are those that take form *in the patient's words, over and beyond what the patient thinks the parents are*. They also differ from those that the analyst imagines on the basis of his theory or the image proposed by the patient. The parents I have in mind are not revealed through introspection, but come to the fore through what the patient says; they constitute the third term with which the patient identifies. This means that it is the patient himself *who at certain moments functions psychically in the very register that is at the origin of his alienating identification*.

I consider that these alienated unconscious identifications are subjected to the regime of narcissistic regulation, a regulation *which ensures its own system of reproduction*. In this sense one can speak of the metapsychological *conditions* of transmission (Faimberg, 1981 [1985]/2005, pp. 17–18). These identifications, of course, exist alongside others; they only occupy the foreground when an early affective experience is reactivated in the transference.

I would now like to examine the functions of appropriation and intrusion in a case published by Micheline Enriquez (1986), the case of Catherine. In order to understand (as Micheline Enriquez did) that Catherine took her interpretations as an intrusion, the analyst had to listen to the way the patient heard them. The analyst's function of 'listening to [the patient's] listening' (Faimberg, 1981/2005 p. 29) enabled her to grasp the function of intrusion. The patient feared that the analyst might be intrusive, just as her mother's delusion had been intrusive. M. Enriquez subtly shows how Catherine confirmed the maternal delusion: the patient put herself in the position of confirming that she owed her life and her death to her mother. I am particularly sensitive to the place granted by M. Enriquez to Aulagnier's ideas to explain the mother's excessive power.

From my perspective, I would like to point out that at the same time as the patient confirms her mother's abusive power, *she assures herself that psychically she does have a mother*. The drama of this kind of alienating narcissistic unconscious identification is that the identification with the mother's history *does not allow the patient to exist psychically in any other register*. This is because the maternal functions of appropriation and of intrusion have deprived Catherine of a psychic space of her own.

It was M. Enriquez's analytic work that allowed the patient to dream that she had established with the analyst a relationship of dependence that was different from the one that bound her to her mother. Once again, the transference is the place of repetition and creation.

From the unspoken to the secret in the transference

We must accept that, in our analytic work, we start out from a very enigmatic situation.

On the one hand, I am saying that, in his countertransference, the analyst must contain the anxiety of not knowing and of not knowing that he does not know. And it will be like this until he understands *après-coup* [*nachträglich*] what portion of the transference was contained in the countertransference. Even when the analyst 'knows' (during the preliminary interview or through what has been said in a session), he actively adopts a position of not knowing in each session. When, in the transference, the unconscious identifications are revealed through the telescoping of generations, this revelation will emerge from the unexpected relationship between known information and the way in which he brings it in as an attempt to solve an enigma posed by the transference.[18]

On the other hand, I hold that it is the patient, and necessarily *he alone,* who reveals by surprise (where neither the patient nor the analyst had suspected it) the narrative which will begin to make it possible to understand *the unconscious identification retrospectively*.

I believe that what the patient does not say obeys certain laws. These laws stem from the functions of appropriation and intrusion which I have discussed elsewhere in connection with the very conditions of the telescoping of generations.

What *makes it possible* for *the unspoken to be put into words*?[19]

I will only concern myself here with the subtle dialectic which is established between *what the patient does not know he knows and what the analyst is completely unaware of*.

I am going to present an extract from an article (Faimberg, 1981 [1985], which became chapter 1 in Faimberg, 2005) which will help us to understand the reflection that will follow.

Mario was a man who gave the impression of having an empty, dead psyche.

The time of 'listening to listening', the time of listening to how my patient heard my interpretations, designated repetitively and inexorably a void. The patient remained inaccessible: he seemed absent and did not recognize my presence. I failed to find any effective interpretative means to make myself present in his psyche which would allow me to interpret his absence. My only merit in such a situation was to contain – in my countertransference – the anxiety of not existing as an analyst in the patient's psyche and therefore of being unable to modify his emptiness, his psychic death.

During the session in question, Mario's anxiety became evident for the first time. He said if things went on like that he would not be able to continue with

---

[18] For the concept of 'enigma posed by the transference', see Faimberg (1992).
[19] For my discussion of the clinical conditions which make the revelation of the telescoping of generations possible, see Faimberg (1981 [1985]/2005, pp. 7–8).

his analysis because he did not have enough money to see him through to the end of the month. He clearly wanted to go on with the analysis, but he was also incapable of taking any economic steps to make this possible. He explained that someone had tried to persuade him to buy dollars and had asked him if he knew how much a dollar was worth. Mario had answered that a dollar was worth two pesos. While he was telling me this, he made a barely perceptible gesture with his hand, as if to make sure that something in his pocket was still there, a loving gesture accompanied by a tender and secret smile. At the same time, with an absent, indifferent attitude, he said that his friend had told him that a dollar was worth 5,000 pesos. He seemed not to realise that he did not know the value of the dollar, nor was he shocked by his own mistake. He seemed to think that it was material reality that was 'wrong'.

Let us recall, as I have already said, that until this session, Mario had never manifested any desire or signs of psychic presence. My difficulty resided in the fact that I was unable to give him any useful interpretation concerning his absence.

The change that emerged during this session was that Mario expressed his wish to continue the analysis as well as his anxiety about having to stop it imminently.

He was absent with regard to what might be called material reality and was unable to protect what he wanted.

I interpreted:

'You must be keeping something very important in your pocket, something secret that demands your attention just when we are talking about the money you need to continue with me. You want to go on with your analysis and you are afraid of losing it. What demands your attention might be connected with the dollars that are worth two pesos. If such is the case, they must belong to some time in the past, perhaps to the forties. *I know nothing about this*, but *if* it were so, have you any idea *who* those dollars *are for*?' [While uttering my interpretation/construction, I realized that at that time Mario had *not yet been born*.]

Needless to say the interpretative construction does not describe a behaviour. Mario's gesture, in the light of everything that had been said, was part of an unconscious chain of meaning which was lacking, and it is this unconscious meaning that makes it possible to speak of interpretation.

Mario's answer came immediately – a prompt, lively and personal answer. He talked with such a feeling of presence that there was no doubt that he was involved in what he was saying. We were engaged. He replied (as if it were natural and evident):

'Yes, I know who those dollars are for. They are for my father's family. My father's family remained in Poland when my father left the country,

in the thirties. My mother told me that my father's character completely changed after the emigration: he just stopped talking, in fact he never really learned Spanish. During the war he started sending money to his relatives in Poland every month, to his parents and his brothers and sisters. Dollars, it was dollars he sent. And a time came when nobody collected the money. I think the whole family had died. Well, my father never talked about them or what could have happened to them. I think he never really got to know what happened. It was my mother who told me all this'.
(Faimberg 1981 [1985]/2005, p. 6)

Let us come back to the question of the dialectic that is established between what the patient does not know he knows and what the analyst is completely ignorant of.

(1) The analyst knows that on the one hand Mario is present in his desire to continue the analysis and in his anxiety about losing it. The analyst also knows that the patient is absent in his relation with the analyst, and at the same time present in a secret space (the tender and secret relationship with the 'two-pesos' dollars). Consequently, *the analyst knows that a part of Mario's discourse is not addressed to her.*

(2) What the analyst does not know is to whom the discourse of the two-pesos dollars is addressed.

(3) The analyst tells the patient what she has understood from his discourse, with its gaps and its anachronisms. This communication from the analyst is *already an interpretation.*

(4) The analyst says something fundamental to the patient – namely, that she, the analyst, does not know what these fragments of discourse mean (the analyst's not knowing is subsequently confirmed: in reality, the analyst did not know).

(5) The analyst invites Mario to interpret the gaps in his own discourse.

She proposes a line of reasoning in a conditional mode: '*If you know*', then I (as I know that this discourse is not addressed to me) ask you the question: 'Do you know who this discourse is addressed to?' This reasoning constitutes the matrix of the interrogative construction. As in every analysis, one cannot put the question directly to the patient, since he does not know that he knows; as in every analysis, one can only make an interpretation/construction, in this case in the interrogative form.

(6) The interrogation implies a virtual point which designates, beyond the presence of the official protagonists, that of an *included third which excludes momentarily the analyst*. This interpretation is *made possible* by the discrepancy between the analyst's countertransference and the patient's manifest discourse. *The interpretation constructs the conditions under which it will be possible to name this third, which is unconscious for the patient and unknown to the analyst.*

(7) This unspoken element can then be interpreted by the patient in the form of a discourse that the analyst will be able to designate, *après-coup* (as I did), as the secret *in the transference* (Faimberg, 1981 [1985]/2005, p. 6).

To sum up, we can consider the secret as already an organisation, an *interpretation* of the unspoken.

I think that the wish to continue the analysis, on the analyst's part as much as the patient's, that was mobilised in the transference–countertransference at this particularly enigmatic moment of the treatment *transforms into interlocution and creation that which hitherto was just repetition.*

Does the telescoping of generations necessarily have its cause in a problem of mourning?

My study has frequently been considered as a logical follow-up to the work of Nicolas Abraham and Maria Torok. The notion of ghost, which is theirs, and the notion of 'living-dead', which I mention, no doubt overlap. The notion of living-dead comes from the essay by Willy Baranger (1961–62), with whom I worked for a long time.

We know that the coincidences between authors who follow their reflections without prior knowledge of each other's respective work have an effect of confirmation. In my case, our coincidences and our divergences have led me to inquire into the genealogy of our respective ideas. This deserves a study of its own.

Speaking about mourning is complex in that it is important to know the place that this concept has in an author's theory. A telling example of what I mean is offered by the concept of the depressive position coined by Melanie Klein. Authors who privilege this position in their way of conceiving psychic functioning grant an important place, in their thinking as a whole, to the notion of mourning.

Another problem can be linked to the last point, namely, that of knowing if the notion of mourning refers to the actual loss through death of a significant person, because it is possible to speak of mourning in other contexts; one can thus imagine a child who has to mourn a mother who has become psychically inaccessible.[20] These multiple scenarios are not the object of my present considerations.

My attention has been particularly drawn to the fact that the work of Abraham and Torok *is centred* on the problem of mourning.

For my part, coming from a psychoanalytic culture which gives central importance to mourning in psychic functioning, I have been keen to think through my subject from other perspectives with the aim of investigating new openings. Thus, I have considered the telescoping of generations, as I explained in my article, while putting between parentheses crucial psychoanalytic concepts such as:

---

[20] A mother can become psychically inaccessible as a result of mourning due to the death of her own mother: see Green (2001, pp. 170–200).

(1) The vicissitudes of the work of mourning.
(2) The works of Freud which deal explicitly with identifications (among other reasons because Freud himself was not satisfied with the way he had dealt with them).
(3) The concept of projective identification.
(4) The articulation of the concepts of splitting, denial and repression.

On the other hand, I have centred my considerations on Freud's writings 'Instincts and Their Vicissitudes' (1915c) (which also has a central place in M. Torok's study; Abraham & Torok, 1978), 'Negation' (1925h), 'On Narcissism: An Introduction' (1914c) and *Totem and Taboo* (1912–13).

Taking into account the way in which my article has been read and understood, I cannot help but ask myself about the *actual* place that the problem of mourning occupies in my thinking, over and beyond my methodological *intentions*.

This questioning has accompanied my reading of the work of Jean Cournut, whose interest in the vicissitudes of the analyst's intrusive activity I share. Likewise, in listening to André Green presenting one of his finest studies, 'The Dead Mother' (2001), I wondered if the figure of the dead mother was *necessarily linked to a mother in mourning*. It goes without saying that André Green quite legitimately chose this perspective without necessarily prejudging other scenarios. We could also wonder how to articulate André Green's concept of the 'dead mother' with the 'appropriation and intrusion functions' I have proposed as being characteristic of the 'narcissistic regulation' of the internal parents.

Can we conceive of a figure of the 'dead mother' who is 'psychically inaccessible'? This inaccessibility could be the consequence of mourning, as André Green says, but also of an alienating narcissistic unconscious identification where there is a telescoping of generations.

In reality, I am raising the more general question of a possible inscription of the problem of mourning within a wider problematic.

If I succeed in setting aside the problem of mourning, and if this concept proves to be inessential to the concept of the telescoping of generations within my argument, then the question of mourning should necessarily be discussed in conjunction with this problematic, which has been the essential object of my study.

If we come back to the line of argument that I am using, in the case of Mario, to define the telescoping of generations, it can be seen that the *key concept is that of the alienating unconscious narcissistic identification which the patient uses to resist, on a narcissistic level, the wound inflicted by the Oedipal conflict* (Faimberg, 1981 [1985]/2005, p. 17)[21] *and more particularly by the recognition of the difference between generations*.

---

[21] [Note added for this publication:] A further development of this concept is given in Faimberg (1993/2005, pp. 50–62).

Mario considers himself unconsciously as the *cause* of his father's history. The psychic crystallisation in frozen time gives Mario the megalomaniac belief that he, Mario, can save the father's family. *The 'two-pesos' dollars that he preserves lovingly and secretly constitute the narcissistic link with an anachronistic history, prior to his birth. Mario's unconscious desire not to recognise his father as father, to resist narcissistically the Oedipal situation, is reinforced by his father's history.*

Mario speaks using his mother's words, which refer in a similar form to the father and to Mario. 'When your father came from Poland, he stopped speaking, and *he was never himself again*', 'When your brother was born, you stopped talking and playing, and *you were never yourself again*'.

Mario's alienating unconscious narcissistic identifications stand in the way of the dialectic between the narcissistic register and the Oedipal register. The telescoping of generations is the *cause* of the narcissistic resistance which manifests itself in the transference.[22]

It emerges from what I have said that *someone resists, and that the narcissistic resistances themselves have a history*. In the case in question, 'someone' is composite because there is a telescoping of generations.

I have designated the psychoanalytic work that is centred on the narcissistic register as the 'narcissistic dimension of the Oedipal configuration,'[23] of which the telescoping of generations is one scenario.[24]

Let us come back to the question of the relation between mourning and the telescoping of generations. I came to the conclusion that 'someone' puts up narcissistic resistances to the wound inflicted by the Oedipus configuration. I have also said that this 'someone' is inscribed in a history. What is the relation between this 'someone' and the notion of mourning?

Clearly, the idea of an *impossible* mourning leaps to the eyes, and the reader sees it *primarily* because, methodologically, I have left it to one side. The advantage of having put the notion of mourning aside is that I did not stop my research when I arrived at the notion of the 'living-dead'. I wanted to inscribe

---

[22] Mario's narcissistic collusion with the history of his father and mother was commented on by a German psychoanalyst during the presentation of my paper in Hamburg: 'Now I understand why I never asked my parents what they did during the war. I didn't ask any questions because unconsciously I knew the answer; I was unconsciously identified with them. It also explains why I have never spoken about this with my analyst.'

[23] [Note added for this publication:] In French 'Le temps narcissique de l'Oedipe' is the original expression by the Argentinian philosopher Guillermo Maci, an expression which is difficult to translate into English as such. It refers to a logical sequence, and not a temporal sequence.

[24] Retrospectively, I reproach myself for not having placed enough emphasis on the patient's unconscious desire, on his psychic activity, in the formation of unconscious identifications.

The reason for this is that I was so impressed by the discovery of the alienating aspect of the patient's subjection to the preceding generations that I stressed the *passive* splitting.

Remember what I wrote in chapter 1 of my book *The Telescoping of Generations* (1981 [1985]/2005, pp. 4–18) – namely, that theorising narcissism does not imply that one shares the patient's narcissistic theories. The fact that the patient *believes* he is free of his drives and free to elaborate psychically the Oedipal situation and its avatars (recognition of sexual difference, generational difference, and otherness) does not imply that psychoanalysts are unaware that *the narcissistic level is also constituted in an instinctual conflict* arising from the *origins of the very constitution of narcissism*.

Mario's unconscious identification with his 'father-who-does-not-acknowledge-the-death-of-his-family-in-Poland' within a wider network – namely, that of refusing to acknowledge the difference between generations.

Is this 'someone' who resists always linked, then, with a 'living dead'?

Is the notion of psychic death, of psychic absence, always linked to the question of mourning?

I leave these questions in abeyance.

Conclusions

In the present paper, a new reading of a previous article, I examine some aspects of the relationship between three generations from a perspective, which, to my knowledge, has not been considered by other authors.

1. I examine the clinical conditions needed to bring out alienating unconscious narcissistic identifications which are partly linked to a history that does not belong to the patient's generation. The telescoping involves three generations.
2. The psychoanalytic pertinence of the concept.
3. Some hypotheses about the conditions of transmission by which this telescoping is established.
4. The telescoping of generations is a universal phenomenon, found in every advanced analysis: this is the central hypothesis.

References

Abraham, N. & Torok, M. (1978). *L'écorce et le noyau.* Paris: Aubier-Flammarion. [*The Shell and the Kernel*, trans. N. T. Rand. Chicago: University of Chicago Press, 1994.]

Aulagnier, P. (1975). *La violence de l'interprétation.* Paris: Presses Universitaires de France. [*The Violence of Interpretation*, trans. A. Sheridan. London: Routledge, 2001.]

Baranger, W. (1961–62). El muerto-vivo, estructura de los objetos en el duelo y los estados depresivos. *Revista Uruguaya de Psicoanálisis*, 4 (4). [The dead-alive: Object structure in mourning and depressive states. In M. Baranger & W. Baranger, *The Work of Confluence.* London: Karnac: 2009.]

Enriquez, M. (1986). Le délire en héritage. *Topique, 38:* 41–67.

Faimberg, H. (1981). Une des difficultés de l'analyse. La reconnaissance de l'altérité. L'écoute des interprétations. *Revue Française de Psychanalyse*, 45 (6): 1351–1367. ['Listening to Listening': An Approach to the Study of Narcissistic Resistances. In *The Telescoping of Generations: Listening to the Narcissistic Links between Generations* (chapter 2). London: Routledge, 2005.]

Faimberg H (1981 [1985]). El telescopaje de generaciones. Genealogía de ciertas identificaciones. *Revista de Psicoanálisis*, 42 (1985): 1042–1056. [The Telescoping of Generations: A Genealogy of Alienated Identifications. In *The Telescoping of Generations: Listening to the Narcissistic Links between Generations* (chapter 1). London: Routledge, 2005.]

Faimberg, H. (1992). L'énigme que pose le transfert [The enigma posed by the transference]. In Jean Laplanche et al., *Colloque international de psychanalyse*. Paris: Presses Universitaires de France, 1994.

Faimberg, H. (1993). The Narcissistic Dimension of the Oedipal Configuration. In *The Telescoping of Generations: Listening to the Narcissistic Links between Generations* (chapter 5). London: Routledge, 2005.

Faimberg, H. (2002). Intergénérationnel. In *Dictionnaire international de la psychanalyse*, ed. A. de Mijolla. Paris: Calmann-Lévy. [Intergenerational. In *International Dictionary of Psychoanalysis*. New York: Macmillan, 2006.]

Faimberg, H. (2005). *The Telescoping of Generations: Listening to the Narcissistic Links between Generations*. London: Routledge.

Faimberg, H., & Corel, A. (1989). Repetición y sorpresa. Una aproximación clínica a la necesidad de la construcción y de su validación. *Revista de Psicoanálisis*, *46*: 717–732. [Repetition and Surprise: Construction and Its Validation. In *The Telescoping of Generations: Listening to the Narcissistic Links between Generations* (chapter 3). London: Routledge, 2005.]

Faimberg, H., Corel, A., & Wender, L. (1982). Psychanalyse en Argentine. In *Histoire de la psychanalyse*, ed. R. Jaccard. Paris: Hachette.

Freud, S. (1912–13). Totem and Taboo. *S.E.*, 13: 1–161.

Freud, S. (1914c). On Narcissism: An Introduction. *S.E.*, 14: 69–102.

Freud, S. (1915c). Instincts and Their Vicissitudes. *S.E.*, 14: 109–117.

Freud, S. (1925h). Negation. *S.E.*, 19: 233–239.

Green, A. (2001). The Dead Mother. In *Life Narcissism, Death Narcissism*, trans. A. Weller. London: Free Association Books.

Lacan, J. (1949). The Mirror Stage as Formative of the Function of the *I* as Revealed in Psychoanalytic Experience. In *Ecrits*, trans. B. Fink. New York: Norton, 2006.

Mijolla, de A. (1986). *Les visiteurs du moi*. Paris: Les Belles Lettres.

Milner, M. (1952). The Role of Illusion in Symbol Formation. In *New Directions in Psychoanalysis*, ed. M. Klein, P. Heimann, & R. E Money-Kyrle. London: Tavistock, 1955; reprinted London: Karnac, 1985.

Rosolato, G. (1967). Trois générations d'hommes dans le mythe religieux et la généalogie [Three generations of men in religious myth and genealogy]. *L'inconscient*, *1*: 71–108.

Tort, M. (1986). L'argument généalogique'. *Topique*: 69–86.

Winnicott, D. W. (1967). Mirror-Role of Mother and Family in Child Development. In *Playing and Reality*. London: Tavistock, 1971.

Winnicott, D. W. (1987). *The Spontaneous Gesture: Selected Letter*. Cambridge, MA: Harvard University Press.

21 'SPEECH IN PSYCHOANALYSIS'
From symbols to the flesh and back[1]

Julia Kristeva

> **Julia Kristeva** is a philosopher and linguist, a full member of the Paris Psychoanalytical Society and professor of literature and semiotics in the University of Paris VII. She has written papers and books on a wide variety of subjects, all of which bear witness to her subtle observation of contemporary society and the changes that occur within it. Her studies of many fields such as art, literature and the theory of language have led her to suggest a re-reading of the psychoanalytic models that we owe to Freud and to Lacan in the light of the new kinds of patient who are the product of the ongoing crisis in value systems in the modern world.
>
> Her psychoanalytic writings include *Soleil noir. Dépression et mélancolie* (Gallimard, 1987) [*Black Sun: Depression and Melancholia* (Columbia, 1992)] and *Les nouvelles maladies de l'âme* (Fayard, 1993) [*New Maladies of the Soul* (Columbia, 1995)]. Her series on *Le génie féminin* [Feminine genius] (Fayard: Hannah Arendt, 1999; Melanie Klein, 2000; Colette, 2002) has attracted considerable interest. She recently published an essay on St Theresa of Avila, *Thérèse mon amour* [Theresa, my love] (Fayard, 2008), which could be seen as the fourth volume in the *Génie féminin* series. In addition, Julia Kristeva has written several novels, including *Les samouraïs* [The Samurais] (Fayard, 1990) and *Meurtre à Byzance* (Fayard, 2004) [*Murder in Byzantium* (Columbia, 2008)].

What do we call 'flesh'?

When the disciplines of phenomenology, and then semiology, were able to lend an ear to the Freudian discovery of the unconscious – but also to the 'gay science' of language brought by the modern 'great writers' – a revolution was, and still is, underway concerning the understanding of what 'speech' means. It

---

[1] This paper was given at the 67th Congress of Psychoanalysis for French-Speaking Analysts in Paris, May 2007, entitled 'La Cure de Parole', and published in the *Revue Française de Psychanalyse*, 71 (2007, no. 5).

involves traversing the surface of the object 'language' made up of signs (words) and predicative syntheses (logic, grammar) in order to reach what Husserl called the *hyle*, the matter left outside the 'bracketing' in the act of signifying. Merleau-Ponty accomplished this upheaval by looking for a 'pre-reflexive' state of thought which enlarges communication with the world (with Being), at the point of intersection (chiasmus) between nature and the mind: a 'transition from the silent world to the speaking world' which the philosopher describes thus: 'The world seen is not "in" my body, and my body is not "in" the visible world ultimately: as flesh applied to flesh, the world neither surrounds it nor is surrounded by it . . . there is a reciprocal insertion and intertwining of one in the other' (Merleau-Ponty, 1964, p. 138). The 'flesh' so defined as a 'chiasmus'[2] between the Ego and the world was to lead him to his *Phenomenology of Perception* (1945).[3] But perception/sensation[4] could only be introduced into the sciences of language when the latter began to be constructed around the 'subject of the enunciation' and, *a fortiori*, around the subject of the enunciation worked on by the unconscious.

Thus when Émile Benveniste, the first linguist, wrote his 'Remarks on the Function of Language in the Freudian Discovery' (1966/1971), concerning himself with the 'contrary meaning of primitive words', it was not at all with the intention of validating the etymological speculations of Carl Abel, in which Freud had sought a basis for his discovery that the unconscious is unaware of negation. Benveniste's article suggests that the same word does not signify two contrary 'meanings', but two perceptions of the same subject of the enunciation who changes his spatial position.[5] And he suggests that primitive languages exist whose vestiges can be found in present modes of communication, which, like the dream and the unconscious (that of the id and not of unconscious representations), convey quasi-sensory signs. The step had now been taken, making it possible to include in the object 'language' the

---

[2] An intersection of terms in which the elements of parallel groups are inverted, following the structure AB/BA. Example: the flesh of the world/the world of the flesh.

[3] This modern return of the term 'flesh' cannot make us lose sight of its Greek tradition: to begin with, flesh, *sarx*, is linked to sensations: Sextus Empiricus (*Against the Professors*, VII, 290, Loeb Classical Library, 382) states that the 'carnal mass' is the seat of the sensations; Plato attributes desire to the body, *soma* (*Phaedo*, 82), which is more 'representable', as the Latin *corpus* would show; but Epicurus returns to the idea of 'pleasure of the body': the flesh aspires to infinite pleasure, which reason *dianoïa* alone can limit. Judaism does not seem unfamiliar with this Epicurean association, but explores it in its own way. In the Bible, the flesh (*basar* or *sherr*) represents the mortal nature of man susceptible of sin, although the struggle between the flesh and the mind is not developed. It is the New Testament that bequeaths us the ambiguous notion of the flesh as sickness of body, weakness of knowledge, a potential stain, which, according to Paul, is nonetheless the bodily condition that must be owned or accepted if one is to really participate, to really believe, in Christ's message. I am employing the term 'flesh' in what follows with reference to Merleau-Ponty, developing it from a psychoanalytic standpoint.

[4] I will not go into the distinction here between *sensation* (reflection in consciousness of external reality due to the sense organs) and *perception* (conscious representation of it).

[5] He is *at the top* of the ladder when he says that a well is *deep*; he is *at the bottom* of the ladder when he determines its *height*.

sensation–perception of a pre- or translinguistic 'acting' [*agir*] of the speaking subject in the world.

Antoine Culioli's (1995, 2000, 2002) linguistic theory[6] was to deepen this perspective by taking up the old notion of the Greek Stoics, the *lekton* – neglected by the 'sign' in Saussure's theory – that is, the signifiable. In effect, the linguistic sign[7] refers not to an opaque object-referent but, through it, to an open ensemble constituted by sensations–affects–drives which manifest the conscious/unconscious negotiation required in the subject's act of signifying. This is reminiscent of the Freudian model of the sign – that is, word-presentations versus thing-presentations – on the condition that we add that the unconscious 'thing' is never 'in itself', but a thing of desire, thus of 'enacting':[8] the 'thing-presentation' is contextualised and acted, and consequently it presents itself from the outset in a 'pre-narrative envelope' (Stern, 1992). The linguist discovers, then, that language itself can function as a predicative articulation of quasi-signs and micro-narratives which are not just metaphors but generate a 'more-than metaphorical' sensorial experience – I would say metamorphic. The 'signifiable' will be a mixture of sensations, affects and cultural memory – for example, 'keeping one's feet on the ground', 'he who sleeps forgets his hunger' or 'having eyes bigger than one's stomach'. All of which creates the charm, the magic of the bond of identity, called the mother or native tongue, but also its power of subjugation, the reverse side of fascination and horror.[9]

The signifiable pushed as far as hallucinatory metamorphosis (of which the speaking subject bears onto- and phylogenetic memory traces) becomes – through the intervention of language – a metaphoricity that is coded and transmissible within the system of language itself. But it is in what our culture considers as a 'literary style' that metaphoricity finds its maximal expansion. Here, the 'simultaneity of the sensory and verbal memory traces' of quasi-signs (meaning-and-sensation) acts in a surprising way, defying the clichés of the national code. Such is the economy of the passage in *La chèvre de M. Seguin*[10] which interested R. Diatkine and L. Danon-Boileau: 'All of a sudden, the wind freshened, and the mountain turned purple. It was evening.' Where the speaking subject does not exist, for Blanchette is annulled by anxiety, it is

---

[6] Antoine Culioli (1924–), a French linguist and English-language specialist, developed a theory known as the 'theory of the enunciative operations', the purpose of which is to study the activity of language in various languages, texts and situations. He was influenced by the Stoics and by the eminent French linguists Emile Benveniste (1966) and Gustave Guillaume (1984). His theory is mainly presented in the three volumes of *Pour une linguistique de l'énonciation* [For a linguistic theory of enunciation] (2000, 2002).

[7] Saussure rehabilitates the linguistic sign at first restrictively, as *signified–signifier* which loses interest in the *referent*, and then in a manner that is more attentive to the unconscious, via the cabalistic network of '*Anagrams*'.

[8] I agree on this point with Widlöcher (1994).

[9] This is reminiscent of L. Danon-Boileau's 'nostalgia' (2007).

[10] In a collection of short stories by Alphonse Daudet entitled *Lettres de mon Moulin*, 1886. [*Trans.*, this volume]

the sensations of the external world into which she projects herself which impose – on the reader – affects of worry, danger and fear. The metaphor metamorphoses the reader by placing him in a chiasmus, in the 'flesh of the world'.

Our [congress] reporter is right to stress the fact that it is not just a question of an arrangement of words, but of a condensation of memory traces which must be brief,[11] even if these 'holes' in the signifying chain can follow on from each other infinitely – as in Proust's sentences and *paperolles*.

Baudelaire, who was fond of coenesthesias,[12] has given a brilliant commentary on this toppling over of the sign into sensation and, via it, into desubjectivation – under the influence of hashish, wine or quite simply, if I may say so, the sublimatory act that we call 'inspiration'. For example: 'Your eye fixes itself upon a tree . . .' – what, in the brain of a poet (meaning, a mediocre one) would only be a very natural comparison, becomes in yours a reality. 'At first you lend to the tree your passions, your desire and your melancholia; its creakings and oscillations become yours, and soon you are the tree' (Baudelaire, 1975, pp. 419–420, 398). I do not write metaphors; I transmit metamorphoses to you, Baudelaire insists in substance. Daniel Widlöcher (1994, p. 88) takes up the term: 'The past in psychoanalysis is not inscribed in time but in an always-there, an infinite universe of metamorphoses.'

I agree with him. When an autistic child turns to jelly in front of a pool of water, he is not expressing himself metaphorically: he is acting a metamorphosis in the sensory chiasmus between a non-ego and the non-world. He is suffering from a failure of signs, a deficiency in 'symbolic thirdness'. He is in the pre-subjective flesh, which Merleau-Ponty calls the 'flesh of the world'.

On the other hand, when the analyst 'verbalises' this immersion in the flesh of the world by means of a metaphor (by thinking and saying that the 'pool' makes the autistic child experience his nameless dread), the autist will perhaps be able – gradually, through transferring his infantile sexuality onto his therapist, and if his 'autistic type' allows him to understand the interpretation – to make his own way towards an experience of quasi-signs.

As for the writer, whose 'power of language' we appreciate, he 'succeeds where the autist fails' (Kristeva, 1994, p. 294). He has experienced 'metamorphoses' in an autistic manner.[13] I am thinking of Proust's narrator enveloped by the scent of lilacs in a urinal, or in the 'cool and rose-pink material' of a stained-glass window (Proust, 1989, p. 449). The author manages, however, to formulate these sensory intensities in the form of metaphors

---

[11] Briefness has a revelatory value, as Heraclitus knew when he wrote 'Oracles neither speak nor conceal but give signs'.
[12] Reciprocal permutations and substitutions involving the five senses: see his sonnet '*Voyelles*' [Vowels] of 1871.
[13] In the sense of the 'latent and endogenous autism' of which Francis Tustin (1986) speaks in *Autistic Barriers in Neurotic Patients*.

which he calls 'transubstantiations'.[14] They are accomplished through the narrative structure, which shelters or lets itself be torn by the insights of the 'unconscious thing' in which – as in the free association of analytic treatment – the sensations compressed in instinctual enacting are conveyed through the narrative envelope. The episode of the '*madeleine*' – in the first drafts, the tasty '*madeleine*' was nothing but a dry 'biscuit' – is over-determined by an interaction of narrative flows: from a scene where the narrator's mother reads a novel by George Sand in which the incestuous mother gives herself the first name Madeleine, to the secretly coded ritual of the homosexuals of that time, who, in order to debase the Catholic communion, savoured biscuits dipped in urine that was called 'tea' in the slang used in the street urinals of the time.[15]

We may also think of Colette: 'one' does not remember the plot of her narratives, commonplace stories of jealousy and adultery, but one recalls the 'tremendous effect' (to use Danon-Boileau's expression), the sensory impact of her metaphors–metamorphoses transporting us from the stratum of the 'linguistic' sign into the sensation of the object evoked, into the pleasure felt from contact with scent or colour, which become as many 'indices'[16] of the affect of solitude and despair: 'Black rose, odorous jam'.[17] 'I am now this solitary and upright woman, like a sad rose, which, after losing its leaves, has a stronger bearing.'[18] You can hear it: the alliterations favour the rupture of the abstract contract between 'signifier' and 'signified', liberating the afflux of the sensory and affective memory.

But it is Artaud, who, from the position of psychosis, insists on the fact that the fine layer of sensations themselves are contiguous with a rebellious instinctual turbulence: 'Feelings are nothing / nor are ideas / everything is in motility / from which like the rest humanity has taken nothing but a ghost.'[19]

Freud's conceptualisations on the facilitation of the memory-trace in the 'Mystic Writing-Pad' (1925a), Derrida's work on writing (*écriture*) – 'trace' or 'impression' prior to vocal language – Green's work on the 'heterogeneity' of the signifier supported by the drive, and others that I cannot mention here, come to mind as we seek to interpret these advances in the *sensory substratum of language* as a relay between *signs* and *drives*. I would like to add my own research into translinguistic 'semiotics' (which I distinguish from the 'symbolic', which comes into being with the acquisition of signs and syntax): the 'semiotic' mode of language condenses and displaces instinctual facilitations

---

[14] See Letter to Lucien Daudet, 27 November 1913, *Correspondence*, Vol. 12, pp. 342–343.
[15] See J. Kristeva, *Le temps sensible* (1994, pp. 13–35).
[16] In the sense of Charles S. Peirce.
[17] Colette, 'Fleurs', 'La treille muscate', in *Prisons et paradis* (Paris: La Pléiade, 1972), Vol. 3, p. 699.
[18] Colette, *La naissance du jour* (Paris: Flammarion, 1928), p. 66.
[19] Cf. 'Note pour une lettre aux Balinais', cited by Kristeva (1974, pp. 154–155/1984, p. 180).

which metamorphose subjective affects in narratives of desubjectivised, or even pre-psychic, sensory experiences.[20]

How do these encounters between the clinical experience of analysts and certain modern approaches of language fit in with Freud's models of language? Or, rather, how do they let themselves be modified by Freud's models of language?

Three models of language according to Freud

I say 'models', because at least three[21] can be distinguished:

- the model of the asymptote
- the optimistic model
- and the model of meaning which underlies language and shows itself to be accessible through it in transference.

A first model, which has its origins in *On Aphasia* (1891b) and *The Origins of Psychoanalysis* (1950 [1887–1902]), points up the inadequacy, the disequilibrium, between the sexual and the verbal. Sexuality cannot be expressed – at least not entirely. And this *asymptote* induces, if not an absence of translation, then at least a deficient translation between unconscious representations (which will become *thing-presentations*) and words (*word-presentations*). This deficiency generates symptoms, which, if they are to be lifted, require an intermediary – to be precise, 'speech in psychoanalysis'. I would like to stress the *heterogeneity*[22] inherent in this 'first model of language', which will be developed later with the theorisation of the *drive* and of its *representability*.

The psychoanalytic model, which I call *optimistic*, appears with the creation of the armchair/couch treatment and its fundamental rule of 'free association', and it is clearly formulated in *The Interpretation of Dreams* (1900a). It is close to the structural conception of language, and it was this model that Lacan was to draw on, except that the structuralist approach to language in psychoanalysis would, curiously enough, keep silent about this Freudian innovation which imposed itself. And yet the invitation made to the patient to provide a *narrative* profoundly modifies the classical conception of language: it is this representation of *acting* and/or its unconscious substratum, *fantasy*, and not *signs* and

---

[20] Cf. Kristeva, *La révolution du langage poétique* (1974, pp. 17–100) and 'La narration en psychanalyse' (2005).
[21] See the study I made of them within the context of my teaching (Kristeva, 1966) and during a conference that I organised with D. Widlöcher and P. Fédida in 1994.
[22] I like to emphasise this heterogeneity of 'speaking', which, for my part, I construct notably from G. Bataille, VIII, Dossier 'Hétérologie' (1970, p. 171) and with reference to A. Green (1971).

syntax, which allows for this modification. What is happening? Because, 'from the outset', language conveys fantasies ('pre-narrative envelopes'), it is charged with something signifiable of which the sciences of language are unaware – namely, *desire* and *drives*. Freud (1923b) says that language is 'preconscious', which implies – already in *The Interpretation of Dreams* – that it is a language of 'contact', as D. Clerc's 2007 report makes clear.

A turning-point in Freud's thought occurred between 1912–1914 which modified profoundly his conception of language and initiated a 'third model', with *Totem and Taboo* (1912–13), 'On Narcissism: An Introduction' (1914c), 'Mourning and Melancholia' (1917e [1915]), the resistances to analysis, the death drive, *Beyond the Pleasure Principle* (1920g), and finally, *Moses and Monotheism* (1939a). Two aspects of this third model are of interest for 'speech in psychoanalysis': first, the *fluidity* of the topographical agencies which promotes both resistances and catastrophes and psychic reorganisations; second, as if to optimise this fluidity, Freud's concern to focus listening and interpretation on the analysis of the paternal function and its unbearable fragility. This is forgetting – or underestimating – the mad endurance of the maternal vocation, but that will be a subject for another congress.

The ego, writes Freud in *The Ego and the Id* (1923b), consists of *verbal traces* and *perceptions*: 'perceptions may be said to have the same significance for the Ego as instincts have for the Id' (pp. 52, 40), this co-presence of perception and verbalisation is posed henceforth as a frontier 'region' or 'province' between the *id* (depths of the unconscious) and the *superego* (conscious), and consequently, as the 'object' *par excellence* of the treatment. As the aim of interpretation is to bring the *ego* into being where the *id* was, we can understand that speech in the treatment – in the transference, which, in the last instance, is Oedipal – is supposed to transform into perception/verbalisation the inexpressible memory-traces of the more or less traumatic 'thing alone' [*la chose seule*]. This means that the formulation will always be a formulation concerning the Oedipus complex, not to be confused with a formulation that can be reduced to the Oedipus complex. From the flesh to signs, or vice versa, and, because he deepens his analysis of the paternal function, Freud constantly sets limits, but also openings–passages–porosities in the signifying process [*signifiance*].

That 'speech in psychoanalysis' is capable – indefinitely – of touching the drives via the sensations is a contention Freud sustains until the last notes of his apophthegm (1941f [1938]) concerning mysticism: 'Mysticism is the obscure self-perception of the realm outside the Ego, of the Id' (p. 300). This testament needs to be set alongside his formula in his *New Introductory Lectures* (1933a, p. 80): 'Perception may be able to grasp [*Erfassen*] happenings in the depths of the Ego and in the Id.' From this we may understand that what distinguishes psychoanalytic treatment from the mystic hole is that, for mystics, the ego has disappeared in favour of the id, which perceives itself. Mystical raptus resides in the vision which operates an *instantaneous* ('*psychoanalysis of the instant*', writes

D. Widlöcher) rent or breach in verbalisation and leaves the thing perceived, and the underlying drive, to act in silence, before Eros starts to become noisy again, leading the mystic to invent a language, a writing. On the contrary, analysis is a *processual event*, temporal and interactive, continually constructing/deconstructing Oedipal ties. *We may ask: what is it that specifically distinguishes speech in psychoanalysis from aesthetic or mystical raptus?*

It is in fact the *guiding thread of the Oedipal destiny* of *Homo sapiens* which will structure both the *ethics of psychoanalysis* that Freud outlines in this period of his work and the analyst's *listening*, and thus his *interpretation*. Thus, retroactively, the *Oedipal destiny with its catastrophes* gives back its meaning – not its ultimate meaning, because it is always evolving and incomplete, but its specific meaning – to what 'speech in psychoanalysis' means. To put it in another way, it becomes clear for Freud that what differentiates 'speech in psychoanalysis' from every other language and theorisation *is dependent on the paternal complex or*, more precisely, the flexibility of the Oedipus complex.

By so enlarging the field of speech in analysis, Freud did not abandon the 'object' language. He made it possible to follow in a new way the process of meaning which makes language not a system of defence, not only – though rarely! – a metamorphic grace, but a dynamic of psychic re-construction.

Thus, faced with the discourse of the patient Ada, saturated with sensations that are inextricably bound up with their 'violence and poetry', faced with the nostalgic defence which bars her from having access to the self-analytic process and imposes on the analysis a seduction which 'castrates listening' by its sensorial ascendancy, the analyst interprets by outlining a *link:* 'Well, there is the dream . . . the scene with Pietro . . . the scene in the café . . . the things your mother said.' To which Ada immediately retorted: 'The link? Oh, you've stumped me there . . .'. This clinical vignette, presented by L. Danon-Boileau, helps us to see that the analysand's speech, compacted with sensations and designed to capture the analyst, is a search for her father who died when she was ten years old. And when, going beyond the end of the session, she opens up a new associative path by mentioning her grandmother – 'She loved me. I don't remember', echoing this missing link – I can hear her analyst thinking: 'The link is that someone is no longer there, someone disappeared too early for you to be able to remember that they loved you.'

If I hear the necessity of including the Oedipal configuration at this moment in the transference, it is because the reminder of 'infantile sexuality', in the vignette, permits me to do so. And because the 'third Freudian model of language' – namely, *signifiance* – has helped us to see that it is the introjection of the primary identification [*Einhülung*] that has been left like a gaping hole in Ada by her father's death. This patient is lacking the *Einhülung* necessary for 'decompacting' the language-sensation that she throws out like a desperate call to the other, for elaborating – in the analyst's listening – a speech that is capable of becoming a psychic transition between the flesh which imprisons her and the scientific excellence which destines her to solitude.

In another way, when D. Clerc's patient 'Pas touche' (Don't touch) complains that he feels nothing for him, due to the 'difference of age', and the analyst interprets tactfully: 'It's true, I could be your mother', the material presented includes the idea, 'I could be your mother, though you need your father so that I don't touch you too much.' It is implied, and only the analyst's tact can decide when and how the fear of the incestuous desire and the call for the thirdness of the father and/or of the analyst can be put into words.

On interpretative speech as question

As Freud developed his theory of the death drive and it became clear that narcissism was powerless to resist it, the *object relation* seemed to be the buttress capable of modulating *unbinding*.[23] Modern psychoanalysis puts much emphasis on this, but perhaps less, I think, on the fact that this movement in Freud's thought is accompanied by the *emergence of signification* [*signifiance*]: identification, working-through, idealisation, superego-isation, sublimation – as many signifying logics which I see as deeper explorations by Freud of his discovery of the 'Oedipus complex', of the *paternal function* inasmuch as, in the speaking animal, it is the regulator of destructiveness.

The Lacanian 'signifier', beyond any linguistic reference, refers to this layering of *the process of signification* (in my terminology), which includes the model of transformation of acts of thinking (such as Bion's system, among others), the model of the *regulation* of processes (metapsychology) (Widlöcher, 2006, p. 32), but both integrated with the *genetic point of view*, which makes the organisation of the psychic apparatus and its agencies depend on the accidents of the Oedipus complex. Indeed, a vigorous revision occurs in this later Freud between the 'genetic point of view' of the stages (oral, anal, phallic and genital), the phases of the Oedipus complex and its differences in men and women, and the object relation which depends on it or defies it. Consequently, as it becomes more refined, it is the *exploration of the paternal function* that links the topographic, dynamic, and economic models with ontogenesis and phylogenesis. Indeed, it is this *process of signification, namely, the narrative, anchored in the destiny of thirdness*, which associates, or subordinates, the model of *transformation* of thoughts (Bion), as well as the model of *regulation* (metapsychology).

For my part, I insist on the Freudian pedestal of signification (*narrative of the fragility of the paternal function*), because this is what gives coherence – indispensable in our clinical work – to these two approaches which otherwise are in danger of becoming isolated in sterile speculation. Rather than referring to the process of translinguistic thought that is transmitted by the third model of

---

[23] A. Green demonstrates this in his work and notably in his latest (2007) book *Pourquoi les pulsions de destruction et de mort?*

speech as Freud invites us as analysts to understand it, as purely genetic or purely historical, I prefer to call it a 'process of signification' [*signifiance*]; for, whatever the stages or strata of it are, signification is rooted in the signs of language as it is constituted by the transference–countertransference. But, in linking the most intimate (the inexpressible 'thing') to historical mutations by means of the evolution of family structures and the regulation of reproduction, *signification* introduces history into what 'speech in psychoanalysis' means.

Freud, who was the least religious man of his century, did not hesitate to postulate, when commenting on the vicissitudes of the paternal function governing the installation of signification and its accidents, 'a superior being in humans' [*das höhere Wesen in Menschen*] (Freud, 1923b, p. 57). Far from betraying some sort of idealistic regression, this theorisation designates the logics of an immanentisation of transcendence, which the founder of psychoanalysis noticed through and in the 'speaking treatment' he invented. Two moments in this Freudian revolution are connected with this linguistic capacity: *primary identification* and the *castration complex*.

The *Einhüllung* of primary identification is prior to loving/hating/knowing (Bion), but constitutes the 'need to believe', the 'expectation coloured by hope and faith' [*Gläubige Erwartung*] which follows fearful anxiety (Freud, 1905b [1890], p. 289), as D. Clerc remarks. A different order of 'objectality' is set up: I do not invest the father as an 'object' of desire, even desire unto death, but the psychic investment of my investment – which this father returns to me if, and only if, he is a loved/loving father.

From this point of view, I have suggested that *negativity* [*Negativität*], the trace of which Freud follows in the oral and anal spheres, is also complemented by *the phallic test* in order to structure the signifying chain. Its binary structure (marked/unmarked phonemes), like a psychosomatic computer, transforms into verbal traces the psychic representations of swallowing and excretion, approbation and rejection.

This means that the acquisition of language, in the last instance, is a negotiation of the *ordeal of castration*, in which the subject takes over appropriation and expulsion in order to construct a signifying chain which will be his ultimate diversion – and distraction – against and with the death drive.

I want to link to the phallic phase, and to the symbolisation of the drives that it completes, a psychic activity to which Freud did not give sufficient attention but which, it seems to me, is foundational for the analytic situation: I am referring to *the allocutory act, par excellence, of questioning*, which challenges the identity and authority of the other (of the real and of the object).[24] The jubilation of the questioning child is still inhabited by the metamorphic (hallucinatory) certitude that all identity is a constructible/deconstructible

---

[24] See Kristeva (1993).

movement or activity of representation [*représentance*],[25] before the ego is subjected to the dictatorship of the conscious and communicational superego – a 'pure culture of the death drive' (Freud, 1923b, p. 53).

Now, some can no longer bear not being able to tolerate symbolic castration, which, through a series of diversions, extricates us from the flesh and installs us in the code, masking severe traumas which have become intolerable by dint of masquerade. These are the ones who become 'analysands': they expect analysis to open Pandora's Box of signification.

So the questioning that occurs in this signifying process of the transference will not be a conscious or philosophical questioning which presupposes an answer. 'Speech in psychoanalysis' challenges this horizontal questioning itself; for, on the vertical axis of the system of language [*la langue*], 'speech in psychoanalysis' ruins the work of language [*langage*] – and, with it, the tyranny of identification with the substitutes of the paternal function. Are not the moments of grace in the treatment those in which every '*self*' proves to be '*false*', or even 'nobody', and where the signs that bind me come into contact with sensitive flesh? 'I' become absent and 'it' speaks. As a result of speaking in this way, I am led to confront silence: the analyst's silence, the silence of anxiety. But as always – as long as the transference lasts – it is a silence of waiting for meaning: the silence of the possible new beginning.

The linking which the analysand becomes capable of through the treatment is none other than that of *investing the process of symbolisation itself*. For the object, whichever it is (sexual, professional, symbolic, etc.), and even if provisionally optimal, can continue to exist if, and only if, the speaking/analysand subject is capable of indefinitely constructing/deconstructing its meaning and the 'thing' [*la chose*].

In short, Freud invented a 'speech', a certain version of language, which is perhaps not its truth, but one of its potentialities, and it is the formidable privilege of psychoanalysis to reveal it. Alongside morality and its ancestor, religion, but also alongside the 'sciences of mind', 'speech in psychoanalysis' opens up another path in our relations to the *signifying process* which constitutes the human. And it is indeed this displacement of speech in relation to itself, this infinitesimal revolution, constitutive of our practice, which worries people. I fear that we are not sufficiently attentive to the exceptional singularity of 'speech in psychoanalysis' – and, worse still, not sufficiently proud of it. For, up till now, it alone has been capable, not of saving us from a culture which psychoanalysis has shown to be a culture of death, but of creating a diversion for the death drive – deferring it, turning it away, diverting it. Endlessly, through the sole experience of language which subtilises language, making it sensitive to the unsayable: back and forth, and vice versa.

---

[25] A general category including different types of representation (psychic representative, ideational representative, representative of the drive, etc.) and which implies the movement, activity, of representation. [*Trans., this volume*]

References

Bataille, G. (1970). *Oeuvres complètes, Vol. 2: Oeuvres posthumes (1922–1940)* [Complete works, Vol. 2: Posthumous works (1992–1940)]. Paris: Gallimard.

Baudelaire, C. (1975). Paradis artificiels [Artificial paradises]. In *Oeuvres complètes* [Complete works]. Paris: Gallimard, La Pléiade.

Benveniste, E. (1966). Remarks on the Function of Language in the Freudian Discovery. In *Problems of General Linguistics* (pp. 65–75), trans. M. E. Meek. Coral Gables, FL: University of Miami Press, 1971. [*Problèmes de linguistique générale* (pp. 75–90). Paris: Gallimard, 1966; first published in *La Psychanalyse* (1956), *1*.]

Clerc, D. (2007). L'écoute de la parole [Listening to speech]. *Revue Française de Psychanalyse*, *71* (5): 1285–1340.

Culioli, A., Stonham, J. T., & Liddle, M. (1995). *Cognition and Representation in Linguistic Theory (Current Issues in Linguistic Theory)*. Philadelphia, PA: John Benjamins.

Culioli A. (2000). *Pour une linguistique de l'énonciation, Vol. 1* [For a linguistic theory of enunciation, Vol. 1]. Paris: Ophrys.

Culioli A. (2002). *Pour une linguistique de l'énonciation, Vols. 2–3* [For a linguistic theory of enunciation, Vols. 2–3]. Paris: Ophrys.

Danon-Boileau, L. (2007). La force du langage [The force of language]. *Revue Française de Psychanalyse*, *71* (5): 1341–1409.

Freud, S. (1891b). *On Aphasia*, trans. E. Stengel. New York: International Universities Press, 1953.

Freud, S. (1900a). *The Interpretation of Dreams. S.E.*, 4/5: 1–621.

Freud, S. (1905b [1890]). Psychical (or Mental) Treatment. *S.E.*, 7: 283–302.

Freud, S. (1912–13). *Totem and Taboo. S.E.*, 13: 1–161.

Freud, S. (1914c). On Narcissism: An Introduction. *S.E.*, 14: 69–102.

Freud, S. (1917e [1915]). Mourning and Melancholia. *S.E.*, 14: 237–260.

Freud, S. (1920g). *Beyond the Pleasure Principle. S.E.*, 18: 1–64.

Freud, S. (1923b). *The Ego and the Id. S.E.*, 19: 3–66.

Freud, S. (1925a). A Note upon the 'Mystic Writing-Pad'. *S.E.*, 19: 227–232.

Freud, S. (1933a). *New Introductory Lectures. S.E.*, 22: 1–182.

Freud, S. (1939a). *Moses and Monotheism. S.E.*, 23: 1–137.

Freud, S. (1941f [1938]). Findings, Ideas, Problems. *S.E.*, 23: 299–300.

Freud, S. (1950 [1887–1902]). *The Origins of Psychoanalysis. S.E.*, 1.

Green, A. (1971). *Le discours vivant*. Paris: Presses Universitaires de France. [*The Fabric of Affect in Psychoanalytic Discourse*, trans. A. Sheridan. London: Routledge, 1999.]

Green, A. (2007). *Pourquoi les pulsions de destruction et de mort?* [Why drives of destruction and death?]. Paris: Panama.

Guillaume, G. (1984). *Principes de linguistique théorique de Gustave Guillaume*. Paris: Klincksieck. [*Foundations for a Science of Language*, trans. W. Hirtle & J. Hewson. Philadelphia, PA: John Benjamins.]

Kristeva, J. (1966). Les métamorphoses du langage dans la découverte freudienne [The metamorphoses of language in the Freudian discovery]. In *Sens et non-sens de la révolte* [The meaning and non-meaning of rebellion]. Paris: Fayard.

Kristeva, J. (1974). *La révolution du langage poétique*. Paris: Le Seuil. [*Revolution in Poetic Language*, trans. Margaret Waller, New York: Columbia University Press, 1984.]

Kristeva, J. (1993). La castration symbolique. Une question. In *Les nouvelles maladies de l'âme* (pp. 135–156). Paris: Fayard. [Symbolic castration. In *New Maladies of the Soul*. New York: Columbia Press, 1995.]

Kristeva, J. (1994). *Le temps sensible*. Paris: Gallimard. [*Time and Sense: Proust and the Experience of Literature*, trans. R. Guberman. New York: Columbia University Press, 1996.]

Kristeva, J. (2005). La narration en psychanalyse [Narration in psychoanalysis]. In *La haine et le pardon* [Hate and forgiveness] (pp. 283–314). Paris: Fayard.

Merleau-Ponty, M. (1945). *Phenomenology of Perception*, trans. C Smith, London: Routledge & Kegan Paul, 1962.

Merleau-Ponty, M. (1964). *The Visible and the Invisible*, trans. A. Lingis. Evanston, IL: Northwestern University Press, 1969.

Proust, M. (1989). *Le temps retrouvé*. In *À la recherche du temps perdu, Vol. 4*. Paris: La Pléiade. [Time Regained. In *In Search of Lost Time, Vol. 6*. London: Cox and Wyman, 1996.]

Stern, D. (1992). The Pre-Narrative Envelope: An Alternative View of 'Unconscious Phantasy' in Infancy. *Bulletin of Anna Freud Centre, 15*: 291–318.

Tustin, F. (1986). *Autistic Barriers in Neurotic Patients*. London: Karnac.

Widlöcher, D. (1994). Psychanalyse de l'instant [Psychoanalysis of the instant]. In *L'inactuel, Vol. 2*. Paris: Calmann-Lévy.

Widlöcher, D. (2006). 'L'inconscient psychanalytique', une question toujours ouverte ['The psychoanalytic unconscious': Still an open question]. *Cahiers de philosophie, 107*.

Section V

THE BODY AND THE DRIVES

V THE BODY AND THE DRIVES
Introduction

Alain Gibeault

In dealing with clinical matters in psychoanalysis, French psychoanalysts have a reputation for constantly insisting on the importance of drive theory. In so doing, they remain faithful to Freud's approach to mental functioning. That said, drive theory is probably the most speculative and abstract element of metapsychology. Freud himself was well aware of that, because in 1933 he commented: 'The theory of the instincts is so to say our mythology. Instincts are mythical entities, magnificent in their indefiniteness' (1933a, p. 95). The theory is nonetheless fundamental, in that the concept of instinctual drives led to the discovery of infantile sexuality and of the key role played by sexuality as a whole – that is, over and beyond its genital aspect. That development of the theory does give rise to some problems because of the shifts in emphasis and the contradictions that emerged in Freud's thinking, particularly as regards the hypothesis of the death drive.

The concept of drive [*Trieb*] entered into Freud's theory through its close connotations with need [*Bedürfnis*] and with instinct [*Instinkt*]; as the word itself makes clear (*Trieb* comes from *treiben*, to push), 'drive' indicates that there is something in the organism that 'pushes', an indeterminate element of activity that leads the organism to accomplish a specific action with a view to obtaining satisfaction. This therefore implies a *quantity* of movement that finds its *quality* in the anatomical zones and aims that are in the service of satisfaction; this led Freud (1905d) to describe four typical features of the drives: a constantly active *thrust* arising from somatic *sources* that has as its objective the fulfilment of an *aim*, satisfaction, with the help of a contingent *object*. This variability with respect to sources, aims and objects led to the idea of component drives, each of which seeks its own satisfaction. That was Freud's way of describing infantile sexuality – that is, a form of sexuality that is wider in scope than the merely genital; this therefore called into question the generally accepted idea that sexuality can only be characterised by reference to a definite aim and object, as the term *instinct* would seem to imply.

In psychoanalysis, the concept of drive has therefore to do with the overall situation of living beings. Several French psychoanalysts have pointed out that Freud (1915c, pp. 121–122) defines drives from a biological point of view: '. . . an "instinct" appears to us as a concept on the frontier between the mental and the somatic, as the psychical representative of the stimuli originating from within the organism and reaching the mind, as a measure of the demand made upon the mind for work in consequence of its connection with the body'.

At other times, Freud described drives as the somatic process itself, which is represented in the mind by 'psychical representatives': the ideational representative and quota of affect. That definition of drives is more consistent with clinical experience, because it gives more emphasis to the actual material of psychoanalytic treatment – representations and affects – so that the idea of drive is brought in only subsequently. This more metapsychological formulation is stricter and more coherent, with the idea that representations and affects have a destiny, correlative with the discovery of the unconscious.

The contradiction in Freud's definition of the concept of drives gave rise to different schools of thought in psychoanalysis, depending on whether the emphasis is put on the biological approach, describing a continuous process from drive to object, which has its representation from birth onwards – Klein's standpoint – or on the metapsychological approach describing a complete break between needs and drives and highlighting in fact a topography of the unconscious in terms of representations and, more precisely, in terms of language-based representations as in Lacan's theory. The danger on the one hand is that of a biological reification of the drives, and on the other a denunciation of the very concept as being a device invented by Freud for conveying a contradictory and untenable parallelism between the organic and mental dimensions; it was that criticism which led Lacan to do away with any reference to affects or the body.

The chapters in this present volume show that it is more interesting to see this conceptual contradiction in Freud's theory as an indication of the articulating and mediating aspects of the concept of instinctual drives. His idea of describing drives in general led him, of course, to attribute an objective content to the concept, thus losing sight of its specific features. He went beyond that positivist outlook, all the same, when he described how the drives emerge from the separation between organic needs and desire for the object. The epistemological approach adopted by many French psychoanalysts gives the idea of drives its true meaning as 'a concept on the frontier between the mental and the somatic' (Freud, 1915c, pp. 121–122) and enables us to give clinical examples of the various psychopathological structures that arise from the vicissitudes of the drives.

According to Freud (1915c), the metapsychological approach to mental phenomena depends on the *topography* of the psychic systems corresponding to the vicissitudes of representations; however, the introduction of the concept of drives implies taking into consideration the *economic* aspect, which, Freud argued, 'endeavours to follow out the vicissitudes of amounts of excitation and to arrive at least at some *relative* estimate of their magnitude' (Freud, 1915c, p. 181). In other words, we have to take into account what, in the destiny of the affects, will either help or hinder the process of symbolisation correlative with the binding of the affects by means of ideational representations.

These topographical and economic aspects are in fact an integral part of the dynamic point of view which corresponds to the fundamental idea of conflict. For Freud, psychic conflicts are always based on a conflict between two great categories of drives. French psychoanalysts interpret this dualism of the drives with reference to the construction of the psychic object. In the psychoanalytic sense, drives are linked to the structural originality of the life of the object. The opposition between narcissistic libido and object-libido is clinically useful, whereas that between the life and death drives has less to do with the description of a conflict between drives than with highlighting one of the fundamental functions of the drives: to underline the contradiction that goes to the very heart of human beings – pleasure coming from the object is always traumatic in comparison to the pleasure individuals try to give themselves.

French psychoanalysts have always been careful to take into account, in evaluating different kinds of mental functioning, the means that the human mind has at its disposal for coping with the trauma linked to the vicissitudes of human sexuality, in the sense of infantile sexuality that is not limited to its genital aspects, as Freud discovered. The 'Paris School of Psychosomatics' – Pierre Marty, Michel de M'Uzan, Christian David and Michel Fain – has highlighted one of these adventures of sexuality when the individual can protect him/herself from a trauma only by rejecting all libidinal cathexes, narcissistic as well as object-related, and by implementing an almost-complete split between mind and body.

Those psychoanalysts, all of them medical practitioners and members of the Paris Psychoanalytical Society, gave a more formal description of their approach in 1963, based on the idea of deficit or inadequacy in mental functioning (fantasy, oneiric or associative); they considered these failures of mental defence to be paradigmatic. That idea tied in with what psychoanalysis had discovered, particularly as far as the economic dimension was concerned: the somatic symptom as such is a-symbolic and non-meaningful, an outlook that gave rise to several major developments.

One of the concepts that has since become indispensable for understanding psychosomatic economics is that of *operational thinking*, developed by Marty and de M'Uzan in their 1963 paper which appears in the present collection (chapter 22). They describe a conscious mode of thought that has no organic link to any real fantasy thinking which can replicate and illustrate actions. It is a form of thinking bereft of associations that appears to be in a direct relationship with sensorimotor aspects, with no reference to a truly alive internal object. It is cut off both from the drives and from the world of objects, so that the individual's fantasy and oneiric life is of poor quality.

> Operational thinking was first described by the founders of the Paris School of Psychosomatics (Marty, de M'Uzan, & David, 1963). It is characterised by a *deficiency in mentalisation* (in fantasy and oneiric activity) and *hypercathexis of factual elements*.

This approach to psychosomatic functioning was illustrated in that same year in a book that has now become a classic text: Marty, de M'Uzan and David's *L'investigation psychosomatique* [Psychosomatic investigations] (1963). In that volume, the authors present seven clinical observations which lend support to the introduction of a new nosography in French psychoanalytic thinking. According to that conception, drive-related excitation that fails to find an outlet in the mind through ideational representations and affects is discharged by means of behaviour and/or of somatisation.

At the end of the 1960s that approach was echoed in Nemiah and Sifneos's (1970) work on alexithymia, in which they describe how difficult it is for these patients to undertake psychoanalytic psychotherapy because they find it difficult to identify and describe their emotions. Such a point of view is close to what Freud said in his description of the actual neuroses; unlike the transference psychoneuroses, these were not suitable for psychoanalytic treatment. The Paris School of Psychosomatics, however, argued that it was possible to treat such patients with psychoanalysis, although there would have to be some technical variations in the setting in both its material and interpretative dimensions.

> **Essential depression** was described by Marty (1968b): no object is involved, and it is not melancholic in nature. Its characteristic features are feelings of incompetence and inadequacy; there are no guilt feelings.

> **Progressive disorganisation** was introduced into psychosomatic theory by Marty (1968a, 1980). It is essentially a phenomenological notion that describes a retrograde movement through the various levels of organisation of psychosomatic functioning, from the highest form to the most primitive.

Thanks to this idea of operational thinking, Marty was able to describe other clinical patterns, among them *essential depression* and *progressive disorganisation*. In his 1968b paper published in this volume (chapter 23), Marty gives an excellent description of the issues involved in 'silent' depression, a 'silent crisis, which often forms the prelude to the establishment of operational life' and brings about a 'functional fragmentation' that corresponds to the death instinct. Marty uses the term 'instinct' rather than 'drive' because his idea is to describe, within the logics of organisation and disorganisation as defined by Hughlings Jackson, 'individual impulses of life and death', which include illness as a manifestation of the logics of what is alive. His theory of somatisation led him – as was the case with Freud in his final theory of the instinctual drives – to include the drives in the overall destiny of life, even if this means losing their dimension of variability as regards both their aims and their objects.

In that period of discovery of psychosomatic 'solutions', it was tempting to hypothesise a linear form of causation between the lack of fantasising, essential depression, operational thinking and somatic disorganisation. Later, Marty (1984) introduced the idea of a *process of somatisation*, thus emphasising the path followed by a series of events leading to somatisation. Further research carried out at the Paris Psychosomatic Institute showed that care had to be taken before attempting to correlate lack of mentalisation with somatic illnesses, as well as in reaching a therapeutic prognosis based on the evolution of mentalisation and that of the illness. For example, in the case of patients with cancer, progress in mentalisation does not necessarily lead to any somatic improvement; this suggests that, at one point, a truly psychosomatic 'divorce' takes place. In a recent paper, Claude Smadja (2006), a follower of Pierre Marty, pointed out that, although operational functioning can be found in many patients, some may suffer from a severe and evolutive somatisation, some from a mild and reversible type and others from no psychosomatic illness at all (p. 42).

Marilia Aisenstein's clinical presentation (1987 – chapter 24, this volume) illustrates both the therapeutic possibilities and the technical difficulties inherent in psychoanalytic work with psychosomatic patients. 'The Man from Burma', the pseudonym she gave to the patient she was treating in psychotherapy, suffered from a severe form of haemorrhagic rectocolitis, typical of a psychosomatic solution. Given that his thought processes were operational, the analyst suggested a setting in which she and her patient would be sitting facing each other, with one therapy session per week; she decided at first not to offer any interpretations, in case they only increased his unbound drive-related excitation and provoked a fresh outbreak of the somatic symptom. They therefore had 'conversations' about seemingly neutral subjects (the weather, politics, professional activity) until, one day, the patient made a slip of the tongue: he spoke of his holiday in 'Burma' instead of 'Bulgaria'.

That provided the opportunity for unveiling a set of split-off traumatic ideas concerning his first wife and for discovering his unconscious identification with her through the somatic symptom; this was confirmed when he recalled a nightmare he had had in the past. From that point on, the analyst was able to take the risk of suggesting interpretations centred more on the patient's mental functioning than on his unconscious fantasies in order to preserve his new-found capacity to make use of the resources of his preconscious, which until that point had been neglected. In this kind of case, the work of mentalisation succeeds in containing the evolution of the somatic illness, but it does not preclude a psychotic breakdown – in this case, a 'professional' paranoia. The delusional solution, all the same, has the advantage of bringing about some binding of excitation in the patient's ideational representations; from that point of view, it is a better mental solution insofar as it implies re-cathexis of objects and of the body.

Aisenstein's clinical case endorsed the metapsychological point of view adopted by Michel de M'Uzan regarding operational thinking. Unlike Marty, who restricted himself more to the phenomenological approach, de M'Uzan (1974) defined that form of thinking as a hypercathexis of the factual sphere that enables the individual to repudiate – in Freud's sense of the word, *Verwerfung* – the return of hallucinatory phenomena. In that view, operational thinking appears to be a primitive defence against psychotic anxiety. Later, de M'Uzan (1998) introduced the concept of **actual psychosis** in order to highlight the close relationship between psychosomatic functioning and psychotic functioning in cases of severe somatic pathology.

> The nosographical concept of **actual psychoses** was suggested by de M'Uzan (1998) in order to enable a more precise description of those entities corresponding to Evelyne Kestemberg's 'cold psychoses' (i.e. non-delusional ones) (Kestemberg, 2001).

Theoretical and clinical thinking about non-neurotic structures such as those explored in these psychosomatic studies led Didier Anzieu (1974) to introduce the concept of the *skin ego*. A member of the French Psychoanalytical Association, Anzieu was the author of a certain number of papers that have proved highly significant for the development of psychoanalysis in France, particularly as regards the sheer spread and variety of the domains he explored and the excellent quality of his clinical illustrations centred around issues involving differentiation between inside and outside. The hypothesis of the skin ego was an attempt at reconciling the two approaches that Freud adopted with respect to the ego, one of which was biological and involved a process of differentiation with respect to the external world given the impact of external excitation, while the other was more mental in scope and corresponded to the identifications that are specific to the various agencies. Anzieu's definition of the skin ego draws on that apparent dichotomy: 'By skin ego, I mean the mental image of which the Ego of the child makes use during the early phases of its development to present itself as an Ego containing psychic contents, on the basis of its experience of the surface of the body. This corresponds to the moment when the mental ego differentiates from the bodily ego on an operative level, while remaining merged with it on the representational level' (1985/1989, p. 40). This involves both what is represented in Freud's concept of the bodily ego, as 'a mental projection of the surface of the body' (1923b, p. 26n) and what enables differentiation between the bodily ego and the ego as a psychic agency. In Anzieu's (2002) words, 'The skin ego develops and is enhanced through the interlocking of the various sensorimotor envelopes. It has a two-layered structure, one of which is turned towards excitation of internal or external origin, while the other is oriented towards communications sent to and received from the environment.'

> The concept of the **skin ego** was introduced by Anzieu (1974). It describes the manner in which the ego seeks support from the body's skin. This operational concept implies that the functions of the ego and those of the bodily envelope (to limit, contain and organise) are homologous.

The ego cannot have access to a new structuration unless it breaks with the primacy of tactile experience and turns into a space for inter-sensory elements. In Anzieu's conceptualisation, that movement is dependent on the prohibition against touching, the forerunner of the Oedipal prohibition. The importance of inter-sensoriality gives a clear impression of what is at stake in the psychoanalytic experience, based on the need to replace tactile contact with words that touch, thereby facilitating the process of symbolisation in the course of an analysis. Anzieu's paper published in the present collection (chapter 25) is one of the fundamental chapters of his book on the skin ego, in which he demonstrates how this notion, which lies between metaphor and concept, highlights the importance of the interface between inside and outside, upon which the relationship between container and contained is built. The main functions of the skin are taken on by the skin ego and, from there, by the ego as a psychic agency. We see here how Anzieu's work echoes that of Bion, Tustin, Esther Bick and Grotstein, each of whom attempted to describe the conditions under which sensations could be transformed into affects and ideational representations.

Analytic work with non-neurotic patients confirms the usefulness of this parallelism between the functions of the skin and those of the ego in making it possible to work with narcissistic disorders using non-verbal communication. Anzieu (1987) gave several clinical examples centred on the reconstruction of the early phases of the skin ego based on what he called 'formal signifiers'. Contrary to fantasy, which is based on visual signifiers, formal signifiers are made up of proprioceptive images – tactile and coenaesthetic, kinaesthetic, postural (equilibration) – thus excluding those sense organs that operate with distance (sight, hearing). The grid of the nine functions of the skin ego enables formal signifiers to be interpreted in such a way as to integrate them, in Anzieu's words, within 'the more general work of psychoanalytic interpretation of psychic containers, and it has a specificity that distinguishes it from work that bears upon the contents' (1987/1990, p. 23). Working on the distortions caused to the setting and on non-verbal material helps compensate for the ego's defective functioning and subsequently facilitates the reconstruction of trauma that occurred in the early mother–infant relationship.

Among the nine functions of the skin ego that are usually positive, Anzieu (1985) writes of a negative function, 'having the aim of self-destruction of the skin and of the ego' (p. 105). He sees manifestations of this in autoimmune diseases, psychosomatic disorders and schizophrenia, and he emphasises the paradoxical nature of these solutions, in which the positive aspect is avoided and replaced by a fascination with the negative aspects. Those psychopathological solutions are quite simply, in André Green's view (2006 – chapter 26, this volume), a confirmation of the hypothesis of the death drive. Green's recent paper gave him the opportunity of opening up a discussion on that highly controversial hypothesis, one that has never been unanimously adopted by psychoanalysts. In his study of the concept, Green asks whether it is both necessary and justifiable to postulate the existence of a death drive; his own view is that it is a concept worth adopting.

Green had already discussed this question in an extremely important paper he read in 1984 to the first scientific symposium of the European Psychoanalytical Federation devoted to that topic; it was subsequently published in his book *The Work of the Negative* (Green, 1993/1999). In that paper, Green had already declared himself to be in favour of the death drive, basing his argument on several clinical examples that testify to the importance of a self-destructive function in the mind and of forms of destruction that can be understood only in terms of a complete unbinding between the life and death drives: melancholic depression and the psychoses in particular reveal underlying anxieties about annihilation or breakdown. Green did all the same point out that 'no clinical argument provides proof of the death drive', adding that 'Although we have not lost sight of the fact that drive theory belongs to the order of concepts and is therefore never completely verifiable by experience, these concepts are designed to elucidate experience and cannot be dissociated from it' (1986/1999, p. 84).

Since clinical experience testifies to the fact that 'the object reveals the drives' (1986/1999, p. 85), which in themselves are not directly knowable, Green introduced an economic hypothesis concerning mental functioning: the life drive, characterised by mechanisms of binding and unbinding, aims at providing an *objectalising function* – that is, cathexis of the object. The death drive, on the other hand, aims at fulfilling a *disobjectalising function* using only unbinding: 'the manifestation characteristic of the destructivity of the death drive is *withdrawal of investment*' (p. 86).

> Green constructed an original theory of the relationship between the life and death drives based on their relation to the object. The aim of the life drive is to preserve an **objectalising function**, not only by enabling relationships to be created with internal or external objects, but also – and above all – by transforming structures into objects, even when no object is directly involved. On the other hand, the death drive has a **disobjectalising function** that attacks not only the object relation but all the substitutes for the object – that is, the ego.

In other words, as relatively stable and well-defined forms, the object and the ego go to make up as it were expressions of libidinal binding and neutralisation of the destructive processes; their inter-relationship, however, reveals a tendency to opposition, to a conflict between the aim of binding with the object (maintaining the relationship with the object) and that of narcissistic unbinding (the relationship with the object is rejected). Hence Green's idea (1993) of supporting the correlative hypothesis of *negative narcissism*, which he described in terms of 'death narcissism', as opposed to positive narcissism, which he called 'life narcissism'.

The advent of the sexual drives, when auto-erotism is linked to the setting-up of an object relation, gives rise to a conflict in which love and hate come respectively from a libidinal drive that binds with the object and from a destructive drive that unbinds. This makes it easier to understand why Freud always spoke in terms of a dualism of the drives, since ambivalence lies at the heart of mental conflict as observed in the clinical work of psychoanalysis: drives are dualistic from the outset, given the dualism involved in object cathexis. For Green, the dualism of the drives is a further manifestation of the death drive, seen as the principle of division and opposition.

In chapter 26, Green describes this conflict in terms of the contrast between internalisation and externalisation; he emphasises the fact that the death drive has to do with the kind of externalisation that Bion called evacuation, without there being necessarily a projective dimension – it is simply a movement of ex-corporation which is in no way aimed at an object. In his final version of drive theory, Freud indeed had introduced the concept of the death drive by locating its tendency to repeat 'beyond the pleasure principle', which functions in terms of the principle of constancy. The drives tend more to follow the principle of inertia insofar as their aim is not only to lessen tension to the lowest level possible, but to abolish all tension completely and bring it down to zero. Hence Green's insistence on starting with the *id* in order to describe the death drive – a force that aims to discharge all excitation – and not with the *unconscious*, which presupposes some binding of excitation through ideational

> The concept of **primary** or **erotogenic masochism** was introduced by Freud in his paper on 'The Economic Problem of Masochism' (Freud, 1924c). Primary masochism is a way of binding the death drive, an admixture of the death and life drives. In this sense, primary or erotogenic masochism has a *positive* role to play in mental life.

representation. The ideas contained in this chapter were developed recently in 'Why Are There Destructive or Death Drives?' (2007), in which Green discusses in more detail the objections raised by the opponents of the idea of a death drive.

The work of the negative corresponding to the death drive includes, Green argues, a *reversal of meaning* in which unpleasure becomes a source of pleasure and the allo-destructiveness internalised in the superego is transformed into a *need for self-punishment*. The theory of the death drive is in fact correlative with the conception of *primary erotogenic masochism*, which is the subject of one of Freud's major writings (1924c). It is that paper which Benno Rosenberg (1982) discusses in chapter 27 in the present volume: it enables us to understand the importance of the hypothesis of masochism as supporting the idea of the death drive in its self-destructive aim.

Rosenberg's chapter is in fact a major exegesis of Freud's (1924c) text. He reminds us that, for Freud, primary or erotogenic masochism represents an important admixture of the death and life drives; part of the death drive is deflected outwards, towards objects in the external world, under the influence of Eros, thereby constituting the sadistic manifestations described by Freud as 'the destructive instinct, the instinct for mastery, or the will to power' (1924c, p. 163). Another part of this self-destructive drive remains within the individual, and, 'with the help of the accompanying sexual excitation [it] becomes libidinally bound there' (p. 163), thus giving rise to masochism. For this reason, primary erotogenic masochism has a positive role to play in mental life because, as Freud points out, it implies the original binding of the death drive by the life drive, hence its function of maintaining 'the self as its object' (p. 164). Just as a Green writes of life narcissism, Rosenberg hypothesises the existence of masochism that is the guardian of life.

When the object can no longer carry out drive binding, masochism becomes deadly and may push the individual towards death, as in the self-destructive behaviour of borderline states, in severe forms of anorexia nervosa and in psychosomatic breakdowns. In *deadly masochism*, the only narcissistic continuity that remains lies in the pleasure of self-destructiveness, thus corresponding to what Green calls negative narcissism.

In that way of looking at the situation, primary masochism has no longer any need to involve the death drive, if we take the latter to be, as in Freud's somewhat speculative hypothesis, the return of living beings to the stability of the inorganic state. On the other hand, it is correlative with the death drive if we understand Freud's final version of the drive theory to be a sign of what he never failed to describe as the opposition between inertia and constancy, between primary and secondary processes, between narcissism and the object which, as an integral part of the sexual drives, organises the continuous binding and unbinding between love and hate.

The debates concerning the death drive have highlighted the difficulty of seeing in the sexual drives the only ones that, from a psychoanalytic perspective, exist. René Roussillon (1999) answers the objections raised by suggesting that we put to one side the alternative 'biological drive' (Green's point of view)/'role of the source-object' (Laplanche's theory) in our attempt to define the origins of sexuality. If we adopt the point of view of a *metapsychology of the processes* involved, it becomes possible to reconcile those who argue in favour of drive theory and those who tend more towards a theory

> Freud (1912–13) made use of the concept of **sexualisation** when referring to animism and magical thinking as bearing witness to the ascendancy of the primary process; the concept of **desexualisation** implies 'an abandonment of sexual aims', 'a kind of sublimation' (Freud 1923b, p. 30). There is, therefore, the organisation of some form of the ego and the actualisation of the secondary process. In sublimation there would seem to be a complementary interplay between **sexualisation** – cathexis of the primary system – and **desexualisation** – cathexis of the secondary system.

of object relations: sexuality could be looked upon as a process of differentiation between inside and outside in a dialectical movement involving both drive and object. Roussillon adopts the idea of *différance*,[1] a notion invented by the philosopher Jacques Derrida (1967), to describe the movement inherent in the concept of process.

The dialectics of drive and object can also be seen in the light of the contrast between **sexualisation and desexualisation**. Roussillon is referring here to the concepts Freud introduced in *The Ego and the Id* (1923b), defining sublimation as the destiny of the drives: 'The transformation of object-libido into narcissistic libido. . . obviously implies an abandonment of sexual aims, a desexualization – a kind of sublimation, therefore' (1923b, p. 30). The idea is to define infantile sexuality, corresponding to the process by which the erotogenic body is appropriated in the mind, without falling into the difficulties that Freud encountered, in his disagreement with Jung, in attempting to explain the movement from sexual to non-sexual, based on the idea of drive renunciation.

Laplanche (1980) suggested that, alongside sublimation linked to repression, there could be a form of sublimation which, staying close to the sources of the libido, does not call upon repression. Sublimation requires that we take into account the dialectics between primary sexualisation, what Roussillon calls the drive cathexis of experience, secondary desexualisation, associated with sublimation, and what he terms non-sexualisation. He agrees with Green's definition of the non-sexualisation that is typical of the death drive as having to do with the disobjectalising function. His conceptualisation therefore leaves open the possibility of both a positive and a

---

[1] *Différance* is a neologism; it is homophonous with the word *différence* [difference]. *Différance* plays on the fact that in French the verb *différer* means both 'to defer, postpone' and 'to differ'. [*Trans.*]

negative destiny for sublimation, a drive-related outcome that, as we know, may also be in the service of lethal tendencies in the individual and in society.

This implies, therefore, that if sublimation is in the service of life rather than of death, when the object is lost the part of object-libido transformed into narcissistic libido in that identificatory movement that Freud called 'a kind of sublimation' (1923b, p. 30) will be immediately re-objectalised through cathecting the sublimated object representation. 'Representation then ceases to be the means or medium by which the drive represents its object; it becomes the very object in which the drive is satisfied' (Roussillon, chapter 28, this volume, p. 538). That point indeed led Roussillon to argue that secondary desexualisation is only 'partial', involving 'the way in which the drives reach fulfilment not the actual basis of the cathexis'. Maintaining a dialectical relationship between the mechanisms of sexualisation and desexualisation is precisely what enables the link between sublimation and infantile sexuality to be preserved, thus highlighting the importance of the work of the sexual drives in mental functioning, even though this may be quite far removed from direct drive satisfaction.

Sublimation may also bring about an unbinding of the drives, thus setting murderous impulses free; that idea had made Freud pessimistic as regards any progress that could be accomplished through civilisation. In the history of drive-related cathexes of reality, we must draw a distinction between narcissistic cathexes and object-cathexes, which Freud conceptualised particularly in terms of the opposition between the narcissistic ego-ideal (the ideal ego) and the post-Oedipal superego. In *Civilization and Its Discontents*, Freud (1930a) showed how the superego creates a link between individual and group psychology, as well as between generations, because the parental superego that is introjected by the child has its origins in the ego of the grandparents. The child's helplessness obliges him or her to submit to the prohibitions laid down by the parents so as not to risk losing their love. Frustration generates aggressiveness and violence that are turned back on the self; Freud saw in this a manifestation of the death drive. This, then, would appear to be a consequence of civilisation, which secretes forces that tend to destroy it.

In his paper, Gilbert Diatkine (1993 – chapter 29, this volume) makes use of Freud's concept of the 'cultural superego' in order to show how it reinforces from outside the action of the individual superego. The importance of narcissism in group psychology leads him to suggest a more explicit definition of what Freud called 'the narcissism of minor differences' (1930a, p. 114): through its shared ideals, a group protects its members, but only its members – all others are rejected and sometimes treated violently in a kind of mass paranoia. The narcissism of minor differences thus turns a fellow-creature into a non-human and reduces to nothing the most elementary of moral commandments. The explanation for this would seem to be that these minor differences call into question the ideal ego of the group; for each member of the group, that ideal ego derives from his or her narcissistic identification with the mother; within that narcissistic identification, the mother's identification of the child with his or her father lies, for the child, at the core of the feeling of belonging to the human species. Diatkine goes on to discuss what this ending of the belief in the inevitability of the civilising process, in which Freud, like almost all of his contemporaries, strongly believed, might mean for psychoanalysis.

References

Aisenstein, M. (1987). Solution psychosomatique – issue psychosomatique. Notes cliniques: L'homme de Birmanie. *Les Cahiers du Centre de Psychanalyse et de Psychothérapie, 14*: 73–97. [Psychosomatic Solution or Somatic Outcome: The Man from Burma – Psychotherapy of a Case of Haemorrhagic Rectocolitis. International Journal of Psychoanalysis, 74 (1993): 371–381.]
Anzieu, D. (1974). Le moi-peau [The skin ego]. *Nouvelle Revue de Psychanalyse, 3*: 195–208.
Anzieu, D. (1985). *Le moi-peau.* Paris: Dunod. [*The Skin Ego*, trans. C. Turner. New Haven, CT: Yale University Press, 1989.]
Anzieu, D. (1987). Les signifiants formels et le moi-peau. In D. Anzieu et al., *Les enveloppes psychiques.* Paris: Dunod. [*Psychic Envelopes*, trans. D. Briggs. London: Karnac, 1990.]
Anzieu, D. (2002). Le moi-peau. In A. de Mijolla (Ed.), *Dictionnaire International de la Psychanalyse.* Paris: Calmann-Lévy.
Derrida, J. (1967). *L'écriture et la différence.* Paris: Editions du Seuil. [*Writing and Difference*, trans. A. Bass. Chicago: University of Chicago Press, 1980.]
Diatkine, G. (1993). La cravate croate. Narcissisme des petites différences et processus de civilisation. [The Croatian cravat: The narcissism of minor differences and the process of civilisation]. *Revue Française de Psychanalyse, 57* (4): 1057–1072.
Freud, S. (1905d). *Three Essays on the Theory of Sexuality. S.E.,* **7**: 125.
Freud, S. (1915c). Instincts and Their Vicissitudes. *S.E.,* 14: 111.
Freud, S. (1923b). *The Ego and the Id. S.E.,* 19: 3.
Freud, S. (1924c). The Economic Problem of Masochism. *S.E.,* 19: 157.
Freud, S. (1930a). *Civilization and Its Discontents. S.E.,* 21: 59.
Freud, S. (1933a). *New Introductory Lectures on Psycho-Analysis. S.E.,* 22: 3.
Green, A. (1986). Pulsion de mort, narcissisme négatif, fonction désobjectalisante. In *Le travail du négatif.* Paris: Editions de Minuit, 1993. [The death drive, negative narcissism and the disobjectalising function (trans. A. Weller). In *The Work of the Negative.* London: Free Association Books, 1999.]
Green, A. (1993). *Le travail du négatif.* Paris: Editions de Minuit. [*The Work of the Negative* (trans. A. Weller). London: Free Association Books, 1999.]
Green, A. (2006). *La pulsion de mort. Sens, objections, substituts* [The death drive: Meaning, objections, substitutes]. Unpublished paper read at a Paris Psychoanalytical Society meeting (21 February).
Green, A. (2007). *Pourquoi les pulsions de destruction ou de mort?* [Why are there destructive or death drives?]. Paris: Panama.
Laplanche, J. (1980). *La sublimation. Problématiques III* [Problematics 3: Sublimation]. Paris: Presses Universitaires de France.
Marty, P. (1968a). A major process of somatization: The progressive disorganization. *International Journal of Psycho-Analysis, 49*: 246–249.
Marty, P. (1968b). La dépression essentielle [Essential depression]. *Revue Française de Psychanalyse, 32* (3): 345–355. [Also in: *Revue Française de Psychanalyse: Textes 1926–2006* (pp. 205–208). Paris: Presses Universitaires de France, 2006.]
Marty, P. (1984). Des processus de somatisation [Processes of somatisation]. In M. Fain, & C. Dejours (Eds.), *Corps malade et corps érotique* [Ill body and erotic body]. Paris: Masson.

Marty, P., & M'Uzan, M. de (1963). La pensée opératoire [Operational thinking]. *Revue Française de Psychanalyse*, *27* (special issue): 345–356.

Marty, P., M'Uzan, M. de, & David, C. (1963). *L'investigation psychosomatique. Sept observations cliniques* [Psychosomatic investigations: Seven clinical observations]. Paris: Presses Universitaires de France.

M'Uzan, M. de (1974). Psychodynamic Mechanisms in Psychosomatic Symptom Formation. (Report on the 2nd International Congress on Psychosomatic Medicine, Amsterdam, 1973.) *Psychotherapy and Psychosomatics*, *23* (1–6): 103–110.

M'Uzan, M. de (1998). Impasses de la théorie, théories indispensables [Impasses in theory, indispensable theories]. *Revue Française de Psychanalyse*, *62* (5): 1459–1463.

Nemiah, J. C., & Sifneos, P. E. (1970). Affect and fantasy in patients with psychosomatic disorders. In O. W. Hill (Ed.), *Modern Trends in Psychosomatic Medicine Vol. 2* (pp. 26–34). London: Butterworths.

Rosenberg, B. (1982). Masochisme mortifère et masochisme gardien de la vie. (Quelques réflexions sur le masochisme érogène tel qu'il est décrit dans 'Le problème économique du masochisme') [Deadly masochism, life-preserving masochism. (Some thoughts on erotogenic masochism as described in 'The Economic Problem of Narcissism')]. In *Masochisme mortifère et masochisme gardien de la vie* [Deadly masochism and life-preserving masochism]. Paris: Presses Universitaires de France, 1991.

Roussillon, R. (1999). Sexualisation et désexualisation [Sexualisation and desexualisation]. *Bulletin du Groupe Lyonnais de Psychanalyse*, *46*: 72–78.

Smadja, C. (2006). Les deux vies de l'opératoire [The two lives of the operational dimension]. *Psychanalyse et psychose*, *6*: 41–52.

22 OPERATIONAL THINKING[1]

Pierre Marty and Michel de M'Uzan

Pierre Marty (1918–1993) was a psychiatrist and a full member and former president of the Paris Psychoanalytical Society. In 1970, when he set up an administrative college within the Society, he initiated a series of significant reforms to the statutes and structure of that organisation. He was keenly interested in contemporary psychosomatic practice, and, with Michel de M'Uzan, he developed the concept of 'operational thinking' and emphasised the importance of economic aspects. In 1963, with Christian David and Michel de M'Uzan, he wrote *L'investigation psychosomatique* [Psychosomatic investigations] (PUF, 1963), and in 1970, with Michael Fain, he set up the Paris Psychosomatic Institute. His two seminal works are: *Les mouvements individuels de vie et de mort* [Individual impulses of life and death] (Payot, 1976), and *L'ordre psychosomatique* [The psychosomatic order] (Payot, 1980); in these books, he explains his conception of mental functioning in adult psychosomatic disorders, a topic that he would later develop with respect to children and babies.

Rosine Debray wrote a concise biography of Pierre Marty for the 'Psychanalystes d'aujourd'hui' series (PUF, 1998).

Michel de M'Uzan is a psychiatrist, a former full member of the Paris Psychoanalytical Society and a former director of the Institute of Psychoanalysis. He is one of the founding members of the Paris Psychosomatic Institute (IPSO) and co-editor of the 'Fil Rouge' series (PUF). He has written some thought-provoking and creative books, characterised by his exceptional aesthetic sensitivity. His work on interpretation and its mutative potentiality, on memory, on the mechanisms of artistic creation and on female sexuality is both original and cohesive.

A list of his writings would include: *De l'art à la mort* [From art to death] (Gallimard, 1977 & 1994) and *La bouche de l'inconscient* [The mouth of the unconscious] (Gallimard, 1994). In his most recent book, *Aux confins de l'identité* [The frontiers of identity] (Gallimard, 2005), he explores, in some depth, issues relating to the sense of identity, drawing a clear distinction

---

[1] This article was presented at the 23rd Congress of Romance-Language Psychoanalysts in Barcelona in 1962 in response to a paper presented by Michel Fain and Christian David, 'Aspects fonctionnels de la vie onirique' [Functional aspects of dream life], which was subsequently published in 1963.

between the non-drive-related *vital-identital* sphere and the psycho-sexual dimension, which has to do with the drives and encompasses narcissism. He has written several works of literature, among which are: *Les chiens des rois* [The kings' dogs] (Gallimard, 1954), *Anthologie du délire* [An anthology of delusion] (Editions du Rocher, 1956), *Le Rire et la Poussière* [Laughter and dust] (Gallimard, 1962), and *Celui-là* [That one] (Grasset, 1994).

Murielle Gagnebin wrote a concise biography of Michel de M'Uzan for the 'Psychanalystes d'aujourd'hui' series (PUF, 1996).

We are glad to echo the praises that will undoubtedly be earned by Michel Fain and Christian David for a report that is remarkable in many respects, and which we consider has the vast merit of remedying a gap. In theoretical and practical terms, it provides us with abundant material for reflection that our contribution in no way proposes to exhaust.

In psychosomatic patients, the absence of phantasmatic activity – at least from the functional viewpoint – goes hand in hand with the development of a completely original form of thinking, which we propose to term *operational thinking*, which will form the main subject of our paper.

The work that we are presenting here is directly connected with the work we are currently carrying out with David, as well as with many exchanges of views with Fain in the course of our shared research activities.

The *operational thinking* that is our theme, and that we will seek to define, does not seem to have attracted attention so far, which is entirely possible since its specific modalities mean that it contains very little to inspire the interest of psychoanalysts. Let us start by noting two key characteristics: it involves a conscious thinking that (1) appears to lack any intrinsic connection with a discernible level of phantasmatic activity and (2) duplicates and illustrates action, sometimes preceding or following it, but in a limited time span. As for the exclusivity of this form of thinking in our subjects, it is not currently possible to assert this categorically; however, we can conjecture that if this existed beyond dispute it would become an original mode of object relations, with a nosographic value comparable to Bouvet's descriptions (1960).[2]

Before dwelling any further on the clinical definition, we would like to present operational thinking, by addressing it, as it were, *in situ*, as it is revealed to us in direct contact with our patients.

The subject who came for a consultation is suffering from some kind of somatic symptoms. He presents his difficulties as a number of isolated facts, with no apparent relational significance. To judge by his attitude, the investigator represents for him merely a function, someone to whom he *submits* his symptoms and from whom he expects nothing but the cure, without any question of an affective involvement on either side. Although the patient

---

[2] Bouvet's point of view to which Marty and de M'Uzan refer concerns the nosographic value of object relations. [*Eds., this volume*]

answers his questions, the investigator is left unsatisfied because there is no real contact, and he feels he is confronted with something we would readily call a 'blank relationship'. Of course, this 'blank relationship' is the kind that the patient deploys constantly, if not exclusively, throughout his life. It is not that the investigation is totally unproductive – for example, it enables the emergence of symptoms to be connected with some specific anecdotal circumstances – but despite the doctor's promptings, it yields nothing, no association that is not linked to the narrowest materiality of the facts or understood in the most limited time span. The atmosphere of the consultation suggests that the patient has the same kind of relations with the investigator as with a raw fact or event, immediate relations that seem to lack either infrastructure or superstructure. As it unfolds, the dialogue might suggest a mechanism of isolation, of an obsessional neurotic nature, but this is not the case. The patient does not distance himself strictly speaking through a mental or verbal manipulation of the material; he is *present*, but *empty*, and it seems difficult to conceive of any obsessional mechanism. We can imagine the investigator's perplexity at such a marked deficiency in the patient's play of identification. Also, if he is not used to it, he will experience some identificatory difficulties and remain baffled as to the possibilities of a psychotherapy.

Although this form of *operational thinking* is electively connected to the 'psychosomatoses', a term we will use to refer to conditions in which the personality is disposed towards the somatic path as a principal exit from conflictual situations, it is probably not alien to certain character neuroses, and it would be interesting to investigate the modalities with which it must be expressed in certain types of psychosis.

Operational thinking can thus be found in a fairly wide range of clinical pictures, but it is useful to consider it in isolation, as a symptom, because it has enough stable characteristics of its own to be identifiable, as we will now seek to demonstrate.

It seems best to start by giving a clinical example. It would not be possible in the limited context of our paper to present a complete observation. However, the verbatim account of a typical sequence will best illustrate the highly specific style of this mode of thinking.

The clinical illustration we will present is drawn from the complete report of a psychosomatic interview conducted at our consultation in Professor Marcel David's service. This is the case of a twenty-five-year-old man, suffering from a complex syndrome: headaches, trembling limbs, memory difficulties and impaired motor coordination. These problems emerged six months after a superficial scalp wound caused by some buckshot that had been fired. The interview extract we are presenting concerns a comparison, partly instigated by the investigator, between the patient and his father.

> 'In the last holidays, I put an insulated roof on my car. For my father, anything goes, but I like every part to be properly joined, although this can be a disadvantage – it

may be less well insulated. Also, the next day we could see that the insulating plates were heating up, but in time they will curve as the roof is convex and they will find a new position and work loose from the metal panel. Then the racks that were inside the car will have to be raised. I had wanted to secure them so they no longer had to be touched, so that they were firm and could be dismantled. For my father, anything goes, whereas I like the job to be finished.

— There is something I haven't understood – whose idea was it to adjust the hardboard?
— Mine.
— And that was a disadvantage?
— I don't know, it's too early to judge.
— How's that?
— Yes, for the next two days, the hardboard still hadn't taken shape; at the ends where it had worked loosest it wasn't hot, but where it touched it had heated up.
— So there was an advantage to it having worked loose?
— Yes.
— So an advantage to not being too meticulous?
— Not necessarily. I reckoned that over time the car's vibrations would bend the plates. That's what's happened; they've come a bit loose but it may not be enough, it may be necessary to put a wedge in.
— You told me that your father did what you wanted, I asked you for an example, and you've given me one in which your success is in fact not conclusive.
— I can't judge yet, it's not finished: as I told you, I don't know what effect that will have, it's an experiment. Before there were pieces of cardboard that insulated and stopped the heat getting through. There is just one difference, the hardboard is closer to the roof than the pieces of cardboard; these allowed the air to circulate above, whereas the hardboard on the supports lets much less air through.
— That's not to your advantage.
— I won't be able to judge for a while. Since it wasn't hot at the ends, and if they didn't heat up, there's no reason for it to heat up elsewhere.'

It seems to us that this example strongly corroborates the definition of operational thinking that we have outlined. The subject's speech only illustrates his action in further detail; it involves no elaboration, and while it refers to a situation of competition with his father, it lacks any connection with a discernible level of phantasmatic activity. The subject remains constantly on the level of his actions; his mode of thinking adheres closely to the materiality of the facts and the utility of the objects; he is stuck in the present situation, and if he manages to project himself into the future or return to the past, it is by transforming these into *pieces of the present*, in which everything is dominated exclusively by the succession of facts. The patient has absolutely nothing in mind but joining the hardboard plates and their distance from the car roof. This thinking is probably well adapted to his task, and even efficient on a practical level, but its adaptation represents the narrow confine of his possibilities for expansion and communication; linear and restricted, it takes its course without opening up to realities of another order, affective or phantasmatic, that might enrich and broaden its operations. It remains without associations. It comes as no surprise then to observe it in direct relationship with sensorimotricity, and that its lack of detachment from *things* is in reality a lack of freedom. Everything happens as if it were imposed on the subject. But its originality consists mainly in the fact that it does not tend to *signify* the action but to *duplicate* it: the verb, here, does nothing but repeat the actions of the hands at work.

This is not to say that operational thinking is necessarily always rudimentary or poor in quality. But even when it is complex and technically productive, such as in the purely abstract domain, it still lacks any reference to an internal object that is truly alive. Thus, for operational thinking, the notion of judgement, as it is usually conceived with its complex set of fundamental factors, is replaced by that of evaluation in only a few dimensions or rather that of scale – hence its aridity and, despite everything, its impoverishment. With no symbolic significance or sublimatory value – it goes without saying that it is incapable of either artistic production or genuine scientific creativity – this form of thinking creates only emblems, the signs of a relationship with time, places and real objects that are experienced as providing security.

The superegoic quality of operational thinking seems evident. But on reflection, it can be observed that it does not in fact exceed the level of conformism. In other words, the subject is almost incapable of anything but superficial identifications, with rules glimpsed through a few individuals. This is a schematic superego, which appears not to be integrated. In the relationship with the investigator, these superficial identifications are expressed in the best of cases in an imitative mode. Other people are, fundamentally, considered identical to the subject and attributed with the same system of operational thinking as his own. As a result, it cannot play any structuring reparative role.

We will give two brief clinical illustrations of the above. The first shows how this impossibility of a subtle identification is compensated not by a projection of the 'id', as in neurotics, but by a comprehensive projection of the subject, in which the object is considered completely identical to the subject and endowed with the same form of thinking. We were asking one patient questions for over half an hour. His system of operational thinking was evident, and at one specific point we made some notes about this in front of him. Trying to encourage him to abandon what might have emerged as a defence mechanism, we explained to him his way of thinking. As the notes we were making did not seem to interest him in the least, we asked him: 'In your opinion, what am I writing down?' Without hesitating, he answered: 'You're writing down someone's name to remind yourself to phone him.' The affective quality of the interview, as well as the interest we were showing in him, seemed to have escaped him entirely. The almost instantaneous reply undoubtedly attested to a phantasy, and reference could have been made to an isolating mechanism, designed to break openly with the relationship established in the interview. But this phantasy was itself isolated. In one hour, no other was demonstrated; his response had no personal tone, it was peremptory and, because of its precision, the patient did not seem to doubt it for a moment. Its resemblance to any obsessional neurotic trait was so weak that it left us entirely perplexed.

The second example will illustrate what we mean by conformism, emphasising the superficial aspect of a superegoic identification, the adherence to decreed rules that have not been integrated.

> One of our patients, whom we were treating in psychotherapy, told us one day on arriving at her session, with strong emotion in her voice, 'My father is dead; what is the form in these cases?' The new situation left her helpless; she had to cling to something that was not included in the relationship with us as psychotherapists but was found in an imposed and socialised rule of behaviour.

Thus, clinging to the present situation as if to a safety-rope, without benefiting from the possibilities of detachment and delay afforded by phantasmatic activity, the subject with only operational thinking at his disposal undergoes reality rather than deeply living it; he only takes part in it empirically. Operational thinking thus seems to us to lack any discernible libidinal quality. It also severely restricts the externalisation of aggression; it is unable to subtend the sado-masochistic dramatisation.

We will not emphasise certain cases in which patients adopt an apparently libidinal or aggressive form of behaviour because this too is in fact a kind of conformism, for they act as if 'under orders'. Neither will we dwell on certain isolated libidinal formulations with a perverse appearance that are sporadically used by some of our patients, which we believe have been addressed by Pasche (1959).

We would now like to adopt another perspective and explain the specific nature of operational thinking by seeking to define its relation to primary and secondary processes. This will lead us to consider its functional value.

In some respects, this might be considered a modality of the secondary process. In fact, it involves the orientation towards a perceptible reality, a concern with causality, logic, and continuity and so on. But the activity of operational thinking essentially applies to *things*, never to products of the imagination or to symbolic expressions. Like the secondary process, it certainly introduces the notion of chronology, but within a limited time-frame. If there is any anticipation, it always relates either to concrete objects or to actions, or to abstract concepts, without ever developing an activity close to that of the secondary elaboration of the dream. This indicates a precarious connection with words – that is to say, an archaic level of the process of cathexis. We associate it with a supplementary phenomenon observed in certain cases that appears as a pseudo-displacement. The subject uses the name of one thing to refer to another, without any possible demonstration of the slightest underlying phantasy that might have connected them by analogy. This manifests a tendency to experience words only as a means of quickly discharging a tension, through lack of ability to maintain it 'in suspense' for long in the way permitted by the energic cathexis in the secondary process. It is therefore not a lapsus in the psychoanalytic sense of the term, but a diminution in the retentive capacity of motor discharge. There is an obvious difference from conscious thought, which apart from its logical coordinating functions, also provides a highly elaborated dramatisation of tensions and their successive unconscious representations. Here, by contrast, the instrumental function of waking life tends to invade the entire field.

If we now examine the relations between operational thinking and the primary process, we see that they initially seem to differ in every respect. We have just seen in fact that because of its links with the concepts of causality, continuity and reality, operational thinking could appear to be an exclusive modality of the secondary process. What is more, operational thinking seems to reveal a kind of hiatus from the primary process, in contrast to the secondary process, which has normally gradually moved away from the primary process towards contact with reality, to be situated in its continuation and in a position of equilibrium with it.

Operational thinking does not take up symbols or words or retrieve any previous phantasmatic elaboration, as the secondary process does, for example, in the secondary elaboration of the dream. Nevertheless, phenomena such as the sudden emergence – apparently unconnected with the context – of perverse or aggressive verbal manifestations such as those we have just mentioned show that operational thinking is not truly cut off from the unconscious, contrary to what might fleetingly be suggested by the attitude of some of these subjects who, living at a distance from an 'id' that has remained unproductive or at least inert, seem to behave like those blind from birth to the unconscious. Needless to say, such a hypothesis does not stand the test of clinical practice, and every note is found on the morbid scale, from these subjects – apparently deprived of primary process, limited to somatic manifestations – to classical neurotics. All that can be stated is that operational thinking makes contact with the unconscious at the lowest, least elaborated level, as beyond the earliest integrative elaborations of the life of the drives. It seems to overstep or bypass any elaborative phantasmatic activity and connect with the early forms of the drives, which can make unexpected returns or generate somatisations or, alternatively, occur under rudimentary appearances in a predominance of the activity–passivity tension that is so common in psychosomatic patients. The investigation should therefore relate to the quality of unconscious phantasies: the most evolved, which assume an audiovisual form, will be retrievable by classical analysis and thus rediscover their broken path towards consciousness; the most archaic will impose therapeutic confrontations in which the verbalisation will long remain very far outside the real relational context.

Thus operational thinking proves unable – as Fain and David have suggested – to ensure the harmonious distribution of the libidinal charges that allows flexible and subtle relations to be established.

At this point in our paper, it seems to us that the positive diagnosis of operational thinking has been sufficiently explained to eliminate any risk of confusion with any other mode of mental activity described in classical terms. Probably in the vast majority of cases, operational thinking will be encountered neither in neurotics nor in subjects who have attained a stage of relationship at what is called the genital level, for the thought that accompanies the action in both these cases always has a quality other than the mere connection with the perceptible, current reality. However, there may be a diagnostic problem in relation to minor obsessional thinking. In fact, we have seen that operational thinking does not allow any distance from the object; the subject maintains superficial contact, and there is apparently nothing other than this contact: as we have said, the subject is present but empty. In both cases, there is certainly a pseudo-mastery of reality, but whereas the obsessional neurotic assures himself of this by actively manipulating a thought that is rich in symbolic or magical properties, the psychosomatic with operational thinking achieves it by directly controlling the sequence of action. For him, the doubt never arises. On the verbal level, words are – as we know – hypercathected in obsessional thinking, acquiring a surfeit of meaning, whereas in operational thinking they are undercathected, merely duplicating the thing or the action, almost eliminating the gap between the signifier and the signified. Finally, the relationship with temporality is very different, since the obsessional patient's thought turns away from action to evolve indefinitely in a time span with very vague limits, whereas the subject with operational thinking is confined in a limited time span that is determined by the concept of succession.

Despite certain appearances, operational thinking is not raw thinking either. The latter is also probably orientated towards reality, but it is another type of reality and it is rooted in it as in a living soil, laden with the past and steeped in meaning. The appearance of operational thinking here is due only to adaptive requirements, but it is still easy to sense the subject's deep relationship with both his preferred objects and the investigator.

We should also say a word about the forms of operational thinking imposed by external pressure, usually professional, when adaptive demands are strong. Forced to resort almost exclusively to this mode of functioning, exhausted by the adaptation to automatic tasks, the subject loses any possibility of personal liberating expression, beyond dream activity, which is in fact also subject to its repercussions. The diagnosis can be difficult when there are somatic manifestations, which is in fact common in these situations. However, after a greater or lesser period of time, the investigation demonstrates the subject's receptivity to affective incentives and the sense of frustration caused him by his way of living, which indicates the traumatic nature of a form of thinking that is externally imposed. It goes without saying that in these cases, the prognosis and the therapy appear in an infinitely better light.

From the preceding discussion, it emerges that operational thinking, given its lack of functional value for integrating the drives, cannot assume any place in the subject's economy. Fain and David (1963) have shown us the economic importance of dream life: from a different viewpoint and following an opposite path, we have been able to assess the economic importance of phantasmatic life in general by studying the very subjects in whom it is lacking.

Our subjects do not dream, or at least they certainly appear incapable of reporting their dreams. When they can, moreover, their accounts also conform to the rules of operational thinking, only mentioning a precise action or series of actions, always closely connected with an existing reality. Of course, such dreams entail a drive cathexis, but the total absence of associations that is usual prevents any assessment of their value. It is perhaps this deficiency in their dream life that makes these patients particularly prone to insomnia. Nevertheless, these periods of insomnia are filled by an operational type of phantasmatic activity in which utilitarian and current representations dominate.

We see what characterises our most typical patients: somatic functions constitute their essential economic path and become the site of morbid sequences; essentially, the economy eludes the mental apparatus, and the psychoanalyst, sensing obstacles to identification on either side, can be disconcerted by the clinical picture and perplexed as to the possibilities of psychotherapy. Finally, the diagnosis of operational thinking is all the more useful to make with certain pictures of character neurosis if it can lead to reserving the prognosis, foreseeing various therapeutic difficulties and confronting them with an appropriate adjustment. Without stopping to consider the technical measures that can be imposed, which in certain cases perceptibly diverge from the classical psychotherapeutic relationship, we should note that it may be necessary to open up the path of mental representations, whatever their quality; it is also important never to interrupt a phantasmatic elaboration in a subject with operational thinking, regardless of the quality of the phantasy and the validity of an intervention concerning the content. In other words, no intervention must hinder the development of a function that has so far been lacking – which, we should note, argues in favour of the analyst's silence.

Given the serious therapeutic task posed by such patients, and the somatic implications that aggravate it, we would wish for the creation of prophylactic measures in the child, appropriate for ensuring a complete functioning for phantasmatic activity.

We are not, of course, in a position yet to pronounce on how to tell which phenomenon can cause an archaic paralysis of the primary process that goes so far as to hinder its evolution even from its earliest stages; on the role at this time of the external factor, as well as its age and its nature; and on the role of the internal factor, for which at such a period the concept of maturation is probably difficult to distinguish from hereditary or congenital dispositions of the personality. We must therefore be satisfied for the time being with getting even a little closer to some answers here.

References

Bouvet, M. (1960). Dépersonnalisation et relations d'objet [Depersonalisation and object relations]. In *La relation d'objet* [Object relations] (pp. 295–435). Paris: Payot, 1967.

Fain, M., & David, C. (1963). Aspects fonctionnels de la vie onirique [Functional aspects of dream life]. *Revue Française de Psychanalyse, 27* (Special Issue): 241–343.

Pasche, F. (1959). Utilisation du matériel onirique en thérapeutique psychanalytique chez l'adulte [The use of dream material in psychoanalytic therapy with adults]. *Revue Française de Psychanalyse, 24* (1).

23 ESSENTIAL DEPRESSION[1]

Pierre Marty

> **Pierre Marty** (1918–1993) was a psychiatrist and a full member and former president of the Paris Psychoanalytical Society. In 1970, when he set up an administrative college within the Society, he initiated a series of significant reforms to the statutes and structure of that organisation. He was keenly interested in contemporary psychosomatic practice, and, with Michel de M'Uzan, he developed the concept of 'operational thinking' and emphasised the importance of economic aspects. In 1963, with Christian David and Michel de M'Uzan, he wrote *L'investigation psychosomatique* [Psychosomatic investigations] (PUF, 1963), and in 1970, with Michael Fain, he set up the Paris Psychosomatic Institute. His two seminal works are: *Les mouvements individuels de vie et de mort* [Individual impulses of life and death] (Payot, 1976), and *L'ordre psychosomatique* [The psychosomatic order] (Payot, 1980); in these books, he explains his conception of mental functioning in adult psychosomatic disorders, a topic that he would later develop with respect to children and babies.
>
> Rosine Debray wrote a concise biography of Pierre Marty for the 'Psychanalystes d'aujourd'hui' series (PUF, 1998).

Psychosomatic depression, which on several occasions I have called 'objectless depression', is ultimately better termed *essential depression* because it constitutes the very essence of depression, namely the reduction in the level of libidinal tonus without any form of positive economic compensation.

The clinical assessment of this depression must be based primarily, as is usual, on the mode of relationship that the patient forms with the investigator.

Initially emerging with difficulty, for good reasons, but gradually perceived in the relationship are some phenomena that do not constitute symptoms within classical psychopathology in the current sense of the term – that is, the expression of tendencies either of defence or of internal impulses.

---

[1] Presented at the Séminaire de Perfectionnement held at the Institute of Psychoanalysis (30 January 1966).

Beyond certain episodes of anxiety – for example, re-emphasising the provisional instability of this depression – the events defy interpretation.

The investigator does not find he has entered any system; neither is he rejected or even distanced by the usual mechanisms of the mental neuroses and the psychoses. The subject presents his case almost if it were someone else, and the psychoanalyst forms the impression that, despite the entirely flexible standpoint of the investigation, he is not even entering what is nevertheless the cold world of his counterpart, that at best he is only a doctor, in the most everyday and professional sense of the term.

The situation does not gradually evolve in the course of conversation, and the psychoanalyst has to wonder what he can do for a patient who in any case is not asking for anything because he is scarcely even suffering.

The absence of an explicit psychopathology means that these patients, those close to them and their unapprised doctors also fail to consider a psychoanalyst. The reason for the initial consultation will have been something of random relevance: tiredness or a somatic incident that often seems benign. The patient has neither chosen nor refused to have the consultation. Everything occurs for him without emotion.

Depression is evident, however, as revealed by the psychoanalytic contact and confirmed by the anamnesis: it resides in the marked reduction in the level of both objectal and narcissistic libidinal tonus. There can be no recourse to anything, either internal or external.

Essential depression thus presents the picture of a silent crisis, which often forms the prelude to the establishment of operational life, a true chronic depression, into which it merges.

It is appropriate, however, to pursue the quest for a clandestine psychopathology that emerges here in the domains of a general lack of coordination and functional fragmentation.

We thus already find, very clearly pronounced, the elimination of key functions from the entire spectrum of mental dynamics. I am referring to identification, introjection, projection, displacement, condensation, the association of ideas and, later on, the definitive elimination of dream and fantasy life. I also wonder if the dynamism of these functions, of which my list is not exhaustive, does not constitute one of the temporal proofs or testimonies of libidinal precedence, a libidinal precedence that is thus particularly submerged in essential depression.

It should be noted, however, that this disorganisation of the subject – a general disorganisation that probably extends beyond the mental domain – and this deep de-systematisation that is entirely distinct from libidinal regression hide behind the mask of social propriety. In this respect, it differs from the other types of depression.

In the study of such cases, it is appropriate, of course, to beware of our own projections as methodical psychoanalysts, which tend under the pressure of the other's painful deficiencies to compensate for his deficiencies on the sound pretext that we are finding all the classical conflicts in his distant past and, in his recent history, an equally classical trauma that has specifically triggered this depression.

In summary, essential depression emerges as a disappearance of both object libido and narcissistic libido, without any economic compensation other than functional fragmentation.

I think these two terms – disappearance of the libido and functional fragmentation – constitute the very definition of the death instinct, on to which we are leading.

I think that essential depression therefore constitutes one of the major clinical manifestations of the precedence of the death instinct.

Here, we do not find what I will provisionally call the 'libidinal recovery' of the other depressions. For although I think that in every form of depression the precedence of the death instinct manifests for a while, either following object loss or by post-traumatic obstruction of the objectal or narcissistic function concerned, I also think that in most cases of depression a true 'libidinal recovery' occurs in an objectal or narcissistic resumption, parallel or regressive in relation to the pre-traumatic starting point.

I call 'libidinal recovery' what is perceptible to us in the various neurotic, or psychotic or sublimatory expressions, whether this concerns objectal intrusion with anxiety, objectal introjection with guilt, whether it is a true relational resumption, objectal or narcissistic, with sado-masochism, or whether it is a sublimatory impulse, with the poetry describing depressive states, for example.

Once again, my list is not exhaustive. But none of that occurs in essential depression, beyond fruitless endeavours for a while. Then calm returns with the death instinct – as master of the scene.

I would point out to you here that essential depression constitutes a less spectacular picture than melancholic depression, but I fear that it may lead more certainly and more naturally to death.

I will also point out, for those of you who are disconcerted by the incomprehensible phenomenon – hard to conceptualise on the economic level – of a loss without compensation or corollary of a libidinal energy, that this is specifically a comparable phenomenon to death, in which the vital energy is lost without compensation or corollary. The essentially depressed thus already seem to bear in them some deathly phenomena.

But remember that we can sometimes have an impact.

★ ★ ★

This concludes my clinical and theoretical outline, this preliminary description of essential depression, and I will not address here either the onset or the psychic, social and economic repercussions of this depression, or the basal organisations that support it, or the detrimental length of time the subject spends in this state.

It is appropriate, however, just to mention two points of interest. First, it should not be believed after my description, scarcely simplified, of those suffering from it, that these are exceptional and therefore rare subjects. Admittedly, most of them do not come to see us, but we still encounter some either in consultation or during the analytic treatment of polymorphous neuroses, without a pronounced mental obsessional or phobic tendency. In each case, it is important to know what must be done, which is always a difficult task.

I will now address the second point. You realise that maintaining the frustrating tension is not a productive approach with an essentially depressed patient. The situation will not evolve. It will therefore be more appropriate to get as close as possible to the patient and facilitate his cathexis of a possible identification, which means one that is scarcely different from him.

To digress a little: if the libido had totally disappeared, the manoeuvre would prove unproductive. But there is almost always an underlying libido, which seems to me only to be extinguished with life itself, barring some exceptional cases. The libidinal debility is considerable though, and, by way of illustration, I will quote this statement by a patient: 'I would like to have some worries, even material ones.'

Reckoning then, as is appropriate, with the ever-present possibility of a libidinal resumption, it is generally a matter of not allowing the essential depression – or rather, the death instinct – time to establish irreversible phenomena of somatic fragmentation.

Here I close the digression.

We need somehow to adhere as closely as possible to a non-existent ego as an agency – another testimony of fragmentation – an ego that seems to be reduced to the dimensions of a collective and current superego. However, we should attempt to open some emergency exit doors, those indicated to us by the patient.

Also, if an error of assessment, a diagnostic error, has been made and if the frustrating tension is not maintained in a case of neurotic or psychotic depression, we know that we are heading for disaster.

I have described the situation and I recommend resolving it in the best possible way by maintaining the classical analytic rule for as long as possible, until you are certain that this is something other than a mental neurosis or a psychosis.

24 PSYCHOSOMATIC SOLUTION OR SOMATIC OUTCOME

The man from Burma – *psychotherapy of a case of haemorrhagic rectocolitis*

Marilia Aisenstein

> **Marilia Aisenstein**'s background was in philosophy. She is a full member and former president of the Paris Psychoanalytical Society and a training analyst of the Hellenic Psychoanalytical Society. Her main interests lie in the mental functioning of psychosomatic and psychotic personalities. She has written several theoretical and clinical papers on the technical approach to the treatment of patients with those kinds of mental organisation and has published, with A. Fine, a monograph on hypochondria. She is a former editor and founding member of the *Revue Française de Psychosomatique*.
>
> Marilia Aisenstein wrote a concise biography of Michel Fain for the 'Psychanalystes d'aujourd'hui' series (PUF, 2000).

> To be protected by madness is worse than to be threatened by it.
> Wiesel (1988)

> Restraint upon motor discharge (upon action), which then became necessary, was provided by means of the process of thinking, which was developed from the presentation of ideas. Thinking was endowed with characteristics which made it possible for the mental apparatus to tolerate an increased tension of stimulus while the process of discharge was postponed. It is essentially an experimental kind of acting, accompanied by displacement of relatively small quantities of cathexis together with less expenditure (discharge) of them. For this purpose the conversion of freely displaceable cathexes into 'bound' cathexes was necessary . . .
> Freud (1911b)

There is no clear reference to somatosis in this pioneering text dating from 1911. A few lines further, Freud goes on: 'With the introduction of the reality principle one species of thought-activity was split off; it was kept free from reality-testing and remained subordinated to the pleasure principle alone. This activity is *phantasying*. . . .' In the space of just nine pages, he gives a masterly description of the vicissitudes of mental functioning and sets out the basic principles whereby acquisitions on the one hand and the working of fantasy on the other will be governed.

The question of a genesis for delusions immediately arises. Two approaches seem to me to be possible:

a. Delusion can be regarded as one of the contingent results of fantasy life mediated by a hypertrophy of the pleasure-ego. The behavioural outcome – diversion of the action which for its part is connected with the thought – would then be a derivative of a hypertrophy of the reality-ego.
b. Alternatively – and here the concept of trauma, and early trauma, assumes its full meaning – it might be the absence, disappearance and crushing of fantasies that is responsible, firstly, for '*delusional solutions*' – re-creations whose principal function is preservation or restoration of the link with the object – and secondly for behavioural or somatic outcomes, thus raising the question of regression to a primitive narcissism, considered not to have existed adequately. Somatic outcomes are to my mind attempts – presumably last-ditch attempts – to mobilise a reparative aim in 'another', whose value as an object is at the relevant time imperceptible and uncertain.

Whichever of these conceptions is chosen, the fields of research converge, and it seems to me that insufficient light has been thrown on the causes: deficiencies, lack of organisation, perhaps disorganisation or catastrophic disruption – all dysfunctions of the preconscious system.

So might it be useful, if not positively appropriate, to invoke the idea of a gradation? It is a commonplace to say that a behavioural outcome or somatic outcomes betray a current, temporal inability to elaborate what we are now accustomed to call a solution – that is, the making of a compromise. However, the word *solution*, according to Webster's Dictionary, is used in two main senses: (a) the action or process of solving a problem; (b) an interruption of continuity:[1] interruption, hiatus or discontinuity.

It is interesting to note that historically, according to the etymological dictionary, the latter sense predates the former. In Latin, *solutio* originally meant dissolution or disaggregation. Later, by a semantic shift, it acquired the connotation of loosening. Seneca was later to use the word in the sense of an explanatory solution, as a culmination, under the heading of intelligibility.

In my view, somatosis is a solution in both of these senses: discontinuity, hiatus, and then outcome and culmination. While delusion falls within the 'internal logic of a mental organisation', illness, and also syndromes, are likewise to be classified as intelligible manifestations, although in a different way.

---

[1] Medicine: solution of normally continuous tissues.

After all, medicine describes them and recognises them as being governed by an internal logic, the logic that is their own.

The difficulty here is how we are to conceptualise this discontinuity, this transition from the words which make up a delusion to the symptoms which appeal to words in order to describe them.

I have chosen in this paper to present fragments of a patient's treatment, not so much because of the alternation of neurotic or delusional solutions and somatic outcomes – which may be said to be a standard feature of clinical practice in the field of psychosomatics – but also because my work with this patient seemed to me to throw light on a particular form of functioning of the psychoanalyst when confronted with somatosis.

Somatic symptoms are essentially opaque and initially unintelligible, because meaning and symbolism are always supplied by deferred action (*après-coup*; see footnote 16 on p. 322); when these symptoms first break out, they appear neither as a compromise nor as a solution. The sick body (Dejours & Fain, 1984; in particular, Fain: 'Du corps érotique au corps malade, la complexité de ce passage') confronts us with a given mental organisation which bothers us 'mind specialists' precisely because of the absence of semiological, psychoanalytic or psychiatric components, as it is often accompanied by an apparent hypercathexis of reality.[2]

What is involved is a new order (Marty, 1980) – or disorder – which is indicative of a recent or old upheaval in the subject's instinctual economy, compelling us to enquire what the mental organisation might have been like previously, what it lacks and what may be found deep within it.

My approach to this kind of work is to invent for myself an arbitrary and imaginary counterpoint, or, rather, to watch out for the emergence of data from which such a counterpoint might arise.

The first meeting with any patient is unique. When the patient is suffering from a serious or even life-threatening disease, one of the particularities of this meeting is that we are like Damocles at the banquet to which he had been invited by Dionysius the Elder[3] (Cicero). The solidity and arrangement of the thread – in Damocles's case, the horsehair – are often impossible to discern. Nevertheless, when faced with exiguous and arid material which evokes little response in us but induces us to associate for two people, to elaborate from the signal anxiety aroused in the analyst and to construct theories and tell ourselves stories, the only course is to wait and see, listening in a manner in tune with the 'anticipatory illusion'.[4]

---

[2] It is by no means the case that all somatic patients present in this way.

[3] Damocles was a courtier of Dionysius the Elder in the 4th century BC. Cicero tells us how the tyrant invited him to a banquet and entertained him regally, but had caused a heavy sword to be suspended above his head by a horsehair to demonstrate to him the fragility of fate.

[4] The 'anticipatory illusion' is a highly fruitful concept of Diatkine & Simon (1972, p. 374). The authors refer to 'primary maternal preoccupation' (Winnicott, 1956) and coin the term 'anticipatory illusion': 'it is the anticipatory illusion which plays a fundamental part in the organisation of the child's mental apparatus'. This idea resembles that of the 'mother's capacity for reverie' (Bion, 1967, p. 116).

When the mind is challenged by the instincts, it has an unlimited range of options open to it, and also an unlimited range of ways of managing conflict. In this sense, notwithstanding somatosis, which is a form of facilitation, the outcome never seems to me to be fixed. This in my view is the factor that allows us to embark on the perilous enterprise of treating a somatic patient.

At moments of despair, I always think that the situation could be different – and not necessarily better – and I sometimes tell myself: 'How unsearchable is the preconscious, and its ways past finding out.'[5] But one day there comes a dream, a silence, a forgetting, which turns out to be the cornerstone of a history, a process.

A psychotherapy, and to an even greater extent a psychoanalysis, is always a thrilling enterprise, as soon as something becomes attached to it. With this particular patient, the enterprise proper began for me fourteen months after the beginning of the treatment, after a parapraxis which induced me to give him the nickname of 'the man from Burma'.

When he telephoned for an appointment, he had indicated that there was no urgency. He had also added that he might perhaps ring back . . . Already he was stealing away. I had seen him as promptly as possible.

It turned out that he was suffering from severe haemorrhagic rectocolitis, which was potentially life-threatening. He had been referred to me by a gastroenterologist and surgery was pending, but had been postponed for the time being; he seemed to be unaware of the nature of the operation he was to undergo. I was subsequently informed by a letter from his doctor that it was a colectomy, probably accompanied by an ileostomy. He himself had not deemed it necessary to look into the matter very closely. 'Everyone has his own field'; the health technicians presumably had their reasons, and he had decided to trust them, as this seemed to him to be the most logical position. Similar considerations had made him agree to consult 'a psychosomaticist'.

He was tall, slim, dark-haired and slightly stooping; his appearance conveyed indifference and immense lassitude at one and the same time. He was nearly 40 years old. His over-politeness barely concealed the fact that he was capable of only fleeting contact. He was a high-calibre scientist with technological leanings, working in the private sector. He said that he was very annoyed by this illness, which had stricken him at a time when he had so many commitments and had to travel so much.

Everything to do with the mind seemed to him to be 'screwy'. He was not accustomed to take an interest in the irrational. All the same, he agreed to the principle of psychotherapy sessions at a frequency of one a week. He could really see no logical reason to turn down a treatment which two professors of gastroenterology had separately recommended to him. Again, it was his wont to complete the tasks assigned to him. He gave himself, and me, a year.

---

[5] 'How unsearchable are [God's] judgements, and his ways past finding out!' (Romans 11:33, commentary by St Augustine).

During the sessions he put on a sceptical and ironic front but appeared, more than anything, ill at ease and even reticent. He presented himself essentially as limited in his concerns; he would answer in the following style: 'States of mind, well, I don't really know what they are', or else 'Unless you can quantify it . . .'. I was also struck by the poverty of his vocabulary and the poor general quality of his language, which contrasted with his cultural level and conceptual intelligence.

He gave me a clear and chronological description of his life in a few sessions. His parents were serious and kindly people, now retired, and he was the elder of two children. His younger sister was a chemist; she suffered from subacute haemorrhagic pancreatitis, which was the only shadow on her life. He was married with no children. He and his wife were very absorbed in their respective careers.

Then came the history of his illness, which bothered him considerably. He described himself as feeling worried in spells, but not fundamentally anxious. The first symptoms had come like 'a bolt from the blue'. All he could remember was a consultation with a view to giving up smoking, followed by a few sessions of acupuncture, as a result of which he had been able to give up his two daily packets of cigarettes overnight. This decision had not been the result of mature reflection or of a wish but had followed from a bet, lightly undertaken, with colleagues. Yet the idea had been his own.

This had been a few months before the onset of the haemorrhagic rectocolitis, for which he had been sent to hospital. We may observe here the construction of a screen-memory that may be interpreted as an attempt to disavow castration: he did not want to know what a colectomy involved – giving up smoking was merely the result of a bet.

It was not long before the time came when he had nothing to say: nothing occurred to him. He was not much in the habit of speaking, still less about himself. Nor could he tolerate silence: he wanted to end the session as soon as I allowed a silence to ensue. I was thus induced to take great pains, using methods of questionable orthodoxy, to bring about and then maintain a trivial conversation ('small talk', as he described it).[6]

We talked at length about the weather and the politics of the day. I questioned him about his work, asking him for a detailed account, which he obligingly supplied, sometimes displaying a certain pleasure. I also asked him about his rare leisure activities. He never read anything other than scientific works; literature seemed to him to be futile. He and his wife seldom went out; they had no friends and felt very little need of any. However, they took part in a variety of sporting activities. On holiday, they went either on tours to faraway places or on trips with organisations like the Club Méditerranée.

---

[6] Marty (1963, chap. 1), 'Progressive Disorganisations', pp. 24–27, on technique, and pp. 45–46: 'talking about precise activities, for the purpose of conflictualisation, in which ideals will not be called into question. . . .' See also Marty (1968a).

At this point I should mention that about a year had passed. The operation had been postponed from one quarter to the next and was still pending. He declined to make any connection between the few symptomatic improvements observed and his exchanges with me – on that, we were agreed. All the same, I suggested to him that we go on, arguing that three quarters of an hour on Saturday mornings could not be much of a bother to him. So we continued.

Shortly afterwards, having launched one day into a comparison of the merits of different Club Méditerranée centres, he told me that the one in Burma was outstanding. I was surprised, alerted by the reference to that country; he corrected himself – he had meant Bulgaria. In the next session, I returned to what he had, oddly, called a 'bloomer'. He put up a prolonged defence, accusing me of obduracy: 'No, Burma does not mean anything to me.' After all, he had never been there. Eventually, however, not without difficulty and in a number of sessions, I came to hear a story that was 'irrelevant because it belongs to the past'.

At university, he had married a fellow student. They had got divorced a few years later. As they had had no children and no property in common, they had never seen each other again. Several years later, while dining at a restaurant with a client, he had met friends of his former parents-in-law. They had told him that his first wife had died two years earlier, in unusual circumstances. She had apparently been murdered in a street in Rangoon, stabbed several times in the abdomen.

Mr L told me that he had been upset for all of a weekend by the news of this particularly horrible and senseless death. He had not known why his ex-wife had been in Burma, but had felt there was no point in asking himself useless questions. For a moment he had considered writing to his former parents-in-law, but had also decided against it: 'Why reopen old wounds?' He had not spoken about this event to his present wife, and had then forgotten it. However, he had had a nightmare, which he had also forgotten, but which had just come back into his mind. He told it to me without apparent emotion, but with a note of hostility towards me: '*My first wife was all covered in blood, and a voice off said that she could be saved with an artificial anus.*'

Noting the collusion between the (old?) dream – at any rate, the fantasy element – and the real (in the present), I decided for the time being to refrain from any comment on the symbolic meaning. I gave him a very 'scientific' explanation of the mechanisms of nightmare and of the sleep–dream system. I was thereby trying to enable him to take an interest, as a scientist, in his mental apparatus, and hence in its functioning – a phase which might precede familiarisation with his own mental productions. I dwelt at length on his account, 'putting the tone back into it': he must have been sad, anxious . . . In this way I was trying to transform the account into a history. He was able to put a date to the nightmare: it had been four months before the consultation about giving up smoking. He remembered very precisely when that had been.

At this point I shall pause, not to mark the onset of a new phase – so much is obvious – but to make a few comments. During the session with the nightmare, I had been profoundly struck by what was missing: some might have spoken of a premonition, while others might have seen it as an example of fate at work. I noted in my patient the absence of any superstition, of any trace of *magical thought* (Freud, 1912–13, mainly chap. III; see also Braunschweig & Fain, 1975, chap. 3), however trivial. This made me think that what was most absent was likely to be what was most countercathected or most suppressed.

Again, this was the meeting point of a number of different lines of thought. What was the significance of the lack – during what I shall call the first period of the psychotherapy – of any mental or character-based defensive structure, certain incipient signs of which had, however, been evident to me from the preliminary interview (his reticence)? Was the relevant organisation lacking, or was he in fact suppressing this semiology in the face-to-face situation, because the latter was felt to reactivate the primal fantasy of *seduction of the child by the adult* and, with it, one of the forms of the threat of castration?

Other questions arising were why Mr L had come into psychotherapy and, in particular, why he had continued with the treatment. Two contradictory hypotheses suggested themselves, although their inconsistency did not imply any differences in the technical handling of the treatment. Both indicated an extreme fragility of the mental apparatus: (a) a conflictuality associated with deficiencies of the preconscious system, or – more likely – (b) failure of this system due to a catastrophic disruption involving the deployment of disavowal. Although it may smack of paradox, I would formulate the situation today as follows: the extreme limit of this patient's reticence was his refusal of reticence, a refusal sustained by negation: 'no, it is not true'. It might also be added that his regression into illness occurred because it was impossible for him, or because he refused, to regress in any other way.

The second phase of the treatment would be moulded by external events: Mr L was to become a father. This coincided with the lifting of his silence about his first wife and with what I shall call *his at times stormy entry into psychotherapy*.

Through his first marriage he and I became able to approach certain themes, which I shall now briefly summarise. His former wife had been his first love; she had been like him and had been a colleague. A radiant personality, bubbling with life, she had had a large number of men-friends. The two of them had gone out a lot, mostly in a group. Both had had the same tastes and had thought it unacceptable to bring children into the world. She had, incidentally, wanted to have her fallopian tubes ligated.

Mr L was not very forthcoming about the reasons why he had come to ask for a divorce, but he indicated that his wife had begun to drink somewhat . . . Eventually she had no longer been 'reliable'. While on a long business trip to the United States, he had decided not to return home. This may be regarded as a tendency to elaborate a phobia (through identification with his wife, seen as unreliable = unfaithful), resulting in avoidance behaviour. The physical details (renting of an apartment, etc.) had been dealt with by his secretary and by telex.

He told me that he was currently very upset because his present wife had just told him that she would like to have a baby. Women, he told me, were unpredictable, incoherent beings. After the separation from his first wife, he had cut himself off. His friends had also been his wife's, and he 'had abandoned them to her', as he had the car and the house. He had apparently immersed himself totally in professional activity, which, while beneficial to his career, had done nothing to shore up his self-regard. He did not feel that he had been depressed or anxious. He had worked long hours and slept a lot. He had sometimes felt tired, but surely this had been natural.[7] He had little memory of this entire period, which he described as 'hazy'.

I see this as a phenomenological description of the 'essential' depression which must have followed the loss of his wife and the collapse (which he himself had caused) of the homosexual buttressing which had probably enabled him until then to experience his cathexes behaviourally.

He was quite unable to say how much time had elapsed in this way, as his references were professional. Mr L had remarried. His present wife was very different from her predecessor; he described her as serious and respectable – home-loving but also with intellectual leanings. They had both wanted a big, beautiful villa and had bought a plot of land for it. The house had taken years to build. Mr L had been its developer, architect and site manager rolled into one.

I concluded from his many anecdotes about this period that he might have emerged from his previous atonic depression by forming new cathexes, which were still behavioural because he was protected from a dangerous passive homosexuality (Fain & Marty, 1960; Marty, 1976, chap. 2) by the presence of his wife and by their common tasks.

Once the house was finished – and it was huge – his wife conceived the outlandish idea of having children. He refused; his arguments were manifestly based on a logic that was as illogical as it was implacable.

This was the background to the encounter in the restaurant, which was to be followed within a few months by his giving up smoking and, shortly afterwards, by the onset of the haemorrhagic colitis (this was Mr L's later chronological reconstruction).

Throughout this period I, for my part, felt that I was in possession of material that was not only interesting but often enthralling. I tried a few forays into the fields of unconscious guilt, identification with his wife, homosexuality and so on. But he put me in a truly desperate position on the counter-transference level. Whatever connection I made, and whatever hypothesis I

---

[7] Cf. Marty (1976): 'Essential depression is a depression without pain, without an object and without guilt; it is characterised by a lowering of libidinal tonus. Feelings of devaluation and of having sustained a narcissistic wound are also lacking and are often replaced by tiredness or overactivity which does not increase self-regard'. An essential depression may precede 'mechanical life', a concept closely resembling Sifneos's 'alexithymia'. See also Marty (1968b).

suggested, he would retort that it was either 'screwy' or incomprehensible, too difficult, too alien to his own field. I was forcing him to play some 'kind of chess game whose rules he did not know'.

He shut himself off like an obstinate child, ending every session with the same sentence: 'Today I understood nothing.' He constantly alternated between categorically refusing to consider what had been said and feeling hurt because he had not understood anything or, even more dramatically, had not even seen the obvious – which he claimed was of no interest anyway. 'I am trapped, you have a weapon that I lack, the struggle is unequal', he told me. In one and the same session, he oscillated between polite hostility and a despair which made him feel '*worthless*'.

One day when I was perhaps somewhat exasperated, I said to him: 'You so often talk about people's respective fields, so you try to imagine me on one of your experimental platforms. What would I do, and would I necessarily be injured by it?' My intervention – which admittedly fell within the sphere of psychodrama[8] – suddenly made him laugh (for the first time ever). With an air of great surprise and amusement, he played with this idea. I think it was the first identificatory meeting he had allowed himself with me – but with me failing.

The sessions from now on became less of a trial, both for him and for me, and more associative. He reported a few dreams. I felt him to be less watchful, because less wounded.

In October, Mr L suddenly announced to me that his wife was four months pregnant. He had been aware of this pregnancy while at the same time pretending to be ignorant of it. He had categorically refused to think about it. Anyway, he had not thought about it at all 'as long as it was not visible'.

I shall now summarise what seemed to me to be a particularly dense session:

He did not like the autumn, he felt cold all the time . . . All the same, he was well, Professor N had told him he was in remission . . . But he felt very tired in the mornings . . . Presumably his insomnia had something to do with that. I pointed out to him that he had not mentioned this to me . . . It was actually of recent date, having started after the summer holidays; it had not occurred to him to refer to it here, but his general practitioner had prescribed sleeping pills for him.

I realised from his answers to two or three questions that he was organising his insomnia meticulously (by a negative bedtime ritual). He foresaw it, took his pills, and then embarked on some activity that demanded attention or application – framing some etchings, performing calculations, etc. – thereby giving rise to paradoxical effects, in turn aggravated by taking more pills in the middle of the night.

---

[8] I have learned a great deal from the practice of psychodrama, particularly for psychotherapeutic work of this kind. I am referring here to role reversal: the exchange of roles between the patient and the co-therapist. See the relevant theoretical considerations in Kestemberg & Jeammet (1987), pp. 33–37 and 58–70.

I suggested that he was thereby preventing himself from sleeping, adding that he might be afraid of his dreams, as well as of his hypnagogic fantasies (I was also thinking of his intolerance of silence with me, but refrained from mentioning it). He replied that my demonstration was 'clever' but must in fact be wrong because he had actually had two dreams, which he had forgotten to bring last time.

The first was very short: '*I was at my first wife's funeral.*' It was absurd: he did not even know if there had been such a ceremony. He accused me of going back to those old stories which he for his part 'would prefer to bury'.

I suggested that having a grave in a precise, known place was very different from a disappearance situation (Marty, 1976, p. 49, n. 68, on an unpublished contribution by Parat; see also Cournut, 1983, and the concept of the crypt in Abraham & Torok, 1972). He replied that his first wife had disappeared twice, first when he had been away at the time of the divorce (this was a condensation on his part), and then when she had disappeared in Asia.

Without any transition, he asked me if I intended to go away for the All Saints Day holiday on 1 November. A few days' holiday would be good for me, he thought.

Now that directly transference-related material had emerged,[9] and assuming that he was associating to the two dreams mentioned together, I asked him to tell me the second.

In slight embarrassment, he told me that in this dream '*he came across one of his secretaries*' – but he did not in fact like this young woman, who was professionally 'unreliable' and neither prepossessing nor pretty. '*We were in an unknown room and . . . in an . . . ambiguous . . . position.*' What made it all the more incongruous was that it would never have occurred to him to meet her outside the office.

I drew attention to the word 'unreliable'. I thus gathered that he suspected her of 'liking a tipple'. This allowed me to remind him that drinking had also been one of his grounds for divorcing his first wife.

He spontaneously suggested a link between the two dreams, which disturbed him and confronted him with his disavowed attachment to his first wife. He would try to think about it. Yet he was anxious: what was his secretary doing in his dreams, while his present wife was pregnant?

I chose this moment to tell him that the assignations he had outside his work situation were actually with me. He blushed crimson and was silent for a few moments.

I was a little worried about the choice and timing of the transference intervention, and I had therefore preferred to make sure of 'taking over' from his first wife before suggesting a connection between his fear of dreaming, his disgust at people who drank (implying a lowering of watchfulness) and the fear I must inspire in him when I asked him to 'imagine'.

---

[9] There was not yet, of course, any transference in the sense of the classical transference neurosis.

At the end of the session I reminded him that I would not be going away for All Saints Day. It was in fact he who telephoned in the following week to cancel his session. Stricken with severe flu, he had taken to his bed; this had not happened to him since he was a child. The interpretation had probably taken insufficient account of the first dream – inhumation – exhumation of memories – mourning – followed by the second: sexual co-excitation connected with mourning.

In view of the hypercondensation manifested in this sequence (All Saints, the day before All Souls, the day of the dead; holidays; vacuity; the pregnancy of his present wife; the unreliability of women; etc.), caution seemed appropriate, as a relative 'strategic' difficulty had to be overcome. While the intention was to open the way to chains of representations, there was a risk of blocking the process by interpretations which, although correct, might be premature and might stoke up the instinctual side before the establishment of a representational system sufficiently fluid to serve as a protective shield against stimuli.

The major changes which ensued were presided over by mourning for his first wife and the birth of his son. He now acknowledged the loss of his former wife. He had lost her three times: when he gave her up, when he heard of her death, and also, in a different way, because she would probably never have made the fatal trip to Burma had he not demanded a divorce. He had lost her, but was finding her again. She often appeared in his dreams, and he also rediscovered her during the sessions when he talked about her with me.

On top of it all, at the same time he was losing his second wife (she was 'mutating' and becoming a woman-as-mother). She was turning away from him in her preoccupation with her pregnancy; he, for his part, averted his eyes, shocked by the 'disharmony' of her body.

Becoming a father is not always easy. For Mr L, it was a prolonged ordeal, during which he was to become severely depressed.

I felt overtaken by unorganised transferences, which betrayed nothing of an infantile neurosis, and by the forthcoming birth of his son – the ultrasound scan had shown that it was a boy: 'That makes it even worse', he said. Confronted with the collusion between, on the one hand, the bringing-back-into-the-present and the resexualisation resulting from the treatment and, on the other hand, the burden of hatred mobilised in the present against the female position – the man's wish for and envy of pregnancy – I felt quite powerless.

The anxiety, however relatively trivial, at the possibility of having a monstrous child, the fruit of attacks on the female body – and hence of old sadistic wishes against the mother – was here mixed up with the whole story of the dead first wife. I experienced the sequence 'ligation of the fallopian tubes – alcoholism – death' as a giddy slope.

Within the sessions he foresaw all kinds of catastrophes, invoking preposterous logic in support of his statements. He got angry either because I was harassing him or because I was silent. He was so furious when I refused point blank to change the time of a session that he went back to the office and picked a quarrel with his new boss. It was on this occasion that I heard of the retirement of the latter's predecessor, to whom Mr L had told me he had been very attached. I made a great deal of use of this dual male representation – in its old and new forms, the good and the bad – in order to steer for a while towards calmer waters. In the midst of all this, his son was born, normal and entire. Mr L appeared for a short time to be relieved, but on my return from holiday in September, I found him sunk in a depression which I was powerless to hold back.

This depression seemed to me to be complex, combining incipient mourning for his first wife, the 'loss' of his present wife, and the confrontation with his son – and hence abandonment of the fantasy of self-begetting. Other factors were the first signs of the transference, and my absence.

He was taking all kinds of drugs, and so I recommended him to have them prescribed by a specialist and referred him to a woman psychiatrist. The consultation was catastrophic. Tranxene set his nerves on edge, while Athymil [Mianserin] prevented him from sleeping. 'That woman is incompetent, or perhaps even a poisoner.' She had disguised her voice on the telephone on the following day so as not to have to answer him . . . The counterpoint of paranoia had for a long time been in the back of my mind, but I had not expected such a clear manifestation.

This splitting of the object between myself and the 'bad' psychiatrist, which I refrained from interpreting too quickly, allowed us to continue the psychotherapy and to embark on what I call the 'third phase'.

It was a period rich in dream material. I was worried about the way he spoke to me about his son – 'three kilos of meat, a little hunk of beef' – and frequently encouraged him to talk about his former boss. Through him, and in the wake of a dream, we were to re-encounter his former father-in-law: 'He was a real gentleman'.

After a lapse of several months, there came a session in which he told me how his son had turned him into a father. Because his wife was away, he had had to take the child to the paediatrician; he had held him during a vaccination and had been suddenly overwhelmed by the baby's gaze, which had sought out and engaged his own.[10]

His discovery of his son – which allowed me to suggest that he too had once been a child – exacerbated the conflict with his new boss. It was at about this time that he one day arrived pale and discomposed: 'My dear lady, you are driving me mad', he said. He had tried to reach me by telephone, but had failed as I had been on holiday. He was having impulse phobias about his son. Yet he

---

[10] See Lebovici (1983): 'It is the child's gaze that makes the mother a mother', and 'the mother is cathected before she is perceived'. Lebovici adds 'and she is created by the baby' (p. 20); see also chap. 10, on father–infant interactions, in the same book.

loved this child; it was incomprehensible and illogical, and he felt he was 'going mad'.

I advised him to find himself a psychiatrist. He chose a young man who suited him; he did not tell me his name.

Later, in a nutshell, I was to note that I knew very little about this patient's childhood, but not for want of reconstructions. He was the eldest son of a much loved, albeit severe, father, while the mother remained oddly absent from his memories. I imagined that there must have been early traumas, but there was for the time being nothing to confirm this hypothesis. I would classify his first marriage under the heading of narcissistic object choice, his wife and himself having shared the 'phobia' of begetting (ligation of the fallopian tubes [*trompes*]). He had apparently tried to elaborate a phobia at the time of his divorce, when he had imagined himself to have been 'deceived' [*trompé*] (and had identified with this wife).

The project for the house with his second wife had a terrible aspect to it: a house is eventually finished. I put this together with his refusal to plan for the child (to think about the pregnancy), which brought back to him his first wife and, with her, the idea of perforation of the abdomen: ligation of the fallopian tubes – colectomy – stabbing in the abdomen – murder.

I would now say that all these contents were on the boundary of the preconscious (cf. the Burma–Bulgaria parapraxis) and blocked by negation (negation – repudiation [*Verwerfung*]), and hence the refusal to accept any information from outside (e.g. reading), which caused him not to inform (the 'small talk' with me).

The impulse phobia broke out as soon as he loved the child; this forced him to rediscover his own childhood and rivalry (his boss) and signified the failure of the phobias he had been unable to construct – that is, an acting out of repression.

Although my case history ends here, the work is still continuing, with rich and complex developments. I would only mention in passing, as a conclusion, a point which again confronted us with the problem of alternation between a delusional solution and a somatic solution or somatic outcomes. In clinical psychosomatics, we are accustomed to those alternating or oscillating movements between a solution on the level of character or delusion and upsurges of symptoms which confront the psychoanalyst with the often distressing and sometimes fruitless need to rethink what has been said.

In this case what occurred was a relatively recent relapse, or 'advance', of the haemorrhagic rectocolitis, for which I feel I must accept some of the blame. By an intervention in the transference, I had displaced Mr L's present conflict with his new boss and brought it back within the analytic setting. Mr L had been on the point of acting out with him. Professionally, things had 'been cleared up again for him', and he thanked me for it. While he was expressing his gratitude, I wondered whether I had thereby prevented him from pursuing a 'professional paranoia' and making a career of it. I asked myself whether this was the case, but was unable to answer the question; however, surely it is more important to ask the questions which arise than to find answers.

The relevant questions remain open for me. I shall end with a thought dear to Freud: *What pleases one agency does not necessarily please another. The pleasure of the other is not always the pleasure of the first* . . . The same, I would add, goes for the analyst.

However carefully one has thought everything through, one is not sheltered from the risk of certain immediate choices. '*Un coup de dés jamais n'abolira le hasard*' ['A cast of dice will never abolish chance']: Mallarmé's fine poem, so entitled, ends with the line '*Toute pensée émet un coup de dés*' ['Every thought produces a cast of dice'].

Chance for the psychoanalyst is made up of the combination of a multiplicity of vicissitudes arising from the confrontation of two preconscious systems throughout the course of a treatment, during which life continues. Our baffled gropings are an essential component in the rich panoply of the enterprise.

References

Abraham, N. & Torok, M. (1972). Introjecter–incorporer. Deuil ou mélancholie. *Nouvelle Revue de Psychanalyse*, 6: 111–122. [Introjection–incorporation: Mourning or melancholia. In *Psychoanalysis in France* (pp. 3–16), ed. S. Lebovici & D. Widlöcher. New York: International Universities Press, 1980.]

Bion, W. R. (1967). *Second Thoughts*. London: Heinemann.

Braunschweig, D., & Fain, M. (1975). *La nuit, le jour*. Paris: Presses Universitaires de France.

Cournut, J. (1983). D'un reste qui fait lien [A remainder that acts as a link]. *Nouvelle Revue de Psychanalyse*, 28:129–149.

Dejours, C., & Fain, M. (1984). *Corps malade, corps érotique* [Sick body, erotic body]. Paris: Masson.

Diatkine, R., & Simon, J. (1972). *La psychanalyse précoce. Le processus psychanalytique chez l'enfant* [Early psychoanalysis: The psychoanalytic process with young children]. Paris: Presses Universitaires de France.

Fain, M., & Marty, P. (1960). The synthetic function of homosexual cathexis in the treatment of adults. *International Journal of Psychoanalysis*, 41: 401–406.

Freud, S. (1911b). Formulations on the two principles of mental functioning. *S.E.*, 12.

Freud, S. (1912–13). *Totem and Taboo*. S.E., 13.

Kestemberg, E., & Jeammet, P. (1987). *Le psychodrame analytique* [Psychoanalytic psychodrama]. Paris: Presses Universitaires de France.

Lebovici, S. (1983). *Le nourrisson, la mère et le psychanalyste* [The infant, the mother and the psychoanalyst]. Paris: Edition Le Centurion.

Marty, P. (1963). *La psychosomatique de l'adulte* [Adult psychosomatics]. Paris: Presses Universitaires de France.

Marty, P. (1968a). A major process of somatization: The progressive disorganization. *International Journal of Psycho-Analysis*, 49: 246–249.

Marty, P. (1968b). La dépression essentielle [Essential depression]. *Revue Française de Psychanalyse*, 32 (3): 345–355. [Also in: *Revue Française de Psychanalyse: Textes 1926–2006* (pp. 205–208). Paris: Presses Universitaires de France, 2006.]

Marty, P. (1976). *Les mouvements individuels de vie et de mort* [Individual impulses of life and death]. Paris: Payot.

Marty, P. (1980). *L'ordre psychosomatique* [The psychosomatic order]. Paris: Payot.

Wiesel, E. (1988). *Twilight*, trans. M. Wiesel. New York: Viking.

Winnicott, D. W. (1956). Primary maternal preoccupation. In *Through Paediatrics to Psychoanalysis* (pp. 300–305). London: Hogarth Press & the Institute of Psycho-Analysis, 1975.

25 FUNCTIONS OF THE SKIN EGO

Didier Anzieu

A graduate of the prestigious École Normale Supérieure and a highly qualified professor of philosophy with a PhD in psychology, **Didier Anzieu** (1923–1999) was a full member of the French Psychoanalytical Association; he was in fact one of its co-founders and became a vice-president of the Association. His psychoanalytic thinking was both highly original and fundamental: he was strongly supportive of research with an epistemological approach to both psychic containers and their contents, developing and applying Freudian concepts and techniques in a whole variety of clinical fields.

With his university background, he was deeply involved in the training of clinical psychologists, creating in 1966 a post-graduate diploma in projective techniques at the Sorbonne. He received the Sigourney Award in 1992.

He was instrumental also in transforming Jacob Moreno's psychodrama technique into a truly psychoanalytic one, and he founded the Centre of French Studies for Training and Active Research in Psychology (CEFRAP). He was the editor of two series with the publisher Dunod: 'Inconscient et culture' (with René Kaës) and 'Psychismes'.

His major works include: *Le psychodrame analytique chez l'enfant et l'adolescent* [Analytic psychodrama with children and adolescents] (PUF, 1956 & 1979); *L'auto-analyse* [Self-analysis] (PUF, 1959, 1975, & 1988); *Les méthodes projectives* [Projective methods] (PUF, 1983 &, with C. Chabert, 1992); *La dynamique des groupes restreints* [Small-group dynamics] (with J. Y. Martin; PUF, 1982 & 1990); *Psychanalyse du génie créateur* [The psychoanalysis of creative genius] (Dunod, 1974); *Le groupe et l'inconscient* (Dunod, 1975) [*The Group and the Unconscious* (Routledge, 1984)]; *Le corps de l'œuvre. Essais psychanalytiques sur le travail créateur* [The body of the work: Psychoanalytic essays on the work of creation] (Gallimard, 1988); *Le moi-peau* (Dunod, 1985 & 1995) [*The Skin Ego* (Yale, 1989)]; *Beckett et le psychanalyste* (L'Aire, 1992) [Beckett and the Psychoanalyst (*Journal of Beckett Studies*, 1994)].

Catherine Chabert wrote a concise biography of Didier Anzieu for the 'Psychanalystes d'aujourd'hui' series (PUF, 1996).

In what follows, I base my thinking upon two general principles. One is specifically Freudian: every psychical function develops by supporting itself upon a bodily function whose workings it transposes on to the mental plane. Jean Laplanche (1970) recommends that the concept of anaclisis be reserved for the support the sexual drives find in the organic functions of self-preservation, but I want to give it a broader interpretation. The psychical apparatus develops through successive stages of breaking with its biological bases, breaks which on the one hand make it possible to escape from biological laws and, on the other, make it necessary to look for an anaclitic relationship of every psychical to a bodily function. The second principle, also known to Freud, is Jacksonian: the development of the nervous system in the course of evolution exhibits a peculiarity not met within other organic systems, namely that the organ which develops last and is the one nearest the surface, the cortex, tends to take over the management of the system, bringing the other neurological subsystems under its overall control. This is also the case with the conscious Ego, which within the psychical apparatus tends to occupy the surface that is in contact with the outside world and to control the functioning of the apparatus. We know also that the skin (the body's surface) and the brain (the surface of the nervous system) derive from the same embryonic structure, the ectoderm.

For a psychoanalyst like myself, the skin is of crucial importance, providing the psychical apparatus with representations both of the nature of the Ego and of its principal functions. This observation fits, in turn, into the framework of the general theory of evolution. The difference between man and the other mammals does not simply lie in the greater size and complexity of the human brain. The skin also loses its hardness and its covering of fur. Body hair hardly remains except on the cranium, where it serves as a further layer of protection for the brain, and around the orifices of the face and trunk, where it adds to the sensibility, and indeed sensuality, of these areas. As Imre Hermann has shown (1930), the infant's clinging drive towards his mother becomes more difficult to satisfy in the human, condemning the representatives of that species to early and prolonged bouts of intense anxiety over the loss of protection or lack of a support object, and to a state of what some regard as 'original distress'. To compensate for this, the attachment drive in the human infant assumes an importance all the greater for the fact that childhood is proportionally longer in humans than in other species. This drive has as its object the identification in the mother, and subsequently in the family group which takes over from her, of signals – including smiles, gentleness of contact, physical warmth of embrace, diversity of sounds, solidity with which the child is carried, how it is rocked, availability of feeding, attention, the presence of others. All these provide clues to external reality and how it is to be dealt with, as well as indications of the affects experienced by the baby's partners, especially in response to its own affects. Here we are no longer concerned with the satisfaction of vital needs of self-preservation (food, breathing, sleep), on which the sexual and aggressive desires will come to constitute themselves anaclitically, but with communication, pre-verbal and infralinguistic, on which linguistic exchange will in due course come to be supported.

The two registers often operate simultaneously: the baby's feeding, for example, provides an opportunity for tactile, visual, auditory and olfactory communication. And it is known that if the vital needs are satisfied in a way that is systematically shorn of these sensory and affective exchanges, it may lead to 'hospitalism' or autism. It is also known that, as the baby grows, greater energies are devoted both by it and by those around it to communication for its own sake, independent of any activities directed towards self-preservation. The original form of communication, both in reality and even more intensely in phantasy, is direct, unmediated, from skin to skin.

In *The Ego and the Id* (1923b), Freud shows that it is not only defence mechanisms and character traits which derive from bodily activities, either as a direct result of these or by their transformation, but that the same is true of the psychical agencies. The psychical drives which constitute the Id derive from biological instincts; what Freud came to call the Super-Ego 'has acoustic roots', and the Ego is initially formed on the basis of the experience of touch. It seems to me that we need to add to this account the existence of a more archaic, perhaps even original, topology in which the subject is aware of the existence of the Self, a Self that corresponds to the auditory and olfactory envelope, a Self alongside which an Ego differentiates itself on the basis of tactile experience, a Self on to whose exterior all the stimuli, whether exogenous or endogenous, are projected. The secondary topology (the Id, the Ego with its appendage the ideal Ego, and the Super-Ego paired with the ideal Ego) comes into being when the visual envelope – particularly under the influence of the primary prohibition on touching – takes the place of the tactile envelope in providing the Ego with essential support, when thing-presentations (mainly visual) become associated in the developing pre-conscious with word-presentations (provided by the acquisition of language) and the subject learns to differentiate between Ego and Super-Ego on the one hand, and between external stimulation and the excitation of the drives on the other.

In my article of 1974 on the Skin Ego, I assigned it three functions: as a containing, unifying envelope for the Self; as a protective barrier for the psyche; and as a filter of exchanges and a surface of inscription for the first traces, a function which makes representation possible. To these three functions, there correspond three representations: the sack, the screen and the sieve. The work of Pasche (1971), 'Le bouclier de Persée' [The shield of Perseus], has led me to consider a fourth function, that as a mirror of reality.

The nine functions of the skin ego

I shall now undertake to establish a more systematic parallel between the functions of the skin and those of the Ego, by attempting to state precisely for each the way in which the organic and the psychical correspond, the types of anxiety connected with the pathology of each function and the forms of disturbance of the Skin Ego revealed by clinical practice. The order I shall follow does not obey any rigorous principle of classification, nor do I claim to provide an exhaustive list of these functions. The list, in fact, remains open.

(1) In the same way that the skin functions as a support for the skeleton and the muscles, the Skin Ego fulfils a function of *maintaining* the psyche. The biological function is performed by what Winnicott calls 'holding', i.e. by the way the mother supports the baby's body. The psychical function develops through the interiorization of this maternal holding. The Skin Ego is a part of the mother — particularly her hands — which has been interiorized and which maintains the psyche in a functional state, at least during waking life, just as the mother maintains the baby's body in a state of unity and solidity. The baby's capacity to maintain itself physically by itself conditions its access to the sitting position, and subsequently to standing and walking. External support from the mother's body leads the baby to learn to support itself internally upon its spinal column, as a solid backbone that allows it to stand upright. One of the anticipatory nuclei of the Ego consists in the sensation/image of an inner maternal, or more generally parental, phallus; this provides the mental space in the process of formation with a first axis, of the order of verticality and of the struggle against gravity, and lays the ground for the experience of having a mental life of one's own. It is by leaning against this axis that the Ego can put into operation the most archaic defence mechanisms, such as splitting and projective identification. But it can only lean upon this support with complete security if it is certain of having in its own body zones of close and stable contact with the skin, muscles and palms of the mother (and of those in its earliest environment) and, on the periphery of its psyche, a reciprocal encirclement (what Sami-Ali, 1974, calls 'mutual inclusion') by the psyche of its mother.

Blaise Pascal, who lost his mother at an early age, developed the theory in physics, then later in psychology and religious apologetics, of the abhorrence of the inner void, long attributed to Nature: the lack of the support object which the psyche needs if it is to find its centre of gravity. Francis Bacon depicts in his paintings deliquescent bodies whose skin and clothing provide them with a superficial unity, but which lack that spinal axis which is the support of body and thought: they are skins filled with a substance more liquid than solid, corresponding quite closely in this to the alcoholic's body image.[1]

---

[1] See my two monographs, 'De l'horreur du vide à sa pensée: Pascal' and 'La peau, la mère et le miroir dans les tableaux de Francis Bacon', reprinted in Anzieu (1981a).

What is evident here is not the phantasied incorporation of the nourishing breast, but the primary identification with a supporting object which the child hugs and which supports it: it is the clinging or attachment drive rather than the libido which finds satisfaction. The face-to-face holding of the child's body against the mother is connected with the sexual drive which finds satisfaction at the oral level in suckling, and in that manifestation of love, the embrace. Adult lovers generally hold each other in this way to satisfy their sexual drives at the genital level. By contrast, primary identification with the supporting background object presupposes a quite other spatial arrangement, occurring in two different but complementary forms which James Grotstein (1981), a Californian disciple of Bion, was the first to define. In one, the child's back is against the stomach of the supporting object (Grotstein's 'Back-ground object'), and in the other, its own stomach is against that object's back.

In the first variant, the child has its back to the background object, which wraps his/her body around it. The child feels protected at the rear, the back being the only part of the body it can neither touch nor see. The nightmare, common in children running a temperature, of a surface full of humps and troughs which folds, buckles and tears, is a figurative expression of damage to the mental representation, a great source of security, of sharing a common skin with the supporting background object. The defective surface may be interpreted by the dreamer as a nest of writhing snakes, but it would be wrong to take this to be simply a phallic symbol. The appearance of several crawling snakes does not mean the same as that of a single upright snake. Grotstein cites one such dream, of a little girl whose mother was a patient of his:

> The daughter apparently awakened in the middle of the night seeing snakes everywhere, including the very floor on which she was walking. She ran to her mother's bedroom and mounted her mother with her back to the mother's abdomen. This was the only place where she could find relief. Although the mother, not the child, was the patient, her associations to the event soon established that she had identified with her child. She was the little girl who wished to lie down on top of me in order to get the 'backing', protection and 'rearing' which she felt deprived of by her own parents.
> (Grotstein, 1981, p. 79)[2]

The second position, with the child stretched out resting the front of its body against the back of the person serving as supporting object, provides the child concerned with the feeling that the most precious and fragile part of its body, its abdomen, is protected by a screen, the original protective shield which the other body now constitutes. This practice generally begins with one or other of the child's parents (or indeed with both); it may continue for quite a long time with a brother or sister with whom the child shares a bed. (Until his

---

[2] I should like to thank Annick Maufras du Chatellier for bringing this passage to my attention.

psychoanalysis with Bion, Samuel Beckett could overcome the anguish of insomnia only by falling asleep lying against the body of his elder brother.) One of my female patients, brought up by violent and quarrelling parents, found inner security this way right up to the prepubertal period, by sleeping against the body of her younger sister with whom she shared a bed. The one who was most afraid would 'be the chair' (their private expression) to receive and squeeze up against the reassuring body of the other. During one whole phase of her analysis, this patient's transference implicitly invited me in turn to 'be the chair': she wanted me to alternate with her in giving my free associations, confessing my thoughts and feelings, my anxieties: she offered to put her body against mine, not understanding why I refused to let her come and sit on my knee. I had first to analyse as a defensive sexualization the hysterical seduction in which she clothed her demand; then we were able to work out the anxiety she felt over the loss of the background object.

Grotstein reports another significant type of example: 'Frequently I have heard dreams from analytic patients in which they were driving a car from the back seat. The associations to these dreams almost invariably led to a notion of having a defective backing and consequently, difficulty with autonomy' (1981, p. 79). Grotstein even proposes a pun here: 'the object *behind* can also be felt to be *underneath*; it therefore becomes the paradigm for the commonly used word, understanding' (p. 80).

(2) To the skin as covering for the entire surface of the body, and into which all the external sense organs are inserted, corresponds the *containing* function of the Skin Ego. This function is set in train primarily by maternal 'handling'. The sensation/image of the skin as sac is awakened, in the very young infant, by the attention to its bodily needs it receives from its mother. The Skin Ego as a mental representation emerges from the interplay between the mother's body and the child's, as well as from the responses the mother makes to the baby's sensations and emotions. These responses encompass both gesture and the voice, for the sound envelope is now added to the tactile, and they are circular in character, the echolalias and echopraxes of the one imitating those of the other, allowing the infant progressively to feel these sensations and emotions for itself without feeling undermined by them. Kaës (1979) distinguishes two aspects of this function: the container [*contenant*], properly so called, is still, stable, and forms a passive receptacle where the baby may store its sensations/images/affects, which in this way are neutralized and preserved. The containor [*conteneur*] corresponds to the active aspect, according to Bion . . . to maternal reverie, or to projective identification, the exercise of the alpha function which elaborates, transforms and restores to the child his sensations/images/affects in a representable form.

Just as the skin envelops the whole of the body, the Skin Ego aspires to envelop the whole of the psychical apparatus, an ambition which proves subsequently to have been overweening, but which is necessary at the outset. At that stage, the Skin Ego is imaginarily represented as an outer shell, the instinctual Id as an inner kernel, the two terms each having need of the other. The Skin Ego cannot function as a container unless it has drives to contain, to localize in bodily sources, and later to differentiate. The drive is only experienced as urge, as motive force, if it encounters limits, specific points of insertion in mental space at which it can deploy itself, and if its source is projected into areas of the body which are particularly open to stimulation. This complementarity of shell and kernel is at the root of the sense of the continuity of the Self.

The failure of this containing function of the Skin Ego results in two forms of anxiety. An instinctual excitation that is diffuse, constant, scattered, non-localizable, non-identifiable, unquenchable results when the psychical topography consists of a kernel without a shell; the individual seeks a substitute shell in physical pain or psychical anxiety: he wraps himself in suffering. In the second case, the envelope exists, but its continuity is broken into by holes. This Skin Ego is a colander: thoughts and memories are only with difficulty retained; they leak away (cf. above the case of Eleanore [1985c, p. 66]). It is a cause of considerable anxiety to have an interior which empties itself, especially of the aggression required for any kind of self-assertion. These psychic holes may find support from the skin's own pores: the case study of Gethsemane given below (1985b, pp. 178–187) shows a patient who perspires during sessions and who thereby unleashes on his psychoanalyst a foul aggression which he can neither hold back nor work over, so long as his unconscious representation of a colander-like Skin Ego has not been interpreted.

(3) The surface layer of the epidermis protects the sensitive layer beneath (where the free nerve-endings and the Meissner corpuscles for touch are located) and shields the organism in general against physical attack, some forms of radiation and an excess of stimuli. As early as his 'Project for a Scientific Psychology' (1950 [1895]), Freud had acknowledged that the Ego fulfils a parallel function as a *protective shield against stimulation* [*Reizschutz*]. In his 'Note upon the "Mystic Writing Pad" ' (1925a), he states clearly that the Ego (like the epidermis, though Freud does not make this point) possesses a dual-layered structure. In the 'Project' of 1895, Freud also hints that the mother serves as an auxiliary 'protective shield' for the baby and does so – I would add – until the baby's growing Ego finds sufficient support upon its own skin to take over that function for itself. In general, we may say that the Skin Ego is a structure potentially present from birth and that it is realized as the relationship between the baby and its primary environment unfolds; the remote origins of the structure seem to go back to the first appearance of living organisms.

Excesses and deficiencies in the protective shield produce very varied figurative representations. Frances Tustin (1972) has described the two body images which pertain to primary and secondary autism respectively: the 'amoeboid' Ego, when none of the functions of the Skin Ego – of support, containment or protective shielding – have been acquired and when the double layer has not begun to take form, and the 'crustacean' Ego, in which a rigid shell replaces the missing container and prevents those functions of the Skin Ego which should develop later from being triggered.

The paranoid anxiety that something is intruding into the psyche takes two forms: (a) they are stealing my thoughts (persecution complex); (b) they are putting thoughts into my head (influencing machine). In these cases, the protective-shield and container functions do distinctly exist, but they are inadequate.

The fear of losing the object fulfilling the role of auxiliary protective shield is most often encountered when the child's upbringing has been entrusted to the mother's own mother (i.e. the maternal grandmother) and when she has taken care of him with such perfection, both qualitative and quantitative, that he has not experienced the possibility or necessity of achieving self-support. Dependence on drugs may then seem to be a solution, to create a barrier of fog or smoke between the Ego and external stimuli.

Support for the protective shield may be sought from the dermis, if the epidermis proves deficient: this is Esther Bick's 'muscular second skin' or Wilhelm Reich's 'character armour'.

(4) The membrane of the organic cells protects the individuality of the cell by distinguishing the foreign bodies to which it refuses entry from the similar or complementary substances to which it grants admission or association. The human skin presents a considerable range of differences as regards grain, colour, texture and smell. These may be narcissistically, or even socially, overvalued. They allow one to identify others as objects of attachment and love and to assert oneself as an individual having one's own skin. In a similar fashion, the Skin Ego performs a function of *individuating* the Self, thus giving the Self a sense of its own uniqueness. The anxiety produced by the 'Uncanny' which Freud described in his paper of 1919 is connected with a threat to the individuality of the Self through a weakening of its sense of boundaries.

In schizophrenia, the whole of external reality (which is imperfectly distinguished from internal reality) is considered dangerous to assimilate, and loss of the sense of reality enables the subject to preserve at any price a sense of the oneness of the Self.

(5) The skin is a surface containing pockets and cavities where the sense organs, apart from those of touch (which are contained in the epidermis itself), are located. The Skin Ego is a psychical surface which connects up sensations of various sorts and makes them stand out as figures against the original background formed by the tactile envelope: this is the Skin Ego's function of *intersensoriality*, which leads to the creation of a 'common sense' (the *sensorium commune* of medieval philosophy) whose basic reference is always to the sense of touch. A defect in this function gives rise to the anxiety of the body being fragmented, or more precisely of it being dismantled (Meltzer, 1975) – that is, of an anarchic, independent functioning of the various sense organs. I shall demonstrate below the crucial role played by the prohibition upon touching in the transition from the containing tactile envelope to the intersensorial space

which lays the ground for symbol formation. In neuro-physiological reality, the coordination of information from the different sense organs is carried out in the encephalon; intersensoriality is therefore a function of the central nervous system, or, to take a more general view, of the ectoderm (from which both the skin and the central nervous system develop at the same moment). In psychical reality, by contrast, such a role is unknown, and there is an imaginary representation of the skin as a background, an original surface upon which sensory interconnections are deployed.

(6) The baby's skin is the object of libidinal cathexis on the part of the mother. Feeding and attention are accompanied by skin contact of a generally pleasurable nature, which prepares for auto-erotism and sets up skin pleasure as a background for sexual pleasures. The latter are localized in certain erectile zones and in certain orifices (protuberances and cavities) where the surface layer of epidermis is thinner than elsewhere and where direct contact with mucus produces an increased level of excitation. The Skin Ego fulfils the function of providing a surface for *supporting sexual excitation*, a surface upon which, in cases of normal development, erogenous zones may be localized, the difference between the sexes recognized and their complementarity sought. The exercise of this function may be sufficient in itself, the Skin Ego drawing in libidinal cathexis over its entire surface and becoming a complete envelope of sexual excitation. (This configuration underlies what is doubtless the most archaic infantile sexual theory, which sees sexuality as entirely restricted to pleasures of skin contact, and pregnancy as resulting merely from embracing and kissing.) Lacking an adequate means of discharge, the envelope of erogenous excitation may be transformed into an envelope of anxiety.

If the cathexis of the skin is more narcissistic than libidinal, the envelope of excitation may be replaced by a gleaming narcissistic envelope, supposedly rendering its owner invulnerable, immortal and heroic.

If sexual excitation is not sustained, the individual will not feel sufficiently secure, on attaining adulthood, to engage in a complete sexual relationship leading to mutual genital satisfaction.

If the sexual protuberances and orifices become the site of algogenic rather than erogenous experience, it may reinforce the imaginary representation of a Skin Ego with holes, increase the level of persecution anxiety and create an inclination towards sexual perversions aimed at converting pain into pleasure.

(7) The skin's function as a surface receiving permanent stimulation of the sensorimotor tonus from external excitations has its counterpart in the Skin Ego's function of *libidinal recharging* of the psychical functioning, the maintenance of internal energetic tension and its unequal distribution among the psychical subsystems (cf. the 'contact-barriers' in Freud's 'Project' of 1895). The failure of this function produces one of two types of antagonistic anxiety: anxiety that the mental apparatus will explode under the pressure of an overload of excitation (e.g. an epileptic fit; cf. Beauchesne, 1980), or Nirvana anxiety, i.e. that one might fulfil the desire of reducing tension to zero.

(8) The skin, together with the tactile sense organs it contains (touch, pain, heat–cold, dermatopic sensitivity), provides direct information about the external world, which is then matched up in the 'common sense' with auditory and visual information, etc. The Skin Ego fulfils a function of *registering* tactile sensory traces, what Piera Aulagnier (1975) sees as a pictogrammic function and what Pasche (1971) describes as the 'Shield of Perseus', sending back a mirror-image of reality. The function is reinforced by the mothering environment to the extent that it fulfils its role of 'object-presenting' (Winnicott, 1962) for the infant. This Skin Ego function develops upon a dual base, biological and social. Biologically, it is upon the skin that a first picture of reality is registered. Socially, an individual's membership of a social group is shown by incisions, scarifications, skin-painting, tattooing, by his make-up and hair-style, and by his clothes, which are another aspect of the same thing. The Skin Ego is the original parchment which preserves, like a palimpsest, the erased, scratched-out, written-over first outlines of an 'original' pre-verbal writing made up of traces upon the skin.

A first form of anxiety related to this function is that of having the surface of one's body marked by shameful and indelible inscriptions emanating from the Super-Ego: rashes, eczema, Bettelheim's 'symbolic wounds' (1954), the infernal machine of Kafka's 'In the Penal Settlement' (1914–19) which inscribes in Gothic letters on the skin of the condemned man the article of the code he has transgressed, until he dies from it. The inverse form of anxiety concerns either the danger of inscriptions being effaced through overloading, or the loss of the capacity to retain traces, e.g. in sleep. The film-skin which allows dreams to unfold reacts in this case by providing the psychical apparatus with the visual image of a Skin Ego restored to its function as a sensitive surface.

(9) All the preceding functions are in the service of the attachment and subsequently the libidinal drive. But is there not a negative function of the Skin Ego, an anti-function so to speak, in the service of Thanatos, having as its goal the *self-destruction* of the skin and the Ego? Progress in immunology, prompted by study of the resistance of the organism to organ transplants, provides a lead here as far as living organisms are concerned. As well as confirming that no two human beings are identical (except in the case of identical twins), the incompatibilities between donors of organs and their recipients have enabled us to grasp the importance of the molecular markers of the 'biological personality'; the greater the similarity of these markers in donor and recipient, the more likely the transplant is to succeed (Jean Hamburger, transplant surgeon). The similarities result from the existence of a plurality of different groups of white corpuscles, from which it appears that it is not merely the corpuscles that are marked, but the personality in its entirety (Jean Dausset, immunologist).

Biologists, without knowing they were doing so, have had recourse to terms analogous to those – such as the Self and the Not-Me [*Non-Moi*] – which some of Freud's successors devised to complete the second topology of the psychical apparatus. In a great number of illnesses, the system of immunological defence can be activated indiscriminately to attack one of the body's own organs as if it were a foreign transplant. These are the so-called auto-immune phenomena, which means, etymologically, that the living organism directs the immunological or immune reaction against itself. The cellular army is designed to reject foreign tissue – what biologists call the 'non-Self' – but it is sometimes so blind as to attack the 'Self', though it respects it totally when it is healthy: this results in auto-immune illnesses which are often very serious.

As an analyst, I am struck by the analogy between the auto-immune reaction on the one hand and, on the other, the turning of drives against oneself, the negative therapeutic reaction, as well as attacks on linking in general and against psychical contents in particular. I note also in passing that the distinction between the familiar and the strange or foreign (Spitz), or between the Ego and non-Ego (or, as Winnicott has it, 'me and not-me'), has biological roots at the level of the cell itself; and I would hazard the hypothesis that the skin as the envelope of the body constitutes the intermediate reality between the membrane of the cell (which collects, sorts and transmits information as to the character, whether foreign or not, of ions) and the psychical interface constituted by the *Pcpt.-Cs.* system of the Ego.

Specialists in psychosomatic illness have described how, in the structure of allergies, the signals of safety and danger are inverted: familiarity, instead of being seen as protective and reassuring, is avoided as bad, and strangeness, instead of being seen as troubling (as in Freud's '*unheimlich* [uncanny]'), is regarded as attractive: hence the paradoxical reaction of the allergy sufferer and also of the drug addict, who avoid what can do them good but are fascinated by what is harmful to them. The fact that the structure of allergy often takes the form of an alternation between asthma and eczema allows us to specify the nature of the Skin Ego involved. Originally, what is at issue is a need to compensate for the inability of the sack Skin Ego properly to delimit an inner psychical sphere of a certain volume, i.e. to pass from a two- to a three-dimensional representation of the psychical apparatus (cf. Houzel, 1985). The two afflictions correspond to the two possible avenues of approach to the surface of that sphere: either from the inside or from the outside. Asthma is an attempt to experience from within the envelope which constitutes the bodily Ego: the sufferer fills himself with air to the point where he experiences from inside the boundaries of his body and confirms the expanded limits of his Self; to preserve this sensation of the Self as a blown-up sac, he holds his breath, at the risk of arresting the rhythm of normal respiratory interaction with the environment and of suffocating. The case study of Pandora below (1985d, p. 116) illustrates this. Eczema is an attempt to feel the corporeal surface of the Self from the outside, in the painful lacerations of the skin, its roughness to the touch and its embarrassing disfigurement, and yet also to feel that surface as an envelope of warmth and diffuse erogenous excitations.

In psychosis, and especially in schizophrenia, the paradox which we see in allergies reaches paroxysm. The mental functioning is dominated by what Paul Wiener (1983) has called the anti-physiological reaction. Confidence in the natural functioning of the organism is either destroyed or has never been acquired. What is natural is experienced as artificial; the living is treated as mechanical; what is good for life and in life is felt to represent mortal danger. Such a paradoxical mental functioning alters, through a circular reaction, the perception of the body's functioning, and its paradoxical nature is thus further reinforced. The underlying paradoxical configuration of the Skin Ego has produced here a failure to master certain fundamental distinctions: between waking and sleeping, dream and reality, animate and inanimate. The case study of Eurydice (D. Anzieu, 1982) provides a limited example of this in a patient who, though not psychotic, feels a threat of mental confusion. The re-establishment of confidence in a natural and felicitous functioning of the organism (on condition that it finds in its environment a sufficient response to its needs) is one of the psychoanalyst's essential tasks with such patients, though it is an arduous and repetitive one, given the patient's unconscious efforts to paralyse the analyst by trapping him in a paradoxical transference (cf. Anzieu, 1975) and dragging him down into the patient's own failure.

Unconscious attacks against the psychical container, which are perhaps based anaclitically upon phenomena of organic auto-immunity, seem to me to originate in parts of the Self that are fused with representatives of the self-destructive instinct inherent in the Id; transported to the periphery of the Self, these parts have become encysted in the surface layer which is the Skin Ego, where they eat into its continuity, destroy its cohesiveness and impair its functions by reversing the goals of those functions. The imaginary skin which covers the Ego thus becomes a poisoned tunic, suffocating, burning, disintegrating. We might therefore speak in this case of a *toxic* function of the Skin Ego.

This list of nine psychical functions of the Ego, which are homologous to biological functions of the skin, is, to my mind, neither immutable nor exhaustive. It provides a grid, open to further elaboration and improvement, against which facts can be tested and which should prove an aid to clinical observation, psychopathological diagnosis, the conduct of psychotherapy and the technique of psychoanalytic interpretation.

To be even more systematic, we may add to this list a number of skin functions not so far mentioned,[3] and with which yet other functions of the Ego may be aligned:

- The storage function (e.g. of fats) can be compared with the function of memory, though the latter arises in the pre-conscious zone of the

---

[3] I have my colleague, the psycho-physiologist François Vincent, to thank for drawing my attention to these.

psychical apparatus and Freud insists that it does not belong to the 'surface' of that apparatus, which is characterized by the Perception–Consciousness system.
- The function of production (e.g. of hair, nails) may be compared with the production of defence mechanisms by the zone (which is also pre-conscious, if not indeed unconscious) of the Ego.
- The function of emission (e.g. of sweat and pheromones) may be compared with the preceding function, projection in fact constituting one of the most archaic of the Ego's defence mechanisms; but this should be articulated with the particular topological configuration I have described as the colander-Skin Ego (cf. the case studies of Eleanore and Gethsemane).

One might also compare, if not certain functions of the Skin Ego then at least certain of its tendencies, with the structural (as opposed to the functional) characteristics of the skin. For example, the fact that the skin has the largest surface and the greatest weight of any of the bodily organs has its counterpart in the Ego's claim to envelop the totality of the psychical apparatus and to weigh heaviest in its functioning. Similarly, the tendency towards interlocking of outer and inner layers in the Skin Ego as in the psychical envelopes (sensory, muscular, rhythmic) appears not unrelated to the intertwining of the layers making up the epidermis, dermis and hypoderm. The complexity of the Ego and the multiplicity of its functions could also be seen as analogous to the numerous important differences of structure and function existing between one point on the skin and another (e.g. the density of the different types of glands, sensory corpuscles, etc.).

A case of perverse masochism

Case study: Monsieur M.

The somewhat exceptional case of Monsieur M., reported by Michel de M'Uzan (1972) before the appearance of my first article on the Skin Ego (1974), does not seem a suitable one for psychoanalytic treatment, and I have only discussed it on two occasions with my colleague. From the perspective provided by the nine functions of the Skin Ego I can now reinterpret the case retrospectively, by showing the impairment of almost all the functions of the Skin Ego (my list of which is thereby indirectly validated) in serious cases of masochism, and the necessity each masochistic subject finds to have recourse to perverse practices to re-establish these functions.

For Monsieur M., who is not by mere chance a radio engineer, the function of supporting the body is artificially ensured by bits of metal and glass inserted everywhere under the skin (this, then, is not a muscular but a metallic second skin) – in particular, needles in the testicles and penis, by two steel rings placed respectively at the tip of the member and at the root of the scrotum, and by having thongs cut out of the skin on his back to allow him to be suspended on butcher's hooks while he is sodomized by a sadist (a realization of the mytheme of the hanged god, mentioned above [1985a, p. 49], in connection with the Greek myth of Marsyas).[4]

The failures of the containing function of the Skin Ego are not only objectivized in the innumerable scars made by burns and cuts, scattered over the whole surface of his body, but by the planing down of certain excrescences (right breast torn off, little toe of the right foot cut off with a metal saw), by the stopping up of certain cavities (navel filled with molten lead), by the artificial enlargement of certain orifices (the anus, the opening of the penis). The containing function is re-established by the creation over and over of an envelope of suffering, using a great diversity of ingenious and cruel techniques and instruments of torture: the phantasy of the flayed skin must be kept permanently alive in the perverse masochist for him to re-acquire a Skin Ego.

The protective-shield function is abused to the point of no return, where the danger becomes fatal to the organism. Monsieur M. has always pulled back from that point (he has suffered neither serious physical illness nor madness), but his young wife, with whom he shared the discovery of masochistic perversions, died of exhaustion from the tortures she endured. Monsieur M. raises the stakes very high in his death-defying game.

The function of individuation of the Self can only be accomplished through suffering both physical (the tortures) and moral (the humiliations); the systematic introduction of inorganic substances under the skin, the ingestion of repugnant substances (urine, the partner's excrement) reveal the fragility of that function; the distinguishing of his own body from those of others is constantly being put in question.

The function of intersensoriality is doubtless the one that is best respected (which explains how Monsieur M. can be so excellently adjusted both socially and professionally).

The functions of sustaining sexual excitation and of libidinal recharging of the Skin Ego are also preserved and activated, but at the cost of the extreme torments mentioned above. And yet Monsieur M. emerged from these sado-masochistic sessions neither down-hearted nor depressed, nor even simply weary: in fact he was invigorated by them. He reached a sexual climax not in

---

[4] The satyr Marsyas is a central figure in two stories involving music: in one, he picked up and played the double flute [*aulos*] that had been abandoned by Athena; in the other, he challenged Apollo to a music contest and lost his hide and his life. In antiquity, literary sources often emphasised the hubris of Marsyas and the justice of his punishment. In the contest between Apollo and Marsyas, the terms stated that the winner could treat the defeated party in any way he wanted. Since the contest was judged by the Muses, Marsyas naturally lost, and he was flayed alive for challenging a god. Apollo then nailed Marsyas' skin to a pine tree, near a lake which was full of the reeds from which the pipes were fashioned. [*Eds., this volume*]

penetrating nor in being penetrated but, initially, by masturbation, and then later by the mere spectacle of perverse scenes (e.g. that of his wife subjected to the cruel attentions of a sadist), accompanied by an excitation of the whole of his skin itself subjected to torture. 'The whole surface of my body could be excited by means of pain.' 'Ejaculation occurred at the moment when the pain was at its height . . . After ejaculation, I felt pain, quite simply' (M'Uzan, 1972/1977, pp. 133–134).

The function of the inscription of signs becomes overactive in the case of Monsieur M. His entire body, apart from his face, is covered with numerous tattoos: e.g. on his buttocks: 'The spot for fine pricks'; on the thighs and belly: 'Long live masochism' and 'I am a living turd', 'Use me like a woman, you'll love it', etc. (M'Uzan, 1972/1977, p. 127). All these inscriptions are evidence of a particular identification with the feminine anatomy, with erogenization of the whole surface of the skin and an invitation to his partner to find pleasure in the various orifices (mouth, anus) through which he himself achieves no pleasure.

Lastly, the function of the Skin Ego which I have termed toxic (i.e. self-destructive) reaches a paroxysm. The skin becomes the source and the object of destructive processes. But the splitting of the libidinal and death instincts is only fleeting – a situation unlike that in psychoses, where it is permanent. At the moment when his dicing with death comes close to suicide, the partner stops tormenting him, the libido makes its 'spontaneous' recovery and Monsieur M. is able to reach orgasm.

He has at least always had enough psychological flair to choose partners who will not go too far: 'the sadist always climbs down at the last moment', he says (M'Uzan, 1972/1977, p. 137). This is a desire for omnipotence, comments de M'Uzan. I would add: for the perverse masochist, the pursuit of omnipotence in destruction is a precondition for access to a phantasm of erotic omnipotence, necessary to trigger his pleasure. The skin is not indeed completely flayed off, and the functions of the Skin Ego are not irreversibly destroyed. Their recovery in extremis, at the very moment when they are being lost, produces a 'jubilatory assumption' much more intense (because at once physical and mental) than that described by Lacan in the mirror phase, but of which the narcissistic economy is equally self-evident.

I hope to have shown that the well-known defence mechanisms (splitting of the drive, reversal and turning against the self, narcissistic hypercathexis of impaired psychical and organic functions) only function with such efficiency in a Skin Ego which has provisionally acquired the nine fundamental functions, which re-enacts again and again a phantasm of having that skin flayed off and the drama of the loss of almost all those functions, in order the more intensely to enjoy the exaltation of finding them again intact. The phantasm (necessary for the evolution towards psychical autonomy) of having a skin of one's own remains ridden with guilt as a result of the earlier phantasm that to have a skin of one's own one has to take it from another, and that it is even better to let it be taken by another to give that other pleasure and, ultimately, to get such pleasure for oneself.

Damp wrapping: the pack, caves

The pack

The pack, a therapeutic technique for treating seriously psychotic patients, derives from the wrapping of patients in damp sheets practised by French psychiatry in the nineteenth century, which has similarities with the African ritual of therapeutic enshrouding or with the icy baths of Tibetan monks. The pack was introduced into France in the early 1960s by the American psychiatrist Michael Woodbury, who added to the practice of physically wrapping the patient in sheets the close encirclement of him by the group of medical personnel. This addition produces an unexpected confirmation of the hypothesis, put forward at the beginning of this work, of the double anaclisis of the Skin Ego: biological, on the surface of the body; social, upon the presence of a unified circle of attendants, who show concern for the experience the patient is undergoing.

The patient, in his underclothes or naked according to his wish, is wrapped up by the attendants in damp, cold sheets. They begin with his arms and legs, wrapping each separately, then they wrap up the whole body tightly, including the arms and legs, but excluding the head. Immediately afterwards, the patient is covered with a blanket so that he can get warm again fairly quickly. He remains lying down for three-quarters of an hour, free to verbalize his feelings or not, as he wishes (in any case, according to the medical staff who often undergo the pack treatment themselves, the sensations and emotions experienced at the time are so intense and extraordinary that words are hardly adequate to express them). The attendants touch the wrapped-up patient, communicate with him with their eyes or reply to what he has to say; they are eager and anxious to know what is going on inside him. The pack creates such a strong group feeling between attendants and patient that it tends to cause jealousy among the rest of the staff. This I take to be a confirmation of my other hypothesis, that the bodily envelope is one of the unconscious psychical organizing factors in groups (Anzieu, 1981b).

After a relatively short phase of anxiety, owing to the impression of being completely surrounded by cold, the patient feels a sense of omnipotence, of physical and psychical fullness. I understand this as a regression to that original unlimited psychical Self which certain psychoanalysts have hypothesized and which seems to correspond to a dissociation of the psychical from the bodily Ego, as experienced by the participants in a group, by mystics, or even by creative artists (cf. Anzieu, 1980). This sense of well-being does not last, but it becomes more durable with repetition of the 'pack' treatment (as with the psychoanalytic model, the complete cure may take years, at a rate of three sessions per week).

The pack provides the patient with a sensation of a double bodily envelope: a thermal envelope (cold, then subsequently warm, as a result of peripheral vasodilation in response to contact with the cold), one which controls the body's internal temperature; and a tactile envelope (the tight, wet sheets which stick to the whole of the skin). This fleetingly reconstructs the patient's Ego as separate from others and at the same time continuous with them, which is one of the topographical characteristics of the Skin Ego. In this regard, one practitioner of the pack, Claudie Cachard (1981), speaks of 'membranes of life' (cf. also de Loisy, 1981).

The pack can also be used with psychotic children and with deaf and blind children whose only access to significant communication with those around them is by means of touch. The pack offers them a structuring 'relief envelope' which can take the place, for a time, of their pathological envelope; thanks to it, they are able also to abandon a part of their defences which consist of motor agitation or of making noise, and to feel unified and still. There is, however, an initial resistance to being wrapped up: to attempt to wrap up such children completely creates an extreme panic reaction and an extraordinary degree of violence.

Three remarks

The experience of the pack and of caves leads me to make three remarks. Firstly, the baby's body does seem to be programmed to experience a containing envelope; if the adequate sensory materials are lacking, it creates this experience nonetheless, with whatever is available: hence the pathological envelopes consisting of a barrage of incoherent noise and of motor agitation; these are there not to allow controlled discharge of instinctual energy, but to enable the organism to adapt for its own survival. Secondly, the paradoxical resistances of people bringing up children are the product of a difference in the level of structuring of their own bodily Egos and those of their children, as well as of the danger they perceive of themselves experiencing a regression which would abolish that difference and produce a state of mental confusion. Thirdly, the therapy of 'relief envelopes' (including not only packs and caves, but also massages, bioenergetics and encounter groups) has only a temporary effect. What we see here is simply an extreme case of a phenomenon observable in normal individuals, who need periodically to reconfirm through practical experience their basic sense of having a Skin Ego. It is also an illustration of the need one finds among those suffering from serious deprivation, to develop substitute and compensatory constructs.

References

Anzieu, D. (1974). Le moi-peau [The skin ego]. *Nouvelle Revue de Psychanalyse, 3*: 195–208.

Anzieu, D. (1975). Le transfert paradoxal [Paradoxical transference]. *Nouvelle Revue de Psychanalyse, 12*: 49–72.

Anzieu, D. (1980). Du corps et du code mystique et de leurs paradoxes [The body, its mystic codes and their paradoxes]. *Nouvelle Revue de Psychanalyse, 22*: 159–177.

Anzieu, D. (1981a). *Le corps de l'oeuvre* [The body of the work]. Paris: Gallimard.

Anzieu, D. (1981b). *Le groupe et l'inconscient. L'imaginaire groupal* (revised edition). Paris: Dunod. [*The Group and the Unconscious*, trans. B. Kilborne. London: Routledge & Kegan Paul, 1984.]

Anzieu, D. (1982). Sur la confusion primaire de l'animé et de l'inanimé. Un cas de triple méprise [On the primary confusion between animate and inanimate: A case of threefold misunderstanding]. *Nouvelle Revue de Psychanalyse, 25*: 215–222.

Anzieu, D. (1985a). The Greek Myth of Marsyas. In *The Skin Ego* (chapter 4), trans. C. Turner. New Haven, CT: Yale University Press, 1989.

Anzieu, D. (1985b). The Olfactory Envelope. In *The Skin Ego* (chapter 13), trans. C. Turner. New Haven, CT: Yale University Press, 1989.

Anzieu, D. (1985c). The Psychogenesis of the Skin Ego. In *The Skin Ego* (chapter 5), trans. C. Turner. New Haven, CT: Yale University Press, 1989.

Anzieu, D. (1985d). Disturbances of Basic Sensori-Motor Distinctions. In *The Skin Ego* (chapter 8), trans. C. Turner. New Haven, CT: Yale University Press, 1989.

Aulagnier, P. (1975). *La violence de l'interprétation. Du pictogramme à l'énoncé*. Paris: Presses Universitaires de France. [*The Violence of Interpretation: From Pictogram to Statement*, trans. A. Sheridan. London: Routledge, 2001.]

Beauchesne, H. (1980). *L'épileptique* [The epileptic]. Paris: Dunod.

Bettelheim, B. (1954). *Symbolic Wounds: Puberty Rites and the Envious Male*. London: Thames & Hudson.

Cachard, C. (1981). Enveloppes de corps, membranes de rêve [Body envelopes, dream membranes]. *L'Evolution Psychiatrique, 46* (4): 847–856.

Freud, S. (1919h). The 'Uncanny'. *S.E.*, 17.

Freud (1923b). *The Ego and the Id. S.E.*, 19.

Freud, S. (1925a). A Note upon the 'Mystic Writing Pad'. *S.E.*, 19.

Freud (1950 [1895]). 'Project for a Scientific Psychology'. *S.E.*, 1.

Grotstein, J. (1981). *Splitting and Projective Identification*. New York: Jason Aronson.

Hermann, I. (1930). *L'instinct filial* [Filial instinct]. Paris: Denoël, 1973.

Houzel, D. (1985). L'évolution du concept d'espace psychique dans l'oeuvre de Mélanie Klein et de ses successeurs [The evolution of the concept of psychic space in the work of Melanie Klein and her successors]. In *Mélanie Klein aujourd'hui*. Lyon: Centurion.

Kaës, R. (1979). Introduction á l'analyse transitionnelle [Introduction to transitional analysis]. In R. Kaës et al., *Crise, rupture et dépassement*. Paris: Dunod.

Kafka, F. (1914–19). In the penal settlement. In *The Complete Stories of Franz Kafka*, ed. N. N. Glatzer. New York: Schocken Books, 1971.

Laplanche, J. (1970). *Vie et mort en psychanalyse*. Paris: Flammarion. [*Life and Death in Psychoanalysis*, trans. J. Mehlman. Baltimore, MD: Johns Hopkins University Press, 1976.]

Loisy, D. de (1981). Enveloppes pathologiques, enveloppes thérapeutiques (le packing, thérapie somato-psychique) [Pathological envelopes, therapeutic envelopes (Packing: A somato-psychic therapy)]. *L'Evolution Psychiatrique, 46* (4): 857–872.

Meltzer, D. (1975). *Explorations in Autism*. Perthshire: Clunie Press.

M'Uzan, M. de (1972). Un cas de masochisme pervers [A case of perverse masochism]. In

La sexualité perverse [Perverse sexuality]. Paris: Payot. Reprinted in *De l'art à la mort* [From art to death]. Paris: Gallimard, 1977.

Pasche, F. (1971). Le bouclier de Persée [The shield of Perseus]. *Revue Française de Psychanalyse*, 35 (5–6): 859–870.

Sami-Ali, M. (1974). *L'espace imaginaire* [The imaginary space]. Paris: Gallimard, 1977.

Tustin, F. (1972). *Autism and Childhood Psychosis*. London: Routledge & Kegan Paul.

Wiener, P. (1983). *Structure et processus dans la psychose* [Structure and process in psychosis]. Paris: Presses Universitaires de France.

Winnicott, D. W. (1962). Ego integration in child development. *The Maturational Processes and the Facilitating Environment*. London: Hogarth Press and the Institute of Psycho-Analysis, 1965.

26 THE DEATH DRIVE
Meaning, objections, substitutes

André Green

A psychiatrist and full member of the Paris Psychoanalytical Society, **André Green** is a former president of that Society and a former director of the Institute of Psychoanalysis. He was Freud Memorial Professor at the University of London (1979–80). A prolific writer, he has published many books and papers on a great variety of subjects: the affects, borderline states, language in psychoanalysis, literature and art. He has been instrumental in bringing together within the confines of a well-defined metapsychology both the main post-Freudian contributions (Winnicott and Bion) and the various trends of French psychoanalysis, including some of Lacan's most interesting ideas.

Several of Green's books have become classics in their own right; in particular: *Le discours vivant. Une conception psychanalytique de l'affect*, (PUF, 1970) [*The Fabric of Affect in the Psychoanalytic Discourse* (Routledge, 1999)]; *Narcissisme de vie, narcissisme de mort* [Life narcissism, death narcissism] (Editions de Minuit, 1983); *La folie privée. Psychanalyse des cas limites* (Gallimard, 1990) [*On Private Madness* (IUP, 1993)]; *Le travail du négatif* (Editions de Minuit, 1993) [*The Work of the Negative* (Free Association Books, 1999)]; *Idées directrices pour une psychanalyse contemporaine* (PUF, 2002) [*Key Ideas for a Contemporary Psychoanalysis* (Routledge, 2005)]; *La lettre et la mort* [Writing and death] (Denoël, 2004), a series of discussions with Dominique Eddé on literature; and he recently wrote a book with the somewhat controversial title *Pourquoi les pulsions de destruction ou de mort?* [Why are there destructive or death drives?] (Panama, 2007).

François Duparc wrote a concise biography of André Green for the series 'Psychanalystes d'aujourd'hui' (PUF, 1996).

An international tribute was paid to him in 2000 via the publication of a book in his honour with papers from several contributors: *Penser les limites. Écrits en l'honneur d'André Green* [Thinking about limits: Essays in honour of André Green] (ed. César Botella; Delachaux et Niestlé, 2000).

The supreme concepts

In the natural sciences, of which psychoanalysis is one, clear-cut general concepts are superfluous, indeed impossible, according to Freud (1925d [1924], pp. 57–58). Freud constantly repeated that the basic concepts of a science cannot be demonstrated. Only their applications must meet this requirement. Such is the case for the concepts of the libido and the drive. While acknowledging, if not his debt, then at least the proximity of his ideas with Schopenhauer's, Freud nonetheless differs with him. He does not contend that the sole aim of life is death. He recognises two basic drives: 'Both instincts [Eros and the death instinct] are from the beginning present together in psychic life and seldom or never appear in pure form but are, as a rule, welded together in various proportions' (Freud & Bullitt, 1967, p. 38).

If fusion and defusion are the ordinary state in which the amalgamation of the life and death drives can be observed, Freud nonetheless suggests that one can, albeit rarely, observe the death drives in the defused state. The satisfaction of the residues of the death drive remaining in the ego seems not to produce feelings of pleasure (Freud, 1940a [1938], p. 154, fn. 1).

Eros and the death drive

The regrouping, in 1920, of the sexual drives under the Platonic entity Eros was no less important than the innovation concerning the death drive. The self-preservative drives, the narcissistic drives, the sexual drives inhibited in their aim, and the uninhibited sexual instincts were henceforth all united under this heading. The relation to self-preservation was thus linked to the ensemble and no longer in antagonism with it. The aim of Eros is to form ever greater unities and its role is fundamentally conservative. The clamour of life proceeds for the most part from Eros, and *its essential function is one of binding together.*

On the side of the destructive drive, Freud (1930a, p. 120) remarks: 'There is an inborn human inclination to "badness", to aggressiveness and destructiveness, and so to cruelty as well.'

As for the observable manifestations of the death drive in clinical experience, according to Freud three major forms may be cited: *masochism, the negative therapeutic reaction and awareness of guilt.*

I will confine myself here to examining these three clinical situations designated by Freud as exemplifying the effects of the death drive. I will not return for the moment, then, to negative narcissism and the disobjectalising function which I have discussed elsewhere, but will limit myself to discussing Freud's line of reasoning in order to throw light on the implications of his thought. Ultimately, the maximal effect of the death drive is to arrive at a lifeless state (a return to organic matter). *Life is a mischief-maker, but peace is death.* It was a highly speculative conclusion that would be the object of much criticism.

The principles

In 'The Economic Problem of Masochism' (1924c), Freud eventually defines three principles of functioning:

1. The principle of Nirvana (introduced by B. Low), whose aim is to attain the level zero of psychic excitation. It characterises the death drive;
2. The pleasure principle, which expresses the claims of the libido;
3. The reality principle, which translates the influence of the external world on the pleasure principle (modified pleasure principle).

These three principles represent the final positions of Freud's metapsychological research. He did not propose any others in his lifetime. 'If the term libido designates the emergence of the sexual drive, we are without a term analogous to "libido" for describing the energy of the destructive instinct', which, like Eros, also proceeds from the id (Freud, 1940a [1938], p. 150).

The ego, sublimation, identification, desexualisation

One of Freud's most disconcerting ideas is his contention that sublimation works in favour of the death drive: 'By thus getting hold of the libido from the object-cathexes, setting itself up as sole love-object, and desexualising or sublimating the libido of the id, the ego is working in opposition to the purposes of Eros and placing itself at the service of the opposing instinctual impulses' (Freud, 1923b, p. 46).

It is a surprising observation: the 'civilising' purpose of sublimation aligns itself with the death drives! What is to be recommended: the satisfaction of the non-sublimated instinctual impulses, the pleasure principle? It too exposes itself to great dangers by ignoring the reality principle.

Freud comes back to this: 'Through its work of identification and sublimation it [the ego] gives the death instincts in the id assistance in gaining control over the libido, but in doing so it runs the risk of becoming the object of the death instincts and of itself perishing' (Freud, 1923b, p.56).

This movement develops with the formation of the superego.

The superego and masochism

The superego is constructed on the paternal model: 'Every such identification is in the nature of a desexualisation or even of a sublimation. It now seems as though when a transformation of this kind takes place, an instinctual defusion occurs at the same time. After sublimation the erotic component no longer has the power to bind the whole of destructiveness that was combined with it, and this is released in the form of an inclination to aggression and destruction' (1923b, pp. 54–55).

In his *New Introductory Lectures* Freud (1933a, pp. 104–105) writes:

> In sadism and masochism we have before us two excellent examples of a mixture of the two classes of instinct, of Eros and aggressiveness; and we proceed to the hypothesis that this relation is a model one – that every instinctual impulse that we can examine consists of similar fusions or alloys of the two classes of instinct. These fusions, of course, would be in the most varied ratios. Thus the erotic instincts would introduce the multiplicity of their sexual aims into the fusion, while the others would only admit of mitigations or gradations in their monotonous trend.

The clamour of life proceeds from Eros, but also the 'medley', the sparkle of colours, the polyphony of sounds, the palette of odours, smells, stimulants of taste, etc.

Freud writes (1924c, p. 164):

> If one is prepared to overlook a little inexactitude, it may be said that the death instinct which is operative in the organism – primal sadism – is identical with masochism. After the main portion of it has been transposed outwards on to objects, there remains inside, as a residuum of it, the erotogenic masochism proper, which on the one hand has become a component of the libido and, on the other, still has the self as its object. This masochism would thus be evidence of, and a remainder from, the phase of development in which the coalescence, which is so important for life, between the death instinct and Eros took place. We shall not be surprised to hear that in certain circumstances the sadism, or instinct of destruction, which has been directed outwards, projected, can be once more introjected, turned inwards, and in this way regress to its earlier situation. If this happens, a secondary masochism is produced, which is added to the original masochism.

Freud engages here in a remarkable temporo-spatial exercise distinguishing between the original form and the secondary form, articulated around the relations inside–outside; the complexity of his thought obliges us to imagine an inside which changes in nature when passing over to the outside, the outside being capable of being reinternalised. In short, inside–outside–inside again.

Conclusion

Freud defends his position: *the concept of the death drive does not depend on an affective need*: 'The death instinct is not a requirement of the heart; it seems to me to be only an inevitable assumption, on both biological and psychological grounds. . . . Thus to me my pessimism seems a conclusion, while the optimism of my opponents seems an a priori assumption' (Freud & Pfister, 1963, p. 133).

However, this reserved judgement retains its currency: 'the distinction between the two classes of instincts does not seem sufficiently assured and it is possible that facts of clinical analysis may be found which will do away with its pretension' (Freud, 1923b, p. 42).

In the same work, he fears undervaluing the part played by Eros (1923b, p. 59). Later, in *Civilization and Its Discontents* (1930a, p. 122) he clarified this doubt by writing that the death instinct 'is not entirely [free from] theoretical objections'. But these are not enough to shake his convictions.

Reflections

Some comments are necessary now for understanding Freud's thinking on the death drive. Freud is not lacking in clinical arguments. He cites them (masochism, negative therapeutic reaction, awareness of guilt). Let it be said without further ado that none of them are decisive, because they can be interpreted in various ways. The death drive belongs in fact to a singular epistemological dimension. It is commonly said that Freud was always marked by his original biological training and only partially freed himself from it. But to give a more complete picture, until the end – that is, until the end of his life – he considered psychoanalysis as a science of nature, even if no one before him had given so much thought to the psychological penetration of the non-conscious layers of the psyche. However, there is a contradiction here – namely, that of wanting obstinately to link psychoanalysis to the sciences of nature by defending the organic foundations of basic psychic phenomena, while at the same time defending fiercely the psychic nature of this psyche which exists in a form that is unknown to us.

In fact, to understand Freud, one has to undertake an analysis of the foundations of his thought. In the beginning is death, and everything will end with death. This death is subject to a principle of Nirvana which strives to bring all forms of excitation back to the level zero. Death is a state of absolute calm, the abolition of all tension, the annihilation of any form of life. Life is marked by the instinctual claims of Eros, a mischief-maker which expresses itself through movement, tension and the search for satisfaction. The clamour of life proceeds from Eros. The death drive seeks to destroy these claims and to establish a return to the absolute calm of death over life. The life drive of Eros and the drive of destruction coexist, are fused, blended and alloyed. When death has not succeeded in evacuating the tensions demanded by Eros, it enters with it into relations of fusion. This results in the appearance, in succession, of internal primordial masochism, primal sadism and secondary masochism through an interplay of interiority, externalisation and re-internalisation. This primary fusion can be accompanied by defusions, in which what has been fused and alloyed can be undone again. If the death drives, which, according to Freud, act in silence, only admit of mitigations in their monotonous trend, the whole diversity of life is linked to the diversity of the sexual aims of Eros. For Eros has an internal power of transformation. In the beginning there is self-preservation, to protect life; then comes narcissism, which unifies what life has succeeded in conserving by preventing the destruction of living substance. Alongside narcissism, there are object-related drives (directed towards the object): some are direct and varied according to diverse sexual aims, while others, inhibited in their aim, do not attain discharge and can conserve an object which they do not consume but to which they express tenderness or friendship. Furthermore, along with the development of the libido, identifications and sublimations appear, all forms of which involve desexualisation and consequently weaken the binding power of Eros. The life-force – the libido – comes from its binding, conservative power, maintaining 'in life' that which has been won over from death. The sole aim of the forces of destruction is that of unbinding, undoing, destroying connections, desexualising. The whole mystery of life resides in these agonistic and antagonistic relations.

Such is Freud's 'vision', which we have some difficulty in accepting. The fact is, unlike Freud, we are not visionaries. Clinical experience has prevailed in our time, and theory is its maidservant. Emphasising our differences can be helpful, though, in order to know where we stand.

Note on certain similarities

If we think about post-Freudian contributions, one cannot fail to be struck by certain resonances. We can see first of all that if the majority of analysts have not been able to agree with Freud on the death drive, almost the whole of contemporary clinical thought is centred on the analysis of the role of destructivity in the clinical situations we are faced with today, especially in non-neurotic structures.

In a recent contribution, Anne Denis (2006) breaks new ground by postulating the existence of a murderous tendency, an 'externalised aspect of the death drive'. Its aim is to kill: the destructive urge – necessary for conservation – also implies the murder of one's fellow man. The murder does not only concern the physical disappearance of the other. This murderous urge is in fact the manifestation of a death-principle which wants to destroy the mind or psyche of the other. Destruction of meaning and destruction of linking coincide. Denis draws support for her ideas from her experience of autistic pathology and borderline cases. In fact, she is concerned with the genesis of the sense of inhumanity, with the origin of psychic pain. She criticises abstract theories of language and grants a place of utmost importance to poetry, a veritable vehicle of linking in which 'symbolicity' is formed and in which the poetic function of psychoanalysis, a true antagonist of the death drive, finds its affirmation.

But the point I am primarily interested in here concerns the correspondence between Freud's ideas of externalisation and Bion's concepts of evacuation. In Freud's work, the death drive aims to undo, to unbind what Eros has succeeded in binding together. This unbinding, which goes hand in hand with a liberation of the death drive, seeks to supplant or indeed eliminate the investments of Eros. How? Through discharge, ejection, the elimination of the sexual drives characteristic of Eros? This is what Freud contends. Remember that in 'Negation' (1925h), Freud identifies the first movement of the psyche through the identity of what is external, the hated and the alien, which are rejected: this is translated by a radical expulsion 'outside the Ego'. No integration is possible. Only the pleasure-Ego can be introjected; the rest, as I have said, is 'excorporation', put outside the body, outside the Ego, because it is unassimilable, unintegratable. Thereafter, the pleasure-Ego and unpleasure will have to be integrated within the problem not of what is good or bad but of what exists or does not exist. It seems to me that this primal question is similar in more than one way to the function of the earliest projective identifications, which cannot retain anything and must be purged of all the disagreeable or uncomfortable consequences of the accumulated frustrations. We are familiar with the fundamental dilemma posed by Bion: frustration is either elaborated or evacuated. It is Bion's view that, in order for elaboration to take place, what has been introjected must first be conserved, maintained and transformed, which evacuation does not permit. With the notion of 'evacuation', elaboration cannot occur. In other words, Eros must prevail over the drives of destruction.

What is happening, then, particularly in psychosis? When the subject resorts to evacuative excorporation, it is not only the frustrating object that is evacuated. By virtue of this manoeuvre, the object is externalised, but the limits of the Ego are externalised too. The Ego pushes back its frontiers even further towards the outside. It constitutes a projective screen which will be able to receive the return of the evacuated stimuli in the form of delusional or hallucinatory projections. As Freud says, that which has been *abolished* on the inside returns from the outside. Henceforth, psychic exchanges no longer take place between an inside (repressed) and an outside, but an inside that has been abolished and externalised, which is now felt to be outside, and an outside which really is outside.

It is a remarkable fact that although Freud and Bion start out from quite different premises, they come to very similar conclusions, justifying them from different angles of clinical experience.

Melancholia and masochism: diverse versions

None of us, whoever we are, can escape living through painful moments, whether the wheel of fortune turns against us, or because we find ourselves in certain circumstances and cannot avoid suffering losses due to the 'facts of life'. In this respect, we are all subject to an age-old experience, that of mourning.

Now, although the experience of mourning plunges those it affects into a profound state of affliction, one cannot fail to notice that the moral pain of the mourner is not directly proportionate to the joy that he or she felt prior to the loved one's death. Before the bereavement, the individual is just going about his normal business, taking care of the person who is going to die (or perhaps it is before the unexpected loss of someone in a deadly accident), often with a heavy heart, without realising that he is mobilising to this end considerable unconscious libidinal energy which he only becomes aware of retrospectively, once his loved object has disappeared for ever. With this loss, a narcissistic haemorrhage occurs in the Ego. A sudden reversal of drive activity takes place. If the joy of living was not apparent before the object disappeared, its 'loss', as Freud saw, is a loss for the Ego (especially when mourning becomes melancholia), something which is inferred *après-coup*, after the event. This is indeed a consequence of the unconscious character of the libidinal investment, whose negativisation indicates indirectly what its positive value was, which is now perceived indirectly in its erotic form. It is drives – affects – much more than unconscious representations, which are remobilised during the work of mourning. Now, mourning is the normal prototype of melancholia, and melancholia, according to Freud's affirmation, is a 'pure culture of the death instinct' (1923b, p. 53).

We are thus brought back to the question of the death drive, which has greatly divided psychoanalysts. Over the course of time I have come to understand better the reservations of the opponents of the death drive without, however, modifying my basic adhesion to this concept. Though Lacan, at the beginning of his work, speaks about it frequently, at the end he hardly ever mentions it. Laplanche also rejects it; Winnicott does not accept referring to its influence in the case of someone who is alive; and Bion seems constantly wary of taking a position on the question. Without adopting Freud's views on the biologisation of the concept (Green, 2000), it seemed to me that one could distance oneself from Freud's formulations while still accepting the validity of the concept. Today I want to suspend, for the time being, the affirmations that I have defended in the past.

The essence of the debate concerns the unquestionable destructiveness we witness in delinquent, psychopathic, psychotic and psychosomatic patients – and especially when we see their symptoms take on a masochistic significance. This is without taking into account the large number of patients, many of whom are borderline cases, who for a long time are unable to benefit from a psychoanalytic treatment and who become champions of the negative therapeutic reaction, of treatments that get bogged down in interminable repetition-compulsions.

None of these findings are deniable, but they are open to different interpretations. Freud was not a man to let himself be tempted by denial to save the theory. He was accustomed to saying: 'Ignorance is ignorance, no right to believe anything can be derived from it' (1927c, p. 32). But, precisely, was the death drive a matter of belief? For him it had become a fact. Melanie Klein, who was more royalist than the king, wanted to hammer the nail home. But with time, she too, like Lacan, gave the impression of avoiding the subject. It seems to me that, instead of blowing on the flames of discord, we would gain by throwing light on the consequences of the turning point of 1920, which saw the introduction of the death drive.

Two fundamental articles are at our disposal for this analysis. The first, which slightly precedes the introduction of the death drive, since it is dated 1919, is 'A Child Is Being Beaten'; and the second, which came after it, is 'The Economic Problem of Masochism' (1924c). The first shows that being beaten by the father means being loved by him. Freud applies a libidinal theory here that is exclusively sexual and envisages masochism as a consequence of excitation. The article on 'The Economic Problem of Masochism' is quite different: it is coloured by Freud's preoccupations on the relations between the pleasure principle – the principle of Nirvana – and the reality principle, which serve as a theoretical basis for his intuition concerning the death drive. Aggressiveness is only the fraction of it that is deflected towards the outside. Now these two articles deal with the same problem, but from the different perspectives of before and after 1920. A comparison may be made with the two conceptions of mourning of 1915 and 1923. In 1923, Freud envisages melancholia as a 'pure culture of the death instinct', which is different from the point of view expressed in 'Mourning and Melancholia' (1917e [1915]).

I want to return now to my observations on the transition from the unconscious representation to the instinctual impulse. I have drawn attention to this deliberate omission by Freud of representation in the id of the second topography and the return in force of the drive, now included as the basis of the psychic apparatus. I have recalled the irrevocable character of Freud's abandonment of the concept 'unconscious', which is no more than a psychic quality. I found it difficult to reconcile myself with the fact that this radical revision was accompanied by the rejection of a theoretical instrument that is so fundamental and so universally recognised by psychoanalysts. If the id is primarily a force, more exactly a conflict of antagonistic forces – dominated by the economic (quantitative) point of view – and ejection is a consequence of this state of affairs, this results in the fragile, precarious nature of all *working-through*. The consequence is a barely restrained expression of the death drive because it is partially fused, and its potential for binding is weak. Unbinding is prevalent here.

This is one way of seeing things, but is it the only one? The place occupied by the drives of destruction, which have come to invade the clinical field, has given rise to objections from those who thought that the field of the erotic libido should not for all that be disinvested. This explains, for example, the insistent reference in J. C. Rolland's work of the interpretation of masochism (1999), linked to the ideas contained in 'A Child Is Being Beaten'. The accumulation of failures by the ego, the search for unconscious sanctions (hospitalisations, confinements, handicapping medications, diverse intensive treatments), are above all evidence for him of the intensity of the unconscious guilt which seeks punishment. This last characteristic, whatever interpretations one gives of it, seem convincing. The failures of the ego – fragmentation, splitting, hallucinatory attacks, etc. – are part of the same mechanism: being beaten by the father.

This position throws light on the clinical case of Schreber (through the figure of Flechsig) (Freud, 1911c [1910]). So what does this drive reversal mean, then? Is it the result (an interpretation that would be somewhat simplistic) of defusion, of the prevalence of sadomasochism? I would say that it is possible to believe that the erotic libido can only be acted out because it lacks diverse forms of assistance: the lack of subjective representation is immediately noticeable. Delusion takes its place. I have already pointed out on many occasions that the absence of intermediate formations – the regression of language (words treated as things) – which makes corporeity unthinkable, the inaccessibility of Lacan's *Nom du Père*, invasion by the imaginary, and the return in force of a foreclosed real (if one accepts that the real is unanalysable horror) are all characteristics that greatly limit the possibilities of analysis and, in fact, make it impossible. In the present case, Freud is more at ease because it is a text that he is interpreting rather than the clinical material of a patient. Here the destruction takes us back to a 'primary erotic libido'. Laplanche (1970) would see in it the confirmation of his hypothesis of 'sexual death drives' – in fact, erotic drives, even in the most elementary form, that cannot be controlled by the ego. And if the ego is itself blinded by the unconsciousness of its defences, it becomes difficult to choose between a primary libidinal drive and a death drive.

An important question remains: that of pleasure. If the id is indeed characterised by the search for satisfaction, then it is erotic and destructive satisfactions that are involved. What becomes of eroticism in those cases where the role of the death drive is invoked? Is it the pleasure of destruction or self-destruction that is involved? We would seem to be dealing with a sort of generalised sadomasochism. This brings us back to the problem of masochistic pleasure, which is the most difficult thing to get patients to acknowledge. On the other hand, many patients belonging to borderline structures openly show affects of hate, envy, rage and so on.

In order to get a clearer picture, we must go back to the theory. The treatment of unconscious affect in Freud's conception continues to cause a lot of ink to flow. For Freud, the affective qualities are conscious; the unconscious affect is *without quality*. Under these conditions, and without it being possible to say how this happens in the unconscious, it is rhythms, intensities and oscillations of tension that are assumed to be operating at this level: movement, and its perception at the level of the body, constitute unconscious affect. Quality, an attribute of consciousness, is not part of it. The main feeling one has is that the patient wavers between states of great instinctual excitation and states of apathy and dejection during depressive periods. Instinctual excitation could be linked to the Lacanian concept of *jouissance* – which cannot be assimilated to pleasure. For Lacan the concept of jouissance is often linked to the horror of raw instinctual satisfaction. Even if one cannot refer here to libidinal Eros, the link with the destructive drives allows little room for this dimension of ecstatic enjoyment. It is important to notice the links between these affects and a narcissism that is devoid of any empathy with the object, rather than what could be said to characterise any given object-relationship. Primary brutality dominates satisfaction here and is as difficult to link to pure destructiveness as to pleasure. The 'unleashing' of the drives – literally speaking – is an activity that seems less bound than absolutely riveted to its blind aim, confining the subject to depersonalisation.

The concept of drive without any other determination implies in itself a reference to an almost unrepresentable force. It is thus not absolutely indispensable to add to it the qualification of a reference to death. Nevertheless, the designation of a so-called drive of death or destruction shows us that the result that the subject is seeking, without always realising it, is his own destruction. There can be no doubt that it is the destruction of the capacity for thinking, for, in this state, the drive cannot lend itself to any activity which implies such elaboration.

This is indeed the conclusion we are bound to come to: binding remains indispensable if the drive is to serve the construction of the psyche. For Winnicott, this is accomplished through play; for Bion, through the work of alpha-function; for Lacan, through the symbolic operations of the signifier. However that may be, Freud had many reasons for situating the foundations of psychic activity – he said it and repeated it on many occasions – in a form we are unfamiliar with, in a substratum that he himself could not imagine, in spite of his great inventiveness. There is indeed a state of psychic life here that is difficult for us to conceive of. This is perhaps, as Lacan contends, because we are speaking subjects.

In other words, the concept unconscious is not superfluous. It may be considered as an indicator of the extent of working-through that has been accomplished, in the form described by its manifestations, while considering at the same time that it is perhaps not the most elementary level of psychic activity but the threshold of what is thinkable of its original state. It is thus both useful and necessary for psychoanalysis and leaves open the question of its origins, of its anchoring in the somatic. The unconscious could then be the result of exchanges between the drive and the object, or indeed between two subjects.

With the id, another level of activity is reached which does not let itself be influenced by the object, any more than one can imagine it being influenced by the functioning of the subject. This is what Freud wanted to say, borrowing the term *Es* from Groddeck: It/Id, not I, but the root from which a subject can come into being. The un-conscious is a negativised form of consciousness. It is not the negativised form of the conscious subject, but the product of a work of the negative, both in relation to the drive and to consciousness. In any case, the unconscious thinks itself, unlike the It/Id, which is only indicated by a subject who only thinks about It/Id.

Bringing into play other modalities of the work of the negative is not, however, a reason for short-circuiting repression. The active role played by desires for destruction should not make us overlook the fact that they, too, are psychic formations, which invite us to think about the role of repression and to seek behind symptoms, and the most openly destructive manifestations, sexual fantasies in which the libido also has its role to play. When this moment is reached in the treatment, sometimes even in the face-to-face situation, the material, at first an object of terror, is then seen with the necessary detachment (J. C. Rolland).[1] In other words, we are invited to recall that all material, of whatever sort, has undergone a distortion due to repression, and we are even obliged to consider that there may be a certain pleasure involved in being ill in order to satisfy a masochistic fantasy. Masochism is without doubt, of all the aspects communicated to the patient, the source of the greatest resistances. The notion of unconscious pleasure, where consciousness reacts with disgust or rejection, already mobilises many resistances, but when it is a question of masochistic pleasure, recognition by the patient is still more difficult to obtain, for accepting it is already going half the way towards recognising the unconscious.

One further argument merits discussion. This is the contention that, in these non-neurotic structures there is insufficient repression, for even this becomes the target of the drives of destruction.

However, reflection swings back and forth like a pendulum from one pole to the other. Having advanced the hypothesis of the 'repressed' libidinal fantasy behind the destructive aspects, we are obliged to pose the question of the change of structure which affects the libido of the masochistic fantasy. It is not enough to interpret destructivity in terms of the idea, entertained by some unconsciously, that to be beaten by the father is to be loved by him. What we must also envisage in the context of a psychotic organisation is the disappearance of certain oppositions. For instance, in this context, loving = killing.

---

[1] This whole exposition owes much to the discussion that took place in the research group of the IPA in 2001, comprising O. Kernberg, W. Grosman, J. Lutenberg, F. Urribarri, E. Spillius, G. Kohon, J. C. Rolland and myself.

But not in the manner of an anal-sadistic problematic which plays on a regression of the libido, saving the ego; this is not the case here. In the present scenario, we observe the transformation of an ego which can no longer play its role as it does in neurosis and normality. Here, loving = killing or being killed, which are considered as equivalents without any differentiation being possible. Changing – a sign of the fact that we are alive – means passing from life to death and vice-versa. It can thus be seen that the hypothesis of a return to the lost libido does not allow us to rediscover it in the form in which we are accustomed to recognising it. So it is clear that it has passed from the unconscious (the fantasy) to the id (the force) – that is, to a state in which opposing impulses coexist and can eventually form compromises, but giving priority to discharge (ejection) with the prevalence of the economic point of view. Conserving means giving oneself the possibility of working-through; evacuating makes all transformation impossible and exposes one to a return of what has been evacuated, through the real, in a hallucinatory form.

However that may be, we are faced again here with the blurring of boundaries at all levels of the psyche between the drives, between the drives and Ego, and between psychic reality and external reality. Working-through takes place around the transference, and the work of interpretation helps to differentiate more clearly the diverse registers of psychic activity. It is here that the countertransference will become the indispensable manifestation for thinking about a transference that cannot be expressed, but which may be the source of affects that are very difficult to tolerate for the analyst, who reacts to the patient's projections while being careful not to interpret them prematurely.[2]

On the signifier, on 'no meaning' and on non-meaning in ordinary thinking

An analyst will readily acknowledge that his work – something Freud had already said – cannot stray from the path which aims at giving a meaning to what is communicated to him by the patient. Initially, Freud's attention was attracted by all the structures of the psyche in which meaning appeared as non-sense or as 'no meaning' ('*pas de sens*', Lacan):[3] dreams, symptoms and more extensively all the manifestations of the unconscious. Was it not an illusion to claim to want to find reasons for the irrational (Jacob, 1976)? After all, a slip of the tongue may be understood as faulty switching of the neurons, and dreams may have no meaning (Hobson, 1989, 2002) or only play the role of a genetic

---

[2] Participation in the International Research Group on borderline states (unpublished).
[3] '*Pas de sens*' involves a play on '*pas*', which means both 'no' and 'step'; thus something that apparently has no meaning at one point may subsequently be seen as a 'step of/towards meaning' at another. [*Trans., this volume*]

reprogramming (Jouvet, 1993); with regard to symptoms, only a disturbance of the neuronal system is really causal (Edelman, 1989). As for the unconscious, there was scarcely any need to encumber it with the jumble of Freudian theory; the unconscious of Pierre Janet, of Saussure, and later on of Lévi-Strauss would free us of the interference of the signified so that once again a solid basis could be found for our demonstrations.

As the arguments were developed which invited us to stop searching for unreasonable reasons for the enigmatic manifestations of the psyche, preferring instead simpler and more easily demonstrable explanations, psychoanalysis pursued its path while discovering that it was not at fault for being too complicated but, on the contrary, for not being complicated enough.

Clinical experience seemed to suggest this more and more each day. Starting out from the neuroses, whose psychic mechanisms remained close to normality, it was constantly discovering new horizons. For example, repression did not suffice to explain all the states of pathology; other functions playing a similar role had to be taken into account: foreclosure, disavowal, and negation. With the first two, we were dealing with rejections outside the sphere of meaning. With splitting, a mode of double play opened up in the ego, which could say yes and no at the same time. As for negation, so deeply rooted in the structure of language, it led one to suspect all language of being a support for a negation.

Clearly, we had passed from the elucidation of these forms of psychic life marked by 'no meaning' [*pas de sens*] to other enigmas which challenged the foundations of ordinary logic. If we consider things from this angle, the whole of the last part of Freud's work is evidence of an extraordinary advance. I will just draw on the example of the death drive which has given rise to so many controversies and raised objections that are widely shared throughout a large part of the analytic world.

At the beginning of Freud's work, owing to a dazzling intuition, the pleasure principle came to occupy a central place that it had not enjoyed hitherto, throwing light on many manifestations in which the unconscious participates. Many analysts, still today, see it as an immovable dogma. But Freud himself was not entirely content with it. After more than twenty years of analytic practice, he discovered a 'beyond the pleasure principle', because of what he had learnt over six years about the role of repetition and acting out, even when no pleasure can be hoped for: the stuckness of the psyche, the bogging down of psychic life which stands still rather than advancing, sterile stereotypes of behaviour, deafness to the other's speech (Oh, come off it!), and, finally, a return to an 'autistic state' that is implicit in this compulsion to repeat.

It is clear, then, that if the pleasure principle had as a consequence the avoidance of unpleasure – namely, that which is threatened by castration as a punishment for transgression – other structures will perpetuate themselves in repetition, as if they were thumbing their noses to the threat of sanction and were even showing utter scorn for it. But behind the scenes a sense of unconscious guilt was operating, which, far from avoiding the sanction, or despising it, seemed unconsciously to be seeking it out. Hence Freud's preference for the expression '*need* for self-punishment'.

So we do not proceed simply to a 'beyond the pleasure principle', but to its reversal. In other words, this pleasure principle is no longer satisfied with simply avoiding unpleasure; it swings round, making unpleasure its pleasure while its pleasure becomes a search for unpleasure, and even pain. Here we are within a hair's breadth of non-meaning. Why is there such a switch of direction?

By making unpleasure switch over towards pleasure, there is certainly a search for self-punishment. But in this transformation apparently devoid of meaning, we can see the effect of identification with the aggressor. Behind the wish to thwart the analyst – who is nonetheless signified as a saviour – we may suspect the derision of his power of sanction. This subversive transformation is accompanied by a negation of a masochistic pleasure of being nothing less than one's own executioner.

It is not impossible that the only condition on which this search can continue calls for a reversal of meaning, in the terms that are associated with them: pleasure is replaced by unpleasure, anxiety by jouissance, avoidance by search, punishment by self-sanction, etc. Thus this switch is a reversal of the direction of meaning so that the idea of direction is maintained, which only has to be negativised for one to be able to continue to refer to it.

The question opens out finally on to the existence (or non-existence) of the meaning of the idea of the death drive, its signification or absurdity, its demonstrable or challengeable character.

This is why it is necessary to return to the question of meaning. I would say: only that which can be bound together has meaning – in other words, that which can tolerate a prior process of linking. Towards what end? Towards the goal of conserving what has been bound together. In order to achieve what? In order to keep the bound groups together. For what purpose? So as to be able to use these ensembles in the service of the pleasure principle, safeguarded by a principle of reality. If the destiny of this pleasure is to transform itself – for example, through sublimation – the principle of reality has to be constructed all the time, since no reference to a fixed or pre-existent entity is sufficient. Thus, if unbinding and destruction are infinite sources of reversal, binding and construction are no less so in respect of a subject who remains the object of knowledge and of a 'real' [*réel*] whose exploration is never completed.

So what we have continued to call fusion and defusion remains, as it were, the respiration of the psyche. One can neither stop it nor control it. Life and death are constantly interweaving their effects.

Trajectories of the drives

Although he had recognised their role and identified their functions at the outset of psychoanalysis, Freud was in no hurry to propose a theory of the drives. Two facts must be noted here: on the one hand, his certainty, which would never vary, with regard to the importance of sexuality, an unmoveable postulate concerning one of the two instinctual poles, whose transformation was confined to the Eros of the drives of life or of love; and, on the other, the aleatory identification of the other pillar of the drive theory, on which his opinion would vary in order to support his equally unmoveable conception of dualism. As it was the opposite of the former, it took Freud a long time to decide to recognise it, before finally adopting the hypothesis of the death drives or drives of destruction. It was a hypothesis that with time became a certainty for him.

In fact it was only with the first of his studies in the *Papers on Metapsychology*, 'Instincts and Their Vicissitudes' (1915c), that Freud elaborated a theory of instinctual (drive) life that was sufficiently articulated to resist the criticisms of his opponents or even of some of his disciples. The richness of this text – recognised by generations of psychoanalysts – is such that I can only take up certain points here to demonstrate my point of view on the last theory of the drives.

So I will just mention briefly the definition, with which everyone is familiar, of the drive as a frontier concept (which implies for Freud the moorings of the drive in the somatic, something he never renounced); the psychic representative of the stimuli arising from within the body and reaching the psyche; and the measure of the demand made upon the mind for work in consequence of its connection with the body (the idea of the psyche as the result of work is essential). It is also necessary to stress the idea of a drive montage (source, pressure, aim, object), which has raised many objections with regard to certain drives. I would just observe that, in his subsequent writings on the subject, Freud did not always go into details and discussed the theme of the drives in the vaguest of terms; however, vagueness is not the sign that he retreated in any way with regard to his view that psychic life is grounded in the drives. What direction are we to take?

Before going any further, we must recall that it is not enough to conceive of the drive – on the basis of pressure alone – as some sort of direct, dynamic, self-propelled life force reaching with the sureness attributed to the instinct its target on its object, realising its aim in an almost automatic manner. If there is indeed a difference between the Freudian '*Instinkt*' and '*Trieb*', it precludes this way of seeing things. Lacan, with his often piercing vision, showed that in reading Freud, the drive, in the text of 1915, should be conceived of as having a more complicated trajectory with a 'reversion from the source to the object' – namely, a trajectory that passes through the stages of the turning round of the drive against the self and the turning round of the drive into its opposite. I have proposed that the articulation of the two drive vicissitudes be called the *double reversal*, which supposes, when one combines them, the formation of a certain frame for drive activity. What I would like to point out here is that these processes, which Freud scarcely took up elsewhere, only seem to be possible because they concern aspects of sexual life (in particular, infantile sexual life). Which means that sexual life, far from letting itself be dominated by repression or tamed by sublimation, circumvents the obstacles that it encounters and succeeds in manifesting itself in the disguised forms offered by the double reversal. In fact, Freud simply applied his 'intellectual impartiality' to the phenomena that clinical experience had put before his eyes or given him to hear.

What are the roots of the unconscious sense of guilt?

In *Civilization and Its Discontents* (chap. VII), Freud develops the consequences of instinctual renunciation (a theme to which he granted a great deal of importance in *Moses and Monotheism*). Now the renunciation of instinctual satisfactions is the source of moral conscience (due to the fact that the superego takes over the renunciation), which, in return, always demands more. 'What happens in [the individual] to render his desire for aggression innocuous? Something very remarkable, which we should never have guessed and which is nevertheless quite obvious. His aggressiveness is introjected, internalised; it is, in point of fact, sent back to where it came from – that is, it is directed towards his own ego' (1930a, p. 123). It is taken over by the superego. Nothing here is comprehensible in Freud's thinking if we omit the idea that the erotic libido is now bound to and woven with the aggressive and destructive libido. And Freud maintains that a considerable quantity of aggression needs to develop in the child towards the authority that prevents him from having his first but nonetheless most important satisfactions. Irrespective of the nature of the instinctual privations that are required of him, he is forced to give up the satisfaction of his vengeful aggressiveness. By means of identification, he takes into himself the unassailable authority.

We can see here the difference with the *Papers on Metapsychology* (1915), which deal with the vicissitudes of the sexual drive. When the death drive makes it possible to form the concept behind the manifestation of the aggressive or destructive drive, it demands something more: the renunciation of instinctual satisfaction and the internalisation which integrates it with the superego. What is involved then is renunciation (letting go, consenting to sacrifice) of vengeful aggression (potentially threatening for 'the life' of the object, and the loss of its love and protection). What comes into play here is not other inventive forms of binding which disguise the primitive instinctual demand, but *unbinding*, a letting-go which is put in the service of the superego. This unbinding now opens up the path to a need for self-punishment. This is the *work of the negative* of the death drive. It will undergo a form of partial re-binding with the superego. But Freud never ceased to stress the fact that binding is not complete; it is not always in a position to bind everything. A portion of aggression remains unbound and is used by masochism against the ego's interests.

Would it still be possible to bind these forms of the work of the negative if they were understood from the perspective of being beaten and loved by the Father? It cannot be entirely excluded, if the Father is elevated to the expression (*Nom du Père*) of a divinity. For to love God is to suffer for him (as is true for any authority of which one becomes a slave). It can be clearly seen that the entanglements of fusion and defusion are inevitable. And how are these hypotheses that I am raising to be reconciled with the observation in *Moses and Monotheism* (1939a [1927–39]) which gives a central place to the murder of Moses as a paradigm of the original parricide, without introducing the death drive? It is worth remembering here that in non-neurotic and psychotic structures, the place of the father (in the mother's mind) is often empty. The omnipotent mother seems to have devoured him and seems to act as if he has no existence for the child. But – let's be fair – the father is party to his neutralisation and seems to have bought his tranquillity by abdicating his paternal power in favour of the mother, who is henceforth androgynous, omnipotent and paradoxically inconsistent behind her phallic mask. At any rate, if anything remains of his vestigial power, it serves to keep everything as it is, to avoid any change, in short, so that his 'little one' always remains an *infans*, through permanently attacking the structural links that he could construct. But ultimately this relational version says nothing about what is going on behind the scenes. In my view, it is instinctual life, the struggle of the Titans between Eros and the drives of destruction and their indomitable character, that will have the last word.

Provisional conclusion

I thus come to a controversial conclusion. Freud made the duality of the drives a postulate. By so doing, he justified the omnipresence of psychic conflict in the most elementary forms. Monopolising instinctual life under the sole angle of Eros is to call into question, is it not, a fundamental Freudian postulate? Why not? Simply because, even if we were to reject the death drive and refer only to the sexual drives, it would not do away with the divisions of the latter, whether from the angle of the antagonisms between the object-drives and the Ego-drives, between external aggressivity and masochistic self-aggression, and even between the constructive and destructive libido, thus freeing us of destruction once and for all. As far as I am concerned, I have tried to enrich the discussion by giving a platform to the detractors of the death drive. Although their ideas have not entirely convinced me, they have forced me to reflect.

If there are subjects in respect of which it is legitimate to hesitate without rushing to conclude, there are others, on the other hand, where doubt is not permitted.

Freud has been reproached – more often than not with reason – for forming a more or less solipsistic idea of the psyche, as if instinctual transformations were sufficient to account for its evolution and eventually for the dysfunctioning which could put a strain on its mental functioning. Since Melanie Klein, the object relation has occupied the foreground. However, the object relation was only a concept of replacement and did not change the basic question in any essential way. For Melanie Klein, like Freud, was interested almost exclusively in the internal world. Freud's drive was progressively dethroned in favour of internal object-relations; external objects played very little part. And it was Winnicott who was the first to study the role of the object (not only the internal object), founding the intermediary area and the creation of transitional objects, the lack of which could be observed in certain patients who often required treatments other than classical analysis.

Since then, the role of the object has been recognised by all but envisaged differently. In any case, the role of the response of the object (Green, 2005) to the instinctual demand was held to be essential. Whether the object's response encourages the emergence of the drives of destruction or whether it is alienating, obliging the child to adopt a false-self, is perhaps of less importance than the fact that the situation allows a fixation to the primary object to occur, with the corollary that the child cannot deal with mourning and so can never achieve separation from the object. This is even more the case when the image of the father places the child in a passive role, making him a witness to exchanges without having the right to speak – at any rate, when the father is not an active agent of separation promulgating prohibitions, facilitating the child's autonomy and recognition of the symbolic function of prohibitions, and participating in the birth of the superego. The role of separation between mother and child is compensated by the offer of another object to love and hate, triangulating the situation, orienting the psyche towards thirdness (Green, 1991).

If it is felt that I am overestimating the role of the Oedipus complex at stages when it is generally considered not yet formed, my answer would be that I am speaking here of a structure 'in germ', which is what Freud says to Fliess in his famous letter of 15 October 1897 (in Masson, 1985), concerning the effect of the tragedy of Sophocles: 'Everyone in the audience was once a *budding Oedipus*' (my italics). Later, in the article 'Psycho-Analysis' (1926f), he stated: 'the most important conflict with which a small child is faced is his relation to his parents, the "Oedipus complex".' Note that Freud says *the most important*, not *the first*, and he situates the Oedipus complex within the wider context of the child's relationship to his parents.

In any case, however the action of the object is envisaged, the active matrix henceforth is no longer the drives alone, nor the omnipotent object, but the drive–object pair, providing the basis for a new way of conceiving the psyche and the subject as effects of the relations of the inside with the outside.

References

Denis, A (2006). Principe de mort, destruction du sens, contresens Principle of death, destruction of meaning, misinterpretation]. In *Le dedans et le dehors* [The inside and the outside]. Paris: Presses Universitaires de France.

Edelman, G. M. (1989). *The Remembered Present: A Biological Theory of Consciousness.* New York: Basic Books.

Freud, S. (1911c [1910]). Psycho-Analytic Notes on an Autobiographical Account of a Case of Paranoia (Dementia Paranoides). *S.E.*, 12: 3.

Freud, S. (1915). *Papers on Metapsychology. S.E.*, 14: 105.

Freud, S. (1915c). Instincts and Their Vicissitudes. *S.E.*, 14: 111.

Freud, S. (1917e [1915]). Mourning and Melancholia. *S.E.*, 14: 239.

Freud, S. (1919e). A Child Is Being Beaten. *S.E.*, 17: 175–204.

Freud, S. (1923b). *The Ego and the Id. S.E.*, 19: 3–66.

Freud, S. (1924c). The Economic Problem of Masochism. *S.E.*, 19, 155–170.

Freud, S. (1925d [1924]). *An Autobiographical Study. S.E.*, 20: 3–74.

Freud, S. (1925h). Negation. *S.E.*, 19.

Freud, S. (1926f). Psycho-Analysis. *S.E.*, 20: 261.

Freud, S. (1927c). *The Future of an Illusion. S.E.*, 21: 3–56.

Freud, S. (1930a). *Civilization and its Discontents. S.E.*, 21: 59–145.

Freud, S. (1933a). *New Introductory Lectures on Psycho-Analysis. S.E.*, 22.

Freud, S. (1939a [1927–39]). *Moses and Monotheism. S.E.*, 23, 1–137.

Freud, S. (1940a [1938]). *An Outline of Psycho-Analysis. S.E.*, 23: 141–205.

Freud, S., & Bullitt W (1967). *Thomas Woodrow Wilson: A Psychological Study.* Boston, MA: Riverside Press.

Freud, S., & Pfister, O. (1963). *The Freud–Pfister Letters: Psychoanalysis and Faith*, trans. E. Mosbacher, ed. H. Meng & E. Freud. (Freud-Pfister Letters.) New York: Basic Books.

Green, A. (1991). De la tierceité [On thirdness]. In *La psychanalyse. Questions pour demain* [Psychoanalysis: Questions for tomorrow]. Monograph of the Paris Psychoanalytic Society. Paris: Presses Universitaires de France.

Green, A. (2000). La mort dans la vie [Life in death]. In *L'invention de la pulsion de la mort* [The invention of the death drive], ed. J. Guillaumin. Paris: Dunod.

Green, A. (2005). *Key Ideas for a Contemporary Psychoanalysis: Misrecognition and Recognition on the Unconscious*, trans. A. Weller. London: Routledge.

Hobson, J. A. (1989). *The Dreaming Brain: How the Brain Creates Both the Sense and the Nonsense of Dreams.* New York: Basic Books.

Hobson, J. A. (2002). *Dreaming: An Introduction to the Science of Sleep?* New York: Oxford University Press.

Jacob, F. (1976). *La logique du vivant.* Paris: Gallimard. [*The Logic of Living.* Princeton, NJ: Princeton University Press, 1993.]

Jouvet, M. (1993). *Le sommeil et le rêve.* Paris: Odile Jacob. [*The Paradox of Sleep: The Story of Dreaming.* Boston, MA: MIT Press, 1999.]

Laplanche, J. (1970). *Vie et mort en psychanalyse.* Paris: Flammarion. [*Life and Death in Psychoanalysis.* Baltimore, MD: Johns Hopkins Press, 1976.]

Masson, J. M. (Ed.) (1985). *The Complete Letters of Sigmund Freud to Wilhelm Fliess, 1887–1904.* Cambridge, MA: Belknap.

Rolland, J.-C. (1999). Eros dolorosus. *Revue Française de Psychosomatique, 15*: 79–85.

27 (EROTOGENIC) MASOCHISM AND THE PLEASURE PRINCIPLE [1]

Benno Rosenberg

Benno Rosenberg is a philosopher, a psychologist and a full member of the Paris Psychoanalytical Society. From 1975 on, he participated in the development of the Centre for Psychoanalysis and Psychotherapy (Mental Health Association, 13th *arrondissement*, Paris) with E. Kestemberg, C. Guedeney and A. Gibeault. His highly original outlook and thorough knowledge of Freud's writings led him to focus on masochism and on the issues that it involves. He has written several articles on the subject, which have formed the basis of his *Masochisme mortifère et masochisme gardien de la vie* [Deadly masochism and life-preserving masochism] (PUF, 1991). The concept of the death drive has given rise to much disagreement among psychoanalysts, but Benno Rosenberg is a strong supporter of the hypothesis because, in his opinion, it helps us to understand more clearly the part played by masochism in mental life.

A. Modification of the pleasure principle in accordance with masochism

1. *The problem*

Masochism, as a clinical fact, poses a twofold problem for the pleasure principle: on the one hand, there is a theoretical problem concerning the *intelligibility* of masochism and of the pleasure principle, by the same token; on the other hand, there is a clinical if not vital problem, 'For if mental processes are governed by the pleasure principle in such a way that their first aim is the avoidance of unpleasure and the obtaining of pleasure, *masochism is incomprehensible*' (Freud, 1924c, p. 159, my italics).

---

[1] This paper first appeared as a part of an article under the title of 'Masochisme mortifère et masochisme gardien de la vie', in *Les Cahiers du Centre de Psychanalyse et de Psychothérapie*, 5 (1982), and in a collection of articles under the same title published by Presses Universitaires de France in 1991. It was translated by Ann Levy.

Given that Freud knew about masochism and wrote about it for twenty years prior to this article, and that he knew about the pleasure principle and had defined it even earlier, how can we explain that it was only in 1924 that he discovered the contradiction between them which rendered their coexistence incomprehensible? The obvious answer is this: until 1924, Freud was essentially speaking about one form of masochism, the so-called feminine or libidinal masochism, objectal masochism, which only posed the problems of (co)excitation and sexual satisfaction. However, in this article, it was no longer only a question of feminine masochism, but that of its two other forms, erotogenic and moral masochism. His emphasis on erotogenic masochism raised a quite different type of problem, that of destructiveness and of self-destruction: Freud was more able to take this vital problem into consideration once he established a basis for it after 1920, when he had introduced the concept of the death drive.[2] Freud made the unintelligibility of the theory explicit in the lines immediately following the above quotation, while completing it with the vital-existential problem: 'If pain and unpleasure can be not simply warnings but actually aims, the pleasure principle is paralysed – it is as though the watchman over our mental life were put out of action by a drug' (p. 159). Here, then, erotogenic masochism was seen to be dangerous for our mental life by putting the pleasure principle out of action. But, there was more: 'Masochism appears to us in the light of a *great danger*, which is in no way true of its counterpart, sadism. We are tempted to call the pleasure principle the watchman over our life rather than merely over our mental life' (p. 159, my italics). If Freud referred here to masochism and not to erotogenic masochism as representing a danger for our mental life and for life itself, it was because erotogenic masochism, while one of the forms of masochism, is finally that from which the other forms are deployed.

To sum up the situation, the problem presented itself in the following way: on the one hand, the fundamental clinical fact of erotogenic masochism; on the other, the (old) theory of the pleasure principle. Freud chose to modify the theory. This choice was important since the pleasure principle was the sovereign law which directly or indirectly (through the intermediary of the reality principle) governed all mental processes; the choice was urgent because in this text the pleasure principle was given the role of a vital warning, which meant that not only were the libidinal aims at stake but, once again, self-preservation.

With that, it would seem necessary to be sensitive to the novelty in Freud's approach expressed in these two introductory pages where he spoke about masochism with respect to the pleasure principle. 'The incomprehensibility' of masochism did not incite him *to construct a theory of masochism* to make it more understandable, as he had done before. On the contrary, this

---

[2] In this paper, the author has deliberately chosen to translate the German term '*Trieb*' by 'drive' in spite of Strachey's preference for 'instinct' in the *Standard Edition*. [*Trans*.]

'incomprehensibility', or the paradox of masochism, was *accepted as such*, and became the starting point for modifying the psychoanalytic theory itself (and the pleasure principle to begin with), implicitly accused of making a clinical fact incomprehensible – that is, of being unable to integrate it. It was thus only in 1924, when 'The Economic Problem of Masochism' was written that masochism, as a fact, accepted and respected in its authentic originality, made its true entrance into analytic theory.

2. *Theoretical modification of the pleasure principle; rehabilitation of excitation*

Before mentioning any modification, Freud begins by restating what used to be his most constant theory concerning the pleasure principle (except for a few isolated doubts): 'It will be remembered that we have taken the view that the principle which governs all mental processes is a special case of Fechner's *"tendency towards stability"*, and have accordingly attributed to the mental apparatus the purpose of *reducing to nothing*, or at least of keeping as low as possible, the sums of excitation which flow in upon it. Barbara Low has suggested the name of *"Nirvana principle"* for this supposed tendency . . .' (p. 159, my italics). This summary does not entirely do justice to Freud for his conceptions concerning the pleasure principle, but it has the merit of posing the question in the most radical form possible, making it easier and clearer to discuss. What was Freud's attitude towards this theory which he supported for a quarter of a century and which he did not entirely abandon? '*But we have unhesitatingly identified the pleasure–unpleasure principle with this Nirvana principle*' (p. 159, my italics). Indeed, Freud goes on to say: 'It seems that in the series of feelings of tension we have a direct sense of the increase and decrease of amounts of stimulus and *it cannot be doubted that there are pleasurable tensions and unpleasurable relaxations of tension*' (p. 160, my italics). It is as if Freud's eyes were opening to clinical facts, or simply to facts of life that he had succeeded (so to speak) in not seeing for a quarter of a century. If we add to that, that 'The state of sexual excitation is the most striking example of a pleasurable increase of stimulus of this sort . . .' (p. 160), we are all the more astonished: indeed, we have a thinker who had placed sexuality at the heart of his theory only to discover that for a quarter of a century, he had not realised that states of sexual excitation were accompanied by pleasure![3] And here is Freud's conclusion to this question: '*Pleasure and unpleasure, therefore, cannot be referred to as an increase or decrease of a quantity (which we describe as "tension due to stimulus")*, although they obviously

---

[3] Cherubino, in *The Marriage of Figaro*, knew this. In the romance ('*Voi che sapete* . . .') which he addressed to the Countess (and to *all* the ladies who awakened his desire), incessant excitation haunted him and was experienced in terms of martyrdom, subjecting him day and night to emotions compared to flames alternating with ice, sighs, palpitations and trembling with no peace to be found. But he knows, in spite of this, that this extremely tense excitation 'is sheer delight':

have a great deal to do with that factor. It appears that they depend not on this quantitative factor, but on some characteristic of it which we can only describe as a qualitative one' (p. 160, my italics). The issue was not to replace one theory by another, but to expound on and enlarge the existing theory, as Freud usually did. Indeed, Freud did not deny – and this will be found in his texts written after 1924 – the affirmation that pleasure–unpleasure is determined, *at least in part*, by the quantity of excitation. But, at the same time, he admitted that both increases in the tension of excitation accompanied by pleasure and unpleasurable relaxations of tensions existed; therefore, the quantitative point of view was not sufficient and had to be completed by a qualitative aspect. Must this be seen as the final abandonment of Freudian scientificity (the exclusively quantitative aspect) and the moment of definitive emancipation, in principle, of psychoanalysis from what was left of the methodology belonging to the experimental sciences? If this is so, we would have to conclude that taking *erotogenic* masochism into consideration was necessary for that.

The astonishment expressed at the idea that it took Freud a quarter of a century to realise that the quantitative point of view of excitation was insufficient to define pleasure–unpleasure does not concern Freud, *the man*. We believe it preferable and more productive to think about the theoretical constellation which can produce certain changes. Indeed, Freud had already expressed, although in isolated instances, certain doubts about defining the pleasure principle according to the quantity of excitation. For example, in *Instincts and Their Vicissitudes*, where this theory seemed to have for him a *hypothetical character*, '. . . unpleasurable feelings are connected with an increase and pleasurable feelings with a decrease of stimulus. We will, however, carefully preserve this *assumption in its present highly indefinite form*, until we succeed, if that is possible, in discovering what sort of relation exists between pleasure and unpleasure, on the one hand, and fluctuations in the amounts of stimulus

> You ladies who know what love is,
> See if it is what I have in my heart.
> All that I feel I will explain;
> Since it is new to me, I don't understand it,
> I have a feeling full of desire,
> Which now is pleasure, now is torment.
> I freeze, then I feel my spirit all ablaze,
> And the next moment turn again to ice.
> I seek for a treasure outside of myself,
> I know not who holds it nor what it is.
> I sigh and I groan without wishing to,
> I flutter and tremble without knowing why.
> I find no peace by night or day,
> *But yet to languish thus is sheer delight.*
> (Lorenzo da Ponte,
> *The Marriage of Figaro*,
> English translation contained in
> the libretto, my italics)

affecting mental life, on the other . . .' (1915c, pp. 120–121, my italics). There are other texts where Freud expresses such doubts. In 'On Narcissism: An Introduction' (1914c), when he evoked hypochondria, Freud asked himself the question: '. . . why this damming-up of libido in the ego should have to be experienced as unpleasurable. I shall content myself with the answer that unpleasure is always the expression of a higher degree of tension, and that therefore what is happening is that a quantity in the field of material events is being transformed here as elsewhere into the psychical quality of unpleasure. *Nevertheless it may be that what is decisive for the generation of unpleasure is not the absolute magnitude of the material event, but rather some particular function of that absolute magnitude . . .*' (p. 85, my italics). And again, this appeared in *Beyond the Pleasure Principle* (1920g), for example. It was therefore not a personal problem but a propitious theoretical constellation which enabled Freud to see what had to be modified in order to define pleasure. This constellation was not put into place until after 1920; there had to be the change in the theory of drives, and the theory of erotogenic masochism had to be elaborated in accordance with this *new theory of drives* in order for the pleasure principle to be modified starting from this new theory of masochism.

Basically, what does Freud tell us? Increasing the tension of excitation is still unpleasurable, but nevertheless it can be experienced as pleasure under certain conditions. *Here, it would seem to me that the model of masochism is a determining factor: this is what teaches us that certain increases in the tension of excitation, which indeed have to do with pain or unpleasure, can be experienced as pleasure.*

By saying this, we are emphasising the importance of the *concept* of the death drive for this renewal. In fact, Freud wrote, 'Every unpleasure ought thus to coincide with a heightening, and every pleasure with a lowering, of mental tension due to stimulus; *the Nirvana principle (and the pleasure principle which is supposedly identical with it) would be entirely in the service of the death instincts,* whose aim is to conduct the restlessness of life into the stability of the inorganic state . . .' (1924c, pp. 159–160, my italics). This means that Freud realised that if he maintained his old definition of the pleasure principle in an absolute and unchanging way, he would be putting it in the service of the death drive, which seemed unacceptable to him, and rightly so. Whether or not we believe in the death drive, it is clear that the *concept* of the death drive was incontestably helpful to the theory at that point.

It is now necessary for us to consider two points related to changes which occurred in the description of the pleasure principle:

1. The theoretical basis that Freud gave to these modifications, which is a description of the genesis of the pleasure principle starting from the drives, or the origin of the pleasure principle in drives.
2. Freud tried to describe, in a hypothetical form, this quality which was added to the quantitative definition of the pleasure principle, and he then introduced the notions of rhythm and, above all, time.

We shall therefore first discuss the origin of the pleasure principle in the drives, and then masochism and its relationship to time.

3. *The theoretical modification of the pleasure principle: its origin in the drives*

The pleasure principle has always been the 'first' starting point, because it characterised the older, primary processes. In 'Formulations on the Two Principles of Mental Functioning', Freud wrote, 'In the psychology which is founded on psycho-analysis we have become accustomed to taking as our starting point the unconscious mental processes, with the peculiarities of which we have become acquainted through analysis. We consider these to be the older, primary processes, the residues of a phase of development in which they were the only kind of mental process. The governing purpose obeyed by these primary processes is easy to recognise; it is described as the pleasure–unpleasure principle, or more shortly the pleasure principle' (1911b, pp. 218–219). The pleasure principle was therefore the first law governing how the mental processes functioned; the reality principle which was a modification of it was developed from this. This situation was changed in the context of 'The Economic Problem of Masochism'. Here is what Freud wrote: 'However this may be, we must perceive that the Nirvana principle, belonging as it does to the death instinct, *has undergone a modification in living organisms through which it has become the pleasure principle*; and we shall henceforward avoid regarding the two principles as one' (1924c, p. 160, my italics).

Thus, in the same way that the reality principle was deduced from the pleasure principle, in the article which interests us here, the pleasure principle itself was secondary, in that it was a modification of the Nirvana principle which 'preceded' it. Of course, we are not referring to temporo-chronological relationships; but, speaking metapsychologically, Freud presented the pleasure principle as a modification of another principle, and we need to understand in what conditions this modification occurred. Freud went on to say, 'It is not difficult, if we care to follow up this line of thought, to guess what power was the source of the modification. *It can only be the life instinct, the libido*, which has thus, *alongside of the death instinct*, seized upon a share in the regulation of the processes of life' (p. 160, my italics). The pleasure principle resulted therefore from a modification made to the Nirvana principle, a modification which the libido brought or imposed on the law of functioning (Nirvana principle) of the death drive. This can be illustrated using the metaphor of a parallelogram of forces: the two forces, the death drive and the life drive, produce a resulting force, the pleasure principle.

This modification could not have been made, of course, without taking into account what has been called a fusion of the drives, where the death drive is bound by the libido.

The pleasure principle thus changed essentially in character. No longer could its functioning be *defined in an absolute way* (absolute starting point) by the quantity of excitation: on the contrary, we can suppose that there are variations from one person to another, and changes occur within the same individual. Indeed, as we know, the fusion of the drives depends on the object: it undergoes a primary elaboration within the framework of the mother–child dyad and is dependent, of course, on the particular conditions of this. There is more: according to how fusions–defusions of drives change in the life of an individual, the functioning of the pleasure principle changes as well. This corresponds to clinical facts. To cite but one example, the claim to pleasure and the conditions for this are fundamentally different for psychotics and for neurotics. We are all familiar with the cases of certain chronically ill psychotics who need to masturbate from morning till night in order to drastically reduce the unbearable tension of excitation (and the anxiety they feel that accompanies it). In this way, they come very close to a *quantitative definition of pleasure as a need to drastically reduce the tension of excitation*, which is not usually the case for neurotics who can relatively better tolerate their excitation (which does not become traumatic). *That the pleasure principle is relative according to individuals, moments and situations gives a basis and an aim to the analytic cure: one of its objectives is a change in the qualitative definition of the pleasure principle of our patients, their claim to pleasure, the urgency with which satisfaction is sought, etc.*

It is necessary to go back to the fusion of drives and the origin of the pleasure principle. What must be understood is the *moment of primary fusions of drives* at the foundation of this principle, not to 'date' it, but to note with what other event it may be contemporary. This will help us to understand, therefore, why these discussions are found in 'The Economic Problem of Masochism'. The other event that Freud referred to is primary erotogenic masochism; he writes, 'This masochism [primary erotogenic] would thus be evidence of, and a remainder from, the phase of development in which the coalescence, which is so important for life, between the death instinct and Eros took place' (p. 164). Masochism and the pleasure principle are the 'products' of this fusion, of this primary fusion–coalescence of drives. *These are the two faces, the two aspects of the same psychic moment*, a formative moment, the first structuring of the archaic ego, constituting itself around the primary erotogenic masochistic nucleus whose governing law is the pleasure principle.

What is the significance of this profound solidarity between masochism and the pleasure principle for the comprehension of masochism and through it of the psychoanalytic notion of pleasure? According to the old definition which identified the pleasure principle and the Nirvana principle, the pleasure principle led to the realisation of the aims of the death drive; pleasure defined as 'reducing' the tension of excitation 'to zero' then paradoxically became the equivalent of extinction, of self-destruction, of death. *It is even probable that such self-destruction cannot be experienced at one or another moment as displeasure, which is an obvious contradiction, inherent in this absolute pleasure.* The influence of masochism on the concept of the pleasure principle enables this self-destructive aspiration towards absolute pleasure to be avoided, and the pleasure principle to be experienced in a more relative way. *Would it be the same to say that Freud modified the pleasure principle according to the 'paradox' inherent in masochism, and that masochistic pleasure became the model for pleasure?* We think so, and believe that this position is in agreement with 'The Economic Problem of Masochism' without being in disagreement with psychoanalytic theory. *Thus, pleasure becomes a combination of pleasure and unpleasure, harbouring within itself a variable but inevitable dose of masochism.* This pleasure–unpleasure, which is pleasure, is variable; at certain times it comes close to (almost) pure pleasure when the component of unpleasure tends towards zero, and, inversely, it is experienced as pure unpleasure when the component of pleasure tends to fade. If pleasure is pleasure–unpleasure, *this is due to a complex and unitary process composed of excitation (unpleasure aspect) as well as discharge (pleasure aspect): discharge 'rubs off' (retroaction) on excitation, which in turn does not totally disappear in discharge.* The old way of formulating the pleasure principle *cut off excitation from discharge*, unpleasure from pleasure, inside the dialectic of pleasure. This 'cut-off' rendered masochism – wherein pleasure and unpleasure are necessarily interdependent – 'paradoxical'. On the other hand, *the internal dialectic of pleasure became manifest in the masochistic pleasure which then appeared, more than any other, as the fundamental model of pleasure.* The old formulation of the pleasure principle, by cutting off excitation from discharge in this way, hypostasised, immobilised two terms linked in a *living process containing both its own temporality and its own internal rhythm* (see above quotation).

The relationship linking masochism, the pleasure principle and time must be examined now.

B. Masochism, the pleasure principle and internal continuity-temporality

As has been shown, Freud modified the exclusively quantitative definition of the pleasure principle by adding a qualitative aspect. Concerning this qualitative characteristic, he set forth a hypothesis: 'If we were able to say what this qualitative characteristic is, we should be much further advanced in psychology. Perhaps it is the rhythm, *the temporal sequence of changes*, rises and falls in the quantity of stimulus. We do not know' (1924c, p. 160, my italics). This text invites us to reflect upon how the pleasure principle and masochism are related to time. The problem here is twofold. First of all, it is necessary to ask what *connection there is between the pleasure principle and temporality*. In other words, why was the question of time and temporality essential to the modification which had to be introduced in the theoretical formulation of the pleasure principle so that it could be adapted to the clinical facts, particularly to the clinical fact of erotogenic masochism? Second, we must ask what *link exists between time and masochism*. We have stated that the change made in formulating the pleasure principle consisted in integrating masochism into its definition. If this is so, we have to know in what way masochism is linked to time and if it is time which changes the understanding of the pleasure principle.

In order to try to answer these two questions, we must go back and reconsider the pleasure principle as it was when it was exclusively defined by the quantity of excitation (or the Nirvana principle). This was not a totally unrealistic assumption. Indeed, it corresponded to a metapsychological reality, since, as we have seen, the Nirvana principle was the law by which the death drive functions before it was linked by the libido, before the fusion of drives changed the nature of the pleasure principle. It might just as well be said that what is being referred to here is a reality corresponding to the functioning of the death instinct before the advent of masochism – that is, a pre-masochistic situation where masochism is the product of this primary fusion of drives.

How does the pleasure principle function in this hypothesis? Let us go back to what Freud said about this: 'It will be remembered that we have taken the view that the principle which governs all mental processes is a special case of Fechner's "tendency towards stability", and have accordingly attributed to the mental apparatus the purpose of *reducing to nothing*, or at least of keeping as low as possible, the sums of excitation which flow in upon it' (1924c, p. 159, my italics). This is as much as saying that, in this hypothesis, the pleasure principle functions in terms of 'all or nothing', and the sooner the excitation is gotten rid of (less excitation means less unpleasure) the better.

Therefore, *it could almost be said that the pleasure principle functions in terms of 'all or nothing', and, if we like, in terms of 'all and right now'*. Of course, this is a hypothesis; the pleasure principle does not ever function in this way. But Freud did consider this, and for quite some time. Hence, in the 'Two Principles of Mental Functioning', he said in a famous note, 'It will rightly be objected that *an organisation which was a slave to the pleasure principle* and neglected the reality of the external world could *not maintain itself alive for the shortest time*, so that it could not have come into existence at all' (1911b, p. 220, my italics).

It must be pointed out that in this passage, concerning the question at hand, both the allusion to time, as well as the allusion to the fact that the mental apparatus would be destroyed if it actually functioned according to an extreme version of the pleasure principle, lead to thinking that such a pleasure principle would prevent the mental apparatus from *lasting* and even from *existing*. This is important since if, as was stated above, the pleasure principle transforms itself in relation to masochism, the *existence and duration of mental organisation would depend on masochism*.

This passage also remarkably illustrates the evolution of Freud's ideas. Indeed, it shows that Freud realised how deathly and destructive the consequences of his conception of the pleasure principle would be, but he was not able to comprehend the meaning that this would have until his new theory of the drives had been formulated and the new theory of masochism which followed from it.

Let us go back to the old form of the pleasure principle. It functions in terms of 'all or nothing' and 'all and right now', in a sort of temporal punctuality, demanding immediate discharge. This would have posed inextricable problems for the mental apparatus; however, only one aspect will be dealt with here: *sexual excitation itself would have been impossible, since it has to do with unpleasure, thus, making even discharge finally impossible*, which is obviously a contradiction within the pleasure principle defined in this way. In order for excitation to be possible, particularly sexual excitation, there has to be a waiting time during which discharge is necessarily postponed. Temporal punctuality must be replaced by the possibility of temporal succession. But any waiting or postponement has to do with excitation and unpleasure. *Now it would seem to us that unpleasure is possible only through masochism, considered here of course in the large sense as the mental capacity to withstand unpleasure.* Postponing pleasure and the ability to withstand unpleasure has, of course, to do with the reality principle. But we believe that the pleasure principle cannot be changed into the principle of reality (both in 'The Two Principles of Mental Functioning' and in the article under study, the reality principle is a modification of the pleasure principle) without having within itself the potential for postponing pleasure – that is, this ability to withstand unpleasure. In other words, it is because the pleasure principle includes masochistic pleasure and because it implies the possibility of pleasure of unpleasure it can transform itself into the reality principle.

In this context, it would be astonishing if we did not mention what was presented by Freud as the nucleus *par excellence* of the postponement of satisfaction that is the hallucinatory satisfaction of wishes. It must therefore be reconsidered in this perspective and in this context. Here is how Freud presented hallucinatory satisfaction as a response to primary distress in 'Formulations on the Two Principles of Mental Functioning' in the note that was quoted above: 'It [the infant] probably hallucinates the fulfilment of its internal needs; *it betrays its unpleasure*, when there is an increase of stimulus and an absence of satisfaction, by the motor discharge of screaming and beating about with its arms and legs, and *it then experiences the satisfaction it has hallucinated*' (1911b, p. 220, my italics). According to this text, hallucinatory satisfaction, while providing the possibility of waiting for satisfaction, does not prevent distress, since the baby 'betrays' his unpleasure *at the same time. Moreover, hallucinatory satisfaction has meaning only in relation to the state of distress and is only possible when and only when distress is experienced.* Thus, there is concomitance between distress and hallucinatory satisfaction. If hallucinatory satisfaction of wishes could prevent a state of distress from existing, whereas it can only diminish it, satisfaction would no longer be necessary (we would all have died from hallucinatory satisfaction . . .) and, paradoxically, nor would hallucinatory satisfaction. According to such an assumption, giving up of hallucinatory satisfaction to which Freud refers in the 'Formulations on the Two Principles of Mental Functioning', would not be understandable: 'It was only the non-occurrence of the expected satisfaction, the disappointment experienced, that led to the abandonment of this attempt at satisfaction by means of hallucination' (1911b, p. 219). It is because the state of distress *continued* at the same time as hallucinatory satisfaction, and that it even increased in intensity, that the disappointment mentioned by Freud is understandable. From this, *the question of withstanding distress remains unresolved, and this (major) unpleasure, like the others, implies that masochism is necessary in order to understand how it is withstood*. The importance of the state of distress in the future development of the individual and his mental apparatus does not need to be demonstrated: it is precisely through the hallucinatory satisfaction of wishes that the development of the phantasy life of the individual is set into motion. But all this is conditioned by *primary erotogenic masochism which, by making distress possible/liveable, permits hallucinatory satisfaction to exist*. When Freud in 'The Economic Problem of Masochism', speaks about a part of the death drive which does not participate in displacement and projection '. . . outwards . . . it remains inside the organism, and with the help of the accompanying sexual excitation . . . becomes libidinally bound there' (1924c, pp. 163–164) thereby founding 'original, erotogenic masochism', he shows us the seed from which mental life develops by making the unpleasure in the state of primary distress possible – like all unpleasure, in fact.

To come back to the question of internal temporality–continuity: without erotogenic masochism, and especially without the primary masochistic nucleus reorientating the pleasure principle so that unpleasure is integrated, all that is not immediate discharge, all postponement, and all temporal successiveness would be impossible because a relative unpleasure would be implied. This may seem far from our clinical concerns. The 'time' which we deal with while listening to our patients is related to the succession of their associations, the unfolding of their memories, perceptions and phantasy life. *Masochism insures the duration, the internal continuity; it is the bridge which joins the timelessness of the id to the specific temporality of the preconscious–conscious system, or, in the new topic, of the conscious and unconscious ego.* Masochism is the condition and the first form of work of preconscious temporality which founds the 'time' that we encounter in our clinical experience. It is the condition for the existence of mental processes and intervenes in the analytic process by the very fact that it can take place – that is, that the patient can stand the session, that he does not interrupt the treatment or, on the contrary, that the analysis does not become interminable. I remember a psychotic (schizophrenic) adolescent whom I had in treatment several years ago, and who, at the beginning of his analysis, could only stay for a few minutes of his session, so much was he overwhelmed by his excitation and by the anxiety that followed it. Little by little, he was able to stay longer, and this as much thanks to a diminishing of his excitation as his having learned to bear it – 'learning' that is essentially masochistic. Certain interruptions of treatment are examples of this, as are the unending treatments by a sort of masochistic hypercathexis of the analytic situation. Successful cures are situated between these two extremes; in these, the primary masochistic nucleus is working in the background and insures the continuity of the analytic process and within this, of psychic working out.

References

Freud, S. (1911b). Formulations on the Two Principles of Mental Functioning. *S.E.*, 12.
Freud, S. (1914c). On Narcissism: An Introduction. *S.E.*, 14.
Freud, S. (1915c). Instincts and Their Vicissitudes. *S.E.*, 14.
Freud, S. (1920g). *Beyond the Pleasure Principle. S.E.*, 18.
Freud, S. (1924c). The Economic Problem of Masochism. *S.E.*, 19.

28 SEXUALISATION AND DESEXUALISATION IN PSYCHOANALYSIS

René Roussillon

> **René Roussillon** is a full member of the Paris Psychoanalytical Society and professor of clinical psychopathology and clinical psychology in the Lumière University of Lyon. He has focused particularly on narcissistic identity disorders and on the way in which these impact on the psychoanalytic setting, particularly in the treatment of borderline patients.
>
> He has written many articles, and five books of his are especially important: *Paradoxes et situations limites de la psychanalyse* [Paradoxes and borderline situations in psychoanalysis] (PUF, 1991); *Logiques et archéologiques du cadre psychanalytique* [Logics and archaeologics of the psychoanalytic setting] (PUF, 1995); *Agonie, clivage et symbolisation* [Agony, splitting and symbolization] (PUF, 1999); *Le jeu et l'entre je(u)* [Playing and interplaying] (PUF, 2008); and *Le transitionnel, le sexuel et la réflexivité* [The transitional, the sexual, and reflexivity] (Dunod, 2008).

The sexual remains one of the crucial themes in contemporary psychoanalysis; it also remains one of the 'shibboleths' of Freudian psychoanalysis. But its central importance is in fact under threat from certain developments in Anglophone psychoanalysis that, especially under the banner of narcissism and 'self' analysis, are strangely diminishing its impact and scope of reference. It is also a theme that has recently returned to 'fashion' through the centenary of the writing of the *Three Essays* (1905d) and more generally in the psychoanalytic literature, in all the discussions concerning the necessity and pertinence of the concept of the drive as it has been developing in the international literature.

Despite these debates, yet perhaps even more so revealed by them, in Francophone psychoanalysis, the sexual remains a major reference point, even a defining one. But is this reference necessarily clear and unambiguous? Although all French psychoanalysts acknowledge its central position in metapsychology, do they agree about what precisely it covers, or does the apparent consensus that seems to unite them under its emblem in fact conceal some divergences as to the essence of what the concept involves?

Often, and the same probably applies to many concepts that have this same defining quality, the sexual and what it covers seems self-evident and to need no definition, as if its mere utterance sufficed to describe it and subdivide its issues.

My reflection starts from the opposite assertion, which is that this is a highly problematic concept that probably still needs to be refined in contemporary psychoanalytic theory and thought, and that there is a real difficulty in the use and reference that can be made of it by psychoanalysts in practical terms.

The problem

First of all, it seems to me important to remember that psychoanalysis is not and could never be a 'sexology' – that is, a field of knowledge concerning the sexual and sexuality – nor a 'psychology' of the sexual or sexuality.

What it means instead is thinking about the role of the sexual in the psychic process and even more specifically in psychic functioning during the session, while taking account of its specific characteristics.

It also seems to me, although of course I will return to this essential point, that the evolutionary trend in the theorisation of the sexual in psychoanalytic metapsychology emphasises sufficiently the effort to adjust the theorisation to the needs of the metapsychology 'of the psychic course of events', as Freud wrote in 1911 – that is to say, of the psychic process, and specifically the psychic process during the session.

In other words, it seems to me that one of the lines of development in the psychoanalytic theorisation of the sexual is increasingly directed at inscribing it in what I call a 'metapsychology of processes'.

This means, more specifically, that the position of the sexual and sexuality in psychoanalytic thought increasingly seems to have to be evaluated by the yardstick of the issues of symbolisation and subjective appropriation that vectorise psychoanalytic practice and the psychic work of the session. It is according to and starting from the position and the role of the sexual in symbolisation and subjectivation that psychoanalysis makes its contribution to an understanding of human sexuality.

This problematic and these difficulties underlie the detours, even bifurcations, that the concept has undergone throughout the history of psychoanalytic thought and its various applications, which seem to me to tend increasingly to separate sexuality as a behaviour from the sexual as a specific psychic process of cathexis.

At the outset, and this is the first aspect of the evolution and therefore also the difficulty, the sexual and sexuality do not overlap, no longer overlap, although they are not totally disconnected either. There is some sexual beyond sexuality, some sexuality apprehended as 'sexual behaviour' and, moreover, there is some non-sexual in sexuality itself, as the sexualisation of certain psychic functions or functioning found in clinical practice sufficiently emphasises.

The same applies to the connection between the sexual and the drive.

Here too there is no exact overlap between terms. Freud was able to define the self-preservative drives that are 'drive-based' but can oppose the 'sexual' drives, in which he was able to describe some forms of transformation of the sexual drives that can themselves 'be desexualised' in their progress and their transposition.

The mere statement of these formulations is enough to convey at the outset the complexity of the issues involved and the subtleties of how they are treated.

I cannot claim to encompass all this complexity in the present framework of reflection, and I would be satisfied for my part with pointing out certain aspects.

I will start with the assertion, presented as my first line of reflection, that *the sexual is not and could never be similar to itself in psychoanalysis*, that it is necessarily the site of a diversion that determines it less 'in itself' than as a form of process that is specifically characterised by its metaphorising capacity, its generative capacity.

In other words, it seems to me that the evolution of psychoanalytic thought leads us to place increasing emphasis on a processual dimension of the sexual, on the sexualisation or desexualisation processes that psychic material is likely to encounter 'in the course of psychic events'.

But before reaching that stage and to be well placed to do so, it is necessary to recall certain points that are essential here.

The identical and the different: Towards the primal scene

Although the drive is born in/of difference, and born of what is non-identical to itself, it tends to restore identity: at its origin, it is pleasure in the same, pleasure in discovering the same, the identical, whether this is 'identity of perception' according to the primary-process model, or 'identity of thought' according to the more relative and moderate secondary-process model.

The sexual is engendered by difference but its primary meaning consists in the desire to reduce difference, the attempt to find the identical in the other, to produce the identical from the other.

It is only in its historical and then intrapsychic course[1] that the drive integrates the need to recognise and accept its own origin, that it can be constituted as a pleasure taken in and by difference, that it 'discovers' difference

---

[1] Cf. R. Roussillon, 'Le rôle charnière de l'angoisse de castration' [The pivotal role of castration anxiety], in *Le mal être (angoisse et violence)* [Malaise (anxiety and violence)], ed. J. Cournut et al. (Paris: Presses Universitaires de France, 1998).

and its organising role, that it discovers that it is the 'product' of this difference, that it discovers and recognises that it is the 'sexual' outcome of a *sexion*.[2]

We know that in this process, the encounter with the question of the father's position – the paternal value and the models it conveys – is essential. It is the father's symbolic function that makes it possible to recognise the value of the pleasure of difference, the pleasure taken in and by difference. It is the paternal metaphor that makes it possible to transcend the mastery of the pleasure in the same; it is this that blocks the return to origins, to the identical, and opens the way to a pleasure taken in and by difference.

From then, the sexual has to combine and dialectise three forms of difference to be organised, so that it can unfold and assume its full meaning.

To state it quickly, and in a concise formula, sexual difference engenders a generational difference that itself then engenders a difference in the sexual, and it is based on the play of this threefold difference that the question of identity then has to be tackled.

It is in the first encounter with the object that the sexual is born within a relationship in which the 'primal separation' of birth is constantly 'reduced' by a relationship 'in duplicate' or 'in the mirror', which is therefore a 'primary homosexual' relationship.

An initial component of the sexual is thus produced in the object's presence, as Freud broadly anticipates when he writes: 'No one who has seen a baby sinking back satiated from the breast and falling asleep with flushed cheeks and a blissful smile can escape the reflection that this picture persists as a prototype of the expression of sexual satisfaction in later life' (1905d, p. 182).

However, this first form encounters some obstacles that also contribute to structuring it. There are some periods of absence of the object, with the discontinuity they introduce into the bond and the subject's need to confront them; we know that this need is the source of the auto-erotisms.

There is also the inevitable encounter in the maternal mode of presence with some heterogeneous aspects that are alien to the baby's psyche, broadly enigmatic to him, and connected with the impact of the mother's adult sexual organisation. It is this heterogeneous element that introduces the question of the father and thus at the same time a difference of sex and the sexual.

But it is only later, in the shaping of the 'primal scene', that these various forms of difference can be represented and organised around the presentation of generational difference.

This is why the 'primal scene', considered not as a fantasy but as an organising 'concept' of the psyche, is so essential to our approach to the sexual, and forms its foundation.

The 'primal scene' structures sexual difference and generational difference in a unified metaphor, but it also integrates at its core the question of the

---

[2] This French term for the establishment of gender also implies a cut, through a play on the French word *section*. [*Trans.*, *this volume*]

child's mode of presence, that of the difference between infantile and adult sexuality.

It integrates in an organised form all the facts relating to the problem posed to the psyche by the sexual; it integrates the question of the identical, one parent at least being of the same sex, as well as that of difference.

With the concept of the 'primal scene', the sexual is thus forged from the differences it organises; it both results from these and produces them. The sexual is then what makes difference 'generative', what allows the generative value of difference to be released.

As has often been observed, the primal scene thus seeks to shape the question of identity based on the presentation of the question of origin.

Origin of the sexual

But the question of the origin of the self is intensified by that of the 'origin of the sexual' itself, which also then has to be reflected in the symbolisation process.

The question of the origin of the sexual is at the heart of the debate that divides proponents of 'source-object' theory (such as Laplanche, in his theory of the enigmatic signifier) from adherents of a theory of the drive that is internal and 'bio-logical' from the outset (as Green, 1998, argued in the debate between these two authors a few years ago).

Does the sexual come 'from within', from the somatic foundation of the psyche, or does it come 'from outside', from the object or from the relationship with it, with its otherness?

It seems to me that this opposition is interesting insofar as it discovers one of the oppositions revealed by clinical practice in connection with various forms of 'sexual theories'. But to assume its entire interest, this opposition must be interpreted or even transcended within a 'metapsychology of processes' that simultaneously posits the origin as undecidable and the sexual as emerging from the meeting point between inside and outside, their chiasmus and the work of their differentiation.

It seems to me that the origin of the sexual can only be well conceived metapsychologically as a process of *différance*,[3] a differentiation process that is carried out starting from an initial amalgam in which self and object are mingled and enmeshed.

The sexual arises when outside and inside, the subject and its object, meet, collide and fuse, 'amalgamate', to produce this 'primary material' of the psyche mentioned by Freud various times in his work from 1900, which is later cathected by the drive impulses.

---

[3] Derrida's term *différance* plays on the meanings of '*différer*' to coin a concept of difference that implies deferral. [*Trans.*, *this volume*]

Although the sexual is initially produced in the encounter between the subject and the other-subject object, it is only manifested as such, understood as such, in its resumption and incorporative internalisation, as indicated by the theory of anaclisis (leaning on) and auto-erotism, or conversely in an evacuation and an excorporation, a subjective discharge.

The internalisation process manifests the drive cathexis of experience, manifests its sexualisation; it makes it perceptible by separating it out from self-preservation.

The oscillation we have just described, the oscillation of an experience between the inside and outside of an internal, internalised experience, characterises a primary level of subjective appropriation of the experience of the sexual.

This in its turn will have to be newly understood, reflected and secondarised. It seems to me that it is the role of the primal seduction fantasy to produce the vagaries of this second resumption.

The seduction fantasy will tend to rock from one side or another the terms of this basic dual polarity; it tends to resolve the undecidability of the origin by assigning a precise origin to the birth of the drive.

A 'sexual' seduction therefore occurs every time one or other of the two amalgamated terms tends to be ousted, whether the sexual is represented only as a biological effect and therefore a kind of 'biological seduction' by the biological, or is conceived only as an effect of the encounter with the object, a seduction by the object.

The sexual 'seduces', just as it must be able to be conceived as seduced; it is perhaps that which is defined only by its overflowing of dichotomous categories, beyond 'simple' oppositions, precisely that which can only be bound with difficulty by bipolar representational systems.

The difficulty I have just indicated also encourages us not to seek a 'positivised' definition of the sexual, not to tackle directly the question of its definition but, rather, to seek to define it from the way in which it functions in the psyche of specific subjects, or from the way in which it has 'functioned' in the history of psychoanalytic thought, the latter seeking to eliminate the impact of the former.

This encourages us to reconsider some markers that are particularly centred around the question of the impact of the sexual in the treatment.

The injured sexual and the diverted sexual

Schematically at the origin of psychoanalytic thought, the sexual is that from which or by which 'we suffer through reminiscence'.

The sexual appears at the outset as an injured sexual, as a traumatised, injured sex, as a suffering sex, even – and we will return to this point later – as a sex in suffering.

The 1895–96 aetiological theory of the neuroses presents the cause of neurosis as the result of an inadequate or incomplete sexuality. It is traumatic precisely to the extent that it has lost its naturalness.

Either its discharge is hindered, as in the theory of hysteria, in which affect remains 'jammed'; or, to the extent that the discharge is inadequate, the malfunctionings of sexuality in current neuroses are presented by Freud as the effect of sexuality in which discharge does not occur in the 'right' place or is carried out 'without an object' beyond the object. In the 1895 theory, Freud presents psychaesthenia as the effect either of onanism or of various forms of incomplete sexuality – 'coitus interruptus' or restricted coitus.

Although the connection with 'genital' sexuality is still very much present, and as we can see this is the lived experience that underlies the symptoms, by contrast the symptomatology already 'metaphorises' sexuality, only evoking it symbolically.

The disconnection of the sexual from sexuality, considered as a genital sexual behaviour, then enters the theorisation with increasing emphasis, without ever becoming completely detached from it.

As the introduction of an infantile 'oral' or 'anal' sexuality confirms still further: anality or orality are only 'sexual', in the sense of sexuality, as a result of their offshoots in the 'preliminary pleasures' of adult sexuality or its forms of perversion; they very quickly overflow the field of sexuality as such to designate relational models.

The idea of a 'phallic' sexuality thus forms the pivotal bridge between 'infantile' and 'genital' sexuality. In the term 'infantile sexuality', its 'sexual' quality is initially defined only as a result of its future evolution into sexuality.

Oral or anal infantile sexuality is only said to be sexual because its traces are later found in adult sexuality or its perversions.

It is indeed always, at least at the outset, adult sexuality that serves as a referent to the sexual, and then, in a second derivation, that which relates to orality or anality is retroactively defined as 'infantile sexual' on this initial foundation.

The sexual and the drive: primary sexualisation

It is this diversion from the sexual that also introduces the idea of 'drive', and which makes it theoretically necessary. The concept of the drive indicates a disparity between the sexual and sexuality itself, a disparity between 'adult' sexuality and infantile sexuality.

Sexuality from this point is nothing more than a specific instance of drive activity, a specific case of the 'sexual' that will instead be better defined by the drive.

But the theory of the drives, the first drive theory, introduces in its turn a disparity between the drive and the sexual, and sexuality. There are the sexual drives and the so-called self-preservative drives, which are not yet 'sexual'. However, the analysis of conflicts such as the hysterical blindness analysed in 1910 demonstrates that self-preservation can be 'sexualised'. In summary, we still suffer from the sexual, but this time it is the sexualisation of a field that is not essentially sexual.

Thus the first drive theory simultaneously restricts the field of the sexual – not everything is sexual – and conceives its possible extension. Although everything is not 'sexual', by contrast everything can be sexualised and thus become sexual through this metaphorising diversion.

Thus we begin to move gradually from a sexual considered as something 'in itself' to a sexual that appears to have issued from a process of 'sexual' cathexis, a mode of functioning or a function that are 'sexualised' as a result of this cathexis. Although everything is not sexual, everything can begin to be 'sexualised' and the model of a conflict that has emerged from this sexualisation can begin to be developed.

The phallic model of sexualisation and integration

As I began to indicate above, the pivot of this 'sexualisation' is so-called 'phallic' sexuality. One of the key characteristics of the 'phallic' organisation is to generalise sexualisation, to apprehend everything, in a concern for integration and completeness, in terms of the binary phallic–castrated opposition, that is to say to interpret and 'sexualise' everything according to this model.

In the infantile economy, this need corresponds to the need to inscribe everything in the orbit of the pleasure–unpleasure principle but also in that of a sexual identity, which is one characterised by difference, thus to enmesh the question of pleasure with that of difference, to transfer gradually from the pleasure of the same, the pleasure of the double, to that of the pleasure of difference, taken in difference.

What matters to us here relates to the fact that this conception of the phallic impulse introduces the concept of a sexualisation process that transcends the sexual–non-sexual opposition, thus considered to oppose 'in itself' categories, to define a process of inscription in the sexual domain as a basic modality of binding and integration, in particular from a metaphorisation process based on sex and the sexual.

Although not everything is sexual, everything will have to be inscribed primarily in the coordinates of the sexual to be libidinised and thus cathected and integrated.

The scope of the shift thus described is enough indication that it contains some fundamental narcissistic issues. It is also probably based on their understanding that the concept of narcissism will be elucidated. Before being fully elucidated as such, narcissism needed to be recognised as phallic-narcissistic.

However, from the point that the sexualisation process is conceived, the first drive theory proves untenable. There can no longer be any opposition between the sexual drives and the self-preservative drives, to the extent that the self-preservative functions must also be 'sexualised' in the process of integration.

As a result, the opposition tends to oscillate within the sexual that then covers the entire field, between the sexual drives of the ego – ego libido – and sexual drives directed at objects – object libido. This becomes the second drive theory, the second because, contrary to what is sometimes asserted, there are in fact three in Freud's work.

The drive is either 'sexual', 'narcissistic-sexual', taking the ego or its attributes as an object, or it is 'objectal-sexual', taking the object as a drive goal. There is no more specificity of the sexual, there is no longer a field reserved to the sexual, at least as concerns the primary cathexis and the functioning of the primary processes.

And the potential question becomes that of desexualisation, then that of non-sexualisation, of the failure of that primary sexualisation.

Without this always being very clear to him or his successors, the evolution of Freud's thinking towards the third drive theory will be carried out in the direction imposed by this implicit theoretical 'constraint'.

To conceive the secondary 'desexualisation' process is to conceive the organisation of secondarity and the problem of the superego, and specifically the post-Oedipal superego; we will return to this question later.

To consider the problem of non-sexualisation, the failure of the primary sexualisation process, is to consider one of the aspects of the death drive, the problem of the failure of drive fusion. The experiences 'beyond the pleasure principle' are ones in which the primary libidinisation process has failed at least in part. The nature of the trauma changes; it is no longer connected only to an overflowing of the drives, it can also be connected with an effraction[4] and a failure of primary binding by the sexual.

The third drive theory – that is to say, the life-drive–death-drive opposition – entails a 'processual' theory of the drives; with this, the picture of the problematic of the sexual in Freudian psychoanalysis is now fully on view. It also involves, and we will return to this point, an analysis of the organisational modalities of the drive.

This is what I must now develop to continue to present my questions.

---

[4] 'Effraction' is a word in common use in French which means a breaking through in material reality (as in a burglary) or metaphorically in psychic reality. The concept here refers to Freud's (1920g) model of trauma: 'We describe as a "traumatic" any excitations from outside which are powerful enough to break through the protective shield' (p. 29). The use of 'effraction' in French can thus be defined as 'a breach in an otherwise efficacious barrier against stimuli' (p. 29). [*Eds., this volume*]

The model of sexualisation by libidinal co-excitation

In this conception, the sexual is no longer only a first and 'constitutional' 'order'; psychic integration rests on the binding capacity of Eros, the life drive, which is revealed particularly in the concept of libidinal co-excitation.

The model of libidinal co-excitation provides a different model for the sexualisation of psychic processes; it extends and amplifies the model of phallic sexualisation. Libidinal co-excitation refers to the process by which a psychic experience is 'sexualised' to be bound at a primary stage, particularly when it does not directly entail satisfaction, or not sufficiently.

The libidinal co-excitation described in relation to masochism only appears then as a particular case of a much more general process, which can be defined as that of the necessity of a primary binding or a primary libidinisation of psychic experiences.

Its description in relation to masochism results from the especially paradoxical shift that it then makes, in which it has the task of converting an experience of initial unpleasure into an experience of pleasure.

But it works progressively on all psychic experiences, and this is an essential characteristic of infantile sexuality; it 'must' be able to work to bind these.

It represents the imperative to inscribe psychic experiences within the pleasure–unpleasure principle, an inscription necessary for integrating and binding these psychically within subjectivity; it represents the fundamental vector of subjective appropriation, its categorical imperative.

From this point, the characteristics of infantile sexuality must be conceived in terms of this fundamental appropriative task, in the direction of the phallic-narcissistic organisation that represents the culmination of this 'entirely sexual' process.

Everything has to go through the sexual to be assimilable, which is why although not everything is sexual, there must be some sexual in everything, such is the constraint of the primary process. But it is also an imperative of subjective appropriation, an imperative of the subjectivation process.

To be able to be subjectivised, the subject's experience must first be inscribed in the sphere of the pleasure principle, and this is carried out by means of its sexualisation.

What eludes this process of integration and binding then appears to be threatened by the mastery of the repetition compulsion, by what are said to be forms of the death drive, beyond the pleasure principle, those which concern what is failing subjective appropriation. We will need to return to this point.

Secondary desexualisation

It is then clear that such a process can only be maintained if, in another psychic system, a secondary desexualisation process simultaneously operates, to which we must return.

Desexualisation does not consist in withdrawing the primary sexual cathexis; it is only 'secondary', concerns only one psychic system, that of the secondary process; it is a partial, relative desexualisation, which concerns only the mode of drive fulfilment, not the foundations of the cathexis.

Classically, the work of desexualisation is carried out under the aegis of the superego, which differentiates its modes of drive fulfilments.

The superego has to differentiate between what can be realised in representation, that which must be realised only in thought or in words, and that which can also be realised in actions.

It raises the possibility of other modes of realisation than those of action (the hallucinatory fulfilment of desire or its interactive equivalents) – that is to say, the possibility of a 'desexualising', even sublimatory, work of metaphorisation.

Sublimation is then conceived as a mode of realisation that takes the representation, the mere representation, as a new and only drive goal. Representation then ceases to be the means or medium by which the drive represents its object; it becomes the very object in which the drive is satisfied.

This process is absolutely fundamental to the organisation of symbolisation; this is what makes the symbolisation work so necessary to the drive economy.

To desexualise is to make do, in the name of the reality principle, with symbolically representing the drive fulfilment; it is to divert the realisation with the aid of successive displacements that provide 'distance' from the first source of the drive, which metaphorise it, change it beyond recognition and repress it. To desexualise is to emerge from the hallucinatory realisation of the desire or its equivalents; it is to emerge from the necessity of the identity of perception to adapt to the identity of thought.

Desexualisation and defusion

We must not therefore confuse this process, which 'secondarises' the drive, with the mode of 'desexualisation' that is only what results from the operation of the death drive, for which the term drive 'defusion' has instead traditionally been used.

This 'desexualisation' is only a form of unbinding, of primary drive defusion. It thus only demonstrates the 'poor quality' of the primary binding by the libidinal co-excitation, a poor quality that prevents its later secondarisation and therefore jeopardises its integration.

The question of this 'poor quality' raises, as we know, the entire question of excess and trauma; it raises the question of an excitation that does not achieve its organisation into a true drive – presupposing a minimal organisation and in particular an object–source differentiation – or its binding into a representable drive form.

This has led to the prevailing idea that the drive is also no longer to be considered as an entity 'in itself' but, rather, as something that results from an organisational mode of excitation. It then becomes theoretically necessary, as I proposed at Cerisy in September (2005), to differentiate various levels of organisation of excitation in the drive and in desire.

In the light of this evolution in the paradigms of the theorisation, we can observe how the first conception of the sexual has evolved. Although we still suffer from the sexual, this is now a sexual that cannot be organised as such, in its process, in its beating, its pulsation.

We still suffer from the sexual, but, although we can always suffer from the excess of the sexual, we also now suffer from the lack of being sexualised.

The processual sexual and the object

It can easily be observed that the understanding of the sexual in terms of the process dynamics of sexualisation–desexualisation 'transcends' a certain number of difficulties connected with a 'naturalistic' definition of sexuality and the sexual; it also transcends, by framing it differently, the genital–pre-genital opposition, leading to a conception of sexuality connected with the work of binding and symbolisation and with its boundaries.

It allows the sexual and sexuality to be connected, but without being trapped in the alternative of a sexual considered as proceeding solely from biology or the object relationship. To the contrary, it is inscribed in a conception that takes the drive–object pair as the fundamental organiser of metapsychology. For such a process implies that the question of the object is posed; it makes it unavoidable.

In fact, whatever the 'achievement' of the psyche's binding and symbolisation capacities, it cannot by itself alone bind the drive impulse in its entirety. Whatever the quality of the sexualisation–desexualisation process, it cannot process the whole of the sexual 'force'. Whatever the quality of the auto-erotisms and 'sublimations', they cannot exhaust the internal tensions.

There is a need for the object, for objects; we need the difference that they alone are capable of introducing. This is where we encounter difference. This also begins to open up the question of sexuality, of the drive exchanges with a different object. Sexuality opens up where the 'binding' sexual is lacking, where intrapsychic erotism is necessarily, inevitably, lacking.

Infantile sexuality, a point on which Freud becomes increasingly assertive, remains fundamentally unsatisfying; it is even in the final analysis what shatters the Oedipus complex. Sexualisation by the primary process leaves an unbindable residue, a lack that engenders a difference in the sexual, *the* difference in the sexual.

The desexualisation operated by the secondary process comes up against this residue that paradoxically 'sexualises' the secondary system, penetrates it and 'claims' the discharge, demands an object 'for' the discharge, another modality for processing the sexual.

It is the non-event of infantile sexuality, its failure to occur, and therefore what is left unbound by it, that claims its place in secondarity, forcing it to reconsider the question of the sexual and to integrate it differently.

It is what could not occur in childhood sexuality that seeks to make its way into secondarity, seeks to be fulfilled in the secondary system and instigates adult sexuality.

This is why it cannot be definable without reference to the negative of childhood sexuality. We repeat, but in the sexual we do not repeat only what might have taken place; it is above all that which has not taken place that we repeat in and through sexuality, we repeat the non-occurrence of ourselves.

Let us move on to the generative process to conclude our reflection.

No object, either, can in itself enable us to bind what is lacking and strives to be discharged; an object of the object is required, another object – that is to say, another subject, a third subject. The unbindable residue engenders an objectalising generativity that is simultaneously a socialising generativity. We know that this can only be maintained and developed if it too can be adequately desexualised at a secondary stage.

Is this pulsation of sexualisation and desexualisation not the essence of what psychoanalysis can bring to a reflection on the sexual in contemporary clinical thought?

The adolescent sexual and the enigma

It is against this background that adolescence then introduces its specific 'revolution' in the sexual. It is in the 'orgasmic potentiality' that it seems to me the revolution specific to adolescence must be most fully understood, but it is also that the sexual will have to find conditions of satisfaction in the resumption of bodily contact with the other-subject object, in conditions that evoke the first physical contact. I have previously (2000) tried to assess the importance and extent of the upheavals incurred by the introduction of sexual maturity into the relationship of adolescence to symbolisation, and I would like to amplify these initial reflections here with some supplementary remarks on the trajectory from the baby's sexuality to that of the adolescent.

The orgasmic potentiality, as the quotation from Freud comparing the baby's satisfaction at the breast with the pleasure of adult sexuality implies, puts the psyche at risk of a confusion between the first hallucinatory experience in found–created and the sexual experience of the orgasm, as if adolescent pleasure 'rediscovered' the baby's first and lost satisfaction. The idea that adolescent and adult sexuality rediscovers the path of primal pleasure, rediscovers the maternal breast, even the very site of their origins, is a highly topical idea in psychoanalysis, and it is probably subtended by the primal fantasy of the 'return to the maternal womb'. But the adolescent's orgasm is not the hallucinatory realisation of the baby's desire, and the amalgam that threatens to be carried out between the two subjective experiences is probably as necessary as it is threatening to the adolescent's psychic organisation.

It is necessary because the amalgam is probably inevitable for psychic integration; it prefigures the work of establishing psychic continuity that is imposed by the crisis undergone at adolescence and the experience of rupture it contains. But at the same time it is accompanied by the threat that the gains of the work of differentiation in childhood, those of the mourning process connected with the elaboration of the Oedipal constellation, and those of the symbolic organisation and the sublimations it makes possible, will be lost on the way, made obsolete by the new potentialities offered by the accession to adult pleasure. The threat is that a short-circuiting from the baby's pleasure to that of the adolescent may be instituted.

Once again, I do not think that a certain part of the short-circuit is entirely avoidable; what matters is that it should be moderated by the maintenance of an adequate cathexis of the factual realities of childhood, that the buffer and the work of differentiation produced by the elaboration of specifically infantile sexuality is interposed between the early sexual of the baby and that of the adolescent.

I should like to conclude these reflections with an observation concerning the adolescent evolution of the enigma incorporated in the object's pleasure for the baby and the child, the 'enigmatic signifiers' described by Laplanche. The discovery of orgasm produces a 'partial lifting' of the enigma of the object's pleasure; it produces a reorganising retroactive operation of the relationship the subject has formed with it, and probably, in the same shift, a reorganisation of the concept of the primal scene. I propose the hypothesis that, furthermore, one of the remarkable revisions thus made possible is a modification in the subject's relationship with the unknown, a reopening of the 'capacity for the negative' (Bion's 'negative capability') that contains the concept of a cathexis and a potential pleasure found in what is unknown, imperceptible. The adolescent's capacity to solve equations with unknown elements, to explore the physical and chemical sciences based on hypotheses beyond the sensory and even perceptible universe (atom, bounds of the universe, etc.), the cathexis of spiritualism common at that age, then for some the cathexis of 'depth psychology', and therefore the acceptance of an unconscious psychic reality, seem to me to stem from and be made conceivable by this profound revision in the relationship to the enigma of pleasure.

There is therefore one final implication that particularly concerns clinicians and takes us back to intersubjectivity, which concerns the form of thought about the unknown and the imperceptible that is contained in the encounter with the concept of the unconscious and specifically that of the object's unconscious. The baby and the child encounter the unconscious of objects with which they have had to construct themselves; they undergo its effects and vagaries; they also organise their psychic life according to the impact of this unconscious. Proponents of 'theory of mind' have rightly emphasised the importance for the socialisation process of constructing a conception of the other's mind, which I would personally formulate as the capacity to imagine that the object is a subject-other, with his own desires, intentions, emotions and so on. But this 'theory' does not engage with the question of the importance for psychic life of an unconscious dimension of the mind – that is to say, the question of the mind's reflexivity and its mode of relationship with itself. I think this capacity is only truly completely acquired at adolescence and in the wake of the above-mentioned revisions concerning the lifting of the enigma of the object's pleasure. The discovery of a pleasure in oneself unknown to oneself ('a pleasure unknown to itself', as Freud said in relation to the Rat Man) opens up the question of a pleasure of the object that is unknown to the object itself; it engages the paradox of an unconscious affect. The accession to the true dimension of intersubjectivity cannot be gained without taking into account the intersubjectivity of this particular characteristic of the human subject: he has an inner shadowy and unknown zone; his messages contain a dimension that eludes him, an unconscious dimension that nevertheless acts and interacts between one subject and another. And what is true of oneself is also true of the object, and the parental objects, which is one of the aspects of the 'murder of the object' encountered in adolescence, with the acquisition of the concept and the right to explore the object's unconscious, a supreme site of psychic transgression.

References

Freud, S. (1905d). *Three Essays on the Theory of Sexuality. S.E.*, 7.
Freud, S. (1911b). Formulations on the Two Principles of Mental Functioning. *S.E.*, 12: 218–226.
Freud, S. (1920g). *Beyond the Pleasure Principle. S.E.*, 28: 7–64.
Green, A. (1998). Le déchaînement du signifiant énigmatique désignifié dans le processus traductif-détraductif autothéorisant. De l'intérêt à bien lire Jean Laplanche. [The unleashing of the enigmatic signifier which loses its meaning in its self-theorizing process of translation non-translation. The benefit of reading Jean Laplanche]. *Revue Française de Psychanalyse, 62* (1): 263–287.
Roussillon, R. (2000). Les enjeux de la symbolisation à l'adolescence [Matters relating to symbolisation in adolescence]. *Adolescence ISAP* (Special issue, October).
Roussillon, R. (2005). Aménagements du cadre psychanalytique [Constructions of the psychoanalytic setting]. In F. Richard & F. Urribarri (Eds.), *Autour de l'oeuvre d'André Green. Enjeux pour une psychanalyse contemporaine* [On the work of André Green: Some issues for contemporary psychoanalysis]. Paris: Presses Universitaires de France.

29 THE CROATIAN CRAVAT
The narcissism of small differences and the process of civilisation

Gilbert Diatkine

> **Gilbert Diatkine** is a psychiatrist, full member and a former president of the Paris Psychoanalytical Society and of the Training Commission of the Institute of Psychoanalysis. He is also associate director of the Psychoanalytic Institute for Eastern Europe (PIEE). His many published papers deal mainly with issues concerning violence and aggressiveness, both in the individual and in conflicts between peoples. In that field he has developed Freud's concept of the cultural superego.
>
> Among his published work are: *Les transformations de la psychopathie* [The transformations of psychopathy] (PUF, 1983); his book on Jacques Lacan in the 'Psychanalystes d'aujourd'hui' series (PUF, 1997); and his Report on the cultural superego read to the 1999 Congress of French-Speaking Psychoanalysts (*Revue Française de Psychanalyse*, 1999, vol. 5).

'They nail a living prisoner to the door of a house, cut his tracheal artery and pull out his tongue through the orifice just created in the form of a cravat. This is how the Serbs pay ironic homage to the invention of this embellishment by the Croats. The agony is prolonged, painful and infinitely agonising.'

This reads like a nightmare reported in a psychoanalytic session, but I am not in my consulting room in Paris. This is Zagreb in 1992. The person talking to me is a cultural affairs expert. Having fully explained to me the 'Croatian cravat' torture invented by the Serbs, he adds that some young history-of-art students at Zagreb University, who had been sent to the front, confessed to their horrified lecturers that having found their comrades tortured in this way on several occasions, after a while they set about inflicting the same treatment on their Serb prisoners. A few months of war turned cultured and peaceful young people into sadistic torturers, protected neither by sublimations, nor culture, nor moral conscience, nor any identification with other people's suffering. At that moment, my friend and I avoided returning to the question of why civilisation is so powerless against the return to barbarism. We both knew that this has gone unanswered ever since the Germany of Goethe and Beethoven invented the 'final solution'. Furthermore, my interlocutor was telling me about events that had just taken place and people he knew. Too direct a confrontation with horror obstructs thinking, instead generating in the listener a functional splitting of the ego (Bayle, 1988). The reported facts are impressed on our inner perception whatever we do, and we must accept that we have to represent them as truly existing. But this acceptance is intolerable, and we simultaneously have to repudiate any psychic reality (Penot, 1989) to the thing-presentations and word-presentations that they risk lifting from repression in us. Otherwise, the connection between the facts reported and our own history would bring what is happening right in front of us fully into our consciousness. The simplest way to prevent this connection from being made is to keep the horrible representations outside our field of perception–consciousness, either by banishing them ('the Balkans aren't part of western Europe') or by bringing them closer while trivialising them ('There are atrocities in all civil wars'). In both cases, the existence of the facts is acknowledged, but we deprive them of the cathexis of psychic reality that would give them a meaning.

Deployed in an emergency, splitting of the ego and disavowal of reality can curb quantities of excitation that would otherwise be intolerable to the ego. A collective reflection can easily mobilise these barricades, which are often rather fragile in subjects without this predisposition. But this would be inadvisable because their disappearance would leave the ego defenceless against dangerous emotional torrents. As long as they are maintained, splitting and denial foster action rather than thought. Also, reflection in these circumstances may encourage aggressors by putting them on the same level as the victims, which would provide excuses to war criminals.

There is an even stronger temptation to postpone reflection to more peaceful times now that the theories that used to give a meaning to violence are in crisis. The confrontation between communism and capitalism during the twentieth century led us to believe that history had a meaning and that violence had a role in it. Before the fall of the Berlin Wall, it was certainly a regrettable time but also one that was indispensable to the progress of civilisation. According to which camp people were in, it promised rosy tomorrows or the curbing of international subversion. The sudden collapse of communism did not put an end to violence, but we have ceased to imagine that it is 'the midwife of every old society pregnant with a new one, that it is the instrument with the aid of which social movement forces its way through and shatters the dead, fossilised political forms' (Marx, quoted by Engels, 1877). The reasoning of conflicts now only deploys nationalism, xenophobia, religious intolerance and racism, without offering any prospect of an advance in civilisation.

Violence and the narcissism of minor differences

Can psychoanalysis nevertheless shed a little more light on this question? Yes, according to at least one of the main parties concerned:

The viewpoint of analysts from the former Yugoslavia

In the countries that have emerged from the former Yugoslavia, as in several others ravaged by violence, there are analysts and psychotherapists today who expect psychoanalysis to help them confront the many traumatic situations they experience, both in the war itself and in the provision of psychological assistance to refugees. Édouard Klain, from Zagreb, and his colleagues have reported in a politically committed book what they have learnt from the war in Croatia and how psychoanalysis has helped them to confront these findings (Klain, 1992). They invite us to join them in reflecting on what has taken place, taking account of the political and historical context, but as psychoanalysts.

The group's return to its 'basic assumptions'

To this purpose, Klain and Moro draw on concepts used by Bion in group psychoanalysis: concerning the current war, they observe that an 'archaic destructiveness, accompanied as always by irrationality, was evident in the actions of extreme groups in both nations. Their treatment of members of the "enemy" nation resembled the actions of primitive tribes, and the basis of their behaviour was provided by the destructive projections of paranoid contents (they felt they were obliged to defend themselves against the threat of torture, killing, cannibalistic massacre, etc.)'. These cruel forms of behaviours are explained by the group's regression to 'basic fight–flight assumptions' (Klain & Moro, 1992, p. 79).

Ethnic cleansing can be conceived as based on a pathological projective identification that eliminates the other in order to take his place. However, a group-based approach that sets to work on regression and projective identification has an application to any war. It does not explain why sadism should be more intense when war brings very close nations into conflict nor why this regression is not instead held in check by another group phenomenon, reciprocal identification, which establishes human rights and rules of engagement in every war. It should oppose the group's 'basic assumptions' even more strongly when the two warring nations belong to the same cultural community. In 'On Identification', Melanie Klein posed the problem of the relation between the capacity to put oneself in another person's place and projective identification, but she remained evasive concerning what can make one person totally prevail over another: 'For the individual to feel that he has a good deal in common with another person is concurrent with projecting himself into that person (and the same applies to introjecting him). These processes vary in intensity and duration and on these variations depend the strength and importance of such identifications and their vicissitudes' (1955, p. 170).

The same objection could be made to the works of René Girard, which initially seem to give an exact description of the current situation in the former Yugoslavia. For Girard, there is only one desire, to imitate the other and to destroy everything that is different about him. *Mimesis* condemns communities to tear themselves apart in ever smaller hostile groups until the sacrifice of an emissary victim puts an end to the chaos. Culture is constructed on the dissimulation of this violence and this sacrifice (Girard, 1972, 1978). However, the impressive concept of *mimesis*, by merging all the forms of identification, eliminates the problem without resolving it.

The hatred of excessive jouissance

Slavoj Žižek, from Paris, works from a Lacanian perspective. He considers that the violence of the conflicts between close nations arises from the fact that the neighbour can always be accused of a secret, perverse sexuality (Žižek, 1992). The accusation is expressed directly if this is malodorous and noisy, or through a reaction formation if instead it is reserved and austere. Through this a specific jouissance materialises without which, Žižek states, the group ideal could not be maintained. According to Lacan, in Žižek's reading, the group ideal is a shared belief: I am Corsican, and I am proud of it because I believe that others are proud of being Corsican. There is no need to explain what it is about being Corsican that inspires pride, except for this specific jouissance that is threatened by the existence in the neighbour of a different jouissance that is considered excessive. Now, Žižek writes, the hatred of excessive jouissance in the other is the projection of the hatred of our own excess of jouissance. Excessive jouissance, according to Žižek, again following Lacan (1969–70), can in certain circumstances be limited by the 'master's discourse'. Minor differences are then easily tolerated. Giving his own view this time, Žižek considers this is what occurs when a nation reaches a state of equilibrium – for example, before the development of capitalism, or if there is a strong state. By contrast, racist violence erupts as soon as capitalism progresses because it 'continually produces excess'. This thesis has the flaw of being contradicted by the facts, since racist violence is entirely compatible with a strong state, as in Tsarist Russia or Hitler's Germany, and with pre-capitalist economic stagnation such as today between Senegal and Mauritania. Furthermore, it is difficult to see how the Lacanian concept of jouissance could dispense with a projection on to the 'Other', whatever the state of society (Laznik-Penot, 1990).

What is the difference between a Serb and a Croat?

In *Civilization and Its Discontents*, Freud demonstrates that the narcissism of minor differences disables the basic moral injunction to 'love your neighbour as yourself'. He seems to describe exactly what happened in the former Yugoslavia. After having confronted each other with extreme cruelty during the Second World War, Serbia and Croatia coexisted peacefully for forty-five years within Yugoslavia. Together they lived through the Communist victory during the Tito–Stalin alliance, then the schism and socialism based on workers' self-management, and they discovered democracy in the same conditions. Serbs and Croats speak the same language and today share the same democratic Christian values. The extension of secondary education substantially raised the cultural level of both populations. Inhabitants of villages that were contested between the two nations attended the same schools and the same sports clubs and worked in the same factories. There were a great many mixed marriages. When the political and economic disagreements between the two states grew, it was long hoped that these could be resolved by negotiation, until war proved inevitable. It might then have been expected that everything that united these very similar communities would limit the destruction to the necessary minimum and that the rules of warfare and human rights would be scrupulously observed. In fact, it is precisely the opposite that occurred: as always when war sets sibling nations against each other, sadism ran riot, with total barbarism.

World views and the application of psychoanalysis to politics

Before continuing, we must ask ourselves if we are not failing to heed Freud's warning against turning psychoanalysis into a 'conception of the world' or a *Weltanschauung*. A *Weltanschauung*, Freud explains, is 'an intellectual construction which solves all the problems of our existence uniformly on the basis of one overriding hypothesis . . . in which everything that interests us finds its fixed place' (1933a, p. 158). We will therefore not turn to *Civilization and Its Discontents* for anything more than a starting point for reflection. In any case, psychoanalysis can be applied to politics and society. Freud engaged in this throughout his life, as is demonstrated by the series of his writings that put forward psychoanalytic interpretations of them. These extend from '"Civilized" Sexual Morality and Modern Nervous Illness' (1908d) to *Moses and Monotheism* (1939a), and include *Totem and Taboo* (1912–13), 'Thoughts for the Times on War and Death' (1915b), 'The Taboo of Virginity' (1918a), *Group Psychology and the Analysis of the Ego* (1921c), *The Future of an Illusion* (1927c), *Civilization and Its Discontents* (1930a), 'The Question of a Weltanschauung' (1933a, Lecture XXXV) and *Why War?* (1933b [1932]).

Of all these works, *Civilization and Its Discontents* is perhaps not the one that speaks to us most today. The actual term 'discontents' is extremely mild for discussing the extermination camps and 'ethnic cleansing'. As Pontalis observes (1983), Freud may have been hindered in this work by the belated recognition he was then receiving, which constrained him to forge a synthesis when his mindset was naturally more analytical. Furthermore, published originally in 1929, *Civilization* appeared in a period of relative political calm. Freud could not have suspected at the time of writing that he was equidistant from two world wars. Despite his pessimism, he trusted in the onward march of the civilising process, and he situated collective violence in such a remote past that he could hardly imagine it at all.

'No matter how much we may shrink with horror from certain situations – of a galley-slave in antiquity, of a peasant during the Thirty Years' War, of a victim of the Holy Inquisition, of a Jew awaiting a pogrom – it is nevertheless impossible for us to feel our way into such people – to divine the changes which original obtuseness of mind, a gradual stupefying process, the cessation of expectations, and cruder or more refined methods of narcotization have produced upon their receptivity to sensations of pleasure and unpleasure' (1930a, p. 89). It is true that even from the second edition of the text, he began to ponder his trust in 'eternal Eros' in a final doubting line (p. 145), unpublished in the French. Other works, directly addressing violence, strike us as closer to our contemporary situation, such as 'Thoughts for the Times on War and Death', in which Freud directs a lucid look at the destruction of our illusions about civilisation by the First World War (1915b, p. 280) or *Moses and Monotheism*, in which the *Anschluss* forces him to recognise that 'We are living in a specially remarkable period. We find to our astonishment that progress has allied itself with barbarism' (1939a, p. 54).

Minor differences and moral conscience

Civilization develops a theory postulated as early as 1918 in 'The Taboo of Virginity': 'It would be tempting ... to derive from this "narcissism of minor differences" the hostility which in every human relation we see fighting successfully against feelings of fellowship and overpowering the commandment that all men should love one another' (p. 199). The concept of the 'narcissism of minor differences' comes from the 'taboo on personal isolation' described by the ethnologist Crawley (1902), who sees it as the origin of feelings of hostility and alienation between individuals. *Civilization* demonstrates in detail how primary aggression and the narcissism of minor differences form an obstacle to reciprocal identification: why would I prefer a stranger to those close to me, why would I love a stranger who is quite ready to hate me and mistreat me? (Freud, 1930a, pp. 48–49). Freud later summarises his pessimism in a famous passage from 'The Dissection of the Psychical Personality' (1933a,

Lecture XXXI): 'Following a well-known pronouncement of Kant's, which couples the conscience within us with the starry Heavens, a pious man might well be tempted to honour these two things as the masterpieces of creation. The stars are indeed magnificent, but as regards conscience God has done an uneven and careless piece of work, for a large majority of men have brought along with them only a modest amount of it or scarcely enough to be worth mentioning' (p. 31). This is the viewpoint adopted by young people from American ghettos who convert the Christian precept 'Do unto others as you would have them do unto you' into 'Do unto others *before* they do unto you' (Wacquant, 1999, p. 153, fn. 20).

What, then, is the source of the spontaneous feeling that generally enables me to recognise someone similar to me in every human being? Freud demonstrates in *Civilization* that its presence is really more remarkable than its absence. It is not a congenital and invariant fact. Contrary to what Freud writes elsewhere, man is not even a wolf to man (1930a, p. 111), because, if he were, congenital inhibiting reflexes would protect him from intraspecies aggression (Lorenz, 1964). We must therefore reconstruct the process by which this fleeting sentiment that forms the basis of moral conscience, human rights and the rules of warfare is constructed. We also have to wonder why 'minor differences' have such a disastrous impact on it. Freud leaves the question unanswered in *Group Psychology and the Analysis of the Ego*, as in *Civilization*: 'We do not know why such sensitiveness should have been directed to just these details of differentiation' (1921c, p. 102).

Moral conscience and the superego

Since moral conscience is a superego function (Freud, 1914c), and in fact an unconscious superego function (Freud, 1923b), the first idea that arises to explain its failure is that the superego is extremely oversensitive to the vicissitudes of narcissism. The superego is the source of unconscious guilt feelings that are among the most formidable elements of resistance to analysis (Freud, 1924c) and interminable analysis (Freud, 1937c). Whereas an unfortunate person can be persecuted by its hatred throughout his life without anything – including analysis – seemingly able to alleviate it, a mere 'minor difference' can throw it completely off course in the only domain where it should have some useful application – namely, social relations!

Group phenomena are not the only narcissistic disorders that can hinder superego functioning. Every day we see hitherto morally irreproachable personalities behaving with fear of neither God nor man following a humiliation of some kind. This is the case with Kleist's hero, Michael Kohlhaas (Kleist, 1808), who sets a whole country ablaze because the magnificent horses he had left as surety with a lord were returned to him in a deplorable state. The superego can be just as easily overturned by another narcissistic disturbance, the state of love. From love for Carmen, Don José, hitherto an impeccable brigadier, abandons military discipline and puts himself at the service of smugglers.

However, this example suffices to show that it is not the superego itself that is 'soluble in love' (Parat, 1973). The smugglers want Don José to enter their ranks precisely because of his professional abilities. Carmen gives Don José some new ideas. He sets out to achieve them with the same seriousness he applied when he was in the army, and his superego persecutes him with the same vigilance if he does not succeed. Similarly, Michael Kohlhaas proves a formidable tactician in his determination to ravage the country, and his superego makes him as excellent a war leader as he had once been a horse dealer. What is most terrifying about 'ethnic cleansing' is that it is implemented by conscientious officials who with zeal, precision and subordination implement a plan that has been prepared and issued in advance. It is likely that their superego torments them if they carry out their horrible task badly.

Carmen replaces the army in the role of ideal ego for Don José. She gives him some new ideas, and he seeks to attain them conscientiously, even becoming an assassin. Although Freud uses the terms 'ideal ego' and 'ego-ideal' interchangeably (Chasseguet-Smirgel, 1973, p. 761), it may be useful to contrast them here. Lagache explains that the ideal ego is linked to the primary identification with the mother (Lagache, 1966, quoted by Chasseguet-Smirgel). How is the ideal ego constituted? What is the connection between 'minor differences' and ego ideals? And, finally, how can a change in the ideal ego involve losing the sense of belonging to a common humanity?

The arbitrariness of minor differences

Minor differences are expressed by variations in pronunciation, in writing and generally in what Marcel Mauss (1924, 1936) calls 'bodily techniques'. These can be reversed or replaced by others while keeping the same meaning. The link that turns an action from everyday life into the symbol of group belonging is as random as that which unites the signifying and the signified aspects of the linguistic sign. The study of minor differences therefore belongs to what Saussure (1986) calls 'semiology' – that is, the science of the 'class of systems based upon the arbitrary nature of the sign' (p. 68).

References

Bayle, G. (1988). Traumatismes et clivages fonctionnels [Trauma and functional splitting]. *Revue Française de Psychanalyse, 6:* 1339–1356.

Chasseguet-Smirgel, J. (1973). Essai sur l'Idéal du Moi. Contribution à l'étude psychanalytique de la 'maladie d'idéalité' [Essay on the ego ideal: Contribution to the psychoanalytic study of the 'disease of ideality']. *Revue Française de Psychanalyse, 37* (5–6): 735–930.

Crawley, A. (1902). *The Mystic Rose: A Study of Primitive Marriage*. London: MacMillan.
Engels, F. (1877). Theory of Force. In *Anti-Dühring. Herr Eugen Dühring's Revolution in Science* (chap. 4), trans. E. Burns. Leipzig.
Freud, S. (1908d). 'Civilized' Sexual Morality and Modern Nervous Illness. *S.E.*, 9.
Freud, S. (1912–13). *Totem and Taboo. S.E.*, 13.
Freud, S. (1914c). On Narcissism. *S.E.*, 14.
Freud, S. (1915b). Thoughts for the Times on War and Death. *S.E.*, 14.
Freud, S. (1918a). The Taboo of Virginity. *S.E.*, 11.
Freud, S. (1921c). *Group Psychology and the Analysis of the Ego. S.E.*, 18.
Freud, S. (1923b). *The Ego and the Id. S.E.*, 19.
Freud, S. (1924c). The Economic Problem of Masochism. *S.E.*, 19.
Freud, S. (1927c). *The Future of an Illusion. S.E.*, 21.
Freud, S. (1930a). *Civilization and Its Discontents. S.E.*, 21.
Freud, S. (1933a). *New Introductory Lectures on Psycho-Analysis. S.E.*, 22.
Freud, S. (1933b [1932]). *Why War? S.E.*, 22.
Freud, S. (1937c). Analysis Terminable and Interminable. *S.E.*, 22.
Freud, S. (1939a). *Moses and Monotheism. S.E.*, 23.
Girard, R. (1972). *La violence et le sacré*. Paris: Grasset. [*Violence and the Sacred*, trans. P. Gregory. Baltimore, MD: Johns Hopkins University Press, 1977.]
Girard, R. (1978). *Des choses cachées depuis la fondation du monde. Recherches avec J.-M. Oughourian et G.Lefort*. Paris: Grasset. [*Things Hidden since the Foundation of the World. Research undertaken with J.-M. Oughourian and G. Lefort*, trans. S. Bann & M. Metteer. London: Athlone Press, 1987.]
Klain, E. (Ed.) (1992). *Psychology and Psychiatry War*. Zagreb: Faculty of Medicine, University of Zagreb.
Klain, E., & Moro, L. (1992). Large and small groups in war. In E. Klain (Ed.), *Psychology and Psychiatry of War*. Zagreb: Faculty of Medicine, University of Zagreb.
Klein, M. (1955). On Identification. In *Envy and Gratitude and Other Works 1946–1963: The Writings of Melanie Klein Vol. III*. London: Hogarth Press.
Kleist H. von (1808). *Michael Kohlhaas: A Tale from an Old Chronicle*, trans. F. H. King. New York: Mondial, 2007.
Lacan, J. (1969–70). *Envers de la psychanalyse*. Paris: Editions du Seuil, 1991. [*The Other Side of Psychoanalysis*, trans. R. Grigg. New York: W.W. Norton, 2007.]
Lagache, D. (1966). La psychanalyse et la structure de la personnalité [Psychoanalysis and the structure of the personality]. *La psychanalyse*, 6.
Laznik-Penot, M.-C. (1990). La mise en place du concept de jouissance chez Lacan [The establishment of the concept of jouissance in Lacan]. *Revue Française de Psychanalyse*, 1: 55–82.
Lorenz, K. (1964). *On Aggression*, trans. M. Latzke. London: Methuen.
Mauss, M. (1924). Rapports réels et pratiques de la psychologie et de la sociologie. In *Sociologie et anthropologie*. Paris: Presses Universitaires de France, 1950. [Real and practical relations between psychology and sociology. In *Sociology and Psychology* (pp. 1–33), trans. B. Brewster. London: Routledge & Kegan Paul, 1979.]
Mauss, M. (1936). Les techniques du corps. In *Sociologie et anthropologie*. Paris: Presses Universitaires de France, 1950.[Techniques of the body. *Economy and Society*, 2 (1973, no. 1): 70–88.]
Parat, C.-J. (1973). Communication à propos du rapport de J. Chasseguet-Smirgel sur l'Idéal du Moi [Communication concerning J. Chasseguet-Smirgel's paper on the ego-ideal]. *Revue Française de Psychanalyse, 33* (5–6): 937–940.
Penot, B. (1989). *Figures du déni. En deça du négatif* [Forms of disavowal. Beyond negativity]. Paris: Dunod.

Pontalis, J.-B. (1983). Permanence du malaise [Persistent malaise]. In *Le temps de la réflexion* [Time for reflection], *Vol. 4*. Paris: Gallimard.

Saussure, F. de (1986). *Course in General Linguistics*, trans. Roy Harris, ed. C. Bally & A. Sechehaye. New York: Open Court.

Wacquant, L. (1999). Inside 'The Zone'. In P. Bourdieu (Ed.), *The Weight of the World*, trans. P. Parkhurst Ferguson. Cambridge: Polity Press.

Žižek, S. (1992). Jouis de ta nation [Rejoice in your nation]. *Lettre Internationale*, *35* (Winter 92/93): 13–17.

Section VI

MASCULINE AND FEMININE SEXUALITY

VI MASCULINE AND FEMININE SEXUALITY

Introduction

Alain Gibeault

In France, the psychosexuality of men and women is a topic that has been addressed via a debate on Freud's theories on the Oedipus complex and on castration. Freud theorised his discoveries on the basis of the psychosexuality of boys; at times he found it much more difficult to describe what happened in girls, and he evoked the existence of a 'dark continent' (Freud, 1926e, p. 212), the exploration of which he left to those who came after him. It is obvious that the inventor of psychoanalysis had never been able to analyse sufficiently the issues raised by his own feminine identifications and the maternal transferences of his patients.

French psychoanalysts have made an important contribution to this debate, particularly with the publication in 1964 of a book – which has since become a classic – edited by Janine Chasseguet-Smirgel: *Recherches psychanalytiques nouvelles sur la sexualité féminine* [Female sexuality: New psychoanalytic views]. One of the chapters of that book is Chasseguet-Smirgel's own paper, 'Feminine Guilt and the Oedipus Complex', extracts from which can be found in the present volume (chapter 30). That book also contains papers by eminent members of the Paris Psychoanalytical Society: Catherine J. Luquet-Parat, Bela Grunberger, Joyce McDougall, Maria Torok and Christian David. Thus it was that male and female analysts came together to review the work that had been done on female sexuality from Freud onwards. The book opens, in fact, with an introduction by Chasseguet-Smirgel in which she provides an overview of the psychoanalytic literature on the subject.

That study highlighted the significant difficulty that exists in understanding the similarities and differences between male and female sexuality. Freud's discovery of infantile sexuality had led him to describe the antecedents of the difference between maleness and femaleness (1923e): between subject and object at the object-stage, between active and passive at the anal-sadistic phase, between the male genital organ and castration in the infantile genital organisation. 'It is not until development has reached its completion at puberty that the sexual polarity coincides with *male* and *female*. Maleness combines [the factors of] subject, activity and possession of the penis; femaleness takes over [those of] object and passivity' (1923e, p. 145). The difference between male and female corresponds to the cathexis of penis and vagina, respectively, contrasting with the preceding phase, that of phallic monism, in which the primacy of the penis was the only characteristic.

It was precisely that developmental sequence that Chasseguet-Smirgel challenged; to a considerable extent she agrees with the standpoints adopted by Ernest Jones and Melanie Klein, who had called into question Freud's hypothesis according to which young girls know nothing of the vagina. What seems in fact to be the case is that, in childhood, the idea of the vagina is misunderstood and pushed aside: penis envy has less to do with a primary desire, as Freud thought, than with a 'feeling of incompleteness' corresponding to a defensive manoeuvre seeking to repress feminine desires in young girls. That misunderstanding could also have a defensive function in boys, because this kind of sexual theory allows them not only to defend themselves against passive homosexuality with respect to the father, but also to evade any envy of the mother in her double function, genital and procreative.

For Freud (1937c), the repudiation of femininity is an 'underlying bedrock', biological in nature, that creates an impasse in psychoanalytic therapy; in women, the wish for a penis and, in men, the rebellion against a passive or feminine attitude towards another man are, in fact, a psychological bedrock. This repudiation of femininity is understood by Chasseguet-Smirgel as a refusal of primitive dependence on the mother, who subjected her child both to her domination as an ambi-sexed imago and to the distress created by her femininity, correlative with her fertility, evocative of maternal castration. It is in this sense that she interprets the theory of phallic monism, saying that any exclusive image of women as a lack, a hole, a wound seems to her to have, to a considerable extent, as its objective the negation of the imagos of the archaic mother, and this in both sexes – in women, all the same, identification with these imagos is, in addition, guilt-ridden. Chasseguet-Smirgel adds that the protective imago of the good, all-powerful mother and the terrifying imago of the bad, omnipotent mother are, in effect, the complete opposite of this representation of the castrated mother (1964). In later papers, Chasseguet-Smirgel (1976, 1988) interpreted this theory as derived from Freud's own need to protect himself against the archaic maternal imago by describing the whole of female sexuality as 'a series of lacks: the lack of a vagina, lack of a penis, lack of a specific sexuality, lack of an adequate erotic object, and finally the lacks which are implied by her being devoid of any intrinsic feminine qualities which she could cathect directly and by her being forced to give up the clitoris' (1976, p. 281). Freud added the relative lack of a superego and of the capacity to sublimate. 'The boy's sexuality is so much more full: he possesses an adequate sexual organ, a sexuality which is specific from the outset, and two love-objects to satisfy the requirements of both tendencies of the Oedipus complex' (Chasseguet-Smirgel, 1976, p. 281).

In her 1964 paper (chapter 30), Chasseguet-Smirgel attempts to highlight certain feminine perspectives in the Oedipal situation, in particular with respect to the issues involved in the change of object. She insists on the importance, in girls, of the defensive idealisation of the father and of her love for him, unlike Freud, for whom this change of object simply gave rise to an exact copy of the relationship she had with the mother. In Chasseguet-Smirgel's view, the wish to have a child by the father is a primary desire linked to the girl's femininity and not, as Freud thought, a secondary desire replacing the wish to have a penis. Female inhibitions can thus be understood not in terms of a narcissistic fear for the ego, but as the effect of a fear of castrating the father, which gives rise to a form of guilt specific to girls.

Freud thought of the girl's entry into the Oedipal situation as a haven of peace bereft of conflict, but Chasseguet-Smirgel sees in this an identification with the father's penis that maintains the girl in a state of infantile dependence. She stresses the difference between the *phallus*, with which women identify in order to be complete and autonomous, and the *penis*, a complementary part that is wholly dependent on the object. Thus she gives that distinction a quite different meaning from that of Lacan, for whom the phallus is the signifier of a lack in the fantasy life of both sexes over and beyond its anatomical presence.

Jean Cournut's idea (1998 – chapter 31, this volume) about the fear that men have of women is similar to what Chasseguet-Smirgel says about the pregenital anxieties in both men and women concerning the *maternal feminine dimension*, describing them as being basically the primal and irrational anxiety of being engulfed by the archaic maternal imago. Cournut emphasises the importance of taking into account the anxieties pertaining to the *erotic feminine dimension* that evokes unlimited sexual pleasure in women, thus giving rise to both fear and envy in men: *'For the erotico-maternal feminine to trigger, as according to Freud, the horror of possible castration, or, worse, confront the man-subject with something unrepresentable, on the path of an unbinding that would threaten him with psychic death, it is necessary that some psychic means of withdrawal, if not support, are organised'* (chapter 31, p. 613; italics in original). Cournut sees these in terms of the possibility of putting a name on what is occurring, representing it in the mind and dialectalising it. He went on to develop these hypotheses in his book that carries the same title as his earlier paper, *Pourquoi les hommes ont peur des femmes* [Why men are afraid of women] (Cournut, 2001), in which he shows how putting forward a phallic and active masculine dimension is in fact a defence against the anxieties aroused by what is unthinkable about sexual pleasure in women, about the phenomena of motherhood and, even worse, about female homosexuality.

In a 1998 book, from which extracts from two articles she had earlier written (1994, 1997) are published in the present volume (chapter 32), Monique Cournut-Janin explores the issues involved in female sexuality. She draws a distinction between 'the feminine' [*le féminin*][1] and 'femininity' [*féminité*]. The latter, included in the unconscious maternal message, consists in cathecting an outside-that-is-displayed which highlights the young girl's body, with all of its adornments; at the same time there is a repression of the cathexis of the vagina and the uterus, which

---

[1] In French, as in English, 'feminine' is used as an adjective. Here, in the original version, it is used as a noun, and we have retained this in the translation in order to make a distinction between, on the one hand, something which is more closely tied to a representation of the inside of the body and biological femaleness and, on the other, something which involves more the external appearance. [*Ed.*]

are typical of an inside-that-remains-hidden, the characteristic feature of the feminine. Cournut-Janin's ideas are close to those of Denise Braunschweig and Michel Fain (1971, 1975), to which she refers in her book, on the importance of the censorship of the woman-as-lover in the maternal transmission of the feminine under the guise of femininity.

It follows that the castration message conveyed by the mother in the name of the father does not concern only the young boy, as Freud had thought, but the young girl also; she is thereby invited to cathect her whole body and to set up a protective phallic lure correlative with the repression of her own sexual organ. Cournut-Janin thus sees in a positive light the young girl's lack of knowledge of her vagina and uterus; she goes on to show how the mother, thanks to her transmission of the Oedipal prohibitions, encourages the future change of object in the young girl: 'Femininity, in the sense that I am proposing, is what a woman displays ("there's something there; there's nothing there") in a hidden–shown that can avert the danger of generating male castration anxiety while simultaneously suggesting enough of the feminine to stimulate desire in the other sex' (chapter 32, p. 634). The idea here is to describe a loving complicity between mother and daughter based on the tenderness that leads to the female Oedipus complex in girls, while at the same time defining the mother as the only woman-as-lover, and 'reserving for herself the ability to have pleasure with the father'. This would be a kind of double game that the mother plays, one which allows an encounter with the Oedipal father while at the same time keeping that encounter away from any incestuous violence.

From that perspective, the psychosexual destinies of boys and girls are different with respect to the visible penis and the invisible element of the female body. They come close together, however, in the primary cathexis of the mother. Cathexis of the maternal feminine dimension can also be seen as a movement towards narcissistic identification with the object. That was probably what Freud had in mind when he described primary identification in terms indicating that projection and introjection were treated as designating the same mental process: '. . . identification is a preliminary stage of object-choice, . . . it is the first way – and one that is expressed in an ambivalent fashion – in which the ego picks out an object. The ego wants to incorporate this object into itself, and, in accordance with the oral or cannibalistic phase of libidinal development in which it is, it wants to do so by devouring it' (Freud, 1917e [1915], pp. 249–250). It is therefore simultaneously that the projective process, which leads to object choice, and the introjective process, represented here as a fantasy of incorporation, take place.

This is not an attempt to diminish the importance of the kind of mental development that makes a greater distinction between projective and introjective components in the work of the mind, at the same time as objectality and objectivity are being set up – this is what Freud meant by the movement from the purified pleasure-ego to the reality-ego. What must be emphasised all the same is that projection as a primal process determines both differentiation and non-differentiation between subject and object: that primal dimension is often represented in Freud's writings by an archaic primary quality. However, that should not make us lose sight of the importance of the process-based aspect of the concepts we use. From that point of view, Klein's introduction of the concept of projective identification had the virtue of confirming the importance of the fundamental 'interaction' between projection and introjection for our understanding of issues involving projection.

The process of differentiation between subject and object is taken up in the concept of *primary homosexuality* as described by Paul Denis (1982 – chapter 33, this volume). The idea is to highlight the importance of the cathexis of the narcissistic 'double' in order to make possible the acceptance of otherness in the difference between the sexes and between generations, and to permit access to secondary identification. The concept of primary homosexuality was introduced by Evelyne Kestemberg (1982, 1984) in order to emphasise the importance in mental work of cathecting 'sameness'. With reference to what Edith Jacobson had written (1964) about the various modalities of projective identification, Kestemberg highlighted the value as a process of the inhibition of drives with respect to their aim as manifested in the experience of tenderness. In this way, the individual becomes able to accept the movement from primary identification, with its quest for *oneness*, to secondary identification. Freud described this as a partial identification with the object pertaining to *likeness*, thereby enabling a relationship with the object that involves *closeness*. As Denis points out, the emergence of tenderness corresponds to a process of relative desexualisation that puts on hold the tendency to drive-related discharge and allows acceptance of difference with respect to the object in terms of sameness; in this way, it makes a vital contribution to the subsequent acceptance of the object's otherness.

Christian David's work on psychic bisexuality throws more light on this development of psychosexuality. In agreement with Freud's discovery of infantile sexuality, David (1973 – chapter 34, this volume) emphasises the fact that, if 'anatomy is destiny', psychic bisexuality is 'anti-destiny', because the child's polymorphous sexuality implies many kinds of sexual satisfaction which Freud theorised on the basis of the concept of the instinctual drives, with their varying aims and objects. It is therefore necessary to take into account the dialectic between the difference between the sexes and issues involving psychic bisexuality, defined by David as 'a bisexualisation process'.

David suggested the concept of bisexualisation in order to describe the integration of masculine and feminine dimensions in the psychosexuality of both men and women. The **bisexualisation process** corresponds, in both sexes, to the possibility of acquiring 'the mental capacity to fantasise, understand and share the sexual and psychosexual experience of someone of the other sex' (David, 1975, p. 836); this implies acceptance of the incompleteness of both sexes, experienced as castration, and not its denial, as we find in actual bisexual behaviour.

The analytic situation enables that dialectic to be processed as it occurs. The regression intrinsic to psychoanalysis calls into question the analysand's psychosexual identity and facilitates recourse to bisexuality experienced as unisexuality. This movement corresponds to what happens in the object relation characterised by 'sameness' and not by difference. As has often been pointed out with respect to narcissistic regression in the course of psychoanalytic treatment, the work of analysis can be seen as the possibility of experiencing moments of controlled depersonalisation that allow for passivity to be integrated in the form of receptiveness; this could just as well be seen as the acceptance, in both sexes, of femininity. As David points out, this has to do with a restoration of the introjection of the difference between the sexes. The clinical and literary examples he describes in his paper illustrate the issues involved in the difference between the sexes and the fact that it is important to relativise that difference if there is to be a true encounter between the sexes.

> The concept of **bisexual mediation** was introduced by David (1975) in order to emphasise the importance of the role played by psychic bisexuality in inter- and intra-subjective relationships. From David's point of view, psychic bisexuality presumes the integration of 'virtual complementarity', one that is potential with respect to the opposite sexuality.

In a later paper, David (1975) introduced the concept of *bisexual mediation* to describe the process that lies between the affirmation of sexual specificity and that of bisexuality: 'The idea of psychic bisexuality implies both a virtual complementarity, one that is potential with respect to the opposite sexuality, the opposite psychosexuality (without which the "coexistence of desire and identification" (Green, 1968), an essential factor in every mental development, would be inconceivable) *and*, given that virtuality, a reminder of the incompleteness linked to sexual specifications. . . . Sexual intercourse exists, relationships between the sexes exist because bisexuality exists' (David, 1975, pp. 834–835)

From that perspective, psychic bisexuality is neither biological bisexuality nor a pathogenic and regressive fantasy, as evidenced in bisexual, transvestite and transsexual enactments; these have to do with the denial of the difference between the sexes and of castration, with the *juxtaposition* of male and female rather than with their *articulation* through the metaphorisation of bodily experience in terms of the wish to penetrate and the wish to be penetrated. The analytic process can thus be thought of as the analysand's identification with the analyst's function as regards this interplay between penetration and receptiveness, in which the parameters of analysis – free association and evenly suspended attention – bear witness to a potential integration between the masculine and feminine dimensions of mental life. In this, psychic bisexuality guarantees creativity and echoes the conditions of the work of symbol-formation.

For Joyce McDougall, too, the criterion of mental health, free of all reference to the normality/abnormality option, is that of creativity, whether emergent or recaptured. The 1978 paper published in the present collection (chapter 35) is the final chapter of McDougall's *Plea for a Measure of Abnormality* (1990), and it is typical of her subversive approach. Born in New Zealand, McDougall began working with Anna Freud and Winnicott before settling in France and becoming a member of the Paris Psychoanalytical Society; that double affiliation goes some way to explaining why she has often challenged the received ideas we sometimes find in psychoanalysis and psychiatry. In her preface to the 1990 English edition of that book, she argues in favour of using the word 'plea' to describe her passionate defence of the cause of psychoanalysis: 'I was also aware of my concern about being imprisoned in time-honoured theoretical concepts that would impede the attempt to find solutions to complex clinical problems. . . . I also questioned the validity of considering neurosis and perversion as connected only in a negative sense, and the view that neurosis and psychosis fall into two totally separated worlds' (pp. viii–ix).

That is why, in McDougall's opinion, the idea of normality is ambiguous, given that it is a mark, simultaneously, of approval and of condemnation: normality evokes ordinariness and conformity, while the idea of abnormality refers to pathology and deviancy. In the examples she gives, McDougall speculates on what it means to be 'normal' on the psychoanalytic stage: she argues that 'normality' can never be an analytic concept. If some people are 'normal', we should ask ourselves what that normality consists of from a psychoanalytic point of view; she wonders also whether sexual normality can ever exist, and questions the very idea of psychoanalytic norms. She argues that a 'good' normality is the outcome of resolving the Oedipal situation. In order to justify a request for analysis, the normal individual must suffer from his or her normality – and this 'bad' normality indicates that something is lacking in that person's fantasy life, with an ever-greater dichotomy opening up as regards the true self. Normality elevated to the rank of an ideal is, in fact, a well-compensated psychosis.

Although she denounces the impasses in which normopaths find themselves, McDougall does not condemn the perverse and psychotic 'deviations', which she refuses to see in terms of 'deviancy', with its moralistic connotations; she acknowledges the importance of the work that the mind of these patients accomplishes in creating unconscious scenarios, even though they are often locked into repetition. The aim is to acknowledge the psychic value of attempts at self-healing with respect to the harrowing conflicts of childhood which could damage sexual life in adulthood. That creativity is preferable to the kind of adaptive normality which evades all self-questioning and involves a subtle form of exclusion from fantasy life.

In her thinking about human sexuality, McDougall takes into consideration various issues that have to do with the relationship between the instinctual drives and the object. The genital sexual function, in both men and women, cannot be dissociated from object-cathexes because, for example, a weak object-cathexis may facilitate an adequate genital experience while, on the contrary, a more sustained object-cathexis could inhibit genital functioning and make it more vulnerable to feelings of guilt and anxiety.

These ideas are close to Evelyne Kestemberg's thinking (1982) about the new forms of pathology that we find in adolescents. In earlier days, as it were, adolescent depression could be hidden behind a whole series of neurotic symptoms, particularly sexual ones; today's adolescents, however, are more likely to present a 'raw' depression focused not on their pleasure or unpleasure at the way in which their body functions, but on intellectual inhibition. This bears witness to a re-sexualisation of mental functioning, which becomes the only form of castration, and to a desexualisation of sexuality, which is then undermined; this is because it is rejected as not being part of the individual's make-up and often faecalised in the vocabulary that these adolescents use. These new forms of pathology represent a challenge to object-cathexis in that they give pride of place to the instinctual drives; they are made all the easier nowadays by changes in social *mores* that encourage freedom of expression in sexuality but testify to the more widespread and diffuse damage done to mental functioning than is the case in classic neurotic structures.

In her plea for calling into question any kind of normative proposal, McDougall does, all the same, specify that she is talking about 'a measure' of abnormality. With that restriction, she attempts to set limits on an approach the intention of which is to take seriously Freud's idea of the instinctual drives as having various kinds of aims and objects, rather than simply taking into account the genital conception of sexuality. McDougall pays close attention to how much damage and suffering these 'abnormal' pathological solutions entail, and to the psychic death faced with which a fragile and childlike being would invent anything at all to escape – in this case, the creations of perverse sexuality. She has always tried to take into account, in the course of any given analysis, the quality of communication with that 'magical narcissistic child', whose development is better assessed in terms of creativity in the analytic process (process goals) rather than through choices in professional and sentimental life (outcome goals), which do not always manage to evade a 'normalising normality'.

References

Braunschweig, D., & Fain, M. (1971). *Eros et Anteros. Réflexions psychanalytiques sur la sexualité* [Eros and Anteros: Psychoanalytic thoughts on sexuality]. Paris: Payot.
Braunschweig, D., & Fain, M. (1975). *La nuit, le jour. Essai psychanalytique sur le fonctionnement mental* [Night, day: A psychoanalytic essay on mental functioning]. Paris: Presses Universitaires de France.
Chasseguet-Smirgel, J. (1964). La culpabilité féminine (De certains aspects spécifiques de l'oedipe féminin). In J. Chasseguet-Smirgel (Ed.), *Recherches psychanalytiques nouvelles sur la sexualité féminine*. Paris: Presses Universitaires de France, 1964. [Feminine Guilt and the Oedipus Complex. In *Female Sexuality: New Psychoanalytic Views*. Ann Arbor, MI: University of Michigan Press, 1970.]
Chasseguet-Smirgel, J. (1976). Freud and Female Sexuality – The Consideration of Some Blind Spots in the Exploration of the 'Dark Continent'. *International Journal of Psychoanalysis, 57*: 275–286.
Chasseguet-Smirgel, J. (1988). *Les deux arbres du jardin* [The two trees in the garden]. Paris: Des femmes.
Cournut, J. (1998). Le pauvre homme ou Pourquoi les hommes ont peur des femmes [The poor man or why men are afraid of women]. *Revue Française de Psychanalyse, 62* (2): 393–414.
Cournut, J. (2001). *Pourquoi les hommes ont peur des femmes* [Why men are afraid of women]. Paris: Presses Universitaires de France.
Cournut-Janin, M. (1994). La boîte et son secret [The box and its secret]. *Revue Française de Psychanalyse, 58* (1): 57–66.

Cournut-Janin, M. (1997). Sous couvert de féminité [Under cover of femininity]. *Revue Française de Psychanalyse*, *61* (2): 387–397.

Cournut-Janin, M. (1998). *Féminin et féminité* [The feminine and femininity]. Paris: Presses Universitaires de France.

David, C. (1973). Les belles différences [The beautiful differences]. *Nouvelle Revue de Psychanalyse*, *7*: 21–45. Also in *La bisexualité psychique* [Psychic bisexuality] (pp. 21–45). Paris: Payot, 1992.

David, C. (1975). La médiation bisexuelle [Bisexual mediation]. *Revue Française de Psychanalyse*, *39* (5–6): 824–845. Also in *La bisexualité psychique* [Psychic bisexuality] (pp. 46–72). Paris: Payot, 1992.

Denis, P. (1982). Homosexualité primaire, base de contradiction [Primary homosexuality: A basis for contradiction]. *Revue Française de Psychanalyse*, *46* (1): 35–42.

Freud, S. (1917e [1915]). Mourning and Melancholia. *S.E.*, 14: 239.

Freud, S. (1923e). The Infantile Genital Organisation: An Interpolation into the Theory of Sexuality. *S.E.*, 19: 141.

Freud, S. (1926e). *The Question of Lay Analysis. S.E.*, 20: 179.

Freud, S. (1937c). Analysis Terminal and Interminable. *S.E.*, 23: 209.

Green, A. (1968). Sur la mère phallique [The phallic mother]. *Revue Française de Psychanalyse*, *22* (1): 1–38.

Jacobson, E. (1964). *The Self and the Object World*. New York: International Universities Press.

Kestemberg, E. (1982). La sexualité des adolescents [Adolescent sexuality]. In *L'adolescence à vif* [Adolescence laid bare]. Paris: Presses Universitaires de France, 1999.

Kestemberg, E. (1984). 'Astrid' ou homosexualité, identité, adolescence. Quelques propositions hypothétiques ['Astrid' or homosexuality, identity, adolescence. Some hypothetical propositons]. In *L'adolescence à vif* [Adolescence laid bare]. Paris: Presses Universitaires de France, 1999.

McDougall, J. (1978). Plaidoyer pour une certaine anormalité. In *Plaidoyer pour une certaine anormalité*. Paris: Gallimard. [*Plea for a Measure of Abnormality*. New York: International Universities Press, 1980; London: Free Association Books, 1990.]

30 FEMININE GUILT AND THE OEDIPUS COMPLEX

Janine Chasseguet-Smirgel

A full member of the Paris Psychoanalytical Society and member of the Philadelphia Psychoanalytic Society, **Janine Chasseguet-Smirgel** (1928–2006) was Freud Memorial Professor at the University of London (1982–83); she was also professor of clinical psychology and psychopathology at the University of Lille.

In 1999, she was awarded the Alexander von Humboldt prize by the Federal Republic of Germany, the first time that this prestigious scientific prize was awarded to a psychoanalyst. In 1964, she edited the first post-war psychoanalytic book on recent developments in the Freudian conception of female sexuality.

Her papers on art, on perversion and on the traces of Nazism in group psychology are known the world over. Her 1973 book on the ego ideal [*The Ego Ideal: A Psychoanalytic Essay on the Malady of the Ideal* (Norton, 1985)], republished under the title *La maladie de l'idéalité* (L'Harmattan, 1999), in which she expands upon her neo-Freudian reworking of the concept of the ego-ideal, has become a classic text. In her most recent book, *Le corps comme miroir du monde* [The Body as Mirror of the World] (PUF, 2003; FAB, 2005), she discusses in her characteristically frank and open-minded manner the strange and sometimes violent mechanisms that emerge in mental life and the modern world.

Dominique Bourdin wrote a concise biography of Janine Chasseguet-Smirgel for the 'Psychanalystes d'aujourd'hui' series (PUF, 1999).

> This is in disagreement with Freud's formidable statement that the concept of the Oedipus complex is strictly applicable only to male children and 'it is only in male children that there occurs the fateful conjunction of love for the one parent and hatred of the other as rival.'[1] We seem compelled here to be *plus royalistes que le roy*. . . . I can find no reason to doubt that for girls, no less than for boys, the Oedipus situation in its reality and phantasy is the most fateful psychical event in life.
>
> Jones ('The Phallic Phase,' 1932)

---

[1] Sigmund Freud, 'Female Sexuality,' 1931.

It is troubling to note that Freudian theory gives the father a central role in the boy's Oedipus complex but considerably reduces that role in the girl's. In fact, in considering Freud's article 'Female Sexuality' (to which Jones replies in his article 'The Phallic Phase') it is suggested that the girl's positive Oedipus complex may simply not exist. If it exists, it is usually an exact replica of her relationship to her mother. Freud says in the same article, 'except for the change of her love object, the second phase had scarcely added any new feature to her erotic life' (this second phase being the positive Oedipus complex).

Freud maintains that it is not because of her love for her father nor because of her feminine desires that the little girl arrives at the positive Oedipal position but because of her masculine desires and her penis envy. She tries to get what she wants from her father, the possessor of the penis. When the Oedipal position is reached, it tends to last some time as it is essentially a 'haven' ('The Dissolution of the Oedipus Complex,' 1924). 'She enters the Oedipus situation as though into a haven or refuge.' As the little girl has no fear of castration, she has nothing to give up, and she does not need a powerful superego.

During the period preceding the change of object, if it occurs at all, the father is 'scarcely very different from an irritating rival' ('Female Sexuality,' 1931), but at the same time the rivalry with the father in the negative Oedipus complex is not so strong and is not in any way symmetrical with the boy's Oedipal rivalry accompanying his desire to possess his mother. The little girl in her homosexual love for the mother does not identify with the father.

If we turn from the study of normal or neurotic behavior to that of psychotics, we note the importance Freud gave to the role of homosexuality in his theories of delusion formation. Desires of passive submission to the father, dangerous for the ego, play the main role in masculine delusions. One of the most important of these wishes is the desire to have a child from the father. It is surprising that Freud, when he considered this desire in the context of a little girl's normal development, did not believe it to be a primary desire arising from her femininity but, on the contrary, a secondary desire, a substitute for penis envy.

Paradoxically, the father seems to occupy a much more important place in the psychosexual development of the boy than of the girl, be it as a love object or as a rival. I would even say that Freud, if one accepts all the implications of his theory, believes the father to be much more important in general for the boy than for the girl. However, Freud, with the open, scientific mind and concern for truth which characterize genius, never considered his studies of femininity to be complete or definitive, and he encouraged his disciples to continue their exploration of 'the dark continent.' One need only refer to the final sentence of one of his last works on the psychology of women: 'If you want to know more about femininity, enquire from your own experience of life, or turn to the poets, or wait until science can give you deeper and more coherent information' (in 'Femininity,' 1932).

My aim in this study is to discuss certain specifically feminine positions in the Oedipal situation which are not found in that of the male. Perhaps I shall be able to reveal a little of their deeper motivation and describe their eventual consequences. Time will prevent our studying in detail many problems of woman's psychosexual life on which this study will inevitably touch, such as penis envy, female masochism, the superego, and the resolution of the Oedipus complex in girls. I shall treat of them only inasmuch as they relate to my central theme. Because of the numerous difficulties involved in this type of study a somewhat artificial presentation becomes unavoidable. I have placed greater emphasis on the particular characteristics of the girl's relation to her father, without taking into consideration, as one should, the significant early history of this relationship; neither have I touched on the particular problems of identification so important in homosexual development. Whenever one discusses 'the specificity' of certain female attitudes one should compare them to male ones. In this study such a comparison can be no more than implied.

Most psychoanalytic authors have noted that women on the road to genital and Oedipal maturity are faced with greater difficulties than men, so much so that Freud, as we know, was led to reconsider his belief in the universality of the Oedipus complex as the nucleus of the neuroses. Those authors who do not agree with Freud generally believe that the difficulties the little girl encounters in her psychosexual development are due mainly to the fears for the ego – *narcissistic anxieties* awakened by the feminine role.

For my part, I shall concern myself with aspects of the female Oedipus complex which have no counterpart in the male, and which are the source of a specific form of feminine *guilt* inherent in a specific moment in woman's psychosexual development: the change of object.

I. Object idealization in the girl's relation to her father

The theories of Freud and those who have followed him, as well as the theories of those who oppose him (Melanie Klein and Ernest Jones in particular), all agree on one point about the girl's development: the *change of object* inherent in the Oedipal development of women is based on *frustration*.

Thus, for Freud, the girl's Oedipus complex is due to a double misapprehension, having to do first with objects, then with her own narcissism. This disappointment is caused mainly by the fact that the little girl discovers her 'castration' – the mother has given her neither the love nor the penis she wanted. According to Freud, this frustrated penis envy, replaced by a desire for a penis substitute, a child, prompts the little girl to turn to her father. Melanie Klein and Ernest Jones, on the contrary, thought that 'the girl is brought under the sway of her Oedipus impulses, not indirectly, through her masculine tendencies and her penis envy, but directly, as a result of her dominant feminine instinctual components' (Melanie Klein, *The Psychoanalysis of Children*,

1932). Most of all the little girl wants to incorporate a penis, not for itself but in order to have a child by it. The desire to have a child is not a substitute for the impossible desire to have a penis (Jones, 'The Phallic Phase,' 1932). These authors, in spite of their refusal to admit the secondary quality of the feminine Oedipus complex, believe that the little girl's Oedipal desire is activated and awakened precociously by the *frustration* caused by the maternal breast, which then becomes 'bad.' It is, therefore, *the bad aspect of the first object* which (in both these views opposing Freud) lies at the basis of the change of object, the little girl seeking a good object capable of procuring for her the object-oriented and narcissistic satisfactions she lacks. The second object – the father or the penis – will be *idealized* because of the disappointment with the first object.

Indeed, a belief in the existence of a good object capable of alleviating the shortcomings of the first one is vital in order for any change of object to take place. This belief is accompanied by a projection of all the good aspects of the primary object onto the secondary object, while at the same time projection onto the original primitive object is maintained (temporarily at least) of all the bad aspects of that (new) object. This splitting is the indispensable condition leading to the change of object which would otherwise have no reason to occur. It is at the base of the girl's triangular orientation. But the splitting of the maternal image implies an *idealization* of the second object, if one may so refer to the projection of qualities all of which are exclusively good.

Several authors have stressed the importance of the idealization of this second object in girls. Thus, in *Envy and Gratitude*,[2] Klein refers to the exacerbation of negative feelings toward the mother, which turn the little girl away from her: 'But an idealization of the second object, the father's penis and the father, may then be more successful. This idealization derives mainly from the search for a good object.'

The idealization process on which the change of object is founded weighs heavily on women's future psychosexual development. In fact it implies an *instinctual disfusion*, each object being, at the time of the change of object, either entirely negatively cathected (the mother, her breast, her phallus) or entirely positively cathected (the father and his penis). Because of this the little girl will tend to *repress and countercathect* the aggressive instincts which exist in her relation to her father in order to maintain this instinctual disfusion. As a result there arises *a specifically feminine form of guilt attached to the anal-sadistic component of sexuality*, which is radically opposed to idealization.

The conflicts the little girl experiences in her relation with her father are, of course, linked to her first experiences with the maternal object as well as the peculiarities of the second object.

If positive experiences and progressively dosed 'normal frustrations' (those which are necessary for the development of a strong and harmonious ego)

---

[2] Melanie Klein, *Envy and Gratitude* (New York, 1957).

prevail in the girl's relation to her mother, if the father's personality offers an adequate basis for the projection of the object's good aspects onto him, and if at the same time he is solid enough, the little girl will be able to go through that change of object when prompted by these frustrations, achieving thereby a nonconflictual identification with the mother without the idealization of the second object becoming unduly important at this particular moment of her development.

The need to make permanent the idealization of the object concomitant with an instinctual disfusion is in this situation less pressing, and feminine psychosexuality can now progress under more satisfactory conditions. On the other hand, if the first attempts turn out badly, and if the second object does not offer the attributes necessary for the projection of good qualities, then character problems, perversions, and psychoses may develop.

Nevertheless, in most cases – and this seems practically inherent in woman's situation – the change of object coincides with dosages of maternal frustration at the wrong times. The father then becomes the last resort, the last chance of establishing a relation with a satisfying object. Indeed, the relation between mother and daughter is handicapped from the start; one might even say intrinsically so, since this state is due to the sexual identity between mother and daughter. Freud himself stressed that the only relation that could avoid 'the ambivalence characterizing all human relations' is that of mother and son. Later, I shall try to show some aspects of the father–daughter relationship which may help to explain why the idealization of the second object can be induced by the paternal attitude itself.

In most cases the father–daughter relation is characterized by the persistence of instinctual disfusion; the aggressive and anal-sadistic components are countercathected and repressed, since the second object must be safeguarded. At the same time the counter-identifications with the bad aspects of the first object are maintained.

The fact that the girl encounters greater difficulties in her psychosexual development than the boy is stressed by all authors. The frequency of female frigidity shows this. The guilt toward the mother alone is not sufficient to explain it; if it were, there ought to be something in the male that corresponds to it.

When Marie Bonaparte says that the cause of frigidity is to be found in the fact that woman has less libidinal energy, while Hélène Deutsch believes it to be linked to 'constitutional inhibitions,'[3] or when other authors believe it to be due to bisexuality, then it seems to me that they are sidestepping the discovery and interpretation of unconscious factors which, as Jones stressed in 'Early Female Sexuality,' form the main part of the analyst's task.

---

[3] 'Our understanding of feminine frigidity ... can be complete only if we take into consideration the fact that there is a constitutional inhibition that has no parallel in men' (*The Psychology of Women*, New York, 1944).

Many writers have noted, on the other hand, that woman's tendency toward idealization of sexuality is commonplace. One has only to think of adolescents or even of mature women who live in a romantic dream à la Madame Bovary waiting for Prince Charming, for eternal love, etc. . . . (In a recent sociological study Evelyne Sullerot mentions that the publishers of romantic pulp sell sixteen million copies a year.) Thus, in *The Psychology of Women*, Hélène Deutsch notes:

> As a result of a process of sublimation, woman's sexuality is more spiritual than man's. . . .
>
> This process of sublimation enriches woman's entire erotic affective life and makes it more individually varied than man's, but it endangers her capacity for direct sexual gratification. The constitutional inhibition of woman's sexuality is all the more difficult to overcome because, as a result of sublimation, it is more complicated (and the conditions for its gratification more exacting) than the primitive desire to get rid of sexual tension that more commonly characterizes masculine sexuality.

Hélène Deutsch stresses the 'spiritualized' character of female sexuality and speaks of 'sublimation' when she refers to it. But if this were a true sublimation the process would not end in inhibition. On the contrary, it seems to me that this is a reaction formation based on repression and countercathexis of those instinctual components opposed by nature to idealization or to anything spiritual or sublime; in other words, the anal-sadistic component instincts.

I shall now try to show the consequences of the repression of the anal-sadistic component for woman's psychosexual development. I shall make no attempt here to reconsider the concepts of activity and passivity, let alone the death instinct, but I would still like to quote certain statements by Freud about these concepts inasmuch as they concern the subject of this paper.

Discussing sexuality in general (not simply masculine sexuality) and referring to the *Three Essays*, Freud says in *Beyond the Pleasure Principle*: 'From the very start we recognized the presence of a sadistic component in the sexual instinct . . . later, the sadistic instinct separates off, and finally, at the stage of genital primacy, it takes on, for the purposes of reproduction, the function of overpowering the sexual object to the extent necessary for carrying out the sexual act.'[4]

In this passage Freud identifies sadism with destructive and death instincts, pointing out that in the sexual act these instincts are subordinated to Eros in order to secure control of the object. This instinctual control explicitly links Freud, in *Three Essays* (1905), to the anal-sadistic stage and to mobility. In the

---

[4] Sigmund Freud (1920), *Beyond the Pleasure Principle*. S.E., 19.

1915 revision he adds: 'It may be assumed the impulse of cruelty arises from the instinct for mastery and appears at a period of sexual life at which the genitals have not yet taken over their later role.'

In *The Ego and the Id*[5] (1923), Freud repeats this idea but this time insists on the importance of instinctual disfusion:

> The sadistic component of the sexual instinct would be a classical example of a serviceable instinctual fusion ... Making a swift generalization, we might conjecture that the essence of a regression of libido (e.g., from the genital to the sadistic-anal phase) lies in a disfusion of instincts. ...

Freud shows, in *Inhibitions, Symptoms, and Anxiety*,[6] that Eros desires contact because it strives to make the ego and the loved object one, 'to abolish all spatial barriers between the Ego and the loved object'; 'the aggressive object cathexis has the same aim.' Here again we see that aggression, according to Freud, is put in the service of Eros, desiring close contact with the object.

In these quotations we can see a sequential chain: mastery–sadism–anality; this chain is indispensable for sexual maturity, and its effective formation is a sign of genital maturation. Does the fact that this chain also has another link, 'activity,' mean that female sexuality is excluded from the Freudian concept of instinctual fusion which I have just mentioned? Once more, it is beyond my purpose to consider the concepts of activity and passivity in general. I merely wish to recall that one can follow Freud's thought and its numerous variations through all his writings on female sexuality in terms of antagonistic pairs of 'masculine–feminine' and 'active–passive.' Whenever Freud attempts to link these pairs of concepts he feels compelled to retract what he has said. In spite of his attempt to avoid equating these terms, other authors have completely identified activity with masculinity, passivity with femininity, and have reached doubtful conclusions as a result, especially as they have taken passivity to mean inertia or inactivity.

Thus, J. Lampl de Groot, in her article 'Contribution to the Problem of Femininity' (1933), equates masculinity with activity and passivity with femininity. She draws a series of conclusions to the effect that 'feminine' women do not know object love, activity under any guise, nor aggression. Since activity and love undoubtedly play a role in maternity, Lampl de Groot makes her famous postulate that it is women's *masculinity* which is expressed in the experience of pregnancy; and as this masculinity is opposed to female sexuality, 'good mothers are frigid wives.' This is not really proved because the postulate with which the article begins is merely repeated throughout in

---

[5] Sigmund Freud (1923), *The Ego and the Id*. S.E., 19.
[6] Sigmund Freud (1926), *Inhibitions, Symptoms, and Anxiety*. S.E., 20.

various tautological ways. Her essay ends with the statement that *introjection*, because it activates aggression, does not exist in truly 'feminine' women.

Hélène Deutsch emphasized[7] the idea of a typically feminine activity 'directed inward,' and the amphimixis of oral, anal, and urethral instincts connected with the vagina during coitus and orgasm. Yet in a symposium on frigidity (1961) at which she presided, she held that orgasmic climax could only occur in men, because it is a sphincter activity typical of the male.

As early as 1930 authors like Imre Hermann, Fritz Wittels, and Paul Schilder had warned against the theoretical and therapeutic dangers of identifying femininity with passivity, or even inertia. Therefore, in order to avoid ambiguity in the use of such terms as 'passivity' and 'activity,' I shall refer instead to the anal-sadistic component, whether it is the aggressive component of incorporative impulses or the aggressiveness linked to all attempts at achievement, for these two seem to me especially charged with conflict for women.

How incorporation becomes charged with conflict

Referring in the *Three Essays* to infantile masturbation Freud states that the girl often masturbates by pressing her thighs together, whereas the boy prefers to use his hand. 'The preference for the hand which is shown by boys is already evidence of the important contribution which the instinct for mastery is destined to make to masculine sexual activity.' In fact I believe that Freud is also indicating the importance this same instinct will have in female sexual activity. In coitus the vagina replaces the hand and like the hand it grasps the penis; this is reflected in the fantasies and problems characteristic for female sexuality, to the point that the anal component in the control of the vagina causes conflict. Psychoanalytic writings frequently refer to man's fear of the vagina (Freud, 'The Taboo of Virginity,' 1918;[8] Karen Horney, 'The Dread of Women,' 1932), but they rarely mention the other side of the problem, which is the attitude of the woman (her superego) toward her own aggression to the penis; if the problem is mentioned, the aggression is usually attributed to penis envy, or to defense against the penis considered dangerous because of certain projections, but the problem is never linked to the anal-sadistic component – as though female sexual desire contained no aggressive or sadistic elements.

In general, women's aggression toward the penis is never seen as a source of guilt. I do not wish in any way to deny the existence of the forms of female aggression which are frequently discussed; but I should like to insist particularly on the problems implied in *a basically feminine wish to incorporate the paternal penis*, which invariably includes the anal-sadistic instinctual components.

---

[7] *Psychology of Women.*
[8] *S.E.*, 11.

One must remember that during sexual intercourse, the woman does actually incorporate the man's penis. Although this incorporation is only partial and temporary, women desire in fantasy to keep the penis permanently, as Freud pointed out in his article 'On Transformations of Instincts as Exemplified in Anal Erotism' (1917).[9]

I shall illustrate the problems connected with wishes of incorporation toward the paternal penis through one case only, though in my experience the same conflicts are to be found in all women's analyses.

The patient whom I shall call Ann had idealized the image of her father. In order to protect this image she split her erotic objects into two very distinct types.

The first, a substitute for the father, is represented by a man, far older than she is, whom she loves tenderly and purely. This man is impotent. He loves her, protects her, encourages her career. She speaks of him in the same terms as she speaks of her father, who would give her a warm stone in winter to prevent the chilling of her fingers while going to school, kiss her tenderly, or sit with her on a bench in front of the house, offering wine to the neighbors passing by. The other man is represented by a Negro, to whom she feels she could show her erotic impulses, which are *linked* to the anal impulses.

During analysis, she says, 'Before, black and white were separate, now they are mixed together.'

Ann is in her forties, she is an opthalmologist, married and with two children, full of vitality and spirit, but paralyzed by deep conflicts which reveal themselves in strong anxieties, depersonalization, and the impulse to throw herself into the river or off a building. The theme of *engulfment* in water is frequent in her associations in the transference.

In the first session she is already very anxious and sees the green wall of my consulting room as an aquarium. *She feels she is in this aquarium herself* and says:

> 'I am very frightened . . . These ideas of aquaria are fetal. . . . I feel I am becoming schizophrenic.'

Several times during the analysis she expressed her anxiety in the following terms:

---

[9] 'I have had occasional opportunities of being told women's dreams that had occurred after their first experience of intercourse. They revealed an unmistakable wish in the woman to keep for herself the penis which she had felt.' I believe that this desire, which Freud thinks is a regressive one, is, in fact, the manifestation of a desire more authentically feminine, that of keeping the penis in order to be *impregnated* by it. The female sexual desire to be penetrated seems to me to be inseparably linked in the unconscious with the biological consequence of that desire – impregnation, that is to say the desire, as E. Jones said, to keep the penis in oneself in order to turn it into a child. Also, the instinctual drive at the level of the primary processes is absolute and unlimited and cannot be set in a spatio-temporal framework. The complementary masculine desire is similar in that it is not limited to penetrating one particular part of the woman's body at a given moment, but, as Ferenczi said in *Thalassa*, it is a desire to return one's whole body to the mother's womb.

> 'I am cracking up, I am *drowning*. I need a branch to save me. Will you be that branch?'

She often expressed the fear that I might become pregnant.

She also suffered from claustrophobia: fear of being alone in a room with no exit, fear of elevators. She dreams she is enclosed in a very tiny and very dark room similar to a coffin from which she cannot escape.

Ann's parents were farmers. She was, along with her sister, brought up by a severe and castrating mother. The father, much older than the mother, was 'gentle and kind.'

> 'My mother bossed him around. She was the ruler of the home. She ruled us all with a rod of iron. . . . Father was good; he forgave her everything. She took advantage of it.'

Ann often recalled incidents which represented the father's castration by the mother. For example, one day her father comes back from the fair where he had been drinking a little, lies down, and goes to sleep. The mother takes advantage of this occasion by stealing his wallet and then accusing him of having lost it. The primal scene which reveals itself through Ann's association is fantasied as a sadistic act during which the mother takes the father's penis.

I cannot give the whole development of Ann's analysis, but her treatment was centered on her difficulty in identifying with her mother. This difficulty was the major obstacle to a satisfactory Oedipal development. It was as though loving her father meant becoming like the castrating mother, sadistically incorporating his penis, and keeping it within her. But her love for her father could not allow her to adopt such a role.

Very early in the analysis, Ann expressed this conflict in the form of a dream:

> 'This is a very frightening dream. *I was* walking with *my mother* (an attempt to identify with the mother) in the river where I had my first impulse to throw myself into the water. We were looking for eel traps. It reminds me of the penis in the vagina (sadistic and castrating aspect of intercourse). My mother was mean to my father. This dream frightens me.'

Another dream of the same night:

> 'My mother was coming back from the river with my father's jacket on her shoulders. She had gone mad. In real life it is I who am afraid of going mad, of giving in to my impulses.'

Behind her impulses of throwing herself into the river or off a building lies the unconscious fantasy of identification with the mother who castrates her father during intercourse (the mother coming back from the river with the father's jacket). She expresses her castration wishes in the transference in many ways, sometimes even in a quasi-delirious way. She feels guilty because she is sure that *by shaking hands with me* (to bid good-bye) *she has strained my wrist* (she associates this with the paternal penis).

The transference expressions of her anal-sadistic impulses directed toward the penis were predominant in her relation with me and were mixed with anxiety and guilt. One day she associated the following recollection with her feeling of cracking up and *drowning:*

> 'In the River Gave there are potholes, you know, and deep eddies. One day my father nearly drowned in one; he was carried away by the current but caught hold of a branch at the last minute. . . . I am afraid of elevators. The elevator could fall in its shaft, and I would fall with it. I have the image of a penis drawn in by a vagina. . . .'

I believe Ann's conflict appears clearly in these associations of her fear of the impulse to throw herself into the river or off a building. The parents' intercourse signified for Ann an aggressive incorporation of the father's penis by the mother (the father's jacket on the mother's shoulders, the eel in the trap, the father engulfed by the eddy). In order to arrive at the Oedipal phase she must identify with the castrating mother, that is to say, *engulf the father's penis* in her vagina.

Yet, behind the patient's symptoms (her phobic impulses) there is a *reverse fantasy:* she is the contents (father's penis or father) of a destructive container (mother or mother's vagina). Her own body or vagina is identified with the mother or the mother's vagina. The destructive feature of the vagina is linked with the sphincteral anal component. The first fantasy hidden behind the symptom is therefore a compromise between the fulfillment of a desire and its punishment.

Ann achieves through guilt in fantasy the genital Oedipal desire to 'engulf' the father's penis (like the mother did), but she does this by *turning the aggression* against herself, her whole body identified with the paternal penis, whereas her destructive vagina, projected onto the outer world, is experienced as a cavity into which she disappears.

The contents and the container are reversed. Ann herself becomes the contents, which have disappeared into the container.

We realize that the first fantasy (the most superficial one), in which the punishment (superego) occurs, resulting in a compromise between the instinct and the defense, merely conceals another more primitive fantasy, which directly expresses the instinct: 'I am the hole in which my father (his penis) is engulfed.'

Her phobic symptom contains a double unconscious fantasy which is in accord with the Freudian theory of symptoms: a compromise concealing a primitive instinct.

It is important to add that one of the precipitating factors in mobilizing Ann's neurosis was her father's death just before her analysis, when she herself was pregnant. When she spoke of her father's death it was always in relation to her pregnancy. It became obvious during the analysis that the fantasy underlying this was that of the father's destruction by incorporation. Her fear that I should become pregnant, her projection of an aquarium onto the green wall of my consulting room, along with her fantasy of fetal regression, manifested the same symptomatic reversal of her fantasy: the fear of being engulfed and shut up inside me, like the fetus in its mother's womb, the fecal stool in the anus, or the penis in the vagina.

Having had a number of female patients with phobias of being engulfed by water, claustrophobia, compulsive ideas of throwing themselves into water or from a great height, vertigo, and phobias of falling, I came to realize that they all had a common meaning. In my experience they signify reversal of contents and container. The patient, by turning the aggression onto herself, experiences the sensation that she is the contents threatened by a dangerous container.

The genital level of these phobias does not mean that the ego is not severely affected; as we have seen the guilt involved in the relation with the idealized father often results from early conflicts with the primary object, since these conflicts are numerous and dangerous.

The sexual problems of these patients are of various kinds. Sometimes the splitting of the desired objects is enough to maintain a normal sexual appearance, but sexual pleasure is often restricted to the *clitoris* only. This particular sexual problem should be related to the same incorporation-guilt that forbids the erotic cathexis of the vagina, the organ of incorporation displacing its cathexis then onto an external organ, the clitoris. The analysis of this incorporation-guilt often allows for a more or less rapid extension of the clitoris's erotic cathexis to the vagina. This happens through the liberation of anal erotic and aggressive drive components which are then invested in the vagina. In some cases active homosexual wishes carry the same meaning of defense when conflict over incorporation is the issue.

A patient suffering from dyspareunia manifested this by a lack of vaginal stricture during intercourse. This symptom, which is in some way the reverse of vaginismus, is relatively frequent, but the patients who suffer from it believe it to be due to their anatomical make-up and become conscious of its psychogenic character only when it disappears during treatment. This symptom is the one which expresses most clearly the countercathexis of the anal-sadistic instinct of control. When this component is well integrated the vagina can allow itself to close around[10] the penis. In Freudian terms, one could say that desire of the Eros to unite with the object is satisfied, due to the instinct of control subordinating itself to the former.

---

[10] '*Epouser*' = 'to take the exact shape of' *and* 'to marry.' [*Trans.*]

Guilt concerning feminine achievement

A girl's guilt toward her father does not interfere merely with her sexual life but extends to her achievements in other fields if they take on an unconscious phallic significance. Inhibition related to this guilt seems to me chiefly responsible for women's place in culture and society today. Psychoanalysts have noticed that Oedipal guilt, linked to the guilt of surpassing the mother, is associated in many intellectual, professional, and creative activities with a feeling of guilt toward the father, a guilt which is specifically feminine. Indeed, I found that in patients suffering from chronic headaches their guilt over surpassing their parents on an intellectual level (which is so often the origin of cephalic symptoms, as though reproducing an autocastration of the intellectual faculties) was usually linked to the father, in both male and female patients. For both sexes successful intellectual activity is the unconscious equivalent of possessing the penis. For women this means they have the father's penis and have thus dispossessed the mother, the Oedipal drama. In addition they have also *castrated the father*. Moreover, the adequate use of such a penis also involves from the unconscious point of view the fecal origin of this image, ultimately, that of retaining an anal penis, which in turn engenders guilt.

One of my patients, a young girl of fifteen and a half who had severe migraine as well as school problems, was particularly poor in spelling and always had low marks on oral tests. When she tried to think, her thoughts blurred. She felt as though she were in a fog. Her ideas would become imprecise, she grew muddled and felt stumped – in other words her ideas lost their anal component. Her headaches began while she was preparing for an examination which she kept failing. The diploma she was trying to obtain was exactly the same as the one her father had.

This inhibition concerning the intellectual field she shared with her father was analyzed in relation to her Oedipal guilt about her mother, but it was soon obvious that interpretations on these levels were insufficient to bring to light the meaning of her symptoms.

She had a dream in which she wanted to hold her hand up, as a sign that she could answer the questions in the tests, but she felt it was 'forbidden'; she had another dream in which she had a snake in her hand which turned into a pen, so she took it to the police station because 'the man to whom it belonged could not write without his pen'; . . . these dreams led to interpretations in relation to her guilt about castrating her father and resulted in the cessation of her school inhibitions as well as a satisfactory Oedipal evolution. Indeed, once her aggression toward the paternal penis was accepted she was able to create fantasies about an Oedipal sexual relation with the father. The last dream she brought was one in which she received an attractive pen as a present from her father and then went with him for a walk along a sunken road, while her mother, who in the dream looked like me, was away on holiday.

Ann, the patient whom I formerly discussed, thought all her problems were due to her professional promotion. 'I am classless,' she would say, 'I am neither peasant nor bourgeois. I would have done better to have stayed working on the farm like father.' With the people who praised her for her professional success she suddenly felt like 'shouting, saying stupid things, acting like a mad woman.' Before her analysis she had had a period of anxiety during which she could not write any prescriptions, all the formulas blurring in her mind. Having a profession meant having a penis which she had stolen from her father just as her mother had done during the primal scene.

This meaning is expressed clearly in the following dream: 'I am beside an operating table. The surgeon is operating on the brain of an elderly man who could be my father. He ablates the whole frontal part of his brain away. I think to myself, "Poor man, he is going to be abnormal." When the surgeon has finished, he addresses the people who are there and says of me: "She is extremely intelligent and an excellent doctor, and she has a very pretty little girl with dark hair."'

Her associations about this dream are:

'I worked for that surgeon when I was a student. He used to congratulate me on doing my medical studies simultaneously with working as a nurse. Oh! *What a headache I've got* . . . I had another dream:

'I was at your place and I was cutting bread. A patient came in. You diagnosed him and phoned the diagnosis to someone. I admired how fast and sure you were in your diagnosis. Then you came up to me and said, "What is the diagnosis?" I gave the same diagnosis as you had. Then I felt embarrassed because it is as though you thought I hadn't overheard your conversation on the phone and that I thought of that diagnosis myself. So for the sake of intellectual honesty I told you that I had overheard your diagnosis. I thought I would have no difficulty in telling you this dream, but on the contrary I feel embarrassed as though I had cheated you. In the dream I had the feeling I was lying, and stealing something. One day I made a girl-friend of mine steal a toy. We were little then. When I said good-bye to you last time I again had the feeling that I had sprained your wrist. I have the feeling you are fragile.'

For Ann professional capability has the meaning of castrating the father, or the analyst in the paternal transference, and this castration represents an identification with the mother who steals the father's power. This is an anal castration as one can see by her feeling that she is telling lies and cheating me, analogous to her fantasy of the primal scene as shown in the screen memories: the mother stealing the father's money after he had come back drunk from the fair, followed by her accusation that the father had lost the money; the mother ordering him about, hiding for hours to frighten him, making him believe that she was working all the time, while in fact she did nothing. She seemed to be like Delilah, taking advantage of Samson's trusting sleep to cut off his hair.

The guilt linked with this desire to identify with the sadistic mother leads Ann to castrate herself (have headaches, fantasies in which she 'loses her mind,' professional inhibitions) and to perform acts which restore what has been taken away (she gives me back the diagnosis she has stolen, she worries about my sprained wrist). This fantasy of possessing a phallus is so conflict-laden that any small intervention touching on it stimulates guilt in women who otherwise seem quite free of work inhibitions.

I had a patient who, before she came to analysis, gave lectures on a rather feminine topic – children's education. At the end of one of her lectures, someone came up to her and said:

> 'All that is very well but, you know, the sight of a woman carrying a briefcase and a whole lot of files – really, that just isn't a woman's role!'[11]

From that day on, this patient never gave another lecture!

Analytic interpretation of these conflicts brings relief to women involved in fields they feel belong to men and which have an obvious phallic meaning (for example, taking exams, driving a car) as well as in those which are specifically feminine, such as pregnancy. Here again guilt toward the mother, the Oedipal rival, is coupled with the guilt of having taken the father's penis in order to make a child with it. This attack against the essence of the love object applied in transformation is experienced as anal guilt.

The symbolic connection 'child–penis' becomes significant in this context. Uncontrollable vomiting during pregnancy, and all the psychosomatic difficulties linked with the problems of accepting motherhood are often related to this guilt, as one can see in the analytic material of pregnant women.

Creativity. It is commonplace that women (with few exceptions) are not great creators, scientific or artistic. Man's creativity has been attributed to a desire to compensate for the fact that he cannot bear children (K. Horney) and thus create life. I believe that this is indeed one of the deep motives of creative work.

Yet creating is a means of alleviating deficiencies at various levels of instinctual maturity, and this results in attempts to achieve narcissistic integrity – represented in the unconscious by the phallus (Grunberger).

The phallic significance of creativity is emphasized in Phyllis Greenacre's 1960 article dealing with women who are creative artists.[12] She believes that this sometimes results in inhibitions due to fear that a phallic achievement

---

[11] It is not sufficient to give purely sociological reasons for women's difficulties in professional or creative fields; we need to seek out the deep unconscious roots of these difficulties. But neither would it be exact to say that there is no sociocultural factor. Women's internal guilt is constantly encouraged by real external factors. Psychoanalysts rightly emphasize the role of these external factors in creating neuroses – by being particularly favorable to unconscious conflicts common to many people.

[12] Phyllis Greenacre, 'Woman as Artist,' *Psychoanalytic Quarterly, 29* (1960): 208–227.

might interfere with the fulfillment of feminine desires. I agree with the author about the phallic meaning of creativity, but I would here again stress the part played by feminine guilt concerning possession of the penis and aggression toward the idealized father.

Women who have not idealized their fathers usually have no urge to create, because creation implies the projection of one's narcissism onto an ideal image which can be attained only through creative work.

If creative work signified only the act of parturition, then women with children would lack any desire to create, but analysis proves this to be untrue. The giving of life is not the same thing as being creative. To create is to do something other and something more than what a mother does, and it is in this respect that we see the phallic meaning of creation and its relation to penis envy.

That so many different achievements are symbolized by the possession and use of a penis results from the unconscious meaning of the phallus for both men and women. Whatever works well is represented in the unconscious by the phallus. Grunberger demonstrates in his essay on 'The Phallic Image' that the phallus is the symbol of narcissistic wholeness. Why is it that valor, creativity, integrity, and power are all, on different levels, symbolized by the male sex organ? In order to attempt to answer to this question we shall consider the problems of castration and penis envy in women.

II. The female castration complex and penis envy

> 'I've got one, and you've got none!'
> Gay little song sung by a three-and-a-half-year-old
> boy to his six-year-old sister

On the subject of penis envy Freud's views are opposed to those of Josine Müller, Karen Horney, Melanie Klein, and Ernest Jones. Freud holds that, until puberty, there is a *phallic sexual monism*, and therefore a total sexual identity between boys and girls up till the development of the castration complex. According to Hélène Deutsch, who agrees with Freud on these points, the little girl has no complete sexual organ from the age of four (age of the castration complex) to puberty – she has only her clitoris, which is seen as a *castrated penis*. She has no vagina as she has not yet discovered it and does not even know of it *unconsciously*.[13] We can understand easily why Freud and those who followed him in his theory on female sexuality believed *penis envy to be a primary phenomenon* and fundamental to women's psychosexuality, since the

---

[13] This assertion was maintained by Freud even in his 'Short Account of Psycho-Analysis' (1924), after many people had opposed him in theory and by clinical observation. Yet in the article Ruth Mack Brunswick wrote with him ('The Pre-Oedipal Phase,' 1940), he seems to have more or less accepted that early sensations do exist in the vagina.

little girl wants to compensate for the instinctual and narcissistic defects which mark most of her childhood.

Authors who do not agree with Freud's theory of female sexuality refuse to consider woman as '*un homme manqué*' (Jones). According to these authors the vagina is the first sexual organ to be libidinally cathected. The little girl is a woman from the start. The cathexis of the clitoris is secondary and serves a defensive function with regard to conflicts concerning genital impulses linked to the vagina: 'The undiscovered vagina is a vagina denied' (Karen Horney).

These authors agree that repression of vaginal impulses is due to narcissistic anxieties concerned with attacks against the inside of the body. Therefore, the erotic cathexis is transferred to the clitoris, a safer, external sexual organ.[14] This throws a new light on the theory of penis envy.

Josine Müller believes that self-esteem is linked to the satisfaction of the impulses peculiar to one's own sex. Penis envy, therefore, is due to the narcissistic wound resulting from unsatisfied genital (vaginal) desires, which have been repressed.

For Karen Horney penis envy results from certain characteristics of the penis (its visibility, the fact that its micturition is in the form of a jet, and so on),[15] but also from a fear of the vagina which exists in both sexes. In the girl such fears are related to her Oedipal desire to be penetrated by the father's penis, which becomes fearful because she attributes to it a power of destruction.

According to Melanie Klein, *the libidinal desire for the penis* is a primary one. It is first of all an oral desire, the prototype of vaginal desire. The fulfillment of this desire is linked to the fantasy of sadistically taking the paternal penis from the mother, who has incorporated it. This results in fear of retaliation from the mother, who might try to wound or destroy the inside of the girl's body. Therefore, penis envy can be related to the following ideas in the girl's unconscious: By using the external organ she demonstrates her fears are unfounded, testing them against reality. She regards the penis as a weapon to satisfy her sadistic desires toward her mother (cleaving to her so as to tear away the penis which is hidden inside her, to drown her in a jet of corrosive urine, etc.). The guilt resulting from these fantasies may make her wish to return the penis which she has stolen from the mother, and thus restitute her by regressing to an active homosexual position for which the possession of a penis is necessary.

Ernest Jones follows Melanie Klein's theory of penis envy in his article 'The Phallic Phase' (1932) centering his ideas on the primary characteristic of the 'receptive' cathexes of all the orifices of a woman's body (her mouth, anus, vagina).

---

[14] I think this transfer of cathexis is due to the guilt associated with the anal-sadistic incorporative drives.
[15] The narcissistic cathexis of these characteristics is linked, according to Grunberger, with the anal-sadistic phase, and thus the only objects of value are those which can be measured, compared, and precisely graded.

All these authors attribute a large part in female psychosexuality to the father and to penis envy, whereas Freud believed the Oedipus complex to be mainly masculine. Ruth Mack Brunswick thought female neuroses lack an 'Oedipus complex' and J. Lampl de Groot claims that the paternal image really exists for the little girl only once she is six, and maintains, that until that age, the relation with the father is the same as the child's relation with any other member of the household: sometimes friendly, sometimes hostile, according to her mood.

In his article on 'Female Sexuality' (1931) Freud argues against the *secondary* nature of penis envy, because the woman's envy is so violent that it can only have drawn its energy from *primary* instincts.

I believe that the fact that there may be primary receptive instincts in women, be they oral, anal, or vaginal,[16] does not prevent penis envy from being primary, too. However, even if one holds that a female sexual impulse exists right from the start, that the little girl has an adequate organ of which she has some certain knowledge, in other words, that she has all the instinctual equipment, yet we learn from clinical experience that from a narcissistic point of view the girl feels painfully incomplete. I believe the cause of this feeling of incompleteness is to be found in the primary relation with the mother and will therefore be found in children of both sexes.

The omnipotent mother

In the article she wrote with Freud, 'The Pre-Oedipal Phase of the Libido Development' (1940), Ruth Mack Brunswick insists on the powerful character of the primitive maternal imago ('She is not only active, phallic, but *omnipotent*'). She shows that *the first activity to which the child is submitted is the mother's*. The transition passage from passivity to activity is achieved by an *identification with the mother's activity*. Because of his dependence on the omnipotent mother

---

[16] Freud not only ignores the vagina but, until the castration complex, that is, the Oedipus complex, he believes the girl's sexuality to be identical with that of the boy. She merely hopes for receptive satisfactions from her mother, but she does not expect them to be phallic and denies the penis as well as the vagina. When she turns to the father wanting a child by him, it is not yet a desire for incorporation of the paternal penis. For Freud, the girl's Oedipus complex occurs without interfering with incorporation desires (or desires of being penetrated in any manner); in a similar way the boy has no desire to penetrate the mother. He is ignorant of her possessing an organ complementary to his own. It is only at puberty that erection of the penis indicates a new aim – the penetration of a cavity. Apart from numerous indications that there are early desires of penetration (which many people have noted), erections are frequent before puberty, and one finds babies having erections, particularly while being suckled. Ernest Jones, Melanie Klein, Josine Müller, Karen Horney, and, more recently, Phyllis Greenacre, in discussing the girl's discovery of the vagina, stress the fact that we are used to talking about external and visible organs without taking deep coenesthetic sensations into consideration. Girl's ignorance of their vaginas does not prove the nonexistence of a genital desire to incorporate the penis, just as a congenital malformation obstructing the mouth would not deny the existence of hunger. Indeed, the impossibility of satisfying the instinct increases guilt, in face of the 'condemned' vagina.

'who is capable of everything and possesses every valuable attribute' the child obviously sustains 'early narcissistic injuries from the mother' which 'enormously increases the child's hostility.'

I believe that a child, whether male or female, even with the best and kindest of mothers, will maintain a terrifying maternal image in his unconscious, the result of projected hostility deriving from his own impotence.[17] This powerful image, symbolic of all that is bad, does not exclude an omnipotent, protective imago (witch *and* fairy), varying according to the mother's real characteristics.

However, the child's primary powerlessness, the intrinsic characteristics of his psychophysiological condition, and the inevitable frustrations of training are such that the imago of the good, omnipotent mother never covers over that of the terrifying omnipotent, bad mother.

It seems to me that when the little boy becomes conscious[18] that this omnipotent mother has no penis and that he, subdued so far by her omnipotence, has an organ which she has not, this forms an important factor in his narcissistic development.

Analysts have mainly stressed the horror (the '*Abscheu*') the little boy feels when he realizes that his mother has no penis, since it means to him that she has been castrated, thus confirming his idea that such a terrifying possibility exists. This in turn may lead to fetishistic perversion and certain kinds of homosexuality. Few people take note of Freud's other statements stressing the narcissistic satisfaction felt by the little boy at the thought that he has an organ which women do not have. Thus, Freud says (in a note on exhibitionism added to the *Three Essays* in 1920): 'It is a means of constantly insisting upon the integrity of the subject's own (male) genitals and it reiterates his infantile satisfaction at the absence of a penis in those of women.' Elsewhere, Freud mentions the little boy's triumphant disdain for the other sex. He believes that this feeling of triumph (a note in *Group Psychology and the Analysis of the Ego*)[19] always arises from a convergence of the ego and the ego ideal. So it is indeed a narcissistic satisfaction, a triumph at last, over the omnipotent mother.

In his 1927 article on 'Fetishism' Freud pointed out the ambivalent role of the fetish. It is supposed to conceal the horrifying castration while it is at the same time the means of its possible reparation. Freud says of the fetishist that 'to point out that he reverses his fetish is not the whole story; in many cases he treats it in a way which is obviously equivalent to a representation of castration,' and at this point Freud refers to the people who cut off braids. When considering the Chinese custom of mutilating women's feet and then venerating them, which he believes to be analogous to fetishism, Freud states:

---

[17] Once frustration has brought the primary narcissistic phase to an end.
[18] Unconsciously, he has probably always known she had no penis just as, unconsciously, he always knew she had a vagina. But this does not exclude representations of a phallic or castrated mother, since the primary processes readily admit contradiction.
[19] S.E., 18.

'It seems as though the Chinese male wants to thank the woman for having submitted to being castrated.'

Countless clinical details relating to both sexes testify to the frequency and wealth of wishes to castrate the mother of her breast and of her phallus. If it were not for this deep satisfaction and its associated horror, the fantasy of the castrated mother would probably be less forceful.

Is it not at this point that myths begin to prevail over scientific thought? Are we not all tempted to talk as Freud did of 'the castrated condition of women,' or of 'the necessity for women to accept their castration,' or as Ruth Mack Brunswick put it, 'The real quality of the representation of the castrated mother and the fantasy quality of the phallic mother,' instead of putting these two representations back under the sway of the pleasure principle?

Images of woman as deficient, as containing a hole or wound, seem to me to be a denial of the imagos of the primitive mother; this is true for both sexes, but in women identification with such an imago leads to deep guilt.

The protective imago of the good omnipotent mother and the terrifying imago of the bad omnipotent mother are both in opposition to this representation of the castrated mother.

Generous breast, fruitful womb, softness, warmth, wholeness, abundance, harvest the earth, all symbolize the mother.

Frustration, invasion, intrusion, evil, illness, death, all symbolize the mother.

In comparison with the ideal qualities attributed to the early mother-image, the fall of the 'castrated' mother appears to result from a deep desire to free oneself from her domination and evil qualities.

The little boy's triumph over the omnipotent mother has many effects on his future relations with women. Bergler[20] points out that man attempts to reverse the infantile situation experienced with the mother and live out actively what he has endured passively, thus turning her into the dependent child he had been. This idea seems to be supported by certain aspects of woman's role, often noted by other authors. One also observes in patients the narcissistic effect of a man's realization that his mother does not possess a penis.

If the little boy has not been traumatized by the omnipotent mother, if her attitude has been neither too restraining, nor too invasive, he will be sufficiently reassured by the possession of his penis to dispense with constant reiteration of the triumphant feeling he once experienced. The need to reverse the situation might be restricted to a protective attitude toward women (this is not necessarily a reaction formation; it might be a way of linking his need for mastery to his love). But if the child was a fecal part-object serving to satisfy the mother's desire for power and authority, then the child's future object-relations with women will be deeply affected.[21]

---

[20] E. Bergler, *Homosexuality: Disease or Way of Life* (New York: Hill and Wang, 1956). [*Eds., this volume*]

[21] Of course other causes also dictate a man's future attitude to women, one of which is an identification with the real father in his relation to the mother.

In analysis we rarely encounter male patients who show defused anal-sadistic impulses in a pure state, nor do we find mothers in *analyses* who satisfy perverse desires through their children. But many male patients present contained sexual and relational problems, linked to a need for a specific form of narcissistic gratification which we regard as being the result of regression to the phallic-narcissistic phase.

It seems that Jones's description of the deutero-phallic phase in boys (with narcissistic overestimation of the penis, withdrawal of object-libido and lack of desire to penetrate sexually) and certain aspects of ejaculatio praecox noted by Abraham are to be found in these narcissistic-phallic men who have been disturbed in their early relation with the mother. They lack confidence in the narcissistic value of the penis and constantly have to put it to the proof; theirs is the 'little penis' complex, they regard a sexual relation as narcissistic reassurance rather than an object relationship of mutual value.[22]

Such men constantly doubt their triumph over women, as they doubt the fact that she has no penis, and are always fearful of finding one concealed in the vagina. This leads to ejaculation *ante portas*, in order to avoid such a dangerous encounter. The fantasy represents not only the paternal phallus but also (as Jones pointed out) the destructive anal penis of the omnipotent mother.[23]

But, in general, possessing the penis proves to be the satisfactory narcissistic answer to the little boy's primary relation with his mother.

Like the boy, the little girl, too, has been narcissistically wounded by the mother's omnipotence – maybe even more than he, for the mother does not

---

[22] See Karen Horney, 'The Dread of Women'. The little boy feels an aggressive desire for his mother. In her role as educator she is obliged to dominate him and frustrate him. He desires to penetrate her, but feels humiliated at being small and incapable of achieving this, which leads to his feeling narcissistically wounded and immensely inferior, but he also feels a violently aggressive desire for revenge, which is projected, along with those desires caused by the first frustrations, onto the mother and her vagina.

[23] One patient suffering from ejaculatio praecox was content in his first sexual relations at the age of twenty-two with merely external contact 'because he did not know' that the vagina existed. Such 'ignorance' is due to frightening sexual fantasies. For him the female organ was a threat, full of fecal content (crumbling caves full of garbage, cow's cloaca blocked with dung 'as hard as granite,' corpses found in rooms, crashed cars spread across an icy road, etc.). Therefore, penetration is dangerous: in order to avoid it one must 'fill the vagina with powdered glass, use it as a chamber pot and fill it to the brim,' think of it as a john where one puts the lid down before urinating or else tries to get rid of the contents first. Thus, at puberty, this patient spent a lot of time disembowelling flies; one of his favorite fantasies was the following: he was master of a harem and ruled women of all ages with a whip. He had established very strict rules in which the women had to defecate by orders and under close scrutiny. This illustrates the child's inversion of sphincter education and his victory over the anal penis of the intrusive mother. (This patient also had fantasies about excision of the clitoris.)

Men fear the mother's power, and her anal penis in particular. Later they try to stop women from using their anal impulses. As woman is guilty about her own anal wishes toward the father, she becomes an accomplice to the man's defenses. This conjunction results in the visible inhibition of women's anality in society: a woman must never swear, spit, eat strong food or wine, and until recently was not allowed to discuss money or business. Charm and grace are on the whole either reaction formations or sublimations of anal impulses (the opposite of vulgarity). At the same time, women are represented as illogical, vague, incapable of the rigors of science, engineering, etc. – all signs of successful integration of the anal components. [*Continues over page*] cathect her daughter in the same way that she cathects her son. But the girl cannot free herself from this omnipotence as she has nothing with which to oppose the mother, no narcissistic virtue the mother does not also possess. She will not be able to 'show her' her independence (I think this expression relates to phallic exhibitionism). So she will envy the boy his penis and say that he can 'do everything.' I see penis envy *not as 'a virility claim' to something one wants for its own sake, but as a revolt against the person who caused the narcissistic wound: the omnipotent mother.*

Clinical experience often shows that penis envy is stronger and more difficult to resolve when the daughter has been traumatized by a domineering mother. The narcissistic wound aroused by the child's helplessness and by penis envy are closely related.

Realization that possession of the penis presents the possibility of healing the narcissistic wound imposed by the omnipotent mother[24] helps to explain some of the unconscious significance of the penis, whether it is that of a treasure of strength, integrity, magic power, or autonomy. In the idea connected with this organ we find condensed all the primitive ideas of power. This power becomes then the prerogative of the man, who by attracting the mother destroyed her power. Since women lack this power they come to envy the one who possesses the penis. Thus, woman's envy has its source in her conflict with her mother and must seek satisfaction through aggression (that is, what she considers to be aggression) toward her love object, the father. Any achievement which provides her with narcissistic pleasure will be felt as an encroachment on the father's power, thereby leading to many inhibitions, as already mentioned. In fact there is often an unfortunate connection between violent penis envy and the inhibition or fear of satisfying this envy. The connection arises because

---

(Owing to the enforced repression it undergoes, the anal instinct may become somewhat 'corrosive.' The weaker muscular structure of women also favors this corrosive aspect of feminine aggression, as it does not allow for adequate motor discharge. Women are said to scratch, bite, or poison, whereas men punch or knock down.) In fact this desire for victory over the omnipotent mother is often displaced by men onto all women. An exception is the daughter, perhaps because she is in a dependent situation. The father projects onto her an idealized image which is opposed to the 'normal lasting contempt' (Freud, Ruth Mack Brunswick, Hélène Deutsch) he feels for other women. His daughter often represents the best part of himself and of the good, primitive object. She is tenderness, purity, innocence, and grace and represents for him a privileged relationship which escapes his ambivalence.

Of course, this relation is not always there, as some men extend their maternal conflicts onto their daughters, too. An obsessional patient suffering from ejaculatio praecox was discussing his six-year-old daughter who was working hard at school in order to attract his attention, a fact he was well aware of: 'I push her away from me but, being truly feminine, she still tries to attract my attention'; but the relation I have described exists frequently enough for it to be noticeable. Three patients told me at the outset of their treatment that one of their reasons for coming to analysis was a desire to help their daughters.

[24] In her article on 'The Pre-Oedipal Phase' (written with Freud), Ruth Mack Brunswick reconsiders the idea that the desire for a child is a substitute for penis envy: the desire for a child expresses mainly the desire to have what the mother possessed: a child.

I believe that if the child's desire is linked both with penis envy and with the omnipotent mother, it is because of a certain connection between penis envy and the omnipotent maternal imago.

penis envy derives from conflict with the mother, giving rise to idealization of the father, which must be maintained thereafter.

I think that women's fear of castration can be explained by this equation of the narcissistic wound and the lack of a penis. Freud could see no reason for the little girl to fear castration as she had already undergone it. This led him to alter his proposition that all anxieties were castration fears to that in *Inhibitions, Symptoms, and Anxiety* (1936), in which he claimed that woman's fear of losing love is the equivalent of castration anxiety.

Jones pointed out that fears of castration do exist in women since they have as many fears about the future as men have; he also stressed the importance of fears about the integrity of their internal organs. In fact, the fears of both sexes are similar (fear of going blind, being paralyzed, becoming mad, having cancer, having an accident, failing, and so on). In the unconscious, all narcissistic fears at any level are equivalent to castration, because of the narcissistic value given to the phallus by both sexes. Thus, women as well as men constantly fear castration; even if they already have lost the *penis*, there are still many other things with a phallic meaning which one might lose. And men as well as women experience penis envy because each attempt to compensate a deficiency implies a phallic acquisition. The fear of loss or of castration centers in the mother as it is from her the daughter wishes to escape, *at the same time that she gives herself a penis and turns to the father.*

During the change of object even though retaining the unconscious image of the phallic mother the daughter fully realizes that *the father is the only true possessor of the penis*. The change of object and the development of the Oedipal situation come about only when the imago of the phallic mother has become that of a mother who has dispossessed the father of his penis. In order to acquire the penis the girl now turns to her father *just as her mother did;* she does this with all the guilt we have discussed earlier, grappling with both her parents at the same time, and also attacking the loved object.

As Freud said, she turns to the father to acquire the penis, but her fears, owing to the temporary split between her libidinal and aggressive cathexes *at the time of the change of object*, are tied to the mother, the guilt to the father.

I believe that it is at this stage that the imago of the phallic mother *who holds in herself the paternal penis* (Melanie Klein) becomes much more important than the imago of the phallic mother who on her own possesses a phallus. Even if this latter imago persists in the unconscious it is not the prevailing one. But the father's penis, the mother's property, loses its genital and positive characteristics and acquires the same intrusive, destructive, anal properties of the phallic mother's own penis, thereby being cathected in the same way as its owner.

If the imago of the phallic mother as possessor of a penis remains the more important one, then the homosexual situation threatens to establish itself permanently, but if the imago of the mother as holder of the paternal penis dominates, the triangular situation begins in outline.

In Freud's view, then, *the girl turns away from her mother in order to acquire a penis;* and by turning to the father enters the positive Oedipus phase.

If, however, *penis envy is caused by the desire to liberate oneself from the mother,* as I propose, the sequence of events is somewhat different: the girl will *simultaneously* be envious of the penis *and* turn to her father, powerfully aided by a basic feminine wish to free herself from the mother. Thus, penis envy and the erotic desire for a penis are not opposed to each other but complementary, and if symbolic satisfaction of the former is achieved this becomes a step forward toward integration of the latter.

In his article on 'Manifestations of the Female Castration Complex' (1920), Karl Abraham states that women who have professional ambitions thereby manifest their penis envy.[25] This can be demonstrated clinically,[26] but I think the desire to fulfill oneself in any field, professional or otherwise, as well as penis envy, spring from the same narcissistic wound, and is therefore an attempt at reparation. Freud in his essay on narcissism states that once the primary stage of narcissism is passed, personal achievement provides narcissistic rewards. It is important to take this into account in analytic treatment. If one interprets desire for achievement as the manifestation of 'masculine demands' (as Abraham did with regard to professional activities), if women's professional desires are invariably interpreted as penis envy, there is a risk of awakening profound guilt feelings. I believe that if one accepts that penis envy is caused by a deep narcissistic wound, then one is able to bind this wound as well as open the way to a normal Oedipus conflict. Sexuality itself is often seen as men's prerogative and, in fact, from a symbolic point of view *normal female sexuality* (a vagina which functions normally) can be regarded as the possession of a phallus, due to the fact that the penis represents wholeness even in regard to orgasm. Certain analysts, basing their views on this fantasy, go so far as to say that normal women never have an orgasm. This is tantamount to acquiescing to the patients' guilt, leading indeed to castration not only of the penis but also of the vagina and of the whole of femininity. Basically, penis envy is the symbolic expression of another desire. Women do not wish to become men, but want to detach themselves from the mother and become complete, autonomous *women.*

Penis envy as a defense and fears for the integrity of the ego

I do not wish to ignore *the role of penis envy* as a feminine defense. I have insisted upon *guilt* because this aspect of female psychosexuality seems to have been more neglected than that of *the narcissistic fears for the ego's integrity.*

---

[25] For Freud (in 'Femininity,' 1932), if a woman comes to analysis in order to be more successful in her profession, she is by the same token displaying her penis envy.
[26] The same is true of men: for a man to achieve his professional ambitions is symbolically to have a penis like the father.

Many women want a penis *to avoid being penetrated*, since penetration is felt as a threat to their integrity;[27] they want to castrate this dangerous penis in order to prevent it from approaching them. But then one wonders, *which* penis?

In the preceding article [in *Female Sexuality*], 'The Change of Object,' Luquet-Parat suggests that, if penetration is desired and imagined as a danger for body as well as ego integrity, that is, if the penis continues to represent exaggerated phallic power (the immense penis the little girl desires, too big in comparison with her, is the heir to the invading, destructive, annihilating phallic power of the *primitive maternal* phallus), then sexual penetration is experienced as an intolerable desire which the ego cannot accept, since it is in contradiction to self-preservation.

I agree with Dr. Luquet-Parat that this destructive penis is the equivalent of the maternal phallus of the anal phase; this, in turn, is linked for the girl with persecution and passive homosexual attitudes and provides the basis for paranoia in women. In these cases I wonder if one can truly speak of a 'change of object' (since emotions concerning the paternal penis are the same as they had been for the mother's phallus). It may be more correct to say that this was already part of the positive Oedipal situation.

The 'transfer' to the father of what was invested in the mother and the fact that these cathexes are equal (as the projections have simply been displaced) seem to point to the creation of a mechanism of defense aimed at escaping the dangerous relation with the phallic mother by establishing a relation with the father. But this mechanism of defense fails because the projections remain the same while the two objects are insufficiently differentiated.

It seems as if in these cases the father did not adequately support the projection of the good aspects of the object, because the primitive object itself was particularly bad. The process of idealization could not be established and thus could not allow for the true triangular situation. Castration as a defense and penis envy which prevents penetration seem to me to be linked mainly to the phallic maternal imago even though they appear to take the father as their aim. The latter does not yet have *the attributes of the paternal role* and only plays the role of a substitute for the mother, who possesses the destructive anal phallus.[28]

Fears for ego integrity are best analyzed from the angle of passive homosexuality and identification and provide a deeper understanding of the meaning of this narcissistic defense against penetration by the penis (unconsciously, the mother's phallus), which causes so many conjugal difficulties. Women who attack and castrate their husbands have unconsciously married the bad mother, and this is often equally true for the husband. Freud noticed that many women marry mother substitutes and act ambivalently toward them.

---

[27] Protecting oneself from penetration is also a way of safeguarding the object. A whole series of aggressive acts toward the father can be understood as an attempt to protect him from *contact*.

[28] Of course, this may also be due to regression.

I believe this results both from Oedipal guilt (one must not take the father from the mother, not incorporate the father's penis) and the repetition compulsion. The issue here is to master the traumatic childhood situation, to live out actively what has been passively experienced, rather than integrated, in relation to the mother. In this case the relationship is homosexual.

It does happen – and this is a proof that the husband does not represent the father in this case – that the idealized paternal imago remains untouched and identical with the ideal portrait created by the little girl.

For example, Adrienne, a young and pretty mother, who has made an important advance in the social and financial scale, has retained a genuine simplicity. She tells me that she married her husband on the spur of the moment. At the time she was 'going out' with a young man whom she loved, but for some reason which she cannot explain she yielded to her present husband's proposal. He is a rather sadistic man who beats her and makes perverse demands upon her. At the same time he is very attentive to her, which gives him an eminently ambiguous position in her eyes. She is full of bitterness toward him and grievances: he deprives her of her freedom; he does not let her gad about, or hum to herself, or whistle; he demands that she wear a girdle, etc. On top of this he is unfaithful to her. It soon became obvious that this husband was an equivalent of Adrienne's mother, who used to take her things away, keep her under her control, force her to work, and never stop pestering her.

When the mother was angry at mealtimes she would throw forks at the children's heads.

From the very beginning this aspect of the mother was projected onto me, and at the outset the analysis was very difficult, especially as she had not come of her own accord but only because her husband insisted on it. Yet she found sufficient satisfaction in the treatment to keep up the analysis despite her pointedly hysterophobic character.

Thus, when she leaves at the end of her session, she feels that she has become very small, her handbag has become a satchel, she senses that I follow her everywhere: into the subway, the streets and even her bedroom. The smell of my flat follows her everywhere, too. I am always behind her, etc. (In spite of the content of her feelings, their relation and structure are not at all paranoiac, there is a true possibility of insight.)

She liked her father but it was always the mother 'who wore the trousers,' who took the father's pay, controlling even the smallest expenditure, shutting him out if he came home late, etc.

Adrienne made an attempt at suicide the day her grandfather had his leg amputated. Later, she visited him in the hospital, went to much trouble for him, pampered him, even wished to become a nurse. To this day, every month she goes and gives her blood at the hospital (the links between the suicide attempt, the grandfather's amputation, and the efforts to put it right only became clear late in the analysis; they came up as separate facts, because they were unconscious). This grandfather is the mother's father whom the mother treats with indifference, hardly bothering or worrying about him, unlike Adrienne. When he died, after a second amputation, Adrienne described her mother's attitude at the grandfather's deathbed (the mother had stolen his cigarettes and his money) in the following words:

> 'How can she think of profiting from him? . . . I can see an animal in the forest, something like a huge wild boar surrounded by hunters. They are trying to strip him of everything he has.'

Her husband had then gone hunting. He had sent her some game which she could not bring herself to eat. Adrienne's attitude to her husband is quite different from her attitude to her father or grandfather. She openly attacks him, forces him to give her money, a personal car, etc., without any inhibition whatsoever. She ridicules him, thinks he looks like a clown and says so in front of him.

One day, the imago she had projected onto her husband became clear:

> 'In his dressing-gown he looks amazingly like my mother-in-law.'

Not long before this, she had a dream in which her mother was dressed up as a priest in a robe.

She sometimes projects onto me the good image of the idealized father, the victim of the mother's castration, at other times the image of the phallic mother, with whom she wishes and fears an anal relation, experiencing once again the intrusive sphincter-training period.

> 'I can still feel you behind me, I am frightened. . . . I don't want to speak. I can feel you're going to interrogate me and I'm frightened. It's stupid; in fact, you never do ask questions . . . or, at least, not in that way. . . . I shall say nothing.'

> 'The image of my husband is haunting me. I keep thinking of him, and yet he infuriates me. I don't want to make love to him. . . . I dreamed of a rat whose claws were pinching my daughter's bottom. . . .'

It seems to me obvious that the relationships to the husband and to me in the transference express a defense against a passive homosexual relation with the phallic mother, whom she attacks, whom she defies, whom she castrates in order to prevent her approach and in order to prove that there is no collusion between them; whereas her relation with her father is based on a counter-identification with the phallic mother and so on an idealization of the paternal image she is trying to restore.

The relation with the phallic husband–mother is connected with *narcissistic fears for the body ego*, whereas the relation to the father–grandfather is connected with guilt.

Feminine guilt and the Oedipus complex 589

III. A conflictual outcome of feminine problems: The daughter's identification with the father's penis

> OEDIPUS. This girl is my eyes, stranger, my daughter.
> ....
> ANTIGONE. Father, we are yours.
> OEDIPUS. Where are you?
> ANTIGONE. Near you, father. (They go toward him.)
> OEDIPUS. Oh, my torches!
> ISMENE.   Of your light, father.
> ANTIGONE. In suffering and in joy.
> OEDIPUS. Let death come, I shall be alone at the time of my extinction, resting on these columns like a Temple.
>
> Translated from Jean Gillibert's French version of Sophocles' *Oedipus at Colonus*

I have tried to show that the idealization of the father, a process which underlies the change of object, can result in a specific conflict for the woman in the area of sadistic-anal instinctual components, thereby rendering difficult the instinctual fusion required for normal sexuality, as well as interfering with any achievement necessary to healthy narcissistic equilibrium.[29]

We have already referred to Freud's idea, in 'On Narcissism, An Introduction,'[30] according to which 'everything a person possesses, or achieves, every remnant of the primitive feeling of omnipotence which his experience has confirmed, helps to increase his self-regard.'

But in the same work Freud also suggested another possibility for narcissistic support: the object's love for us: 'In love relations not being loved lowers the self-regard, while being loved raises it.' It seems that many women unconsciously choose Freud's second solution to the need for narcissistic gratifications, because they cannot freely and without guilt fulfill themselves through their personal achievements.

I do not think this choice necessarily implies an incapacity for object love. Indeed, according to Freud ('Instincts and Their Vicissitudes'),[31] 'If the object becomes a source of pleasurable feelings, a motor urge is set up which seeks to bring the object closer to the ego and to incorporate it into the ego. We then

---

[29] Space prevents our considering here the child's role as a narcissistic support. Joyce McDougall noted that penis envy plays as important a role in mothers as in women who are childless.

It is a fact that many mothers castrate their children psychologically, which indicates that their penis envy is not satisfied by maternity.

It is no solution to the problem to say that in these cases the women have not been able to transform their desire for a penis into a desire for a child.

Having a child may mean possessing what the omnipotent mother had (Ruth Mack Brunswick), but it does not yet mean having *something different* from what she had, and this, I believe, is the true aim of narcissistic achievements.

[30] *S.E.*, 14.
[31] *S.E.*, 14.

speak of the "attraction" exercised by the pleasure-giving object, and we say that we "love" that object.'

Thus, love is first of all a response to satisfaction, that is, an answer to the love which the object gives us. The two states – loving and being loved – are therefore correlative, and loving implies the desire to renew, to perpetuate the agreeable experience and the love one has received, by incorporating the object in the ego. In fact one often gives love in order to be loved by the object. Further discussion of this subject would lead us to examine the essence of love itself, but that would take us far beyond our present purpose. Here I wished to state above all that the conflictual outcome, when partly based on guilt, necessarily implies consideration for the object, and therefore love, even if the aim is at the same time to find satisfaction for narcissistic needs.

I believe this to be a very common female attitude, and one which can be interpreted as an identification with the part-object, the father's penis. I am not referring to woman's identification with an *autonomous phallus*, but to an identification with the *penis* as such, that is a complementary and totally dependent part of the object.

Identification of oneself with an autonomous phallus results in a pathological form of secondary narcissism. The ego is libidinally overcathected and shielded from external objects without which the link with reality is broken. Favreau (personal communication) stresses the importance of the narcissistic characteristics peculiar to this situation: the woman who identifies with the phallus *desires only to be desired*. She establishes herself as a phallus; this implies impenetrability and therefore withdrawal from any relation with an external erotic object. Some of these characteristics can be compared with those found in masculine narcissistic-phallic regression.

This sort of phallic identification is traceable in models ('mannequins'), ballerinas (though, of course, many other components make up a true artist's character), vamps, etc. The phallus woman resembles, more than any other woman, what Freud described as the narcissistic woman whose fascination, similar to that of a child, is linked with her '*inaccessibility*' like 'the charm of certain animals *which seem not to concern themselves about us*, such as cats and the large beasts of prey' ('On Narcissism, An Introduction,' 1925). Further on Freud mentions the 'enigmatic nature' and the 'cold and narcissistic' attitude these women have toward men. Rather than seeing in this the essence of women's object relations, I see it as an identification with an autonomous phallus. Is it not true that men admire the phallus in these women more than the women themselves?

If I have dwelt at such length on this description of woman's identification with the autonomous phallus, it is because I wish to avoid confusing it with the position I am now going to discuss – that of the paternal-penis woman. Far from being autonomous with regard to the object, she is closely dependent on it and is also its *complement*. She is the *right hand*, the assistant, the colleague, the secretary, the auxiliary, the inspiration for an employer, a lover, a husband, a father. She may also be a companion for old age, guide, or nurse. One sees the basic conflicts underlying such relationships in clinical practice.

The autonomous phallus-woman is similar to the woman described in Conrad Stein's article 'La Castration comme négation de la féminité' (*Revue Française de Psychanalyse*, 1961). Stein relates this problem to bisexuality and to the dialectic of 'being' and 'having.' I think it is necessary to distinguish in metapsychology between 'being' as identification with the total object one would like to 'have,' and 'being' the other person's 'thing,' as an identification with the part-object. This latter position seems to be linked with the subject's reparative tendencies and results from a counter-identification with the mother's castration of the father during the primal scene. In this case the daughter remains closely dependent on the object she makes complete.

Alice is a thirty-eight-year-old woman, small, lively, and full of humor. She is the best friend of a colleague who entrusted her to me, saying that she was 'the apple of his eye.'

In Alice's case this expression was full of meaning. Alice came to analysis after undergoing an operation for the removal of a neoplastic tumor. The illness naturally aroused deep narcissistic fears, but even more important was the fact that the seriousness of her illness had allowed her to do something for herself for once. Her marriage situation suddenly became unbearable. She was an only child. Her mother was a severe and demanding school teacher, her father a kind and sentimental man who grew flowers and vines in his garden and wrote naïve and delicate poems. He would say to Alice when she was little, 'You are the prettiest little girl in the world.' Even today Alice sometimes wakes up and asks her husband if she really is 'the prettiest little girl in the world.'

But Alice did not recognize her love for her father. She said her father 'revolted' her, she did not like his kisses, he annoyed her, she felt like pushing him down the stairs, especially when he had had a bit too much homemade wine. 'At those times,' said Alice, 'his eyes were very very small.' He was clumsy and missed the glass as he poured out the wine. Alice did not understand why she felt irritated by this father whose love could also bring her to tears.

Alice's relation with her mother was based on a mixture of fear and the desire to be held on her lap again and have body contact with her as she was when very small. Alice avoided telling her mother that she had a malignant tumor because her mother despised illness and weakness. When Alice was little she never dared complain nor tell her mother for instance that her sweater made of rough wool itched nor that her socks were too tight.

Alice's fantasy of the primal scene was a sadistic one, the mother playing the role of a castrating and sadistic person.

She studied at the National Academy of Music and married a gifted composer. Once married she gave up her career, saying that 'one artist in the family is enough.'

She suffered from eczema, particularly at her son's birth; she feels the need for a nonconflictual fusion with the object (the analyst in the transference; the 'allergic object relation' described by Pierre Marty[32]). At one point in the treatment she expressed the need for fusion in the following fantasy:

She is on a lake in a foam-rubber boat with an opening only big enough to let in a little air. But when she thinks of this opening she sees flies and insects coming to bother her.

It became clear that these were her aggressive instincts which she had to leave outside the world of fusion. She associated the boat with a cradle and the mother's womb. But on the level of the triangular relationship the fusion was between her and the gentle, kind father (heir to the mother upon whose lap it was so nice to sit), the mother representing her own aggressive instincts which needed to be repressed. Before and at the beginning of the analysis. Alice dreamed of empty flats; she associated them with the parcels she used to receive from her father's house, which annoyed her and which she did not want to open. Yet one day, opening a parcel from her father, she cried because she was so touched and thus expressed the pleasure she could have felt at accepting her father's love and presents. It became obvious that her rejection of her father was only a superficial defense and that her difficulties with incorporation (empty houses) were not related solely to narcissistic fears of damage.

I cannot give a detailed account of Alice's analysis, but she did express strong guilt about her anal-sadistic instinctual impulses toward the father and his penis. Thus, she dreamed she had a shrimp-child which had dried up between the pages of a book. She felt very guilty at having killed him. She associated this with her father's body. In another dream a baby put in her mother's care was dying of dehydration. After a frantic race she managed to arrive just in time to save him. She noticed her mother was feeding the baby with a bottle full of dirty water. Etc.

This guilt became increasingly obvious in the transference. For example, she thought of offering me a reproduction of a painting by Chagall which represented a rooster. She associated this with childhood fantasies in which a woman wandered the roads with a rooster on a leash. In the sessions I am about to discuss this appears as a penis which has to be restored to the father.

For some time Alice had been feeling guilty toward me, thinking she was not paying me enough money. Her husband, also in analysis, was paying a much higher fee. Alice arrives at her session at 11:30, lies down, and wonders if she is on time. Is her session at 11:20 or 11:40? She cannot remember even though she has come at the same time since the beginning of her analysis and is on time today. She continues by listing a series of things 'which are not going well.' The windows in her apartment are broken, and she cannot get the caretaker to send someone round to repair them (this question of windows has

---

[32] P. Marty, 'The Allergic Object Relationship.' *International Journal of Psychoanalysis*, 39 (1958): 98–103.

taken up a great deal of the analysis lately); with her husband things are not going well, she cannot stand it any longer. She fails in what she attempts. She asks me if she has arrived early or late. I say: 'It seems as if one of us must give up something (ten minutes from you or ten minutes from me) and you are trying to show me that it is *you* who loses, that you are diminished by everyone in every way.'

At the next session Alice gets muddled about the time of her appointment and arrives half an hour early. After going away and coming back at the usual time she lies down and says:

> 'One of my eyes is running, it stings. By the way my eye always runs when I come here.' Silence. 'Oh! Well what do you know! But I never told you that my father had his eye put out, right in front of me when I was little. I don't remember how old I was . . . maybe eight. We used to go together in the fields and he suddenly put his foot down on some barbed wire which flew in the air and hit him in the eye. How amazing that I never told you about that. My running eye is on the same side as my father's. Now I suddenly understand why I was fascinated for so long by the Galton portrait game, in which one glues both left sides and both right sides together. Because of his eye my father has two very different profiles. When I was little I used to imagine the story of a little girl who had one dark and one light eye.' Her dark eye was due to the fact that she went to school by a path sunk between two very dark walls and the light eye was due to the fact that these walls suddenly gave way to a dazzling courtyard full of bits of glass, etc. . . .

This session was one of the most important in Alice's analysis as it allowed her to understand better and experience certain aspects of her object relations through the specially symbolized details in her fantasy (her love of big, transparent, amber pearls, her worry about the windows in her flat, her hatred of symmetry, etc.). This historical event is important inasmuch as it 'crystallized' a series of emotions linked to the father and his penis; the event was traumatic because Alice's aggressive fantasies had been confirmed in reality.

Her annoyance with her father, with his 'small eyes' when he was drunk, with his clumsiness (Alice never associated the 'small eyes' with the event of his eye being put out), were struggles against guilt: 'It is not my fault my father had this accident, in fact there was no accident, he had only drunk a little and that is why he had those "small eyes." He can see perfectly well, he is only clumsy. I must not approach him, accept his love, because any contact between us is dangerous. I must reject my father, that is the only desire I have toward him.' But unconsciously all Alice's object relations are dominated by the desire to *heal* her father, as an atonement for her guilty desires toward him.

Alice, who never took full advantage of her musical knowledge, is very clever with her hands and can achieve amazing things in carpentry and handiwork. She is proud of these activities, even though she deprecates herself in so many others. During her analysis, she thinks of taking up some professional activity. At the beginning of his career her husband had written some commercial songs to earn money. She had contributed the main ideas for these, so he now suggested that she write her own songs. But she says she is incapable of doing that – she could never be inspired *unless the song could be considered as his creation.*

During one session the unconscious meaning of her handicraft becomes clear. First of all she mentions her present difficulty over driving a car, a difficulty in total contrast to the facility with which she drove her father in a car, since he was incapacitated by the accident to his eye. 'Daddy was very proud of me then.' She associated this with her difficulty in remembering what I had told her during the previous session, yet she had fully understood what I had said. She said that if I were to repeat the beginning of what I had said, she would remember the rest of it. In other words, if I were beside her she could drive but she could not take the initiative alone: that would have meant driving for oneself, and she could not do that any more than she could write a song if it were not to become her husband's.

Then she mentioned a disagreeable woman who had annoyed her the previous day until she had suddenly learned that this woman did a lot of handicraft. 'All my irritation with her vanished, she did not seem aggressive or disagreeable any more. I thought she was very sweet.' In Alice's mind handicraft seemed to make the lady as *innocent* as it made Alice herself.

One of her fantasies clarified the meaning of her attitudes and activities. She was going to Lourdes to sell miraculous, pious objects, virgins with luminous eyes. She also invented medicines for sick animals. One can see that Alice's activities are aimed at *replacing the eye lost by her father.* She is entirely involved in her prothetic function. She can only create, act, live, *for* someone of whom she becomes the complementary part, the penis.

Her love for her father meant that she could not take on an identification with the mother, castrating the father during the primal scene. All activity, all means of existing which could be symbolized in the unconscious as a penis, were forbidden her. Indeed, acting for oneself, being autonomous, creating for oneself meant possessing the paternal penis and thus castrating the father. Alice has disfused her instinctual impulses, countercathected her aggression, and offered herself as a replacement for the lost paternal penis, thus making the loved object complete. The position is therefore a *reaction formation.*

Alice's sexuality follows the same pattern. She seems free, but her choice of erotic objects shows that she is not. She is loved by several charming, cultivated gentlemen, much older than herself. They court her in a slightly discreet melancholic way. Alice only shows them kindness and friendship. One of them, who is married, has even decided, with his wife's agreement, to adopt her as his daughter.

Thinking about these 'affairs,' Alice remembers that ten years ago, while being courted by one of these men, she went to the cafe where they usually met and encountered some young men, her 'little brothers,' seeing them for an obvious sexual purpose. These adventures always occurred during her father's absence from Paris. This is a classical defense against the Oedipus complex. But another fact more precisely locates the level of this defense: these gentlemen, Alice realizes, are nearly all Jewish. In fact she only gets on well with Jews. Even a badly educated man, if he is Jewish, attracts her. Perhaps it is because of their sense of humor, or their sadness, or their persecution. Sometimes, when Alice sees beggars, she is very upset. Once, with a lump in her throat, she gave one a lot of money, the notes rolled up into a ball. Then she realized he looked like her father.

These conflicts were analyzed at great length. Alice, whose dream life had been poor, as though paralyzed, suddenly began to have many dreams and started recalling all her childhood. One series of dreams is particularly important. Having recalled the erotic games of her childhood, especially her favorite one of taking people's temperatures,[33] she remembers an adolescent dream: she was looking at the stars with her mother, and one constellation looked like an agitated man. She was the only one to see this in the stars and she was going to go mad because her head kept flopping onto her shoulder. She associated this with the memory of witnessing a friend's epileptic fit. She feared that she too might have those terrible convulsions.

Next, a transference dream. A faith healer noticed that she was emitting an excessively dangerous electric vibration. The next night the healer died, very probably of this vibration.

Thereafter, every night Alice dreamed of corpses. The first one was that of the kindest of her old gentlemen; he was all broken up and was about to die when Alice called for a doctor. Strangely, the dying man was taken to a sordid barn; the next night she dreamed that her husband was taken to a sinister clinic on the outskirts of Paris, with the side of his body all black. The following night she dreamed that she was crying during a session while I was explaining that the police were coming, and I showed her a man's corpse which I kept in a coffin. The police arrived and, quite unexpectedly – that was the worst punishment of all – they took away her father while she cried, and then she had to see him die in a prison cell, while she stood by powerless, seeing his abject poverty.

This dream, in which the id disguises itself as the superego in order to fulfill the desire of anally incorporating the paternal penis, was followed by a number of memories: sex play with a farm-hand who had shown her his penis, games with a cousin in the hayloft, the exciting smell of the granaries and cellars where the hams were hung and the cheese and wines matured. At the same time Alice tells me that, for some incomprehensible reason, she has deliberately omitted telling me one fact: a good-looking rag-and-bone man, with dark eyes, came to empty their cellar. He made advances to her, but although she refused them she was not indifferent to them. As the price he was asking for emptying her cellar was too steep, she decided to do it herself. Once the cellar was empty, there was a huge carpet rolled up on the ground. With a great effort

---

[33] Taken anally in France. [*Trans.*]

Alice unrolled the carpet and very cleverly managed to hang it vertically from the cellar ceiling and leave it there.

Of course I cannot discuss here all the material from this series of sessions nor give details of the transference. I shall merely recount the two dreams which followed this last session, as they show in an abbreviated form the shape of her development.

Alice is going up the staircase in my building. She meets a handsome man who flirts with her. He is my husband. He asks her when he can see her again, and Alice replies: 'I come here three times a week.'

The following night Alice dreams that her father and mother are sleeping in her flat. In the middle of the night Alice's mother throws the father out of her room and he goes and sits on a stool in the kitchen. Grieved because he cannot spend the whole night there, Alice offers to let him sleep with her.

As the anal-sadistic incorporative desires toward the father's penis become conscious a true Oedipal situation is able to develop. The disfused instinct begins to appear under its own disfused aspect only to merge with the cluster which makes up genital primacy.

When the sadistic-anal instincts of incorporating the paternal penis result in guilt (as discussed at the beginning of this article) they increase the possibility of the girl's identifying with the father's penis. As we have shown, there is then an inversion of content and container, the woman identifying herself with the penis in the dangerous vagina – dangerous because of the sadistic-anal component, the fecal stool in the rectum. (This inversion is the main symptom of claustrophobia; it also exists in other structures.) The girl thus becomes the father's anal penis, she is a part of him and offers herself to his handling and mastery. Mastery, possession, or domination of the father, or of his substitutes (generally masculine ones), are forbidden to her. Thus, Alice, asked to compose the music for a ballet, is very pleased and says:

> 'The person who asked me to do it is a friend; I know his taste. There will be no problem in doing it. But I would never dare accept a job from a stranger. He might not like what I did. I would never dare impose my taste on anybody.'

I would readily see this as the source of one of woman's main conflicts, that of being *relative* to men, just as nearly all of woman's cultural or social achievements are. Women are said to produce few original works; they are often the brilliant disciple of a man or of a masculine theory. They are rarely leaders of movements. This is surely the effect of a conflict specific to women.

I believe it is important, both from a clinical and from a technical point of view, to discuss this position which can be scotomized because of the countertransference it causes. (I am here thinking of my own clinical experience.) Certain patients, and this seems to be peculiar to women – for when this happens in men the conflictual aspect of it is immediately obvious – are cured of their symptoms only in order to make publicity for their analyst; they feel they are a successful product, and experience their analysis as though the future and the reputation of the analyst depended on it. (The aggression toward the object becomes self-destructive.)

Thus, one of my patients imagined she was a sandwichman advertising my name and address. This reminded her of a brand of coffee whose advertising had taken the form of men disguised as coffee packets walking through Paris.

Certain aspects of *female masochism* seem to be related to this position. One of the main aspects of the masochistic character is the role of being 'the other person's thing.' 'I am your thing. Do whatever you want to with me,' says the masochist to his partner. In other words I am your fecal stool and you can deal with me as you wish. One explanation of female masochism is to be found in its link with the guilt of incorporating the penis in a sadistic-anal way, as though women, in order to achieve this incorporation, had to pretend to offer themselves entirely, in place of the stolen penis, proposing that the partner do to her body, to her ego, to herself, what she had, in fantasy, done to his penis.

Grunberger had based his study of masochism (in both sexes) on the guilt associated with anal introjection of the paternal penis, but the mechanism he discussed is not quite the same as the one I am here describing.

The woman's superego seems also to be linked to her identification with the paternal penis. Without entering the discussion of whether her superego is stronger than man's (Melanie Klein), or weaker (Freud), or quasi-nonexistent (J. Lampl de Groot), I wish to discuss one of the aspects of the female superego described by Freud. He states that woman's superego is more impersonal than man's. This is a common observation. Women have, at least in appearance, a superego which constantly changes, taking on new aspects, giving up old ones, according to their sexual partners. One frequently says that women are easily influenced, that they have no fixed opinions, that they readily change their principles. One of my patients, the one who gave up her lectures because of a disagreeable criticism, seems to be this type of woman who judges her acts and thoughts according to the object's judgments. She seems to hear only the rules she is told of, while being ignorant of the law. But this 'malleable' character of her thought is linked only to her conscious guilt. Beyond these variations, the internalized prohibitions are very strong. One of them dominates all the others, as if it were some sort of Eleventh Commandment: 'You may not have your own law – your law is your object's law.' It seems as though many women have internalized this commandment, making them eternally dependent.

Here again, man's conflict with the omnipotent mother and woman's conflict with the cathexis of the loved object both contribute to this situation in which woman plays the role of a part-object.[34]

Conclusion

The cases which I have chosen to discuss, despite different nosological data, all have one feature in common: the mother was sadistic and castrating, the father

---

[34] This is similar to the situation described by Simone de Beauvoir in *The Second Sex* (New York, 1952).

was good and vulnerable. Of course, many families do not have this structure. There are families where the opposite is true, where the mother is the good element and the father the sadistic one. It is interesting that in these latter cases the paternal figure becomes ambiguous and is identified once again, in woman's unconscious, with the phallic mother. Therefore, the family structure, in the cases discussed here, even though it seems exaggerated, is nevertheless an objective one inasmuch as it represents the normal unconscious structure at the time of the change of object, the bad object being projected onto the mother, the good onto the father. When reality cannot correct this unconscious image, severe problems are bound to arise. Then the primal scene represents a mixture of the destructive bad object and the good object which must be safeguarded, or, in other words, a terrifying fusion of the aggressive and erotic instincts. To deny the necessity of instinctual fusion in female sexuality corresponds to ignoring men's terrifying fantasies about femininity and women's guilty fantasies about their instinctual impulses, which is rather like trying to transform black Eros into a cherubic cupid.

It seems to me that one cannot base all female conflicts with the father and his penis on primitive conflicts with the mother and her breast; that would be shortcircuiting the total transformation which occurs during the change of object inherent in the path to womanhood.

Freud has shown that the little girl's Oedipus complex, caused by penis envy, is a *haven* for her inasmuch as the girl, whose castration has already been effected, has nothing more to fear from the mother. This results in *a tendency to prolong the Oedipal situation*. It is interesting that the female Oedipus complex is not resolved in the way that the male Oedipus complex is. (Parents readily say that 'a son's your son till he gets a wife; a daughter's your daughter all her life.')

Is this not related to the fact that the girl, in seeking to free herself from the mother during the change of object, and in her need to safeguard the father, offers herself to him as a part-object, protected from the mother, loved by the father, and forever dependent?

It seems as if the girl who prolongs this situation feels it to be a *haven* only inasmuch as she is not taking the mother's place beside the father because she is not identifying with her and because she stays a child rather than becomes a woman. I believe that she is, at the same time, protecting herself from castration threatened by the mother by refusing to take her place. An Oedipal situation in which the girl truly identifies with the mother in order to take her place beside the father is never a comfortable one. The obstacles which the girl encounters in her love for her father and in the rivalry with her mother are frightening enough for the girl's Oedipus complex to be just what the boy's Oedipus complex was, 'the crux of neuroses.'

Man and woman are born of woman: before all else we are our mother's child. Yet all our desires seem designed to deny this fact, so full of conflicts and reminiscent of our primitive dependence. The myth of Genesis seems to express this desire to free ourselves from our mother: man is born of God, an idealized paternal figure, a projection of lost omnipotence. Woman is born from man's body. If this myth expresses the victory of man over his mother and over woman, who thereby becomes his own child, it also provides a certain solution for woman inasmuch as she also is her mother's daughter: she chooses to belong to man, to be created *for* him, and not for herself, to be a part of him – Adam's rib – rather than to prolong her 'attachment' to her mother. I have tried to show the conflicts which oblige so many women to choose between mother and husband as the object of dependent attachment.

Editors' added bibliography

Abraham, K. (1920). Manifestation of the female castration complex. *International Journal of Psychoanalysis*, *3* (4): 467–472.
Beauvoir, S. de (1952). *The Second Sex*. New York.
Bergler, E. (1956). *Homosexuality: Disease or Way of Life*. New York: Hill & Wang.
Deutsch, H. (1944). *The Psychology of Women*. New York: Grüne & Stratton.
Freud, S. (1914c). On Narcissism, an Introduction. *S.E.*, 14.
Freud, S. (1915c). Instincts and Their Vicissitudes. *S.E.*, 14.
Freud, S. (1917). On Transformations of Instincts as Exemplified in Anal Erotism. *S.E.*, 17.
Freud, S. (1918). The Taboo of Virginity. *S.E.*, 11.
Freud, S. (1920). Beyond the Principle of Pleasure. *S.E.*, 18.
Freud, S. (1920). Three Essays on the Theory of Sexuality. *S.E.*, 7.
Freud, S. (1921c). Group Psychology and the Analysis of the Ego. *S.E.*, 18.
Freud, S. (1923). The Ego and the Id. *S.E.*, 19.
Freud, S. (1924). A Short Account of Psycho-Analysis. *S.E.*, 19.
Freud, S. (1926). Inhibitions, Symptoms and Anxiety. *S.E.*, 20: 75–174.
Freud, S. (1927). Fetishism. *S.E.*, 21.
Freud, S. (1931). Female Sexuality. *S.E.*, 21.
Freud, S. (1932). On Femininity. *S.E.*, 22.
Greenacre, P. (1960). Woman as artist. *Psychoanalytic Quarterly*, *29*: 208–227.
Horney, K. (1932). The dread of woman. Observations on a specific difference in the dread felt by men and by women respectively for the opposite sex. *International Journal of Psychoanalysis*, *13* (3): 348–360.
Jones, E. (1932). The phallic phase. In *Papers on Psycho-analysis*. London: Baillière, Tindall & Cox, 1948.
Klein, M. (1932). *The Psycho-Analysis of Children*. London: Hogarth Press and Institute of Psycho-Analysis.
Klein, M. (1957). *Envy and Gratitude: A Study of Unconscious*. London/New York: Tavistock.
Lampl de Groot, J. (1933). Problems of femininity. *Psychoanalytic Quarterly*, *2* (3–4): 489–518.
Luquet-Parat, C. (1970). The change of object. In J. Chasseguet-Smirgel (Ed.), *Female Sexuality*. University of Michigan Press.
Mack Brunswick, R. (1940). The pre-oedipal phase of the libido development. *Psychoanalytic Quarterly*, *9* (2–3): 293–319.
Marty, P. (1958). The allergic object relationship. *International Journal of Psychoanalysis*, *39*: 98–103.
Stein, C. (1961). La castration comme négation de la féminité. *Revue Française de Psychanalyse*, *25* (2): 221–242.

31 POOR MEN – OR WHY MEN ARE AFRAID OF WOMEN

Jean Cournut

> A psychiatrist, full member and former president of the Paris Psychoanalytical Society, **Jean Cournut** (1929–2003) was for some eight years the co-editor of the *Revue Française de Psychanalyse*.
>
> With his great independence of mind, he explored drive-related phenomena in some depth and emphasised the importance of quantitative factors in the way that the mind works. He also studied the relationship between men and women in their love life.
>
> He is the author of: *L'ordinaire de la passion* [Everyday passion] (PUF, 1991); *Epître aux oedipiens* [Epistle to the Oedipans] (PUF, 1997); and *Pourquoi les hommes ont peur des femmes* [Why men are afraid of women] (PUF, 2001). With Monique Cournut-Janin, he wrote the Report on the 1993 Congress of French-speaking Psychoanalysts on 'Castration and the Feminine in Both Sexes' (*Revue Française de Psychanalyse*, 1993, 6).

Genesis – new version

Adam was almost happy. With food and shelter, and naked, he was perfectly self-sufficient in his earthly paradise. For the pleasures of the flesh, he gave himself satisfaction; for the delights of the mind, he had his own conversation. Not yet having a superego, he had created God in his own image, which led him to perpetuate the best of all worlds, a flawless Eden, a goalless Nirvana. No problems, then? Yes – Adam was bored.

Then Adam said to God, 'Create me some otherness'. So God took a small part of Adam out of himself and undertook to make an other for him. God could quite simply have replicated Adam, cloned him, and created for him a mass of similar others among whom Adam would have encountered himself as in so many mirrors. But no; identity – God alone knows why – was rejected, and the rest is history: God created difference.

Eve appeared opposite Adam. They stared at each other in surprise: compared with all the variety of creation, they were the same; and yet, not completely the same . . . Adam could not understand it at all; this thing or rather this lack of a thing on Eve's body disturbed him, as did the fact that Eve seemed to want to do something with his thing. So the best thing to do was to accept this small difference and live with it . . .

Then Adam told Eve to take care of the household; during this time he would reflect and would protect her. But despite everything, Adam was not at peace; he felt mistrustful.

Universal assertions throughout culture and history

- The most widespread thing in the world, more so than common sense, is *sexual difference*. A few rare aberrations apart, being of one sex, everywhere and for all time, is apparently simple: man or woman, anatomy is destiny . . .
- Another assertion, the corollary of the above, everywhere and for all time, in every social organisation, *men dominate women*.
- From St Paul to Benoîte Groult, not forgetting the 'holy family' of Marx and Engels, male supremacy is exalted or condemned, but works on the subject only ever explain the *how* while scarcely touching on the *why*. Why this domination?
- Hypothesis: men are afraid of women. Not some men, or some women, or men in general, or in a specific situation, but on a fundamental level. The hypothesis proposed is therefore: *men dominate women because they are afraid of them*, they do everything they can, by every means, from the most rational to the most magical, to defend themselves against these feared dangers.
- Question: *why this fear?* Of what and of whom are men afraid in women or as a result of women? Why this high valuation of the male sex and this devaluation of the female, which is in fact also praised, adorned and adored (and then again, by whom and why . . .)?
- Observation: in contrast with the objectifying descriptions formulated in 'how' terms, the questions posed here will concern 'why', seeking a cause, a hypothesis, an interpretation. This mode of questioning, suspect to scientists, is also that used by children concerning the 'big' questions (life, death, origins, sexuality).
- Approach: in seeking to answer the question 'why are men afraid of women?', we will use what we have learnt from psychoanalytic experience, which specifically operates in the living and active residues of the adult's childhood past and thus explores the child in the adult.

Simple causalities

Male domination is said to be physical, social, political, economic and so on, but it is rarely pointed out that each term is only explained by another and vice versa! If we consider anatomical sex, we may think that the female sexual organs are hardly visible, and therefore mysterious, and that by contrast the visible male sexual organ is both a symbol of power and a point of vulnerability. But what is threatening it, with what and why . . .? In individual and collective thought systems, men's fear of women is hardly recognised, often denied and more often still not even consciously felt. On the contrary, the dominant discourse is deliberately 'macho'. The quest is also suspect; outside the paths of enquiry that are usually trodden, it can scarcely take anything but byways and realign the tracks as just another series of questions. For instance, matrilineal but not matriarchal societies are known. Men have muscles, while women have a belly; men hunt standing up, while women bend down to pick things. Lucy[1] was smaller than the other skeletons next to her. Women are mothers, but men are leaders, or their deputies; they are hierarchical, whereas women are submissive. Colloquial language hesitates between 'the fair sex' and 'the weaker sex'; or it refers to the 'backside' and at least everyone knows of what . . . it turns round. From the back, the difference is less glaring. So difference is formulated in terms of 'having or not having', a way of founding the phallic order on a denial, and conceiving a social order as if it were a natural order, so that the dominated party (race, colonial, woman, etc.) is also deeply convinced of it. Alienation, dispossession, voluntary servitude: in Athens, women do not have citizenship (Nicole Loraux, 1981); over the centuries in our culture, plates in the anatomy books have promulgated the belief in a single sex, the male sex, of which the female is the obverse, the negative, the concave form (Laqueur, 1990), in an ideological anatomy based on the infant's sexual theory of the universal penis (Freud, 1908c). More recently, the *MLF*[2] observed that 'every other man is a woman' and politicians have drawn up quotas. There is also the familiar African saying: 'The man loves the woman, he is proud to protect her: the woman loves the man, she is proud to serve him.'

Sex and difference

It is obviously necessary to examine other disciplines, the biology of the unconscious, the philosophy of difference, sociology, history, anthropology and so on. This reveals that women are adored and despised; sometimes as saints, more often as witches; they are held even further at a distance given that women's oestrus means they are constantly available and thus potentially predatory. So what is to be done but keep them captive . . .

[1] While correcting the proofs of this text I found, written in the margin, the following sentence: 'Recent hypotheses strongly suggest that in fact Lucy will be [sic] male.' I leave the responsibility for this information about Lucy (the skeletal remains discovered at Hadar in 1974) to whomever it may concern, but I appreciate, I must admit, what this 'will be' indicates to us concerning Lucy's future. Altogether, contrary to Aragon's (1963) prediction ('*la femme est l'avenir de l'homme*' [woman is man's future]), it is the man who 'will be' the woman's future, and it is therefore necessary to review the prehistory of . . . the masculine.

[2] Mouvement de Libération des Femmes – the women's liberation movement in France.

Let us set out here just a few main themes for our observations:

- Human sexuality is not animal sexuality (or physiological bisexuality) with some added psychological factors. It is characterised by the recognition of sexual and generational difference.
- For modern anthropology, sexual difference is the prototype of every difference. Difference separates but it produces. It is because there is a cut that there can be a copulation. Furthermore, again according to anthropologists, every difference implies the notion of a valuation (and a domination) of one element over another.
- Male or female gender (psychological and social givens) does not necessarily correspond to anatomical sex. 'Gender identity' (Robert Stoller) is not congruent with the male or female condition.
- Psychoanalysis makes the same assertions but adds an interpretation. It states that observations and myths of fusion, non-differentiation, origin or eternal recurrence have their fundamental model in the physical contact and subsequent separation of mother and child. It states that the assertion of sexual and generational differences has emotional repercussions. It posits that before the 'there's something there; there's nothing there', men tell themselves stories about castration. It considers the Oedipus complex and the castration complex as organisers of the human being, such that otherness and separation imply a third that de-merges and structures (that structures because it de-merges).

Relevance and irrelevance of psychoanalysis

Confronted more specifically here with the question of why men feel a fundamental fear of women, we will emphasise several specific psychoanalytic perspectives:

- Psychoanalysis comes close to the indictment of irrelevance to the extent that it claims to hold a universal discourse about the human being based on a highly specific experience of recent and disputed invention, which is invariably practised without witnesses behind closed doors.
- It proposes an enquiry into the world similar to that of children, not only in terms of '*how*' (how does that work, how are children made . . .) but above all in terms of '*why*', examining desires more than functioning (why are children made?).
- One of the major questions of its theoretical corpus concerns 'representability'. In other terms: *it is what the man does not manage to transpose into affect-charged, repressible and symbolisable representations that triggers his fear, anxiety and terror.*

- It emphasises the identificatory processes that enable otherness and difference to be negotiated. However, *'minor differences'* disturb narcissism; hence the hypothesis that men are afraid of women because they are 'the same–not the same', resembling them apart from one small difference. It remains to be explored in what respect and why *this small difference disturbs men; self-'representation' may be such a difficult undertaking that they end up feeling attacked, identifying with the aggressor and even attacking the aggressor.*

The Freudian response

This can only be summarised in a highly schematic way:

- Men's fundamental fear is the fear of castration (except when they succeed, through the castration complex, in converting it into signal anxiety that triggers repression).
- Every fear, anxiety, terror (of death, injury, illness etc.) relates back to the fear of losing that most excitable and most highly cathected bodily organ, and thus refers to the fear of castration.
- The infantile sexual theory of the universal penis divides human beings into two categories: those who have a penis 'normally' and those whose penis has been cut off.
- The masculine is the culmination of the 'active, sadistic, phallic' sequence, whereas the feminine is the culmination of the 'passive, masochistic, mutilated' sequence.
- Men experience women as castrated (when, in 1908c, Little Hans refers to castration, his father and the teacher express their horror by explaining to the unfortunate little boy that, mutilated, he would be 'so to speak like a woman') and potentially castrating (see, among other texts, 'The Taboo of Virginity', 1918a); they reject the feminine – that is, they relegate women and disclaim their own femininity.

Masculine femininity according to Freud

Feeling or being recognised by others as 'a bit' feminine can be a male characteristic. However, at a stage beyond this, the question of homosexuality arises. To be passive, masochistic and mutilated is to be like a woman and, consequently, to desire men; altogether, it is to be homosexual by identification with the woman-aggressor (and mother – see below). The caution, pertinence and frequency with which Freud addressed the theoretical and clinical questions posed by male homosexuality are well-known. This is why we are first presenting the Freudian viewpoint here, even though a few modifications will be proposed later.

In 1922, in a text entitled 'Some Neurotic Mechanisms in Jealousy, Paranoia and Homosexuality', Freud (1922b) gives a detailed explanation (clarifying that given in the text on Leonardo da Vinci) that could be summarised as follows:

- intense fixation on the mother in the identificatory mode;
- quest for love objects in which the subject can find himself and whom he can love as his mother loved him;
- tendency towards narcissistic object-choice;
- overvaluation of the penis and incapacity to relinquish its presence in the love object;
- contempt, aversion and disgust towards the woman's sexual organs because she does not possess a penis.

To this picture, Freud adds early seduction by an adult and fraternal rivalry, in which hatred then turns to love. Later on here we will return to some definitions of male homosexuality, but let us state immediately that we should add to the Freudian description the common absence of a father and the son's propensity to experience himself as the mother's penis and to think that he is completing her in this way. It is also observed that in this instance Freud draws no distinction between the father's mother and his wife.

Critique of 'castration'

Does the fear of castration as presented by Freud explain . . . everything, and in particular men's fear of women? There are several counter-arguments, as well as some persisting questions that cast doubt on the Freudian assertion.

Anxieties

Does castration anxiety cover every modality of anxiety? There is a traumatic paralysis of the psychic apparatus that cannot elaborate the subject's influx of excitations, helplessness – or what remains of it and has not yet 'got over it' (in the sense that we say in astonishment: 'well, I just can't get over that!') – emotional flooding, somatic expression, counter-cathexes to massive, elemental fantasmatic scenarios such as unconscious body-and-soul identification with the aggressor or the rescuer (it's not him, or her, it's I who . . . etc.) or the projective impulse rejecting externally everything 'bad' (it's not me, it's he, or she who . . . etc.). In the 'good cases', it is castration anxiety that serves as a signal that reconnects the psychic elaboration; in the 'bad cases', signal anxiety and repression are inoperative; then it is the unfolding of nameless anxieties about unbinding that we seek to . . . bind by describing them as fragmentation, effraction, annihilation and so on.

The disagreement of women

The critique of the central place Freud accorded to castration must also take account of the fact that, except when they adhere excessively to the dominant phallocentrism, women do not agree with the Freudian meaning of the feminine, and on several counts. For them, and they are very clear:

- The feminine is not something mutilated. A woman is a complete being, not a deficient man (a woman is a man like the others, and vice versa!). A woman's narcissism can be termed phallic (Catherine Parat, 1964) precisely when she feels complete and uses her penis envy to good purpose (see some of the more recent works by Jacques André, 1994, 1995; Monique Cournut-Janin, 1998; Sylvie Faure-Pragier, 1997, 1999; Jacqueline Godfrind, 2001; Florence Guignard, 1996, 1997; Michèle Perron-Borelli, 1993, 2001; Jacqueline Schaeffer, 1997).
- Passivity is not shameful; it can be considered a receptive activity, but – more deeply – when it is genuine passivity, it offers a certain number of advantages in the form of increased pleasure.
- Masochism is not only a perversion; more fundamentally, it helps to integrate pain and pleasure and thus contributes to jouissance.
- However, the question of penis envy remains. Do women want one in order to have it and not to be mutilated, as Freud states, or do they only want one to have pleasure with it? Whichever answer is preferred, this will lead men to fantasise and to be afraid.

The disagreement of some men

Some men appear not to reject the feminine and seem to identify with female behaviours. However, three concepts need to be discussed: bisexuality, ambivalence and homosexuality:

- The concept of *bisexuality*. It must be firmly emphasised that, unlike embryological and physiological facts, the concept of bisexuality in psychoanalysis only concerns identificatory phenomena that are usually unconscious: the subject simultaneously identifies with behaviours or people of the opposite sex.
- *Ambivalence*. It is that of the Wolf Man: 'two contrary currents side by side, of which one abominated the fear of castration while the other was prepared to accept it and console itself with femininity as a compensation' (Freud, 1918b, p. 85). Despite his terror, the Wolf Man is fully prepared to accept castration in order to be like his father's wife, in the

feminine position. However, Freud certainly seems to subscribe to a more fundamental fear of castration since, having demonstrated ambivalence, he emphasises the existence of a 'third current, the oldest and deepest, which did not as yet even raise the question of the reality of castration' (p. 85). It is a matter, beyond repression and ambivalence, of what *has been rejected* [*Verwerfung*] – 'he would hear nothing of repression' – and can only 'return' in the form of hallucination. It is just after having mentioned this third trend, this radical rejection of castration, that Freud describes the hallucination that occurred when the Wolf Man was five years old and he momentarily believed he had severed one of his fingers.

- *Male homosexuality and the death drive*. We have seen above Freud's definition of this in 1922, so we will emphasise only one point, which in fact supports the Freudian thesis while appearing to contradict it. This concerns the relationship between homosexuality and the death drive. It is stated in 1923 and 1937 that the intensity of the homosexual drive force and its intensive repression combine to generate some fatal unbinding (Freud, 1923b, 1937c). This reference to the death drive in connection with latent homosexuality is interesting to note to the extent that it does not invalidate Freud's general explanation in terms of castration anxiety – which is an explanation of homosexuality, a general interpretation of relations between men and women and, very specifically, the rejection of the feminine.

Altogether, Freud gives an unequivocal answer to the universal question 'what are men really afraid of?': men are afraid of castration – we should add: all the more so when it induces fatal unbinding effects, including and especially in their relationships with women. However, castration anxiety does not comprise all the modalities of anxiety; women devalue neither the feminine nor the 'passive, masochistic, mutilated' sequence – and some men do not systematically reject the feminine.

Female jouissance

Whereas for Freud, then, female signifies passive, masochistic, mutilated, subject to coitus and childbirth (1924c, 'The Economic Problem of Masochism'), we are justified in posing a question, or rather posing it from both its aspects:

- If this is true, what does it imply?
- And if the feminine does not signify being passive, mutilated and so on, what in men's experience could it be? In other words, are men telling themselves stories about castration and fear to avoid being confronted with something else that the feminine would unconsciously evoke for them? But if so, what?

To the question posed in both its forms, someone replies:

- *Schreber*: in fact, Schreber wants the exact opposite of what men are generally supposed to fear. We remember his very first sentence: 'after all it really must be very nice to be a woman submitting to the act of copulation' (Freud, 1911c, p. 13). Beyond any castration, what he wants is to be a woman, a mother, submitting to coitus, pregnant, giving birth, but also passive, prostrate, penetrated, beaten, humiliated. He wants to be possessed to the extent of being dispossessed of himself, collapsing and dissolving like a woman in an infinite orgasm, whore of God and mother of a new race, all in a continuous jouissance, a bliss that is not male (merely cerebral, he says) but female – that is, in a total, complete exquisite pleasure, without interruption, limit or end.

The erotic feminine

There is little reference in psychoanalytic theory to this erupting drive onslaught that men suspect women of feeling. Nevertheless, even if only *a contrario*, this jouissance raises some questions for treatment and practice, during the inhibitions, even panics, that are often engendered by its prospect. It also poses them just as much from the theoretical viewpoint in positive terms, when it appears, calm or wild, as a felicitous emotional upheaval.

In fact, men know little about women's jouissance when it occurs, stated by Tiresias to surpass men's pleasure by a proportion of nine to one. At best, as devoted companions, they induce and contain it, the loving cathexis then recovering the tenderness of a time swept by torment in which unconscious identifications are surrendered, as it were, to our heart's content. At worst, the malicious voyeur looks on, the passing warrior moves on, the premature ejaculator makes a quick escape, and the rest become monks or sailors, unless a cold sympathy comes to restore at least some equilibrium to the partners in this enterprise.

As for women, they say nothing about it. Freud says not a word about this silence; Lacan acknowledges it but then suddenly refers only to mystics; as for female analysts, they practise its metapsychology. Two questions then arise: why do women say nothing about their jouissance; and what do men imagine about this Tiresian–Schreberian Parousia?

The indescribable: With women firmly saying nothing about this extreme of their possible pleasure, we might suppose that this is a fiercely guarded secret. But no, if it were a secret it would certainly end up being known. It concerns something that is probably more elemental and more protopathic. Orgasm is a paroxystic psychophysiological phenomenon: it is excitation and energic discharge in the almost pure state, so intense that perhaps in certain cases (good cases?) the overwhelmed psychic apparatus is unable to 'translate' the physiological phenomenon, to integrate it psychically, to transpose it into inscribed and memorisable representations. Women say nothing about their jouissance because it is indescribable, unrepresented and possibly too intense to be 'representable' and memorisable in the sense that some representations could 'return'. It is probably necessary to construct the psychoanalytic hypothesis of a bodily memory, more precisely: non-psychised mnemic traces, very close to the physiological, instincts and satisfactions; excitational traces rather than memory of that which, coming from the body, could have been translated and described but in its intensity was not.

The maternal feminine

Moreover, these women are mothers; the first woman in every man's life is his mother. What a strange character in a man's life is this woman whose son he is – as 'the fruit of her womb'; surprisingly, fundamentally, definitively familiar, but strange.

Forget the anatomical plates for a moment and what you have learnt in the 'natural sciences' and listen as you read to what you're feeling inside; admit that you don't begin to understand it! It seems that he has been made in her belly. He is born, he is told, in pain. Fused with her, and vice versa, they formed a single entity, with the same blood, same womb, same sexual organs. When he began to separate from her, she started to reign over him. She was everything for him; she had everything but he soon realised that this was through him. He completed her, he fulfilled her, he was what he did not know that she lacked. In exchange, she gave him everything, taught him everything, put everything in order for him: smile, words, sphincters. Her image helps him to symbolise the landmarks of his own life: the Fates, the Madonna, the Furies, the pin-up, the Pietà.

'Maternal madness' (Green) is the term that has been used to refer to this set of incredible events that follow each other from conception, pregnancy, birth and so on: visceral madness of the maternal feminine that is as protopathic as the orgasmic 'fury' of the erotic feminine. The comparison is all the more valid given that to experience this maternal madness, this mother has had 'to do the same thing as the whore'. For this mother has betrayed her son from the outset, from the origins, with a third figure, his own father. He has tried to make a saviour of this rival; he offers him the femininity that she has instilled in him; he identifies with her as much as she allows him.

Furthermore, it is not true that she is omnipresent; she is present at times, absent at others; stimulating excitation by excess and by default. More or less good enough, attentive but alternating, she is seductive – the first one – then she goes away, then omnipresent only in his dreams and daydreams. But she leaves him a message: if he gets too excited by thinking too much about her, the retaliation will be harsh. He understands this, but he needs to see it to believe it; then he renounces, constructs his own forbidden meanings, but probably never completely believes in them. Moreover, who is this mad mother, whore and messenger? When Little Hans asks his own: 'Mummy, have you got a widdler too?' the mother's answer is surprisingly ambiguous: 'Of course. What did you think?' (Freud, 1907c, p. 134). In fact, Little Hans's mother says nothing; she explains nothing, either about her sex, her identity or her desire.

The son has no understanding of his mother's maternal feminine dimension, and he is betrayed by her erotic feminine dimension. With one, it's madness; with the other, it's fury. Strange ambiguity: what does a woman want, what does a mother want? He is all alone. In search of the lost object, he identifies, trying out motherhood and the feminine. But he still needs to be able to tolerate being like his mother, as woman and mother. It is difficult because they are simultaneously the same and not the same.

So, another solution presents itself: since this mother is a forbidden woman, to choose another; but this other woman also bleeds, has pleasure and then becomes a mother, as if everything were beginning all over again. No, not everything: the erotic feminine has some advantages, and also the maternal feminine does not only have disadvantages. In any case, it is about preserving for the erotic feminine as many desirable springs as possible, for one day the son observes that his mother is becoming very small again, and that she is fading away. Then he would feel even more alone.

Radical misunderstandings

It has been said that difference, any difference, disturbs the subject, his integrity, the representation he forms of himself and his narcissism; it forces him to work psychically on the excitations, interrogations and distresses caused by the inescapable acknowledgement of these differences. We will therefore not forget this paradox of the mother–son relationship: for him, the closest, indispensable, primal person, the object of his every appeal and desire, is a fundamentally different creature from him. They do not have the same sexual organs; they are not from the same generation. She is everything for him, while he is not everything for her; for him, she is his entire relational universe, whereas in fact, however cathecting she may be, she is partly elsewhere, with the third figure in this otherness. If she is too close to him, he will experience her as too stimulating, stifling and devouring; if she is absent, this will be his despair and psychic agony. So it is better to think that she is forbidden; to this crazy business, a meaning imperatively must be given, even a forbidden and guilt-inducing meaning, giving rise to retaliation if necessary . . .

We also know that what causes men difficulty is of two orders: the situations that he can represent to himself and that have a meaning, and those that remain unrepresentable and mad to him. In the first case: the danger is explicit, recognised, identified, it can – in a matter of urgency – be transposed into representations that are affect-charged, repressible and symbolisable. At the opposite extreme are situations, phenomena, processes that the man can just about understand intellectually and even study but cannot integrate, of which he can only create representations as it were at one remove, provided with borrowed affects, which he represses as far as possible, unless he endeavours to symbolise them, like children who tell themselves 'anything at all' when they do not 'know' and they are frightened in the dark.

Vital question: is it possible to move from the second category to the first (as will be observed, this is also the entire question of psychoanalytic treatment: to make something representable where it is lacking?). The Freudian answer is that it is possible but we stumble on a rock, the rejection of the feminine, because the feminine is about passivity, masochism and above all mutilation, which, except in the event of signal anxiety, triggers the terror of castration and paralysis of the psychic apparatus. And we can add here that this explains men's fear of women: they evoke castration, because they are castrated and castrating! The answer is worth . . . what it is worth, but it has the vast merit of remaining in the register of representation. *This story of women's castration is in doubtful taste; it is a scenario of lack, but – true or false – it is coherent, intelligible, reasonable and representable.*

New question: what if the feminine is not a mutilation with which men are confronted? If the erotico-maternal feminine does not evoke castration but, rather, a fury of jouissance, if this great madman Schreber guessed right, if Little Hans's mother persists in her ambiguous answers, if the Wolf Man's mother does not really appear to suffer during the siesta from the 'coitus *a tergo*, three times repeated' (Freud, 1918b, p. 37), then we understand that men are even more afraid of women than when they imagine they are mutilated. They do not know what to imagine, and psychoanalysts themselves remain extremely hard put to define a status of the feminine.

It is difficult for women too, but not in the same way: it is simplest for them, too, to think, as they were taught, in a phallic system, and to make do with an envy of the penis that men think they want to take away from them, whereas they only want to enjoy it, but amply. Otherwise, beyond the phallic order, they say nothing, nothing of what they experience as women and as mothers; nothing because it is experienced and not spoken about. But men? There some psychic work is absolutely necessary for them to formulate, stage, in vivid and reasonable scenarios what seems to them mad, unimaginable, I was going to say, without head or tail! Apologies, but nevertheless that is after all what it is about . . . thinking requires some penis on the body, of one and not on the body of the other, and some phallus in both heads.

Precautions against the erotico-maternal feminine

The 'maternal' denotes the aspects of a woman that essentially relate to her child, thus to generational difference, and in accordance with specific situations such as conception, pregnancy, childbirth, breastfeeding, care given and so on. This maternal *de facto* includes a man – a father, even if only in the . . . mother's head, knowing that she has had a father. By contrast, the feminine is defined in relation to sexual difference without prejudging any maternal quality in the woman, or in the man.

The distinction is conceptually necessary, but is it enough to reassure men? *For the erotico-maternal feminine to trigger, as according to Freud, the horror of possible castration, or, worse, confront the man-subject with something unrepresentable, on the path of an unbinding that would threaten him with psychic death, it is necessary that some psychic means of withdrawal, if not support, are organised. We will try to identify them, starting from the most immediate to the most historically constituted.*

In a matter of urgency, there are several strategies for averting danger: naming, illustrating and dialectising it.

- *Naming*: this is a path of elemental and fundamental psychic restructuring. The lost cathexis of things returns through the recathexis of word-presentations that designate them. Also, to say 'castration' but equally to say 'madness' or 'fury' already permits an emergence of representability that the psychic apparatus will be able to elaborate.
- *Illustrating*: if the Medusa head is a classical illustration of castration, we might for example observe that in Christian culture the Virgin Mary is the paragon of a purely maternal feminine, whereas Mary Magdalene embodies a feminine with a strong erotic propensity. The Greek–Latin opposition would be between Hera–Juno and Aphrodite–Venus; with Athena too, denying eroticism and motherhood, cathecting intelligence and, probably on that basis, protecting the heroes.
- *Dialectising*: there is a strong temptation to use one definition of the feminine to discredit another and altogether to soothe, however slightly, this fear men have of women. It will be noticed in general that these recovery attempts are made rather to the benefit of a motherhood that seems to have a better reputation than the feminine. For example, a 'full' motherhood may be opposed to a hollow, if not mutilated, femininity. We might also make motherhood an attribute that completes a deficient femininity or alternatively isolate a non-erotic motherhood, even if by later transferring this eroticism conceptually into the mother–child relationship. There is also the high valuation of the 'mother-goddess' – that is, a primal motherhood that precedes any difference; complete and omnipotent, she has sons but no need of a father-man to produce them.
- *In analytic practice*: we also encounter, of course, these temptations to escape the feminine through motherhood and sometimes the reverse.

The analyst's theoretical choices, his own training, his 'drive preferences' (to use Freud's term) will direct his listening and his interpretations. For example: a patient tells her analyst that a couple she knows are going to adopt a child. 'I envy them', she says, 'adopting a child is absolute love.' Sceptical, the analyst repeats the word: 'absolute?' 'Yes', replies the patient, 'without physical contact.' The analyst asks her to explain: 'So you think that absolute love is love without maternal contact, without physical contact between mother and child?' As she reports what she said, her supervisor thinks to himself that he would instead have asked: 'So you think absolute love is love without making love?' He communicates to the analyst his own choice, ready to discuss it. But the analyst then tells him what the patient replied to her 'maternal' choice: 'No, without physical contact, that means without the disadvantages of pregnancy. My friend is on a diet to lose weight, she doesn't want to lose her figure; she sets great store by her image. . . .' The signifier 'physical contact' thus had the potential to designate motherhood, eroticism or phallic narcissism. The technical problem of interpretation consisted in choosing one but holding the others in reserve, ready to use if they proved pertinent.

Vicissitudes of identifications

If we consider the feminine as truly mutilated or difficult to understand in the erotico-maternal obscurity, then we also always have a possible recourse – to identification, or rather various modes of identification, conscious and especially unconscious, in psychic elaboration, fantasmisation or – failing that – in behaviour. The method is not unproblematic, however – particularly if men, fearing the feminine, defend themselves with a female identification; this is in fact an identification with the aggressor, which complicates the life of homosexuals and . . . the metapsychology of homosexualities.

Male homosexualities

We will broadly differentiate, both in clinical practice and from the theoretical perspective, at least three varieties.

Dyadic homosexuality

This form, or this style, operates an identification with the mother, without a father. There is a total narcissistic identification with a complete, maternal, erotic mother. The father is absent, devalued, denigrated; the mother's erotic feminine is either transferred to its maternal aspect or scattered to the wind in adventures that are witnessed by the dazzled but still fatherless son. In this form of male homosexuality – the most productive – the Oedipal triangulation is blurred and the castration problematic is avoided. Whether as cause or consequence, the narcissistic atmosphere prevails, not far removed from narcissistic neurosis. Because there is no castration complex, the wounds are not partial but total, and the suicidal tendency is frequent.

In fact, the analyst shows that the identification is very often with the object of the mother's desire, occasionally the father, sometimes the mother's father, more often the mother's mother, the subject's grandmother. And sometimes we observe caricatural identifications with feminine styles in fashion forty years earlier or some imperative obligations to repair or expiate a sin thought to have been committed two generations earlier.

Triadic homosexuality

In this variety, the identification is not with the mother but with the father's wife, in a sense without the mother. This is the erotic female position in relation to the prevailing father. The maternal feminine seems to be elided; this is the 'paternal' problematic of the Wolf Man. Even if the fantasy of having the father's child, like the mother, is evidently present – persistence of the identification with the maternal feminine – what predominates is the wish to take pleasure like a woman from the father and for his good pleasure. This form of homosexuality accentuates – if truth be told – the so-called inverted Oedipus complex, with the father desired and the mother at a distance. Anyway, it is difficult to overstate the danger of systematising; the two forms are enmeshed in highly variable proportions. The same applies to the third variety.

Failed homosexuality

This is unrealised because of moral and social prohibitions and phobic behaviours. In fact, what dooms this form of homosexuality to failure is that the identification with the mother is itself experienced as incestuous. In principle, forced to relinquish the prohibited object, the subject identifies with it, replacing having it with being it. This occurs when the Oedipal prohibition is so oppressive that it impedes any displaced fulfilment and identification is the last resort. However, this identification itself continues to be suspected as transgressive and its homosexual realisation is forbidden, as with any other Oedipal wish.

The fetishistic solution

If the feminine is mutilation then, according to Freud, what is lacking is replaced by the fetish. Faced with the fear of castration that is so easily triggered by the differences, absences, wounds and cuts, the fetishistic solution is there, ready-made; a denial suffices. No, they lack nothing; women are men like the others.

Spectacular in the sexual pervert, the fetish is not in fact only an object. An excitational trace from the past, a possibly exclusive brilliant phallic or dark anal fixation, the fetish strictly speaking does not replace but rather *is* what is lacking. Materialising the denial of a castration, more than an object, in everyday life is a scenario that plays and replays presence and absence, the 'there's something there; there's nothing there'. It assumes varying forms, from the classical metonymy of the shoe to the scintillating metaphor: it is then the female body completely exalted. But it is also the theoretical corpus that is constructed within the gaps in knowledge, the argument that is brandished, the unswerving belief, essentially the logos as a generalised fetish, crutch of the human condition.

Exclusion, excision, exhibition

A fantasy, a behaviour or an ideology can have the status of a fetish. But sometimes it is inadequately established. The fetish compensates for castration; it responds poorly to the unrepresentable, especially if it concerns the unrepresentable erotico-maternal feminine. And again, aren't the questions asked about motherhood usually more or less closed by everything that culture conveys about maternal love, the instinct of the same name, filial love and so on? Is the erotic feminine more formidable to confront?

'Ardent lovers or austere scholars', admiring, sometimes unsettled, always surprised – when men look, notice or contemplate women's jouissance, they may have the fantasy of an infinite orgasm: women sail the high seas, while men are left on the shore, possibly envious, in any case at a loss. This unknown pleasure of the other only increases the sense of a difference that is both infinitesimal and vast, as if women possessed not a knowledge or a power but a mystery, an unutterable bodily secret that has sprung from the depths of the ages and defies any symbolisation. Something emerges from the unrepresentable maternal feminine: it is totally incomprehensible but it produces children! This unrepresentable erotic feminine, however, produces nothing; it is a fury and nothing more. Measures therefore have to be taken: this torrent cannot be prohibited, but it can be limited, confined and obstructed.

Despite the intensity of their own sensations and the identificatory phenomena, the fact that men feel they are surpassed by a quantity and quality of pleasure to which they remain relatively alien is certainly a factor in the exclusion measures to which, for all time and everywhere, women have been subjected. Exclusion takes multiple forms, from ostracisation to accusations of witchcraft. An even more radical form, applied to the very body of women, is the circumcision practised on 2 million little girls every year, adding to the

120 million worldwide who have already undergone the procedure.³ Another possible form of female exclusion because of misplaced jouissance is exhibition. Men tell themselves that this woman is gifted, exceptional, but if beyond a certain point she makes too much of it, is she mad, ill, nymphomaniac? . . . But no, there's Barbarella who explodes the machines for measuring jouissance or Emmanuelle who counts her orgasms to know exactly when she will be going too far.

The necessity of primal fantasies

Within the forms and vagaries of identification, beyond the fetishes that men create to reduce their fear of castration, the stories they tell themselves to explain an erotico-maternal feminine that is completely incomprehensible to them, the behaviours that they contrive to dominate women, respect mothers and circumscribe their own femininity, the psychic apparatus – or, if you like: the human condition – also elaborates, or rather already elaborates, some primal fantasies.

These are unconscious imaginary scenarios that give meaning to human realities. These fantasies are termed primal to the extent that they answer children's 'why' questions, their questions about origins, their parents' desires and the imaginary, identity-related and symbolic networks. For these same reasons, they are organisers of psychic life.

Every individual embroiders these fantasies in his own way according to his biological and cultural attributes, his generational prehistory and his own childhood history. However, whatever their modes of expression, there are four of these fantasies: seduction, primal scene, castration, return to the maternal womb. Like infantile sexual theories, they are all the same for every individual. In fact, to the extent that they answer the major questions of humanity, it can be observed that each implies the necessity of the next and that there is not in fact any other conceivable answer.

- The child's fantasy of seduction by the adult 'represents' (psychises) in generational difference the inherent excitations of the early physical and affective contact between the child and his mother, thus called 'the first seductress'.
- The primal-scene fantasy: in relation to the above fantasy, this introduces the father into a primal scene of parental coitus of which the subject is the director, capable of identifying simultaneously with all the characters, their desires and their roles. It is an ineluctably violent scene; at this Big Bang of origins, the subject projects his still unpsychised excitation, his own desire to be there already and his frustration at not being there yet.

---

³ According to the UN: *Le Monde*, 10 August 1997.

He also projects on to it the question of his parents' desire and his own identity: why are they doing that – for their own pleasure, or to produce me, me and none other?

- The castration fantasy: order, cohesion and meaning have to be wrought from the chaos of the primal scene. The castration fantasy, which instigates the complex of the same name, proposes a structured scenario: three people, desire, a prohibition, a threat, something heard, something seen, a well-founded and redemptive renunciation, and the internalisation of the prohibition in the form of an agency constantly at work – a vigilant, protective superego that is productive for the work of culture because it is prohibitive towards the individual.

The phallic order

Equipped with a good organisation of positive primal fantasies, we might hope that men would be less afraid of women, to the extent that they are well provided and capable of transposing this unrepresentable erotico-maternal feminine into representations and meaning. In fact, they erotise the excessive stimulus of the maternal relationship and create something representable with a seduction scenario in which the mother is responsible and the child is innocent. They then construct a scene of madness and fury in which the feminine is both ardently erotic and maternal. Finally, they dramatise (in the theatrical sense of enacting) an 'action' that leads to sexual latency in children, to policing families and a drive renunciation with a civilising quality. The order thus restored is inscribed in the very phallic order that produces culture.

In fact, as will have been observed, all three of these primal fantasies, especially the second and even more so the third, are centred on the phallic. If we retained the naïve imagery of the child's chance observation of parental coitus, we would say there is some penis; if we symbolise the human imaginary in relation to the main themes of its condition, we will say there is some phallus. Evidently, since it is what constitutes the outrage of difference that enables difference to be conceived.

The outrage

Now there is one relationship that men, despite their cogitations, completely fail to picture accurately because it denies difference, and this is the *mother–daughter relationship*, and more generally the relationship between women. It seems that there is an erotico-maternal feminine that is even more incomprehensible. Although we can imagine women caressing each other or tearing each other apart, and understand the mother and daughter loving or hating each other, it is only up to a certain point. For beyond a certain threshold, the question of women's jouissance among themselves arises. What do they do it with? It is impossible to imagine them without a thing, a prosthesis, without an illusory method (just as it is difficult to imagine homosexuals without sodomy).

In fact, the question 'what do they do it with?' breaches the phallic order. Female homosexuality is inconceivable for men; they can only imagine them doing the same as men. From the same perspective, *mother–daughter incest is a meaningless term. No difference, no copulation for penetrating, no opening to think about, the same on the same: now that is probably the radical unrepresentable* . . .

A secret envy

To summarise: the castration fantasy seeks to explain the feminine as best it can: it does not, in fact, succeed either for full, abundant motherhood or for infinite jouissance, less still in imagining a fusion without any opening or copulation. So, men, like women, should not confuse these matters. Ultimately, whether or not it is passive, masochistic or mutilated, the feminine is perhaps neither pejorative nor catastrophic. On the contrary: it is indeed, moreover, as Schreber says, in wanting to know and experience the 'female state of bliss' (Freud, 1911c, p. 29), certainly superior to and more delicious than the insipid and cerebral male one. Schreber wants everything: to be passive, beaten, eviscerated, submitting to coitus, giving birth, mother of a new race, and all with pleasure in a jouissance that is . . . infinite.

This leads to another question: what if behind men's fear of women, which leads them to dominate them, in the background of this anxiety about the unrepresentable erotico–maternal feminine, a secret envy was burning? In other words: *what if a Schreber lay dormant in every man?*

Not rejecting the feminine would mean knowing and experiencing what can be only felt in passivity and what, in the heat of action, activity stifles; it would be to connect pain and pleasure and vice versa; it would be no longer to set ourselves up in the uncertainty of outcome but instead to let ourselves go in receiving; it would be to abandon ourselves, most happily, on a very young woman's breast, even on pain of death: this is what is depicted by Michelangelo's *Pietà* at St. Peter's in Rome; this is the fourth primal fantasy, the return to the mother's womb.

This desire is nevertheless fraught with dangers:

- Good passivity, by not moving, becomes deadly.
- Masochism is inexhaustible; the guardian of life to a certain extent, beyond a certain threshold it turns into self-destruction.
- When fear of castration does not function (or ceases to function) as signal anxiety, it is and remains (and returns to being?) the terror of being

mutilated, like an amputated Narcissus who loses his self-image and his life.
- When the separation from the maternal object is not mediatised by a castration complex that sacrifices a part to save the whole – as is very generally the case with the girl in relation to her mother – the relationship is at full throttle, symbiotic; total love, as well as hatred, can flourish and be conveyed there. The lost maternal object becomes invasive, from one generation to the next. A functional equivalent of the castration complex in men, penis envy would then enable women to cover the melancholic core of this fundamental loss (Cournut-Janin, 1998). It is in this sense that the castration complex and penis envy struggle in some against the nameless dread of a partial loss and in others against the even more nameless dread of a total loss. From this perspective, we might think that the phallic order and men's domination of women renders women a service by helping them to relativise their loss; but this must not be said . . . for it would lead to the rather politically incorrect notion that women's servitude towards men renders them the service of rescuing them from their mothers. Perhaps they even deliberately frighten men so that they can serve as a superego for them – a paternal superego, of course.

The community protects

If by chance men, one by one, stopped restraining their secret envy of the erotico-maternal feminine and did not forestall the risks to which it would expose them, external intervention would be necessary. Fortunately, the community intervenes, that of men, these linguistic and social beings; it does not tolerate solitary jouissance, first because it is dangerous, then because it is unproductive. Society requires active arms, inventive minds and productive sexual organs. If the erotico-maternal feminine that men find incomprehensible makes them envious, then it is necessary to reject and exclude it, dominate the women who embody it, confine them to the gynaeceum, separate mothers and daughters by extolling the exogamy that banishes daughters while keeping mothers, silence the children who pose unfathomable questions, exclude the homosexuals who pretend, foster penis envy in men, brandish the fan of castration and promote every form of fetish – fine speeches, beautiful machines, beautiful women who do not inspire fear . . .

A woman who is an actress and writer is told:

– Men love you because you're beautiful.
– No, because I'm something worse.
– Are men afraid of you?
– Yes, because I like them too much . . .

New version of Genesis – closing sequel

Adam was afraid because he still did not understand. God had nevertheless told Eve: 'Your husband will rule over you' and, furthermore, 'You will bear children in pain'. Eve still said nothing and from time to time seemed to be leaving, with a cry, for the high seas; or else – with what, how, why – she played with her daughters (those daughters hardly mentioned in Genesis). One day, unable to bear it any more, Adam said to God, 'Reveal to me the woman's states of bliss'. And God made known to him the female states of bliss.

These were such that he sank into nameless and imageless delights, savouring the astonishing amalgam of pain and pleasure; he ceased to move. His sons, who bustled around, fought and had children, came to reproach him for his state: the community cannot tolerate an individual enjoying pleasure all alone, being inactive, not reproducing. But Adam was raving with joy, he said: 'My child, my sister, think of the rapture, of living together there!' It was then that God told Adam: 'Be careful, if you let yourself go, you will go too far'. But Adam continued to rave: 'Of loving at will, of loving till death, in the land that is like you! . . .' Then God regretted having created otherness and said that for Adam now it was the beginning of unbinding.

Adam died; then the others laid the table for the totemic meal, between men.

References

André, J. (1994). La sexualité féminine [Feminine sexuality]. Paris: Presses Universitaires de France.

André, J. (1995). *Aux origines féminines de la sexualité* [At the female origins of sexuality]. Paris: Presses Universitaires de France.

Aragon, L. (1963). *Le fou d'Elsa* [Elsa's fool]. Paris: Gallimard.

Cournut-Janin, M. (1998). *Féminin et féminité* [The feminine and femininity]. Paris: Presses Universitaires de France.

Faure-Pragier, S. (1997). *Les bébés de l'inconscient. Le psychanalyste face aux stérilités féminines aujourd'hui* [The babies of the unconscious. The psychoanalyst dealing with female infertility today]. Paris: Presses Universitaires de France.

Faure-Pragier, S. (1999). Le désir d'enfant comme substitut du pénis manquant. Une théorie stérile de la féminité [The wish for a child as a substitute for the absent penis. An unproductive theory of femininity]. In J. Schaeffer, M. Cournut-Janin, S. Faure-Pragier, & F. Guignard (Eds.), *Clés pour le féminin* [Keys to femininity] (pp. 41–55). Paris: Presses Universitaires de France.

Freud, S. (1907c). The Sexual Enlightenment of Children. *S.E.*, 9.

Freud, S. (1908c). On the Sexual Theories of Children. *S.E.*, 9.

Freud, S. (1911c). Psycho-Analytic Notes on an Autobiographical Account of a Case of Paranoia (Dementia Paranoides). *S.E.*, 12.

Freud, S. (1918a). The Taboo of Virginity. *S.E.*, 11.

Freud, S. (1918b). From the History of an Infantile Neurosis. *S.E.*, 17.

Freud, S. (1922b). Some Neurotic Mechanisms in Jealousy, Paranoia and Homosexuality. *S.E.*, 18.

Freud, S. (1923b). *The Ego and the Id. S.E.*, 23: 12–66.

Freud, S. (1924c). The Economic Problem of Masochism. *S.E.*, 19.

Freud S. (1937c) Analysis Terminable and Interminable. *S.E.*, 23: 216–253.

Godfrind, J. (2001). *Comment la féminité vient aux femmes* [How women acquire femininity]. Paris: Presses Universitaires de France.

Guignard, F. (1996). *Au vif de l'infantile. Réflexions sur la situation analytique* [At the heart of childhood: Reflections on the analytic situation]. Lausanne: Delachaux et Niestlé.

Guignard, F. (1997). *Epître à l'objet* [Epistle to the object]. Paris: Presses Universitaires de France.

Laqueur, T. (1990). *Making Sex: Body and Gender from the Greeks to Freud*. Cambridge, MA: Harvard University Press. [French edition: *La fabrique du sexe*. Paris. Gallimard, 1992.]

Loraux, N. (1981). *Les enfants d'Athena. Idées athéniennes sur la citoyenneté et la division des sexes*. Paris: Maspero. [*The Children of Athena: Athenian Ideas about Citizenship and the Division between the Sexes*, trans. C. Levine. Princeton, NJ: Princeton University Press, 1994.]

Parat, C. (1964). Le changement d'objet. In J. Chasseguet-Smirgel (Ed.), *Recherches psychanalytiques nouvelles sur la sexualité féminine* (pp. 115–127). Paris: Payot. [The Change of Object. In *Female Sexuality: New Psychoanalytic Views*. London: Virago, 1981.]

Perron-Borelli, M. (1993). L'investissement phallique. Fonction symbolisante pour les deux sexes [The phallic cathexis. Symbolizing function for both sexes]. *Revue Française de Psychanalyse, 57* (special issue): 1617–1629.

Perron-Borelli, M. (2001). *Les fantasmes* [Fantasies]. Paris: Presses Universitaires de France.

Schaeffer, J. (1997). *Le refus du féminin* [The repudiation of the feminine] (4th edition). Paris: Presses Universitaires de France, 2003. New edition: *Le refus du féminin (La sphinge et son âme en peine)* [The repudiation of femininity (The Sphinx and its lost soul)]. Paris: Presses Universitaires de France, 2008.

32 THE FEMININE AND FEMININITY

Monique Cournut-Janin

> A psychiatrist, full member of the Paris Psychoanalytical Society, and former co-director of the Jean Favreau Centre for Psychoanalytic Consultation and Treatment, **Monique Cournut-Janin** was instrumental in facilitating communication between psychoanalysts on an international level, in particular by organising meetings between French and British analysts. A major part of her work deals with female sexuality; many of her papers on the subject were published in *Féminin et Féminité* [The feminine and femininity] (PUF, 1998). She contributed to a book co-edited by J. Schaeffer, S. Faure-Pragier and F. Guignard, *Clés pour le féminin. Une femme, mère, amante et fille* [Key concepts in understanding the feminine: Wife, mother, lover and daughter] (PUF, 1999).

The box and its secret

Preliminary remarks

Between Dora's jewel box and the secret that Winnicott's little girl knows how to keep,[1] the metaphor of a box is constructed, with what it conceals inside: the female body, rich inside with 'transposable' contents (penis, faeces, child . . . jewels, buttons[2] – not forgetting blood, promising periods).

The clasp

The metaphor of the box also evokes the secret clasp (hymen is the technical term); we posit that it belongs to the father and the mother is its keeper.

---

[1] 'Unless a girl can keep a secret she cannot become pregnant' (Winnicott, 1988, p. 46).
[2] See L. Andréas-Salomé (1980), on the feminine type.

The feminine[3] hidden inside; femininity shown on the outside

Following on from some ideas close to those of other authors, I have proposed that femininity is what the woman displays – attractive in her finery, make-up, everything that makes her 'beautiful' . . . and deflects the gaze from the genital organs. As we know, the sight of these corresponds to the boy's first encounter with what triggers his castration anxiety and its complex.

Accordingly, femininity displays the entire body adorned, distancing the male gaze from what would make him flee in anxiety. Femininity can therefore be understood as the unconscious organisation of a lure.[4] This forms part of the great game of psychosexuality: the object of desire, but also of the prohibition relayed by fear, is always 'on the body of the other'.

Message of castration to the feminine

This preamble may help us to reconstruct what happens between a mother and her baby daughter. We are of course envisaging a mother whose psychic life is organised by her own Oedipus complex, whose motherhood is an experience of perceptual, affective, cathecting, binding and unbinding violence. Denise Braunschweig and Michel Fain have clearly identified what is at stake in this crisis: for this mother, the intrapsychic proximity between the real child and the child of Oedipal desire gives rise to Oedipal guilt. So this mother simultaneously transmits desire and prohibition to the child of either sex. The child must therefore be considered to have a psychogenetic predisposition, and on several levels:

- a capacity to identify with the mother while also gradually cathecting her as a love object;
- an ability to receive her implicit or stated messages.

This mother was once a baby daughter who wanted to take into herself, eat and incorporate everything she cathected. In this sequence of 'objects', her father's penis occupied a particular place. This incorporative voracity – oral, anal, loving, jealous but also hateful – that she used to feel is still present in her unconscious. Now she is the mother of a daughter, it generates in her a counter-cathectic mechanism that is massively projected on to this daughter. This is an implicit message that could be simplified as follows: 'Your sexual

---

[3] In French as in English, feminine is an adjective, which Monique Cournut-Janin uses here as a noun to make a distinction between '*le féminin*' and '*féminité*' as two different constructions of femininity. It was decided to follow this in the translation and make feminine into a noun. [*Eds. & Trans., this volume*]

[4] There is an obvious similarity here between this feminine organisation and the masculine one that strives to establish a fetish.

organs should not desire to take and incorporate your father's sexual organ; you must not enjoy it or risk destroying it.' Thus the maternal unconscious, fearful of having destroyed the coveted object, encounters the castration anxiety that is always present in the father's unconscious. This unspoken maternal message passes, as we have seen, through the cathexis of the little girl's entire body: so the specific cathexis of her sexual organs is shifted, displaced, annulled and repressed.

Denise Braunschweig and Michel Fain give a more metapsychologically exact theoretical construction, which explains this relegation of the female sexual organs with the term 'primary repression of the vagina'.[5] But what concerns us here is the specific nature of the mother's message to the daughter, which we think organises the transmission of femininity as a protective phallic lure.

The price to be paid, the marginalisation of the female sexual organs as such in the little girl, therefore paves the way for a compromise between drive and defence: as a girl, she is recognised, loved as such, attractive, even seductive and as non-anal as possible: a hole being a hole, anality might evoke the genitals, and this must remain silent. Cathected by the mother, she is – but in a different way from the boy, who is recognised and loved as the bearer of the penis. She, however, is 'entire; entirely phallic'; we imagine the mother's gaze enveloping the daughter's body, a child of the loved man. Thus the maternal and paternal gazes meet around this girl child. For the father too, it is entirely (including intact hymen) that his daughter represents (equivalent according to Freud's 1917c formulation) his own cathexis of his sexual organs and the cathected body of the child's mother. As for her sexual organs, we suppose that castration anxiety – always present in the unconscious – prevents both partners from discovering these except during sexual relations.

Underneath femininity, the feminine

To return to the girl: under cover of this caution against revealing men's castration anxiety, in the physical contact with her mother, sucking the breast and desiring and undergoing penetrating care of her body, she structures and prepares the organisation that incorporates her psychosexual life, with its essentially centripetal tropism. The little boy experiences the same agitations, the same penetrating excitation of his erogenous zones, but his penis, cathected by him and by the others, partly draws outside (penetrating, piercing holes everywhere: Freud, 1908c) that which in the girl presses to be taken inside.

---

[5] But not the clitoris, which tends to foster the phallic lure ('that will grow' . . . for example!). For the man, it is a matter of avoiding his castration anxiety being aroused in this way; for the woman, of not risking being decathected in that event: for Freud, the girl's fear of not being loved corresponds to the boy's castration anxiety (Braunschweig & Fain, 1971).

'Attract your father, but not with your sexual organs'

How are we to understand this maternal tendency, too common to be construed as perverse, to encourage daughters to be attractive to their fathers, as anything other than a compromise? In the identification, 'attract your father as I liked to attract mine, but your sexual organs as such should remain sidelined', this is the price paid to the incest prohibition.

The feminine Oedipus complex, under cover of femininity

Freud proposes a completely different destiny for the girl's Oedipus complex from its explosive destruction through the impact of the castration complex described in the boy.

The construction we have just considered may have some similarities with Freud's ideas on the subject: protected by the mother, distanced from her sexual organs, the girl may undergo an Oedipus complex that is more protracted.

In fact, early on and constantly, the mother induces in the girl a counter-cathexis of her vagina. The girl's penis envy – and, as several authors have suggested,[6] beyond the desire to penetrate the mother – serves to reinforce the counter-cathexis in question: 'No, I don't have (don't want to have) a vagina that would place me in a position of rivalry with you, my mother; I prefer to believe that there is only one, supremely enviable, sexual organ – the male one.'

Mother–daughter complicity: one secretly feminine, the other entirely phallic

This involves a complicity based on a lure that is the precondition of its possibility. The mother teaches her daughter a game of finery: a pretty dress and a nice hairstyle, ways of being and appearing, including the girl's game of being 'like a boy'.[7] Thus, again excluding the sexual organs, an erotically cathected complicity is in play. The feminine then is transmitted unknown and unspoken; the girl can learn from her mother to love herself as feminine (in the sense of both femininity and the feminine); the promise of a child, via the doll, prepares the way for the other crisis: the inevitable acute rivalry between women. If this emerges only after a period of shared tenderness, it will be relatively easy to negotiate . . . The fact remains that then abandoning the part to preserve the whole precisely when she perceives herself as 'complete' and 'entire' is a less easy process than it is for the boy, and it can overbalance into the 'all' of loss: no longer being loved, no longer being anything.

---

[6] Maria Torok (1970), in particular.
[7] *Comme des garçons*' ['Like boys'] is a fashionable brand of women's clothing, not at all in the 'tomboy' style but instead deriving its success from the 'game' with the phallic.

While I do not seek to deny the many paths that the transaction can then take in the form of various renunciations, they are nevertheless generally at the extremes of all or nothing.

In the tracks of the Freudian female Oedipus complex

Is the girl confronted less clearly and less suddenly than the boy with the Oedipal prohibition? Perhaps ... if so, it is through these adaptations, this lure that we have envisaged.

Accordingly, the repression of her sexual organs sometimes allows her, until the post-adolescent stage, to deploy a bisexual seduction: a girl, but without a hole and phallic: 'like a boy', but complete. The real issues are then ineluctably found; I have previously described these loving adolescent couples in which this arrangement temporarily suits both girl and boy (Cournut-Janin, 1989).

'A little girl is being raped'

Is it because the girl is cathected by herself and by others as 'entirely phallic' that her commonest anxiety is usually about penetration? If this desire to be penetrated (and possess an appropriate organ) is revealed too early, it risks destroying the compromise described. I have also tried to demonstrate the role played by these rape fantasies in the progressive integration of this desire for receptive activity (Parat, 1995), with its requisite elaboration of sadistic primal-scene fantasies. The fantasies around this theme also allow the full richness of bisexual identifications: penetrating, being penetrated.

In the above description, have I painted too theoretical and above all too idyllic a portrait of the girl's accession to the feminine? Perhaps: I have chosen to emphasise one particular mode of adaptation: 'totally phallic'. It is of course not the only one, but I have often observed its frequency and its characteristic integration of a harmonious bisexuality.

Although I have not referred explicitly to female homosexuality here, I think I have described some of its aspects.

The feminine, dark version

It is in violence – in certain analyses from the outset, later on for others – that the physical contact of the female homosexual transference appears in the form of a flight from an excessively frightening drive dimension, a depleting hatred of oneself and the other, from the horror of a mixture in which self and other become undifferentiated, are lost, in which thought cannot be autonomous, can even cease to function.

The fantasies that connect the erogenous zones with the mother are too archaic not to trigger a horrified rejection: having the buttocks or sexual organs washed, being given an enema and so on (Troisier, 1992).

The more Oedipal desire to take the father's place in order to penetrate the mother and give her a child is not entirely peaceful either, even if it takes over from the deeper buried desire to expect a child from her. But is the price of a 'successful' analysis not the integration, the toleration, the defusion of these infantile agitations, repressions, even splittings, or at least the massive counter-cathexes or major inhibitions they have caused?

So many women, despite being wives and mothers, spend years on the couch making a cathected link between the various excitable zones of their body and the capacity to conceive of them as their own.

The crises

The discovery of fertility: the first period

Whether it is anticipated or comes as a surprise, this is a critical point at which everything radically changes. Many women on the couch mention their shame when their mother spoke the ritual words, addressed to their fathers: 'Your daughter is now a big girl.' On closer examination, this entails the long-term discovery of her feminine and maternal role. But it also brings a strange new closeness to the father, as well as a distancing: 'You're becoming a woman, so you can't play with your father, your brothers and so on any more as you used to do.' A sort of ambiguous message, both a promise and a prohibition. Instead of a 'Dr X' to cut whatever it may be, a form of taboo is established[8] – for example, 'I didn't dare climb onto his knees any more'.

The fear, sometimes of being pregnant, if the taboo on touch is infringed clearly indicates what is at stake here: the incest prohibition. Not getting on to Daddy's knees, so as not to risk being pregnant: desire and prohibition.

And what if periods, too, were part of the 'treasure'?

Much has been written about the revulsion inspired by periods, but very little about the opposite. Do women analysts perhaps more often receive confidences about this?

I am referring to the pride, the liking for the hot smell, the rich, sticky liquid, the sensation of heaviness, of weight verging on pain, that gives the little girl a different, deeper perception of her abdomen. She is soon aware, from a few signs known only to her, such as more sensitive nipples, when that rich, intimate flow, very much her own, will return month after month, with the promise of a future child . . . and vague sadness that is it as yet only a promise. It is also, and in this respect very different from faeces, a spontaneous occurrence,

---

[8] A taboo comparable to the threat to Little Hans from his mother: 'If you do that, I shall send for Dr. A. to cut off your widdler' (Freud, 1909b). [*Eds., this volume*]

at her own rhythm, independently of her mother. 'I've got my period': the possessive clearly indicates this new sense of self-belonging. And when, many years later, the menopause comes, it is not only the eternally possible child that has to be mourned but the periods as well.[9]

This enriching 'crisis', like any crisis, can come unstuck and organise an experience of real castration: no longer being able to 'do everything' or, specifically, having to renounce being 'like a boy'. But, generally, periods belong to the treasure in the box and do nothing to tarnish its veneer. Splitting? No, but various levels of psychic functioning. The emergence from this 'excess' requires no renunciation of femininity or the feminine. The idea of penetration remains latent. In this adaptive mode, periods do not involve the vagina . . . and, as 'totally phallic', she is only all the more complete for having her periods.

In the good cases!

The filiation to the father's femininity

Aren't 'feminine filiations' in both sexes also a complex game of identification with the mother's feminine and with her bisexuality – that is, with her own paternal identification? But here I should like to emphasise one further aspect of these multiple identifications. I want to discuss the girl's identification with the feminine component presented by her father: this is sometimes the opportunity for a very useful identificatory support.

Hilda had a violent mother, very womanly and highly unfeminine, and a father whose feminine identifications, in particular with his daughter's femininity, allowed a playful atmosphere: on the couch, she reconstructed the subtle complexity of the effects on her of a paternal gaze that she felt to be clearly male, designating her as a daughter, and as the granddaughter of a grandmother whom she had never known. This grandmother seems to have protected her father in his phallic anxiety: spontaneously, Hilda had taken that over: with her, the maternal message of femininity as protective against male castration anxiety had been somewhat lacking. Her father, unconsciously, had provided it: she remembered what might be considered a message of castration when, very little, she was 'touching' herself: 'Don't touch, little one, you might hurt yourself.' She had been a robust child, 'like her mother', she said, and she realised that she had always heard this sentence, spoken gently and tenderly, as a paternal request: 'Don't touch what might hurt *me*.'

Among others, Hilda confirmed my idea that for women it is men's castration anxiety and the concern to avoid generating it in them that strongly characterise the form of relationship they establish with their own psychosexuality.

[9] The current medical support for the menopause can maintain menstruation for a while: the pleasure of 'feeling them flow' is mentioned much more often than the apparent renunciation of a so-called 'curse'.

Pregnancy stories

I will keep to the essential facts about Celia: she was a very young woman, with rich potentialities, and in pieces. She only felt alive at top speed, alternately idealising and abandoning the object. When she stopped, she lost any sense of existing at all. She was feminine, but this involved narcissistic reassurance more than any mechanism deeply bound to the object; she was intelligent but could not really pursue a piece of work or research. After a period of attending psychotherapy that gradually assumed real importance for her, I would like to report how a wanted pregnancy with a man she loved allowed a form of crystallisation process to occur. She seemed to me to be constructing herself precisely along with the baby as it was growing in her womb. Some real identifications appeared, helping to give a sense of reality to her existence; she perceived herself as a woman in the process of becoming a mother. She was expecting a daughter. Unlike some patients whose pregnancy helped them to rediscover their own childhood, Celia seemed to construct herself around this future girl-child, without this identification prevailing over what was for her the new mode of the beginnings of a loving, protective maternal relationship. The 'crisis' of motherhood prolonged in her an adolescent crisis that had not been concluded before this pregnancy. Celia's psychic organisation in terms of the second topography became clearly conceivable for me.

With other patients, at lower intensity, the 'crisis' of motherhood appeared to me as the opportunity to complete a game of identification that had not yet concluded: to be a mother, to perceive a baby in oneself, instigates a role, a place in the filiation of women and the succession of generations. Even if the price has to be paid through the acceptance of ageing and death, time assumes a new meaning and plenitude.

With Judith, rather than a physical pregnancy, there was a cathexis of a feminine filiation in rebuilding the connection, hitherto disregarded, between her work as a journalist and a book written by her grandmother: another form of maternal and feminine filiation and an accession to what she could experience as fertility.

How to conclude except by attesting the richness of identifications with both sexes as both an openness and a balm to the suffering, never totally appeased, from being only a woman . . . or a man?

From mother to daughter, from one woman to another, what if it were no more than that? From mother to daughter, because the father is the third, designated by the mother, resuming her own childhood history.

From paternal grandmother to granddaughter, and between them the person without whom the filiation would lose its meaning and its spark . . .

Under cover of femininity

Transmission

Women are said to be unable to resist succumbing to hubris. The feminine is equated with madness; and if not the feminine, then motherhood. Temptress, witch, anti-social woman, contaminating feminine ... The feminine designates excess, irrationality and lawlessness ... and Freud, concerning the weakness of the superego in women, seems to adduce to the case a serious – because metapsychological – argument: in short, the woman, and her femininity, inspire distrust on many counts.

Freud further explains (1937c) that this rejection of the feminine is encountered not only in men – for them it is a matter of course – but also in women ...

This raises the question of a mother–daughter transmission of what might be called a *strategy* for making the feminine tolerable, in terms of female psychosexuality, for the woman herself and in her object-relationships.

On the body of the other, the difference

As Freud clearly posits in 'On the Sexual Theories of Children' (1908c), it is through the *gaze* at the body of the other that the human being of either sex discovers what supremely constitutes *the* difference. For the boy, the effect is traumatic and forces him, when it is supplemented by the *understood* threat, to repress his Oedipal desires to safeguard the part of himself that is so narcissistically cathected: his penis.

For the girl too, the *sight* of this penis that she does not have herself is traumatic; it triggers envy, and this envy plays an essential role both in the elaboration of the primary relationship with the mother, with the desire to penetrate her as the father does, and in the temporary avoidance of the rivalry with her.

The object: herald of castration

Freud did not propose an equivalent, for the girl, to mother's threat of castration in the name of the father towards the little boy. Less evident, it is suggested rather than stated, but it is nonetheless a conceptual tool that it is helpful to postulate, perhaps following the example of this unconscious stage that Freud (1919e) includes between the first and the third phase of the 'child is being beaten' fantasy.

Female fantasies

Let us briefly consider the significance of this second phase, in the girl's case: 'My father is beating me, exciting me and punishing me at the same time, on the part of my body I can't see, behind me, *any more than I can see inside* my sexual organs, but which is the surface, *visible* to others, that is closest to these strong, diffuse, even overwhelming but vague sensations felt *inside* me'. We can observe that the voyeur's position is at the core of this fantasy, whereas in the first and third phase, it is the subject of the fantasy who is looking . . .

For both the boy and the girl, 'a child is being beaten' involves the presentation of the father's violent *contact* with their own body, which may indicate the important psychic transition from the turmoil linked with the stimulating maternal care to that caused by the excitation linked with this fantasised physical encounter with the father: this is a feminine phase in both sexes that seems to correspond to what Cathérine Parat (1995) identifies as a structuring masochistic *shift* in the girl towards her father (Thierry Bokanowski, 1993, has addressed the equivalent in the boy).

To the 'child is being beaten' fantasy is added the rape fantasy, apparently occurring later, but the psychic apparatus is known to function in a constant revision, from one retroactive operation to the next, which qualifies any scalar presentation. The psychic future of these fantasies may form the matrix of what the little girl, having later become a mother, will be led, in the mode of projected counter-cathexis, to deliver as a message of castration to her daughter. The rape fantasy in fact completes – in the work of the preconscious – what could be realised by 'a child is being beaten'. The zone concerned is this time clearly *internal*; it is about *penetration* and, as in 'A Child Is Being Beaten' (1919e), the *father* or his substitute is its active agent. When the psychic apparatus functions enough on the side of Eros rather than the pure repetition compulsion, these fantasies accomplish an identificatory game with the various protagonists of the drama, contributing to the psychic exploration of bisexuality and the integration of reciprocal identifications.

This is not the place for a detailed consideration of the psychic impulses that inevitably occur in a woman who is expecting a child, brings it into the world and finally abandons for its sake, temporarily, every narcissistic cathexis of her own, placing herself entirely at the child's disposition. This, preconsciously, even consciously, is transposed into behaviour and in no way excludes the complex revisions that affect the emergence of drive impulses that were previously repressed and adequately counter-cathected.

Penis equals child, and this child, in a regressive impulse on the mother's part, can represent a penis stolen both from her father and from the child's father, even from her own mother. The baby, unconsciously linked to the child of incestuous desire, then triggers maternal anxiety by his very existence. Much has been written about the day baby and the night baby (Braunschweig & Fain, 1975), the censorship of the woman-as-lover leading the infant, in her absence, to create his own auto-erotisms; I will not address these processes here.

The exhibition of the little girl

It is by extending this research that I will situate my theme, by giving special consideration to the *gaze*. The baby girl, showing and exhibiting herself seductively to her love objects, causes agitation, even signal anxiety, in her mother. Her naked little daughter, happy to be so and to be *seen* in the other's *gaze* – especially the father's – *re*presents in her mother's eyes what she herself once felt, a pleasure in exhibiting herself. Retroactively led to feel guilty, she had sought and perhaps found in her own father a response, the erotic quality of his response being covered by repression: and it became a smack on the bottom given to the little girl who had disobeyed. What in fact could she have disobeyed, if not the Oedipal law, taken up again in an organising retroactive operation? – 'Only Mummy can be *touched sexually* by Daddy.' The child, conceived and brought into the world, does not suspend every form of castration anxiety – quite the opposite – that in her time the little girl may have experienced in terms of her own sexual body, with more or less displacement. Now, with her narcissism projected on to the child, it is this extension of herself that she perceives to be in danger.

The child of incestuous desire

Pregnancy, the crisis of childbirth, then mothering seem to have brought about this madness of mastery, this glory of omnipotence – namely, a child of one's own, only separated in the maternal psyche from the dream of the child of incestuous desire by the fragile membrane of censorship. On this basis, that of the Oedipus complex, the female child, like the boy, is a prohibited child, in danger of disappearing under the impact of a sentence from the superego. In this psychic crisis, it is often re-sexualised and projected on to the child's father. It might further be wondered if such a mechanism, which has some affinities with Freud's pessimism concerning the female superego, may not subsist in the mother's psychic apparatus, at the very least as concerns the child: he or she is always to some extent for her a transgressive child and at the same time is threatened, according to Michel Fain (1982), by the monstrous sodomising and castrating penis of an archaic father. To place herself and the child under the real father's authority then constitutes for the mother a refuge from the paternal law that is tantamount to rebellion. The worry that seems to come from outside often without an object, with which every mother educates and protects her child, bears the trace of this unconscious guilt linked to incestuous desire and to its ever-fragile counter-cathexis. The father's role is rarely mentioned insofar as he is – does he always know it? – summoned at the baby's arrival to be not only a father but also maternal with the young mother: he is to provide her with a hollow, a container, for her and her baby.

The love of the object in person

The fear of loss of love is certainly present in human beings of both sexes; Freud, moreover, has deemed this the female equivalent of the male castration anxiety that she specifically fears arousing. Traces of oral, anal and genital drive impulses to appropriate this highly valued sexual organ subsist in the female unconscious.

Woman and mother as messenger

It seems to fall to the woman to lower the threshold of the man's castration anxiety, and her own fear of mutilating him and being deprived of love and punished in her body and her psychosexuality, or through her children. It is in the father's name that she seeks to protect her son, as much from the rivalry with his father as from the sharing of erotic agitations with him, in any case those linked to her own genital sexuality. The message she conveys to him can be translated as: 'Don't excite the two of us with your sexual organ.'

She also intervenes with her daughter in the same terms ('don't excite us'), but this is also through a counter-cathexis massively projected on to her. Implicitly, this would mean: 'Your sexual organs should not desire to take and incorporate your father's sexual organ; you must not enjoy it or risk destroying it.' The mother's unconscious, fearful of destroying the envied object, encounters the father's unconscious, in which castration anxiety is always present.

It is in the cathexis of the little girl's entire body that the precise cathexis of her sexual organs can be concealed, displaced and repressed.

Entirely phallic

The girl's cathexis of the 'entirely phallic' mode is one of the forms assumed by the mother's precaution of placing her under the father's aegis. Thus the little girl is narcissistically cathected, entirely, in the way the mother cathects the father as bearer of the penis; as for him, his eyes can envelop the little girl in one look, narcissising for him, because she represents his phallic power and for a while does not evoke anything feminine but sex as a marker of gender, rather than the site in which the sign of lack could resurface.

The game of hidden–shown

Femininity, in the sense that I am proposing, is what a woman displays ('there's something there; there's nothing there') in a *hidden–shown* that can avert the danger of generating male castration anxiety while simultaneously suggesting enough of *the feminine* to stimulate desire in the other sex. It is in a game of identification with the mother, instigated by her, that this femininity can be transmitted, cathected and introjected; we must then suppose a preconscious dual game in the mother, encouraging her daughter to counter-cathect the vagina and the desire for penetration, while reserving for herself the ability to have pleasure with the father. This is a dual game that we may consider a characteristic of female psychosexuality.

Do the drive destinies, albeit under the primacy of genitality, often maintain a greater intimacy with and proximity to the body, even perhaps the drives, in the woman? With a more direct engagement of hormonal intermediaries, and at every stage of life? When a daughter gives birth, her mother feels inside her own body what used to be called *after-pains*. . . . We could cite countless examples. Freud is said to have referred to somatic compliance; can we also refer to hysteria – might we add 'normal hysteria'?

Gradiva, the lizard and the rift

The most feminine woman in the Freudian oeuvre, with whom every woman analyst readily identifies, is Gradiva. Freud took this figure from Jensen at a time when the castration complex had not yet assumed its later self-evidence to him. Let us recall the description of the *bas-relief*: 'With her head bent forward a little, she held slightly raised in her left hand, so that her sandaled feet became visible, her garment which fell in exceedingly voluminous folds from her throat to her ankles' (Jensen, 1993, p. 4). To show, discover, hide; the young archaeologist was certainly attracted, but protected by the displacement operated by the stimulating sight of the living Zoe walking over the – immobile and therefore reassuring – Roman woman in the *bas-relief*. If the archaeologist unconsciously needed to distance himself as far as possible – geographically and temporally – from his childhood friend who was now a woman, the 'strangely obscure' dream' that Jensen tells us he had in Pompeii, where in the novel he met the young woman, gives us the key: 'Somewhere in the sun Gradiva was sitting, making *a snare out of a blade of grass to catch a lizard in*' (Freud, 1907a, p. 25). At this point in his elaboration, Freud does not consider the aspect of the dream that transposes the dreamer's castration anxiety: the capture of the lizard simply refers then to the young man's conquest, admittedly in the form of a lizard-sexual organ penetrating a rift (the slipknot is not addressed or analysed in relation to disturbing female sexual organs). As for the Gradiva aspect, the importance accorded to her walk, to the side of the dress that reveals . . . let us go no further! – the way the fetishist's gaze stops at the part of the body or clothing that he glimpsed just before the traumatic discovery of female castration. Thus, what I have proposed to term *femininity* is the encounter offered to the male gaze so that he can avoid or displace on to that which covers, clothes and conceals; the gleaming make-up, clothes and jewels evoke, show *and* hide. We are dealing with a female psychic mechanism that induces a behaviour and probably fulfils an ambiguous and complex unconscious agenda:

- To reassure male desire by distancing from the gaze that which would evoke the threat, a mechanism that resembles the fetishist's staging of castration.
- But also, through the *hidden–shown*, to attract the gaze, thus signalling the *feminine desire to please* and to be loved.
- To obtain some narcissistic reassurance (at a phallic level that there is every reason to believe still exists in the unconscious), which also resembles the fetish; the underlying thought, originating from the historic frustration at not having a penis, would be: 'I may not have this envied sexual organ, but altogether what I display is cathected by me, and not only do I not inspire fear, but I please.'
- Finally, to share this narcissistic game with other women, following the mother; secondary homosexuality, as far as *femininity* is concerned, also plays on the third, which is absent but incorporated in the very mechanism of femininity. Unlike the homosexuality of male groups, female homosexuality, cathected in this way, remains under the sign of the male third.

The necessary third

Let us return to the little girl. Under the cover of femininity, the identification with *the feminine* in her mother can then be accomplished, but more clandestinely. I will return to this point. Femininity is constructed, as we have seen, in relation to the father, by the vital interest in considering him above all else. The mother–daughter relationship does not exclude the stimulating cares, any more than the mother–son relationship does; its more diffuse erotism exposes the little girl to a particularly strong relationship of love and identification with the mother. The predominance in her of centripetal drives, much less mitigated than in the boy by centrifugal drive impulses, increases the risk of clinging, of imprisonment in Russian dolls; this is not even then a matter of mother–daughter incest but of being in a place beyond all prohibition, in a psychotic fusional world.

By instituting, through the game of femininity, a loving mother–daughter complicity with regard to the father, the mother inscribes the supremacy of the paternal order and works to prepare for the little girl's future change of object. These impulses induced by the mother contain a certain ambiguity, or even a dual game: is there some feminine duplicity even in the maternal function? Probably – even if this involves a welcome unconscious dual game and ambiguity; what is in fact the naked truth can be the height of naivety, even sadism, in the sexual sphere . . .

Incest and its repetition

How are we to understand the psychic functioning of women who do not protect their daughters, even provoke their incestuous encounters with their fathers? Analysis can bring to light a repetition, with the daughter reviving the mother's own incestuous history in the next generation. When the maternal imago cannot be connected in the psyche with the father, through a primal scene that can be elaborated, it blocks the elaboration of a desire that must confront the law, which sometimes only leaves the act as a drive outcome.

What could Jocasta transmit to her daughters? As far as Antigone was concerned, she was no more able to accept abandoning her incestuous objects than her mother – or Laius, in his time – had been able to do.

Being a mother is, among other things, about transmitting prohibitions, which Braunschweig and Fain (1971) have also demonstrated through the training surrounding anality; a hole is a hole, and the vagina is only separated from the anus by a thin membrane, definitely physical but also psychic. For the mother, toilet-training is already a means of subjugating the little girl to the paternal law.

Let us return to the feminine that is more easily transmitted under cover of what I have sought to describe with the term *femininity*. This previously experienced Oedipal guilt and narcissistic shame that led the mother to deliver the message of castration to the feminine will have to be re-lived by the little girl on her own account, in her psychic apparatus and with her body, exploring each of them, exploring one through the other, adequately separated from her mother by the father, but also by what the message will have induced, thus clearly introduced in the name of the father, in terms of psychic separation from her first object. In the play of the finery, the hairstyling, and in the transition through the doll, the physical contact between mother and daughter is dramatised by multiple mirrors from which the father's gaze is not excluded.

Father and daughter, in adolescence

The mother constantly intervenes in her daughter's psychosexual development. A key point is the onset of periods. In our work following on from Freud, we have wondered about the ambiguity of the maternal messages, the classic example being 'Mummy, have you got a widdler too?' – eliciting the response: 'Of course. What did you think?' (1907c, p. 134). The way in which the mother announces to the father that her daughter has started her periods – 'Your daughter has become a woman!' – persists, to judge by what is heard from many women on the couch, as the disturbing moment of a dual message, both *offering* the father this completely new *feminine* in her daughter and awakening a new form of the incest prohibition.

As we have seen, the daughter's virginity *belongs* to the father; it used to represent his honour – his phallic completeness – which is something that the evolution of mores has probably done nothing to change at the unconscious level.

No, that's not sexual!

All parents tend to negate their child's sexuality, which is linked to repression of their own infantile sexuality, until puberty appears, sometimes very violently, to remind them that the child's sex is not only a matter of gender. This type of functioning would resemble: 'No, that's not sexual.' Some adolescent girls cannot accept this body that becomes round, with visible breasts and hips, this body that designates them as women: sex as a marker of gender has become sexual in everyone's eyes.

Jocasta exemplifies this maternal dual register because, from one moment to the next, she knows, or does not want to know, that she lives in transgression; it is this knowing-not-knowing that drives a 'good-enough' mother to be, in her turn, the messenger of castration towards her children.

Touch, sight and hearing

I should like to emphasise the importance of three types of sensory perception that we have to consider. The most primitive is *touch*, which is involved in three primal fantasies; the mother – as Green (1997) observed – being the only one necessarily in contact with both father and child. The prohibition on touch in her case can only, as we have seen, be displaced on to a repression of the sexual valency, under the father's aegis. Is this so very different from a 'normal' hysteria?

Sight, in relation to our present concern with the consequences of the traumatic perception of sexual difference, is the sensory function deployed by the most fundamental narcissistic and objectal adaptations. I will briefly relate a recent interview with a young woman, whom I had met a few years earlier, who complained of being unwell since her husband had left her for someone else: 'I'm ugly and I'm doing nothing about it' she said, adding that she used to know how to *show herself* [sic] so as to attract people. This complaint – 'I'm ugly' – is new to her: she *perceives herself* as 'ugly', as no longer pleasing *him*, her husband's gaze being the guarantee of her existence as a lovable woman. This abandonment was immediately followed by a regression; in fact, while she ceased to accord herself any attention or interest, she transferred her entire narcissistic cathexis to her young child; I remember what I had already ascertained in her that was very ordinary, two years earlier, when this child was born. She was, she told me, no longer anything by herself: she was entirely dependent on the judgement made by the bearer of the penis. I had already observed this female tendency to refer, for a criterion of existence, entirely to the man, whereas he, in the event of a break-up, instead tends to question his sexual organs, his phallic power, and feels mutilated by his partner's desertion.

The last sense involved is evidently *hearing*, since it is through language that the Oedipal prohibitions are transmitted and that the message of castration triggers the process of repression, putting infantile sexuality into latency.

A drive with a centripetal goal

The feminine and femininity: it is *femininity* that is displayed and *elevated* as an unconscious defence to deal with the anxieties of both sexes. *The feminine* seems to be more clandestinely constituted, under the cover of femininity, lending a complex and at least dual aspect to female identity. While femininity concerns the surface and the gaze, with a phallic reference, the feminine concerns the hollow, of genital, anal and buccal erogenous zones, of the drive with a centripetal goal, taking inside, as described by Klein, everything enviable that comes from the mother or the father. It is not easy clearly to distinguish what is feminine from what is maternal in that which is thus constructed in the girl child; the Oedipal rivalry with the mother clashes with the identification with her, and it is impossible to disagree with Freud's assertion that the girl's relationship with this first object goes on to characterise every subsequent relationship. The discourse on the couch seems to play on two misunderstandings: concerning the vagina and, albeit in a totally different way, the uterus; faeces, penis and child seem not only interchangeable but also impossible to relate clearly to very specific organs. This is obviously not theoretical knowledge but a form of knowledge that can in no way be based on the gaze: this is an essential difference from the boy, who can see his sexual organs and their modification according to his level of excitation. The faeces alone, including in their erotic valency, can clearly be observed to emerge from *her* body for the female child.

Accordingly, the feminine appears close to the unconscious, and the young mother's drive upsurge only tends to confirm this. I referred to the pubertal stage and the announcement so often made to the father; periods, according to what is in play, in particular with the mother, mark the programmed entry into the adult world, the promise of fertility, but also sometimes the invasion by anal shame. In analysis, it is very often through anality that we can work, gradually discovering the means of both connecting and differentiating between what is anal and what is genital, what is self from what is the mother's body or psyche. But perhaps the relative obscurity of the contours of self and other persists more easily and often more tolerably in a woman than in a man, even if the analysis of the feminine in him conditions the access to bisexuality . . . But that is another story.

A dual key: Femininity is a way of playing with the phallic by borrowing its logic

In the minefield that human beings have to navigate to tame their mother's feminine as far as possible, in which most are led by their sex towards identification or the object relationship, femininity offers comedy rather than tragedy. It spares no one the violence of the Oedipal tragedy, even if a certain mother–daughter complicity has been established and the mother's femininity has offered the boy's fantasies a means of playing, more or less, for a longer or shorter period, and with more or less freedom, with feminine characteristics.

Is the music of femininity therefore always played on two staves, with the phallic order in the key signature on one side, differently harmonised according to each person's psychic organisation, and the feminine on the other?

References

Andréas-Salomé, L. (1980). *L'amour du narcissisme* [The love of narcissism]. Paris: Gallimard.

Bokanowski, T. (1993). Destins au féminin chez l'homme [Feminine destinies in men]. *Revue Française de Psychanalyse, 57* [Special Congress Issue].

Braunschweig, D., & Fain, M. (1971). *Eros et Anteros. Réflexions psychanalytiques sur la sexualité* [Eros and Anteros: Psychoanalytic thoughts on sexuality]. Paris: Payot.

Braunschweig, D., & Fain, M. (1975). *La nuit, le jour. Essai psychanalytique sur le fonctionnement mental* [Night, day: A psychoanalytic essay on mental functioning]. Paris: Presses Universitaires de France.

Cournut-Janin, M. (1989). La même et l'autre [The same and the other]. *Adolescence, 1*.

Fain, M. (1982). Le désir de l'interprète [The desire of the interpreter]. In *La psychanalyse prise au mot* [Psychoanalysis taken at its word]. Paris: Aubier-Montaigne.

Freud, S. (1896c). The Aetiology of Hysteria. *S.E.*, 3.

Freud, S. (1907a). *Delusions and Dreams in Jensen's 'Gradiva'*. *S.E.*, 9.

Freud, S. (1907c). The Sexual Enlightenment of Children. *S.E.*, 9.

Freud, S. (1908c). On the Sexual Theories of Children. *S.E.*, 9.

Freud, S. (1909b). Analysis of a Phobia in a Five-Year-Old Boy. *S.E.*, 10.

Freud, S. (1917c). On Transformations of Instinct as Exemplified in Anal Erotism. *S.E.*, 17.

Freud, S. (1919e). A Child Is Being Beaten. *S.E.*, 17.

Freud, S. (1937c). Analysis Terminable and Interminable. *S.E.*, 23.

Green, A. (1997). *Les chaînes d'Éros* [The chains of Eros]. Paris: Odile Jacob.

Jensen, W. (1993). *Part I. Gradiva: A Pompeiian Fancy*. In S. Freud, *Jensen's Gradiva*. Los Angeles: Sun & Moon Press.

Parat, C. (1995). L'affect partagé [Shared affect]. In *Le fait psychanalytique* [The psychoanalytic fact]. Paris: Presses Unversitaires de France.

Torok, M. (1970). The Significance of Penis Envy in Women. In J. Chasseguet-Smirgel (Ed.), *Female Sexuality: New Psychoanalytic Views* (pp. 135–171). Ann Arbor, MI: University of Michigan Press, 1970.

Troisier, H. (1992). L'empreinte érotique de la mère sur la fille [The mother's erotic imprint on the girl]. *Bulletin of the Paris Psychoanalytical Society, 25*.

Winnicott, D. W. (1988). *Human Nature*. London: Free Association Books.

33 PRIMARY HOMOSEXUALITY
A foundation of contradictions

Paul Denis

> **Paul Denis** is a psychiatrist, full member of the Paris Psychoanalytical Society, former director of the *Revue Française de Psychanalyse*, and editor of two series published by the Presses Universitaires de France: 'Le Fil Rouge' and 'Psychanalystes d'aujourd'hui'. He has written many articles, focusing more particularly on issues involving power in the behaviour of human beings, including extremely destructive violence; this led him to update to a significant degree what Freud had referred to as the 'instinct for mastery'.
>
> Among his writings are: *Emprise et satisfaction, les deux formants de la pulsion* [Mastery and satisfaction: The two formants of the drive] (PUF, 1997) and *Sigmund Freud, T. 3: 1905–1920* [Sigmund Freud, vol. 3: 1905–1920] for the 'Psychanalystes d'aujourd'hui' series (PUF, 2000).

The term 'primary homosexuality' seems to originate from Fenichel, who introduced it in relation to female homosexuality: 'The first object of every human being is the mother; all women, in contradistinction to men, have had a primary homosexual attachment, which may later be revived if normal heterosexuality is blocked' (1946, p. 338). This primary homosexual attachment is therefore the girl's prerogative. However, what about the baby boy, who only feels any sexual difference through its indirect effects? Does he experience a form of 'primary heterosexuality', or, as we are inclined to think, does he experience an undifferentiated primary sexuality as concerns sex, with a partner perceived as similar to him, which is then a primary homosexuality for the boy just as much as for the girl?

This is the conception of primary homosexuality, common to both sexes, that Kestemberg (1984)[1] proposes and invites us to elaborate on. It is a 'conception' of early relations and certain modalities of mental functioning, a

---

[1] The idea of a 'primary homosexuality' was put forward by Evelyne Kestemberg at a seminar that took place long before the publication of her own paper on the subject in 1984. She asked the author to propose a theory for the notion, and this paper, originally published in 1982, is the result of her invitation.

conception in Freud's sense in the *New Introductory Lectures*, when he explains this term by saying: 'But it is truly a matter of conceptions—that is to say, of introducing the right abstract ideas, whose application to the raw material of observation will produce order and clarity in it' (1933a, p. 81).

In 'A Case of Paranoia Running Counter to the Psycho-Analytic Theory of the Disease', Freud gives a theory of the patient's homosexuality that relates to the primal relationship with the mother: the 'powerful emotional attachment to her mother', the 'homosexual dependence on her mother', is transposed on to 'the elderly superior', and it is this bond that is at the root of the difficulties. Freud further explains that: 'The manifestation of the neurotic reaction will always be determined, however, not by her present-day relation to her actual mother but by her infantile relations to her earliest image of her mother' (1915f, p. 268). The concept of primary homosexuality, in the case of girls, is therefore implicit in Freud, but it is observation that reveals a 'homosexual' relationship between a boy and his mother. This applies in the case of Louis, aged five years. He is restive; he plays Tarzan on the shower curtains; with feet and hands pressed to either side of the corridor, he runs along it at two metres above the floor, to the great detriment of the wallpaper, and his general behaviour is unstable, refreshing and inventive. One day, he began a session by saying: 'My mother is Tarzan. You know, she wants to kill me, my mother does. She wants to get rid of me; she can't stand me any longer. She says, "I've had enough of that kid; I'm going to send him to boarding school." You know why it's called a boarding school? Because they hang people there.'[2] We can undoubtedly point here to the terrifying mother image and adduce mechanisms of identification with the aggressor in Louis's behaviour. We can also observe that Louis identifies his mother with the same omnipotent character, Tarzan, with which he identifies, and that the relationship between Louis and his mother is in some respects a homosexual one. Anatomical sex is therefore not adequate to define the relational modalities; here we are dealing with an age at which the knowledge of sexual difference has already been attained, and, if primary homosexuality exists, it forms the bedrock of the developing relational system. We will first take an ontogenetic perspective and consider a stage in the development of the psychic apparatus that presupposes the subject–object distinction but precedes the perception of sexual difference. In *The Ego and the Id*, Freud states his view that 'before a child has arrived at definite knowledge of the difference between the sexes, the lack of a penis, it does not distinguish in value between its father and its mother' (1923b, p. 31n.). In the first object relationship, considered from the viewpoint of the child's psychic apparatus, comprising the subject–object distinction, the first sexual relationship is established with a mother figure, or 'parental' figures, whom we can suppose the child conceives as similar to himself and each other.

---

[2] Louis is making a connection between the word '*pension*' [boarding school] and '*on pend*' [they hang]. [*Trans.*, this volume]

It is this mode of identification that Jacobson has described with the term '*likeness*'. According to her: 'in general the maternal image will continue for some years to be only an extension of the child's image of his self' (1954, p. 99). Primary sexuality is therefore addressed to an object that is sexually undifferentiated but similar – that is to say, sexually similar – to the subject. The prefix 'homo-' in homosexuality refers to the similarity between the partner and the subject; it is therefore legitimate to refer to homosexuality when adopting the perspective of early relations, for which 'primary homosexuality' is strictly the more accurate term. It is then not solely a matter – as in Fenichel's formulation – of a process that is specific to the girl, but of relational modalities common to both sexes. It is therefore an entire important part of early development that needs to be reformulated in terms of primary homosexuality. This specific relational register extends from primary identification to the recognition of sexual difference.

The transition from primary identification to primary homosexuality involves the establishment of a transaction with the object, a transaction that comes to replace the feeling of unity with the object. Freud refers to the regressive transition from homosexuality to identification: 'We can see by what means the girl had freed herself from her homosexual dependence on her mother. It was by means of a small piece of regression: instead of choosing her mother as a love-object, she identified herself with her' (1915f, p. 269). In the same register, Fenichel writes: 'we distinguish between object relationship and identification and we assume that understanding for the real object stops where identification becomes the means of the relationship' (1946, p. 84). Primary homosexuality is thus a relational modality and consequently later an alternative modality of mental functioning in relation to primary identification. The establishment of the primary homosexual relationship involves some modifications that can also be envisaged from the viewpoint of narcissism and from the viewpoint of the theory of auto-erotism. 'At a time at which the first beginnings of sexual satisfaction are still linked with the taking of nourishment, the sexual instinct has a sexual object outside the infant's own body in the shape of his mother's breast. It is only later that the instinct loses that object, just at the time, perhaps, when the child is able to form a total idea of the person to whom the organ that is giving him satisfaction belongs. As a rule the sexual instinct then becomes auto-erotic' (Freud, 1905d, p. 222). With this quotation from Freud, another can be connected: 'Originally, at the very beginning of mental life, the ego's instincts are directed to itself and it is to some extent capable of deriving satisfaction for them on itself. This condition is known as narcissism and this potentiality for satisfaction is termed auto-erotic' (1915c, p. 134). There can be considered to be two phases in auto-erotism, one corresponding to primary narcissism and comprising no reference to the object, a form of primary auto-erotism, the other corresponding to a recognition of the external object and being exercised in terms of its loss. It is then inscribed in a dialectical impulse, of which the two terms are the erotic transaction with the object and the auto-erotism that compensates for its loss. In the libidinal impulse that can be classified under 'primary identification', the object is perceived without any 'affect of difference' from the subject (Kestemberg, 1981) and the satisfaction arising from the object relationship has an auto-erotic quality for the child's psychic apparatus. Conversely, in the libidinal impulse corresponding to primary homosexuality, otherness, difference from the object, becomes affect-laden and erotism becomes differentiated from auto-erotism. The mastery and development of this transaction involve 'consideration for the object' (Fenichel) or, in other terms, the development of tenderness.

Freud indicates on various occasions that tender affective ties originate from impulses that had sexuality as their object. For him, the current of tenderness proceeds from the earliest years of childhood and corresponds to the child's primary-object choice. He indicates that this tender current has formed on the basis of the interests of the self-preservative drive, and he accords an important role to the parents' tenderness; it does a great deal to increase the share of erotism in the cathexes of the ego drives. He emphasises the 'tender fixations' that have the capacity to bring with them some erotism that is consequently diverted from its sexual aims. However, it is in the *Three Essays* that Freud clearly links the emergence of tenderness with the period that concerns us here, the early relations with the mother. In the paragraph devoted to 'The sexual object during early infancy', Freud writes:

> even after sexual activity has become detached from the taking of nourishment, an important part of this first and most significant of all sexual relations is left over, which helps to prepare for the choice of an object and thus to restore the happiness that has been lost. All through the period of latency children learn to feel for other people . . . which is on the model of, and a continuation of, their relation as sucklings to their nursing mother. There may perhaps be an inclination to dispute the possibility of identifying a child's affection and esteem for those who look after him with sexual love.

He goes on to describe the relationship between the mother's behaviour, the mother's tenderness and the awakening of the child's sexuality and demonstrates that 'an excess of parental affection does harm by causing precocious sexual maturity', adding that 'neuropathic parents, who are inclined as a rule to display excessive affection, are precisely those who are most likely by their caresses to arouse the child's disposition to neurotic illness' (1905d, pp. 222–223).

So it may be thought that the tender current is born of a gradual desexualisation of the relations between the child and his caregivers. Fain's conception that the baby's auto-erotism is triggered by the mother's recathexis of her own sexuality supports this idea (Braunschweig & Fain, 1975; Fain, 1971 – see chapter 16, this volume). This would indicate a concordance between the development of the capacity for tenderness and the development of auto-erotism. The evolution of pleasure in suckling can serve to illustrate this shift towards desexualisation. The formidable discharge of energy observed in feeding gradually cedes to the less intense pleasure of the spoon, and it is in auto-erotism that the child will seek discharge, in the auto-erotism of thumb-sucking and then anal auto-erotism. Thus the 'self-preservative drive' becomes largely desexualised; any residue of oral erotism is attenuated and constitutes the portion of tenderness that will remain attached to the alimentary exchanges. The development of the cathexis of 'appetition behaviours' described by René Diatkine (1972) and of everything that allows deferral of satisfaction forms part of this shift. The mother's tenderness – tenderness because her main sexual cathexis is not to the baby – thus leads to a diminution in the quantity of energy involved in the physical exchanges with the child, reducing the amount of excitation and the tendency to discharge. The field of exchanges, involving no major excitation of the erogenous zones, extends to games, verbal exchanges and so on. The corollary of these exchanges that entail frustration as regards discharge is the development of auto-erotism and the fantasmatic life that is related to it.

We therefore see the two currents – the tender and the sensual – becoming differentiated, with the sensual current continuing to cathect the erogenous zones (and the auto-erotism relating to them) and maintain the tendency to discharge. Thus the aim-inhibition of the drives in the primary homosexual relationship is constitutive of tenderness, just as the aim-inhibition of secondary homosexuality is constitutive of social ties. The link between the development of tenderness and sublimatory capacities, emphasised by Freud, thus has an early origin. The 'asexual' quality of tender relations stems from both the desexualisation process and their origin in primary homosexuality, prior to the establishment of sexual difference.

It is the recognition of sexual difference and its accession to the centre of psychic life that puts an end to primary homosexuality. Direct observational data show that perceptual elements relating to sexual difference appear early and are progressively amplified. The baby's reactions to differences in voice, contact, smell, the way in which he is carried and so on are clear to an observer, but this does not mean that it is these differences that organise the child's psychic apparatus, which at this stage is mainly established on the basis of 'good' and 'bad' projections. The perceptions of difference linked to sexual difference are quickly amplified and play the role of precursors until one further element brings a Copernican upheaval that leads to all the differences being organised in terms of a single one that becomes fundamental – sexual difference. This recognition of anatomical sexual difference then assumes a considerable dynamic quality that reorganises the whole of mental functioning. The direct perception, the sight of the genital organs of the opposite sex, assumes a particular role in this shift; if it happens too early it remains meaningless, whereas later it is recognised as the key to differences, the key to understanding. The refusal to accord it its true status will involve, in some children, a distortion in the development of thought. So there is a link between fetishism, perversion and the persistence of thought systems that have emerged from primary homosexuality and structure differences in terms of elements other than sexual difference and that seek to deny this or eliminate any importance to it. It is perhaps here that we might situate Chasseguet-Smirgel's (1975) suggested link between religion and perversion; certain modalities of religious thought may be related to the refusal to accord sexual difference its true status: the immaculate conception is a dogma. As long as sexual difference is not recognised, the mother is a woman only for herself; for the child's psyche, the mother is a woman only retroactively.

The parents' attitude towards the baby's sex plays its well-known fundamental role in the early determination of sexual identity, just as the baby's bodily experience is probably perceptibly different according to whether it possesses a penis or a vulva–vagina–clitoris constellation. However, all these fundamental elements are only retroactively structured in a causative way in the child's psyche with the perception of sexual difference – that is to say, according to the evolution of the Oedipus complex and the castration complex. Until then and whatever the child's bodily experience, whatever the attitude of the parents who predestine it for a masculine or feminine role, the child builds its erotic exchanges with people whose perceptible differences are essentially qualitative and serve as a support to the play of projections; it may be that psychic bisexuality is structured around the reorganisation of these early experiences. Bisexuality emerges when sexual difference introduces a break in the succession of memories. The androgynous state no sooner appears than it is torn apart. In other words, the theory of androgyny is only retrospective.

According to our theory, there is a time for both the boy and the girl when the first love object changes its nature. The first, primary homosexual, object – undifferentiated sexual or polymorphously sexual – is differentiated, becomes female, and 'the parents' become the father and the mother. Heterosexuality and secondary homosexuality emerge together; the effect of the retroactive operation creates a past for them. The difference between the boy and the girl, in terms of their sexual development, is therefore not the way in which the girl has to change sexual object to move from the mother to the father, while the boy keeps the same object. The difference is that the change in the object's nature produces different retrospective meanings for the girl and for the boy: homosexual (in the secondary sense of the word) for the girl, and heterosexual for the boy.

To describe this development in terms of primary homosexuality may allow a different formulation of the organisation of male or female homosexuality and different modalities of mental functioning. As Freud writes in the Schreber case, those 'who are manifest homosexuals in later life have, it may be presumed, never emancipated themselves from the binding condition that the object of their choice must possess genitals like their own; and in this connection the infantile sexual theories which attribute the same kind of genitals to both sexes exert much influence' (1911c, p. 61). The narcissistic homosexuality described by Freud here is connected then with primary homosexuality; the first object, the mother, being implicitly endowed with the same sexual possibilities as the child, the subject, choosing a sexual partner similar to himself, seeks to maintain – at least in one area of his life – the relational modalities of primary homosexuality. This is a homosexuality that is addressed to someone similar – that is, a child of the same sex, often the brother – and avoids the vagaries of the homosexual relationship to the father with his adult and therefore 'different' genital organs. Thus in his theory of paranoia, Mallet (1966) considers that the relationship with the elder brother plays a key role for the paranoiac. When early relations have not allowed the development of a primary homosexuality and an adequate desexualisation to establish a capacity for tenderness in the child, there is a persistent tendency to maintain or re-establish a mode of relationship with an object similar to the subject or still undifferentiated and chosen precisely for this reason. A tendency to discharge is constantly maintained and manifested, leading to the sexualisation of social ties and of the ego's activities. Accordingly, there is a large number of adult pathological states in which it will prove apposite to consider the earlier vicissitudes of the primary homosexual relationship and the changes it undergoes in development.

In the psychotic states in which, as Freud states, 'the weak spot in their development is to be looked for somewhere between the stages of auto-erotism, narcissism and homosexuality' (1911c, p. 62), the concept of primary homosexuality may have a particularly strong heuristic value.

References

Braunschweig, D., & Fain, M. (1975). *La nuit, le jour. Essai psychanalytique sur le fonctionnement mental* [Day, night: A psychoanalytic essay on mental functioning]. Paris: Presses Universitaires de France.
Chasseguet-Smirgel, J. (1975). Perversion, idealization and sublimation. *International Journal of Psychoanalysis, 55* (3): 349–358.
Diatkine, R., & Simon, J. (1972). *La psychanalyse précoce. Le processus analytique chez l'enfant* [Psychoanalysis with young children]. Paris: Presses Universitaires de France.
Fain, M. (1971). Prélude à la vie fantasmatique [The prelude to fantasmatic life]. *Revue Française de Psychanalyse, 35* (2–3): 291–364.
Fenichel, O. (1946). *The Psychoanalytic Theory of Neurosis.* London: Routledge & Kegan Paul.
Freud, S. (1905d). *Three Essays on the Theory of Sexuality. S.E.,* 7.
Freud, S. (1911c). Psychoanalytic Notes on an Autobiographical Account of Paranoia (Dementia Paranoides). *S.E.,* 12.
Freud, S. (1915c). Instincts and Their Vicissitudes. *S.E.,* 14.

Freud, S. (1915f). A Case of Paranoia Running Counter to the Psycho-Analytic Theory of the Disease. *S.E.*, 14.

Freud, S. (1923b). *The Ego and the Id. S.E.*, 19.

Freud, S. (1933a). *New Introductory Lectures on Psycho-Analysis. S.E.*, 22.

Jacobson, E. (1954). The Self and the Object World. *Psychoanalytic Study of the Child*, 9: 75–127.

Kestemberg, E. (1981). 'L'appareil psychique' et les organisations psychiques diverses [The 'psychic apparatus' in various mental structures]. In *La psychose froide* [Cold psychosis] (pp. 179–199). Paris: Presses Universitaires de France, 2001.

Kestemberg, E. (1984). 'Astrid' ou homosexualité, identité, adolescence. Quelques propositions hypothétiques ['Astrid' or homosexuality, identity, adolescence: Some hypothetical propositons]. In *L'adolescence à vif* [Adolescence laid bare]. Paris: Presses Universitaires de France, 1999.

Mallet, J. (1966). Une théorie de la paranoia [A theory of paranoia]. *Revue Française de Psychanalyse, 30*: 63–68.

34 THE BEAUTIFUL DIFFERENCES

Christian David

> A philosopher, poet, artist, medical practitioner and psychoanalyst, **Christian David** became a full member of the Paris Psychoanalytical Society in 1965. Co-editor of the *Revue Française de Psychanalyse* and of the 'Fil Rouge' series (PUF), he was one of the founders in 1972 of the Paris Psychosomatic Institute.
>
> His innovative work has dealt with being in love, representation of affects, psychic bisexuality, emotional perversion and mourning the loss of one's self. With an emphasis on interlacing soul and body before language becomes possible, he has presented his ideas in many different ways: writings, university lectures, contributions to several books, articles, poetry and exhibitions of his paintings. Among his major works are: *L'état amoureux* [Being in love] (Payot, 1992) and *La bisexualité psychique* [Psychic bisexuality] (Payot, 1992).
>
> Laurent Danon-Boileau wrote a concise biography of Christian David for the 'Psychanalystes d'aujourd'hui' series (PUF, 1998).

The unconscious is said to have no knowledge of time. However, there are many signs that some fairly striking characteristics of our own are the progressive attenuation of conventional manifestations of sexual difference, even a trend towards the complete reversal of masculinity and femininity, hand in hand with a strange bisexual claim. The more of a stake this claims, the more it seems that sexually specific characteristics – which are undoubtedly among these 'beautiful differences of nature' that Freud deplored Groddeck for seeking to disparage 'in favour of tempting unity' (Letter of 5 June 1917, in Freud, 1961, p. 324) – tend to diminish, even disappear.

Does the half made-up, grotesque and disturbing countenance of the hero of Stanley Kubrick's sinister 1971 film *A Clockwork Orange* bring together in one hard-hitting, symbolic opening shot these recent psychosexual vicissitudes in our society? Does the strange expression that emanates from these ill-matched eyes, one with long mascara-coated lashes and fully adorned with make-up, and the other completely undecorated, contain something more than an ambiguous provocation – namely, the hidden meaning of a defusion of the drives? Does the conjunction of homosexual and heterosexual attitudes and behaviours, readily considered a feat and an achievement by certain naïve witnesses, in fact involve an insidious negation of sexuality, like a challenge to Eros, in the guise of an unleashing of erotism?

On the other hand, leaving the uncanny register of disturbing strangeness for what I would call wonderful strangeness, I will gladly make an opposite symbol of a countertenor voice heard the other evening. This presented to the listener not only through its unique inflections and timbre but through all it conveyed of the artist's inner nature, an indescribable mixture of masculinity and femininity. Now Alfred Deller,[1] through his stature, his face and his words, appears an eminently 'virile' character, and the quality of his voice, however close to the castrati of bygone days, is the fruit – if we are to believe some recent impromptu comments by the singer himself on television – of patient and exciting work intended to 'bring out' and develop to its point of perfection the 'head voice' that every man capable of singing has available potentially but without knowing it, without daring to use it or without thinking of doing so.

These are landmark images, key moments, of the kind also encountered in analysis, in which a world of affects and meanings is obscurely condensed, and I would like to convey its resonance so that at least on a preliminary basis this slightly over-abstract approach to the disturbing problematic presented here does not resemble an impossible detachment.

I

Whether this is a question of sexual difference or bisexuality, an incontestable ambiguity – probably in connection with the constitutive duality of every drive – characterises the elaboration of these facts in Freud's work. Based on the anatomy and embryology of his day, Freud draws out the 'psychological implications' of some elements that are inherently alien to psychology. Thus he regards bisexuality as a biological concept, which he extrapolates into a postulate of psychoanalytic treatment; however, in parallel, albeit from an entirely different perspective, he writes to Fliess – his well-known source of inspiration in this case – that he is getting used to 'regarding every sexual act as a process in which four individuals are involved' (Letter of 1 August 1899, in Masson, 1985, p. 364). As for this 'bisexual constitution' that everyone is said to possess, how is it manifested psychically? Through the masculinity and femininity of attitudes . . . Moreover, although sexual difference assumes the

---

[1] Alfred Deller (1912–1979), an English singer and a musicologist, was one of the main figures in popularising the use of the countertenor voice in Renaissance and Baroque music, a voice that had been forgotten since the castrati of the sixteenth and seventeenth centuries. [*Eds., this volume*]

status of 'destiny', there is still no strict concordance between sex, psychosexual characteristics and the type of object choice. What is more: 'We speak, too, of "masculine" and "feminine" mental attributes and impulses, although, strictly speaking, the differences between the sexes can lay claim to no special psychical characterization' (Freud, 1913j, p. 182). In fact, all that can ultimately be claimed is that activity and passivity are involved; now apart from the fact that these are inadequate connotations, they do not concern the drives themselves but the nature of their goals, and their 'regular association . . . in mental life reflects the bisexuality of individuals' (p. 182).

Has this argument not become somewhat circular? Freud never allowed himself to be impressed by obstacles of that kind: he always treated them with a sovereign disregard and a cool audacity. 'But psycho-analysis cannot elucidate the intrinsic nature of what in conventional or in biological phraseology is termed "masculine" and "feminine" '. If only! . . . 'it simply takes over the two concepts and makes them the foundation of its work . . .' (1920a, p. 171).

Admittedly, this was an inspired move, but also because these 'works' simultaneously found other and better foundations, and above all perhaps because between the foot and the summit a real metamorphosis has occurred, from which it seems that we have only recently departed, having explained the full importance and theoretical implications. I am thinking in particular here of the definition of the drive in relation to instinct, and even more of the determination of the many effects of the extension of the notion of sexuality – this brilliant speculative master-stroke. We cannot in fact address the sexual psychoanalytically in clinical or theoretical terms without having made this extension *our own*. Certainly we must avoid being dragged here on to the path of a spiritualism that would not dare speak its name, neglecting the somatic basis and 'scandalous' aspects of sexuality, but we must also remember that its conceptual extension is – like a difficult realisation fleetingly effected during the treatment – an acquisition that is permanently under threat. This can easily be seen with the creator of psychoanalysis himself, when its temporary overshadowing sometimes gives rise to a certain wavering in thought. Laplanche seeks to explain these eclipses as the inevitable confusion caused by 'a scientific revolution which suddenly enlarges the meaning of a concept [and] sweeps away, we might say, its very ground. Such is the case for Freud himself: at which point we see him taking refuge in the hopes for a biological, chemical, or hormonal definition of sexuality . . . or we see him simply repeating, as though he could progress no further, the reasons which force him to *assimilate* the domain he discovered to sex in the popular, "genital" sense of the word' (Laplanche, 1976, p. 28). We must also be wary of overemphasising this similarity, as well as subjugating ourselves too narrowly to scientific advances, *on pain of losing the benefit of an epistemological leap through which the unconscious can be indicated as sexual and sexuality as psychic.*

The sexual certainly originates from far beyond the psychic, but analysis proposes to address the way in which it is represented. This is the case with anatomical sexual difference, which, as the object of conscious and unconscious representations, is introduced into analysis as a difference between psychosexualities. Then what about bisexuality? Certainly, we may think that Freud would have hesitated to introduce it into his theory if he had not believed he could give it a biological foundation, based primarily on the embryology of his era. But there again, bisexuality is linked in psychoanalysis not to the vestigial presence in an individual of a particular sex of certain characteristics of the other sex, but to psychic organisations that depend on many other factors. It is even certain that, as something psychic, it has only the most tenuous connection with these vestiges: one proof of this is that the advances made since Freud in the field of embryology (notably, imposing the concept of an embryonic differentiation that occurs not from a bisexual preliminary stage as previously thought but is absolutely phenotypically female) only seem to have to involve *ipso facto* abandoning the concept of bisexuality in psychoanalysis if the psychoanalytic dimension is seriously underestimated.[2] Although it may also be highly instructive as an analyst to study the psychic repercussions of a particular anatomico-physiological bisexual characteristic (true hermaphroditism, pseudo-hermaphroditism, transsexualism and so on), it is nonetheless true that psychic bisexuality is absolutely independent of the existence of such aberrations or other equivalents (endocrine malfunctioning). Bisexuality, as a coexistence of opposite psychosexual dispositions, some conscious and others unconscious, in each of us, proceeds – whatever its biological connections – from psychic processes. How otherwise, moreover, can we explain the universality of its role and how can we recognise that fundamentally 'we can only see that both in male and female individuals masculine as well as feminine instinctual impulses are found, and that each can equally well undergo repression and so become unconscious' (1919e, p. 202). Also, when in 1914 Freud reverses the determining priority in relation to repression that he had previously attributed like Fliess to bisexuality, and in respect of which he tried, as early as the Wolf Man case, to demonstrate how it is the ego that instigates the repression to the advantage of one of the sexual orientations, can it be said that he is finally giving bisexuality its specific psychoanalytic status? Is it not, in fact, highly revealing that it should be on this point alone that his position should have changed throughout all his works?

This subordination of sexuality to conflict is decisive, and this is probably what best elucidates the connection between sexual difference and bisexuality. Their relationship emerges as essentially dialectical. This is what I should like to emphasise in the course of the pages that follow.

To be born a girl or born a boy is – even more broadly and more decisively than being summoned to live the castration complex in one way or another – to be promised, as Green (1972) persuasively demonstrates, to a certain sexual

---

[2] As was the case, for instance, with S. Rado as early as 1940, E. Bergler (1956) and more recently M. J. Sherfey (Rado, 1940; Sherfey, 1972).

destiny, according to an inescapable sexual reality: a man will never give birth and a woman will never impregnate, which are truths that are more comprehensive than the anatomical facts but equally restrictive. However, to be a man with certain female tendencies, or a woman with some male tendencies, *is to possess a potential sexual otherness and consequently to bear some indeterminacy*. If, therefore, on the one hand anatomy is destiny, then on the other sexual reality, or sexual destiny, we might say, *bisexuality is – or may be – anti-destiny*. The formula may be less surprising if we recall that the extended concept of bisexuality stems from that of sexuality. As with pregenital sexuality, there are grounds for conceiving of a pregenital bisexuality. The early relations with the mother entail a close relationship between the emergence of desire, the genesis of fantasy and the internal object, and the emergence of a psychosexual bipotentiality (e.g., receiving or giving pleasure in one mode or another), although admittedly this will be specified only later and in stages of bisexuality in the current analytic sense of this term. Furthermore, is it not part of the logic of sexuality, which is difference and division, that it promotes itself from one bipartition to the next, from one opposition to the next? Bisexuality testifies to the internalisation of the active–passive polarity and the progressive introjection of sexual polarity. It is through these internalisations of difference that some *play* can intervene from the outset in the evolution of sexuality: in parallel with the maturational activity that prepares the integration of sexual identity, what I will call *an unconscious bisexualisation process* seems to be quietly at work, a process that clinical observation suggests does not necessarily involute when the specific psychosexuality is fully established.

Being closely connected with the configuration of identifications and their vicissitudes, the Oedipus complex provides the theory of bisexuality (and the problem of its connection with sexual difference) with its only means of achieving coherence and adequate clarity. Rather strangely, Freud does not seem to have resolved to make full use of this resource to elucidate the concept of bisexuality and to determine its integration in drive theory. I would again readily point to his biologism here ... However, on the nature and development of bisexuality, there are really two discernible lines of thinking in his work, which are difficult to reconcile. Often, Freud sees bisexuality as a primal and universal disposition, clearly morbid when it is very pronounced,[3] which has the natural (i.e. biological) destiny – depending on the consecutive demands at the primacy of genitality – of a gradual diminution in the course of libidinal development. Ultimately, it 'normally' no longer consists in anything but subtle individual traits, aim-inhibited desires or capacities for socialisation and sublimation. Even if the orientation of the object choice is subject to discrepancies in relation to anatomical destiny, psychosexual identity – in the

---

[3] Accordingly, Freud (1908a) regards the bisexual nature of many hysterical symptoms as 'an interesting confirmation of my view that the postulated existence of an innate bisexual disposition in man is especially clearly visible in the analysis of psychoneurotics' (pp. 165–166).

vast majority of cases – is finally integrated in accordance with the person's own sex: this presupposes the successful repression of the initial bisexuality. In other words, the more sexual difference is asserted, the more bisexuality becomes involuted and virtualised. Nevertheless, however dominant this genetic and dynamic correlation may be in Freud's conception of bisexuality, it has another non-biologistic aspect that may generally be understated. According to this, the differential integration of sexuality, far from excluding an active psychic bisexuality, and far from necessarily requiring its entirely successful repression in accordance with prevailing norms, can (in some cases even should) go hand in hand with an authentic bisexual fulfilment – if not in relation to the erotic choice of object and fulfilment, at least as concerns personal psychic characteristics and functioning. This viewpoint is eloquently illustrated in 'The Psychogenesis of a Case of Homosexuality in a Woman' (1920a), where Freud clearly indicates that: 'in normal sexuality also there is a limitation in the choice of object' (he does not refer to more hidden restrictions but to even more important ones that concern 'psychical sexual characteristics' in general). He assigns the psychoanalytic treatment of homosexuality the goal of 're-establishing a complete bisexual function' while emphasising the difficulties of such a result, an ideal outcome for which we can only strive. He clearly states on several occasions that, especially in men, psychic hermaphroditism is independent of physical hermaphroditism of whatever nature and degree, as well as that these two sequences are independent of the type of object choice. The three characteristics vary independently of each other and occur in combination in the most diverse fashion in different individuals. It would be making a concession to the layperson and adopting his frequent conformism to favour the modalities of object choice and also to fail to recognise that 'In all of us, throughout life, the libido normally oscillates between the male and the female object' (p. 158); it would also be attaching little importance to unconscious sexuality and losing sight 'of the general bisexuality of mankind' (p. 143).

This second aspect of the Freudian conception seems to me to be the only one to do justice both to the meaning shift in the concepts of bisexuality and sexuality in psychoanalysis and to the reformulation of the psychosexual problematic in accordance with the Oedipal structural model (the 'complete' Oedipus complex with all its implications and resonances). It is also the only one to account for the compatibility of sexual difference with bisexuality and to point towards any possible resolution – at least in part – of the divergence of their respective dynamisms. Finally, it is the only model that enables us to imagine their functional association, according to an ideal goal, beyond their many conflictual potentialities.

II

The sexual is not the sole object of analysis, but is its constant object. The transference in the analytic situation could be said to correspond to the principle of libidinal co-excitation postulated by Freud as a consequence of the possible extension of erogeneity to the entire human body. There is in fact nothing in the field this defines that cannot and must not be considered an effect – proximate or remote, pure or combined – of the transference, whether in the strict or broad sense of the word. There is nothing, then, that cannot be considered a sign of the drives and consequently, given the actual conjunction represented by every psychic phenomenon, a sign of sexuality. What is expressed and lived and, in the process, disguised and neglected in the analysand is impelled by a sexual dynamic (even if it is never the only thing in play), pursues the satisfaction of desire and is perpetuated in accordance with an ever-recurrent dissatisfaction. Just as the essence of sexuality could be said to reside in the very impulse that separates the sexual drive from the vital function on which it is based, it is equally legitimate to regard the inherent restrictive conditions in the analytic treatment as a form of experimental reproduction and, consequently, *an enforced intensification of this fundamental separation*. It is not from the vital function that the sexual dynamic tends to extricate itself here, but from the discharge function. And just as the genesis of sexuality involves its perversion (human sexuality always bears at least some traces of this origin), so the channelling of the drive expression solely according to the possibilities of the analytic transference brings an artificial increase in these first conditions, leading innate perverse sexuality ultimately to become an 'affective perversion'.[4]

These general observations are connected with the more specific aspects of our problem. In fact, this capacity for separation revealed by the libido, a sign of its plasticity, applies not only to that from which it separates but also in regard to itself. 'It is my belief that, however strange it may sound, we must reckon with the possibility that something in the nature of the sexual instinct itself is unfavourable to the realization of complete satisfaction' (1912d, pp. 188–189), writes Freud. This contains the bold but suggestive and productive hypothesis of an intra-libidinal negativity. Thus, irrespective of the fact that the libido follows a particular specific developmental destiny according to whether it animates an anatomically male or female being, there pre-exists in it a potential internal division, the beginning of a splitting that could be seen as both the mark and the origin of a primitive '*sexion*'[5] (Lewinter, 1969).

---

[4] This notion was presented in 1977 in a lecture I gave at the British Psychoanalytical Society; it could briefly be defined as the psycho-affective fetishism of an internal object or as a kind of intimate and repetitive fantasy scenario.

[5] This term for the establishment of gender also implies a cut, through a play on the French word *section*. [*Trans., this volume*]

It is clear where this is leading: the very close affinity in the sexual between the positivity of desire and the negativity of inhibition altogether represents a prefiguring of bisexuality and the herald of sexual difference. In other words, the duality, a contrasting dynamic duality, emerges as their common principle, but when this intrinsic antagonism is externalised into a trans-individual sexual dichotomy, then it promotes itself less visibly by establishing an intra-individual psychosexual polarity. This gives rise to two major lines of conflict in sexual life, which are, of course, inseparably intermingled, one relational and the other intrasubjective. Introjection and projection enmesh them from the outset on a canvas on to which the destructive drives are also placed, to which I am deliberately only referring to the extent that they reinforce intra-libidinal negativity.

Within a psychoanalysis, such a reinforcement, as I have emphasised, intensifies solely under the impact of the transference and the elective appeal of 'psychical participation' (Freud, 1905d).

This enforced internalisation is never a smooth process; however, we can consider that *the analytic situation intrinsically consists in a testing of psychosexual characteristics and identity and simultaneously a stimulation of psychic bisexuality*, in which regression always generates some psychosexual de-differentiation. Everything occurs as if this dual incitement must temporarily find its response if a redistribution of the drive economy is to be achieved; as if a quasi-experimental amplification of the potential for psychosexual indeterminacy had to occur for new choices and a better functioning to become possible at a secondary stage. But this manifestly implies that the activation of bisexuality generated by the treatment can have a destructuring effect. Against this, various defence reactions are instigated that can form resistances that are difficult to lift or alternatively barriers that are too fragile to allow time for a re-elaboration of psychosexuality to mature for the benefit of the complete development of the analytic process.

> 'When I come in here, there's always a smell of perfume or eau de Cologne, never the smell of tobacco, or smoke! . . . Ah! If only you smoked a pipe. You're colourless, odourless and tasteless . . . No! It's not true what I said just then . . . It's when I think about what you have and what I would like to have that I get sad. Sometimes I even feel a desire to tear you to pieces.' – '*To emasculate me.*' – 'Oh! I see things in a less clear, less localised and more general way. It is more about power. It is that I can't simply desire a man I like; I immediately have to imagine appropriating for myself the thing by which he would seduce me if I followed my first impulse, if I could let myself be charmed . . .'

It was in this context that at the end of the session, of which I have just approximately transcribed the initial phase, this young person, whose female status has constantly represented a painful problem ever since she attained self-awareness, directly raised the question of sexuality in the analytic situation:

'Altogether, it's as if neither you nor I had a sex here, don't you think? Yes, really, what difference can it make that I'm a woman and you're a man?' – '*You regret this though*' – 'That, I've no idea . . . Oh! I'm thinking back to the interview I had with an analyst, to ask her advice and possibly for a referral to a therapist. I made it very clear at the start that if a psychoanalysis was recommended for me, I would only consider doing it with a man. She reacted in what I felt was rather an impulsive way, replying curtly that once the analysis started it made no difference at all whether it was conducted by a man or a woman. I argued that in my view with my current state of mind, it wasn't the same thing at all and that it was very important to me to undertake my analysis, if I decided to do this, with a man. With a woman, the whole thing seemed impossible, intolerable. That was a while ago, and now I realise that this analyst was right! In reality, in fact, what difference can it make that you're a man?'

Beyond the obvious defensive impact of this negation of the role of sex and sexuality in the analytic situation, this patient is both right and wrong at the same time. She is wrong because in spite of the strong predominance of projections over perceptions in her relationship with me, her transference experience incorporates an aspect that belongs not to the revival of past affects but to current turmoil in which my sexual identity, my voice and my character as she perceives them during the sessions play a distinct role. She is also wrong in the sense that sporadically she reacts to my presence with an erotic excitation or tender emotions that she wishes to forget, but, above all, in the sense that within the fabric of her discourse (including of course the sequence reported here and even – as we see – when the sexual and sexual difference are being revoked) everything that she says – and does not say – is inscribed in the psychosexual dimension (in which genitality only represents a privileged component); only she has an acute resistance to recognising that inscription. She is right, on the other hand, to the large degree to which the analytic situation and the incomparable relational modes it establishes hardly depend on the analyst's sex, even often play with sexual difference, while actively appealing to each protagonist's bisexuality. The fundamental rule has the dual and contradictory quality of a barrier raised before incest *and* of an almost provocative systematic seduction of the sexual fantasmatic. 'Here again is the present–absent, accessible–elusive, lost–found object of your desire', the analyst implicitly states in every session. Such is the 'liberty' that he proposes for the associative process: we imagine that he must be responding to this with evenly suspended attention, in-difference, some suspension of the drives and a maximum of bisexual availability. It is in particular through this availability, as Cathérine Parat pointed out (during some work that clearly demonstrated the primacy of psychosexuality and fantasy over external reality and the sexual in the 'popular' sense) that analysts find themselves undergoing, by assuming some of their patients' fantasies, affective experiences that they would never have been able to have in any other situation because of their sex (Luquet-Parat, 1962).

Closer examination of the sequences just reported initially reveals an active and passive castration fantasy. Now, this fantasy is explicitly related to a bisexual conflict, emerging in all its acuity. Let us note here the dual ambiguity of the standpoint from which the question of the role of sexuality in the analytic situation is formulated: both a negation of my masculinity *and* an acknowledgement that she feels me to be male (the paternal transference is currently fairly intense); accordingly, a masochistic assertion of her female position in terms of the phallic illusion (fully in play in her at this point in the treatment) of the assimilation of femininity to a castration that has been effected *and* a rejection of this position by the admission of her current incapacity to adopt a passive attitude that is nevertheless desired (forcing her to attempt a narcissistic retreat). Given the excessive ambiguity of the situation at the point that the question with which we are concerned arises, it is hardly surprising that this question itself should be posed in a fundamental uncertainty, in a great indeterminacy: that today it is no longer at all important in her view – she says – that we should be of different sexes, even that we should have a sex at all, although she used to imagine that it took place altogether differently. Admittedly neither the unconscious nor the analyst take account of this opposition between present and past, particularly given that a latent homosexual desire is implicitly outlined that intensifies the disappointment and pique created by the analytic frustration. *Another impulse to negate sexual difference can be seen to instigate the awakening of bisexuality here.*

This is evidenced by the dream that she presented fairly soon afterwards:

> 'A young man is visiting a blonde, curly-haired woman who is clearly older than him. She is an enchantress. In the large, rather dark room in which she is standing, the windows are open. On a nearby table is a bottle of perfume, opened. Affected by the aroma of this perfume, the young man loses his head, feels an upsurge of anxiety, until it becomes intolerable. No longer able to stand it, he suddenly throws himself out of the window.'

The associations – the reader will not have failed to notice in passing certain parallels between the dream text and the above session report – reveal very clearly that this young man represents her, while I am the enchantress. The reversal of our respective genders, as a product of the dream work, can easily be related to the conscious and vigilant expression of her desire to appropriate for herself, 'the thing by which a man would seduce her if she allowed herself to be charmed', and therefore also to her emphasis on my lack of certain specifically masculine signs (smoking a pipe, for instance). It can be noticed that the simultaneous negation of the erotic atmosphere of the session and the role of the analyst's sex is accompanied here by a perception of me as effeminate or, in the dream, overtly feminised. In parallel, she often states that she is feeling uneasy in her women's clothes. She therefore projects on to me her own feeling of castration by condemning us both to a sort of amorphous undifferentiated destiny that excludes any sexual attraction. For this to be exerted she considers it necessary for sexual difference to be strongly in evidence, but because of her unresolved conflicts she rejects her female 'destiny' while also contesting my masculinity, and she inadvertently instigates all the resources of her unconscious homosexuality in order to rid her relationship with me of any eroticism; at least, this is how things are proceeding at this stage of her analysis. She exhibits a sexuality that she feels is weak: she is not the boy her parents wanted and that she would have liked to be; neither is she 'a real woman'. Moreover, she is exasperated by women who are regarded as highly feminine. As for me, rather than being the masculine man for whom she hoped, I am someone fragile and ambiguous.

Here we see again the effects of the unconscious androgynous fantasy: elimination of sexual difference and diminution of the sexual drive. Psychic bisexuality is then in functional opposition with psychosexual specificity. It is from difference that the drive seems to draw its energy, whereas the emphasis on analogies and reciprocal exchanges only weakens it. From this perspective – but it is not, as I have already indicated, in any sense the only one – in which bisexuality 'works' to diminish sexual differences and *seems to be directed at the mythical realisation of a form of unisexuality*, it constitutes a factor of erotic impoverishment, a source of degeneration of male and female, a kernel of de-eroticisation, de-differentiation – in short, of lethal desexualisation. While it is true that a man's desire to be a woman responds to a woman's desire to be a man, this commonality of the desire to be the other is a very long way from founding an entire, less still an exclusive, similarity . . .

Also, in contrast to the picture I have just presented, clinical experience often provides the opportunity to observe how, through the realisation and integration of latent homosexuality, and non-apparent and more or less effectively repressed femininity or masculinity, as well as through the reconciliation of conflicting identifications, the re-establishment of the bisexual function instead tends to liberate energy, an irreplaceable innovatory factor in relational modalities that also enriches the functioning of the psychic apparatus. Now, such a re-establishment is antinomical to the defensive implementation of a hermaphrodite fantasy, of realised ambisexuality: it certainly presupposes its transcendence and dissolution. At the conclusion of these felicitous analyses, both the repudiation of femininity and the overvaluation of phallicity will have been recognised as reactions linked to misunderstanding and illusion, whereas the progressive perception and acceptance of neglected psychosexual potentialities, of unknown desires and pleasures, will have entailed a more accurate and deeper appreciation of masculinity and femininity. The process that led to such a result does not tend towards de-differentiation – which was nevertheless required in the early phases of the analysis – but this time in a resumption of the introjection (in the Ferenczian sense of the term) of differences. Admittedly, its completion is never achieved, but this is not necessary for the subject's specific sexuality to be harmonised with his psychic bisexuality, or for him to find and develop his own sexual formula, which is moreover oscillating because alive. Such a successful outcome does not involve the unconditional and massive disengagement of the thwarted psychosexual pole, but only its qualified reintegration in the various directions. Furthermore, it assumes *neither the abolition nor the exacerbation of sexual difference but its relativisation*, and it requires the resumption of what I have called the unconscious bisexualisation process (totally incompatible with unisexualising goals) in the service of establishing what Freud terms the 'full bisexual function' (1920a, p. 151).

III

Although because of its length and its teeming abundance, the story of Ḳamar-ez-Zemán and Princess Budoor, one of the most delightful in the *Thousand and One Nights*,[6] contains too much 'material' to be used satisfactorily in the context of an article, I cannot resist the pleasure of referring to it here – which will at least introduce a note of colour into the grey tones of the picture. Both its content (manifest and latent) – which in my view gives an opportune illustration of the dialectic of sexual difference and bisexuality – and above all the trajectory taken by the many twists and turns of a story that always starts again seem to me *to demonstrate the possibility of a precedence of libidinal plasticity over anatomical destiny and the key role of bisexuality in this precedence*. To demonstrate this, I will first summarise this never-ending tale, strangely enlivened by what I am inclined to call the *sexual romance*.

King Sháh-Zemán, at an advanced age, belatedly has a son, Ḳamar-ez-Zemán, who is so perfectly beautiful that he is known as 'the Moon of the Age'. He loves him so much that he cannot part from him for a moment, even at night. However, worried about his lack of descendants, he then decides to arrange a marriage for this son. Fiercely misogynistic, the son categorically refuses to do this. At his failure, the father – with a heavy heart – finally imprisons him in a tower – with very little idea of what will happen there – in the hope that the isolation will make him reflect. In this prison, haunted by jinns – male and female – of the air and the earth, Meymooneh, illustrious among all the daughters of the jinns, surprises Ḳamar-ez-Zemán in his sleep. She is captivated by his beauty and therefore immediately decides to take the young man under her protection to defend him against any male jinn who, attracted by his charms, might wish to exploit them. Then she meets Dahnash, an evil jinn, who tells her how in the great El-Ghayoor's kingdom in China, he happened to discover Budoor, the monarch's adored daughter, in identical circumstances: indescribably beautiful, she too is rejecting

---

[6] The summary of this story is based on the French translation by Dr. J. C. Mardrus (1990, vol. 5). Quotations are from Lane (1883).

every marriage proposal her father conveys to her: 'O my father, I have no wish at all to marry; for I am a princess, and a queen, ruling over men, and I desire not a man to rule over me' (p. 82). She threatens to kill herself if her father tries to force her to take a husband. So El-Ghayoor also has her imprisoned in a tower.

The two jinns then make a bet that the object of their respective discoveries is unsurpassably beautiful. Meymooneh immediately leads Dahnash to Ḳamar-ez-Zemán's bedside. He concedes he has never in fact seen so many perfections in an adolescent's body but adds that the mould that made him only broke after producing a female version, Princess Budoor. He sets off to send for her so that Meymooneh can compare them. She first observes that the resemblance between the two young people is so perfect that they would be taken for twins if they did not differ in their environment and origins. The same moon-like face, the same delicate waist, the same rounded behind . . . and on Budoor the breasts advantageously replace the embellishing penis that she lacks. However, Meymooneh tells Dahnash that anyone would have to be blind or mad not to agree that the male surpasses the female. They then appeal to the arbitration of a third person (from the brotherhood). Having acknowledged that the young people are equal in beauty and only different in sex, he suggests a way of determining who should win the bet: it is enough to awaken and then put back to sleep first one then the other young person, having brought them together: 'the one who shall be most inflamed with love for the other shall be confessed to be the inferior in beauty and loveliness' (p. 87) because he will have recognised the superior attractions of his companion. Initially conquered by the beautiful Budoor, Ḳamar-ez-Zemán soon finds he cannot resist the desire to penetrate her, when suddenly it occurs to him that this may be a ruse of his father's to force him into marriage. He therefore resolves to defer his satisfaction and only puts a ring on the young girl's finger. As for her, once she has been awoken, after a moment of fright and confusion, she behaves as if under a spell. With increasing emotion, soon, no longer worrying about anything, she becomes bolder, discovers Ḳamar-ez-Zemán's penis and immediately understands its specific purpose because, we are told, just as desire in women is much more intense than in men, so their intelligence is infinitely quicker to grasp the relations between the organs of pleasure. Meymooneh therefore wins the bet.

Having returned to their prisons, the two protagonists utter loud cries for their partner of the night. They are both thought to be mad. Ḳamar-ez-Zemán, however, provides some tangible evidence of his story so that his father, convinced, then leaves with him for an island to lament 'their' misfortune there. But Budoor meanwhile does not manage to persuade her father. Believing her to have gone mad, he imprisons her and promises her hand in marriage to anyone who can cure her of her madness. Budoor then gets her foster brother, Marzawán, to leave in search of the mysterious lover from the tower. Through a combination of circumstances, he arrives at King Sháh-Zemán's court because fate has decreed that he should cure Ḳamar-ez-Zemán of his melancholy. Marzawán, who is also astounded by his foster-sister's resemblance to the prince, reveals to him his mission, which is enough to bring him immediately back to life. Using a ploy to leave his father, who would not spontaneously allow him to leave, he leaves the country with Marzawán to rejoin his beloved in El-Ghayoor. Having arrived, he disguises himself as a wizard and easily manages to get a letter transmitted to Budoor into which he has inserted her ring (for she also put one on his finger). The princess comes back to life in turn. Ḳamar-ez-Zemán reveals his identity to everyone and tells their story to general astonishment. The marriage is celebrated with no further ado. After a honeymoon, one night Ḳamar-ez-Zemán has a dream in which his father is in tears. He convinces Budoor to accompany him to her father-in-law's court. On their journey, the prince – contemplating his young wife asleep one evening – discovers an extraordinary cornaline jewel hidden in her pubic hair. When he has made it glitter between his fingers, a bird swoops down from the sky, snatches it from him with his beak and takes it away. Ḳamar-ez-Zemán rushes after it, in vain . . . for ten days, he dares not return to Budoor without her jewel. This quest finally leads him to an island where he is greeted by an old gardener, who takes him to help, becomes attached to him as to a son, and showers him with gold when he dies not long afterwards.

Meanwhile the princess, in despair at having lost the object of her desire again, disguises herself as a man to make her journey. When she arrives several days later at King Armánoos's court, she pretends to him that she is Ḳamar-ez-Zemán. Armánoos, with an only daughter Hayát-en-Nufoos, is overcome by the exceptional beauty of this young Adonis, not guessing his cross-dressing, and he immediately asks him to accept both his succession and Hayát-en-Nufoos's hand. Budoor realises that there is no question of refusing if she wants to stay alive. The marriage is celebrated. The night after the wedding night, Armánoos and his wife, furious that the marriage has not been consummated, make some alarming threats with regard to the false Ḳamar-ez-Zemán. Budoor therefore tells her young companion about the situation and with her tender agreement, they simulate the defloration with a chicken's blood. The royal couple having been comforted, Budoor continues to share Hayát-en-Nufoos's bed but, we are told, less innocently than before.

In the meantime, Ḳamar-ez-Zemán miraculously finds the lost cornaline and hides it at the bottom of an earthenware jar. This jewel, which he had planned to take away with him when he could leave his island, ends up without him at Armánoos's court because of a missed departure. Having asked for the cargo of the boat that transported the jar, Budoor finds the cornaline in it and faints. The captain is then asked about its owner and he reveals that it belonged to a gardener's assistant who fled in fear of being punished for having cruelly sodomised one of his chef's assistants. On royal orders, the alleged cook is then seized: Ḳamar-ez-Zemán clearly has no idea what is happening to him when he feels a hand placed on his shoulder. Once he is facing Budoor in men's clothing, he does not recognise her and believes that the young sovereign is a great lover of handsome boys . . . Despite the extreme reticence that he shows towards her, Budoor becomes more and more insistent, and finally entreats him to spend the night with 'him'. To persuade him better, she says she wants him to play the active role. Ḳamar-ez-Zemán, believing he must play along with this if he wants to save his skin, only asks his tyrant to at least do him the honour of agreeing that the act should take place once only, in hope of showing him that he would do much better to embrace heterosexuality. When the moment arrives, Ḳamar-ez-Zemán discovers – to his great surprise! – that his seducer is a woman and that this is none other than Budoor. The joyous reunion follows. The reunited couple reveal the whole truth to Armánoos who, in a generous impulse, offers his daughter again – still a virgin – in marriage, this time to the real Ḳamar-ez-Zemán: she will be, if he likes, his second wife. This suggestion is accepted happily by everyone, including Budoor and Hayát-en-Nufoos themselves. The two women continue to live in harmony, giving their nights to their husbands but granting themselves the daytime hours together. And they lived happily ever after.

Quite apart from all the general reasons against it, there could be no question here of subjecting this dry summary of a luxuriant narrative[7] to an actual interpretation. I merely offer it to the reader's associations (I hope, inspiring him to read or return to the text) and will only present some of mine in the form of a few observations.

Anatomical in manifest content, and more complex undoubtedly in the latent content and symbolic import of this story, sexual difference plays a decisive role here since it constitutes – constantly we might say – the impetus of the story. However, from the outset, bisexuality is an equally strong theme in the strong indication of the father's latent homosexuality towards the son and that of the son towards the father, as well as in the way that Ḳamar-ez-Zemán's misogyny, just like Budoor's androphobia, become associated, in both of them, with an intense and touchy narcissism in which fantasmatic bisexuality plays a part. Auto-erotic retreat and father fixation are only transcended by the impact of a dual trauma inflicted on narcissism by the exhortation that is successively external and internal towards heterosexual union. It should also be noted that the connection is made here in favour of the extreme resemblance and equal beauty of the two protagonists, who resemble twins. Can we not perceive there an echo of the myth of Plato's *Symposium*[8] in the idea of the mould that made Ḳamar-ez-Zemán only having broken after producing a female version, Princess Budoor? This 'split' represents the origin of sexual differentiation, but this has been experienced in the bisexual mode of Oedipal identifications and narcissistic fantasies long before the irruption of desire and the breakthrough of

---

[7] In particular, the story contains various poems that I have not taken into account.
[8] The myth of the origin of love and sexuality, according to which the human being was originally a male and female creature that was split by the gods into two halves, each of which has ever since been in search of its counterpart.

the feeling of incompleteness instigate the quest for the lost complementary object.

According to the same phallocentric tendency that leads Meymooneh to state that with equal beauty it would be mad not to recognise the male's superiority to the female, the particular intensity of Budoor's desire, in her initial contact with Ḳamar-ez-Zemán, is presented by the arbiter jinn as proof of the princess's inferiority. Does this not raise doubts as to the unconscious motivations for this highly Platonic criteriology: what male envy in regard to female desire and pleasure, what denial of the unknown,[9] what precarious repression of femininity do they not conceal? Whatever the answer, there are grounds from this perspective for recalling that the day after the crucial night when the two heroes are brought together, the young man's father immediately shares his melancholy, and his impetus towards a narcissistic and homosexual retreat, whereas El-Ghayoor will hear none of his daughter's 'madness' and temporarily banishes her. It will certainly be said that the oscillations between male and female continue to occur incessantly at every level throughout this extravaganza, as in everyday life. If the young people were able to spend their auto-erotic isolation in the deliberate pursuit of the object, no sooner found than lost, it is indeed through the brilliance of the other's desire, but it is also because this otherness is the object of a recognition, a reminiscence – a term as dear to Freud as to Plato – because the other's mute, hidden internal and internalised presence is re-externalised and largely re-projected. *The possibilities of psychic bisexuality combine here to accomplish the 'sexual destiny'.*

Reading – in Mardrus's text – the story of Ḳamar-ez-Zemán and Budoor, it is soon obvious that everything happens as if the circulation of libidinal and loving cathexes were always occurring through the presence of small mediating objects, which have a symbolic as well as a quasi-transitional quality that is gradually imposed on the mind. This particularly involves rings and jewels that are gradually discovered, transmitted, lost and found, each event accentuating the long erotic apprenticeship of the hero and heroine. Thus Budoor 'recognises' her lover without seeing him when, in a message he transmits to her, she finds the ring she had given him; the same thing happens later when, after many trials and tribulations, she identifies her lost cornaline, which Ḳamar-ez-Zemán placed at the bottom of a precious jar. However obvious the sexual symbolism of these objects may appear, there is nevertheless a sense that they cannot always be assigned a fixed and unequivocal meaning.

Every time the loving encounter finally occurs, the witnesses marvel and the story of the adventures and wonders that have taken place give the signal of the festival – the festival of the reunion of the separated halves – but the satisfaction and joy born of the long-anticipated union are only said to endure at the end

---

[9] During one of the princess's initial descriptions (in the Mardrus version), it is mentioned that the sleeves of her blouse were embroidered with the lines: 'Three things prevent her from granting men a look that says "yes": the fear of the unknown, the horror of the known and her beauty.'

of the story (perhaps because an end has to be put to it after all). Otherwise, once the honeymoon is over, a gnawing dissatisfaction is seen to re-emerge. On two occasions, this is the act of Ķamar-ez-Zemán: scruples about his father and regret for his absence, or curiosity about Budoor and the acute blame directed at the consequences of this curiosity. Thus the primacy of genital heterosexuality, under the dual sign of pleasure and fertility, does not long stifle the aspirations and desires linked to each character's bisexuality. It is because Ķamar-ez-Zemán does not find in Budoor the complete fulfilment of his wishes – he would vainly seek there his father, with whom he has always shared a very close bond – that he risks losing for a second time the long-concealed object of his desire. As for Budoor, she pines for her young spouse at Armánoos's court, but this does not prevent her benefiting from the opportunities presented to her by her cross-dressing to involve Hayát-en-Nufoos in some homosexual games that do not long remain 'innocent'. Rather, having rediscovered the object of her strongest love, she does not baulk at sharing him with a rival whose erotic partner she will also happily continue to be. Far from weakening them, the satisfaction of the heterosexual drives thus intensifies the homosexual drives. Admittedly this is merely an oscillation, more or less rapid and intense, in the object cathexis, but do the latent resonances of our tale not invite a duplication of what occurs in this order with analogous oscillations in others: in both protagonists' relationship to themselves following the fluctuations of their narcissistic cathexes and their psychosexual characteristics, as relatively independent of the type of object choice and even the modalities of their object relationships?

In any case, it is obvious that the trajectory followed by the unfolding of the entire story (even if proven to be the result of successive additions over time, that would not change anything from our point of view) is jointly and constantly determined by the inherent incompleteness of sexual difference and by a complex and variable combination of homosexuality and heterosexuality, a combination that can only be conceived with the help and in terms of psychic bisexuality. Is it not also remarkable that through so many trials and tribulations of all kinds, a progression or, better, an expansion is emphasised and confirmed, from the initial phobogenic fixations to the supple complexity of the ultimate polygamous situation? There would probably be a great deal to say in passing on the role of cross-dressing and make-believe in this development. A particular character's disguise in fact regularly contributes to the resolution of conflicts and the mobility of situations. It simultaneously provides, under the cover of usurped external fulfilments, authentic affective and sexual accomplishments.

By taking into account some recompense for homosexuality – especially female – and polygamy, here the expression of a tradition, while also reserving its place to a constant freeing of the latent from the manifest, is it not finally rather tempting to see this ambiguous extravaganza as an illustration – both naïve and esoteric – of the 'full accomplishment of the bisexual function'? Is it not significant from this perspective that in the closing scene in which Ḳamar-ez-Zemán is supposed to have to submit to his tyrant's homosexual demands, his intense surprise on noticing in 'his' partner the absence of the anticipated penis (an absence presented, let us recall, at the beginning of history as equivalent to a real lack of being) then becomes the marvelling rediscovery – of a wonder that this time is just as great as Budoor's in the episode of the tower – of the entire female body and especially the vagina, described as a 'paradise regained'?

The economy of each person's sexuality (to give the word the full wealth of meaning that psychoanalysis confers on it) is based on an ever-fragile relationship between the assertion of bisexuality and the assertion of sexual specificity. Reckoning with the oscillation between femininity and masculinity – a constant in our psychic life – with the highly composite nature of the concept of sexual difference and with the fact that the individual psychosexual position – I mean each person's position on the infinitely varied spectrum of concrete sexualities – is the result of a long and hazardous drive-related and personal evolution, it becomes evident that the 'psychic participation' has transformed human sexuality into an extremely plastic and polymorphous reality. Admittedly, sexual reality indisputably limits this plasticity, this polymorphism, but is it not counterbalanced, at its very core, by another reality that is potentially antagonistic: the sexual fantasmatic, with its powerful modulating effects?

When psychosexuality, in a subject or a group, submits to a costly and contrived effort with a view to compartmentalising sexual choices and attitudes and is pledged to a highly contrasting simplification of the inherent vocations and characteristics of each of the sexes, libidinal tension will probably be increased and perhaps the species – at least its reproduction – will benefit; but the living communication between people, genuine exchanges between men and women, are compromised: an end is made to potential similarities and affinities, as well as opportunities for agreement and unity.

However, if the opposite transpires (might this be the case today in some of our societies?), if 'bisexualisation' stimulates an opening up of the male and female universes and an attenuation of sexual difference as the source of insurmountable conflicts, in short if the commonality between men and women increases, libidinal tension probably loses by it, and there is even a risk of a certain involution of sexuality occurring, but communication becomes livelier and more complete . . .

Unless, of course, the economic equilibrium is broken by an excessively strong bisexualisation, for, from then, the vulnerability of Eros to the destructive drives becomes more pronounced, the drive defusion is facilitated, and soon what it seemed could only extend or create communication breaks it down, and the happy introjection of the other sexuality turns into a narcissistic androgynous fantasy that is toxic in nature: then an end is made to those effective and beautiful differences!

References

Bergler, E. (1956). *Homosexuality: Disease or Way of Life*. New York: Hill and Wang.
Freud, S. (1905d). *Three Essays on the Theory of Sexuality. S.E.*, 7.
Freud, S. (1908a). Hysterical Phantasies and Their Relation to Bisexuality. *S.E.*, 9.
Freud, S. (1912d). On the Universal Tendency to Debasement in the Sphere of Love. *S.E.*, 11.
Freud, S. (1913j). The Claims of Psychoanalysis to Scientific Interest. *S.E.*, 13.
Freud, S. (1914c). On Narcissism: An Introduction. *S.E.*, 14: 73–102.
Freud, S. (1919e). A Child Is Being Beaten. *S.E.*, 17.
Freud, S. (1920a). The Psychogenesis of a Case of Homosexuality in a Woman. *S.E.*, 18: 147–172.
Freud, S. (1961). *Letters of Sigmund Freud, 1873–1939*, ed. E. L. Freud. New York: Basic Books.
Green, A. (1972). Aggression, Femininity, Paranoia and Reality. *International Journal of Psychoanalysis*, 53 (2).
Lane, E. W. (Trans). (1883). *The Thousand and One Nights: Commonly Called, in England, the Arabian Nights' Entertainments, Vol. 2*, ed. E. S. Poole. London: Chatto & Windus.
Laplanche, J. (1976). *Life and Death in Psychoanalysis*, trans. J. Mehlman. Baltimore, MD: Johns Hopkins University Press.
Lewinter, R. (1969). Preface. In G. Groddeck, *La maladie, l'art et le symbole* [Illness, art and the symbol] (pp. 290–309). Paris: Gallimard.
Luquet-Parat, C. (1962). Réflexions sur le transfert homosexuel dans le cas particulier d'un homme analysé par une femme [Reflections on the homosexual transference in the particular case of a man analysed by a woman]. *Revue Française de Psychanalyse*, 5.
Mardrus, J. C. (Trans). (1990). *Mille et une Nuits* [A thousand and one nights]. Paris: Ed. de la Revue Blanche.
Masson, J. M. (Ed.) (1985). *The Complete Letters of Sigmund Freud to Wilhelm Fliess, 1887–1904*. Cambridge, MA: Belknap Press.
Rado, S. (1940). A Critical Examination of the Concept of Bisexuality. *Psychosomatic Medicine*, 4.
Sherfey, M. J. (1972). *The Nature and Evolution of Female Sexuality*. New York: Random House.

35 PLEA FOR A MEASURE OF ABNORMALITY

Joyce McDougall

Joyce McDougall is a full member of the Paris Psychoanalytical Society and a member of the New York Freudian Society. Very much the cosmopolitan, she learned a lot from the various conflicts that arose within the British and French psychoanalytical Societies, but remained aloof from any dogmatic standpoint. She has written mainly on psychosomatic disorders, perversion and the neo-sexualities. Her talent as the stage director of the drama that takes place in every psychoanalytic treatment enables her readers – now spectators – to participate meaningfully in the psychic phenomena that are being played out.

Joyce McDougall's publications include the following: *Plaidoyer pour une certaine anormalité* (Gallimard, 1978) [*Plea for a Measure of Abnormality* (IUP, 1980)]; *Théâtres du Je* (Gallimard, 1982) [*Theatres of the Mind* (Free Association Books, 1986)]; *Théâtres du corps* (Gallimard, 1989) [*Theatres of the Body* (Free Association Books, 1989)]; and *Eros aux mille et un visages* (Gallimard, 1996) [*The Many Faces of Eros* (Free Association Books, 1995)], which won the prestigious Gradiva Award.

Ruth Menahem wrote a concise biography of Joyce McDougall for the 'Psychanalystes d'aujourd'hui' series (PUF, 1997). More recently, Philippe Porret has written of the life and intellectual itinerary of this outstanding practitioner of psychoanalysis: *Joyce McDougall, une écoute lumineuse* [Joyce McDougall, an illuminating listening] (Campagne première, 2005).

I was once invited to take part in a psychoanalytic colloquium on the following theme: 'Pathological and Pathogenic Aspects of Normality' – a provocative title – raising an important question, if only for the fact that the participants were stimulated to assess the concept of normality. What is 'normality' from a psychoanalytic viewpoint? And, supposing we manage to define such a commodity, could it be endowed with varying qualities: a 'good' normality and a 'bad' one? No sooner had I begun to reflect upon the problem, than I became aware that over and beyond the attempt to define 'abnormal' normality I was far from being able to conceptualize the structure of 'normal' normality. In the midst of these questionings one further doubt clouded my mind, a matter rather delicate to formulate. For several years I have spent much of my time with *analysts* (and of course, with analysands); could I be sure I even knew what constitutes a 'normal' person? My colleagues have never appeared to me to be eminently 'normal' people; as for myself, I feel quite at home with them. Who are we, who am I, to judge what is normal or abnormal?

The more I thought about it, the more I became convinced that 'normality' is not, and never could be, *a psychoanalytic concept*; the very notion is unequivocally anti-analytic.

For an analyst to speak of normality is like trying to describe the dark side of the moon. We can imagine it of course, even send up a rocket and take some photos and, on this basis, build up theories about how it *ought* to look. But where does that lead us? It is not our country, scarcely even our planet. The neuroses with their secret psychotic center, the psychoses with their thick neurotic fringe – this is our family, our terrain, where we all speak, with certain variations of dialect, the same language. But this apart, we must ask the question whether something called a 'normal personality structure' could really exist. And even if it exists, why must we leave our familiar analytic field, so comfortably abnormal, to search for traces of the normal? So that we may explain to these 'normal' people how sick they really are? There is the further complication that those who proclaim themselves normal – though we may consider their normality pathological or even pathogenic – do not want any truck with us. Not only do they escape our contact, they are indeed suspicious of us. I am reminded of a time when I offered a bunch of asparagus to the elderly farm-hand who had helped to till the soil in my country garden. He vigorously refused my offer. 'You don't care for asparagus?' I asked. 'Couldn't rightly say,' he replied, 'never tasted 'em. Folks around here don't eat stuff like that'! It is possible that analysts are a luxury item, like asparagus; you need to have developed a taste for it. That we may consider ourselves highly edible changes nothing – and in any case is not specific to analysts. One of life's overall aims is to possess something that others may need or desire, so, why should we concern ourselves with these 'normals' who want nothing to do with analysts? Our narcissism (normal? pathological?) sees to it that those who ask *nothing* of us, hold little interest for us. But let us put aside our prejudices and let us aim for the moon.

Although it is conceivable that an analyst might oppose 'normal' and 'neurotic' it is equally feasible to suggest that it is 'normal to be neurotic.' This brings us face to face with two distinct dimensions of the concept of normality. To say that neurosis is a normal phenomenon is to refer to an idea of *quantity:* the *statistical norm*. If on the contrary we seek to contrast 'normal' and 'neurotic,' this is based on the notion of *quality:* a 'normally acceptable' idea of the norm for a given society – and for which I propose the term *normative norm* (in contrast to the statistical norm) with a view to maintaining the distinction between attributes of quantity and quality. The normative norm designates a state of being toward which one tends and wherein is included the notion of an *ideal*. So now we have statistical normality and normative normality over and above our elusive pathological normality.

The quantifiable, the statistical norm, indubitably has sociological research value, but its psychoanalytic interest is relatively unimportant. What is of interest to psychoanalysis is normality from the normative aspect (which, we are well aware, includes a vagueness of limits and shifting superego elements). From this vantage point the analyst might be tempted to formulate a number of questions. I have chosen a few which are of interest to me:

- Are there any 'normal' analysts?
- Is there such a thing as 'normal' sexuality?
- Are there any 'psychoanalytical norms'?

Let us leave the terra firma of the quantifiable, with its statistical curves (and their built-in *trompe-l'oeil*) for the shifting sands of the normative and see whether we may begin to map out its contours. But now we are back at the beginning: What is a normal human being? My dictionary (Webster's) informs me that 'normal' means: conforming to rules, regular, average, or ordinary. Might this help us to track down the pathogenic 'regulars' and the 'ordinary' pathologicals? The 'regular guy' is everywhere; those who desire above all to 'conform to the rules,' the 'good children,' are constantly with us also; many people wish to appear to conform, at least in the eyes of others. But who, in his heart of hearts, aspires to be 'average' or 'ordinary'?

Without leading us too far astray this short excursion into lexical erudition highlights the fundamental *ambivalence* attached to the concept of normality – that is to say, approbation and condemnation at the same time. If one finds it unenticing to be 'ordinary,' this does not mean that one wishes to be thought *abnormal*. The ambiguity implicit in the term might already indicate to us that it pertains to two different sectors of our psychic being, one that seeks to obey the laws, and another that seeks to circumvent them. But quite apart from this inherent ambivalence, the normative is always a subjective value. The idea that each person has formed of his own 'normality' can only be understood in relation to reference points: normal as compared with what? In the eyes of whom? Whether one judges oneself, or others, to be normal or abnormal, this judgment is obligatorily relative to a *preexistent norm*. The earliest conception of all future norms is furnished, obviously, by the family. For the child (and there is very little difference for the adult) the 'normal' is that which is *heimlich*, the recognizable, that which is accepted *at home*. Das Unheimliche, the disquieting unfamiliar, the *uncanny*, so vividly described by Freud (1919h), is the essence of the 'abnormal,' that which arises from within and in so doing casts its dark shadow upon the familiar background – that which will or will not be *accepted by the family*. *Das Unheimliche*, that which does not belong 'at home,' represents, as Freud demonstrated, a special category of that which is familiar, recognizable, normal. The apparent opposition fades away. The wish to escape conformity is the desire to transgress the family-transmitted laws, whereas the contrary wish, to 'be normal,' is fundamentally aimed at deserving the parents' love by respecting their rules and adopting their ideals – a narcissistic goal destined to be embodied in an ego ideal which in turn will leave its imprint on the instinctual aims. Children make valorous efforts to behave 'normally.' I am reminded of a certain little boy and his father on a visit to the zoo. The child did everything he should not do – he leaned too far over the bear-pit, he threw pebbles at the seals, and pushed his way rudely among the other visitors. Finally, the exasperated father shouted: 'How many times must I tell you – behave like a human being!' The little boy looked at his father sadly: 'Daddy, what do you have to do to become a human being?' How does one fit into the norm? The answer is evident – for every child, the norm is the identification with the parents' desires. This family norm will therefore be 'pathogenic' or 'normative' according to its coincidence with or derivation from the norms of the society to which the parents belong.

In psychoanalytic theory this norm is defined in terms of the concept of an 'oedipal organization' within each individual, a *normalizing structure* in the sense that it pre-exists the birth of the child and is destined to structure psychically the child's future intra- and interpersonal relations. Is the solving of the oedipal conflict the factor that will bring forth 'good' normality? But everybody finds some kind of 'solution' to the unacceptable oedipal situation. Whether it be a neurotic, psychotic, perverse, or psychosomatic solution, or a mixture, the task of distributing these according to a normative scale is an exceedingly delicate one. Certain psychoanalytic writings would seem to incarn some such ideal in a mythical being who displays a 'genital character' – that is, someone who loves his neighbor as much as he loves himself; and he is compared with a less highly esteemed small brother known as a 'pregenital character' (but the latter has the privilege of also being able to hate his neighbor). And now we have, in inverse position, yet another – the subject of our discussion – he who is *afflicted with normality*, who suffers from a normality symptom. What are the manifestations of this affliction? We might suppose that these 'normal' people are the ones who would give the impression of 'conforming to the rules,' of 'fitting into the norm,' the 'regular guys' – that is, they would appear to be free of psychological symptoms except that they might suffer from psychosomatic symptoms or subtle character pathology. At first glance there is nothing *unheimlich*, nothing uncanny about these people. The normality symptom, invisible to the naked eye, hides behind an asymptomatic screen. I tried to draw a psychological portrait of analysands of this kind (McDougall, 1978) and named them 'robot analysands' in that they functioned with an unshakable system of preconceived ideas which prevented any further thought and gave to the ego structure the force of a programmed robot. This infallible thought structure enables these patients to maintain a certain psychic equilibrium in face of unrecognized archaic anxieties. They are often tempted to undertake an analysis for reasons other than psychological suffering, but nevertheless present themselves as authentic neurotic sufferers (in which they are not mistaken), although their symptoms do not truly interest them. Once engaged in an analytic relationship, it is the analyst who suffers; he is disavowed as a separate being, as though any recognition of difference would bring the threat of castration and death. The analyst is treated as though he might attack the patient's most vital defenses. But these are not the patients I wish to discuss here. Others, who resemble them in certain respects but who proclaim themselves to be *normal*, also seek psychoanalysis these days, frequently to please some other person.

Mrs. N (for Normal) seats herself comfortably in the armchair facing mine (not perched on the edge of it, as many patients are in their first interviews). Slim and elegant, she holds her head high and looks calmly into my eyes. The thought crosses my mind that she is more at ease than I am, and I have an urge to say, 'Now tell me what's wrong!' as though to create a balance of power, but she takes the initiative.

Mrs. N: No doubt you're wondering why I've come to see you. Well, my Doctor told me I should do an analysis. My marriage has been going badly for some time, and I'm really tired out. We're both forty-five, and we have three children. I love my husband and my daughters, but lately he has been making life impossible. He's always in a bad mood . . . complains about the slightest thing . . . drinks a bit much . . . and recently I discovered he has a mistress. It's quite intolerable . . . particularly since there is absolutely no reason [Mrs. N stops as though she has now given me all the basic elements of the situation].
JM: You do not feel you have contributed anything yourself to the problems between you and your husband?
Mrs. N: Frankly, I don't. I've looked into it, but I haven't changed at all. I don't see what more I could have done. I love him. There's no problem.
JM: You feel that he is the one with the problem?
Mrs. N: Well – yes I do, rather.
JM: And yet it is you who has come to see me. Do you feel you might have some problems that could be talked over?
Mrs. N: Me? No, not really. No. In fact I've always felt quite good about myself – always felt confident you might say.

Attempts to explore the possibility that the changes in her husband might have made her feel less confident led us nowhere. During my own two interviews with Mrs. N, this phrase constantly recurred: 'I've always felt rather good about myself.' Effectively, Mrs. N did seem to feel rather good and confident about herself; if problems there were, they were somewhere outside, external to herself. What was Mrs. N seeking? What did she really want – that what went on outside herself should be as ordered, as well arranged, as she was inside herself?

What more can I say about Mrs. N? Member of a wealthy upper-class family, religiously oriented without bigotry, affectionate without excess, patriotic but not chauvinistic, slightly aligned with the intellectual left – Mrs. N felt worthy of her family lineage. Like the other women of the family, she was a good housekeeper, concerned herself with her servants, her children, and her husband. To the latter, she was faithful, and she was not frigid. In winter she went skiing, in the summer to the seaside. She kept up numerous civic and social activities. During her second interview she went as far as to say that she could not see what psychoanalysis could do for her. I was rather of her opinion, but I must admit asking myself if it were possible that some people might feel *too good* about themselves.

But what does this mean? Too good for analysis? Or for the analyst? Mrs. N was a 'normal' woman, in her own eyes as well as those of her family, her neighbors, and her friends. What more could one ask? It seems that the psychoanalyst asks for something more. As analysts we cannot avoid the troubling impression that something is lacking in these so-called 'normal personalities.' Our only hope (and however could we justify it?) would be that this normal person should *come to suffer from his normality*. As long as Mrs. N remains incapable of putting herself in question, in no matter what dimension of her daily existence or personal history – incapable of asking herself what she genuinely thinks of her married life and her partner, of facing up to what her husband may feel about her, of putting in question the foundation for her feelings, impressions and convictions, finally of asking herself whether there might be a measure of illusion in her way of seeing her world, perhaps even a lack of imagination on her part – then she remains in my opinion unanalyzable.

We must ask ourselves, however, *whether it is normal to put oneself in question in this manner*. Is it normal to put in doubt one's object choices, one's rules of behavior, one's religious and political beliefs, even one's esthetic tastes? Surely not, no more than it would be to doubt one's own identity. 'Who am I?': A question for philosophers and fools. To be a witness to one's own division, to seek for sense in the nonsense of symptoms, to doubt all that one is or has ever been – these are the signs by which a person reveals himself as an eventual candidate for a psychoanalysis – precisely in virtue of these 'abnormal' questions. Those who consider themselves normal, who create no such problems for themselves, who do not doubt their good sense or their essential goodness, nevertheless come too, nowadays, seeking analysis. To what end? What is even more troubling is the fact that we analysts regard them as armor-plated and *ill* people! An illness for which psychoanalysis can do nothing. Whence comes this illness? Does it arise from feeling 'too good' about oneself? Are such people 'ill' simply because they suffer less than we do?

It should be pointed out that if the psychoanalyst considers the too-well-adapted with suspicion, they from their side do not consider the psychoanalyst as one of them either. What sort of figure does the analyst cut in the eyes of 'normal' mortals? No doubt we can be fitted into a statistical curve, but we do not readily fit into the normative norm of these normal others. In this respect I would like to recount a story that dates back some fifteen years ago. A fourteen-year-old girl whose parents were analysts, like many adolescents, considered herself well fitted to judge the adult world. In her school there was considerable talk about psychoanalysis, and the students even wrote papers on different aspects of the subject. For the first time, her parents' professional work took on a certain value in her eyes. She asked if she could, like a grown-up, meet some of the analyst friends about whom she had heard so much. Her mother suggested she come to the country the following Sunday and take part in a luncheon to which she planned to invite an assortment of analysts of varying persuasions. The friends came, ate well, drank well, talked at length – about sex and perversion, about their colleagues and the Psychoanalytic Society – until late in the day. That evening the parents asked the girl for her impressions. 'Well,' she said, 'your friends are a fair bunch of creeps.' Her parents invited her to be a little more precise. 'Do you ever listen to yourselves?' she asked. 'Have you ever noticed that you only have two subjects of conversation? Analysts don't talk about anything but the penis and the Psychoanalytic Society! You find that *normal*, huh?'

When thinking about it, I realized that, normal or not, there was a certain truth to this young lady's opinion. Analysts in social gatherings do not talk like other people. One might even wonder if, when they talk of 'the penis and the Psychoanalytic Society,' it might not be one and the same thing. A more disquieting fact I have observed is that, as the years go by, the established analysts talk more and more about the Society and less and less about the penis. Is this a 'normal' development? Whatever the answer may be, there is little evidence that analysts belong to a 'normal' category of persons. It is indeed interesting to note that the writings of American colleagues, in spite of a culture pattern that sets high value on the capacity for adaptation, conformity, and decision-making, have been the most insistent in warning against the danger of accepting 'normal' people as candidates for psychoanalytic training. It would appear that the 'too-well-adapted-to-life' citizens do not make gifted analysts. Those who recognize within themselves neither symptom nor psychic suffering, who have never been touched by the torture of self-doubt or the fear of the Other, are perhaps little apt to understand these psychic ills in other people.

So much for the 'normality' of analysts. What about sexuality? Is there such a thing as a 'normal sexual pattern'? This would appear to be a thoroughly 'psychoanalytic' question. From 1905 on Freud underlined the fact that the frontier between so-called normal sexuality and deviant sexuality was difficult to distinguish. Having characterized neurosis as the 'negative' and perversion as the 'positive' of one and the same complex of sexual conflicts, he then added: '... in the most favorable cases, which lie between these two extremes, they may by means of effective restriction and other kinds of modification bring about what is known as normal sexual life' (Freud, 1905b). It is clear that Freud considered man's sexual life to be the target of many hazards, and a successful sexual life as something of a luxury. In contrast, he found that the credulity of love and the overestimation of the charms and perfections of the love object were of a remarkable banality. In this respect, Freud made a distinction between the erotic life of antiquity and that of the our epoch – or rather of his, since the sexual mores have changed considerably. The Greeks, he claimed, glorified the drive to the detriment of the object, whereas modern man idealizes the object and looks upon the drive with contempt. We might, of course, question the ancient 'glorification' because of the nostalgia and fantasy it contains, but we might likewise question the overestimation of the sexual object today. Certain musical comedies, the ubiquitous sex shops, pornographic films and the like, would all appear to idealize the *drive* as such, in all its different erotic forms, while the *object* has become indistinct or interchangeable.

In psychoanalytic practice, we observe changes that tend in the same direction. A few years ago, we found on the analyst's couch numerous patients suffering from diverse neurotic sexual problems, frequently in a context in which the sexual object was loved and highly esteemed. 'I love her, yet I cannot make love to her.' Today there are more analysands who say: 'I make love with her, but I do not love her.' Here are two clinical vignettes that highlight, in condensed fashion, these two positions in relation to the objects of desire.

Gabriel, thirty-eight, has suffered for many years from persistent sexual impotence. 'Last night, I tried to make love to her. Nothing worked! And to think that makes three years I've been in love with her. I'm so afraid of losing her. I said, "Look, I want to make love to you, but it [indicating his penis] doesn't want to." '

Pierre-Alain has been coming for two years, twice a week, for psychotherapy. I am still not sure whether he would be capable of accepting an analysis with its more rigid conditions. He is a typical young man of the times. His long hair is held in place by a hairband; he talks of 'grass' and 'acid,' and of the paintings of Vasarely, which, with the 'babes,' seems to fill up the empty spaces of his existence. Twenty-seven years old, he sought therapy because of severe work inhibitions in an intellectual field, but also because of his unsatisfactory relationships and his feeling of loneliness. He has four or five girl friends with whom he maintains sexual relations, but complains that he is incapable of loving any of them – except on rare occasions when wandering through one of his sought-after chemical paradises. There he meets signs, so he feels, of his unconscious life and the impression of being in love. One day he recounted: 'I had sex yesterday afternoon with Pascale, and then last night I took Francine to bed. I made love to her too, but only because I had an erection. She doesn't excite me very much – but neither does Pascale. Still, I'm not a homosexual. I tried it once with a guy. Stupid! I'll stick to women!'

Gabriel lays emphasis on the *importance of the drive* and finds his symptom arises in his sexual activity, whereas Pierre-Alain places it on the side of the object and finds his symptom in his object relations. Their two problems might be subsumed by the remark each one made about his penis. Gabriel: '*I* want to, but *it* doesn't.' Pierre-Alain: '*It* wants to, but *I* don't.' One complains of an executive lack and the other an affective lack. Everyone would say that Gabriel has a sexual problem, whereas Pierre-Alain, who has not the slightest functional difficulty, might be considered by some as symptom-free. Gabriel dreams of a sexual activity like Pierre-Alain's.

Statistically, with respect to his age and socio-cultural group, the sexual preoccupations of Pierre-Alain are within the norm, yet most analysts would probably agree that beneath his 'normal' sexual appearance this patient conceals problems that are more complex than those of Gabriel. They would say that an object relationship in which erotism is linked to feelings of love is the more normal. Is this a countertransference prejudice? The norm, sexual or otherwise, always has a sociotemporal dimension. The recent rebellion of homosexuals against the discrimination from which they suffer may seem abnormal to certain people, whereas others, particularly young adults, consider the 'gay liberation front' perfectly normal. Why, they exclaim, should anyone accept persecution simply because he does not practice the same sexuality as the 'old man'? In point of fact, are these questions truly *psychoanalytic* problems? I do not think so. It is not the analyst's function to decide what his analysands are to do with their lives, their children, or their sex.

If Gabriel, impotent, and Pierre-Alain, incapable of love, are both psychoanalytic 'cases,' it is not because of their sexual behavior, but because *they put themselves in question*. If judgment there be, it can only be concerned with the analyzability of the patients who seek help, and the form of analytic help best suited to their needs. The patients discussed here have quite different psychic structures. Gabriel's repressed fantasies, impregnated with anxiety and phallic castration fears, find expression within the body, thereby mastering the fantasied danger in symbolic fashion. For Pierre-Alain the fantasied danger is a more global one, a sort of 'primary' castration anxiety of a global kind. Pierre-Alain resembles a baby who has lost the breast and is frantically trying to find it through drugs, other people, and his genital apparatus. He has a 'thirst' for others, and his penis functions to this effect. It enables him to make some form of contact with the Other. Moved by his own particular castration fantasy, he hurtles himself across the space that separates him from others – like a trapeze artist circling toward unknown hands – with only one demand to make of them: *they must be there*. My observations and reflections on changing sexual mores lead me to conclude that (quite apart from the question of basic differences of psychic structure between one individual and another) *sexual norms change continually, but castration anxiety remains. It has simply found new disguises.*

Of what consists the normality of so-called normal people? Is a normal person someone who needs analysis or someone who does not? Some authors have suggested, and not without reason, that a person needs to be in excellent psychic health if he hopes to be able to make use of a classical psychoanalysis. People who 'need' analysis, as popular parlance would put it, are not necessarily analyzable (as every analyst has discovered to his dismay). Although the experience of psychoanalysis theoretically should benefit most 'normal neurotics,' this must be predicated on the desire of the patient to undergo this experience, because he believes that he harbors problems to which psychological answers might be found. However, if it is statistically normal to be neurotic, it is even more normal to be unaware that this is so, or to acknowledge neurotic failings even when these appear evident. I come back therefore to the question formulated earlier: is it *normal* (not only statistically but also normatively) to put oneself in question, to question one's cherished beliefs and their origins, to examine attentively the established orders and all one has been taught to accept without question – that is, to question the order that reigns within ourselves, within our family backgrounds, or within the social group to which we belong? Most people, it must be admitted, do not ask themselves such questions. The viewpoint of the analyst as well as the analysand does not fit within the norm. We evolve, with our patients, in a rarefied atmosphere. Why should we become preoccupied with those who call themselves normal, particularly if their sole motivation for seeking analysis arises from the idea that 'it is normal to be psychoanalyzed'? The major aim of such an analysis could only be to bring to light psychic pain, which till then had not been recognized as such, and to make the patient capable of suffering. Do we wish to bring the plague to the whole world?

Normality when glorified as an ideal is certainly to be regarded as a symptom; but what of the prognosis? Is it curable? Man is not easily cured of his character traits. No doubt we all harbor chimeric beliefs to which we cling more dearly than to life itself. Might 'normality' be nothing more than a chimera? Is the 'normal man' a creature of the imagination who believes he is self-evident, to be found everywhere, a well-established reality, convinced of his conformity? This state of self-esteem might conceivably enable a person to maintain his psychic equilibrium; it might also make him inaccessible to analysis. It may be added that of all the narcissistic character traits that man may construct for himself, the reputation for being 'normal' is probably the one that brings the largest number of secondary benefits! However, even if the belief that some people have in their normality is for analysts a sign of pathology, this does not give us the right to try at all costs to open their eyes, to force them to face the deceits and disguises of the human spirit. Analysis leads us after all to come to know all that we have passed our lives in wishing *not* to know; to recognize all that is most painful and most scandalous in the depths of our being – not only the forbidden erotic desires, but also our infantile avidity for what we do not possess, our unsuspected selfishness, our childlike narcissism, and our murderous aggression. Why should anyone seek to possess this knowledge? Who wants to question all that he knows, all that he is? Let the analyst keep for himself this questionable treasure, proclaim those who live at a comfortable distance from their unconscious.

Might one of the side benefits of analysis be that it enables us to live with 'normal' people? We are a marginal minority, and as such are interested in other marginal people who resemble us. Indeed, should psychoanalysis one day cease to be a marginal discipline that seeks to question the established order of beliefs and prejudices (should it cease to be 'beyond the norm'), then it shall have ceased to fulfill its function.

If the conviction of 'being normal' is a character defense that blocks the liberty of individual thinking, why are people so afflicted in such large numbers? What are the signs and what is the cause of this affliction? Permit me to narrow the question by pointing out certain signs to the contrary, since it is frequently easier to appreciate what an entity is not rather than what it is. I would willingly contrast the so-called normal personality, from a statistical as well as a normative standpoint, with what might be called the creative personality (irrespective of neurotic, psychotic, or characterological symptoms). Most people are sadly uncreative in the commonly accepted sense of the word (artistic or intellectual creation, political or scientific genius, etc.). But in a larger perspective, it must be recognized that man *always creates something* in the space that separates him from the Other or from the fulfillment of his desires. These diverse 'creations' require as much energy, passion, and innovation as the socially recognized ones. They may take the form of a neurotic symptom, a perversion, a psychosis, a criminal career, a work of art, or an intellectual production. The important clinical differences that distinguish these various inventions is not in question here, for that has to do with the specific 'abnormality' which is the domain of psychoanalysis. My interest is centered for the time being on those individuals who appear to create nothing either sublime or pathological. But they do in fact create the protective shield we call normality. Such a person respects the ideas that have been handed down to him as he respects the rules of society; there is no apparent conflict, for the wish to transgress these rules of thought and behavior does not appear, even in imagination. The nostalgic fragrance of Marcel Proust's *madeleine* awakens no remembrance of things past, and he will waste no time in searching for *les temps perdus*. Yet he too has lost something precious. In the construction of his solid wall of normality, the richness of fantasy seems to be lacking; or perhaps it would be nearer the truth to say that this restraining wall keeps the subject *out of contact with himself and his imaginative life*.

Children who vociferously question every perception that is new to them, who imagine the unimaginable with facility before becoming 'normalized,' are, in contrast to most adults, authentically innovative and formulate creative questions. I have in mind a faraway memory of my son, aged three, watching me pouring tea. 'Hey Maman, what makes the tea stand up in the cup when you pour it out of the pot?' I looked, as though for the first time, at that column of tea which effectively 'stood up' between the teapot and the cup. Moreover I was incapable of providing a plausible explanation. Why does this childlike questioning eye with its passionate vigilance become lost to the majority of adults? At what moment do the shutters fall into place, and what determines their subsequent transparence or opacity? Fall they must, because the curious gaze of children is quickly apprehended as transgression. The astonished concentration of the little boy on the column of tea *has become detached from his mother's body* and its mysteries. He has begun to understand that one no longer asks questions about the columns of water that pour from human bodies; and even less about the phallic column of his father, its lack in his mother, and the unimaginable conjunction between the parents. Should he fail to find new symbolic links to the objects of his passionate curiosity by turning his eyes elsewhere, he risks losing forever the open-eyed questioning attitude of the child and henceforth will keep his eyes on the ground. We all have within us locked doors and dark areas where no light may fall and no doubt may penetrate, so that new and unusual connections of ideas and perceptions will not arise. How many adults are capable of questioning the obvious? How many are able to draw with the serious and sophisticated naivety of children? Or see in everyday objects something fantastic that the others no longer see? An Einstein? a Picasso? a Freud?

A handful only – artists, musicians, writers, scientists – escape the icy shower of *normalization* that the world pours upon them. Indeed each child must pass this way, must take his place in the order of things; but does it have to be at the price of the loss of that magical time when all thoughts, fantasies, and feelings were at least thinkable, representable? To hold fast to the hope that all might be questioned, that each desire may be fulfilled, that everything can be transformed into its opposite or even cease to exist, is to defy the laws and challenge the logic upon which human relations are built and regulated. Thus all art, every invention, each new thought is at the same time an act of transgression. Small wonder that new and curious connections become forbidden. How many of us can even equal in our waking lives the creativity of our own dreams? Men of genius and certain madmen perhaps.

Others no longer even know how to dream. If the psychotic wipes out the distinction between inner and outer, between desire and its fulfillment, the most affected of our so-called normal folk block all interpenetration between the world within and perceptions of the outside world; the fluid of psychic life no longer flows. The unusual, the unknown, and the unexpected will not light a fire in conscious thought; they may even pass unperceived. Rather like *Das Unheimliche* – that Freud derived from its opposite, the familiar – normality, following the same trajectory, comes ever closer to its opposite, the 'abnormal,' in this respect. This ego quality, this good common sense that never confuses inner and outer, nor desire and realization, leaves the imaginary world behind to concentrate exclusively on external reality with its concreteness and its mastery over emotion. Such clinging to the factual world may go so far as to *cripple symbolic functioning*, thus opening a dangerous door to the explosion of the imaginary in the soma itself.

Obviously the child, who does not yet know the 'norms' life imposes, must submit, little by little, to the normalizing effect of his environment and family structure, with their ideals and interdictions, if he hopes to take his place one day as an adult among adults. But to be caught in the grip of an overly powerful social ego, over-reasonable and overadapted, is no more desirable than the dominance of unleashed instinctual forces. The point at which the 'norm' becomes the straitjacket of the soul and the cemetery of imagination is a delicate one to define. No doubt it originates in that primordial relationship with the breast-mother, the baby's universe, wherein evolve his first creative psychic acts – his capacity to hallucinate this mother-universe and eventually to recreate her inside himself to help support the intolerable reality of her absence and otherness. It is possible that some, even many, renounce too early the magical omnipotence of their infantile megalomania, give up too early their transitional objects, resolve too readily, perhaps too well, their incestuous oedipal longings?

Faced with the difficulty of 'becoming a human being' it is always possible to respond by an over-adaptation to the world of external reality, by becoming 'supernormal.' Thereafter the feverish forces of life may become entrapped in a closed-circuit system; these forces, to become creative, must be filtered through the representational symbolic world or their effects may become purely destructive, and when conflict goes unnoticed, even put life itself in danger. What lies beneath this solid protective wall of the 'too-well-adapted-to-life' people? A budding psychosis? Is it possible that when 'normality' is worshipped as an ideal state it serves the function of maintaining a well-compensated psychotic state? There is a growing body of evidence to support the hypothesis that both psychotic and psychosomatic accidents are cloaked for many years in unimpeachable 'normality,' and that the maintenance of this character defense is something of a hazard to health in the event of sudden environmental stress.

Even though such people rarely turn to psychoanalysis, I would not say that our science can do nothing for the 'supernormal.' The analytic process is itself a *creative process*, and these individuals carry within themselves all the elements for creating *their* analyst and *their* psychoanalytic adventure, like everybody else. If once engaged in this adventure nothing happens to transform their way of experiencing themselves and the world, it may be that *we* have failed to understand their communication and to detect their cry of distress.

We must also admit in respect to 'normal' people that they are the pillars of society and that without them the social structure would be in imminent peril. The normal man will never overthrow the Monarchy and he will willingly die for the Republic. But analysts, beware! For whom tolls the bell? For them, for me, for you? We may likewise run the risk of dying locked in our identity as 'analyst.' This is a fate that pursues us all. The analyst who believes himself to be 'normal,' and capable of deciding on 'norms' of behavior for his patients, runs the risk of being extremely detrimental to the creative unfolding and self-discovery they seek. No analyst, according to Freud (1910d), may hope to take his patients beyond the point at which he can no longer put *himself* in question.

References

Freud, S. (1905d). *Three Essays on the Theory of Sexuality. S.E.*, 7: 125–231.
Freud, S. (1910d). The Future Prospects of Psycho-Analytic Therapy. *S.E.*, 11: 141–151.
Freud, S. (1919h). The 'Uncanny'. *S.E.*, 17: 219.
McDougall, J. (1978). The Anti-Analysand in Analysis. In *Plea for a Measure of Abnormality*. New York: International Universities Press, 1980.

Section VII

PSYCHOSIS

VII PSYCHOSIS
Introduction

Alain Gibeault

After the Second World War, several French psychoanalysts became interested in the psychoanalytic treatment of patients whose mental functioning could be described as psychotic. One of the most important of those analysts was without a doubt Francis Pasche. The paper of his published in the present volume, on the metaphor of Perseus's shield (chapter 36), has become a classic text in French psychoanalysis and bears witness to the way in which psychoanalytic work with psychotic patients can be envisaged, taking into account the theory of ideational representation.

In the dialectic between psychic reality and external reality, Freud showed that access to reality depends on a drive-related movement in which reality is not simply accessible from the outset but is, in fact, an objective that has to be attained, the result of a conquest. This takes us into a clearly psychoanalytic view of the drives, in which the object is the means by which a drive obtains satisfaction. Here the developmental hypothesis becomes highly meaningful: the emergence of a wish is related to real functions that depend on self-preservation through anaclisis and, at the same time, involves the problem of access to reality, of the gradual construction of the libidinal object – and this implies mourning the loss of archaic objects of a narcissistic or anaclitic type, and of prohibited objects that are incestuous in nature.

It is that adventure of the mind which Pasche (1971), an expert in psychosis, explores through the metaphor of Perseus's shield. According to mythology, Perseus was able to defeat the gorgon Medusa by never looking at her directly – as that would risk being turned into stone – but by observing her reflection in his shield. Perseus's shield therefore has a twofold function: that of *protection*, given that it is a barrier which separates mother and child and prevents their being merged together, and that of a *mirror* which sends out images – that is, reflections. In psychosis, the individual has to deal with anxiety about non-differentiation, which Pasche (1975) describes in terms of fantasies of incorporation and threats of re-incorporation by the mother: 'The image of the devouring and intrusive mother leads to *non-figurability*, because it is impossible to imagine an object – or oneself – simultaneously penetrating completely inside another object and being completely penetrated by that object' (Pasche, 1975, p. 49).

From that perspective, the psychotic is exposed to the Medusa's petrifying and immobilising stare because he or she does not have available that protective shield against stimuli represented by Perseus's shield. Pasche (1971 – chapter 36, this volume) describes that annihilation anxiety as being both an 'effraction' of the external world and a 'threat of internal explosion due to the drive overload' involving decathexis of the external world. In order to cope with the void that then overcomes the individual, he or she has to construct a delusional neo-reality, which Pasche compares to the 'phantasmagorias . . . so well described by Klein', a whole series of terrifying serpents that are typical of the Medusa and compensate for the 'horror of the lack'. In a clearly Freudian approach, Pasche describes psychosis as a decathexis of the outside world in order to break free of a non-representable confusion with the imago of the archaic mother and as an attempt to re-cathect the world through the creation of a delusional neo-reality. The origins of psychosis lie in deficiencies of the ego as a bodily ego – a topic that would later be taken up by Didier Anzieu (1985) in his study of the skin ego.

Pasche again (1975) makes use of the metaphor of Perseus's shield in his description of the conditions under which subject and object can be differentiated. He draws a comparison between the shield as an inanimate substance and the *tangible material* (skin appendages, clothes, jewellery) that infants place between themselves and their mother, and between themselves and their self, as a condition of their autonomy. They can thereupon break free of the threat posed by maternal desire; as Pasche quite correctly observes: 'Finding an inanimate substance, one that is soul-less – i.e. with no psychic reality – enables infants to spread out their cathexis so as not to jeopardize their self-preservation and their identity, as well as to satisfy their drives at little cost and with less risk' (1975, p. 52).

Perseus's shield as inert matter is therefore at the heart of the construction both of the fetish and of the transitional object. Pasche observes that the 'fetish' may well be a shield, an inanimate thing that enables the individual to face up to maternal castration, but it is not a mirror, which would be able to reflect the mother's gaze. In the manner in which he explores the metaphor of the mirror, Pasche is closer to Winnicott than to Lacan, because in the experience of the mirror stage, Pasche emphasises the importance of the mother's gaze in which the infant can give him/herself a representation both of the self and of the world. The metaphor of the reflection in the mirror is illustrative of the importance of the function of representation as a means of surmounting the anxiety about non-differentiation that is a characteristic feature of psychosis.

As regards these studies of psychosis, Evelyne and Jean Kestemberg were also part of the group of pioneers who explored in some depth what is involved in psychotic functioning and the conditions under which psychoanalytic work can be done with such patients. At the beginning of the 1970s, the Kestembergs were instrumental in founding the Centre for Psychoanalysis and Psychotherapy under the aegis of the Mental Health Association of the 13th *arrondissement* in Paris. This treatment and research centre for psychotic and borderline patients has contributed

> The concept of **blank psychosis** was suggested by Donnet and Green (1973) and has to do with a latent psychotic structure that may appear to be borderline but is in fact the starting-point, the very nucleus, of a psychosis. The concept of **cold psychosis** was put forward by the Kestembergs as a result of their work with patients suffering from anorexia nervosa (Kestemberg, Kestemberg, & Decobert, 1972), who are drawn into a kind of auto-erotic withdrawal which excludes projection into the object, their only recourse being to erotogenic masochism expressed as physical aggression against their own bodies.

to the publication of many papers on psychosis, particularly in the annual review *Psychanalyse et Psychose* [Psychoanalysis and psychosis].[1]

Jean-Luc Donnet and André Green introduced the concept of '**blank psychosis**' in their description of mental functioning in certain borderline states (Donnet & Green, 1973). Evelyne Kestemberg, Jean Kestemberg, and Simone Decobert (1972) added that of '**cold psychosis**' when describing non-delusional psychoses, with reference to the kind of projection that leaves room only for an economic aspect characterised by self-destructive or allo-destructive enactments, in which erotogenic masochism is prevalent. These non-delusional psychoses differ from their delusional counterparts in that the latter include the object in the work of projection; even though this projection de-humanises the world by transforming it into abstract entities, it does preserve a link with the object even if the price to pay is the creation of that neo-reality we call a delusion.

Drawing on her considerable experience with cold psychoses, of which anorexia nervosa is one example, Evelyne Kestemberg (1978 – chapter 37, this volume) describes a particular kind of relationship that is set up between the psychotic patient and the psychoanalyst: an extension of the idea of the fetish, viewed not in terms of an inanimate object that supports the denial of castration, as in Freud's way of thinking (a substitute for the penis or some other object), but as applied to the analyst as a person, devitalised, ossified, perennated. In that fetishistic relationship with the object, the patient projects onto the analyst an ambi-sexed maternal imago, thereby ensuring sufficient narcissistic continuity to be able to face up to an object relationship that until then had been too disorganised. For Kestemberg, this kind of object relationship is similar to what Melanie Klein called projective identification, although she does emphasise the immutable and devitalised aspect of the process.

Kestemberg (1981) went on to argue that the fetishistic object relationship is a product of the self, corresponding in her view to the original organised patterning of the mental apparatus, as it emerges from the mother–infant unit (1981, p. 188). That concept enables us to understand the issues involved in the construction of

---

[1] In 2001, *Psychanalyse et Psychose* took over from an earlier biannual publication, *Les Cahiers du Centre de Psychanalyse et de Psychothérapie* [Journal of the Centre for Psychoanalysis and Psychotherapy], founded in 1980 by E. Kestemberg. That journal enabled those working in this field in France to develop a psychoanalytic approach to psychotic functioning, taking as their basis a certain number of concepts that research in this domain had highlighted: splitting of the ego, negation, erotogenic masochism, moral masochism, delusional solutions, etc.

auto-erotism before the differentiation between subject and object takes place when, to quote Lebovici's (1961, p.151) famous dictum, 'the object is cathected before being perceived'. Hypercathexis of the self in non-delusional psychoses leads to a denial of reality with respect to an internal object distinct from the individual, so that, most of the time, the only recourse is erotogenic masochism. From that point of view, the fetishistic object relationship enables the patient to restore communication with the object, thus rescuing him or her from self-destructiveness – although the price to be paid is that of devitalising the object. A parallel could be drawn between that notion and Kohut's idea of the grandiose self, as long as we include the link with the instinctual drives, an element that is not included in the overall theory of self-psychology (Kohut, 1977).

In a similar connection, Paul-Claude Racamier has written several papers on the psychoanalytic treatment not only of the psychoses but also of narcissistic perversions and, above all, on the process that links these two pathologies together; their pathogenesis is considered to be normal and particularly creative. The psychoses are a kind of inflexible straitjacket, but when some degree of mobilisation can be achieved this leads to perverse narcissistic manifestations which are less fossilised and more open to ambiguity and creativity.

In his paper, Racamier (1991 – chapter 38, this volume) explores mental suffering, with its analogy to physical suffering, mainly as regards the silent wounds that may be inflicted on the ego when it has to cope with unachievable tasks while at the same time being deprived of any narcissistic support. Finding itself in such peril, its only objective is to survive. Survivance is a true principle of mental life presented along with its complement, the principle of elimination, and with its own means of defence. '**Paradox** is one of those means of defence, described by Racamier in terms similar to the 'double bind' as defined by the Palo Alto school: it is a 'psychic formation that indissolubly links and constantly relates two propositions or impositions that are irreconcilable and nevertheless unopposable' (Caillot, 2002). Racamier goes on to suggest an extension of the paradox, which he calls *paradoxicality*, describing it as an original and essential modality of mental life, the most apt at playing a specific role in the birth of the ego and in its survival when faced with a situation of extreme mental peril – the death of the psyche. It is on that basis that survival is the very organiser of schizophrenic existence.

Although there is a link between this concept and Winnicott's paradox of the 'found–created' object, Racamier focuses more on the problem of the paradox involved in the denial of origins and of temporality in psychosis; his hypothesis as regards the primary psychotic breakdown is extremely interesting. With a point of view similar to that of Pasche, Racamier (1987) explores what is involved in the catastrophe that is psychosis, through his description of the fantasy of self-procreation – a non-fantasy fantasy – that is marked more by sensory feeling than by representation:

> The notion of **paradox** was first introduced by the anthropologist Gregory Bateson and his colleagues in the 1950s, to describe a form of communication they termed the 'double bind'. In France it was developed in particular by Anzieu (1975) and Racamier (1973).

Introduction 687

What to me seems both obvious and highly significant is that the activation of that 'fantasy' [of self-procreation] brings about an extremely rare modification in the individual's state of mind. It constitutes what I would call a *blank psychic event* (and I do mean *psychic*). Blank – something that lights up as in a flash of lightning, creating an explosion all around, and blinds you. I may as well say it now: that psychic event corresponds exactly to the primal catastrophe. And thus we have in the history of a delusion a process that is different from and more precise than simple decathexis. Of course, it does require massive denial – but there is more to it than just denial: there is the constitution and activation of this fantasy which is extraordinarily *seductive* in nature. And I say that all the more because self-procreation is directly related to *narcissistic seduction*. Any person who reaches that particular dimension will be exposed to the 'blank' event, both fascinating and terrible, which will empty everything out of his mind; the only way to recover from it is via the creation of a delusion.

(1987, p. 38)

Paradoxicality would therefore seem to be a very powerful defence against this experience of 'blank'-ness. Among other issues, Racamier has developed his thinking on this psychotic experience in one of his best-known books, *Le génie des origines* (1992).

Piera Aulagnier's work on psychosis can be seen as a further exploration of that psychotic catastrophe based on the splitting of sensations and the destruction of intersensoriality. In the paper published in the present collection, Aulagnier (1985 – chapter 39, this volume) returns to her hypotheses concerning the primal dimension in order to describe what is at issue in the 'retreat into hallucination' and the similarities it shares with autistic withdrawal. That paper was delivered as the conclusion to an international symposium on autism held in Monaco in June 1984 in which several well-known psychoanalysts took part who specialised in treating autistic and psychotic patients: Frances Tustin, Donald Meltzer and Martha Harris from the United Kingdom; and Annie Anzieu, Colette Chiland, René Diatkine, Florence Guignard, Geneviève Haag, Serge Lebovici and Roger Misès from France.

Aulagnier goes back to the theory that she had first set out in her 1975 book *La violence de l'interprétation* about the relationship between the primal, the primary and the secondary dimensions, which describes the movement from sensations and affects to fantasies and then to thoughts and concepts. She compares the experience of hallucination to the sensation of a hand grasping a rocky outlet, the absorption in the sensation of the hand/rock the last defence against sliding into a void of non-representation and self-annihilation. Once sliding into the vertiginous whirlwind of the void, the only solution is to produce delusional images, particularly of pursuing persecutors, or to dash headlong into unpredictable actings-out that are either self-destructive or allo-destructive in order not to sink down into that endless descent bereft of all representation. Aulagnier theorises psychotic experience and its accompanying affect of terror in terms of her conception of the primal process, '*the image of the complementary object-zone*', i.e. the 'pictogram' (1975/2001, p. 25), in her view the earliest and most primitive representation of psychic life.

When auto-erotism is set up, the role of the mental apparatus is to represent itself on the basis of the junction between an erotogenic zone and an object that is a source of excitation; psychotic rejection aims at setting up a movement of self-mutilation of the organ and of the sensory function, and attempts to destroy the objects of excitation (Aulagnier, 1975/2001, p. 37). This, as in Racamier's theory, involves a relationship of self-generation.

> Green (1980) has suggested that we make a distinction between **madness**, which is a component part of human beings and marks the victory of the life drive, and **psychosis**, which, on the contrary, indicates the triumph of the destructive drives. On the one hand, there is a link to Eros; on the other, the unbinding of the death drive, the only way to escape from a fusional relationship with the primary object.

The annihilation anxiety experienced by psychotics is correlative with a decathexis of the body and its sensations, in addition to that of all links with the object. In their description of the decathexis that is a typical feature of the loss of the object in psychosis (Freud, 1924e), French psychoanalysts make use of different concepts in order to elucidate the same experience of mental paralysis and breakdown: fragmenting dissociation (Pasche), disobjectalising function (Green), dazzling experience of blankness (Racamier), hallucination of a complementary object from an erotogenic zone corresponding to a sensory perception (Aulagnier) (see **madness** and **psychosis** definition).

The case of the schizophrenic patient who had committed murder, presented by Alain Gibeault (2008 – chapter 40, this volume), illustrates these theoretical conceptions of psychotic functioning. That patient himself evoked an experience of 'going blank', meaning both a kind of dazzling white-out as well as an experience of emptiness that he described as 'nothingness'.[2] It was at that point in the splitting of his watertight ego that he committed the murder; he was subsequently unable to explain this other than in terms of 'getting caught up in something' – a mechanism, therefore, over which he himself had no control whatsoever.

Gibeault's patient, hospitalised under the relevant section of the mental health legislation, had been in psychiatric care for several years before he began individual psychodrama at the Evelyne and Jean Kestemberg Centre for Psychoanalysis and Psychotherapy. Psychodrama itself was invented by Moreno, but the technique was later adopted by French psychoanalysts and used particularly in the treatment of psychotic patients. Individual psychoanalytic psychodrama introduces certain variations in setting and in technique, based on playing out a scenario. The paradox inherent in analytic psychodrama is that it consists in systematically prescribing in the form of play what is otherwise considered to be an obstacle to the development of the analytic process – especially the facilitation of lateral transference and of enactments, either physical or verbal. It is true that the playful mode avoids

---

[2] *Blanc* means both 'white' and 'blank'. [*Trans.*]

the kind of resistance that these defences usually generate – with actings-out as the consequence – and transforms the situation into one that actually facilitates working-through in patients who would otherwise be unable to tolerate a transference relationship focused on a single analyst. The motive force behind the process – the transference – and its objective are the same as in the classic form of psychoanalytic treatment; in psychodrama, the only differences have to do with the setting.

Psychoanalytic psychodrama, as theorised in the 1950s by Serge Lebovici, René Diatkine and Evelyne and Jean Kestemberg (Lebovici, Diatkine & Kestemberg, 1969–1970; Kestemberg & Jeammet, 1987) and more recently by Jean Gillibert (1985) and Philippe Jeammet (Jeammet & Kestemberg, 1981; Kestemberg & Jeammet, 1987), provides the economic and topographical conditions that enable interpretations to be listened to without their being experienced as intrusive and, consequently, to be introjected. The psychodrama is focused on a single patient, with a group of therapists comprising the play director, who has the task of interpreting the material, and a number of co-therapists – at least four, with equal numbers of men and women – who are also potential participants in the play scenario. There is one session per week, which lasts for approximately half an hour.

Individual psychoanalytic psychodrama, with its specific setting, can be offered to child or adult patients who, in general, present major forms either of excitation or of inhibition; these are often characteristic features of psychotic functioning or of some major change in life – adolescence, for example, or the period immediately before pre-adolescence. The range of personalities – the play director with the other members of the psychodrama team – enables any excessive transference cathexis to be fragmented, thus lightening the economic burden of that excitation. Alternating interpretations within the play scenario and outside it lead in the best of cases to a focusing of material, displaced and ambivalent, on the play director; at that point it can be dealt with in the same way as in the classic form of psychoanalytic treatment with a single psychoanalyst.

In fact, the tactics of interpretation have less to do with systematically analysing the transference than with facilitating the work of representation corresponding to the installation of formal and topographical regression. From that perspective, the distribution of transference cathexes throughout the group of psychodrama therapists enables the organisation of an analytic process; it is only after this, and thanks to temporal regression, that it may become possible to interpret the transference with respect to the play director. This technical approach is different from that adopted by British analysts in the post-war years (Bion, Herbert Rosenfeld, Hanna Segal) in the treatment of schizophrenic patients: their technique maintained the same kind of setting (five sessions per week) and same interpretative approach (interpretation of projective identification and in particular of the negative transference) as in the psychoanalytic treatment of neurotic patients.

Evelyne Kestemberg, who was a close friend of Hanna Segal, suggested a very different psychoanalytic approach. She challenged the idea that the psychotic state should be replaced by a transference psychosis, following the model of the transference neurosis, with the idea of resolving it at the end of the treatment. 'On the contrary, my impression is that we ought to avoid as much as we can setting up a transference psychosis and work at neuroticising any manifestations of a psychotic transference. It is only that gradual neuroticisation which will help us recover with our psychotic patients that narrow margin between fantasy and reality which, as Nacht pointed out, is what we can work on' (Kestemberg, 1958, p. 45). She argued also in favour of varying the setting with psychotic patients, recommending psychotherapy in which patient and analyst sit facing each other, with one or two 45-minute sessions per week, or individual psychoanalytic psychodrama with one 30-minute session per week. 'If we replace the psychotic state with a transference psychosis, this transference is a delusional construction the defensive character of which we can no longer effectively point out, because the analyst is an integral part of that construction; the analyst is in fact the devoured and devouring reality against which the patient is struggling, a reality that prohibits any autonomous action on the patient's part other than this kind of defence which, in its extreme form, would lead to autism or suicide' (p. 45).

The first psychodrama session with 'John', a schizophrenic patient, is a good illustration of this psychoanalytic approach based on the symbolising function of the psychodrama setting (see chapter 40). One of the psychiatric symptoms presented by this patient was the feeling of *déjà vu*; indeed, in that first session, he wanted to re-experience in exactly the same way the memory he had of a situation dating from when he was much younger, so as to be protected as much from a breakthrough by the object as from the sheer violence of his own instinctual drives. After imagining that the therapists might have a persecutory effect, he entered fully into the treatment, which helped him to break free of the perplexity entailed by the splitting of his ego and, after only six months, to face up to the shame and guilt that weighed heavily on him. It then became possible to consider letting him leave the psychiatric hospital, although with fairly intensive psychiatric care as an outpatient. The disappearance of his *déjà vu* defence after only two months of psychodrama bears witness to the value of that technique, which is a characteristic feature of French psychoanalysis.

That approach is correlative with the possibility of facilitating the processes of symbol-formation, which other French psychoanalysts have described in terms of processes of subjectivation (Cahn, 1991, 1998). Symbolisation can indeed be defined as the procedure thanks to which something will come to represent something else for someone. That could appear to indicate one object being substituted for another, but it is above all the outcome of a process that presupposes the capacity to *represent* an absent object as well as that of realising that the symbol is *not* the object symbolised. Symbol-formation is thus correlative with imaginative play, encouraging both the establishment of a capacity to fantasise and the organisation of mental space. It is therefore, above all, an anti-depressive mechanism which contributes to the binding of affects by representations. In the *principle* of symbolism, we discover the reciprocal connections between distinct elements, the combining of which becomes meaningful – more specifically, in the formations of the unconscious, the connection between two representations or ideas (the symbol and what is symbolised), the purpose of which is to bind an affect which otherwise would remain free-floating.

Over and beyond the relationship of substitution between two elements, symbolisation also denotes the reflexive mediation between subject and object, between psychic reality and external reality, and between past and present; it is therefore concomitant with the purpose of the sublimatory process in its function of acknowledging and sharing social reality and its values. Hanna Segal has explored in some depth this *effect* of the symbolisation process, with its aim of introducing an intra- and inter-subjective system of exchange. It is interesting to compare the French and British approaches on this point: in spite of their differences in theoretical and clinical conceptualisations as well as in technique, they share the same objective – to facilitate the symbolisation process in the psychoanalytic treatment of psychotic patients by emphasising the importance of the work the patient accomplishes in looking inside him/herself, the better to discover the object in all of its otherness.

References

Anzieu, D. (1985). *Le Moi-peau*. Paris: Dunod. [*The Skin Ego*, trans. C. Turner. New Haven, CT: Yale University Press, 1989.]

Aulagnier, P. (1975). *La violence de l'interprétation. Du pictogramme à l'énoncé*. Paris: Presses Universitaires de France. [*The Violence of Interpretation: From Pictogram to Statement*, trans. A. Sheridan. London: Routledge, 2001.]

Aulagnier, P. (1985). Le retrait dans l'hallucination. Un équivalent du retrait autistique? [Retreat into hallucination: An equivalent of the autistic retreat?]. In *Un interprète en quête de sens* [An interpreter in search of meaning]. Paris: Ramsay, 1986.

Cahn, R. (1991). Du sujet [The subject]. *Revue Française de Psychanalyse*, 55 (6): 1353–1490.

Cahn R. (1998), *L'adolescent dans la psychanalyse. L'aventure de la subjectivation* [The adolescent in psychoanalysis: The adventure of subjectivation]. Paris: Presses Universitaires de France.

Caillot, J.-P. (2002). Paradox. In *Dictionnaire international de la psychanalyse*, ed. A. de Mijolla. Paris: Calmann-Lévy.

Donnet, J.-L., & Green, A. (1973). *L'enfant de ça. Psychanalyse d'un entretien. La psychose blanche*. [The child of that/of the id. The psychoanalysis of an interview: Blank psychosis.] Paris: Editions de Minuit.

Freud, S. (1924e). The Loss of Reality in Neurosis and Psychosis. *S.E.*, 19: 183.

Gibeault, A. (2008). Schizophrénie et meurtre d'âme. Le psychodrame psychanalytique de 'Jean', l'homme au 'ça sur le dos'. [Schizophrenia and soul murder: Psychoanalytic psychodrama with 'John', the man 'saddled with that/the id']. *Psychanalyse et psychose*, 8: 131–143.

Gillibert, J. (1985). *Le psychodrame de la psychanalyse* [The psychodrama of psychoanalysis]. Paris: Champ Vallon.

Jeammet, P., & Kestemberg, E. (1981). Le psychodrame psychanalytique. Technique, spécificité, indications [Psychoanalytic psychodrama: Technique, specificity, indications]. *Psychothérapies*, 2: 85–92.

Kestemberg, E. (1958). Quelques considérations à propos de la fin du traitement des malades à structure psychotique [Thoughts on ending treatment with patients presenting a psychotic structure]. In *La psychose froide* [Cold psychosis] (pp. 15–54). Paris: Presses Universitaires de France, 2001.

Kestemberg, E. (1978). La relation fétichique à l'objet [The fetishistic object relationship]. In *La psychose froide* [Cold psychosis] (pp. 77–101). Paris: Presses Universitaires de France, 2001.

Kestemberg, E. (1981). 'L'appareil psychique' et les organisations psychiques diverses [The 'psychic apparatus' in various mental structures]. In *La psychose froide* [Cold psychosis] (pp. 179–199). Paris: Presses Universitaires de France, 2001.

Kestemberg, E. & Jeammet, P. (1987). *Le psychodrame psychanalytique* [Psychoanalytic psychodrama]. Paris: Presses Universitaires de France.

Kestemberg, E., Kestemberg, J., & Decobert, S. (1972). *La faim et le corps* [Hunger and the body]. Paris: Presses Universitaires de France.

Kohut, H. (1977). *The Restoration of the Self*. New York: International Universities Press.

Lebovici, S. (1961). La relation objectale chez l'enfant [Object relationships in children]. *Psychiatrie de L'enfant*, *3* (1): 147–226.

Lebovici, S., Diatkine, R., & Kestemberg, E. (1969–70). Bilan de dix ans de pratique psychodramatique chez l'enfant et l'adolescent [Ten years of psychodrama practice with children and adolescents – an assessment]. *Bulletin de Psychologie*, *23* (13–16, no. 285): 839–888.

Pasche, F. (1971). Le bouclier de Persée ou psychose et réalité [The shield of Perseus, or psychosis and reality]. In *Le sens de la psychanalyse* [The meaning of psychoanalysis]. Paris: Presses Universitaires de France, 1988.

Pasche, F. (1975). Réalités psychiques et réalité matérielle [Psychic reality and material reality]. In *Le sens de la psychanalyse* [The meaning of psychoanalysis]. Paris: Presses Universitaires de France, 1988.

Racamier, P.-C. (1987). De la dépossession du moi à la possession délirante ou: A la recherche du nouveau monde [From dispossession of the ego to delusional possession, or In search of the New World]. *Les Cahiers du Centre de Psychanalyse et de Psychothérapie*, *14*: 29–50.

Racamier, P.-C. (1991). Souffrir et survivre dans les paradoxes [Suffering and surviving in paradoxes]. *Revue Française de Psychanalyse*, *55* (4): 893–909.

Racamier, P.-C. (1992). *Le génie des origines. Psychanalyse et psychoses* [The genius of origins: Psychoanalysis and the psychoses]. Paris: Payot.

36 THE SHIELD OF PERSEUS OR PSYCHOSIS AND REALITY

Francis Pasche

> **Francis Pasche** (1910–1996) trained in psychiatry and in philosophy; he was a full member of the Paris Psychoanalytical Society and president of the Society from 1960 to 1964. He is best known for his original and significant contributions to the clinical manifestations of psychosis and depression; he introduced the concept of anti-narcissism, a centrifugal cathexis in which the individual tends to relinquish his or her self, in contrast with the centripetal cathexis that is typical of narcissism. Other highly remarkable papers that Pasche wrote deal with anxiety, the superego and issues that arise in psychoanalytic treatment, including ethical ones.
>
> The following can be thought of as essential reading: *A partir de Freud* [Starting with Freud] (Payot, 1969); *Le sens de la psychanalyse* [The meaning of psychoanalysis] (Payot, 1988); and *Le passé recomposé* [The past reconstructed] (PUF, 2000).
>
> Michèle Bertrand wrote a concise biography of Francis Pasche for the 'Psychanalystes d'aujourd'hui' series (PUF, 1997).

To divert his mother Danae from the gallant ventures of Polydectes, Perseus undertakes to bring to him the head of Medusa. He accomplishes this feat through his cunning and his courage, as well as through the aid of Hermes and Athene, one of whom provides him with the weapon, a bill-hook, the other with a shield. But given the Medusa's extraordinary weapon – a gaze that petrifies every living creature that comes face to face with her, even accidentally – this will be a shield of a highly specific nature and use. Polished like a mirror, its protective intervention will enable Perseus to locate Medusa and decapitate her without ever facing her: so he will have been able to look at her without any danger.

How did this stratagem work? By depriving Medusa of a magical dimension of which the metaphor is the third dimension – depth – the dimension into which her snakes of hair, her outstretched tongue, her bulging eyes and her gaze are pointed. This is all flattened in the mirror despite the illusion of perspective because the reflective surface makes this irreducibly two-dimensional, with an impenetrable frontal plane. Perseus can now act; the adversary has become definitively parallel to him, at the closest possible tangent. Reality is alongside him. In this way a space is established, a real one in which he can stand still or flee, or move forward, a path he can choose to take: the margin of his liberty.

To this is opposed the enchanted space that entraps Medusa's victims, who, along the imaginary lines that connect them to her, can only be sucked in or assailed by the Gorgon, if they are not turned to stone. In this direction, it is impossible to stop and the monster cannot be stopped. This is the rule of necessity, the domain of the continuum. With the aid of the mirror, however, Medusa will not only be reached but seen. Hardly glimpsed, frozen by her gaze, and the mirror has extinguished her, like a crystal with concentrated light: she is finally perceived, that is to say, can be apprehended, through the successive infinity of her profiles; now a profile is always seen in a frontal plane. Medusa has become an integral part of external reality, seen in the mirror; for an instant, she is reborn in the world from which Athena's curse had banished her. Stripped of her magical omnipotence, she – first – regains her liberty; she could in fact have defended herself and perhaps triumphed if she had not been sleeping, if Athena had not given Perseus the shield and guided his arm.

Medusa has therefore become an image of reality, the reality that we would readily define as that which lies beyond a surface, made of juxtaposed contingencies or, more precisely, made of the liberty of the living and the contingency of things and events.

We should now consider the nature of this miraculous device that protected Perseus from the spell and exorcised Medusa. This shield is reminiscent of another apparatus with which we are familiar, the protective shield of the perception–consciousness system. It is the surface, projection of a surface, characteristic of the ego (Freud, 1923b), and the excitations of external origin slide over him without leaving any trace, in contrast to the underlying region in which the primary material of memories sinks to be deeply imprinted, but, as if in compensation, this fleeting contact gives rise to consciousness.

This is the consciousness not only that something is happening at the periphery of his being but, essentially, that something exists outside him in a particular place, at a particular distance, in a particular form and colour and, if the approach is tangential, of a particular weight and substance. It returns him to whence he came so that, as Kant stated, 'Point O is perceived at point O'. Freud indicates to us, and we will return to this, that this shield is made of dead matter like the metal of Perseus's shield.

Are we to say that Perseus, his shield, Medusa[1] – in other words the subject, the perception–consciousness system and external reality, interconnected – all

---

[1] It would probably be worthwhile to resume the critical examination of Platonic idealism based on a parallel between this mythical sequence and the cave allegory in *The Republic*, and also to consider the prohibition in Orthodox churches of any three-dimensional representation of the deity and the absence of perspective in the icons of the Middle Ages.

three combine to form a structure, a system of interdependent elements subject to the inflexible law of a unifying organisation? It is the opposite argument that we will be making.

This device is precisely what breaks every causal link, undoes every suture, tears apart the stitches of every cloth woven according to the symbolic, for it puts things and people back in their place in a free space.

This is a free space, that of perception, which necessity does not contract into a tightly woven fabric; and it matters little to us that this fabric is made of causes and effects, each designed to fold into the other like the tubes of opera-glasses, or signifiers that cluster ever closer according to metaphor and metonymy until the real gains its substance. The space of perception is discontinuous, heterogeneous and lacunary, and it is in these holes, these gaps, these blank spaces that Perseus and many others can move around, not necessarily to kill but also, for example, to embrace.

This leads us to wonder about the cathexis of objects in the external world at the time of perception.

Perceiving is truly going out of oneself, but specifically not to bring something back to oneself, according to the amoeba metaphor.[2] Quite the opposite! It is to leave oneself there, which presupposes staying there as long as the object is there, and focusing in the visual sense on its distance. It is perception, and also love (possibly the same in nature), that have made the concept of anti-narcissism appear ineluctable to us. Here it should be emphasised that the fusional modalities of this anti-narcissistic cathexis are in the service of the percept.

Our thesis is that the psychotic is the person who does not have a shield of Perseus, the person who is made anxious and immobilised by Medusa's gaze, to the point of being turned to stone.

She therefore terrifies him at the outset. Freud (1924e) explains this anxiety as the pressure of reality itself on the ego, a reality that I think the face of Medusa illustrates rather well. All this bristling of reptiles and organs expresses very well the effractive potential represented by the external world for the psychotic. Any kind of reality attacks him as soon as it appears to him and immediately ceases to be truly perceived because the sensory data it contains can no longer be perceived as anything but threatening. Only the shield given by Athena, as the adoptive mother, the mother without a man, could protect him, and this is precisely what he lacks. She has not given him, or he has not been able to receive, the aegis that would enable him to confront

---

[2] The narcissistic phase of libido fixation was also illustrated by the metaphor of an amoeba capable of putting forth extensions (pseudopodia) that can in due course be withdrawn once more, this primitive distribution of the libido being reestablished during sleep. This analogy, first used by Freud in 'On Narcissism' (1914c, p. 75), was repeated frequently between *Beyond the Pleasure Principle* (1920g) and *An Outline of Psycho-Analysis* (1940a [1938]). Pasche's theory of perception implies that the libido is not withdrawn onto the ego. [*Eds., this volume*]

'the formidable external forces'. This maternal deficiency, this lack, has been mentioned by Freud in another form; he tells us that the hypertely of Medusa's head is intended to disguise an absence, a hole, the absence of the maternal phallus, which is felt as castration, but we know this is both preceded and prefigured by the separation from the mother. It is therefore not the absence of the shield that distinguishes the Medusa–victim relationship from the Medusa–Perseus relationship, but the presence of the absence of the shield; here, too, there are three terms that exist together in contradiction – Medusa, the shield and Perseus: this is a structure with interdependent terms. We know the outcome of their interaction: to imprison in itself the being transfixed by the Medusa's gaze. The Greek verb from which the word 'Medusa' derives means to measure, to measure out, to maintain in the limits of its dimensions, in other words to petrify, since to perceive and to act are precisely to leave the spatial confines of one's body. Medusa reduces her prey to their congruent portion; she imprisons them in themselves.

This perfect self-enclosure presupposes that Medusa, fate having taken its course, no longer exists for a paralysed victim for whom there is nothing left but the void:[3] the subject has incorporated what Freud interpreted as the erection of raised penises (*Medusa's head*), but by neutralising their dynamism, their impetus, by his own opposite impetus, by joining as a passive double in this activity, as female to this masculinity, thus realising the immobility of catatonia through the confrontation of opposite forces (death drive and life drive) or – to refer to Tausk – through the mutual blocking of agonists and antagonists. Is this an introjection? Not if we mean by this taking an image or a representation into ourselves. For the representation can only derive from a perception; now reality ceases to be perceived as soon as it irrupts into the world of the psychotic. We could equally well say that it is absorbed by the subject or that it invades him; in any case, it becomes installed in him in its entirety, outright, it becomes ensconced there; it takes its place in the internal space designed to leave some room for the freedom it eliminates. And it is because this reality has been included that it will be able to re-emerge from there in the form of projection (hallucinations and so on); it returns whence it came. It is therefore not a case of repression; the subject has to some extent become external 'reality'; he does not simply possess its image; it is not surprising that this image cannot be found because it is the three-dimensional model that is inside him, forming an integral part of him. Reality is therefore not foreclosed but incorporated, and, since it is manifested as an intention (to assail), the subject makes this intention his own. He is possessed; it is narcissistic identification. This presence of an impulse of unknown origin inside him, in his innermost depths, and of a body, this second embodied 'will' that he also assumes, forms the basis of psychic dissociation, the division of the I that

---

[3] Lot's wife was turned into a salt statue for having wanted to see Sodom and Gomorrah again, concerning which it is only known that they concealed male desires (erections) directed at angels.

defines psychosis. Two Is are therefore present, riveted to each other, stamped inside each other, all deprived of this void that resembles the inner threshold of the project of the I, in the Heideggerian sense. The 'object', the other subject, fills this void, this void that is found beyond the site of their pairing, around them, and no longer between them, separating them. Everything is in the body and no longer leaves it.

A parallel with melancholic depression (which is not a psychosis) will help to explain our theme. Whereas the melancholic introjects the shadow of the object, the psychotic introjects the living body of the object. The melancholic has a hierarchically organised structure, and it is into a localised area of himself that he introjects the object to deliver it to the higher agency; the two are at different levels, a difference that the melancholic precisely tends to make infinite, deifying the superego and vilifying the ego. In psychosis, the two Is brought together by incorporation share the same status and rank: Schreber is the worthy wife of God, for here everything is on the same level, that of the body-ego. Finally, while for the depressive the perception of the external world subsists, for the psychotic it is ultimately eliminated.

The form of bond, indivisible and exclusive of any other between the two 'persons', thus created is the prototype of every psychotic relationship.

Everything happens between these two poles and nowhere else: attraction–repulsion, eating–eaten, tearing apart–torn apart, castrating–castrated, penetrating–penetrated, persecuting–persecuted, beating–beaten, seeing–seen. There it is true that the subject is not in himself but in the entire process, and there alone, in psychosis. We discover the Kleinian universe of paranoid and depressive phases, but also the sadomasochistic and voyeuristic–exhibitionistic play, although no real partner is involved. Here the relationship is immediate and inescapable; time and space contract to the point of the blink of an eye, and it is at the speed of light that the thought or action of the pseudo-others reaches that of the two protagonists, temporarily proclaiming the status of I. So that in reality there is no longer any movement, but a succession of instantaneous changes of view, flashes. Nothing really moves in the psychotic universe.

In any case, there is only one dimension in this space: the third, which joins these two 'people' trapped together in an irreducibly *sagittal* space. This space can be neither superimposed nor connected with the space of perception (space in which a subject with some scope is distinguished from his objects), and its exploration cannot teach us anything about him, it is not the truth of the other; psychosis is not the truth of the perceived world, contrary to the argument of anti-psychiatry. Let us quickly say that the psychotic becomes conscious of another truth that escapes perception, that of the unconscious intentions and desires of the included object to the extent that they target it, an extension of the insight that is indispensable to the psychoanalyst, but which must not exclude a correct perception.

This struggle in pairs, in which one is always or alternately the victim of the other, immediately evokes the primal scene. I believe in fact that the mnemic schema of this scene that is more or less revived by circumstances informs this intrapsychic relationship. I believe that whereas the non-psychotic can experience this as a spectacle, witness it as a third party even if he participates in it, the psychotic must enter into it and no longer emerge from it, as if he is sucked in by the space empty of one of the partners; the Medusa head, with the void (scar of castration, vulva) from which it appears and that no shield exorcises, illustrates a primal scene. But consequently, the stone statues must also be interpreted as primal scenes, but frozen ones. Should we recall that the dragon's teeth sown by Cadmos gave birth to pairs of warriors who killed each other and that the stones thrown by Deucalion and Pyrra gave birth to pairs of women and men who copulated?

Now this primal scene is characterised by the fact that no change occurs in one of the partners that does not modify the other, or is not his act. There we have defined the structure. The primal scene is in fact the prototype, the constitutive atom, of every structure.

It is therefore the same with psychosis, and, far from resulting in a sort of hole in the symbolic, this instead carries out its fulfilment; the psychotic becomes lodged in the primal scene and thus completes the system *without leaving anything outside it*.

The psychoses must in fact be conceived as various inadequate attempts to weaken the attachment of the couple in the primal scene, which nevertheless remains imprisoned in a single body. The vastest delusional space (it sometimes claims to be infinite) keeps within the bounds of our skin. Freud's (1915f) persecuted patient gathered together in her body the woman she had loved with the suitor and his accomplices, for the camera click that was to record her shame turned out to be the erection of her own clitoris, and this to be the instrument of her persecutors.

This leads us to pose the problem of the origin of psychosis.

Let us refer to Freud's distinction between a reality ego and a pleasure ego, the latter succeeding and having issued from the former.

We must suppose that something has been lacking in the future psychotic's reality ego; this something is the shield given by Athena, a present that is both a protective envelope and a mirror:

- a protective envelope that makes it possible to resist external forces and in particular to curb the fearsome aspect of the mother (Medusa) and consequently to remain one and to achieve autonomy;
- a mirror that makes it possible to recognise and evaluate the outside, the external world 'according to good objective criteria' but also to cathect it sufficiently, which removes any need for this paroxysm of anxiety triggered by the mutual confrontation of the two instincts in the presence of the objectal void.

This gift is only an appendage of Athena, a sort of exoskeleton; the transitional object is its vestige. This extension of the maternal body is made of dead matter, which means that it is not the bearer of maternal desires directed at the child. It is a support with which she has provided him. Now this is lacking for the future psychotic. This void in its place is the absence of the mother that prefigures castration, and it is because this absence is always against the background of sensory data that these constitute a fracturing reality, or, to be more precise, one that is apprehended as fracturing.

This effraction is indissociable from the threat of internal explosion due to the drive overload, which itself results from the total decathexis of the external world and the accumulation of energy inside that brings the tendency to defusion to culmination point.

The threat of invasion by the head of Medusa – that is to say, by a reality deserted by the mother – is connected with the imminence of fragmenting dissociation. The eight-month-old's anxiety before an unknown face illustrates this.

Why this decathexis or this impossibility of cathexis at the reality-ego stage? What is lacking? Does it involve a specific attitude on the mother's part?

1. An overprotective mother does not allow the emanation of that carapace, nor would an over-absent mother; an atmosphere of average concern is necessary, but all that is too vague. Reference is required to the alternative, acute analyses made by Fain (1971; Braunschweig & Fain, 1975), who emphasises the mother's turning away from the child towards the father, a mother who then takes up for her own attire the component of her own narcissism with which she had anointed the child, who only takes it up having deadened it at the very outset. Fain illustrates the formative properties of this intermittent disaffection.
2. Is it the imperfect development of atavistic models, which have been thought to found the representation of the external world?
3. Is it ultimately due to a form of congenital hyperaesthesia, a drive defusion that compromises the establishment of the anti-narcissism that we have found to be so important in perception?

These three factors exist in conjunction.

In any event, what remains, with all reality eliminated, is the void, the absence, the lack that generates anxiety in its pure form, anxiety about nothing in particular. The phantasmagorias immediately created, so well described by Klein, are in some respects – like the Medusa's fearsome appendages – nothing but palliatives, as Freud said, to mitigate the horror of the lack. What the mother must allow to the child when she leaves him, when she stops feeding him, attending to him, is probably the hallucinatory fulfilment of a desire, but what must be emphasised is the word 'hallucinatory' – that is, the evocation of a presence irrespective of the satisfaction it promises.

The mother is not only what gratifies or frustrates, adapting more or less to desires, but also a material reality, a surface, a surface of skin, the skin of the world. And it is a piece of this skin, stuffed, that Athena offers Perseus. Psychosis is less about the drives than the ego's deficiencies as the projection of a surface. This is probably what Hartmann (1939) sensed and put to such poor use.[4] Perseus can also look at himself in the shield, and even if he only found his reflection there, that would be enough to destroy Medusa's magical power over him. It seems that the cathexis of one's own image is the ultimate defence against psychosis.

Clinical experience provides some convincing evidence. I am thinking primarily of the conditions that trigger paranoia, which generally consist in breaking a link (more or less desexualised) with an object of the same sex.[5] It is the resemblance to the subject, sex being only one element of this resemblance, which protected him against madness, with the object compensating for the incapacity to look at himself, *to have a representation of himself*. Coming together with a complementary being, a heterosexual experience (cf. Freud) triggers by contrast anxiety and dissociation. Unpublished cases of two psychotics, one treated by Monnot, the other by Brémont, have recently provided further confirmation of these views.[6]

Someone with this predisposition keeps hold of himself if he manages to recreate the illusion of a mirror with help from others, as in these music-hall acts in which a stooge plays the reflection. How can this fail to evoke the mirror stage? We are not seeking to deny its interest, but we believe that it only illustrates one of the phases of an evolution, the first of which is the cathexis of the mother's body as a primary model, as the visible example of the unification and differentiation of the body, as a mirror. The mother's body is the first mirror.

But does having a representation of himself not first require that he is looked at, perceived by his mother? This means that he must feature not only in maternal fantasies with the risks that have been well demonstrated to us by Piera Aulagnier (1964) and Maud Mannoni (1967) but also outside them. What is decisive for the evolution of the future psychotic is not only the position he occupies in these fantasies and the role he plays there but that he should be there alone, that he should be absent from the world perceived by the mother, from the real world for the mother.

---

[4] According to Heinz Hartmann (1894–1970), one of the founders and principal representatives of ego psychology, the ego is an 'autonomous' and innate device which includes perception, language, memory, thought, motor development, etc. The autonomous ego does not depend on its instinctual sources nor on its relationship with the id and the superego but on its relationship with the external reality. For Pasche, the ego necessarily implies the reference to the drives.

[5] See Pasche's (1958) and Mallet's (1963, 1966) authoritative contributions on the genesis of paranoia.

[6] Drs Françoise Monnot and R. Brémont were two psychiatrists and psychoanalysts who were close collaborators of Francis Pasche at the Centre des maladies mentales et de l'encéphale [Centre of Mental Illnesses and of the Encephalon] of Sainte-Anne psychiatric hospital (Paris, 14th arrondissement).

Why these representations of a headless body if not because is he thereby signifying that he was reduced there to looking at himself without the aid of a mirror, without the aid of the mother's body looking at him?

This shield that the mother gives the child is indeed the barrier that separates them, which opposes their re-fusion, which prohibits the child from returning to the mother's womb, prevents him from entering fully into the maternal structure, the maternal system.

We have not entirely finished with the mirror–shield. It has the particular characteristic of returning the images, the visual aspects of things as he has received them; it displays them a second time, it duplicates them, it reflects them. This is a capacity we do not have, but there are some sensory messages over which we have this power – those that we hear – for we are capable of exactly reproducing a spoken sentence. It is easier for us to be an echo than a source. We are in fact on the journey of speech, a transitional point, a stopping place at which our answers to the questions are then articulated; whereas in a certain sense an object image remains stuck in our throat, the word itself can enter through our ear and emerge through the mouth. This is very close to the one-dimensional space of psychosis (Pasche, 1969).

What is specific to language, as Freud has shown, is that it translates the relations of the real; certain contemporary linguisticians seek to demonstrate that language is essentially nothing but intrinsic relations. 'To spell', as Monnot's patient says, 'is to explain.'

Now if the primal scene is the unity of a *represented* structure, the feeling of interdependence in a unified whole, the founding intuition is given to us by our body. The psychotic cathects words rather than things and uses 'the language of the body', because, being unable to look at the surface of his body, or that of others, he is reduced to identifying with his internal structure and reconstructing a world inside it for better or for worse – a world that is modelled on functional correlations within the organism. The verbal image is much more appropriate there than the object image, one that always contains an excess of signifier for the use that is sought from it, which is just there in its facticity as duplicate of the thing that exists.

This language that moves so easily through the channel of our body, which is so easily converted from a sensory message into motricity, nevertheless remains an object of perception; it can be spread out before us, like our own image if we are speaking, and thus take the place of a shield – unless it is a mirror, when the aspect of our own body is rather blurred, perhaps lost, and the perception of the external world somewhat modified.

To consider the defence against the vision of a mother who is frightening because deprived of a phallus is to address the problem of fetishism. In relation to the advertising images of objects that can easily be taken as fetishes – shoes, tights, underwear and so on – it has been found that the fetish is always presented so as to illustrate with the fragment of the body that wears it a conjunction of genital organs, a summary of the primal scene; I think there is material there for research and reflection.

It should first be observed that all fetishes without exception are envelopes, enveloping surfaces, skins (even the 'sheen' on the nose mentioned by Freud) – satin, leather, rubber, hair – and that they are all made of dead or inanimate material. A hollow penis? In any case, a phallus, if the phallus signifies a symbol of power, for the fetish is in our view the vestige of a maternal *power*: that of procuring this protective shield for the subject.

This hypothesis does not prejudge any other meanings of the fetish (penis and faeces), nor does it invalidate the role of the father, whose deficiency allows it to be maintained or necessitates its emergence, but its origin seems to us to lie beyond its anal and penile meanings and to be their foundation. It also seems to us that the fetish is constituted, is pre-formed, before the father emerges as sexed and as a vehicle of the law; the child perceives the external world before he has located the maternal emblems and attributes.

There is no doubt that the fetish, with its support, mimics the primal scene, in fantasies, the to-ing and fro-ing, this game of hide-and-seek, concealment and exhibition, presence and absence, idealisation and faecalisation, adoration and mistreatment – a primal scene in which the fetishist participates with a total mastery.

But what of the fetish itself, the envelope, the lid placed over this hole – the site of lack, that of the mirror-shield, the maternal penis, the protagonist of the primal scene and the father? We would argue that it results from the transposition and rotation of the sagittal plane of the primal scene (itself modelled on the interrelations of the organism) into a frontal plane, raised opposite, and as a result perceptible. The subject has stepped out of the picture and placed it in front of himself.

What about the canvas? It is still made of inanimate matter that used to be alive, or a product of something living – leather, silk, cotton, latex, hair and its imitation – a dead structure that retains the skeleton of its organisation. The petrifaction by Medusa is the perfect metaphor for the constitution of a fetish: the victim keeps his shape, and for ever. The fetish can readily be seen as an autoscopic image, an X-ray portrait of the subject.

Should we venture to suggest that reductive systems – mechanistic, dialectical, structuralist – when they exclude every contingency, result from the 'stuffing', the fetishisation, of the real?[7] Perseus can make bad use of his trophy; it is a weapon of the tyrant or the terrorist.

The fetish is only a shield; it is not a mirror, a skin without a gaze.[8] The fetishist can find in it the model of his internal organisation, but he cannot allow it the least breath of life on pain of seeing it transformed into an

---

[7] As previously, this is in the sense in which dead animals are stuffed.
[8] This importance of the gaze and the skin has not escaped Racamier in his substantial 1962 article, 'Propos sur la réalité dans la théorie psychanalytique' [Statements on reality in psychoanalytic theory].

'influencing machine' and himself turned into a psychotic, which is the very outcome from which the fetish should protect him.

This is why the fetish – whether stockings, pants, an essay on epistemology or a work of sculpture or music – must be distinguished from the object of beauty and from the intellectual or aesthetic masterpiece to which it is in fact so akin (as I have tried to show elsewhere) but that it could not become without a deep mutation, a true metamorphosis.

What is lacking is the reflection – in other words, the mother's gaze. It is a specific gaze that I have attempted above to define, in the order of which the child is seen and situated, neither desired, nor hated, simply seen and held in place, considered, a gaze in which he sees himself and the rest of the world, for this gaze keeps nothing back for itself, it scrupulously renders everything it receives – including the air that circulates between things – and it shows all these things to him; finally, as a result of this and above all, it gives him his freedom.

Reality is discovered in pairs; narcissism can no longer apprehend it as anything but the agent of its destruction. The object relationship (with its narcissistic and anti-narcissistic components), perception, fixation of the subject in its place and freedom go together.

Narcissism, denial of reality, ubiquity of the I (which, being all over the place, is ultimately nowhere) and necessity (fate) also go together.

Psychoanalysis has the specific task of demonstrating procedures and mechanisms, but it must result in the exposure of what we have called the personal symbol – in other words, the material form of each person's contingency, since the work of art is only such if an essential and unique contingency is revealed there.

The other path is that indicated to us by the man–machine. Now, however marvellous its arrangement, this rigged mirror is the inductive image of a destiny that Freud condemned as one of our two deepest temptations: the return to the inorganic state, towards which the bulging face leads us.

Perseus was certainly guilty of pulling Medusa's head from his bag to make use of it; the psychoanalyst must be a penitent Perseus.

References

Aulagnier, P. (1964). Remarques sur la structure psychotique. I. Ego spéculaire, corps phantasmé et objet partiel [Remarks on the structure of psychosis. I: Specular ego, phantasy body and part-object]. *La Psychanalyse, 8*: 47–66.

Braunschweig, D., & Fain, M. (1975). *La nuit, le jour. Essai psychanalytique sur le fonctionnement mental* [Day, night: A psychoanalytic essay on mental functioning]. Paris: Presses Universitaires de France.

Fain, M. (1971). Prélude à la vie fantasmatique [Prelude to a fantasmatic life]. *Revue Française de Psychanalyse, 35* (2–3): 291–364.

Freud, S. (1914c). On Narcissism: An Introduction. *S.E.*, 14.

Freud, S. (1915f). A Case of Paranoia Running Counter to the Psycho-Analytic Theory of the Disease. *S.E.*, 14: 263–272.

Freud, S. (1920g). *Beyond the Pleasure Principle. S.E.*, 18.

Freud, S. (1923b). *The Ego and the Id. S.E.*, 14.

Freud, S. (1924e). The Loss of Reality in Neurosis and Psychosis. *S.E.*, 19.

Freud, S. (1940a [1938]). *An Outline of Psycho-Analysis. S.E.*, 23.

Hartmann, H. (1939). Ich-Psychologie und Anpassungsproblem. *Internationale Zeitschrift für Psychoanalyse und Imago, 34*: 62–135. [*Ego Psychology and the Problem of Adaptation*. New York: International Universities Press, 1958.]

Mallet, J. (1963). De l'homosexualité psychotique [On psychotic homosexuality]. *Revue Française de Psychanalyse* (1964), *28* (5–6).

Mallet, J. (1966). Une théorie de la paranoia [A theory of paranoia]. *Revue Française de Psychanalyse, 30*.

Mannoni, M. (1967). *L'enfant, 'sa maladie' et les autres. Le symptôme et la parole* [The child, 'his illness' and others: The symptom and the word]. Paris: Editions du Seuil.

Pasche, F. (1958). Réactions pathologiques à la réalité [Pathological reactions to reality]. *Revue Française de Psychanalyse, 22*.

Pasche, F. (1969). L'anti-narcissisme [Anti-narcissism]. In *À partir de Freud* [Starting from Freud]. Paris: Payot.

Racamier, C. (1962). Propos sur la réalité dans la théorie psychanalytique [Statements on reality in psychoanalytic theory]. *Revue Française de Psychanalyse, 26* (6).

37 THE FETISHISTIC OBJECT RELATIONSHIP
Some observations

Evelyne Kestemberg

> A full member and former president of the Paris Psychoanalytical Society, **Evelyne Kestemberg** (1918–1989) directed the Centre for Psychoanalysis and Psychotherapy of the Mental Health Association of the 13th *arrondissement* in Paris and edited the *Revue Française de Psychanalyse*. She played a major role in the development of psychoanalysis in France and, with R. Diatkine and S. Lebovici, created individual psychoanalytic psychodrama, an excellent technique for adolescents who suffer from anorexia nervosa and for patients whose mental functioning is psychotic.
>
> Among her published works are: *La faim et le corps* [Hunger and the body] (PUF, 1972 – a seminal psychoanalytic study of anorexia nervosa, which she wrote with Jean Kestemberg and Simone Decobert) and *La psychose froide* [Cold psychosis] (PUF, 2001).
>
> Liliane Abensour wrote a concise biography of Evelyne Kestemberg for the 'Psychanalystes d'aujourd'hui' series (PUF, 1999).

Before presenting here some of the reflections that have led Jean Kestenberg and me to elaborate some specific modalities of the object relationship we have defined as fetishistic,[1] I should probably start by indicating how it diverges from Freud's conception of fetishism while also being deeply rooted in it, as well as in the current sense of this term. There is no need to return here to Freud's definition of fetishism (Freud, 1927e). We need only recall that it is based on the denial of castration, in which the fetish represents the lost or potentially lost penis and therefore guarantees the individual's corporeal integrity. Freud clearly demonstrates how such a denial of reality involves and translates a splitting of the ego and entails a psychic functioning that no longer conforms to the neurotic organisation. In short, castration anxiety can find no other adaptations than its own negation, certainly through the mechanism of disavowal, but also through the projection on to a *thing* of the quality of

---

[1] Presentation at the Congress of Romance Language Psychoanalysts on bisexuality (E. Kestemberg & J. Kestemberg, 1975).

narcissistic integrity that is necessary to the psychic apparatus. If we wish – as we have not omitted to do – to extrapolate from the terrain of the sexual perversions as such, with which the concept of fetishism is connected, to a broader domain of psychic functioning, it appears, even in this early description by Freud, that the fetish is in some sense simultaneously animated by the component of the projection of narcissistic integrity that it contains and disanimated by the fact that this narcissistic integrity is devolved on to *a thing*. Essentially, there is a shift from the person to the thing, and the internal psychic object incorporated in narcissism becomes an object in the material sense of the term outside the subject. It is on this basis that we will later return to the fetishistic object relationship involving the same animated/disanimated ambiguity,[2] but in a shift that is simultaneously opposite and essentially similar and that consists, in a relationship with a favoured person, in making it seem disanimated to ensure its perpetuity and to cathect it as a guarantee of the subject's narcissism.

Moreover, turning to Littré's *Dictionnaire de la langue française* definition of the fetish, we find the same ambiguity: 'object of nature, animal deity, wood, stone, crude idol' and, from Littré, to quote Voltaire: 'when my mother sold me for ten patagons on the coast of Guinea, she said to me, "My dear child, bless our fetishes; adore them forever; they will make thee live happily" ' (Voltaire, 1918, p. 80). From there the fetish naturally becomes the object of a veneration, adoration and magical power that is well-known. As for fetishism, it is defined – still by Littré – either as the worship of fetishes, or as 'the blind adoration of a person, his faults, his whims and also of a system'.[3] It should be noted that the term 'fetishism' is in fact fairly recent since it is owed to President Desbrosse.[4] We should also explain that the etymology of the word 'fetish', initially relating to fairies, witches and sorcery (Spanish: *hechizo*), has been contested and there has been an attempt to trace it back to *factum, facticium*, meaning factitious. In fact if we return to the fetish object in the Freudian sense of the term, this is very much a factitious penis that nevertheless serves to support the psychic apparatus in its sense of integrity. This latter sense of fetish has had a particularly remarkable fate in the psychoanalytic literature since many authors (too well-known to need naming here)[5] have emphasised this factitious quality that conveys both falsity and fabrication. In other words, the fetish becomes a product of the subject with the anal connotation implicit

---

[2] 'Animated' should be understood here with reference to the Latin *anima*.
[3] Fetish: 'objet naturel, animal divinisé, bois, pierre, idole grossière'; and fetishism: 'l'adoration aveugle d'une personne, de ses défauts, de ses caprices et aussi d'un système'.
[4] Charles de Brosses (1709–1777), a French magistrate and writer, was the first president of the Dijon Parliament. He introduced the term 'fetishism' in 1760 in his book *Du culte des dieux fétiches ou parallèle de l'ancienne Religion de l'Egypte avec la Religion actuelle de Nigritie* [The worship of the fetishistic Gods or parallel between the ancient Religion of Egypt and the present Religion of Nigritie]. The word fetishism was thus created to describe the objects of worship in primitive civilisations. [*Eds, this volume*]
[5] The most recent work to my knowledge is that of Grunberger (1976).

in the term 'product'; hence the notion of faecalisation that attaches to the fetish.

Let us conclude these preliminary remarks by noting that it is only very recently in history that fetishism has come essentially to denote a modality of sexual perversion.

If we briefly consider the evolution of this term I have just broadly outlined, it is impossible not to observe how the meaning of fetish has narrowed in scope, with its understanding remaining as rich as it is ill-defined.

I am adopting here in some sense an opposite approach, which seeks to restore to the fetish – or the fetishistic impulse – a much wider meaning than that of a projection on to an external object of qualities of perenniality, immutability, even magical power (megalomania) that usually form part of the subject's unconscious phantasies about himself in his relationship with his internal objects. It is therefore obvious that the fetish is the result of the idealising impulse intrinsic in the psychic apparatus, and fetishism is one of the modalities of this idealising impulse.

In his early article on 'The Fetish', Pontalis (1970) observed that fetishism was a distinct and specific order of world view and not only the result of the denial of castration, if we take this latter term in its most precise sense.

We follow Pontalis entirely in this regard and are inclined to think that the fetishistic impulse is a mode of being in the world and being towards the world that assumes, according to various psychic organisations, a greater or lesser economic value, one that is itself signifying and significant of the quality of each individual's psychic organisation. The spectrum of these fetishistic impulses is in fact very broad. It is first revealed in the privileged thing from which the subject never separates, a sort of habitual talisman, blessed not by witches and gods but by himself, which he cathects simultaneously as bearer of his object libido – loving and becoming attached to it – and of his narcissistic continuity in that it protects him from misfortune and death. Now, who among us can proclaim they are immune to such an impulse?

We easily find an equally common variety in the work of mourning, where the things that belonged to the deceased assume a quality of his presence and are intended to staunch the narcissistic and libidinal haemorrhage caused by loss of the loved object, as well as the loss of a part of oneself that this induces.

A more unusual expression of this is provided – based on which we have elaborated our reflection – by the quality of narcissistic guarantee devolved to the analyst by his patients, who at a particular moment in the treatment and even in the most absolutely neurotic organisations need *solely* to reassure themselves of the analyst's presence to assure themselves not only of his existence but above all of their own. Beyond this ordinary observation that could come from any analytic treatment, it is a fact that in various psychotic organisations this verification impulse necessary to the patient's survival assumes a major economic importance and occurs in the very earliest level of the relational modalities established between analyst and analysand.

It is hardly necessary to indicate at this early stage the introjective difficulties that this impulse conveys, since it is the presence of an external object that assures the presence of the internal object, even serves as one.

To the contrary, it should be emphasised that it is purposely that I have referred above to the relations between patient and analyst rather than to the transference, for we think that this modality of cathexis of the analyst cannot be merged with the transference in the sense that, although it may well be the fruit of repetition, it could not in my view have the connotation of imagoic displacement implicit in the transference concept – if we are to keep to the necessary precision of this term.

I realise how contestable this point is on the grounds that such a displacement of the imago is contained in the patient's projection of his internal objects on to the analyst. However, the critical question is then for us to define this imago and the extent to which it is the fruit of elaborated object relations, objects that are first internalised and then re-projected into the analyst. In other words, can we consider that in such a relationship the subject is the bearer of evolving identifications with differentiated and sexed imagos, or is it, rather, only a question of an indistinct ambi-sexed archaic imago that is somehow included in the patient's narcissistic cathexes, poorly distinguished from him and, furthermore, poorly organised as an object?

From another angle, I am also aware of the similarity between the psychic impulse outlined above and that which institutes the transitional objects described by Winnicott,[6] as well as the famous *fort-da* game. We should note, however, that they all contain a high proportion of narcissistic cathexes, since the first two are, according to the author, the meeting point between the child's projected narcissism and the imago, while in the other – the *fort-da* game – the child's capacity to make the bobbin return as a substitute for the absent mother plays not the slightest role in the degree of narcissistic reassurance and pleasure he derives from it.

Both these impulses ultimately concern the mother imago, but a mother who in my view at that point in the organisation of the psychic apparatus is poorly distinguished from the father, whom of course it contains but without according the latter a precise and objectally diverse status. Whatever the case may be, the mother is experienced there, essentially it seems not so much as a privileged love object but as the love object of which the loss constitutes a psychic danger – that is to say the disorganisation of the ego – in other words, an object included in the narcissistic experience.

My practice and my attempt at theoretical understanding of various

---

[6] In the same issue of the *Nouvelle Revue de Psychanalyse* as Pontalis's paper 'The Fetish', Bak (1970) emphasises this affinity in his paper. By contrast, Winnicott, as we know, emphasises the distinction between transitional objects and fetish objects. I essentially share Winnicott's view that transitional objects are the result of an objectalising 'animation' of these things, whereas the fetish objects (in the sense of the fetish penis) instead attest a 'disanimation' – in the precise connotation given above to the animated/disanimated pair.

psychotic organisations, which now extend over many years and for which, first with Jean Kestenberg and Simone Decobert (Kestemberg, Kestemberg, & Decobert, 1972), then with Jean Kestenberg and René Angelergues,[7] we developed the concept of cold psychosis, have led us to detect in subjects with such an organisation a modality of transference or pre-transference relationship that seemed to conform to this fetishistic impulse that I have briefly outlined above.[8] It is probable that other psychotic organisations and schizophrenics in particular have a tendency to 'exclude' the internal object, as Racamier (1978) observes, or alternatively to concentrate it, as in paranoia, into one or more persecutors, each external to the subject, to avoid in either case invasion for some, or persecution for others, by internal objects – and there is probably an analogy here with the fetishistic organisation of the analyst-object that occurs in cold psychosis. It seems, however, that it is worth determining and defining more closely this unusual status of the object in relation to other forms of exclusion.

In our work on anorexia nervosa (Kestemberg, Kestemberg, & Decobert, 1972), we described the immutable archaic imago bearing the patient's ego ideal that is represented by the analyst, and in our earlier article on bisexuality[9] we referred in the narration of a clinical example to the 'fetishisation' of the analyst discerned in this treatment. Since then, many clinical examples have led us to observe the presence of such a relational modality in the tentative analyses conducted with patients with a psychic organisation of the kind that we term 'cold psychosis'.

Despite the invariably rather unpredictable and debatable nature of clinical illustrations, I shall endeavour to provide an account of this that seems likely to elucidate our theme.

To do this, I am choosing a supervised treatment that was provided by a young colleague, which has a rather spectacular aspect that does not detract from its similarity to other apparently less eloquent and therefore probably more convincing cases. This choice is due to the fact that it would be difficult to report them for various reasons, such as an imperative for discretion or the excessively lengthy narration required for the limited framework into which this work has to fit.

This is the case of a young man aged around thirty years whose first name I do not know but whom I will call François.

---

[7] René Angelergues (1922–2007), a psychiatrist, had been General Director of the Mental Health Association of the 13th Arrondissement of Paris and Associate Professor at the faculty of medicine of the Pitié-Salpétrière Hospital. A good friend of Jean and Evelyne Kestemberg, he contributed to the development of the concept of cold psychosis corresponding to non-delusional psychotic states which are near the borderline states. He published two important books which show the close relationships between psychiatry and psychoanalysis: *La psychiatrie devant la qualité de l'homme* [Psychiatry in front of the quality of man] (Paris, Presses Universitaires de France, 1989), and *L'homme psychique* [The psychic man] (Paris, Calmann-Lévy, 1993). [*Eds, this volume*]

[8] A relationship that is probably fairly akin to what J. Gillibert (1977) terms 'the magical transference'.

[9] 'On the Misuse of Bisexuality' (E. Kestemberg & J. Kestemberg, 1975).

He has come to see the analyst because he is, he says, a fetishist. Moreover, he is suffering from a vague unease, an incapacity for relations with other people, for which he does not even really see any need. He also complains of sexual impotence, which preoccupies him all the more because he is totally apragmatic on this level and, finally, he wonders if he might be homosexual. However, he is interested only in his fetishism, or at least what he calls his fetishism. And this is what it consists in: at the age of thirteen years, when he was suddenly separated from his parents because of a journey they were making, he was taken to a tailor and, after being given his new clothes, he looked in the mirror, did not recognise himself and an employee told him he was no longer the same person. In fact, since then he has been a different person or to be more precise, according to what he says, he was born in the tailor story. He no longer has any memory of his childhood; ultimately, the very fact of having existed previously is open to doubt. In short, he no longer lives on anything but what he calls the 'tailor story'.

In this first meeting, he presents 'the tailor story' – which in the course of the treatment assumes various qualities in succession and sometimes simultaneously – as the basis of what he calls his fetishism, which consists in thinking about 'the tailor story' and masturbating. It is also not very clear whether these are masturbatory actions or only pleasure in conjunction with the evocation of this fixed image. The context, which is later better known, tends to support the second hypothesis. This is what displeases him, but he does not question the fact of being born in 'the tailor story'. This patient's psychic organisation at this point can only generate an extreme perplexity. However, it seems legitimate to suppose that it does not fit the precise framework of a sexual perversion and that it also exceeds that of a neurotic organisation. François is in fact in a state of extreme tension, suffers from acute anxiety that is inadequately focused on his 'masturbation', has difficulties in working and lives with his family – consisting of an aunt, two younger sisters and his parents – but in extreme isolation; he has only very infrequent and limited contact with his contemporaries, and he wishes to be quickly relieved of his unease.

Whatever the case may be, and without it being possible or perhaps even necessary to postulate a precise diagnosis, it seemed justified to form the hypothesis of a psychotic organisation, for which an analytic treatment proved to be unpredictable, if not impossible. However, François found face-to-face psychotherapy hard to tolerate, and it was difficult to determine how a psychoanalytic psychotherapy could be at all effective. It was therefore decided to try the analytic venture even if making recourse – if necessary – to some rather different technical modalities from those used in the classical treatment. This undertaking has now been in progress for around four years, and it has been deeply instructive for François, his analyst and me. It goes without saying that we could not relate its full complexity and abundance here, and we will be restricted to some moments and shifts that seem to us especially significant for our theme.

As could be predicted, during the first stage of his analysis – lasting nearly eighteen months – François manifested a major disorganisation on the couch, being invaded by an almost indescribable fantasmatic torrent. He fended it off and translated it as an extraordinarily abstract uninterrupted discourse with alternating disjointed thoughts, repeated references to an 'absolute body' (meaning his own) and . . . 'the tailor story', related in a fixity and a repetition that were simultaneously remarkable and wearying.

However, he never wearied of it, but kept going over it in every possible way while deliberately asserting that this was his only reality and that the analyst was an ear into which he would pour 'the tailor story'. It should be noted that 'pour' is not the word used by François (it is mine), for it is much too corporeal to be tolerable to him. Corresponding to the 'absolute body' are 'others' whose nature is in fact unknown to him, except in that it is 'normal' to be interested in 'others' or to enter into relationships with 'others'. But he does not know what the 'norm' really is, nor in fact why he should conform to it.

Moreover, if all that existed we would have to postulate that he has a desire, whereas 'he has no desire *over* other people', neither does he know what desire is or what others are. What he wants is to be able to relate 'the tailor story' to an ear. He cannot tolerate the slightest manifestation of the analyst's presence, and he drowns the few rare interpretations attempted (relating to the narcissistic reassurance provided him by the immutability of his memory of the tailor and that of the analyst himself) in an increasingly confused, abstract discourse into which some bizarre neologisms sometimes find their way. The analyst, however, persists by holding back and listening tirelessly to a burgeoning discourse that he finds extremely difficult to determine, in which it is difficult to elucidate the fixed themes that I have just indicated. However, François attends his sessions with absolute regularity, even gradually managing to stop getting up at times and adopting a recumbent posture. He never looks at his analyst, even in the short walk from the waiting room to the office. Little by little, however, his discourse becomes structured, and he comes to express repetitively – while maintaining the constant replication of the 'tailor story' – that if the analyst had his own external existence, if he were really a person, then he himself would have his own existence, would be a person, which is something he finds totally intolerable. He tries to express this suffering by rationalising it through the 'norm' to which he does not intend to be reduced, and the analyst takes advantage of this to show him the inherent contradiction in wanting not to exist while according himself an extraordinary singularity by comparison with all other human beings.

This interpretative elucidation of an internal contradiction initially generates in François an immediate response in the form of some minor acting out, then a flight impulse (brief interruption of the analysis), but in fact it entails a significant economic modification in the long term. This is initially characterised by such an intense anxiety that François becomes unable to lie down on the couch. This institutes a period of face-to-face analysis during which François untiringly clings to the impossibility of constituting either the analyst or himself as two separate people and also to the non-existence for him of any past prior to the tailor scene. He intends firmly to maintain that his interlocutor is only an ear by hoping – already an important shift, since he can imagine and say it – that he is not a receptacle. In his own terms, it is important that nothing he says should be remembered because then again this would be intolerable; it would mean that each of them existed separately in his own right. What he needs is for both of them to exist only through 'the tailor story' in its fixity, in the absence of any desire on either side, on the clear understanding that he remains an 'absolute body'. At that point in the treatment there is a minor incident: François encounters his analyst in the metro, does not talk about it right away, but suddenly outside the privileged, incorporeal place that he has organised in the framework of his analytic sessions, he perceives that his analyst has a real bodily existence.

He is deeply shaken by this observation. The analyst firmly but delicately insists that he can only act as he did. François then expresses the need he feels to break off the analysis. He came to tell 'the tailor story'. If it is about something else, he does not want any part of it. Besides, now he has told that story, nothing has changed and nothing can change, so why continue? It is possible at that moment to show François that it is he who constructed the tailor scene and also why he constructed it. In fact, its fixity and its oppressive presence enabled François to ignore everything about himself, while assuring himself, without saying or even perhaps knowing it, of his continuity; just as ignoring the analyst's bodily reality, his existence as a separate person, enabled him to ensure his analyst's continuity and to come regularly to sessions to verify it.

François said he was and wanted to be a fetishist. And although he is not one in the usual sexual sense of fetishism, he is nevertheless right, we think, in that this self-definition translates his intuition of his modality of object relationship.

In fact, if we reconsider, without dwelling on this too much further, how the analyst is cathected by this young man, the complex characteristics of the fetish and the fetishistic impulse are unmistakable there.

The analyst is strangely disanimated (even splintered), reduced to an ear, dehumanised and bearing the projection *on to* him rather than *into* him of the subject's latent fantasies – simultaneously included and erased by 'the tailor scene' – this scene on which the patient in its fixity and its constant presence confers the status of that by which he gave birth to himself – which thus confers life on him, ensures his narcissistic continuity (we recall that the patient constructed this scene to alleviate his parents' absence). However, he does not recognise that he produced or constructed it, he experiences it as something *external* to him, ever available, there to be picked up and resumed, even giving him a sexual *jouissance* (all qualities that are invariably reminiscent of the fetishistic accessory of the sexual perversions).

It should be noted that if François had stopped there, we would in fact have been able to consider whether this was an unusual form of sexual fetishism, without an Other. However, his unease, his anxiety, his desire – expressed in the negative – about relations with others, his need to assert his refusal to enter the 'norm', to be like others (which reveals in contrast something akin to the sense of the uncanny) enable us to perceive a distinct, more complex psychic organisation that is more psychotic than perverse and closer to a form of autism than to hysteria (we will return later, fairly briefly, to this last point).

He makes recourse to others – the analyst – whom he comes to see at his own initiative and gradually – while maintaining the tailor scene – displaces on to the analyst the same qualities that he had devolved to this – fixed, depersonalised, immutable in the regularity of the sessions, but above all the witness and bearer of his narcissistic continuity – a projection of the patient's megalomaniac magical powers.

It therefore seems to me that it is entirely accurate to refer here to a fetishisation of the analyst by the patient, intended to provide an adequate distance from the internal object (a latent imago that is still obscure) while using it without actually causing any narcissistic *disruption* – as would occur if an autonomous sexed existence were conferred on him – as well as a guarantee of that same narcissistic continuity because of the magical power that, in its non-mortal quality, is conferred on him.

The strangely intertwined and reversible pair – animated/disanimated – is certainly present in this relational modality, and the omnipotence of thoughts certainly plays a role.

I believe that by maintaining such a relationship for as long as necessary, the analyst provided an adequate narcissistic foundation to enable François to tolerate the irruption of an internal object into his previously closed universe (cf. the encounter in the metro and its consequences in the course of the treatment).

I will not dwell on what followed this privileged elaborative period (which was in fact fairly extensive) except to indicate that from then on François said painfully that if he had to relinquish that situation, this meant he had a history, that he had existed before he was thirteen years old, that he was his mother's and his father's son and that this was totally intolerable, that it reduced him to being like everyone else, in 'the norm' – that is, not existing – that this finally led him to relinquish a family romance that he suddenly remembered (or at least reported remembering), a completely ordinary family romance in fact – in which, of course, he was not his parents' son – but that he recognised had slightly preceded the tailor scene.[10] It was then easy to show him that having first changed his parents, he then changed himself in the tailor's mirror.

The analysis then took a different turn, essentially in that François could abandon his abstract and confused discourse for increasingly long periods.

---

[10] It would also be interesting elsewhere to compare and contrast this 'memory' and 'screen memories'.

He even rediscovered some early childhood memories and, in particular, of his mother enjoying dressing up her son, attaching great importance to her own dress, often changing her clothes. As for his father, François essentially rediscovered him through his timidity, his weakness and possibly his fear of seeing him die. François's 'absolute body' and his analyst's bodily non-existence were actually a highly effective and immutable guarantee against his own and his parents' mortality.

Here I will close the account of this case, which has since been greatly enriched in François's recovery of his capacities for neurotic functioning; his analysis, although still very arduous and uncertain for both protagonists, is now being conducted within more usual parameters. He has reached the point of wondering if he comes to his analyst to get dressed in the way that he used to be by his mother.

From this highly condensed and to that extent even rather inaccurate observation, we will draw some points that illustrate or serve our current purpose.

First of all, as concerns diagnostic considerations, we need to distinguish François's organisation from a schizophrenic state that cannot be excluded as a possibility. However, although many elements support this hypothesis, it does not seem – except by over-extending this nosographic concept – to be truly tenable.[11] In fact, in his current state, François's words cannot strictly be defined as the emanation of a delusional construction that would constitute a new version of reality that substitutes for the repressed reality that he finds intolerable. Although the 'absolute body' – his own and the other's non-existence as separate entities, the negation of their respective corporealities – are loudly proclaimed by François and are indispensable to his economic equilibrium, it is nevertheless the case that they do not involve a total belief on his part that would divorce him – outside the analytic setting – from the perception of his reality. Just as there are no signs of any dissociative processes, there is no invasion by the object that characterises schizophrenia. He fears it, but does not experience it as having occurred.[12]

We know little about François's behaviour beyond what he reports or, rather, hardly reports in the context of his sessions, but we are justified based on the few elements that he does relate in supposing that his mode of existence must be 'ordinary' enough for the gravity of his psychic mis-organisation to be only faintly apparent rather than severely disabling (currently he is working,

---

[11] Perhaps towards the end of his adolescence there was a period of 'floating' akin to an incipient schizophrenic state. It can be detected but not considered to have occurred and healed. The question can also be raised as to the evolution of a psychosis or an infantile pre-psychosis.

[12] I ought also to refer here, in contrast, to hysteria. I will not do so, though, to avoid expanding this work excessively. Besides, it seems to us sufficiently obvious that François's organisation could not fit into the framework of anxiety hysteria or conversion hysteria. This would require recourse to a concept of 'hysterical psychosis' that in our view is not very enlightening. However, this young man's hysterical potentialities should not be overlooked.

and his activity requires a coherent psychic functioning that is free enough for him to be able to carry it out efficiently).

If I have used the term 'mis-organisation' above, this is because precisely, despite the intensity of the anxiety, the vagueness of the discourse and the few neologisms to which I have referred, it is impossible to believe we are confronted with a more or less cataclysmic or chaotic disorganisation, any more than a reorganisation within a delusional activity that is sufficiently structured to justify any reference, it seems to us, to schizophrenia. The economic value of the fixed and constantly present memory of the tailor scene, like the use of the 'absolute body' fantasy and the negation of any common characteristic between him and other mortals, resides precisely in a highly specific defensive adaptation that consists in a fantasmatic or, better put, a conscious phantasmagoria designed to keep any conflict repressed and provide the hedonism of a conviction close to delusion, *which nevertheless remains in the order of the wish, of the possible but not of realism*. More explicitly, I do not think that François truly believes that he has no body other than an 'absolute body', that his analyst does not exist in flesh and blood, and that he really had no history before the age of thirteen. But if that were possible – and it is uncertain that it is not – he would be able, as he perseveres in doing, to avoid the Oedipal conflict (he was not born of a father and a mother, he has forgotten that his mother liked dressing him up, that she attached importance to his clothes, that his father was retiring, sickly and so on). He would be his own creator (he was born in 'the tailor story') and finally since he had no birth, he is not doomed to confront death, any more than his parents or his analyst are. Neither is he like any other human being (he is outside the 'norm'). We can see fairly well how this satisfies his megalomania and his pleasure in this kind of self-creation and how *this imaginary possibility that is both believed and known to be not entirely true* also enables him to preserve a flow of neurotic-style functioning: the intensity of his extreme but not invasive anxiety, the fear of homosexuality, the unease at having no relationship with his fellow human beings or his parents or brothers and sisters – all these elements testify to some unconscious return of the repressed. Altogether, all other things also being unequal, the immutable, fetishised (as he says himself) tailor scene comes to replace in some way the family romance – neurotic in nature – that he had constructed before being forced to resort to this conscious phantasmagoria to which he has clung and that has also enabled him to survive. To take up his own text, after the tailor scene, established almost as a 'machine for functioning', he did not completely lose himself in the mirror; it is more that he found he was different without any longer being easily able to know what he was.

This type of organisation that I have just described in François seems to me to be precisely characteristic of cold psychosis, with its components of disavowal, obvious splitting of the ego, but also non-restructuring into a richly elaborated delusional solution, whether stable or disorganising. There is also this particular recourse to a fantasmatic that is always fixed – almost immutable

– which allows the conflict to be obscured with imagos and confers a particular status on the object in its indeterminacy.

Moreover, the affinity with Freud's account of perversion, if we want to extend this concept beyond sexual perversion as such to that of the perverse organisation, seems to us to be equally well illustrated in François's observation, albeit only – apart specifically from its characteristic disavowal and splitting – through two distinct but compatible observations. One, which is major, is François's specific manipulation of his analyst, the ease with which he expresses his sadism by erasing him, for example, and by subjecting him to the harsh test of his discourse (all this without blame); the other, the masturbatory *jouissance*, also devoid of blame and conflictuality, leaving room only for a certain feeling of shame or, rather, of narcissistic inadequacy.

Returning now to my initial theme, I hope to have shed some light through the narration of François's treatment on the specific modalities of his transference or rather pre-transference relations with his analyst, at least during the long period preceding the economic mutation I have indicated.

Although I believe I have sufficiently clarified the fetishistic quality of the tailor scene, through which François verified both his narcissistic continuity – since he had given birth to himself – and his permanence, I believe I must place more emphasis on the modalities of cathecting his analyst that presided at the establishment and in an entire long section of the progress of this treatment. In fact, François needed to see his analyst as an incorporeal and ageless *duplication* of himself that was therefore immutable and eternal, which he verified without knowing or telling himself through the very regularity of the sessions. In a rather lapidary metaphor, we might say that he came here to touch his analyst as we touch wood in a conjuratory and magical verification without any obsessional thinking having truly been established. His analyst thus had indeed assumed the quality of a fetish – a talisman created, in this function, by the power of the subject who wears it, but also bearer of its creator's narcissistic continuity. The very attitude of the analyst who was able to submit to this mode of relationship by refraining from interpretative intrusions, nevertheless hypothetically possible, relating to differentiated or elaborated imagos, enabled François to feel, over time, secured enough in his narcissistic foundations to be able to move towards a less deeply regressive psychic organisation and, in direct consequence, to establish a true transference relationship primarily in the register of the maternal imago. We might say, however, that in reality the analyst, internally, even externally, behaved like this 'surrogate mother' guaranteeing narcissism as discussed by Winnicott.

In fact, François's words – probably induced largely by the regressive function of the analytic situation – well conveyed what can be imagined of the mother–child unity that presides at the origin of the organisation of the functioning of the psychic apparatus. It is in fact at this level and on this basis that we want to add some theoretical elements of a kind that we think explain the organisation of such a fetishistic object relationship – which we have detected in many other patients and of which François is only one of several illustrative examples.[13]

It is debatable here whether there is any need to name this fetishistic object relationship, which could be reduced to the projective identification described by Klein. It is in fact very close to it and shares many of its characteristics, to which, however, are added *a restrictive factor of immutability and a disanimated object quality that constitute its distinctiveness*. Neither of these two elements – neither the eternal quality nor the disanimation – is incorporated in the concept of projective identification. Furthermore, the analyst is not experienced as a container for receiving the patient's projected drives – it is only belatedly that François reached this point when he expressed the fear of his being a receptacle – but much more as an object *on to* which he projected his anxieties, even his unnamed desires – to use his own expression.

The proximity to Freud's description of narcissistic identification seems to have to be indicated, but probably – at least on the manifest level – in the opposite sense and in a more complex modification. In fact, François does not appropriate the qualities of the analyst-object. He lends it those that he attributes to himself: immortality, absolute singularity and incorporeality – or, rather, those that he wants himself, in order later, verifying them outside himself, to be able to reappropriate them.

All these elements seem to us specific enough in their conjunction to define a particular mode of ego functioning that presents a heuristic value in psychoanalytic clinical practice, even within metapsychology, and, as a result, some technical inferences.

To give a metapsychological basis to the fetishistic relationship just described, I must return to a hypothesis that I first advanced with Jean Kestemberg in our paper at the 26th Congress of the Romance-Language Psychoanalysts (J. Kestemberg & E. Kestemberg, 1966), revised and amplified in *La faim et le corps* (Kestemberg, Kestemberg, & Decobert, 1972), which concerns the self[14] and is specified in the current elaboration as follows.

We think in fact that *the self constitutes the first organised configuration of the psychic apparatus that emanates from the mother–child unity and succeeds it*. It represents that which at the level of the subject – the mother's object – belongs to the subject itself, at an extremely early stage, before the subject–object distinction is established. This implies that at the level of primary auto-erotism, at the level of the organisation of narcissistic continuity, the object relationship is included, by the very fact that the subject – the child – is an object for the

---

[13] We have also detected it at certain times in the analysis of subjects with character neuroses.
[14] In the context of this work, I cannot detail the similarities and differences from the self described by Winnicott nor by Kohut. Besides, the reader will probably have noticed them himself.

mother and that the latter's fantasies modulate the beginnings of the child's psychic organisation.[15]

The self is thus an organised psychic configuration in which the child can discharge and express an excitation, while exercising his own capacity to subdue this excitation, in the mother's presence or absence. Accordingly, this is an auto-erotic organisation that contains the object without its being represented or imagined as separate there. The contribution of this object to this psychic configuration stems from the fact that in the mother–child unity, the child is an object for the mother.

The psychic apparatus and the capacity to hallucinate pleasure are already organised at the level of this first configuration that is the self.[16] At this level, however, it seems that the self is not strictly an object of representation for the child, but that feelings or particular affects take root there that differ from those that emanate from what comes from the mother or from outside. In that capacity, they prefigure the distinction between ego–I and the object before the internal object is experienced as such (i.e. as different from the subject), and then the imagos that are differentiated within the ego come to be organised. *This self cannot be identified with the ego, which both remains the organising agency and represents within that same agency the source of the feeling of the I.* Furthermore, this psychic configuration, which coincides neither with the ego nor with the object, endures throughout existence. It probably does not give rise to a precise figuration but becomes the anchor of particular feelings and affects that are experienced and probably not represented as such, although articulated,[17] which in their destiny will evolve in various directions and introduce a different weight in the psychic apparatus according to both the vagaries of existence and the modalities of various psychic structurings.

Known by its products, which I am going to enumerate briefly, the self represents the subject's narcissistic continuity within an auto-erotic operation

---

[15] It seems superfluous to indicate that I am basing this essentially on Freud's 'Formulations on the Two Principles of Mental Functioning' (1911b), but also on an entire tradition of works and experiences in child psychoanalysis that today no longer permit any doubt as to the importance of modalities of the mother's cathexis of the child for the organisation of the latter's psychic apparatus.

[16] The modalities and qualities of the mother's cathexis of the child and the way in which he responds to them – that is, internalises them – are entirely obvious from bodily exchanges, touches, looks and so on, and direct observations convey them eloquently. They are now well known. Moreover, I am glad to mention here an encounter with the thought of Pasche who, at the 38th Congress of Romance-Language Psychoanalysts in Florence in 1978 postulated that one of the aporias of psychosis was due to the fact that the child is a fetishistic subject for the mother. Thus, starting from the mother, he discovers a hypothesis close to our own, and we think that specifically in the case of the schizophrenics to whom he refers, the quality of the mother's cathexes burdens the organisation of the child's self. In our forthcoming work (E. Kestemberg, 1981), we also propose to study at length both the contribution of the mother's cathexes for the organisation of the self and, above all, in the course of the destiny of the self, the different status assumed by the object, which is specific to the various organisations of psychosis (schizophrenia, paranoia, etc.).

[17] This poses the problem of the representation of the self at the preconscious level. It is impossible to address it here, but this problem will be discussed by us in the above-mentioned work (E. Kestemberg, 1981).

in which the object, not represented or perceived as such, is included in some sense 'in outline' and can constantly be shaped by the subject.

One of the products of this self is the pleasure of functioning that is first expressed in the hallucinatory satisfaction that is constitutive of the psychic apparatus. I will not dwell on this because it is described at length in Kestemberg and Kestemberg (1966).

Another form of the destiny of the self during development is transcribed, it seems to me, in the 'personisation' process described by Racamier (1965), who puts more emphasis on the structured developmental aspects. We can also to a certain extent relate to the self the organisation of the ego-ideal that is overdetermined by the pleasure of functioning, the subject's many representations of his body images and the sense of himself that underlies them – that is to say, the organised, developmental and evolving representation of his person.

The fetishistic object relationship described above is also one of the products of the self and contributes to organising the ego-ideal.

If I may use metaphorical language – with both the affinity and the simplification of metaphor – it seems that from the self, the subject expels[18] the object outside himself, but an object that is not separate from him and whose external existence attests his own. This fetish object is not the mirror of the subject because he does not see himself in it; it is, rather, the external duplication of the subject through which he verifies both his existence and his ideality (which makes it bear the subject's megalomania and acquire an imperishable quality). As we have shown, this duplication includes an immutable, eternal, incorporeal quality and alleviates the effraction constituted for the psychotic subject by the very existence of an internal object that invades him or breaks his narcissistic continuity.

This modality of organisation of the relationship to *the internal object, not instituted as such, both outside the subject and representing it*, is one of the adaptations of the impasse into which every psychotic individual is driven. I even think that in a great many cases, as, for instance, for François, *this particular modality of object relationship makes it possible to dispense with the delusion – while retaining its defensive and hedonic quality – or with a cataclysmic disorganisation*.

However, I would not restrict to psychotics the capacity for a fetishistic object relationship, nor the recourse to the self implicit in such a relationship. Although its benefit and economic value seem obvious for a better understanding of the horrifying universe of the autistic child, it seems to me that there is

---

[18] A certain similarity will be observed here with the exclusion process described by Racamier, with one slight difference that the author refers to an organised internal object, whereas we are dealing with an object included in the self, experienced as a part of the subject. Furthermore, there is probably some proximity to the externalisation process proposed by A. Freud (1965) and Judith S. Kestenberg (1968). However, the difference is noteworthy because these authors are basing this externalisation on the superego – projected externally – whereas the process we describe occurs in development long before the organisation of the superego – heir to the Oedipus complex. However, Judith Kestenberg's standpoint is, in my view, more subtle and complex than that of Anna Freud's in this respect.

no individual who cannot – whatever the stability of his psychic organisation – make recourse to it either on a minimal basis – as, for example, with the lucky-charm object – or in a more complex way at a particular moment in his life. This amounts to putting forward the hypothesis that, in the order of object relations, particular modalities are organised and endure that were established early within primary auto-eroticism, in which the object, included in the subject rather than perceived as separate, can be excluded from it, rejected externally, and can retain the status of the subject's narcissistic guarantee. It finds itself in some sense by its very qualities taking on *within* the subject the 'surrogate-mother' role described by Winnicott, which is its internal reflection but bears neither its precise configuration nor its name. It is therefore inalienable, whatever the subject's affects of hatred and destructive potentialities. It is also not destroyed by his love, love and hatred being obscurely merged in this external projection of the subject's internal excitation. This capacity for auto-erotic and nevertheless objectal modification of the externally projected internal object seems to be able to serve as a point of access to the fixation within the psychic apparatus to which the subject could have recourse in a regression that is either temporary or very prematurely stabilised. It is provisional, for example, in a psychic trauma or during a psychoanalytic treatment and is prematurely stabilised, for example, in anorexia nervosa. When prematurely stabilised, it obviously translates a splitting of the ego, in a breakdown of exchanges with internal objects and relations with the fetish object, but it also provides the possibility of a 'free' functioning of the ego in what is often a rather large area, even the possibility of apparently rather unaltered relations with objects that seem to represent *imagos* and that are often, nevertheless, only *reflections* or *images* of them. This seems to be the case for individuals who have organised a cold psychosis.

Ultimately, the fetishistic object relationship that refers to the self seems to represent a mode of being in the world that is simultaneously close to and distinct from the narcissistic universe, which it nevertheless broadly attests in economic terms, while also being infiltrated by the objectal universe that has organised it, which in a highly specific way it organises in turn.

It is in this respect that its specific nature seems to me to have to be defined. I think this contains the foundations of the fantasy of fusion with the mother that is constantly observed in clinical practice, as well as a theoretical account of the symbiotic relationship with the mother, which differs from that proposed by Mahler (1968).

Within the ego, the self and the internal object – depending on age, various stages of life and their vagaries and the diverse psychic organisations that have been structured – find an adaptive modality that enables them to avoid or bypass the Oedipal conflict that is ineluctably inscribed there, which proves inaccessible to certain subjects and at certain times. The retreat to the heart of auto-erotic functioning, albeit with some recourse to the object that does not speak its name, allows I believe a useful, even restrictive 'transaction' for reducing the intensity of the anxiety (even extinguishing it) that is necessary for the subject's survival. It does not omit, however, to incorporate a triumphant *jouissance* – the component of pleasure without which the life of the psychic apparatus is impossible – at least in the fortunate cases. This same triumphant *jouissance* can lead, in other cases, to an *exhilaration with immortality* that leads to the 'Herostratus suicide',[19] but then the fetish object itself has been swept away and only the *jouissance* of immortality has remained active.

In summary, the concept of self and the hypothesis of a fetishistic type of object relationship seem to explain various modalities of narcissistic cathexes, amplifying the problematic concept of primary narcissism, both in its structuring quality and in its fatal aspects, from the moment that – inordinately 'enlarged' and hypercathected, economically stabilised in its immutability and its importance – it comes to crush and clasp the subject in his relationship to himself, the object and its shadow, its 'outline' existence having been erased.

In addition, considering the existence of such a relationship has significant technical implications in that recognising and respecting it, as long as the subject cannot help but make recourse to it, enables the necessary conditions to be established for an authentic transference organisation that is modifiable for those to whom it remains intrinsically closed either for a long period or intractably. In this latter case, such a relationship fairly often fosters, at least in our experience, a possibility of maintaining a modality of being in the world that is less detrimental and fearsome than the unshaken narcissistic retreat.

References

Bak, R. C. (1970). Le fétichisme [Fetishism]. *Nouvelle Revue de Psychanalyse*, 2: 65–76.
Freud, A. (1965). *Normality and Pathology in Childhood*. New York: International Universities Press.
Freud, S. (1911b). Formulations on the Two Principles of Mental Functioning. *S.E.*, 12.
Freud, S. (1927e). Fetishism. *S.E.* 21.
Gillibert, J. (1977). De l'auto-érotisme [On auto-eroticism]. *Revue Française de Psychanalyse*, 41 (5–6): 774–949.
Grunberger, B. (1976). Essai sur le fétichisme [Essay on fetishism]. *Revue Française de Psychanalyse*, 40 (2): 235–264.
Kestemberg, E. (1981). 'L'appareil psychique' et les organisations psychiques diverses. ['The psychic apparatus' and the various psychic organisations]. In: *La psychose froide* [Cold psychosis] (pp. 179–199). Paris: Presses Universitaires de France, 2001.
Kestemberg, E. (2001). *La psychose froide* [Cold psychosis]. Paris: Presses Universitaires de France.
Kestemberg, E., & Kestemberg, J. (1975). Du mésusage de la bisexualité [On the misuse of bisexuality]. *Revue Française de Psychanalyse, 39* (5–6). 875–883

---

[19] To immortalise his name, Herostratus set fire to the temple of Ephesus on the same night that Alexander the Great was born; the Ephesians tried to thwart Herostratus by swearing death to anyone who mentioned his name, but the decree only gave increasingly wide publicity to his act.

Kestemberg, E., Kestemberg, J., & Decobert, S. (1972). *La faim et le corps. Une étude psychanalytique de l'anorexie mentale* [Hunger and the body. A psychoanalytic study of anorexia nervosa]. Paris: Presses Universitaires de France.

Kestemberg, J., & Kestemberg, E. (1966). Contribution à la perspective génétique en psychanalyse. Quelques propos en guise d'introduction [Contribution to the genetic perspective in psychoanalysis: A few remarks as an introduction]. *Revue Française de Psychanalyse, 30* (5–6).

Kestenberg, J. S. (1968). Outside and inside, male and female. *Journal of the American Psychoanalytic Association, 16*: 457–520.

Mahler, M. S. (1968). *On Human Symbiosis and the Vicissitudes of Individuation. Volume I: Infantile Psychosis*. New York: International Universities Press.

Pasche, F. (1978). L'aporie ou l'angoisse et la première défense contre [Aporia or anxiety and the first defence against it]. *Revue Française de Psychanalyse, 42* (5–6): 987–990.

Pontalis, J.-B. (1970). Le fétiche. *Nouvelle Revue de Psychanalyse, 2*: 5–15.

Racamier, P.-C. (1965). Le moi, le soi, la personne et la psychose. Essai sur la personnation [The ego, the self, the person and the psychosis: About personisation]. *L'Evolution Psychiatrique, 28; 72* (2007): 659–679.

Racamier, P.-C. (1978). *Paradoxes des schizophrènes* [Paradoxes of schizophrenics]. *Revue Française de* Psychanalyse, *42* (5–6): 877–969.

Voltaire, F.-M. (1918). *Candide*. New York: Modern Library.

38 SUFFERING AND SURVIVING IN PARADOXES

Paul-Claude Racamier

Paul-Claude Racamier (1924–1996) was a full member of the Paris Psychoanalytical Society and a former director of the training Institute of the Society. One of the leading figures behind the College for Family and Group Psychoanalysis, he was also the first and foremost French analyst to treat psychotic patients, reformulating how treatment should be undertaken and with what outlook; these developments can be seen throughout his published work: *Le psychanalyste sans divan* [The psychoanalyst without a couch] (Payot, 1970); *Les schizophrènes* [Schizophrenics] (Payot, 1980); *Anti-oedipe et ses destins* [Anti-Oedipus and its vicissitudes] (Payot, 1989); *Le génie des origines. Psychanalyse et psychoses* [The genius of origins: Psychoanalysis and the psychoses] (Payot, 1992); and *L'inceste et l'incestuel* [Incest and the incestual] (Payot, 1995).

They have wounds to their soul, which bleed in silence. They have undergone devastations of the ego in which the suffering itself has been devastated. They emerge from it like walking wounded of the psyche.

They have almost perished. However, they are surviving. They are not truly living in this life; we do not feel they are entirely of this world.

They come to us, sometimes caparisoned with psychotic defences and proliferations, sometimes instead almost naked in a skinless ego, with almost nothing to express but their difficulty in living, and are thus even more moving. Sometimes they even appear shrivelled inside, as if they were ashamed of their suffering; in fact, they hardly know it because it remains so obscure and almost imperceptible. It is as if they chiefly fear confronting an unfathomable void or losing a treasure that is so deeply buried that it has become almost inaccessible to them.

They come with the faintest flicker of hope. When we receive them, we feel the shadow of an obscure malaise. It is true that survivors are not always easy to be near to.

Is it even the case that to greet them fully, there may be a few missing links in the mesh of our psychoanalytic understanding?

Wounds

There are in fact some patients who make us wonder how they have managed to survive. They are not the ones who are obviously suffering; they have no obvious discernible traumas (cf. Racamier, 1991) or even 'traumatosis' (Carel, 1990). These patients have been very silently wounded both in their libido and in their narcissism.

They have been stricken in these essential needs for narcissistic confirmation, formation and for free space, of which the basic satisfaction is indispensable to the very constitution of the ego. (They have therefore undergone what I call 'specific ego frustrations' – cf. Racamier, 1979, 1991).

These may have occurred through maternal 'abandonments' that were too protracted to allow the ego to maintain the continuity of its narcissistic cathexis, or fundamental and inassimilable inconstancies of these maternal objects that I call 'dual-aspect objects', which blow hot and cold without any connection appearing comprehensible or even imaginable; or they may have occurred through the persistent imposition of insoluble dilemmas, the clandestine transmission of uncompleted mournings, or early narcissistic and sexual seduction, but in all these secret cases, and many others besides, the developing ego is put into a *state of suffering*. While its narcissistic equipment and support are lacking, it is subjected to impossible tasks. Neither repression, nor ambivalence, nor even splitting, which early on form part of the ego's 'toolbox', can deal with these demands (cf. Racamier, 1991).

They exceed the capacity of the ego (by 'capacity of the ego', I mean the area covered by this ego and everything that it is able to 'work on').

The psyche is then inhabited by something that Tustin (1986) has termed a 'black hole'. It is in a state of suffering. I would like to adopt this concept of ego suffering in a sense close to that used in reference to the suffering of the organism. This organic suffering can remain diffuse, extensive and mute: it is as if there is a deficiency in living rather than too much to tolerate. The organism enters a state of suffering as soon as it is confronted with a task that it is far from able to accomplish; it lacks glucose, red blood cells, oxygen; it has too many poisons, urea, lactic acid and so on. It may even have received too many wounds; but extensive suffering is what predominates.

It seems obvious that these secret wounds of the ego, these hidden sufferings of the psyche not only require our full attention as clinicians and therapists (a task to which Bégoin, 1979, 1990, in particular has already and very opportunely devoted himself) but even require a theoretical complement.

In favour of a second principle of psychic life

At this point, I must now make a detour into metapsychology: it will be brief, and I will only present it in general terms. In fact, the struggling psyche's efforts for its own survival can assume such an amplitude that we are led to propose the hypothesis of a principle at work within psychic life of survival or survivance.

Survivance will designate the principle by which the psyche strives and works for its own survival. It is self-evident that such a principle could only assume its meaning, place and function with regard to the pleasure principle and in complementary opposition to it.

In fact, it will have been clearly understood that survivance does not work purely and simply for survival: to be is not a postulate but an outcome, the outcome of the discovery of the object and thus of the self; of the invention of meaning and what is thinkable, of the establishment of a sphere for its expansion. Survivance consists in all these things. And already we see dawning what will soon appear to us: it is impossible to find the object without losing it; to formulate thoughts without encountering the unthinkable; to expand without setting limits for ourselves. We already understand that survivance cannot proceed without an antagonist.

As for the origins of the forces at work, our theory is more familiar with those that work in the service of pleasure than in the service of survival: it goes without saying that for this, the preservation instinct, auto-erotism, the ego libido and the narcissism of life are summoned, but this is too vast a question to be debated here.

It is evidently the survival of the psyche that is threatened by the suffering of the ego. It is to its survival that this ego will devote the sum of energies that are still accorded to it. Confronted with life, non-life goes into hiding; confronted with survivance, annihilation. Should we not also consider that the survivance principle has its own indispensable corollary, which consists in a *principle of annihilation or elimination*? Here the complementary principle that we have already observed has appeared and been named. Some important works, starting of course with Freud, prove to us that the metapsychology of this dual principle (essentially narcissistic, and of life or death) is at our disposal.

One further essential detail: when the psyche has not suffered too much, the dual principle works smoothly; the object is invented, reality is established, pleasure is instigated, boundaries are born. (This is what I call a 'well-tempered anti-Oedipus'.) But when the psyche is damaged, when survival mechanisms, already striving for power, are elevated to omnipotence, only the mobilisation of narcissistic omnipotence seems able to safeguard the survival of an ego threatened with perdition. It is then that the defences rage. Let us start to present them in more detail.

Survival defences

While the libido pours forth at the source of excitations, reality serves as a model for limitation, and anxiety emanates from an excessive plenitude, which when it is not overwhelming gives a signal, and when finally the object has been discovered and the real is located, it is indeed pleasure that directs, followed like its shadow by the real. But when the ego remains to be found or preserved, when the object is elusive, when the anxiety is that of non-life and can culminate in *psychic agony* (cf. Racamier, 1985), it is survivance that must enter the scene. Whereas the quest for pleasure and its satisfaction are not too difficult to conceive, if only because they occur and run for a long period, by contrast the processes for inventing and safeguarding the ego have an entirely different complexity, if only because here the passage of time is far from running in a single direction, and it even seems permissible for it to run in the opposite direction.

In fact, it would be simplistic to take the view that Eros worked solely in the service of survivance and Thanatos in the service of its opposite. It would be another equally damaging simplification to believe that the principle of elimination only brings self-destruction. *Its elimination means as much to the ego as its survivance* (see Racamier, 1989, concerning anti-Oedipus, the complementary aspects of self-procreation and destruction). I will even go so far as to say without too much hesitation that the ego that suffers is one that is overwhelmed both in its survivance *and* in its elimination: it is an ego that cannot tolerate being erased without risking its own destruction; insomnia and the incapacity to dream both form an intrinsic part of this intolerance.

As for the *economy*: just as there are various economies of pleasure, of which there is a pathology (in the neuroses and the erotic perversions), there are also various economies of survivance, again with their own pathology (in the psychoses and states of 'parapsychotic' suffering). Survivance is mobilised under different pressures and distinct intensities – whether with violence in situations of defeat in which the endangered psyche has to defend its existence, or in the universal situation (less dramatic but no less acrobatic) of the discovery of self in which the psyche in labour invents an existence for itself. (It is in fact this conflict of origins that I have set out to formulate by studying *Anti-Oedipe*; Racamier, 1972.)

These new details concerning the issues, the bipolarity and the economies of survivance enable us to present its elective defence mechanisms. Most of these are well-known and have already been mentioned. Even if they are encountered in an attenuated form in more recent contexts, they show some remarkable common characteristics here.

They tend *to mobilise the entire psyche*: it is true that they work on matters of life and death.

They operate by *expulsion*, exportation (like massive projection and violent identificatory projection) and by *amputation*, like splitting and denial: in order to escape better the psyche gets rid of everything that encumbers it and might threaten it; it jettisons it; the more threatened it feels, the more it jettisons. This extends to amputating some of its own domains – even some highly valuable ones. This is how 'reason' and 'reality' come to be thrown overboard; it is then that the manifest 'madness' appears in its most unusual light: as a means of self-preservation for a psyche on the point of being lost. It is true that the coherence of the secondary process of thought matters less than survival; and if thought itself justifiably comes to appear as a death threat, then: away with thought!

Here a new feature thus appears: survival mechanisms are essentially mobilised *as a matter of urgency*. They also lead less often to compromises as we usually understand this (and in which every opposing force finds some advantage) than to *expedients*, whatever means happen to be at hand, destined in the best of cases to be replaced.

Final characteristic: the elective defences of survivance have the shared characteristic of *instantly summoning aid from the entourage*: they not only operate internally, they operate between the inside and the outside; it is for the entourage (chosen, found and designated as soon as fantasised, and even before being truly fantasised), it is for it to accommodate the projections, confirm the denials, absorb the madness . . .

One of the methods of safeguarding the endangered psyche combines all the characteristics we have just seen, even surpasses them. It is in fact the most complex of all; capable of protecting as a matter of urgency, it is also capable of being organised over the long term and thus of staying the course; it seeks to save the psyche, but knows how to work for its own discovery; it can be mobilised *en masse* but also work with subtlety. In short, it seems to manage better than any other to combine survivance and elimination.

So it is time to present this form of masterpiece of the psyche: paradoxicality.

An introduction to paradoxes

Everything is in place now to introduce the register of paradox.

It is likely that we have come to know it already. But do we yet know how to make full use of its positive characteristics? In fact, whereas paradox designates an unusual psychic formation, the paradoxical characterises a general modality of organisation of psychic life (what I call paradoxicality). Moreover, if the paradoxical extends to an individual's psychic life, it can extend to the life and relationships of an entire family or a group. Finally, although paradox can play a role in humour, we find it mainly and most powerfully exercised in confronting the most catastrophic anxieties: the danger of the death of the psyche.

Definition

The overview I have just outlined might suggest that paradox exists to some extent everywhere, and consequently nowhere. So we should return to some basic definitions.

Strictly speaking, paradox is defined as a 'psychic formation that indissolubly links and constantly relates two propositions or impositions that are irreconcilable and nevertheless unopposable' (Racamier, 1978, 1980, etc.).

What can be observed in this definition (that it will easily be imagined has terms that have been fairly carefully considered) is both the complexity of this psychic formation and its perfect originality. I will venture to assert that it resembles nothing else. Is paradox an amalgam? Not at all: the terms it combines (for example, and to simplify: near/far, alive/dead, yes/no, etc.) are definitively opposed. Does paradox therefore establish a categorical opposition, an absolute discord? Not at all: although the terms are irreconcilable, they cannot be opposed: neither ambivalence and its compromises, nor splitting or splintering and its fractures are apposite here. Does paradox therefore allow without challenge or contradiction the coexistence of assertions (of logic or fantasy) that initially seem contrary (as can clearly be seen in the ambiguity of the so-called transitional object, which is without argument simultaneously held to be mine and not mine)? Not at all: the 'propositions' are not adjacent, they do not adjoin, they constantly refer to each other ('if it's mine, it must be yours – but no, since this thing of yours is mine', etc.). It appears that ultimately paradox is that which organises the insoluble. Should we therefore abandon a quest that proves to be fundamentally impossible? Not at all: paradox, provided that it is fully accomplished, continues to appear in a relationship of dependency, which it locks in place by prohibiting its evasion: a perfect enigma, both inevitable and insoluble.

Towards the paradoxical

There is therefore not just one path to the paradoxical: there are several.

We might, as we have just done, adopt that which comes from the depths of the ego's misery. Paradox then takes over from the *discredits* incurred by a devastated, confused, splintered ego. Does it inflict blows on this ego with no response? So it might be thought; this might be perceived as a sophisticated way of disqualifying the ego, when we see it imposing some of these fundamentally insoluble enigmas we have encountered, which discredit first some and then other means that the ego ordinarily has at its disposal to accomplish its tasks, for this enigma is constructed so as to defy all logic and then tends to demobilise the entire secondary process, whereas it calls with the greatest insistence on the work of reason to condemn to inanity the transition through affect, fantasy, dreams or any other path that belongs to the primary process. Is it not, then, as if paradox, playing one register off against the other in the psyche and *vice versa*, far from bringing them together, paralyses them both, striking a double blow and making the ego turn on itself like a spinning top, having lost that highly valuable recourse of asking for mercy by saying 'pax!'.

However, while it is true that paradox, through this sort of double game with the strategy I have just outlined, constantly overwhelms the ego in some fairly skilful torments, it also knows, in danger and in the shadows, how to work for survival: against the defeat of the ego, paradox constitutes a supreme defence.

We find the most pleasing illustration of this in *humour*. (It is, in fact, through this humorous aspect that I previously undertook for the first time in France the psychoanalytic study of the paradoxical register; Racamier, 1972.) It is no coincidence that death and survival are explicitly implicated there. Freud had clearly demonstrated that in humour the ego pretends to appear weak in order ultimately to rejoice more in its victory. The impetus of survivance plays its part in humour on two counts: the ego puts itself in danger and goes right to the point of being thrown off balance before recovering itself like a plane coming out of a dizzying nose-dive at the last minute, in a final burst of energy. Previously I compared this humour to a daredevil. Steeped in paradoxical thinking, humour, this perfect sublimated offshoot of the principle of survivance and elimination, operates in a subtly pleasing way the staging of the death and survival of the psyche.

Plumbing the depths of the psyche, we could still address paradox starting from the *origins of the ego*. For everything tends to suggest that the ego (or the I) emerges from a founding paradox, a paradox that could be described as native, just as we refer to a metal – gold, silver or copper – as native. To formulate it in words, and thus risk giving it away, this native paradox consists in nothing less than supposing the object to have been discovered before having found it. Do we remember, however, that in the order of survivance the flow of time does not necessarily obey its ordinary inclinations? Our origins are certainly constructed from a natural, native paradox (cf. Racamier, 1990).

This should therefore come as no surprise: *we will rediscover some paradox every time the question of origins is poignantly raised.*

Paradoxicality

Three registers for the paradoxical

What we have so far observed through a series of glances is now going to emerge in its coherence. For it is highly evident that paradox, considered in isolation, is only one fragment of psychic life; it interests us less in itself than as a model: the model of a general functioning that I have proposed to call paradoxicality.

As we already know, paradoxicality simultaneously defines a mode of thought, a defensive system and a relational mode that resemble each other and are all modelled on paradox.

Since I have been working to construct this clinical concept and argue for its psychoanalytic value, it is the present work that enables us to situate paradoxicality as the main psychic organisation designed to ensure, in case of a substantial danger, the survivance of the psyche. It will be easily understood that it has the qualities we have already attributed to the survival defences.

Above all, it is comprehensive; it extends to the individual's entire psychic life; it is capable of being extended to those around him and of being applied to entire families.

It is initially *thought* that is governed by paradoxicality. We have seen how it exercises a sort of mental fascination that can extend to tying up the play of thought entirely in a paralysing net. Absurdity appears as the product of a defence; behind endless arabesques catastrophic anxieties are secretly lurking. If, as we have seen, paradoxical thought excludes the register of contradiction, it will equally eliminate the register of the passage of time. The question 'How in the unconscious?' may be asked. One nuance should be recalled, however, and it is critical. The unconscious is atemporal, while paradoxicality plays with time, for by denying that all things have an origin and an end, it denies the progress of time: it is anti-temporal. (Have we not observed among the properties of the survivance defences this literally reversing dimension, which is admittedly particularly difficult to conceive?) What is to be said of the weight of the real in a thought that can ultimately eliminate the passage of time? And above all, what is to be said of fantasy (as well as the dream) before the paradoxical? Paradoxicality is probably the only organisation of the psyche that can radically immobilise the circulation of fantasies without paralysing it completely. We can easily tell ourselves that an important therapeutic game has been won from the moment that a fantasy reappears from the imbroglio of fantasies that was stifling it.

Paradoxicality will not stop in its tracks: it organises the *relationship*; it is seen in the paradoxical transference (Anzieu, 1975) in which every exchange comes to seem to lack an outcome, in which the therapeutic alliance reverses into its opposite, in which the object is summoned only to be denied, in which the projective endeavour does not even seem necessary for attraction to revert to repulsion.

This is the place to mention (although the space allocated here will not enable us to develop its vast domain) the capacities of *familial* and even group *extension* of paradoxicality. I do not know any organisation as capable as paradoxicality of organising psychic life, the relational and defensive system of an entire family, even an entire group. Thoughts without origins or terms can be seen circulating there, without their internal contradictions and fundamental absurdities being apparent or even possible to locate: nothing is true, nothing is false, nothing belongs to anyone, everything belongs to everyone. And what is the reason for this system so strongly organised in its apparent absurdity, this system from which, an essential fact, any individual or collective fantasy is forcibly excluded – why, if it is not by the struggle against catastrophic anxieties about birth and separation, in short: psychic death (cf. the works of Anzieu, 1985; Decobert, 1985; Caillot & Decherf, 1985; Racamier, 1985).[1]

For finally, paradoxicality is organised as a *defensive system*, one of the most powerful known; I think I have shown elsewhere that this defence is exercised simultaneously against conflictuality and ambivalence, against individualisation, separation and mourning (Racamier, 1980).

Deep within the paradoxical ligatures, what is always obscurely and tenaciously in play is the anxiety about the wrench, death, including the inevitable uprooting represented by psychic birth, as well as the endless birth constituted by growth (it is too often forgotten that growth is a mourning, as Bégoin, 1990, rightly reminded us).

An unusual form of psychic binding

We are familiar with the order of opposites in psychic life: with ambivalence at the level of the drives, *conflict* at the level of the ego, and contradiction at the secondary-process level. Paradoxicality does not belong to that order; it not only differs from it, it opposes it; it is anti-ambivalent, anti-contradictory and anti-conflictual.

We also know in psychic life the order of intractable antagonisms; insoluble oppositions; we know splitting and, worse still (cf. Racamier, 1980), splintering; in short, we know (cf. Bion, 1959) the order of the *broken bonds* in the psyche. Paradoxicality does not belong to that order either: it distorts but does not break.

It belongs to an order of its own that is totally original. If it could be defined in only one word, it would be *knotting*. The characteristic of the paradoxical is the knotting, sometimes to the point of inextricability, of irreconcilable psychic propositions; *the art of the paradoxical is that of the bond inside the non-bond*: a psychic formation that is neither binding, nor breaking, but simultaneously conjunction and disjunction.

Will that suffice to remind us that the paradoxical is situated in a highly specific way between the life and the non-life of the psyche?

It is well known that there are several forms of psychic energy and, in particular, that some are free and others are bound: should another category of *knotted* energies be allowed?

---

[1] These authors worked together, and they participated in a congress on family psychoanalysis in Toulouse in 1985; their papers were published in a special issue of *Gruppo, Revue de Psychanalyse Groupale*.

Paradoxes and schizophrenia

No one is unaware of it and everyone knows it: a knot can be more or less tight. Its tightness varies according to the importance of the function devolved to it. The same applies to paradoxes and paradoxicality.

At the point we have now reached, we have understood one thing: between conjunction and disjunction, paradoxicality organises a specific form of the psyche's struggle for its survivance. What we now easily understand is that the paradoxical knotting will be all the tighter, the more burdensome and difficult the issue of survivance has been.

An open paradox, a paradoxical knotting that allows some play, is the one we have encountered in humour: the ego plays with its defeat, which it is capable of imagining and even staging, to triumph over it; to that end, and in memory of every possible and past defeat, it uses the paradoxical mode. A fantasy circulates; a choice continues to be proposed; a sphere of play is demarcated; an exchange is possible.

It is an entirely different matter when the psyche is defending its life, confronted with essential anxieties that constantly torment it. Nothing will be able to confront this but a tight paradoxicality; here it is a matter of immersing the ship, battening down the hatches, blocking the exits and preventing the suffusion of past anxieties. Paradoxicality is exercised in a tight way. Nothing in the psyche may escape it. The typically paradoxical struggle against conflictuality is exerted with the greatest intensity. It is simultaneously, as we have seen, a struggle against ambivalence, against any idea of ending, against separation, against mourning. At the depths of everything, it is a struggle against non-life.

But paradoxicality is not so simple that it only puts survivance in play. It should therefore come as no surprise here that non-existence is employed by paradoxicality to be placed in the service of existence, as we can clearly see: what health (as in humour) hums in a low voice, pathology shouts at the top of its voice.

For as we have clearly understood, we have just imperceptibly entered the register of the schizophrenias – a domain so well-trodden by me that here I will merely cross it in long strides; we are fully prepared for understanding its complex detours.

It is not only conflictuality (internal conflictuality, of course) that will need to be combated, determinedly countered simultaneously in its origins, its appearances and its outcomes; ambiguity will also be subverted by paradoxicality (Racamier, 1985). This ambiguity is, as we know, characteristic of the transitional object and allows the simultaneous assertion that it is mine and not mine: paradox, by contrast – and this is a key difference – operates through a double denial.

In accordance with its nature, paradoxicality is exercised in *all* domains of psychic life: thought, the thought of the real, the relationship, the family, the defences. It even affects what is essential: existence. I have already shown (1978, 1980) that a schizophrenia attains the heights of paradox by succeeding in that of being while not being. It seems to me that this feat is elucidated by some observations on survivance.

Supreme luxury: schizophrenics manage to reintroduce some pleasure into the exercise of a defence of which the first function consisted initially in surviving.

Like every question of survivance, that raised by schizophrenia is a question of *urgency*. It must be asked: urgency of doing what, in a psychosis that is known to be built to last, as I often recall? There are, however, some chronic urgencies, and this is not the least . . . paradox of schizophrenias.

In fact, psychotic paradoxicality only manages to reign over the psyche by dint of a fairly solid arsenal: the same one that is obtained by the energy of survivance, reinforced by anxiety about disappearance and further reinforced by the full potential of primitive megalomania. For it is this omnipotence that enables the subject to make himself absolute master, in his innermost heart, of his origins (cf. Racamier, 1989).

Origins

Although in this denial of any capacity of origins, we hold the key to paradoxical organisations, although we know their effects and consequently we know very well the mass of aggressive energies that fuel it, and the force of unbinding it has available (like every type of denial), we are left with one more question: why this denial of originability and to what purposes? Might it be a way of mastering origins to deny not only that these do exist but even that any possibly might exist?

Let us be more explicit and more precise: I believe that it is those of our patients who have the strongest need to deny any kind of origins, who devote the most energy to this denial and who in order to adhere to it consent to so many sacrifices of thought, who remain racked by an inexpressible anxiety relating to their own origins. Have they only been given birth? With biological life, have they been bequeathed some beginning of a family romance? Have they been given that grain of primal fantasy that in turn would have enabled their own sense of origins to assume a form and grow in the same way as pearls? Parents who are much too set on denying their own sexuality, stifling it to the point of denying their own Oedipal roots, are parents who prove incapable of bequeathing this essential imaginary heritage to their child. They exercise a sort of intellectual disavowal of paternity or 'parenthood'. As for the child, a gap will be left in the hollow of his soul, which he will incessantly try to fill, to imprison deep inside himself and finally to deny radically. To the disavowal of parenthood that leaves him gaping in this way, the subject will respond – if he even has enough strength left to respond – by radically denying his own origins.

At the root of the denial of origins (of which the proliferation of paradoxes is one of the consequences) resides a suffering from not having been psychically engendered. (On this point, I share the thought and observations of Piera Aulagnier (1985 – chapter 39, this volume), who had deep experience of psychotic patients.)

Without entirely knowing whether I have succeeded in this (but do we ever know these things?), I believe I have done what I can to present the schizophrenias not from the perspective (usually the commonest) of an absolute strangeness, but certainly at the extremes (hardly liveable and yet liveable) of an essential, universal and necessary principle of the psyche: that of survivance. In short, to present them as a simultaneously unremitting and complex, absolutist and advanced means of defending while attacking a psychic survivance that is constantly under threat.

Will I thus have managed to reinscribe these psychoses and these patients in a double and necessary dimension of singularity and universality?

It is precisely the idea of this (formidable) universality that will lead me to make a visit that our path does not allow me to avoid: ultimate recreation, or supreme teaching, I don't know which . . .

Medusa, again . . .

There is, in fact, one visit I make almost every time I address the question of paradoxes: it is the visit to Medusa. Every visit to this exemplary monster brings us one further enlightenment concerning the throes of the psyche grappling with the most harrowing anxieties.

The first visit, in the company of Freud, had shown us in Medusa a paralysing personification of the horror of castration: does that forest of penises madly erected on her head not represent the fearsome negation of a formidably feared castration? To this infinitely multiplied symbol, we must add the terrible profusion of the tongue pushing out such a phallus, pointed from a mouth that splits the face on a horizontal rather than a vertical axis, as would be suggested by the image of the genital slit. But the penises have proliferated in vain: Medusa does not yet cease to paralyse, and this last image gives no encouragement to erotism.

Moreover, Medusa is terrifying not only because she is castrated; a second visit in the company of Pasche (chapter 36) showed us that the terror she inspires is that of very raw reality as long as its impact is not filtered by this mediating mirror that enables Perseus to see her without being pierced by her.

A third visit (in my own company) will have revealed to us in Medusa the incarnation of paradoxical powers; some opposites coexist in her that absolutely cannot be opposed, extremes that are eternally irreconcilable but eternally inseparable. Medusa elevates herself not only to the encounter of femininity and all sexuality, but more still to the encounter with ambivalence and thereby to the encounter with all opposites; it is thus that she concentrates into her murky gaze the paralysing omnipotence of paradoxes.

But beyond the horror of castration, beyond the paralysing impact of a reality without mediators, beyond the knotting and ligaturing grip of paradoxes, is there an even more fundamental horror? Further on, towards nonsense, towards unbinding, a new visit imposes itself, which will be the last. It must be made in the company of Vernant (1985): the Gorgon, Gorgô, this Hellenist knows her: he has taken the full measure of her terrifying strangeness.

Nothing fits with anything else in this monstrous body; hardly has one fragment begun to assume a meaning than it is immediately denied, demolished: un-bound. The author has clearly seen it: everything in the primitive Gorgô, everything is 'characterised by the unusual and by strangeness'; 'ordinary parameters appear blurred and syncopated'; male–female, celestial–infernal, high–low, inside–outside, 'all the categories overlap, intersect and merge'. Should we imagine (as we have just done) that the tongue projected completely outside the mouth, itself stretched like a split, represents the phallic sexual organ lacking in the female sex? Probably, and, I will say, simply yes: for this tongue comes from the womb, the split is horizontal, it opens the face from side to side, and it is through the neck that Medusa gives birth after her death. The Medusa is not only a repaired or altered anatomy but a broken anatomy; this is not even a dismembered body; it is an impossible body: what we imagine about it is immediately shattered by contradictions.

I believe I am translating rather than traducing the Hellenist's thought by saying that, considered right up to its final entrenchments, the Gorgon, masterpiece of the unusual and strange, of absurdity and monstrosity, embodies the unthinkable.

For this final visit, Medusa reveals to us a secret that is worth its weight in gold or horror: paradox is also a form of binding; beyond this machine for thinking without thinking, there is something worse, and this worse takes us back to the first few pages of this work – it is the unthinkable . . .

References

Anzieu, D. (1975). Le transfert paradoxal [The paradoxical transference]. *Nouvelle Revue de Psychanalyse*, *12*: 49–72.
Anzieu, D. (1985). Illusion groupale [Group Illusion]. *Gruppo, Revue de Psychanalyse Groupale*, *1* (Special Congress Issue): 110–113.
Aulagnier, P. (1985). Le retrait dans l'hallucination. Un équivalent du retrait autistique? [Retreat into hallucination: An equivalent of the autistic retreat?]. In *Un interprète en quête de sens* [An interpreter in search of meaning]. Paris: Ramsay, 1986.
Bégoin, J. (1979). L'angoisse catastrophique. Aspects nouveaux de la théorie psychanalytique de l'angoisse [Catastrophic anxiety. New aspects of the psychoanalytic theory of anxiety]. *Revue Française de Psychanalyse*, *43* (1): 89–96.

Bégoin, J. (1990). Vers une révision de la notion de souffrance psychique. Les problèmes de la croissance psychique [Towards a revision of the concept of psychic suffering. The problems of psychic growth]. *Psychiatrie Française, 5*: 7–16.

Bion, W. (1959). Attacks on linking. *International Journal of Psychoanalysis, 40* (4): 308–315.

Caillot, J.-P., & Decherf, G. (1985). La position narcissique paradoxale: la défense par l'oscillation contre les angoisses catastrophiques [The paradoxical narcissistic position: defence through the oscillation against catastrophic anxieties]. *Gruppo, Revue de Psychanalyse Groupale, 1* (Special Congress Issue): 47–67.

Carel, A. (1990). Le traumatisme à la naissance et les dysfonctionnements précoces au sein du groupe-famille [Birth trauma and early dysfunctions within the family group]. In A. Carel, J. Hochmann, & H. Vermorel (Eds.), *Le nourrisson et sa famille* (p. 99–112). Lyon: Césura.

Decobert, S. (1985). Spécificité de la thérapie familiale psychanalytique [Specificity of the Psychoanalytic Family Therapy]. *Gruppo, Revue de Psychanalyse, 1 (Special Congress Issue)*: 87–102.

Racamier, P.-C. (1972). *Anti-Œdipe* [Anti-Oedipus]. Paris: Ed. Minuit.

Racamier, P.-C. (1973). Entre humour et folie [Between humour and madness]. *Revue Française de Psychanalyse, 37* (4): 655–668.

Racamier, P.-C. (1978). Les paradoxes des schizophrènes [Paradoxes of schizophrenics]. *Revue Française de Psychanalyse, 42* (5–6): 877–969. Reprinted in *Les Schizophrènes*. Paris: Payot, 1980; revised edition, 1990.

Racamier, P.-C. (1979). Les frustrations du moi [Frustrations of the ego]. In: *De psychanalyse en psychiatrie*. Paris: Payot.

Racamier, P.-C. (1980). *Les schizophrènes* [Schizophrenics]. Paris: Payot (2nd edition, 1983; revised and expanded edition, 1990).

Racamier, P.-C. (1985). Ambiguïté, paradoxalité [Ambiguity and paradoxicality]. *Gruppo, Revue de Psychanalyse Groupale, 1* (Special Congress Issue): 114–121.

Racamier, P.-C. (1989). *Antœdipe et ses destins* [Anti-Oedipus and its vicissitudes]. Paris: Apsygée.

Racamier, P.-C. (1990). Schizophrénie et psychanalyse. Un éclairage en profondeur [Schizophrenia and psychoanalysis. An in-depth study]. In B. Boffet, *Œdipe et neurones. Psychanalyse et neurosciences – un duel* [Oedipus and neurones: Psychoanalysis and the neurosciences – a duel] (pp. 152–157). Paris: Autrement.

Racamier, P.-C. (1991). Blessures du moi et séduction narcissique [Wounds of the ego and narcissistic seduction]. *Bulletin du Groupe Lyonnais de Psychanalyse, 20*.

Tustin, F. (1986). *Autistic Barriers in Neurotic Patients*. London: Karnac.

Vernant, J.-P. (1985). *La mort dans les yeux* [Death in the gaze]. Paris: Hachette.

39 RETREAT INTO HALLUCINATION
An equivalent of the autistic retreat?

Piera Aulagnier

After qualifying as a psychiatrist, **Piera Aulagnier** (1923–1990) trained as a psychoanalyst under Jacques Lacan, joining him in 1963 and becoming one of the founder members of the Freudian School of Paris in 1964. She left that Society in 1969 when, with F. Perrier and J.-P. Valabrega in particular, she founded the Quatrième groupe (OPLF: Organisation psychanalytique de langue française), in which she played a leading role. With the Presses Universitaires de France publishing house, she was instrumental in setting up two journals: *L'Inconscient* (1967–68) and *Topique* (from 1969).

In her work, her initial inspiration was Lacan, but she gradually distanced herself from him and devised a metapsychological model that enabled a new approach to the psychoses. Her main focus was on three topics: issues raised by the psychoanalytic discourse, a metapsychological model for understanding the psychotic patient's relationship to language, and the practice and ethics of psychoanalysis as well as the conditions under which it can be handed down.

Among other books, she wrote: *La violence de l'interprétation. Du pictogramme à l'énoncé* (PUF, 1975) [*The Violence of Interpretation: From Pictogram to Statement* (Routledge, 2001)]; *Les destins du plaisir – aliénation, amour, passion* [The vicissitudes of pleasure – alienation, love, passion] (PUF, 1979); and *L'apprenti-historien et le maître-sorcier. Du discours identifiant au discours délirant* [The apprentice historian and the master sorcerer: From identifying discourse to delusional discourse] (PUF, 1984).

Hélène Troisier wrote a concise biography of Piera Aulagnier for the 'Psychanalystes d'aujourd'hui' series (PUF, 1998).

Clinical aspects

The rich dialogue between Frances Tustin and Donald Meltzer inspired me to study some of their works on autism. As I read and reflected on them – a retroactive process – one question was constantly in my mind: in my analyses, past and present, of adults presenting a schizophrenic problematic, which 'signs' or phenomena seemed to me to resemble most closely the experiences of 'autistic retreat' attested by these two authors in young children who also present a schizophrenic picture? This is a retreat that presupposes the abandonment, marginalisation and temporary 'dismantling' of defences that indicate schizophrenia and the 'retraction' of the psyche into preserved islets, these autistic enclaves. From my own theoretical standpoint, I would regard the equivalent of these experiences as consisting in a very specific type of 'hallucinated sensation': I hope that my proposed example will shed some light on the theoretical hypotheses to follow.

Hallucinatory phenomena are almost invariably present in the schizophrenic's experience and speech: they can be either predominant or unobtrusive, either constant or sporadic; sometimes we will discover them only long after our analytic work has begun. They generally emerge in the form of these 'voices' that accuse the subject of being homosexual, criminal, condemned to die or chosen for a sacrificial function. This is an accusation that is sometimes clearly 'heard', and sometimes interpreted from what the subject has 'seen' in a particular look, attitude or sign in other people or in the world at large. Another common type of hallucination concerns the olfactory and proprioceptive register: waves, pressures or impulses of decomposition that he feels inside his body, a bad smell he emits, which he may be the first and only one to perceive, or which he infers from the expression of disgust or remoteness he causes in those around him.

It is not this type of phenomenon that I am going to discuss, but an experience that can occur *during the session* in phases that do not include any hallucinatory activity. However, even if it were present, the type of experience that I am going to analyse is different and does not form part of the same structure.

All of a sudden, while the subject is talking to you, a total silence sets in; his facial expression changes, freezing, and there often seems to be a change in his breathing rate. Equally specific is the reaction triggered by these phenomena in the analyst, or at the very least, in my own psychic space: these are not the familiar anxiety feelings, fight-or-flight impulses, or – conversely – the excessively protective or approaching impulses we sometimes feel towards this type of patient. I would be unable to define this experience in any other terms than the sense of being struck by *a verdict of non-existence*. Having the feeling, confronted with a schizophrenic, that he cannot conceive of us as a separate subject from himself, distinct and distinguishable, as an Other corroborating the existence of another time and space, forms one of our familiar experiences. Less common but not so very rare is also this impression that we are at times – as Klein recalls – nothing more for the subject than an object that forms part of the furniture. To explain what I mean by a 'verdict of non-existence', what springs to mind is a term borrowed from Orwell's *1984*: we become an 'unperson'. Alternatively, I would say that we are 'struck' by a status that is in one sense mentally inconceivable for us; we become an *imperceptible* object. What is happening for our counterpart? Before trying to understand the position he occupies at these moments, I will explain why they can only be 'moments'. In fact, either the analyst, confronted with this subjectively untenable position, succeeds through his words, a gesture, or his behaviour in making a new effraction into the sensory world, imposing on his counterpart a perceptual reaction that makes him recognise that a thing, if not a subject, occupies a fragment of the space of the room he is in and the time in which he is living; or this 'moment' signals the subject's transition into an acute phase of his delusion and, above all, into a delusional mode that momentarily breaks any relationship and any possibility of communication between him and us. If we ask the subject what he can tell us about the experience he has just had, often he will say nothing about it, and the experience may have been so fleeting that he and the analyst each regain their existent status by 'erasing' this brief digression from their memories. At other times, he will talk about it spontaneously if it has been preceded by a long period of analysis – and thus if there is already an affective bond between the two partners – but even then, it is generally induced by the analyst.

What, then, has taken place? A 'noise' rather than a meaningful utterance, an indefinable smell, a proprioception concerning the inside of his own body, have suddenly irrupted into the psychic space and totally invaded it: the subject is no longer, can no longer be, has no longer been, anything but this auditory, olfactory or proprioceptive *perceptual function* that is indissolubly linked to the percept: the subject *is* this noise, this smell, this sensation, and he is *jointly* this fragment, and this fragment alone, of the sensory body, mobilised and stimulated by the percept.

It is in one sense the opposite situation of the splintering of sensory perceptions and functions described by Meltzer. The entire focus is on one zone or, rather, one sensory point that becomes the metonymic representative of all the zones and all their functions, just as the 'percept' that is self-generated by the psyche (hallucinated) becomes the metonymic representative of the world's objects. We witness a marginalisation of the ideational representation and the fantasmatic representation in favour of the pictographic representation of *a complementary object-zone*.[1] However, we must wonder here about the affect that accompanies the invasion of the psychic scene by this representation alone – an affect attested by the subject's expression, our own reaction and what he can tell us about it, once the thread of his fantasmatic and ideational activity has been retrieved and the other functions of the psychic apparatus have been remobilised. We will then discover that this type of experience was preceded and followed by a highly specific affective experience: it cannot be defined either as anxiety or as a feeling of depersonalisation, or as a persecutory experience – it goes beyond this or, rather, it is different in nature.

Imagine someone who has suddenly fallen into a precipice and is clinging with only one hand to the only fragile piece of rock jutting out. During this time, he will be only this conjunction between the palm of his hand and the

---

[1] We will see shortly how I am defining these terms.

piece of stone, and he must be nothing more than that if he wants to survive. As long as this tactile perception endures, he is assured that he is alive, that he has not started falling down into the void. In order not to fall, he has to avoid thinking of himself as 'himself falling' or fantasising the omnipotence of a persecutor wanting to hurl him down into the void. The tension of his hand and his grip similarly manifest the irruption into the psychic space of a 'hand-rock' representation, as the only thing present, and the sum of psychic work expended to maintain the exclusion, the marginalisation, of the fantasmatic representation and the ideational representation of the experience he is undergoing. This is a double exclusion that can never be extended because it presupposes the loss or dissolution of any external support on to which the psyche could project its relationship to the internal or 'internalised' object.[2] It is a momentary return to that which precedes any possibility of imagining the existence of something beyond oneself as the cause of the affect that is experienced, 'clinging' to the pictographic representation by which the psyche self-represents itself only through and as this capacity to feel the positive or negative affect, present in its space. The affective experience that is indissociable from its representation is the first 'existent sign' of itself that the psyche can constitute: the absence of this sign would simply presuppose the non-functioning of psychic activity.

To illustrate what I mean by 'existent sign', I will give the analogy of the relationship between an unused film and the image that is imprinted on its surface. For this impression to be transformed into a photograph visible to the eye, the film has to undergo a set of operations and procedures necessary to its development. I will also say that this affect that 'imprints' the intact psyche and this impression that then combines to set it in motion only become perceptible to the I through this developmental work that allows the transition from the pictographic representation to the fantasmatic production – a primary-process task – and from this to the ideational formulation – a secondary-process task. But let us imagine now that, by some manufacturing error, the film is not 'impressionable': it is nothing more than an amorphous substance, a 'piece of a thing', without use or purpose. It would be the same for the psyche if affect could not 'impress' it and make appear on it a representation that returns to the psyche its first and inaugural self-representation. Confronted with the irruption of an affect that eludes the conditions that would make it conceivable, as well as those that would make it fantasisable, and faced with a marginalisation of the primary and secondary processes, the psyche can only avoid its own annihilation, I mean the loss of every 'existent attribute', by hallucinating not an object but a *sensory perception*:[3] it will hallucinate the

---

[2] In the French text, Aulagnier, writing in 1985, explains in the footnote that this is 'an English term for the psychic mechanism that constructs the psychic representative of the external object'. [Eds, this volume]

[3] This is probably very close to Frances Tustin's concept of the *autistic shape*.

complementary object of an erogenous zone, more precisely a 'stand-in for the object' that only exists through its sole capacity for excitability. When the subject comes through this experience and can talk to us about it, we will observe in the process the remobilisation of this *enmeshed primary–secondary process*, through which it can apply a label and a meaning to an experience that has already occurred (I take the opportunity here to recall that there is always a time-lag between the hallucinatory experience and the discourse by which the subject explains it: either the hallucination is in process and the subject cannot talk about it, or he talks about it but always as if about the interpretation of a phenomenon that has already occurred). And what does the schizophrenic tell us about his hallucinations? *They* (the persecutors, in the sense this term assumes in schizophrenia, are always more vague and anonymous than in paranoia), *they* effract into his psychic space through this noise, this smell, this movement of his organs: the sensory experience will from then on be addressed in his speech as evidence of the existence of a persecutor: the sensory testimony becomes the evidence of the truth of the delusional construction. This is shown by this brief clinical example, taken from a book that has just been published.[4] Here are the terms in which one of my patients reported to me the beginning of the crisis that had led two months earlier to a delusional period that required her hospitalisation.

She: You've never asked me how my crises begin. I'd like to tell you what happened last time. A friend had brought me a dress of hers to try on; as soon as I put it on, I felt as if I had another skin on my body, I was frightened, threatened by a danger, I could no longer move; it wasn't anxiety. I know anxiety very well, I often feel it. It was the certainty of a danger, the experience of terror.

I: How is anxiety different for you from this sense of danger?

She: Anxiety happens there (she points to inside her body on a level with her breasts). Anxiety is a feeling of fright, the fear of a failure, of no longer being able to do anything. What I'm talking about is something completely different. It's something that proceeds from the anus, spreads from there like rays throughout the body; that's how anal haemorrhages begin (her first hospitalisation coincided with her sister's suicide who had had rectal surgery). What happens to me has to do with my body, I'm no longer thinking, it happens in my body; it turns into something else, something I don't know. What I feel can't be described, but it is close to terror.

I: Terror at the thought of dying?

She: I can't answer that. I don't know if I'm thinking about death at that moment. I re-live in my body . . . I don't know what I re-live in my

---

[4] Piera Aulagnier, *L'apprenti historien et le maître sorcier* [The apprentice historian and the master sorcerer] (Paris: Presses Universitaires de France, 1984), p. 164.

body, but definitely something horrible. Everything becomes anus or perhaps everything just becomes rays. Some people at the hospital talk about hallucinations, but this isn't a hallucination; it's something else, I don't see anything, it's something I feel. It's as if my body were experiencing that image; it's inexplicable.

Listening carefully to how this young woman rediscovers and reconstructs this event, we can distinguish two 'moments': what happens when she puts on the dress, 'the feeling of another skin covering her body' (she cannot speak about this fleeting sensation; it is something intrinsically inconceivable and inexplicable); for an instant, she *is*: a skin that does not belong to her? A skin that is no longer anything but this possibility of feeling contact with another separate skin? A content without a skin, flayed alive? We do not know; nonetheless, in this type of experience the frozen dimension of the body and psyche is a constant (unless it triggers acting out and is resolved by this). The next moment, 'terror' appears: the inside of the body, but also the inside of the psyche, are represented as invaded spaces, dissolved by rays; or we might suggest that they have been absorbed, incorporated by the (anal) erogenous zone that radiates throughout the entire psychosomatic space, which becomes this totality.

The patient's account of this, long afterwards, in the session, which addresses the themes of the delusional phase that followed this moment of 'hallucinatory retreat', relates her attempt to reintegrate this experience into a fantasmatic structure: the fantasy of anal haemorrhages, the cause of her sister's suicide, her own terror, often expressed in the session, when she is overwhelmed by the conviction of having cancer or by her delusional conviction of having been pregnant and miscarried in the night (the evidence being a small blood stain found on her sheets in the morning) – terror because she knows she will be punished for her 'childhood crimes'. The affect that accompanies these delusional themes is the same as that evinced by her expression when, in the session extract that I have reported, she tells me about the 'beginning' of her crises: terror faced with the inexplicable, faced with an 'emotion' that cannot be formulated. The analyst confronted with this context has every reason to suppose that the subject is re-experiencing the affects that accompany the early experiences of distress and murderous rage that are undergone by the newborn.

However, there is another possible scenario, as I was told by this same young woman and by other patients: having undergone this type of experience, the subject will tell us that during this 'out of time' experience, of a duration that he would be quite incapable of defining, he was nothing but a 'pure sound', a 'shining light', a 'caressed surface'. But this was also a sound, light or tactile sensation that incorporated the entire universe: he was only 'that', but 'that' was everything. What little the subject manages to express about it enables us in this case to deduce that these moments were accompanied by the return of that state of conjunction and 'identity' with the world that are specific to the inaugural experience of pleasure, at this moment when mouth and nipple, body and psyche, are inseparable in the real satisfaction of need.

Now, one fact merits special consideration: at the time, these experiences are impossible to formulate. The psyche is nothing but this inseparability between the experiencing subject and the experience itself, this *representation* (a term I will adopt again shortly) that was and is accompanied by an affect – pleasure or suffering – in its most radical and most extreme form. But, whatever the nature of the affect accompanying the phenomenon (the intensity does not vary), when the subject can remobilise his fantasmatic activity and his ideational activity and reinstigate the primary process and the secondary process, *in either case* he will fantasise and conceive this 'past experience' as an experience of terror, of nothingness. He is confronted with this experience in the position of a subject who realises that he has been hanging over an abyss into which he was very nearly sucked: it matters little to him, therefore, to know which face it was he glimpsed on the surface of the bottom of the abyss.

However, this interpretation only applies in the register of psychosis. This is why this type of phenomenon has to be distinguished from a very similar one that some subjects have the possibility, and perhaps we should say the good fortune, of experiencing: the feeling that accompanies certain inspired states connected with aesthetic emotion.

In this case as well, the subject is temporarily nothing more than this function of gaze–seen, ear–music, perceiver–percept, a moment located 'outside time', always in silence, in a 'spell' (in the former and strong sense of the term) that can only be broken with its formulation into thought or words. It is afterwards that the subject will be able – *if he is gifted* – to reflect on his experience, explain it to himself and, possibly, find an equivalent in the register of fantasy.

At the time of the experience, he will be nothing but this sensory function, inseparable from the object that is at its source: the concept of projection has no place here, nor does projective identification. The subject is moved by an impulse that takes him *beyond* the everyday sensory world, which confronts him with what he did not know would be revealed as a possible form, quality or presentation of this world, and thus of his relationship to this world and therefore in one sense of himself.

To differentiate this type of experience from that described above, imagine a subject who decides to go to an art exhibition. This presupposes, unless it is a professional duty, a certain frame of mind, a form of anticipation of something that is not exactly known. And there this same subject suddenly finds himself opposite a picture whose light strikes him, opposite a 'percept' that reveals to him . . . Nothing can be said in general, except that he contemplates, understands and perceives some previously unknown aspect of a colour, something previously unknown in an encounter with something *unexpected* that fulfils an expectation that he did not know he was carrying inside him.[5] I am using these terms to try to formulate what can only be the retroactive reconstruction of an inherently elusive moment of emotion.

Now imagine a subject who – to flee enemies on his trail – also takes refuge in a museum. The pursuit continues and he is cornered at the end of a room, with his back to the enemy and facing the same picture. He may then attempt to forget the hand that is about to strike by trying no longer to be anything but this gaze that will remain the gaze of a living person as long as the picture remains visible to him. I very much doubt that the experience is the same for these two subjects, and if the second succeeded in 'retreating' into this sensory experience, in curling up into this 'enclave' of pure sensoriality, I am certain that once he had escaped death, this 'experience', this 'moment', would become inconceivable – retroactively – except as an experience of terror.

In the first scenario, a sensory emotion comes to express what thought cannot formulate (thinking–speaking requires the preservation of this gap that enables the 'thinker' to reflect on the 'thought' object), but this new expression–experience–discovery, far from harming him, enriches his 'thinking power'. In these moments of silence and quiescence, thought contemplates what may become the *future* object of its knowledge.

In schizophrenia, not only is the picture 'hallucinated' by a percipient who can no longer find an object in the world to cathect, but for him it is no longer a matter of acquiring a new expression but of making recourse to the only manoeuvre that can assure his psyche that it has preserved its 'living' state despite this moment of *void* that has dispossessed the scene of the world of any object that could become the support of a fantasmatic projection, of any object that can meaningfully be present or absent.

This is why I accord a particular status to these fleeting borderline experiences that occur during the session and undoubtedly also outside it. But in this case we will not be informed of this: it is only at the moment of 'awakening' that the subject can possibly talk about it, thanks to a presence, our own, that has taken part in this 'awakening' by managing to impose on him the external presence of something perceptible. In other cases, I am convinced that as with certain dreams the awakening includes the erasure of the representation and its accompanying affect, or, alternatively, as I suggested earlier, the way out of this moment that cannot last as it is, barring psychic death, will go hand in hand with its metabolisation by the primary process, which will produce it in a fantasy of sadistic rape, a primal scene or a violent intrusion into the subject's own body, and with the remobilisation of the secondary process that will come

---

[5] Unknown anticipation not of an object – even an eternally lost first breast – but a *state*, a relationship of identity to oneself, to the object, to the world; a state that eliminates any possibility of conflict, any doubt, any question. A highly illuminating and original analysis of this anticipation and its motivations can be found in Michel Artières's text entitled 'Menace d'objet et saisie du motif' (*Topique, 33*, Sept. 1984).

to construe it by reading there and presenting to the other the evidence of mutilations imposed on his own body or shackles that fetter his own psyche.

A metapsychological interpretation

This brings me to the metapsychological interpretation of these phenomena that I am presenting to you: it will be for you, and above all for the specialists present here, to judge whether or not it can enrich the theoretical and therapeutic approach to autism. Despite the different theoretical standpoints of the authors who have privileged this clinical picture in their research, they all agree in interpreting it as a mode of mental organisation that is closest to that thought to be present when the psychic apparatus begins to function. To be more precise, autism and its variants are the comprehensible and visible consequences of an elusive and invisible cause situated in this inaugural period.

Analytic experience demonstrates that the earlier the causes of our psycho-pathology appear, the more dangerous are the consequences that may ensue in the short or long term for the whole of psychic functioning, and the more the analyst, who cannot dispense with this causal link either theoretically or clinically, will be obliged to deploy constructions in which his theoretical, imaginative and inventive contribution will take precedence. In his account of autism, Meltzer tells us the story of the foetus's last few months of intrauterine life, a plausible account that is partly confirmed by recent findings in neurophysiology. Tustin tells us the story of the struggle made by the genotype for the survival of the species in protecting itself from predators. This is another plausible account that is partly confirmed by biological research. However, these two authors are too analytic to be unaware of the limits of what they can expect from these findings borrowed from other disciplines, of which the value is nevertheless incontestable.

I am in turn going to tell you the story of representation. It, too, will be plausible, I hope: I will leave aside what I have drawn from the information sciences, but admittedly it will mainly be from a similar perspective.

My historical construction testifies to a boundary that is lacking from those of both Meltzer and Tustin for one very simple reason: I can conceive of a prelude to the fantasmatic representation of the baby's relationship to the breast, as well as a prelude to a child–mother relationship, characterised by the former's accession to language, but I cannot strictly conceive of a prelude to representation (except in foetal life perhaps, but I admit to having such difficulty understanding what occurs afterwards and often so long afterwards that I have believed and still believe it preferable not to venture into these domains). With apologies to Meltzer for summarising one of his hypotheses so briefly, I will formulate it in these terms: birth coincides with the baby's encounter not only with a sensory world but a world of stimuli that are initially accompanied by an emotionally painful affective charge, for its intensity and excess disable his capacity for toleration and containment. This failure just as immediately generates the quest for a 'containing-receiving' object capable of converting the beta-elements back into alpha-elements. Through this, the baby discovers the capacity to produce cathectable dreams (Meltzer's use of the term 'dream' in this context is hard to distinguish from what Freud defines as hallucinated satisfaction). Meltzer thus seems to share Bion's hypothesis of a preconception, an anticipation or advance intuition of an object that is very quickly transformed into what he terms an 'aesthetic object', if it is not one already. It is the latter that will become the support of the baby's projective impulses and the source of his question concerning the possible hiatus between the erogenous pleasure exuded by its presence and the feelings of persecution and distress aroused by its disappearance and its excessively rapid departure. This brief reminder of one of Meltzer's hypotheses illustrates a point of convergence between our conceptions of the onset of psychic activity: what he defines as a 'symbolic object' occupies a similar position to the 'psychic being' that I have termed 'representation'. But our conceptions diverge in relation to the referent of the symbol or, in my terms, the figuration of the represented, and the same applies concerning the evolution of this first creation of psychic activity. I will try to summarise as clearly as possible what I mean by pictogram, the complementary object-zone and the self-generative relationship that pertains between the representative and the represented. This construction seems to me to account better for certain characteristics that indicate the schizophrenic's relationship to his own body. I will start from this postulate: representational activity is the psychic equivalent of the metabolisation work that characterises organic activity. The characteristic of the psyche is to metabolise – into elements of self-information – excitations with a bodily source, such as the stimuli that reach it from the external world.

This is self-information that, in this phase of psychic activity, can only concern the self-representation that the psyche forges of itself as a *capacity to feel* the affect resulting from its encounter with the bodily space and the space of the world (the first representative of these two spaces returning us, of course, to what is at work and what is manifested in and from the maternal psychic space). The only quality specific to these two spaces of which the psyche can be informed is the quality of pleasure or suffering that accompanies their encounter and, since in this inaugural phase the existence of an elsewhere is totally neglected, pleasure and suffering will be conceived as self-generated by the representative itself. The essential and specific characteristic of the primal process is therefore to posit the experiencing subject as generating the emotion that affects the psychic space.

Let us now consider what we can conceive and, more precisely, imagine of these representations in the figurative sense of the term. My experience in treating psychoses has led me to propose the hypothesis that the primal process draws the elements and organisation of its pictograms from the sensory model. The beginning of somatic life, like psychic life, coincides with the encounter between a sensory organ and an external object with a capacity for stimulation in its regard. It is this sensory model that the primal process adopts in its constructions: this is what I call 'the complementary object-zone', the representation of a state of conjunction, identity and continuity between the erogenous zone (oral cavity, auditory zone, visual zone, tactile surface . . .) and the source-object of an excitation that was a source of pleasure in an inaugural encounter. As for the affect of unpleasure (or suffering, a more eloquent term), it will be experienced every time the object fails in its pleasure-giving function: the perceptual function self-presents itself from then on as generating its state of suffering. The consequence is that the psyche can only flee such an emotion by mutilating and decathecting itself as a perceiving zone-function. Before the activity of the primary process and its fantasmatic production begin to operate and, very soon afterwards, if not jointly, the first gains that are due to the secondary process, and to its sense-making work, this state of suffering is only compatible with psychic survival because the outside world (the surrounding psychic milieu and more generally the mother) will periodically re-offer the erogenous zones a pleasure-giving object that enables the psyche to represent itself, again, as able to generate its own pleasure. In the opposite scenario, the decathexis activity that characterises the death drive puts an end to all life. There is not much more I can say about the primal process. An extremely important factor is the irradiative capacity specific to each erogenous zone; every pleasurable sensation of an erogenous zone is only such because it radiates throughout all the erogenous zones. There we have the precondition for integrating the body as a future unity, but also the cause of an extension of the mutilation that generates an anxiety about fragmentation involving a disintegration of the representation of the body that is understood. As long as we remain in the primal sphere, every affective experience will be represented by a pictogram that is indissociably a representation of the affect and an affect of the representation. The affect as an experience of the primal is represented by a bodily action and, more precisely, by the action of attraction or reciprocal rejection of the zone and the object, an action that reflects the relationship of attraction or rejection between the representative and the represented. These two relationships are the pictographic illustration of the two basic emotions that are colloquially called love and hatred. Every positive impulse of the representative towards the world will be depicted by an action-figuration of swallowing, every negative impulse by one of rejection. This is why it merits this repetition: every experience of suffering jointly involves a self-mutilating impulse of the organ and the sensory function and a destructive impulse towards the corresponding objects of excitation.

    The relationship of identity between self–world and psyche–body has as a premise this self-representation of a psychic activity that presents itself as generating the source-objects of excitation and as thereby generating the state of pleasure or the state of suffering present in an undifferentiated psyche–soma space.

The arrival on the scene of the primary process and the fantasmatic production it generates is the consequence of the recognition imposed on the psyche of the presence of another body and thus of an 'elsewhere'. It is true that this fantasmatic representation is simultaneously a recognition of the separation and a challenge to its consequences. The characteristic of the fantasy is to present two bodies, two parts of the body, two psychic spaces, which are nevertheless subjected to the desire for a single one. To take a simple example, I will say that the fantasy of fusion realises the fulfilment of the desire of a fantasising subject who would be able to appropriate and merge with an object whose separate status has been perceived, however fleetingly. What is denied in this fantasy concerns the object's capacity to oppose this fusion, this continuity of two desires, by which the fantasising subject eliminates any distance, any difference, any disparity between two desiring subjects, two bodies, two psyches.

I will not refer here to what is constituted by the onset of functioning of the secondary process that accompanies the emergence of these linguistic functions (observation, reflection, memorisation) that will work to make sense of the affective experiences undergone by the I, make them possible to formulate, communicate and share. This accession to the ideational representation, or alternatively the possibility and necessity for the I to express its desires and goals through *meanings*, results from the operation of the reality principle in the ordering of the semantic capital that constitutes our conscious thought. The primary process will not be excluded from it on that basis, but between the moment that signals the child's accession to language and that other moment that signals or should signal his exit from the Oedipus complex and, thereby, establish a more autonomous relationship between him and his parents, between his thought and theirs, between his own identificatory project and that of which his parents dreamt for him, we will witness a reversal of the power balance between these two processes. This reversal does not involve the exclusion of one or the other, but the supremacy that the secondary process and the reality principle should manage to safeguard in the sectors of conscious thought and action. This brings me to the final point: the evolution of these three processes during the development of the psychic apparatus. They can be defined in one word: by their *persistence*.

Primal process, primary process, secondary process or alternatively pictographic, fantasmatic and ideational representations of our affective experiences will remain active from the first to the last day of our existence. We have seen that it is the characteristic of the fantasmatic representation to deny the autonomy of desire and the autonomy of the cathected external object, but also to acknowledge its existence. This is why the fantasy is supremely *projectable* on to the external object (referent of the internal object-representation), which means that the threads of its fabric will always share in the 'linguistic threads' by which the I forges the representation of its relationship to the external object, to reality, to the world.

The same does not apply to the pictogram: the self-generative postulate rules out any projection on to an external support, a projection that would presuppose the primal process taking account of something existing beyond the psyche. This is a structural impossibility. But the effects on the I or, if you prefer, on the subject of this activity, with its productions that are distinct from those of the primary process (fantasies) that will be partly revealed by the analytic work, will constitute this 'representative content' that, beyond the field of psychopathology, will be manifested by these elusive feelings that language translates with highly illuminating metaphors ('feeling good in yourself', 'feeling physically shattered', 'having an exploding head'). In the register of psychosis, this representative content may at times come to the forefront of the scene. It is not that the pictogram as such becomes figurable for and by the I, but this latter will be confronted with the extreme endeavour, within the bounds of possibility, to become aware of the emotions that originate from the representation of a world that is no longer anything more than the reflection of a body being swallowed, mutilated and rejected. These moments are rarely absent from the psychotic's experience of the I: they can underlie the actions that we define as acting out, which signal these moments in which the marginalisation of the primary and secondary activity reflects a representation of the world that is close to the primal. Moments and acts during which what is played out on the world stage generates an impulse of maximal decathexis; at this time the scene becomes the site of the void, of nothingness. The affect caused by this catastrophic decathexis then comes into resonance with the affect accompanying what is played out on the original scene: the space of the world and the space of the body find their only and final psychic representative, their ultimate existent status in a pictographic representation that excludes the I, depriving it of any identificatory reference-point. This explains the paralysing effect of these 'hallucinatory phenomena' that I described at the beginning of this paper. I began by stating that the consequences can be either their 'erasure' or their resumption into a delusional problematic; I added this third possibility – acting out – understood as the sudden, unforeseeable, irrepressible action manifested by an acted-out drive that is always destructive of self or other.

The metapsychological construction I have just proposed has a direct application to our clinical practice. In the majority of cases, the phenomena at work in psychosis can and must be interpreted with reference to projective phenomena, to what we know or suppose about all early mother–baby relations, the 'anticipatory effect' of the mother's desire, the catastrophe that his mother's incapacity to tolerate his projections and to foster his desire for proximity can constitute for the young child. But, faced with certain instances of the psychotic experience, which are probably isolated but may well prove to have catastrophic consequences, we must renounce this type of interpretation and succeed in 'thinking' in images of bodily things about what is played and tested out for the subject, to make describable for us and him a relationship of union or repulsion, cathexis or decathexis, love or hatred, life or death, which he has – I would say – *in fact* generated himself in the sense that it is the first psychic presentation of this radical structural conflict in and through which the psyche is born. It is a conflict that opposes the life drive to the death drive, Eros to Thanatos; the pleasure principle is a reality principle that is initially imposed by the subject's own body.

I will not pronounce on the applicability of such a model to the autistic phenomena that may appear in early infantile psychosis, but I will attest to its positive results in my affective comprehension–participation in certain psychotic phenomena in the adult subject. It remains for me to hope that some of you will be inclined to put this model to the test in the treatment of autism . . .

40 SCHIZOPHRENIA AND SOUL MURDER

Psychoanalytic psychodrama with 'John', the man 'saddled with that/the id'

Alain Gibeault

The Freudian adventure could be seen as a quest for the mechanisms specific to psychosis without being in contradiction with those of neurosis. Freud initially (1924b [1923]) described psychotic breakdown as a total denial of reality that lay at the origin of delusions; however, he then went on, in his *Outline of Psycho-Analysis* (1940a [1938], pp. 201–202), to say that the denial of reality was never actually complete: 'The problem of psychoses would be simple and perspicuous if the ego's detachment from reality could be carried through completely. But that seems to happen only rarely or perhaps never. . . . One learns from patients after their recovery that at the time in some corner of their mind (as they put it) there was a normal person hidden, who, like a detached spectator, watched the hubbub of illness go past him.' That contradiction in Freud's writings should be seen in the context of his research into psychosis, particularly as regards the discovery of narcissism. It is true that he emphasised the role of delusion in psychosis, but at the same time he referred to a kind of ego organisation – splitting of the ego – different from that of neurotic patients, and he highlighted the prevalence of narcissistic cathexes and undercurrents.

The history of the concepts of dissociation and splitting, as described by Kapsambelis (2007), bears witness to Freud's wish to maintain some connection between the mechanisms of neurosis and those of psychosis. Bleuler (1911), on the other hand, who introduced the concept of schizophrenia into classical psychiatry, was, it is true, faithful to some extent to Freud's ideas, but he did reify the process of psychosis; for Bleuler, *Spaltung* is a side-effect of a primary deficit corresponding to an actual disintegration of mental processes. In that way of looking at things, there is a deep – indeed, an insurmountable – hiatus between neurosis and psychosis.

That opposition between neurosis and psychosis can be found in Freud's writings (1924b [1923], 1924e), where it is presented in such a way that repression and denial could appear to be two completely different mechanisms. The concept of foreclosure [*forclusion*] introduced by Lacan also assumes that there is a clear 'separation' between these two mechanisms. Denial, however, can be seen as a specific kind of repression that concerns not only representations and affects but also the manner in which the ego functions. As Jean Gillibert (1977) pointed out, 'The repressing ego is itself repressed'.

This helps us to understand differences in the use of projection: in the neuroses, there is a projection of *aspects* of the ego, preserving the difference between ego and non-ego, whereas in the psychoses there is a projection of *parts* of the ego, thereby undermining the frontiers between ego and non-ego, as we see in pathological projective identification (Gibeault, 2004).

In fact, those theories which postulate the existence of a hiatus between neurosis and psychosis belong more to phenomenology than to psychoanalysis. They ignore not only one of the three dimensions of metapsychology – the economic aspect (in other words, the economy of narcissistic cathexes and object-cathexes) – but also the importance of the affects in their relationship with representations. If we place the emphasis on the economy of narcissistic and object cathexes, there is no longer any real hiatus between various kinds of mental organisation. Splitting can then be seen as an economic extension of a mechanism of defence and of the organisation of the primary ego.

In the classic form of repression that we encounter in neurotic structures, it always remains possible to make a connection between representations and affects. In the psychoses and perversions, where narcissistic cathexes predominate, there is a modification of the economy and a failure of counter-cathexis. The ego loses its synthesising function and can no longer create associative connections between two contradictory positions; it is forced into denial and splitting of the ego, and into juxtaposing two contradictory and parallel positions in its thinking, in order to contain the annihilation anxiety that submerges it.

It is interesting to note that this continuity between neurosis and psychosis helps us to understand why, in his *Outline of Psycho-Analysis*, Freud (1940a [1938]) spoke of splitting of the ego in his discussion of the neuroses: 'Just as the id is directed exclusively to obtaining pleasure, so the ego is governed by considerations of safety. The ego has set itself the task of self-preservation, which the id appears to neglect. It [the ego] makes use of the sensations of anxiety as a signal to give a warning of dangers that threaten its integrity' (p. 199).

Rosenberg (1980) pointed out that this anxiety specific to the ego is triggered when its own integrity is threatened. He went on to say: 'Neurotics may feel that threat when their internal conflictuality becomes excessive and polarised, and when their ability to synthesise and compromise is about to collapse' (p. 26). In Rosenberg's view, the anxiety that we find in the syndrome of depersonalisation has to do with the loss of one's unity and self-identity, not with the apparition of a split in the ego. Although splitting of the ego may not exist as such in the neuroses, the *potentiality* for splitting of the ego is present in every human mind.

On the other hand, psychosis bears witness to the fact that splitting of the ego has indeed occurred – not one that is completely watertight, all the same, so that psychotic anxiety can be seen as the potentiality for transforming splitting of the ego into a mental conflict. That is why, paradoxically enough, it is in cases of perversion that splitting of the ego reaches its highest point; because of that, these patients are less likely to experience anxiety about losing their sense of unity. The process of psychosis can be defined with reference to denial and splitting of the ego, while psychotic anxiety can confront the individual with what Racamier (1992) called 'the complex of de-being' which lies 'at the very birth of the mind, where we find the original dehiscence between the I and the object'. Nevertheless, psychosis carries within itself the possibility of re-finding the path that leads to the object, because it bears witness to an internal conflictuality that has not been entirely evacuated. The example of 'John', a young schizophrenic patient who had committed murder, will allow me to illustrate what is involved in dissociation or splitting of the ego in adolescence, with the outcome being either a delusional projection or an act of violence – in this case, murder.

First interview: an encounter

At the time of this first interview, John had been in a psychiatric hospital, sectioned under the relevant mental health provisions, for the previous eighteen months. He was referred to me by V. Kapsambelis, who was seeing him in consultation once a week for psychiatric treatment. During that time, Dr Kapsambelis felt that the patient was simply repeating the same thing over and over again; he thought that a more psychoanalytic form of treatment might help to improve John's mental functioning.

   The patient's history is a tragic one. At that time 29 years of age, he had lived all his life in a small village with his father, an alcoholic, and his mother, who let herself be sadistically abused by her husband. John had had a psychotic breakdown when he was 18; he was hospitalised at that point, and neuroleptic medication was prescribed. When he recovered somewhat, he decided to move to Paris and train in hotel work and catering. He did not, however, take his medication on a regular basis, so that he had a relapse, this time with a delusional aspect that meant he had to be hospitalised in S____. His thought processes were completely disorganised, and he refused the psychiatric follow-up that Dr Kapsambelis offered him. That was the first time he had met Dr Kapsambelis, and John said to him somewhat enigmatically: 'I managed to find you now, so I'll know how to find you again.'

   Subsequently, he would visit on a regular basis Arlette, an old lady who lived alone; she was a friend of John's grandmother and about the same age as she was. Arlette made meals for him and gave him some money to buy cigarettes. Arlette's family were worried about this, and one of her sons-in-law told John that they did not like that situation at all. John thought he would lose Arlette, and it was in that context that he stabbed her to death. Detained for a year in the hospital wing of a prison, he was later transferred to S____ hospital, where he 'found Dr Kapsambelis again'.

In the interview with me, John spoke willingly of the loneliness and despair that lay at the heart of his mental disorganisation. 'What happened after that was that I moved to Paris, and there, for the next three years, I would cry every day, yes, every day, every single day, I couldn't stop crying. And I was imagining crazy things about my family, or my friends, or the people I knew in Paris.' 'Crazy things' about his parents before he moved to Paris were expressed particularly through the feeling of not recognising his mother any more; this could indicate a denial of perception, but perhaps on a deeper level it was a denial of filiation, a disowning of his origins.

He associated to the distress he felt in the period when he killed Arlette. He spoke quite openly – but without guilt – about what he called 'the drama' or 'the homicide', expressing both his perplexity and his wish to understand what had happened. The psychiatrist had suggested that perhaps he had killed Arlette so as not to have to do without her; John explained: 'It's quite easy to understand when it's put like that, but inside the person who is doing the killing or who ... I'm just speaking for myself, of course, but it's something that comes on you little by little, you get caught up in something, it's the snowball effect. Suddenly a problem grew up between me, Arlette and her daughters – and it was as though at one point I found myself all alone, the pillar if you like, with her daughters on one side with their husbands and Arlette on the other, it's as though I'm trying to get closer to her and suddenly, to solve the problem, I go all the way up to Arlette and kill her, you see. It's hard to ... it's the way one thing led to another, you get caught up in something, if you like, I don't know if you can follow what I'm saying.'

It is remarkable that, in what he said, the only solution that John could think of at that point to cope with the loss of Arlette was to kill her. The only way he could 'solve the problem', as he put it, was to make the object of the problem disappear. Splitting of the ego is obvious in his description of a drive-related impulse that acted without his realising it, as if it were something mechanical, with his 'getting caught up in something' [*s'engrène*], carrying him along without leaving him any possibility of controlling what was happening. Could what John was saying be an example of what Racamier (1992) called *engrènement* – being enmeshed in something and swept along by it?[1] The idea behind that way of putting it is to illustrate 'the sequence in which an individual's experience finds itself directly connected – with no mental intermediary – to the experience and acts of someone else: it is a kind of short-circuit, an impressive example of forced interaction' (Racamier, 1992, p. 140). In that view, the murder of Arlette would be seen as the tragic consequence of the non-fantasy fantasy concerning the incestual 'spiral' between John and Arlette,

---

[1] In French, there is a certain degree of homophony between the word used by the patient, '*s'engrène*', and Racamier's term *engrènement*. [*Trans., this volume*]

echoing over the generations the incestual relationship with his grandmother and with his mother.

At another point in that first interview, John showed that he wanted to be sure that I understood what had happened. 'Even today there are questions, I don't always know how to answer them, there are things that . . . If they asked me directly "Why did you do that?", I would say out of hate, but hate is just a word, just a little word, out of hate . . . I don't mean out of revenge, but I can't push what words mean too far either, I can't . . . Either I can't find the words, or else all I say is that it is getting caught up in something [he uses the same words as before] as I told you, it all just snowballed. . . .'

It is particularly interesting to observe the fact that this patient found it impossible to establish any link between words and affects, just as he spoke of an enactment in which he 'got caught up in something' without his realising it – an enactment of which he was the agent without any sense of agency. This split in his ego led to the court's decision that he was unfit to plead. As regards John's mental functioning, the murder could be seen as the impossibility he found himself in of imagining the absence of the object at a point in time when the perceived object was suddenly experienced as being separate from him, with the threat that he would no longer be able to have any contact with Arlette. For John, the loss of Arlette represented an intolerable threat to his narcissistic continuity; he therefore had to destroy her in order to reinstate that continuity. In a paradoxical manner, the murder of the object aims to preserve the existence of the object (cf. Balier, 1988, 1996).

In his quest for an explanation of the murder he had committed, John went on to tell me about the many deaths over the previous five years of people close to him: his paternal grandmother, his uncle, his father, his maternal grandfather and his maternal grandmother to whom he was very attached; she died just three months before he killed Arlette. Arlette, indeed, had lived in the village from which John came, and she had known him as a little boy. The snowball effect that John talked about had to do with that series of unbearable deaths. When, in the course of that interview, I acknowledged the pain he must have felt, I pointed out to him that crying every day when he was in Paris was perhaps a way of shedding tears over all these deaths. John said: 'But I cried before they died – even before they died, I was crying, because there's a problem I talked to the psychiatrist about – a *déjà vu*, I've already seen what is actually taking place, I've already felt the feelings. It's a kind of retroactive effect: when you find yourself somewhere, in a room, for example, or outdoors, it sometimes happens that you think you're once again in a situation you've been in before, that it's happening all over again. I was told that it happens quite often to people who are this or that, but so far nobody's been able to explain to me why this happens.' The feeling of '*déjà vu*' was interpreted by Freud (1914a) as being the recollection of a fantasy or unconscious day-dream; for John, however, it was his way of denying loss. In that interview he gave me an example of what he called '*déjà vu*': the almost-hallucinatory experience of his father's presence in the flat in Paris when he (John) first moved there. '*Déjà vu*' thus contributed to overcoming the confusion evoked by his father's absence, which for John was impossible to process.

The impossibility he found himself in of coping with any loss of the object led John to speak of the early stages of his illness, the frequent losses of girlfriends from adolescence onwards, and the emergence of delusions of betrayal involving his brother, his parents and his friends; there was also the non-recognition of his mother, which led to the delusional reconstruction of another mother – a female cousin, an aunt or his mother's twin sister. This disowning also involved his brother, older than John by five years. Only his father – we later learned that John was his father's favourite – escaped non-recognition.

Psychosis has to do with a de-cathexis of the object or disobjectalisation in order to fight against the anxiety of not being differentiated from it; at the same time, it is a kind of break-up, which Freud (1940e [1938], p. 276) described as 'a rift in the ego', the expression he used for describing the splitting of the ego. That rift is often experienced as a *blank*, and, in the course of that first interview, John, in an attempt to explain what he had experienced, put it thus: 'There were times in my life *when it all went blank*, I felt completely lost. For example, I can't remember what I did between age 21 and 22, I don't remember at all what happened that whole year, where I was, what I was doing during all that time, was I still living with my Mum or Dad, my parents I mean, was I living in my own flat, or living with somebody – I can't remember.' As Racamier (1992) quite correctly points out, 'the adjective blank evokes, through the interplay of images, both the overheating of the economy and a vacuity of fantasy.[2] ... *An event of that nature and of that magnitude gives an experience of ecstasy and produces a catastrophe*: the psychotic catastrophe' (p. 171).

I pointed out to John that you can feel very anxious when things go blank like that. He then said: 'Yes, nothingness, that's what it amounts to'. When I asked him to think about the need to cope with nothingness, John explained: 'What got attached to that was the "*déjà vu*" feeling, because the blank that I had when I arrived in Paris – when I said to myself, hey, this is the second time I've been in this flat – maybe it was the same blank that I'd had in my head for some time, maybe it was there already, and everything got all mixed up. . . .' Thus the aim of the '*déjà vu*' feeling is to avoid finding oneself in a blank and to facilitate being reunited with a familiar object; this is the same objective as we find in the delusional solution, which amounts, as Freud said, to a kind of recovery on the patient's part.

I then attempted to get some idea about John's capacity for dreaming. He reported a recurrent dream from his childhood. 'Dreams, well, there are dreams I had when I was just a little boy, really very young, and I have never forgotten

---

[2] The French word *blanc* means both 'white' and 'blank'. In the present example, 'overheating' would imply making something 'white-hot'. [*Trans., this volume*]

them. It was my parents' bedroom, like here if there was a bed and so forth, with lights, you know what I mean? Chandeliers, big lights hanging from the ceiling, and on the walls, I see tomato ketchup, running down the walls like blood. That's a dream I had when I was really very young, maybe 5 years of age, 5 or 6, and it's something I've never, never, never forgotten – a dream that I've never forgotten.' What could we say about the psychic status of that repetitive childhood dream? I was impressed by the fact that the primal scene immediately awakened in him a sense of murderous violence: the parents are dead, and there are traces on the wall – blood is running down the wall. They have killed each other – or, rather, they have been murdered by the patient himself. Then John spoke of the nightmares he had been having recently; he could not remember what they were about, but he wondered if they could have anything to do with the interview that he was due to have with me. Obviously that scheduled interview had given rise to persecutory anxiety which he was, all the same, able to overcome in order to have this discussion about what was going on in his mind.

John himself gave some indication of that when he spoke of the nightmares he was having at that time, nightmares that he could not remember. In a very apposite way, he wondered if they might have something to do with me; as someone unknown to him, I might well evoke in him some unbearable persecutory and violent feelings. Our interview, nonetheless, enabled him to set up a tolerable form of contact: even though I was not an *acquaintance* of his – he did not, of course, know me at all – an *encounter* had indeed been possible, and that, in my view, is what a preliminary interview is all about. I felt that he did have the capacity to want to communicate something about the tragic side of his life and the wish to understand his psychic reality. I thought, therefore, that he could get quite a lot out of psychoanalytic work, and I suggested to him that we think along the lines of psychodrama.

Symbolisation and psychodrama

In fact we began the preliminary stage of the psychodrama a few months later than had been planned after the initial interview. During that interval, John had contacted the secretary's office to find out when psychodrama would begin, thereby showing that he really did want to begin the treatment.[3]

At the first session, after hesitating for quite some time over what kind of scenario he could find, John suggested that the group play out a memory he had of something that had occurred when he was about 20 years of age. One day his maternal grandmother gave John and his brother a cheque for 10,000

---

[3] The psychodrama team consisted of nine psychodramatists (Clément Bonnet, Anne Enguerrand, Murielle Gagnebin, Monique Israël, Marina Loukomskaïa, Pierre Mattar, Laurent Muldworf, Brigitte Reed-Duvaille and Martha Villarino), plus myself as play director.

francs each after the sale of the business that the grandparents owned. In the play scenario, John showed how pleased he was to receive that gift; he was going to put the money in the bank because he was thinking about the future. He added that it would open doors for him as far as his future work was concerned. We could see in that comment an anticipation of how John saw his future in the work of the psychodrama. The psychodramatist who was playing the part of John's brother said that he wanted to spend the money right away – he would buy a car, thereby giving the impression of being something of a daredevil. That imagined scenario did not quite match up with the brother's internal reality; John described him as being reserved, while the daredevil aspect was more like John himself. That sequence showed that John was able to make use of the projective function of psychodrama.

In his free associations at the end of the session, John immediately said that he felt ill at ease because of the difference between his actual memory of that event, the 'gift of 10,000 francs', and 'the script', because 'it didn't happen like that'. Obviously he was somewhat worried by the fact that he could not simply rely on a '*déjà vu*', but had to deal with imagining. That imaginary dimension could turn out to be a source of persecutory anxiety for him, given that he could not control at the same time the reactions of other people and his own drive-related impulses which could give rise to destructiveness. As he himself said, it can be unsettling 'when you don't know the rhythm yet, the mechanics of how it works'. In fact, when I asked him what he had felt during that session, pleasure or fear, he answered with a question of his own: 'That's what I don't know, because is the aim of it to help me or is there some other more direct aim that I'm not supposed to know about?' In an attempt to rule out the other, potentially persecutory, option, I told him that the aim was to help him. John then said: 'Yes, by offering me something that will be different.' That comment showed that John was sensitive to the symbolising function of the psychodrama set-up. It did not, however, stop him from voicing his unease: 'There's a frustrating side to it, because that's it, the end, maybe because it's the first time, I don't know. And it's a bit frustrating when I'm asked, for example, to play out a scene and it doesn't happen the way it actually did or the way you might have imagined it; so that's a bit, a bit restrictive, disturbing, difficult to take on board, I don't quite know. . . .'

As in every psychoanalytic situation, there is the idea that one has to accept the gap between what is *real* – what John called 'concrete things' – and what is *imaginary*, which has more to do, as he put it, 'with things that are not concrete', hence the need to distance oneself from the control that perception allows. John emphasised the fact that 'we started off at the beginning with a scene that I'd like to see again', but at the end of that first session he understood that there is no set text on which everything can be based; he realised that psychodrama 'requires improvisation, and a lot of . . . I think that you have to be level-headed to . . .'. Indeed, one does have to be able to control one's violent and murderous impulses and have the support of an adequate measure of self-esteem. That indeed was what I said to John to help him think about how the psychodrama could be followed up. 'It's important in life to feel that we have something good inside us . . . because it gives us a positive image of ourselves, good self-esteem, and that encourages us to go on doing things.' Even though John had committed murder in a moment of psychotic breakdown, he ought to be able to get back in touch with a positive image of himself and look forward to a future other than one in which he would spend the rest of his life – as he himself put it – 'going round in circles in a psychiatric hospital'.

The 'drama'

After several months in which John played out scenarios often centred on his past family life, he told us, in the final session before the summer break, that that particular day was the anniversary of the 'drama' – that is, of Arlette's murder. He was especially relieved to be able to talk to us about it more openly. He suggested a scenario involving John and his mother, in which he would play the part of himself. He mentioned his wish to go to the village cemetery with her in order to meditate at his father's grave and at Arlette's. He had the idea of writing to Arlette's daughters in order to apologise for what he had done; his mother had been against that idea in the past, but this was no longer the case. He wondered whether he had been pushed into committing murder because he had drunk some wine that day – or perhaps it was something in the wine. That hypothesis gave him, for a time, some relief as regards possible feelings of guilt. In that session, which took place just before we would be separated for several weeks, John gave a picture of the distress he had felt long before the 'drama' had occurred: he had been unable to open up his sofa bed, so that, feeling completely neglected and abandoned, he had lain down on the floor, like a thing or a wounded animal.

Violence and guilt feelings

When we came back together again in September, John said for the first time that he felt guilty about the 'homicide' – the word he used along with that of 'drama', rather than 'murder' or 'assassination'. The way he put it was 'I'm saddled with that', evoking something 'mechanical' that he could not quite grasp but which swept through him without his realising it, particularly when he travelled on public transport.

That was when he felt claustrophobic anxiety, which he associated to the fear of the dark he used to experience as a young boy. Because of that, up to the age of six or seven, he had to have a night-light. In a discussion with me about his associations to all of this, John spoke of his anxiety when his parents quarrelled; he was afraid that his mother would drive off in the middle of the night and that he would never see her again. There are images engraved in his memory – for example, when his mother said to him: 'Your father is so aggressive that I have the feeling he'll kill me one of these days.' This was John's description of those terrifying scenes: 'It happened once, he threw a plate at the wall! I don't remember if I told you this before, but . . . One day my mother took down the shotgun and pointed it at him, and I said at that point we're completely losing any idea of . . . there's no love any more. . . . And that day, I took the shotgun from my mother's hands very very quickly, and I took her into my arms and told her that I loved her.'

That violence between his parents was internalised by John and subsequently led him to be violent in his delusional phases, when he thought that his brother or a friend had betrayed him with his 'ex-girlfriend'. 'I couldn't figure out the truth, so I was punching walls and breaking up chairs. I broke one of the garden chairs by kicking it . . . I broke a photo frame in my bedroom, the photo of an Indian, it was in my room. I took a punch at it! And when I got to Paris, it happened all over again.'

John went on to tell us that, after the previous session, he had witnessed on the metro 'an aggression, two people bumping into each other'. He had no idea what it was all about, and he had not even wanted to turn round and look at what was going on. I suggested that we play out that scene. John chose two other passengers, a man and a woman. He himself stayed somewhat in the background, but the woman passenger, played by a female psychodramatist, exclaimed: 'Well, you'll be able to give support to each other, but as for me, I'm just so scared, so scared! I'm scared because I feel I just might kill somebody.' John was initially surprised by that reaction, but then he associated as follows: 'It makes you want to thump somebody, but, well, there's a difference between that and killing somebody.' He went on: 'I don't feel relaxed about any of this . . . because what that lady is saying out loud is what I have inside myself.' The only solution he could find to that situation of violence was to turn his head away and adopt an attitude of withdrawal, because, as he put it: 'I don't want to be saddled with that too' – in other words, as in his childhood, to be exposed to the violence of other people as well as to his own; that would only increase the feelings of guilt that he was beginning to experience at that point.

The scene on the metro, with 'two people bumping into each other' and all that screaming and shouting going on, cannot but evoke the violent primal scene of his childhood, when he was afraid that his parents would kill each other – as when the image of murderous hatred made him shout out 'there's no love any more'. That day, he took the shotgun – which, he said, was in fact not loaded – from his mother's hands; but the murder of Arlette may, in that sense, have been an actualisation of the murder of one of his parents by the other, and, beyond that, the 'soul murder' imposed on a child terrified by the violence of his parents. In his delusion, Senatspräsident Schreber had built up a picture of a 'soul murder' carried out by his doctor, Fleschig, thus harking back to the terror of his childhood experiences (Freud, 1911c, p. 38). We could see in this a metaphor of the self-destructive and allo-destructive processes in psychosis.

This enables us to understand retroactively the representation that lies within the repetitive dream that John had as a child. He had indeed witnessed traumatic and violent quarrels between his parents, and these may have awakened in him echoes both of his own murderous impulses and of the impossibility he had found himself in to process in fantasy the loss of the object. Unable to face up to the primal scene, he attempted to control it through an image (the night-light in his bedroom was displaced onto the lights in his parents' bedroom), and he represented the murder of his parents as blood running down the walls.

As an adolescent, the patient had had a schizophrenic breakdown. The dream, which in some ways is reminiscent of a scene from a horror film, could be seen as a pre-psychotic dream similar to the *pavor nocturnus* of childhood. As Racamier (1976) points out, it could foreshadow the onslaught of psychosis while simultaneously protecting John himself. The dream is both complex and repetitive, and it bears witness to the patient's attempts to control the annihilation anxiety that threatens to overwhelm him. Hence the hypothesis that, although he does have some capacity to represent what lies behind that anxiety, there are significant defects in the dream space and in its function.

The psychodrama stage thus allowed John to represent in a play scenario his violence and guilt feelings and to have more control over his murderous impulses than had been the case before. When he evoked the anxiety that he had felt on the metro, we were at one point afraid that, after his psychodrama sessions, he might commit some sort of murderous attack on himself, one that would result from deep-seated depression. However, the confidence that John had in the psychodrama group and in the psychiatric team was strong enough for us to put aside the fear of a suicide attempt on his part.

Conclusion

Thanks to the psychodrama and the psychiatric team who continued to take care of John, he was no longer in the dark imagining that the worst was about to happen. He was beginning to understand that his past history could to some extent determine how he felt about things in his adult life. It is indeed interesting to note that, after a few months of psychodrama, John no longer mentioned to the hospital staff his obsession with '*déjà vu*' – the only psychiatric symptom that remained, and indeed the one that prevented his leaving the hospital (his hallucinations and delusions had significantly decreased thanks to neuroleptic medication). After six months of psychodrama, he could look forward to leaving the hospital, to re-cathecting life and to accepting the offer made by the psychiatric team of a place in a therapeutic hostel in Paris. Although that idea frightened him at first – because it meant going back to the place where he had felt so distressed and had committed murder – John was able to see that new experience as a potential opening towards communication with other people that would not always involve the threat of narcissistic disruption.

Splitting of the ego had led John into a murderous outburst, and it is worth noting that that experience of subjective dis-owning was still reflected in the structure of his speech and in the words that he used. Instead of using the first-person pronoun 'I', he often preferred to use a more impersonal way of expressing himself: 'it was externalised', 'that didn't give me a feeling of safety', 'that couldn't correspond to anyone', 'that said it', 'that spoke', 'that pushed back' in referring to drive-related impulses – all expressions that point to his being acted upon from the inside.[4] John's language mirrored a break-through of the id, as Freud described it (1940a [1938], p. 148): 'No such purpose as that of keeping itself alive or of protecting itself from dangers by means of anxiety can be attributed to the id.' What John said would often come up against a barrier – we could sense that a word evocative of an affect was being replaced by another one, more neutral. Here is one example: 'A scene that would have to be forced a bit . . . It took place between my mother, my brother and me.' In that instance, the idea was to talk together about the murder and therefore to face up to the fact of being 'saddled with that', an eloquent expression that John used to convey both his violence and the guilt feelings that weighed heavily on him. The psychodrama set-up could, of course, have put him back into a world of people and objects who persecute him through his projection of the 'mechanics' and 'upheaval' that he experienced from the inside; however, thanks to the psychodrama play, John began to own his drives and to catch a glimpse of a new life awaiting him in the place where he had earlier had no option other than being overwhelmed by despair.

The symbolising function of psychodrama enabled John to transform the actual violence of the dramatic incident with Arlette – which for him was impossible to represent – into a fantasy scene in which images and words were able to bind the drive-related excitation that until then was unbearable unless evacuated through an act of murder. The *space for playing* in psychodrama could thus replace the *space for dreaming*, to which, indeed, it is very similar. Some time later, this would enable John to report a dream during a session, thanks to the capacity that he by then possessed to make use of topographical and formal regression.

Psychoanalytic psychodrama thus materialises a dream space and a dream screen that are defective; it thereby enables psychotic patients to have dreams that are guardians of sleep rather than, following Racamier's hypothesis (1976),

---

[4] In all of these examples, the patient uses the word '*ça*' as an indeterminate pronoun ('that' or 'it'); as pointed out earlier (p. 138), this is also the technical term, in French, for the 'id'. [*Trans., this volume*]

being themselves dreams. According to Racamier, instead of *having* dreams, psychotics *are* dreams: they are the incarnate dreams of their object and live off the insistent though erratic existence of which dreams are made. John's analytic adventure thus shows that it is possible for patients to open up to the imaginary dimension and to the unknown, without being terrified of drive-related violence overwhelming them. Psychodrama allows patients like John, who cannot say to themselves, 'It was just a dream', the opportunity of saying, 'It was just play-acting', and thereby go beyond the annihilation anxiety that up to that point could not be put into words.

References

Balier, C. (1988). *Psychanalyse des comportements violents* [The psychoanalysis of violent behaviour]. Paris: Presses Universitaires de France.

Balier, C. (1996). *Psychanalyse des comportements sexuels violents* [The psychoanalysis of violent sexual behaviour]. Paris: Presses Universitaires de France.

Bleuler, E. (1911). Dementia praecox, oder die Gruppe der Schizophrenien. In: *Handbuch der Psychiatrie*. Leipzig: F. Deuticke. [*Dementia Praecox, or, The Group of Schizophrenias*. New York: International Universities Press, 1969.]

Freud, S. (1911c). Psycho-Analytic Notes on an Autobiographical Account of a Case of Paranoia (Dementia Paranoides). *S.E.*, *12*: 3–82.

Freud, S. (1914a). Fausse Reconnaissance (déjà raconté) in Psycho-Analytic Treatment. *S.E.*, *13*: 201–207.

Freud, S. (1924b [1923]). Neurosis and Psychosis. *S.E.*, *19*: 149

Freud, S. (1924e). The Loss of Reality in Neurosis and Psychosis. *S.E.*, *19*: 183.

Freud, S. (1940a [1938]). *An Outline of Psycho-Analysis. S.E.*, *23*: 141

Freud, S. (1940e [1938]). Splitting of the Ego in the Process of Defence. *S.E.*, *23*: 273

Gibeault, A. (2004). La projection dans la cure. Introduction théorique [Projection in psychoanalytic treatment: A theoretical introduction]. In *Projection dans la cure* (46th Continuous Education Seminar, Société Psychanalytique de Paris, pp. 8–24). Paris: Paris Psychoanalytical Society (internal publication).

Gillibert, J. (1977). De l'auto-érotisme [On auto-eroticism]. *Revue Française de Psychanalyse*, *41* (5–6): 774–949.

Kapsambelis, V. (2007). La dissociation et ses histoires [Dissociation and its histories]. *Psychanalyse et psychose*, *8*: 15–39.

Racamier, P.-C. (1976). Rêve et psychose. Rêve ou psychose [Dreams and psychosis: Dreams or psychosis]. *Revue Française de Psychanalyse*, *40* (1): 173–193.

Racamier, P.-C. (1992). *Le génie des origines. Psychanalyse et psychoses* [The genius of origins: Psychoanalysis and the psychoses]. Paris: Payot.

Rosenberg, B. (1980). Quelques réflexions sur la notion de clivage du Moi dans l'œuvre de Freud [Some thoughts on the notion of splitting of the ego in Freud's writings]. *Les Cahiers du Centre de Psychanalyse et de Psychothérapie*, *1*: 9–32.

GLOSSARY

Acted scansion [*scansion agie*]

The concept of acted scansion concerns the changes that Lacan introduced into the psychoanalytic treatment setting in the early 1950s. His intention was to promote the idea of variable-length sessions and the interpretative value for the analyst of ending sessions unexpectedly. This challenge to the idea of fixed-length sessions – usually of 45 or 50 minutes – led to Lacan's introduction of short and/or shortened sessions, particularly in training analyses. This in turn triggered the principal schisms that agitated psychoanalytic institutions in France – first in 1953, when Lacan left the Paris Psychoanalytical Society to found the French Psychoanalytic Society, then in 1963, when that association was disbanded and Lacan founded the Freudian School of Paris. Lacan justified his choice by refusing to adopt a conformist and dogmatic approach based on an objectified setting that, for him, evoked restrictions linked to the imaginary identifications that are at work in groups. The general criticism of psychoanalysis as an institution that underlay this advocacy of variable-length sessions found support in what Lacan felt was the importance of a topographical model of the unconscious centred on language, and in the dynamic and interpretative value of ending a session according to whether what the analysand was saying was 'empty' or 'full'. That interpretative option in acted scansion was paralleled in his rejection of the economic point of view in the analytic process, on the basis that it was an alibi for the psychoanalyst's own resistances.

In practical terms, acted scansion led to a shift from variable-length sessions to short sessions – a radicalisation, as it were, in the direction of brevity. In the subsequent development of Lacanian psychoanalytic societies, not all of them agreed with Lacan on this point, choosing instead a theoretical and practical compromise: some, for example, offer sessions lasting on average from 20 to 30 minutes, while continuing to maintain the principle according to which the analyst has the right to put an end to any given session whatever its actual length.

Many French psychoanalysts (cf. Donnet, 1995) have denounced what they see as subverting the analytic setting and have stressed the fact that it calls into question the fundamental rule and the very principle of free association. Acted scansion has been seen as a misuse of power that jeopardises the analyst's and the analysand's commitment to the third-party function of the analytic setting and encourages feelings of omnipotence and arbitrariness in the analyst. The concomitant intensifying of suggestion and seductiveness in the analytic process has been pointed out.

The practice of scanning[1] sessions and making them shorter is understood by its opponents to contribute significantly to multiplying the number of analysts in the Lacanian movement through encouraging identification with the analyst as seducer-aggressor, in an unanalysable narcissistic context. Acted scansion is seen as an acting-out that short-circuits any processing in fantasy of the transference relationship.

---

[1] 'Scanning' ('scander') as in 'to scan verse', describes punctuating or interrupting the analysand's discourse.

Reference

Donnet, J.-L. (1995). *Le divan bien tempéré* [The well-tempered couch]. Paris: Presses Universitaires de France.

Actual psychoses [*psychoses actuelles*]

The nosographical concept *actual psychoses* was suggested by Michel de M'Uzan (1998) in order to enable a more precise description of those clinical entities corresponding to Evelyne Kestemberg's 'cold psychoses' (i.e. non-delusional ones) (Kestemberg, 2001). In this clinical picture, we find in close relationship a denial of internal reality, a lack of mentalisation (deficiency in fantasy and oneiric activity) and a disqualification of libidinal energy for cathexis. These 'actual psychoses' are as much in contrast to paraphrenia and delusions of imagination as the *actual neuroses* (in which the symptoms have no meaningful value) are to the *psychoneuroses* (hysterical, phobic and obsessional).

References

Kestemberg, E. (2001). *La psychose froide* [Cold psychosis]. Paris: Presses Universitaires de France.

M'Uzan, M. de (1998). Impasses de la théorie, théories indispensables [Impasses in theory, indispensable theories]. *Revue Française de Psychanalyse, 62* (5): 1459–1463.

Bisexualisation process [*processus de bisexualisation*]

Christian David suggested the concept of bisexualisation in order to describe the integration of masculine and feminine dimensions in the psychosexuality of both men and women. For Freud, the recognition of the difference between the sexes is the outcome of a developmental process that gives access to other sorts of difference: between subject and object at the object stage, between activity and passivity at the anal-sadistic stage, and between the male sexual organ and castration in the infantile genital organisation phase. The idea of a bisexualisation process implies that the difference between masculine and feminine is seen not simply as the outcome of a certain development – of sexual maturation at puberty – that makes the difference between the sexes meaningful in the fullest sense of the word, but indeed as the very principle behind that development. From that perspective, the process is seen as a dialectical movement between psychic bisexuality, related to the narcissistic issues involved in the identificatory path leading from primary to secondary identification, and the acceptance of the difference between the sexes, which is more libidinal and object-related in nature. This bisexualising movement corresponds to the internalisation of psychosexual difference based on a primary intersubjectivity through which the infant gains access to the beginnings of differentiation between masculine and feminine in the emergence of auto-erotism and in primary identification with the maternal feminine dimension. 'The sexual dimension becomes auto-sexual and at the same time bisexual or, if preferred, pre-bisexual' (David, 1975, p. 840). That internalisation includes splitting because it has the potential for gradually accepting differences, in particular the difference between the sexes and between generations. The bisexualisation process thus corresponds, in both sexes, to the possibility of acquiring 'the mental capacity to fantasise, understand and share the sexual and psychosexual experience of someone of the other sex' (p. 836); this implies acceptance of the incompleteness of both sexes, experienced as castration, and not its denial, as we find in actual bisexual behaviour.

Reference

David, C. (1975). La bisexualité psychique. Eléments d'une réévaluation [Psychic bisexuality: Material for a re-evaluation]. *Revue Française de Psychanalyse, 39* (5–6): 824–845.

Bisexual mediation [*médiation bisexuelle*]

The concept of *bisexual mediation* was introduced by Christian David in order to emphasise the importance of the role played by psychic bisexuality in inter- and intra-subjective relationships and to distinguish it both from a pathogenic factor in psychosexual development and from a regressive fantasy corresponding to the denial of the difference between the sexes and of castration. From David's point of view, psychic bisexuality presumes the integration of 'virtual complementarity, one that is potential with respect to the opposite sexuality, the opposite psychosexuality. . . . By that very virtuality it is a reminder of the incompleteness linked to sexual specifications' (David, 1975, pp. 834–835). The very possibility of fantasising about and sharing the experience of the other sex *in a virtual manner* is precisely what enables sexual relationships to exist. The concept of mediation thus implies a division and an encounter between the sexes, a dynamic synergy between psychic bisexuality and castration anxiety. This in turn implies dissociation of the opposition between masculine and feminine, male and female – in other words making a distinction between, on the one hand, the *mental representation of the body*, which is more a fantasised body than a real one, a drive-related body that gives pride of place to what is felt and cannot be immediately depicted, and, on the other, the *objective body, spatialised anatomically*, which is more based on what can be seen and on the external apprehension of the difference between the sexes.

Bisexual mediation is thus proof of a creative process within the mind and represents one of the objectives of the psychoanalytic process: the integration of the masculine–feminine polarity in both sexes through a metaphorisation of the functions of penetration and receptiveness.

Reference

David, C. (1975). La bisexualité psychique. Eléments d'une réévaluation [Psychic bisexuality: Material for a re-evaluation]. *Revue Française de Psychanalyse, 39* (5–6): 824–845.

Blank psychosis, cold psychosis [*psychose blanche, psychose froide*]

The concept of *blank psychosis* was suggested by Jean-Luc Donnet and André Green (1973) as a result of their work with a patient whom they called 'Z'. That patient is also known as 'The child of that', because of the words with which he began the interview: 'Well, my mother slept with her son-in-law, and I'm the child of that' (p. 34). For Green and Donnet, blank psychosis is a syndrome that is not easy to describe or to define. 'In fact, it is an invisible structure, seldom encountered as such, always falling short of or going beyond what the name itself attempts to circumscribe. It could quite easily be taken for a more or less neurotic depression or for a borderline syndrome; it may even lurk behind a clinical presentation evocative of a psychotic process without there being any obvious signs of this' (pp. 263–264). Blank psychosis, therefore, has to do with a latent psychotic structure that may appear to be borderline but is in fact the starting-point, the very nucleus, of a psychosis, somewhere between autistic withdrawal and an attempt at recovery through delusion. The main symptoms are feelings of emptiness, dejection, affect-less depression and inhibition of thinking. On the metapsychological level, Green and Donnet's description of this psychotic state is based on three elements: (1) The Oedipal organisation is in fact a false triangulation – the relationship with the mother and father figures amounts to nothing more than one with good and bad objects; (2) Object relationships are characterised by the patient's inability to be alone in the mother's presence (Winnicott 1958); (3) In keeping with Bion's concept (1959), there is an attack on thinking as regards both external reality and drive representation, i.e. fantasy.

The concept of *cold psychosis* was put forward by Jean and Evelyne Kestemberg as a result of their work with patients suffering from anorexia nervosa (Kestemberg, Kestemberg, & Decobert, 1972). There is a certain analogy with the idea of blank psychosis: both are attempts at dealing defensively with drive-related excitation in cases where there is no capacity for representation, including by means of delusional activity. The Kestembergs focused more on the psychic-economy situations that draw such patients into the kind of auto-erotic withdrawal which excludes projection into the object; their only recourse is to erotogenic masochism, expressed principally as physical aggression against their own body. In this psychic structure, hypercathexis of erotogenic masochism and the pleasure that results from this 'almost completely wipe out any pleasure that could be taken in interacting with the object', which is to all intents and purposes reduced to a mere shadow (Kestemberg, 1981, p. 195). The grandiose ideal ego can be seen in self-destructive or allo-destructive enactments and, in particular, in repeated suicide attempts. Evelyne Kestemberg compares these to the glorious but ultimately suicidal gesture of Herostratus, who set fire to the Temple of Artemis at Ephesus in his quest for fame. The concept of cold psychosis has been compared with borderline states in an attempt to define a kind of non-delusional and auto-erotic psychotic functioning, as distinct from that which is delusional and allo-erotic.

References

Bion, W. R. (1959). Attacks on Linking. *International Journal of Psychoanalysis*, *40*: 5–6.

Donnet, J.-L., & Green, A. (1973). *L'enfant de ça. Psychanalyse d'un entretien. La psychose blanche* [The child of that/of the id. The psychoanalysis of an interview: Blank psychosis]. Paris: Editions de Minuit.

Kestemberg, E. (1981). 'L'appareil psychique' et les organisations psychiques diverses. In *La psychose froide* [The 'psychic apparatus' and the various psychic organisations. Cold psychosis]. Paris: Presses Universitaires de France.

Kestemberg, E., Kestemberg, J., & Decobert, S. (1972). *La faim et le corps* [Hunger and the body]. Paris: Presses Universitaires de France.

Winnicott, D. W. (1958). The Capacity to Be Alone. *International Journal of Psychoanalysis*, *39*: 416

Chimera [*chimère*]

The chimera is a theoretical and clinical concept introduced by Michel de M'Uzan (1994) to designate a new kind of organism that emerges from the encounter between two unconscious systems, that of the analysand and that of the analyst: it appears as a monster that possesses its own ways of functioning. The development of this fabulous/mythical child is affected by various influences that originate in its creators. Some of these have to do with the analysand's psychic structure, but those that depend on the analyst must also be taken into account; they come from a particular predisposition to primary identification and from a capacity to tolerate experiences of depersonalisation.

Reference

M'Uzan, M. de (1994). *La bouche de l'inconscient* [The mouth of the unconscious]. Paris: Gallimard.

Enigmatic message [*message énigmatique*]

This concept was introduced by Jean Laplanche (1987) in his description of what he called the 'fundamental anthropological situation' corresponding to a fundamental asymmetry between adult and infant as regards the act of communication. Laplanche called into question Freud's abandonment of the theory of seduction and suggested a theory of *generalised seduction*, in which the mother becomes the seducer who addresses to her infant messages that are pregnant with unconscious sexual significations. These messages are just as enigmatic for the infant who receives them as they are for the adult who sends them. Laplanche first proposed the concept of *enigmatic signifier* to describe this presence of the adult's unconscious; he later changed this to *enigmatic message* or message compromised by the adult's unconscious. The issue for the infant is to control, translate and symbolise these enigmatic messages. The unconscious residues that remain untranslated are defined as *source-objects of the drives*. Laplanche's theory fits in well with those other explorations in French psychoanalysis which have highlighted unconscious fantasy transmission from adult to infant, and in particular those of Michel Fain and Denise Braunschweig on the 'censorship of the woman-as-lover' (see chapter 16, this volume). This tradition focuses on a very different maternal function from that of Bion's 'maternal reverie' in which the mother is receptive to her infant's message rather than communicating her own unconscious dilemmas.

Reference

Laplanche, J. (1987). *Nouveaux fondements pour la psychanalyse*. Paris: Presses Universitaires de France. [*New Foundations in Psychoanalysis*, trans. D. Macey. Oxford: Blackwell, 1987.]

Essential depression [*dépression essentielle*]

Essential depression was described by Pierre Marty (1968): no object is involved, and it is not melancholic in nature. Its characteristic features are feelings of incompetence and inadequacy; there are no guilt feelings. This kind of depression is typical of severe psychosomatic disorders. *Essential depression* and *operational functioning* of the mind tend to go hand in hand.

Reference

Marty, P. (1968). La dépression essentielle [Essential depression]. *Revue Française de Psychanalyse, 32* (3): 345–355. [Also in: *Revue Française de Psychanalyse: Textes 1926–2006* (pp. 205–208). Paris: Presses Universitaires de France, 2006.]

The feminine [*le féminin*]

French psychoanalysts, who always go back to Freud, have not entirely rejected Freud's view of femininity and feminine development as have others in the Anglo-Saxon world who think that Freud was wrong in his view that the little girl starts 'as a little man' with no knowledge of the vagina, no heterosexual desires and that femininity arises out of penis envy. However, Chasseguet-Smirgel and her colleagues questioned some of these assumptions, considering penis envy to be essentially defensive rather than primary, and suggesting that the vagina is repressed because of 'incorporation guilt' (Chasseguet-Smirgel, 1964 – chapter 30, this volume).

Others have developed and added to the Freudian theory. Monique Cournut-Janin (1998) makes a distinction between femininity [*fémininité*], which concerns the *external* phallic-narcissistic investment of the little girl, and the feminine ['*le féminin*'], which concerns her *internal* investment of the vagina and uterus (see chapter 32, this volume). She suggests that femininity develops from an unconscious prohibition from the mother to the daughter asking her to cathect the outside of her body, to adorn it, as a phallic lure, and at the same time to repress her sexual organ in order not to arouse the father's castration anxiety. This complicity between mother and daughter is a kind of double game that the mother plays, one which allows an encounter with the Oedipal father while at the same time keeping that encounter away from any incestuous violence.

'The feminine' is a concept used by French analysts to describe feminine identification, not only in girls but also in boys. Florence Guignard (1997) differentiates in these early identifications two psychic spheres, the 'primary maternal' and the 'primary feminine': the former corresponds to the first three months of life during which the mother's 'reverie' (Bion) contributes to her infant's capacity for symbolisation and promotes communication between human beings; the latter, subsequent, phase contributes to the organisation of primary feminine identifications in children of both sexes and to the first observable triangulation in human beings. She refers to Melanie Klein's descriptions of the primary feminine phase.

Jacqueline Schaeffer (1997) has also discussed the question of the feminine dimension. She uses the term to designate both the primary identification with the mother – the maternal feminine aspect – and the movement leading to the secondary identifications with the mother as a woman – the erotic feminine aspect. Jean Cournut (1998) makes use of a similar demarcation. The first phase, that of the 'maternal feminine', is inseparable from the fantasy-related integration of masochism as a libidinal co-excitation of receptiveness and the process of differentiation from the mother. The second phase implies a displacement of the masochistic impulses towards the father; erotogenic masochism leads the girl to want to be penetrated by the father's penis: 'A young girl will only turn into a woman if she can resist the maternal feminine dimension of her mother' (p. 148). Therefore, for Schaeffer, the feminine dimension involves not only the 'primary maternal' aspect, but also the difference between the sexes. The libidinal genital 'feminine' dimension is not complete at puberty, nor once the young woman has had her first experience of sexual intercourse, as Freud (1905d) thought; it is achieved thanks to the kind of intercourse that gives rise to *jouissance* – that is, intense sexual pleasure or ecstasy. It is this which leads to a second change of object, from the Oedipal father to the 'lover-for-ecstatic-pleasure' [*amant de jouissance*]. This shift from the phallic-castrated couple to the masculine–feminine couple enables the woman to break free of her primitive relationship with the mother figure.

In their descriptions of 'the feminine', these authors refer to the fact that the mother must be able to set up some compromise between her maternal and her feminine cathexes linked to what Braunschweig and Fain (1975) have described as the censorship of the woman-as-lover (i.e., that she is able to turn away at times from the infant, to become the lover of the father of the infant). This process leads to the integration of psychic bisexuality in both sexes as described by Christian David (1975) as a capacity for each sex to identify with the psychosexuality of the other sex.

References

Braunschweig, D. & Fain, M. (1975). *La nuit, le jour. Essai psychanalytique sur le fonctionnement mental* [Night, day: A psychoanalytic essay on mental functioning]. Paris: Presses Universitaires de France.

Chasseguet-Smirgel, J. (1964). La culpabilité féminine (De certains aspects spécifiques de l'oedipe féminin). In J. Chasseguet-Smirgel et al. (1964). *Recherches psychanalytiques nouvelles sur la sexualité féminine*. Paris: Presses Universitaires de France. [Feminine guilt and the Oedipus complex. In *Female Sexuality. New Psychoanalytic Views*. Ann Arbor, MI: University of Michigan Press, 1970.]

Cournut, J. (1998). Le pauvre homme ou Pourquoi les hommes ont peur des femmes [Poor men – or why men are afraid of women]. *Revue Française de Psychanalyse*, 62 (2): 393–414.

Cournut-Janin, M. (1998). *Féminin et féminité* [The feminine and femininity]. Paris: Presses Universitaires de France, pp. 68–89.

David, C. (1975). La médiation bisexuelle [Bisexual mediation]. In *La bisexualité psychique. Eléments d'une réévaluation* [Psychic bisexuality: Material for a re-evaluation]. *Revue Française de Psychanalyse*, 39 (5–6): 824–845. Also in *La bisexualité psychique* [Psychic bisexuality] (pp. 46–72). Paris: Payot, 1992.

Freud (1905d). *Three Essays on the Theory of Sexuality. S.E.*, 7.
Guignard, F. (1997). *Epître à l'objet* [Epistle to the object]. Paris: Presses Universitaires de France.
Schaeffer, J. (1997). *Le refus du féminin* [The repudiation of femininity] (4th edition). Paris: Presses Universitaires de France, 2003. New edition: *Le refus du féminin (La sphinge et son âme en peine)* [The repudiation of femininity (The Sphinx and its lost soul)]. Paris: Presses Universitaires de France, 2008.

Figurability [*figurabilité*]

French psychoanalysts are careful to make a distinction between *Darstellung* which involves an image, and *Vorstellung* which is a thought and is not necessarily visual. 'Figuration' is used as the translation of Freud's *Darstellung*, a pictorial representation. *Darstellbarkeit* in French is '*la prise en considération de la figurabilité*'. In the English *Standard Edition* of *Interpretation of Dreams*, it becomes 'considerations of representability', with reference to the dream work.

In the *Standard Edition*, *Vorstellung* is usually translated by idea or presentation and *Darstellung* by representation; however, in the English psychoanalytic literature this distinction between *Darstellung* and *Vorstellung* is not usually made, and both are translated by representation.

The notion of figuration refers to the description given by Freud of the process of the dream work according to the three dimensions of *regression*: topographical, formal and temporal. What is involved here is the destiny of the libido as Freud defined it with respect to the way in which the psychic apparatus functions. Regression is *topographical* when it has to do with re-cathexis of the *Pcpt.–Cs.* (perception–consciousness) system, as in hallucinations and dreams; it is also *formal* when unconscious thoughts are transformed into images. It can be *temporal* according to three modalities: *object-related*, by going back to objects of the past; *libidinal*, when erotogenic zones correlative with the phases of the libido are re-cathected; and *narcissistic*, in a return to non-differentiated unity with the mother.

From the point of view of the theory of representation, a capacity to use topographical and formal regression – that is, the 'conditions of figurability' – is essential in order for a temporal regression to be possible; this issue is particularly important in the psychoanalytic treatment of non-neurotic organisations.

This concept of *regression* is thus different from a use of the term which has more to do with a psychopathological *disorganisation*.

The notion of '*figurabilité*' is important in French psychoanalysis. 'Figuration (or presentation) is the operation which transforms the latent content into a hallucinatory production through the work of the dream: unconscious desire is thus presented visually, that is figuratively, through a specific movement of formal regression using primary process mechanisms' (Bourdin, 2009, p. 543).

The focus is on the work of figuration, which obeys the conditions of representability.

Botella and Botella (2005) use the neologism of 'figurability' in the English translation of their book (*The Work of Psychic Figurability*) thus bringing the term to the English-speaking world; for them the work of figurability represents not only the foundation of the dream, but a general tendency of psychic life, which in the analytic process gives the analyst the possibility to represent what was already in existence in the patient as a non-representable state. This point of view is very close to what Michel de M'Uzan (1976) has described as the analyst's paradoxical thoughts, which in the analytic process contribute to the formulation of the interpretation (see **paradoxical system**).

References

Botella, C., & Botella, S. (2005). *The Work of Psychic Figurability: Mental States without Representation*, trans. A. Weller, with M. Zerbib. London: Routledge.

Bourdin, D. (2009). Figurabilité [Figurability]. In *Dictionnaire Freudien*, ed. C. Le Guen. Paris: Presses Universitaires de France.

M'Uzan, M. de. (1976). Contre-transfert et système paradoxal. *Revue Française de Psychanalyse*, 40 (2): 575–590. [Countertransference and the Paradoxical System. In S. Lebovici & D. Widlöcher (Eds.), *Psychoanalysis in France*. New York: International Universities Press, 1980.]

Madness and psychosis [*folie et psychose*]

Freud described psychosis as a decathecting of the object accompanied by a narcissistic withdrawal into the ego; he saw in delusions 'an attempt at recovery' (Freud, 1911c, p. 71) because of the movement towards re-cathecting the object and creating a neo-reality. André Green (1980) has suggested that we make a distinction between *madness*, which is a component part of human beings and marks the victory of the life drive, and *psychosis*, which, on the contrary, indicates the triumph of the destructive drives. On the one hand, there is a link to Eros, a link that can be identified in Norbert Hanold's hysterical delusion (Freud 1907a [1906]) and even in Daniel Paul Schreber's paranoid delusion (Freud, 1911c). On the other, there is the unbinding of the death drive, the only way to escape from a fusional relationship with the primary object: this is what Green (1980/1993, p. 243) calls the 'conjuration of the object' in psychosis. French psychoanalysts who have treated patients presenting a psychotic form of functioning have attempted to theorise that primal psychotic division. Francis Pasche (1971 – chapter 36, this volume) talks of the break-up of the alliance between object-related and narcissistic cathexes – which he calls the imbrication of narcissism with anti-narcissism – because in psychosis the object is an enemy that constantly threatens to suck in and engulf the self, given the very fact of its being cathected. Destructive violence against the object is thus the only way of escaping from that anxiety; this exposes the self to experiences of *blankness*, as described by Racamier (1992) in which sensoriality is omnipresent and evacuated into external reality. This helps us understand psychotic projection as defined by Freud (1911c, p. 71) in terms of the suppression of a perception experienced as a bodily sensation that is virtually part of the ego and its hallucinatory return to external reality. The therapeutic solution recommended by French psychoanalysts is not a direct confrontation between the internal space of the mind and external space, but indirect therapeutic modalities that facilitate the move, as Racamier puts it, from the *space for delusion* to *transitional space*: 'The reality that we invoke so readily as a panacea is not a remedy for delusion. The best remedy would be play (in the sense in which Winnicott uses the word)' (Racamier, 2000). Pasche, for his part (1971), suggests that we learn the lessons of Perseus's shield in order to be able to deal with the attacks coming from the Medusa-ing and petrifying object! Playing with images and with words, as in psychoanalytic psychodrama, is one of these highly productive therapeutic creations that have allowed us a 'conjuration' of the object in the service of life and of pleasure in mental functioning.

References

Freud, S. (1907a [1906]). *Delusions and Dreams in Jensen's* Gradiva. *S.E., 9*: 3.
Freud, S. (1911c). Psycho-Analytic Notes on an Autobiographical Account of a Case of Paranoia (Dementia Paranoides). *S.E., 12*: 3.
Green, A. (1980). Passions et destins des passions. Sur les rapports entre folie et psychose [Passions and their vicissitudes: On the relation between madness and psychosis]. In *La folie privée*. Paris: Gallimard, 1990. [*On Private Madness*. Madison, CT: International Universities Press, 1993; London: Karnac, 1996.]
Pasche, F. (1971). Le bouclier de Persée ou psychose et réalité [The shield of Perseus, or psychosis and reality]. In *Le sens de la psychanalyse* [The meaning of psychoanalysis]. Paris: Presses Universitaires de France, 1988.
Racamier, P-C. (1992). *Le génie des origines. Psychanalyse et psychoses* [The genius of origins: Psychoanalysis and the psychoses]. Paris: Payot.
Racamier, P-C. (2000). Un espace pour délirer [A space for being delusional]. *Revue Française de Psychanalyse, 64* (3): 823–829.

Negative narcissism [*narcissisme négatif*]

André Green's concept of *negative narcissism* is a clarification of his idea of the disobjectalising function of the death drive. The regressive movement that decathects every significant cathexis, following the principle of inertia or Nirvana principle described by Freud, is seen here as attempting to discharge all excitation and reduce it to zero. This negative movement is expressed as an attack not only on cathexes of objects or their substitutes, but also on the objectalising process itself (Green, 1993). Green's concept of negative narcissism can be compared to Herbert Rosenfeld's *destructive narcissism*, which implies, according to Rosenfeld, 'that some active destructiveness is involved ... not only against objects but against parts of the self' (Rosenfeld, 1987, p. 109). Green, however, emphasises the fact that these attacks are aimed particularly at the individual's capacity for representation; this is not the case with Rosenfeld's concept, which, from a Kleinian perspective, assumes that this capacity is preserved: several of Rosenfeld's clinical illustrations show that his patients retained their capacity for dreaming in spite of the importance of their self-destructive behaviour. For Green, who, with Jean-Luc Donnet, introduced the concept of blank psychosis, the aim of negative narcissism is to eradicate all capacity for representation and fantasising. Green has also described this negative narcissism as *death narcissism*, the return to 'absolute' primary narcissism, which he contrasts with *life narcissism*, related to secondary narcissism and the construction of the ego, which has preservation and representation as its objectives. This conception of narcissism is thus related to Freud's final theory of the instinctual drives.

References

Green, A. (1993). *Le travail du négatif*. Paris: Editions de Minuit. [*The Work of the Negative*, trans. A. Weller. London: Free Association Books, 1999.]
Rosenfeld, H. (1987). *Impasse and Interpretation*. London: Routledge.

Objectalising function/disobjectalising function [*fonction objectalisante/fonction désobjectalisante*]

The concepts of objectalising function and disobjectalising function were introduced by André Green to clarify his conception of the relationship between drive and object. Although he highlighted the fundamental role of the object in mental life, calling it the 'revealer of the drives', he theorised that dialectic on the basis of Freud's final theory of the instinctual drives. Green constructed an original theory of the relationship between the life and death drives based on their relation to the object. The aim of the life drive is to preserve an *objectalising function*, not only by enabling relationships to be created with internal or external objects, but also — and above all — by transforming structures into objects, even when no object is directly involved. Green thus goes further than object relations theories which, in his view, are too restricted to the object *as such*; for Green, 'it is the investment itself that is objectalized' (Green, 1993/1999, p. 85), hence the work of mental transformation concerning sublimation and symbolisation.

On the other hand, the death drive has a *disobjectalising function* that attacks not only the object relation but all the substitutes for the object – that is, the ego. That is why that function of the death drive implies decathexis of mental life, the manifestations of which can be seen in the destructiveness that is intrinsic to psychotic functioning and psychosomatic disorganisation.

In reaching that conclusion, Green took into account theories concerning the processes of subjectivation and de-subjectivation (Cahn, 1991), adding to the idea of objectalising that of *subjectalising* and to that of disobjectalising that of an 'unbinding of the subject' by the ego; this corresponds to an operation of the ego the aim of which is to disconnect the very basis of subjectivity, particularly through splitting of the ego.

References

Cahn, R. (1991). Du sujet [The subject]. *Revue Française de Psychanalyse, 55* (6): 1353–1490.

Green, A. (1993). *Le travail du négatif*. Paris: Editions de Minuit. [*The Work of the Negative*, trans. A. Weller. London: Free Association Books, 1999.]

Operational thinking [*pensée opératoire*]

Operational thinking is a kind of mental functioning that was first described by the founders of the Paris School of Psychosomatics (Marty, M'Uzan, & David, 1963). It is characterised by a *deficiency in mentalisation* (in fantasy and oneiric activity) and *hypercathexis of factual elements* – that is, those which are the most concrete in external reality. This kind of mental functioning is typical of severe psychosomatic disorders.

Reference

Marty, P., M'Uzan, M. de, & David, C. (1963). *L'investigation psychosomatique. Sept observations cliniques* [Psychosomatic investigations: Seven clinical observations]. Paris: Presses Universitaires de France.

Paradox and paradoxical transference [*paradoxe et transfert paradoxal*]

Racamier defines a *paradox* as a 'psychic formation that indissolubly links and constantly relates two propositions or impositions that are irreconcilable and nevertheless unopposable' (Racamier, 1980, p. 145).

The notion of paradox was first introduced by the anthropologist Gregory

Bateson and his colleagues in the 1950s, to describe a form of communication they termed the 'double bind'. In the United States the work of Harold Searles (1959) bears witness to the influence of these researchers in the understanding of schizophrenia. In France it was developed in particular by Anzieu (1975) and by Racamier (1973). Anzieu discusses it within the psychoanalytic situation as a manifestation of the work of the negative when the patient puts the psychoanalyst into a paradoxical situation. Racamier extends this to describe it as a defensive organisation in the schizophrenic patient, while Roussillon (1991) contrasts it with 'transitionality', the transitional modality described by Winnicott (the opposite of the irreconcilable).

References

Anzieu, D. (1975). Le transfert paradoxal [Paradoxical transference]. *Nouvelle Revue de Psychanalyse, 12*: 49–72.

Racamier, P.-C. (1973). Entre humour et folie [Between humour and madness]. *Revue Française de Psychanalyse, 37* (5–6): 871–885.

Racamier, P.-C. (1980). *Les schizophrenes* [Schizophrenics]. Paris: Payot.

Roussillon, R. (1991). *Paradoxes et situations limites de la psychanalyse* [Paradoxes and borderline situations in psychoanalysis]. Paris: Presses Universitaires de France.

Searles, H. F. (1959). The effort to drive the other crazy – an element in the aetiology and psychotherapy of schizophrenia. In *Collected Papers on Schizophrenia and Related Subjects* (pp. 254–283). London: Hogarth Press and the Institute of Psycho-Analysis, 1965.

Paradoxical system and paradoxical countertransference
[*système paradoxal & contre-transfert paradoxal*]

De M'Uzan's notion of 'paradoxical system and paradoxical functioning' is taken from the term '*sommeil paradoxal*' (paradoxical sleep), which refers to REM (rapid eye movement) sleep. He uses the term 'paradoxical' in a very different way from Racamier, Anzieu and Roussillon, who describe a mode of communication with irreconcilable messages. De M'Uzan refers to the sleep cycle which paradoxically is favourable to the process of dreaming.

The *paradoxical system* is a mode of mental functioning in the analyst described by Michel de M'Uzan (1976). During the session, the analyst is invaded by strange representations, unexpected phrases, abstract formulae, coloured images, reveries that have been more or less processed, etc. These thoughts, images and words give rise in the analyst to a kind of momentary alienation, corresponding to as yet undetected mental processes that are taking place in the analysand. The fundamental feature of this phenomenon is that the analyst is some steps ahead both of what can be understood from the material and of the fantasies that the patient is able to formulate. De M'Uzan designates this phenomenon as *paradoxical countertransference*.

Reference

M'Uzan, M. de (1976). Contre-transfert et système paradoxal. *Revue Française de Psychanalyse*, 40 (2): 575–590. [Countertransference and the Paradoxical System. In S. Lebovici & D. Widlöcher (Eds.), *Psychoanalysis in France*. New York: International Universities Press, 1980.]

Pictogram [*pictogramme*]

The term 'pictogram' was used by Piera Aulagnier (1975) to describe a primal form of representation. It is not a representation of the object as such, but of the partial experience of an encounter between a sensory zone and an object that perhaps will make it complete. This is what Aulagnier calls a 'complementary object-zone', in which the dimension of feelings and sensations prevails over that of object-representation. Looked at from the individual's point of view, the concept has to do with the beginnings of the self-reflexive capacity and with the possibility, at a primal level, of self-representation and self-procreation of the mind as it 'takes into itself/throws out'; this corresponds to what Freud described as primary splitting. Although Piera Aulagnier does take into account Lacan's idea of specularisation in the experience of the mirror stage, she focuses more on the reflexive movement that mental activity operates on itself rather than on the idea of a representation of the self, which, at such an early stage in development, does not exist separately from the object. The pictogram therefore does not correspond to the Freudian idea of the graphic sign that is correlative with ideographic writing and its figurative capacity; that classic conception excludes any movement which may be inherent in that kind of writing, concentrating solely on stylised figurative drawing. Aulagnier's concept of the pictogram does have dynamic connotations and contributes more to defining the primary modality of a human being's encounter with his or her environment (the primal dimension), with its force of attraction that we see in psychotic functioning; this will be followed by access to representation in the true sense of the word and to phantasy (the primary dimension), and thereafter to thinking and language (the secondary dimension).

Reference

Aulagnier, P. (1975). *La violence de l'interprétation. Du pictogramme à l'énoncé*. Paris: Presses Universitaires de France. [*The Violence of Interpretation: From Pictogram to Statement*, trans. A. Sheridan. New Library of Psychoanalysis. London: Routledge, 2001.]

Primary erotogenic masochism [*masochisme primaire érogène*]

The concept of primary or erotogenic masochism was introduced by Freud in 1924 in his paper on 'The Economic Problem of Masochism' (Freud, 1924c) and contributed to the development of his thinking on the structural model of the mind and his final theory of the drives. Primary masochism is a way of binding the death drive, an admixture of the death and life drives. Part of the death drive, defined as a self-destructive drive, is diverted on to objects in the outside world through the influence of the life drive and takes the form of sadistic manifestations which Freud calls 'the destructive instinct, the instinct for mastery, or the will to power' (1924c, p. 163). Part of this self-destructive drive, however, remains within the self and is bound libidinally with the help of sexual co-excitation, thus constituting masochism. In this sense, primary or erotogenic masochism has a *positive* role to play in mental life, because it testifies to an initial binding of the death drive by the life drive; its functioning, as Freud emphasises, 'still has the self as its object' (p. 164). The clinical work of French psychoanalysts with borderline patients has enabled them to verify the heuristic value of the concept: as the object is decathected, the hypercathexis of erotogenic masochism in self-destructive attacks is an ultimate solution that can be put in the service of death by destroying anything that would be projective as regards the object. In such cases, the work of analysis attempts to reintroduce a link with the object by underlining the sadism that is implied in erotogenic masochism and thus reviving a possibility of opening up to life. In addition to erotogenic masochism defined as pleasure in physical pain, Freud described two other kinds of masochism: moral masochism, with its eroticisation of guilt feelings, and feminine masochism, corresponding to the fantasy in men of 'being castrated, or copulated with, or giving birth to a baby' (p. 162). Although these two kinds of masochism have their drive-related base in erotogenic masochism, they bear witness to the self's capacity to make use of projection by means of representations involving the object.

Reference

Freud, S. (1924c). The Economic Problem of Masochism. *S.E.*, *19*: 157.

Primary homosexuality [*homosexualité primaire*]

The concept of *primary homosexuality* was introduced by Evelyne Kestemberg (1984) to account for the transition from *primary identification*, defined by Freud as a complete and identical identification with the object and 'the earliest and original form of emotional tie' (Freud, 1921c, p. 106), to *secondary identification*, corresponding to a partial identification with the object as a result of cathecting it. In both sexes, primary homosexuality can be defined as cathecting the maternal object in a first attempt at differentiation in terms of a 'double', thus enabling the beginnings of a dialectical relationship between being like the object and loving the object, between 'identification with' and 'cathexis of'. The idea is to facilitate the shift from a relationship with an identical object to one with a *similar* object through cathecting an *affect of tenderness*; Freud had said of tenderness that it encourages the inhibition of the drives as regards their aim – the tendency to immediate discharge of drive-related excitation. From that point of view, the psychosexual destiny of girls can be seen as being easier than that of boys, since, unlike boys, girls do not have to dis-identify with the maternal body – they can therefore *be* like their first love object and *love* it at the same time.

References

Freud, S. (1921c). *Group Psychology and the Analysis of the Ego. S.E., 18*: 65.
Kestemberg, E. (1984). 'Astrid' ou homosexualité, identité, adolescence. Quelques propositions hypothétiques ['Astrid' or homosexuality, identity, adolescence: Some hypothetical propositions]. In *L'adolescence à vif* [Adolescence laid bare]. Paris: Presses Universitaires de France, 1999.

Progressive disorganisation [*désorganisation progressive*]

This notion was introduced into psychosomatic theory by Pierre Marty (1963, 1968, 1980). It is essentially a phenomenological notion that describes a retrograde movement through the various levels of organisation of psychosomatic functioning, from the highest form to the most primitive.

References

Marty, P. (1963). *La psychosomatique de l'adulte* [Adult psychosomatics]. Paris: Presses Universitaires de France.
Marty, P. (1968). A major process of somatization: The progressive disorganization. *International Journal of Psycho-Analysis, 49*: 246–249.
Marty, P. (1980). *L'ordre psychosomatique. Les mouvements individuels de vie et de mort*, Vol. 2 [The psychosomatic order: Individual impulses of life and death]. Paris: Payot.

Real, Imaginary and Symbolic [*Réel, Imaginaire & Symbolique*]

This trilogy was introduced by Lacan in the 1950s when he described his conception of the topography of the mind and his structural approach to the unconscious 'structured as a language'. The concept of the *Real* dimension is a reference both to the philosophical notion of the thing-in-itself that cannot be known and to Freud's concept of psychic reality. Lacan (1954a) defined it as a real thing, impossible to symbolise, that had to do with primitive anxiety concerning the maternal sex organ; it is therefore the *locus* of madness. In psychosis, which for Freud is characterised by the repudiation [*Verwerfung*] of external reality and for Lacan by the foreclosure [*forclusion*] of the fundamental signifier, that of the paternal function, the Real dimension represents that 'other place' which cannot be integrated into the unconscious.

The *Imaginary* dimension, conceptualised by Lacan (1949 – chapter 3, this volume) as early as 1936 based on his work on the specular image, designates a dual relationship with a visual likeness [*semblable*]; it is the *locus* of the ego with its phenomena of illusion, alienation and deception correlative with narcissistic identification with the mother. That imaginary relationship may result in psychosis unless it is mediated by a relationship with the father, a notion that led Lacan immediately to conceptualise the third element of his trilogy.

The concept of the *Symbolic* dimension was introduced by Lacan (1953, 1954b) when he drew a parallel between the structure of the unconscious and that of language. The perspective he adopted was close to that of structural linguistics (Ferdinand de Saussure) and structural anthropology (Claude Lévi-Strauss). The term Symbolic thus involves a *structure*, the elements of which are to be described not in themselves but through their reciprocal relationships, like signifiers in language; it designates the register to which that structure belongs – that is, the *Symbolic order*. Freud's reference to *the* symbolism of dreams had to do with the semantic dimension of symbols based on a one-to-one relationship between the symbol and what is symbolised, whereas Lacan set out to emphasise the idea of *The Symbolic*, used as a masculine noun, following a syntactic approach to symbols in which the idea is to make reference to a *law* of functioning. That is why seeing the unconscious in terms of the structure of language is taken as a model for describing both mental functioning and the shift from an imaginary relationship with the mother to one with the *symbolic father* (the *Nom-du-Père* [Name-of-the-Father]). The symbolic father is not reducible to the real or the imaginary father; it represents the law that governs the relationship between human beings as regards their desires. Although that Lacanian trilogy does to some extent echo Freud's description of the Oedipus complex and of the structuring role of the primal fantasies, Lacan in fact emphasises the hiatus between the Imaginary and Symbolic dimensions; this is on a par with the idea of an insurmountable gap between neurosis and psychosis, the mechanisms in either of which are irreducible to those of the other.

References

Lacan, J. (1953). Fonction et champ de la parole et du langage en psychanalyse. In *Ecrits* (pp. 237–322). Paris: Editions du Seuil, 1966. [The Function and Field of Speech and Language in Psychoanalysis. In *Ecrits* (pp. 197–268), trans. B. Fink. New York: W. W. Norton, 2002.]

Lacan, J. (1954a). La topique de l'imaginaire. In *Le séminaire, Livre 1: Les écrits techniques de Freud* (pp. 87–102). Paris: Editions du Seuil. [The Topic of the Imaginary. In *The Seminar of Jacques Lacan, Book 1* (pp. 73–88), trans. J. Forrester, ed. J.-A. Miller. New York: W. W. Norton, 1991.]

Lacan, J. (1954b). L'ordre symbolique. In *Le séminaire, Livre 1: Les écrits techniques de Freud* (pp. 245–258). Paris: Editions du Seuil. [The Symbolic Order. In *The Seminar of Jacques Lacan, Book 1* (pp. 220–234), trans. J. Forrester, ed. J.-A. Miller. New York: W. W. Norton, 1991.]

Sexualisation and desexualisation [*sexualisation & désexualisation*]

Freud (1912–13) made use of the concept of sexualisation when referring to animism and magical thinking as bearing witness to the ascendancy of the primary process; the concept of desexualisation refers to the 'transformation of object-libido into narcissistic libido' and implies 'an abandonment of sexual aims', 'a kind of sublimation' (Freud, 1923b, p. 30). There is, therefore, the organisation of some form of the ego and the actualisation of the secondary process. That economic approach to the difference between what is sexual and what is sublimated has given rise to a great deal of debate and laid the foundations for the metapsychological status of sublimation: the hypothesis of complete desexualisation in the sublimatory process would fail to take into account the link between sublimation and the vicissitudes of the sexual drives. Studies of symbol-formation have enabled us to overcome the aporia inherent in Freud's economic approach to sublimation. After Jones (1916) and Ferenczi (1913), Melanie Klein (1930) showed that there is an initial stage of treating objects as symbolically equivalent, thus contributing to the infant's exploration of the world of objects and culture; this to all intents and purposes is a sexualisation of thinking. Symbol-formation in the strict sense of the term requires that, after this initial stage, distinctions can be made so that the equivalence between symbol and symbolised object can be rejected. Symbol-formation thus contributes to conceiving of a hiatus, necessary for mental functioning, between sexualisation and desexualisation, between object-cathexis and cathexis of the ego, between the primary and secondary processes. In sublimation there would seem to be a complementary interplay between sexualisation – cathexis of the primary system corresponding to the activation of a libidinally charged unconscious fantasy – and desexualisation – cathexis of the secondary system – which contributes to the change of aims and objects that is typical of sublimation. That dialectic, however, leaves open the possibility of both a positive and a negative outcome for sublimation – either the link between these two processes is maintained and sublimation is in the service of life, or they are split apart, thus generating deadly impulses both within the self and in society as a whole.

References

Ferenczi, S. (1913). Entwicklungsstufen des Wirklichkeitssinnes [Stages in the development of the sense of reality]. In *The Selected Papers of Sandor Ferenczi, Vol. I. First Contributions to Psychoanalysis*, trans. E. Jones. London: Hogarth Press, 1952.
Freud, S. (1912–13). *Totem and Taboo*. *S.E.*, 13: ix.
Freud, S. (1923b). *The Ego and the Id*. *S.E.*, 19: 3.
Jones, E. (1916). The Theory of Symbolism. In *Papers on Psychoanalysis*. London: Baillière, Tindall & Cox, 1920.
Klein, M. (1930). The Importance of Symbol-Formation in the Development of the Ego. *International Journal of Psychoanalysis*, 11: 24–39.

Skin ego [*moi-peau*]

The concept of the skin ego was introduced by Didier Anzieu (1974). It describes the manner in which the ego seeks support from the body's skin and highlights how the ego can then be built up so as to constitute both a psychic envelope and the *locus* where contact with the external world is established. This operational concept implies that the functions of the ego and those of the bodily envelope (to limit, contain and organise) are homologous. The idea that the ego and the skin are structured in an interface relationship offers a whole new dimension to notions such as boundaries, limits and containers from a psychoanalytic perspective. Anzieu described several functions of the skin ego that are related to concepts such as Bion's container–contained relationship, Winnicott's holding and handling, and Bick's studies of the importance of the skin in early relationships: holding, containing, protecting against excitation, individuation of the self, inter-sensoriality, support for sexual excitation, libidinal recharging and registering tactile sensory traces. The conceptual richness of the notion of the skin ego enables a better understanding of complex clinical cases, emphasising the reconstruction of the early stages of the skin ego and their influence on the organisation of the mind – particularly in psychoanalytic work with borderline states. In his subsequent development of these topics, Anzieu introduced the concept of the *formal signifier*: psychoanalytic work with borderline patients aims, to some extent, to put words on these formal signifiers, which correspond to proprioceptive, tactile, coenaesthetic, kinaesthetic and postural images, thereby enabling the skin ego to be differentiated from the thinking ego (Anzieu, 1987).

References

Anzieu, D. (1974). Le moi-peau [The skin ego]. *Nouvelle Revue de Psychanalyse*, 3: 195–208.

Anzieu, D. (1987). Les signifiants formels et le moi-peau [Formal signifiers and the skin ego]. In *Les enveloppes psychiques*. Paris: Dunod. [*Psychic Envelopes*, trans. D. Briggs. London: Karnac, 1990.]

Spectrum of identity [*spectre d'identité*]

The '*spectrum of identity*' is a concept invented by Michel de M'Uzan (1994) to define the various positions that narcissistic libido may take up – or, more precisely, the *loci* and quantities cathected by narcissistic libido, from an internal pole to an external one, which coincides with the representation of the other person. Thus the 'I' is not in the ego, nor completely in the other person – it is distributed all along the fringes of this spectrum of identity. A parallel could be drawn here with Winnicott's 'intermediate area of experience', which calls into question the idea of boundaries between subject and object and encourages the development of creativity.

Reference

M'Uzan, M. de. (1994). *La bouche de l'inconscient* [The mouth of the unconscious]. Paris: Gallimard.

Specular image [*image spéculaire*]

Specular image refers to the experience Lacan (1949 – chapter 3, this volume) described in his classic paper, first read in 1936, on the 'mirror stage': between the age of six and eighteen months, infants – who are still in a state of motor helplessness because of their neoteny – anticipate in an imaginary manner being in control of their bodily unity through the perception of their own image in a mirror and by identification with the image of a visual likeness [*semblable*] in terms of a whole unit. That image in the mirror is therefore a specular image which enables infants to go beyond the image of their body as fragmented, in a perspective that recalls the shift from auto-erotism to narcissism as described by Freud. The infant's primary identification with his or her image in the mirror is not simply a cognitive experience, as the psychologist Henri Wallon (1934) thought (it was thanks to Wallon that Lacan became aware of that experience), but a libidinal experience that lies at the heart of the construction of a form of the ego. It is a narcissistic identification that Lacan calls *imaginary*, because the child identifies with a '*double*' of him/herself; the image is not actually the infant, but allows the child some form of self-recognition. That experience highlights the need to differentiate between the *subject* and the *ego*; although the ego can thus envision its unity, it runs the risk of being drawn into an illusion of autonomy and of falling victim to mis-recognition. In this sense, the ego is imaginary, while the subject is 'a speaking being'.

References

Lacan, J. (1949). Le stade du miroir comme formateur de la fonction du Je telle qu'elle nous est révélée dans l'expérience psychanalytique. In *Écrits*. Paris: Editions du Seuil, 1966. [The Mirror Stage as Formative of the Function of the *I* as Revealed in Psychoanalytic Experience. In *Ecrits*, trans. A. Sheridan. London: Tavistock, 1977.]
Wallon, H. (1934). *Les origines du caractère chez l'enfant* [The origins of character in children]. Paris: Presses Universitaires de France, 1987.

Subjectivation and de-subjectivation [*subjectivation & désubjectivation*]

The concept of subjectivation was introduced into psychoanalytic thinking in France in the early 1990s by Raymond Cahn (1991) in his description of the psychoanalytic treatment of adolescents – adolescence is the time in life when the idea of the subjective owning of one's psychic reality is at its most acute. In the 1950s, Lacan (1957) had already insisted on the importance of differentiating between 'the subject' and 'the ego'; he conceptualised the philosophical and logical notion of 'the subject' in the context of his theory of the signifier, transforming the subject of consciousness into a subject of the unconscious, of knowledge and of desire. However, Lacan's linguistic approach led him to dispossess the concept of subject of any link with the body and affects. Many other French-speaking psychoanalysts who went on to explore narcissistic issues found that the concept of 'the *subject*' was especially useful – indeed necessary – for describing a process of *subjectivation* correlative with the construction of a mental space differentiated on the basis of links with the *object*. The actualisation and acknowledgement of this process-related subject is the ultimate aim of any psychoanalytic undertaking. Psychosis, on the other hand, confronts the individual with a process of *de-subjectivation* because of the splitting of the ego, which deprives the subject of any possibility of experiencing him/herself in a relationship of narcissistic continuity with the self. The subjective owning of mental space, as described by this new concept, is closely related to the concept of symbolisation and to what Winnicott defined as the construction of a potential space for play. Without being entirely novel, this approach does have the virtue of encompassing in a single concept several processes that participate in the formation of the individual as a separate being.

References

Cahn, R. (1991). Du sujet [The subject]. *Revue Française de Psychanalyse*, 55 (6): 1353–1490.

Lacan, J. (1957). L'instance de la lettre dans l'inconscient ou la raison depuis Freud. In *Ecrits* (pp. 493–528). Paris: Editions du Seuil, 1966. [The Instance of the Letter in the Unconscious or Reason since Freud. In *Ecrits* (pp. 412–542). New York: W. W. Norton, 2002.]

'Vital-identital' [vital-identital]

The concept of *'vital-identital'* was introduced by Michel de M'Uzan (2005) and corresponds in part to Freud's concept of self-preservation. On the terminological level, the concept is a necessary one, since self-preservation is not drive-related. The word *drive* should be applied only to what involves the psycho-sexual domain. De M'Uzan prefered the word *'identital'* to the more usual French word *'identitaire'*, which is very close, in order to show the reciprocity with the term *'sexual'* introduced into French by Jean Laplanche (2007). In addition, self-preservation as an activity or mechanism is only one of the responsibilities incumbent upon an essentially genetic programme, triggered by the encounter between male and female gametes and scheduled to last for a predefined length of time.

References

Laplanche, J. (2007). *Sexual. La sexualité élargie au sens freudien, 2000–2006* [Sexual: A broader concept of sexuality in Freud's sense, 2000–2006]. Paris: Presses Universitaires de France.

M'Uzan, M. de. (2005). *Aux confins de l'identité* [The frontiers of identity]. Paris: Gallimard.

Work of the negative [travail du négatif]

The *work of the negative* is one of the major concepts of André Green's thinking; it is indeed the title of one of his most important books (Green, 1993/1999). The work of the negative has to do with all the negative and destructive manifestations of the mind which Green explored through his clinical work as a psychoanalyst: negative or death narcissism, pathological negative hallucination, blank psychotic nucleus, dead mother. However, in parallel with the destructive effect, Green emphasises the positive role of the negative dimension in the mind as an effect of the unconscious; he shows (chapter 17, this volume) that the capacity for representing and fantasising is related to that of setting up a *negative hallucination* of the perceived object as well as a framework structure enabling representation to take place. The hypothesis of the *work of the negative* is a fundamental aspect of Green's theory: the infant has to negativise the mother's presence in order to create an empty space in which representations can be set up. That conception of mental functioning can be likened to Bion's idea that the self has first of all to acquire an apparatus for thinking thoughts if thoughts, fantasies and dreams are to exist. Green (1997) has pointed out the potential parallels between his idea of the work of the negative and Winnicott's intuition concerning the role of the negative dimension in the final 1971 version of his famous paper 'Transitional Objects and Transitional Phenomena' (Winnicott, 1953) particularly as regards not-me possession, the transitional object as not being the breast and the decathexis of the representation of an object.

References

Green, A. (1993). *Le travail du négatif*. Paris: Editions de Minuit. [*The Work of the Negative*, trans. A. Weller. London: Free Association Books, 1999.]

Green, A. (1997). The Intuition of the Negative in *Playing and Reality*. *International Journal of Psychoanalysis, 78*: 1071–1084.

Winnicott, D. W. (1953). Transitional objects and transitional phenomena. In *Playing and Reality*. London: Routledge, 1971.

INDEX

'a priori', transcendental, Kant's 274
abandonment, maternal 725
abnormality, 'a measure of' 561
abreaction 122
absent mother 346, 700, 709
'absolute' primary narcissism 777
abstinence 77, 82; rule of 129
acted scansion 138, 766
acting out 129, 162, 165, 170, 171, 219, 236, 262, 475, 509, 712, 743, 750
active defence 122
actual neuroses 439, 767
actual psychoses 440, 767
adolescence, sexual in 540–2
adolescent depression 560
adolescents, psychoanalytic treatment of 57, 787
affect(s): role of 3, 8, 17, 20, 32, 272; and feeling 91; and idea 4, 17, 34, 37, 268, 271; instinctual 292; and phantasy 33; primacy of 3; quota of 268, 437; and representation, Freud's distinction between 4, 33; and representations 17, 30, 33, 437; of tenderness 26, 782; of unpleasure 293; unconscious 505, 506, 542; and words 106
affective memory 425
affective perversion 655
aggressor, identification with 295, 510, 606, 614, 642
agieren 162, 262, 263; *see also* acting out
agony, psychic 611, 727
agoraphobia 127, 321
Aha-Erlebnis 98
alexithymia 439, 470
alienated unconscious identifications 412
alienating narcissistic unconscious identification 412, 417
alienation, paranoic 102

allergy 362, 487
allo-destructiveness 444
allusive interpretations 145
alpha: elements 91, 747; function 30, 165, 482, 506
alterity 239, 246, 247, 377–82
ambi-sexed maternal imago 686
ambivalence 143, 179–80, 275, 282, 304, 361, 400, 443, 567, 584, 607, 608, 670, 725, 729, 732, 733, 735
aménagement 116
amnesia, infantile 181, 182
amnesic memory 164
amoeboid ego 483
anaclisis 273, 276, 478, 492, 533, 684; *see also* Anlehnung
anaclitic relation 289
anaclitic stage 289, 289–93, 294
anal auto-erotism 645
anal castration 576
anal erotism 228
anal phase 304
anality 534, 569, 583, 625, 637, 639
anal-sadistic stage 568, 767
analysing situation 167–9
analysis: constructions in 150, 256, 278; final stages of 120; free 79; tactical conception of 146; terminable, immanence of 168; termination of 371; training 18, 78
analyst: benevolent neutrality of 141, 147, 149, 246; as guardian of the enigma 149; as guardian of play 140; identification with 120, 559, 766; immutability of 118; implication of [in analysis of character 227–30; and countertransference 148, 220]; introjection of 142, 145, 184; invisibility of 225; as mirror 146, 199, 406; neutrality of 92; transference of 147, 215; unconscious

analyst – *Contd*.
  participation of 151, 260; *see also* psychoanalyst
analytic method: definition of 155; and fundamental rule 155–71; key aspects of 155–9
analytic procedure, and fundamental rule 159–61
analytic process, finality of, in child 182–84
analytic sessions, variable-length 4
analytic site 138, 141, 142, 146, 167, 168
analytic situation: vs. analysing situation 139; concept of 163–7; countertransference in 225–7; narcissistic aspects of 190–9; use of tact in 124
analytic space 43, 146, 147, 211, 214, 215
analytic third 30
analytic unbinding 245
anamnesis 219, 460
animism 379, 380, 384, 445, 784; primitive 384
animistic double 379–85
animistic thinking 384
Anlehnung 273; *see also* anaclisis
'Anna O.' 310, 397
annihilation 34, 357, 500, 607, 688, 726, 741; anxiety 277, 278, 442, 685, 689, 753, 762, 764; principle of 726; sense of 317
anorexia nervosa 403, 444, 686, 706, 710, 721, 769
Anspruch 264
anthropological situation, fundamental 149, 771
anthropology, structural 325, 783
anthropomorphism 356
anticipatory illusion 465
anti-narcissism 694, 696, 700, 776
anti-physiological reaction 488
anxiety(ies): annihilation 277, 278, 442, 685, 689, 753, 762, 764; archaic 83, 671; castration 183, 342, 469, 585, 631, 672, 676; claustro-agoraphobic 42; death 379; eighth-month 293; fragmentation 305; masculine 23; neurosis 191; Nirvana 485; persecutory 758, 759; pregenital 24, 556; primitive, archaic (unthinkable) 36, 277; projected 129; projective 119; prototypes of 288; psychotic 42; separation 22, 42
APF: *see* French Psychoanalytical Association
aporia 148, 215, 784

apparatus for thinking 35, 789
après-coup 3, 20, 29, 148, 150, 156, 158, 167, 405, 409, 413, 415, 503; descriptive 21; dynamic 21; *see also* deferred action; *Nachträglichkeit*
archaic anxieties 83, 671
archaic maternal imago 555, 556
archaic mother 555, 685; imago of 685
archaic primitive ego 358
'armchair strategy' 222
asthma 275, 347, 348, 487; infantile 362
Athena 490, 613, 695, 696, 699, 700, 701
attachment(s) 16, 129, 157, 158, 257, 328, 472, 478, 481, 484, 486, 600, 641, 642, 699; denial of 6; erotic 35; theory 14
attacks on linking, in psychotic functioning 39, 487
autism 286, 346, 348, 424, 479, 688, 691, 714, 738, 746, 751; primary and secondary 483
autistic enclaves 739
autistic patients 424, 501, 509, 688, 720, 738, 739, 741*n*, 751, 769
autistic phenomena, metapsychological interpretation 746–51
autistic withdrawal 688, 769
auto-erotic double 380–3
auto-erotic functioning 721
auto-erotic phantasy 34
auto-erotic satisfaction 274, 334
auto-erotic stage, of oral phase 298
auto-erotic withdrawal 686, 770
auto-erotism 34, 273–5, 322, 332–6, 345–52, 443, 485, 531, 533, 539, 632, 643–7, 687, 689, 726, 768, 786; anal 645; object-related 281; pre-object 281, 282; primary 347, 643, 718, 721; secondary 377, 380
autohypnosis 311
auto-immune diseases 442
auto-immune phenomena 487
automatism, psychic 253, 254
autonomous ego 57, 90–3, 294, 308, 701*n*

barbarism 543, 547, 548
basic assumptions, fight–flight 545
Bedürfnis 436
Befriedigung 333
behaviourism 44, 70
benevolent neutrality 141, 147, 149, 246

benign neurosis 192
beta elements 91, 747
binding 29, 34, 35, 168, 207, 262, 270, 275, 351, 352, 437, 440, 444, 497, 501–6, 510, 512, 535–9, 624, 646, 691, 736, 781; libidinal 443; primary 536, 537, 538; psychic 732; *see also* unbinding
biological bisexuality 559
biology 208
bipersonal field 44, 147, 149
birth, trauma of 288
bisexual mediation 559, 768–9
bisexualisation 653, 660, 666; concept of 558, 767; process of 558, 767
bisexuality 567, 592, 604, 627, 629, 632, 639, 706n; biological 559; concept of 607, 652, 653; fantasmatic 663; literary example 660–6; pregenital 653; psychic 23, 42, 95, 558, 559, 646, 649–67, 773, 767
black hole 725
blank dreams 290, 363
blank psychic event 688
blank psychosis(es) 44, 138, 155, 277, 363, 686, 769–70, 777
blank psychotic nucleus 276, 789
blank relationship 451
blank thought 364
blankness 776; dazzling experience of 689
bodily ego 441, 685
bodily envelope 441, 492, 493, 785
body 435–46; ego 14; fragmented ['*corps morcelé*'] 13, 89, 90, 101; image 14; significance of 3
body ego 14, 15, 380, 381, 589; boundary of, skin as 15
body image 480; unconscious 24
borderline pathology/states 25, 26, 39, 41, 42, 94, 115, 139, 263, 355, 367, 372, 444, 496, 501–5, 528, 685, 686, 745, 769, 770, 781, 785
borderline patient(s) 41, 42, 139, 263, 528, 685, 781, 785
Borromean knots 67, 90
bracketing 223, 422
breast, feeding 34, 289; maternal 24, 271–4, 288, 289, 334, 345, 346, 541, 566, 643; as signifier 333
British psychoanalysis 5, 12, 23
British Psychoanalytical Society 2, 74, 140, 655
buccolingual directional reflex 289

cadre 4, 42, 43, 528; *see also* setting
cancellation, as mechanism of obsessional neurosis 101
cannibalistic massacre 545
castrated mother 555, 581, 582
castration: anal 576; anxiety 23, 24, 183, 202, 204, 206, 208, 342, 469, 530, 557, 585, 606, 608, 624, 625, 629, 631–5, 672, 676, 706, 768, 772 [Freudian concepts of, women disagreement on 607]; auto-, 575; complex 24, 202, 305, 352, 430, 564, 604–8, 615, 617, 619, 620, 626, 635, 646, 652 [female, and penis envy 578–89]; denial of 686, 706, 708; fantasy 618, 619, 658, 676; female 578, 635; genital 308; male 557, 629, 634; maternal 555, 685; paternal 572, 772; primordial 24; symbolic 24, 431
catastrophic decomposition 36
catatonia 697
catharsis 4, 310
cathexis(es): displacement of 187; of ego 303, 308, 644, 784; of factual realities of childhood 541; of internal objects 183; libidinal 178, 485; narcissistic 143, 187, 195, 196, 214, 277, 279, 308, 446, 579, 632, 638, 665, 696, 709, 722, 725, 752, 753, 776; of object 279, 299, 303, 308, 443, 757; oral, of maternal object 297–8; of 'sameness' 558; transference 690
causality 100, 150, 270, 334, 454, 455
censorship 43, 194, 329, 339; between consciousness and preconscious 145; ego 262; of lover 341, 343, 347, 348, 349, 350, 352; of woman-as-lover 275, 276, 557, 632, 633, 771, 773
censure de l'amente 34
central ego 305
Centre for Psychoanalysis and Psychotherapy, Paris 516, 685, 689, 706
character neurosis(es) 119, 187, 451, 457, 718n
character resistance 227
characteropathic shell 228
child(ren): development 300; finality of analytic process in 182–4; importance of play 142; magical narcissistic 561; object relationships of 286–308; polymorphous sexuality of 558; psychoanalysis of 7, 24, 69, 76, 142, 173–88, 719n; psychotherapy of 142, 184–8; psychotic 187, 188, 300, 493; specificity of psychoanalytic process in 175–81

Index 793

chimera 145, 147, 677, 770
chimèra/chimère 44, 770
circumcision, female 616
claustro-agoraphobic anxieties 42
claustrophobia 572, 574, 597
clitoris 325, 555, 574, 578, 579, 583, 625, 646, 699
coenaesthetic proprioceptive images 442
co-excitation, libidinal 537, 538, 655, 773
cognitivism 70
coitus interruptus 534
cold psychosis(es) 39, 45, 440, 686, 710*n*, 716, 721, 767, 769–70
coming-into-being 99
communication: extra-verbal 302; linguistic 213; non-verbal 281, 442; pre-symbolic, semiotic 17; pre-verbal 301, 302; semantification of 302; symbolic 17; theories of 20, 299, 301, 303, 306; verbal and non-verbal 281
communion 109, 110
complementary object-zone 282, 688, 740, 747, 748, 780
complex of de-being 754
compulsion to represent 165
conceptual memories 271
condensation 41, 177, 226, 328, 348, 374, 424, 460, 472
conditioned reflexes 303
conflict-free area 92
conflicts, unconscious 116, 577
confrontation 2, 3
confusion of tongues 279
conjuration of object 775
conscience, moral 378, 512, 543, 549 [and minor differences 548–9; and superego 549–50]
constancy: vs. inertia 444; principle of 245, 270, 443
construction in psychoanalysis 148, 150, 256, 278; and/or reconstruction 148
container(s): and contained 441; maternal 43; psychic 442, 477, 488
containment 34, 225, 245, 483, 747
continuity-temporality, internal, and masochism and pleasure principle 523–7
contre-transfert paradoxal 779; *see also* paradoxical countertransference
controlled depersonalisation 42, 45, 95, 143, 559
Controversial Discussions 29
coprophagia 303

corps morcelé 13, 14; *see also* fragmented body
couch: and lying-down position 214; use of 41, 42, 43, 69, 70, 93, 136, 137, 139, 140, 143, 155, 165, 166, 169, 191, 192, 205, 237, 241, 426, 628, 629, 637, 639, 712, 724
counter-cathexis(es) 176, 262, 275, 276, 342, 606, 626, 628, 632, 633, 634, 753
counter-identification(s) 259, 567, 589, 592
countertransference 43, 44, 71, 77, 94, 123, 139, 145–51, 158, 162, 168, 175, 197, 210–31, 236, 240, 243, 244, 259, 260, 280, 367, 371, 380, 383, 384, 386, 408–16, 430, 470, 508, 597, 676; analyst's implication 148, 220; in analytic situation 225–7; as demand 230; etymological composition of term 219; extensive theory of 221; homosexual 373, 375; negative 145; paradoxical 20, 144, 145, 278, 779, 780; precession of 218–19; and psychoanalytic thought 218–31; and reflective thinking 230–1; restricted meaning of 219–20; role of 210–17; and thinking 231
cravat, Croatian 543
creativity 8, 16, 91, 166, 391, 453, 559, 560, 561, 577, 578, 679, 687, 786
crypts 279
cultural superego 446, 543
cure: psychoanalytic 159, 174, 178, 181, 183; talking 92, 271; -type 41
cure, la 40
cybernetics 20
cyclothymic patient 106

damp wrapping 492–3
Darstellbarkeit 4, 33, 36, 774; *see also figurabilité*; representability
Darstellung 4, 33, 36, 45, 269, 774; *see also* figuration; representation
'day baby' 276, 632
daydream(s)/daydreaming 145, 252, 311, 321, 327, 328, 329, 330, 336, 610
dead mother 19, 259, 276, 277, 417, 789
deadly masochism 444
death: anxiety 379; denial of 378; drive 25, 29, 30, 31, 35, 44, 63, 64, 231, 245, 276, 305, 348, 351, 355, 427–31, 436, 438, 442–46, 496–514, 516, 517, 520–26, 536, 537, 538, 608, 689, 697, 748, 751, 775, 777, 778, 781 (and Eros 497); instinct 29, 31, 35, 38, 39, 102, 311, 339, 341, 344, 439, 461, 462, 491, 497–504, 521, 522, 524, 568; narcissism 29, 276, 355, 443, 496, 777, 789; of psyche 687,

728; psychic 279, 379, 413, 419, 556, 561, 613, 732, 745
de-being, complex of 754
decathexis 126, 294, 341, 345, 348, 352, 688, 748, 750, 751, 778, 789; of body 689; of external world 685, 700; of object 31
de-centred subject 9
decompensation, catastrophic 36
deep regression 195
defence(s) 11, 26, 39, 90, 95, 116, 118, 177, 228, 237, 247, 275, 276, 277, 291, 315, 316, 329, 332, 356, 372, 428, 459, 468, 487, 556, 560, 625, 639, 656, 687, 688, 691, 701, 702, 731, 732, 734, 753; active 122; analysis of 6, 124; of ego 102; interpretation of 120; manic 170, 183; mechanisms 128, 294, 453, 479, 480, 489, 491, 727; mental 438; obsessional 195; pathological 315; penis envy as, and fears for integrity of ego 586–9; primitive 440; by reality 313; of splitting 20; supreme 20, 730; survival 20, 726–8
defensive narcissism 15
defensive working-through 275
deferred action 21, 150, 322, 465; see also après-coup, Nachträglichkeit
defusion, and desexualisation 538–9
déjà vu 383, 386, 691, 756, 757, 759, 762
délire d'interprétation 197
delusion(s) 10, 39, 201, 277, 346, 359, 364, 365, 366, 412, 450, 464, 475, 564, 686, 688, 716, 720, 740, 752, 757, 761, 762, 767, 769; hysterical 775; paranoid 192, 775; space for 776
delusional solutions 464, 465, 686n
demarcation signifiers 262
denial 322; of castration 686, 706, 708; of death 378; by fetishisation 353
depersonalisation 94, 117, 130, 131, 144, 145, 151, 202, 203, 205, 206, 260, 278, 506, 740, 753, 771; controlled 42, 45, 95, 143, 559
depression 12, 186, 390, 391, 399, 400, 474, 694, 762, 769; adolescent 560; essential 38, 45, 439, 459–70, 771–2; maternal, and formation of identity 19; melancholic 442, 461, 698; neurotic 769; objectless 459; psychotic 38, 462; silent 439
dépression essentielle 38, 771; see also essential depression
depressive mother 303
depressive neuroses 119

depressive position, Kleinian concept of 12, 17, 37, 401, 416
depth psychology 541; psychoanalysis as 61
derealisation 203, 373
désaide 58; see also helplessness, Hilflosigkeit
descriptive après-coup 21
desexualisation 258, 308, 498, 501, 558, 561, 644, 645, 647, 659, 784; and defusion 538–9; secondary 445, 446, 538; and sexualisation in psychoanalysis 528–42
désexualisation 784; see also desexualisation
desobjectalisation 28
désorganisation progressive 782; see also progressive disorganisation
destructive drive(s) 179, 276, 357, 360, 443, 444, 497, 506, 512, 656, 666, 689, 775, 781
destructive instinct 444, 488, 498, 781
destructive narcissism 29, 777
de-subjectivation 57, 778, 787
désubjectivation 787; see also de-subjectivation
deutero-phallic phase 583
developmental psychoanalysis 56, 272
developmental psychology 98
devenir 99
différance 445, 532
différence 445; differentiated object relations, stage of 295–6
differentiation 532
Ding-Vorstellungen 4, 269
disanimation 709n, 718
disavowal 356, 360, 361, 469, 509, 544, 706, 716, 717, 734
discourse, unconscious 262
disobjectalising/disobjectalisation 28, 31, 757; function 276, 443, 445, 497, 689, 777–8
disorganisation: progressive 35, 38, 439, 782; psychopathological 774; somatic 439
disorientation 143, 191
displacement(s) 13, 162, 177, 180, 226, 256, 273, 328, 396, 431, 460, 463, 526, 538, 633, 635, 709, 773; of cathexis 187; as mechanism of obsessional neurosis 101; psychic 229; symbolic 117
dissociation: of consciousness 311; fragmenting 689, 700
dissolution, of transference 139, 149, 237, 247
distance, concept of 115–33 (case material 125–33)
diverted sexual 533–4
dizziness 143
'Dora' [Freud's patient] 223, 225, 241, 623

Index   795

'double' 89, 90, 278, 782, 787; animistic 379–85; auto-erotic 380–3; dynamic of 378–82; narcissistic 277, 381, 383, 558 ('material', 380–1); specular 277; working as 14, 44, 45, 367–86 (clinical example) 372–77; and Freudian theory 368–72)
double bind 20, 687, 779
dream(s): blank 290, 363; formation 33; hallucination 36; hallucinatory aspect of 140; imagery 36; images 269; interpretation of 156; life 38, 449, 457, 596; logical relationships in 269; pathogenic 322; repetitive 762; screen 34, 35, 363, 763; space 762, 763; symbolism of 783; theory 140, 271; transference 117, 122, 596; traumatic 275; -work 145, 269, 339, 368, 384, 774
dreaming, operational 38
drive(s) [*passim*]: binding 444; concept of 73, 268, 275, 436, 437, 506; death *see* death instinct; definition 436; destructive 179, 276, 357, 360, 506, 656, 666, 689, 775; dualism of 438, 443; economic aspect 437; functioning 144, 206; genitalisation of 117, 118; importance of 3, 29; vs. instinct 27; instinctual 81, 82, 83, 143, 297, 298, 435–46, 571 [concept of 436, 437]; introjection of, Ferenczi's concept of 391–6; libidinal 29, 39, 179, 298, 443, 486, 505; life 29, 443, 444, 500, 521, 537, 689, 697, 751, 775, 777, 781; oral 273, 350; origin of pleasure principle in 521–3; psychic representative of 271; -related excitation 276, 439, 440, 763, 769, 782; renunciation 445, 618; representations 36; representative 431; revealer of 777; self-destructive 444, 781; self-preservative 25, 144, 276, 497, 530, 535, 536, 644, 645; and sexual, primary sexualisation 534–5; as somatic process 437; splitting of 350, 491; theory of 25, 28, 436, 442, 443, 444, 445, 511, 520, 524, 535, 536, 653, 781 [first 535, 536; second 536; third 536; Freud's 30]; trajectories of 511–13; *see also* pulsion, *Trieb*
Durcharbeiten 176; *see also* working through
dyadic homosexuality 614–15
dynamic *après-coup* 21

eating 273, 331, 395, 396, 403, 698
École de la cause freudienne (ECF) 69
École freudienne de Paris (EFP) 1, 11, 67, 68, 69, 71; *see also* Freudian School

economic function of mother 275
economic model, Freud's 27
eczema 486, 487, 593
EFP: *see* École freudienne de Paris
ego 57, 63, 498; amoeboid 483; autonomous 57, 90, 92, 93, 308, 701*n* (sectors of 294); bodily 441, 685; breakdown 95; cathexis of 303, 308, 644, 784; central 305; conceptualisation of, Lacanian 13; defences of 83, 102; development of 14, 292, 296, 305, 334, 378; frustrations, specific 725; functions 31, 107, 113, 753; hieratic- 373, 374, 375; -ideal 90, 187, 196, 378, 446, 550, 581, 671, 710, 720 (*see also* ideal ego); infant's, structuring 299; integrity of, fears for, penis envy as defence against 586–9; internal destructive 305; libidinal 305; libido 536, 726; narcissistic haemorrhage in 503; pleasure 352, 464, 502, 557, 699; primitive, archaic 358; as psychic agency 441; psychology 5, 7, 8, 10, 12, 14, 15, 56, 57, 67, 88, 90, 216, 272; reality 352, 353, 464, 557, 699, 700; repressing 753; rudimentary 291, 308; splitting of 15, 349, 544, 691, 706, 716, 721, 752, 753, 754, 757, 778, 787; structure of 94, 363 [primary 305]; and superego 180–5; verbal traces and perceptions 427; wounds of 725
eighth-month anxiety 293
Einbildung 313
Einbildungskraft 311
Einspruch 264
elaboration, through interpretation 175, 178, 179, 184
elation 143, 179, 192–4, 198
elimination, principle of 687, 727
empathy 151, 257, 258, 260, 273, 506
empiricism 2, 406
empiricist psychology 270
enactments 93, 559, 689; self-destructive or allo-destructive 686, 770
encephalopathy 300
end-of-session syndrome 192–3
engulfment 90, 571
enigmatic message 19, 29, 34, 149, 242, 771
enigmatic other 19
enigmatic signifier(s) 149, 248, 532, 541, 771
enigmatic unconscious 43
enunciative operations, theory of 423
envelope: bodily 441, 492, 493, 785; protective 699
environment, facilitating 8

environmental modifications 184
Epictetus' basket 215
epileptic fit 485, 596
epoché 223, 411; *see also* bracketing
Erfassen 427
erogeneity 307, 334, 655
erogenous zones 29, 206, 334, 335, 485, 625, 627, 639, 645, 748
Eros 25, 30, 35, 338, 350, 360, 428, 444, 497–502, 506, 511, 513, 522, 537, 548, 568, 569, 574, 599, 632, 650, 666, 668, 689, 727, 751, 775
erotic attachments 35
erotic feminine dimension 556, 609–11
erotic masochism 23
erotico-maternal feminine 556, 612, 613, 616–18, 619, 620
erotism: anal 228; intrapsychic 539
erotogenic masochism 381, 444, 499, 687, 773; hypercathexis of 770, 781; and pleasure principle 516–27; primary 781
erotogenic zones 275, 304, 307, 335, 380, 774; excitation of 274
essential depression 38, 45, 439, 459–62, 470, 771, 772
ethnic cleansing 545, 548, 550
euphoria 65, 193, 198
European Psychoanalytical Federation 73, 141, 173, 405, 442
evacuation 36, 443, 502, 533
evenly suspended attention, analyst's 138, 141, 144, 145, 156, 212, 559, 657
event, and structural schema 273
excitation: drive-related 276, 439, 440, 763, 769, 782; of erotogenic zone 274; external 315, 316, 441; overload of 485; rehabilitation of, and pleasure principle 518–21; sexual 315, 335, 444, 485, 490, 518, 525, 526, 785
excorporation 358, 359, 502, 533
exhibitionism 335, 581, 584
existentialism 103
experience of satisfaction 19, 29, 140, 336
exquisite corpse, fantasy of, and pain of mourning 400–3
extermination camps 548
external reality, vs. psychic reality 136, 508, 684, 692
extra-verbal communication 302

facilitating environment 8
factual, hypercathexis of 339, 440

faeces 20, 129, 350, 623, 628, 639, 703
failed homosexuality 615
false self 15, 18
family romance 313, 714, 716, 734
fantasmatic bisexuality 663
fantasmatic life 338–53
fantasmatic representation 740, 741, 746, 749
fantasy(ies): etymological root of 253; female 631–2; of incorporation 331, 395, 396, 401, 557; metapsychological status of 329, 336; original 323, 324, 325, 330, 335; and origins of sexuality 310–37; paranoid 325; vs. phantasies 327; primal 90, 274, 275, 325, 330, 331, 339, 341, 345, 346, 347, 469, 541, 617, 618, 619, 638, 734, 783 [necessity of 617–18]; (*see also Urphantasien*); regressive 120, 129, 559, 768; of seduction 320, 326; structure of 333; unconscious 25, 95, 176, 177, 178, 181, 193, 323, 327, 328, 331, 336, 440, 572, 573, 771, 784; wish- 331; *see also* phantasy(ies)
father: castration of 572, 772; femininity of, filiation to 629; law of 16, 20, 92; name of 20, 22, 557, 631, 637; *see also Nom-du-Père*; penis of 24, 345, 347, 556, 566, 572, 573, 575, 577, 579, 585, 588, 624, 773 [daughter's identification with 590–8]; relation of girl to, object idealization in 565–78; rivalry with 564; role of 3, 24, 295, 703; seduction by 316; symbolic 22, 783
feeding 34, 272, 289, 291, 298, 334, 335, 345, 346, 350, 478, 479, 593, 645, 700
female castration 578, 635 (complex, and penis envy 578–89)
female homosexuality 556, 627, 636, 641, 646
female masochism 565, 598
female Oedipus complex, Freudian 627
female sexuality 22, 23, 201, 449, 554–6, 563, 568–70, 578, 579, 586, 599, 623
femaleness 554, 556
féminin, le 556, 623, 624, 772; *see also* feminine
feminin érotique 23
feminin maternal 23
feminine 92, 607, 772–3; achievement, and guilt 575–8; erotic 609–10; erotico-maternal 556, 612–20; and femininity 623–40; maternal 556, 557, 610–11, 613, 615, 616, 773, 768; work of 23
feminine development 92, 772
feminine dimension 92, 556, 557, 611, 773, 768; erotic 556, 611

feminine guilt, and Oedipus complex 563–600
feminine identifications 92, 554, 629, 772
feminine masochism 517, 781
feminine Oedipus complex 566, 626
feminine problems, conflictual outcome of 590–8
feminine sexuality 22, 23
fémininité: *see* femininity
femininity 371, 555, 556, 557, 559, 564, 569, 570, 586, 599, 607, 610, 613, 617, 649, 650, 658, 659, 664, 666, 735; and feminine 623–40; Freud's view of 92, 772; masculine 605–6; phallic/narcissistic 23; primary 23; refusal of 145
feminism 15
fertility, discovery of: first period 628
fetish 23, 581, 615, 616, 620, 624, 636, 685, 686, 702–8, 713, 717, 720, 721, 722
fetishisation 703, 710, 714; denial by 353; primary 341, 351
fetishism 342, 350–3, 581, 646, 655, 702, 706, 708, 711–14; clinical example 710–27; concept of 706; primary 351
fetishistic object relationship 686, 687, 706–22
fetishistic solution(s) 352, 615–16
fiction, Freudian 333
fight–flight assumptions 545
figurabilité 4, 36, 44, 367, 381, 774, 775; *travail de* 45; *see also* figurability
figurability 36, 45, 269, 278, 367, 370–4, 382, 384, 386, 684, 774–5; hallucinatory 382
figuration 4, 33, 36, 45, 261, 269, 278, 373–6, 719, 747; semiotic 261
figurative regression 166
Fiktion 333
filled-in transference 149
fixation: and illness of mourning 396–7; narcissistic 194
flight into health 137
flight response 287
foetalization 101
folie 355, 496, 775; *see also* madness
fonction désobjectalisante 777; *see also* disobjectalising function
fonction objectalisante 777; *see also* objectalising function
forclusion 322, 752, 783; *see also* foreclosure
foreclosure 356, 360, 509, 752, 783; identity, formation of and maternal depression 19

formal regression 41, 44, 45, 140, 141, 145, 278, 382–6, 763, 774–5; and topographical regression 151, 690
formal signifier 282, 442, 785
fort–da game 349, 709
found–created 16, 139; object 92, 166, 168, 170, 540, 687
fragmentation, functional 38, 439, 460, 461
fragmentation anxiety 305
fragmented body 13, 89, 90, 101; *see also corps morcelé*
fragmenting dissociation 689, 700
frame, guardian of, analyst as 169
France: history of psychoanalysis in 53–86; lines of advance in psychoanalysis in 73–85; post-war, psychoanalytic scene in 5, 9–12, 17, 42, 55, 56, 57, 65, 88, 93, 136, 563; psychoanalytic culture in 80–5; psychoanalytic practice in, evolution of 73–85
free analysis 79
free association(s) 37, 40, 43, 136, 138, 141–4, 155–60, 167, 196, 212, 381, 382, 425, 426, 482, 559, 759, 766; patient's 212, 216; principle of 766
free listening 226
French–British reciprocal influences 5–9
French-Language Psychoanalytic Group (OPLF) 69, 738
French psychoanalysis, philosophical foundations of 33
French Psychoanalytic Society (SFP: Société française de psychanalyse) 1, 11, 28, 66, 70, 97, 766
French Psychoanalytical Association (APF: Association psychanalytique de France) 1, 2, 4, 5, 11, 68, 73, 233, 251, 310, 441, 477
French school of psychosomatics 31
Freudian concepts, of sexuality 605
Freudian female Oedipus complex 627
Freudian fiction 333
Freudian metapsychology 12, 18, 37, 245, 269; return to 12–13
Freudian models of language 426–29
Freudian School of Paris (EFP: École freudienne de Paris) 1, 11, 24, 67, 70, 97, 738, 766
Freudian theory 19, 21, 92, 118, 244, 292, 334, 364, 502, 509, 514, 564, 568, 573, 581, 609, 772; castration complex 605–6; death drive 500; evolution of, and the double 368–72

frustration 58, 94, 110, 119, 120, 132, 194, 211, 215, 226, 253, 254, 290, 296, 333, 360, 382, 457, 502, 565, 566, 567, 581, 617, 636, 645, 658; capacity to tolerate 35, 290
frustrator, identification with 295
functional fragmentation 38, 439, 460, 461
functioning, operational 38, 440, 772
fundamental anthropological situation 149, 771
fundamental rule 43, 138, 139, 140, 143, 230, 244, 357, 381, 426, 657, 766; and analysing situation 155–71
fusion 106, 107, 108; with mother 26, 721; protective 307; with object 33, 37, 593

Gegenstand 256
Gegen-Übertragung 219; *see also* countertransference
generalised seduction 149, 771
generations, telescoping of 279; and mourning 416–19; psychoanalytic pertinence of 405–19; and transmission of history 411–12
Genesis, new version of 601–2, 621
genetic regression 319
genital castration 308
genital object relation 117, 118
genital-Oedipal transference 130
genital penis 24
genital sexuality 25, 304, 396, 634
genitalisation of drives 117, 118
German Psychotherapy Society 64
Gestalt 98, 99, 100, 289, 290, 297, 298, 334, 350
ghosts 279
girl, relation of to father, object idealization in 565–78
Gradiva 327, 635
grandiose self 687
gratification, capacity to delay 31
guardian: of enigma, analyst as 149; of frame, analyst as 169; of play, analyst as 140
guilt: awareness of 497, 500; feminine, and Oedipus complex 563–600; and feminine achievement 575–8; Oedipal 575, 588, 624, 637

haemorrhagic rectocolitis 440, 463, 466, 467, 475
hallucinated satisfaction 333, 747
hallucination(s) 29–36, 99, 140, 143, 244, 254, 258, 263, 269, 275–7, 311, 322, 351, 526, 608, 688–9, 697, 762, 774; dream 36; negative 31, 35, 277, 361–6, 374–7, 380, 385 [pathological 276, 789]; of object 31, 271; positive 277; primal 333; retreat into 688, 738–51; of satisfaction 271, 275
hallucinatory activity of infancy 32
hallucinatory figurability 382
hallucinatory fulfilment 165, 538, 700
hallucinatory phenomena 440, 750
hallucinatory projection 378
hallucinatory regression 401
hallucinatory satisfaction 150, 171, 295, 332, 340, 398, 525, 526, 720
hallucinatory vision, and speech 150
hallucinatory wish-fulfilment 31, 150, 271, 272
hallucinatory work 271
health, flight into 137
Hegelian murder 103
Hegelian philosophy 9, 18, 64, 103, 243, 356
heimlich 234, 670
helix 248
Hellenic Psychoanalytical Society 463
helplessness 58, 89, 253, 292, 316, 446, 584, 606, 786; primal 253; *see also désaide, Hilflosigkeit*
here-and-now: interpretations 21, 147; relationship 21, 139, 160, 229; situation 139, 146, 161, 164, 219, 224, 230, 382, 383, 385
hermaphroditism 652, 654
Herostratus suicide 770
heteromorphic identification 100
heterosexuality 21, 641, 663, 665
hidden–shown 557, 634, 636
hieratic-ego 373, 374, 375
Hilflosigkeit 58, 253; *see also désaide*, helplessness
history: of psychoanalysis in France 60–71; transmission of, and telescoping of generations 411–12
hollowed-out transference 149, 234, 246, 247, 248, 249
homeomorphic identification 100
homosexual countertransference 373, 375
homosexual relationship, primary 643, 645, 647
homosexual transference 368, 369, 371, 375, 383, 627
homosexualité primaire 781; *see also* primary homosexuality

homosexuality 21, 197, 364–76, 380–3, 470, 531, 555, 564, 565, 574, 579, 581, 585–9, 605–8, 619, 650, 654, 658, 659, 663–6, 676, 711, 716, 739; dyadic 614–15; failed 615; female 556, 627, 636, 641, 646; male 608, 614–15; primary 14, 26, 278, 558, 641–7, 781; triadic 615
hospitalism 479
humour 55, 236, 374, 728, 730, 733
hunger 289, 297, 333, 395, 396, 580; perception of, interoceptive 289
hyle 422
hypercathexis 347, 491, 527; erotogenic masochism 770, 781; of factual 339, 438, 440, 465, 778; of self 687; of thing-presentation 32, 269; of unconscious thoughts 269
hypnosis 4, 136, 140, 194, 311, 357
hypnotic suggestion 70, 139
hypochondria 191, 463, 520
hypochondriac patient 143, 192
hysteria 30, 40, 101, 193, 195, 271, 315, 316, 318, 327, 364, 534, 635, 638, 714; Freud's theory of 39
hysterical acting 165
hysterical delusion 775
hysterical depressive conditions 187
hysterical identification 386
hysterical psychosis 715*n*
hysterical repression 102
hysterical symptoms 33, 268, 271, 319, 653
hystero-phobic neuroses 122

I function 90
id 26, 28, 57, 63, 101, 103, 138, 155, 182, 185, 256, 296, 305, 306, 332, 340, 341, 345, 356–9, 363, 422, 427, 443, 455, 498, 504–8, 526, 596, 752, 753; Freud's conceptualisation of 35; impulses 30, 165; projection of 453; resistance of 145, 275
idea, vs. perception 276
ideal ego 90, 383, 446, 550, 770
idealisation 18, 20, 359, 429, 555, 703
idealised transference 127, 132
idealistic regression 430
ideation 4, 276, 277, 282
ideational capacity 276
ideational representation 437–44, 684, 740, 741, 749
ideational representative 268, 431, 437
identification(s): with aggressor 295, 510, 606, 614, 642; with analyst 120, 559, 766;
disengaging from 226; *en abîme* 410; feminine 92, 554, 629, 772; with frustrator 295; heteromorphic 100; homeomorphic 100; hysterical 386; interlocking 410; kinds of 199–200; mirror stage as 98; narcissistic 89, 274, 417, 446, 557, 614, 697, 718, 783, 787; partial 558, 782; paternal 629; primary 26, 92, 151, 278, 340–6, 349, 379, 386, 428, 430, 481, 550, 557, 558, 643, 644, 771, 773, 767, 781, 786; projective 6, 15, 19, 90, 147, 295, 358, 360, 417, 480, 482, 502, 545, 558, 686, 690, 718, 744, 753 [interpretation of 690; pathological 545, 753]; secondary 278, 558, 767, 782; unconscious 149, 279, 280, 407–13, 418, 440, 609 [alienated 412, 417; intergenerational 150]; vicissitudes of 614–15; work of 498
identificatory processes 89, 168, 605 (primitive 168)
identificatory projection 727
identitaire 201, 206, 207, 788; *see also* identity
identity: masculine/feminine 15; perceptual 140, 141, 150, 231, 370, 371, 375, 383; problems of 26; psychosexual 558, 653; scandal of 207; spectrum of 144, 786; thought 140, 141, 150, 231, 382, 383
ideographic writing 780
ideoverbal associations, preconscious 178
illusion, anticipatory 465
image spéculaire 786; *see also* specular image
Imaginaire 57, 782; *see also* Imaginary register
imaginary 13, 235; vs. specular 91
Imaginary register 5, 21, 57, 90, 91, 274, 782–3
imago 99; parental 180, 181, 187
immanence 155, 169, 225, 282
immutability, of analyst 118; of terminable analysis 168
impasse 20, 128, 132, 133, 158, 318, 352, 353, 357, 402, 555, 720
incest 619, 626, 628, 636, 637, 657, 724; taboo 20, 22
incestuous desire 429, 632, 633
incorporated object 279, 304, 305, 388, 392, 395
incorporation 123, 132, 273, 296, 304, 307, 358, 388, 391–401, 580, 593, 598, 698; conflict in 570–4; fantasy(ies) of 298, 331, 335, 395, 396, 401, 557, 684; of guilt 772; of object 279
Independent Group, in British Psychoanalytical Society 140

individual psychotherapy 136
inertia: vs. constancy 444; principle of 270, 276, 443, 776
infans [pre-verbal child] 3, 16, 99, 513
infant and mother, transitional relations between 293
infantile amnesia 164, 181, 182, 362
infantile asthma 362
infantile dependency, stage of 304
infantile development 35
infantile genital organisation phase 767
infantile masturbation 320, 570
infantile neurosis 111, 140, 371, 383, 385, 398, 473
infantile omnipotence 37
infantile pre-psychosis(es) 715*n*
infantile projections 34
infantile sexuality 254, 273, 274, 384, 424, 428, 438, 446, 485, 512, 605, 617, 638, 639, 647; importance of in mental life 55; and Oedipus complex 318–20; oral and anal 534; origins of sexuality 314, 318–24, 330, 333, 534; phallic monism in 24, 25; and sublimation 446; theory of 73, 270, 318, 322, 333, 436, 445, 537, 539–41, 554, 558
infantile transitivism 102
infinity, experience of 143
information theory 299, 303
ingesting food 273
injured sexual 533–4
Innenwelt vs. *Umwelt* 100–1
inner reality, denial of 183
insight, intuitive 116
insomnia 275, 341, 343, 344, 349, 457, 471, 482, 727
instinct 3, 5, 26, 27, 331, 333, 334, 394, 511, 517, 569, 570, 573, 574, 580, 584, 597, 616, 641, 643, 651, 655, 726; death 29, 31, 35, 38, 39, 311, 339, 341, 344, 439, 461, 462, 497, 499, 500, 503, 504, 521, 522, 524, 568; destructive 444, 488, 498, 781; life 29, 35, 521; maternal 344–5; theory of 436
instinctual affect 292
instinctual drive(s) 57, 81–3, 112, 116, 122, 143, 144, 268, 279, 292, 293, 297–8, 305, 435–46, 558, 560, 561, 571, 687, 691, 777 (concept of 436, 437)
Instinkt 436, 511
Institut de Psychanalyse de Paris 66
Institute of Psychoanalysis 105, 201, 286, 355, 449, 459, 496, 543

integration and sexualisation, phallic model of 535–6
intergenerational relationship 409
intergenerational unconscious identifications 150
interlocking identifications 410
intermediate area of experience 16, 147, 786
internal conflicts, unconscious 77
internal continuity-temporality, masochism and pleasure principle 523–7
internal destructive ego 305
internal object(s) 94, 116–7, 180, 268, 401, 438, 453, 514, 653, 655, 687, 708–10, 714, 719–21, 749; cathexis of 183; concept of 280
internal parents 280, 409, 411, 412, 417
internal reality, denial of 767
internal setting 140
International Association for Child and Adolescent Psychiatry and Allied Professions 286
International Association for the History of Psychoanalysis 54, 60
International Psychoanalytical Association (IPA) 1–5, 8, 11, 13, 55, 56, 60, 65–8, 73, 78, 82, 88, 89, 93, 105, 115, 155, 272, 286, 405, 507
interoceptive receptivity 292
interpretation(s): allusive 145; as confrontation 239; of defence 120; elaboration through 175, 178, 179, 184; here-and-now 147; mutative 21, 123, 139, 145, 151; of projective identification 690; psychoanalyst's 140, 161; of regressive fantasy 129; reversed 120, 129; role of 216; tactics of 690; timing of 124; transference 83, 139; verbal 92
interpretative speech, as question 429–31
intersensoriality 441, 484, 485, 490, 688, 785
intersubjectivist school 147
intersubjectivity 80, 83, 273, 406, 407, 541, 542, 768
intrapsychic erotism 539
intrapsychic tombs 279
intrauterine life 274, 746
introjection 22, 171, 203, 271, 296, 317, 318, 360, 388, 401–4, 428, 446, 460, 461, 499, 502, 512, 557–9, 570, 598, 635, 653, 659, 666, 690, 697; of analyst 142, 145, 184; concept of 391–3; of desires 279, 395; of drives, Ferenczi's concept of 391–6; of

introjection – *Contd.*
    good object 311; of Oedipal image 178; of psychoanalyst 178, 180, 184
introjective process 398, 401, 557
intrusion(s) 2, 18, 43, 60, 124, 125, 128, 311, 317, 318, 400, 408, 410, 411, 412, 413, 417, 582, 745, 717; objectal 461
intuitive insight 116
inversion, as mechanism of obsessional neurosis 101
investment, withdrawal of 31, 374, 384, 443
IPA: *see* International Psychoanalytical Association
isolation, as mechanism of obsessional neurosis 101

jouissance 506, 510, 607–12, 616, 617, 619, 620, 713, 717, 722; *amant de* 773; excessive, hatred of 546; female 608–9

kinaesthetic proprioceptive images 442
knotting 732–6

labile ego structure 127
Lacanian model, and history of psychoanalysis in France 60–71, 80–5
langage 426, 431
language [*passim*]: acquisition of 8, 18, 430, 479; -based representations 437; conception of, Freudian 32; of contact 282; development of 8, 16, 17, 270, 293, 299; as function of preconscious 32; importance of 3; models of, Freudian 426–9; and sensoriality 283; sensory substratum of 281, 425; sign system of 8; structuring power of 77; as symbolic agency 255; unconscious structured like 32, 57
langue 69, 202, 431, 738; *see also* language
latency period 180–4, 618, 639, 644
lateral transference 236, 249, 689
law of the father 16, 20, 92
legendary psychasthenia 100
'Leonardo' [Freud's analysis of] 241, 606
libidinal binding 443
libidinal cathexis 178, 485
libidinal co-excitation 538, 655, 773; and sexualisation 537
libidinal development 304, 333, 349, 557, 653
libidinal drive 30, 39, 179, 298, 443, 486, 505
libidinal ego 305
libidinal life 38
libidinal object 179, 289, 292, 294, 334, 684

libidinal recovery 461
libidinal regression 141
libido [*passim*]: aggressive and destructive 512; and death instinct 311; erotic 340; hypothesis of 304; increase in 389, 390, 391, 396, 397; narcissistic 102, 144, 346, 348, 438, 445, 446, 461, 784, 786; object- 438, 445, 446, 583, 784; oral 395primal 258; primary erotic 505; sexual 102; theory 366, 392
life: drive(s) 438, 442, 497, 500, 537, 689, 697, 751, 775, 777, 781; instinct 29, 35, 38, 521; narcissism 443, 444, 776 (as guardian of 92); operational 38, 339, 341, 439, 460
linguistic communication 213
linguistic signs 151, 281
linguistic structuralism 13
linguistic theory 21, 423
linguistics 10, 30, 57, 65, 68, 280; structural 4, 20, 30, 783
linking 29, 171, 431, 501, 510; attacks on, in psychotic functioning 39, 487
listening: free 226; to listening 407, 408, 413; neutral 226
'Little Hans' [Freud's patient] 174, 605, 611, 612, 628
'living-dead' 416, 418
loss, metapsychological moment of, reconstruction of 397–400
lost object 94, 150, 279, 303, 333, 334, 392, 394, 395, 611, 689, 757, 762
Lösung 237, 247; *see also* transference, dissolution of
ludeln 335; *see also* sucking
lying-down position 214

madness 103, 155, 357, 463, 490, 610–13, 618, 631, 633, 661, 664, 689, 701, 728, 760, 783; vs. psychosis 775–76
'magical narcissistic child' 561
magical thinking 445, 784
male castration 557, 629, 634
male homosexuality 614–15
maleness 554
malignant regression 41
mania, normal 390–1, 396
manic defences 170, 183
manic-depressive patients 304
Marxist thought 68, 91
masculine anxieties 23
masculine dimension 92, 556
masculine femininity 605–6

masculinity 23, 569, 649, 650, 658, 659, 666, 697
masochism 92, 335, 461, 513, 537, 612; deadly 444; erotic 23; erotogenic 381, 444, 499, 517, 519–26, 687, 773 [hypercathexis of 770, 781; and pleasure principle 516–27; primary 781]; female 565, 598; feminine 517, 781; internal primordial 500; and melancholia 503–8; moral 517, 686n, 781; perverse (clinical example) 489–93; primary 31, 444; secondary 499, 500; and superego 498–9
masochisme primaire érogène 781; see also primary erotogenic masochism
masturbation 193, 332, 349, 491, 711; infantile 320, 570; Oedipal 349; pre-pubertal 332
maternal abandonment 725
maternal behavioural matrixes 303
maternal breast 24, 271, 273, 274, 288, 345, 346, 541, 566
maternal castration 555, 685
maternal container 43
maternal depression, and formation of identity 19
maternal environment, impact of 34
maternal feminine 556, 557, 610–11, 613, 615, 616, 773, 768
maternal imago 580, 584, 587, 637, 717; ambi-sexed 686; archaic 555, 556
maternal instinct 344, 345
maternal object, oral cathexis of 297–8
maternal phallus 17, 18, 587, 697
maternal primary preoccupation 16
maternal reverie 31, 482
maternal seduction 28, 206
maternal signals 303
maternal subjectivity 19
maternal transferences 554; pregenital 193
maternal unconscious 18, 19, 34, 625
maternal womb, return to 541, 617
maturational process 194
Maxwell demon 356
meaning: question of 510; reversal of 444, 510
méconnaissance 12, 14, 90, 102, 103; see also misrecognition
médiation bisexuelle 768; see also bisexual mediation
Medusa 34, 613, 684, 685, 694–704, 735, 736, 776
megalomania 680, 708, 716, 720, 734

melancholia 12, 38, 389, 390, 397, 424; and masochism 503–8
melancholic depression 442, 461, 698
memory(ies): amnesic 164; childhood, traumatic 147; conceptual 271; and desire, refraining from 41; vs. perception 270, 277; of satisfaction 272, 332; screen- 169, 321, 467; -traces 32, 33, 270, 291, 292, 294, 324, 336, 383, 423, 424, 427 [re-cathecting of 271]
men, fear of women of 601–21
menopause 403, 629
menstruation 628
mental functioning [*passim*]: associative 438; conscious and unconscious 177; economic hypothesis 443; fantasy 438; French conceptualisation of 32; oneiric 438; psychoanalytic comprehension of 173; psychoanalytic understanding of 281
mentalisation 38; deficiency in 438, 778; failure of 35; lack of 439, 767; work of 440
merycism 275, 348–51
message énigmatique 771; see also enigmatic message
metamorphosis 345, 423, 424, 651, 704; and metaphor 281
metaphor 14, 34, 77, 101, 164, 406, 424, 441, 521, 616, 694, 703, 717, 720, 762; amoeba 696; of box 623; from chivalry 228; vs. metamorphosis 281; of mirror 685; paternal 531; of Perseus's shield, 684, 685 (*see also* Perseus, shield of); semiotic 261; of theatre 43; topographical 180; of train journey 160
metaphorical capacity of words 37
metaphorisation 535, 538, 559, 769
metaphysics 108
metapsychology 12, 18, 37, 245, 269, 328, 341, 355, 429, 436, 445, 496, 528, 529, 532, 539, 592, 609, 614, 718, 725, 726, 753
methodic unreason 155
metonymy 81, 616, 696
mimesis 252, 258, 546
mind, topographic model of 10, 26, 57, 151, 766
minor differences, and semiology 550
mirror: experience 90; and formation of I 97–104; function of analyst 163, 199, 406; as identification 98; maternal 684, 685; metaphor of 685; and mother's face 91; role of analyst 191, 212; -shield 703; stage

Index 803

mirror – *Contd.*
    13–15, 21, 89, 90, 91, 97, 98, 101, 406, 685, 701, 780, 786
'mirroring', in analytic relationship 235
misrecognition 14, 26, 102, 244
mnemic traces 262, 347, 610
mnesic symbol of trauma 321
moi-peau 14, 477, 785; *see also* skin ego
monadology 243
money as symbol 79
moral conscience 378, 512, 543; and minor differences 548–9; and superego 549–50
moral masochism 517, 686*n*, 781
morcellement fonctionnel 38; *see also* functional fragmentation
morphological mimicry 100
mother [*passim*]: absent 346, 700, 709; archaic 555 [imago of 685]; castrated 555, 581, 582; –child relationship 8, 14, 16, 17, 296, 297, 326, 349, 522, 613, 717, 718, 719; –child unity 717, 718, 719; –daughter relationship 618, 619, 631, 636, 640; dead 19, 259, 276, 277, 417, 789; depressive 303; economic function of 275; face of, as mirror 91; fusion with 26, 721; gaze of 91, 625, 685, 704; good, all-powerful 555; –infant relationship 442, 696; –infant system, dyadic 298; narcissistic identification with 274, 446, 783; Oedipal 377, 403; omnipotent 24, 513, 555, 580–90, 598; over-absent 700; overprotective 700; phallic 344, 582, 585, 587, 589, 599; pre-genital 26; primary identification with 343, 550, 773; primitive 90, 582; primitive dependence on, refusal of 555; as protective shield 275, 340–53, 473, 481–4, 490, 536, 685, 695, 703; reverie 31, 34, 91, 276, 328, 330, 360, 465, 482, 771, 772; sadistic 344; separation from 92, 697
mourning 6, 7, 12, 44, 163, 261, 373, 410, 416–19, 473, 474, 504, 514, 541, 649, 684, 732, 733; denial of 258; illness of 278, 388–405 [and fixation 396–7; and vicissitudes of transition 403–4]; pain of, and fantasy of exquisite corpse 400–3; pathological 279; work of 37, 279, 392, 397, 400, 401, 402, 417, 503, 708
murder: Hegelian 103; of object 542, 756
mutative interpretations 21, 123, 139, 145, 151
mutilation 357, 612, 615, 689, 748
mutual inclusion 480

mysticism 254, 427
myth, concept of 318

Nachträglichkeit 20–1, 322; *see also après-coup*
Name-of-the-Father 20, 22, 57, 557, 631, 637, 783; *see also Nom-du-Père*
nameless dread 36, 91, 277, 424, 620; Bion's concept of 36
narcissism [*passim*]: anti- 694, 696, 700, 776; concept of 535 [Freud's 34]; death 29, 276, 355, 443, 496, 777, 789; defensive 15; destructive 29, 777; as guardian of life 92; imbrication of, with anti-narcissism 776; life 92, 443, 444, 777; negative 276, 443, 444, 497, 776; non-defensive 15; phallic 15, 614; positive 92, 443; primary 14, 17, 41, 90, 92, 102, 141, 143, 219, 340, 378, 379, 643, 722 ['absolute' 777; normal 27]; primitive 464; secondary 27, 591, 777
narcissisme de mort 355, 496; *see also* death narcissism
narcissisme de vie 355, 496; *see also* life narcissism
narcissisme négatif: *see* negative narcissism
narcissistic aspects, of analytic situation 190–9
narcissistic cathexis 143, 187, 195, 196, 214, 277, 279, 288, 308, 446, 579, 632, 638, 665, 696, 709, 722, 725, 752, 753, 776
narcissistic disorders 442, 549
narcissistic double 277, 381, 383
narcissistic ego-ideal 446
narcissistic elation 143, 179, 193
narcissistic envelope 485
narcissistic fixation 194
narcissistic gratification 199, 583
narcissistic identification 89, 274, 417, 446, 557, 614, 697, 718, 783, 787; with mother 274, 446, 783
narcissistic libido 102, 144, 346, 348, 438, 445–6, 461, 784, 786
narcissistic 'material' double 380–1
narcissistic neurotic patients 192
narcissistic object 95, 143, 279, 410, 475, 606; regulation 279, 410
narcissistic omnipotence 24, 195, 196, 726
narcissistic pathology 15
narcissistic perversion 199, 687
narcissistic projection 196
narcissistic regression 15, 33, 37, 41, 42, 141, 143–6, 192–5, 278, 379, 380, 559
narcissistic seduction 688
narcissistic self-image 15

narcissistic stage 287–90, 293
narcissistic unbinding 443
narcissistic unconscious identification, alienating 412, 417
narcissistic wound 24, 216, 300, 470, 579, 584–6
Narcissus 15, 190, 191, 620
narcoanalysis 194
Nazi regime 55, 56, 64, 84, 88, 375
Nebenmensch 255
negation 24, 35, 170, 263, 295, 302, 335, 356, 376–7, 381, 422, 469, 475, 509, 555, 650, 658, 706, 715, 716, 735
negative: concept of 30; conceptualisation of 39; theory of 35; work of 30, 31, 276, 277, 356–61, 444, 507, 512, 513, 779, 788, 789
negative capability 156, 541
negative countertransference 145
negative hallucination 31, 35, 276, 277, 361–6, 374–7, 380, 385, 789; pathological 276, 789
negative judgement 358
negative narcissism 276, 443, 444, 497, 776
negative Oedipus complex 564
negative therapeutic reaction 31, 276, 357, 361, 487, 497, 500, 504
negative transference 143, 179, 182, 195, 197, 231, 690
Negativität 430; *see also* negativity
negativity 102, 212, 430, 655, 656
Neubeginn 198
neurobiology 272, 298
neuroleptic medication 754, 762
neurophysiology 245, 746
neurosis(es) [*passim*]: actual 439, 767; aetiology of 315; anxiety 191; benign 192; character 119, 187, 451, 457, 718n; depressive 119; hystero-phobic 122; infantile 111, 140, 371, 383, 385, 398, 473; obsessional 101, 119–22; psycho- 439, 767; transference 81, 110–23, 132, 139, 140, 145, 161, 168, 182, 192, 211–15, 230, 382, 383, 472, 690 [dissolution of 115]; trauma as origin of 315
neurotic depression 769
neurotic disorders 54, 159
neurotic patient(s) 31, 41, 42, 192, 304, 323, 393, 453, 455, 456, 522, 677, 690, 752; regressed 119
neurotic symptoms 268, 328, 560
neuroticisation 691
'neutral benevolence' 175

neutral listening 226
neutralisation 292, 308, 443, 513
neutrality 110, 131, 137, 146, 211, 212, 229; of analyst 92; benevolent 147, 246 [analyst's 141, 149]; rule of 111
New York Freudian Society 668
'night baby' 276, 632
nightmare 362, 374–6, 385, 403, 440, 468, 469, 481, 543
Nirvana: anxiety 485; principle 276, 498, 500, 504, 518, 520–2, 524, 776
no meaning and non-meaning 508–10
'*Noein*' of Parmenides 112
Nom-du-Père 16, 22, 505, 513, 783; *see also* Name-of-the Father
non du père, vs. *Nom-du-Père* 22
non-conflictual regression 143
non-defensive narcissism 15
non-delusional psychoses 39, 686, 687
non-differentiation 34, 288, 379, 557, 604, 684, 685
non-linear time 21
non-representation 36, 277, 278, 377, 379, 380, 385, 688
non-verbal communication 281, 442
non-verbal relationship 89 (in psychoanalytic treatment 105–13)
non-verbal representation 32
non-verbal unconscious-to-unconscious relationship 111
non-verbal and verbal signifiers 149
normal mania 396
'normalising normality' 561
normality 247, 508, 509, 559, 560, 561; abnormal 668–81; 'pathology, concepts of 174
nucleus, unconscious 311

object(s): cathected before being perceived 272, 296, 687; cathexis 275, 279, 281, 298–9, 303, 308, 379, 381, 443, 446, 498, 560–1, 569, 665, 753, 757, 784; decathexis of 31; found–created 92, 166, 168, 170, 540, 687; fusion with 33, 37, 593; hallucination of 31, 271; idealization, in girl's relation to father 565–78; incestuous 684; incorporation of 304, 305, 388, 391–5; internal 94, 116–17, 180, 183, 268, 280, 401, 438, 453, 514, 653, 655, 687, 708–10, 714, 719–21, 749; -libido 438, 445, 446, 583, 784; loss 94, 150, 303, 334, 394, 689, 757, 762; murder of 542, 756; narcissistic

object(s) – *Contd.*
   95, 143, 279, 410, 475, 606; part- 14, 273; regulation, narcissistic 279, 410; -related auto-erotism 281; -related regression 141; -related transference 143; representation 446 (unconscious 31); stage 287, 293–95, 767; symbolic 747; -zone, complementary 282, 688, 740, 747, 748, 780; whole 273

object relation/relationship [*passim*]: in children 286–308; differentiated, stage of 295–6; fetishistic 686, 687, 706–22; genetic study of 287–307; genital 117, 118; kinds of 116–18; pregenital 117–18; theory 19, 26, 35; and variations in technique 118–21

objectal intrusion 461
objectalisation 28, 35, 206
objectalising function 443, 777–8
objective reconstruction, vs. subjective construction 150
objectivisation 157
objectless depression 459
objectual transference 195
Objekt-Vorstellungen 269
obsessional defences 195
obsessional mechanisms 451
obsessional neurosis 101, 119–22, 451, 454, 456
obsessions 17, 127, 131
Oedipal analysis 194
Oedipal configuration 21, 279, 418, 428; of parents 19
Oedipal conflict 118, 192, 296, 347, 417, 671, 716, 721
Oedipal constellation 541
Oedipal desire 566, 573, 579, 624, 628
Oedipal father 282, 557, 772, 773
Oedipal feeling 122
Oedipal guilt 575, 588, 624, 637
Oedipal identifications 180, 663
Oedipal image, introjection of 178
Oedipal masturbation 349
Oedipal mother 377, 403
Oedipal organization 769
Oedipal phase 21, 261, 573
Oedipal position 564
Oedipal situation 90, 128, 130, 132, 283, 347, 411, 418, 555, 556, 560, 565, 585, 587, 597, 599
Oedipal structure 6, 83, 230
Oedipal triad 36
Oedipal triangle 179

oedipification, fantasies of 295
Oedipus complex 3, 20–2, 24, 83, 102, 180–3, 193–4, 318–20, 324–5, 374, 393, 427–9, 514, 539, 554, 557, 604, 615, 624, 633, 646, 653–4, 749, 783; 'classical' conception of 25; early 25; female, Freudian 627; feminine 626 (guilt 563–600); negative 564
Oedipus myth 6
Oedipus structure 324
omnipotence 6, 63, 491–2, 581–4, 590, 600, 633, 680, 695, 714, 734, 736, 741, 766; illusion of 16, 198; infantile 37; loss of 24; narcissistic 24, 195, 196, 726; symbiotic 359
omnipotent mother 24, 513, 555, 580–90, 598
omnipotent wish 332
onanism 534
oneiric regression 140
operational dreaming 38
operational functioning 38, 440, 772
operational life 38, 339, 341, 439, 460
operational thinking 32, 38, 438–40, 449–59, 778
OPLF: *see* French-Language Psychoanalytic Group
oral cathexis, of maternal object 297–98
oral drive 273, 350
oral phase/stage 304, 306; auto-erotic stage of 298; object-stage of 298
oral sexual drives 273
orality 256, 534
organ pleasure 334
Organlust 334
orgasm 247, 396, 398, 399, 491, 540, 570, 586, 609, 616–discovery of 541
original fantasy 323–5, 330, 335
Other: enigmatic 19–role of, in the formation of unconscious 18–21
outcome goals 40, 561

pack (damp wrapping) 492–3
pain, psychic 501, 677
pansexualism 55
paradox(es) 20, 76, 139, 147, 218, 221, 246, 488, 518, 523, 542, 611, 687, 689, 728–36, 778; concept of 728–30; register of 728; and schizophrenia 733–4; suffering and surviving in 724–36
'paradoxality' 20, 687, 688
paradoxe 778; *see also* paradox(es)

paradoxical countertransference 20, 144, 145, 278, 779, 780
paradoxical functioning 779
paradoxical sleep 779
paradoxical system 144, 775, 779
paradoxical transference 20, 488, 731, 778
paradoxicality 728, 730–4
paranoia 364, 474, 475, 587, 647, 710, 742; mass 446; 'professional' 440
paranoic alienation 102
paranoid delusions 192, 775
paranoid fantasies 325
paranoid-schizoid position, Kleinian 20
paranoid thinking, meaning of 10
paraphrenia 767
parapraxis 466, 475
parapsychotic suffering 727
parental imagos 180, 181, 187
parents: internal 280, 409, 411–12, 417; Oedipal configurations of 19
Paris Institute of Psychoanalysis 88, 105
Paris Psychoanalytical Society (SPP: Société psychanalytique de Paris) 1–7, 11, 24, 55–6, 60, 64, 66, 68, 70, 88–9, 97, 105, 115, 147, 155, 173, 190, 201, 205, 210, 218, 280, 286, 338, 341, 355, 367, 388, 405–6, 410, 421, 438, 449, 459, 463, 496, 516, 528, 543, 554, 559, 563, 601, 623, 641, 649, 668, 694, 706, 724, 766
Paris Psychosomatic Institute 201, 338, 439, 449, 459, 649
Paris School of Psychosomatics 92, 275, 438, 439, 778
partial identification 558, 782
part-objects 14, 273, 272, 292, 295, 305, 307, 346, 582, 591, 592, 598, 599
'pas de sens' 508, 509
paternal complex 364, 428
paternal function 427, 429, 430, 431, 783
paternal identification 629
paternal metaphor 531
paternal penis 350, 570–3, 575, 579, 580, 585, 587, 595–8
paternal superego 620
paternal transference 576, 658
pathogenic dream 322
pathological defence 315
pathological mourning 279
pathological negative hallucination 276, 789
pathological projective identification 545, 753
pathological regression 194
pathological vertigo 143
pavor nocturnus 762
Pcpt.-Cs system 268, 271, 487
penis [*passim*]: envy 92, 396, 555, 564, 565, 570, 578–80, 584–5, 590–99, 607, 620, 626, 772 (as defence and fears for integrity of the ego 586–9); father's/paternal 24, 345, 347, 350, 556, 566, 570–80, 585–91, 595–8, 624, 773 [daughter's identification with 556, 590–8]; genital 24; hollow 703; *see also* phallus
pensée opératoire 38, 39, 778; *see also* operational thinking
perception: –conscious (*Pcpt.–Cs.*) system 140; –consciousness system 103, 695; of faces 272; vs. idea 276; vs. memory 270, 277; vs. sensation 33, 271; sensory 263, 638, 689, 741
perceptual identity 141, 150, 231, 370, 371, 375, 383; and thought identity 140
periodicity 370
permanence 82, 112, 270, 273, 292, 295, 311, 333, 717
persecutory anxiety 758, 759
Perseus 380, 479, 486, 735; shield of 34, 684, 685, 694–704, 776
personality: irrational zones of 216; neurotic organisation of 321; psychotic parts of 42
personisation 720
perverse masochism (clinical example) 489–91
perverse sexuality 546, 561, 655
perversion(s) 17, 24, 94, 205, 316, 348, 490, 534, 560, 563, 567, 581, 607, 646, 649, 668, 674, 678, 708, 727, 753, 754; affective 655, 687; narcissistic 199; sexual 485, 707, 708, 711, 713, 717
phallic exhibitionism 584
phallic model of sexualisation and integration 535–6
phallic monism 23, 24, 555
phallic mother 344, 582, 585, 587, 589, 599
phallic narcissism 15, 614
phallic/narcissistic femininity 23
phallic-narcissistic phase 583
phallic order 603, 612, 618, 619, 620, 640
phallic phase 23, 304, 430, 583
phallic sexualisation 537
phallic stage 180; Freudian 22
phallic symbol 343, 481
phallic test 430
phallocentrism 607

phallus 22–4, 480, 556, 566, 577–8, 582, 583, 585, 586, 587, 591, 592, 612, 618, 697, 702, 703, 735; maternal 17, 18, 587, 697; *see also* penis
Phantasie(n) 311, 327, 330
phantasieren 241, 252, 253, 256, 257, 327
phantasmagorias 685, 700
phantasy(ies): auto-erotic 34; as concomitant of drives 36; vs. fantasies 327; primal 19; primary 34, 331; and representation(s) 33–5; scene-making capacity of 36; unconscious 29, 44, 166, 311, 385, 455, 708; *see also* fantasy(ies)
phantasying 464
phenomenology 28, 90, 282, 421, 753; Husserl's 223
Philadelphia Psychoanalytic Society 563
philosophy, and psychological field 221
phobia 17, 128, 132, 174, 183, 263, 469, 475
phobic patient 122
phobic situation 120
phylogenesis 323, 324, 336, 379, 429
pictogram 36, 282, 688, 738, 747, 748, 750, 780
pictogramme 738, 780
Platonic idealism 695*n*
play: capacity to 8; vs. game 140; guardian of, analyst as 140; material 177, 178; potential space for 16, 56, 276, 788
pleasure-ego 352, 464, 502, 557, 699
'pleasure premium' 333
pleasure principle 143, 150, 164, 176, 195, 235, 269, 275, 287, 305, 312, 394, 443, 463, 498, 504, 509–10, 536–7, 582, 726, 751; and erotogenic masochism 516–27; origin of in drives 521–3; –unpleasure 290, 518–23, 535, 537 [principle 518, 521, 535, 537]
politics, application of psychoanalysis to 547–8
polymorphous sexuality 558
positive hallucination 277
positive narcissism 92, 443
positive transference 120, 127
post-analytic transference 249
posthumous primary process 315
post-Oedipal superego 446, 536
postural proprioceptive images 442
potential space for play 56, 276, 788
pre-analytic transference 249

preconscious 38, 41, 57, 145, 151–2, 259, 262, 264, 269, 270, 326–9, 372, 427, 440, 464, 466, 469, 475–6, 489, 526, 632, 635; –conscious system 268, 270, 526; language as function of 32
preconscious ideoverbal associations 178
preconscious thinking 270
preconscious word-presentations 151
pre-genital anxieties 24, 556
pre-genital bisexuality 653
pre-genital fixations 25
pre-genital maternal transference 193
pre-genital mother 26
pre-genital object relation 117, 118; gestalt, pre- 301, 307
pre-genital regressions 180
pregenitality 24
pre-gestalt 301, 307
pregnancy 99, 131, 348, 471, 473, 475, 485, 569, 574, 577, 610, 613, 614; clinical example 630
prehistory 274, 321, 324, 603, 617
premature sexual stimulation 317
premonition 469
pre-narrative envelopes 427
pre-object 272–5, 290–2, 301, 306, 307; auto-erotism 281–2; stage 272, 273 (vs. object stage 272)
pre-psychosis, infantile 715*n*
pre-pubertal masturbation 332
presentation(s): thing- 32, 151, 259, 262, 268–71, 423, 426, 479, 544; word- 32, 151, 259, 262, 268–71, 423, 426, 479, 544, 613
présentation 269
pre-symbolic communication, semiotic 17
pre-transference relations 717
pre-verbal communication 301, 302
pre-verbal experience 20
pre-verbal relationships 272
pre-verbal thinking 270
primaeval man 324
primal catastrophe 688
primal cavity 291, 307, 350
primal dimension 557, 688, 780
primal fantasy(ies) 90, 274–5, 325, 330–1, 336, 339, 341, 345–7, 469, 541, 638, 734, 783; necessity of 617–19
primal father 324
primal hallucination 333
primal helplessness 253
primal phantasy 19
primal repression 275, 330

primal scene 24–5, 260, 274–5, 317, 321–6, 336, 340, 352, 541, 572, 576, 592, 595, 599, 617–8, 627, 637, 699, 702, 703, 745, 758, 761–2; identical and different 530–2; symbolic representation of 177
primal separation of birth 531
primary auto-erotism 347, 643, 718, 721
primary binding 536, 537, 538
primary dimension 780
primary erotic libido 505
primary erotogenic masochism 781
primary feminine phase 772
primary femininity 23
primary fetishisation 341, 351
primary fetishism 351
primary homosexual relationship 643, 645, 647
primary homosexuality 14, 26, 278, 558, 641–7, 781
primary identification 26, 92, 151, 278, 340–6, 349, 379, 386, 428, 430, 481, 550, 557–8, 643–4, 771, 773, 781–2, 786
primary masochism 31, 444
primary narcissism 14, 17, 41, 90, 92, 102, 141, 143, 219, 340, 378, 379, 643, 722; 'absolute' 777; normal 27
primary phantasy(ies) 34, 331
primary process 32, 145, 177, 195, 231, 244–5, 269, 278, 300, 330, 333, 444–5, 454–5, 457, 521, 530, 536–9, 571, 581, 729, 741, 744–5, 748–50, 775, 784; posthumous 315
primary psychotic breakdown 687
primary and secondary processes: enmeshed 742; and operational thinking 454
primary seduction 149
primary sensoriality 351, 353
primary sexualisation 445, 534, 536; sexual and drive 534–5
primary splitting 780
primitive animism 384
primitive defence 440
primitive drive representations 36
primitive ego, archaic 358
primitive identificatory processes 168
primitive mother 90, 582
primitive narcissism 464
primordial castration 24
principle of annihilation 726
principle of constancy 245, 270, 443
principle of elimination 687, 727
principle of inertia 270, 276, 443, 776
process goals 561

process of bisexualisation 558, 767
processual sexual, and object 539–40
processus de bisexualisation 767; *see also* process of bisexualisation
progressive disorganisation 35, 38, 439, 782
projected anxieties 129
projection(s) [*passim*]: destructive 361, 545; hallucinatory 378; of id 453; infantile 34; narcissistic 196; patient's 213, 508; psychotic 776; in transference 120
projective anxiety(ies) 119
projective identification 6, 15, 19, 90, 147, 295, 358, 360, 480, 482, 502, 686, 744; concept of 417, 558, 718; interpretation of 690; pathological 545, 753
projective process 557
proprioceptive images 442
protective fusion 307
protective shield: auxiliary 483, 484; mother as 275, 340–53, 473, 481, 490, 536, 685, 695, 703
provision-of-food-and-in-the-mouth 291
pseudo-automatism of repetition 305
pseudo-displacement 455
pseudo-hermaphroditism 652
psychaesthenia 534; legendary 100
psyche, death of 687, 728
psychic agency, ego as 441
psychic agony 611, 727
psychic apparatus, model of 63, 269
psychic automatism 253, 254
psychic binding 732
psychic bisexuality 23, 42, 95, 558, 559, 646, 649, 652, 654, 656, 659, 660, 664–7, 773, 767
psychic container 442, 477, 488
psychic death 279, 379, 413, 419, 556, 561, 613, 732, 745
psychic displacement 229
psychic life 3, 30, 251, 288, 297, 347, 380, 497, 506, 509, 511, 542, 617, 624, 645, 666, 679, 688, 725–33, 747, 775 (second principle of 725–6)
psychic object 271, 375, 384, 438, 707
psychic pain 501, 677
psychic reality 81–84, 163, 178, 179, 225, 336, 361, 411, 536, 541, 544, 685, 758, 787; vs. external reality 136, 508, 684, 692; Freud's concept of 274, 783
psychic representations 37, 430
psychic representative 268, 431, 511, 741*n*, 750 (of drives 271)

Index 809

psychic trauma 721
psychische Triebrepräsentanz 268
psychoanalysis: advances in, in France 73–85; application of, to politics 547–8; child 7, 24, 69, 76, 142, 173–88, 719*n* [and adolescent 66, 141, 272; importance of play in 142]; construction and/or reconstruction in 148; as depth-psychology 61; developmental 56, 272; evolution of 74–85; extramural 240; Freud's definition of 159; history of in France 53–86 [distinctive features of 60–72]; *hors cure* 240; vs. psychotherapy 41, 75, 136, 137, 140, 142, 179; relevance of to sexual difference 604–5; repetition in 240; role of speech in 32, 280, 421–31; sexualisation and desexualisation in 528–42; sexuality as object of 655–60; therapeutic aims of 40
psychoanalyst [*passim*]: introjection of 178, 180, 184; *see also* analyst
psychoanalytic culture, French 80–5
psychoanalytic cure 159, 174, 178, 181, 183
psychoanalytic field: limits and contradictions of 222–3; specificity of 222
psychoanalytic practice in France, evolution of 73–85
psychoanalytic process 40–5 (specificity of, in child 175–81)
psychoanalytic psychodrama 136, 286, 689–91, 706, 752, 763, 776; *see also* psychodrama
psychoanalytic psychotherapy 136, 185, 439, 711
psychoanalytic relaxation therapy 136
Psychoanalytic Society for Research and Training (SPRF: Société psychanalytique pour la recherche et la formation) 1, 4
psychoanalytic space 146, 210
psychoanalytic technique: considerations for 121–4; variations in, and object relations 118–21
psychoanalytic thought: and countertransference 218–31; historical development of, and countertransference 223–4
psychoanalytic treatment: of adolescents 57; aims of 57, 81, 83; non-verbal relationship in 89, 105–13; vicissitudes of 106
psychodrama 41, 45, 139, 286, 471, 477, 689–91, 706, 752, 758–63, 776; psychoanalytic 136, 286, 689–91, 706, 752,
763, 776; and schizophrenia (clinical example) 752–64
psychological field, and philosophy 221
psychological trauma 314, 316
psychology, developmental 98
psychoneuroses 382–4, 439, 767; transference 140, 137, 439
psychopathological disorganisation 774
psychopathological structures 119, 122, 305, 327, 437
psychose(s) 39, 44, 138, 155, 286, 706, 769, 775; *actuelles* 767; (*see also* actual psychosis); *blanche* 39, 44, 138, 155, 769; (*see also* blank psychosis); *froide* 769; (*see also* cold psychosis); *see also* psychosis(es)
psychosexual identity 558, 653
psychosexuality 554, 558–9, 567, 578, 580, 586, 624, 629, 631, 634–5, 653, 656–7, 666
psychosis(es) [*passim*]: actual 440, 767; blank 44, 138, 155, 277, 363, 686, 769–70, 777; cold 39, 45, 440, 686, 710*n*, 716, 721, 769–70; deep 318; hysterical 715*n*; vs. madness 775–6; non-delusional 39, 686, 687; pre-, infantile 715*n*; and reality 694–704; white 45
psychosomatic disorders 17, 39, 45, 92, 275, 440, 442, 449, 459, 487, 668, 772, 778
psychosomatic disorganisation 778
psychosomatic economics 438
psychosomatic functioning and psychotic functioning 440
psychosomatic illness 35
psychosomatic patient 38
psychosomatic regression 39
psychosomatic solution or somatic outcome (clinical example) 463–76
psychosomatic states 45
psychosomatic theory 439, 767
psychosomaticians 17, 34, 35
psychosomatics 37–9, 85, 94, 465, 475; French school of 31
psychotherapy 45, 71–7, 83, 127, 191, 195, 216, 440, 451, 454, 457, 463, 466, 469, 474, 488, 630, 675, 691, 711; child 142, 184–8; individual 136; vs. psychoanalysis 41, 75, 136–7, 140, 142, 179; psychoanalytic 136, 185, 439, 711
psychotic anxieties 42
psychotic breakdown 440, 687, 752, 754 (primary 687)
psychotic children 187, 188, 300, 493
psychotic depression 38, 462

psychotic functioning 32, 39, 138, 140, 277, 685, 689–90, 770, 778, 780 (and psychosomatic functioning 440)
psychotic nucleus, blank 276, 789
psychotic parts of personality 42
psychotic patients 10, 39, 42, 66, 492, 684–92, 724, 735, 738, 763
psychotic projection 776
psychotic transference 690, 691
puberty 315, 316, 318, 319, 320, 396, 554, 578, 580, 583, 638, 767, 773
pulsion 26–31, 35, 38, 73, 355, 429, 496, 641; *de mort*: *see* death drive, death instinct; *see also* drive(s), instinct(s)

quantum physics 208
Quatrième groupe (OPLF: Organisation psychanalytique de langue française) 1, 68, 738
question, interpretative speech as 429–31

rapprocher 94, 116–33
reaction formation 176, 177, 178, 546, 568, 582, 595
Real 21, 57, 91, 274, 411, 782–3; register 90
Realitäteinspruch 254
reality: -ego 352, 353, 464, 557, 699–700; principle 103, 143, 150, 176, 253, 312, 463, 498, 504, 510, 517, 521, 525, 538, 749, 751; psychic 81–84, 136, 163, 178–9, 225, 274, 336, 361, 411, 508, 536, 541, 544, 684, 685, 692, 758, 783, 787; -testing 239, 312, 463
re-cathecting of memory traces 271
rectocolitis, haemorrhagic 440, 463, 466, 467, 475
reduplication, as mechanism of obsessional neurosis 101
Réel 57, 782; *see also* Real
reflective thinking 230 (and countertransference 230–1)
refusement 58; *see also* frustration, *Versagung*
regressed neurotic patients 119
regression [*passim*]: during analytic treatment 192; deep 195; figurative 166; formal 41, 44–45, 140–1, 145, 278, 382–6, 763, 774–5 (and topographical 151, 690); genetic 319; idealistic 430; libidinal 141; malignant 41; narcissistic 15, 33, 37, 41–42, 141–6, 192–5, 278, 379–80, 559; non-conflictual 143; object-related 141 (and conflictual 143); oneiric 140; pathological 194; pre-genital 180; prevention of 41; psychosomatic 39;

temporal 141, 145, 151, 690, 774 [libidinal 774; narcissistic 774; object-related 774]; topographical 140, 141, 145, 151, 261, 690, 774 (formal and temporal 774); total 199; transference 214
regressive fantasy 120, 129, 559, 768; interpretation of 129
regressive transference neurosis 137; reification, of object 280
Reiz 245n
rejection 360
relaxation therapy, psychoanalytic 136
relief de stature 99
REM sleep 144, 779
remembering, work of 167, 371
'rendering conscious what is unconscious' 182
repetition: compulsion 164, 195, 235, 275, 370, 504, 509, 537, 588, 632; pseudo-automatism of 305; tendency 176, 177; transference 148–9, 164
repetitive dream 762
representability 36, 278, 363, 426, 604, 613, 775; considerations of 4, 774; *see also Darstellbarkeit*
représentance 165, 431
representation(s) [*passim*]: absence of 4, 363; and affects 4, 17, [Freud's distinction between 33]; concept of 31–7; drive, primitive 36; and emotional experience 32; failure of 35–6, 39; fantasmatic 740, 741, 746, 749; ideational 437, 439, 440, 442, 444, 684, 740, 741, 749; lack of 44, 335; language-based 437; mental 252, 457; non-verbal 32; object 446 (unconscious 31); and phantasy 33–5; primal form of 282, 780; psychic 37; relationship of 263; repressed 263; and symbolisation 36–7; unconscious 31, 35, 223, 255, 262, 263, 264, 422, 426, 455, 483, 503, 504, 652; visual 36, 363; work of 36, 44, 690
représentation 269; *see also* representation
representative: of drive 431; ideational 268, 431, 437; psychic 268, 431, 511, 741n, 750; repressed, return of 13, 202, 398, 716
repressed representation 263
repressed unconscious 262, 358
repressing ego 753
repression(s) 3, 13, 19, 26, 122–3, 132, 171, 176, 178, 188, 244, 247, 255, 263, 268, 271, 305, 315–7, 322, 328–32, 348, 356–60, 362, 365, 374, 376, 384, 391–404, 409, 417, 445,

Index 811

repression(s) – *Contd.*
    475, 507, 509, 512, 544, 556–7, 568, 579, 584, 605–8, 625–8, 633, 638–9, 652, 654, 664, 697, 725, 752, 753; hysterical 102; lifting of 151, 269; primal 275, 330; secondary 182, 330
repudiation 23, 253, 322, 371, 440, 475, 544, 555, 659, 783; *see also Verwerfung*
resistance(s) 74, 77, 115, 121, 147, 148, 163, 183, 186, 213, 214, 226, 236, 271, 276, 357, 406, 418, 427, 493, 507, 656, 766; character 227; of id 145, 275; to interpreting 161; transference 18, 193, 198
retrospective fantasies 318, 322
return to Freud 10, 12–13, 18, 21, 27, 32, 56, 57, 58, 67, 73, 84, 85, 151
return of the repressed 13, 202, 398, 716
reverie, 31, 360, 465, 482 (function of 34, 91, 276, 328, 330, 360, 465, 482, 771, 772)
reversed interpretation 120, 129
Rücksicht auf Darstellbarkeit 4; *see also* representability, considerations of
rudimentary ego 291, 308

Sach-Vorstellungen 4, 269; *see also* thing-presentations
sadism 335, 401, 517, 545, 547, 568, 569, 636, 717, 781; primal 499, 500
sadistic mother 344
sadomasochism 111, 505
'sameness' 26, 558, 559; cathecting 558
satellite signifier 151, 261–4
satisfaction: experience of 19, 29, 140, 336; hallucination of 271, 275; hallucinatory 150, 171, 295, 332, 340, 398, 525–6, 720; memory of 272, 332
scansion 56, 138, 211, 766
scansion agie 766; *see also* acted scansion
schematic superego 453
schizoid cases 119
schizoid patients 304
schizoid position 20, 305
schizophrenia 20, 119, 126, 442, 484, 488, 710, 715–16, 739, 742, 745, 779; and paradoxes 733–4; and psychodrama (clinical example) 752–64
schizophrenic patient(s) 221, 526, 571, 687–91, 710, 734, 738, 747, 754, 762
School of the Freudian Cause 69, 97; *see also* École de la cause freudienne (ECF)
Schreber [Freud's case] 346, 364, 365, 366, 505, 609, 612, 619, 646, 698, 761, 775

scotomisation 123
screen, dream 34, 35, 363, 763
screen-memory(ies) 169, 181, 321, 330, 467, 576
séances scandées 4
second skin 484, 490
second topography 10, 30, 504, 630
secondary auto-erotism 377, 380
secondary desexualisation 445, 446, 538
secondary dimension 780
secondary identification 278, 558, 767, 782
secondary narcissism 27, 591, 777
secondary process 32, 138, 145, 177, 231, 269–70, 300, 330, 371, 444–5, 455, 530, 538, 540, 728–9, 732, 741, 744–5, 748–9, 784 (and operational thinking 454)
secondary repression 182, 330
seduction 29, 43–44, 170, 177, 226, 229, 233–4, 241–5, 326, 330, 404, 428, 469, 482, 533, 606, 617–8, 627, 657; direct 225; by father 316; fantasies of 320, 326; generalised 149, 771; maternal 28, 206; narcissistic 688; primary 149; 'restrained' 242; scene 315, 322; sexual 315, 725; theory 18–19, 149, 234, 243–5, 314–22, 336, 771 (Freudian 18); traumatic 274, 275
self-analysis 158, 183, 211, 314, 319, 369, 370
self-annihilation 688
self-destructive or allo-destructive enactments 686, 770
self-destructive drive 444, 781
self-destructive function in mind 442
self-destructiveness 444, 687
self-image, narcissistic 15
self-preservation 144, 201, 207, 238, 242, 287, 478–9, 497, 501, 517, 533, 535, 587, 684–5, 728, 753, 788 (Freud's concept of 788)
self-preservative drive 25, 144, 276, 497, 530, 535, 536, 644, 645
self-procreation 687, 688, 727, 780
self-psychology 687
self-representation 282, 373, 741, 747, 748, 780
self-torture 401
semantification, of communication 302
semblable 89, 783, 786; *see also* visual likeness
semiology 94, 151, 258, 421, 469, 550 (and minor differences 550)
semiotic figuration 261
semiotic pre-symbolic communication 17
semiotics 34, 151, 280, 281, 421, 425; translinguistic 281

812   *Index*

sensation, vs. perception 33, 271
sensoriality 282, 344, 745, 776, 785; and language 283; primary 351, 353
sensorimotricity 350, 453
sensory perception 263, 638, 689, 741
sensory substratum of language 281, 425
separation: anxiety 22, 42; from mother 92, 697; necessity for 113; primal, of birth 531; unbearable 31
sessions: fixed-length 138, 766; frequency of 78–9, 84, 88, 105, 137, 142, 146, 259, 468, 493, 690, 691; rhythm of 93, 142; state of 381–3
setting, psychoanalytic: classical 44; internal 140; overall arrangement of 139; and process 40–5
sexual: in adolescence 540–2; diverted 533–4; and drive, primary sexualisation 534–5; injured 533–4; origin of 532–3
sexual deviations 26
sexual difference 384, 418, 531, 602–4, 613, 638, 641–3, 645–6, 649–60 (literary example 660–6)
sexual drives 28, 244, 272, 276, 443–6, 478, 481, 497, 502, 513, 530, 535–6, 784 (oral 273)
sexual excitation 315, 335, 444, 485, 490, 518, 525, 526, 785
sexual perversion 485, 707–8, 711, 713, 717
sexual seduction 725 (theory of 315)
sexual stimulation, premature 317
sexual trauma 21, 315
sexual unconscious 19
sexualisation 344, 445–6, 530, 533–40, 560, 647, 784; and desexualisation, in psychoanalysis 528–42; and integration, phallic model of 535–6; and libidinal co-excitation 537; phallic 537; primary 445, 536 [sexual and drive 534–5]
sexualité 22, 25, 73, 233
sexuality 21–6, 58; female 22, 23, 201, 449, 554–6, 563, 568–70, 578–9, 586, 599, 623; feminine 22, 23; genital 25, 304, 396, 634; infantile 24–25, 55, 73, 270, 274, 318–24, 333, 424, 428, 436, 438, 445–6, 534, 537, 540, 541, 554, 558, 638, 639; male vs. female 22, 554; as object of psychoanalysis 655–60; origins of, and fantasy 310–37; perverse 546, 561, 655; 'phallic' 534, 535; polymorphous 558; role of 436
sexuel, le 25, 528

SFP: *see* French Psychoanalytic Society (SFP: Société française de psychanalyse)
shield of Perseus 694–704
signifiance 427–30; *see also* signification
signification 100, 149, 165, 290, 300, 431; emergence of 429; process of 429–30
signifier(s) 22, 33, 41, 57, 81, 82, 83, 161, 171, 244, 252, 256, 274, 326, 423–5, 429, 456, 506, 508–10, 556, 614, 696, 702, 783; breast as 333; demarcation 262; enigmatic 149, 248, 532, 541, 771; formal 282, 442, 785; function of 259–64; of language 262; non-verbal and verbal 149; satellite 151, 261–4; visual 442
signifying process 427, 431
silence 11, 12, 71, 82–3, 92, 118, 165–70, 211–5, 225, 229, 255, 260, 351, 362, 373, 374, 403, 428, 466–9, 609, 620, 724, 739, 744–5; of analyst 43, 165, 168, 170, 215, 431, 457; in analytic relationship 109; dropping into 109; intolerance of 472; in psychoanalytic treatment 105–13
silent depression 439
situation analysis 165–7
situation analytique 165–7
skin: ego 441, 442, 685, 785–6 (functions of 477–93); functions of 15, 441, 442, 488, 785; second 484, 490
slip of tongue 440, 508
social smiling-response 293
Society for Group Analytical Psychotherapy 76
solipsism 246
solution, delusional 464, 465, 686*n*
somatic disorganisation 439
somatic outcome, or psychosomatic solution (clinical example) 463–76
somatic symptoms 450, 465
somatisation 38, 439–40; theory of 439
somatosis 463–6
sommeil paradoxal 144, 779; *see also* paradoxical sleep
space 270; for play 16, 56, 276, 788; potential 56, 276, 788
Spaltung 752; *see also* splitting
speaking, and renouncing 251–64
specific ego frustrations 725
spectre d'identité 786; *see also* spectrum of identity
spectrum of identity 144, 786
specular, vs. imaginary 91
specular double 277

specular image 89, 99, 378, 783, 786–7
speech: and hallucinatory vision 150; interpretative, as question 429–31; role of in psychoanalysis 32, 280, 421–31
spermatozoa 366
spitting out 358, 359
splitting [*passim*]: as defence 20; of drive 350, 491; of ego 15, 349, 544, 691, 706, 716, 721, 752–4, 757, 778, 787; of object 179; primary 780; topographical 277
SPP: *see* Paris Psychoanalytical Society
SPRF: *see* Psychoanalytic Society for Research and Training
squiggle game 139
stade du miroir 9, 13–15, 406; *see also* mirror stage
stage of differentiated object relations 295–6
state of session 381–3
structural anthropology 325, 783
structural linguistics 4, 20, 30, 783; theory 21
Structural Marxism 68
structural model of mind 10, 30, 57, 654, 781
structural schema, and event 273
structuralism 68, 98; linguistic 13
structuralist view of the unconscious 280
subject, de-centred 9
subjectivation 15, 25, 57, 529, 537, 691, 778, 787–8
subjective construction, vs. objective reconstruction 150
subjective disparity 245
subjectivity: concept of 9; technical 158
sublimation 230, 250, 258, 281, 292, 429, 445–6, 498, 501, 510, 512, 538, 539, 541, 543, 568, 583, 653, 777, 784, 785
sucking 28, 256, 290, 291, 304, 332–9, 625, 645
suffering and surviving in paradoxes 724–36
suicide 103, 204, 491, 588, 691, 722, 742, 743, 762, 770
superego [*passim*]: cultural 446, 543; and ego 180, 183, 185; ideal 170; and masochism 498–9; moral conscience and 549–50; parental 446; paternal 620; post-Oedipal 446, 536; schematic 453; severe 197
supreme defence 20, 730
Surrealism 64
Surrealists 55, 100
survival defences 20, 726–28
survivance 687, 726–35
surviving in paradoxes 724–36

symbiotic omnipotence 359
symbol-formation 147, 559, 691, 784
Symbolic 57, 90, 91, 262, 274, 782–3
symbolic activity 16, 41
symbolic capacity 24
symbolic castration 24, 431
symbolic communication 17
symbolic development 345
symbolic displacement 117
symbolic equation 37, 139
symbolic father 22, 783
symbolic function 14, 514, 531
symbolic functioning 6, 37, 680
symbolic object 747
symbolic order 22, 83, 274, 275, 324, 339, 348, 351, 352, 783
symbolic organisation 346, 351, 541
symbolic reduction 101
symbolic register 90
symbolic thinking/thought 37, 118
symbolic thirdness 424
Symbolique 57, 782; *see also* Symbolic
symbolisation 6, 8, 16, 25, 32, 41, 90, 171, 247, 273, 322, 358, 430, 431, 437, 441, 528, 529, 532, 538–40, 616, 691, 692, 777, 788; absence of 279; capacity for 772; and psychodrama 758–64; and representations 36–7
symbolised object 784
symbolism, principle of 691
symptom formation 183
système paradoxal 779; *see also* paradoxical system
systems, unconscious, preconscious and conscious 57, 326

tact 198, 228, 429; use of, in analytic situation 124
tactile proprioceptive images 442
talking cure 92, 271
technical subjectivity 158
teeth 272, 403, 699
telescoping of generations 279, 405–10, 413–9
temporal regression 141, 145, 151, 690, 774
temporality 3, 21, 169, 405, 456, 523, 526, 687
tenderness 317, 501, 558, 584, 609, 626, 644, 645, 647; affect of 26, 782
termination, of analysis 371
Thanatos 350, 486, 727, 751
theatre, metaphor of 43
therapeutic alliance 175, 731

814 *Index*

therapeutic deadlock 139
therapeutic relationship 8, 142
thing-presentations 29, 32, 34, 37, 151, 252, 259, 262, 268–71, 423, 426, 479, 544 (unconscious 151, 269)
thinking: apparatus for 35, 789; capacity for, development of 31; operational 32, 38, 438, 439, 440, 449–59; paranoid, meaning of 10; preconscious 270; pre-verbal 270; reflective, and countertransference 230–1; symbolic 37
thirdness 91, 156–9, 162–9, 424, 429, 514; analytic 30; creating 159, 164, 167, 169; symbolic 424; *see also* triangulation
thought: animistic 231, 382; identity 140, 141, 150, 231, 382, 383 (and perceptual identity 140); meaning of 231; religious 231, 646; scientific 231, 582; symbolic 118
time 270 (non-linear 21)
tombs, intrapsychic 279
topique 5, 10; *see also* topography
topographic model of mind 10, 26, 57, 151, 268, 766
topographical barrier 329
topographical regression 140, 141, 145, 151, 261, 690
topographical splitting 277
topography 5, 94, 270, 274, 296, 437, 483, 782 (second 10, 30, 35, 504, 630)
torture 490, 491, 543, 545
training analysis 18, 78
transactional relationship 302
transcendence 234, 242, 247, 282, 430, 659
transcendental *a priori*, Kant's 274
transference(s) [*passim*]: actualisation 162, 171; analysis of 83, 227; of analyst 147, 215; 'basic' 236; cathexes 690; countertransference dynamic/interplay 94, 139, 146, 147, 150, 158, 168, 218, 229, 280, 367, 371, 410, 416, 430; desire for 199; dialectics of 163; diplopia of 247; disposition for 215; dissolution of 139, 149, 237, 247; dream 117, 122, 596; dynamics of 165, 211, 248; fear of 198; 'filled-in' 149, 234, 247; and fundamental rule 161–3; genital-Oedipal 130; -hate 235; hollowed-out 149, 234, 246–9; homosexual 368–71, 375, 383, 627; idealised 127, 132; interpretations 7, 83, 139, 237; kinds of 249; lateral 236, 249, 689; -love 164, 235; maternal 554 [pregenital 193]; negative 143, 179, 182, 195, 197, 231, 690; neurosis 81, 110–16, 120–3, 132, 139, 140, 145, 161, 168, 182, 192, 211–15, 230, 382, 383, 472, 690 [dissolution of 115; regressive 137]; -object 163, 167 [-related 143]; objectual 195; as obstacle 223; 'ordinary' 234, 235, 241 (and 'extraordinary', 234); originary 234, 247; paradoxical 20, 488, 731, 778; paternal 576, 658; positive 120, 127; post-analytic 249; projection in 120; provoked by analyst 233–50; psychoneuroses 137, 140, 439; psychotic 690, 691; rapport 199; readiness 199; regression 214; relationship 5, 133, 143, 312, 690, 717, 766; repetition in 148, 149, 164; resistance 18, 193, 198, 236, 237; on to speech 166; symptoms 162; transference of 234, 236, 247, 249; transferring of 149; unspoken and secret in 413–16; vicissitudes of 158
transfert paradoxal 778; *see also* paradoxical transference
transgenerational 280, 409
transition, vicissitudes of, and illness of mourning 403–4
transitional, Winnicott's register of 20
transitional object(s) 16, 30, 56, 295, 304, 360, 407, 514, 680, 685, 700, 729, 733, 789
transitional phase 31
transitional phenomena 37
transitional space 16, 34, 43, 144, 407, 776
transitionalité 16
transitionality 138, 276, 779
transitivism, infantile 102
'translation' theory 248
translinguistic semiotics 281
transsexualism 26, 652
transubstantiations 425
trauma: of birth 288; mnesic symbol of 321; as origin of neurosis 315; psychic 721; psychological 314, 316; sexual 21, 315
traumatic dreams 275
traumatic memories dating from childhood 147
traumatic seduction 274, 275
traumatic situations 126, 545
traumatosis 725
travail: en double 44, 367, 372, 375; du feminin 23; *de figurabilité* 45; *du négatif* 355, 496, 788
triadic homosexuality 615
triangulation 91, 296, 306, 346, 615, 769, 772; *see also* thirdness

Index 815

Trieb(e) 26, 331, 336, 436, 511, 517; *see also* drive(s)
Triebanspruch 253
Triebrepräsentanz, psychische 268
trouvé-créé 16; *see also* found-created
true self 18

Übertragungswiderstand 236
Umwelt vs. *Innenwelt* 100, 101
unbearable separation 31
unbinding 30, 35, 39, 357, 429, 442–6, 501–4, 510, 512, 538, 556, 607, 608, 613, 621, 624, 689, 734, 736, 775, 778; analytic 245; narcissistic 443
uncanny, the 141, 143–5, 201–8, 234, 278, 378, 382, 385, 487, 650, 670, 671, 714
unconscious: concept of 504; creations of 77; discovery of 270, 323, 421, 437; enigmatic 43; hypothesis of 268; Lacan's concept of 32; maternal 18, 19, 34, 625; repressed 262, 358; role of Other in formation of 18–21; sexual 19; structuralist view of 280; structured as language 32, 57, 274, 783; topographical model of 57, 151, 766
unconscious affect 505, 506, 542
unconscious conflicts 116, 577
unconscious desire 19, 143, 261, 278, 328, 329, 342, 418, 775
unconscious discourse 262
unconscious fantasy(ies) 25, 95, 176, 177, 181, 193, 323, 327, 328, 331, 336, 440, 572, 573, 771, 784 (interpreting 178)
unconscious identification 149, 279, 280, 407–13, 418–19, 440, 609; alienated 412; intergenerational 150; narcissistic, alienating 412, 417
unconscious internal conflicts 77
unconscious nucleus 311
unconscious object-representation(s) 31
unconscious participation, analyst's 151, 260
unconscious phantasy 29, 44, 166, 311, 385, 455, 708
unconscious processes 3, 10, 28, 38, 111, 156, 247, 312
unconscious representations 31, 35, 223, 255, 262–4, 422, 426, 455, 483, 503, 504, 652
unconscious thing-presentations 151, 269
unconscious thoughts, hypercathexis of 269
unconscious wishes 313–4
unheimlich 201–2, 234, 487, 671; *see also* uncanny
Unheimliche, das 670, 679; *see also* uncanny

unpleasure 31, 269, 272, 274, 287–90, 294, 303, 316–7, 444, 502, 509–10, 516–26, 535, 537, 548, 560, 748; affects of 293
Urmensch 324
Urphantasien 274, 323, 330, 336; *see also* primal fantasies
Urszenen 321; *see also* primal scenes
Urvater 324
Urverdrängung 330

vagina 23, 342, 345, 555–7, 570–4, 578–83, 586, 597, 625–6, 629, 635, 637, 639, 646, 666, 772; denial of 24
verbal interpretations 92
Verleugnung 322
Verliebtheit 235
Verneinung 103; *see also* negation
Versagung 58; *see also* frustration; *refusement*
Verständigung 300
vertigo 368, 369, 574; pathological 143
Verwerfung 360, 440, 475, 608, 783; *see also* repudiation
violence, and narcissism of minor differences 545–50
visual hallucinations 365
visual likeness 89, 274, 783, 786; *see also semblable*
visual representation 36, 363
visual signifiers 442
vital-identital 144, 201, 207, 450, 788
vomiting 256, 348, 359, 395, 396, 577
Vorstellung 4, 268, 269, 774; *see also* representation(s)
Vorstellungrepräsentanz 32, 268; *see also* thing-presentation
voyeurism 70, 335

white psychosis 45
whole objects 273
Winnicottian theory in France 16–18
wish: -fantasy(ies) 331; -fulfilment 363 (hallucinatory 31, 150, 271, 272); omnipotent 332; unconscious 313, 314
Witz 264
'Wolf Man' [Freud's patient] 322, 360–3, 607–8, 612, 615, 652
woman-as-lover, censorship of 275, 276, 557, 632, 771, 773
women, men's fear of 601–21
word-presentation(s) 29, 32, 37, 151, 252, 259, 262, 268, 269, 271, 423, 426, 479, 544, 613 (preconscious 151)

words, metaphorical capacity of 37
work of the negative 30, 31, 276, 277, 356–61, 444, 507, 512, 513, 779, 788, 789
work of representation 36, 44, 690
working, as double 44, 45, 372, 381, 384, 386
working alliance 168, 170
working through 40, 42, 151, 161, 176, 260, 429, 504, 506, 508, 690; defensive 275
World Association for Infant Psychiatry and Allied Disciplines 286
Wort-Vorstellungen 269

wounds, narcissistic 24, 470, 579, 584–6 (and libido 725)
Wünschen 332
Wunscherfüllung 333
Wunschphantasie 331

Yugoslavia, former, violence in 545

zero principle 245
Zurückphantasieren 318, 322; *see also* retrospective fantasies